7th IEEE International Conference on
Computer Vision
September 20 - 27, 1999
Kerkyra, Greece

ICCV'99

Volume II

THE PROCEEDINGS OF THE

Seventh IEEE International Conference on Computer Vision

September 20 – 27, 1999

Kerkyra, Greece

Sponsored by

The IEEE Computer Society Technical Committee on
Pattern Analysis and Machine Intelligence

IEEE
COMPUTER
SOCIETY

Los Alamitos, California

Washington • Brussels • Tokyo

IEEE Computer Society Order Number PR00164
ISBN 0-7695-0164-8
ISBN 0-7695-0165-6 (case)
ISBN 0-7695-0166-4 (microfiche)
Library of Congress Number 99-65067

Additional copies may be ordered from:

IEEE Computer Society
Customer Service Center
10662 Los Vaqueros Circle
P.O. Box 3014
Los Alamitos, CA 90720-1314
Tel: + 1-714-821-8380
Fax: + 1-714-821-4641
E-mail: cs.books@computer.org

IEEE Service Center
445 Hoes Lane
P.O. Box 1331
Piscataway, NJ 08855-1331
Tel: + 1-732-981-0060
Fax: + 1-732-981-9667
mis.custserv@computer.org

IEEE Computer Society
Asia/Pacific Office
Watanabe Bldg., 1-4-2
Minami-Aoyama
Minato-ku, Tokyo 107-0062
JAPAN
Tel: + 81-3-3408-3118
Fax: + 81-3-3408-3553
tokyo.ofc@computer.org

Editorial production by Bob Werner

Cover art production by Alex Torres

Printed in the United States of America by Technical Communication Services

Table of Contents

International Conference on Computer Vision — ICCV'99

Volume I

Vision and Graphics

Real-Time Active Vision and Computer Interfaces

Motion Analysis

Volume II

Physics-Based Vision

Segmentation, Grouping, and Feature Extraction

Matching, Recognition, and Indexing

Vision and Learning

Preface

Welcome to the 7th IEEE International Conference on Computer Vision held this year on the beautiful island of Corfu (Kerkyra, in Greek), Greece, September 20-27, 1999.

The conference continues in the tradition of ICCV being a single-track conference. Among the benefits of a single-track conference is an important detractor. The competition is unreasonably constrained due to available presentation time and as a result many papers that deserve inclusion can not be included. There were 575 papers submitted and the 78 Program Committee members and many additional reviewers took the task of reviewing very seriously. The result is that we accepted 177 papers, 46 for oral presentation and 131 for poster presentation. Both oral and poster presentation papers have the same amount of space in the proceedings; the order of presentation in the proceedings is determined by topic and not by presentation mode. Proceedings will appear in both paper and CD-ROM format and all registrants will receive one copy of each. The CD-ROM version will contain color images.

All assignments of reviewers, reviewing and PC decision-making were done blind. Papers were reviewed by three or four people and final decisions were made by a 12-person sub-committee of the Program Committee. The Program Committee has put in very significant effort to ensure that any paper that is rejected is done so carefully with sufficient review feedback so that authors may improve their work and presentation for their next submission. We thank all members of the program committee and all reviewers for their efforts.

The David Marr Prize process is governed by the General Chair and Program Co-Chairs of the conference and the winning papers will be announced at the conference. Microsoft Corporation has generously donated the cash prizes.

A conference such as this is impossible without the dedication and hard work of many people. Mrs. Marina Haloulos was instrumental in all aspects of the organization. Stavria Mathiou, Chakra Chennubhotla, Alex Vasilescu, W. James MacLean, Konstantinos Derpanis, Florin Cutzu, Jimmy Konandreas, Andrea Levin, Laura Wood, John Midgely, Rainer Herpers, Allan Jepson, Michael Jenkin all played important roles and provided assistance at various stages of the process. Special thanks go to Steve Shafer and Keith Price of the IEEE PAMI Technical Committee for their guidance throughout. We thank IEEE Conference Services especially Mary-Kate Rada and Maggie Johnson for all their advice and assistance. Mr. Byron Tsonakis of the Corfu Holiday Palace provided greatly appreciated guidance on many local arrangements issues. Finally, we acknowledge the financial and logistical support of the Research Committee of the University of Patras, the Ministry of Education of Greece, the Ministry of Development of Greece, the Ministry of Culture of Greece, and the University of Toronto.

John K. Tsotsos, Andrew Blake, Yuichi Ohta, Steven W. Zucker

Organizing Committee

General Chair
John K. Tsotsos, University of Toronto

Program Co-Chairs
Andrew Blake, University of Oxford
Yuichi Ohta, University of Tsukuba
Steven W. Zucker, Yale University

Local Arrangements Committee
Lefteris Kirousis, University of Patras
Marina Haloulos, University of Toronto
John K. Tsotsos, University of Toronto

General Secretary
Marina Haloulos, University of Toronto

Administrative Assistants
Stavria Mathiou, University of Patras
Chakra Chennubohtla, University of Toronto
Alex Vasilescu, University of Toronto

Program Committee

Australia
Les Kitchen, University of Melbourne
Terry Caelli, Curtin University

Belgium
Luc Van Gool, Katholieke Universiteit Leuven

Canada
Gregory Dudek, McGill University
James Elder, York University
Frank Ferrie, McGill University
David Fleet, Queen's University
Michael Jenkin, York University
Allan Jepson, University of Toronto
Jim Little, University of British Columbia
David Lowe, University of British Columbia
Demetri Terzopoulos, University of Toronto
John Tsotsos, University of Toronto

China
Roland Chin, The Hong Kong University of Science and Technology

Czech Republic
Vaclav Hlavac, Czech Technical University

Finland
Ollie Silven, University of Oulu

France
Nicholas Ayache, INRIA, Sophia Antipolis
Patrick Bouthemy, Institut de recherche en informatique et systèmes aléatoires
Olivier Faugeras, INRIA, Sophia Antipolis
Radu Horaud, INRIA, Rhône-Alpes
Roger Mohr, INRIA, Rhône-Alpes

Germany
Heinrich Bülthoff, Max-Planck-Institute for Biological Cybernetics
Wilfried Enkelmann, Fraunhofer-Institut IITB, Karlshuhe
Wolfgang Förstner, University of Bonn
Hans-Hellmut Nagel, Fraunhofer-Institut IITB, Karlsruhe
Bernd Neumann, University of Hamburg

Greece
Lefteris Kirousis, University of Patras

Israel
Shmuel Peleg, Hebrew University
Amnon Shashua, Technion
Shimon Ullman, Wiezmann Inst.

Italy

Alessandro Verri, Istituto Nazionale di Fisica Nuleare — Genova
Guilio Sandini, University of Genova

Japan

Takashi Matsuyama, Kyoto University
Naokazu Yokoya, Agency of Industrial Science &Technology Nara
Yoshiaki Shirai, Osaka University
Masahiko Yachida, Osaka University
Ken-ichi Kanatani, Gunma University
Katsushi Ikeuchi, University of Tokyo
Jun-ichi Hasegawa, Chukyo University
Hiromi Tanaka, Ritsumeikan University
Kokichi Sugihara, University of Tokyo
Fumiaki Tomita, Electrotechnical Laboratory
Naoki Mukawa, Nippon Telegraph & Telephone Data
Takeshi Shakunaga, Okayama University
Yuichi Ohta, University of Tsukuba

Korea

Hyun Seung Yang, Korea Advanced Institute of Science and Technology

The Netherlands

Jan Koenderink, University of Utrecht

New Zealand

Reinhard Klette, The Auckland University

South Africa

Gerhard de Jager, University of Cape Town

Sweden

Stefan Carlsson, Royal Institute of Technology
Tony Lindeberg, Royal Institute of Technology

Switzerland

Guido Gerig, Eidgenössische Technishe Hochschule Zurich

UK

Andrew Blake, University of Oxford
Bernard Buxton, University College London
Roberto Cipolla, University of Cambridge
David Hogg, University of Leeds
Steve Maybank, University of Reading
David Murray, University of Oxford
Andrew Zisserman, University of Oxford

Reviewers

Keiichi Abe

Lourdes Agapito

Manoj Aggarwal

Tal Arbel

Carloine Baillard

Peter Bajcsy

Simon Baker

Nick Barnes

Ronen Basri

Sumit Basu

Paul Beardsley

Francois Belair

Stephen M. Benoit

Nels Eric Benson

David Beymer

Volker Blanz

Robert Bolles

Eric Bourque

Jeffrey E. Boyd

Edmond Boyer

Barry Brumitt

Lee Campbell

Rodrigo Carceroni

Francois Chaumette

Rama Chellappa

Tanzeem Choudhury

James Clark

Brian Clarkson

Isaac Cohen

Antonio Criminisi

Ross Cutler

Kristin Dana

Madirakshi Das

Tom Davis

Richard Dearden

Doug DeCarlo

Herve Delingette

David Demirdjian

Frèdèric Devernay

Joyoni Dey

Zachary Dodds

Chitra Dorai

Gregory Dudek

Rakesh Dugad

Rahul Bhotika

Toshio Endo

Moshe Ben-Ezra

Georgy Gimel'farb

Nicola J. Ferrier

Martin A. Fischler

Andrew Fitzgibbon

Yoram Gdalyahu

Joshua Gluckman

Patrick Gros

Efstathios Hadjidemetriou

Michal Haindl

Steven Haker

Mei Han

Allen R. Hanson

David Harwood

Janne Heikkile

Rainer Herpers

Shinsaku Hiura

Keith Hoepfner

Lei Huang

Naoyuki Ichimura

Michal Irani

Lee Iverson

Yoshio Iwai

Hidehiko Iwasa

Martin Jagersand

Tony Jebara

Nebojsa Jojic

Farhana Kagalwala

Masayuki Kanbara

Takekazu Kato

John Kender

Yakov Keselman

Hojoon Kim

Z. Kim

Fumitaka Kimura

Reinhard Koch

Pierre Kornprobst

Hiroyasu Koshimizu

John Krumm

Yoshinori Kuno

C.C. Kuo

Takeshi Kurata

Takio Kurita

Andrea Kutics

Kiriakos Kutulakos

Inso Kweon

Michael Langer

B. Leroy

Guy Lorette

Larry Lu

Q.-Tuan Luong

Jianbo Ma

Brian C. Madden

Yasushi Mae

Shyjan Mahamud

Gregoire Malandain

Raghavan Manmatha

Richard Mann

Russell Manning

Riccardo Manzotti

Eric Marchand

Mauricio Marengoni

Index of Authors

Accurate Motion Flow Estimation with Discontinuities*

Lionel Gaucher and Gérard Medioni
Institute for Robotics and Intelligent Systems
University of Southern California
Los Angeles, CA 90089-0273
{lgaucher,medioni}@iris.usc.edu

Abstract

*We address the problem of motion flow estimation for a scene with multiple moving objects, observed from a possibly moving camera. We take as input a (possibly sparse) noisy velocity field, as obtained from local matching, produce a set of motion boundaries, and identify pixels with different velocities in overlapping layers. For a fixed observer, these overlapping layers capture occlusion information. For a moving observer, further processing is required to segment independent objects and infer structure. Unlike previous approaches, which generate layers by iteratively fitting data to a set of predefined parameters, we instead find boundaries first, then infer regions and address occlusion overlap relationships. All computational steps use a common framework of **tensors** to represent velocity information, together with saliency (confidence), and uncertainty. Communication between sites is performed by convolution-like tensor **voting**. The scheme is non-iterative, and the only free parameter is the scale, related to neighborhood size. We illustrate the approach with results obtained from synthetic sequences and from real images. The quantitative results compare favorably with those of other methods, especially in the presence of occlusion.*

1 Introduction

We seek to determine accurate optical flow from a motion sequence. Early methods have relied on local, raw estimates of the optical flow field to produce a partition of the image. This leads to severe limitations, as the flow estimates are known to be very poor at boundaries, and cannot be obtained in uniform areas. In addition, the calculation of optical flow is a coupled problem. The determination of accurate flow requires prior knowledge of discontinuities at motion boundaries where smoothness constraints must be relaxed. But locating discontinuities presupposes knowledge of the flow.

Past methods have investigated the usefulness of Markov Random Fields (MRF) in treating discontinuities in the optical flow[12]. Regularization techniques which preserve discontinuities by weakening the smoothing of areas which demonstrate strong intensity gradients have also been used[13]. More recently, significant improvements have been achieved by casting the problem in terms of layered descriptions[1][2][3][4]. This novel formalism has many advantages. It is a natural way to accomodate discontinuities present in the motion field. Also, it allows information transfer between spatially separated regions, and may resolve local uncertainties.

But the actual mapping of pixels to layers is difficult. Many current methods use common motion to group regions, usually performing a parameterized fit to motion data[5][6]. Weiss[7] provides a good overview of the difficulties involved in this estimation process, which range from inadequate representation of motion as rigid and non-planar, to the overfitting and instabilities resulting from higher-order parameterizations.

Weiss performs image segmentation using a variant of the Expectation-Maximization (EM) algorithm[8], where a dense smooth flow field is fit to multiple layers. But methods dependent strictly upon a mathematical fitting can be limited by a lack of higher-level analysis. It is possible for unrelated regions to be accidentally merged into a single layer simply because of similar motion profiles, despite the presence of conflicting evidence (e.g. occlusion). The merging of spatially diffuse regions is more appropriately the domain of higher-level processing.

Within the same layered description framework, we present here a completely different approach in which we first detect boundary elements between smooth velocity fields. We then locally group these into curves. The velocity fields near these boundaries are then refined.

The determination of motion boundaries prior to the refinement and smoothing of the velocity field bordering these boundaries effectively decouples the problem of determining accurate optical flow. After refining the boundaries and the velocity fields near them, occlusion relationships between regions are determined. Pixels with different velocities in separate layers are easily identified.

All of the computational steps, from local boundary detection to velocity refinement, are implemented in a common framework which involves voting and tensor calculus[15]. This non-linear methodology is non-iterative, does not depend upon critical thresholds, and is robust in the presence of local irregularities in the motion field.

Section 2 presents an overview of the methodology, as well as a flowchart illustrating the algorithm. Section 3 presents the proper background for understanding the ten-

---

*This research is supported by contract DAAB07-97-C-J023, funded by DARPA, and monitored by U.S. Army, Fort Monmouth, NJ.

sor voting formalism which is used throughout the study. Section 4 describes the acquisition of the initial velocity input. The next four sections present the details of the steps. Section 9 shows results of the method on motion sequences, and Section 10 presents conclusions.

2 Our Approach

Figure 1 illustrates the steps of our method. The input is a field of velocity vectors, derived via a three-frame maximum cross-correlation technique. We then generate a dense tensor velocity field, which encodes not only velocity, but also estimates of confidence (saliency) and uncertainty. We then extract discontinuities from this field, which are found as locations of maximal velocity uncertainty using the tensor voting formalism. Interpreting these uncertain velocity locations as local estimates of boundaries of regions, tensor voting is used again to both align tangents along these boundaries, and to join these tangents into region boundaries.

Having segmented the motion field, tensor voting is used again between pixels not separated by boundaries to accurately estimate the velocities at the borders of these objects (which are inherently uncertain in the presence of occlusion).

With coherent velocities at the borders of these objects, a *local* representation of occlusion is found by determining which region's velocity field dominates in both future and past frames. From this analysis, the locations of pixels with multiple velocities are determined.

3 Tensor Voting and Saliency

We propose to augment the traditional representation of local information (here, a displacement vector) by two critical components, *saliency* which expresses the degree of confidence associated with the measurement, and *uncertainty*. This compound information can be conveniently expressed by an ellipsoid (ellipse in 2-D), where the *shape* of the ellipsoid conveys the direction and uncertainty, and its absolute *size* expresses saliency. Mathematically, it is known as a (second-order, symmetric) tensor[10].

A useful statistical representation of an ellipsoid is as the covariance matrix S derived from a distribution of points on its surface.

$$S = \begin{bmatrix} \hat{e}_1 & \hat{e}_2 & \hat{e}_3 \end{bmatrix} \begin{bmatrix} \lambda_1 & 0 & 0 \\ 0 & \lambda_2 & 0 \\ 0 & 0 & \lambda_3 \end{bmatrix} \begin{bmatrix} \hat{e}_1^T \\ \hat{e}_2^T \\ \hat{e}_3^T \end{bmatrix} \quad (1)$$

The eigenvalues $\lambda_1, \lambda_2, \lambda_3$ (where $\lambda_1 \geq \lambda_2 \geq \lambda_3$) correspond to each of the principal directions $\hat{e}_1, \hat{e}_2, \hat{e}_3$. The eigenvalues determine the shape of the ellipsoid while the eigenvectors determine the orientation (Figure 2). Since

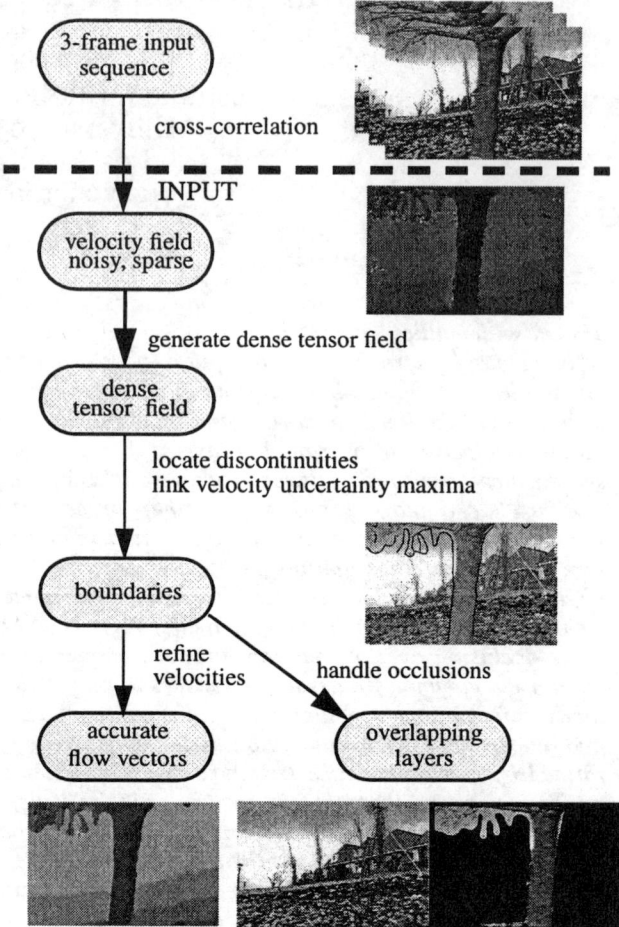

Figure 1 Determination of Image Layers

the eigenvalues determine the shape and size of the ellipsoid, they also convey saliency and uncertainty information.

A simple rearrangement of (1) yields the following:
$$S = (\lambda_1 - \lambda_2)\hat{e}_1\hat{e}_1^T + (\lambda_2 - \lambda_3)(\hat{e}_1\hat{e}_1^T + \hat{e}_2\hat{e}_2^T)$$
$$+ \lambda_3(\hat{e}_1\hat{e}_1^T + \hat{e}_2\hat{e}_2^T + \hat{e}_3\hat{e}_3^T) \quad (2)$$

The first term represents a "stick" component of the saliency tensor S, with complete dominance by a single orientation. The second and third terms represent "plate" and "ball" components. In the plate component, two equal eigenvalues co-dominate. In the ball component, all eigenvalues are equal; no orientation is favored.

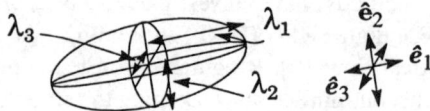

Figure 2 Ellipsoid and Eigensystem

Given a (possibly sparse and noisy) set of velocity vectors as input, we can generate a dense tensor field by allowing active sites to communicate with their neighbors. This communication is performed by a convolution-like operation, and produces a tensor at every location.

It is necessary to provide a voting function $V(S,p)$ which provides the value of the tensor field for a saliency tensor S at a location p relative to the tensor's coordinate system. The strength of the field should decrease with distance and be orientation-independent.

In addition, the linear nature of the voting field allows us to exploit the component expansion of S given above to provide fields for the stick, plate, and ball components. Some linear combination of these is sufficient to represent any saliency tensor. Furthermore, the orientation-independence of the field allows each of the three fields to be calculated once and stored for all future uses. Application can then be in the form of a convolution mask properly oriented to suit the originating saliency tensor's principal axis.

The functional form of the ball field used in this work is $V(S, p) = \exp(-p^2/\sigma^2)\hat{p}\hat{p}^T$, where σ is a scale factor. This functional form obviously satisfies the symmetry and decay requirements of the ball field. The stick field used is the same 2-D extension field of Guy and Medioni[9][14], whose work provides detailed functional forms.

Following tensor voting, the eigenvalues and eigenvectors of the saliency tensor at each voted site are determined. The saliency tensor at the recipient site can then be divided into the stick, plate, and ball components. Accordingly, the saliency of each of these is $(\lambda_1-\lambda_2)$, $(\lambda_2-\lambda_3)$, and λ_3 respectively. Features corresponding to each of these components are then located at the local maxima of the corresponding saliency, and extraction is performed by non-maximal suppression on the feature saliency map[14]. (For example, local extrema of the plate tensor correspond to surface discontinuities.)

4 Velocity Field from Three Frames

The raw velocity field which is provided as input should be as accurate as possible. In recent work[15], a standard two-frame maximum cross-correlation coefficient technique was used. While this two-frame technique gives adequate values for the motion field where velocities vary slowly, areas in which differently moving objects are simultaneously found within the convolution mask are more troublesome. Even worse are the results in areas of the first frame which are about to be occluded in the second frame, since there can be no meaningful correlation detected in this case. In these areas in particular, it is very difficult to determine either the correct motion field or the proper boundaries between objects.

Making a few reasonable assumptions about the nature of the observed object motion suggests that a cross-correlation calculation in which *three* consecutive frames

are used, leads to more accurate results. It can generally be assumed at the *local* level that most occlusion events involve only two conflicting motion boundaries. Further assuming that the objects in a scene are locally convex and demonstrate negligible acceleration between frames, one can conclude that an area at time t which is about to be occluded at time $t + \Delta t$, was probably also visible at time $t - \Delta t$. In other words, an object which is being occluded in forward time is likely to be in the process of being uncovered (disoccluded) in reverse time.

Since disoccluding events pose less trouble than occluding events during determination of the motion field, this suggests that a more accurate estimate of the local velocity can be attained by choosing the best cross-correlation match in either forward or reverse time, negating the velocity in the case where the reverse time cross-correlation is larger.

Since the correlation mask has finite extent, there will still be weaker cross-correlation where an object boundary crosses the mask. But, most importantly, these areas of weak cross-correlation are now roughly *symmetrically* distributed around the true motion boundary, rather than being considerably more extended into the object undergoing occlusion in forward time. This enables the tensor-voting formalism to more accurately locate the motion boundary. The cross-correlation coefficient also offers a measure of strength to be used in the tensor-voting process.

5 From Velocity Field to Tensor Field

The first step of the process is to convert the input flow field into a dense tensor field. Figure 3(a) shows a frame from the "Flower Garden" sequence, and Figure 3(b) shows the horizontal and vertical components of the input velocity field. Note that velocities near the motion boundaries are incoherent and the boundaries are irregular.

At each point, the displacement vector $(v_x\ v_y)^T$ between P_t and P_{t+1} is the projection onto the xy plane of the 3-D vector $(v_x\ v_y\ \Delta t)^T$. Assuming the sampling rate is constant (and set to 1), this flow can be represented by two variables. As explained in Section 3, we want to encode saliency as the size of the tensor, so we map the velocity vector $(v_x\ v_y)^T$ to $(v_x\ v_y\ 1)^T$, but scaled down to a *unit* vector. Note that such a representation does not introduce any motion bias, and that the null flow maps to the unit vector $(0\ 0\ 1)^T$. Similarly, given a tensor with a long axis given by $(a\ b\ c)^T$, the length $\sqrt{a^2 + b^2 + c^2}$ represents the saliency, and the corresponding image velocity is $(a/c\ b/c)^T$.

This technique, which represents velocity vectors of varying lengths as unit vectors in a higher dimensional space, prevents high velocities from disproportionately influencing the tensor-voting process. The weight of the unit vectors can be modulated by a confidence measure.

5.1 Initial Vote

We now allow all the sites with velocity information to communicate with each other, and with empty sites. This is performed as a convolution with a ball field, which is the simple scaled Gaussian field already described.

Intuitively, each site broadcasts its current motion to its neighbors, but allows deviations from it. The result is a true tensor field, encoding velocity information, saliency, and uncertainty. Adjacent sites with similar motion increase saliency, whereas adjacent sites with different motions increase uncertainty.

(a) A Frame   (b) Input X- and Y-velocities
Figure 3 Flower Garden Sequence

6 Segmentation of the Motion Field

6.1 General Description

Assuming that the interiors of moving regions exhibit smoothly varying velocity field values, boundaries between moving objects can be detected by extracting curves of relative maxima in the *uncertainty* of the velocity. These areas of maximal uncertainty result from the fact that boundaries between neighboring regions with different velocities are influenced by both of these regions during voting.

6.2 Regions of Maximally Uncertain Velocity

Following our first vote, and diagonalization of its co-variance matrix, each tensor is then characterized by a principal axis (representing an encoded velocity), and eigenvalues λ_1, λ_2, and λ_3, where $\lambda_1 \geq \lambda_2 \geq \lambda_3$. We use as a measure of velocity uncertainty the quantity λ_2/λ_1, which will approach unity as uncertainty increases. (See Figure 4a.)

This uncertainty measure varies smoothly across the image. Relative maxima in the uncertainty will occur along "ridges" which represent boundaries between regions of differing velocity. These locations are found by a modified version of the Marching Square algorithm[9][11].

6.3 Determination of Component Boundaries

These boundary curves of maximally uncertain velocity lie between regions of differing velocities. These curves are later used to determine which pairs of pixels may communicate during a velocity refinement procedure. It is therefore advantageous to complete these boundaries to the greatest extent possible by finding the most likely curves passing through these regions.

First, we assign a tangent to the pixels in these maximally uncertain regions. The 2-D extension field[9][14] is ideally suited for this purpose. At each pixel judged to be maximally uncertain, other such pixels vote for prospective tangents. These tangents are derived from unit vectors parallel to segments joining the voting pixel to the recipient pixel. Voting is restricted to maximally uncertain pixels, resulting in a sparse 2-D tensor field. The principal axis of the pixel's diagonalized covariance matrix determines the resultant tangent direction. The strength of the tangent vote is taken to be the magnitude of the stick component of the 2-D tensor, $\lambda_1 - \lambda_2$.

The result of this 2-D convolution-like operation is a dense 2-D field of 2-D tensors (ellipses) where the shape represents uncertainty and the size saliency. We extract curves from the dense field as maxima of the stick component, once again using a modified Marching Square procedure.

These edges represent the boundaries of the desired regions. The velocity field is therefore segmented into regions of coherent velocity. (See Figure 4b.)

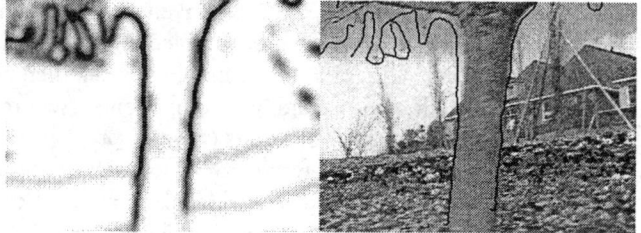

(a) Uncertainty Map   (b) Region Boundaries
Figure 4 Determination of Boundaries

7 Region Refinement

7.1 General Description

With the initial segmented description now complete, we go from a pixel-level representation to a region-level representation. A *local* determination of occlusion between regions will be made based upon velocities present near region boundaries. In the presence of an occlusion event, however, these velocities are the most uncertain. A more elaborate local analysis is therefore necessary.

7.2 Region-Level Velocity Refinement

Near the boundary between two regions moving differently, the velocity information is necessarily inaccurate and corrupted, as it is estimated from a mixture of velocities. Furthermore, occlusion of a region by another in time also alters the true velocity in the occluded area. Now that we have boundaries between regions, we can overcome these problems by another round of tensor voting, with some slight changes.

In this round, voting is only permitted between pixels which can be connected with a straight line which does not cross a region boundary. And the strength of a pixel's velocity vote is proportional to $1 - \lambda_2/\lambda_1$, where λ_1 and λ_2 are the eigenvalues resulting from the diagonalization of that pixel's covariance matrix during first stage voting.

The quantity $1 - \lambda_2/\lambda_1$ is a measure of the certainty of that pixel's velocity. The more certain velocities of the region supplant the less certain ones near the region boundaries. This has the effect of refining the velocity field within each region, and compensating for a lack of reliable velocity information near region boundaries.

It should be noted that the refined velocities near region boundaries are still *locally* influenced, and are not averaged over the entire region. This allows for accurate representation of objects which exhibit variations in velocity, such as rotating or slowly deforming objects.

Results of the velocity refinement as applied to the Flower Garden sequence are shown in Figures 5(a) and 5(b), the horizontal and vertical components, respectively, of the refined velocity field.

 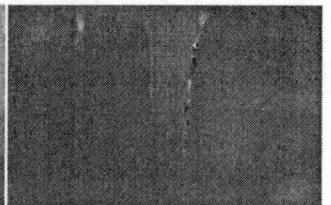

    (a) Refined X-velocities   (b) Refined Y-velocities
Figure 5　Refined Velocity Field

At this level of processing, we have provided a higher level of description for the image which preserves discontinuities in the motion field at region boundaries, but still permits further refinement within individual regions.

In this way, we have effectively circumnavigated the coupled nature of the problem of solving for the optical flow. Restricting the tensor voting to occur on only one side of a region boundary allows refinement of the velocity field subject to the boundary conditions imposed by the presence of discontinuities at the region borders.

Despite the presence of smoothly coherent velocity fields within these regions, no attempt is made at this point to partition the set of regions into meaningful objects. This process requires determination of other higher-level relationships between regions. By postponing the merging of regions until further information (e.g. occlusion, or even higher-level semantic relationships) is computed, the methodology avoids the pitfalls of relying on a low-level mathematical fit for determining when regions can be merged.

8 Handling Occlusion

8.1 General Description

At this point, the motion field has been refined and the uncertain velocities near the component boundaries have been replaced by more accurate estimates. Using the refined velocity field at time t_0, and assuming the absense of any occluding components, the velocity field at time $t_1 = t_0 + \Delta t$ can be predicted. Region pixels simply translate in time to their new positions.

But in the presence of occlusion, the velocity field at time t_1 will depend upon which regions at time t_0 occlude others. When pixels from two regions at time t_0 are predicted to project into the same location at time t_1, the occluding region will determine the velocity at the new location. Therefore, to the extent that two "conflicting" pixels in separate t_0 regions differ in their velocities, the refined velocity field at time t_1 can be used to determine occlusion orderings between the regions at time t_0. It should be noted that the availability and reliability of such time-projected conflict information depends heavily upon the accuracy of the velocity refinement process previously described.

Unfortunately, such predictive capability does not exist with boundaries which *uncover* regions. The portion of a region occluded at time t_0 cannot predict a velocity at time t_1 since velocities in the t_0 occluded region are not available. Since resolution of this velocity conflict at time t_1 is necessary to determine the nature of the occlusion, no occlusion ordering information can be gained in this case. (See Figure 6.)

region to be occluded   region being uncovered

time = t_0 time = $t_0 + \Delta t$
Figure 6 Uncertain Occlusion Boundaries

But occlusion classifications are invariant to time-reversal, and an uncovering event in forward time becomes an occlusion event in reverse time. Therefore, detection of occlusion in both forward and reverse time flow detects all occlusion events.

8.2 Criteria for Classification of Occlusion

We detect occlusion *locally* as follows. A *first* pixel is propagated from the previous (future) frame forward (backward) using the refined velocity field in that frame. This new *second* pixel in the present frame is then propagated back, using its refined velocity, to the previous (future) frame to arrive at a *third* pixel.

If the *second* pixel in the present frame has *not* just occluded a pixel from another layer in either forward or reverse time, the *first* pixel will be the same as the *third* pixel in both cases (or at least they will not be separated by a motion boundary). Otherwise, in either forward or reverse time, the *first* pixel will be separated from the *third* pixel by a motion boundary. This allows us to locate pixels in the present frame which have dual values. The two velocities are easily determined, as is the order of the occlusion based on the refined velocity of the *second* pixel.

Figure 7 shows which pixels in the central frame of the Flower Garden sequence are dual valued. Clearly, this procedure depends heavily on having accurate (or at least consistent) placement of motion boundaries. Using the partial

Figure 7 Dual-velocity Pixels

order of occlusion derivable from this data, a separation into layers can be effected. Propagating background pixel velocities from several frames allows reconstruction of the background image, shown in Figure 8. Figure 9 shows a

Figure 8 Flower Garden Layers

segmentation of a random dot motion sequence into overlapping layers. The accuracy of the segmentation is resistant to gradual distortions of the component objects.

Figure 9 Random Dot Motion Sequence

9 Additional Results

In addition to the previously shown results from the analysis of the Flower Garden sequence, we also present results from the analysis of five other three-frame sequences.

First, in order to demonstrate an ability to accurately obtain optical flow in regions undergoing some distortion, Figure 10 shows the results obtained from analysis of a synthetic sequence in which a disk composed of random dots undergoes expansion in front of a similarly-textured background. The disk border moves radially at 5 pixels/frame.

Figure 10(a) shows the second-frame disk in a three-frame sequence after final segmentation. Figure 10(b) shows the error in the refined velocity field, where darkness grows linearly with error.

Here, the error measure used is the "angular" error measure used by Barron, Fleet, and Beauchemin[16]. A velocity $\hat{v} = (v_1, v_2)^T$ is represented as the 3-D unit vector

$$\hat{v} \equiv (v_1, v_2, 1)^T / (\sqrt{v_1^2 + v_2^2 + 1})$$

in space-time coordinates. A 2-D velocity is then completely characterized by the orientation of this unit vector. The error measure used is $\theta_{error} = cos^{-1}(\hat{v}_c \bullet \hat{v}_e)$ where $\hat{v}_c$ is the correct velocity and $\hat{v}_e$ is the estimated velocity.

The average error found for the expanding disk is $4.05° \pm 5.85°$ for full 100% field coverage. Figures 10(c) and 10(d) show the refined horizontal and vertical components of the motion field, respectively.

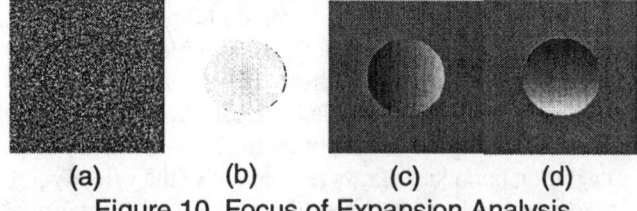

(a)   (b)   (c)   (d)

Figure 10 Focus of Expansion Analysis

The velocities near the boundaries of the disk have been faithfully reproduced by the refinement voting. Distortion resulting from dissimilar rates of expansion have little effect on the refined velocity field. The method has no bias toward *constant* velocity motion in the image plane.

Figure 11 shows a similar analysis for a disk rotating counter-clockwise at approximately 12° per frame. In this case, the measured "angular" error is $8.80° \pm 13.8°$ for full 100% field coverage. The area near the center of rotation provides a weak correlation since its motion cannot be approximated linearly. Some error is also incurred by virtue of the fact that rotation necessarily includes acceleration between frames. But, in particular, boundaries are very accurately found.

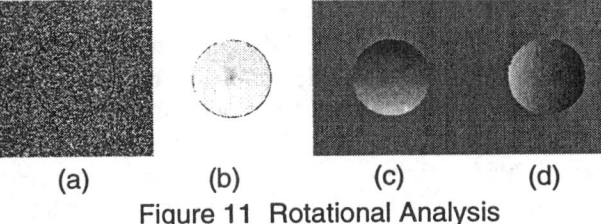

(a)   (b)   (c)   (d)

Figure 11 Rotational Analysis

Figure 12 shows three frames from a sequence in which a block mounted on a post is allowed to translate and rotate in front of a speckled background. The analysis is performed on the central frame. Figure 13(a) shows the horizontal component of the initial noisy velocity field. Figure 13(b) shows the scaled horizontal component of the motion field after the refinement voting procedure. The local nature of the tensor voting procedure easily accomodates variations in velocity along the border of the block resulting from its rotation.The accuracy of the edge placements and refined velocity field makes possible a realistic representation of occlusion in the scene..

Figure 12 Rotating Block Sequence

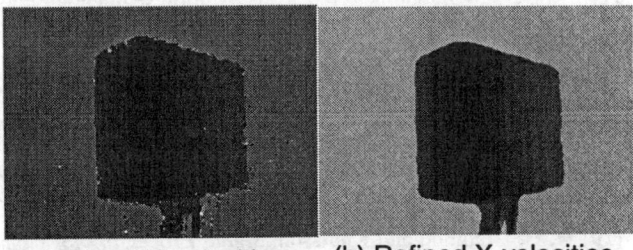

(a) Input X-velocities   (b) Refined X-velocities

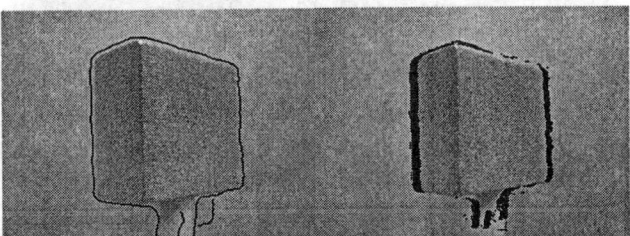

(c) Boundaries   (d) Dual-velocity Pixels

Figure 13 Rotating Block Analysis

Figure 13(c) shows the resulting boundaries derived from the uncertainty map, superimposed on the original image. The boundaries accurately reflect the true motion boundary of the block, except at the top of the block where

a lack of texture in a portion of the background has caused this portion to be merged with the block. Figure 13(d) shows the occlusion analysis applied to the rotating block sequence. The dual-velocity pixels are accurately placed due to the precision of edge determination and velocity refinement.

An analysis of three frames of the Yosemite sequence (without sky) is shown in Figure 14. Figure 14(a) shows the central frame of the three-frame subsequence used. Figure 14(b) shows the "angular" error map. The average error obtained is $8.83° \pm 10.6°$ for 100% field coverage, and $2.12° \pm 0.92°$ for 34% field coverage. Figures 14(c) and 14(d) show the refined horizontal and vertical components of the velocity field, respectively.

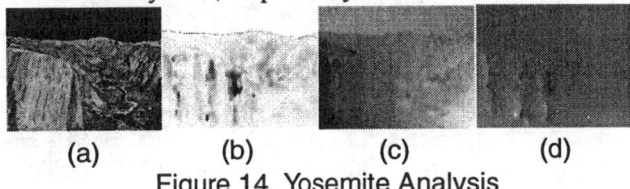

(a)   (b)   (c)   (d)

Figure 14 Yosemite Analysis

The Yosemite sequence calculation was performed with only three frames of the sequence, but it could have been performed with only *two* since there is no appreciable occlusion present. Since the strength of this methodology is its ability to treat sequences presenting a substantial degree of occlusion, performance on this sequence does not completely convey the power of the technique.

Table 1

Sequence	Error (degrees)	Density
Expanding Disk	4.05 +/- 5.85	100%
Expanding Disk	2.32 +/- 0.87	70%
Expanding Disk	1.54 +/- 0.48	32%
Rotating Disk	8.80 +/- 13.8	100%
Rotating Disk	4.45 +/- 2.18	66%
Rotating Disk	2.81 +/- 1.35	37%
Yosemite	8.83 +/- 10.6	100%
Yosemite	3.71 +/- 2.07	61%
Yosemite	2.12 +/- 0.92	34%

Table 1 presents an error analysis for the sequences studied which have available ground truth data. It reports "angular" error for specific levels of coverage of the motion field. These results compare very favorably with those in the current literature[16].

As another example, the SRI Tree sequence is analyzed. Figure 15 shows the three frames used in the analysis. Figure 16(a) shows the horizontal component of the noisy input velocity field, while Figure 16(b) presents the same component after refinement. . With the exception of the admittedly more difficult lower half of the foreground tree, the boundaries and velocities derived in the upper half are fairly accurate. Incorporation of monocular data in the analysis would obviously improve the results.

Figure 15 SRI Tree Sequence

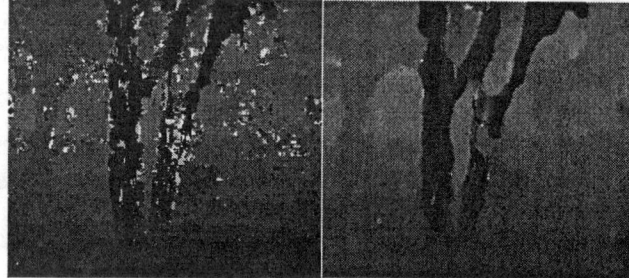

(a) Input X-velocities   (b) Refined X-velocities

Figure 16 SRI Tree Analysis

10 Conclusions and Future Work

We have presented some preliminary results of a novel methodology to address the issues of accurate optical flow computation using motion information *only*. It explicitly addresses the classical limitation that velocity information is necessarily inaccurate around motion boundaries, and that pixels may have multiple velocities.

Most importantly, it effectively demonstrates an ability to simultaneously determine motion boundaries and accurate optical flow without resorting to iterative global optimization techniques. This ability can be viewed as an important foundation upon which higher levels of image sequence processing can be based.

While these preliminary results are very encouraging, there is considerable room for improvement. For example, the stability of the method can be greatly improved by incorporating the coherence which exists between frames. All results presented here are obtained with only *three* frames.

In addition, the localization of motion boundaries can be made more accurate by the inclusion of monocular information (e.g. edges). This is particularly true for motion boundaries between occluding/occluded pairs in which the only difference between velocities on both sides of the boundary is an out-of-plane projection (e.g. boundaries of non-translating rotating objects).

Also, additional investigation is needed to determine how to combine information acquired at the local level (motion boundaries, occlusion evidence, and, eventually, edges) into a complete partitioning of the image into indi-vidual regions with coherent velocity. This will likely require merging of information sources with very different characteristics.

Further study must also be undertaken to determine criteria for grouping partitioned regions with similar motion profiles into the same layer. This process, which is usually performed in other techniques as the result of a mathematical fit at the pixel level, is more properly performed at a higher level of processing where characteristics of macroscopic entities (e.g regions, etc.) can influence the outcome. These are the topics of our ongoing research.

11 References

[1] T. Darrell and A. Pentland, "Robust estimation of a multilay-ered motion representation", *Proc. IEEE Workshop on Visual Motion,* Princeton, 1991, pp. 173-178.

[2] A. Jepson and M. J. Black, "Mixture models for optical flow computation", *Proc. IEEE Conf. Comput. Vision Pettern Recog.,* New York, 1993, pp. 760-761.

[3] S. Hsu, P. Anandan, and S. Peleg, "Accurate computation of optical flow by using layered motion representation", *Proc. 12th Int'l Conf. Pattern Recog,* 1994.

[4] S. Ayer and H.S. Sawhney, "Layered representation of motion video using robust maximum likelihood estimation of mixture models and MDL encoding", *Proc. Int'l Conf. Comput. Vision,* 1995, pp. 777-784.

[5] M. Irani and S. Peleg, "Image sequence enhancement using multiple motions analysis", *Proc. IEEE Conf. Comput. Vision Pattern Recog.,* Champaign, Illinois, 1992, pp. 216-221.

[6] J. Y. A. Wang and E.H. Adelson, "Representing moving images with layers", *IEEE Trans. on Image Processing Special Issue: Image Sequence Compression,* Sept. 1994, 3(5): pp. 625-638.

[7] Y. Weiss, "Smoothness in Layers: Motion segmentation using nonparametric mixture estimation", *Proc. IEEE Conf. Comput. Vision Pattern Recog.,* Puerto Rico, 1997, pp. 520-526.

[8] A. P. Dempster, N.M. Laird, and D.B. Rubin "Maximum likelihood from incomplete data via the EM algorithm", *J.R. Statist. Soc. B,* 39:1-38, 1977.

[9] G. Guy and G. Medioni, "Inferring Global Perceptual Contours from Local Features", *IJCV,* vol. 20, no. 1/2, Oct 1996, pp. 113-133.

[10] G. H. Granlund and Knutsson, *Signal Processing for Computer Vision,* Kluwer Academic Publishers, 1995.

[11] W. E. Lorensen and H.E. Cline, "Marching Cubes: A High Resolution 3-D Surface Reconstruction Algorithm", *Computer Graphics,* vol. 21, no. 4, July, 1987.

[12] F. Heitz and P. Bouthemy, "Multimodal Estimation of Discontinuous Optical Flow Using Markov Random Fields", *PAMI,* vol. 15, no. 12, Dec. 1993, pp. 1217-1232.

[13] S. Ghosal, "A Fast Scalable Algorithm for Discontinuous Optical Flow Estimation", *PAMI,* vol. 18, no. 2, Feb. 1996, pp. 181-194.

[14] G. Guy and G. Medioni, "Inference of Surfaces, 3-D Curves and Junctions from Sparse, Noisy 3-D Data", *PAMI,* vol. 19, no. 11, Nov. 1997, pp. 1265-1277.

[15] L. Gaucher, G. Medioni, and J. Wilson, "Accurate Motion Flow Estimation Using a Multilayer Represenation", *CVPR Workshop on the Interpretation of Visual Motion,* June 22, 1998, Santa Barbara.

[16] J. L. Barron, D. J. Fleet, and S. S. Beauchemin, "Performance of Optical Flow Techniques", *IJCV,* vol. 12, no. 1, February 1994, pp. 43-77.

Real-Time Motion Analysis with Linear-Programming *

Moshe Ben-Ezra   Shmuel Peleg   Michael Werman

Institute of Computer Science
The Hebrew University of Jerusalem
91904 Jerusalem, Israel
Email: {moshe, peleg, werman}@cs.huji.ac.il

Abstract

A method to compute motion models in real time from point-to-line correspondences using linear programming is presented. Point-to-line correspondences are the most reliable motion measurements given the aperture effect, and it is shown how they can approximate other motion measurements as well.

Using an L_1 error measure for image alignment based on point-to-line correspondences and minimizing this measure using linear programming, achieves results which are more robust than the commonly used L_2 metric. While estimators based on L_1 are not theoretically robust, experiments show that the proposed method is robust enough to allow accurate motion recovery in hundreds of consecutive frames. The entire computation is performed in real-time on a PC with no special hardware.

1 Introduction

Robust, real-time recovery of visual motion is essential for many vision based applications. Numerous methods have been developed for motion recovery from image sequences, among them are algorithms that compute the motion directly from the grey level or general local measures [7, 11, 9, 2]. A second class of algorithms use feature points to recover motion [4, 8]. A probabilistic error minimization algorithm [15] can be used to recover motion in the presence of outliers. Another class of algorithms use explicit probability distribution of the motion vectors to calculate motion models [13].

Most of the methods cited above have problems when computing high-order motion models (e.g. an affine motion model or a homography): either they are sensitive

*This research was funded by DARPA through the U.S. Army Research Labs under grant DAAL01-97-R-9291, Supported by Esprit project 26247 - Vigor

to outliers, or the execution speed is very slow. An algorithm is presented to recover such high-order motion models from point-to-line correspondences using linear-programming. Point-to-line correspondences are robust in the sense that they are largely insensitive to aperture effects and to T-junctions, unlike the common point-to-point correspondences. Point-to-line correspondences can also approximate other measurements as well, such as point-to-point correspondences, correspondences with uncertainty, and spatio-temporal constraints.

The L_1 metric ($\sum |a_i - b_i|$) can be used with the point-to-line correspondences, and is much more robust then the L_2 metric ($\sqrt{\sum (a_i - b_i)^2}$), for example, the median minimizes the L_1 metric, while the centroid (average) minimizes the L_2 metric. L_1 estimators are not considered truly robust [5, 14] as they can be sensitive to leverage points. However, our experiments show that linear-programming, minimizing an L_1 error measure is, robust enough to compute accurate motion of hundreds of frames, even with large moving objects in the scene. Moreover, this is done in real-time on a regular PC.

The linear programming solver does not need an initial guess, which is required for iterative re-weighted least-square algorithms (such as M-estimators). The re-weighting stage, which is similar to motion-segmentation, is sometimes as hard as the motion recovery itself. Comparisons between estimators based on the L_1 metric and the robust LMS (Least Median of Squares) estimators show that global motion analysis using the L_1 estimator is only slightly less robust than the LMS estimator, but the L_1 computation is much faster.

The alignment process has two steps. (i) Computing correspondences and representing them as point to line correspondences, is described in Sec. 2. (ii) Converting the alignment problem into a linear program using the point to line correspondences, and solving it, described in Sec. 3. Sec. 4 describes experimental results and comparisons with other methods. Sec. 5 gives concluding remarks. Appendix A

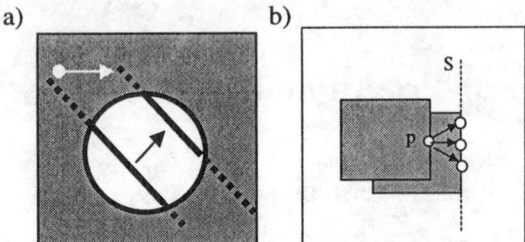

Figure 1. Aperture Effect. a) The white arrow represents the actual motion, while the black arrow represents the apparent motion. b) Point to line correspondence.

describes a possible explanation for the experimental insensitivity of L_1 motion estimators to leverage points.

2 Point to Line Correspondences

Point to line correspondence are used for their insensitivity to the aperture effect. This section describes the aperture effect, and the use of point to line correspondences to represent normal flow and uncertain correspondences.

2.1 Aperture Effect

Fig. 1.a describes the aperture effect: The apparent motion of a line when viewed through a small aperture is normal to the line. Therefore, the motion of point p in Fig. 1.b is defined only up to a line. The constraint on the displacement (u, v) such that point $p = (x, y)$ in the first image has moved to the straight line $S(x + u, y + v)$ in the second image and is defined by the line equation:

$$S(x + u, y + v) \equiv A(x + u) + B(y + v) + C = 0 \quad (1)$$

Without loss of generality we assume for the rest of the paper that $A^2 + B^2 = 1$ by normalization.

2.2 Normal Flow

A constraint on the optical flow in every pixel can be derived directly from image intensities using the gray level constancy assumption. This optical-flow constraint is given by [7, 11]:

$$uI_x + vI_y + I_t = 0 \quad (2)$$

where (u, v) is the displacement vector for the pixel, and I_x, I_y, I_t are the partial derivatives of the image at the pixel with respect to x, y and time.

Eq. (2) describes a line, which is the aperture effect line. When $I_x^2 + I_y^2$ are normalized to 1 the left hand side of Eq. (2) becomes the Euclidean distance of the point (x, y) from the line passing through $(x + u, y + v)$, which is also called the normal flow [1].

2.3 Fuzzy Correspondence

An optical flow vector between successive images in a sequence represents the displacement between a point in one image to the corresponding point in the second image. While it is difficult to determine this point to point correspondence accurately from the images automatically, a correspondence is usually assigned to the most likely point. For example, given a point in one image, the corresponding point in the second image will be the one maximizing some correlation measure. However, such correspondences are error prone, especially when other points in the second image have a local neighborhood similar to the real corresponding point.

A possible solution to this problem is to postpone the determination of a unique correspondence to a later stage, and to represent the uncertainty as given by the correlation values. In this case the correspondence will not be a unique point, but a fuzzy measure over a set of possible corresponding points.

The fuzzy correspondence of a point p can be represented as a matrix $M(p)$ (the fuzzy correspondence matrix). Each cell (i, j) of $M(p)$ corresponds to the probability that point p has a displacement of (i, j) [13]. In many cases the fuzzy correspondence matrix has a dominant compact shape: points on corners usually create a strong compact peak while edges form lines. A common case is an ellipse. While the fuzzy correspondence matrix contains all correspondence uncertainty, utilizing this information to its full extent is difficult.

To enable computation of global motion with linear programming, we propose an approximation of the fuzzy correspondence matrix by two point to line correspondences. This approximation is given by two lines: $S_i(x, y) \equiv (A_i x + B_i y + C_i) = 0 \quad (i = 1, 2)$ with two associated weights, W_i. Fig. 2.a-b show a distance map of each point from a line. The weighted sum of both distances forms an L_1 "cone". Each equidistant line on the cone is an L_1 "ellipse" with eccentricity proportional to the weights of the two lines, as shown in Fig. 2.c

This approximation can also be used to express point-to-point correspondence: $(x, y) \to (x', y')$ can be approximated by two point to line correspondences: between point (x, y) and the line $(x = x')$, and between point (x, y) and the line $(y = y')$, with weights $W_1 = W_2$.

Given a fuzzy correspondence matrix, the approximation by the sum of distances from two lines can be computed using a Hough transform as described in [3]. The following constraint can be used in the linear programming for the displacement for point (x, y):

$$W_1 S_1(x + u, y + v) + W_2 S_2(x + u, y + v) = 0 \quad (3)$$

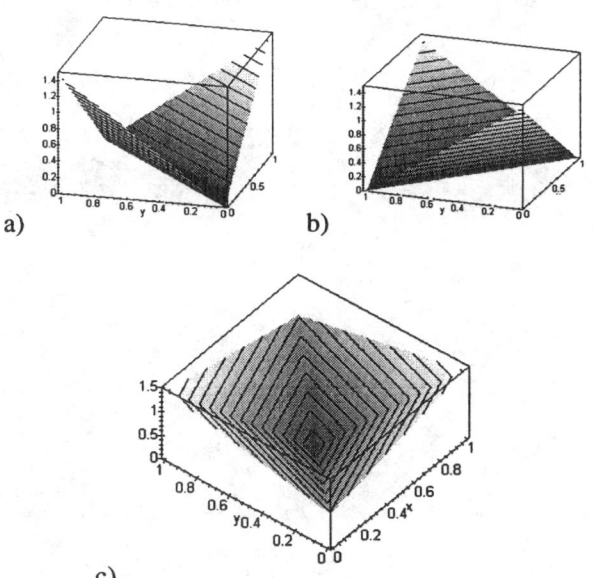

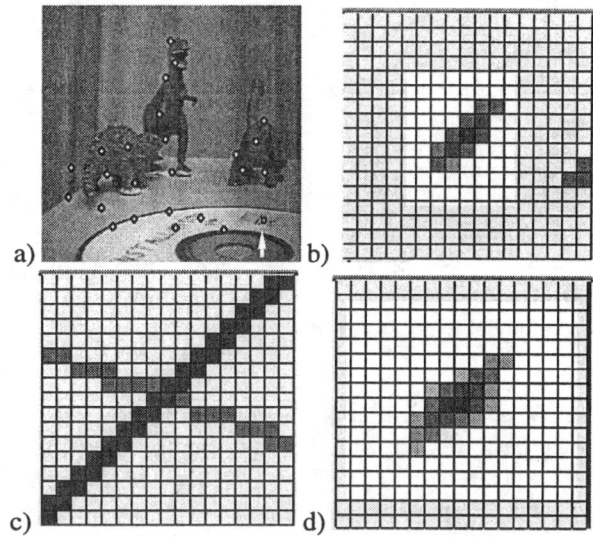

Figure 2. Approximation of an L_1 "ellipse" using two lines. a) Distance surface from one line. b) Distance surface from a second line. c) Weighted sum of distances from both lines, with weights of 2 from the first line and of 1 from the second line. Each equal-distance line is an L_1 "ellipse".

Figure 3. Approximations for fuzzy correspondences. b) The fuzzy correspondence matrix between successive images for the point that is marked with a white arrow in (a). c) The lines used to approximate the fuzzy correspondence matrix. Intensity corresponds to weight. d) Weighted sum of city-block distance from the two lines in (c) is used as the approximation of the fuzzy correspondence matrix in (b).

3 L_1 Alignment Using Linear Programming

The alignment process has two steps: (i) Computing correspondences and representing them as point-to-line correspondences. (ii) Converting the alignment problem into a linear-program using the point-to-line correspondences, and solving it. The first step was detailed in Sec. 2, and in this section the second step is described. In particular, we show how to compute an eight parameter 2D homography, which corresponds to the transformation between different views of a planar surface.

A homography H is represented by a 3×3 matrix, whose i'th row is designated H_i. A 2D point $p = (x, y, 1)^t$ (in homogeneous coordinates) located at image I_1 is mapped by the homography H into the 2D point p' in image I_2 as follows:

$$p' = \left(\frac{(H_1 \cdot p)}{(H_3 \cdot p)}, \frac{(H_2 \cdot p)}{(H_3 \cdot p)}, 1 \right)^t \qquad (4)$$

The Euclidean distance of point p' from constraint line $S = (Ax + By + C)$, using Eq. (4), is given by the following equation which is zero when the alignment is perfect.

$$d(p', S) = \left(\frac{A(H_1 \cdot p)}{(H_3 \cdot p)} + \frac{B(H_2 \cdot p)}{(H_3 \cdot p)} + C \right) \qquad (5)$$

Multiplying Eq. (5) by $(H_3 \cdot p)$ (which is non-zero for a finite size image) gives the following linear equation for the *residual error* of point p.

$$r(p', S) = d(p', S)(H_3 \cdot p) = A(H_1 \cdot p) + B(H_2 \cdot p) + C(H_3 \cdot p). \qquad (6)$$

Since, in order to get a linear equation, we multiply the geometrical distance $d(p', S)$ by the (unknown) value $(H_3 \cdot p)$, the coordinates of p should be normalized to avoid bias [6]. Setting the residual error $r(p', S)$ to zero gives a linear constraint on the elements of the homography H that states that point p is mapped to point p' which is on the line S.

In order to recover the eight parameters of the 2D homography H, at least eight such point-to-line correspondences are required. Each point-to-line correspondence gives one point-to-line equation, and each point to two-lines correspondence (the linear approximation to fuzzy correspondence) gives two point-to-line equations. When more than eight point-to-line correspondences are given, H can be recovered using L_1 by solving the following minimization problem:

$$Minimize: \sum_{i=1}^{n} W_i |r(p_i', S_i)|. \qquad (7)$$

This error minimization problem is converted into the following linear program, where one constraint equation is written for each point-to-line correspondence:

$$min: \sum_{i=1}^{n} W_i(Z_i^+ + Z_i^-)$$
$$s.t.$$
$$A_i(H_1 \cdot p_i) + B_i(H_2 \cdot p_i) + C_i(H_3 \cdot p_i) + (Z_i^+ - Z_i^-) = 0$$
$$Z_i^+, Z_i^- \geq 0$$

The expression $(Z_i^+ + Z_i^-)$ is the absolute value of the residual error, $r(p_i', S_i)$. The is the result of the use in linear programming of only positive values [10]. Each residual error is represented by the difference of two non-negative variables: $r(p_i', S_i) = (Z_i^+ - Z_i^-)$, one of which is always zero at the above minimum.

Notes:

1. When the constraints are of the form $Ax - b + Z = 0$, a basic feasible solution that satisfies the constraints is given by $x = 0, Z = b$. This enables the use of an efficient one-phase simplex algorithm to solve the problem.

2. This linear program can be used to minimize any linear equation: $Min(Ax - b)$. Parameter normalization or an additional constraint may be needed to avoid a zero root if $b = 0$.

3. If L is an $(M \times N)$ matrix, M is the number of constraint equations and N is the number of parameters $(M > N)$, then the linear program will have a total of $2(M + N)$ variables: $2N$ variables for the variable vector x, and $2M$ variables for the slack variable vector Z. The factor of two is needed since in linear programming each variable is represented by a difference of two non-negative variables.

4. The slack variable vector Z contains the error measures for each point and can be used for motion segmentation.

5. Additional linear constraints can be added to the recovered model. For example we can define a motion model that is more general than similarity but has bounded affine/projective distortions.

4 Experiments and Comparisons

To compare our model to existing point-to-point methods, we converted each point-to-point correspondence to two point-to-line correspondences according to Section 2.3. The panorama example used point-to-line correspondences computed from fuzzy correspondence matrices.

4.1 Mosaicing with Similarity Model

A panoramic image was created in real-time (10-12 frames / second) using a PC, as shown in Fig. 4.b. While the camera was scanning the scene, a large pendulum was

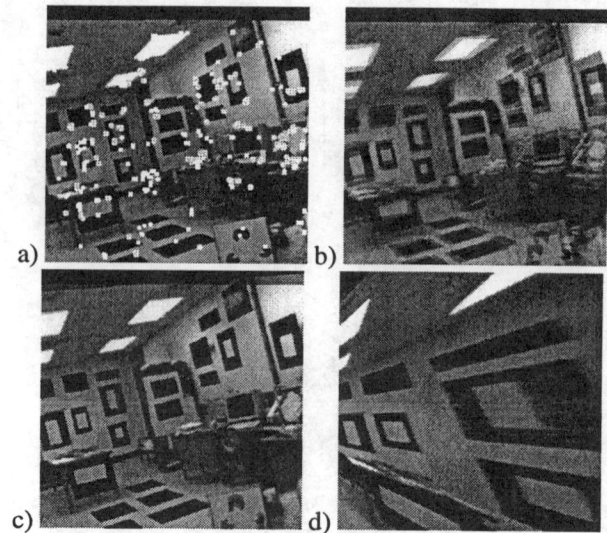

Figure 5. Computing homography using L_2 registration compared to L_1 registration. The same feature points were used in the L_1 minimization and the L_2 minimization. Both examples are single iteration output, no segmentation and no re-weighting were used. a) Selected feature points are marked on one images. b) The sum of the two original images to show their misalignment. c) The sum of the images aligned with the homography obtained using linear programming. d) Warping the second image towards the first image with the homography obtained using a least-square method.

swinging. The size of the pendulum was large enough to create about 15% outliers among the feature points. Since the stabilization algorithm used only frame to frame motion recovery, *any* error will cause the panorama to fail. Fig. 4 shows the pendulum (and its shadow) appearing/disappearing several times due to the swinging motion. However *all* frames were correctly aligned with a similarity model as can be seen by the objects that were not occluded by the pendulum.

4.2 Homographies: Comparison with L_2

This experiment compares the computation of a 2D homography using L_1 registration to the least-squares method for point-to-point registration. Given two images, the feature points were selected automatically from a bi-directional optical-flow field. Each selected point had a strong intensity gradient, and the optical flow from the first to the second image agreed with the optical flow from the second to the first image. Selected points are shown in Fig. 5.a.

The homography that minimizes the L_2 distance between the computed correspondences is shown in Fig. 5.d. It is completely useless due to outliers.

a) b)

Figure 4. Mosaicing examples. a) Point selected for motion computation. Four of the thirty points are located on the moving pendulum. b) Panoramic image that was created while a pendulum was swinging. The alignment was not affected by the outliers.

The L_1 alignment used the same data, but converted each point-to-point correspondence into two point-to-line correspondences (point (u, v) is converted to the two lines $(x = u)$ and $(y = v)$). Fig. 5.c shows the sum of the two images after alignment. The alignment is now very good, and can be compared to Fig. 5.b where the two images were added before alignment.

4.3   Computing Affine Motion from Normal Flow

An affine alignment between two images can be computed from normal flow by an iterative method. In this example 112 points residing on strong edges and spread evenly across the image were selected automatically. The iterations were as follows:

1. The normal flow is computed from spatio-temporal derivatives and represented by a line constraint as described in Sec. 2.2.

2. An affine motion model was computed using linear programming from the linear constraints.

3. The second image was warped toward the first image using the affine model.

4. Repeat steps 1-3 until convergence.

The iterations are necessary in this case since the accuracy of the normal flow depends on the accuracy of the spatio-temporal derivatives, which increases as the motion estimate becomes better. Fig. 6 shows the registration results for the L_1 registration by normal flow lines.

4.4   Efficiency Considerations

The linear programming approach is compared to the following well known probabilistic algorithm [15]:

Input: N matched pairs (either point to point or point to line).

Output: A linear motion model M^* of rank k that minimizes the sum of the absolute values of the residual errors.

Algorithm :

1. k pairs are selected randomly.

2. The motion model M is computed from the k selected pairs.

3. The sum of residual L_1 errors is computed from all pairs, using the recovered model.

4. The last three steps are repeated for t iterations.

5. Of all examined models, the model M^* having minimal error is selected.

If the probability of choosing an outlier is q, then in t iterations the probability P of having at least one perfect guess, with no outliers in all k selected points, is given by:

$$P = 1 - \left[1 - (1 - q)^k\right]^t. \tag{8}$$

Given the desired probability of success P, the number of necessary iterations t is given by

$$t = ln(1 - P)/ln(1 - (1 - q)^k). \tag{9}$$

The number of iterations required to reach a certain level of confidence is exponential in k and in q, and therefore this method is very expensive in these cases. The complexity of the linear program is polynomial in the number of constraints, which equals the number of correspondences. In most practical cases, however, the complexity is known to be nearly linear.

4.4.1   Synthetic Performance Experiment

In this test we tried to compare the actual performance of the two algorithms. The test consisted of the following synthetic data:
Number of matched pairs: 100 point to point correspondences.

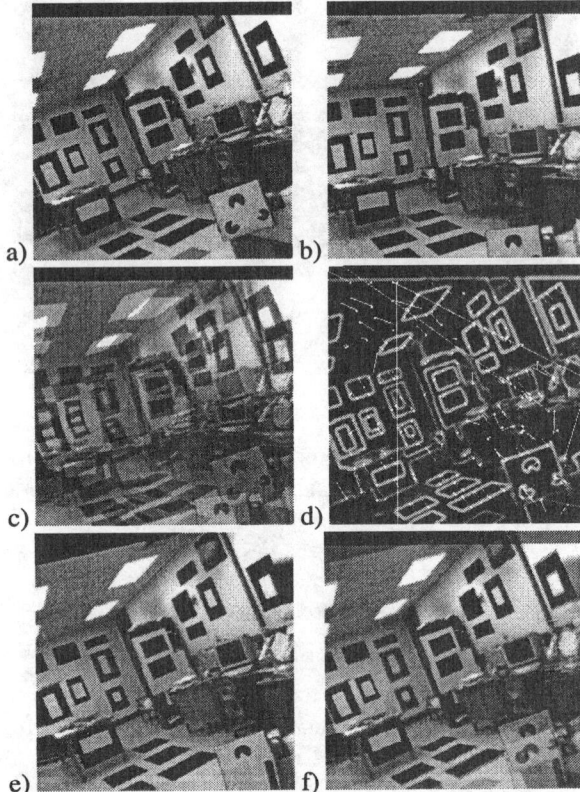

Figure 6. Normal-flow point-to-line L_1 registration. a) First image. b) Second image. c) Summation of (a) and (b) shows the displacement between the two images. d) Magnified Normal flow of the selected points at the last iteration, displayed over a gradient map. The outliers are easy to spot. e) (b) warped towards (a) using the affine model computed by L_1 alignment. f) Summation of (a) and (e) shows good alignment in most of the scene.

Rank of linear model: $k = 4$.

Outliers probability: $q = 0.4$ (three motion models, matched pairs are distributed as follows: 20, 60, 20).

Added Noise: Normal distribution with zero mean and variance is 5% of the range. Even though the probabilistic algorithm was able to execute 7000 iterations during the time the single-iteration linear programming executed, the results obtained were inferior to linear programming as seen in Fig. 9.

4.4.2   Real-Time Performance

Programs for video mosaicing and for image stabilization were written based on fuzzy correspondences (Sec 2.3). Execution on a PC using windows NT with no special hardware an image sequence was directly processed from the camera at 10-12 frames per second. The panoramas in Fig. 4 were created in real-time using this program.

5   Concluding Remarks

This paper presented a new approach for real-time motion analysis by converting image measurements into point-to-line correspondences, and computing the motion model using linear programming. The presented approach was shown in many experiments to be resistant to outliers, efficient, and enables real-time performance on a regular PC.

Although other estimators, e.g. the LMS estimator, may be superior to the L_1 estimator, the L_1 estimator is recommended for many applications which have a large number of parameters. An analysis regarding the effects of leverage points on the L_1 metric in the image analysis domain is described in the Appendix, as well as a comparison between a least L_1 estimator and LMS.

References

[1] Y. Aloimonos and Z. Duric. Estimating the heading direction using normal flow. *IJCV*, 13(1):33–56, September 1994.

[2] P. Anandan. A computational framework and an algorithm for the measurement of visual motion. *Int. J. of Computer Vision*, 2:283–310, 1989.

[3] M. Ben-Ezra, S. Peleg, and M. Werman. Robust real-time motion analysis. In *DARPA98*, pages 207–210, 1998.

[4] O. Faugeras, F. Lustman, and G. Toscani. Motion and structure from motion from point and line matching. In *Int. Conf. on Computer Vision*, pages 25–34, 1987.

[5] R. P. Hampel F.R., Ronchetti E.M. and S. W.A. *Robust Statistics: The Approach based on influence Functions*. New York: John Wiley, 1986.

[6] R. Hartley. Minimizing algebraic error in geometric estimation problems. In *ICCV98*, pages 469–476, 1998.

[7] B. Horn and B. Schunck. Determining optical flow. In *AI*, volume 17, pages 185–203, 1981.

[8] T. Huang and A. Netravali. Motion and structure from feature correspondences: A review. *PIEEE*, 82(2):252–268, February 1994.

[9] M. Irani and P. Anandan. Robust multi-sensor image alignment. In *ICCV98*, pages 959–966, 1998.

[10] H. Karloff. *Linear Programming*. Birkhäuser Verlag, Basel, Switzerland, 1991.

[11] B. Lucas and T. Kanade. An iterative image registration technique with an application to stereo vision. In *IJCAI81*, pages 674–679, 1981.

[12] P. Meer, D. Mintz, and A. Rosenfeld. Analysis of the least median of squares estimator for computer vision applications. In *CVPR92*, pages 621–623, 1992.

[13] Y. Rosenberg and M. Werman. Representing local motion as a probability distribution matrix and object tracking. In *DARPA Image Undersading Workshop*, pages 153–158, 1997.

[14] P. Rousseeuw. Least median of squares regression. *Journal of American Statistical Association*, 79:871–880, 1984.

[15] P. Torr and D. Murray. Outlier detection and motion segmentation. In *SPIE*, volume 2059, pages 432–443, 1993.

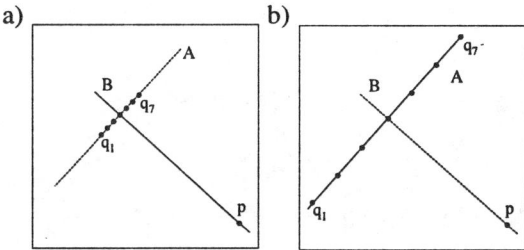

Figure 7. Leverage points for line regression.

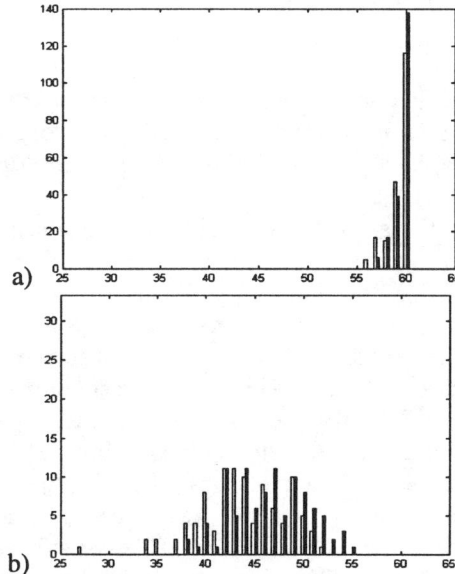

Figure 8. Monte-Carlo comparison between least L_1 and LMS. The histograms show the number of correct classifications. White bars corresponds to the L_1 recovered model. Black bars corresponds to the LMS recovered model. a) Low noise level. b) High noise level.

A L_1 Leverage Points in Motion Analysis

The L_1 metric has a breakpoint zero. This means that even a single outlier point can flip the recovered model very far from the real model. Such points are called leverage points. An example of a leverage point is shown in Fig. 7.a. Line A is the real model, points $q_1..q_7$ are located on line A. Point p satisfies: $L_1(p, A) > \sum_{i=1}^{n} L_1(q_i, B)$, where $L_1(a, b)$ represents the L_1 distance between a and b. This causes the model to flip into line B. Figure 7.b describes a very similar setup with points $q_1..q_7$ spread along the line A. This time there is no single point in the bounded-rectangle that qualifies as a leverage point. There is no "room" for a "lever" long enough to flip the model. In this particular case the breakpoint of the L_1 metric is larger than zero - we then refer to line A as the "dominant line".

In practice, the background of a scene usually forms a

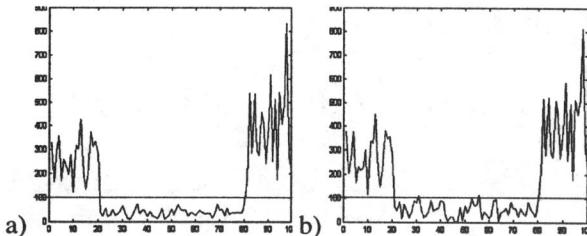

Figure 9. Comparing performance of linear-programming and a probabilistic algorithm running for the same time. 60 of the 100 points are in the desired model ($q = 0.4$). a) Error plot for the linear programming solution. clean separation is obtained. b) Error plot for the probabilistic algorithm solution. Separation between inliers and outliers is possible, but not for all points.

large model that is spread across the image, and thus is not subject to leverage points within the image boundaries. This behavior was confirmed by hours of testing in real-time rate (10-12 fps) and by synthetic Monte-Carlo tests presented in Sec. A.1.

A.1 Comparing L_1 and LMS Estimators

The Least Median of Squares (LMS) estimator is a well known robust estimator [12, 14] which has a theoretical model breakpoint of 0.5 (i.e. it can tolerate up to 50% outliers). This is better than the theoretical breakpoint of the least L_1 estimator, which is zero.

Fig. 8 shows the results of comparing LMS with least L_1 on synthetic data using a Monte-Carlo method. Given two similar linear transformations (4 by 4 matrices), a single test consisted of randomly selecting 100 points (3D projective points), transforming 60 points with one model and 40 points with the second model, and then adding random noise to the transformed points. Given this data, the linear transformation was recovered one time using LMS and one time using a least L_1 estimator. The accuracy of a recovered transformation was computed by counting the number of correct classifications: The transformation was applied to the original points, and the points were sorted based on their error from the transformed points. In perfect conditions, all 60 points having lowest error should come from the first model. The "correct classifications" is the number of points actually coming from the first model among the 60 points having lowest errors. The test was performed 200 times, each time with a new set of points. The histogram in Fig. 8 shows for each number of correct classifications how many times it occurred among the 200 tests. as can be seen, the LMS has a shift to the right which means that it has more correct classifications. Therefore the LMS is better that the least L_1, but only slightly in the global motion analysis domain.

Multi-View Subspace Constraints on Homographies

Lihi Zelnik-Manor   Michal Irani

Dept. of Computer Science and Applied Math
The Weizmann Institute of Science
76100 Rehovot, Israel
Email: {lihi,irani}@wisdom.weizmann.ac.il

Abstract

The motion of a planar surface between two camera views induces a homography. The homography depends on the camera intrinsic and extrinsic parameters, as well as on the $3D$ plane parameters. While camera parameters vary across different views, the plane geometry remains the same. Based on this fact, we derive *linear* subspace constraints on the relative motion of multiple (≥ 2) planes across multiple views.

The paper has three main contributions: (i) We show that the collection of all relative homographies of a *pair* of planes (homologies) across *multiple* views, spans a 4-dimensional linear subspace. (ii) We show how this constraint can be extended to the case of *multiple planes* across *multiple views*. (iii) We suggest two potential application areas which can benefit from these constraints: (a) The accuracy of homography estimation can be improved by enforcing the multi-view subspace constraints. (b) Violations of these multi-view constraints can be used as a cue for moving object detection. All the results derived in this paper are true for *uncalibrated cameras*.

1 Introduction

Homography estimation is used for $3D$ analysis [8, 9, 11, 4, 2, 6, 7], mosaicing [5], camera calibration [12], and more. The induced homography between a pair of views depends on the camera intrinsic and extrinsic parameters, and on the $3D$ plane parameters [1]. While camera parameters vary across different views, the plane geometry remains the same. In this paper we show how we can exploit this fact to derive multi-view *linear* subspace constraints on the relative motion of multiple (≥ 2) planes.

Linear subspace constraints on homographies have been previously derived by Shashua and Avidan [10]. They showed that the collection of homographies of *multiple planes* between a *pair of views*, spans a 4-dimensional linear subspace. This constraint requires the number of planes in the scene to be greater than 4. In this paper we first derive a "dual" constraint,

for a *pair* planes over *multiple (> 4) views* (Section 3). This constraint is then extended to a constraint on homographies of *multiple planes* across *multiple views* (Section 4).

Algorithms for $3D$ analysis which are based on the use of multiple homographies (in scenes with *multiple planes*) have been suggested (e.g., [8, 9, 13, 7]). Most of these algorithms rely on *accurate* precomputation of the homographies. However, in scenes containing multiple planes, the image region corresponding to each plane may be small. In such cases, the homography estimation tends to be highly inaccurate [11] (i.e, when applied to small image regions). In this paper we show how the accuracy of homography estimation can be improved by employing the multi-view subspace constraints (Section 5.1). We also show how *violations* of these multi-view constraints can be used as a cue for moving object detection (Section 5.2).

All the results derived in this paper are true for *uncalibrated camera*.

2 Homographies - Basic Notations

Let $\vec{Q} = (X, Y, Z)^t$ and $\vec{Q'} = (X', Y', Z')^t$ denote a scene point with respect to two different camera views, respectively. Let $\vec{q} = (x, y, 1)^t$ and $\vec{q'} = (x', y', 1)^t$ denote the corresponding points in the two images. We can write:

$$\vec{q} \cong C\vec{Q} \quad , \quad \vec{q'} \cong C'\vec{Q'} \tag{1}$$

where $\cong$ denotes equality up to a scale factor. C and C' are 3×3 matrices [1] (composed of camera internal parameters and projection).

Let π be a planar surface with plane normal $\vec{n}$, then $\vec{n}^t\vec{Q} = 1$ for all points $\vec{Q} \in \pi$ ($\vec{n} = \frac{\vec{m}}{d_\pi}$, where $\vec{m}$ is a unit vector in the direction of the plane normal, and d_π is the distance of the plane from the first camera center). The transformation between the $3D$ coordinates of a scene point $Q \in \pi$ in the two views, can be expressed by:

$$\vec{Q'} = G\vec{Q} \tag{2}$$

710

where

$$G = R + \vec{t}\vec{n}^t \tag{3}$$

R is the rotation matrix and $\vec{t}$ is the translation of the camera. Therefore, the induced transformation between the corresponding *image* points is:

$$\vec{q'} \cong H\vec{q} \tag{4}$$

where

$$H = C'(R + \vec{t}\cdot\vec{n}^t)C^{-1} \tag{5}$$

is the induced homography between the two views of the plane π. From Eq. (4) it is clear that when H is computed from image point correspondences, it can be estimated only up to a scale factor.

3   Multi-View Two-Plane Constraint

Let J be a "reference" image, and let $K^1, \ldots, K^F$ be F other images of the same scene taken from different views. Let π_r, π_p be two planar surfaces in the scene with plane normals $\vec{n}_r$ and $\vec{n}_p$, respectively. Let H_r^f and H_p^f denote their corresponding homographies between the reference image J and an image K^f ($f = 1, \ldots, F$). Composing the homography of π_p with the *inverse* of the homography of π_r yields a "relative homography":

$$H_{pr}^f = (H_r^f)^{-1} H_p^f \tag{6}$$

This is also known as a "plane homology" [3, 7]. Some properties and invariants of planar homologies have been discussed in [3], and used in [7]. Here we present a different set of constraints on homologies.

Using Eq. (5) and the Sherman-Morisson formula[1] [14], it can be shown that, for rigidly moving planes π_r and π_p, the matrix H_{pr}^f has the form:

$$
\begin{aligned}
H_{pr}^f &= I + \vec{v}^f \vec{n}_{pr}^t \\
&\equiv \begin{bmatrix} 1+h_1 & h_2 & h_3 \\ h_4 & 1+h_5 & h_6 \\ h_7 & h_8 & 1+h_9 \end{bmatrix}
\end{aligned} \tag{7}
$$

where $\vec{v}^f = C \frac{R^{f-1}\vec{t}^f}{1+\vec{n}_r^t R^{f-1}\vec{t}^f}$, $\vec{n}_{pr} = (\vec{n}_p - \vec{n}_r) C^{-1}$, I is a 3×3 identity matrix and $\vec{t}^f, R^f$ are the camera translation and the camera rotation matrix, between the reference image J and the image K^f. C is the camera

---

[1]For a square matrix A, and two column vectors $\vec{u}$, $\vec{w}$, the Sherman-Morrison formula gives:

$$(A + \vec{u}\vec{w}^t)^{-1} = A^{-1} - \frac{(A^{-1}\vec{u})(\vec{w}^t A^{-1})}{I + \vec{w}^t A^{-1}\vec{u}}$$

projection matrix at the reference view J. Note that C^f (i.e., the projection matrix of K^f) is eliminated by the composition. Note that $\vec{v}^f$ is view-dependent, i.e., is common to all rigidly moving planes between a pair of views J and K^f, whereas $\vec{n}_{pr}$ is plane-dependent, i.e., is common to all views for a pair of planes π_r and π_p.

Rearranging the components of the relative-homography (3×3) matrix H_{pr}^f in a single (9×1) column vector $\vec{h}_{pr}^f$, we can rewrite Eq. (7) as:

$$
\vec{h}_{pr}^f = \mathcal{N}_{pr} \begin{bmatrix} v_X^f \\ v_Y^f \\ v_Z^f \\ 1 \end{bmatrix} = \mathcal{N}_{pr} \begin{bmatrix} \vec{v}^f \\ 1 \end{bmatrix} \tag{8}
$$

where

$$
\mathcal{N}_{pr} = \begin{bmatrix}
n_{pr_X} & 0 & 0 & 1 \\
n_{pr_Y} & 0 & 0 & 0 \\
n_{pr_Z} & 0 & 0 & 0 \\
0 & n_{pr_X} & 0 & 0 \\
0 & n_{pr_Y} & 0 & 1 \\
0 & n_{pr_Z} & 0 & 0 \\
0 & 0 & n_{pr_X} & 0 \\
0 & 0 & n_{pr_Y} & 0 \\
0 & 0 & n_{pr_Z} & 1
\end{bmatrix} \tag{9}
$$

In practice $\vec{h}_{pr}^f$ are estimated only up to an unknown scale factor λ_{pr}^f (see Eq. (4)). Hence, the *computed* relative homographies, denoted by $\tilde{\vec{h}}_{pr}^f$, are

$$\tilde{\vec{h}}_{pr}^f = \lambda_{pr}^f \vec{h}_{pr}^f \tag{10}$$

We now consider *multiple* views $K^f, f = 1 \ldots F$. Since the matrix $\mathcal{N}_{pr}$ depends only on plane normal parameters, and on the camera calibration of the *reference* view, it is common to all views $f = 1 \ldots F$, whose homographies are estimated relative to the reference frame J. Hence, we can stack all computed relative homography vectors in a $9 \times F$ matrix $\mathcal{H}_{pr}$, where each column corresponds to a single image view K^f (relative to the reference view J):

$$
\begin{aligned}
[\mathcal{H}_{pr}]_{9 \times F} &= \begin{bmatrix} \tilde{\vec{h}}_{pr}^1 & \cdots & \tilde{\vec{h}}_{pr}^F \end{bmatrix}_{9 \times F} = \\
[\mathcal{N}_{pr}]_{9 \times 4} &\begin{bmatrix} \vec{v}^1 & \cdots & \vec{v}^F \\ 1 & & 1 \end{bmatrix}_{4 \times F} \begin{bmatrix} \lambda_{pr}^1 & & 0 \\ & \ddots & \\ 0 & & \lambda_{pr}^F \end{bmatrix}
\end{aligned} \tag{11}
$$

The dimensionality of the matrices on the right hand side of Eq. (11) implies that the matrix $\mathcal{H}_{pr}$ is of rank 4 at most[2]. Hence the collection of all relative-homographies of the two planes across all images, resides in a 4-dimensional linear subspace. This constraint is complementary to the constraint shown by Shashua and Avidan [10]. There, it was shown that the collection of homographies of *multiple* (> 4) *planes* between a *pair* (2) *of views*, spans a 4-dimensional linear subspace. In contrast, here we derived a rank-4 constraint for a *pair* (2) of planes over *multiple* (> 4) *views*.

4 Multi-View Multi-Plane Constraints

As explained above, homographies are determined only up to a scale factor. This scale factor differs for every pair of planes and for every pair of views. Therefore, the extension of the two-plane multi-view factorization (Section 3), or the two-view multi-plane factorization [10], into a *multi-view multi-plane* factorization is not straightforward. To extend the low-dimensionality linear subspace constraint to multiple-planes, we constrain the scale factors, denoted by λ_{pr}^f, to be a product of two scalars: one of which is view-dependent and one which is plane-dependent. This can be done with no calibration information.

Let $\pi_1, \ldots, \pi_P$ be P planar surfaces with normals $\vec{n}_1, \ldots, \vec{n}_P$, respectively. Let $H_1^f, \ldots, H_P^f$ be their corresponding homography matrices between the reference view J and the other views $K^f (f = 1 \ldots F)$. Let π_r be a *reference plane* (e.g., could be chosen as the plane occupying the largest image region in the reference image). Assuming the relative homographies $H_{pr}^f (f = 1, \ldots, F; p = 1, \ldots, P)$, with respect to the reference plane π_r and the reference image J, have been computed and are known up to a scale factor, we can arbitrarily set one of the six off-diagonal entries in the *relative homographies* H_{pr}^f to be equal to 1 (i.e., h_2, h_3, h_4, h_6, h_7 or h_8; See Eq. (7)), while the other entries are scaled accordingly. This results in a scale factor λ_{pr}^f, for the relative homographies, which can be factored into a bilinear product of two scalars:

$$\lambda_{pr}^f = \alpha^f \cdot \beta_p$$

where α^f is view-dependent, and β_p is plane-dependent (e.g., if we choose $h_3 = 1$, then we get: $\lambda_{pr}^f = \frac{1}{h_3} = \frac{1}{v_x^f} \cdot \frac{1}{n_{prz}}$, i.e., $\alpha^f = \frac{1}{v_x^f}$ and $\beta_p = \frac{1}{n_{prz}}$). Note that α^f is common to all planes and β_p is common to all views. Since all planar surfaces π_p share the same $3D$ camera motion between a pair of views, we get from Eq. (11):

---

[2]In practice the actual rank may be even lower than 4, e.g., in cases of degenerate camera motion.

$$\mathcal{H} = \left[\begin{array}{c} \mathcal{H}_{1r} \\ \vdots \\ \hline \mathcal{H}_{Pr} \end{array} \right]_{9P \times F} = B \cdot \mathcal{N} \cdot V \cdot A \qquad (12)$$

where,

$$
\begin{aligned}
B &= \left[\begin{array}{ccc} \beta_1 & & 0 \\ & \ddots & \\ 0 & & \beta_P \end{array} \right]_{9P \times 9P} \\
\mathcal{N} &= \left[\begin{array}{c} \mathcal{N}_{1r} \\ \vdots \\ \hline \mathcal{N}_{Pr} \end{array} \right]_{9P \times 4} \\
V &= \left[\begin{array}{ccc} \vec{v}^1 & \cdots & \vec{v}^F \\ 1 & & 1 \end{array} \right]_{4 \times F} \\
A &= \left[\begin{array}{ccc} \alpha^1 & & 0 \\ & \ddots & \\ 0 & & \alpha^F \end{array} \right]_{F \times F}
\end{aligned}
\qquad (13)
$$

The dimensionality of the matrices on the right hand side of Eq. (12) implies that, the matrix $\mathcal{H}$ is of rank 4 at most.

This implies that when solving for the homographies while consistently setting one of the six off-diagonal entries of the relative homographies to be 1, we are guaranteed that the collection of all relative homographies, of *all planes* across *all views*, lies in a 4-dimensional linear subspace. This scaling of the relative homographies is possible only when at least one of the six off-diagonal entries is different from zero for all planes, in all views. An example where this fails to exist is the identity matrix, which is the case of no motion.

5 Applications

In this section we present two different potential uses of the multi-view subspace constraints presented in Sections 3 and 4. In Section 5.1 it is shown how the accuracy of two-view homography estimation can be improved by constraining it with information from multiple images, using the multi-view subspace constraints. In Section 5.2 we show how *violations* of the multi-view subspace constraints can be used as a cue for detection of moving objects.

The purpose of this section is to convey the strength and potential use of these constraints, and *not* to present a particular algorithm.

5.1 Constrained Homography Computation

Homography estimation techniques perform well when the planar surface captures a large image region.

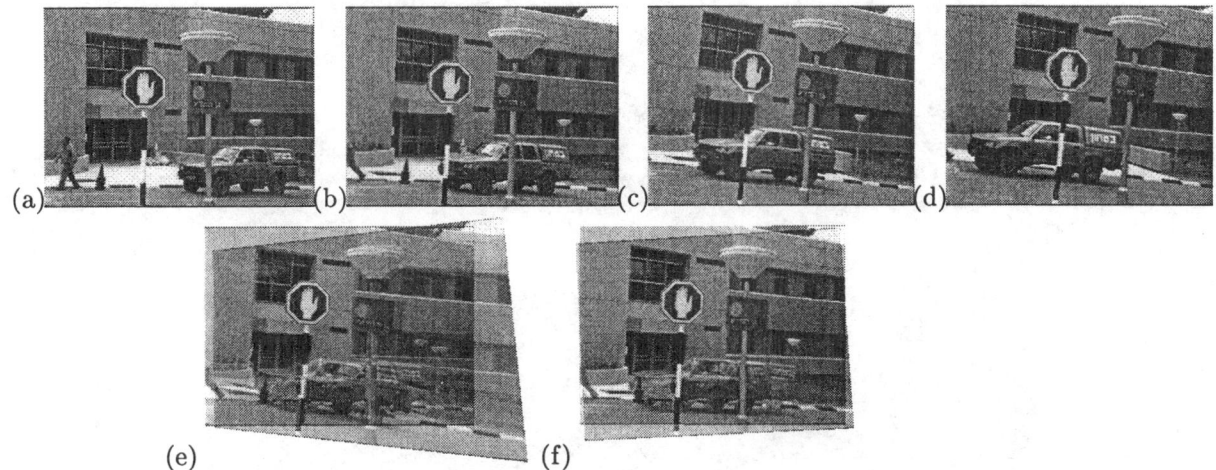

Figure 1: Constrained homography estimation. *(a,b,c,d) sample images from a collection of 25 images obtained from different camera positions. Image 1.b was used as the reference image. (e) Example of bad results from unconstrained two-view homography estimation of the stop sign region. The homography was estimated between the reference view 1.b and view 1.c. All the point correspondences were located on the sign itself and none on the pole. The displayed result is an overlay of the two images after registration according to the unconstrained homography. Although the stop-sign appears aligned, the rest of the image is completely distorted. Note that the pole of the stop-sign is already misaligned, although it lies on the same plane as the sign, and is very close to the region of analysis. (f) The corresponding result from applying the constrained two-plane multi-view homography estimation scheme, to the same region of analysis. The building was used as a reference plane (see text). The stop-sign is well aligned, including the pole, and the building displays accurate 3D parallax. For color images see CD-ROM version.*

However, they tend to be highly inaccurate when applied to small image regions [11], as is often the case in scenes with *multiple* planar surfaces.

While each independent homography computation is unreliable, all homographies of all planes, across all views must satisfy the multi-view subspace constraints. These constraints can therefore be used to compensate for insufficient spatial information.

Below we suggest one possible approach for taking advantage of the multi-view subspace constraints in the homography estimation:

(i) Define one image as the reference image J. Use any existing method to estimate initial homographies, for all planes and all images, with respect to the reference image.

(ii) Define one of the planes to be a reference plane π_r (e.g., choose π_r to be the plane with the largest image region in J, or the one with the most reliable initial homographies). Compute all the *relative homographies* (homologies, see Eq. (6)), of all other planes for all images, with respect to it.

(iii) If the number of planes $= 2$, do *not* perform any scaling. Otherwise ($\#planes > 2$) examine the entries $h_2, h_3, h_4, h_6, h_7, h_8$ of all relative homographies and choose the one which consistently differs from zero in all of them. Scale the relative homographies such that the chosen entry becomes 1.

(iv) Stack all relative homographies into a $9P \times F$ matrix $\mathcal{H}$ (see Eq. (12)).

(v) Project the columns of the matrix $\mathcal{H}$ onto a low-dimensional linear subspace, by constraining its rank to be ≤ 4. This gives a matrix $\hat{\mathcal{H}}$. (The choice of the actual rank of $\hat{\mathcal{H}}$, which may be even smaller than 4, can be done by examining the rate of decay of the matrix singular values).

(vi) Refine the estimation of the individual homographies by computing: $H_p^f = H_r^f \hat{H}_{pr}^f$, where $H_r^f =$ *reference* homography and $\hat{H}_{pr}^f =$ is the subspace-projected *relative* homography (both in the regular 3×3 matrix form).

(vii) If you're using an iterative framework to solve for the homographies, repeat steps (i) to (vi) at each iteration.

Fig. 1 shows a comparison of applying *two*-view and *multi*-view homography estimation to small image regions. 25 images were taken from different viewing positions. Because the camera is imaging the scene from a short distance, and because its motion contains a translation, different planar surfaces (e.g., the building, the stop-sign, etc.) induce different homogra-

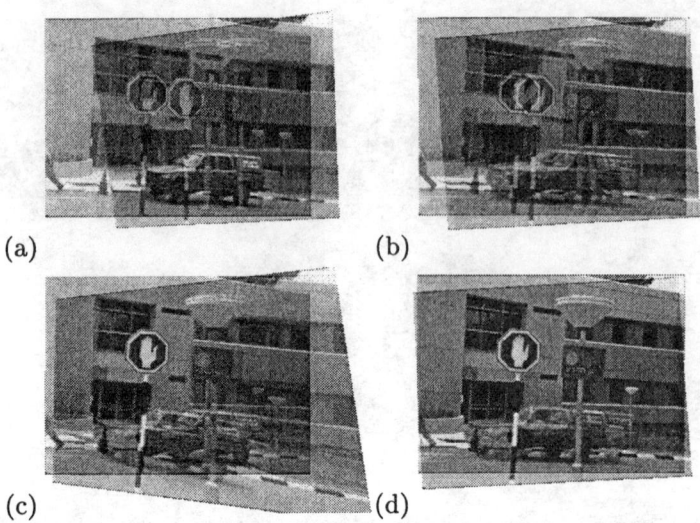

(a)　　　　　　　　　(b)

(c)　　　　　　　　　(d)

Figure 2: Moving object detection.　　(a) Example of unconstrained two-view homography estimation of the car region, between the reference view 1.b and view 1.c. The car appears well aligned after registration and overlay of the two images according to the unconstrained homography. (b,c) The corresponding results from applying the constrained multi-plane multi-view homography estimation scheme, to the car and the stop-sign simultaneously, using the building as a reference plane. Since the car motion is inconsistent with those of the stop-sign and building motion, applying the multi-plane multi-view constraint spoils the homography estimation of both the car (shown in (2.b), where the car is no longer aligned), and the stop-sign (shown in (2.c), where the pole is not aligned). (d) In contrast, the corresponding result from applying the constrained multi-plane multi-view homography estimation scheme, to the stop-sign and the other road-sign simultaneously. The stop-sign is now well aligned, and the rest of the image displays accurate 3D parallax.

phies. The induced homographies of the building were first estimated, using a two-view estimation method. Since it occupies a large image region, these were computed accurately enough. The building was chosen as the reference plane, hence, its computed homographies were used as inputs for constraining the estimation of the homographies corresponding to the other planes in the scene, using the approach described above. Because the stop-sign occupies a very small image region, an unconstrained *two-view* homography estimation of the stop-sign gave distorted results (see Fig. 1.e). The *two-plane multi-view* homography estimation, on the other hand, gave good results for all images, eventhough applied to the same small region (see Fig. 1.f). For the purpose of these experiments the homographies where estimated using Least-Squares fit to precomputed point correspondences.

5.2　Moving Object Detection

The multi-view subspace constraints of Sections 3 and 4 are true only for planar surfaces moving rigidly with respect to each other. Planar surfaces with different 3D motions will not necessarily comply with these constraints. Given two planar surfaces (π_r and π_p), we can construct the matrix $\mathcal{H}_{pr}$ of their relative homographies (see Eq. (11)) and examine its rank. If $rank(\mathcal{H}_{pr}) > 4$ then the two planes cannot be rigid with respect to each other. Note that this is a *sufficient* condition, but not a necessary one. In the case of *multiple* planes, we can do the same with the matrix $\mathcal{H}$ of Eq. (12), after appropriate scaling (see Section 4).

In the presence of noise, however, the rank of the matrix $\mathcal{H}$ may appear to be larger than 4 even for rigid planes. To avoid misinterpretation due to errors in the homography estimation, and to detect rank violations which are truly due to inconsistent 3D motion, we take the following approach: We apply the multi-view rigidity scheme presented in Section 5.1 to *improve* the estimation of the individual homographies and their relative-homographies, as if the planes were rigid with respect to each other. If the planes are in fact rigid with respect to each other, (i.e., have the same 3D motions across all views) then this process will improve their homography estimation. (This can be verified e.g., by comparing the accuracy of alignment before and after applying the rank estimation). If, on the other hand, the planes are not rigid with respect to each other (i.e., have different 3D motions across *some* views), then forcing the multi-view low-dimensionality constraint will *spoil* the homography estimation, leading to larger misalignment errors. This is detected as a case of inconsistent $3D$ motion.

Fig. 2 presents the results of applying the multi-plane multi-view homography estimation to non-rigidly moving objects. The scene contains a car, moving independently of the camera motion. Using the previously computed homographies of the building region as a reference plane, we applied the multi-plane multi-view scheme, of Section 5.1, to the car and the stop-sign simultaneously (this time using the parameter scaling of Section 4). Since the car is not moving rigidly with respect to the stop-sign and the building, applying the constrained estimation resulted in *worse* homography estimation for the car as well as for the stop-sign, than those found by two-view unconstrained process (See Figs. 2.b and 2.c). In contrast, the same *multi-plane* multi-view scheme, was applied simultaneously to the stop-sign and the *other* road-sign. Accurate homography estimation is now achieved (See Fig. 2.d). Hence, the degradation in the homography estimation observed in Figs. 2.b and 2.c, indicates that the car is moving $3D$-inconsistently with respect to the other planes (the building and the two signs).

6 Concluding Remarks

In this paper we showed that the collection of homologies of multiple planar surfaces across multiple views, are embedded in a low dimensional linear subspace. We further showed that these constraints can be used to improve homography estimation in multiplanar scenes, and serve as a cue for moving object detection. While the paper presented the core constraints and the core elements of such approaches, the integration of these elements into a single end-to-end algorithm remains a task for our future research.

References

[1] Olivier Faugeras. *Three-Dimensional Computer Vision – A Geometric Viewpoint*. MIT Press, Cambridge, MA, 1996.

[2] A.W. Fitzgibbon and A. Zisserman. Automatic camera recovery for closed or open image sequences. In *European Conference on Computer Vision*, pages 310–326, 1998.

[3] Van Gool, L. Proesmans, and A. Zisserman. Grouping and invariants using planar homologies. In *In Workshop on Geometrical Modeling and Invariants for Computer Vision*, 1995.

[4] M. Irani, P. Anandan, and D. Weinshall. From reference frames to reference planes: Multi-view parallax geometry application. In *European Conference on Computer Vision*, pages 829–845, 1998.

[5] Michal Irani, P. Anandan, and S. Hsu. Mosaic based representations of video sequences and their applications. In *International Conference on Computer Vision*, pages 605–611, Cambridge, MA, November 1995.

[6] K. Kanatani. Optimal homograhpy computation with a reliability measure. In *Proc. of the IAPR Workshop on Machine Vision*, Makuhari, Chiba, Japan, November 1998.

[7] P. Pritchett and A. Zisserman. Matching and reconstruction from widely separated views in 3d structure from multiple images of large-scale environments. In *LNCS 1506*, Springer-Verlag, 1998.

[8] Q.T.Luong and O.Faugeras. Determining the fundamental matrix with planes. In *IEEE Conference on Computer Vision and Pattern Recognition*, pages 489–494, New York, June 1993.

[9] A. Shashua. Projective structure from uncalibrated images: Structure from motion and recognition. *IEEE Transactions on Pattern Analysis and Machine Intelligence*, 16:778–790, 1994.

[10] A. Shashua and S. Avidan. The rank 4 constraint in multiple ($\geq$3) view geometry. In *European Conference on Computer Vision*, 1996.

[11] R. Szeliski and P.H.S Torr. Geometrically constrained structure from motion: Points on planes. In *European Workshop on 3D Structure from Multiple Images of Large-Scale Environments*, pages 171–186, Freiburg, Germany, June 1998.

[12] Bill Triggs. Autocalibration from planar scenes. In *European Conference on Computer Vision*, pages 89–105, 1998.

[13] T. Vieville, C.Zeller, and L.Robert. Using collineations to compute motion and structure in an uncalibrated image sequence. *International Journal of Computer Vision*, 20:213–242, 1996.

[14] W.T. Vetterling W.H. Press, S.A. Teukolsky and B.P. Flannery. *Numerical Recipes in C*. Cambridge University Press, Cambridge, MA, 1992.

3D Articulated Models and Multi-View Tracking with Silhouettes[1]

Quentin Delamarre and Olivier Faugeras

RobotVis Project - I.N.R.I.A

2004 route des Lucioles - BP 93

06902 Sophia-Antipolis Cedex FRANCE

Email: Quentin.Delamarre, Olivier.Faugeras@sophia.inria.fr

http://www-sop.inria.fr/robotvis/personnel/qdelam/

Abstract

We propose a method to estimate the motion of a person filmed by two or more fixed cameras. The novelty of our technique is its ability to cope with fast movements, self-occlusions and noisy images. Our algorithms are based on the latest works on calibration and image segmentation developed in our lab. We compare the projections of a 3D model of a person on the images to the detected silhouettes of the person, and by creating forces that will move the 3D model towards the final estimation of the real pose. We developed a fast algorithm that computes the motion of the articulated 3D model. We show that our results are good, even if the cameras are not synchronized.

1. Introduction

Tracking a person in a sequence of images has many potential applications such as man-machine interaction, security, virtual studio, ... Using computer vision to perform these kinds of tasks would increase the flexibility of these applications, but this is a difficult problem.

Our final goal is to be able to analyze the gait of persons filmed by two or more cameras to answer such questions as: are they running or walking? Where are they going? or to identify them from the study of the time variation of the parameters of the 3D model.

For gait analysis, one needs to recover not only the general location and orientation of the body, but also the pose of the legs and the arms. For this purpose we use an articulated 3D model of human.

Many recent model-based methods have been proposed as described in [1] and in [6]. They depend upon the amount of precision required by the applications and upon the number of cameras. Gavrila and Davis [7] use a best-first local

search after a segmentation of images. Bregler and Malik [3] use twists and exponential maps to model the orthographic projection of the 3D model, in order to perform a local search for pose estimation.

Most of the methods using a 3D model for tracking have some drawbacks: they can only handle small motions because they use a differential theory and perform a local search around an estimated solution, and they need images of good quality to perform a segmentation.

In order to get away from this problem, the idea in our work is to create forces between the 3D model and the image contours of the moving person. These forces are applied to each rigid part of the model (whereas Kakadiaris and Metaxas [8, 9] use forces for estimating also a better shape of the 3D model). Since we only need to recover the state parameters of the 3D model, we use an approximate model of a human, and show that it is sufficient for our purpose.

2. Pose estimation from two or more points of view: Theory

We present our method based on the use of two or three cameras, a silhouette extractor from images, a 3D model of what we want to track and the forces that will attract the image projections of this 3D model to the contours.

2.1. Input data

A single camera is too constraining: depth cannot be well estimated (except if you have a very precise model of what you are tracking, as described in [13], [10] or [4] for the hand), the background generates false matches, occlusions are hard to manage, etc. However, two points of view of an object yield 3D information that is easier to recover. If the cameras are well calibrated, the depth of the object of interest can be in general estimated. We have studied previously the case of two cameras with a small baseline and

---

[1]This work was partially supported by the European Project ESPRIT ltr 23.515: IMPROOFS (www.esat.kuleuven.ac.be/~konijn/improofs.html)

vergence and computed a 3D reconstruction of the tracked object (see [5] about hand tracking). Here we tackle the alternative case where the vergence angles are more than 45 degrees and the baseline is about five meters: fig. 1 shows an example of simultaneous images taken by three cameras. See also the mpeg sequence "Movie 1".

Figure 1. Three points of view of a running man. See Movie 1.

The cameras are calibrated through the software package TOTALCALIB developed in our lab ([2]) The three sequences of images have been synchronized manually.

2.2. 3D model of a person

The 3D model consists of truncated cones (arms and legs), spheres (neck, joints and head) and right parallelepipeds (hands, feet and body). It has 20 degrees of freedom (DOF). A frame is attached to each rigid part, and is easily related to others by rotations and translations thanks to the hierarchical structure of the model (see fig 2) .

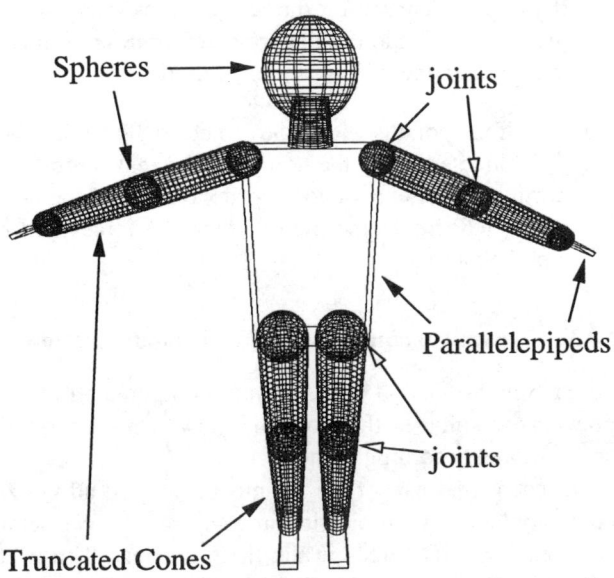

Figure 2. 3D model of a person

This model is adapted to the kind of data the contours

Figure 3. Final results (black lines) at the convergence of the active contour around the silhouette of the running man. See Movie 2.

extractor provides us with. It is simple enough to make quick calculations based on the data possible, and complex enough to capture the pose of our person well.

2.3. External contours extractor

We use an algorithm based on geodesic active contours. The contours evolve according to a PDE that incorporates optical flow and intensity measures and converge towards the silhouette of the moving person (see fig 3). For more details, see [11] and [12].

2.4. How to make the images of the 3D model converge towards the contours?

We assume that the initial pose of the person is known. The initialization has been done manually in the first frame for the examples of this paper.

The 3D model has then to track the person in the remaining of the sequences. For this purpose, we create forces that attract the images of the 3D model towards the contours found in the images. We currently initialize the pose of the 3D model at time t with the estimation computed at time t-1. Prediction based, e.g. on a Kalman filter, can easily be incorporated.

2.4.1 Projecting the 3D model into images

In order to compare the pose of the 3D model and the real pose of the person, the 3D model is projected into the image plane of each camera (using the pinhole model). The difference between the projected and the real contour will give our algorithm the ability to estimate the difference between the pose of the 3D model and the pose of the real person. Having several views will resolve most of the depth and self-occlusion ambiguities.

Each rigid part of the 3D model is projected into the image planes. We then compute the union of the resulting polygons (see fig. 4).

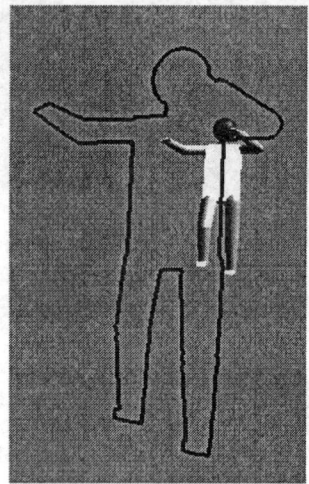

Figure 4. The black curve is the contour of the projection of the 3D model in the image plane of one of the cameras. See Movie 3.

2.4.2 Forces between the projected 3D model and the contours in the images

Matching the two sets of contours is a well known problem in computer vision. We want the projection of the 3D model to move inside the real silhouette, because the silhouettes are supposed to be an enlarged version of the images of the person. In each image, the contour of the projected 3D model is moved towards the interior normals to the real contour. More precisely, we use a technique developed in [16]: the Maxwell's demons. When points chosen on the real contour are within the projected contour, a force is created directed along the normal, to move the 3D model in the inside direction (see fig. 5).

If the two contours don't intersect each other, a different kind of forces has to be applied. One solution to this problem is the ICP algorithm (Iterative Closest Points [18]). In its simplest form, points are chosen on one curve. Then, at each step, and until convergence, a force f_i similar to those created by a spring is created between each of these points and its closest point on the other curve. The sum of these forces is then applied to the 3D model (see fig. 6). This forces the projection of the 3D model to intersect the real contours.

So, at each iteration of the process to fit the model contours to the real ones, forces f_i are created in the following way:

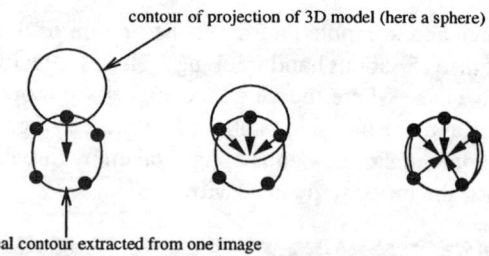

Figure 5. Two steps of Maxwell's demons algorithm: compute normals f_i, move 3D model according to Σf_i.

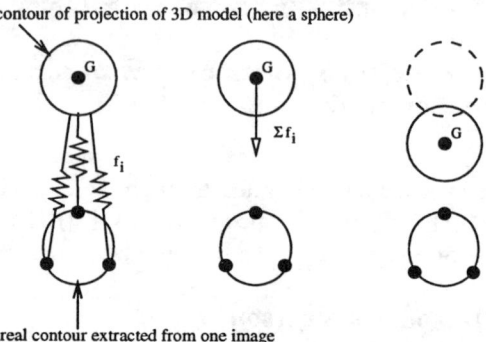

Figure 6. One step of the ICP algorithm: choose points, compute forces f_i and move the 3D model according to Σf_i. See Movie 4.

- if the point chosen on the real contour is not within the current position of the projected contour of the 3D model, then the ICP algorithm is used,

- else, if the point is within the projected 3D model, then f_i is directed along the normal to the real contour. Its norm is taken to a value near the average of the norm of the ICP forces (so the two kinds of forces will be well balanced).

2.4.3 Dynamical equations of the 3D model motion

For each iteration, and once we have computed all the 2D forces in each images, the problem is now to move correctly the 3D model according to them.

For each rigid part of the 3D model, we add all the 2D forces applied to its projection in each image. We obtain three resulting 2D forces in the three images. Those 2D forces are then simply added in the (3D) scene frame. The resulting 3D force is then applied to the rigid part we consider (see fig. 7 for an example with only one sphere). We follow this scheme for each rigid part of the 3D model.

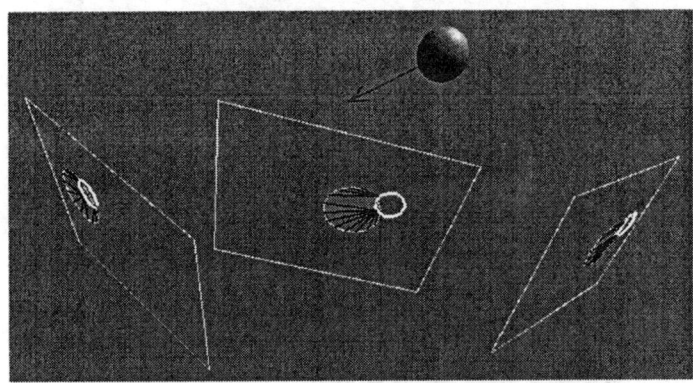

Figure 7. The 2D forces are added from the 3 cameras, and applied on the 3D model (here a simple sphere). The black arrow is the resulting 3D force applied onto the sphere. This force will move the 3D model towards its estimated real pose. See Movie 5.

Because the 3D model is articulated, computing its motion when submitted to the above forces is not easy. Considering the dynamical equations, there are 6 unknown positional parameters for each of the 20 rigid parts of the model, so we have to invert a 120x120 matrix at each iteration, not counting all the constraints of the joints! Fortunately, the dynamics of systems of rigid objects has been addressed before by the robotics community [17]. Schwertassek and Roberson explain in their book [14, 15] how to compute the accelerations of articulated objects in time O(N), N being the number of rigid parts (20 in our case). They show how we can simplify the computation of the motion by taking into account the constraints (or modes of motion) applied at each joint, in a recursive way along the tree-configured system of rigid parts. Solving the dynamical equations becomes equivalent to inverting a 6x6 matrix for the general pose of the model, and a DxD matrix for each joint with D degrees of freedom (that is to say: four 3x3 matrices and four numbers only).

Note that the dynamical equations introduced here have nothing to do with the real dynamics of the motion of the person. It is just a way to minimize the distance between the contours of the projected 3D model and the real contours in one frame. The kinetic energy is set to zero, so that solving the dynamical equations is equivalent to minimizing the potential energy between the 3D model and its real pose. Of course this O(N) system can also be used to predict the movement (using a Kalman filter for example).

3. Experimental results

We present the results of the convergence of the edges of the projections of the 3D model to the edges of the real silhouettes extracted from the images. Movies are available on the ICCV99 ftp site: ftp.cs.toronto.edu/pub/iccv99/in.coming/. They are referenced as "Movie x" in the following sections and in the captions of the figures, where x is the number of the mpeg movie.

3.1. Contours of the real silhouettes

We have found that the quality of the contours extracted from the images was sufficient to retrieve useful information like the general location of the the person, pose of the legs, head, and sometimes arms. See fig. 3.

3.2. Comparing the pose of the 3D model with the real contours

We initialize the pose of the 3D model in the first frame. We then use our algorithm to estimate its pose in the next frame.

Fig. 8 is an example of the 2D forces created between the projected model and a contour from one camera. See also "Movie 2".

3.3. Convergence of the 3D model

If the initialization of the pose of the 3D model is not completely different from the real one, convergence is correct and fast (about 0.1 second without any optimization). Our method allows a sizeable motion between frames. In figs. 9 and 10 we show some results of our system with a real sequence of images. Fig. 9 shows the convergence of our algorithm in frame 32. Fig. 10 shows the final result for frames 18 to 23 seen from camera 1, and an example of self-occlusion for frames 33 to 35 seen from all cameras. See also the mpegs "Movie 6" and "Movie 7".

There are two difficulties for this sequence. The first one is due to the poor calibration of the cameras due to the bad image quality and the lack of a calibration grid. The second one is to track the fast moving person with an approximate 3D model.

But our results are good, given the data available. The estimation of the general pose of the person is correct. The legs are tracked well, despite the self-occlusions and the lack of a model of movement. The pose of the arms is less precise due to the fact that we only use the external contours of the silhouette.

Figure 8. Continuous black lines are the edges of the silhouette of the projected 3D model. Dotted black lines are those of the real silhouette. White lines are the 2D forces: ICP if the force links the two contours, Maxwell if the force is directed along the interior normal to the real contour.

4. Future developments

We are currently working on the following points in order to obtain an operational person tracker:

- Create some sequences of specific actions and study how our algorithm performs the tracking.

- Implement a Kalman filter to improve the speed of convergence, and to smooth the estimated time variation of the angular parameters to perform gait analysis.

- Add constraints to the joints in order to prevent impossible poses of body. A simple way to do that is to add external torques to every joint of the 3D model, or to add forces between parts of the 3D model.

- Solve the bootstrapping problem: the general location of the person and his direction can be deduced from the general movement of the contours in the first two or three images, but we are looking for a more robust and more precise first pose estimation.

- Study the tracking of other 3D models like a hand or a robot arm, since our algorithm can manage any kind of 3D model.

Figure 9. Results at the convergence of our algorithm for the frame of fig. 1. Top: new real contours of person, initial pose of the 3D model and forces between them. Middle: eighth iteration. Bottom: final results after ten iterations. See Movie 6.

5. Conclusion

We have presented a new method for tracking persons in video images by extracting silhouette contours. The results are sufficient to extract informations about the person: is he/she walking or running? Where is he/she going? Our al-

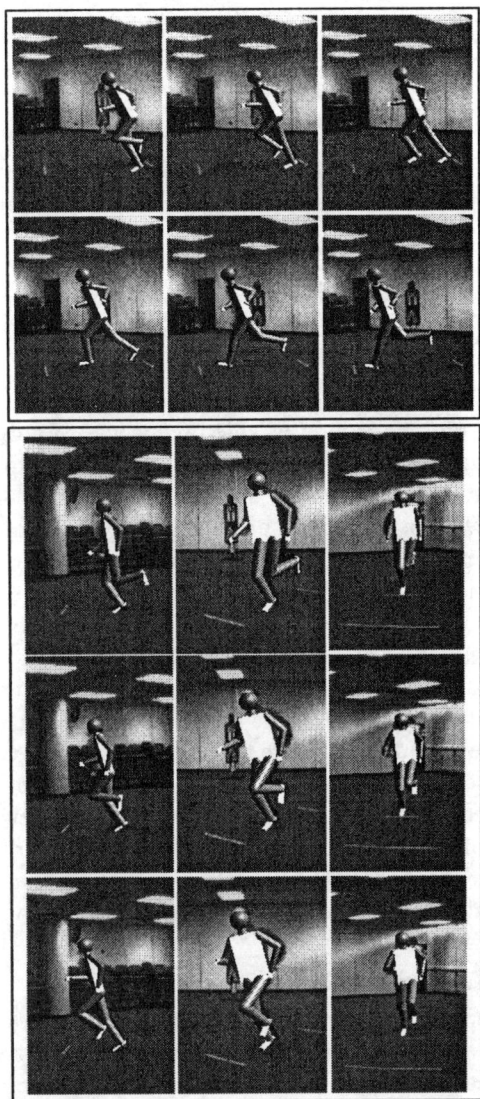

Figure 10. Top: final results of our algorithm for the beginning of the sequence for camera 1. Bottom: in case of self-occlusion (the left leg), our algorithm doesn't fail thanks to the multi-view approach (each column corresponds to a camera). See Movie 7.

gorithm can deal with fast movements and self-occlusions, but also with changing lights and moving clothes without needing a very precise 3D model of the person, since we only use the silhouette contours.

References

[1] J. Aggarwal and Q. Cai. Human motion analysis: A review. *IEEE Proc. Nonrigid and Articulated Motion Workshop*, pages 90–102, June 1997.

[2] S. Bougnoux and L. Robert. Totalcalib: a fast and reliable system for off-line calibration of images sequences. In *CVPR*, June 1997.

[3] C. Bregler and J. Malik. Tracking people with twists and exponential maps. *Proc. of IEEE Conference on Computer Vision and Pattern Recognition, Santa Barbara, USA*, pages 8–15, June 1998.

[4] Q. Delamarre. Modelisation de la main pour sa localisation dans une sequence d'images. Technical Report 0198, I.N.R.I.A., December 1996.

[5] Q. Delamarre and O. Faugeras. Finding pose of hand in video images: a stereo-based approach. *IEEE Proc. of the third International Conference on Automatic Face and Gesture Recognition (FG'98) in Japan*, pages 585–590, April 1998.

[6] D. M. Gavrila. The visual analysis of human movement: A survey. In *Computer Vision and Image Understanding*, volume Vol. 73, Number 1, pages 82–98. Academic Press, January 1999.

[7] D. M. Gavrila and L. Davis. 3D model based tracking of humans in action: a multi-view approach. *Proc. of IEEE Conference on Computer Vision and Pattern Recognition, San Francisco*, pages 73–80, 1996.

[8] I. Kakadiaris and D. Metaxas. 3D human body model acquisition from multiple views. *Proc. of IEEE International Conference on Computer Vision, Cambridge*, pages 618–623, 1995.

[9] I. Kakadiaris and D. Metaxas. Model based estimation of 3D human motion with occlusion based on active multiviewpoint selection. *Proc. of IEEE Conference on Computer Vision and Pattern Recognition, San Francisco*, pages 81–87, 1996.

[10] J. Kuch and T. Huang. Vision based hand modeling and tracking for virtual teleconferencing and telecollaboration. *Proc. of IEEE International Conference on Computer Vision, Cambridge*, pages 666–671, 1995.

[11] N. Paragios and R. Deriche. A PDE-based Level Set approach for Detection and Tracking of moving objects. In *ICCV*, pages 1139–1145, Bombay, India, 1998.

[12] N. Paragios and R. Deriche. Unifying Boundary and Region-based Information for Geodesic Active Tracking. In *CVPR*, Colorado, USA, 1999.

[13] J. Rehg and T. Kanade. Model-based tracking of self-occluding articulated objects. *Fifth Int. Conf. on Computer Vision ICCV*, pages 612–617, June 1995.

[14] R. Roberson and R. Schwertassek. *Dynamics of Multibody Systems*. Springer-Verlag, 1988.

[15] R. Schwertassek and W. Rulka. Aspects of efficient and reliable multibody systems simulation. In *NATO ASI Series F: Computer and Systems Sciences: Real-Time Integration Methods for Mechanical System Simulation*, volume 69, pages 55–96. E. Haug and R. Deyo Springer-Verlag, 1990.

[16] J.-P. Thirion. Non-rigid matching using demons. *Computer Vision and Pattern Recognition*, June 1996.

[17] J. Wittenburg. *Dynamics of Systems of Rigid Objects*. B. G. Teubner Stuttgart, 1977.

[18] Z. Zhang. Iterative point matching for registration of free-form curves and surfaces. *International Journal of Computer Vision*, 13:119–152, 1994.

Three-Dimensional Scene Flow

Sundar Vedula†, Simon Baker†, Peter Rander†‡, Robert Collins†, and Takeo Kanade†

†The Robotics Institute, Carnegie Mellon University, Pittsburgh, PA 15213

‡Zaxel Systems Inc., Ten 40th Street, Pittsburgh, PA 15201

Abstract

Scene flow is the three-dimensional motion field of points in the world, just as optical flow is the two-dimensional motion field of points in an image. Any optical flow is simply the projection of the scene flow onto the image plane of a camera. In this paper, we present a framework for the computation of dense, non-rigid scene flow from optical flow. Our approach leads to straightforward linear algorithms and a classification of the task into three major scenarios: (1) complete instantaneous knowledge of the scene structure, (2) knowledge only of correspondence information, and (3) no knowledge of the scene structure. We also show that multiple estimates of the normal flow cannot be used to estimate dense scene flow directly without some form of smoothing or regularization.

1 Introduction

Optical flow is a two-dimensional motion field in the image plane. It is the projection of the three-dimensional motion of the world. If the world is completely non-rigid, the motions of the points in the scene may all be independent of each other. One representation of the scene motion is therefore a dense three-dimensional vector field defined for every point on every surface in the scene. By analogy with optical flow, we refer to this three-dimensional motion field as *scene flow*.

In this paper, we present a framework for the computation of *dense, non-rigid* scene flow directly from optical flow. Our approach leads to efficient linear algorithms and a classification of the task into three major scenarios:

1. Complete instantaneous knowledge of the structure of the scene, including surface normals and rates of change of depth maps. In this case, only one optical flow is required to compute the scene flow.

2. Knowledge only of stereo correspondences. In this case, at least two optical flows are needed to compute the scene flow, but more improve robustness.

3. No knowledge of the surface. In this case, several optical flows can be used in a reconstruction algorithm to estimate the scene structure (and then scene flow).

For each scenario, we propose an algorithm and demonstrate it on a collection of video sequences of a dynamic, non-rigid scene. We also show that multiple estimates of the normal flow cannot be used to estimate scene flow directly, without some form of regularization or smoothing.

One possible application of scene flow is as a predictor for efficient and robust stereo. Given a reconstructed model of the scene at a certain time, one would like to obtain an estimate of the structure at the next time step using minimal computation. This would allow: (1) more efficient computation of the structure at the next time step because a first estimate would be available to reduce the search space, and (2) more robust computation of the structure because the predicted structure can be integrated with the new stereo data. Other applications of scene flow include various dynamic rendering and interpretation tasks, from the generation of slow-motion replays, to the understanding and modeling of human actions.

1.1 Related Work

Computing the three-dimensional motion of a scene is a fundamental task in computer vision that has been approached in a wide variety of ways. If the scene is rigid and the cameras are calibrated, the three-dimensional scene structure and relative motion can be computed (up to a scale factor) from a single monocular video sequence using *structure-from-motion* [Ullman, 1979]. If the scene is only piecewise rigid, extensions to structure-from-motion algorithms can be used. See, for example, [Zhang and Faugeras, 1992a] and [Costeira and Kanade, 1998].

Although restricted forms of non-rigidity can be analyzed using the structure-from-motion paradigm [Avidan and Shashua, 1998], general non-rigid motion cannot be estimated from a single camera without additional assumptions about the scene. However, given strong enough *a priori* assumptions about the scene, for example in the form of a deformable model [Pentland and Horowitz, 1991] [Metaxas and Terzopoulos, 1993] or the assumption that the motion minimizes the deviation from a rigid body motion [Ullman, 1984], recovery of three-dimensional non-rigid motion from a monocular view is possible. See [Penna, 1994] for a recent survey of monocular non-rigid motion estimation, and the assumptions used to compute it.

Another common approach to recovering three-dimensional motion is to use multiple cameras and combine stereo and motion in an approach known as *motion-stereo*. Nearly all motion-stereo algorithms assume that the scene is rigid. See, for example, [Waxman and Duncan, 1986], [Young and Chellappa, 1999], and [Zhang and Faugeras, 1992b]. A paper which explicitly combines two optical flow fields is that of [Shi *et al.*, 1994]. In this paper, both the analysis and implementation are only applicable to certain simple motions of the camera (i.e. translations).

A few motion-stereo papers do consider non-rigid motion, including [Liao *et al.*, 1997] and [Malassiotis and Strintzis, 1997]. The former uses a relaxation-based algorithm to co-operatively match features in both the temporal and spatial domains. It therefore does not provide dense motion. The latter uses a grid which acts as a deformable model in a generalization of the monocular approaches mentioned above. Besides requiring *a priori* models of the scene, most deformable-model based approaches to motion-stereo would be too inefficient for our stereo-prediction application.

2 Image Formation Preliminaries

Consider a non-rigidly moving surface $f(x, y, z; t) = 0$ imaged by a fixed camera i, with 3×4 projection matrix $\mathbf{P}_i$, as illustrated in Figure 1. There are two aspects to the formation of the image sequence $I_i = I_i(u_i, v_i; t)$ captured by camera i: (1) the relative camera and surface geometry, and (2) the illumination and surface photometrics.

2.1 Relative Camera and Surface Geometry

The relationship between a point (x, y, z) on the surface and its image coordinates (u_i, v_i) in camera i is given by:

$$u_i = \frac{[\mathbf{P}_i]_1 (x, y, z, 1)^{\mathrm{T}}}{[\mathbf{P}_i]_3 (x, y, z, 1)^{\mathrm{T}}} \tag{1}$$

$$v_i = \frac{[\mathbf{P}_i]_2 (x, y, z, 1)^{\mathrm{T}}}{[\mathbf{P}_i]_3 (x, y, z, 1)^{\mathrm{T}}} \tag{2}$$

where $[\mathbf{P}_i]_j$ is the jth row of $\mathbf{P}_i$. Equations (1) and (2) describe the mapping from a point $\mathbf{x} = (x, y, z)$ on the surface to its image $\mathbf{u}_i = (u_i, v_i)$ in camera i. Without knowledge of the surface, these equations are not invertible. Given f, they can be inverted, but the inversion requires intersecting a ray in space with the surface f.

The differential relationships between $\mathbf{x}$ and $\mathbf{u}_i$ can be represented by a 2×3 Jacobian matrix $\frac{\partial \mathbf{u}_i}{\partial \mathbf{x}}$. The 3 columns of the Jacobian matrix store the differential change in projected image co-ordinates per unit change in x, y, and z. A closed-form expression for $\frac{\partial \mathbf{u}_i}{\partial \mathbf{x}}$ as a function of $\mathbf{x}$ can be derived by differentiating Equations (1) and (2) symbolically. The Jacobian $\frac{\partial \mathbf{u}_i}{\partial \mathbf{x}}$ describes the relationship between a small change in the point on the surface and its image in

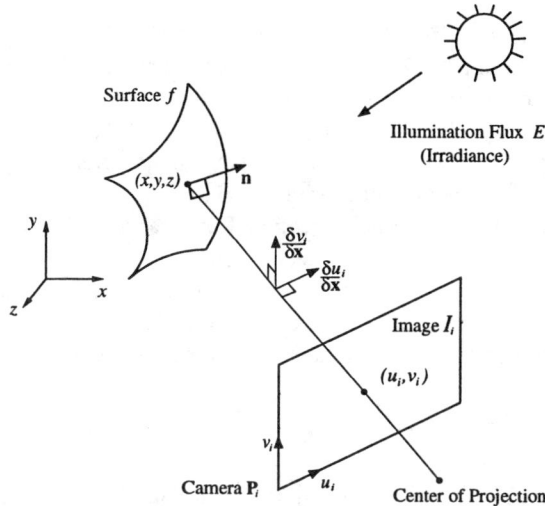

Figure 1: A non-rigid surface $f(x, y, z; t) = 0$ is moving with respect to a fixed world coordinate system (x, y, z). The normal to the surface is $\mathbf{n} = \mathbf{n}(x, y, z; t)$. The surface is assumed to be Lambertian with albedo $\rho = \rho(x, y, z; t)$ and the illumination flux (irradiance) is E. The ith camera is fixed in space, has a coordinate frame (u_i, v_i), is represented by the 3×4 camera matrix $\mathbf{P}_i$, and captures the image sequence $I_i = I_i(u_i, v_i; t)$.

camera i via $\Delta \mathbf{u}_i \approx \frac{\partial \mathbf{u}_i}{\partial \mathbf{x}} \Delta \mathbf{x}$. Similarly, the inverse Jacobian $\frac{\partial \mathbf{x}}{\partial \mathbf{u}_i}$ describes the relationship between a small change in a point in the image of camera i and the point it is imaging in the scene via $\Delta \mathbf{x} \approx \frac{\partial \mathbf{x}}{\partial \mathbf{u}_i} \Delta \mathbf{u}_i$.

Since image co-ordinates do not map uniquely to scene co-ordinates, the inverse Jacobian cannot be computed without knowledge of the surface. If we know the surface (and its gradient), the inverse Jacobian can be estimated as the solution of the following two sets of linear equations:

$$\frac{\partial \mathbf{u}_i}{\partial \mathbf{x}} \frac{\partial \mathbf{x}}{\partial \mathbf{u}_i} = \begin{pmatrix} 1 & 0 \\ 0 & 1 \end{pmatrix} \tag{3}$$

$$\frac{\partial f}{\partial \mathbf{u}_i} = \frac{\partial f}{\partial \mathbf{x}} \frac{\partial \mathbf{x}}{\partial \mathbf{u}_i} = \nabla f \frac{\partial \mathbf{x}}{\partial \mathbf{u}_i} = (\,0\ 0\,). \tag{4}$$

Equation (3) expresses the constraint that a small change in $\mathbf{u}_i$ must lead to a small change in $\mathbf{x}$ which when projected back into the image gives the original change in $\mathbf{u}_i$. Equation (4) expresses the constraint that a small change in $\mathbf{u}_i$ does not lead to a change in f since the corresponding point in the world should still lie on the surface.

The 6 linear equations in Equations (3) and (4) can be decoupled into 3 for $\frac{\partial \mathbf{x}}{\partial u_i}$ and 3 for $\frac{\partial \mathbf{x}}{\partial v_i}$. Unique solutions exist for both $\frac{\partial \mathbf{x}}{\partial u_i}$ and $\frac{\partial \mathbf{x}}{\partial v_i}$ if and only if:

$$\left(\frac{\partial u_i}{\partial \mathbf{x}} \times \frac{\partial v_i}{\partial \mathbf{x}} \right) \cdot \nabla f \neq 0. \tag{5}$$

Since ∇f is parallel to the surface normal $\mathbf{n}$, the equations are degenerate if and only if the ray joining the camera center of projection and $\mathbf{x}$ is tangent to the surface.

2.2 Illumination and Surface Photometrics

At a point $\mathbf{x}$ in the scene, the irradiance or illumination flux measured in the direction $\mathbf{m}$ at time t can be represented by $E = E(\mathbf{m}; \mathbf{x}; t)$ [Horn, 1986]. This 6D irradiance function E is what is described as the *plenoptic function* in [Adelson and Bergen, 1991].

We denote the net directional irradiance of light at the point (x, y, z) on the surface at time t by $\mathbf{s} = \mathbf{s}(x, y, z; t)$. The net directional irradiance $\mathbf{s}$ is a vector quantity and is given by the (vector) surface integral of the irradiance E over the visible hemisphere of possible directions:

$$\mathbf{s}(x, y, z; t) = \int_{S(\mathbf{n})} E(\mathbf{m}; x, y, z; t) \, d\mathbf{m} \qquad (6)$$

where $S(\mathbf{n}) = \{\mathbf{m} : \|\mathbf{m}\| = 1 \text{ and } \mathbf{m} \cdot \mathbf{n} \leq 0\}$ is the hemisphere of directions from which light can fall on a surface patch with surface normal $\mathbf{n}$.

We assume that the surface is Lambertian with albedo $\rho = \rho(\mathbf{x}; t)$. Then, assuming that the point $\mathbf{x} = (x, y, z)$ is visible in the ith camera, and that the intensity registered in image I_i is proportional to the radiance of the point that it is the image of (i.e. image irradiance is proportional to scene radiance [Horn, 1986]), we have:

$$I_i(\mathbf{u}_i; t) = -C \cdot \rho(\mathbf{x}; t) [\mathbf{n}(\mathbf{x}; t) \cdot \mathbf{s}(\mathbf{x}; t)] \qquad (7)$$

where C is a constant that only depends upon the diameter of the lens and the distance between the lens and the image plane. The image pixel $\mathbf{u}_i = (u_i, v_i)$ and the surface point $\mathbf{x} = (x, y, z)$ are related by Equations (1) and (2).

3 Two-Dimensional Optical Flow

Suppose $\mathbf{x}(t)$ is the 3D path of a point on the surface and the image of this point in camera i is $\mathbf{u}_i(t)$. The 3D motion of this point is $\frac{d\mathbf{x}}{dt}$ and the 2D image motion of its projection is $\frac{d\mathbf{u}_i}{dt}$. The 2D flow field $\frac{d\mathbf{u}_i}{dt}$ is usually known as optical flow. As the point $\mathbf{x}(t)$ moves on the surface, it is natural to assume that its albedo $\rho = \rho(\mathbf{x}(t); t)$ remains constant; i.e. we assume that

$$\frac{d\rho}{dt} = 0. \qquad (8)$$

(For a deformably moving surface, it is only the surface properties like albedo that distinguish points anyway). The basis for optical flow algorithms is then the equation:

$$\frac{dI_i}{dt} = \boldsymbol{\nabla} I_i \cdot \frac{d\mathbf{u}_i}{dt} + \frac{\partial I_i}{\partial t} = -C \cdot \rho(\mathbf{x}; t) \frac{d}{dt}[\mathbf{n} \cdot \mathbf{s}] \quad (9)$$

where $\boldsymbol{\nabla} I_i$ is the spatial gradient of the image, $\frac{d\mathbf{u}_i}{dt}$ is the optical flow, and $\frac{\partial I_i}{\partial t}$ is the instantaneous rate of change of the image intensity $I_i = I_i(\mathbf{u}_i; t)$.

The term $\mathbf{n} \cdot \mathbf{s}$ depends upon both the shape of the surface ($\mathbf{n}$) and the illumination ($\mathbf{s}$). To avoid explicit dependence

upon the structure of the three-dimensional scene, it is often assumed that:

$$\mathbf{n} \cdot \mathbf{s} = \int_{S(\mathbf{n})} E(\mathbf{m}; \mathbf{x}; t) \, \mathbf{n} \cdot d\mathbf{m} \qquad (10)$$

is constant ($\frac{d}{dt}[\mathbf{n} \cdot \mathbf{s}] = 0$). With uniform illumination or a surface normal that does not change rapidly, this assumption holds well (at least for Lambertian surfaces).

In either scenario $\frac{dI_i}{dt}$ goes to zero, and we arrive at the *Normal Flow* or *Gradient Constraint* Equation, used by "differential" optical flow algorithms [Barron *et al.*, 1994]:

$$\boldsymbol{\nabla} I_i \cdot \frac{d\mathbf{u}_i}{dt} + \frac{\partial I_i}{\partial t} = 0. \qquad (11)$$

Using this constraint, a large number of algorithms have been proposed for estimating the optical flow $\frac{d\mathbf{u}_i}{dt}$. See [Barron *et al.*, 1994] for a recent survey.

4 Three-Dimensional Scene Flow

In the same way that optical flow describes an instantaneous motion field in an image, we can think of scene flow as a three-dimensional flow field $\frac{d\mathbf{x}}{dt}$ describing the motion at every point in the scene. The analysis in Section 2.1 was only for a fixed time t. Now suppose there is a point $\mathbf{x} = \mathbf{x}(t)$ moving in the scene. The image of this point in camera i is $\mathbf{u}_i = \mathbf{u}_i(t)$. If the camera is not moving, the rate of change of $\mathbf{u}_i$ is uniquely determined as:

$$\frac{d\mathbf{u}_i}{dt} = \frac{\partial \mathbf{u}_i}{\partial \mathbf{x}} \frac{d\mathbf{x}}{dt}. \qquad (12)$$

Inverting this relationship is, again, impossible without knowledge of the surface f. To invert it, note that $\mathbf{x}$ depends not only on $\mathbf{u}_i$, but also on the time, indirectly through the surface $f = f(\mathbf{x}; t)$. That is $\mathbf{x} = \mathbf{x}(\mathbf{u}_i(t); t)$. Differentiating this expression with respect to time gives:

$$\frac{d\mathbf{x}}{dt} = \frac{\partial \mathbf{x}}{\partial \mathbf{u}_i} \frac{d\mathbf{u}_i}{dt} + \frac{\partial \mathbf{x}}{\partial t}\bigg|_{\mathbf{u}_i}. \qquad (13)$$

This equation says that the motion of a point in the world is made up of two components. The first is the projection of the scene flow on the plane tangent to the surface and passing through $\mathbf{x}$. This is obtained by taking the instantaneous motion on the image plane (the optical flow $\frac{d\mathbf{u}_i}{dt}$), and projecting it out into the scene using the inverse Jacobian $\frac{\partial \mathbf{x}}{\partial \mathbf{u}_i}$.

The second term is the contribution to scene flow arising from the three-dimensional motion of the point in the scene imaged by a fixed pixel. It is the instantaneous motion of $\mathbf{x}$ along the ray corresponding to $\mathbf{u}_i$. The magnitude of $\frac{\partial \mathbf{x}}{\partial t}\big|_{\mathbf{u}_i}$ is (proportional to) the rate of change of the depth of the surface f along this ray. A derivation of $\frac{\partial \mathbf{x}}{\partial t}\big|_{\mathbf{u}_i}$ is presented in Appendix A.

There are three major ways of computing scene flow, depending upon what is known about the scene at that instant:

$t = 1$ $t = 2$ $t = 3$ $t = 4$ $t = 5$

Figure 2: A sequence of images that show the scene motion. For lack of space, we only present scene flow results for $t = 1$ in this paper. The extended sequence is presented to help the reader visualize the three-dimensional motion.

1. Completely known instantaneous structure of the scene, including surface normals, depth maps, and the temporal rate of change of these depth maps.

2. Knowledge only of stereo correspondences. Since we are working in a calibrated setting, this is equivalent to having the depth maps. However, it does not include the surface normals and the temporal rates of change of the depth maps.

3. Completely unknown scene structure. We do not even know correspondence information.

Each of these cases leads to a different strategy for estimating the scene flow. It seems intuitive that less knowledge of scene structure requires the use of more optical flows, and indeed this result does follow from the amount of degeneracy in the linear equations used to compute scene flow. We now describe algorithms for each of the three cases. We also demonstrate their validity using flow results computed from multiple image sequences (captured from various viewpoints) of a non-rigid, dynamically changing scene. One such image sequence is shown in Figure 2.

4.1 Complete Knowledge of Surface Geometry

If the surface f is completely known (with high accuracy), the surface gradient ∇f can be computed at every point. The inverse Jacobian $\frac{\partial \mathbf{x}}{\partial \mathbf{u}_i}$ can then be estimated by solving the set of 6 linear equations in Equations (3) and (4). Given the inverse Jacobian, the scene flow can be estimated from the optical flow $\frac{d\mathbf{u}_i}{dt}$ using Equation (13):

$$\frac{d\mathbf{x}}{dt} = \frac{\partial \mathbf{x}}{\partial \mathbf{u}_i} \frac{d\mathbf{u}_i}{dt} + \frac{\partial \mathbf{x}}{\partial t}\bigg|_{\mathbf{u}_i}. \tag{14}$$

Computing $\frac{\partial \mathbf{x}}{\partial t}\big|_{\mathbf{u}_i}$ requires the temporal derivative of the surface depth map, and is described in Appendix A.

Complete knowledge of the scene structure thus enables us to compute scene flow from one optical flow, (and the rate of change of the depth map corresponding to this image.) These two pieces of information correspond to the two components of the scene flow; the optical flow is projected onto the tangent plane passing through $\mathbf{x}$, and the rate of change of depth map is mapped onto a component along the ray passing through the scene point $\mathbf{x}$ and the center of projection of the camera.

Figure 3: The horizontal and vertical optical flows at $t = 1$ for the same camera used in Figure 2. Darker pixels indicate motion to the left and top of the frames respectively.

Note that we assume that the surface is locally planar when computing the inverse Jacobian. Since the surface is known, it is possible to project the "flowed" point in the image and intersect this ray with the surface. We currently do not perform this to save an expensive ray-surface intersection for every pixel.

If only one optical flow is used, the scene flow can be computed only for those points in the scene that are visible in that image. It is possible to use multiple optical flows in multiple cameras for better visibility, and for greater robustness. Also, flow is recovered only when the change in depth map is valid - that is, when an individual pixel sees neighboring parts of the surface as time changes. If the motion of a surface is large relative to its size, then a pixel views different surfaces, and flow cannot be computed.

Consider the scene shown as a sequence in Figure 2. For lack of space, we only present scene flow results for time $t = 1$ in this paper. The scene flow is computed using depth maps from the model obtained from the volumetric merging of multiple range images, each computed using stereo, as described in [Rander *et al.*, 1996]. Another input is the optical flow shown in Figure 3, which was computed using a hierarchical version of the Lucas-Kanade optical flow algorithm. The final input is the temporal rate of change of the depth map, estimated from the difference between two independently computed volumetric models.

Figure 4 shows the result of computing scene flow for the visible set of points on the model. The original points are shown in light grey. The points that the original points have "flowed to" by adding the scene flow are shown in black. The darker points therefore represent a prediction

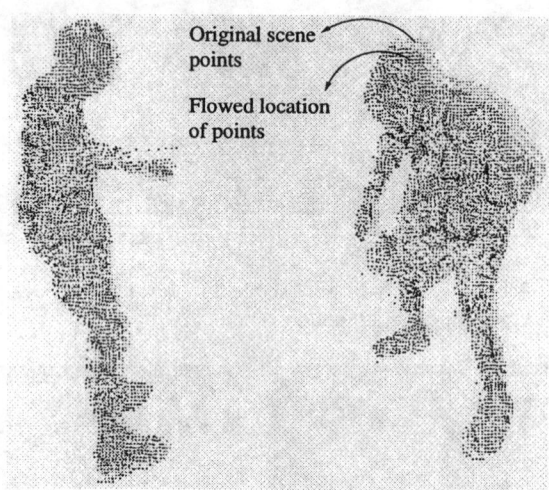

Original scene points

Flowed location of points

Figure 4: The computed scene flow. The original points on the model are shown in grey. The locations that these points have "flowed" to are shown in black. These flowed points form a prediction of the model at time $t = 2$.

of the model at time $t = 2$. They could be used to enhance the efficiency and robustness of shape recovery. In Figure 4, it is seen that the bending motion of the player on the right (the player with the ball) is recovered, as is the downward (and somewhat sideways) motion of the ball. The major motion of the player of the left (the player facing the ball) is the upward motion of his left arm, which is partially recovered. No flow is recovered for some points on the arm because the arm moves very fast relative to its size. Many pixels see completely different surfaces even during one time-step. Therefore the rate of change of depth information for the points on those surfaces is invalid yielding no flow estimate for those points.

4.2 Known Image Correspondences

The second major case is when the structure of the scene is not completely known, but correspondences between images are available. In our calibrated setting, correspondences can be used to compute depth maps, but these depth maps may be too noisy to estimate surface normals and temporal rates of change. This situation is common. For example, it is typical in image based modeling and rendering problems. While these problems typically only consider static scenes, scene flow can be used as a means of extending image based modeling methodologies into the temporal domain for dynamic scenes.

If the surface is not completely known, it is not possible to solve for $\frac{d\mathbf{x}}{dt}$ directly from one camera. Instead, consider the implicit linear relation between the scene and the optical flow, as described by the Jacobian in Equation (12).

This set of equations provides two linear constraints on $\frac{d\mathbf{x}}{dt}$. Therefore, if we have $N > 2$ cameras, we can solve for $\frac{d\mathbf{x}}{dt}$, by setting up the system of equations $\mathbf{Bx} = \mathbf{U}$,

Figure 5: The magnitude of the scene flow is displayed for points on the model (the locations of which are obtained by projecting depth maps from 4 cameras into the scene). The magnitude of the scene flow is displayed as intensity. It can be seen that the largest motion occurs on the ball and the arm of the person at the rear, while the smallest motion is near the feet of the players.

where:

$$\mathbf{B} = \begin{bmatrix} \frac{\partial u_1}{\partial x} & \frac{\partial u_1}{\partial y} & \frac{\partial u_1}{\partial z} \\ \frac{\partial v_1}{\partial x} & \frac{\partial v_1}{\partial y} & \frac{\partial v_1}{\partial z} \\ \cdot & \cdot & \cdot \\ \cdot & \cdot & \cdot \\ \frac{\partial u_N}{\partial x} & \frac{\partial u_N}{\partial y} & \frac{\partial u_N}{\partial z} \\ \frac{\partial v_N}{\partial x} & \frac{\partial v_N}{\partial y} & \frac{\partial v_N}{\partial z} \end{bmatrix}, \quad \mathbf{U} = \begin{bmatrix} \frac{\partial u_1}{\partial t} \\ \frac{\partial v_1}{\partial t} \\ \cdot \\ \cdot \\ \frac{\partial u_N}{\partial t} \\ \frac{\partial v_N}{\partial t} \end{bmatrix} \quad (15)$$

This gives us $2N$ equations in 3 unknowns, and so for $N \geq 2$ we have an overconstrained system and can find an estimate of the scene flow. (This system of equations is degenerate if and only if the point $\mathbf{x}$ and the N camera centers are co-linear.) A singular value decomposition of $\mathbf{B}$ gives the solution that minimizes the sum of least squares of the error obtained by re-projecting the scene flow onto each of the optical flows.

We implemented the above algorithm and applied it to the same sequence that was used in the previous section, but without using the surface normal or rate of change of the depth map. We used optical flows from 15 different cameras. The use of this many optical flows ensures that every point at which we desire to compute scene flow is viewed by at least 2 or 3 cameras.

Figure 5 shows the magnitude of the computed scene flow. The absolute values of the computed flows in the x, y, and z directions are averaged and displayed as the intensity for each point. Since image correspondences along with camera calibration give us depth maps, the scene flow is computed for a set of points, the locations of which are obtained by projecting depth maps from 4 widely separated cameras into the scene. It is seen that the motion of the ball,

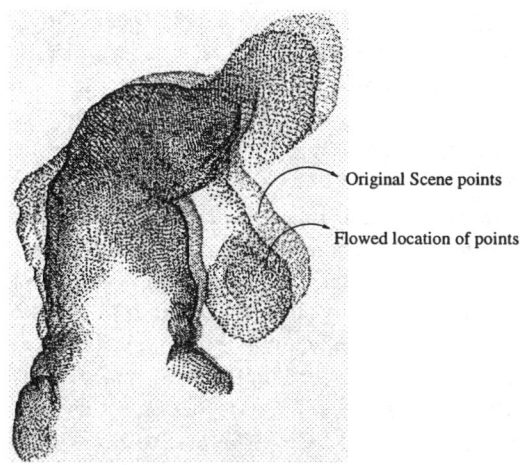

Figure 6: The initial point cloud is shown in light grey, while the set of points that these points have flowed to are shown in black. As can be seen, there is significant three-dimensional motion of the player downwards and to their right.

and the vertical motion of the left arm of the person at the rear are the most significant.

A close up of the player holding the ball is displayed in Figures 6 and 7. In Figure 6, the light grey points represent the model at $t = 1$, which are displaced by the estimated scene flow to give the darker colored points. The same *flowed* points are shown in Figure 7, except that the light grey points now represent the model at $t = 2$, computed independently using stereo and volumetric merging [Rander *et al.*, 1996]. The figures clearly show that the displacement of points using the scene flow results in them moving almost exactly onto the "true" model. Hence, scene flow may be used as a predictor for the structure of the scene at subsequent time intervals.

4.3 No Knowledge of the Surface

If the point x lies on the surface, Equation (12) must hold for every camera i. Therefore, it is possible to use the degree to which Equation (12) is consistent across cameras as information for a flow-based reconstruction algorithm. Such an approach would, however, be very susceptible to outliers. A single large magnitude flow which was wrong could always make the equations inconsistent. We therefore take a slightly different approach.

The solution of Equation (12) can be written in the following form:

$$\frac{d\mathbf{x}}{dt} = \left(\frac{\partial \mathbf{u}_i}{\partial \mathbf{x}}\right)^\star \frac{d\mathbf{u}_i}{dt} + \mu \, \mathbf{r}_i(\mathbf{u}_i) \qquad (16)$$

where $\left(\frac{\partial \mathbf{u}_i}{\partial \mathbf{x}}\right)^\star$ is the pseudo-inverse of $\frac{\partial \mathbf{u}_i}{\partial \mathbf{x}}$, $\mathbf{r}_i(\mathbf{u}_i)$ is the direction of a ray through the pixel $\mathbf{u}_i$ (see Appendix A), and μ is an unknown constant that depends upon instantaneous properties of the surface f. (Equation (16) holds because

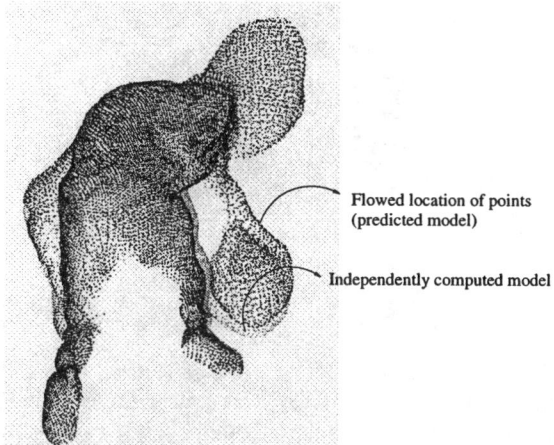

Figure 7: A comparison of the flowed points (black) with an independently computed model at the next next time instant (light grey). It is seen that the flowed points are a good approximation of the model at the next time instant.

$\mathbf{r}_i(\mathbf{u}_i)$ is in the null-space of $\frac{\partial \mathbf{u}_i}{\partial \mathbf{x}}$). Therefore, we have the following constraint on the the scene flow:

$$\mathbf{m}_i(\mathbf{x}) \cdot \frac{d\mathbf{x}}{dt} \equiv \left[\left(\frac{\partial \mathbf{u}_i}{\partial \mathbf{x}}\right)^\star \frac{d\mathbf{u}_i}{dt} \times \mathbf{r}_i(\mathbf{u}_i)\right] \cdot \frac{d\mathbf{x}}{dt} = 0 \quad (17)$$

where $\mathbf{m}_i(\mathbf{x}) = \left(\frac{\partial \mathbf{u}_i}{\partial \mathbf{x}}\right)^\star \frac{d\mathbf{u}_i}{dt} \times \mathbf{r}_i(\mathbf{u}_i)$ is a vector which is perpendicular to the plane defined by the camera center and the optical flow in the image plane. Hence, if $\mathbf{x}$ is actually a point on the surface, the vectors $\mathbf{m}_i(\mathbf{x})$ should all lie in a plane (the one perpendicular to the scene flow $\frac{d\mathbf{x}}{dt}$). We form a measure of how coplanar the vectors are by computing the 3×3 matrix:

$$M(\mathbf{x}) = \sum_i \hat{\mathbf{m}}_i \hat{\mathbf{m}}_i^T \qquad (18)$$

where $\hat{\mathbf{m}}_i$ is $\mathbf{m}_i$ normalized to a unit vector. The normalization makes the algorithm less susceptible to incorrect large magnitude flows. The smallest eigenvalue $\lambda = \lambda(\mathbf{x})$ of M is a measure of non-coplanarity. We therefore use $N - \lambda(\mathbf{x})$ as a measure of the likelihood that $\mathbf{x}$ lies on the surface. (N is the number of cameras.)

We discretize the scene into a three-dimensional array of voxels, as was done in the Voxel Coloring algorithm of [Seitz and Dyer, 1997]. We then compute $N - \lambda(\mathbf{x})$ for each voxel, ignoring visibility as in [Collins, 1996]. Ignoring visibility in this way does not significantly affect the performance because our coplanarity measure is not significantly affected by outliers. (This algorithm could be extended to keep track of the visibility in a similar manner to [Seitz and Dyer, 1997] if so desired.)

We present the results of this algorithm in Figure 8. We used the data from all 51 cameras of the CMU Virtualized Reality dome [Narayanan *et al.*, 1998] (Some of the data

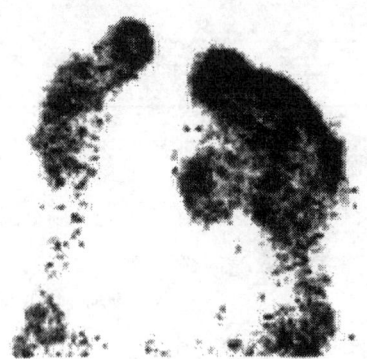

Figure 8: A volume rendering of the coplanarity measure $N - \lambda(\mathbf{x})$. As can be seen, the gross scene structure is recovered fairly well. Note, however, that this algorithm only recovers structure where the scene is moving. Hence, certain parts of the scene, such as the legs, are not recovered as well as others. The information provided by $N - \lambda(\mathbf{x})$ could be combined with traditional sources of information to further enhance the robustness of stereo.

from one camera is presented in Figure 2). For all 51 cameras, we computed the optical flow from $t = 1$ to $t = 2$. The measure of coplanarity $N - \lambda(\mathbf{x})$ was then computed for each voxel and thresholded. Figure 8 contains a volume rendering of the results. As can be seen, the gross structure of the scene is recovered. Note, however, that this flow-based reconstruction algorithm can only recover structure where the scene is actually moving. This is the reason that certain parts of the scene, such as the legs of the people, are not fully recovered.

4.4 Three-Dimensional Normal Flow Constraint

Optical flow $\frac{d\mathbf{u}_i}{dt}$ is a two dimensional vector field, and so is often divided into two components, the *normal flow* and the *tangent flow*. The normal flow is the component in the direction of the image gradient ∇I_i, and the tangent flow is the component perpendicular to the normal flow. The magnitude of the normal flow can be estimated directly from Equation (11) as:

$$\frac{1}{|\nabla I_i|} \nabla I_i \cdot \frac{d\mathbf{u}_i}{dt} = -\frac{1}{|\nabla I_i|} \frac{\partial I_i}{\partial t}. \quad (19)$$

Estimating the tangent flow is an ill-posed problem. Hence, some form of local smoothness is required to estimate the complete optical flow [Barron *et al.*, 1994]. Since the estimation of the tangent flow is the major difficulty in most algorithms, it is natural to ask whether the normal flows from several cameras can be used to estimate the 3D scene flow without having to use some form of regularization.

The Normal Flow Constraint Equation (11) can be rewritten as:

$$\nabla I_i \cdot \left[\frac{\partial \mathbf{u}_i}{\partial \mathbf{x}} \frac{d\mathbf{x}}{dt} \right] + \frac{\partial I_i}{\partial t} = 0. \quad (20)$$

This is a scalar linear constraint on the components of the scene flow $\frac{d\mathbf{x}}{dt}$. Therefore, at first glance it seems likely

that it might be possible to estimate the scene flow directly from three such constraints. Unfortunately, differentiating Equation (7) with respect to $\mathbf{x}$ we see that:

$$\nabla I_i \frac{\partial \mathbf{u}_i}{\partial \mathbf{x}} = -C \cdot \nabla \left(\rho(\mathbf{x}; t) \left[\mathbf{n}(\mathbf{x}; t) \cdot \mathbf{s}(\mathbf{x}; t) \right] \right). \quad (21)$$

Since this expression is independent of the camera i, and instead only depends on properties of the scene (the surface albedo ρ, the scene structure $\mathbf{n}$, and the illumination $\mathbf{s}$), the coefficients of $\frac{d\mathbf{x}}{dt}$ in Equation (20) should ideally always be the same. Hence, any number of copies of Equation (20) will be linearly dependent. In fact, if the equations turn out not to be linearly dependent, this fact can be used to deduce that $\mathbf{x}$ is not a point on the surface. (See Section 4.3.)

This result means that it is impossible to compute 3D scene flow independently for each point on the object, without some form of regularization of the problem. We wish to emphasize, however, that this result does not mean that is it not possible to estimate other useful quantities directly from the normal flow, as for example is done in [Negahdaripour and Horn, 1987] and other "direct methods."

5 Conclusions

Three-dimensional scene flow is a fundamental property of dynamic scenes. It can be used as a prediction mechanism to build more robust stereo algorithms, and for various scene interpretation and rendering tasks. We have presented a framework for computing scene flow from optical flow, assuming various instantaneous properties of the scene are known. We intend to extend our framework to incorporate knowledge of structure computed independently at the next time instant. We also plan to investigate other algorithms for computing scene flow that do not use optical flow, and develop methods of quantitatively evaluating their accuracy.

A Computing $\frac{\partial \mathbf{x}}{\partial t}\big|_{\mathbf{u}_i}$

The term $\frac{\partial \mathbf{x}}{\partial t}\big|_{\mathbf{u}_i}$ is the 3D motion of the point in the scene imaged by the pixel $\mathbf{u}_i$. Suppose the depth of the surface measured from the ith camera is $d_i = d_i(\mathbf{u}_i)$. Then, the point $\mathbf{x}$ can be written as a function of $\mathbf{P}_i$, $\mathbf{u}_i$, and d_i as follows. The 3×4 camera matrix $\mathbf{P}_i$ can be written as:

$$\mathbf{P}_i = [\mathbf{R}_i \, \mathbf{T}_i] \quad (22)$$

where $\mathbf{R}_i$ is a 3×3 matrix and $\mathbf{T}_i$ is a 3×1 vector. The center of projection of the camera is $-\mathbf{R}_i^{-1}\mathbf{T}_i$, the direction of the ray through the pixel $\mathbf{u}_i$ is $\mathbf{r}_i(\mathbf{u}_i) = \mathbf{R}_i^{-1}(u_i, v_i, 1)^{\mathrm{T}}$, and the direction of the camera z-axis is $\mathbf{r}_i(0) = \mathbf{R}_i^{-1}(0, 0, 1)^{\mathrm{T}}$. Using simple geometry, (see Figure 9) we therefore have:

$$\mathbf{x} = -\mathbf{R}_i^{-1}\mathbf{T}_i + d_i \left[\frac{\|\mathbf{r}_i(0)\| \, \mathbf{r}_i(\mathbf{u}_i)}{\mathbf{r}_i(0) \cdot \mathbf{r}_i(\mathbf{u}_i)} \right]. \quad (23)$$

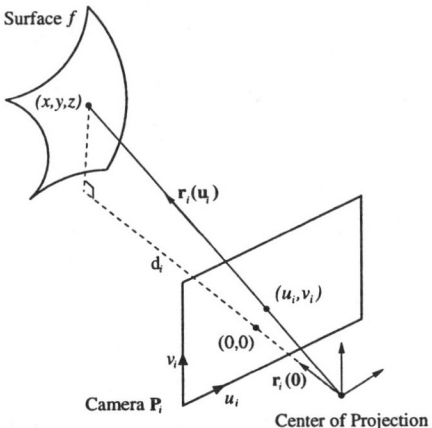

Surface f

(x,y,z)

$\mathbf{r}_i(\mathbf{u}_i)$

d_i

(u_i,v_i)

$(0,0)$

v_i

$\mathbf{r}_i(0)$

Camera $\mathbf{P}_i$ u_i Center of Projection

Figure 9: Given the camera matrix $\mathbf{P}_i$ and the distance d_i to the surface, the direction of the ray through the pixel $\mathbf{u}_i$ and the direction of the z-axis of the camera can be used to derive an expression for the point $\mathbf{x}$. This expression can be symbolically differentiated to give $\frac{\partial \mathbf{x}}{\partial t}\big|_{\mathbf{u}_i}$ as a function of $\mathbf{x}$, $\mathbf{P}_i$, and $\frac{\partial d_i}{\partial t}$.

(Care must be taken to choose the sign of $\mathbf{P}_i$ correctly so that the vector $\mathbf{r}_i(\mathbf{u}_i)$ points out into the scene.) If camera $\mathbf{P}_i$ is fixed, we have:

$$\frac{\partial \mathbf{x}}{\partial t}\bigg|_{\mathbf{u}_i} = \left[\frac{\|\mathbf{r}_i(0)\| \, \mathbf{r}_i(\mathbf{u}_i)}{\mathbf{r}_i(0) \cdot \mathbf{r}_i(\mathbf{u}_i)}\right] \frac{\partial d_i}{\partial t}. \qquad (24)$$

So, the magnitude of $\frac{\partial \mathbf{x}}{\partial t}\big|_{\mathbf{u}_i}$ is proportional to the rate of change of the depth map and the direction is along the ray joining $\mathbf{x}$ and the center of projection of the camera.

References

[Adelson and Bergen, 1991] E. Adelson and J. Bergen. The plenoptic function and the elements of early vision. In Landy and Movshon, editors, *Computational Models of Visual Processing*. MIT Press, 1991.

[Avidan and Shashua, 1998] S. Avidan and A. Shashua. Non-rigid parallax for 3D linear motion. In *Proc. of the DARPA IUW*, 1998. (To appear in CVPR '99).

[Barron et al., 1994] J.L. Barron, D.J. Fleet, and S.S. Beauchemin. Performance of optical flow techniques. *IJCV*, 12(1):43–77, 1994.

[Collins, 1996] R.T. Collins. A space-sweep approach to true multi-image matching. In *Proc. of CVPR '96*, pages 358–363, 1996.

[Costeira and Kanade, 1998] J.P. Costeira and T. Kanade. A multibody factorization method for independently moving objects. *IJCV*, 29(3):159–179, 1998.

[Horn, 1986] B.K.P. Horn. *Robot Vision*. McGraw Hill, 1986.

[Liao et al., 1997] W.-H. Liao, S.J. Aggrawal, and J.K. Aggrawal. The reconstruction of dynamic 3D structure of biological objects using stereo microscope images. *Machine Vision and Applications*, 9:166–178, 1997.

[Malassiotis and Strintzis, 1997] S. Malassiotis and M.G. Strintzis. Model-based joint motion and structure estimation from stereo images. *CVIU*, 65(1):79–94, 1997.

[Metaxas and Terzopoulos, 1993] D. Metaxas and D. Terzopoulos. Shape and nonrigid motion estimation through physics-based synthesis. *IEEE PAMI*, 15(6):580–591, 1993.

[Narayanan et al., 1998] P.J Narayanan, P.W. Rander, and T. Kanade. Constructing virtual worlds using dense stereo. In *Proc. of the Sixth ICCV*, pages 3–10, 1998.

[Negahdaripour and Horn, 1987] S. Negahdaripour and B.K.P. Horn. Direct passive navigation. *PAMI*, 9(1):168–176, 1987.

[Penna, 1994] M.A. Penna. The incremental approximation of nonrigid motion. *CVGIP*, 60(2):141–156, 1994.

[Pentland and Horowitz, 1991] A.P. Pentland and B. Horowitz. Recovery of nonrigid motion and structure. *IEEE PAMI*, 13(7):730–742, 1991.

[Rander et al., 1996] P.W. Rander, P.J Narayanan, and T. Kanade. Recovery of dynamic scene structure from multiple image sequences. In *Proc. of the 1996 Intl. Conf. on Multisensor Fusion and Integration for Intelligent Systems*, pages 305–312, 1996.

[Seitz and Dyer, 1997] S.M. Seitz and C.M. Dyer. Photorealistic scene reconstrcution by space coloring. In *Proc. of CVPR '97*, pages 1067–1073, 1997.

[Shi et al., 1994] Y.Q. Shi, C.Q. Shu, and J.N. Pan. Unified optical flow field approach to motion analysis from a sequence of stereo images. *Pattern Recognition*, 27(12):1577–1590, 1994.

[Ullman, 1979] S. Ullman. *The Interpretation of Visual Motion*. MIT Press, 1979.

[Ullman, 1984] S. Ullman. Maximizing the rigidity: The incremental recovery of 3-D shape and nonrigid motion. *Perception*, 13:255–274, 1984.

[Waxman and Duncan, 1986] Allen M. Waxman and James H. Duncan. Binocular image flows: Steps toward stereo-motion fusion. *IEEE PAMI*, 8(6):715–729, 1986.

[Young and Chellappa, 1999] G.S. Young and R. Chellappa. 3-D motion estimation using a sequence of noisy stereo images: Models, estimation, and uniqueness. *IEEE PAMI*, 12(8):735–759, 1999.

[Zhang and Faugeras, 1992a] Z. Zhang and O. Faugeras. *3D Dynamic Scene Analysis*. Springer-Verlag, 1992.

[Zhang and Faugeras, 1992b] Z. Zhang and O. Faugeras. Estimation of displacements from two 3-D frames obtained from stereo. *IEEE PAMI*, 14(12):1141–1156, 1992.

Registration of Multiple Point Sets Using the EM Algorithm

Jacob Goldberger

The Weizmann Institute of Science

Rehovot, 76100 ISRAEL

jacob@wisdom.weizmann.ac.il

Abstract

In this paper we address the problem of global registration between multiple d-dimens-ional point patterns with a given correspondence. The actual overlapping is not necessarily between pairs. Instead, it can be between any number of patterns. It is assumed that each pattern is a portion of an image of an unobserved object under a distinct rigid transformation. We derive an iterative solution for the problem of global registration of the patterns in order to reconstruct the original object. Our solution is based on the EM algorithm and it generalizes the well known solutions for the two-pattern case. We also suggest a very efficient method to implement the proposed algorithm. Experimental results demonstrate the improved performance of the proposed method.

1 Introduction

In computer vision applications the following mathematical problem is encountered. A set of rigid transformations (i.e. rotation and translation) is simultaneously applied to an object in the d-dimensional space. Each transformation creates an image which is a reflection of the object in its own local coordinate system. A noise is added to each point of each image and only a portion of the image is observed. Our target is to reconstruct the original object from the noisy images. The problem of finding the motion parameters of a rigid object using two point patterns is a special case of this problem. This special case has been extensively studied over the past decade [1] [5] [6] [12]. Arun, Huang and Blostein [1] proposed a method that utilizes the singular value decomposition to find the transformation parameters that give the least mean square error between the two point pattern. This method is incorporated in our algorithm and it is reviewed in section (3). In the special case when $d = 3$, it is possible to

exploit the isomorphism that exists between the group of rotations and the group of quaternions of unit norm. Faugeras and Hebert [5] and Horn [7] proposed methods for fitting two point sets, based on quaternions. An overview of the techniques for two sets registration can be found in [10]. It was found [11] that no one algorithm is superior in all cases to the other ones. The problem of registration of multiple patterns is much more difficult. A widely used approach is to sequentially apply a pairwise registration until all the images are combined. This scheme does not use all the available information during each registration step. It remains essentially a local approach and it can cause a cumulation of registration errors as pointed out in [2] [3]. Benjemaa and Schmitt [2] proposed an iterative global registration method for the case $d = 3$ which generalizes the quaternions based solution. Their method first finds the rotation part of the transformations. Then, the translations are found by solving a linear system.

This paper proposes a solution for the registration problem that is based on the EM algorithm [4]. We analyze the situation where there is overlapping between any number of patterns and not just the simpler situation of overlapping between pairs of patterns. In the next section we present a complete statistical model that describes the noise included in the observation as a Gaussian white noise. The unknown object and transformation set are viewed as parameters of the density function of the observed patterns. Section (3) reformulate the solution for the problem of two sets registration using the singular value decomposition. In order to implement the EM algorithm, we present in section (4) a modified model which we call "two step model". This model is closely related to the original model and it serves as a technical tool. The two step model enables us to view our problem as an estimation problem in a manner such that the EM algorithm can be easily applied to find the maximum-likelihood (ML) estimation of the model parameters. The iterative registration algorithm is presented in section (5).

Methods for efficient time computations and accelerating the convergence rate are considered in section (6). Finally, experimental results are shown in section (7).

2 A Formal Statement of the Problem

Following is a formal presentation of the problem stated above. Let $Q = \{q_1, ..., q_n\}$ be a set consisting of n points in the d-dimensional space. The set Q can be considered a discrete description of an object in the space. Let $S = \{S_1, ..., S_m\}$ be a set of rigid Euclidean transformations. Each transformation S_i consists of a rotation matrix R_i and a translation vector t_i. Denote :

$$p(j, i) = S_i(q_j) + \epsilon_{ij} = R_i q_j + t_i + \epsilon_{ij} \qquad (1)$$

$$i = 1, .., m \quad , \quad j = 1, .., n$$

The point $p(j, i)$ is a noisy image of q_j under S_i. We assume that ϵ_{ij} is a Gaussian random vector with a zero mean and a scalar covariance matrix $\sigma^2 I$ such that I is the $d \times d$ identity matrix. We further assume that the random vectors $\{\epsilon_{ij}\}$ are mutually independent. In real situations, not all the object points are reflected in all the image sets. Suppose that for each object point q_j there is a subset of $\{1, ..., m\}$, denoted by c_j, such that only the image points $\{p(j, i), i \in c_j\}$ are observed. In other words, the point q_j is only reflected in the images indexed by a member of c_j. We shall assume without any loss of generality that for each j, the size of c_j, denoted by $|c_j|$, is at least 2. Denote $P_i = \{p(j, i) \mid i \in c_j\}$. The set P_i is a noisy image of a portion of the original object Q under the transformation S_i. Denote $P = \{P_1, ..., P_m\}$. In our problem we only observe the noisy images $P_1, ..., P_m$. The original object Q and the transformation set S are unknown. Our target is to reconstruct the object Q. The solution we shall present also reconstructs the transformation set S which defines the global registration of the images.

From a statistical point of view, S and Q can be considered as parameters of the density function of the observed images. We shall find a maximum likelihood (ML) estimation for S and Q.

$$\log f(P|Q, S) = -\frac{1}{2} d \log(2\pi\sigma^2) \sum_{j=1}^{n} |c_j| \qquad (2)$$

$$-\frac{1}{2\sigma^2} \sum_{j=1}^{n} \sum_{i \in c_j} \|p(j, i) - S_i(q_j)\|^2$$

The ML estimate for the variance of the noise can be found by setting the partial derivative with respect to σ^2 to zero.

$$\hat{\sigma}^2 = \frac{\sum_{j=1}^{n} \sum_{i \in c_j} \|p(j, i) - \hat{S}_i(\hat{q}_j)\|^2}{d \sum_{j=1}^{n} |c_j|}$$

such that $\hat{S}_i$, $\hat{q}_j$ are the ML estimates of S_i and q_j. From equation (2) we derive that whether σ^2 is known or not, in order to find the ML estimates for S and Q we need only to minimize the following expression :

$$L(S, Q) = \sum_{j=1}^{n} \sum_{i \in c_j} \|(p(j, i) - S_i(q_j)\|^2 \qquad (3)$$

$$= \sum_{j=1}^{n} (|c_j| \|\hat{q}_j(S) - q_j\|^2 + \sum_{i \in c_j} \|S_i^{-1}(p(j, i)) - \hat{q}_j(S)\|^2)$$

$$\text{such that :} \qquad \hat{q}_j(S) = \frac{1}{|c_j|} \sum_{i \in c_j} S_i^{-1}(p(j, i)) \qquad (4)$$

Therefore, given an estimated transformation set S, the best prediction of the original point q_j is the empirical average of the preimages of the noisy images of q_j. Denote $\hat{Q}(S) = \{\hat{q}_1(S), ..., \hat{q}_n(S)\}$. The set $\hat{Q}(S)$ is the reconstruction of Q given S. Substituting equation (4) in equation (3) yields :

$$L(S) = L(S, \hat{Q}(S)) = \sum_{j=1}^{n} \sum_{i \in c_j} \|p(j, i) - S_i(\hat{q}_j)\|^2 \qquad (5)$$

Hence the ML estimate for the unknown transformation set can be found by minimization the following expression :

$$\sum_{j=1}^{n} \sum_{i \in c_j} \|S_i^{-1}(p(j, i)) - \frac{1}{|c_j|} \sum_{k \in c_j} S_k^{-1}(p(j, k))\|^2 \qquad (6)$$

Equation (6) has the following intuitive motivation. The only information conveyed in the given point sets P is that for each j the points $p(j, i), i \in c_j$ are images of the same unobserved point q_j. In a noiseless environment we could expect that for the true transformation set, for each j the pre-images of $p(j, i), i \in c_j$ will coincide to the same point. In our noisy model we expect, at least, that under the true transformation set, the empirical variance of the pre-images will be as small as possible. Equation (6) is the formal presentation of this intuition.

We are still left with the main estimation problem considered in this paper, namely how to find the ML estimation of the transformation set. In the general case this cannot be done analytically. In the special case where we have only two images of the object there is a well known solution. It shall be reviewed in the next section.

3 Fitting of Two Point Sets

The following problem is fundamental in many computer vision applications. Two noisy point patterns are given in a d-dimensional space and we want to find the transformation parameters (rotation and translation) that yield the least mean square error between these sets. This problem can be obtained from our problem as a special case where m is equal to 2. We continue the analysis performed in the previous section and show that in this special case we can obtain a closed form solution. This solution is based on the singular value decomposition [1].

Recalling equation (6), we want to minimize $L(S)$. In the case $m = 2$ we obtain :

$$L(S) = \sum_{j=1}^{n} \|S_1^{-1}(p(j,1)) - S_2^{-1}(p(j,2))\|^2 \quad (7)$$

Due to a degree of freedom in the problem statement we can assume, without loss of generality, that S_1 is the identity transformation. Hence in this case :

$$L(S) = \sum_{j=1}^{n} \|S_2(p(j,1)) - p(j,2)\|^2 \quad (8)$$

It was shown by Huang et al. [9], that the translation t_2 can be easily found. Setting the partial derivative of $L(S)$ according to t_2 to zero reveals :

$$\hat{t}_2 = \frac{1}{n} \sum_{j=1}^{n} (p(j,2) - \hat{R}_2 p(j,1)) = \bar{p}_2 - \hat{R}_2 \bar{p}_1 \quad (9)$$

such that : $\quad \bar{p}_i = \frac{1}{n} \sum_{j=1}^{n} p(j,i) \quad i = 1,2$

substituting definition (9) in expression (8) yields :

$$\hat{R}_2 = \arg \max_{R_2} \sum_{j=1}^{n} (p(j,2) - \bar{p}_2)^T R_2 (p(j,1) - \bar{p}_1) \quad (10)$$

Arun et al. [1] used the singular value decomposition technique (SVD) to solve this maximization problem in the following way. Let UDV^T be the SVD of the covariance matrix $\sum_{j=1}^{n} (p(j,1) - \bar{p}_1)(p(j,2) - \bar{p}_2)^T$, then $\hat{R}_2 = VU^T$.

This algorithm is not guaranteed to return a rotation matrix, and may instead, when the data is very noisy and corrupted, return a reflection matrix. Umeyama [12] has improved the algorithm so that it always returns a rotation matrix. In [9], [1] and [12] there is an implicit assumption that the noise is only present in one of the two point sets. Goryn and Hein [6] observed

that under the assumption that both sets are noisy, the estimation problem has the same form as if one of the sets was not noisy. In this section we gave a statistical explanation for this fact.

4 The Two Step Model

This section describes another modeling interpretation for the registration problem. The advantage of the new model is that the EM algorithm can be utilized in order to find the ML estimation of the model parameter. We shall first show that the ML estimates of S and Q in the two models coincide. This enables us to solve the minimization problem presented in equation (6). For each object point q_j fix an index $I_j \in c_j$ (for example define I_j to be the smallest index in c_j). Denote $P_0 = \{p(j, I_j) \mid j = 1, ..., n\}$. P_0 is a set constructed from the observed images in such a manner that each point from the original object is represented exactly once. In the model stated in section (2), the points q_j serve as parameters in the density function. In contrast, in the model we shall now describe, the points q_j are assumed to be Gaussian random vectors with mean $S_{I_j}^{-1}(p(j, I_j))$ and variance $\sigma^2 I$. The points in P_0 are no longer considered as observed data. Instead, $p(I_j, j)$ are parameters that define a prior distribution on the original object point q_j. Sampling the data according to this model is, therefore, composed of two steps :

1. Sampling the object Q. Each of the original object points q_j is independently sampled according to the normal distribution $N(S_{I_j}^{-1}(p(j, I_j)), \sigma^2 I)$.

2. Sampling $P \backslash P_0$. Each point $p(j, i)$ is independently sampled according to the distribution $N(S_i(q_j), \sigma^2 I)$.

We name this interpretation "Two step model". In this model, P_0 is a known parameter and the observed data is $P \backslash P_0$. The likelihood of the observations according to the two step model is :

$$f(P \backslash P_0 | P_0, S) = \int_Q f(Q | P_0, S) f(P \backslash P_0 | Q, S) \, dQ$$

$$(11)$$

$$= \prod_j \int_{q_j} f(q_j | p(j, I_j), S) \prod_{i \in c_j \backslash I_j} f(p(j,i) | q_j, S_i) \, dq_j$$

Direct algebraic manipulation reveals that for each $j = 1, .., n$:

$$\sum_{i \in c_j} \|p(j,i) - S_i(q_j)\|^2 = |c_j| \|q_j - \hat{q}_j(S)\|^2 + \quad (12)$$

$$\sum_{i \in c_j} \|S_i^{-1}(p(j,i)) - \hat{q}_j(S)\|^2$$

and therefore : $q_j | P, S \sim N\left(\hat{q}_j(S), \frac{\sigma^2}{|c_j|} I\right)$ (13)

Relation (12) enables us to obtain the following closed from expression for the integral (11) :

$$\log f(P\backslash P_0 | P_0, S) = c - \frac{1}{2\sigma^2} \sum_{j=1}^{n} \sum_{i \in c_j} \|S_i^{-1}(p(j,i)) - \hat{q}_j(S)\|^2$$

such that c is a constant that only depends on σ^2. Hence, in order to find the ML estimate of S in the two step model we have to solve the following minimization problem :

$$\min_{S} \sum_{j=1}^{n} \sum_{i \in c_j} \left\|S_i^{-1}(p(j,i)) - \frac{1}{|c_j|} \sum_{k \in c_j} S_k^{-1}(p(j,k))\right\|^2$$

This is exactly the same minimization problem we faced in our original model in equation (6). Therefore, the ML estimation of the transformation set S in the two models is identical.

From equation (13) it can be seen that the maximum aposteriory estimation for Q given P and S is exactly the ML estimation of Q that was computed in equation (4). From a more general point of view, there is a close relation between the two models. The two density functions, $f(P|Q,S)$ in the first model, and $f(Q, P\backslash P_0 | P_0, S)$ in the two step model, are identical.

5 Applying the EM Algorithm to the Two Step Model

In this section we apply the EM algorithm to find ML estimation of the parameter set of the two step model presented in section (4). As we have already shown, this parameter set is also ML estimation for the model presented in section (2).

Using the EM terminology, we shall refer to $y = P\backslash P_0$ as the observed incomplete data. $x = Q \cup P\backslash P_0$ is the complete data. The missing data is, therefore, the original object Q which was sampled in the first step but was not reported. We shall see that parameter estimation in the complete data framework is indeed much simpler. The unknown parameter is the set S. P_0 is a known parameter. Denote the current value of the parameters set by $S_0 = \{S_{01}, ..., S_{0m}\}$.

$$\log f_X(x; S, P_0) = c - \frac{1}{2\sigma^2} \sum_{j=1}^{n} \sum_{i \in c_j} \|S_i^{-1}(p(j,i)) - q_j\|^2$$

such that c is a constant that depends only on the variance σ^2. c will be ignored in the sequel. The EM auxiliary function in this case is:

$$Q(\theta, \theta_0) = E(\log f(Q, P\backslash P_0; S, P_0 | P\backslash P_0; S_0, P_0))$$

$$= -\frac{1}{2\sigma^2} \sum_{j=1}^{n} \sum_{i \in c_j} E(\|S_i^{-1}(p(j,i)) - q_j\|^2 | S_0, P)$$

Note that given P and S_0, the only undetermined element inside the conditional expectation expression is the original object Q. Denote

$$\hat{q}_j(S_0) = \frac{1}{|c_j|} \sum_{i \in c_j} S_{0i}^{-1}(p(j,i)) \qquad j = 1, ..., n$$

Denote also $\hat{Q}(S_0) = \{\hat{q}_1(S_0), ..., \hat{q}_n(S_0)\}$. From equation (13) we derive :

$$E(q_j | S_0, P) = \frac{1}{|c_j|} \sum_{i \in c_j} S_{0i}^{-1}(p(j,i)) = \hat{q}_j(S_0)$$

$$E(q_j^T q_j | S_0, P) = \frac{d\sigma^2}{|c_j|} + \hat{q}_j^T(S_0)\hat{q}_j(S_0)$$

Therefore :

$$Q(\theta, \theta_0) = c - \frac{1}{2\sigma^2} \sum_{j=1}^{n} \sum_{i \in c_j} \|S_i^{-1}(p(j,i)) - \hat{q}_j(S_0)\|^2$$

This completes the E-step. In order to perform the maximization step we first observe that we can now maximize $Q(\theta, \theta_0)$ separately for each S_i. This is the main reason for using the EM to solve the original problem. Hence :

$$\hat{S}_i = \arg\min_{S_i} \sum_{\{j | i \in c_j\}} \|S_i^{-1}(p(j,i)) - \hat{q}_j(S_0)\|^2$$

Therefore $\hat{S}_i$ is the most likely rigid transformation from the relevant portion of $\hat{Q}(S_0)$ to P_i. In section (3) we reviewed the solution for this problem using SVD. This completes the M-step.

To summarize the EM iteration :

1. E-step : Given the current estimation of the transformation set S_0, reconstruct the original object Q :

$$\hat{q}_j(S_0) = \frac{1}{|c_j|} \sum_{i \in c_j} S_{0i}^{-1}(p(j,i)) \qquad j = 1, .., n$$

2. M-step : given the current reconstructed object $\hat{Q}(S_0)$ reestimate the transformation set in the following way. Denote :

$$\bar{q}_i(S_0) = \frac{1}{|P_i|} \sum_{\{j | i \in c_j\}} \hat{q}_j(S_0) \qquad (14)$$

$$\bar{p}_i = \frac{1}{|P_i|} \sum_{\{j | i \in c_j\}} p(j,i)$$

$$H_i = \frac{1}{|P_i|} \sum_{\{j | i \in c_j\}} \hat{q}_j(S_0)(p(j,i) - \bar{p}_i)^T$$

Let $U_i D_i V_i^T$ be the SVD of the covariance matrix H_i. The reestimation of the transformation $S_i = (R_i, t_i)$ is :

$$R_i = V_i U_i^T \quad , \quad t_i = \bar{p}_i - R_i \bar{q}_i(S_0) \qquad i = 1, ..., m$$

As mentioned in the case of two images, there is a degree of freedom in the solution for our problem. We can apply a global transformation to all the transformations in the suggested set $\hat{S}$. This is so because we do not have any knowledge about the coordinates of the real world where the object Q is located. In other words, the reconstruction of Q is unique up to a rotation and translation of the object.

A good initialization of the EM-algorithm is crucial in order to reach the global maximum of the likelihood function. The widely used approach of sequential applying a pairwise registration until all the images are combined can be used for initial values of the transformations set. Any other global registration method that have been suggested in the literature can be used to initiate the EM iteration as well.

6   Acceleration Methods

A major problem in the implementation of the iterative algorithm, presented in the previous section, is the need to go over all the data points during each iteration. In real situations, where there are millions of data points, this cannot be done in a reasonable time. The main computational effort during one EM iteration is spent on computing the matrices H_i defined in equation (14). We shall now show that after a preproccesing on the data, the complexity of computing the matrices H_i in each iteration can be significantly reduced. Direct algebraic manipulation on the definition of H_i reveals :

$$
\begin{aligned}
H_i &= \frac{1}{|P_i|} \sum_{\{j|i \in c_j\}} \hat{q}_j(S_0)(p(j,i) - \bar{p}_i)^T \\
&= \frac{1}{|P_i|} \sum_{\{j|i \in c_j\}} \frac{1}{|c_j|} \sum_{k \in c_j} S_{0k}^{-1}(p(j,k))(p(j,i) - \bar{p}_i)^T \\
&= \frac{1}{|P_i|} \sum_{k=1}^{m} \sum_{\{j|i,k \in c_j\}} \frac{1}{|c_j|} S_{0k}^{-1}(p(j,k))(p(j,i) - \bar{p}_i)^T \\
&= \sum_{k=1}^{m} R_{0k}^{-1}(X_{ik}^1 - t_{0k} X_{ik}^2)
\end{aligned}
$$

such that :

$$X_{ik}^1 = \frac{1}{|P_i|} \sum_{\{j|i,k \in c_j\}} \frac{1}{|c_j|} p(j,k)(p(j,i) - \bar{p}_i)^T$$

$$X_{ik}^2 = \frac{1}{|P_i|} \sum_{\{j|i,k \in c_j\}} \frac{1}{|c_j|}(p(j,i) - \bar{p}_i)^T$$

It can be easily seen that X_{ik}^1 and X_{ik}^2 depend only on the observed data. Therefore, they can be computed once in advance. The rotation element of the transformation S_i can be obtained from H_i using the SVD technique. The translation element of the rigid transformation can be efficiently computed in a similar manner.

Until now we have shown how to efficiently perform one EM iteration. The iterative algorithm eventually convergences to a local maximum point of the likelihood function. It is well known, however, that the rate of convergence of the EM algorithm is very slow. We shall now propose the following modification in order to accelerate the convergence. In the EM algorithm, all the transformations are being updated simultaneously. In contrast, in the modified algorithm, after a transformation is reestimated, the new value can be immediately used in the updating of the next transformation. This enables us to propagate the influence of the updated transformation on the other ones much more rapidly. In this modified algorithm there is a monotone decrees of $L(S)$ and therefore it implies a monotone improvement of the likelihood function.

Yet another acceleration step can be done. As it was mentioned in section (3), H_i is actually a technical step in order to solve the maximization problem defined in equation (10) :

$$\hat{R}_i = \arg \max_{R_i} \sum_{\{j|i \in c_j\}} (p(j,i) - \bar{p}_i)^T R_i \hat{q}_j(S_0) \qquad (15)$$

$$= \sum_{k=1}^{m} \sum_{\{j|i,k \in c_j\}} \frac{1}{|c_j|}(p(j,i) - \bar{p}_i)^T R_i R_{0k}^{-1}(p(j,k) - t_{0k})$$

We can now plug into this expression the unknown value of R_i instead of the old value R_{0i}. In this way we do not involve the current inaccurate estimation in the reestimation step. Then, for the case $k = i$ we obtain :

$$\sum_{\{j|i \in c_j\}} \frac{1}{|c_j|}(p(j,i) - \bar{p}_i)^T R_i R_i^{-1}(p(j,i) - t_{0i}) =$$

$$\sum_{\{j|i \in c_j\}} \frac{1}{|c_j|}(p(j,i) - \bar{p}_i)^T (p(j,i) - \bar{p}_i)$$

This expression is constant and has no influence on the maximization operation. We can, therefore, eliminate the case $k = i$ from the summation (15). The updating formulae for S_i, therefore, become :

$$H_i = \sum_{k \neq i} R_k^{-1}(x_{ik}^1 - t_k x_{ik}^2) \qquad (16)$$

$$R_i = V_i U_i^T \quad s.t. \quad U_i D_i V_i^T \text{ is the SVD of } H_i$$

$$t_i = \bar{p}_i - R_i \sum_{k \neq i} R_k^{-1}(y_{ik}^1 - t_k y_{ik}^2)$$

such that :

$$x_{ik}^1 = \frac{1}{|P_i|} \sum_{\{j|i,k \in c_j\}} \frac{1}{|c_j-1|} p(j,k)(p(j,i) - \bar{p}_i)^T$$

$$x_{ik}^2 = \frac{1}{|P_i|} \sum_{\{j|i,k \in c_j\}} \frac{1}{|c_j-1|} (p(j,i) - \bar{p}_i)^T$$

$$y_{ik}^1 = \frac{1}{|P_i|} \sum_{\{j|i,k \in c_j\}} \frac{1}{|c_j-1|} p(j,k)$$

$$y_{ik}^2 = \frac{1}{|P_i|} \sum_{\{j|i,k \in c_j\}} \frac{1}{|c_j-1|}$$

These formulae can be made much simpler in cases of pairwise overlapping or full overlapping between the images. Updating the transformation S_i according to this algorithm has the following geometric intuition. Suppose a transformation set S_0 is given and we want to update the estimation of the transformation S_i. First, reconstruct the original object from all the images except P_i using the current transformation set S_0. The updated value of S_i is the best rigid transforma-

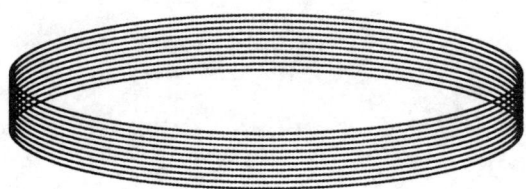

Figure 1. original object

7 Experimental Results

Experiments of global registration were performed using synthetic data. The object we wanted to reconstruct is a cylinder with radius of 1 and height of 0.1. The object was constructed from 4000 points. The original object is shown in Figure 1. The cylinder was segmented in a circular manner into 20 parts, such that each part overlaps with its two neighbors. A random

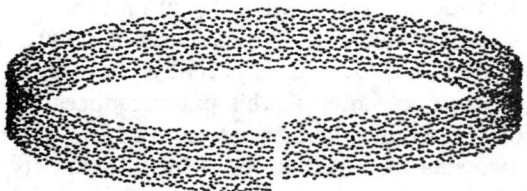

Figure 2. reconstruction results of the sequential registration.

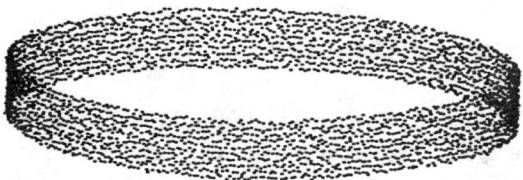

Figure 3. reconstruction results after iterative global registration.

rigid transformation was applied to each part and a noise with $\sigma = 0.01$ was added to each point of each image. First, we have applied the sequential registration algorithm. The results are shown in Figure 2. As can be seen, the quality of registration between the first part and the last one is poor. The average distance between these two parts after the registration is 0.05. The transformation set produced by the sequential registration was used as an initial guess for the iterative algorithm summarized in equations (16). In this experiment we found that 10 iterations (such that in each iteration the entire transformation set is updated) are enough to achieve convergence of the likelihood function. The results of the global registration are shown in Figure 3. In this reconstruction the registration error is homogeneously distributed.

8 Conclusion

We have presented here an iterative solution for the problem of global registration of noisy images. We have shown the stability of the iterative process by illustrating that it can be considered an example of the EM algorithm. The general theory of the EM algorithm assures that each iteration improves the quality of the reconstructed object. We have also suggested an initialization for the iterative algorithm that can improve the chance that the local maximum point, that the algorithm approaches, is actually a global one. The algorithm presented in this paper reduces the general problem of multiple registration to the simpler problem of two sets registration. In order to explicitly demonstrate our method, we adopted Arun et al. [1] method that uses the singular value decomposition to solve the problem of two set registration. Any other existing method can be plugged into the maximization step of the EM algorithm instead. A major element of the presented method is the efficient computation of the iterations.

Acknowledgments

I wish to thank Tamir Shalom for presenting me the global registration problem and for many helpful discussions. Part of the work was done while the author was with the CogniTens Ltd. Israel.

References

[1] K. S. Arun, T. S. Huang and S. D. Blostein, "Least-squares fitting of two 3-D point sets", *IEEE Trans. Pattern Anal. Machine Intell.*, PAMI-9, pp. 698-700, 1987.

[2] R. Benjemaa and F. Schmitt, "A solution for the registration of multiple 3D point sets using unit quaternions", *Proc. of the Fifth European Conference on Computer Vision Freiburg, Germany*, vol 2,pp 34-50, 1998.

[3] R. Bergevin, M. Soucy, H. Gagnon and d. Laurendeau, "Towards a general multi-view registration technique", *IEEE Trans. Pattern Anal. Machine Intell.*, PAMI-18, pp. 54-547, 1996.

[4] A. P. Dempster, N. M. Laird and D. B. Rubin, "Maximum likelihood estimation from incomplete data", *Journal of the Royal Statistics Society*, vol 39, pp 1-38, 1977.

[5] O. D. Faugeras and M. Hebert, "A 3-D recognition and positioning algorithm using geometrical matching between primitive surfaces", *Proc. Eighth Int. Joint Conf. Artificial Intell. Karlsruhe, Germany*, pp. 996-1002, 1983.

[6] D. Goryn and S. Hein, "On the estimation of rigid body rotation from noisy data", *IEEE Trans. Pattern Anal. Machine Intell.*, PAMI-17, pp. 1219-1220, 1995.

[7] B. K. P. Horn, "Closed-form solution of absolute orientation using unit quaternions", *J. Opt. Soc. Amer.*, vol. 4, pp. 629-642, 1987.

[8] B. K. P. Horn, "Closed-form solution of absolute orientation using orthonormal matrices", *J. Opt. Soc. Amer.*, vol. 5, pp. 1127-1135, 1987.

[9] T. S. Huang, S. D. Blostein and E. A. Margerum, "Least squares estimation of motion parameters from 3D correspondences", *Proc IEEE Conf. Computer Vision and Pattern Recognition*, 1996.

[10] K. Kanatani, "Analysis of 3D rotation fitting" *IEEE Trans. Pattern Anal. Machine Intell.*, PAMI-16, pp. 543-549, 1994.

[11] A. Lorusso, D. Eggert and R. Fisher, "A comparison of four algorithms for estimating 3D rigid transformations", *British Machine Vision Conference*, pp 237-246, 1995.

[12] S. Umeyama, "Least-squares estimation of transformation parameters between two points patterns", *IEEE Trans. Pattern Anal. Machine Intell.*, PAMI-13, pp. 376-380, 1991.

New Algorithms for Two-Frame Structure from Motion

J Oliensis
NEC Research Institute
4 Independence Way
Princeton, NJ   08540

Yakup Genc
Department of Computer Science
University of Illinois
Urbana, IL   61801

Abstract

We describe two new algorithms for two–frame structure from motion from tracked point features. One is the first fast algorithm for computing an exact least–squares estimate. It exploits our observation that the rotationally invariant least–squares error can be written in a simple form that depends just on the motion. The other is essentially as accurate as the least–squares estimate and is more efficient, probably faster, and potentially more robust than previous algorithms of comparable accuracy. We also analyze theoretically the accuracy of the optical–flow approximation to the least–squares error.

1 Introduction

The most accurate current structure–from–motion (SFM) algorithms minimize the least–squares image error in the structure as well as the motion. This makes them slow, since the minimization is in many variables. There exists a faster but non–optimal 2–frame algorithm that minimizes the coplanarity error in the five motion unknowns. Recently, [7][15] have shown that a standard version of this second approach, which we refer to as the **weighted–coplanarity** algorithm or **WC,** gives results that are almost as accurate as those of the full minimization. **WC** typically give results for the translation direction differing by *fractions* of a degree from those of the full minimization.

Also, [7][6][11] have shown that two–frame algorithms have less of a problem with local minima and give better results than previously believed. Combined, the results of [7][6][15][11] show that two–frame algorithms can be at once fast, robust, and accurate, and should be considered important tools for SFM.

This paper describes two new two–frame algorithms. The first, A_1, is based on our observation that the least–squares, rotationally–invariant error can be written in a simple form that depends on the motion alone. By minimizing this error in the motion unknowns, we obtain the first fast algorithm that computes a true least–squares reconstruction. Our second

algorithm, A_2, is targeted for increased speed, at a small cost in accuracy. It is based on the optical–flow approximation to the least–squares error. We analyze this approximation theoretically and show that it is typically a good one. Experimentally, we show that A_2 is as accurate as the weighted–coplanarity approach [15][7] and thus nearly as accurate as the least–squares estimate. It is also more efficient and probably faster[1] than either A_1 or **WC**, and it is potentially more robust.

A_2 minimizes over the motion unknowns, but it reorganizes the minimization to make it more efficient. Like some previous approaches, it alternates between solving for the rotation and the translation direction $\hat{T} \equiv T/|T|$. But, in contrast with these, its computation of $\hat{T}$ is insensitive to first–order rotation errors, so that it is guaranteed to converge to the correct reconstruction when it starts nearby. The algorithm gives accurate results for $\hat{T}$ even when the rotation still has a large error, and typically it requires just a few cycles of rotation/translation recovery to compute $\hat{T}$ accurately. Also, its rotation–recovery step is purely linear and thus fast, while its translation recovery is also relatively fast since it involves a nonlinear minimization just in the two unknowns corresponding to the translation direction. In fact, much of the translation–recovery step can be reduced to a minimization in a single variable, and for roughly forward translations one can do the full minimization *exactly* with little computational cost [11].

Since the core of A_2 consists of a minimization in one or two unknowns, it should be significantly faster than **WC** or A_1. Also, since [6] suggests that local–minimum problems occur mainly when the focus of expansion (FOE) lies within the image, and since for these cases A_2 can find the global–minimum solution for the translation [11], A_2 should also be more robust than **WC** or even a full minimization as in A_1.

---

[1] We have not compared explicit timings for the algorithms, since this depends crucially on the implementation and our current implementations are non–optimal.

One disadvantage of $\mathbf{A}_2$ is its lack of generality: it cannot deal with arbitrarily large translations. But theory and experiment confirm that this is a mild restriction. Our experiments show that even very large translations do not cause problems.

2   Algorithm $\mathbf{A}_1$

Let the unit vectors $\hat{\mathbf{p}}_{0i}$ and $\hat{\mathbf{p}}_{1i}$ represent image points in the first and second image corresponding to the 3D point $\mathbf{P}_i$, and let R and $\mathbf{T}$ be the rotation and translation. We represent the structure $\mathbf{P}_i$ in the coordinate system of the first image. Consider the *rotationally invariant* least–squares error

$$E_{LS\theta,i} \equiv \left| \frac{\mathbf{P}_i}{|\mathbf{P}_i|} - \hat{\mathbf{p}}_{0i} \right|^2 + \left| \frac{R(\mathbf{P}_i - \mathbf{T})}{|R(\mathbf{P}_i - \mathbf{T})|} - \hat{\mathbf{p}}_{1i} \right|^2 . \quad (1)$$

The least–squares error in the image plane (Section 3) is more standard. But the two errors are almost equal for moderate field of view (FOV), and it is not clear which is more realistic. $E_{LS\theta}$ seems to accord better with the physics of lenses and with an assumption that the scene is independent of viewing angle.

Assume R and $\mathbf{T}$ are given. Rewrite the second term in (1) as $\left| (\mathbf{P}_i - \mathbf{T}) / |\mathbf{P}_i - \mathbf{T}| - R^{-1}\hat{\mathbf{p}}_{1i} \right|^2$. $P_i / |\mathbf{P}_i|$, $(\mathbf{P}_i - \mathbf{T}) / |\mathbf{P}_i - \mathbf{T}|$, and $\mathbf{T}$ lie on a great circle which we characterize by its normal $\hat{n}$. Neglecting the positive–depth constraints as usual, one can select $P_i / |\mathbf{P}_i|$ and $(\mathbf{P}_i - \mathbf{T}) / |\mathbf{P}_i - \mathbf{T}|$ anywhere on this great circle. Thus $E'_{LS\theta,i} \equiv \min_{\mathbf{P}_i} E_{LS\theta,i}$

$$= \min_{\hat{n} \perp \mathbf{T}} \left(|\hat{n} \cdot \hat{\mathbf{p}}_{0i}|^2 + |\hat{n} \cdot R^{-1}\hat{\mathbf{p}}_{1i}|^2 \right)$$
$$= \min_{\hat{n} \perp \mathbf{T}} (\hat{n}^T S_\theta \hat{n}) , \quad S_\theta = \hat{\mathbf{p}}_{0i}\hat{\mathbf{p}}_{0i}^T + R^{-1}\hat{\mathbf{p}}_{1i}\hat{\mathbf{p}}_{1i}^T R.$$

Since $\hat{n} \perp \mathbf{T}$, one can compute $E'_{LS\theta,i}$ explicitly as the least eigenvalue of a 2×2 matrix

$$E'_{LS\theta,i} = A_\theta/2 - \sqrt{A_\theta^2/4 - B_\theta} ; \quad (2)$$

$$A_\theta \equiv \hat{\mathbf{p}}_{0i}^T \left(1 - \hat{\mathbf{T}}\hat{\mathbf{T}}^T \right) \hat{\mathbf{p}}_{0i} + \hat{\mathbf{p}}_{1i}^T R \left(1 - \hat{\mathbf{T}}\hat{\mathbf{T}}^T \right) R^{-1}\hat{\mathbf{p}}_{1i}$$

and $B_\theta \equiv \left(\hat{\mathbf{T}} \cdot \hat{\mathbf{p}}_{0i} \times R^{-1}\hat{\mathbf{p}}_{1i} \right)^2$.

Algorithm $\mathbf{A}_1$ minimizes $E_{LS\theta}(\mathbf{T},R) \equiv \sum_i E'_{LS\theta,i}$ over $\mathbf{T},R$ using the simple expression (2). $E_{LS\theta}$ is the correct least–squares error under the rotationally symmetric error model, except for our neglect of the positive–depth constraints.[2] The main advantage of the exact form (2) over the approximate errors of $\mathbf{WC}$ or $\mathbf{A}_2$ is that it gives better results when $\mathbf{T}$ is close to an image point, see below and [15].

---

[2] We know of no work to date which properly incorporates the positive–depth constraint into the least–squares error. It may not be difficult to incorporate these constraints into (2), due to its simplicity.

3   Algorithm $\mathbf{A}_2$

Algorithm $\mathbf{A}_2$ minimizes the optical–flow approximation to the least–squares error. We first analyze this approximation.

The standard image–plane least–squares error

$$E_{LS,i} \equiv \left| \frac{[\mathbf{P}_i]_2}{Z_i} - \mathbf{p}_{0i} \right|^2 + \left| \frac{[R(\mathbf{P}_i - \mathbf{T})]_2}{[R(\mathbf{P}_i - \mathbf{T})]_z} - \mathbf{p}_{1i} \right|^2 ,$$

where now $\mathbf{p}_{0i}$ and $\mathbf{p}_{1i}$ are 2D image points. We use the notation $[\mathbf{V}]_2$ to denote a 2D vector consisting of the first 2 components of the vector $\mathbf{V}$.

First assume zero rotation. As before, one can compute $E'_{LS,i} \equiv \min_{\mathbf{P}_i} E_{LS,i}$ neglecting the positive–depth constraints:

$$E'_{LS,i} = A/2 - \sqrt{A^2/4 - B},$$
$$A \equiv \left(|\mathbf{p}_{0i} - \mathbf{e}|^2 + |\mathbf{p}_{1i} - \mathbf{e}|^2 \right) /2,$$

$B \equiv |(\mathbf{p}_{0i} - \mathbf{e}) \times (\mathbf{p}_{1i} - \mathbf{p}_{0i})|^2$. Here the epipole $\mathbf{e} \equiv [\mathbf{T}]_2 / T_z$, and for 2D vectors V, V', the notation $V \times V'$ signifies $V_x V'_y - V_y V'_x$. Expanding $E'_{LS,i}$ in the parameter $\alpha_i \equiv 4B/A^2$ yields

$$E'_{LS,i} = E'_{0,i} \left(1 + \alpha_i/4 + o\left(\alpha_i^2\right) \right) ,$$
$$E'_{0,i} \equiv B/(2A) .$$

We have $E'_{0,i}/E'_{LS,i} = \frac{1}{2}\alpha / \left(1 - \sqrt{1-\alpha} \right)$, so $1 \geq E'_{0,i}/E'_{LS,i} \geq 1/2$, and $E'_{0,i}/E'_{LS,i}$ is a slowly decreasing function of α_i. Explicitly, $\alpha_i = 4\sin^2(\theta)\rho^2 / \left(1 + \rho^2 \right)^2$, where θ is the angle between $(\mathbf{p}_0 - \mathbf{e})$, $(\mathbf{p}_1 - \mathbf{e})$ and $\rho \equiv |\mathbf{p}_1 - \mathbf{e}| / |\mathbf{p}_0 - \mathbf{e}|$. α_i is small and thus $E'_{0,i}$ is an excellent approximation to $E'_{LS,i}$, except very near the special configuration where $\mathbf{p}_{0i}$, $\mathbf{e}$, $\mathbf{p}_{1i}$ form an approximate isosceles right triangle. For a general image, no matter where $\mathbf{e}$ is, this configuration occurs for at most a small fraction of the image points. For moderate translations, it occurs only for $\mathbf{e} \sim \mathbf{p}_{0i}$. Thus $E_0 \equiv \sum_i E'_{0,i}$ gives an excellent approximation to $E_{LS} \equiv \sum_i E'_{LS,i}$, especially for moderate translations.

For zero rotations, the optical–flow error corresponds to

$$E'_{F,i} \equiv B / \left(2 |\mathbf{p}_{0i} - \mathbf{e}|^2 \right) .$$

$E'_{F,i}$ gives a good approximation to $E'_{0,i}$ whenever $|\mathbf{e} - \mathbf{p}_{0,1i}| \gg |\mathbf{p}_{0i} - \mathbf{p}_{1i}|$. Since $E'_{0,i}$ gives a good approximation to $E'_{LS,i}$ under these circumstances, so does $E'_{F,i}$. For example, if $|\mathbf{e} - \mathbf{p}_{1i}| > 6 |\mathbf{p}_{0i} - \mathbf{p}_{1i}|$, the maximum of $\left| E'_{0,i} - E'_{LS,i} \right| / \left| E'_{LS,i} \right|$ is about .007 and that of $\left| E'_{F,i} - E'_{LS,i} \right| / \left| E'_{LS,i} \right|$ is about 0.18. Since

$E'_{F,i}$ can give a poor approximation to $E'_{F,i}$ only for image points near $\mathbf{e}$, the sum $E_F \equiv \sum_i E'_{F,i}$ typically gives a good approximation to E_{LS}.

We sketch how this result extends for small, nonzero rotations. Assuming N_p image points, consider the length–N_p vector $\boldsymbol{\Upsilon}$ with elements

$$\Upsilon_i \equiv (\mathbf{p}_{0i} - \mathbf{e}) \times (\mathbf{p}_{1i} - \mathbf{p}_{0i}) / |\mathbf{p}_{0i} - \mathbf{e}|.$$

The optical–flow error for nonzero rotations, which is the one used by $\mathbf{A}_2$, is

$$E_F(\mathbf{T}) = \boldsymbol{\Upsilon}^T \bar{\mathbf{P}}_3 \boldsymbol{\Upsilon}/2, \qquad (3)$$

where $\bar{\mathbf{P}}_3$ is a $N_p \times N_p$ projection matrix defined to annihilate the first–order rotation contribution to Υ_i. (That is, $\bar{\mathbf{P}}_3$ annihilates all vectors of the form $(\mathbf{p}_{0i} - \mathbf{e}) \times \mathbf{r}_i / |\mathbf{p}_{0i} - \mathbf{e}|$, where $\mathbf{r}_i$ is a rotational flow.) $\bar{\mathbf{P}}_3$ causes $E_F(\mathbf{T})$ to be rotation invariant to first order.

For moderate FOV and small rotations, $E_{LS,i} \approx$

$$\tilde{E}_{LS,i} \equiv \left| \frac{[\mathbf{P}_i]_2}{Z_i} - \mathbf{p}_{0i} \right|^2 + \left| \frac{[\mathbf{P}_i - \mathbf{T}]_2}{(\mathbf{P}_i - \mathbf{T})_z} - R^{-1}\mathbf{p}_{1i} \right|^2,$$

and $\min_R E_{LS}(\mathbf{T},R) \approx \min_R \tilde{E}_{LS,i}(\mathbf{T},\mathbf{R}) \equiv \tilde{E}_{LS,i}(\mathbf{T},\mathbf{R}_{\min})$. Our previous discussion for zero rotation, plus the fact that $E_F(\mathbf{T})$ is first–order rotation invariant, implies that the optical flow error continues to be a good approximator for small rotations: $E_F(\mathbf{T}) \approx \min_R E_{LS}(\mathbf{T},R)$.

3.1 Algorithm $\mathbf{A}_2$: Description

$\mathbf{A}_2$ cycles between recovering the translation and rotation. In the translation–recovery step, we assume that the rotation has already been recovered and compensated for up to a small error. Our current technique for recovering $\hat{\mathbf{T}}$, described in [5] and briefly below, is based on a steepest–descent minimization of (3). It can be supplemented by the global method of [11].

3.2 Rotation Recovery

We assume that the previous step of the algorithm has recovered $\hat{\mathbf{T}}$ up to small corrections and describe how to recover the rotation. With focal length 1, the image displacements between the two images neglecting noise are

$$\mathbf{d}_i \equiv \mathbf{p}_{1i} - \mathbf{p}_{0i} = \frac{Z_i^{-1}(T_z \mathbf{p}_{0i} - [\mathbf{T}]_2)}{1 - Z_i^{-1} T_z} + f_i(R, \mathbf{p}_{1i}), \quad (4)$$

where f_i is the rotational displacement. (4) is exact with no optical–flow approximation. Let $\mathbf{p}_{0i} \equiv (x_i, y_i)^T$, and let $\bar{\mathbf{r}}_i^1 \equiv (-xy, -(1+y^2))_i^T$, $\bar{\mathbf{r}}_i^2 \equiv$

$(1 + x^2, xy)_i^T$, $\bar{\mathbf{r}}_i^3 \equiv (-y, x)_i^T$ denote the first–order rotational flows. For small rotations, f_i is approximately given by

$$f_i \approx \sum_{b=1:3} \omega^b \bar{\mathbf{r}}_i^b + o\left(\omega^2, \omega Z |T|\right). \qquad (5)$$

Define three length–N_p vectors $\bar{\mathbf{V}}^{(1,2,3)}$, where $\bar{\mathbf{V}}^{(b)}$ has elements

$$\bar{\mathbf{V}}_i^{(b)} \equiv \frac{\mathbf{p}_{0i} - \mathbf{e}}{|\mathbf{p}_{0i} - \mathbf{e}|} \times \bar{\mathbf{r}}_i^{(b)}. \qquad (6)$$

Let $\bar{\mathbf{V}} \equiv [\bar{\mathbf{V}}^{(1)}, \bar{\mathbf{V}}^{(2)}, \bar{\mathbf{V}}^{(3)}]$. From (4) and (5),

$$\boldsymbol{\Upsilon}_c = \bar{\mathbf{V}}_c \boldsymbol{\omega} + o\left(\omega^2, \delta \hat{\mathbf{T}} Z^{-1} |\mathbf{T}|\right), \qquad (7)$$

where the subscript c indicates that the quantities are calculated for the current $\hat{\mathbf{T}}$ estimate, and $\delta \hat{\mathbf{T}}$ denotes the error in the recovered $\hat{\mathbf{T}}$. For a moderate field of view (FOV) with $\theta_F < 90°$, solving $\bar{\boldsymbol{\Upsilon}}_c \approx \mathbf{V}_c \boldsymbol{\omega}$ directly for $\boldsymbol{\omega}$ would give a result biased toward $\boldsymbol{\omega} \sim \hat{\mathbf{z}}$, since the third column of $\mathbf{V}_c \sim o(x,y)$ while the other columns are $o(1)$. Thus we actually compute $\boldsymbol{\omega}$ by solving

$$\bar{\boldsymbol{\Upsilon}}_c = \mathbf{V}'_c \boldsymbol{\omega}'$$

in the least–squares sense for $\boldsymbol{\omega}'$, where

$$\mathbf{V}'_c \equiv [\bar{\mathbf{V}}_c^{(1)}, \bar{\mathbf{V}}_c^{(2)}, \lambda^{-1} \bar{\mathbf{V}}_c^{(3)}], \quad \boldsymbol{\omega}'^T \equiv (\omega_1, \omega_2, \lambda \omega_3),$$

and

$$\lambda \equiv \left(N_p^{-1} \sum_{i=1}^{N_p} \left(x^2 + y^2\right)_i \right)^{1/2}.$$

Once we have computed $\boldsymbol{\omega}$ in this way, we rotate the second image to compensate for this recovered rotation and then reapply the translation–recovery step.

3.3 Initializing the Iteration

To start the iteration described above, we have considered two methods for providing initial estimates of the translation and rotation. The first is the standard linear "8–point" algorithm [4] as improved by Hartley [2]. It can deal with motions of any size but works best for large motions [10]. The second, an improved version [5] of the original approach of [3], also requires just linear–algebra computations. It assumes that the translational motion is not very large.

We have arbitrarily used the second method in many of our experiments. But it cannot deal with planar scenes, and, somewhat surprisingly, our experiments indicate that the "8–point" algorithm does essentially as well as the second technique even for small translations. Thus for practical implementations of our algorithm one should probably initialize using the "8–point" algorithm.

3.4 Details of the Translation Recovery

Due to the bas–relief ambiguity [1][8] [12], the initial linear estimate for $\mathbf{T}$ usually determines the $\mathbf{T}$–$\hat{\mathbf{z}}$ plane accurately, where $\hat{\mathbf{z}}$ is the viewing direction, but does not compute $\hat{\mathbf{T}}$ reliably within this plane. Thus, as described in [5], after this initial estimate, we first minimize $E_F(T)$ just within the plane of $\hat{\mathbf{z}}$ and the initial estimate for $\hat{\mathbf{T}}$. This typically accomplishes most of the work of recovering $\hat{\mathbf{T}}$, and, since it is a minimization in a single variable, it is faster than doing the full minimization in two variables.

The two–frame error function has a characteristic local minimum which is intrinsic to Euclidean SFM [6]. We also use the stage of single–variable minimization to avoid this local minimum, by minimizing in $\hat{\mathbf{T}}$ separately on both sides of the viewing direction [5].

Following the single–variable minimization, we use the full two–variable minimization of $E_F(T)$ to refine the $\hat{\mathbf{T}}$ estimate.

This iterative–minimization technique is important mainly for FOE lying outside the image. For FOE within or near the image, one can compute the exact–minimum solution for $\hat{\mathbf{T}}$ as in [11]. We used the iterative method in all the experiments below.

3.5 Experiments

3.5.1 Synthetic Sequences

In the following experiments, the rotations were chosen randomly up to a maximum of about $22°$. The structure consisted of 30 randomly selected points, and the noise was 1 pixel Gaussian, assuming a 512×512 image and the specified FOV. For each translation tested, we created 30 sequences, with different structures, rotations, and noise for each sequence. The error reported for each $\mathbf{T}$ represents the average result over these 30 sequences.

We compared our approach $\mathbf{A}_2$ to $\mathbf{WC}$, which gives close–to–optimal results [15][7]. Figure 1 shows results for a FOV of $60°$ and 3D points with $20 \leq Z \leq 100$. For five different directions of the true $\mathbf{T}$, we plot the average angular error in the recovered $\mathbf{T}$ as a function of the magnitude of $\mathbf{T}_{\text{true}}$ as $|\mathbf{T}_{\text{true}}|$ varies from 0.75 to 16 units. For the most part, the results of $\mathbf{A}_2$ and $\mathbf{WC}$ are indistinguishable. $\mathbf{A}_2$ appears to do slightly better for the more difficult small–translation trials, at least when translation direction is near $\hat{\mathbf{z}}$. Both algorithms do poorly in these trials, however. The performance of $\mathbf{A}_2$ could have been improved by using the exact method of [11] to avoid local minima.

Figure 2 shows how the algorithms' performance varies as a function of the translation direction. The FOV and depth range were as before. Again, $\mathbf{A}_2$ does

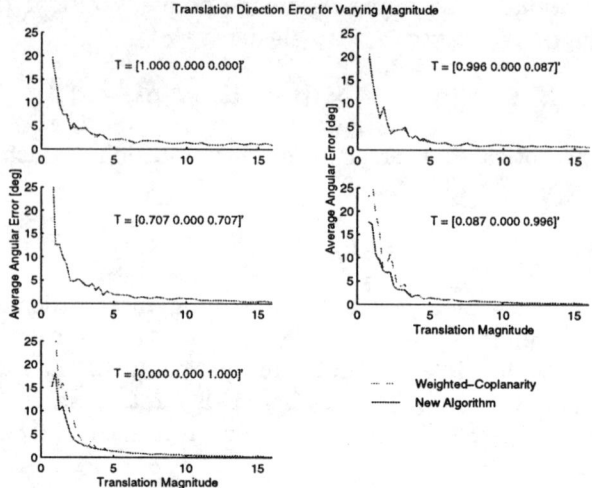

Figure 1: Angular error in recovered translation directions for varying magnitudes at fixed directions ($\hat{T} = (\cos\theta, 0, \sin\theta)^T$ with $\theta = 0°$, $\theta = 5°$, $\theta = 45°$, $\theta = 85°$ and $\theta = 90°$).

slightly better than $\mathbf{WC}$ when $|\mathbf{T}|$ is small and $\hat{\mathbf{T}} \sim \hat{\mathbf{z}}$, but otherwise gives identical results.

We also studied the convergence behavior of our algorithm. For the experiments in Figure 1, the bottom plot in Figure 4 shows how many cycles of rotation/translation recovery our algorithm needed to converge. Convergence typically takes less than 4 cycles even for large translations. For an additional set of experiments, the top plot in Figure 4 shows how the error in the recovered $\hat{\mathbf{T}}$ decreases with the number of iterations. The error shown is the average result over 300 trials with random translations varying in slant between $0°$ and $90°$ and in magnitude between 0.75 and 16. The FOV and depth range were as before. Typically, just 2–3 iterations are enough to give a good estimate of the translation direction.

We also tested our initial linear estimator from [5] against the "8-point" algorithm. Figure 5 shows the results for a variety of translation directions and magnitudes. The FOV and depth range were as before. As expected, the "8–point" algorithm does better at large translations. But, unexpectedly, it also does as well as our linear estimator even for small translations, except for $\hat{\mathbf{T}} \sim \hat{\mathbf{z}}$. We also compared an iterative version of our linear estimator to the "8-point" algorithm. For this version, we repeat a two–step cycle of linear rotation recovery followed by linear translation recovery, until convergence. Figure 6 shows that this iterated approach again does slightly better than (a single run of) the "8-point" algorithm for $\hat{\mathbf{T}} \sim \hat{\mathbf{z}}$ but otherwise performs nearly identically.

Figure 2: Angular error in translation direction recovery for varying translation directions ($\hat{T} = (cos(\theta), 0, sin(\theta))^T$, $\theta \in [0°, 90°$

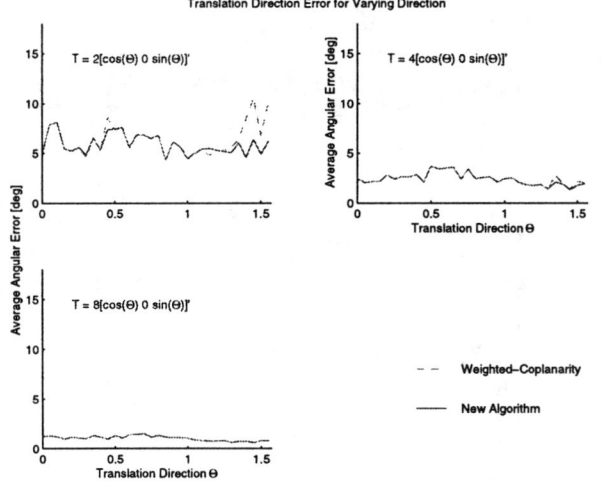

Figure 3:) at fixed translation magnitudes of 2, 4 and 8.

Figure 4: Number of iterations for convergence in the new algorithm.

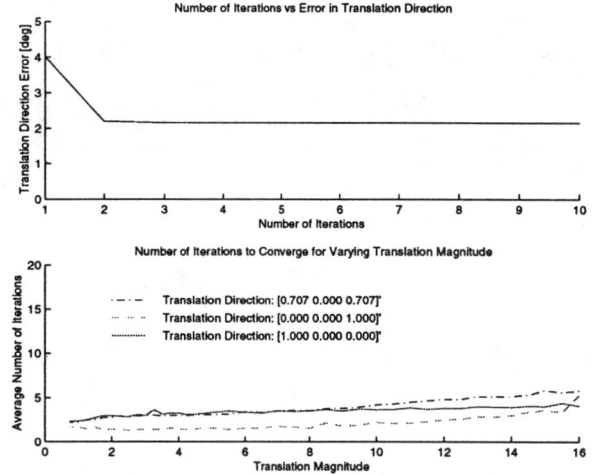

We tested the two algorithms on planar scenes. The planes were chosen with random tilts, with random slants between 20° and 75°, and so that the minimum depth of the 3D points was 20. The FOV was 60°. Figure 7 shows the results.[3] When $\hat{T} \sim \hat{z}$, A_2 again does slightly better than **WC** for small $|\mathbf{T}|$, but it now appears to do slightly worse for large $|\mathbf{T}|$. For other $\hat{T}$ directions, its performance is nearly the same. Surprisingly, our algorithm achieved the same converged results whether started with the "8–point" algorithm or our initial linear estimator. Since our initial estimator gives poor results for planar scenes, this indicates that our approach converges quite stably for these scenes.

We also tested the algorithms with very large motion to the side of the scene. For each image pair, we chose the depths of the 3D points in the range $\bar{d} - 40$ to $\bar{d} + 40$, where $\bar{d}$ varied from 50 to 70 for different pairs. The translation was $\left(4 \left(\bar{d} + W_{max}\right) \quad 0 \quad - \left(\bar{d} + W_{max}/2\right) \right)^T$, where W_{max} characterizes the width of the structure. The rotations were in the range 60°–90°. Figure 8 shows the results for 1000 image pairs created in this way.

---
[3]To account for the well known two–fold ambiguity in reconstructing planar scenes, the error plotted in this Figure is computed as the minimum of the two errors between the recovered $\hat{T}$ and the two valid possibilities for the ground truth $\hat{T}$.

A_2 gives results close to those of **WC** even for this large translational motion. Surprisingly, it again converged to the same results when started from either initial linear estimator, indicating its stability.

Finally, we conducted experiments with varying FOV (Figure 9) and scene depth (Figure 10). For the FOV test, we created 1000 image pairs in the same way as in the first two experiments except that the FOV varied randomly in the range 50°–80°. We also chose the translations randomly with magnitudes of 2–6 units. For the varying scene–depth test, we kept the field of view fixed at 60°, again varied the translations in the range $2 \leq |\mathbf{T}| \leq 6$, and randomly chose $\bar{d}$ in the range 50–80 units. (As before, for any given sequence we chose the 3D depths in the range $\bar{d} - 40$ to $\bar{d} + 40$.) Note that the average error does not decrease with the FOV, though larger FOV makes it easier to distinguish rotations from translations. This is due to the fact that we scaled the size of the image noise by the FOV [13].

3.5.2 Experiments on Real Images

We have also run A_2 and **WC** on the CASTLE data set (available from CMU). This sequence consists of 11 images with 28 feature points tracked over the sequence. From the provided calibration, we calculated that the FOV was 9.2°. Based on a multi–frame reconstruction and the provided ground truth, the 3D points vary in depth from 90–104, in units where the maximum translation from the first camera position was 4 units. Figure 11 shows one of the images with the tracked feature points marked. Figure 12 shows

Figure 5: Angular error in translation direction recovery with linear algorithms for varying translation magnitudes at fixed translation directions ($\hat{T} = (\cos\theta, 0, \sin\theta)^T$ with $\theta = 0°$, $\theta = 45°$ and $\theta = 90°$).

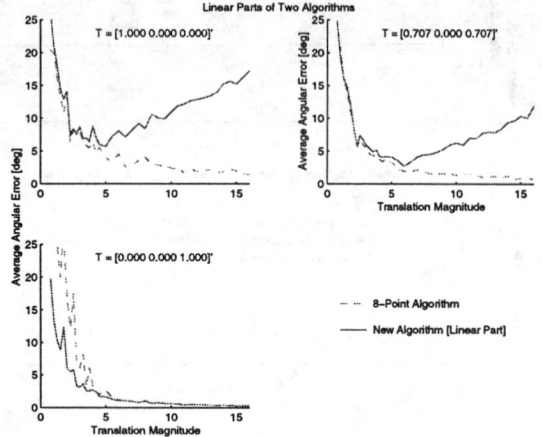

Figure 6: Angular error in translation direction recovery with linear algorithms (iterative for the new approach) for varying translation magnitudes at fixed translation directions ($\hat{T} = (\cos\theta, 0, \sin\theta)^T$ with $\theta = 0°$, $\theta = 45°$ and $\theta = 90°$).

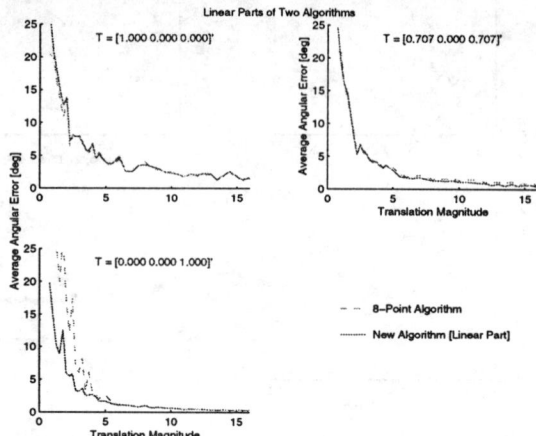

the results[4] obtained by **WC** and A_2 for the angular errors in the recovered $\hat{T}$ for all 55 distinct image pairs. The two algorithm perform essentially identically. Over all pairs, the average error in $\hat{T}$ is 1.35° and the standard deviation is 1.44°.

4   Conclusion

We presented two new algorithms for 2–frame structure from motion and experimentally evaluated the second. The first, A_1, computes a true least–squares reconstruction by minimizing an error just in the motion. The second, A_2, is approximate but more efficient. Our experiments show that the efficiency of A_2 comes at little cost in accuracy: it usually gives the same results as **WC** and in some cases does better. Applying the exact method of [11] would have improved A_2's robustness.

A_2 may be more robust than **WC** or even than a full minimization of the least–squares error such as in A_1. This is because A_2 minimizes a simpler error function, whose properties are easier to analyze. It is the simplicity of this error function that makes possible the fast global search technique of [11], using which A_2 can avoid all local minima for forward **T**. The simplicity also makes possible the analysis of [6], which shows how to avoid local minima for non–forward **T**.

Though A_2 starts from a small–translation assump-

tion, it can give accurate results even for very large translations when initialized using the "8–point" algorithm. As shown in [10], the "8–point" algorithm gives accurate and reliable results when the translation is large and the depth range of the scene is not too small. The translation–recovery step in A_2 can deal with arbitrarily large translations as long as the rotation is known accurately enough: if the rotation is zero, minimizing $E_F(\mathbf{T})$ gives **T** *exactly* up to noise, even for large translations. Thus, when the translation is large, typically the "8-point" algorithm will compute the rotation accurately, and A_2 will accurately compute the translation after compensating for this rotation.

We have not yet studied how to optimize the convergence schedule for A_2. We expect it to be faster than **WC** or A_1 at least for the initial convergence toward the correct reconstruction. At a later stage of refining the reconstruction, A_1 and A_2 might be equally fast.

References

[1] P. Belhumeur, D. Kriegman, and A. Yuille "The Bas–Relief Ambiguity," *CVPR* 1060–1066, 1997.

[2] R. I. Hartley, "In Defense of the Eight–Point Algorithm," **PAMI** 19:580–593, 1995.

[3] A.D. Jepson and D.J. Heeger, "Linear subspace methods for recovering translational direction," in **Spatial Vision in Humans and Robots**, Cambridge, 39–62, 1993.

---

[4]Since the motion in this sequence is almost purely translational, for our algorithm we did not compensate for the rotation. Compensating for the rotations gives similar results; the difference in average is just 0.08°.

Figure 7: Angular error in translation direction recovery for planar scenes. The translation directions are given by $\hat{T} = (\cos\theta, 0, \sin\theta)^T$, with $\theta = 0°$, $\theta = 45°$ and $\theta = 90°$.

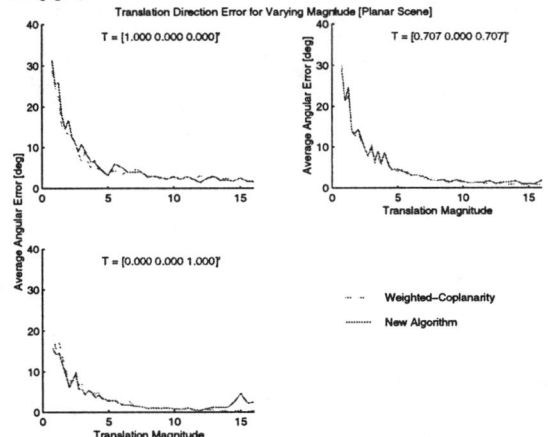

Figure 8: Angular error in translation direction recovery for a motion to the side of the scene.

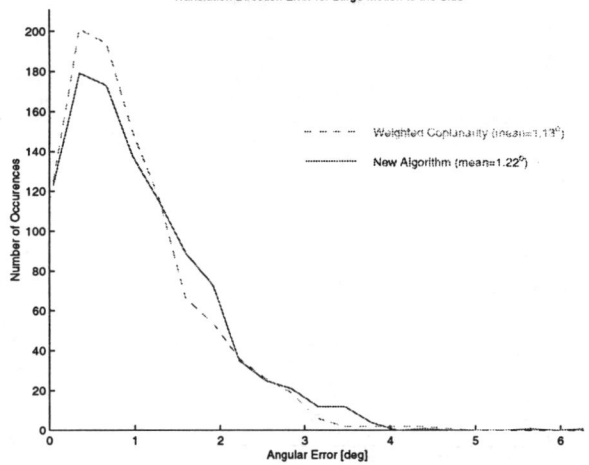

[4] H. C. Longuet–Higgins, "A computer algorithm for reconstructing a scene from two projections," **Nature**, 293:133–135, 1981.

[5] J. Oliensis, "Computing the Camera Heading from Multiple Frames," *CVPR* 1998, 203–210.

[6] J. Oliensis, "A New Structure from Motion Ambiguity," *CVPR* 185–191, 1999

[7] J. Oliensis, "A Multi–frame Structure from Motion Algorithm under Perspective Projection," **IJCV**, to appear.

[8] J. Oliensis, "Structure from Linear and Planar Motions," *CVPR* 335–342, 1996.

[9] J. Oliensis, "A Critique of Structure from Motion Algorithms," NECI TR, 1997.

[10] J. Oliensis, "Rigorous Bounds for Two–Frame Structure from Motion," *ECCV* 1996, pp. 184–195.

[11] S. Srinivasan, "Extracting Structure from Optical Flow Using the Fast Error Search Technique," University of Maryland CAR-TR-893, 1998.

[12] R. Szeliski and S.B. Kang, "Shape ambiguities in structure from motion," **PAMI** 19, 506–512, 1997.

[13] T. Y. Tian, C. Tomasi, and D. J. Heeger, "Comparison of Approaches to Egomotion Computation" *CVPR*, pp. 315–320, 1996.

[14] C. Tomasi and T. Kanade, "Shape and motion from image streams under orthography: A factorization method," **IJCV** 9:137-154, 1992.

[15] Zhengyou Zhang, "On the optimization criteria for two–frame structure from motion," **PAMI** 20, 717-729, 1998.

Figure 9: Angular error in translation direction recovery for varying field of view.

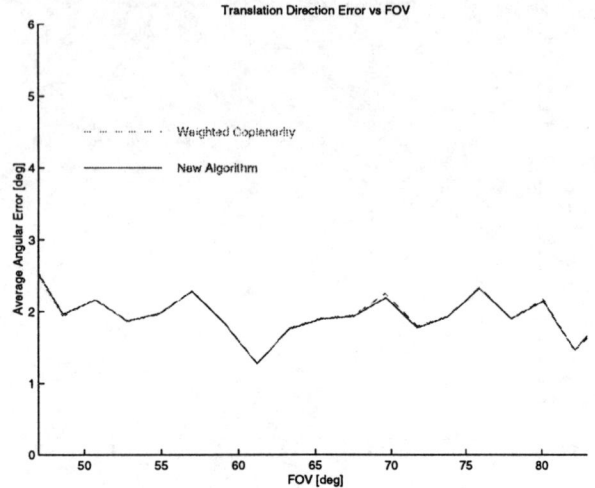

Figure 10: Angular error in translation direction recovery for varying scene depth.

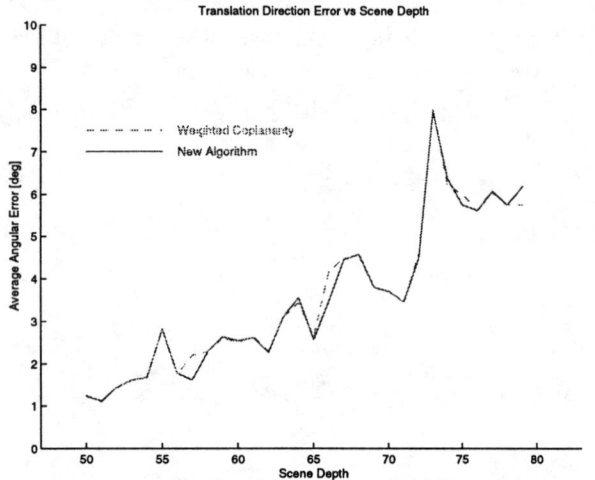

Figure 12: Performance of approximate and the full minimization algorithms on CASTLE data.

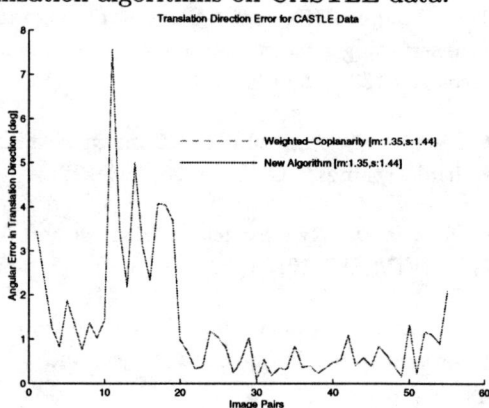

Figure 11: A frame in CASTLE data with overlayed feature points.

Fast and Accurate Self–Calibration

J. Oliensis

NEC Research Institute

4 Independence Way

Princeton, NJ 08540

Abstract

This paper describes new techniques for self–calibration and for recovering the motion from a projective reconstruction when the calibration is known. We show that our approach deals with the ambiguities in self–calibration produced by special motions. We extend our techniques to deal with varying calibration parameters. In passing, we prove convergence for the iterative projective–reconstruction algorithm of Sturm/Triggs and Berthilsson/Heyden/Sparr.

1 Introduction

This paper describes new techniques for self–calibration and for recovering the motion from a projective reconstruction when the calibration is known. We discuss how our approach can deal with the ambiguities in self–calibration produced by special types of motions. In passing, we prove convergence for the iterative projective–reconstruction algorithm of Sturm/Triggs [18][21] and Berthilsson/Heyden/Sparr [1][6] (the STBHS algorithm).

Our approach is two–fold. First, we present simple, fast techniques for motion recovery and self–calibration that work by minimizing standard error functions. Second, we describe how these errors functions can be improved to give better approximations to the correct least–squares image error. Our experiments on real and synthetic images demonstrate that the first class of techniques gives good results but that the second significantly improves on them.

2 Preprocessing: STBHS Algorithm

To generate the initial projective reconstruction, any method could be used. We use the iterative STBHS algorithm [18] [21] [6] to recover the projective reconstruction where, as in [21][6], we start the iteration by taking all projective depths to be 1. This approach gives nearly perfect results for small camera motions, since the exact projective depths can then be chosen very close to 1 and even the first iteration is guaranteed to return a good approximation

to the maximum–likelihood projective reconstruction [21]. Also, this algorithm is guaranteed to converge. Since this result has not appeared in the literature, we show it here.

Definitions. Let the image sequence consist of N_I images and N_p points. We denote the projective depths as Δ_n^i where $i = 1 \ldots N_I$ and $n = 1 \ldots N_p$. Define the homogenous image points $\mathbf{I}_n^i \equiv \begin{pmatrix} x_n^i & y_n^i & 1 \end{pmatrix}^T$, where x_n^i, y_n^i are the image coordinates, and let $\bar{\mathbf{I}}(\Delta)$ be the $3N_I \times N_p$ matrix consisting of the $\mathbf{I}_n^i$ multiplied by the projective depths: $\bar{\mathbf{I}}_n^i = \Delta_n^i \mathbf{I}_n^i$. Given $\bar{\mathbf{I}}(\Delta)$, let $\bar{\mathbf{I}}_4(\Delta)$ be its best rank–4 approximation. Define the error $E \equiv \|\bar{\mathbf{I}}_5\|_F / \|\bar{\mathbf{I}}\|_F$, where $\bar{\mathbf{I}}_5 \equiv \bar{\mathbf{I}} - \bar{\mathbf{I}}_4$ and $\| \|_F$ denotes the Frobenius norm.

Proposition. E is nonincreasing over each full iteration of the STBHS algorithm. The algorithm converges to a minimum value for E.

Proof sketch. Each iteration consists of two steps. Step 1 computes the best rank–4 approximation to the current $\bar{\mathbf{I}}$, that is, the $\bar{\mathbf{I}}_4$ minimizing $\|\bar{\mathbf{I}} - \bar{\mathbf{I}}_4\|_F = \|\bar{\mathbf{I}}_5\|_F$. Since this step does not change $\bar{\mathbf{I}}$, the ratio $\|\bar{\mathbf{I}}_5\| / \|\bar{\mathbf{I}}\|$ is clearly nonincreasing during this step.

Step 2 recomputes $\bar{\mathbf{I}}_n^i \equiv \Delta_n^i \mathbf{I}_n^i$ for the current $\bar{\mathbf{I}}_4$ by computing the projective depths that minimize $\left| \Delta_n^i \mathbf{I}_n^i - \bar{\mathbf{I}}_{4n}^i \right|^2$. We first ask what choice of the Δ_n^i minimizes E or, equivalently, E^2. We have

$$E^2 = \frac{\sum_{i,n} \left| \Delta_n^i \mathbf{I}_n^i - \bar{\mathbf{I}}_{4n}^i \right|^2}{\sum_{i,n} \left| \Delta_n^i \mathbf{I}_n^i \right|^2}.$$

Wlog, we minimize E^2 under the constraint $\sum_{i,n} \left| \Delta_n^i \mathbf{I}_n^i \right|^2 = \sum_{i,n} \left| \mathbf{I}_n^i \right|^2$. Enforcing the constraint by a Lagrangian multiplier α, we find

$$\Delta_n^i = \frac{\mathbf{I}_n^i \cdot \bar{\mathbf{I}}_{4n}^i}{\left| \mathbf{I}_n^i \right|^2 \left(1 - \alpha \sum_{i,n} \left| \mathbf{I}_n^i \right|^2 \right)}.$$

If we ignore the overall scale[1] $\alpha' \equiv \left(1 - \alpha \sum_{i,n} \left| \mathbf{I}_n^i \right|^2 \right)$, these are exactly the values for Δ_n^i computed in Step

---

[1] Explicitly,

2. Thus this Step returns $\bar{\mathbf{I}} \equiv \alpha' \bar{\mathbf{I}}'$, where $\bar{\mathbf{I}}'$ minimizes E for the current $\bar{\mathbf{I}}_4$. At least for $\bar{\mathbf{I}}'$, E is not larger than it was after Step 1.

Now we reapply Step 1 for the new $\bar{\mathbf{I}}$. Since the scale α' factors out, the result for E after this step is the same whether we use $\bar{\mathbf{I}}$ or $\bar{\mathbf{I}}'$. Since E for $\bar{\mathbf{I}}'$ is non-increasing in all steps, E for $\bar{\mathbf{I}}$ cannot have increased since the previous Step 1. Thus E is nonincreasing over the full iteration.

Because $E \geq 0$, the sequence of E returned by the algorithm must converge to a minimum value. In Step 2, if E (for $\bar{\mathbf{I}}'$) remains constant rather than decreasing, then this Step leaves $\bar{\mathbf{I}}$ unchanged and the iteration has actually converged to a fixed point. Thus the algorithm converges. ∎

3 Recovering the Motion from a Projective Reconstruction

Even with known calibration, a projective reconstruction can be a useful first step in computing a Euclidean one. For instance, for small motions the STBHS algorithm [18][6] gives excellent projective reconstructions and, for known calibration, it is straightforward to extend these to a Euclidean result. We describe below a simple linear method for this extension.

A projective reconstruction consists of N_I 3×4 motion matrices M^i, N_p homogeneous structure 4–vectors S_n, and the Δ_n^i, with $\Delta_n^i \begin{pmatrix} x_n^i & y_n^i & 1 \end{pmatrix}^T = M^i S_n$. For known calibration,

$$M^i \mathbf{P} = \mu_i \begin{bmatrix} R^i & -R^i \mathbf{T}^i \end{bmatrix}, \tag{1}$$

where $\mathbf{P}$ is a 4×4 projective transform, the μ_i are unknown scales, R^i are rotations, and $\mathbf{T}^i$ are translations. The problem we address in this section is to recover the μ_i, R^i, $\mathbf{T}^i$, and $\mathbf{P}$ from the recovered M^i, S_n. Since $\mathbf{T}^i$ is arbitrary, the only constraint available for computing these quantities is the orthogonality of the rotation matrices R^i. Let $\mathbf{P}_{1:3}$ denote the first three columns of $\mathbf{P}$. Then

$$M^i \mathbf{P}_{1:3} \mathbf{P}_{1:3}^T M^{iT} = \mu_i^2 \mathbf{1}_3 \tag{2}$$

where $\mathbf{1}_3$ is the identity matrix. We define the symmetric 4×4 matrix $\Pi \equiv \mathbf{P}_{1:3} \mathbf{P}_{1:3}^T$ and solve for it by minimizing $E_{\text{euc}} =$

$$\sum_i \text{tr}\left(\left(M^i \Pi M^{iT} - \mu_i^2 \mathbf{1}_3 \right) \left(M^i \Pi M^{iT} - \mu_i^2 \mathbf{1}_3 \right) \right) \tag{3}$$

subject to the constraint that $\text{trace}\left(\Pi^2 \right) = 1$. In [20], Π has been called the absolute quadric.

$\alpha' = \left(\sum_{i,n} \left(\left(\mathbf{I}_n^i \cdot \bar{\mathbf{I}}_{4n}^i \right)^2 / \left| \mathbf{I}_n^i \right|^2 \right) \right)^{1/2} / \left(\sum_{i,n} \left| \mathbf{I}_n^i \right|^2 \right)^{1/2}$.
Thus $\alpha' \geq 0$.

Because $\Pi \equiv \mathbf{P}_{1:3} \mathbf{P}_{1:3}^T$, it must be non–negative definite ($\mathbf{v}^T \Pi \mathbf{v} \geq \mathbf{0}$ for any $\mathbf{v}$) and at most rank 3. Conversely, when Π satisfies these two constraints it can always be written in the form $\Pi \equiv \tilde{\mathbf{P}}_{1:3} \tilde{\mathbf{P}}_{1:3}^T$ for some 4×3 matrix $\tilde{\mathbf{P}}_{1:3}$. The rank 3 constraint amounts to a single equality constraint on Π, $\det(\Pi) = 0$.

Neglecting this single constraint, (3) is *quadratic* in the unknowns, which we can thus solve for linearly. Differentiating (3), and imposing the constraint that $\text{tr}\left(\Pi^2 \right) = 1$ by means of a Lagrangian multiplier λ, we find the following equations[2] for Π and the μ_i

$$\sum_i \left(\mathcal{M}^i \Pi \mathcal{M}^i - \mu_i^2 \mathcal{M}^i \right) - \lambda \Pi = 0,$$

$$\text{tr}\left(M^i \Pi M^{iT} - \mu_i^2 \mathbf{1}_3 \right) = 0,$$

where $\mathcal{M}^i \equiv M^{iT} M^i$. This yields

$$\sum_i \mathcal{M}^i \Pi \mathcal{M}^i - \frac{1}{3} \mathcal{M}^i \text{tr}\left(\Pi \mathcal{M}^i \right) - \lambda \Pi = 0.$$

This can be rewritten as an eigenvalue equation $(A - \lambda)\pi = 0$, where π is a vector containing the 10 unknowns from Π (the upper–diagonal elements) and A depends on the elements of the $\mathcal{M}^i$. We recover π as the eigenvector of A with the smallest eigenvalue, since λ equals the minimum value of (3). Given Π, we compute $\mathbf{P}_{1:3}$ as the best rank 3 approximation to its square root. $\mathbf{P}_{1:3}$ is ambiguous up to a rotation. One way to eliminate this ambiguity is to select the coordinate system of one of the images to represent the reconstruction. The rotation must be the identity for this image, which fixes $\mathbf{P}_{1:3}$. Similarly, the fourth column of $\mathbf{P}$ is fixed (up to scale) from the requirement that the translation be zero for this image.

Since typically the image data overdetermine the motion matrices, and since the motion matrices in turn overdetermine Π, the Π recovered as above will generally be close to the correct one and thus nonnegative–definite. For the same reason, the recovered Π typically satisfies $0 = \det(\Pi)$ to a good approximation. If Π does have negative eigenvalues, our approach has failed. We have not encountered this problem in our experiments.

A standard linear analysis [3] implies that the error in the recovered Π is proportional to the ratio of the smallest eigenvalue of A to the next smallest. If A has a single, isolated small eigenvalue, this implies that the determinant constraint does not strongly affect the computation of Π. This is the usual case, since the

---

[2] Assuming Π is non–negative definite, the second equation below always gives a non–negative solution for μ_i. Thus we need not consider the alternative solution $\mu_i = 0$.

determinant constraint is only one compared to the $6N_I$ constraints from (2).

For the full self–calibration problem, the $\det(\Pi) = 0$ constraint is important for some special types of motions (Section 4, [16][17]). We do not know if this is also true for known calibration. If it is, A will have two small eigenvalues when the constraint is important. As discussed in Section 4, we can then recover the correct Π by taking the linear combination of the two least eigenvectors of A such that the combination corresponds to a Π satisfying $\det(\Pi) = 0$.

3.1 Improving the Motion Recovery

Though the linear technique gives a fast technique for minimizing (3), we have not yet considered whether this is the appropriate error. Here we define an improved error which still depends on the same small number of unknowns, so that it can be minimized quickly, but whose minimum yields a better approximation to the "optimal" motion estimate (minimizing the least–squares image error). The error is

$$\tilde{E}_{\text{euc}} \equiv \mathcal{R}^T C^{-1} \mathcal{R}, \tag{4}$$

where the residual $\mathcal{R}$ is a length–$6N_I$ vector, whose elements are the independent entries of the residual matrices $\mathcal{R}^i_{\text{mat}} = M^i \Pi M^{iT} - \mu_i^2 \mathbf{1}_3$, and C is the covariance of $\mathcal{R}$. $\tilde{E}_{\text{euc}}$ correctly represents the properties of the least–squares image error to first order.

To compute the covariance C, one must first compute the covariances for the motion matrices M^i. Suppose that we have decomposed the homogeneous image–data matrix $\bar{\mathbf{I}} \approx \bar{M} \bar{S}^T$ such that $\bar{S}$ is orthogonal. Here the $3N_I \times 4$ matrix $\bar{M}$ consists of all the motion matrices M^i arranged in a block column, and the $N_p \times 4$ matrix $\bar{S}$ contains the homogenous structure vectors as its rows. To first order [3], the error in $\bar{M}$ is $\delta\bar{M} \approx (\delta\bar{\mathbf{I}}) \bar{S}$, and the covariance is

$$\langle M^{ia}_\mu M^{kb}_\nu \rangle \approx \sum_{nm} \langle \bar{\mathbf{I}}^{ia}_n \bar{\mathbf{I}}^{kb}_m \rangle \bar{S}_{\mu n} \bar{S}_{\nu m}.$$

The error $\delta\bar{\mathbf{I}}$ comes from the direct error in the image coordinates and from $\delta\Delta^i_n$, the error in recovering the projective depths. To first order,

$$\sum_{nj} \langle \bar{\mathbf{I}}^{ia}_n \bar{\mathbf{I}}^{kb}_m \rangle \approx \eta^2 \delta_{ik} \delta_{nj} (\delta_{ab} - \delta_{a3}\delta_{b3}) \tag{5}$$

$$+ \sigma_\Delta^2 \delta_{ik} n^{ia}_n n^{ib}_n,$$

where we have assumed that the errors $\delta\Delta^i_n$ are approximately independent and all have roughly zero mean and standard deviation σ_Δ. η represents the standard deviation of the noise. Since the image data

overconstrain the recovery of the Δ^i_n and since the $\Delta^i_n \sim 1$ [21], σ_Δ should not be much larger then the direct image noise η. Also, for typical fields of view $|x^i_n, y^i_n| \ll 1$ for most image points. Thus we can approximate the second term in (5) by $\sigma_\Delta^2 \delta_{ik} \delta_{a3} \delta_{b3}$. Since the $\bar{S}$ are orthogonal, this means that

$$\langle M^{ia}_\mu M^{kb}_\nu \rangle \approx \delta_{ik} \delta_{\mu\nu} c_{ab},$$
$$c_{ab} \equiv \left(\eta^2 (\delta_{a1}\delta_{b1} + \delta_{a2}\delta_{b2}) + \sigma_\Delta^2 \delta_{a3}\delta_{b3} \right).$$

To first order, therefore, $C^{iaa'}_{kbb'} \equiv \left\langle \mathcal{R}^i_{\text{mat},aa'} \mathcal{R}^k_{\text{mat},bb'} \right\rangle$

$$\approx \delta_{ik}\text{sym}\left(\left(M^i \Pi^2 M^{iT} \right)_{a'b'} c_{ab} \right), \tag{6}$$

$\text{sym}(f_{ab,a'b'}) \equiv f_{ab,a'b'} + f_{a'b,ab'} + f_{ab',a'b} + f_{a'b',ab}$. To compute (6), we must estimate the ratio of η and σ_Δ. We do this from the discrepancy between the product $\bar{M}\bar{S}^T$ computed in the initial reconstruction and $\bar{\mathbf{I}}$.

Using (6) for C, our improved algorithm minimizes $\tilde{E}_{\text{euc}}$ in the $\mathbf{P}_{1:3}$, μ_i starting from the initial reconstruction. Note that C does not depend on the μ_i: given $\mathbf{P}_{1:3}$ or Π, $\tilde{E}_{\text{euc}}$ is quadratic, and one can compute its minimum in the μ_i linearly. Thus the nonlinear minimization of $\tilde{E}_{\text{euc}}$ only involves the 9 unknowns[3] of $\mathbf{P}_{1:3}$. As before, one must fix the overall scale during the minimization. One simple way to do this is to introduce a soft constraint favoring $\text{tr}(\Pi^2) = 1$. Alternatively, one can strictly enforce $\sum_i \mu_i^2 = N_I$ using a Lagrangian multiplier.

We refer to our algorithm minimizing (4) as the **weighted algorithm** (Euclidean version).

3.2 Euclidean Experiments

We ran our algorithms on three real image sequences: the Rocket [2] and PUMA [14][15] sequences from UMASS, and the CMU castle sequence [23]. Table 1 shows the results. For the Rocket sequence, the camera translation is approximately along a line. The row labeled $\delta\hat{\mathbf{T}}$ in the Table gives our algorithms' errors in recovering the translation direction compared with the Euclidean maximum likelihood estimates (MLE) from [11]. The depth results for the Rocket sequences summarize the errors for 9 of the 11 points with known ground truth. The remaining two points are both distant and close to the focus of expansion (FOE) and have inaccurate reconstructions. Including these two points, the mean depth errors divided by the mean depth are 0.23, 0.20, and 0.07 for our linear and weighted algorithms and the MLE ([11]).

Our weighted algorithm usually improves on the linear one except for the PUMA results. The PUMA

---

[3]Fixing the rotational ambiguity eliminates 3 of the unknowns in $\mathbf{P}_{1:3}$.

	Rocket	PUMA
$\delta\hat{\mathbf{T}}$	$3.4°$, $1.2°$, $2.2°$	
$\frac{\langle|\hat{\mathbf{T}}-\hat{\mathbf{T}}_G|\rangle}{|\hat{\mathbf{T}}_{max}|}$	$.071$, $.063$	$.060$, $.059$
$\frac{\langle|Z-Z_G|\rangle}{\langle Z\rangle}$	$.087$, $.079$, $.052^*$	$.121$, $.126$
δR	$2.9°$, $3.3°$, $1.1°$	$2.0°$, $2.1°$
	Castle	
$|\vec{X}-\vec{X}_G|$	0.28mm , 0.19 mm , $.3$mm	

Table 1: Motion–recovery results for three real–image experiments. In each slot, the first and second entries show results for the linear and weighted algorithms. The third gives the MLE error (Rocket sequence, from [11]) or the ground truth error (Castle). $\delta\hat{\mathbf{T}}$ is the angular error in recovering the translation direction. $\langle|\hat{\mathbf{T}}-\hat{\mathbf{T}}_G|\rangle/|\hat{\mathbf{T}}_{max}|$ is the mean error in the recovered translations normalized by the size of the maximum translation. $\langle|Z-Z_G|\rangle/\langle Z\rangle$ is the mean depth error normalized by the ground truth mean. $|\vec{X}-\vec{X}_G|$ is the mean error in the positions of the 3D points. All errors are computed following a scaling (and, for the Castle sequence, a rotation and translation) of the recovered values to the ground truth.

Figure 2: Puma Image

sequence is difficult: since the translations are almost parallel to the image plane, the reconstruction is strongly affected by the bas–relief ambiguity. However, even though our algorithms start from a projective reconstruction, they do better on the PUMA sequence than the purely Euclidean (non–optimization) algorithm of [11], at least for the rotations where we can easily compare results. Our results on the Rocket sequence are also comparable to those of [11].

Figure 3: Castle image.

Figure 1: Rocket sequence.

3.3 Euclidean Reconstruction: Varying Focal Length

Our algorithms are easily modified to deal with a calibration that is known except for a varying unknown focal length. For this case, $\mathbf{1}_3$ in (2) is replaced by $\mathrm{diag}(f_i^2, f_i^2, 1)$, leading to 4 constraints on Π per image:

$$\left(M^i \Pi M^{i^T}\right)_{i>j} = 0,$$
$$\left(M^i \Pi M^{i^T}\right)_{11} = \left(M^i \Pi M^{i^T}\right)_{22}.$$

It is straightforward to solve this linear system for Π. We applied this algorithm to a modified version of the castle sequence, generated by multiplying each image by an arbitrary scale varying from 1 to 10. Our algorithm recovered the structure with an average error[4] of 5.9 mm per point. This error is reasonable but much larger than for our reconstruction with known calibration. One reason for this is the following. We have shown [10] that varying, unknown focal lengths strongly enhance the effects of the bas–relief ambiguity. This ambiguity is already important for the Castle sequence due to the distance of the scene from the camera and the small motions. Thus the worse recovery is explained in part by the enhancement of the bas–relief effects.

4 Self–Calibration

In this section we extend our techniques to self–calibration. (1) is now replaced by

$$M^i \mathbf{P} = \mu_i K \begin{bmatrix} R^i & -R^i \mathbf{T}^i \end{bmatrix},$$

where the calibration matrix K has the standard form

$$K \equiv \begin{pmatrix} f_1 & s & x_c \\ 0 & f_2 & y_c \\ 0 & 0 & 1 \end{pmatrix}.$$

The $f_{1,2}$ are focal lengths, s is the skew, and $\begin{pmatrix} x_c & y_c \end{pmatrix}$ is the image center. The orthogonality of the rotations R again yields the only constraints

$$M^i \Pi M^{iT} = \mu_i^2 K K^T.$$

Define $Q \equiv K K^T$. Our initial algorithm solves for Q and Π by minimizing[5]

$$\sum_i \mathrm{tr}\left(\left(\hat{M}^i \Pi \hat{M}^{iT} - Q\right)\left(\hat{M}^i \Pi \hat{M}^{iT} - Q\right)\right), \quad (7)$$

---

[4]After scaling, translating and rotating to the ground truth.

[5]It would be more correct to minimize the error corresponding to (3)—i.e., the error (7) but with each summand multiplied by μ_i^4. This would be easy to do. We chose not to for convenience and also because μ_i is typically very close to 1, as we discuss below, so that factors of μ_i should make little difference in the reconstruction.

where $\hat{M}^i \equiv \mu_i^{-1} M^i$. For this minimization, we relax the constraint that $Q_{33} = 1$ and fix the scales by requiring $\mathrm{tr}\left(\Pi^2\right) = 1$ and $\sum_i \mu_i^{-2} = N_I$, which we impose by Lagrangian multipliers.

The error (7) is quadratic in the Q and Π for fixed μ_i. Thus one can solve linearly for the Q, Π given the μ_i. Similarly, for fixed Q, Π, (7) is quadratic in the inverse scales $\nu_i^2 \equiv 1/\mu_i^2$, and one can solve linearly for these. Our algorithm consists of alternating between minimizing in the Q, Π for fixed ν_i and in the ν_i for fixed Q, Π. Each minimization is linear and fast, and the overall iteration must converge to a minimum of (7). Typically, few iterations are required.

[20] described a generalized constrained optimization approach[6] for minimizing an error similar to that of (7). In contrast to [20], our approach is to use a simple, fast technique for minimizing (7), while we reserve the full–blown optimization approach for minimizing the more complex (and accurate) error defined below. Besides being simple, our approach has the advantage of a natural starting point for iteration (see the end of this section), which reduces its problem with local minima. Also, because our approach is quasi–linear, we can use linear analysis to estimate the nature and size of the errors in its reconstructed calibrations.

As in the Euclidean case (Section 3), our technique for minimizing (7) neglects the single $\det\left(\Pi\right) = 0$ constraint. But when the camera moves on a sphere fixating its center, neglecting this constraint produces an artificial ambiguity in recovering the calibration [16][17]. This ambiguity is easily detectable. When we recover Π, Q for fixed μ_i, we do so by finding the least eigenvector of a matrix $A\left(\mu_i\right)$. For motions on a sphere, the artificial ambiguity causes A to have two small eigenvalues rather than the usual one, indicating the one–parameter ambiguity in self–calibration. It is easy to adapt our method to handle this: we simply recover Π, Q as a linear combination of the two least eigenvectors of $A\left(\mu_i\right)$, where the combination is determined by the $\det\left(\Pi\right) = 0$ constraint. Our experiments below show that our adapted approach gives accurate self–calibrations for spherical motions. For more general motions, they show that neglecting the $\det\left(\Pi\right) = 0$ constraint does not significantly affect the reconstruction.

Other types of motion cause real ambiguities in self–calibrating; [17][16] contain a complete catalog. We have verified that our approach can deal with the

---

[6]Some past work on self–calibration [8] constrains Π to depend on Q, giving a technique related to Kruppa's equations [9]. This approach neglects the error in one of the images and should give less accurate self–calibration than the absolute quadric approach [20] which we follow here.

generic cases. For instance, when the camera rotates about a single axis, there is a one–parameter ambiguity in recovering the calibration, which again causes $A(\mu_i)$ to have two small eigenvalues. But, in contrast with the artificial ambiguity produced by neglecting the $\det(\Pi) = 0$ constraint, the two least eigenvectors both correspond to approximately rank-3 Πs, i.e., to possible calibrations. The true $Q = KK^T$ is given by $\alpha_1 Q_1 + \alpha_2 Q_2$, where the $Q_{1,2}$ are computable but α_1/α_2 is indeterminate. We show below for a real image sequence that one can accurately recover the subspace generated by the $Q_{1,2}$, despite the ambiguity of recovering Q itself. The error in recovering the subspace can be estimated from the ratio of the second–least eigenvalue to the third–least [3].

Similarly, when the camera only translates and does not rotate, the calibration cannot be recovered except for the plane at infinity. This ambiguity causes $A(\mu_i)$ to have 6 small eigenvalues. We verified in synthetic and real experiments [23] that the plane at infinity is computable from the least eigenvector of $\sum_k \Pi_k$, where the sum is over the 6 Π_k corresponding to the small eigenvalues.

In intermediate cases, for instance if the rotations are small or mainly around one axis, the eigenvalues of $A(\mu_i)$ have intermediate values. This causes some components of Q to have relatively large errors. We can estimate these erorrs in our approach: if Q_k corresponds to an eigenvector of $A(\mu_i)$ with eigenvalue a_k, the expected error in determining the Q_k component of Q is inversely proportional to a_k [3].

We initialize our algorithm with $\mu_i^2 = 1$. An argument similar to that of [21] for the STBHS algorithm [18][6] shows that μ_i^2 will be very close to 1 if the motion is not too large. Thus, for moderate motion, our approach should find the the correct self–calbration at the global minimum of (7).

Essentially, [21] notes that the third components of

$$K \begin{bmatrix} R & -R\mathbf{T}/\bar{Z} \end{bmatrix} \begin{bmatrix} \frac{X}{Z} & \frac{Y}{Z} & 1 & \bar{Z}/Z \end{bmatrix}^T \quad (8)$$

are exactly 1 when the rotations R are around the z axis and the translation $R\mathbf{T}$ has zero z–component. ($\bar{Z}$ is the average depth.) The third components can be taken as the projective depths, giving $\Delta_n^i = 1$ for such motions. Similarly, the Δ_n^i will be close to 1 assuming small motions, with $|\mathbf{T}|/\bar{Z} \ll 1$, and a moderate field of view[7], with $|(X,Y)/Z| \leq 1$.

Thus, for small motions, (8) with $\mu_i = 1$ yields $\Delta_n^i \approx 1$, while the STBHS gives a projective reconstruction which also has $\Delta_n^i \approx 1$. This implies that

the μ_i reconstructed from the STBHS result also satisfy $\mu_i^2 \sim 1$. Our experiments confirm this.

4.1 Improved Self–Calibration

As in Section 3.1, we can improve the self–calibration by minimizing an error that better reflects the statistics of the true least–squares image error. The error can be derived as in Section 3.1 and is

$$\tilde{E}_{\text{calib}} \equiv \mathcal{R}_{\text{calib}}^T C^{-1} \mathcal{R}_{\text{calib}}, \quad (9)$$

where C is exactly as in (6) but now $\mathcal{R}_{\text{calib}}$ is a vector composed of the elements of the residuals $\left(M^i \Pi M^{iT} - \mu_i^2 Q\right)$. The next section reports experimental results obtained using both our approaches.

4.2 Self–Calibration: Experiments

We tested our algorithms in five synthetic experiments, where each experiment consisted of 97–99 sequences with 10 images and 30 points. The results are shown in Table 2. For each sequence, we selected 3D points[8] with the Z chosen uniformly from $Z \subset [20, 100]$ for Experiments 1–4 and $[30, 100]$ in Experiment 5. Similarly, we selected the X, Y from intervals matching the FOVs shown in the Table. For Experiments 1–3 and 5, we chose the camera positions such that $\left|\left(T^i - T^1\right)_{x,y,z}\right| \leq T_{\max}$, where Table 2 shows the values for $T_{\max}$. Also, in these experiments we added random rotations up to maximums of about $20°, 14°, 7°$ and $30°$, respectively.[9] For Experiment 4, instead, we generated the motions by rotating the scene around a point on the optical axis by up to $15°$. For all sequences, we added Gaussian noise of 1 pixel assuming a 512×512 image.

For stable reconstruction, one should always scale the image coordinates so that they and the effective K are $o(1)$. For our synthetic sequences, we generated the final images by multiplying the image obtained as above by such a K, with $(f_1, f_2, s, x_c, y_c) = (1.1, .9, 0, .2, .15)$. The error reported in the Table represents the angular difference between the recovered direction of this length–5 vector compared to the true one.

The weighted projective algorithm (minimizing $\tilde{E}_{\text{calib}}$) improves on the quasi–linear results except in Experiment 4, where the results are already accurate. The improvement is most signficant for Experiment 3, for which self–calibration is relatively difficult due to the smallness of the FOV and translations. There is also significant improvement in Experiment 5

Note that in Experiment 4 the motion is exactly the type for which one needs the $\det(\Pi) = 0$ constraint.

---

[7] The Δ_n^i will remain near 1 for large FOV if the rotations are sufficiently small.

[8] In the coordinate system of the first image.

[9] The size of the rotations should not affect the results sigificantly, as long as they are small compared to $90°$ [19].

The quasi–linear results shown in Table 2, obtained by combining the two lowest singular vectors of $A\left(\mu_i\right)$ as described in the previous section, verify that our algorithm can handle this type of motion.

We claimed that the scales μ_i^2 were typically close to 1. For 100 sequences as in Experiment 3, the largest values of $\Delta_n^i/\Delta_{n'}^{i'}$ and $\mu_i^2/\mu_{i'}^2$ were 1.08 and 1.12, respectively.[10] For 100 sequences as in Experiment 4, the relatively large motions caused some scatter in the Δ_n^i, with $\max\left(\Delta_n^i/\Delta_{n'}^{i'}\right) = 1.64$, while $\max\left(\mu_i^2/\mu_{i'}^2\right) = 1.18$. Because of the Δ_n^i scatter, the STBHS algorithm gives a worse approximation to the maximum likelihood projective reconstructions as input for our self–calibration. Nevertheless, the Table shows that self–calibration works well.

The large motions also cause scatter in the Δ_n^i and μ_i^2 in Experiment 5. For 100 similar noise-less sequences, $\max\left(\Delta_n^i/\Delta_{n'}^{i'}\right)$ ranges up to 1.37 and $\max\left(\mu_i^2/\mu_{i'}^2\right)$ up to 2.05. Because of the variation in the projective depths, noise causes the STBHS algorithm to converge very slowly in this experiment— even at our cut–off of a thousand iterations, it often appears not to have reached a fixed point. This may explain in part why the self–calibration results are worse here than in Experiment 1, even though one would expect the larger translations to produce more image information and better self–calibration. (A comparison of Experiments 1 and 2 suggests that larger translations do help.) Since the μ_i^2 have large scatter also, one might expect our algorithms starting from $\mu_i^2 = 1$ to sometimes encounter local minima. But this is not apparent in the errors summarized in the Table, which seem to have no outliers.[11]

Finally, note that the $C = 1$ results in Table 2 are *worse* than for our quasi–linear approach, even though they are obtained by minimizing (7) with a more correct weighting.[5] This remains to be explained.

We also ran our algorithm on a real image sequence (Figure 4). We took 12 1536×1024 images, discarding 4 that appeared dark or had motion blur. We ran the point–correspondence algorithm of Z. Zhang [22] on successive image pairs of the remaining 8 using default settings for its parameters. Of the correspondences returned by this algorithm, 41 points were tracked consistently over the entire 8–image sequence. We ran our algorithms on these. The quasi–

Expt	θ_F	$T_{\max}$	Lin	Wt	$C = 1$
1	60	4	1.6° (3.9°)	1.4° (2.8°)	1.6° (3.6° s)
2	60	1	1.7° (4.4°)	1.5° (3.3°)	2.3° (40.4°)
3	30	1	7.9° (23.8°)	4.2° (13.0°)	8.1° (48.4)
4	30	*	.55° (1.6°)	.63° (2.1°)	.60° (1.4°)
5	60	10	3.8° (11.0°)	2.7° (6.2°)	3.7° (9.9°)

Table 2: Self–calibration errors for five synthetic experiments. **Lin**, **Wt** label the quasi–linear and weighted approaches. The $C = 1$ results were obtained by minimizing (9) neglecting the covariance, i.e., with C given by the identity matrix. θ_F is the FOV. Each slot shows the mean and maximum (in parentheses) of the self–calibration error over roughly 100 sequences.

Figure 4: Image from real calibration sequence, with automatically detected correspondences.

---

[10]For noiseless images, these numbers were slightly lower .

[11]The μ_i scatter could also make our quasi–linear algorithm give worse approximations to the MLE, due to our choice to weight the error fuction by μ_i^{-4} (See Footnote 5). However, since the $C = 1$ algorithm uses the correct weightings and gives similar results, this does not seem an important factor.

linear and weighted algorithms computed $(757, 509)$ and $(773, 486)$ for the image center, compared to the ground truth of $(768, 512)$. For the FOV, they gave $45.1° \times 31.1°$ and $46.9° \times 32.3°$, respectively, compared to the true $51° \times 38°$. For the skew, they gave values for $2s/(f_1 + f_2)$ of .0010 and .0025. For the overall error measure used in our synthetic experiments, they gave $4.07°$ and $3.51°$—the weighted algorithm again does better. Both approaches give good accuracy, considering that we used only 41 points and that there was no manual intervention apart from our vetoing four images initially (with no feedback from the tracking). For this experiment, the STBHS algorithm took 92 iterations and our quasi–linear approach took 13 to converge to a tolerance of 10^{-7}.

We also ran our quasi–linear algorithm on the **PUMA** sequence. Since all rotations in this sequence are around a single axis, we can recover the calibration only up to a one–parameter ambiguity [17]. As expected, the ambiguity manifests itself in our approach in the occurrence of two small singular values for the matrix $A(\mu_i)$. From the two corresponding singular vectors, we recovered a 1D subspace of 3×3 matrices that approximately contain the true $Q = KK^T$.

To measure the error in recovering this subspace, we selected from it the Q_{best} that is closest to the ground truth value. The corresponding K_{best} satisfies

$$K_{\text{best}}^{-1} K_{\text{true}} = \begin{pmatrix} 1.04 & -.003 & -.133 \\ 0 & 1.06 & -.003 \\ 0 & 0 & 1 \end{pmatrix}.$$

Thus our quasi–linear algorithm accurately recovers the 1D subspace containing Q_{true}, except for a moderate error in the image center. However, we already noted that the PUMA sequence suffers severely from the bas–relief ambiguity. This ambiguity makes it hard to recover the image center accurately, for exactly the same reasons that it causes difficulties in distinguishing rotations from translations. Our difficulty in recovering the image center may be intrinsic to this sequence.

References

[1] R. Berthilsson, A. Heyden, G. Sparr, "Recursive Structure and Motion from Image Sequences using Shape and Depth Spaces," *CVPR* 444–449, 1997.

[2] R. Dutta, R. Manmatha, L.R. Williams, and E.M. Riseman, "A data set for quantitative motion analysis," *CVPR*, 159-164, 1989.

[3] G. Golub and C. F. Van Loan, *Matrix Computations*, John Hopkins Press, Baltimore, Maryland, 1983.

[4] R. Hartley, "Kruppa's Equations Derived from the Fundamental Matrix," **PAMI** 19 133–135, 1997.

[5] A. Heyden, "Projective Reconstruction from Image Sequences using Factorization Methods–A Generic Approach," Lund University technical report.

[6] A. Heyden, "Projective structure and motion from from image sequences using subspace methods," *SCIA* II 963–968, 1997.

[7] A. Heyden and K. Astrom, "Euclidean reconstruction from image sequences with varying and unknown focal length and principal point," *CVPR* 438–443, 1997.

[8] A. Heyden and K. Astrom, "Euclidean reconstruction from constant intrinisic parameters," *ICVPR* I 339–343, 1996.

[9] S. Maybank and O. Faugeras, "A theory of self calibration of a moving camera," **IJCV** 8(2):123–151, 1992.

[10] J. Oliensis, "A Multi-frame Structure from Motion Algorithm under Perspective Projection," **IJCV**, to appear.

[11] J. Oliensis, "Structure from Linear and Planar Motions," *CVPR* 335–342, 1996.

[12] M. Pollefeys, R. Koch, and L. Van Gool, "Self–Calibration and Metric Reconstruction in spite of Varying and Unknown Internal Camera Parameters," *ICCV* 90–95, 1998.

[13] M. Pollefeys , L. Van Gool, M. Proesmans, "Euclidean 3D Reconstruction from Image Sequences with Variable Focal Lengths," *ECCV* 1, 31–42, 1996.

[14] H. S. Sawhney, J. Oliensis, and A. R. Hanson, A "Description and Reconstruction from Image Trajectories of Rotational Motion", *ICCV*, 494-498, 1990.

[15] H.S. Sawhney and A.R. Hanson, "Comparative results of some motion algorithms on real image sequences," *IUW*, 307-313, 1990.

[16] P. Sturm, Phd Thesis 1997.

[17] P. Sturm, "Critical motion sequences for monocular self–calibration and uncalibrated euclidean reconstruction," *CVPR* 1100–1105, 1997.

[18] P. Sturm and B. Triggs, "A factorization based algorithm for multi–image projective structure and motion," *ECCV* 709–720, 1996.

[19] T. Y. Tian, C. Tomasi, and D. J. Heeger, "Comparison of Approaches to Egomotion Computation" *CVPR* 315–320, 1996.

[20] B.Triggs, "Autocalibration and the absolute quadric," *CVPR* 609–614, 1997.

[21] B. Triggs, "Factorization methods for projective structure and motion," *CVPR* 845–851, 1996.

[22] Z. Zhang, R. Deriche, O. Faugeras, and Q.-T. Luong, "A Robust Techniques for Matching Two Uncalibrated Images Through the Recovery of the Unknown Epipolar Geometry," **AI Journal**, 78:87–119, 1995.

[23] CMU CIL-0001 castle image sequence, available at http://www.cs.cmu.edu/~cil/cil-ster.html.

Removal of Translation Bias when using Subspace Methods

W. James MacLean

Department of Computer Science,
University of Toronto,
Toronto, Ontario M5S 3H5
maclean@vis.toronto.edu

Abstract

Given estimates of the motion field (optic flow) from an image sequence, it is possible to recover translational direction, $\vec{T}$, using a variety of techniques. One such technique, known as "subspace methods," generates constraints which are perpendicular to $\vec{T}$, so that two distinct constraints allow a solution for $\vec{T}$. In practice many constraints are used in a least-squares solution, but it has been observed that the recovered estimates for $\vec{T}$ are biased towards the optical axis. While the cause of the bias is well known, previous attempts to remove it have been flawed. This paper outlines a new method which removes the bias. The technique is simple to apply and computationally efficient.

1 Introduction

In the analysis of image sequences in which the observer moves relative to a static background, the recovery of the observer's motion parameters (termed *egomotion*) has long been a central problem. A variety of methods have been introduced to accomplish this: methods have been introduced by Bruss and Horn [1], Rieger & Lawton [16], Longuet-Higgins & Prazdny [14, 19], and Jepson & Heeger [7, 9, 10, 8, 11].

The subspace methods allow one to recover translational motion $\vec{T}$ using a linear method [11]. However, it is immediately apparent that for the case of noisy flow as input, a significant bias in the estimate for $\vec{T}$ is seen. This occurs as a result of the fact that isotropic noise in flow measurements used as input lead to anisotropic noise in constraints which are central to the subspace methods. The bias is consistently towards the optic axis.

Two different approaches have been used to compensate for the bias. Jepson & Heeger [11] suggest a *dithering* method in which more noise is added to the constraints with the goal of making the resulting noise isotropic in nature. Kanatani [12, 13] takes the approach of subtracting the anisotropic covariance matrix prior to estimating $\vec{T}$, in a process term *renormalization*. Since subtraction is being used it is necessary to correctly estimate the scale of the subtracted covariance matrix.[1]

---

[1] Kanatani's analysis is with respect to constraints on $\vec{T}$ de-

In this paper the author presents a new method for dealing with the bias. This method involves rescaling the linear constraints from the subspace methods according to the covariance matrix for the constraints. Since the re-scaling is done through a multiplication, we eliminate the need to estimate the scale of the covariance matrix.

In this paper the theory of subspace methods and the cause of the bias are presented, the rescaling method for bias removal is introduced, and results from a synthetic image sequence (for which the "ground-truth" motion are known) are presented.

2 Theory

This paper considers the case of planar receptor surfaces. The coordinate system (see Figure 1) is right-handed and aligned so that the z-axis aligns with the optical axis of the camera. The origin of the coordinate system is placed at the optical centre of the camera, so the receptor surface is the plane $z = f$. The receptor surface is placed in front of the optic centre to avoid the need to reflect coordinates.

A point $\vec{X}$ in 3-D space images to point $\vec{x}$ in the image place. Under perspective projection we have

$$\vec{x} = \frac{f}{X_3}\vec{X} \ . \tag{1}$$

We are interested in the movement of $\vec{x}$, which has been termed the *motion field*. Assuming

$$\vec{V} = \frac{d\vec{X}}{dt} = \vec{T} + \vec{\Omega} \times \vec{X}$$

where $\vec{T}$ is the translational motion and $\vec{\Omega}$ the rotational motion of $\vec{X}$, then we can write

$$\vec{u} = \frac{d\vec{x}}{dt} = \begin{bmatrix} 1 & 0 & -x_1/f \\ 0 & 1 & -x_2/f \\ 0 & 0 & 0 \end{bmatrix} \left(\frac{f}{X_3}\vec{T} + \vec{\Omega} \times \vec{x} \right) \ . \tag{2}$$

The vector $\vec{u}$ represents the motion of $\vec{x}$ in the image plane. The measurement of motion of image points is often referred to as *optic flow*.

---

rived using the essential matrix methods, so the bias problem is not exclusive to the subspace methods.

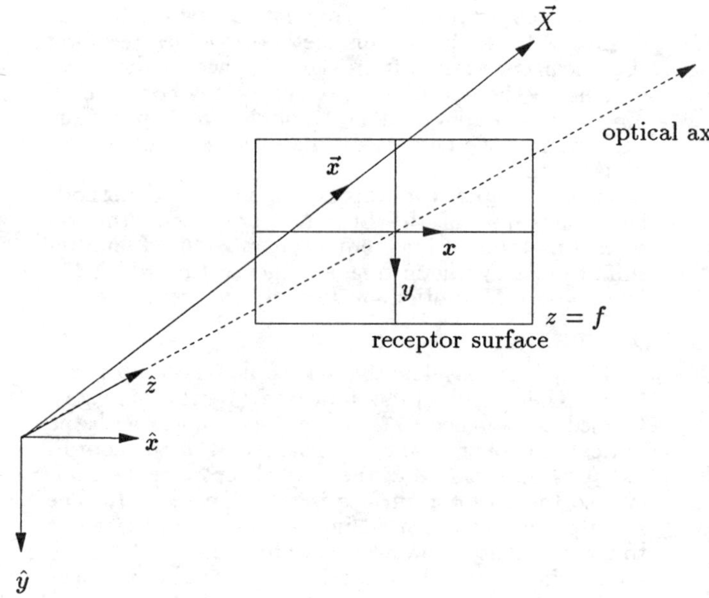

Figure 1: A right-handed coordinate system is attached to the imaging system. The origin coincides with the nodal point of the imaging system, and the z-axis with the optical axis. The planar receptor surface lies in the $z = f$ plane. A point $\vec{X}$ in the 3-D world is imaged to a point $\vec{x}$ in the image plane. Under perspective projection the relation is $\vec{x} = \frac{f}{\vec{X}^T \hat{z}} \vec{X}$.

Knowledge of the motion field can be used to estimate the values of $\vec{T}$ and $\vec{\Omega}$ if the motion field arises from a single underlying motion.[2] Techniques for recovering motion parameters have included methods based on orthographic projection [18], the essential matrix [14, 19], methods which require the detection of planar surfaces in the image [17, 2], and *subspace methods*. The latter probably begins with work by Rieger & Lawton [16] and was further developed by Heeger & Jepson [7, 9, 10, 8, 11].

A simple algebraic manipulation of Eq. 2 leads to the following *bilinear constraint* on translation and rotation:

$$\vec{T}^T (\vec{x} \times \vec{u}) + (\vec{T} \times \vec{x})^T (\vec{x} \times \vec{\Omega}) = 0 . \qquad (3)$$

One such constraint can be written for each $\vec{u}$. Nonlinear methods must be applied to a set of bilinear constraints to recover the values of $\vec{T}$ and $\vec{\Omega}$. It is worth noting that Eq. 3 can be rewritten more simply as $\vec{T}^T(\vec{a} + B\vec{\Omega})$ where B is a 3×3 matrix-valued quadratic function of image position $\vec{x}$ and $\vec{a} = \vec{x} \times \vec{u}$.

A *linear constraint* can be constructed from 7 or more bilinear constraints. Noting that B is a quadratic value function, it is possible to compute a set of coefficients $\{c_k\}$ which are orthogonal to all quadratic forms in $\vec{x}$, and when applied to the bilinear constraint effectively annihilate the B terms, leaving

$$w\vec{\tau} = \sum_{k=1}^{K} c_k [\vec{u}(\vec{x}_k) \times \vec{x}_k] . \qquad (4)$$

The unit-vector $\vec{\tau}$ is guaranteed to be orthogonal to $\vec{T}$. Thus 2 or more linear constraints can be used to obtain a linear solution for $\vec{T}$. Specifically, if we construct $D = \sum_{i=1}^{N} w_i^2 \vec{\tau}_i \vec{\tau}_i^T$ then the eigenvector corresponding to the minimum eigenvalue of D is the recovered direction for $\vec{T}$.[3]

In the absence of noise the linear subspace constraints are exact [11]. Unfortunately optic flow estimates tend to be very noisy, so it is necessary to consider the effect this has on the resulting $\vec{\tau}$ vectors. Jepson & Heeger [11] report a bias in the estimates of $\vec{T}$ when using a motion field with isotropic noise added to generate the linear constraints. The cause of the bias lies in the fact that the noise in the linear constraints is anisotropic.

Consider the noisy constraint vector $\tilde{\tau} = \vec{\tau} + \vec{n}$ where $E\{\vec{n}\} = 0$, and

$$E\{\vec{n}\vec{n}^T\} = \sigma^2 \begin{bmatrix} 1 & 0 & -x \\ 0 & 1 & -y \\ -x & -y & x^2 + y^2 \end{bmatrix} \qquad (5)$$

---

[2] There are techniques for recovering motion parameters from a motion field which arises from multiple underlying motions, but these are not central to the point of this paper, and as such are not discussed here.

[3] Note that we cannot recover the magnitude of $\vec{T}$, just its direction. This is inherent to the problem itself and not just in the particular case of subspace methods.

where (x, y) is the average image location of the bilinear constraints used to construct $\vec{\tau}$. This covariance matrix for the noise vectors is derived assuming isotropic, zero-mean noise in the optic flow. Recalling the construction of our D matrix,

$$\tilde{D} = \sum_{i=1}^{N} w_i^2 \tilde{\tau}_i \tilde{\tau}_i^T$$

$$= \sum_{i=1}^{T} w_i^2 (\vec{\tau}_i \vec{\tau}_i^T + \vec{\tau}_i \vec{n}_i^T + \vec{n}_i \vec{\tau}_i^T + \vec{n}_i \vec{n}_i^T) ,$$

we see that the expected value for $\tilde{D}$ becomes

$$E\{\tilde{D}\} = D + E\{\sum_{i=1}^{N} w_i^2 \vec{n}_i \vec{n}_i^T\}$$

$$= D + \sigma^2 M$$

where

$$M = \sum_{i=1}^{N} w_i^2 \begin{bmatrix} 1 & 0 & -x_i \\ 0 & 1 & -y_i \\ -x_i & -y_i & x_i^2 + y_i^2 \end{bmatrix} .$$

We see that the noise adds a term to the expected value of $\tilde{D}$, and as such we expect it to affect the eigenvectors of $\tilde{D}$.

An intuitive explanation as to why the estimate for $\vec{T}$ is biased towards the centre of the image is as follows. While the $\vec{\tau}$ are orthogonal to $\vec{T}$, we see that for small angular extent of the imaging receptor, the constraints are also roughly orthogonal to the optic axis, since the $\vec{\tau}$ constraints are constructed as the sume of terms involving $\vec{u}_i \times \vec{x}_i$ and the $\vec{x}_i$ used to construct each constraint do not vary largely. In this case translational direction estimates near the optical axis are 'favoured'. We expect that as angular extent of the image is decreased that the bias will become worse, and this is indeed what happens[11].

Jepson & Heeger [11] suggested a dithering method to make the noise in the $\vec{\tau}_i$ isotropic, thereby removing the bias. While this approach is effective, it is not an intuitively satisfying approach since it involves adding more noise. Note that the bilinear constraints themselves do not suffer from the bias, so another approach is to get an initial (biased) estimate for $\vec{T}$ using the linear constraints, and then improve this estimate through a small number of iterations to solve the bilinear constraints.

Kanatani [13] suggests a method called *renormalization* for removal of the bias. Recalling that $E\{\tilde{D}\} = D + \sigma^2 M$, it is possible to construct $\hat{D} = \tilde{D} - \sigma^2 M$. This leads to $E\{\hat{D}\} = D$. This however requires an estimate not only of M but of its scaling factor σ^2, which is related to the noise in the optic flow. By contrast, the proposed re-scaling method does not require an estimate for σ^2.

2.1 Removing the Bias

We have derived the form of the noise covariance matrix for the linear constraints. In general we will not know the scaling of the noise, *i.e.* we won't know the value of σ, so it is not feasible to subtract $\sigma^2 M$ from $\tilde{D}$, as suggested by Kanatani [13]. However, it is possible to *re-scale* the $\vec{\tau}_i$ into a space where the noise is isotropic. If $\vec{T}$ is estimated in this re-scaled space the bias will have been removed. Finally, the estimate for $\vec{T}$ can be converted back to the original space.

In order to understand how this works, note that adding a scaled version of the identity matrix to D does not change the eigenvectors: if $\tilde{D} = D + \sigma^2 I_3$, then $D\vec{x} = \lambda\vec{x} \rightarrow \tilde{D}\vec{x} = (\lambda + \sigma^2)\vec{x}$. The eigenvectors of the two matrices are identical, and the ordering of the eigenvalues is preserved. Re-scaling is achieved by pre- and post-multiplying $\tilde{D}$ by the inverse square-root of the covariance matrix M. This gives us $M^{-1/2}DM^{-1/2} + \sigma^2 I_3$, which has the same eigenvectors as $\hat{D} = M^{-1/2}DM^{-1/2}$. This operation is sometimes called *pre-whitening* [5]. Choose the eigenvector $\vec{x}$ that corresponds to the minimum eigenvalue of $\hat{D}$, namely $M^{-1/2}DM^{-1/2}\vec{x} = \lambda\vec{x}$. The new estimate for the translational direction is $\vec{T} = M^{-1/2}\vec{x}$.

Note that $M^{-1}D(M^{-1/2}\vec{x}) = \lambda M^{-1/2}\vec{x}$. This means the estimate for $\vec{T}$ is an eigenvector of $M^{-1}D$, not D. However, since D represents the noise-free constraints, its minimum eigenvalue is 0. This guarantees that pre-multiplying D by M^{-1} will not change the corresponding eigenvector. Therefore the estimate $\vec{T}$ corresponds to the noise-free estimate, and the bias has been removed. It can be shown that this is also the maximum-likelihood (ML) estimate. It will not be possible to completely remove the bias in practice, as the form M depends on isotropic noise in the flow estimates, and will not be exact for any case of anisotropy in the noise.

It is worth noting that once $M^{-1/2}$ has been computed, its application involves three matrix multiplications, and therefore is computationally inexpensive. Computing M can be done in advance if the constraint weights are assumed to be equal.

3 Results

The rescaling technique developed in the previous section is now applied to a synthetic image sequence. The first task is to estimate the covariance form matrix, M, which will be used in the re-scaling step.

One possibility is to compute the "average image location" of the constraints, $\vec{x}_{av}$, and compute M as

$$M_{av} = \begin{bmatrix} 1 & 0 & -x_{av} \\ 0 & 1 & -y_{av} \\ -x_{av} & -y_{av} & x_{av}^2 + y_{av}^2 \end{bmatrix} .$$

It might be argued that this will always be at the centre of the image, but since many $\vec{\tau}$ constraints will be rejected due to low SNR, it in general will not be. It would also be possible to weight the constraint location vectors by each constraint's SNR in order to get a

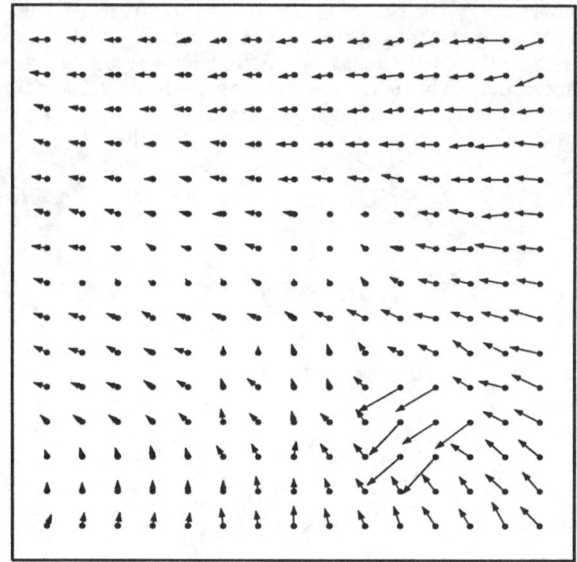

Figure 3: This figure shows synthetic optic flow generated from the depth maps shown in Figure 2. The observer is moving with a translational velocity of $\vec{T} = [1\ 0\ 1]^T$ with respect to the background. The cube is falling, and has a translational velocity of $\vec{T} = [0\ 1\ 0]^T$. A rotation has been added to simulate the observer fixating a point near the centre of the image. 10% noise has been added.

Figure 2: On top is a depth-map (Z-buffer) from a computer generated image of an office. Below is a depth-map for a cube. These two depth-maps have been used to generate a synthetic flow field containing an independently moving object.

"centre of mass" type of average image position. This is referred to as 'Method 1.'

A second method would be to compute M as the average of the M_i for each constraint, where M_i is given by Eq 5. This method will be referred to as 'Method 2.' Again, this average could be weighted by the SNR of individual constraints. Results from both methods are demonstrated.

Motion field estimates were generated by applying a known $\vec{T}$ and $\vec{\Omega}$ to the depth-map (Z-buffer) for the synthetic image (see Figure 2). The translational and rotational motions were chosen such that the back of the chair was "fixated". This has the effect of improving SNR for the resulting linear constraints [15]. The depth map is shown in Figure 2, and the resulting (noisy) flow is shown in Figure 3.[4]

Random noise was added to the optic flow in a series of 5 trials. The noise is added as $\hat{u}(\vec{x}) = \vec{u}(\vec{x}) + \vec{n}$. The noise component $\vec{n}$ is chosen from a 2-D isotropic normal distribution having a standard deviation equal to 10% of $\|\vec{u}(\vec{x})\|$. The noisy flow field is shown in Figure 3. Note that this noise is multiplicative in nature, but this has been suggested as an appropriate model for optic flow recovery [4, 6]. Linear constraints were computed from the flow using a 7×7 convolution mask

---

[4] The flow and motion estimates were generated as part of a project on segmenting multiple 3-D motions from optic flow. Results shown in this paper are for the background motion only.

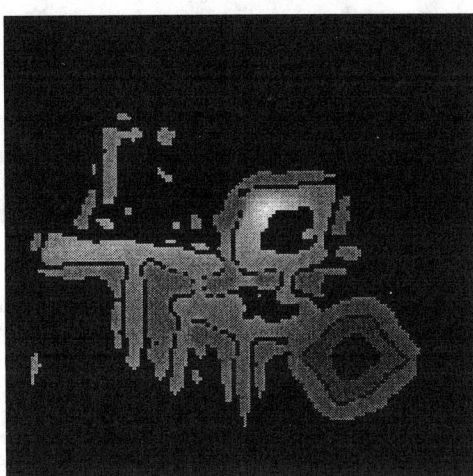

Figure 4: This is a plot of the magnitudes of the $\vec{\tau}$'s recovered from Figure 3. Regions containing depth-discontinuities give rise to the largest constraints. Constraints having an SNR of less than 5 were removed.

	True	Uncorrected	Method 1	Method 2
$\vec{\tau}$	$\begin{bmatrix} 0.7071 \\ 0.0000 \\ 0.7071 \end{bmatrix}$	$\begin{bmatrix} 0.6316 \\ 0.0005 \\ 0.7737 \end{bmatrix}$	$\begin{bmatrix} 0.7236 \\ 0.0037 \\ 0.6890 \end{bmatrix}$	$\begin{bmatrix} 0.7196 \\ 0.0035 \\ 0.6932 \end{bmatrix}$
error	$0.0°$	$5.7523°$	$1.4172°$	$1.0907°$

Table 1: This table shows the results of correcting for the anisotropic nature of the noise on the estimated translational direction. The results are tabulated over 5 trials, each of which uses a different seed to the random number generator to add noise to the optic flow. Both Method 1 and Method 2 provide considerable improvement over the uncorrected case.

[11] (see Figure 4) and estimates for $\vec{T}$ were computed both with and without the re-scaling method. The results are shown in Table 1.

The "true" (noise-free) direction for $\vec{T}$ is $[0.7071 \; 0 \; 0.7071]^T$. This corresponds to translation which is forward and to the right. The estimate of $\vec{T}$ recovered without bias-correction has an error of $5.7523°$, and is biased towards the centre of the image as expected.

From Table 1 we see that both Method 1 and Method 2 offer substantial improvement over the uncorrected solution, with Method 2 performing somewhat better. The exact form used for C is therefore important, and should be made the subject of further study. Note that the value of M used in both methods is only an approximation to the form we require, so it is not expected that the bias will be completely removed.

4 Conclusion

Estimation of egomotion parameters from image sequences is an important pursuit in computer vision. The development of linear methods for estimating translational direction is an important step towards fast estimation, but comes with an inherent problem in the form of biased estimates.

While a number of methods have been proposed for solving this bias problem, they require either adding more noise, which is intuitively un-appealing, or attempting to estimate the scale of the covariance matrix, which is difficult unless *a priori* information about the amount of noise in the flow estimates is available.

The author has presented a new method for removing the bias which only requires knowledge of the form of the covariance matrix, that is knowledge of the covariance matrix up to a scale factor. Removal of the requirement that the scale is known is a significant improvement, since this parameter is difficult to estimate.

Further results from the re-scaling method presented in this paper may be found in [3] and the method is shown to outperform both dithering and renormalization. Earnshaw & Blostein [3] suggest a further improvement which requires an iterative solution.

Results are presented for optic flow from a synthetic image sequence. Use of a synthetic sequence allows knowledge of the "ground truth" egomotion parameters, demonstration of the bias effect, and demonstration of the efficacy of the technique for its removal. Two different methods are suggested for estimating the covariance matrix (up to a scale factor) associated with the subspace linear constraints. Since the estimates for the form of the covariance matrix are not exact the bias was not completely removed, but was significantly reduced.

5 Acknowledgements

The author would like to thank Allan Jepson, who made many suggestions and contributions to this work, and to NSERC for providing financial support.

References

[1] Anna R. Bruss and Berthold K. P. Horn. Passive navigation. *Computer Vision, Graphics and Image Processing*, 21:3–20, 1983.

[2] Trevor Darell and Alexander Pentland. Robust estimation of a multi-layered motion representation. In *Proceedings of the IEEE Workshop on Visual Motion*, pages 173–177, Princeton, New Jersey, October 1991.

[3] A. Mark Earnshaw and Steven D. Blostein. The performance of camera translation direction estimators from optical flow: Analysis, comparison, and theoretical limits. *IEEE Transactions on Pattern Analysis and Machine Intelligence*, 18(9):927–932, 1996.

[4] David J. Fleet. *Measurement of Image Velocity*. Kluwer Academic Publishers, Boston, Massachusetts, 1992.

[5] Simon Haykin. *Adaptive Filter Theory*. Prentice-Hall, Englewood Cliffs, New Jersey, 1986.

[6] David J. Heeger. Optical flow from spatiotemporal filters. In *Proc. Int. Conf. on Computer Vision, ICCV-87*, pages 181–190, 1987.

[7] David J. Heeger and Allan Jepson. Simple method for computing 3d motion and depth. In *3rd International Conference on Computer Vision*, pages 96–100, Osaka,Japan, December 4–7 1990.

[8] David J. Heeger and Allan D. Jepson. Subspace methods for recovery of rigid motion I: Algorithm and implementation. *International Journal of Computer Vision*, 7(2):95–117, 1992.

[9] Allan D. Jepson and David J. Heeger. Subspace methods for recovering rigid motion, part II: Theory. Research in Biological and Computational Vision RBCV-TR-90-36, University of Toronto, November 1990.

[10] Allan D. Jepson and David J. Heeger. A fast subspace algorithm for recovering rigid motion. In *Proceedings of the IEEE Workshop on Visual Motion*, pages 124–131, Princeton, New Jersey, October 1991.

[11] Allan D. Jepson and David J. Heeger. Linear subspace methods for recovering translational direction. In L. Harris and M. Jenkin, editors, *Spatial Vision in Humans and Robots*. Cambridge University Press, 1993. See also: Research in Biological and Computational Vision, Department of Computer Science, University of Toronto, RBCV-TR-90-40, Apr. 1992.

[12] Kenichi Kanatani. *Geometric computation for machine vision*. Clarendon Press, Oxford, England, 1993.

[13] Kenichi Kanatani. Renormalization for unbiased estimation. In *Proceedings of the 4th International Conference on Computer Vision*, pages 599–606, Berlin, Germany, May 11–14 1993.

[14] H. C. Longuet-Higgins and K. Prazdny. The interpretation of a moving retinal image. *Proceedings of the Royal Society of London B*, 208:385–397, 1980.

[15] W. James MacLean. *Recovery of Egomotion and Segmentation of Independent Object Motion Using the EM Algorithm*. PhD thesis, University of Toronto, 1996.

[16] J. H. Rieger and D. T. Lawton. Processing differential image motion. *J Opt Soc Am A*, 2(2):354–359, 1985.

[17] D. Sinclair. Motion segmentation and local structure. In *Proceedings of the 4th International Conference on Computer Vision*, pages 366–373, Berlin, Germany, May 11–14 1993.

[18] Carlo Tomasi and Takeo Kanade. Factoring image sequences into shape and motion. In *Proceedings of the IEEE Workshop on Visual Motion*, pages 21–28, Princeton, New Jersey, October 1991.

[19] Juyang Weng, Thomas S. Huang, and Narendra Ahuja. Motion and structure from two perspective views: Algorithms, error analysis, and error estimation. *IEEE Transactions on Pattern Analysis and Machine Intelligence*, 11(5):451–476, 1989.

Densities and Maximum Likelihood Estimation of Matching Constraints*

R. Berthilsson
Centre for Mathematical Sciences
Lund University
P.O. Box 118, S-221 00 Lund, Sweden

Abstract

In this paper we present a theory for obtaining densities that are important for computer vision. As a result of the theory we compute the exact and novel density of the slope of a line fitted to image points. This density makes it possible to obtain confidence intervals for the slope or to make hypothesis testing about if two intersecting lines form a corner or not. The theory also lets us derive a novel technique for maximum likelihood estimation, that can be used for computing the fundamental matrix, conics, or any other constraint that can be expressed by polynomials of degree 2. We present exact and novel densities for the fundamental matrix and conic constraints, that are needed for the estimation. Experiments show how the results can be used in practise to compute maximum likelihood estimates of the fundamental matrix.

1 Introduction

Whenever processing real data there is a need for estimating the impact of noise to the computations. This can be treated in a firm way by introducing a probability space and then treating a measurement as an observation of a random variable X on this probability space. A simple, but yet often good model is obtained by letting the probability space be normal, i.e. Gaussian. Now a measurement can for example be the slope of a line fitted to image points. The probability space can be the set of possible locations of image points together with a measure P of how likely these outcomes are. The slope is then a random variable X on this probability set. However, even if the probability space is normal, the density X_*P, which is the density of measurements values, need not be close to being normal.

It is obvious that in order to draw conclusions from a measurement X it is advantageous to know the density X_*P. The assumption of normality of P makes it possible to compute the density X_*P for a number of random variables that occur frequently in image analysis and computer vision. In this paper we will derive some such densities and also present estimation techniques for matching con-

straints. The theory is based on the theory of quadratic forms of normal random variables. For a treatment of this subject see for example [8].

Estimation techniques for matching constraints, in computer vision, has been studied to a large extent, e.g. [1, 10, 9, 11, 12, 13, 14, 15, 17], and range from first order approximations to the so called bundle adjustment method. Under the assumption of normal distribution, the bundle adjustment method gives a maximum likelihood (ML) estimate of the constraint parameters. The ML-estimation is obtained by optimizing the likelihood of the location of the image points, while fulfilling the constraint.

Here we present a novel estimation technique that directly optimizes the likelihood that the matching constraint is fulfilled. This is a very natural approach to the estimation problem, since fulfilling the constraint is the objective of the fitting. Furthermore, the technique allows ML-estimates when the assumption of normally distributed image points is relaxed. The points do not even have to be independently distributed. However, we require that the constraint can be expressed by a set of second order polynomials. Such constraints include for example the fundamental matrix and conic constraints.

It is also interesting to know the density of the estimated parameters. In this paper we present exact and novel densities for the slope angel of the line when estimating a straight line from image points the locations of which have uncertainty in all directions. The fitted line is obtained by solving for least squares. Several other methods exist for geometric fitting of straight lines, see for example [2, 7, 16, 6, 4, 5]. We remark that especially straight lines are very important image features, since many man made environment have linear boundaries. This motivates its study in computer vision and in particular the statistics that are involved.

The basic theory is presented in Section 2, while Sections 3 and 4 provide relevant examples that show how the theory can be used in computer vision. We stress that Sections 3 and 4 do not in any way exhaust the possible applications of the theory. An experiment is also included where we compute an ML-estimate of the fundamental matrix. Finally, we include a section that explains the involved

*This work has been done within the VISIT program of Swedish Foundation for Strategic Research (SSF) and ESPRIT Reactive LTR project 21914, CUMULI.

numeric computations.

2 Preliminaries

This section is somewhat technical and can be skipped at a first read through.

Let $(\Omega, \mathcal{A}, P)$ be a probability space and let $X : \Omega \to \mathbb{R}^n$ be a random variable. The density of the values of X is given by the (probability) measure X_*P, where $*$ denotes the push forward operation on measures. The terms probability measure and density function are equivalent here and both expressions will be used. The measure X_*P is defined by the identity

$$\int_\Omega f(X(\omega))P(\omega) = \int_{\mathbb{R}^n} f(X)X_*P,$$

which should hold for all $f : \mathbb{R}^n \to \mathbb{R}$, such that $f \circ X \in L^1$, i.e. absolutely integrable according to the measure P.

For convenience, introduce the notation

$$(x, y) = \sum_1^n x_k y_k$$

for $x, y \in \mathbb{C}^n$. Note that this is not a scalar product on $\mathbb{C}^n$. In the same spirit let $(x, c) = c \sum_1^n x_k$, when $x \in \mathbb{C}^n$ and $c \in \mathbb{C}$.

The Fourier transformation of X_*P is given by $\mathcal{F}X_*P = E(e^{-i(\omega, X)})$, where E denotes the expectation. The term characteristic function is also widely used for $\mathcal{F}X_*P$. We will also use the notation $\widehat{X_*P} = \mathcal{F}X_*P$. The Fourier transformation of a function $u \in L^1(\mathbb{R}^n)$ is defined by

$$\hat{u}(\omega) = \int_{\mathbb{R}^n} e^{-i(\omega, x)} u(x) dx, \omega \in \mathbb{R}^n,$$

and if $\hat{u} \in L^1$, then

$$u(x) = (2\pi)^{-n/2} \int_{\mathbb{R}^n} e^{i(\omega, x)} \hat{u}(\omega) d\omega.$$

The notation $A = \{a_{j,k}\}_1^n$ may be used for an $n \times n$ matrix with elements $a_{j,k}$. By the support $\mathrm{supp}(f)$ of a function f is meant the smallest closed set Ω such that $f(x) = 0$, when $x \notin \Omega$.

If not otherwise stated the measure P is always a normal probability measure, and $P_{m,c}$, where $m \in \mathbb{R}^n$, $c \in \mathbb{R}^{n \times n}$, denotes the normal probability measure on $\mathbb{R}^n$, with mean m and positive definite covariance matrix c. If $x = (x_1, \ldots, x_n) \in \mathbb{R}^n$ is a random variable with probability measure $P_{m,c}$, with $c = \{c_{j,k}\}_1^n$ being diagonal, then

$$P_{m,c} = \prod_{j=1}^n P_{m_j, c_{j,j}}$$

and x_j and x_k are independent when $j \neq k$.

Proposition 2.1. *Let $(\mathbb{R}^{n_1}, \mathcal{B}, P_{m,c})$ be a normal probability space and let $p : \mathbb{R}^{n_1} \to \mathbb{R}^{n_2}$ be a polynomial of degree ≤ 2. Then, $\widehat{p_*P_{m,c}}$ can be computed analytically.*

In fact, let

$$q(\omega, x) = i(\omega, p(x)) + \frac{1}{2}\left((x - m), c^{-1}(x - m)\right). \quad (1)$$

Then

$$\widehat{p_*P_{m,c}}(\omega) = E\left(e^{-i(\omega, p(x))}\right)$$
$$= (2\pi)^{-n_1/2}(\det c)^{-1/2} \int_{\mathbb{R}^{n_2}} e^{-q(\omega, x)} dx,$$

converges since p is real valued. Note that (1) can be written

$$q(\omega, x) = \sum_1^{n_2}\left((x - m_k), i\omega_k A_k(x - m_k)\right)$$
$$+ \frac{1}{2}\left((x - m), c^{-1}(x - m)\right) + d,$$

where A_k are real symmetric $(n_1 \times n_1)$-matrices and $d \in \mathbb{C}$ is a constant. This comes from the fact that p is quadratic polynomial. Thus,

$$q(\omega, x) = \left((x - \tilde{m}), \tilde{A}(\omega))(x - \tilde{m}\right) + \tilde{d}.$$

for some $n_1 \times n_1$ matrix valued function $\tilde{A}(\omega)$. By an orthogonal change of variables it follows that

$$E(e^{(-i\omega, p(x))}) = 2^{-n_1/2} e^{-\tilde{d}}(\det(\tilde{A}(\omega)c))^{-1/2} \quad (2)$$

Formula (2) is of fundamental importance here. If for example p is a real valued polynomial of degree 2 on $\mathbb{R}^n$ and ϕ is the density function of the values of p, then the Fourier transformation $\hat{\phi}$ can be obtained by (2). Furthermore, from $\hat{\phi}$, the density of ϕ can be computed by the inverse Fourier transformation. This can be computed by numeric integration or preferably by more effective methods as explained in Section 5.

Remark. Although (2) is only valid for normal probability measures, it is easy to extend the calculus to non normal measures. In fact, let P be a probability measure, and let $\{P_{m_k, c_k}\}_{m_k, c_k}$ be a set of normal probability measures for some means m_k and covariance matrices $c_k, k = 1, 2, \ldots, n$. Then, we can approximate P by a linear combination of P_{m_k, c_k}, i.e.

$$P \approx \sum_k \alpha_k P_{m_k, c_k}.$$

For any random variable X it follows that

$$\widehat{X_*P} \approx \sum_k \alpha_k \widehat{X_*P}_{m_k, c_k}.$$

Furthermore, the size of the error made in the approximation is bounded by the error of the original measure, i.e. $\|X_*P - X_*P_{m_k, c_k}\| \leq \|P - \alpha_k P_{m_k, c_k}\|$. ∎

3 Geometric fitting of lines by least squares

Fitting a line to measured data is important in many areas like for example computer vision. The angle between two intersecting lines is an important feature and can be used to decide whether the intersection is a corner or not. Often the line fitting is done by extracting some image points and finding a least square estimate. If the image point locations are treated as random variables, there is a problem to determine the density of the parameters of the line. Below we compute the density function of the angle or slope of the line relative to the x-axis.

Let $(x_j, y_j) \in \mathbb{R}^2$ be independent normal random variables, corresponding to measures P_{m_j, c_j}, where $m_j \in \mathbb{R}^2$ and $c_j = \sigma_j^2 I$, $j = 1, \ldots, n$. Note that each point is regarded as a geometric point with uncertainty in all directions, and not as a function value with uncertainty along only one axis.

We fit a line to the points by minimizing the sum of squared **orthogonal** distances from the points $x_j \in \mathbb{R}^2$ to the line.

A general line in $\mathbb{R}^2$ can be expressed by the equation $\cos(\theta)x_1 + \sin(\theta)x_2 + l = 0$, for some real θ and l. The orthogonal distance from $x \in \mathbb{R}^2$ to the line is given by $|(x - p, v)|$, where p is any point on the line and $v = (\cos(\theta), \sin(\theta))$. By selecting $p = -lv$, it follows that $|(x - p, v)| = |\cos(\theta)x_1 + \sin(\theta)x_2 + l|$. Thus, we find the minimum of the sum of squared orthogonal distances from the points to the line by minimizing

$$Q(\theta, l) = \sum_{j=1}^{n} (\cos(\theta)x_j + \sin(\theta)y_j + l)^2.$$

It is seen that the slope vector $v = (\cos(\theta), \sin(\theta))$ is orthogonal to the line and has length 1. A straight forward, but tedious, computation gives that

$$l = -\frac{1}{n}(\cos(\theta)(x, 1) + \sin(\theta)(y, 1)),$$

and that

$$\tan(2\theta) = \frac{2(x, 1)(y, 1) - 2n(x, y)}{n(|y|^2 - |x|^2) + (x, 1)^2 - (y, 1)^2}.$$

Before stating the result we introduce the notation

$$\delta_{a,b} = \begin{cases} 1, & a = b, \\ 0, & a \neq b, \end{cases}$$

where the equality sign is taken in rather general interpretation. For example, we have that $\delta_{2k, \text{even}} = 1$ for all $k \in \mathbb{Z}$.

Theorem 3.1. *Let $P_{m,c}$ be a normal probability measure on $\mathbb{R}^{2n}$, where*

$$m = (m_{x_1}, m_{y_1}, \ldots, m_{x_n}, m_{y_n})^T \in \mathbb{R}^{2n}$$

and $c = \sigma^2 I$. Set

$$\theta : \mathbb{R}^n \times \mathbb{R}^n \ni (x, y)$$
$$\to \frac{1}{2} \arctan\left(\frac{2(x, 1)(y, 1) - 2n(x, y)}{n(|y|^2 - |x|^2) + (x, 1)^2 - (y, 1)^2}\right) \in \mathbb{R}.$$

Then the density of the angle of the fitted line is given by

$$(-\pi/4, \pi/4) \ni \theta \to \theta_* P_{m,c}$$
$$= \int_{\mathbb{R}} \phi(\gamma \tan(2\theta), \gamma)|\gamma|(2 + 2\tan(2\theta)^2)d\gamma,$$

where

$$\hat{\phi}(\omega) = e^{-(m,m)/(2\sigma^2) + (m, A(\omega)^{-1}m)/(4\sigma^4)}$$
$$(\det A(\omega))^{-1/2}(2\sigma^2)^{-n/2}$$

and the matrix $A(\omega_1, \omega_2) = \{a_{j,k}\}_1^{2n}$ is given by

$$\frac{i}{2}\omega_1\left(\delta_{j-k, odd} - \delta_{|j-k|, 1}\delta_{\max(j,k), even}2n\right)$$
$$+ i\omega_2\left(n\delta_{j,k}(-1)^k + \delta_{j, odd}\delta_{k, odd} - \delta_{j, even}\delta_{k, even}\right)$$
$$+ \frac{1}{2\sigma^2}\delta_{j,k}.$$

This result follows in principle directly from (2) together with the computation of a marginal density.

Note that in order to obtain the density of the slope angle θ relative the x-axis, as given by $\theta_* P_{m,c}$, we must first compute ϕ from $\hat{\phi}$ numerically and then compute a 1-dimensional integral numerically. The latter problem is simple and the former is dealt with in Section 5. The density of θ can be used for obtaining confidence intervals and for hypothesis testing concerning the slope of a fitted line. If two lines are fitted to two disjoint sets of normal random variables $O_k = \{x_{j,k} \in \mathbb{R}^2\}_j$, $k = 1, 2$, such that a and b are independent whenever $a \in O_1$ and $b \in O_2$, then the densities of θ_1 and θ_2 can be used for computing confidence intervals and hypothesis testing concerning the intersection angle of two fitted lines.

Note that the assumption of normal measure $P_{m,c}$ can be relaxed by the remark in Section 2.

4 Estimating the fundamental matrix

Consider the problem of estimating the fundamental matrix, cf. [3, 14, 17]. This matrix plays an important role for the epipolar geometry of two uncalibrated cameras. Given two images of an ordered set of object points, the fundamental matrix F is a 3×3 matrix of rank 2, that fulfills

$$\begin{pmatrix} x_{j,1} & x_{j,2} & 1 \end{pmatrix} F \begin{pmatrix} y_{j,1} \\ y_{j,2} \\ 1 \end{pmatrix} = 0, \tag{3}$$

where $x_j = (x_{j,1}, x_{j,2})$ and $y_j = (y_{j,1}, y_{j,2})$ are points number j in the first and second image respectively, $j = 1, \ldots, n$. The fundamental matrix F is uniquely defined by the equations (3) if 8 or more corresponding points in general position are available, where uniqueness of course is only given up to the scale of F. When 8 points are available, the well known eight point algorithm can be used. This algorithm solves a simple linear problem, by finding the nullspace of a matrix containing image measurements data. If more than eight points are available, the set of equations do not in general have a solution, since the image measurements are usually not exact.

Here we present a novel method for obtaining an optimal estimate of the fundamental matrix when image data are not exact. This is done under the assumption that the density of the image point locations is known or can be estimated. In short the method gives an ML-estimate of F by maximizing the likelihood of the event that the constraint (3) is fulfilled.

Theorem 4.1. *Let (x_1, x_2, y_1, y_2) be a normal random variable, with probability measure $P_{m,c}$, where $m = (m_{x_1}, m_{x_2}, m_{y_1}, m_{y_2})^T \in \mathbb{R}^4$ and $c = \sigma^2 I$ is a 4×4-matrix. Furthermore, let $F = \{f_{j,k}\}_{j,k=1}^3$ be a 3×3 matrix and introduce the random variable*

$$\zeta : \mathbb{R}^4 \ni (x, y) \to (x_1 \quad x_2 \quad 1) F \begin{pmatrix} y_1 \\ y_2 \\ 1 \end{pmatrix} \in \mathbb{R}.$$

Then

$$\widehat{\zeta_* P_{m,c}}(\omega; F)$$
$$= \frac{1}{4\sigma^4} e^{-i\omega f_{3,3} - \frac{1}{2\sigma^2}(m,m) + (v, Av)} (\det A)^{-1/2},$$

where

$$A(\omega) = \frac{1}{2\sigma^2} I + \frac{i\omega}{2} \begin{pmatrix} 0 & 0 & f_{1,1} & f_{1,2} \\ 0 & 0 & f_{2,1} & f_{2,2} \\ f_{1,1} & f_{2,1} & 0 & 0 \\ f_{1,2} & f_{2,2} & 0 & 0 \end{pmatrix},$$

and

$$v = -\frac{1}{2} A^{-1} \left(i\omega (f_{1,3}, f_{2,3}, f_{3,1}, f_{3,2})^T - \frac{1}{\sigma^2} m \right).$$

Theorem 4.2. *Let P be a probability measure on $\mathbb{R}^{n_1}$, and let $f : \mathbb{R}^{n_1} \times A \to \mathbb{R}^{n_2}$ be a continuous function, where A is compact. Set*

$$\mathbb{R}^{n_2} \times A \to \hat{\psi}(\omega; t) = \widehat{f(x;t)_* P}.$$

If $\omega \to \hat{\psi}(\omega; t) \in L^1$, for all $t \in A$, then an ML-estimate t of $f(x;t) = 0$ exists and is given by any solution to

$$\max_{t \in A} \int_{\mathbb{R}^{n_2}} \hat{\psi}(\omega; t) d\omega. \tag{4}$$

Note that a restriction $g(x;t) = c$ can be written $f(x;t) = g(x;t) - c = 0$, to which Theorem 4.2 can be applied.

In order to obtain an ML-estimate of the fundamental matrix, when measurements are observations of normal random variables, we can use (3) together with Theorems 4.1 and 4.2.

Since the equation for any conic in $\mathbb{R}^2$ can be written as

$$(x_1 \quad x_2 \quad 1) A \begin{pmatrix} x_1 \\ x_2 \\ 1 \end{pmatrix} = 0,$$

the same method can be used for finding the ML estimate of the matrix A.

The following theorem gives the density for the conic constraint.

Theorem 4.3. *Let $(x_1, x_2) \in \mathbb{R}^2$ be a normal random variable, with probability measure $P_{m,c}$, where $m \in \mathbb{R}^2$ and $c = \sigma^2 I$ is a 2×2-matrix. Furthermore, let $A = \{a_{j,k}\}_{j,k=1}^3$ be a symmetric 3×3 matrix and introduce the random variable*

$$\zeta : \mathbb{R}^2 \ni x \to (x_1 \quad x_2 \quad 1) A \begin{pmatrix} x_1 \\ x_2 \\ 1 \end{pmatrix} \in \mathbb{R}.$$

Then

$$\widehat{\zeta_* P_{m,c}}(\omega; A) = \frac{1}{2\sigma^2} e^{-i\omega a_{3,3} - \frac{1}{2\sigma^2}(m,m) + (v, Mv)} (\det M)^{-1/2},$$

where

$$M(\omega) = \frac{1}{2\sigma^2} I + i\omega \begin{pmatrix} a_{1,1} & a_{1,2} \\ a_{1,2} & a_{2,2} \end{pmatrix},$$

and

$$v(\omega) = -\frac{1}{2} M^{-1} \left\{ 2i\omega (a_{1,3}, a_{2,3})^T - \frac{1}{\sigma^2} m \right\}.$$

It can often be assumed that the probability measure $f(x;t)_* P$ on $\mathbb{R}^{n_2}$ in Theorem 4.2 is independent, i.e.

$$f(x;t)_* P = \prod_{k=1}^{n_2} P_k(y_k; t), \qquad y \in \mathbb{R}^{n_2}$$

in which case (4) reduces to

$$\max_{t \in A} \prod_{k=1}^{n_2} \int_{\mathbb{R}} \hat{\psi}_k(\omega; t) d\omega,$$

where $\hat{\psi}_k(\omega; t) = \hat{P}_k(y_k; t)$.

We will now use Theorems 4.1 and 4.2 to compute an ML-estimate of the fundamental matrix F under the assumption that the measurement of the image points are normally and independently distributed.

Since F is a rank 2 matrix, only given up to scale, the ML-estimate (4) is given by the solution of the constrained optimization problem

$$\max_{\substack{\|F\|=1 \\ \det F=0}} \int \hat{\psi}(\omega; F)\,d\omega.$$

From the fact that measurements are independent, it follows that $P_{m,c} = \prod_1^n P_{m_k,c_k}$, where m_k and σ_k have to be estimated. In the example below we let $m_k = (x_{k,1}, x_{k,2}, y_{k,1}, y_{k,2}) \in \mathbb{R}^4$ be the actually performed measurement of correspondence point number k in each image, and the 4×4 covariance matrix is given by $c_k = 0.02^2 I$. Thus, the ML-estimate reduces to

$$\max_{\substack{\|F\|=1 \\ \det F=0}} \prod_{k=1}^n \int_{\mathbb{R}} \hat{\psi}_k(\omega; F)\,d\omega, \qquad (5)$$

where $\hat{\psi}_k(\omega; t) = \widehat{\zeta_* P_{m_k,c_k}}(\omega; F)$ is given by Theorem 4.1.

5 Experiments and numerical considerations

5.1 Experiments

An experiment was performed on synthetic data. An ordered 12 point configuration $\mathcal{X} \in \mathbb{R}^3$ was generated, with points in general position. Figure 1 shows two projective images of $\mathcal{X}$ after normal and independent noise with covariance matrix $\sigma = 0.02^2 I$ and mean $m = (0,0)$ has been added to the points, where I is the 2×2 identity matrix.

The bundle adjustment method, can be used to obtain en estimate of the fundamental matrix. Under the assumption of normal density $P_{m,c}$ of the image points it gives an estimate F_{bundle}. Let $m_{x_j} = (m_{x_{j,1}}, m_{x_{j,1}}) \in \mathbb{R}^2$ and $m_{y_j} = (m_{y_{j,1}}, m_{y_{j,1}}) \in \mathbb{R}^2$, $j = 1, \ldots, n$, be the unknown means of the n image points in the left and right image, respectively. Furthermore, let x_j and y_j, $j = 1, \ldots, n$, be the measured image points in the left and right image, respectively. Then, the bundle adjustment estimate is given by the solution to

$$\max_m \prod_{j=1}^n P_{m_{x_j},c_{x_j}}(x_j) P_{m_{x_j},c_{x_j}}(y_j),$$

subject to $(m_{x_j}, 1) F (m_{y_j}, 1)^T = 0$ and $\operatorname{rank} F = 2$, $j = 1, 2, \ldots, n$. Note that the optimization is performed over both m and F. In our experiment

$$F_{\text{bundle}} = \begin{pmatrix} -0.0158 & 0.4108 & -0.8760 \\ -0.2723 & -0.0380 & 0.1646 \\ 0.8686 & -0.0807 & -0.0922 \end{pmatrix}, \quad (6)$$

where $\|F_{\text{bundle}}\| = 1$ in operator norm. The likelihood that constraint (3) is fulfilled with $F = F_{\text{bundle}}$ is given by

$$\psi(0; F_{\text{bundle}}) = \prod_{k=1}^n \int_{\mathbb{R}} \hat{\psi}_k(\omega; F_{\text{bundle}})\,d\omega = 1.83 \cdot 10^{13}.$$

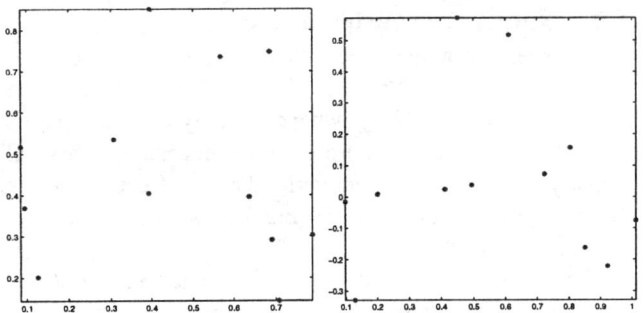

Figure 1. Two images of a 12 point configuration in $\mathbb{R}^3$ with added noise. The standard deviation of the noise is $\sigma = 0.02$.

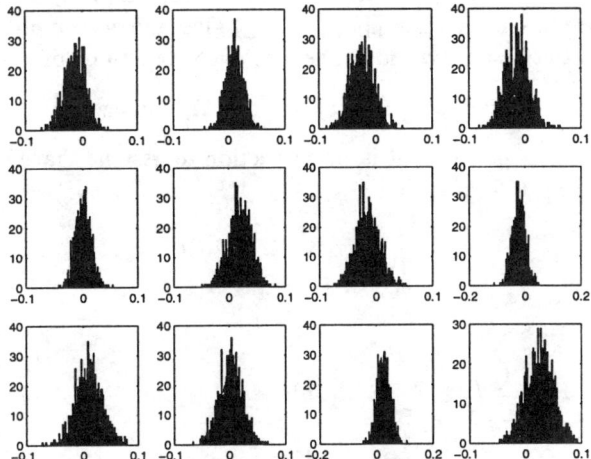

Figure 2. Histograms for F_{ML}.

An ML-estimate of F can be obtain by using F_{bundle} as starting value for a descent algorithm. The so obtained ML-estimate of F is given by

$$F_{ML} = \begin{pmatrix} -0.0397 & 0.6181 & -0.7684 \\ -0.2829 & -0.0360 & 0.1637 \\ 0.8116 & -0.1872 & -0.1007 \end{pmatrix}, \quad (7)$$

where $\|F_{ML}\| = 1$ in operator norm. The likelihood is F_{ML} is given by $\psi(0; F_{ML}) = 7.86 \cdot 10^{13}$, i.e. an improvement over F_{bundle} by a factor ≈ 4.3.

We stress that this method is fundamentally different from bundle adjustment. Here we aim directly at maximizing the likelihood of the event that the constraint is fulfilled. Furthermore, by the remark in Section 2, it is easy to relax the assumption of normal measure P by approximating P as a linear combination of normal measures P_{m_k,c_k}, $k = 1, 2, \ldots, m$.

5.2 Numerical considerations

In order to obtain the densities in some of the examples, it is necessary to compute the inverse Fourier transformation $y_* P_{m,c} = \mathcal{F}^{-1}\widehat{y_* P_{m,c}}$, where y is polynomial of degree ≤ 2 and $P_{m,c}$ is a normal probability measure. This will usually have to be done numerically. An effective method for doing this is obtained by using the fast Fourier transformation (FFT).

To this end, assume that $u \in L^2(\mathbb{R})$ and that $\text{supp}(u) \subseteq [a,b] = \Omega$. The interval Ω can be estimated either by theoretical arguments or by Monte-Carlo simulations for obtaining histograms of outcomes. Let the density function $\psi_k(t;F)$, $k = 1,2\ldots,12$, be given by the inverse Fourier transformation of $\hat{\psi}_k(t;F)$ in (5). Figure 2 gives an estimate of the 12 densities $\psi_k(x;F_{ML})$, and thus their supports, where F_{ML} is given by (7). The matrix F_{ML} should be chosen such that $\prod_k \psi_k(0,F_{ML})$ gives the maximum.

Set $T = b - a$ and define $\bar{u}$ by cyclic repetition of u, i.e.

$$\bar{u}(x+nT) = u(x), \qquad x \in \Omega, \ n \text{ integer}.$$

As $\bar{u}$ is periodic, it is no restriction to assume that $\Omega = [0,T]$. It follows that

$$\bar{u}(x) = \sum_{j=-\infty}^{\infty} c_j e^{2\pi i x j/T}, \tag{8}$$

where

$$c_j = \frac{1}{T} \int_0^T e^{-2\pi i x j/T} \bar{u}(x)dx$$
$$= \frac{1}{T} \int_{-\infty}^{\infty} e^{-2\pi i x j/T} u(x)dx = \frac{1}{T}\hat{u}(2\pi j/T).$$

Thus c_j is readily obtained from $\hat{u}$. By approximating the summation (8) by a finite summation and rearranging the terms we get $\tilde{c}_j$ instead of c_j and

$$\bar{u}\left(\frac{kT}{N}\right) = \sum_{j=0}^{N-1} \tilde{c}_j e^{2\pi i jk/N},$$

which can be computed effectively by FFT, when $N = 2^n$. Thus, there is no need to compute the inverse Fourier transform for continuous parameter numerically.

The extension to functions $L^2(\mathbb{R}^n)$ for $n > 1$ is straight forward, but gets notationally more complex.

6 Conclusions

In this paper we have computed novel densities for line fitting and derived a novel method for estimating parameters in matching constraints. An experiment is included, where a maximum likelihood estimate of the fundamental matrix is computed. The theory applies for normal random variables but it is shown that this assumption can easily be relaxed. Further applications of the theory are likely to exist, and will be subject for continued research.

References

[1] F. Bookstein. Fitting conic sections to scattered data. *Computer Graphics Image Process*, 9(1):56–71, 1979.

[2] M. Creasy. Confidence limits for the gradient in the linear functional relationship. *J. of the Royal Statistical Society, Series B*, 18:65–69, 1956.

[3] R. Hartley. In defence of the 8-point algorithm. In *Proceedings of the 5th International Conference on Computer Vision*, pages 1036–1040, 1995.

[4] B. Kamgar-Parsi and N. Netanyahu. A nonparametric method for fitting a straight line to a noisy image. *Pattern Analysis and Machine Intelligence*, 56(5):424–432, 1994.

[5] K. Kanatani. *Statistical Optimization for Geometric Computation: Theory and Practice*. Elsevier Science, 1996.

[6] N. Kiryati and M. Bruckstein. What is in a set of points. *Pattern Analysis and Machine Intelligence*, 14(4):496–500, 1992.

[7] A. Madansky. The fitting of straight lines when both variables are subject to error. *J. of American Statistical Association*, 54:173–205, 1959.

[8] A. Mathai and S. Provost. *Quadratic Forms in Random Variables*. Marcel Dekker, 1992.

[9] T. Nagata and K. Tamura, H. an Ishibashi. Detection of an ellipse by use of a recursive least-squares estimator. *Journal of Robotics Systems*, 14(4):496–500, 1985.

[10] Y. Nakagawa and A. Rosenfeld. A note on polygonal and elliptical approximation of mechanical parts. *Pattern Recognition Letters*, 40(2):79–94, 1979.

[11] J. Porrill. Fitting ellipses and predicting confidence envelopes using a bias corrected kalman filter. *Image Vision Comput.*, 8(1):37–41, 1990.

[12] P. Rosin. A note on the least squares fitting of ellipses. *Pattern Recognition Letters*, 14(10):799–808, 1993.

[13] P. Rosin and G. West. Nonparametric segmentation of curves into various representations. *Pattern Analysis and Machine Intelligence*, 17(12):1140–1153, 1995.

[14] P. Torr and D. Murray. The development and comparison of robust methods for estimating the fundamental matrix. *IJCV*, 24(3):271–300, 1997.

[15] B. Triggs. Optimal estimation of matching constraints. In *3D Structure from Multiple Images of Large-Scale Environments, SMILE'98*, pages 63–77, 1998.

[16] I. Weiss. Line fitting in a noisy image. *Pattern Analysis and Machine Intelligence*, 11(3):325–329, 1989.

[17] Z. Zhang. Determining the epipolar geometry and its uncertainty: A review. *IJCV*, 27(2):161–195, 1998.

Recovery and Tracking of Continuous 3D Surfaces from Stereo Data Using A Deformable Dual-Mesh

Yusuf Sinan Akgul and Chandra Kambhamettu

Video/Image Modeling and Synthesis(VIMS) Lab
Department of Computer and Information Sciences
University of Delaware
Newark, Delaware 19716
{akgul|chandra}@cis.udel.edu
http://www.cis.udel.edu/~vims

Abstract

We propose a novel method for continuous 3D depth recovery and tracking using calibrated stereo. The method integrates stereo correspondence, surface reconstruction and tracking by using a new single deformable dual mesh optimization, resulting in simplicity, robustness and efficiency. In order to combine stereo correspondence and structure recovery, the method introduces an external energy function defined for a 3D volume based on cross-correlation between the stereo pairs. The internal energy functional of the deformable dual mesh imposes smoothness on the surfaces and it serves as a communication tool between the two meshes. Under the forces produced by the energy terms, the dual mesh deforms to recover and track the 3D surface. The newly introduced dual-mesh model, which is one of the main contributions of this paper, makes the system robust against local minima and yet it is efficient. A coarse-to-fine minimization approach makes the system even more efficient. Tracking is achieved by using the recovered surface as an initial position for the next time frame. Although the system can effectively utilize initial surface positions and disparity data, they are not needed for a successful operation, which makes this system applicable to a wide range of areas. We present the results of a number of experiments on stereo human face and cloud images, which proves that our new method is very effective.

1 Introduction

The first step of a traditional stereo analysis system is to extract a disparity map from the stereo image pair. The subsequent analysis steps use this disparity to perform their tasks. A few of the many examples of this approach are by Terzopoulos[17] and Blake and Zisserman[3], who fit a surface to a readily available depth information by minimizing a spline function, by Wildes[18] and Devernay and Faugeras[7], who calculate local differential properties from the disparity map. The common problem with these methods is that the main analysis, such as surface reconstruction and extraction of differential properties, is done separately from the extraction of 3D data, i.e., extraction of disparity map. This results in sequential systems where erroneous or noisy results of the first step have to be used in subsequent steps. In addition, the subsequent steps can not help the first step by feeding back additional constraints, such as smoothness, that can be useful in producing better results from the first step.

In order to address the above problem, there have been a number of proposals to integrate the main analysis phase with the extraction of 3D data. Hoff and Ahuja[11] and Fua[9] combine the steps of stereo matching and surface reconstruction. Kambhamettu et. al.[13] couple motion estimation analysis with stereo matching problem. Faugeras and Keriven[8] pose the stereo problem as a variational problem to drive partial differential equations, which are solved by level-set methods in a single step.

Following the research trend on integration of stereo correspondence and surface reconstruction, in this paper we present a novel method to unify stereo correspondence, continuous surface reconstruction and tracking at the same step using a deformable dual mesh. Although we find Hoff and Ahuja[11], Fua[9], and Faugeras and Keriven[8] closest to our work, our system is fundamentally very different in the assumptions and in the basic methods used.

The basic similarity between the above three systems and our system is that all four of them are formulated as an optimization framework. Hoff and Ahuja's surface reconstruction is based on fitting planar and quadratic patches after a matching process between the stereo pair. The results of matching are used as initial positions for the planar and quadratic patches. Similarly, Fua's work has an initialization phase where a correlation process is used for stereo matching to determine initial local surface positions. In contrast, our system does not perform any explicit matching between the stereo pair and it does not need any initial mesh positions to start optimization. Another fundamental difference is the optimization methods used. Hoff and Ahuja use Hough transforms and standard least-square fitting as their main optimization tools. Fua uses conjugate gradient as the optimization tool, which requires derivatives of the objective function. On the contrary, we use a novel optimization method that is based on energy information flow between the two meshes, which is robust against local minima and is computationally efficient. In spirit, the system of Faugeras and Keriven[8] is the most similar one to our system. Both systems are formulated as one single step optimization without any initialization steps. In addition, both systems recover a smooth surface after this optimization. However, the optimization methods are fundamentally very different as will be explained in later sections.

Although we assume a continuous surface, we note that the ideas presented in this paper can be applied to discontinuous surfaces with proper modifications and additions, such as detecting the discontinuities first and applying our method on several 3D surfaces. Further details of the differences and contributions of our work will be mentioned in later sections.

Our system first forms a 3D array with cells representing the 3D spatial locations. This array is filled with correlation values as explained in section 2.2. The resulting 3D array is used by the potential energy in the deformable mesh energy formulation. Then we form two deformable meshes parallel to each other; one is at the nearest depth position (camera side in Figure 2) and the other is at the farthest depth position. The internal energy of the deformable mesh is used to impose smoothness and as a communication tool between the two meshes. The deformation occurs under the internal forces as well as the external forces produced by the 3D array. Our new minimization method guarantees that the dual mesh finds the same position by introducing additional forces that push the dual mesh towards each other. When the two meshes find the same position, we take the mesh element positions as the assigned depth values to the 3D surface. The system does not use or extract any explicit disparity data. However, the disparity data can be obtained at the end of the deformation without any computational overhead. This whole process is done in a coarse to fine scheme as explained in Section 3.2.

Tracking of the deformation of the surface in time is tackled by utilizing the usual deformable model tracking proposed by Kass *et. al.*[14]. We take the recovered surface from a time frame and use it as the initial surface position in the next time frame. Using our minimization method, the dual mesh is allowed to deform, thus recovering and tracking the 3D surface. Although our tracking does not achieve point correspondences between the tracked surfaces, there are advantages of using this method as explained in Section 4.

2 The Deformable Mesh

In this section, we give the formal definition and the energy functional for the deformable mesh. A deformable mesh, M, with l columns and k rows is a set of horizontally and vertically connected points in 3D space in a mesh form.

$$M = \begin{bmatrix} m_{11} & m_{12} & \dots & m_{1l} \\ m_{21} & m_{22} & \dots & m_{2l} \\ \vdots & \vdots & \vdots & \vdots \\ m_{k1} & m_{k2} & \dots & m_{kl} \end{bmatrix}$$

where m_{kl} represents the element at the kth row and l^{th} column. Each element of the mesh represents a point in the 3D space. The column and row of a mesh element will represent x and z positions. In addition, each mesh element will hold a depth value as its y dimension. See Figure 1 for the orientation of our coordinate system.

The energy functional of a mesh is written in terms of spatial positions of the two meshes, as our system is based on a dual mesh formulation. Given the two meshes N and M, the energy associated with the deformable mesh M is written as

$$E_{Mesh}(M, N) = \tag{1}$$
$$\sum_{i=1}^{k} \sum_{j=1}^{l} \alpha E_{Smo}(m_{ij}) + \beta E_{Comm}(m_{ij}, n_{ij}) + \gamma E_{Ext}(m_{ij})$$

where α, β, and γ are the weighting parameters, and n_{ij} is an element of the other mesh N.

2.1 Internal Energy

Internal energy of Equation(2) is the weighted sum of smoothness term and the communication term. We do not measure the continuity on the mesh because it is already assumed by the definition of the deformable mesh.

The smoothness energy term $E_{Smo}(m_{ij})$ is based on the summation of 3D dot vector products in both horizontal and vertical mesh directions and it is proportional to the angles between these 3D vectors. Formally,

$$E_{Smo}(m_{ij}) = $$
$$\left(1 - \frac{\overrightarrow{m_{i-1j}m_{ij}} \cdot \overrightarrow{m_{ij}m_{i+1j}}}{|\overrightarrow{m_{i-1j}m_{ij}}| \, |\overrightarrow{m_{ij}m_{i+1j}}|} \right) + $$
$$\left(1 - \frac{\overrightarrow{m_{ij-1}m_{ij}} \cdot \overrightarrow{m_{ij}m_{ij+1}}}{|\overrightarrow{m_{ij-1}m_{ij}}| \, |\overrightarrow{m_{ij}m_{ij+1}}|} \right).$$

For the mesh elements where the above formula is not valid, e.g, elements at the edge of the mesh, we use the smoothness term of the nearest mesh element that has a valid smoothness value.

The communication term $E_{Comm}(m_{ij}, n_{ij})$ is not always active. It is activated only if one or both of the meshes stop deforming without finding the same 3D surface. This is a mechanism to address attraction by local minima which is a serious problem in optimization methods. The details of this term will be explained in Section 3.1.

2.2 External Energy

The external energy is the only mechanism that links the deformation of the dual mesh to the stereo image pair. Given a mesh element position m_{ij} in 3D space, a smaller value of $E_{Ext}(m_{ij})$ indicates that m_{ij} is likely to be on a 3D surface.

$$E_{Ext}(m_{ij}) = 1 - V(x, y, z) \qquad (2)$$

where x, y, z are the positions of m_{ij} on the main axes of 3D space. V is a 3D array that holds the correlation values that are computed as described below. Any

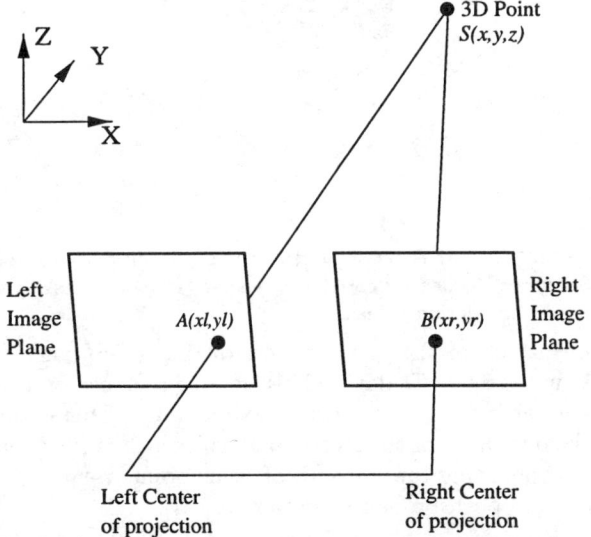

Figure 1: Projection of 3D scene points on the image planes

point $S(x, y, z)$ in 3D space that is visible in both calibrated left and right cameras will be projected on left and right image planes, producing two image intensity pixels $A(xl, yl)$ and $B(xr, yr)$ (Figure 1). If the point $S(x, y, z)$ lies on a physical surface and it is visible by both cameras, then classical assumption of stereo analysis states that the 2D regions around the projection points A and B should produce a high correlation value. Using this principle, for each 3D point $S(x, y, z)$ we calculate the image locations $A(xl, yl)$ and $B(xr, yr)$ and we run the

following normalized mean and variance correlation on the regions centered around 2D points A and B and assign the resulting value to $V(x, y, z)$

$$V(x, y, z) = \frac{\sum_{i,j}(A_{ij} - \overline{A})(B_{ij} - \overline{B})}{\left[\sum_{i,j}(A_{ij} - \overline{A})^2\right]^{\frac{1}{2}} \left[\sum_{i,j}(B_{ij} - \overline{B})^2\right]^{\frac{1}{2}}} \qquad (3)$$

where $\overline{A}$ and $\overline{B}$ are the mean values of the regions centered around the points A and B, and A_{ij} and B_{ij} are the elements of these regions. Since the above correlation cannot be larger than 1.0, which is the perfect matching case, the external energy term (Equation 2) cannot be smaller than 0.0.

The process of filling the correlation values of V may seem to be similar to what Fua[9] does for filling the 3D buckets in the initialization phase. What we fill in the 3D array is the result of correlation values without any interpretation of whether the 3D point is part of a surface or not. On the contrary, Fua calculates some initial surface points from the correlation values and these points are filled into the 3D buckets. The rest of Fua's algorithm depends on these initial surface points. The filling process of V resembles the construction of the initial volume before the space carving begins in Kutulakos and Seitz[15] and the filling of "u-v-d" volume before the extraction of disparity surface in Chen and Medioni[5]. Kutulakos and Seitz[15] has a number of pointers for systems utilizing scene-space algorithms. In the above two methods, the surface reconstruction do not have any explicit surface model. On the other hand, our system extracts the underlying surface by using a deformable surface model which imposes more constraints on the extraction process to make it more robust and efficient.

As apparent from Figure 1 and the filling process of V, our system does not need the images to be rectified because filling V does not involve any search processes that require a rectified stereo pair. Since the external energy is the only mechanism that relates the optimization process to the stereo data, our system does not need rectified images. We only need the precise positions of the cameras used, that is we need a calibrated stereo pair. However, using a rectified stereo pair makes the formulations simpler and it is relatively easier to calculate the dimensions of the 3D volume that is visible from both cameras. For the sake of a clear presentation, we will assume rectified stereo pairs in this paper.

It is trivial to extend this system to work with more than two views by modifying the filling process of the 3D array V. If we are using trinocular images, then for a 3D point $S(x, y, z)$ we will have three image points that we can run correlations in combinations. In other words, we can take the correlation values between points one and two, between points two and three, and between points one and three. Finally, we can put the weighted sum of these correlation results to the 3D array position $V(x, y, z)$. Another possibility is to keep only the maximum of these correlation values into the 3D array.

One may argue that our calculation of the external energy is computationally expensive because it involves many unnecessary correlation operations to fill the 3D array V. However, this is not the case. First, producing a correlation value for a given 3D point $S(x, y, z)$ corresponds to the epipolar constraint, which prevents many unnecessary correlation operations. Second, when we are running the filling process, we know the depth of the point $S(x, y, z)$. If this depth value is not possible to be a part of 3D surface, then we simply do not calculate the correlation and we do not assign any values to $V(x, y, z)$, which is initialized with a negative number to push the mesh away. This constraint corresponds to the search window constraint on the epipolar conjugate in the rectified stereo pair. Finally, our algorithm uses a coarse to fine scheme, which was used in many computer vision systems including stereo analysis. First we start with a coarse 3D array, which requires much lesser number of correlation calculations. Then we minimize the mesh energy functional using this coarse 3D array. After the minimization, we calculate a finer 3D array around the minimized mesh locations and the process continues on. At the coarser level, we use larger image templates for correlation around image points A and B and the meshes are also coarse. At finer levels we use smaller templates and finer meshes, which greatly increases efficiency. As a result of the above reasons, we argue that our calculation of external energy is very efficient.

Figure 2-(b) shows the visualization of the 3D array V produced from the rectified stereo pair shown in Figure 2-(a). Only three perpendicular slices of the volume are shown for visibility. The camera side of the volume is marked on the figure. Darker color represent high correlation areas. For visualization purposes, we filled in every element of the array with the corresponding correlation values. In usual filling process, most of the array elements are not filled due to the coarse to fine scheme and the constraints we use, as shown in Figure 3.

3 Surface Recovery and Deformable Model Optimization

One may consider using the 3D array V shown in Figure 2-(b) as a real 3D data such as Magnetic Resonance Imaging (MRI) data or Computed Tomography (CT) data. This gives us the possibility of using a volume segmentation algorithm such as the one used by Cohen and Cohen [6] or by McInerney and Terzopoulos [16], which are based on deformable models. However, the assumption of considering the 3D array V as an MRI image is not valid because inherently V holds only the depth in-

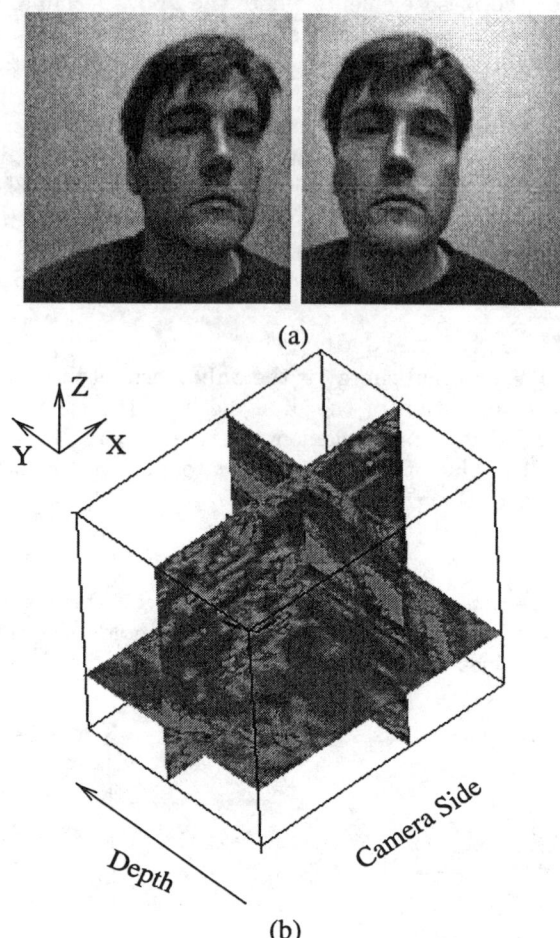

(a)

(b)

Figure 2: (a) A rectified stereo pair (b) Visualization of the 3D array V filled by correlation values. Darker colors represent higher correlation values.

formation of the image points of the stereo pair and it is not a real 3D data. Therefore, direct use of volume segmentation algorithms is not possible. This is due to the definition of the stereo analysis, which is the problem of calculating the distance of scene points relative to the camera position or the viewer [12, 11].

We propose using a deformable mesh to recover the surface inside a volume, such as the one shown in Figure 2. The mesh will be large enough so that the projections of the mesh elements will cover all the image pixels on both images. The mesh deforms under the energy forces produced by Equation (2) with a restriction that the mesh elements can move in the depth dimension only so that it is always visible from all the image points during the deformations. At the end of the deformation, we will have the assigned depth values to the stereo image pixels by projecting mesh points on both image planes and the deformed mesh will give us the structure of the surface recovered. Our work should be distinguished from the methods that use snakes to perform the stereo correspondence such as Cham and Cipolla[4] and the original snake formulation[14].

The deformations described above will place the mesh into a position that minimizes the mesh energy defined by Equation(2). This kind of minimization can be performed using a gradient descent optimization technique, that uses energy functional gradient information to guide the search process. However, this approach is sensitive to initial mesh positions and local minima is a serious problem especially with noisy data. The external energy contains a large amount of noise because of the inherent stereo analysis problems such as noise, occlusions, inaccuracies in the correlation process, etc. Moreover, a good initial position is not always available for most applications. Alternatively, an exhaustive enumeration that iterates on all possible mesh element positions would be computationally prohibitive. Exhaustive mesh minimization methods based on dynamic programming with a polynomial running time, such as the one proposed by [1], might be feasible. However, they are still not as efficient as we need. As a result, we needed to develop a new minimization technique to fit the needs of our application to minimize Equation(2).

3.1 Dual Mesh Optimization

A greedy minimization algorithm is an iterative approach that checks the possible locations for a single mesh element at a time and chooses the location that produces lowest energy. It performs this process for all mesh elements iteratively and the process continues until there is no improvement in the mesh energy. Due to its greedy nature, it is very fast. However, it is extremely sensitive to local minima for the same reason. Williams and Shah [19] use this approach to minimize a deformable contour energy for a 2D application. They argue that it is fast and the extracted contours are reliable. Applying such a minimization algorithm to the minimization of Equation(2) seriously suffers from the local minima due to the noise in the external energy mentioned in the previous section.

In order to address the local minima problem, we propose to use a dual mesh instead of just one mesh as our deformable model. We initialize one of the meshes at the smallest possible depth location, and we call it the near mesh, NM. The initial position of this mesh assigns the smallest depth values to all the pixels of stereo images. The other mesh, the far mesh FM, is initialized at the greatest depth location. Similar to NM, initially FM assigns greatest possible depth values to all of the pixels of the stereo pair(Figure 3). The greatest and smallest possible depth values are generally available in stereo analysis problems. The size of the search window in a classical stereo system assumes the same information as in the form of minimum and maximum possible dispar-

ity. If greatest and smallest possible depth values are not available, we use zero as the smallest and a large value as the greatest.

After the initialization phase the optimization continues by the following steps.

1. Let the initial dual mesh deform independently and simultaneously under the forces produced by Equation(2) ignoring the communication term, $E_{Comm}(m_{ij}, n_{ij})$. Due to their greedy nature, the dual mesh will be attracted by local minima and will stop deforming.

2. After the deformations stop, the energy of each mesh element is compared with the corresponding element in the other mesh ignoring the $E_{Comm}(m_{ij}, n_{ij})$ value. That is, the energy of NM_{ij} is compared with FM_{ij} for all i, j. If one of the mesh element energies is lower, that mesh element is more likely to find the global minima and the higher energy mesh element should be pushed towards the other mesh. This is accomplished by turning on the internal energy term $E_{Comm}(m_{ij}, n_{ij})$ for the high energy element. If m_{ij} is the high energy mesh element then

$$E_{Comm}(m_{ij}, n_{ij}) = |depth(m_{ij}) - depth(n_{ij})|.$$

E_{Comm} returns zero for the lower energy mesh element n_{ij} in this case. The value of E_{Comm} is updated after each greedy iteration so that it reflects the change when m_{ij} gets closer to n_{ij}.

3. After the energy comparison and E_{Comm} setting step, we again let the dual mesh deform under the energy forces, this time with E_{Comm} turned on, which pushes the meshes together.

4. When they stop deforming, we check if they found the same location. If they did not, we turn the E_{Comm} forces off and let the dual mesh deform again until they stop deforming.

5. We repeat the above energy comparison in step 2, turn E_{Comm} on and repeat the whole process until both of the meshes find the same position. We also increase the forces that push the meshes together at each iteration step. This guarantees that they will find the same position after a finite number of steps.

We found that the dual mesh approach is robust against local minima. This is because when one of the meshes is caught by a minima, we immediately know whether it is a local minima by comparing the mesh energies. If it is a local minima, we know which way to push the mesh in order to beat the local minima. We also argue that the dual mesh minimization does better than many gradient descent optimization methods for our application. In a gradient descent algorithm, it is not trivial to know if the current minima is local or global because the gradient vectors do not show which direction to move in that case.

We also found our approach very efficient because it is based on a greedy algorithm and both meshes are guaranteed to find the same position.

Our work on dual mesh is motivated by our previous work [2], which in turn was motivated by Gunn and Nixon[10]. Gunn and Nixon use a dual active contour to extract contours in noisy images robustly. The user has to supply the initial positions of the dual contour because they use a gradient descent algorithm in their minimization. The minimization stops when the dual contour finds the same position. Although the basic idea is to overcome the local minima, our approach is fundamentally different because it works on meshes and it does not need initial mesh positions. Another important difference is that, in our method we always know the correspondences between the two meshes. This gives us the possibility of comparing the local energies and changing the communication energy locally, which will result in robustness in capturing the global minima. On the other hand, Gunn and Nixon do not describe a way of establishing correspondences between the contours. As a result, the whole contour has to be pushed towards the other lower energy contour. This may cause the system to miss the global minima because the high energy contour may locate the global minima contour position partially and pushing it towards the other contour may move the contour from this partial global minima position.

3.2 Coarse to Fine Scheme

In order to make the system more efficient, we use a coarse to fine scheme that starts with a coarse 3D array V and a coarse dual mesh. Figure 3 shows a coarsely initialized 3D array V. The dark colored plane shows the initial position of the near mesh and the light colored plane shows the initial position of the far mesh.

Figure 4-(a) shows the two meshes initialized at the coarsest level before the minimization to recover the surface of the subject's face shown in Figure 2-(a). After the initialization, the dual mesh starts deforming under the energy forces. Figure 4-(b,c) shows the two planes deforming at the coarsest level. The final position of the dual mesh at the coarsest level (Figure 4-(d)) is used to determine the initial positions of the near mesh and the far mesh at the finer level by shifting it in positive and negative directions along the depth dimension (Figure 4-(e)). When the optimization ends at this fine level(Figure 4-(f)), the process is repeated in the same way at a finer level. The final recovered surface (Figure 5), which is the result of the optimization at the finest level, shows the

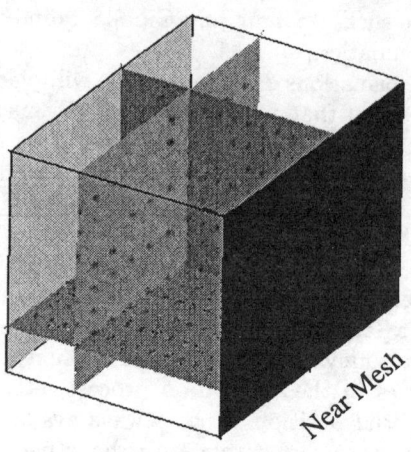

Figure 3: A coarsely initialized 3D array V. The dark and light planes show the initial positions of near and far mesh, respectively.

accuracy of our system, especially at the occluded areas near the sides of the subject's nose. There was a considerable amount of noisy correlation values at the occluded areas which affected the external energy. However, the internal forces were able to estimate a smooth surface for those areas. We found the dual mesh mechanism to be very successful at these situations in order to come up with the optimal result. The viewing angle of the face in Figure 5 is intentionally chosen to show the robustness of the system near the occluded areas. The recovery of the surface shown takes about 300 seconds on an SGI Octane.

4 Tracking

In order to handle the tracking problem, we use the usual tracking method of deformable models, which was first proposed by Kass et. al.[14]. We take the recovered surface from a time frame, use it as an initial estimate for the next time frame and let the mesh deform under a new potential energy. Although this kind of tracking will not give us point correspondences on the 3D surfaces between time frames, it is very useful in a number of ways. First, it is efficient because we know what part of the 3D space we should perform the search for global minima. Second, the recovered surfaces will be more accurate because the deformations will be much less than what it would be without initial positions. As a result, it is more likely to find the global minima.

Figure 6 shows the tracking results of Hurricane Luis by our system for three frames. We cannot show more frames due to space limitation. Although there are small discontinuities, we assumed that the cloud surfaces are continuous in order to test our system's robustness

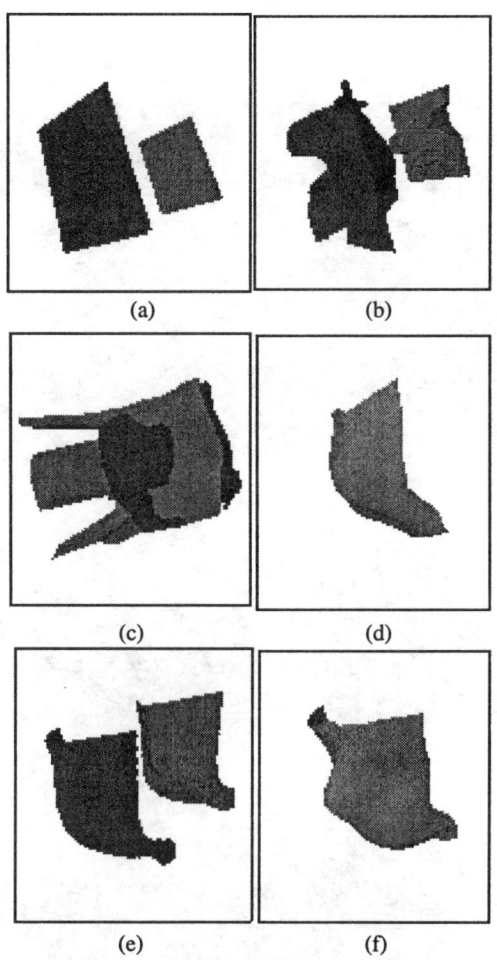

(a) (b)

(c) (d)

(e) (f)

Figure 4: The deformation process of the dual mesh using a coarse to fine scheme. The initial stereo pair is shown in Figure 2. See the text in Section 3.2 for explanations.

against these kinds of surfaces. We confirmed the results by numerically comparing the computed disparity values with the ground truth which was obtained by infrared (IR) images; IR is a good approximation for the opaque cloud-top heights. The experiments show that our system is consistently within less than 1 pixel disparity error range. We also confirmed the results by manually measuring the disparity on the cloud images for a number of pixels.

As expected, the tracking of a single cloud pair takes about 20% less CPU time compared to surface recovery where no initial frame is supplied. From the experiments, we found that the performance of our system is very promising.

5 Conclusions

We presented a new method for integrating stereo correspondence, continuous 3D surface recovery and track-

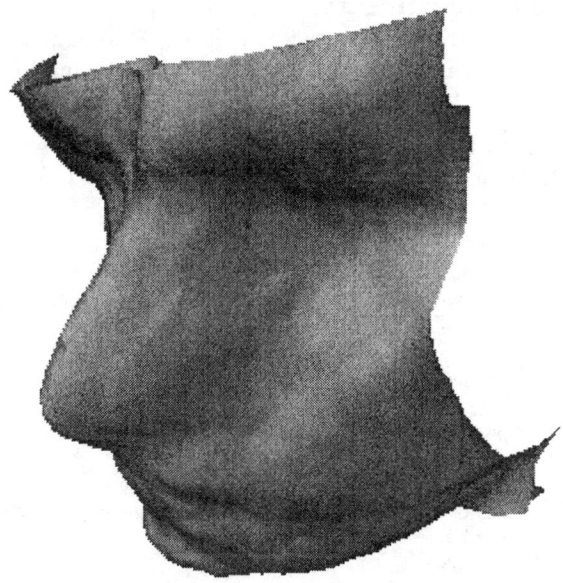

Figure 5: The recovered surface from the finest level (The mesh is shaded for better visualization)

ing in a single deformable dual mesh optimization process. The system introduces a number of novel ideas that would be valuable for stereo reconstruction, tracking and deformable model optimization research. The stereo correspondence and the surface recovery is unified by using the external energy mechanism of the deformable models in a novel way. The optimization of the deformable model is performed by a newly introduced dual mesh method, which showed that it is robust against local minima and efficient by a number of surface recovery and tracking experiments. By combining main stereo analysis steps in an efficient deformable optimization process, we achieved an easy to implement and simple system without sacrificing performance. Although we assumed a continuous surface, the system can be conveniently adapted for a system that can handle discontinuities.

There are many practical applications for this work. We are working on a framework that uses this system to analyze human facial expressions by tracking 3D features. We will embed constraints from the facial expression analysis into our deformable model to increase the system performance. For example, the nose can be assumed to be less rigid than the cheek. This information can be embedded into the optimization process by imposing more rigidity for the nose area mesh elements, resulting in a more robust and efficient stereo analysis system.

Acknowledgments

This work is supported by NSF CISE Research Infrastructure Grant CDA-9703088 and NSF Grant No. IRI 961924.

References

[1] Yusuf Sinan Akgul, Chandra Kambhamettu, and Maureen Stone. Analysis of the tongue surface movement using a spatiotemporally coherent deformable model. In *Proc. IEEE Workshop on Applications of Computer Vision*, pages 109–114, 1998.

[2] Yusuf Sinan Akgul, Chandra Kambhamettu, and Maureen Stone. Extraction and tracking of the tongue surface from ultrasound image sequences. In *CVPR*, pages 298–303, 1998.

[3] A. Blake and A. Zisserman. *Visual Reconstruction*. MIT Press, 1987.

[4] T.J. Cham and R. Cipolla. Stereo coupled active contours. In *CVPR*, pages 1094–1099, 1997.

[5] Q. Chen and G. Medioni. A volumetric stereo matching method: Application to image-based modeling. In *CVPR99*, pages I:29–34, 1999.

[6] L.D. Cohen and I. Cohen. Finite-element methods for active contour models and balloons for 2-D and 3-D images. *PAMI*, 15(11):1131–1147, November 1993.

[7] F. Devernay and O.D. Faugeras. Computing differential properties of 3d shapes from stereoscopic images without 3d models. In *IEEE Computer Vision and Pattern Recognition*, pages 208–213, 1994.

[8] O.D. Faugeras and R. Keriven. Variational-principles, surface evolution, pdes, level set methods, and the stereo problem. *IEEE Transactions on Image Processing*, 7(3):336–344, March 1998.

[9] P. Fua. From multiple stereo views to multiple 3-D surfaces. *International Journal of Computer Vision*, 24(1):19–35, August 1997.

[10] Steve R. Gunn and Mark S. Nixon. A robust snake implementation; a dual active contour. *PAMI*, 19(1):63–68, January 1997.

[11] W. Hoff and N. Ahuja. Surfaces from stereo: Integrating feature matching, disparity estimation, and contour detection. *PAMI*, 11(2):121–136, February 1989.

[12] R.C. Jain, R. Kasturi, and B.G. Schunck. *Machine Vision*. McGraw-Hill, 1995.

[13] C. Kambhamettu, K. Palaniappan, and A.F. Hasler. Coupled, multi-resolution stereo and motion analysis. In *Symposium on Computer Vision*, pages 43–48, 1995.

[14] M. Kass, A. Witkin, and D. Terzopoulos. Snakes: Active contour models. In *ICCV*, pages 259–269, 1987.

[15] K.N. Kutulakos and S.M. Seitz. A theory of shape by space carving. Technical Report 692, University of Rochester CS, May 1998.

[16] T. McInerney and D. Terzopoulos. A finite element model for 3d shape reconstruction and nonrigid motion tracking. In *ICCV93*, pages 518–523, 1993.

[17] D. Terzopoulos. Regularization of inverse visual problems involving discontinuities. *PAMI*, 8(4):413–424, July 1986.

[18] R.P. Wildes. Direct recovery of three-dimensional scene geometry from binocular stereo disparity. *PAMI*, 13(8):761–774, August 1991.

[19] D. J. Williams and M. Shah. A fast algorithm for active contours and curvature estimation. *Computer Vision, Graphics, Image Processing*, 55:14–26, 1992.

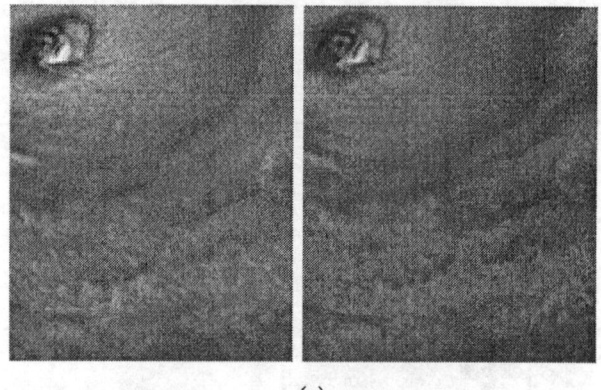

(a)

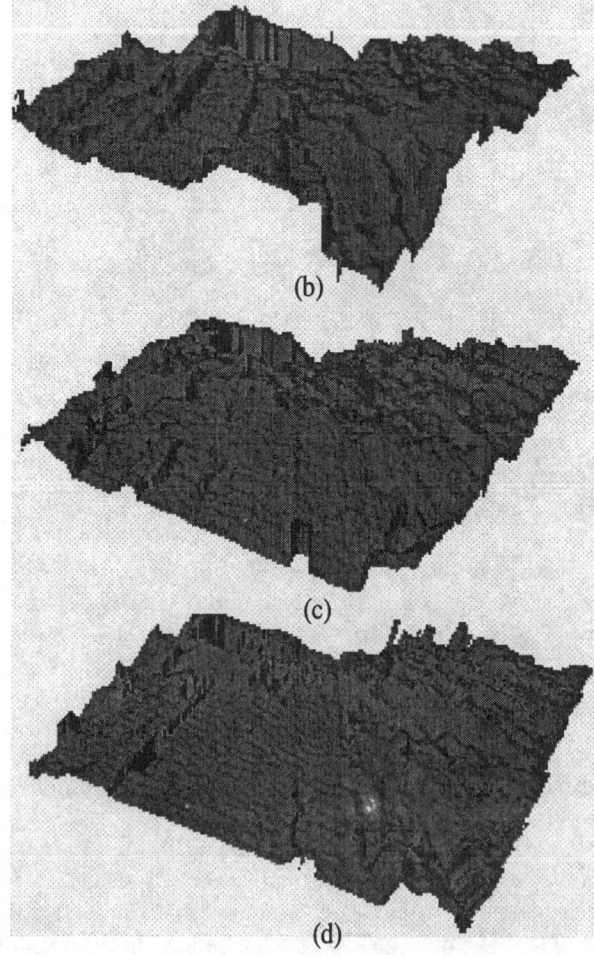

(b)

(c)

(d)

Figure 6: Tracked cloud surfaces. (a) Stereo image pair of the first frame (b) Recovered surface for the first frame (c-d) Tracked surfaces for the second and third frame

Euclidean Reconstruction and Reprojection Up to Subgroups

Yi Ma[†]   Stefano Soatto[‡]   Jana Košecká[†]   Shankar Sastry[†]

† UC Berkeley, Berkeley - CA 94720   ‡ Washington University, St.Louis - MO 63130

Abstract

The necessary and sufficient conditions for being able to estimate scene structure, motion and camera calibration from a sequence of images are very rarely satisfied in practice. What exactly can be estimated in sequences of practical importance, when such conditions are not satisfied? In this paper we give a complete answer to this question. For every camera motion that fails to meet the conditions, we give explicit formulas for the ambiguities in the reconstructed scene, motion and calibration. Such a characterization is crucial both for designing robust estimation algorithms (that do not try to recover parameters that cannot be recovered), and for generating novel views of the scene by controlling the vantage point. To this end, we characterize explicitly all the vantage points that give rise to a valid Euclidean reprojection regardless of the ambiguity in the reconstruction. We also characterize vantage points that generate views that are altogether invariant to the ambiguity. All the results are presented using simple notation that involves no tensors nor complex projective geometry, and should be accessible with basic background in linear algebra.

1. Introduction

Reconstructing spatial properties of a scene from a number of images taken by an uncalibrated camera is a classical problem in computer vision. It is particularly important when the camera used to acquire the images is not available for calibration, as for instance in video post-processing, or when the calibration changes in time, as in vision-based navigation. If we represent the scene by a number of isolated points in three-dimensional space and the imaging process by an ideal perspective projection, the problem can be reduced to a purely geometric one, which has been subject to the intense scrutiny of a number of researchers during the past ten years. Their efforts have led to several important and useful results. The problem is that *conditions for a unique Euclidean reconstruction are almost never satisfied in sequence of images of practical interest*. In fact, they require as a necessary condition that the camera undergoes rotation about at least two independent axes, which is rarely the case both in video processing and in autonomous navigation [14].

In this paper we address the question of *what exactly can be done when the necessary and sufficient conditions for unique reconstruction are **not** satisfied*. In particular:

(i) For all the motions that do not satisfy the conditions, to what extent can we reconstruct structure, motion and calibration?

(ii) If the goal of the reconstruction is to produce a new view of the scene from a different vantage point, how can we make sure that the image generated portrays a "valid" Euclidean scene?

On our way to answering these questions, we pause to reflect on the nature of multilinear constraints. While constraints involving two images at a time (fundamental constraints) are well understood and involve clean notation and geometric interpretation, muti-linear constraints are more difficult to work with and to interpret. It seems therefore natural to ask the following question

(iii) Do multilinear constraints carry geometric information on the camera system that is not contained in bilinear ones?

1.1. Relation to previous work

The study of ambiguities in Euclidean reconstruction **(i)** arises naturally in the problem of motion and structure recovery and self-calibration from multiple cameras. There is a vast body of literature on this topic, which cannot be reviewed in the limited space allowed. Here we only comment on some of the work that is most closely related to this paper, while we refer the reader to the literature for more details, references and appropriate credits (see for instance [4, 8, 10, 13, 19, 20, 21] and references therein).

It has long been known that in the absence of any *a priori* information about motion, calibration and scene structure, reconstruction can be performed at least up to a projective transformation [6]. Utilizing additional knowledge about the relationship between geometric entities in the image (e.g., parallelism) one can stratify the different levels of reconstructions from projective all the way to Euclidean

[3, 5, 6, 18]. At such a level of generality, the conditions on the uniqueness and existence of solutions are restrictive and the algorithms are computationally costly, often exhibiting local minima [12].

The nature of the constraints among images of the same point in different cameras has been studied extensively, and is known to be multilinear (see for instance [7, 10, 20]). The algebraic dependency among constraints (iii) has been established by means of elimination [21] or other algebraic geometric tools [9]. However, an explicit characterization of how the information is encoded in different constraints - which is crucial in the design of robust estimation algorithms - is hard to derive by such means.

Recently, Sturm [19] has proposed a taxonomy of critical motions, that is motions which do not allow a unique reconstruction. However, not only the given taxonomy is by no means intrinsic to Euclidean reconstruction (see [14]), but also no explicit characterization of the ambiguities in the reconstructed shape, motion and calibration has been given. A natural continuation of these efforts involved the analysis of cases where the motion and/or calibration were restricted either to planar or linear motion [2, 18] and techniques were proposed for affine reconstruction or up to one parameter family.

Several techniques have been proposed to synthesize novel views of a reconstructed scene (ii): in [1], trilinear constraints have been exploited to help generate reprojected images for a calibrated camera. In the case of a partially uncalibrated camera, such a method has to face the issues of whether the reprojected image portrays a valid Euclidean scene.

1.2. Outline of this paper and its contributions

As we anticipated in the previous section, the answer to question (iii) has been established before on an algebraic footing – the algebraic ideals generated by trilinear and quadrilinear constraints (as polynomials of image coordinates) are necessarily contained in that generated by bilinear ones [9]. However, in order to give a complete account of ambiguities in 3D Euclidean reconstruction (especially for self-calibration and motion recovery), it is crucial to know how the information on the Euclidean configuration of a camera system is encoded in the multilinear constraints. In section 2 we give a novel, complete and rigorous proof that unveils how the information encoded in trilinear and quadrilinear constraints depends on that in bilinear ones. There we also discuss the role of multilinear constraints with regards to singular configurations of points.

The well-known - but conservative - answer to question (i) is that structure can at least be recovered up to a global projective transformation of the three-dimensional space. However, there is more to be said, as we do in section 3 for the case of constant calibration.[1] There, we give explicit formulas of exact ambiguities in the reconstruction of scene structure, camera motion and calibration with respect to all subgroups of the Euclidean motion. In principle, one should study ambiguities corresponding to all critical configurations as given in [14]. However, it is only the ambiguities that exhibit a *group structure* that are of practical importance in the design of estimation algorithms. In such a case, not only can the analysis be considerably simplified but also clean formulas for all generic ambiguities can be derived. Such formulas are important for 3D reconstruction as well as for synthesizing novel 2D views.

Question (ii) is then answered in section 4, where we characterize the complete set of vantage points that generate "valid" images of the scene regardless of generic ambiguities in 3D reconstruction.

These results have great practical significance, because they quantify precisely to what extent scene structure, camera motion and calibration can be estimated in sequences for which many of the techniques available todate do not apply. Furthermore, the analysis clarifies the process of 2D view synthesis from novel viewpoints. In addition to that, we give a novel account of known results on the role of multilinear constraints and their relationship to bilinear ones.

Granted the potential impact on applications, this paper is mainly concerned with theory. We address neither algorithmic issues, nor do we perform experiments of any sort: the validation of our statements is in the proofs. We have tried to keep our notation as terse as possible. Our tools are borrowed from linear algebra and some differential geometry, although all the results should be accessible without background in the latter. We use the language of (Lie) groups because that allows us to give an explicit characterization of all the ambiguities in a concise and intuitive fashion. Traditional tools involved in the analysis of self-calibration involved complex loci in projective spaces (e.g., the "absolute conic"), which can be hard to grasp for someone not proficient in algebraic geometry.

2. Dependency of multilinear constraints revisited

We model the world as a collection of points in a three-dimensional Euclidean space, which we represent in homogeneous coordinates as $q = (q_1, q_2, q_3, 1)^T \in \mathbb{R}^4$. The perspective projection of the generic point onto the two-dimensional image plane is represented by homogeneous coordinates $\mathbf{x} \in \mathbb{R}^3$ that satisfy

$$\lambda(t)\mathbf{x}(t) = A(t)g(t)q, \quad t \in \mathbb{R} \quad (1)$$

where $\lambda(t) \in \mathbb{R}$ is a scalar parameter related to the distance of the point q from the center of projection and the non-

---

[1]In fact, even in the case of time-varying calibration, in principle, the best one can do is an affine reconstruction, not just a projective one!

774

singular matrix $A(t)$ - called "calibration matrix" - describes the intrinsic parameters of the camera. Without loss of generality we will re-scale the above equation so that the determinant of A is 1. The set of 3×3 matrices with determinant one is called Special Linear group denoted by $SL(3)$. The rigid motion of the camera $g(t)$ is represented by a translation vector $p(t) \in \mathbb{R}^3$ and a rotation matrix $R(t)$, that is an orthogonal matrix with determinant equal to one. Such matrices form a group called Special Orthogonal group and indicated by $SO(3)$; $g(t) = (R(t), p(t))$ belongs to $SE(3)$, the special Euclidean group of rigid motion in $\mathbb{R}^3$. The action of $g(t)$ on the point q is given by $g(t)q = R(t)q + p(t)$. In equation (1) we will assume that $\mathbf{x}(t)$ is measured, while everything else is unknown.

When we consider measurements at n different times, we organize the above equations by defining

$$M_i \doteq (A(t_i)R(t_i), A(t_i)p(t_i)) \in \mathbb{R}^{3 \times 4} \qquad (2)$$

which we will assume to be full-rank, that is $rank(M_i) = 3$ for $i = 1, \ldots, n$. So we have

$$\begin{pmatrix} \mathbf{x}(t_1) & 0 & \cdots & 0 \\ 0 & \mathbf{x}(t_2) & \cdots & 0 \\ \vdots & \vdots & \ddots & \vdots \\ 0 & 0 & \cdots & \mathbf{x}(t_n) \end{pmatrix} \begin{pmatrix} \lambda(t_1) \\ \lambda(t_2) \\ \vdots \\ \lambda(t_n) \end{pmatrix} = \begin{pmatrix} M_1 \\ M_2 \\ \vdots \\ M_n \end{pmatrix} q$$

which we re-write in a more compact notation as $\mathbf{X}\vec{\lambda} = Mq$. We call $M \in \mathbb{R}^{3n \times 4}$ the *motion matrix* and $\mathbf{X}$ the *image matrix*.

2.1. Constraints on multiple images

Let $\vec{\mathbf{m}}_i \in \mathbb{R}^{3n}, i = 1, \ldots, 4$ denote the four columns of the matrix M and $\vec{\mathbf{X}}_i \in \mathbb{R}^{3n}, i = 1, \ldots, n$ be the n columns of the matrix $\mathbf{X}$. Then the coordinates $\mathbf{x}(t_i)$ represent the same point seen from different views only if they satisfy the following wedge product equation:

$$\vec{\mathbf{m}}_1 \wedge \vec{\mathbf{m}}_2 \wedge \vec{\mathbf{m}}_3 \wedge \vec{\mathbf{m}}_4 \wedge \vec{\mathbf{X}}_1 \wedge \cdots \wedge \vec{\mathbf{X}}_n = 0. \qquad (3)$$

This constraint, which is multilinear in the measurements $\mathbf{x}(t_i)$ simply expresses the fact that the columns of M and $\mathbf{X}$ are linearly dependent. Constraints involving four images are call *quadrilinear*, constraints involving three images are called *trilinear*, and those involving two images are called *bilinear* or *fundamental*. In general, the coefficients of all the multilinear constraints are minors of the motion matrix M. As it has been shown (see, for instance, Triggs in [20]), constraints involving more than four frames are necessarily dependent on quadrilinear, trilinear and bilinear ones. In this section we go one step further to discuss how trilinear and quadrilinear constraints are dependent on bilinear ones.

When studying the dependency among constraints, one must distinguish between *algebraic* and *geometric* dependency. Roughly speaking, algebraic dependency concerns the conditions that a point in an image must satisfy in order to be the correspondent of a point in another image. Vice versa, geometric dependency is concerned with the information that corresponding points give on the operator that maps one to the other. The two notions are related but not equivalent, and the latter bears important consequences when one is to use the constraints in optimization algorithms to recover structure and calibration. While the geometric dependency of multilinear constraints has been established before under the assumption of constant calibration [10], we give a novel, simple and rigorous proof that is valid under the more general assumption of time-varying calibration.

2.2. Algebraic vs. geometric dependency

To clarify the relation between algebraic and geometric dependency[2], note that in general we can express a multilinear constraint in the form: $\sum_j \alpha_j(M)\beta_j(\mathbf{X}) = 0$ where α_j are some polynomials of entries of M and β_j polynomials of entries of the image coordinates, with M and $\mathbf{X}$ defined as before. α_j's are called the *coefficients* of multilinear constraints. Studying the *algebraic dependency* between constraints then corresponds to fixing the coefficients α_j and asking whether there are some additional constraints among the image coordinates $\mathbf{X}$ generated by three and four views[3]. This problem has been studied many researchers and an elegant answer can be found in [9] by explicitly characterizing the *primary decomposition* of the ideal (in the polynomial ring of image coordinates $\mathbf{x}_i$'s) generated by the bilinear constraints in terms of that generated by trilinear ones or quadrilinear ones.

Geometric dependency, on the other hand, investigates whether, given the image coordinates $\mathbf{X}$, the coefficients α_j corresponding to motion parameters in additional views can give additional information about M. These two different types of dependencies were previously pointed out (see for instance the work of Heyden [10]). For both types of dependencies, the answer is negative, *i.e.*, trilinear and quadrilinear constraints in general are dependent of bilinear ones. We here give a simple but rigorous study of the geometric dependency. The results will also validate the ambiguity analysis given in following sections.

Consider the case $n = 3$ and, for the moment, disregard the internal structure of the motion matrix $M \in \mathbb{R}^{9 \times 4}$. Its columns can be interpreted as a basis of a four-dimensional subspace of the nine-dimensional space. The set of k-dimensional subspaces of an m-dimensional space is called a Grassmannian manifold and denoted by $G(m, k)$. Therefore, M is an element of $G(9, 4)$. By just

---

[2]This subsection is for the benefit of the reader already familiar with existing work on the algebraic dependency among multilinear constraints. The reader who is not at ease with algebraic geometry or unfamiliar with the existing literature can skip this subsection without loss of continuity

[3]In other words, it addresses the dependency among algebraic ideals associated with the three types of multilinear constraints.

re-arranging the three blocks M_i, $i = 1, \ldots, 3$ into three pairs, (M_1, M_2), (M_1, M_3) and (M_2, M_3), we define a map ϕ between $G(9, 4)$ and three copies of $G(6, 4)$

$$\phi : G(9, 4) \rightarrow G(6, 4) \times G(6, 4) \times G(6, 4)$$

$$\begin{pmatrix} M_1 \\ M_2 \\ M_3 \end{pmatrix} \mapsto \left(\begin{pmatrix} M_1 \\ M_2 \end{pmatrix}, \begin{pmatrix} M_2 \\ M_3 \end{pmatrix}, \begin{pmatrix} M_1 \\ M_3 \end{pmatrix} \right).$$

The question of whether trilinear constraints are independent of bilinear ones is tightly related to whether these two representations of the motion matrix M are equivalent. Since the coefficients in the multilinear constraints are homogeneous in the entries of each block M_i, the motion matrix M is only determined up to the equivalence relation:

$$M \sim M' \text{ if } \exists \lambda_i \in \mathbb{R}^*, M_i = \lambda_i M_i', \quad i = 1, \ldots, n \quad (4)$$

where $\mathbb{R}^* = \mathbb{R} \setminus \{0\}$. Thus for multilinear constraints the motion matrix is only well-defined as an element of the quotient space $G(3n, 4)/ \sim$ which is of dimension $(11n - 15)$, [4] as was already noted by Triggs [20].

We are now ready to prove that coefficients α_j's in trilinear and quadrilinear constraints depend on those in bilinear ones.

Theorem 1 (Geometric dependency) *Given three (or four) views, the coefficients of all bilinear constraints or equivalently the corresponding fundamental matrices uniquely determine the motion matrix M as an element in $G(9, 4)/ \sim$ (or $G(12, 4)/ \sim$) given that $Ker(M_i)$'s are linearly independent.*

Proof: It is known that between any pair of images (i, j) the motion matrix: $\begin{pmatrix} M_i \\ M_j \end{pmatrix} \in G(6, 4)$, is determined by the corresponding fundamental matrix F_{ij} up to two scalars λ_i, λ_j: $\begin{pmatrix} \lambda_i M_i \\ \lambda_j M_j \end{pmatrix} \in G(6, 4)$, $\lambda_j \in \mathbb{R}^*$. Hence for the three view case all we need to prove is that the map:

$$\tilde{\phi} : (G(9, 4)/ \sim) \rightarrow (G(6, 4)/ \sim)^3$$

is injective. To this end, assume $\tilde{\phi}(M) = \tilde{\phi}(M')$; then we have that, after re-scaling, $\begin{pmatrix} M_1' \\ M_2' \end{pmatrix} = \begin{pmatrix} \lambda_1 M_1 \\ M_2 \end{pmatrix} G_1$, $\begin{pmatrix} M_2' \\ M_3' \end{pmatrix} = \begin{pmatrix} \lambda_2 M_2 \\ M_3 \end{pmatrix} G_2$, $\begin{pmatrix} M_1' \\ M_3' \end{pmatrix} = \begin{pmatrix} M_1 \\ \lambda_3 M_3 \end{pmatrix} G_3$ for some $\lambda_i \in \mathbb{R}^*$ and $G_i \in GL(4)$,[5] $i = 1, 2, 3$. This yields $M_1(\lambda_1 G_1 - G_3) = 0, M_2(\lambda_2 G_2 - G_1) = 0, M_3(\lambda_3 G_3 - G_2) = 0$. Therefore there exist $U_i \in \mathbb{R}^{4 \times 4}, i = 1, 2, 3$ with each column of U_i is in $Ker(M_i)$ such that:

$$G_3 - \lambda_1 G_1 = U_1, \quad G_1 - \lambda_2 G_2 = U_2, \quad G_2 - \lambda_3 G_3 = U_3.$$

---

[4] The Grassmannian $G(3n, 4)$ has dimension $(3n - 4)4 = 12n - 16$. The dimension of the quotient space is $n - 1$ smaller since the equivalence relation has $n - 1$ independent scales.

[5] $GL(4)$ is the general linear group of all non-degenerate 4×4 real matrices.

Combining these three equations, we obtain:

$$(1 - \lambda_1 \lambda_2 \lambda_3)G_1 = \lambda_2 \lambda_3 U_1 + \lambda_2 U_3 + U_2.$$

The matrix on the right hand side of the equation has a non-trivial null-space since its columns are in $span\{Ker(M_1), Ker(M_2), Ker(M_3)\}$ which has dimension three. However, G_1 is non-singular, and therefore it must be $\lambda_1 \lambda_2 \lambda_3 = 1$. This gives $\lambda_1 G_1 - G_3 = -\lambda_1(\lambda_2 G_2 - G_1) - \lambda_1 \lambda_2(\lambda_3 G_3 - G_2)$. That is, the columns of $\lambda_1 G_1 - G_3$ are linear combinations of columns of $\lambda_2 G_2 - G_1$ and $\lambda_3 G_3 - G_2$. But $Ker(M_i), i = 1, 2, 3$ are linearly independent. Thus we have $\lambda_1 G_1 = G_3, \lambda_2 G_2 = G_1, \lambda_3 G_3 = G_2$. This implies

$$\begin{pmatrix} M_1' \\ M_2' \\ M_3' \end{pmatrix} = \begin{pmatrix} \lambda_1 M_1 \\ M_2 \\ \lambda_1 \lambda_3 M_3 \end{pmatrix} G_1.$$

which means that M' and M are the same, up to the equivalence relation defined in equation (4). Therefore, they represent the same element in $G(9, 4)/ \sim$, which means that the map $\tilde{\phi}$ is injective.

In the case of four views, in order to show that coefficients in quadrilinear constraints also depend on bilinear ones, one only needs to check that the obvious map from $G(12, 4)/ \sim$ to $(G(9, 4)/ \sim)^4$ is injective. This directly follows from the above proof of the three frame case. ∎

Comment 1 *As a consequence of the theorem, coefficients α_j's in trilinear and quadrilinear constraints are functions of those in bilinear ones. While the above proof shows that the map $\tilde{\phi}$ can be inverted, it does not provide an explicit characterization of the inverse. Such an inverse can in principle be highly non-linear and conditioning issues need to be taken into account in the design of estimation algorithms. We emphasize that the geometric dependency does not imply that two views are sufficient for reconstruction! It claims that given n views, their geometry is characterized by considering only combinations of pairs of them through bilinear constraints, while trilinear constraints are of help only in the case of singular configurations of points and camera (see comment 2). For four views, the condition that $Ker(M_i), i = 1, \ldots, 4$ are linearly independent is not necessary. A less conservative condition is that there exist two groups of three frames which satisfy the condition for the three view case.*

Theorem 1 requires that the one-dimensional kernels of the matrices $M_i, i = 1, \ldots, n$ ($n = 3$ or 4) are linearly independent. Note that the kernels of M_i for $i = 1, 2, 3, 4$ are given by $(-p_i^T R_i, 1)^T$, where the vector $R_i^T p_i \in \mathbb{R}^3$ is exactly the position of the ith camera center. Hence the condition of the theorem is satisfied if and only if the centers of projection of the cameras generate a hyper-plane of dimension $n - 1$. In particular, when $n = 3$, the three camera centers form a triangle, and when $n = 4$, the four camera centers form a tetrahedron.

Comment 2 (Critical surfaces and motions) *Although we have shown that the coefficients of multilinear constraints depend on those of bilinear ones, we have assumed that the latter (or the corresponding fundamental matrices) are uniquely determined by the epipolar geometry. However, this is not true when all the points lie on critical surfaces. In this case, as argued by Maybank in [15], we may obtain up to three ambiguous solutions from the bilinear constraints. This is one of the cases when trilinear and quadrilinear constraints provide useful information. On this topic, see also [16]. Also, when the camera is undergoing a rectilinear motion (i.e., all optical centers are aligned), trilinear constraints provide independent information in addition to bilinear ones. This fact has been pointed out before; see for instance Heyden in [11].*

3. Reconstruction under motion subgroups

The goal of this section is to study all "critical" motion groups that do *not* allow unique reconstruction of structure, motion and calibration. While a *classification* of such critical motions has been presented before (see [14]), we here go well beyond by giving an *explicit characterization* of the ambiguity in the reconstruction for each critical motion. Such an explicit characterization is crucial in deriving the ambiguity in the generation of novel views of a scene, which we study in section 4.

In this section, we characterize the generic ambiguity in the recovery of (a) structure, (b) motion and (c) calibration corresponding to each possible critical motion. A subgroup of $SE(3)$ is called *critical* if the reconstruction is not unique when the motion of the camera is restricted to it. For the purpose of this section, we assume that the calibration matrix A is constant.

3.1. Some preliminaries

So far the only restriction we have imposed on the constant calibration matrix A is that it is non-singular and is normalized as to have $\det(A) = 1$. However, A can only be determined up to an equivalence class of rotations, that is $A \in SL(3)/SO(3)$.[6] For more detail, please see [14]. The unrecoverable rotation in our choice of A simply corresponds to a rotation of the entire camera system. We borrow the following statement directly from [14]:

Theorem 2 (Necessary and sufficient condition for a unique calibration) *Given a set of camera motion $\{(R_i, p_i)\} \subset SE(3)$ where none of the rotation component R_i is of the form $e^{\hat{u}_i k \pi}$ with $\|u_i\| = 1, k \in \mathbb{Z}$, then the camera calibration A as an element in $SL(3)/SO(3)$ is uniquely determined if and only if at least two of the axes u_i's are linearly independent.*

---

[6] Here take left cosets as elements in the quotient space. A representation of this quotient space is given, for instance, by upper-triangular matrices; such a representation is commonly used in modeling calibration matrices by means of physical parameters of cameras such as focal length, principal point and pixel skew.

Although the necessity of the independence of the rotation axes has been long known in the literature (see e.g. [13]), the sufficiency is not proven till recent [14]. This theorem states a very important and useful fact: the condition for a unique calibration has nothing to do with translation (as opposed to the results given in [19])! See [14] for the detail. Due to this theorem, all proper continuous subgroups of $SE(3)$ except $SO(3)$ are critical for self-calibration. So the first step in our analysis consists in classifying all continuous Lie subgroups of $SE(3)$. It is a well known fact that a complete list of these groups (up to conjugation) is given by [7]:

> Translational Motion: $(\mathbb{R}^3, +)$ and its subgroups
> Rotational Motion: $(SO(3), \cdot)$ and its subgroups
> Planar Motion: $SE(2)$
> Screw Motion: $(SO(2), \cdot) \times (\mathbb{R}, +)$
> Planar + Elevation: $SE(2) \times (\mathbb{R}, +)$

We are now ready to explore to what extent scene structure, camera motion and calibration can be reconstructed when motion is constrained onto one of the above subgroups. In other words, we will study the *generic* ambiguities of the reconstruction problem. In what follows, we use $q(t) = (q_1(t), q_2(t), q_3(t))^T \in \mathbb{R}^3$ to denote the 3D coordinates of the point $q = (q_1, q_2, q_3, 1)^T \in \mathbb{R}^4$ with respect to the camera frame at time t: $q(t) = (R(t), p(t))q$. To simplify notation, for any $u \in \mathbb{R}^3$ we define $\hat{u}$ to be a 3 skew-symmetric matrix such that $\forall v \in \mathbb{R}^3$ the cross product $u \times v = \hat{u}v$.

3.2. Generic ambiguities in structure, motion and calibration

Translational motion ($\mathbb{R}^3$ and its subgroups). The coordinate transformation between different views is given by $Aq(t) = Aq(t_0) + Ap(t), p(t) \in \mathbb{R}^3$. According to Theorem 2, the calibration $A \in SL(3)$ cannot be recovered from pure translational motion, and therefore the corresponding structure q and translational motion p can be recovered only up to the unknown transformation A. We therefore have the following

Theorem 3 (Ambiguity under $\mathbb{R}^3$) *Consider an uncalibrated camera described by the calibration matrix $A \in SL(3)$, undergoing purely translational motion $\mathbb{R}^3$ (or any of its nontrivial subgroups) and let B be an arbitrary matrix in $SL(3)$. If the camera motion $p \in \mathbb{R}^3$ and the scene structure $q \in \mathbb{R}^4$ are unknown, then B, $B^{-1}Ap$ and $B^{-1}Aq$ are the only generic ambiguous solutions for the camera calibration, camera motion and the scene structure respectively.*

Note that this ambiguity corresponds exactly to an affine reconstruction [18].

---

[7] The completeness of this list can be shown by classifying all Lie subalgebras of the Lie algebra $se(3)$ of $SE(3)$ and then exponentiate them.

Rotational motion ($SO(3)$). The action of $SO(3)$ transforms the coordinates in different cameras by $Aq(t) = AR(t)q(t_0)$, $R(t) \in SO(3)$. According to Theorem 2, the calibration A can be recovered uniquely, and so can the rotational motion $R(t) \in SO(3)$. However, it is well known that the depth information of the structure cannot be recovered at all. We summarize these facts into the following:

Theorem 4 (Ambiguity under $SO(3)$) *Consider an uncalibrated camera with calibration matrix $A \in SL(3)$ undergoing purely rotational motion $SO(3)$ and let λ be an arbitrary (positive) scalar. If both the camera motion $R \in SO(3)$ and the scene structure $q \in \mathbb{R}^3$ are unknown, then A, R and $\lambda \cdot q$ are the only generic ambiguous solutions for the camera calibration, camera motion and the scene structure respectively.*

Planar motion ($SE(2)$). While the previous two cases were of somewhat academic interest and the theorems portray well-known facts, planar motion arises very often in applications. We will therefore study this case in some more detail.

Let $e_1 = (1,0,0)^T$, $e_2 = (0,1,0)^T$, $e_3 = (0,0,1)^T \in \mathbb{R}^3$ be the standard basis of $\mathbb{R}^3$. Without loss of generality, we may assume the camera motion is on the plane normal to e_3 and is represented by the subgroup $SE(2)$.

Let A be the unknown calibration matrix of the camera. As described in section 3.1 we consider A as an element of the quotient space $SL(3)/SO(3)$. According to [14], any possible calibration matrix $A_0 \in SL(3)/SO(3)$ is such that the matrix $S = A_0^{-T}A_0^{-1}$ is in the *symmetric real kernel* ($SRKer$) of the Lyapunov map for all $C = A^{-T}R^T A^T$, $R \in SE(2)$:

$$L : \mathbb{C}^{3 \times 3} \to \mathbb{C}^{3 \times 3}; \quad X \mapsto X - CXC^T. \quad (5)$$

By the choice of e_1, e_2, e_3, the real eigenvector of R is e_3. Imposing $S \in SL(3)$, we obtain $S = A^{-T}D(s)A^{-1}$, where $D(s) \in \mathbb{R}^{3 \times 3}$ is a matrix function of s:

$$D(s) = \begin{pmatrix} s & 0 & 0 \\ 0 & s & 0 \\ 0 & 0 & 1/s^2 \end{pmatrix}, \quad s \in \mathbb{R} \setminus \{0\}. \quad (6)$$

Geometrically, this reveals that only metric information within the plane can be recovered while the relative scale between the plane and its normal direction cannot be determined. If we choose an erroneous matrix A_0 from the set of possible solutions for calibration, then $A_0 B = A$ for some matrix $B \in SL(3)$. Since $A_0^{-T}A_0^{-1}$ is necessarily in $SRKer(L)$, we further have that, for some $s \in \mathbb{R}$,

$$A_0^{-T}A_0^{-1} = A^{-T}D(s)A^{-1} \Rightarrow B^T B = D(s). \quad (7)$$

A solution of (7) is of the form $B = HD(s)$ with $H \in SO(3)$ and $s \in \mathbb{R}$. Let us define a one-parameter Lie group

$G_{SE(2)}$ as:

$$G_{SE(2)} = \{D(s) \mid s \in \mathbb{R} \setminus \{0\}\}. \quad (8)$$

Then the solution space of (7) is given by $SO(3)G_{SE(2)}$. The group $G_{SE(2)}$ can be viewed as a natural representation of ambiguous solutions in the space $SL(3)/SO(3)$.

Once we have a calibration matrix, say A_0, we can extract motion from the fundamental matrix $F = A^{-T}R^T A^T \widehat{p'} \in \mathbb{R}^{3 \times 3}$ as follows: we know that $A = A_0 B$ for some $B = HD(s) \in SO(3)G_{SE(2)}$. Then we define $E = A_0^T F A_0$ and note that, for $R = \exp(\widehat{e_3}\theta)$, we have that $D(s)$ commutes with R i.e., $D(s)RD(s)^{-1} = R$. Then E is an essential matrix since $E = H^{-T}D^{-T}(s)R^T \widehat{p}D^{-1}(s)H^{-1} = HR^T H^T \widehat{HD(s)p}$. The motion recovered from E is therefore $(HRH^T, HD(s)p) \in SE(3)$, where $(R,p) \in SE(2)$ is the true motion. Note that $(HRH^T, HD(s)p)$ is actually a *planar motion* (in a plane rotated by H from the original one). The coordinate transformation in the uncalibrated camera frame is given by $Aq(t) = ARq(t_0) + Ap(t)$. If, instead, the matrix A_0 is chosen to justify the camera calibration, the coordinate transformation becomes:

$$A_0 Bq(t) = A_0 BRq(t_0) + A_0 Bp(t) \Rightarrow$$
$$HD(s)q(t) = HRH^T(HD(s)q(t_0)) + HD(s)p(t).$$

Therefore, any point q viewed with an uncalibrated camera A undergoing a motion $(R,p) \in SE(2)$ is not distinguishable from the point $HD(s)q$ viewed with an uncalibrated camera $A_0 = AD^{-1}(s)H^T$ undergoing a motion $(HRH^T, HD(s)p) \in SE(2)$. We have therefore proven the following

Theorem 5 (Ambiguity under $SE(2)$) *Consider a camera with unknown calibration matrix $A \in SL(3)$ undergoing planar motion $SE(2)$ and let $B(s) = HD(s)$ with $H \in SO(3)$ and $D(s) \in G_{SE(2)}$. If both the camera motion $(R,p) \in SE(2)$ and the scene structure $q \in \mathbb{R}^3$ are unknown, then $AB^{-1}(s) \in SL(3)$, $(HRH^T, B(s)p) \in SE(2)$ and $B(s)q \in \mathbb{R}^3$ are the only generic ambiguous solutions for the camera calibration, camera motion and scene structure respectively.*

Comment 3 *Note that the role of the matrix $H \in SO(3)$ is just to rotate the overall configuration. Therefore, the only generic ambiguity of the reconstruction is characterized by the one parameter Lie group $G_{SE(2)}$.*

Subgroups $SO(2)$, $SO(2) \times \mathbb{R}$ and $SE(2) \times \mathbb{R}$. We conclude our discussion on subgroups of $SE(3)$ by studying $SO(2)$, $SO(2) \times \mathbb{R}$ and $SE(2) \times \mathbb{R}$ together. This is because their generic ambiguities are similar to the case of $SE(2)$, which we have just studied. Notice that in the discussion of the ambiguity $G_{SE(2)}$, we did not use the fact that the translation p has to satisfy $p_3 = 0$. Therefore, *the generic reconstruction ambiguities of $SO(2) \times \mathbb{R}$ and $SE(2) \times \mathbb{R}$ are* exactly the same as that of $SE(2)$. The only different case is $SO(2)$. It is readily seen that the ambiguity of $SO(2)$ is the "product" of that of $SE(2)$ and that of $SO(3)$ due to the fact $SO(2) = SE(2) \cap SO(3)$. As a consequence of Theorem 4 and Theorem 5 we have:

Corollary 1 (Ambiguity under $SO(2)$) *Consider an uncalibrated camera with calibration matrix $A \in SL(3)$ undergoing a motion in $SO(2)$ and let $B(s) = HD(s)$ with $H \in SO(3)$, $D(s) \in G_{SE(2)}$ and $\lambda \in (R^+, \cdot)$. If both the camera motion $R \in SO(3)$ and the scene structure $q \in \mathbb{R}^3$ are unknown, then $AB^{-1}(s) \in SL(3)$, $HRH^T \in SO(3)$ and $\lambda \cdot B(s)q \in \mathbb{R}^3$ are the only generic ambiguous solutions for the camera calibration, camera motion and scene structure respectively.*

From the above discussion of subgroups of $SE(3)$ we have seen that generic ambiguities exist for any proper subgroup of $SE(3)$. Therefore all subgroups of $SE(3)$ are critical with respect to reconstruction of scene structure, motion and camera calibration. Furthermore, such ambiguities - which have been derived above based only on bilinear constraints, are not resolved by multilinear constraints according to Theorem 1.

4. Reprojection under partial reconstruction

In the previous section we have seen that, in general, it is possible to reconstruct the calibration matrix A and the scene's structure q only *up to a subgroup* - which we call K, the ambiguity subgroup. For instance, in the case of planar motion, an element in K has the form $D(s)$ given by equation (6). Therefore, after reconstruction we have

$$\tilde{q}(K) = Kq, \quad \tilde{A}(K) = AK^{-1}. \quad (9)$$

Now, suppose one wants to generate a novel view of the scene, $\tilde{\mathbf{x}}$ from a new vantage point, which is specified by a motion $\tilde{g} \in SE(3)$ and must satisfy $\lambda \tilde{\mathbf{x}}(K) = \tilde{A}(K)\tilde{g}\tilde{q}(K)$. In general, the reprojection $\tilde{\mathbf{x}}(K)$ depends both on the ambiguity subgroup K and on the vantage point $\tilde{g}$ and there is no guarantee that it is an image of the original Euclidean scene.

It is only natural, then, to ask *what is the set of vantage points that generate a valid reprojection*, that is an image of the original scene q taken as if the camera A was placed at some vantage point $g(K)$. We discuss this issue in section 4.1. A stronger condition to require is that the reprojection be independent (*invariant*) of the ambiguity K, so that we have $g(K) = \tilde{g}$ regardless of K; we discuss this issue in section 4.2.

4.1. Valid Euclidean reprojection

In order to characterize the vantage points - specified by motions $\tilde{g}$ - that produce a valid reprojection we must

find $\tilde{g}$ such that: $\tilde{A}(K)\tilde{g}\tilde{q}(K) = Ag(K)q$ for some $g(K) \in SE(3)$. Since the reprojected image $\tilde{\mathbf{x}}$ is $\lambda \tilde{\mathbf{x}}(K) = \tilde{A}(K)\tilde{g}\tilde{q}(K) = Ag(K)q$, the characterization of all such motions $\tilde{g}$ is given by the following Lie group:

$$R(K) = \{\tilde{g} \in SE(3) \mid K^{-1}\tilde{g}K \subset SE(3)\}. \quad (10)$$

We call $R(K)$ the *reprojection group* for a given ambiguity group K. For each of the generic ambiguities we studied in section 3, the corresponding reprojection group is given by the following

Theorem 6 *The reprojection groups corresponding to each of the ambiguity groups K studied in section 3 are given by:*
1. $R(K) = (\mathbb{R}^3, +)$ for $K = SL(3)$ (ambiguity of $(\mathbb{R}^3, +)$).
2. $R(K) = SO(2)$ for $K = G_{SE(2)} \times (\mathbb{R}^+, \cdot)$ (ambiguity of $SO(2)$).
3. $R(K) = SE(2) \times \mathbb{R}$ for $K = G_{SE(2)}$ (ambiguity of $SE(2), SO(2) \times \mathbb{R}, SE(2) \times \mathbb{R}$).
4. $R(K) = SE(3)$ for $K = I$ (ambiguity of $SE(3)$).

Even though the reprojected image is, in general, not unique, the family of all such images are still parameterized by the same ambiguity group K. For a motion outside of the group $R(K)$, *i.e.*, for a $\tilde{g} \in SE(3) \setminus R(K)$, the action of the ambiguity group K on a reprojected image cannot simply be represented as moving the camera: it will have to be a more general non-Euclidean transformation of the shape of the scene. However, the family of all such non-Euclidean shapes are minimally parameterized by the quotient space $SE(3)/R(K)$.

Comment 4 *[Choice of a "basis" for reprojection] Note that in order to specify the viewpoint it is not just sufficient to choose the motion $\tilde{g}$ for, in general, $g(K) \neq \tilde{g}$. Therefore, an imaginary "visual-effect operator" will have to adjust the viewpoint $g(K)$ acting on the parameters in K. The ambiguity subgroups derived in section 3 are one-parameter groups (for the most important cases) and therefore the choice is restricted to one parameter. In a projective framework (such as [6]), the user has to specify a projective basis of three-dimensional space, that is 15 parameters. This is usually done by specifying the three-dimensional position of 5 points in space.*

4.2. Invariant reprojection

In order for the view taken from $\tilde{g}$ to be unique, we must have

$$\lambda \tilde{\mathbf{x}} = \tilde{A}(K)\tilde{g}\tilde{q}(K) = AK^{-1}\tilde{g}Kq \quad (11)$$

independent of K. Equivalently we must have $K^{-1}\tilde{g}K = \tilde{g}$ where K is the ambiguity generated by the motion on a subgroup G of $SE(3)$. The set of $\tilde{g}$ that satisfy this condition is a group $N(K)$, the so called *normalizer* of K in $SE(3)$. Therefore, all we have to do is to characterize the normalizers for the ambiguity subgroups studied in section 3.

Theorem 7 *The set of viewpoints that are invariant to re-projection is given by the normalizer of the ambiguity subgroup. For each of the motion subgroups analyzed in section 3 the corresponding normalizer of the ambiguity group is given by:*

1. $N(K) = I$ for $K = SL(3)$ (ambiguity of $(\mathbb{R}^3, +)$).

2. $N(K) = SO(2)$ for $K = G_{SE(2)} \times (\mathbb{R}^+, \cdot)$ (ambiguity of $SO(2)$).

3. $N(K) = SO(2)$ for $K = G_{SE(2)}$ (ambiguity of $SE(2), SO(2) \times \mathbb{R}, SE(2) \times \mathbb{R}$).

4. $N(K) = SE(3)$ for $K = I$ (ambiguity of $SE(3)$).

For motions in every subgroup, the reprojection performed under any viewpoint determined by the groups above is unique.

5. Conclusions

When the necessary and sufficient conditions for a unique reconstruction of scene structure, camera motion and calibration are not satisfied, it is still possible to retrieve a reconstruction up to a global subgroup action (on the entire configuration of the camera system). We characterize such subgroups explicitly for all possible motion groups of the camera. The reconstructed structure can then be re-projected to generate novel views of the scene. We characterize the "basis" of the reprojection corresponding to each subgroup, and also the motions that generate a unique reprojection. We achieve the goal by using results from two view analysis [14]. This is possible because the coefficients of multilinear constraints are geometrically dependent of those of bilinear constraints. Therefore, the only advantage in considering multilinear constraints is in the presence of singular surfaces and rectilinear motions. Our future research agenda involves the design of optimal algorithms to recover all (and only!) the parameters that can be estimated from the data based upon their generic ambiguities. The reconstruction and reprojection problem studied in this paper is for a constant calibration matrix. We will present generalized results for the time-varying case in future work.

Acknowledgment

This work is supported by ARO under the MURI grant DAAH04-96-1-0341.

References

[1] S. Avidan and A. Shashua. Novel view synthesis in tensor space. In *Proc. of IEEE Conference on Computer Vision and Pattern Recognition*, pages 1034 – 1040, 1997.

[2] P. Beardsley and A. Zisserman. Affine calibration of mobile vehicles. In *Europe-China Workshop on Geometric Modeling and Invariants for Computer Vision*, 1995.

[3] B. Boufama, R. Mohr, and F. Veillon. Euclidean constraints for uncalibrated reconstruction. In *ICCV*, pages 466–470, Berlin, Germany, 1993.

[4] S. Carlsson. Multiple image invariance using the double algebra. In *Applications of invariance in computer vision*, 1994.

[5] S. Christy and R. Horaud. Euclidean shape and motion from multiple perspective views via affine iterations. *IEEE PAMI*, 18(11):1098–104, November 1996.

[6] O. Faugeras. What can be seen in three dimensions with an uncalibrated stereo rig? *INRIA Research Report*, No. 3225, July, 1997.

[7] O. Faugeras and T. Papadopoulo. Grassmann-Cayley algebra for modeling systems of cameras and the algebraic equations of the manifold of trifocal tensors. In *Proc. of the IEEE workshop of representation of visual scenes*, 1995.

[8] R. Hartley. Lines and points in three views; and integrated approach. In *Proc. of the Image Understanding Workshop*, 1994.

[9] A. Heyden and K. Åström. Algebraic properties of multilinear constraints. *Mathematical Methods in Applied Sciences*, 20(13):1135–1162, 1997.

[10] A. Heyden, G. Sparr, and K. Åström. Perception and action using multilinear forms. In G. Sommer and J. Koenderink, editors, *Algebraic Frames for the Perception-Action Cycle*, pages 54–65. Springer-Verlag, 1997.

[11] A. Heyden. Reduced multilinear constraints – theory and experiments. In *International Journal of Computer Vision*, vol. 30, no. 2, pages 5-26, 1998.

[12] Q.-T. Luong and O. Faugeras. Self-calibration of a moving camera from point correspondences and fundamental matrices. *IJCV*, 22(3):261–89, 1997.

[13] Q.-T. Luong and T. Vieville. Canonical representations for the geometries of multiple projective views. *ECCV*, pages 589–599, 1994.

[14] Y. Ma, R. Vidal, J. Košecká, and S. Sastry. Camera self-calibration: Geometry and Algorithms. *Submitted to IEEE transactions on PAMI and also see UC Berkeley Technical Report* UCB/ERL No. M99/32, June 1999.

[15] S. Maybank. *Theory of Reconstruction from Image Motion*. Springer-Verlag, 1993.

[16] S. Maybank and A. Shashua. Ambiguity in reconstruction from images of six points. In *ICCV*, pages 703–8, Bombay, India, 1988.

[17] S. Maybank and O. Faugeras. A theory of self-calibration of a moving camera. *IJCV*, 8(2):123–152, Aug 1992.

[18] T. Moon, L. Van Gool, M. Van Dients, and E. Pauwels. Affine reconstruction from perspective pairs obtained by a translating camera. In J. L. Mundy and A. Zisserman, editors, *Applications of Invariance in Computer Vision*, pages 297–316, 1993.

[19] P. Sturm. Critical motion sequences for monocular self-calibration and uncalibrated Euclidean reconstruction. *CVPR*, pages 1100–1105, 1997.

[20] B. Triggs. The geometry of projective reconstruction I: Matching constraints and the joint image. *International Journal of Computer Vision*, to appear.

[21] M. Werman and A. Shashua. The study of 3D-from-2D using elimination. In *Proc. of Europe-China Workshop on Geometrical Modeling and Invariants for Computer Vision*, pages 94–101, Xi'an, China, 1995.

Prediction Error as a Quality Metric for Motion and Stereo

Richard Szeliski

Vision Technology Group, Microsoft Research
One Microsoft Way, Redmond, WA 98052-6399

Abstract

This paper presents a new methodology for evaluating the quality of motion estimation and stereo correspondence algorithms. Motivated by applications such as novel view generation and motion-compensated compression, we suggest that the ability to predict new views or frames is a natural metric for evaluating such algorithms. Our new metric has several advantages over comparing algorithm outputs to true motions or depths. First of all, it does not require the knowledge of ground truth data, which may be difficult or laborious to obtain. Second, it more closely matches the ultimate requirements of the application, which are typically tolerant of errors in uniform color regions, but very sensitive to isolated pixel errors or disocclusion errors. In the paper, we develop a number of error metrics based on this paradigm, including forward and inverse prediction errors, residual motion error, and local motion-compensated prediction error. We show results on a number of widely used motion and stereo sequences, many of which do not have associated ground truth data.

1 Introduction

The ability to quantitatively evaluate the performance of competing algorithms is important in many branches of computer science, e.g., speech recognition, information retrieval, and machine learning. Quantitative evaluation allows us to measure progress in our field and motivates us to develop better algorithms. It allows us to carefully analyze algorithm characteristics and to improve overall performance by focusing on sub-components. It allows us to ensure that algorithm performance is not unduly sensitive to the setting of "magic parameters". Furthermore, it enables us to design or tailor algorithms for specific applications, by tuning these algorithms to problem-dependent cost or fidelity metrics and to sample data sets.

Unfortunately, computer vision does not have a very strong tradition of quantitative evaluation. In part, this is unavoidable, since computer vision encompasses some very ambitious goals such as general scene understanding. For more specific problems, such as *edge detection*, there is a tendency to evaluate the quality of results by visual inspection, which leads to subjective decision by experimenters or readers (but see, e.g., [10] for an attempt to quantify performance).

Two of the most widely studied problems in computer vision are motion estimation (sometimes called *optic flow*) and stereo correspondence. The goal in both problems is to place pixels in two or more images into correspondence so as to extract a dense (per-pixel) low-level description of the scene.

The availability of quantitative results for motion estimation improved a few years ago with the publication of Barron *et al.*'s comparative paper on optic flow estimation [5]. Since then, most motion estimation papers publish at least one quantitative result based on the Barron *et al.* data set. In stereo correspondence, it is still relatively rare to see quantitative evaluation (but see, e.g., [8]). Most papers that include comparative results tend to just publish depth maps for two or more algorithms, and leave it to the reader to gauge their relative quality.

One reason for this situation is that it is relatively difficult to get accurate ground truth results, when what is required is the exact motion vector or depth estimate at *each* pixel. (Some attempt has been made to provide ground truth at a *sparse* set of pixels [7], but as we argue below, this does not reflect the typical requirements of a lot of modern applications.) In motion estimation, the most widely used "realistic" motion data set (with ground truth) is the *Yosemite* data set, which is actually computer-generated, based on a texture-mapped digital terrain model. A less widely used data set [36] is a relatively simple scene made of textured marble blocks whose motion was labeled by hand. In stereo matching, a recent hand-labeled data set [33] is starting to be used, but the accuracy of the data is only to the nearest integer disparity level. Some synthetic test sequences have been developed for stereo matching [19, 17], but comparative quantitative results have not been reported.

A second problem with using ground truth data for evaluating motion or stereo algorithms is that it is unclear why overall root-mean square (RMS) deviation from ground truth should be a good predictor of a motion or stereo algorithm's utility. Is it, for example, necessary to be equally accurate in low-texture areas, where motion or stereo is difficult, as it is in textured areas? Are regions near discontinuities more or less important in evaluating algorithms?

781

In this paper, we propose an alternative to evaluating correspondence algorithms on the basis of their error from ground truth. Our suggestion is to measure how accurately the motion or depth estimates (combined with the original image) can *predict* the appearance of an image from a *novel* view or at a future time, i.e., the appearance of an image that was *not* used to compute the motion or depth estimate. We want to emphasize that this is *not* the same as motion-compensated prediction in video coding. Instead of being given two images and being asked to predict the second from the first (which is not that hard to do, given a general flow field), we are asked to predict novel views, not used in the matching.

Our approach has two advantages over measuring ground truth error. First, it is much easier to acquire datasets for which algorithms can be evaluated in this manner. For example, given any collection of three or more images, motion or stereo can be computed on a subset (two or more) of the images, and tested on the remaining images. (Another possibility would be to measure the *self-consistency* of estimates computed using different pairs of images [26].)

Second, prediction error is a useful indicator of the expected quality and utility of motion or stereo algorithm when used in newer application areas such as virtual reality, image-based rendering, and video editing or special effects [23, 6]. Examples of such applications include view interpolation [11] and view morphing [38], frame-rate conversion [35], and de-interlacing [13].[1] Many of these applications require the estimates to be accurate at *every* pixel (or sometimes even fractions of a pixel [44, 2]), since even small errors show up as "halos" or scintillating pixels.

The idea of partitioning data into *training* and *testing* subsets is common in many areas of computer science such as speech recognition. It is also a commonly used technique in statistics, where it is called *cross-validation* [12, 46], and can be used to recover unknown internal parameters and to prevent overfitting. Unlike many of these tasks, which involve classifying the inputs or producing a concise description, we propose a complete image prediction problem, where a large amount of data (several images) is used to estimate a large number of unknowns (the motion estimates), which in turn are used to predict another large set of data (the test images).

The remainder of this paper is structured as follows. We begin in Section 2 with a brief review of stereo and motion representations and estimation. In Section 3 we introduce our novel family of view prediction metrics. In Sections 4 and 5, we propose a number of novel view generation algorithms and a set of potential quality (cost) metrics. In Section 6 we use some simple experiments to demonstrate these metrics, and then show some results on standard data sets (with and without ground truth) using our new metrics. We close with a discussion of our results and some ideas for future work.

---

[1] We haven't included video compression as an application, since this also requires coding the motion itself, and hence would add additional cost terms to our quality metric.

2 Motion and stereo representations

Dense stereo or motion estimation can be formulated as follows. Given two or more images, find a per-pixel *correspondence* that matches each pixel in a given *reference image* to corresponding pixels in the other images. In general 2-D motion estimation, motion vectors can be in any direction. (If more than two images are used, it is common to assume that motion vectors are constant in time, i.e., that there is no acceleration.) In stereo matching, an *epipolar geometry* is usually computed ahead of time, which restricts the search for matching pixels to a 1-D *epipolar line* for each pixel. (Stereo matching naturally generalizes to multiple frames, without any restrictions on camera placement or motion, by associating a separate epipolar geometry (camera matrix) with each image.) Descriptions of commonly used stereo and motion estimation algorithms can be found in computer vision textbooks [3, 20, 34, 15] and in a number of survey articles [4, 1, 14, 9, 5, 32].

A single depth or motion map associated with a chosen reference image is just one possible representation for shape or motion. Single-valued depth/motion maps do not normally capture the full information available in a sequence of images, e.g., regions not visible in the reference image (due to occlusion or cropping to the image boundary) are not represented, and cannot be reproduced. For this reason, a number of alternative representation have be proposed in recent years.

One possibility is to estimate more than one depth value per pixel. Such a multivalued representation can be thought of as a *volumetric* description of the scene (under some projective resampling of three dimensions). Stereo algorithms based on this representation have been developed [39, 44, 24], as well as novel image-based rendering algorithms [40]. Another possibility is to represent the scene as a collection of potentially overlapping *layers* [47, 48, 2]. Three-dimensional surface models are another possibility [18, 16]. Finally, motion or depth maps can be associated with more than just one image [43], and then used for novel view generation using image-based rendering [11] or bi-directional motion interpolation [27].

3 Prediction error as a quality metric

As we mentioned in the introduction, a traditional way to evaluate the quality of such algorithms is to measure the deviation in motion or depth estimates from *ground truth* motion or depth [5, 36, 33, 8]. Since such data sets are hard to come by, we propose using the input images themselves as both "training" and "test" data.

Given three or more images in a motion or stereo data set, we select a proper subset as input to our estimation algorithm (the "training" phase). We then predict the appearance of the remaining images (Section 4), and compute the difference between the predicted and actual images using some error metric (Section 5).

In general, we expect to see different kinds of errors for

 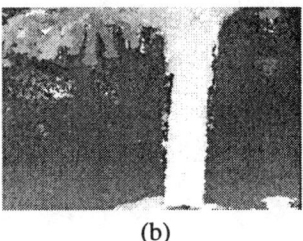  

(a)   (b)   (c)   (d)

Figure 1. Flower garden sequence: (a) original frame 2, (b) estimated depth map, (c) frame 2 extrapolated (forward warped) to frame 10, (d) frame 10 inverse warped to frame 2. Note the different behavior of the occluded region behind the tree.

interpolating a novel view or frame which lies *between* the images chosen as input vs. *extrapolating* a view or frame *beyond* the set of input images. The first kind of error is more indicative of the expected performance of an algorithm in view interpolation, image-based rendering, and motion-compensated frame rate conversion applications, since it is in general dangerous to extrapolate from a given set of images (e.g., there may be disoccluded regions where no data exists).[2] On the other hand, extrapolation error will behave more like *ground truth* error metrics, since errors in uniform color regions will eventually contaminate extrapolated views, while they may not show up in interpolated views.

4 Novel view generation

Given an image and its associated depth or motion map, how do we generate a novel view or frame in order to compare it against a real image? In general, there is no single right or optimal answer, and the answer is highly dependent on the representation chosen. In fact, this question lies at the heart of current research into image-based rendering [40].

One possibility is to use texture-mapping hardware (or software) to paint the novel image as a collection of teeny-tiny triangles (two or four per input pixel or quad of pixels). Given a depth map, a 3D surface can be created (optionally mapping from projective depths to Euclidean coordinates), and then rendered from a novel viewpoint, using the original image as a texture map [30, 42]. Given a 2-D motion map, the reference image can again be drawn using a texture-mapped computer graphics rendering algorithm, with the triangles drawn at their displaced locations. However, in this case, the actual order of rendering may affect the final results, since there is no third dimension to correctly resolve visibility issues. This is an endemic problem with general 2-D motion interpolation (or extrapolation), and cannot be solved without making layering information explicit [47]. For better visual quality (less aliasing), bilinear or higher order texture interpolation should be used.

A second possibility is to use a forward-mapping or *splat-*

ting algorithm [49]. Here, each pixel is painted at the location where it would land in the novel image (in the case of depth maps, a back-to-front ordering can be enforced [31]). Overwriting the nearest pixel results in a poor quality rendering (a lot of aliasing and gaps). Therefore, most splatting algorithms use a soft kernel that increments several adjacent pixels. This kind of operation may require a post-processing stage to renormalize colors, or may result in order-dependent artifacts [40].

A third possibility is to use a two-pass algorithm, where a depth map or flow map is first created for the novel view [40]. Since depth or motion maps tend to vary smoothly (at least, away from discontinuities), a nearest neighbor (single pixel) splat can often be used in this stage, followed by single-pixel gap filling. The new depth or motion map can then be used to perform an *inverse* warping algorithm, i.e., to find the interpolated pixel value in the reference image that corresponds to each (non-empty) novel pixel. Figure 1c shows an image produced with this two-pass algorithm. Note how the regions behind the tree show up as gaps with "empty" pixels (no values).

In general, all of these forward mapping algorithms have to deal with a number of thorny issues. One of these issues is the question of discontinuities: when a break occurs in a motion or depth map, do we interpolate across the break, or leave the disoccluded area blank? In the latter case, do we fill with some background color, or flag these pixels as special and adjust the error metric accordingly? And how does an algorithm estimate the discontinuities in the first place? Another issue is the appropriate resampling/interpolation function. We know that bilinear interpolation of intensities/color is better than nearest neighbor, but how much better are the results with higher order interpolators? Do we still want to use higher order filters near image edges and discontinuities?

An alternative to these forward mapping algorithms is to directly perform an inverse warping of the actual novel view, i.e., to resample the new image so that it conforms (as best as possible) to the reference image. While this breaks the spirit of our train and test (prediction) paradigm, it can still give us useful quality metrics, as we will show in the experimental section of this paper. Figure 1d shows an example of inverse warping. Note how the pixels in regions that become occluded

---

[2]In fact, Seitz [37] proves that for a photoconsistent reconstruction [24], interpolated views *will* be rendered correctly, except for regions partially or fully occluded in the input views.

in later frames are painted with colors from the occluding foreground object (the tree).

So far, we have only discussed novel view generation algorithms for the simplest case of a single reference image with an associated depth or motion map, as this is the case we focus on in this paper. Other motion or shape estimation representations and algorithms entail their own associated view generation algorithms. For example, a volumetric data set can be visualized using a back-to-front warping and compositing algorithm [25, 44]. Layered representations can be rendered by first warping (rendering) each layer separately, and then compositing the resulting images in back-to-front order (which enables a better prediction of mixed foreground/background pixel values [2]). 3-D surface models can be rendered using texture-mapping algorithms. Multiple sets of colored depth or motion maps can be rendered using image-based rendering techniques that blend rendered images while preserving visibility relationships.

The quality estimates produced by the error metrics discussed in the next section depend heavily on the choice (and quality) of the prediction or resampling algorithms. This can be mitigated somewhat by fixing the rendering algorithm while varying the estimation algorithm or its parameters. To a certain extent, however, viewing the estimation and rendering algorithms as part of a complete system whose end-to-end performance is being optimized may be unavoidable and probably even desirable.

5 Error metrics

Once we have synthesized the appearance of predicted images, how do we measure their fidelity? The simplest method is to compute the root mean square (RMS) difference between the two images, expressed in gray levels. However, depending on the acquisition hardware, individual images may be differently exposed. It is therefore prudent to compute a global bias and gain (additive and linear) correction to apply to one of the two images before measuring RMS error. (Ideally, we would like to use perceptually-based error metrics [28], but the state of research in this field is still not very advanced. This is likely to be an important area of future research.)

Even once we have compensated for exposure effects, we still often find that the error is far from being identically distributed Gaussian noise. In fact, the magnitude of the brightness error is strongly correlated with the amount of local intensity variation. Simoncelli *et al.* [41] explain that this can arise because the gradient estimates used in most flow estimation techniques are themselves noisy. Other sources of error include sub-pixel shifts in the digitization process [30], mis-estimation of the epipolar geometry which can result in *vertical parallax*, and general re-sampling (interpolation) errors due to poor quality (e.g., bilinear) filters or aliasing during image acquisition.

Given that these problems are endemic, would it be fairer to

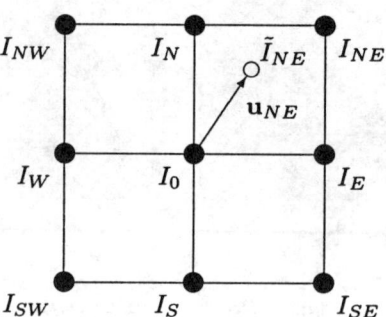

Figure 2. Residual flow computation and value compensation.

down-weight the squared error at each pixel by some term that includes the local intensity gradient [41]? If we do this, then are we still getting good estimates of the perceptual quality of an estimation / rendering combination?

5.1 Residual motion estimation and compensation

A better option is to estimate the *residual flow* [22], which is the per-pixel estimate of flow required to register the predicted and actual novel image. We can then compute the RMS residual flow magnitude as well as the RMS intensity error after residual motion compensation, in order to get a feel for how much of the prediction error is due to small mis-registrations.

In our current implementation, since we do not want regions with little texture variation to contribute to the residual flow measure, we compute residual flow as follows (see Figure 2). For each pixel I_0 in the image to be corrected, we examine each of the four quads of pixels surrounding I_0. We use the nearest two neighbors to form a linear approximation to the interpolated intensity, e.g.,

$$\tilde{I}_{NE} = I_0 + (I_E - I_0)u_{NE} + (I_N - I_0)v_{NE}. \quad (1)$$

We find the residual flow vector $\mathbf{u}_{NE} = (u_{NE}, v_{NE})$ that minimizes

$$\|\tilde{I}_{NE} - I_1\|^2 + \lambda\|\mathbf{u}_{NE}\|^2, \quad (2)$$

where I_1 is the corresponding pixel in the image we are correcting against, and the second term suppresses the computation of spurious residual flow vectors in region with little texture or color variation (see [41] for a probabilistic justification).[3]

We clip the four candidate flow vectors to lie within the quad being examined (which means that many of the vectors get clipped to $(0, 0)$), and compute a better interpolated color value $\tilde{I}$ using *bilinear* interpolation. We then pick the residual

---

[3]Minimizing the above cost is similar to a one-pixel version of the Lucas-Kanade flow estimation algorithm [29], and essentially computes normal flow. For all of our experiments, we set $\lambda = 16 \cdot (\#bands)$, where $\#bands$ is the number of bands (3 for color images, 1 for monochrome).

flow vector with the lowest $\|\tilde{I} - I_1\|$ value (or $(0,0)$ if none of these errors beats $\|I_0 - I_1\|$), and set the corrected pixel value to $\tilde{I}$. Some examples of estimated residual flows and corrected images are given in the next Section.

5.2 Outliers and invisible pixels

Two other issues that arise in computing error statistics are outliers (robust statistical estimates), and invisible pixels (i.e., pixels for which there are no corresponding pixels in other images). Traditional statistical measure such as the standard deviation of the intensity errors can be heavily affected by outliers, which may be caused by occlusions, variation of brightness with viewpoint, and residual motion errors. In order to get a more robust set of error statistics, we compute a robust measure of the standard deviation using $\sigma = 1.4826 \, \text{med}|I_1 - I_0|$ [21]. We also compute the percentage of outliers, i.e., the number of pixels for which $|I_1 - I_0| > 3\sigma$. These statistics are reported along with the more traditional RMS (root mean square) error.

In order to compensate for pixels that are invisible in other images (e.g., pixels whose correct motion has carried them outside the image frame), we modify our forward and inverse warping algorithms to flag pixels as *invisible* when their source is outside the image (inverse warping), or when no pixels map to a given pixel after gap filling (forward warping). These pixels do not participate in the computation of RMS or robust statistics, but their percentage is reported in the experimental section.

6 Experiments

Because of space limitations, we only have room to present a few simple experiments to demonstrate the behavior of our error metrics. We are currently undertaking a more comprehensive set of comparative experiments, focusing in particular on dense two-frame stereo matching [45].

6.1 Synthetic flow error

To get a sense of the behavior of our error metrics, we first generated a synthetic motion field by taking an image from the flower garden video (Figure 1), and using $(u, v) = (k/16, k/8), k = 0 \ldots 4$ as motion field estimates (the true motion is $(0, 0)$). Figure 3a shows a variety of error metrics as a function of frame number k (increasingly erroneous flow estimates). The raw RMS error increases linearly as a function of k, as does the robust estimate of σ. Figure 3c shows the uncompensated difference image for $k = 4$, and Figures 3d–e show the horizontal and vertical components of the residual flow estimates. Notice how there is little flow in untextured areas, but that the flow is in general quite noisy. (Remember that no area-based averaging is used to compute these flows—they are used solely to reduce the difference error. It may be fruitful to compute residual flows over larger areas, as is done in [22]) After compensation, the RMS error (and robust error)

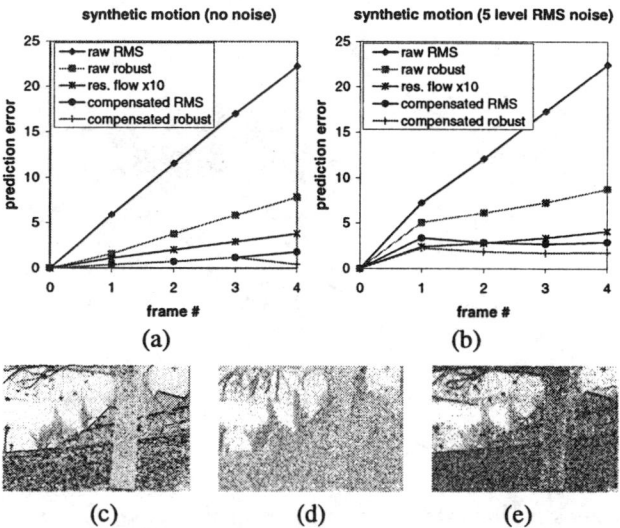

Figure 3. Synthetic motion errors: (a) no noise, (b) $\sigma = 5$. (c) uncompensated difference image, (d–e) horizontal and vertical residual flow estimates.

are both very small (imperceptible in the difference image, which is not shown).

To generate these plots, we used inverse warping, optionally followed by residual flow estimation and image compensation. The image being compensated was always the *original* and not the *warped* image. This ensures that the two images compared have been resampled the same number of times. If we interchange the sense of which image is compensated, we find that there is very little improvement in the RMS error after compensation. On a smoother image (e.g., the SineC sequence used in [5]), this asymmetry goes away. However, for realistic images, it is very important to compare apples to apples, i.e., to try to ensure that resampling errors are similar between images being compared.

If we add synthetic noise to the images in the sequence, the overall noise estimates go up. Figure 3b shows the error plots when Gaussian noise with $\sigma = 5$ was added. While the uncompensated difference does not change much (which indicates that motion error dominates), the compensated difference is now much higher, with a standard deviation of about 2.5 (which indicates that residual motion compensation is removing about half of the imaging noise).

6.2 Sequences with ground truth

To demonstrate the behavior of our metrics when ground truth motion is known, we chose the Yosemite sequence. (Table 1 and Figure 6 list some more image sequences for which ground truth motion or disparity is known.) Using the ground truth flows for the middle frame (frame 7), we computed the raw RMS and robust error metrics, the residual flow, and the compensated RMS error metric. Figure 4a shows these plots, along with the percentage of invisible pixels. As the sequence

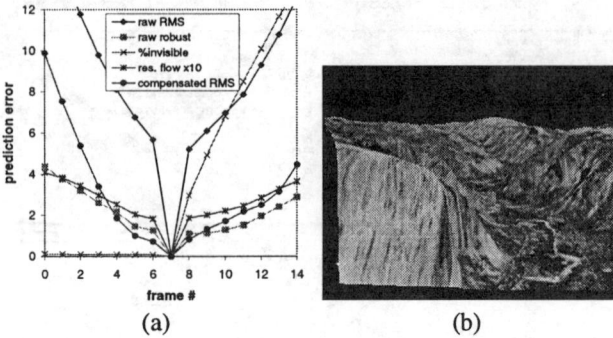

Figure 4. Yosemite sequence: (a) plots of prediction errors; (b) frame 14 inverse warped to frame 7 (note the missing pixels along the lower left edge).

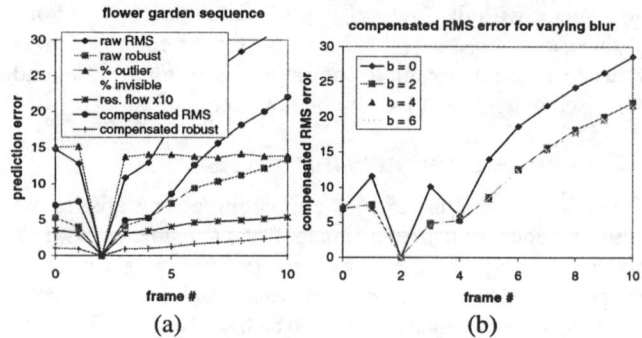

Figure 5. Flower garden sequence: (a) plot of prediction errors based on motion estimated from frames 0, 2, and 4; (b) plots error for various amount of blurring

progresses, the lower left section of the image moves out of view, so that more an more pixels become invisible during backward warping (Figure 4b).

The plots show that the error continuously increases as we move away from the reference frame. By looking at the frames inverse warped toward the central frame, we have observed that the ground truth motion does not accurately predict the appearance of frames far from the center. In fact, because the motion is looming, the flows have a significant acceleration, which shows up as a "swinging" motion on the foreground object. Using a rigid motion model (with known disparities) should alleviate a lot of this problem.

6.3 Sequences without ground truth

Figure 5a shows the error metrics applied to a disparity field computed from frames 0, 2, and 4 of the flower garden sequence (Figure 1). The stereo algorithm used was a simple plane sweep algorithm, which is functionally equivalent to a robustified sum-of-squared-differences (SSD) algorithm. Instead of aggregating information over a square window, iterative convolution with a binomial kernel was used before the min-picking stage.

Since the motion was computed on the first three even frames, we might expect the prediction error to be lower at these frames than at other frames. On the other hand, there is a tendency for prediction error to increase systematically away from the reference frame, both due to errors in motion estimation, and other effects such as disocclusions, sampling artifacts, and photometric effects. Figure 5a shows that both of these effects are indeed present. The raw RMS and robust errors increase monotonically away from the reference frame, while the compensated error is slightly higher at the two interpolated frames (1 and 3) than at the two frames used in the stereo computation (2 and 4).

To see whether cross-validation could be used to automatically tune one of the stereo algorithm parameters, we re-ran our algorithm with a varying number of blurring steps after the initial per-pixel cost computation. Figure 5b shows the compensated RMS error for various choices of b (the number of blurring iterations). Not using any blurring results in significantly worse estimates, whereas there is not much difference between the other choices. However, observe that if we were given just four frames from the sequence (e.g., frames 0, 1, 2, and 4), we could use the prediction error for frame 1 to tune b for the three-frame stereo algorithm being run on the other three frames. Figure 5b shows that this would give us a good choice of b, since the interpolation error at frame 1 is a good predictor of the relative prediction errors at other frames. We are currently applying this kind of analysis to other stereo algorithm parameters, such as window size and the amount of regularization [45].

7 Discussion and Conclusions

In this paper, we have introduced prediction error as a novel quality measure for evaluating and designing motion and stereo correspondence algorithms. Prediction error is much easier to obtain than ground truth data for multi-image sequences. It also more closely matches modern requirements for motion and stereo algorithms. We have shown how raw prediction error depends on the interaction between motion errors and local intensity gradient structure, and suggested a means (residual flow compensation) for mitigating this factor.

Quantitative evaluation is essential if we are to continue making progress in the development of motion and stereo algorithms. Not only does it enable us to judge when an advance is truly worthwhile, but it also enables us to dissect existing algorithms and approaches to learn which components are responsible for their good (or bad) behavior, and to determine how sensitive they are to internal parameters. It also holds out the hope that algorithms can themselves discover (*learn?*) internal parameter values, using generalized cross-validation to see whether their outputs accurately predict images that have intentionally been held back.

The work presented in this paper is just a first step towards what we hope will become an accepted framework for research in this area. Our models to date do not incorporate any notion

Marble blocks   Lab scene   SRI trees   NASA (Coke)   Rubik

CIL Town   Parking meter   Baseball   Calendar   Coast guard

Figure 6. Images from some commonly used multi-image sequences

of perceptual quality or perceptual similarity. Adding such models should prove to be very usuful, although the state of research in this area is still not very advanced. An interesting question this bring up is: is it better for an algorithm to *look good* (i.e., to have no visible artifacts), or to *be good*, i.e., to accurately predict the geometric and photometric appearance of a scene.

Other variants on prediction error should also be explored. For instance, given a 3D reconstruction of a scene from stereo, it should be possible to excise foreground elements or insert mid-ground elements. Algorithms that mis-classify pixels near object boundaries will produce "halos" when such element insertion is performed. It should be possible to structure the acquisition process to add and remove scene elements. It would also be interesting to compare our new methodology with the self-consistency metric proposed in [26].

One question that comes up when considering prediction error as a quality metric is: *why not just directly optimize the 3D scene description with respect to how closely it matches the input images?* While this approach is at the heart of many newer stereo algorithms, it fails to take into account that algorithms will often happily overfit their input data, unless some data is held back to "keep them honest".

In current work, we are starting to apply our methodology to a number of stereo algorithms, in order to evaluate their quality, refine their behavior, and shed more light on desirable properties of quality metrics [45]. It is our hope that our approach will lead to a marked increase in the quantitative evaluation of low-level vision algorithms. Rather than providing yet another mechanism for researchers to bag "bragging rights" about their latest results, we hope that this will help increase our general understanding of the nature and behavior of low-level motion and structure estimation algorithms.

Name	Source	# img.	motion	grnd. truth
Yosemite	Quam [5][1,2]	15	rigid[6]	flow/Z
Marble block	Otte [36][3]	31	rigid[7]	flow
Lab scene	Nakam. [33]	25	rigid	Z
SRI Trees	Bolles [5][1]	21	rigid	-
NASA	NASA [5][1]	37	rigid	-
Rubik	Szeliski [5][1]	21	non-rig.	-
CIL town	Matth. [30][4]	60	rigid	-
Park. meter	CMU[4]	25	rigid	-
Baseball	Kanade [23][5]	51	rigid[8]	-
Flower grdn	MPEG-4	150	rigid	-
Calendar	MPEG-4	300	non-rig.	-
Coast guard	MPEG-4	300	non-rig.	-

1. ftp://csd.uwo.ca/pub/vision/TESTDATA
2. http://www.parc.xerox.com/spl/members/black
3. http://i21www.ira.uka.de/image_sequences
4. http://www.ius.cs.cmu.edu/idb
5. http://www.cs.cmu.edu/afs/cs/project/VirtualizedR/www
6. clouds are non-rigid; 7. one block moves non-rigidly; 8. 51 *movies*.

Table 1. List of some commonly used multi-image sequences

References

[1] J. K. Aggarwal and N. Nandhakumar. On the computation of motion from sequences of images—a review. *Proceedings of the IEEE*, 76(8):917–935, Aug. 1988.

[2] S. Baker, R. Szeliski, and P. Anandan. A layered approach to stereo reconstruction. In *CVPR'98*, pp. 434–441, June 1998.

[3] D. H. Ballard and C. M. Brown. *Computer Vision*. Prentice-Hall, Englewood Cliffs, New Jersey, 1982.

[4] S. T. Barnard and M. A. Fischler. Computational stereo. *Computing Surveys*, 14(4):553–572, Dec. 1982.

[5] J. L. Barron, D. J. Fleet, and S. S. Beauchemin. Performance

of optical flow techniques. *Intl. J. Comp. Vis.*, 12(1):43–77, Jan. 1994.

[6] L. Blonde *et al.* A virtual studio for live broadcasting: The Mona Lisa project. *IEEE Multimedia*, 3(2):18–29, 1996.

[7] R. C. Bolles, H. H. Baker, and M. J. Hannah. The JISCT stereo evaluation. In *Image Under. Work.*, pp. 263–274, 1993.

[8] Y. Boykov, O. Veksler, and R. Zabih. A variable window approach to early vision. *IEEE Trans. Patt. Anal. Mach. Intell.*, 20(12):1283–1294, Dec. 1998.

[9] L. G. Brown. A survey of image registration techniques. *Computing Surveys*, 24(4):325–376, Dec. 1992.

[10] J. Canny. A computational approach to edge detection. *IEEE Trans. Patt. Anal. Mach. Intell.*, PAMI-8(6):679–698, Nov. 1986.

[11] S. Chen and L. Williams. View interpolation for image synthesis. *SIGGRAPH'93*, pp. 279–288, Aug. 1993.

[12] P. Craven and G. Wahba. Smoothing noisy data with spline functions: Estimating the correct degree of smoothing by the method of generalized cross-validation. *Numerische Mathematik*, 31:377–403, 1979.

[13] G. de Hann and E. B. Beller. Deinterlacing—an overview. *Proceedings of the IEEE*, 86(9):1839–1857, Sept. 1998.

[14] U. R. Dhond and J. K. Aggarwal. Structure from stereo—a review. *IEEE Trans. Sys. Man Cyber.*, 19(6):1489–1510, Nov./Dec. 1989.

[15] O. Faugeras. *Three-dimensional computer vision: A geometric viewpoint.* MIT Press, Cambridge, Massachusetts, 1993.

[16] O. Faugeras and R. Keriven. Variational principles, surface evolution, pdes, level set methods, and the stereo problem. *IEEE Trans. Im. Proc.*, 7(3):335–344, Mar. 1998.

[17] T. Frohlinghaus and J. M. Buhmann. Regularizing phase-based stereo. In *ICPR'96*, volume A, pp. 451–455, Aug. 1996.

[18] P. Fua and Y. G. Leclerc. Object-centered surface reconstruction: Combining multi-image stereo and shading. *Intl. J. Comp. Vis.*, 16:35–56, 1995.

[19] W. Hoff and N. Ahuja. Surfaces from stereo: integrating feature matching, disparity estimation, and contour detection. *IEEE Trans. Patt. Anal. Mach. Intell.*, 11(2):121–136, Feb. 1989.

[20] B. K. P. Horn. *Robot Vision.* MIT Press, Cambridge, Massachusetts, 1986.

[21] P. J. Huber. *Robust Statistics.* John Wiley & Sons, New York, New York, 1981.

[22] M. Irani, B. Rousso, and S. Peleg. Detecting and tracking multiple moving objects using temporal integration. In *ECCV'92*, pp. 282–287, May 1992.

[23] T. Kanade, P. W. Rander, and P. J. Narayanan. Virtualized reality: constructing virtual worlds from real scenes. *IEEE MultiMedia Magazine*, 1(1):34–47, Jan.-Mar. 1997.

[24] K. N. Kutulakos and S. M. Seitz. A theory of shape by space carving. In *ICCV'99*, Sept. 1999.

[25] P. Lacroute and M. Levoy. Fast volume rendering using a shear-warp factorization of the viewing transformation. *SIGGRAPH'94*, pp. 451–457, July 1994.

[26] Y. G. Leclerc, Q.-T. Luong, and P. Fua. Self-consistency: A novel approach to characterizing the accuracy and reliability of point correspondence algorithms. In *DARPA Image Understanding Workshop*, Nov. 1998.

[27] D. Le Gall. MPEG: A video compression standard for multimedia applications. *Comm. of the ACM*, 34(4):44–58, Apr. 1991.

[28] J. Lubin. A human vision system model for objective picture quality measurements. *IEE Conference Publications*, 1(447):498–503, 1997.

[29] B. D. Lucas and T. Kanade. An iterative image registration technique with an application in stereo vision. In *IJCAI-81*, pp. 674–679, 1981.

[30] L. H. Matthies, R. Szeliski, and T. Kanade. Kalman filter-based algorithms for estimating depth from image sequences. *Intl. J. Comp. Vis.*, 3:209–236, 1989.

[31] L. McMillan. A list-priority rendering algorithm for redisplaying projected surfaces. Technical Report 95-005, University of North Carolina, 1995.

[32] A. Mitiche and P. Bouthemy. Computation and analysis of image motion: A synopsis of current problems and methods. *Intl. J. Comp. Vis.*, 19:29–55, 1996.

[33] Y. Nakamura, T. Matsuura, K. Satoh, and Y. Ohta. Occlusion detectable stereo - occlusion patterns in camera matrix. In *CVPR'96*, pp. 371–378, June 1996.

[34] V. S. Nalwa. *A Guided Tour of Computer Vision.* Addison-Wesley, Reading, MA, 1993.

[35] O. A. Ojo and G. de Haan. Robust motion-compensated video upconversion. *IEEE Trans. Cons. Elec.*, 43(4):1045–1056, Nov. 1997.

[36] M. Otte and H.-H. Nagel. Optical flow estimation: advances and comparisons. In *ECCV'94*, volume 1, pp. 51–60, May 1994.

[37] S. M. Seitz and C. M. Dyer. Toward image-based scene representation using view morphing. In *ICPR'96*, volume A, pp. 84–89, Aug. 1996.

[38] S. M. Seitz and C. M. Dyer. View morphing. In *SIGGRAPH'96*, pp. 21–30, Aug. 1996.

[39] S. M. Seitz and C. M. Dyer. Photorealistic scene reconstrcution by space coloring. In *CVPR'97*, pp. 1067–1073, June 1997.

[40] J. Shade, S. Gortler, L.-W. He, and R. Szeliski. Layered depth images. In *SIGGRAPH'98*, pp. 231–242, July 1998.

[41] E. P. Simoncelli, E. H. Adelson, and D. J. Heeger. Probability distributions of optic flow. In *CVPR'91*, pp. 310–315, June 1991.

[42] R. Szeliski. Video mosaics for virtual environments. *IEEE Computer Graphics and Applications*, pp. 22–30, Mar. 1996.

[43] R. Szeliski. A multi-view approach to motion and stereo. In *CVPR'99*, pp. 157–163, June 1999.

[44] R. Szeliski and P. Golland. Stereo matching with transparency and matting. In *ICCV'98*, pp. 517–524, Jan. 1998.

[45] R. Szeliski and R. Zabih. An experimental comparison of stereo algorithms. In preparation, 1999.

[46] G. Wahba. Bayesian "confidence intervals" for the cross-validated smoothing spline. *J. Roy. Stat. Soc.*, B 45(1):133–150, 1983.

[47] J. Y. A. Wang and E. H. Adelson. Representing moving images with layers. *IEEE Trans. Im. Proc.*, 3(5):625–638, Sept. 1994.

[48] Y. Weiss. Smoothness in layers: Motion segmentation using nonparametric mixture estimation. In *CVPR'97*, pp. 520–526, June 1997.

[49] G. Wolberg. *Digital Image Warping.* IEEE Computer Society Press, Los Alamitos, California, 1990.

Rigid and Articulated Motion Seen with an Uncalibrated Stereo Rig

Andreas Ruf *   Radu Horaud*

Andreas.Ruf@inrialpes.fr   Radu.Horaud@inrialpes.fr
GRAVIR-IMAG, INRIA Rhone-Alpes
655, avenue de l'Europe
38330 Montbonnot St.Martin, France

Abstract

This paper establishes a link between uncalibrated stereo vision and the motion of rigid and articulated bodies. The variation in the projective reconstruction of a dynamic scene over time allows an uncalibrated stereo rig to be used as a faithful motion capturing device. We introduce an original theoretical framework – projective kinematics – which allows rigid and articulated motion to be represented within the transformation group of projective space. Corresponding projective velocities are defined in the tangent space. Most importantly, these projective motions inherit the Lie-group structure of the displacement group.

These theoretical results lead immediately to nonmetric formulations of visual servoing, tracking, motion capturing and motion synthesis systems, that no longer require the metric geometry of a stereo camera or of the articulated body to be known. We report on such a nonmetric formulation of a visual servoing system and present simulated experimental results.

1 Introduction

In this paper we address the problem of representing and controlling the motion of robot manipulators or, more generally, of articulated mechanical devices using image measurements and continuous feedback from an uncalibrated stereo camera pair - a stereo rig. It is well-known that such a camera pair can recover the 3D projective structure of an observed object from point-to-point matches between the two images - this result has been simultaneously shown by Faugeras [5] and Hartley [8]. The relationship between the projective structure thus recovered has been further investigated by a number of authors: Zisserman revealed how to upgrade projective structure to metric if the stereo rig

undergoes a general displacement [18] and to affine if the rig undergoes planar motion [1], Devernay & Faugeras revealed important algebraic properties associated with the similarity between rigid and projective motion [3]. Horaud & Csurka devised a closed-form solution for computing the internal parameters from general motion [11], and from a single planar motion [2].

In parallel other authors investigate the relationship between a stereo rig and the visual control of a robot manipulator. Hollinghorst and Cipolla considered an affine approximation of the perspective camera model [10] and Hager et al. investigated both, the representation of alignments using projective invariants and the sensibility of stereo-based visual control in the presence of coarse calibration [7].

Therefore, based on the current state-of-the-art, a possible solution for stereo-guided visual servoing using uncalibrated cameras would be to calibrate the stereo rig first and then to use the classical Euclidean robot to establish a visual control law [4].

The work described in this paper takes a different approach, where neither internal camera parameters, nor Euclidean robot representations are required anymore. Since the motions of a robot are combinations of elementary rotations (revolute joints) or translations (prismatic joints), we introduce two special projective transformations, namely, *projective rotations* and *projective translations*. These transformations are special parameterizations of 4×4 homographies that arise when a weakly calibrated stereo rig observes either rotations or translations. We reveal the Lie-group structure of these transformations and we analyze the action of these groups onto 3D projective space. We explicitly devise the projective tangent operators associated with them. Next, we establish the projective forward kinematics and inverse models of a robot manipulator. Note that this model applies to articulated motion in general. Moreover, we devise the projective velocity associated with such an articulated motion and we explicitly

---

*The authors are very grateful towards the European Commission for financial support through the Marie-Curie fellowship FMBICT972281, and the Esprit LTR project VIGOR 26247.

derive the relationship between the joint velocities and the 2D velocities observed in the two images. Finally, we introduce the concept of non-metric (projective) visual servoing, where no Euclidean representations (neither of the cameras nor of the robot) are required.

1.1 Notation

Bold type $\mathbf{H}, \mathbf{T}$ is used for matrices, bold italic $\boldsymbol{M}, \boldsymbol{k}$ for vectors, calligraphic $\mathcal{F}, \mathcal{P}$ for frames, and Roman a, b, θ for scalars, angles etc. Vectors $\boldsymbol{k}$ are column vectors, and row vectors are written by the transpose $\boldsymbol{h}^T$. "$\simeq$" denotes equality up to scale.

We give without proof a well-known matrix identity

$$\exp(\mathbf{A}^{-1}\mathbf{X}\mathbf{A}) = \mathbf{A}^{-1}\exp(\mathbf{X})\mathbf{A}. \qquad (1)$$

2 Projective reconstruction

A calibrated stereo rig is modeled as two pinhole cameras which have intrinsic parameters $\mathbf{K}, \mathbf{K}'$, and which are rigidly linked by $(\mathbf{R}', \boldsymbol{t}')$. A point N in Euclidean space projects onto the points $\boldsymbol{m}$ and $\boldsymbol{m}'$ in the left and right projective image plane $\mathbb{P}^2$ [6]. Solving the projection constraints (2) for N yields a *Euclidean reconstruction* in the *Euclidean camera frame* $\mathcal{E}$

$$\boldsymbol{m} \simeq \begin{bmatrix} \mathbf{K}|\boldsymbol{0} \end{bmatrix} N, \qquad \boldsymbol{m}' \simeq \begin{bmatrix} \mathbf{K}'\mathbf{R}'|\mathbf{K}'\boldsymbol{t}' \end{bmatrix} N. \qquad (2)$$

A weakly calibrated stereo rig is modeled as a pair of cameras whose epipolar geometry $\mathbf{F}$ is supposed to be known [9]. This allows two projection matrices $\mathbf{P} = [\mathbf{I}|\boldsymbol{0}]$ and $\mathbf{P}'$ to be calculated, such that the corresponding *projective reconstruction*, solving

$$\boldsymbol{m} \simeq \mathbf{P}M, \qquad \boldsymbol{m}' \simeq \mathbf{P}'M \qquad (3)$$

for M, is relative to a *projective camera frame* $\mathcal{P}$. The frame $\mathcal{P}$ is defined by $\mathbf{F}$ and can be thought of as five rigid points attached to the stereo rig [8], [13].

If the stereo rig remains fixed, i.e. constant $\mathbf{K}, \mathbf{K}'$, and $(\mathbf{R}', \boldsymbol{t}')$, the so-called *projective-Euclidean link (PE-link)* $\mathbf{H}_{PE}$ is the well-defined homography

$$N \simeq \mathbf{H}_{PE}M, \quad \mathbf{H}_{PE} \simeq \begin{bmatrix} \mathbf{K}^{-1} & \boldsymbol{0} \\ \boldsymbol{a}^T & 1 \end{bmatrix}, \qquad (4)$$

that upgrades the projective reconstruction (3) in $\mathcal{P}$ to a Euclidean one (2) in $\mathcal{E}$. The PE-link completely encapsulates the geometry of the stereo camera, and recovering $\mathbf{H}_{PE}$ amounts to metric calibration [18], [3].

Throughout this paper, we consider a stereo camera observing and reconstructing a dynamic scene containing rigid and articulated motion. We assume a fixed but unknown stereo geometry $\mathbf{H}_{PE}$ (4).

3 Metric rigid motion

At a time instant t, generic points N on a rigid body have coordinates $\boldsymbol{N}(t) = [X(t), Y(t), Z(t), 1]^T$ with respect to the Euclidean camera frame $\mathcal{E}$. The trajectory of a *rigid motion* is described by

$$N(t) = \mathbf{T}_{RT}(t)N(0), \qquad \mathbf{T}_{RT}(t) = \begin{bmatrix} \mathbf{R}(t) & \boldsymbol{t}(t) \\ \boldsymbol{0}^T & 1 \end{bmatrix}, \quad (5)$$

where $\mathbf{T}_{RT}(t)$ is a differentiable trajectory in the displacement group $SE(3)$. Therefore, *spatial point-velocities* are defined by the tangent

$$\dot{N}(t) = [\dot{X}, \dot{Y}, \dot{Z}, 0]^T = \dot{\mathbf{T}}_{RT}(t)N(0), \qquad (6)$$

where $\dot{N}$ as well as N are relative to the frame $\mathcal{E}$. Moreover, the Lie-group structure of $SE(3)$ allows a *spatial body-velocity* to be defined by the tangent operator

$$\hat{\mathbf{T}}_{RT}(t) = \dot{\mathbf{T}}_{RT}(t)\mathbf{T}_{RT}^{-1}(t), \qquad (7)$$

which indeed yields the motion tangent $\dot{\mathbf{T}}_{RT}(t)$ and the point-velocity of $N(t)$ by simple left-multiplication

$$\dot{N}(t) = \hat{\mathbf{T}}_{RT}(t)N(t) = \dot{\mathbf{T}}_{RT}(t)N(0). \qquad (8)$$

The instantaneous body-velocity as written in (7) is a matrix representation of the Lie-Algebra $se(3)$ of $SE(3)$. It has generally the form

$$\hat{\mathbf{T}}_{RT}(t) = \begin{bmatrix} 0 & -\omega_z & \omega_y & v_x \\ \omega_z & 0 & -\omega_x & v_y \\ -\omega_y & \omega_x & 0 & v_z \\ 0 & 0 & 0 & 1 \end{bmatrix}, \qquad (9)$$

which is geometrically interpreted as follows. The vectors $\boldsymbol{w} = [\omega_x, \omega_y, \omega_z]^T$ and $\boldsymbol{v} = [v_x, v_y, v_z]^T$ are the instantaneous angular- and linear velocity of the camera frame $\mathcal{E}$ as if it were rigidly moving with the body at instant t [14]. This has to be distinguished from the common usage of kinematic screws, where the above vectors represent the velocity of a rigid body in its own, body-fixed frame and not in a spatial reference frame; here the camera frame $\mathcal{E}$.

4 Projective Rigid motion

In this section, we no longer assume a calibrated stereo camera and the Euclidean frame $\mathcal{E}$, but consider an uncalibrated rig. The reconstruction then can only be projective, and is relative to the projective camera frame $\mathcal{P}$. Nevertheless, the PE-link (4) between the points $N(t)$ and their projective coordinates $M(t)$ allows us to define the notions of **projective kinematics**.

4.1 Projective displacements

The projective coordinates $M(t)$ and $M(0)$ of rigidly moving points are related by a 4×4 homography matrix $\mathbf{H}_{RT} \in PGL(3)$ – the three-dimensional projective group – which can be calculated from at least 5 such point and their correspondences

$$M(t) \simeq \mathbf{H}_{RT}(t)M(0). \tag{10}$$

Such homographies are algebraically similar to a displacement by the PE-link up to the scalar γ

$$\mathbf{H}_{RT}(t) = \gamma \, \mathbf{H}_{PE}^{-1} \, \mathbf{T}_{RT}(t) \, \mathbf{H}_{PE}. \tag{11}$$

By similarity, the trace and the determinant of $\mathbf{H}_{RT}$ determine γ and allow normalizing it to unit scale

$$\gamma = sign(trace(\mathbf{H}_{RT}))(|\mathbf{H}_{RT}|)^{1/4}. \tag{12}$$

We refer to normalized homographies $\mathbf{H}_{RT}$ that have the form (11) and $\gamma = 1$ as *projective displacements (p-displacement)*. It is straight forward to see that they form a subgroup of $PGL(3)$, modulo a fix matrix $\mathbf{H}_{PE}$ embodying the stereo geometry. What is more, thanks to normalization, equation (11) is a well-defined differentiable homeomorphism from $SE(3)$ into $PGL(3)$, such that the p-displacements inherit this structure and become a subgroup, moreover a Lie-subgroup in $PGL(3)$. They are simply a matrix representation of $SE(3)$ in $PGL(3)$, which we will denote as $PSE(3)$.

4.2 Projective body-velocity

In analogy with equation (7), a notion of *projective body-velocities* can be defined as

$$\hat{\mathbf{H}}_{RT}(t) = \dot{\mathbf{H}}_{RT}\mathbf{H}_{RT}^{-1}. \tag{13}$$

Geometrically, these are spatial velocities with respect to the projective frame $\mathcal{P}$. Algebraically, they are a matrix representation of $PSE(3)$'s Lie-Algebra, denoted $pse(3)$, and generally have the form

$$\hat{\mathbf{H}}_{RT}(t) = \mathbf{H}_{PE}^{-1} \begin{bmatrix} 0 & -\omega_z & \omega_y & v_x \\ \omega_z & 0 & -\omega_x & v_y \\ -\omega_y & \omega_x & 0 & v_z \\ 0 & 0 & 0 & 0 \end{bmatrix} \mathbf{H}_{PE}. \tag{14}$$

4.3 Orbit of projective points

From the PE-link(4), a scale factor ρ can be identified in the homogeneous coordinates M of a projective point, that is related to the unknown vector $[a^T 1]$ that represents the plane at infinity.

$$\rho N = \mathbf{H}_{PE}M_\rho, \qquad \rho = [a^T 1]M_\rho. \tag{15}$$

All vectors M_ρ have ρ as an implicit property, which we call *height*. Neither a^T, nor the height are known, but the *height is invariant* under p-displacements.

$$\mathbf{H}_{RT}M_\rho = \mathbf{H}_{PE}^{-1}\mathbf{T}_{RT}\mathbf{H}_{PE}M_\rho = \mathbf{H}_{PE}^{-1}\mathbf{T}_{RT}\rho N = \rho \mathbf{H}_{PE}^{-1}N' = M_\rho'.$$

So M_ρ's orbit under the action of $PSE(3)$ lies entirely within the hyperplane $[a^T 1]M_\rho = \rho$ of $\mathbb{R}^4$. Hence ρ is its *orbital height*.

4.4 Projective point-velocity

For a point on such a rigid orbit $M_\rho(t)$, a *projective point-velocity* is well-defined by $\dot{M}_\rho(t)$. It is related to its metric velocity (6) up to its fix but unknown height

$$\rho \dot{N} = \mathbf{H}_{PE}\dot{M}_\rho. \tag{16}$$

Finally, applying a projective body velocity $\hat{\mathbf{H}}_{RT}(t)$ to a point-vector $M_\rho(t)$, yields again its point-velocity

$$\begin{aligned} \hat{\mathbf{H}}_{RT}(t)M_\rho(t) &= \dot{\mathbf{H}}_{RT}(t)M_\rho(0) \\ &= \mathbf{H}_{PE}^{-1}\dot{\mathbf{T}}_{RT}(t)\,\mathbf{H}_{PE}\,\rho\,\mathbf{H}_{PE}^{-1}N(0) \\ &= \rho\mathbf{H}_{PE}^{-1}N(0) = \dot{M}_\rho(t). \end{aligned}$$

5 Articulated projective motion

In this section, the projective motions arising from revolute and prismatic joints are derived, then the projective motions of articulated chains are composed from these projective joint motions.

5.1 Projective revolute joints

Projective revolute joints are represented by means of a projective formulation of pure rotational twists [14]. Geometrically, a *general pure rotation* is a revolution around an axis at a general position in space. It can no longer be represented by $\mathbf{R}(\theta) \in SO(3)$ (special orthogonal group), since this would constrain the axis to go through the origin. Instead, it has a linear representation in $SE(3)$

$$\mathbf{T}_R(\theta) = \mathbf{T}^{-1} \begin{bmatrix} \mathbf{R}(\theta) & \mathbf{0} \\ \mathbf{0}^T & 1 \end{bmatrix} \mathbf{T}, \tag{17}$$

where the position of the joint is specified by means of its displacement $\mathbf{T}$ away from the origin.

We define a *projective rotation (p-rotation)* to be

$$\mathbf{H}_R(\theta) = \mathbf{H}_{PE}^{-1} \, \mathbf{T}_R(\theta) \, \mathbf{H}_{PE}, \tag{18}$$

the p-displacement (11) corresponding to the general pure rotation $\mathbf{T}_R(\theta)$.[1] Its definition in (18) yields immediately the canonical *Jordan decomposition of a p-rotation*

$$\mathbf{H}_R(\theta) = \mathbf{H}_{PE}^{-1}\mathbf{T}^{-1} \begin{bmatrix} \cos\theta & -\sin\theta & 0 & 0 \\ \sin\theta & \cos\theta & 0 & 0 \\ 0 & 0 & 1 & 0 \\ 0 & 0 & 0 & 1 \end{bmatrix} \mathbf{T}\mathbf{H}_{PE} \quad (19)$$

$$\mathbf{H}_J^{-1} \qquad \mathbf{J}_R(\theta) \qquad \mathbf{H}_J, \quad (20)$$

Geometrically, this decomposition is achieved by writing $\mathbf{R}(\theta)$ in (17) w.l.o.g.[2] as a rotation around the z-axis. Algebraically, all p-rotation form a similarity class and are hence have the Jordan matrix $\mathbf{J}_R$. This implies their *rotation angle* to be determined by

$$\cos(\theta) = 1/2(\text{trace } \mathbf{H}_R - 2). \quad (21)$$

However, there is a whole family $\mathbf{H}_J = \mathbf{C}_R\mathbf{T}\mathbf{H}_{PE}$ of decompositions like (20), which is spanned by the commutator group $\mathbf{C}_R$ of the Jordan matrix $\mathbf{J}_R$.

$$\mathbf{C}_R = \begin{bmatrix} a & -b & 0 & 0 \\ b & a & 0 & 0 \\ 0 & 0 & c & d \\ 0 & 0 & e & f \end{bmatrix}, \qquad rank(\mathbf{C}_R) = 4. \quad (22)$$

This ambiguity is undesirable, since $\mathbf{H}_J$ encapsulates the projective geometry of the joint. Nevertheless, consider an arbitrary $\mathbf{H}_J$ and denote its jth row as $\boldsymbol{h}_j^T$ and the ith column of $\mathbf{H}_J^{-1}$ by $\boldsymbol{k}_i$.

Remember that the Jordan matrix $\mathbf{J}_R(\theta)$ is the $SE(3)$ representation of z-rotations, i.e. a 1D Lie-subgroup of $SE(3)$. It is generated over the trivial Lie-Algebra with elements $\theta\hat{\mathbf{J}}_R$:

$$\mathbf{J}_R = \exp(\theta\hat{\mathbf{J}}_R), \qquad \hat{\mathbf{J}}_R = \begin{bmatrix} 0 & -1 & 0 & 0 \\ 1 & 0 & 0 & 0 \\ 0 & 0 & 0 & 0 \\ 0 & 0 & 0 & 0 \end{bmatrix} \in se(3). \quad (23)$$

As soon as (23) is substituted into (20), we have a differentiable homomorphism from $SE(3)$ to $PSE(3)$. Therefore, the p-rotations form a family of 1D Lie-subgroups of $PSE(3)$, modulo an axis position and a fixed stereo geometry, both embodied in $\mathbf{H}_J$.

Formally applying the matrix identity (1) to $\mathbf{H}_J^{-1}\exp(\theta\hat{\mathbf{J}}_R)\mathbf{H}_J$ yields the *exponential form* of a p-rotation and its *generator* $\hat{\mathbf{H}}_R$:

$$\mathbf{H}_R = \exp(\theta\hat{\mathbf{H}}_R), \qquad \hat{\mathbf{H}}_R = \mathbf{H}_J^{-1}\hat{\mathbf{J}}_R\mathbf{H}_J. \quad (24)$$

So, the *generator* $\hat{\mathbf{H}}_R$ of a p-rotation can be written as

$$\hat{\mathbf{H}}_R = \boldsymbol{k}_2\boldsymbol{h}_1^T - \boldsymbol{k}_1\boldsymbol{h}_2^T, \quad (25)$$

Despite of the ambiguity in $\mathbf{H}_J$ (22), $\hat{\mathbf{H}}_R$ itself is unique, since $\mathbf{C}_R$ commutates also with $\hat{\mathbf{J}}_R$ (24), (23).

---

[1] a joint can be positioned w.l.o.g. relative to frame $\mathcal{E}$

[2] since $\mathbf{T}$ allows for free reorientation of the axis

We now prove the *Rodriguez' form* of p-rotations

$$\mathbf{H}_R(\theta) = \mathbf{I} + \sin\theta\hat{\mathbf{H}}_R + (1 - \cos\theta)\hat{\mathbf{H}}_R^2. \quad (26)$$

Notice that $-\hat{\mathbf{H}}_R^2 = \boldsymbol{k}_1\boldsymbol{h}_1^T + \boldsymbol{k}_2\boldsymbol{h}_2^T$ since $\boldsymbol{k}_i\boldsymbol{h}_j^T = \delta_{ij}$. Substitute $(\mathbf{J}_R - \mathbf{I}) + \mathbf{I}$ into (20), expand in the sum, and collect the rows and columns corresponding to $\sin\theta$ and $(\cos\theta - 1)$ to obtain (26) – q.e.d.

On the one hand, given the joint angle θ, the Rodriguez form (26) allows us to analytically calculate the projective motion caused by a revolute joint. Its projective geometry is uniquely represented by the generator $\hat{\mathbf{H}}_R$ of the corresponding Lie-subgroup of $PSE(3)$. This result is used lated to express the projective forward kinematics.

On the other hand, given a single p-rotation $\mathbf{H}_R$, calculated from a trial motion of the revolute joint (Fig. 3), the *logarithm of a p-rotation*

$$\hat{\mathbf{H}}_R = \frac{1}{2\sin\theta}(\mathbf{H}_R - \mathbf{H}_R^{-1}), \quad (27)$$

allows us to recover its generator in $pse(3)$. C.f. $\frac{1}{2\sin\theta}(\mathbf{R} - \mathbf{R}^T)$ to go from $SO(3)$ to $so(3)$. This results is used later to identify a projective model of an articulated body.

5.2 Projective prismatic joints

The projective motion of prismatic joints is derived along the lines of section 5.1. It is only summarized here and can be found in greater detail in [15]. Starting from a pure translation of $\tau = 1$ along the z-axis, the *Jordan decompositions of p-translations* have the form

$$\hat{\mathbf{H}}_T(q) = \mathbf{H}_{PE}^{-1}\mathbf{T} \begin{bmatrix} 1 & 0 & 0 & 0 \\ 0 & 1 & 0 & 0 \\ 0 & 0 & 1 & \tau \\ 0 & 0 & 0 & 1 \end{bmatrix} \mathbf{T}\mathbf{H}_{PE} \quad (28)$$

$$\mathbf{H}_J^{-1} \qquad \mathbf{J}_T(q) \qquad \mathbf{H}_J. \quad (29)$$

They form a 1D Lie-subgroup of $PSE(3)$, modulo the translation direction and the affine stereo geometry, both embodied by $\mathbf{H}_J$.

The *generator* $\hat{\mathbf{H}}_T$ of p-translations is the product of the coordinate vectors $\boldsymbol{k}_3$ representing their vanishing point, and $\boldsymbol{h}_4^T$ representing the plane at infinity:

$$\hat{\mathbf{H}}_T = \mathbf{H}_J^{-1} \begin{bmatrix} 0 & 0 & 0 & 0 \\ 0 & 0 & 0 & 0 \\ 0 & 0 & 0 & 1 \\ 0 & 0 & 0 & 0 \end{bmatrix} \mathbf{H}_J, \qquad \hat{\mathbf{H}}_T = \boldsymbol{k}_3^T\boldsymbol{h}_4. \quad (30)$$

Their *exponential form* and *logarithm* are trivial, where unit τ has the length of the trial motion $\mathbf{H}_T$

$$\mathbf{H}_T(q) = \exp(q\hat{\mathbf{H}}_T) = \mathbf{I} + \tau\hat{\mathbf{H}}_T, \quad \hat{\mathbf{H}}_T = \mathbf{H}_T - \mathbf{I}.$$

5.3 Projective motion of articulated chains

Projective articulated motion is expressed by means of a projective generalization of the twist model of articulated chains and the product-of-exponentials expansion of their zero-reference kinematic model [14],[17]. In particular, we concisely prove this projective model of an articulated chains' kinematics using merely the notions developed within the projective kinematic framework.

Consider an articulated chain whose elements are serially linked by either revolute or prismatic joints. Consider further a stereo rig rigidly fixed with respect to one end of the chain. This end is called the *base* of the chain, whereas the opposite end is called its *tip*. The n joints are indexed with $i = 1 \ldots n$ in base-to-tip order, and the element linking joint i with joint $i + 1$ is indexed with i.

This convention allows us to uniformly cover both, the independent-eye case, where the robot and the stereo rig are independently but rigidly installed in the workspace, and the eye-in-hand case, where the rig is rigidly mounted on the robot hand, which is now taken as the base of the chain. To help intuition, focus on a six-axes robot manipulator moving in front of a stereo rig.

A vector $q = [q_1 \ldots q_n]^T$ of joint variables q_i, which stand for θ_i or τ_i depending on whether the ith joint is revolute or prismatic, describes the *configuration* of the chain relative to its *zero-reference*: an arbitrary configuration chosen as the origin $q = 0$ of joint-space. Now, assign to generic points on the ith element the coordinates $M_i(0)$ in zero-reference, and $M_i(q)$ in configuration q. The p-displacement $\mathbb{H}_i(q)$ of the ith element, and such for all the elements, represent the *articulated projective motion* corresponding to a joint-space motion q (Fig. 1)

$$M_i(q) = \mathbb{H}_i(q)M_i(0). \tag{31}$$

The projective motion of a single articulation $\mathbf{H}_i(q_i)$ is directly expressed using the Lie-algebra $\hat{\mathbf{H}}_i(q_i)$ of the respective joint, since the zero-reference fixes for each joint a specific position in space. More precisely, moving only the ith joint to q_i results in either a p-rotation $\mathbf{H}_{Ri}(q_i)$ or a p-translation $\mathbf{H}_{Ti}(q_i)$, that is generated either by $\hat{\mathbf{H}}_{Ri}$ or by $\hat{\mathbf{H}}_{Ti}$, depending on the type of joint. The generators encapsulate the projective geometry of the joint in the zero-reference.

$$M_i(q_i) = \mathbf{H}_i(q_i) M_i(0). \tag{32}$$
$$\mathbf{H}_i(q_i) = \exp(q_i \hat{\mathbf{H}}_i), \quad \hat{\mathbf{H}}_i = \hat{\mathbf{H}}_{Ri} \text{ or } \hat{\mathbf{H}}_i = \hat{\mathbf{H}}_{Ti}. \tag{33}$$

Given an articulated chain and the projective representation $\hat{\mathbf{H}}_i$ of its joints, the p-displacement of the ith element can be written as a product-of-exponentials (Fig. 1):

$$\mathbb{H}_i(q) = \exp(q_1 \hat{\mathbf{H}}_1) \cdots \exp(q_i \hat{\mathbf{H}}_i). \tag{34}$$

The argument is a simple induction. The points on the 1st element are affected only by the motion of the 1st joint: $M_1(q) = \mathbf{H}_1(q_1)M_1(0)$. Thus the hypothesis is that the elements preceeding the ith one move like (34). Now, points on the ith element move like $M_i(q_i) = \mathbf{H}_i(q_i)M_i(0)$ if only the ith joint is actuated. And after the ith joint is locked to q_i, the points $M_i(q_i)$ on the ith element move rigidly with element $i - 1$. Conclusively, we can apply the hypothesis for $i - 1$, to see that elementary joint motions have to be left-multiplied in tip-to-base order (34). – q.e.d.

Since each $\mathbf{H}_i(q_i)$ in (34) is expressed w.r.t. to frame $\mathcal{P}$, their conjugate forms (19), (28) can be substituted into (34). Since the inner pairs $\mathbf{H}_{PE}\mathbf{H}_{PE}^{-1}$ cancel out, $\mathbb{H}_i(q)$ is in fact the p-displacement of the ith element's articulated motion:

$$\mathbb{H}_i(q) = \mathbf{H}_{PE}^{-1} \exp(q_1 \hat{\mathbf{T}}_1) \cdots \exp(q_i \hat{\mathbf{T}}_i) \mathbf{H}_{PE}. \tag{35}$$

Here, the $\hat{\mathbf{T}}_i$ in the Euclidean POE are the twists (14) representing the zero-reference of each joint w.r.t. $\mathcal{E}$. It is essentially this particular modelling of the chain's geometry, that allows us to directly exploit the correspondence between the Euclidean and projective motion.

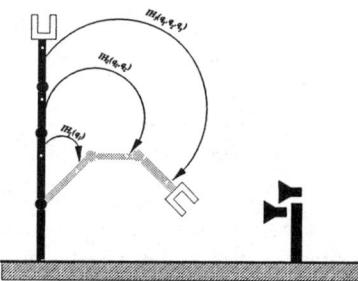

Figure 1: Zero-reference model of articulated chain.

5.4 Projective velocity of articulated chain

The instantaneous motion of an articulated body along a differentiable trajectory $q(t)$ in joint space is characterized by the projective body velocities $\dot{\mathbb{H}}_i$ of its elements. Consider a time instant t, at which the chain instantaneously has the configuration $q = q(t)$ and the joint-space velocity $\dot{q} = \dot{q}(t)$.

We obtain the *motion tangent* $\dot{\mathbb{H}}_i(q, \dot{q})$ from the temporal derivative of the POE-formula (34)

$$\dot{\mathbb{H}}_i(\boldsymbol{q}, \dot{\boldsymbol{q}}) = \frac{d\mathbb{H}_i(\boldsymbol{q})}{d\boldsymbol{q}} \, \dot{\boldsymbol{q}} = \sum_{k=1}^{i} \dot{q}_k \, \frac{\partial \mathbb{H}_i(\boldsymbol{q})}{\partial q_k} \qquad (36)$$

$$\frac{\partial \mathbb{H}_i}{\partial q_k} = \mathbf{H}_1(q_1) \cdots \hat{\mathbf{H}}_k \exp(q_k \hat{\mathbf{H}}_k) \cdots \mathbf{H}_i(q_i) \qquad (37)$$

The *projective body-velocity* $\hat{\mathbb{H}}_i(\boldsymbol{q})$ of the ith element

$$\hat{\mathbb{H}}_i(\boldsymbol{q}, \dot{\boldsymbol{q}}) = \dot{\mathbb{H}}_i(\boldsymbol{q}, \dot{\boldsymbol{q}})\mathbb{H}_i^{-1}(\boldsymbol{q}) \qquad (38)$$

$$= \sum_{k=1}^{i} \dot{q}_k \left(\underbrace{\mathbb{H}_{k-1}(\boldsymbol{q}) \, \hat{\mathbf{H}}_k \, \mathbb{H}_{k-1}^{-1}(\boldsymbol{q})}_{\hat{\mathbf{H}}_{k,q}} \right). \qquad (39)$$

follows from definition (13). The expression $\hat{\mathbf{H}}_{k,q}$ in (39) follows by inserting (34) (37) into (38). It represents the projective motion of the kth joint for its new position in configuration $\boldsymbol{q}$. Consequently, the body velocity as written in (39) can be seen as the joint-wise linear superposition of projective motions $\hat{\mathbf{H}}_{k,q}$ weighted by the joint-velocities q_k.

Finally, points $\boldsymbol{M}_i(\boldsymbol{q})$ rigidly moving with the ith element have the *projective point-velocity*

$$\dot{\boldsymbol{M}}_i(\boldsymbol{q}, \dot{\boldsymbol{q}}) = \hat{\mathbb{H}}_i(\boldsymbol{q}, \dot{\boldsymbol{q}})\boldsymbol{M}_i(\boldsymbol{q}) = \hat{\mathbb{H}}_i(\boldsymbol{q}, \dot{\boldsymbol{q}})\boldsymbol{M}_i(\boldsymbol{0}), \qquad (40)$$

$$= \sum_{k=1}^{i} \dot{q}_k \, \hat{\mathbf{H}}_{k,q} \boldsymbol{M}_i(\boldsymbol{q}) = \sum_{k=1}^{i} \dot{q}_k \frac{\partial \mathbb{H}_i(\boldsymbol{q})}{\partial q_k} \boldsymbol{M}_i(\boldsymbol{0}),$$

$$= \sum_{k=1}^{i} \dot{q}_k \, \frac{\partial \boldsymbol{M}_i(\boldsymbol{q})}{\partial q_k}. \qquad (41)$$

Equation (40) agrees with direct differentiation of (34). Again, (41) rewrites is as a joint-wise linear superposition of respective velocity components.

6 Non-metric Visual Servoing

In this section, we introduce a *non-metric formulation* of the visual servoing paradigm, based on the projective representation of articulated motions. Classically, this paradigm consists in servoing the end-effector to a target position by means of aligning its velocity screw with the difference between the current and the target image of its features. To fix ideas, consider a gripper mounted on a six-axis robot arm that is moving under visual control of a stereo rig.

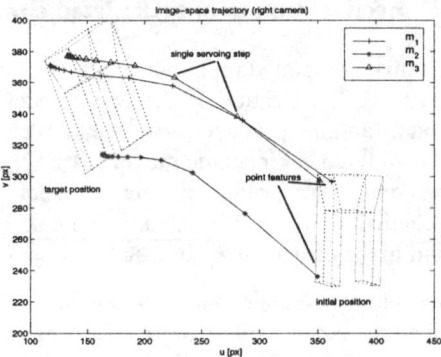

Figure 2: Initial and target image of the gripper and the feature trajectories over the iterations of the control loop.

We call our formulation non-metric for three reasons: First, generally speaking, the geometry of the entire system is modeled w.r.t. the projective camera frame $\mathcal{P}$. Metric frames do not appear anymore. Second, no a-priori knowledge about the geometry of the system is required. The camera geometry, $\mathbf{P}, \mathbf{P}'$, the geometry of gripper features $\boldsymbol{M}_6$, and the robot geometry in terms of $\hat{\mathbf{H}}_i$ are acquired on-line. Third, the actual control law no longer servos the robot's Cartesian velocity, but servos the manipulator's joint-velocities. Therefore, we seek to derive a Jacobian that relates image-velocities $\dot{s}$ to joint ones: $\dot{s} = \mathbf{J}(\boldsymbol{q}, \boldsymbol{M}_6)\dot{\boldsymbol{q}}$.

Most important is to understand the *Jacobian as an analytic expression* in $\boldsymbol{q}, \boldsymbol{M}_6$, which ensures its soundness over the robot's entire configuration space. In contrast to existing systems, it is neither an on-line estimated linear model [12], nor an a-priori given approximation around the target [4], [7]. First of all, for each joint k, its projective motion is developed around the current configuration $\boldsymbol{q}$, i.e. for its current position in space. The calculation is that of $\hat{\mathbf{H}}_{k,q}$ in (39). Second, for each point $\boldsymbol{M}_6$ on the gripper and for each joint k, a point-velocity component $\hat{\mathbf{H}}_{k,q} \cdot \boldsymbol{M}_6$ is developed around $\boldsymbol{q}$ and the current position $\boldsymbol{M}_6$ of the point. Now, their superposition (41) can be expressed by a Jacobian matrix $\mathbf{J}_H$

$$\dot{\boldsymbol{M}}_6(\boldsymbol{q}, \dot{\boldsymbol{q}}) = \mathbf{J}_H(\boldsymbol{q}, \boldsymbol{M}_6)\dot{\boldsymbol{q}} \qquad (42)$$

$$= \left[\frac{\partial \boldsymbol{M}_6(\boldsymbol{q})}{\partial q_1} \cdots \frac{\partial \boldsymbol{M}_6(\boldsymbol{q})}{\partial q_6} \right] \dot{\boldsymbol{q}}. \qquad (43)$$

$$\frac{\partial \boldsymbol{M}_6(\boldsymbol{q})}{\partial q_k} = \hat{\mathbf{H}}_{k,q} \cdot \boldsymbol{M}_6 \qquad (44)$$

Finally, the camera Jacobian $\mathbf{J}_C$ between spatial velocity $\dot{\boldsymbol{M}}_6$ and image velocity $\dot{s}$ is developed around the point's current image $\boldsymbol{m} = \mathbf{P}\boldsymbol{M}_6$ in the projective plane $\mathbb{P}2$. This first step has the trivial Jacobian $\mathbf{P}$. The map $C : \boldsymbol{m} \to \boldsymbol{s} = [m_1/m_3, m_2/m_3]^T$ from $\mathbb{P}^2$ onto the pixel plane describes the actual perspective projection, which has Jacobian $\mathbf{J}_C(\boldsymbol{m})$

$$\dot{s} = \mathbf{J}_C\left(\boldsymbol{m}\right)\dot{\boldsymbol{m}}, \quad \mathbf{J}_C\left(\boldsymbol{m}\right) = \begin{bmatrix} \frac{1}{m_3} & 0 & -\frac{m_1}{m_3^2} \\ 0 & \frac{1}{m_3} & -\frac{m_2}{m_3^2} \end{bmatrix}. \quad (45)$$

Finally, the Jacobian $\mathbf{J}$ is a function of $\boldsymbol{q}$ and M_6

$$\begin{bmatrix} \dot{s} \\ \dot{s}' \end{bmatrix} = \begin{bmatrix} \mathbf{J}_C(\mathbf{P}\,M_6)\ \mathbf{P}\ J_H(\boldsymbol{q},M_6) \\ \mathbf{J}_C(\mathbf{P}'M_6)\ \mathbf{P}'\ J_H(\boldsymbol{q},M_6) \end{bmatrix}\dot{\boldsymbol{q}}, \quad (46)$$

where the projective geometry of the system is encapsulated in $\mathbf{P}, \mathbf{P}'$ and in the $\hat{\mathbf{H}}_i$.

We now report on *simulations* of such a non-metric visual servoing system. The metric geometry of the simulated setup is roughly a stereo system having $20cm$ baseline, 20° vergence angle, a $3/4''$ CCD, and $12.5mm$ lenses, capturing over time the motion of a PUMA-like robot from $1m$ distance. The latter has an arm with links of $36cm$, $48cm$, and $40cm$ length, and carries a gripper of $10cm$ in size. In contrast, the only inputs used by the non-metric system are joint angle measurements and image projections of gripper features. To take into account real imaging conditions, independent Gaussian noise with $\sigma = 1px$ is added, whereas joint angle are supposed to be accurate.

Figure 3: Robot in zero-reference and trial motions.

During the *acquisition phase* (Fig. 3) , six joint-wise trial-motions $[30, 20, 30, 40, 60, 60]^T$ are acquired through the p-rotation homographies $\mathbf{H}_i$ estimated for 7 point features M_6 on the gripper. In a first step, the generators $\hat{\mathbf{H}}_i$ are calculated algebraically (27), but have to be refined using a non-linear numerical method to obtain stable and accurate results in presence of noise. The method employed has already proved its performance on **real image data** [15], [16].

During the *servoing phase*, three points on the visible face of the gripper are tracked, and the point-wise stack of the error vectors from their current images s, s' to

their goal images s_*, s'_* constitutes the overall image-error. This stack is used to invert the Jacobian relation (46) for joint-velocities $\dot{\boldsymbol{q}}$. This proportional control law causes the image-error to decrease exponentially [4].

$$\begin{bmatrix} \dot{q}_1 \\ \vdots \\ \dot{q}_6 \end{bmatrix} = -\mathbf{J}^+ \begin{bmatrix} s - s_* \\ s' - s'_* \\ \vdots \end{bmatrix} \quad (47)$$

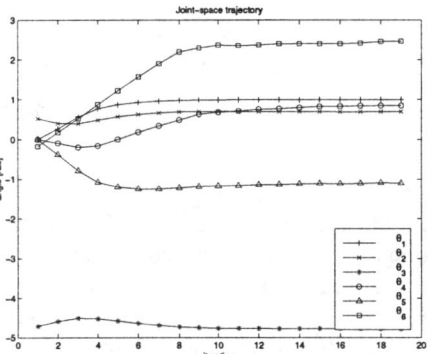

Figure 4: Joint-space trajectory

We show the result for a servoing task which translates the gripper by $82cm$ and rotates it by 88°. The goal was attained after 20 iterations. In joint-space (Fig. 4), a smooth, almost monotonous trajectory covers a distance of $\boldsymbol{q} = [57, 10, 5, 51, -60, 158]^T$ and attains the target to within $\Delta\boldsymbol{q} = [0.04, 0.15, 0.23, 0.31, 0.10, 1.5]^T$ for $0.5px$ image noise, and to within $\Delta\boldsymbol{q} = [0.01, 0.04, 0.09, 0.19, 0.21, 0.35]^T$ for $0.1px$ image noise. In the image (Fig. 2), the approximately linear trajectory covers a distance of about $220px$. The image error (Fig. 5) shows exponential decay in all its components until convergence is attained with the residual error below the noise levels.

7 Summary and Conclusions

We have shown how an uncalibrated stereo rig sees rigid and articulated motion.The introduced original formalism of *projective kinematics* has proven to be almost as powerful as classical kinematics in a metric space. In detail, projective formulations for displacements, for body- and point-velocities, as well as for revolute and prismatic joints have been introduced. Most importantly, a projective model for the geometry of an articulated chain has been presented that leads immediately to an original approach for "non-metric visual servoing", which has been formulated without any knowledge about the metric geometry of the system, at all.

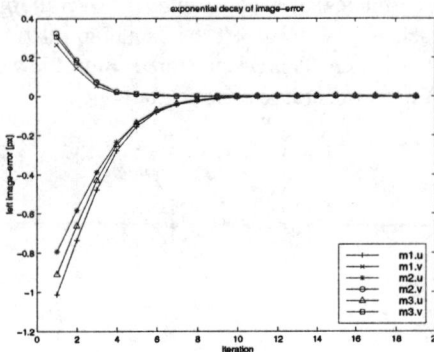

Figure 5: Exponential convergence in image-error.

We hope this work will give foundations and motivations for the integration of uncalibrated visual sensors into perception-action cycles. We judge the present simulations and formerly published practical experiments very promising. Future work will hence concentrate on further developing the practical and numerical means to better validate the contribution of non-metric systems in practice.

References

[1] P. A. Beardsley, I. D. Reid, A. Zisserman, and D. W. Murray. Active visual navigation using non-metric structure. In *Proc. 5th ICCV*, pages 58–64. IEEE Computer Society Press, June 1995.

[2] G. Csurka, D. Demirdjian, A. Ruf, and R. Horaud. Closed-form solutions for the euclidean calibration of a stereo rig. In *Proc. 5. ECCV*, volume I, pages 426–442. Springer, 1998.

[3] F. Devernay and O. Faugeras. From projective to Euclidean reconstruction. In *Proc. IEEE Conf. CVPR*, pages 264–269, San Francisco, CA., June 1996.

[4] B. Espiau, F. Chaumette, and P. Rives. A new approach to visual servoing in robotics. *IEEE Transactions on Robotics and Automation*, 8(3):313–326, June 1992.

[5] O. D. Faugeras. What can be seen in three dimensions with an uncalibrated stereo rig. In G. Sandini, editor, *Computer Vision – Proc. 2. ECCV*, pages 563–578. Springer Verlag, May 1992.

[6] O. D. Faugeras. *Three Dimensional Computer Vision: A Geometric Viewpoint*. MIT Press, Boston, 1993.

[7] G. D. Hager. A modular system for robust positioning using feedback from stereo vision. *IEEE Transactions on Robotics and Automation*, 13(4):582–595, August 1997.

[8] R. I. Hartley. Euclidean reconstruction from uncalibrated views. In M. Z. Forsyth, editor, *Applications of Invariance in Computer Vision*, pages 237–256. Springer Verlag, Berlin Heidelberg, 1994.

[9] R. I. Hartley. In defence of the 8-point algorithm. In *Proc. 5. ICCV*, pages 1064–1070, Cambridge, Mass., June 1995. IEEE Computer Society Press.

[10] N. Hollinghurst and R. Cipolla. Uncalibrated stereo hand-eye coordination. *Image and Vision Computing*, 12(3):187–192, March 1994.

[11] R. Horaud and G. Csurka. Self-calibration and euclidean reconstruction using motions of a stereo rig. In *Proc. 6. ICCV*, pages 96–103. IEEE Computer Society Press, January 1998.

[12] M. Jagersand and R. Nelson. Aquiring visual-motor models for precision manipulation with robot hands. In Buxton-Cipolla, editor, *Proc. 4. ECCV*, volume II, pages 603–612. Springer, April 1996.

[13] Q.-T. Luong and T. Viéville. Canonic representations for the geometries of multiple projective views. *Computer Vision and Image Understanding*, 64(2):193–229, September 1996.

[14] R. Murray, Z. Li, and S. Sastry. *A Mathematical Introduction to Robotic Manipulation*. CRC Press, 1994.

[15] A. Ruf, G. Csurka, and R. Horaud. Projective translations and affine stereo calibration. In *Proc. IEEE Conf. CVPR*, pages 475–481. IEEE Computer Society Press, June 1998.

[16] A. Ruf and R. Horaud. Projective rotations applied to a non-metric pan-tilt head. In *Proc. IEEE Conf. CVPR, accepted*, June 1999.

[17] J. Selig. *Geometrical Methods in Robotics*. Springer, 1996.

[18] A. Zisserman, P. A. Beardsley, and I. D. Reid. Metric calibration of a stereo rig. In *Proc. IEEE Workshop on Representation of Visual Scenes*, pages 93–100, June 1995.

Detecting salient motion by accumulating directionally-consistent flow

L. Wixson   M. Hansen

Sarnoff Corporation

Princeton, NJ 08543

{lwixson,mhansen}@sarnoff.com

Abstract

Motion detection can play an important role in many vision tasks. Yet image motion can arise from "uninteresting" events as well as interesting ones. In this paper, salient motion is defined as motion that is likely to result from a typical surveillance target (e.g., a person or vehicle traveling with a sense of direction through a scene) as opposed to other distracting motions (e.g., the scintillation of specularities on water, the oscillation of vegetation in the wind). We propose an algorithm for detecting this salient motion that is based on intermediate-stage vision integration of optical flow. Empirical results are presented that illustrate the applicability of the proposed methods to real-world video. Unlike many motion detection schemes, no knowledge about expected object size or shape is necessary for rejecting the distracting motion.

1 Introduction

Motion detection can play an important role in many vision tasks, especially those related to detection and tracking for surveillance. Depending on the specific scene conditions, the difficulty of these tasks can vary widely. Some of the most challenging domains are those in which motion is being exhibited not just by the objects of interest, but also by other non-salient objects such as vegetation, shadows cast by vegetation, and specularities on water [3, 19].

Non-salient motions of this type are a common source of false positives for most simple motion-detection schemes, which either detect areas of frame-to-frame intensity change [1, 4, 15, 11, 24], or areas of intensity change with respect to some reference representation [9, 3, 23, 6].[1] When the reference represen-

---

[1]These are by no means all the work in this area. A more thorough listing of past work can be found in [20].

tation is a learned probability distribution of intensities at each pixel, the system can, over time, learn not to report non-salient change, but it will still give rise to false positives until the reference representation has been learned [9]. Motion-based methods for change detection, such as the one presented in this paper, have the potential to be much more stable than those that rely on intensity representations.

Typical approaches for suppressing false positive detections are based on their aspect ratio, size, or magnitude of the frame-to-frame flow or normal flow [11, 6]. These approaches are not satisfying, since it is easy to construct counterexamples to such heuristics, such as the example we will present in Figure 3. For example, the frame-to-frame motion of the non-salient objects may be larger than that of the salient objects, especially if the non-salient objects are significantly closer to the camera or if the salient object is moving very slowly to avoid detection.

A more sound approach is to filter out false positives based on some aspect of the distance traveled by the object. Branches on a tree will stay roughly in the same place (or at least within some area) over time. The key problem is how to perform the tracking. Typically vegetation gives rise to many regions of change that are not constant in extent or motion from frame to frame, and which are therefore difficult to instantiate and track with a higher-level vision process. Some researchers have begun to examine ways of performing this detection using lower-level processing. For example, one approach uses multiple frames to construct "XT" or "YT"' spatiotemporal intensity slices from a sequence of frame-to-frame change images, and then to extract lines from these slices [13, 16] or even from the XYT spatiotemporal volume. An issue with this approach is how to select the image rows or columns to be used to construct the slice. For example, in scenes with extensive motion, it is not sufficient to simply project all the image columns onto a single X-

797

row in order to form the XT image. Another approach uses spatiotemporal filtering [19, 20]. However, this introduces an assumption that the object is moving with a certain velocity due to the velocity-dependent nature of the spatiotemporal filters.

In this paper, we take salient motion to be motion that tends to move in a consistent direction over time. We propose an approach that works by integrating frame-to-frame optical flow over time so that for each pixel it is possible to compute a rough estimate of the total image distance it has moved. On each frame, we update a salience measure that is directly related to the distance over which a point has traveled with a consistent direction. Because we use sub-pixel optical flow, the algorithm can track an object even if it is moving extremely slowly, and we can maintain our salience even if the object comes to a stop. (Of course, it may in some cases be desirable to suppress the salience of objects that stop for an extended time.) The algorithm is designed to minimize the salience of both easily-tracked oscillatory motion, such as a lone branch without leaves swaying periodically, as well as complicated assemblies of branches with fluttering leaves and occlusions. There are no user-controlled parameters relating to object size or intensity contrast; all parameters are related to velocity or distance traveled. Furthermore, the algorithm is not especially sensitive to these parameters; the same parameter settings are used for all the examples in this paper.

A related approach has recently been proposed in [17] to deal with detecting low-contrast moving objects in video from a moving airborne camera. Their approach, which uses normal flow to temporally propagate change energy, has been motivated by similar goals, but does not use consistency of direction as a filter.

2 Algorithm input

We shall denote an image at time t as either I_t or, when it is necessary to denote a specific image point $\mathbf{p}$, $I_t(\mathbf{p})$.

The computation of the salience measure takes as input a set of frame-to-frame optical flow fields. Let $\mathbf{F}(\mathbf{p}) = (F_x(\mathbf{p}), F_y(\mathbf{p}))$ denote an optical flow vector field that defines a 2D vector at each pixel location $\mathbf{p} = [x \ y]$. Such a flow field can be used to warp an image $I_t(\mathbf{p})$ to yield a new image. Let the function that performs such a warp be denoted as

$$warp(I_t, \mathbf{F}, \mathbf{p}) = I_t(\mathbf{p}')$$

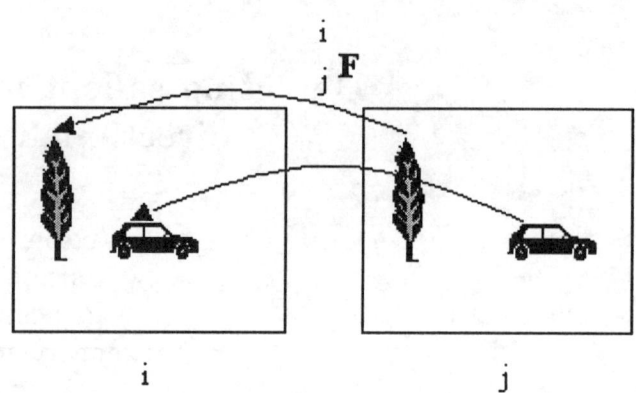

Figure 1. Illustration of notation used for flow fields. Flow field $_j^i\mathbf{F}$ maps coordinates in image j to image i. Flow field $_i^j\mathbf{F}$ maps coordinates in image i to image j.

where

$$\mathbf{p}' = \mathbf{p} + \mathbf{F}(\mathbf{p})$$

(It should be noted that when $\mathbf{F}$ has been computed to subpixel precision, then the x' and y' components of $\mathbf{p}'$ will not be integer values. Therefore $I_t(\mathbf{p}')$ must be computed using image interpolation [22]. We use bilinear interpolation in practice.) The result of applying the *warp* function at all pixel locations $\mathbf{p}$ shall be written as $warp(I, \mathbf{F})$.

The warp function also can be used to warp a 2D vector field $\mathbf{V}$. In this case, the warp function is applied to each component of the vector field individually:

$$warp(\mathbf{V}, \mathbf{F}, \mathbf{p}) = \left[\begin{array}{c} warp(V_x, \mathbf{F}, \mathbf{p}) \\ warp(V_y, \mathbf{F}, \mathbf{p}) \end{array} \right]. \quad (1)$$

Given two images I_i and I_j, the optical flow field that maps each pixel in I_j to a coordinate in I_i will be denoted as $_j^i\mathbf{F}$. This notation, developed by Craig [5], is illustrated in Figure 1. For images taken at two successive time instances t and $t + 1$, the flow field $_{t+1}^t\mathbf{F}$ can be used to warp I_t into alignment with I_{t+1}, yielding a new image $^{t+1}I_t = warp(I_t, {}_{t+1}^t\mathbf{F})$.

In practice, we compute flow using a multi-resolution least squares technique [14, 2].[2] There are other variations [18] of this technique with better accuracy. However, since in general the motion in the scene will be complicated and non-rigid, it is unlikely that the

---

[2]In practice, there are well-known situations where the flow cannot be recovered if the image patch contains gradients in only one direction. Our algorithm handles this by computing only the normal flow in regions where only one image gradient is dominant.

specifics of the flow estimation will significantly impact the algorithm.

The difficulty of recovering perfect flow vectors is well-known [10]. In locations where there is occlusion, where the temporal sampling used for digitization is not fast enough to keep up with motion in the scene, or where there is insufficient texture, the computed flow vectors can be incorrect. We identify such flow vectors between two frames t and $t + 1$ by performing forwards-backwards checking [8, 12] using the flow fields ${}^t_{t+1}\mathbf{F}$ and ${}^{t+1}_t\mathbf{F}$. The forwards-backwards checking examines whether the flow vectors in the two flow fields map to the same points. If not, the flow vector is set to 0. More specifically, ${}^t_{t+1}\mathbf{F}(\mathbf{p})$ is reset to $[0\ 0]$ if $\|{}^t_{t+1}\mathbf{F}(\mathbf{p}) + {}^{t+1}_t\mathbf{F}(\mathbf{p} + {}^t_{t+1}\mathbf{F}(\mathbf{p}))\| > k_c$. I.e., the two flow vectors should cancel each other. The constant k_c is the pixel distance by which the two flow vectors can differ. Generally, when flow vectors are incorrect this distance will be large, so in practice $k_c = 3$ produces adequate checking.

3 Cumulative flow and salience

Theoretically, given perfect frame-to-frame flow fields and perfect image warping, one could track an image point from I_i to I_j by using the frame-to-frame flow fields ${}^t_{t+1}\mathbf{F}$ for $t = i, \ldots, j-1$. More specifically, the frame-to-frame flow fields could theoretically be combined into a "cumulative" flow field ${}^i_j\mathbf{C}$, as shown in Figure 2. This can be defined as

$$
{}^i_j\mathbf{C} = \begin{cases} {}^i_j\mathbf{F} & \text{if } j = i+1 \\[2ex] \boldsymbol{\Delta}_j + warp({}^i_{j-1}\mathbf{C}, {}^{j-1}_j\mathbf{F}) & \text{if } j > i+1 \end{cases} \tag{2}
$$

where $\boldsymbol{\Delta}_j$ is the contribution, to the cumulative flow, of the frame-to-frame flow from frame $j-1$ to frame j. Theoretically, $\boldsymbol{\Delta}_j$ is simply ${}^{j-1}_j\mathbf{F}$, but this will change for the measures we develop below.

The cumulative flow field defined above can be used to measure the distance between each image point's location in a reference image I_i and its location in a subsequent image I_j. We will now develop a variation on this measure that accumulates the distance that each point travels in a consistent x- or y-direction, and relate this to a measure of salience. This measure will also be a vector field over the image, and will be denoted $\mathbf{S}_j$.

Our desired cumulative measure must have two properties. First, it must take on values that, for each point, are proportional to the distance that point has traveled in a consistent x- or y- direction. Second, since a flow field is rarely perfect, and since a salient object may temporarily pass behind small occlusions,

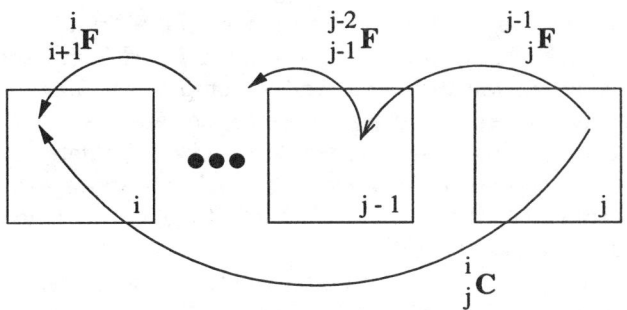

Figure 2. Given perfect frame-to-frame flow fields $\mathbf{F}$, the theoretical cumulative flow field $\mathbf{C}$ would be identical to that obtained by composing the individual frame-to-frame flow vectors.

we would like the accumulation to be tolerant of small temporal gaps in the frame-to-frame tracking of a point where the frame-to-frame flow is incorrect.

3.1 The salience field

We now define a vector-valued salience measure $\mathbf{S}_j$ with the first property, i.e. it takes on values that, for each point, are related to the distance that point has traveled in a consistent x- or y- direction. This measure is similar to the theoretical cumulative flow field, except that we augment the system with a method of resetting the salience to 0 when the direction of each tracked point's flow reverses course, and use an "extended" flow field ${}^{j-1}_j\mathbf{E}$ rather than the original flow field ${}^{j-1}_j\mathbf{F}$ for each new frame j. The extended flow field is introduced to handle errors and occlusions that occur in real flow fields and will be explained in the next section; for the time being it suffices to consider it identical to the original flow field.

Given a new frame j, the computation of the salience measure is divided into three steps. The first simply updates an intermediate measure $\mathbf{S'}_j$ in the same manner as the theoretical cumulative flow updating shown in Equation 2, using the extended flow field:

$$
\mathbf{S'}_j := \begin{cases} \mathbf{0} & \text{if } j = 0 \\[2ex] \boldsymbol{\Delta}_j + warp(\mathbf{S}_{j-1}, {}^{j-1}_j\mathbf{E}) & \text{otherwise} \end{cases} \tag{3}
$$

The second and third steps detect locations that have reversed direction, and reset their salience to zero. Detecting direction reversals is non-trivial, as it is common for a point's flow to reverse course slightly on some frames either due to errors in flow computation or occasional small backwards movement. Therefore, to detect reversals in course we maintain a "maximum salience" 2D vector field that holds for each point the maximum value of the x- and y- components that the point's salience has taken on since the salience at that point was last reset. Direction reversals are detected when the maximum salience of a point is above some threshold k_s but the point's current salience is below some fraction k_r of the maximum.

We reset the salience separately for motion in the x- and y-directions, so that the overall salience magnitude at a point is not reset to 0 if the point reverses course in one direction but not the other (for example a person zigzagging while running forward).[3]

Let us now turn to the specifics of the second and third steps. In step two, the maximum cumulative flow field $\mathbf{M}_j$ is computed by warping it from the previous frame and updating those locations at which the one component of the salience vector is directionally consistent with the maximum cumulative flow vector and has a larger magnitude than the corresponding component of the maximum cumulative flow vector. Specifically, the x-component of the maximum cumulative flow vector on frame j, $M_{j,x}$, is updated at each point $\mathbf{p}$ as follows. Let m_x be the value of the x-component of the maximum cumulative flow vector at point $\mathbf{p}$'s location in the previous frame $j-1$, i.e. $m_x = \mathbf{M}_{j-1,x}(\mathbf{p} + {}_j^{j-1}E(\mathbf{p}))$. Then

$$
M_{j,x}(\mathbf{p}) := \begin{cases} S'_{j,x}(\mathbf{p}) & \text{if } \mathrm{sign}(S'_{j,x}(\mathbf{p})) = \mathrm{sign}(m_x) \text{ and} \\ & |\, S'_{j,x}(\mathbf{p})\,| > |\, m_x\,| \\ \\ m_x & \text{otherwise} \end{cases}
$$
(4)

The y-component, $M_{j,y}$, is updated similarly.

Finally, the third step detects direction reversals and resets the appropriate x- or y- component of the salience measure accordingly. The x-component of the salience measure, $S_{j,x}$, is assigned as follows.
$S_{j,x}(\mathbf{p}) :=$

$$
\begin{cases} 0 & \text{if } |\, M_{j,x}(\mathbf{p})\,| > k_s \text{ and} \\ & |\, S'_{j,x}(\mathbf{p}) - M_{j,x}(\mathbf{p})\,|\, /\, |\, M_{j,x}(\mathbf{p})\,| > k_r \\ S'_{j,x}(\mathbf{p}) & \text{otherwise} \end{cases}
$$
(5)

If $S_{j,x}(\mathbf{p})$ is reset to 0, $M_{j,x}(\mathbf{p})$ is also reset to 0.

The y-component of the salience measure, $S_{j,y}$, is computed similarly. Typically the minimum salience k_s is set to 8 to ensure that some minimal salience has a chance to accumulate before it can be reset to 0. The fractional change k_r is typically set to .1, indicating

---

[3]This can in some situations mean that zigzagging movement while running along the image diagonal may have slightly different resetting properties than those moving along image axes, but we have not observed any difficulties to date.

that if the cumulative flow drops to 90% of the largest value previously observed, a direction change is occurring. The precise setting is not particularly important, since in general pixels on vegetation will exhibit direction reversals that represent large percentage changes relative to their maximum value.

3.2 The extended flow field

To achieve robustness to errors in computed flow and temporal gaps created when a moving object temporarily passes behind small occlusions, we update the salience measure using an "extended" flow field ${}_j^{j-1}\mathbf{E}$ rather than the original flow field ${}_j^{j-1}\mathbf{F}$ for a new frame j. The extended field is derived from the original by checking for each point $\mathbf{p}$ in the original flow field, whether there exists a scalar multiple s of the original vector ${}_j^{j-1}\mathbf{F}(\mathbf{p})$ that extends the vector so that it connects to a location with large salience. More precisely, suppose we have $\mathbf{S}_{j-1}$, the salience measure from the previous frame. Then the vector-valued salience measure $\mathbf{g}$ at point $\mathbf{p}$'s location in the previous frame, assuming an extension by a factor of s, is $\mathbf{g} = \mathbf{S}_{j-1}(\mathbf{p} + s\,{}_j^{j-1}\mathbf{F}(\mathbf{p}))$. We test whether there exists an $s > 1$ that meets the following five criteria:

1. The flow vector to be extended must be large enough to be significant. Specifically, $\|\, {}_j^{j-1}\mathbf{F}(\mathbf{p})\,\| \geq k_f$, where k_f is a user-specified distance (typically 1).

2. The extended flow vector can't be more than k_e pixels longer than the original vector. Specifically, $\|\, s\,{}_j^{j-1}\mathbf{F}(\mathbf{p}) - {}_j^{j-1}\mathbf{F}(\mathbf{p})\,\| < k_e$ where k_e is a user-specified distance (typically 6).

3. The point to which the flow is to be extended must have a reasonably large salience. Specifically, $\|\, \mathbf{g}\,\| \geq k_g$, where k_g is a user-specified salience (typically 15).

4. The salience magnitude resulting from the extension must be more than the salience that would be obtained without an extension. Specifically, $\|\, \mathbf{g}\,\| > \|\, \mathbf{S}_{j-1}(\mathbf{p} + {}_j^{j-1}\mathbf{F}(\mathbf{p})) + {}_j^{j-1}\mathbf{F}(\mathbf{p})\,\|$.

5. The vectors ${}_j^{j-1}\mathbf{F}(\mathbf{p})$ and $\mathbf{g}$ must lie in the same quadrant (i.e., the signs of their components must be identical).

If all of the above criteria are met, then we select the s that maximizes $\|\, \mathbf{g}\,\|$ and assign:

$$
\begin{aligned} {}_j^{j-1}\mathbf{E}(\mathbf{p}) &:= s\,{}_j^{j-1}\mathbf{F}(\mathbf{p}) \\ \mathbf{\Delta}_j(\mathbf{p}) &:= \mathbf{0} \end{aligned}
$$

This has the effect of setting the flow vector to be the extended flow vector, but the salience update term to 0. Intuitively, this allows the salience value of the tracked point to remain the same as that of the point to which it has been linked by the extension, but not to increase. The motivation for this policy is that since the flow was not actually observed, it should not increment the salience.

If not all of the criteria for extending the flow vector are met, then the extended flow and salience update is identical to the original flow:

$$
\begin{aligned}
{}_{j}^{j-1}\mathbf{E}(\mathbf{p}) &:= {}_{j}^{j-1}\mathbf{F}(\mathbf{p}) \\
\mathbf{\Delta}_j(\mathbf{p}) &:= {}_{j}^{j-1}\mathbf{F}(\mathbf{p})
\end{aligned}
$$

4 Empirical studies

Figure 3 illustrates the algorithm on a challenging video sequence in which camouflaged soldiers are visible as very small objects while bushes in the foreground are large and sway wildly. To the human eye, the people are not visible in still frames from the sequence, and can only be seen when the sequence is played as a movie. Column 2 of the figure shows the x-component of the frame-to-frame flow. The regions corresponding to the salient objects (people at a distance) has been circled. The frame-to-frame velocity of the people varies from .6 to 2.5 pixels/frame, while that of the vegetation varies from 0 to 12 pixels/frame. Clearly the people cannot be distinguished from the foreground clutter on the basis of their size or their frame-to-frame motion magnitude. Column 3 of the figure shows the evolution of the x-component of the salience measure, $S_{j,x}$. Over time, $S_{j,x}$ for pixels on the soldiers increases (on the rightwards-moving soldier) or decreases (on the leftwards-moving soldier).

Notice that salient objects leave a streak behind them in the salience imagery. This is because the salience of a pixel location persists indefinitely until it is reset by a direction reversal. This policy has the benefit that it allows the salience measure to be largely unaffected by variations in the object velocity, even if the object comes to a stop. The trail could even be useful for further analysis or display of the object's history. On the other hand, in applications where objects paths cross or where an accurate delineation of the object is desired, further techniques can be applied to cause the trail to decay where it does not lie on the salient object. This will be discussed further below.

The magnitude of the salience is shown in Column 4. Over all the frames in the sequence, the salience magnitude found on the vegetation is no more than 55. In the first frame shown, (frame 37), the salience magnitude of the object is 31, so it would not yet be distinguishable from vegetation by thresholding. But by the second frame (frame 70), its salience magnitude is 60. Until this point in the sequence, the salience has increased slowly compared to the actual distance traveled by the object (160 pixels). This is because the object is so small that it is difficult to extract reliable flow vectors and so the flow vector extension is being used heavily, which does not increase salience. After frame 70, however, the object increases slightly in size and flow can be more reliably computed, so salience increases directly in proportion to the distance traveled. By the time the object reaches its leftmost position in the final frame (frame 150), its salience is 140. A second object also becomes visible, moving leftwards, in the third frame (frame 113). Its salience increases rapidly, since its flow is reliable. (The small linear extension protruding ahead of the object is the person's shadow on the ground.)

Figure 4 provides more examples of the algorithm on three other sequences. *Identical algorithm parameters were used for all four sequences.* In the top example, a person walks right to left while a fan blows the leaves of a potted plant at the left side of the image. The largest computed salience magnitude on the leaves was 25, while that of the person quickly rises with the distance traveled. In the frame shown, the person has traveled approximately 150 pixels and the typical salience of a pixel on the person is 140.

In the middle example a person walks upper-left to lower-right against a background of gently-swaying tree branches. The largest computed salience magnitude on the branches was 14, while that of the person rises quickly. In the frame shown, the person has traveled 126 pixels and his salience is approximately 122.

In the bottom example a person walks top to bottom while the branches on the tree sway violently in a strong wind. Furthermore, a car is visible for a brief period in the upper left corner as it moves from behind the tree and off the top edge of the frame. The largest computed salience magnitude on the tree was 35. Again, the salience of the person and vehicle rises quickly. In the frame shown, the person has traveled 48 pixels and his salience is approximately 45. His salience increases further as he travels further in subsequent frames.

5 Temporal decay

As noted above, salient objects leave a streak behind them in the salience image. In many applications, it may be desirable to add a mechanism that allows the salience to either decay gradually over time or rapidly be set to 0 once the object has moved past. For example, this might be desirable if one wished to use the salience magnitude to delineate the object. The appropriate approach depends on the application. Here we report one possible mechanism, whose goal is to reset the salience of a pixel to 0 when the moving object no longer is imaged in the pixel.

We achieve this goal by determining, for each pixel $\mathbf{p}$, whether there exists another pixel $\mathbf{p}'$ within some distance k_d whose frame-to-frame flow magnitude exceeds that of $\mathbf{p}$ by more than some factor k_a. If so, then $\mathbf{S}_j(\mathbf{p})$ and $\mathbf{M}_j(\mathbf{p})$ are reset to $\mathbf{0}$ before the next new frame is processed. The intuition behind this scheme is that if there is nearby motion that is substantially larger than the motion at this pixel, then this this is likely to have happened because the object has moved off this image pixel.

This approach usually gives good results (see the bottom two examples in Figure 4). However, there are some scenarios where it does not suffice. Consider, for example, an intruder crawling slowly beneath waving tree limbs. The proximity to the tree limbs might result in the suppression of the intruder's salience. Obviously, there exist a gamut of variations that might be appropriate, such as basing the reset on whether the salience at $\mathbf{p}$ changes by some amount within a user-specified time window.

6 Discussion

This paper has outlined a salience measure that at each pixel is based on the straight-line distance that the pixel has moved in a consistent direction. Our examples have shown that objects moving in a straight line rapidly take on salience magnitudes that are significantly larger than that of vegetation. This suggests that for surveillance tasks, it might be possible to trigger a detection alarm at a pixel when the magnitude of its salience exceeds a threshold, and that it will be possible to choose a threshold that results in significantly fewer false positives than more conventional change detection schemes. This threshold would be based on the expected amount of side-to-side movement of vegetation in the scene. Alternatively, other more sophisticated analysis techniques might be applied to the salience "trails" left by objects.

The algorithm has some further advantages. It does not need to explictly detect and track hypothetical targets to assess their salience. It does not make assumptions about the size or intensity contrast of salient objects. Because it uses multi-resolution optical flow it is applicable to a broad range of image velocities, and can even handle image stops. Of course, it still is possible for salient objects to move either so slowly or so quickly that the flow is not reliable. To handle very slow-moving objects, it may be necessary to select among various temporal scales when computing flow. However, in surveillance scenarios involving objects that move by only a small fraction of a pixel per frame, shape change as recovered from stereo [7] is a more appropriate cue than motion.

The algorithm also has some weaknesses. An object that moves in a straight line but oscillates forwards and backwards, such as taking two steps forward and then one backward would have low salience. Again, in surveillance scenarios where subjects are actively trying to fool the salience measure, it is probably necessary to supplement this motion-based method with a shape-based method such as stereo. Another issue is computational expense. However, this issue is only temporary; as flow-warping hardware becomes widely available, the salience computation will rapidly become tractable.

Finally, optical flow has received widespread criticism as being inaccurate and error-prone. However, our results show that it can nonetheless be used to define effective salience measures. Future work, therefore, may examine its use in other grouping measures, such as those of Williams [21].

References

[1] C.H. Anderson, P.J. Burt, and G.S. van der Wal. Change detection and tracking using pyramid transform techniques. In *SPIE Vol. 579 - Intelligent Robots and Computer Vision*, pages 72–78, 1985.

[2] James R. Bergen, P. Anandan, Keith J. Hanna, and Rajesh Hingorani. Hierarchical model-based motion estimation. In *Proceedings of the European Conference on Computer Vision*, 1992.

[3] T. Boult, R. Michaels, A. Kerkan, P. Lewis, C. Powers, C. Qian, and W. Yin. Frame-rate multi-body tracking for surveillance. In *Proceedings of the DARPA Image Understanding Workshop*, 1998.

[4] P. J. Burt, J. R. Bergen, R. Hingorani, R. Kolczynski, W. A. Lee, A. Leung, J. Lubin, and H. Shvaytser. Object tracking with a moving camera: An application of dynamic motion analysis. In *Proceedings of the IEEE Workshop on Motion*, March 1989.

[5] J. Craig. *Introduction to Robotics: Mechanics and Control.* Addison-Wesley, 1989.

[6] R. Cutler and L. Davis. View-based detection and analysis of periodic motion. In *International Conference on Pattern Recognition*, 1998.

[7] C. Eveland and K. Konolige. Background modeling for segmentation of video-rate stereo sequences. In *IEEE*

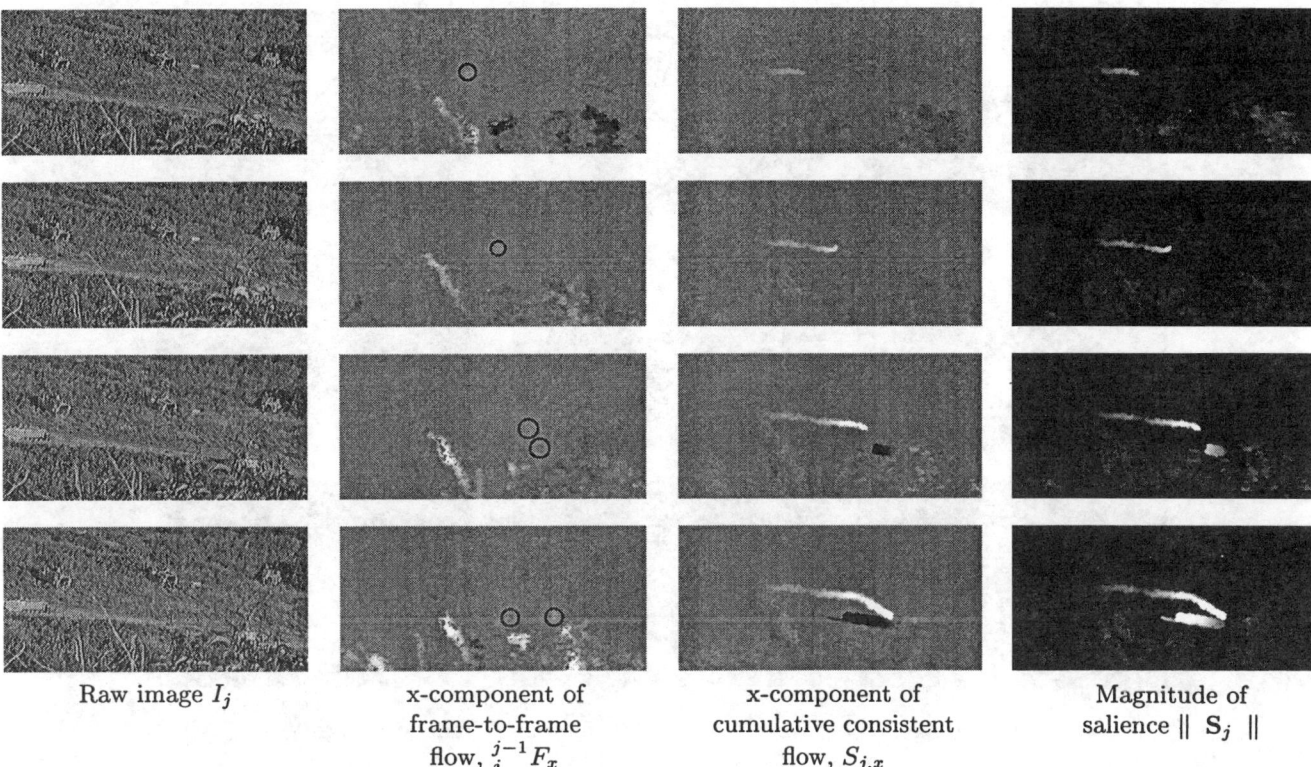

Raw image I_j	x-component of frame-to-frame flow, $_j^{j-1}F_x$	x-component of cumulative consistent flow, $S_{j,x}$	Magnitude of salience $\| \mathbf{S}_j \|$

Figure 3. Illustrative example of salience detection on four frames from a challenging video sequence, proceeding temporally downward. The center two columns contain signed imagery, so medium gray represents 0. Column 2 contains the x-component of the frame-to-frame flow (after zeroing of those flow vectors that fail the forwards-backwards check). The frame-to-frame flow corresponding to the salient objects (people at a distance) has been circled. Clearly the people cannot be distinguished from the foreground clutter on the basis of their size or their frame-to-frame flow magnitude. See text for details.

Conference on Computer Vision and Pattern Recognition, 1998.

[8] P. Fua. A parallel stereo algorithm that produces dense depth maps and preserves image features. *Machine Vision and Applications*, 6 (1), 1993.

[9] W.E.L. Grimson, C. Stauffer, R. Romano, and L. Lee. Using adaptive tracking to classify and monitor activities in a site. In *IEEE Conference on Computer Vision and Pattern Recognition*, 1998.

[10] G. Halevi and D. Weinshall. Motion of disturbances: Detection and tracking of multi-body non-rigid motion. In *IEEE Conference on Computer Vision and Pattern Recognition*, 1997.

[11] A. Lipton, H. Fujiyoshi, and R. Patil. Moving target classification and tracking from real-time video. In *Workshop on Applications of Computer Vision*, 1998.

[12] James J. Little and Walter E. Gillett. Direct evidence for occlusion in stereo and motion. In *Proceedings of the European Conference on Computer Vision*, 1990.

[13] F. Liu and R. Picard. Finding periodicity in space and time. In *Proceedings of the International Conference on Computer Vision*, 1998.

[14] B.D. Lucas and T. Kanade. An iterative image registration technique with an application to stereo. In *DARPA Image Understanding Workshop*, 1981.

[15] F. Meyer and P. Bouthemy. Region-based tracking using affine motion models in long image sequences. *CVGIP : Image Understanding*, 60(2), September 1994.

[16] S. Niyogi and E. Adelson. Analyzing and recognizing walking figures in xyt. In *IEEE Conference on Computer Vision and Pattern Recognition*, 1994.

[17] R Pless, T. Brodsky, and Y. Aloimonos. Independent motion: The importance of history. In *IEEE Conference on Computer Vision and Pattern Recognition*, 1999.

[18] Joseph Weber and Jitendra Malik. Robust computation of optical flow in a multi-scale differential frame-

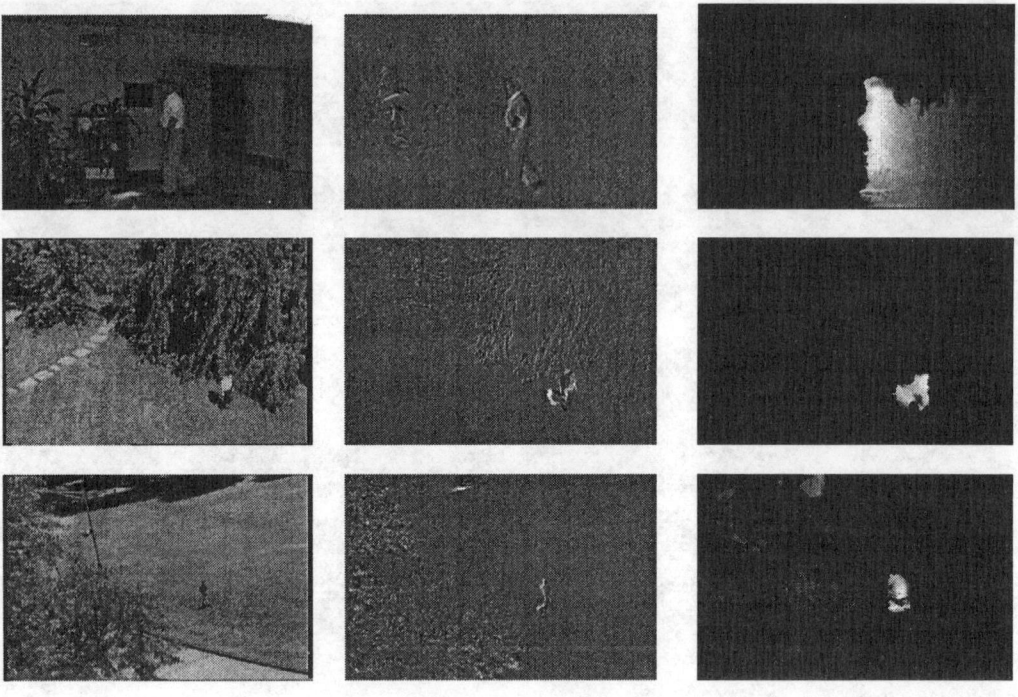

Example raw image.　　　Frame-to-frame difference.　　Salience magnitude, $\| \mathbf{S}_j \|$

Figure 4. Salience measures from three other video sequences. The bottom two rows contain the salience magnitude after supressing the salience trails, as described in Section 5.

work. In *Proceedings of the International Conference on Computer Vision*, 1993.

[19] R. Wildes. A measure of motion salience for surveillance applications. In *IEEE International Conference on Image Processing*, 1998.

[20] R. Wildes and L. Wixson. Detecting salient motion using spatiotemporal filters and optical flow. In *Proceedings of the DARPA Image Understanding Workshop*, 1998.

[21] L. Williams and K. Thornber. A comparison of measures for detecting natural shapes in cluttered backgrounds. In *Proceedings of the European Conference on Computer Vision*, 1998.

[22] G. Wolberg. *Digital Image Warping*. IEEE Computer Society Press, 1992.

[23] C. Wren, A. Azarbayejani, T. Darrell, and A. Pentland. Pfinder: Real-time tracking of the human body. *IEEE Transactions on Pattern Analysis and Machine Intelligence*, 19, July 1997.

[24] S. Yalamanchili, W.N. Martin, and J.K. Aggarwal. Extraction of moving object descriptions via differencing. *Computer Graphics and Image Processing*, 18:188–201, February 1982.

Monocular Perception of Biological Motion - Detection and Labeling

Yang Song[†], Luis Goncalves[†], Enrico Di Bernardo[†] and Pietro Perona[††]

† California Institute of Technology, 136-93, Pasadena, CA 9112 5, USA

‡ Università di Padova, Italy

{yangs,luis,dibe,perona}@vision.caltech.edu

Abstract

Computer perception of biological motion is key to developing convenient and powerful human-computer interfaces. Successful body tracking algorithms have been developed; however, initialization is done by hand. We propose a method for detecting a moving human body and for labeling its parts automatically. It is based on maximizing the joint probability density function (PDF) of the position and velocity of the body parts. The PDF is estimated from training data. Dynamic programming is used for calculating efficiently the best global labeling on an approximation of the PDF. The computational cost is on the order of N^4 where N is the number of features detected.

We explore the performance of our method with experiments carried on a variety of periodic and non-periodic body motions viewed monocularly for a total of approximately 30,000 frames. Point-markers were strapped to the joints of the subject for facilitating image analysis. We find an average of 2.3% labeling error; the experiments also suggest a high degree of viewpoint-invariance.

1. Introduction

Being able to extract the position and motion of humans ('biological motion' in the literature of human vision) from images is very useful for human social interactions and is a most important technology for developing convenient and effective human-computer interfaces. Our visual system has developed a very strong ability in perceiving biological motion, even from monocular low resolution noisy data, e.g. NTSC television.

A striking demonstration of the capabilities of the human visual system is provided by the experiments of Johansson [8]. In his experiments, Johansson demonstrated that biological motion may be accurately perceived even from very poor data. We postulate that this is true because the degrees of freedom of the problem are highly constrained, both by the kinematics and dynamics of the body, and, more importantly, by the fact that humans move in stereotypical and predictable ways. *It is our belief that defining and estimating perceptual models of human motion is the key to automating biological motion perception.*

Much progress has been made recently in tracking the human body [12, 11, 6, 2, 7, 4] under a number of conditions: static background, periodic motion, stereo-scopic vision, hand-initialization. In all these schemes the body is segmented into parts which are independently tracked – the final estimate is obtained by enforcing the body's kinematic constraints and simple statistical models of motion (e.g. first order random walks). No use is made of dynamic and/or perceptual models of body motion. We believe that in order to achieve self-initializing trackers that will work against unmodelled backgrounds in the presence of general motions of the human body, models of how the body 'tends to move' have to be used.

In this paper we address the problem of defining and estimating a perceptual model of biological motion and use it for detecting the human body and labeling it in monocular image sequences. By 'labeling' we mean assigning to each region in the image a label that corresponds to the body part (shoulder, elbow etc) that is imaged in that region. We choose not to address the issue of detecting and classifying pictorial features that are associated to the body parts – for the time being this has been sufficiently explored by [1, 9, 5, 10]. Therefore our experimental setup is identical to Johansson's experiments: we suppose that a number of markers are attached to the body of an actor. At every frame we need to attach labels to a subset of the features (some may be caused by noise; some may have been missed). We approach the problem as a learning problem: we observe the subject moving about in order to estimate a model of his/her stereotypical motions. This model, which we formulate as the joint probability density function (PDF) of the position and motion of the body, is used to select the best labeling.

2. Approach and Notation

We choose to characterize body pose and motion by the joint probability density of the position and velocity of its parts. Our goal is to interpret monocular image sequences, hence we use part position and velocity in the image plane (Figure 1). In our Johansson scenario each part appears as a single dot (marker) in the image plane. Therefore its iden-

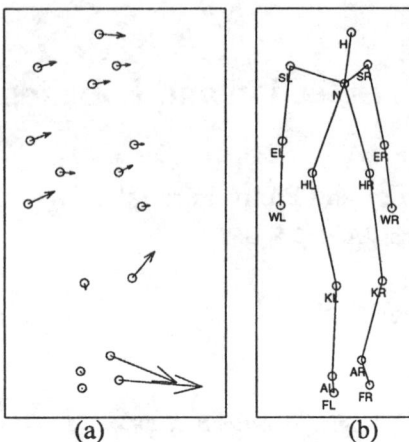

Figure 1: **The labeling problem:** Given the position and velocity of body parts in the image plane (a), we use a probabilistic model to assign the correct labels to the body parts (b). 'L' and 'R' in label names indicate left and right. H:head, N:neck, S:shoulder, E:elbow, W:wrist, H:hip, K:knee, A:ankle and F:foot.

tity is not revealed by cues other than its relative position and velocity.

Let $V = \{v_1, \ldots, v_m\}$ be the set of candidate markers in an image. Let $\mathcal{L} = \{L_1, L_2, \ldots, L_N\}$ be the set of N labels representing body parts such as head, neck, left elbow, etc. Since candidate markers can be wrongly detected, and some body parts may be missing due to occlusion, m is not always equal to N. If we assume that there are no missing points, then $N \leq m$. Therefore, the labeling problem is to find the mapping $f : \mathcal{L} \longrightarrow V$ such that $f(L_i) \neq f(L_j)$ for $i \neq j$ and the $Prob\{body\ part\ L_i\ is\ in\ marker\ f(L_i), 1 \leq i \leq N\}$ is maximized.

Three problems face us at this point: (a) What is the structure for the probability/likelihood function to be maximized? (b) How do we estimate its parameters? (c) How do we address the combinatorial search problem of finding the optimal labeling? Problems (a) and (c) need to be addressed together: the structure of the probability density function must be such that it allows efficient optimization.

A brute force solution to the optimization problem is to search exhaustively among all $(m)_N \overset{\text{def}}{=} m * (m - 1) * \cdots * (m - N + 1)$ possible f's and find the best one. The search cost is exponential with respect to N. Assume $N = m = 16$ (this is the case without missing points and wrong detections), then the number of possible mappings is 2×10^{13} which is computationally prohibitive.

It is useful to notice that the body is a kinematic chain: the wrist is connected to the body indirectly via the elbow and the shoulder. It is a reasonable approximation to assume that the position and the motion of the wrist are, therefore, independent of the position and velocity of the rest of the body once the position and velocity of elbow and shoulder are known. This intuition may be generalized to the whole body: once the position and velocity of a set S of body parts is known, the behavior of the body parts above and below (left and right) of S is independent. This approximation of course needs to be validated experimentally.

Our intuition on how to decompose the problem may be expressed in the language of probability: consider the joint probability function of 5 random variables $P(ABCDE)$. It may be expressed as $P(ABCDE) = P(ABC)P(D|ABC)P(E|ABCD)$. If these random variables are conditionally independent as described in the graph of Figure 3, then

$$P(ABCDE) = P(ABC)P(D|BC)P(E|CD) \qquad (1)$$

Thus, if the body parts can satisfy the appropriate conditional independence conditions, we can express the joint probability density of the pose and velocity of all parts as the product of conditional probability densities of n-tuplets. This approximation makes the optimization step computationally efficient as will be discussed below.

What is the best decomposition for the human body? What is a reasonable size n of the groups of body parts? We hope to make n as small as possible to minimize the cost of the optimization. But as n gets smaller, conditional independence may not be a reasonable approximation any longer. There is a tradeoff between computational cost and algorithm performance. In this paper we use models with $n = 3$ as described in Figure 2. Optimization on triangulated graphs such as these may be efficiently performed using Dynamic Programming [13].

Estimation of the conditional probability densities from training data and the dynamic programming algorithm are described in the next section.

3. Algorithms

We characterize each triplet $\{L_i, L_j, L_k\} \subset \mathcal{L}$ (corresponding to one triangle in Figure 2) with a 10-dimensional feature vector

$$X = (v_{ix}, v_{jx}, v_{kx}, v_{iy}, v_{jy}, v_{ky}, p_{ix}, p_{kx}, p_{iy}, p_{ky}) \qquad (2)$$

The first three dimensions of X are the x-direction (horizontal) velocity of body parts (L_i, L_j, L_k) , the next three are the velocity in the y-direction (vertical), and the last four dimensions are the positions of body parts L_i and L_k relative to L_j. If the data are normalized for scale, it would be reasonable and convenient to assume that X is jointly Gaussian-distributed. Then

$$
\begin{aligned}
p(L_i, L_j, L_k) &= p(X) \\
&= \frac{\exp[-\frac{1}{2}(X - \bar{X})^T \Sigma^{-1} (X - \bar{X})]}{(2\pi)^{d/2}|\Sigma|^{1/2}} \\
&= \frac{\exp[-\frac{1}{2}\sum_i \frac{Y_i^2}{\lambda_i}]}{(2\pi)^{d/2}\prod_i \lambda_i^{1/2}} \qquad (3)
\end{aligned}
$$

where $\bar{X}$ is the mean value of X; Σ is the covariance matrix of X; d is the dimensionality of X ($d = 10$ here); $Y = \Phi^T(X - \bar{X})$; Φ is the unitary eigenvector matrix of Σ; and $\Lambda = diag(\lambda_1, \lambda_2, \ldots, \lambda_{10})$ is the corresponding diagonal matrix of eigenvalues [3]. Φ and Λ can be obtained from singular value decomposition (SVD) of the training set. After the joint probability is computed, the conditional one can be obtained accordingly:

$$p(L_i | L_j, L_k) = \frac{p(L_i, L_j, L_k)}{p(L_j, L_k)} \qquad (4)$$

where $p(L_j, L_k)$ can be obtained by estimating the joint probability of the vector $\{v_{jx}, v_{kx}, v_{jy}, v_{ky}, p_{kx}, p_{ky}\}$.

Suppose there are m markers available for a frame, then for each triangle in Figure 2, we can compute the (conditional) probabilities of all possible $(m)_3$ combinations of markers and rank them. The bigger the probability is, the more likely they are the right markers for the triangle.

If out of all the possible combinations the one with the correct markers always produces the highest probability, the labeling problem can be solved easily by picking the highest ranked combination for each triangle individually. In practice, since the data are noisy and we only have available an approximation of the true probability density functions, this will not work. In fact, since all triangles share at least one edge (and thus two vertices) with at least one other triangle, picking the top combination for each triangle individually won't even produce a consistent set of labels. What is needed is an algorithm that will search through all the legal labelings and find the one that maximizes the global joint probability. By the decomposition in equation (1), we know that dynamic programming can be used to solve this problem efficiently. The key condition for using dynamic programming is that the problem exhibits optimal substructure, namely, if equation (1) holds, then

$$\max_{A,B,C,D,E} P(ABCDE) = \max_{A,B,C}(P(ABC) \cdot \max_D(P(D|BC) \cdot \max_E P(E|CD)))$$

If we take the probability as the cost function, a dynamic programming method similar to that described in [13] can be used, which requires the triangulated body graph to be decomposable. If all the cliques in a graph are of size three, then the decomposable property means that there always exists a free vertex to delete and the remaining subgraph is again a collection of triangles until only one triangle is left. A vertex is free when it is only contained in one triangle. Figure 2 shows two decomposable graphs of the whole body, along with the order of successive elimination of cliques.

If the decomposed body graph is decomposable and the corresponding conditional independence holds, then,

$$p(L_1, L_2, \cdots, L_N) = \prod_{t=1}^{N-3} p(l_t | a_t b_t) p(l_{N-2} l_{N-1} l_N) \qquad (5)$$

where $(l_1, l_2, \ldots, l_{N-3})$ are the body parts to be deleted in order in stage $t = 1, 2, \ldots, N-3$; (l_{N-2}, l_{N-1}, l_N) is the triangle in the final stage $T = N - 2$; and $(a_t b_t)$ are the two vertices connected to l_t when l_t is deleted. Let

$$\Psi_t(l_t, a_t, b_t) = -\log p(l_t | a_t b_t), \ for \ 1 \leq t \leq T-1 \qquad (6)$$
$$\Psi_t(l_t, a_t, b_t) = -\log p(l_{N-2}, l_{N-1}, l_N), \ for \ t = T \qquad (7)$$

be the cost function associate with each triangle.The dynamic programming algorithm can be described as follows:

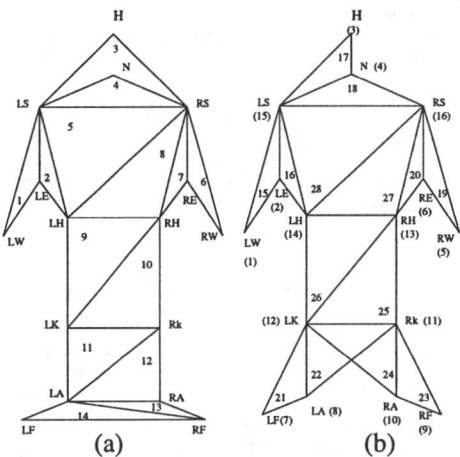

Figure 2: **Two decompositions of the human body into triangles.** The label names are the same as in Figure 1. The numbers inside triangles give the index of triangles used in the experiments. In (a) they are also the order in which the vertices are deleted. In (b) the numbers in brackets show the order.

Stage 1: for every pair (a_1, b_1),

Compute $\quad \Psi_1(l_1, a_1, b_1) \quad$ for all possible l_1,

Store $\quad \begin{cases} l_{1[a_1,b_1]}^* \\ \Psi_1(l_{1[a_1,b_1]}^*, a_1, b_1) \end{cases}$

where $\quad l_{1[a_1,b_1]}^* \quad$ minimizes $\quad \Psi_1(l_1, a_1, b_1)$

Stage t, $2 \leq t \leq T$: for every pair (a_t, b_t),

Compute $\quad \Psi_t(l_t, a_t, b_t) \quad$ for all possible l_t

Compute the total cost so far (till stage t):

– Let $\quad T_t(l_t, a_t, b_t) = \Psi_t(l_t, a_t, b_t) \quad$ the total cost so far

– If edge $\quad (l_t, a_t) \quad$ is contained in a previous stage and τ is the latest such stage, add the cost $T_\tau(l_{\tau[l_t,a_t]}^*, l_t, a_t)$ (or $T_\tau(l_{\tau[a_t,l_t]}^*, a_t, l_t)$ if the edge was reversed) to $T_t(l_t, a_t, b_t)$

– Likewise, add the cost of the latest previous stage containing edges (l_t, b_t) and edges (a_t, b_t) to $T_t(l_t, a_t, b_t)$

Store $\quad \begin{cases} l_{t[a_t,b_t]}^* \\ T_t(l_{t[a_t,b_t]}^*, a_t, b_t) \end{cases}$

where $\quad l_{t[a_t,b_t]}^* \quad$ minimizes $\quad T_t(l_t, a_t, b_t)$

When stage T calculation is complete, $T_T(l_{T[a_T,b_T]}^*, a_T, b_T)$ includes the value of each Ψ_t, $1 \leq t \leq T$, exactly once. Since the Ψ_t's are the logs of conditional (and joint) probabilities, then

$$T_T(l_{T[a_T,b_T]}^*, a_T, b_T)$$
$$= -\log(\text{joint probability density of the entire graph})$$

Thus picking the pair (a_T, b_T) that minimizes T_T automatically maximizes the joint probability.

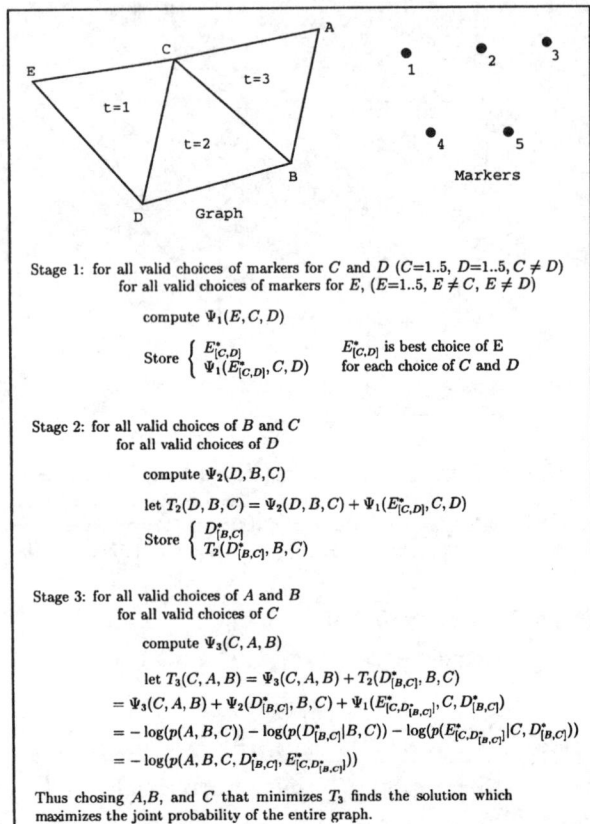

Stage 1: for all valid choices of markers for C and D ($C=1..5$, $D=1..5$, $C \neq D$)
     for all valid choices of markers for E, ($E=1..5$, $E \neq C$, $E \neq D$)

     compute $\Psi_1(E,C,D)$

     Store $\begin{cases} E^*_{[C,D]} & E^*_{[C,D]} \text{ is best choice of E} \\ \Psi_1(E^*_{[C,D]},C,D) & \text{for each choice of } C \text{ and } D \end{cases}$

Stage 2: for all valid choices of B and C
     for all valid choices of D

     compute $\Psi_2(D,B,C)$

     let $T_2(D,B,C) = \Psi_2(D,B,C) + \Psi_1(E^*_{[C,D]},C,D)$

     Store $\begin{cases} D^*_{[B,C]} \\ T_2(D^*_{[B,C]},B,C) \end{cases}$

Stage 3: for all valid choices of A and B
     for all valid choices of C

     compute $\Psi_3(C,A,B)$

     let $T_3(C,A,B) = \Psi_3(C,A,B) + T_2(D^*_{[B,C]},B,C)$
     $= \Psi_3(C,A,B) + \Psi_2(D^*_{[B,C]},B,C) + \Psi_1(E^*_{[C,D^*_{[B,C]}]},C,D^*_{[B,C]})$
     $= -\log(p(A,B,C)) - \log(p(D^*_{[B,C]}|B,C)) - \log(p(E^*_{[C,D^*_{[B,C]}]}|C,D^*_{[B,C]}))$
     $= -\log(p(A,B,C,D^*_{[B,C]},E^*_{[C,D^*_{[B,C]}]}))$

Thus chosing A,B, and C that minimizes T_3 finds the solution which maximizes the joint probability of the entire graph.

Figure 3: **An example of dynamic programming algorithm applied to a simple graph**

The best labeling can now be found tracing back through each stage: the best (a_T, b_T) determines l^*_T, then the latest previous stages with edge respectively (l^*_T, a_T), (l^*_T, b_T), and/or (a_T, b_T) determine more labels and so forth.

A simple example of this algorithm is shown in Figure 3.

The above algorithm is computationally efficient. Assume N is the number of body part labels and m is the number of candidate markers, then the total number of stages is $T = N - 2$ and in each stage the computation cost is $\mathcal{O}(m^3)$. Thus, the complexity of the whole algorithm is on the order of $N * m^3$.

4. Experiments

We trained our model and tested the performance of the algorithm on data obtained filming a subject moving freely in 3D; 16 light bulbs were strapped to the main joints of the subject's body. In order to obtain ground-truth the data were first acquired, reconstructed and labeled in 3D using a 4-camera motion capture system operating at a rate of 60 samples/sec. Since our goal is to detect and label the body directly in the camera image plane, a generic camera view was simulated by orthographic projection of the 3D marker coordinates. In the following sections we will indicate with viewing angle the azimuth viewing angle: a value of 0 degrees will correspond to a right-side view, a

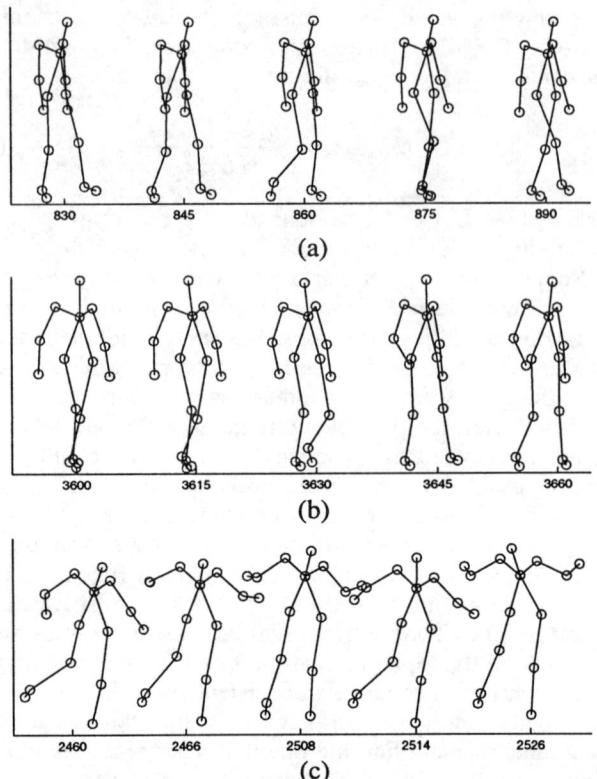

Figure 4: **Sample frames** for the **(a)** walking sequence W3; **(b)** happy walking sequence HW; **(c)** dancing sequence DA. The nubmers on the horizontal axes are the frame numbers.

value of 90 to a frontal view of the subject. Five sequences were acquired each around 2 minutes long. In the next sections they will be referred as follows: Sequences W1 (7000 frames), W2 (7000 frames): relaxed walking forward and backwards along almost straight paths (with ±20 degree deviations in heading); W3 (5305 frames): relaxed walking, with the subject turning around now and then (Figure 4(a)); Sequence HW (5210 frames): walking in a happy mood, moving the head, arms, hips more actively (Figure 4(b)); Sequence DA (3497 frames): dancing and jumping (Figure 4(c)), with the subject moving his legs and arms freely and much faster than in the previous four sequences. Given that the data were acquired from the same subject and that orthographic projection was used to simulate a camera view, our data were already normalized in scale. The velocity of each candidate marker was obtained by substracting the positions in two consecutive frames.

Among the above five sequences, walking sequences W1 and W2 are the relatively simple ones, so W1 and W2 were first used to test the validity of the probability model and the performance of two possible body decompositions (Figure 2). Since the heading direction of W1 and W2 was roughly along a line, performance under changing viewing angles was also investigated. Then experiments were conducted using W3, HW and DA to see how the model worked for more violent and non-periodic motions.

4.1. Detection of individual triangles

In this section, the performance of the probabilistic model for individual triangles is examined. In the training phase, the joint Gaussian parameters (mean and covariance) for each triangle in Figure 2 were estimated from walking sequence W1. In the test phase, for each frame in W2, each triangle probability was evaluated for all possible combinations of markers ($16 \times 15 \times 14$ different combinations). Ideally, the correct combination of markers should produce the highest probability for each respective triangle. Otherwise, an error occured. Figure 5(a) shows how well each triangle's joint probability model detects the correct set of markers. Figure 5(b) shows a similar result for the conditional probability densities of triangles, where for each triangle conditional probability density $p(L_i|L_j, L_k)$, we computed the probability of L_i for all the possible markers (14 choices), given the correct choice of markers for L_j and L_k. Figure 5 shows that the Gaussian model is very good for most triangles (in the joint case, if a triangle is chosen randomly, then the chance of getting the correct one is 3×10^{-4} and the probability models do much better than that).

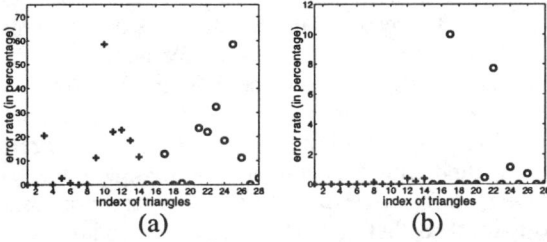

Figure 5: **Local model error rates** (percentage of frames for which the correct choice of markers did not maximize each individual triangle probability). Triangle indices are those of the two graph models of Figure 2. '+': results for decomposition Figure 2(a); 'o': results for decomposition Figure 2(b). **(a)** joint probability model **(b)** conditional probability model

It is not surprising that the performance of some triplets is much worse than others. The worst triangles in Figure 5(a) are those with left and right knees, which makes sense because the two knees are so close in some frames that it is even hard for human eyes to distinguish between them. Therefore, it is also hard for the probability model to make the correct choice.

Further investigation of the behavior of the triangle probabilities revealed that, for frames in which the correct choice of markers did not maximize a triangle probability, that probability was nevertheless quite close to the maximal value. Figure 6 shows the ratio of the probabilities of the correct choice over the maximizing choice for the two worst behaving triangles, over the set of frames where the errors occured. Figure6(a) shows the ratio of the joint probability distribution for triangle 10 (consisting of right hip, left knee, and right knee, as in figure 2(a)). Figure 6(b) shows the ratio of the conditional probability distribution for triangle 17 (head, neck, and left shoulder). Although these two triangles had the highest error rates, the correct marker com-

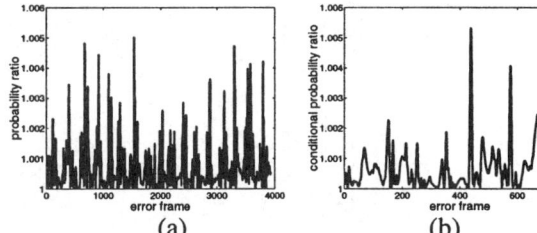

Figure 6: **probability ratio (correct markers vs. the solution with the highest probability when an error happens.)** The horizontal axis is the index of frames where error happens. **(a)** joint probability ratio for triangle 10 or 25 (RH, LK, RK) **(b)** conditional probability ratio for triangle 17 (H, N, LS)

bination was always very close to being the highest ranking, always less than a factor of 1.006 away. This is a good indication that the individual triangle probability models encode the distribution quite well.

4.2. Performance of different body graphs

We did experiments on the two decompositions in Figure 2. The training sequence W1 and the test sequence W2 were under the same viewing angle: 45 degrees, which is between the side view and the front view. Table 1 shows the results. The *frame-by-frame error* is the percentage of frames in which errors occurred, and *label-by-label error* is the percentage of markers wrongly labeled out of all the markers in all the testing frames. Label-by-label error is smaller than frame-by-frame error because an error in a frame does not mean all the markers are wrongly labeled.

decomposition model	(a)	(b)
frame-by-frame error	0.27%	13.13%
label-by-label error	0.06%	1.61%

Table 1: **Error rate using the models in Figure 2**

The performance of the algorithm using the decomposition of Figure 2(a) is almost perfect and much better than that of (b), which is consistent with our expectation (by Figure 5, the local performance of decomposition Figure 2(a) is better than that of Figure 2(b)). We used the better model in the rest of the experiments.

4.3. Viewpoint invariance

In the previous sections the viewing angle for training and for testing was the same. Here we explore the behavior of the method when the testing viewing angle is different from that used during training. Figure 7 shows the results of three such experiments where walking sequence W1 was used as the training set and W2 as the test set .

The solid line in Figure 7(a) shows the percentage of frames labeled correctly when the training was done at a viewing angle of 90 degrees (subject facing the camera) and the testing viewing angle was varied from 0 degrees (right

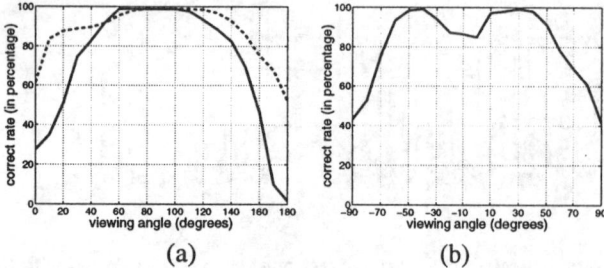

(a)   (b)

Figure 7: **Labeling performance as a function of viewing angle.** (a) Solid line : percentage of correctly labeled frames as a function of viewing angle, when the training was done at 90 degrees (frontal view). Dashed line: training was done by combining data from views at 30, 90, and 150 degrees. (b) Labeling performance when the training was done at 0 degrees (right side view of walker). The dip in performance near 0 degrees is due to the fact that from a side view orthographic projection without inter-body occlusions it is almost impossible to distinguish left and right.

side view) to 180 degrees (left side view) in increments of 10 degrees. When the viewing angle was between 60 to 120 degrees almost all frames were labeled correctly, thus showing that the probabilistic model learned at 90 degrees is insensitive to changes in viewpoint by up to 30 degrees.

The solid line in Figure 7(b) shows the results of a similar experiment where the training viewpoint was at 0 degrees (right side view) and the testing angle was varied from -90 degrees (back view) to 90 degrees (front view) in 10 degree increments. A noticeable dip in the performance centered around 0 degrees is visible in the plot. Inspection of the errors which occurred at these viewing angles revealed that they consisted solely of confusions between homologous left-right leg parts ; i.e., the two hips were sometimes confused, as were the knees, the ankles, and the feet. Considering that an orthographic projection of the 3-D data was used to create the 2-D views, this result is not surprising; given an orthographic side view of a person walking (with no intra-body occlusions) a person viewing the motion is unable to distinguish the left and right sides of the body. Thus, modulo this left-right ambiguity, the model learned at 0 degrees viewing angle is insensitive to changes in viewpoint of up to 40 degrees.

The dashed line in Figure 7(a) shows the results of an experiment to try to increase the invariance of the probabilistic model with respect to changes in viewpoint. The same 3-D training sequence was used to generate three 2-D data sequences with viewing angles at 30, 90, and 150 degrees. The three 2-D sequences were combined, and used all together to learn the probability density functions of the graph triangles. As shown in the plot, this procedure does in fact improve the labeling accuracy. At 0 degrees, the only errors were the above mentioned left-right ambiguity within the legs. Between 10 and 60 degrees, besides left-right errors, also the feet and ankles were confused. From 120 to 180 degrees, the errors once again consisted solely of swapped left and right body parts.

4.4. Performance with different motions

The previous sections show that for simple motions very good results can be achieved using the probabilistic model. Here we want to investigate how the method works for more general sets of motions. We did experiments on walk sequence W3, happy walking sequence HW and dancing sequence DA. Each sequence was divided into four segments for a total of twelve segments. To test a segment, frames from all the other eleven segments were used as the training set. The error rates for different sequences are obtained by averaging the results of the corresponding segments.

test set	ALL	W3	HW	DA
frame error	6.81%	3.02%	4.49%	15.95%
label error	0.69%	0.38%	0.50%	1.45%

Table 2: **Error rates for different sequences.** Frame error means *frame-by-frame error* and label error means *label-by-label error*. ALL: average over all three sequences; W3:walking sequence; HW: walking in happy mood; DA: dancing sequence

Table 2 shows the error rates for different sequences. The first column is the average result for all the three sequences, and the next three columns show the error rates for walking sequence W3, happy walking sequence HW and dancing sequence DA respectively. The results for walking sequence W3 and happy walking sequence HW are very good, with *frame-by-frame error* less than 5% and *label-by-label error* no more than 0.5%. It is not surprising that the error rates of dancing sequence are higher than the walking sequences because the motions in the dancing sequence are more random and agitated and therefore it is harder to model. Another possible reason is that the dancing sequence is shorter than the other sequences, so the motion of dancing has relatively less weight in the training set.

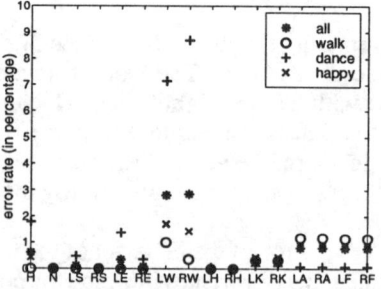

Figure 8: **Error rates for individual body parts.** 'L' and 'R' in label names indicate left and right. H:head, N:neck, S:shoulder, E:elbow, W:wrist, H:hip, K:knee,A:ankle and F:foot.

Figure 8 shows the error rates of each individual body part for each of the sequences. Notice that most errors occur at the left and right wrist (LW and RW) in the dancing sequence. This is because in the dancing sequence wrists are very close to hips in some frames, and the program wrongly took hips as wrists. The reason why the program wouldn't take wrists as hips is that hips have better motion constraints than wrists. In our decomposed body graph Figure 2(a), both left and right hip (LH and RH) appear in five triangles, but the wrists (LW and RW) are only in one triangle each.

5. Dealing with missing body parts

The labeling method discussed so far assumed that all body parts were detected. However, when dealing with real images, this is not always true. As a first step towards being able to handle missing data, we extended our algorithm to the case where individual triplets may have up to one marker missing. This is done by adding a new special point v_0 (that represents a missing marker) to the set of candidate markers. The definition of joint and conditional probability density for the triplets is extended to include the case where one of the body parts is the missing marker v_0.

Consider the generic triplet (L_1, L_2, L_3). Let $\bar{q}_m$ denote L_m $missing$, and q_m denote L_m $present$ for $m = 1, 2, 3$. If none of the body parts is missing, then for $i \neq 0$, $j \neq 0$ and $k \neq 0$,

$$
\begin{aligned}
& p(L_1 = v_i, L_2 = v_j, L_3 = v_k, q_1, q_2, q_3) \\
= \ & p(L_1 = v_i, L_2 = v_j, L_3 = v_k | q_1, q_2, q_3) p(q_1, q_2, q_3)
\end{aligned}
$$

where $p(L_1 = v_i, L_2 = v_j, L_3 = v_k | q_1, q_2, q_3)$ is the 10-dimensional probability density function we used in previous sections and $p(q_1, q_2, q_3)$ is the prior probability of all the three body parts present, which can be learned through the training set.

If body part L_1 is missing, then for $i \neq 0$ and $j \neq 0$,

$$
\begin{aligned}
& p(L_1 = v_0, L_2 = v_i, L_3 = v_j, \bar{q}_1, q_2, q_3) \\
= \ & p(L_1 = v_0, L_2 = v_i, L_3 = v_j | \bar{q}_1, q_2, q_3) p(\bar{q}_1, q_2, q_3) \\
= \ & p(L_1 = v_0 | \bar{q}_1) p(L_2 = v_i, L_3 = v_j | q_2, q_3) p(\bar{q}_1, q_2, q_3)
\end{aligned}
$$

The second equality can hold because L_1 is missing and therefore it is reasonable to assume that L_1 and other body parts are independent. In the above equation the prior probability $p(\bar{q}_1, q_2, q_3)$ and $p(L_2 = v_i, L_3 = v_j | q_2, q_3)$ can be obtained from the training set. And $p(L_1 = v_0 | \bar{q}_1)$ can be estimated as a uniform density covering an ellipsoid in the 4-dimensional sub-space which describes the position and velocity of L_1 in the original 10-dimensional pdf space. The size of the ellipsoid is chosen to be such that, if the body part were present, it would be inside the ellipsoid some high percentage (say 99%) of the time. Therefore, the uniform density can be computed by scaling with an appropriate constant the inverse of the square root of the determinant of the corresponding 4-dimensional sub-matrix of the covariance matrix of the original distribution.

By the same idea, $p(L_1 = v_i, L_2 = v_0, L_3 = v_j, q_1, \bar{q}_2, q_3)$ or $p(L_1 = v_i, L_2 = v_j, L_3 = v_0, q_1, q_2, \bar{q}_3)$ can be estimated. Similarly, the lower dimensional case can also be handled.

Two experiments were performed to test the extended algorithm. In the first experiment, the exact same data as in section 4.4 were used, so the results with the extended algorithm could be directly compared to the previous ones.

Table 3 shows the resulting error rates. The possibility that markers may be missing increases the error rate only slightly for the walking sequences, but dramatically for the dance sequence. The reason is that for the difficult cases such as some frames in the dancing sequence, even if the ground truth has the highest probability, the probability itself may not be high. So when the missing points are allowed, the configuration with missing points get higher probability than the ground truth.

test set	ALL	W3	HW	DA
frame error	15.75%	3.8%	8.89%	43.84%
label error	2.25%	0.48%	0.83%	7.04%

Table 3: **Error rates for different sequences (using the algorithm that allows for missing markers).** Frame error means *frame-by-frame error* and label error means *label-by-label error*. ALL: all the three sequences; W3:walking sequence; HW: happy walking sequence; DA: dancing sequence

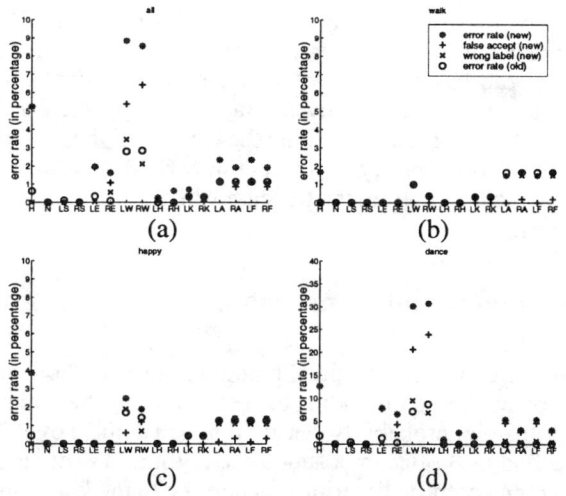

(a)   (b)

(c)   (d)

Figure 9: **Comparison of the extended algorithm (new: allowing missing points) with the original (old: without considering missing points).** The exact same sequences were used with the two algorithms (all markers present in all frames). The error rates of the new algorithm can be decomposed into **false accept** (missing marker chosen instead of correct real marker) and **wrong label** (the wrong real marker is chosen). Horizontal axis labels denote individual body parts. **(a)** ALL: average performance of all the three sequences **(b)** walking sequence W3 **(c)** happy walking sequence HW **(d)** dancing sequence DA

Figure 9 sheds more light on this result by decomposing the error rates into different categories on a label-by-label basis. Note that with the inclusion of missing markers, there are three types of errors that can occur – false accept: the missing marker is chosen but the real point is there; false reject: some marker is chosen but actually it's missing (can't occur in this experiment since all markers were always present); wrong label: an incorrect point is chosen instead of the ground truth. Notice that for the dancing sequence the majority of errors occur in the labeling of the wrists, with the most common type of error being that the wrists are deemed missing when in fact they are

811

test set	ALL	W3	HW	DA
frame error	16.32%	5.87%	9.63%	42.01%
label error	2.28%	0.7%	0.97%	6.61%

Table 4: **overall error rates for different sequences (using the algorithm allowing missing point, and all the sequences with at most one missing point).** Frame error means *frame-by-frame error* and label error means *label-by-label error*. ALL: all the three sequences; W3:walking sequence; HW: happy walking sequence; DA: dancing sequence

present. This error may arise as the combination of three effects. First, only one triangle in the graph models contains the wrists, whereas most other body parts are represented in multiple triangles. Second, in the dancing sequence the arms moved quite randomly in relation to the rest of the body (even with respect to the elbows), so that the estimate of the wrists' probability density is not as 'tight' as the one corresponding to other body parts. Finally, the dancing sequence was shorter than the other two sequences, so that it accounted for only approximately one-seventh of the training data.

The second experiment tested the performance of the algorithm when some body part was missing in the data. The program run 16 times on all the sequences, each time a different body part was removed. Table 4 shows the resulting average error rates including the case of all the markers present and the case of one marker removed. The results are not much different from the test case when no markers were removed.

6. Summary and Conclusion

We have built a perceptual model for solving the labeling problem based on finding the set of labels which maximizes the joint probability density function defined over the entire body. By decomposing the body into a decomposable graph composed of triplets according to the kinematic-chain structure of the human body, dynamic programming has been used to find the globally optimal solution in an efficient manner. For each triplet of the graph a Gaussian model of the mutual positions and velocities of the body parts is learned. When these PDFs are composed together, they define the joint probability density function of the entire body.

Experiments done on a frame-by-frame basis indicate that the learned probability models for triplets of body parts are reliable, although care needs to be taken in choosing the triplets. The method was tested on several types of motions and has an overall label-by-label error rate of 0.7% (without considering missing points), although very vigorous and random motions of wrists were not modeled as well as the rest of the body. The method is robust to point of view, having good performance with variations of viewpoint up to 30 to 40 degrees from that of training. An initial extension of the method able to handle the occurrence of missing markers (with up to one missing marker per triplet) also showed good labeling capability, with an overall label-by-label error rate of 2.3%.

Our model may be applied to body detection and labeling in markerless monocular image sequences by detecting image features and regions using the techniques described in [1, 9, 5, 10]. The position, motion and photometric characteristics of these features and regions would be inserted into the joint probability density function that describes the set of 'typical' body postures and motions. Extensions to the current model include training on a larger set of motions, testing different probability density functions that are more sophisticated than the Gaussian, dealing with different persons and different scales, extending viewpoint invariance to 360^0, enforcing certain constrains to reduce the computational cost and using a temporal model to further decrease labeling errors.

References

[1] A.Jepson and M.J.Black. Mixture models for optical flow computation. In *Proc. IEEE CVPR*, pages 760–761, 1993.

[2] E. D. Bernardo, L. Goncalves, and P. Perona. Monocular tracking of the human arm in 3d: Real-time implementation and experiments. In *International Conference on Pattern Recognition*, August 1996.

[3] B.Moghaddam and A.Pentland. Probabilistic visual learning for object representation. *IEEE Transactions on Pattern Analysis and Machine Intelligence*, 19:696–709, 1997.

[4] C. Bregler and J. Malik. Tracking people with twists and exponential maps. In *Proc. IEEE CVPR*, pages 8–15, 1998.

[5] C.Wren, A.Azarbayejani, T.Darrell, and A.Pentland. Pfinder: Real-time tracking of the human body. *IEEE Transactions on Pattern Analysis and Machine Intelligence*, 19:780–785, 1997.

[6] L. Goncalves, E. D. Bernardo, E. Ursella, and P. Perona. Monocular tracking of the human arm in 3d. In *Proc. 5th Int. Conf. Computer Vision*, pages 764–770, Cambridge, Mass, June 1995.

[7] I. Haritaoglu, D.Harwood, and L.Davis. Who, when, where, what: A real time system for detecting and tracking people. In *Proceedings of the Third Face and Gesture Recognition Conference*, pages 222–227, 1998.

[8] G. Johansson. Visual perception of biological motion and a model for its analysis. *Perception and Psychophysics*, 14:201–211, 1973.

[9] J.Shi and C.Tomasi. Good features to track. In *Proc. IEEE CVPR*, pages 593–600, 1994.

[10] M.Yang and N.Ahuja. Extracting gestural motion trajectories. In *International Conference on Face and Gesture Perception*, pages 10–15, Nara, Japan, April 1998.

[11] J. Rehg and T. Kanade. Digiteyes: Vision-based hand tracking for human-computer interaction. In *Proceedings of the workshop on Motion of Non-Rigid and Articulated Bodies*, pages 16–24, November 1994.

[12] K. Rohr. Incremental recognition of pedestrians from image sequences. In *Proc. IEEE Conf. Computer Vision and Pattern Recognition*, pages 8–13, New York City, June, 1993.

[13] A. Y.Amit. Graphical templates for model registration. *IEEE Transactions on Pattern Analysis and Machine Intelligence*, 18:225–236, 1996.

Physics-Based Vision

Polarization-based Decorrelation of Transparent Layers:
The Inclination Angle of an Invisible Surface

Yoav Y. Schechner   Joseph Shamir   Nahum Kiryati[†]

Department of Electrical Engineering,
Technion - Israel Institute of Technology,
Haifa, Israel 32000

yoavs@tx.technion.ac.il
jsh@ee.technion.ac.il

[†]Dep. of Electrical Engineering - Systems,
Faculty of Engineering, Tel-Aviv University,
Ramat Aviv, Israel 69978

nk@eng.tau.ac.il

Abstract

When a transparent surface is present between an observer and an object, an image reflected by the surface may be superimposed on the image of the observed object. We present a new approach to recover the scenes (layers) and to classify which is the reflected/transmitted one, based on imaging through a polarizing filter at two orientations. Estimates of the separate layers are obtained by weighted pixel-wise differences of these images, inverting the image formation process. However, the weights depend on the angle of incidence, hence on the inclination of the transparent (invisible) surface. This angle is estimated by seeking the angle-value which (through the weights) leads to decorrelation of the estimated layers. Experimental results, obtained using real photos of actual objects, demonstrate the success of angle estimation and consequent layer separation and labeling. The method is shown to be superior to earlier methods where only raw optical data was used.

1. Introduction

In the computer vision and image processing fields, it has usually been assumed that at each point of the image the intensity is single valued. However, the situation in which several (typically two) linearly superimposed contributions exist is often encountered in real-world scenes. For example [4, 8, 10], looking out of a car (or room) window, we see both the outside world (termed *real object* [6, 7, 8]), and a semi-reflection of the objects inside, termed *virtual objects* (Fig. 1). The term *transparent layers* has been used to describe such situations [2]. The combination of several unrelated layers is likely to degrade the ability to analyze and understand them (for example, it can certainly confuse aut-

ofocusing devices [8]). The detection of the phenomenon is of importance itself, since it indicates the presence of a clear (invisible), transparent surface in front of the camera, at a distance closer than the actual imaged objects [6, 8].

Earlier approaches to reconstruct each of the layers relied mainly on motion [2], stereo [9], and focus [8]. These methods essentially assume that the superimposed layers lie at significantly different optical distances from the camera [8], and the reconstruction of the low spatial frequency components was ill conditioned [8] (while the DC component was ill posed). Other fundamental ambiguities in the solutions obtained by motion and stereo were discussed in [9, 12].

An approach based on polarization can avoid these problems. Polarimetric imaging has recently drawn interest [5, 11, 14], particularly for removal of specular reflections superimposed on diffuse scattering from opaque surfaces [5, 13]. Suppressing the virtual layer by incorporating a polarizer into the imaging system is a common photographic technique [10]. Some previous works attempted to remove the virtual layer by using just the raw output of a polarization analyzer (Fig. 1) in front of the camera [4, 6]. These methods suggested taking several images of the scene at different states of the polarizer, and picking one of them as the reconstruction of the real layer. However, optical filtering eliminates the reflected (virtual) layer only at a specific incidence angle, called the *Brewster angle* [1, 10], which is $\approx 56°$ for glass (and at which good filtering was demonstrated in [6]). Away from this angle, polarization filtering may improve the visibility of the real object, but cannot eliminate the crosstalk with the virtual layer. Independent components analysis of polarization filtered images was used for this purpose, and demonstrated the potential of polarization as an initial step for separation achieved by signal post processing [3], but the intensities are evaluated up to an unknown factor.

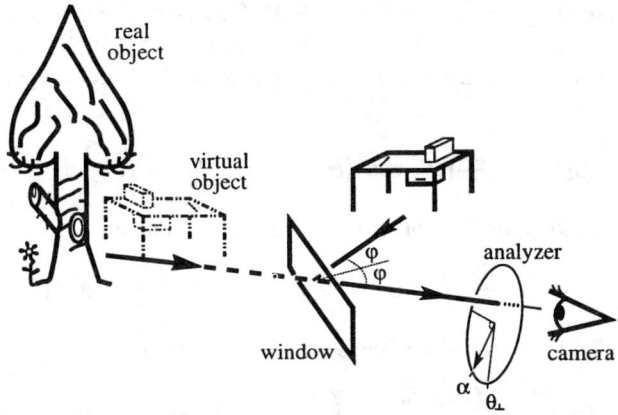

Figure 1. The image of a real object is partly transmitted through a transparent window inclined at an angle φ. The window also creates a virtual image by partly reflecting the image of another object. The combined scene is viewed through a polarization analyzer (filter) at angle α. The plane of incidence includes the incident ray and the normal to the window. The best transmission of the polarization component perpendicular to this plane is when the analyzer is oriented at some value of α denoted $\theta_\perp$.

The most significant disadvantage of the previous works is that they could not determine which of the reconstructed images is of the real object and which is of the virtual one (beside Ref. [6] which attempted the use of the raw images to determine the real layer, and Ref. [7] where the surface had to be curved). Moreover, they did not extract information about the invisible semi-reflecting surface itself, in particular, the angle of incidence (AOI) remained unknown.

In this work we suggest and demonstrate a novel method for separation of the transparent layers and their automatic labeling as virtual or real, together with determination of the angle of incidence (the inclination angle of the invisible semi-reflecting surface). It is based on the physical image formation process, i.e., the combination of two image sources, when viewed through a polarization analyzer. Internal (secondary) reflections within two-surfaced reflecting media (e.g., glass windows) are taken into account.

Initial separation is obtained using the raw output of a polarization analyzer (filter) in front of the camera. Weighted differences between the acquired images yield estimates of the images of the real and the virtual objects. The weights are derived from the reflection and transmission processes determined by the optical properties of the transparent interface. These properties depend on the geometry of the setup, in particular, the angle of incidence (inclination). To estimate it, we seek the weights that lead to *decorrelation* of the estimated layers, based on the as-

sumption that the real object is unrelated to the virtual one.

In contrast to simplistic use of a polarizer, the presented approach allows operation away from Brewster's angle and gives far better results than those achievable by using only raw optical data. Unlike methods that rely on stereo, motion or defocus, it is not ill-conditioned at the low frequencies, it resolves the DC component, and labels the layers as virtual/real. It does not require the layers to have different depths or motion fields.

2. Image formation

The ray incident on a surface (e.g., a face of a window) is partly reflected from the surface, and partly transmitted through it (Fig. 2). All rays lie in the *plane of incidence* (POI). We divide the intensity to two components: $I_\|$, for which the polarization is *parallel* to the POI, and $I_\perp$, for which the polarization is *perpendicular* to it. Each component has, respectively, reflectivities $R_\|, R_\perp$ and transmissivities $T_\|, T_\perp$.

For a single-surface medium (e.g., water in a lake), the reflectivities are [1]

$$R_\| = \frac{\tan^2(\varphi - \varphi')}{\tan^2(\varphi + \varphi')} \quad , \quad R_\perp = \frac{\sin^2(\varphi - \varphi')}{\sin^2(\varphi + \varphi')} \quad , \quad (1)$$

where φ is the AOI. φ' is the angle of the ray refracted within the medium (Fig. 2), which is related to φ by Snell's law [1]. Cases of reflection from double-surfaced media are, however, by far more common. Typical examples are glass or polycarbonate windows and covers of pictures. Eqs. (1) also apply to a ray passing from the dense medium (e.g. glass) to the air. As the light ray within the window is refracted to the air at the back surface (Fig. 2), part of it is reflected back to the front surface, from which refraction occurs again, and so on. For each polarization component the total reflectivity is

$$\tilde{R} = R + T^2 R \sum_{l=0}^{\infty} (R^2)^l \quad . \quad (2)$$

We neglected the absorption within the medium, and assumed that the spatial shift between the significant reflection orders is small relative to the variations in the image. The latter assumption usually holds since, due to the typically small value of R, only the first two orders are significant and since most parts of a typical image are smooth. Thus, the total reflectivities are

$$\tilde{R}_\| = \frac{2}{1 + R_\|} R_\| \quad , \quad \tilde{R}_\perp = \frac{2}{1 + R_\perp} R_\perp \quad , \quad (3)$$

and the transmissivities are

$$\tilde{T}_\| = \frac{1 - R_\|}{1 + R_\|} = 1 - \tilde{R}_\| \quad , \quad \tilde{T}_\perp = \frac{1 - R_\perp}{1 + R_\perp} = 1 - \tilde{R}_\perp \quad .$$

$$(4)$$

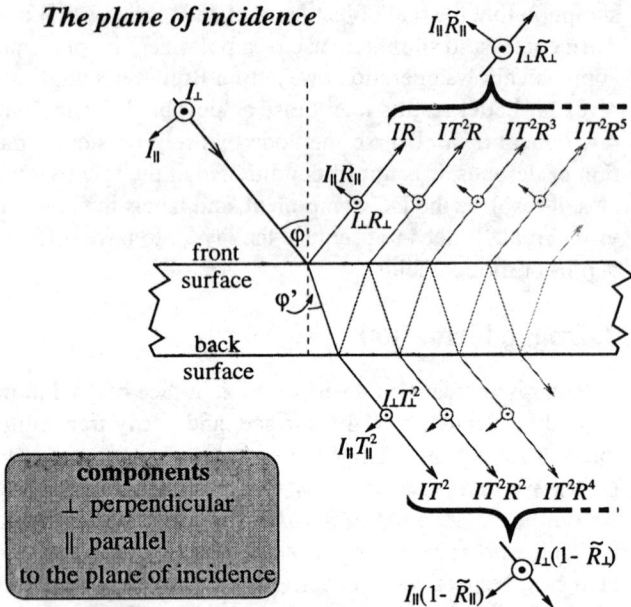

The plane of incidence

Figure 2. Each component of a light ray incident on any of the window surfaces undergoes reflection and refraction (transmission) with coefficients R and T, respectively. Internal reflections within the window give rise to orders of reflected/transmitted rays with decreasing intensities.

We define the *polarizing effect* (PE) of reflection by the degree of polarization it induces on unpolarized light. For a window it is $\mathrm{PE}_R \equiv |\tilde{R}_\perp - \tilde{R}_\parallel|/|\tilde{R}_\perp + \tilde{R}_\parallel|$. As in a single-surface medium, it is full ($\mathrm{PE}_R = 1$) at the Brewster angle, in which the parallel component vanishes [1]. It is zero for 0° and 90°. For transmission $\mathrm{PE}_T \equiv |\tilde{T}_\perp - \tilde{T}_\parallel|/|\tilde{T}_\perp + \tilde{T}_\parallel|$. It is easy to show that

$$\frac{\mathrm{PE}_T}{\mathrm{PE}_R} = \frac{\tilde{R}_{\mathrm{av}}}{\tilde{T}_{\mathrm{av}}} \ , \tag{5}$$

where $\tilde{R}_{\mathrm{av}} = (\tilde{R}_\perp + \tilde{R}_\parallel)/2$ and $\tilde{T}_{\mathrm{av}} = (\tilde{T}_\perp + \tilde{T}_\parallel)/2$ are the reflectivity and transmissivity of unpolarized light, respectively. Therefore, *neglecting the degree of polarization induced on the transmitted light* (PE_T) *is equivalent to neglecting the reflection phenomenon (which is invalid in the cases discussed in this work).*

Let I_T be the intensity (at a certain pixel) of the image of the real object without the window. Let I_R be the intensity (at the same pixel) of the image of the virtual object, had there been a perfect mirror instead of the window. For an arbitrary cylindrical coordinate system, whose axis is parallel to the optical axis of the camera, let $\theta_\perp$ be the orientation of the polarization analyzer for best transmission of the component perpendicular to the POI. Generally, the orientation of the analyzer is some angle, α. Assuming initially unpolarized natural light, the contribution of the reflected scene is

$$f_R(\alpha) = \frac{I_R}{2}[\tilde{R}_\perp \cos^2(\alpha - \theta_\perp) + \tilde{R}_\parallel \sin^2(\alpha - \theta_\perp)] \tag{6}$$

and the contribution of the transmitted scene is

$$f_T(\alpha) = \frac{I_T}{2}[\tilde{T}_\perp \cos^2(\alpha - \theta_\perp) + \tilde{T}_\parallel \sin^2(\alpha - \theta_\perp)] \ . \tag{7}$$

The total intensity is the sum of these contributions,

$$f(\alpha) = \left(\frac{f_\perp + f_\parallel}{2}\right) + \left(\frac{f_\perp - f_\parallel}{2}\right)\cos[2(\alpha - \theta_\perp)] \ , \tag{8}$$

where

$$f_\perp = f(\theta_\perp) = (I_R \tilde{R}_\perp/2 + I_T \tilde{T}_\perp/2) \tag{9}$$

$$f_\parallel = f(\theta_\perp + 90^o) = (I_R \tilde{R}_\parallel/2 + I_T \tilde{T}_\parallel/2) \ . \tag{10}$$

Note that $f_\perp - f_\parallel = 0.5(\tilde{R}_\perp - \tilde{R}_\parallel)(I_R - I_T)$. Thus, if $I_T = I_R$, the light leaving the reflecting medium (Eq. (8)) is unpolarized. Since $R_\perp \geq R_\parallel$ [1], it can be shown that $\tilde{R}_\perp \geq \tilde{R}_\parallel$. Thus, if the real object is brighter than the virtual one ($I_T > I_R$, e.g., when looking out of the room window during daylight), the intensity $f(\alpha)$ would be *minimal* at $\alpha = \theta_\perp$. Thus the polarization of the transmitted light, rather than the reflected one, may be dominant in the determination of the overall polarization. Hence, generally one cannot associate $\theta_\perp$ with the highest output of the polarization analyzer when imaging transparent scenes.

3. Reconstruction

3.1. For a given angle of incidence

Suppose now that the geometry of the setup, that is, the POI (hence $\theta_\perp$) and the AOI φ, is known or estimated. Note that $f_\perp$ and $f_\parallel$ are not sensitive to small errors in the estimation of $\theta_\perp$, since

$$\left.\frac{\partial f}{\partial \theta_\perp}\right|_{\alpha = \theta_\perp, \theta_\perp + 90^o} = 0 \ . \tag{11}$$

In this case $\tilde{R}_\perp(\varphi)$ and $\tilde{R}_\parallel(\varphi)$ are known. Thus Eqs. (9,10) together with (4) yield

$$\hat{I}_T(\varphi) = \left[\frac{2\tilde{R}_\perp(\varphi)}{\tilde{R}_\perp(\varphi) - \tilde{R}_\parallel(\varphi)}\right]f_\parallel - \left[\frac{2\tilde{R}_\parallel(\varphi)}{\tilde{R}_\perp(\varphi) - \tilde{R}_\parallel(\varphi)}\right]f_\perp \tag{12}$$

and

$$\hat{I}_R(\varphi) = \left[\frac{2 - 2\tilde{R}_\parallel(\varphi)}{\tilde{R}_\perp(\varphi) - \tilde{R}_\parallel(\varphi)}\right]f_\perp - \left[\frac{2 - 2\tilde{R}_\perp(\varphi)}{\tilde{R}_\perp(\varphi) - \tilde{R}_\parallel(\varphi)}\right]f_\parallel \tag{13}$$

Hence if the AOI is the Brewster angle [1] (for which $\tilde{R}_\| = 0$), $\hat{I}_T$ can be directly associated with $f_\|$, as demonstrated in [6]. However, even at that angle, $\hat{I}_R$ is not proportional to $f_\perp - f_\|$, in contrast to [6]. In any case, operation at Brewster's angle is a rare situation, and one should generally use Eqs. (12,13). The reconstructions become unstable as $(\tilde{R}_\perp - \tilde{R}_\|) \to 0$, that is, at very low or high AOI.

Mechanical rotation of the analyzer causes small image distortions, leading to false polarization readings at image edges [5, 14]. Here, this results in false edges in the reconstructed layer in locations where true edges exist in the other layer. To mitigate that, we align the raw images such that, locally, the gradients in the resulting reconstructed (difference) images are minimized. No blurring operator is used. It turns out that small local translations lead to better results than a global translation. Note that the presence of genuine edges is typically preserved by this alignment process.

3.2. Estimating the angle of incidence

Changing the analyzer's angle α modulates sinusoidally the intensity at each point (8). This modulation is determined by the point intensities I_R and I_T, and by the reflection coefficients - which in turn depend on the AOI, φ. Since I_R and I_T are unknown, pointwise data analysis provides little information (if at all) on the AOI.

To estimate the AOI, an assumption related to multiple points is needed. *We assume that the real and virtual layers are uncorrelated.* This is reasonable since they usually originate from unrelated scenes.

Inserting Eqs. (9,10), that are based on the true AOI φ_{true}, into Eqs. (12,13), which assume φ, we obtain that

$$\hat{I}_T(\varphi) = (1 - \rho)I_T + \rho I_R$$
$$\hat{I}_R(\varphi) = (1 - \tau)I_R + \tau I_T \,, \qquad (14)$$

where

$$\rho(\varphi_{\text{true}}, \varphi) = \frac{\tilde{R}_\perp(\varphi)\tilde{R}_\|(\varphi_{\text{true}}) - \tilde{R}_\perp(\varphi_{\text{true}})\tilde{R}_\|(\varphi)}{\tilde{R}_\perp(\varphi) - \tilde{R}_\|(\varphi)}$$
$$(15)$$

$$\tau(\varphi_{\text{true}}, \varphi) = \frac{\tilde{T}_\perp(\varphi)\tilde{T}_\|(\varphi_{\text{true}}) - \tilde{T}_\perp(\varphi_{\text{true}})\tilde{T}_\|(\varphi)}{\tilde{T}_\perp(\varphi) - \tilde{T}_\|(\varphi)} \,.$$
$$(16)$$

Loosely speaking, for a range of values of φ traces of the virtual layer will remain in $\hat{I}_T$, resulting in positive correlation between the estimated layers. For other values of φ negative traces of the virtual layer will be left in $\hat{I}_T$, leading to a negative correlation between the estimated layers. By using the correct AOI in Eqs. (12,13) zero correlation between the estimated images is obtained.

Our approach is thus to search for the zero crossing of the correlation between the estimated images

$$\hat{\varphi} = \{\varphi : Corr[\hat{I}_T(\varphi), \hat{I}_R(\varphi)] = 0\} \,. \qquad (17)$$

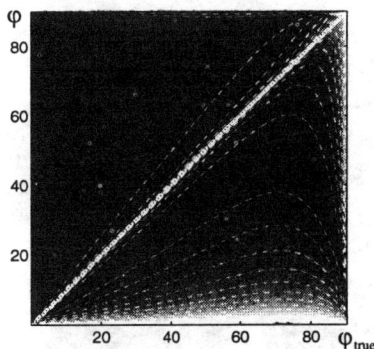

Figure 3. The brightness depicts $|\log|\tau(1 - \rho)||$. Zeros of $\tau(1 - \rho)$ appear only for $\varphi_{\text{true}} = \varphi$.

For any images p and q the cross-correlation is

$$Corr(p, q) = Cov(p, q)/\sqrt{Var(p) \cdot Var(q)} \qquad (18)$$

where Var denotes the (spatial) variance. The covariance is estimated in the N-pixels images by

$$Cov(p, q) \simeq \langle p - \mu_p, q - \mu_q \rangle/N \,, \qquad (19)$$

where μ_p is the mean of p. Of course, the zero crossing of the correlation occurs at the zero crossing of the cross-covariance (19), which can also be used to estimate φ. However, note that assuming a constant 'image' as a solution for any layer will satisfy the zero covariance criterion. To reject such possibilities the zero correlation criterion is used. Assuming no correlation between I_R and I_T,

$$Cov(\hat{I}_T, \hat{I}_R) = \tau(1 - \rho)Var(I_T) + \rho(1 - \tau)Var(I_R) \,.$$
$$(20)$$

If $\varphi = \varphi_{\text{true}}$, then $\rho, \tau = 0$, nulling Eq. (20). Other than in this case, $[\tau(1 - \rho)]$ has no zero (Fig. 3), so we can write Eq. (20) as

$$Cov(\hat{I}_T, \hat{I}_R) = \tau(1-\rho)Var(I_R) \left[\frac{Var(I_T)}{Var(I_R)} - \eta \right] \,, \quad (21)$$

where

$$\eta(\varphi_{\text{true}}, \varphi) = -\frac{\rho(1 - \tau)}{\tau(1 - \rho)} \,. \qquad (22)$$

Thus, beside the wanted zero-crossing, a zero value of the cross-covariance at a wrongly assumed AOI is possible if and only if $\eta > 0$. We note that if φ is allowed to take values arbitrarily close to 90°, η can take any positive value. Thus if φ is not bounded by some practical limit, the ambiguity is inevitable for any combination of I_R and I_T. The white domains in Fig. 4 mark the range of AOI on glass for which the possibility of error exists. Note that if it is *a priori* known that the AOI φ_{true} is smaller than the Brewster angle, the ambiguity is removed since in these cases

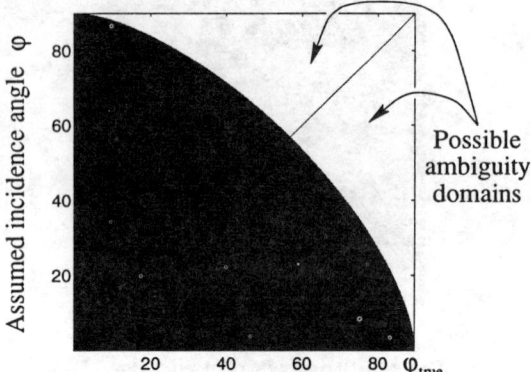

Figure 4. For each φ_{true} there are domains (white) where a zero of the correlation exists at a wrong angle (beside the correct one).

Fig. 4 indicates that the wrong angle of decorrelation will always be at $\varphi > \varphi_{\text{true}}$. Generally, possible ways to bypass this problem may be based on comparison of the results obtained for different image parts having different variances, or for different color bands, or for shifts between the images prior to the correlation estimation.

An alternative method for estimating the AOI, can be based on the assumption that the statistical dependence of the real and virtual layers is small. Thus, if the layers are correctly separated, each of the estimates contains a minimum of information about the other. The use of mutual information as a criterion for separation is now being studied.

4. Reconstruction experiment

We imaged several objects through an upright glass window. The window semi-reflected another scene. The combined scene is shown (contrast-stretched for clarity, as are all the images here) in Fig. 5(a). The optical distance between the camera and both scenes was $\approx 3.5m$. A linear polarizer was rotated in front of the camera between consecutive image acquisitions. For good demonstration quality, 5 frames were averaged at each analyzer state.

The POI was horizontal, thus it was easy to obtain $\theta_\perp$ and take images of $f_\perp$ and $f_\parallel$[1], shown in Fig. 5. The reflected layer is attenuated by the polarizer in $f_\parallel$. Still, a significant disturbance due to this scene remains since $\varphi_{\text{true}} = 27.5^o \pm 3^0$ was far from the Brewster angle. Thus optics alone does not solve the problem.

The AOI φ to be estimated, was assumed to be between 5° and 85° (to avoid instabilities at the singular angles 0° and 90°). For each assumed angle, the cross-correlation

---

[1]More details, and the raw images database can be linked through $http : //www.ee.technion.ac.il/ \sim yoavs/PUBLICATIONS$.

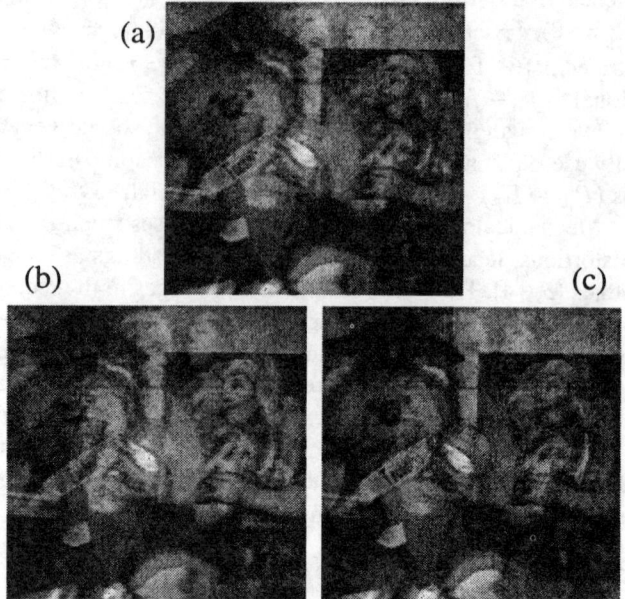

Figure 5. (a): The combined scene. (b): $f_\perp$. (c): $f_\parallel$. Although the reflected component is weaker in $f_\parallel$, the image is still unclear.

between the images was estimated. At $\varphi = 27^o$ the estimated layers are decorrelated (Fig. 6). This is in excellent agreement with the angle used in the physical experimental setup. A second zero-crossing of the correlation coefficient exists at 84°. This result is also in agreement with the theory, since for this φ_{true}, the threshold for the appearance of this crossing (Fig. 4) is 80°.

We operated Eqs. (12,13) on each point in the images shown in Figs. 5(b,c) using the estimated AOI $\varphi = 27^o$. To eliminate false edges, the results were 'fine-tuned' by the alignment procedure described above. The results shown in the top row of Fig. 7 can be compared with the "ground-truth" shown in the bottom row of this figure.

5. Discussion

Real and virtual objects superimposed by a reflecting surface can be well separated and labeled by the proposed method. The method significantly extends the useful range of incidence angles for polarization-based clearing of transparent disturbances. In addition, it automatically provides the inclination of the invisible surface that lies between the camera and the visible objects. It may be a basis for useful and practical techniques in amateur and professional photography, and enable scene understanding in the presence of semi reflections.

We believe that mutual information may be a better measure than decorrelation for correct separation, especially

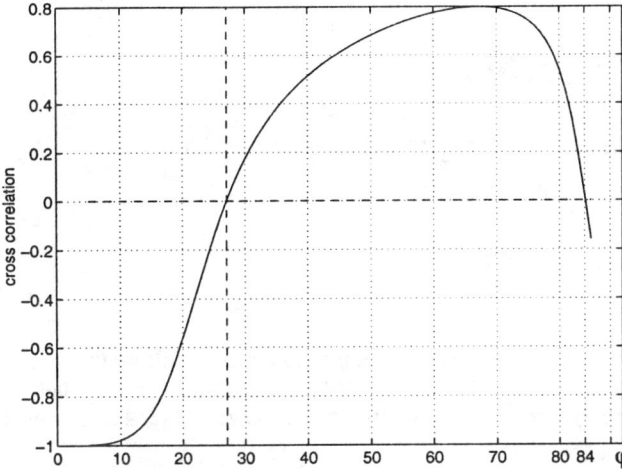

Figure 6. At the estimated angle $27°$ the estimated layers are decorrelated.

Figure 7. [Top row]: The reconstructed real (left) and virtual (right) layers, based on the automatic detection of the angle of incidence. [Bottom left]: The real object photographed without the interfering glass window. [Bottom right]: The virtual object photographed by removing the objects behind the glass window.

when there is some correlation between the scenes, or when the scene contains opaque objects beside transparent ones. This measure is being studied. Other issues we consider are the effects of noise and curvature of the reflecting surface across the field of view. The observed objects may partially polarize the light before its incidence on the semi-reflecting medium (e.g., by specular reflections from dielectrics). We expect this to somewhat degrade the performance of the current method, motivating further improvements in the approach.

This research was carried out in the Ollendorff Center of the Department of Electrical Engineering, Technion, and in the Department of Electrical Engineering - Systems, Faculty of Engineering, Tel-Aviv University. It was funded in part by the Israeli Ministry of Science.

References

[1] M. Born and E. Wolf, *Principles of optics*, 5th ed., (Pergamon, Oxford, 1975).

[2] J. R. Bergen, P. J. Burt, R. Hingorani and S. Peleg, "Transparent motion analysis" Proc. ECCV, pp. 566-569, 1990.

[3] H. Farid and E. H. Adelson, "Separating reflections and lighting using independent components analysis," Proc. CVPR, Vol-I, pp. 262-267, 1999.

[4] H. Fujikake, K. Takizawa, T. Aida, H. Kikuchi, T. Fujii and M. Kawakita, "Electrically-controllable liquid crystal polarizing filter for eliminating reflected light," Optical Review **5**, pp. 93-98, 1998.

[5] S. K. Nayar, X. S. Fang and T. Boult, "Separation of reflection components using color and polarization," Int. J. Comp. Vis. **21**, pp. 163-186, 1997.

[6] N. Ohnishi, K. Kumaki, T. Yamamura and T. Tanaka, "Separating real and virtual objects from their overlapping images," Proc. ECCV, Vol-II, pp. 636-646, 1996.

[7] M. Oren and S. K. Nayar, "A theory of specular surface geometry," Proc. ICCV, pp. 740-747, 1995.

[8] Y. Y. Schechner, N. Kiryati and R. Basri, "Separation of transparent layers using focus," Proc. ICCV, pp. 1061-1066, Mumbai, 1998.

[9] M. Shizawa, "On visual ambiguities due to transparency in motion and stereo," Proc. ECCV, pp. 411-419, 1992.

[10] W. A. Shurcliff and S. S. Ballard, *Polarized light* (Van Nostrand, Princeton, 1964).

[11] R. Walraven, "Polarization imagery," Opt. Eng. **20**, pp. 14-18, 1981.

[12] D. Weinshall, "Perception of multiple transparent planes in stereo vision," Nature **341**, pp. 737-739, 1989.

[13] L. B. Wolff, "Using polarization to separate reflection components," Proc. CVPR, pp. 363-369, 1989.

[14] L. B. Wolff, "Polarization vision: a new sensory approach to image understanding," Image and Vision Computing **15**, pp. 81-93, 1997.

Vision in Bad Weather *

Shree K. Nayar and Srinivasa G. Narasimhan

Department of Computer Science, Columbia University
New York, New York 10027
Email: {nayar, srinivas}@cs.columbia.edu

Abstract

Current vision systems are designed to perform in clear weather. Needless to say, in any outdoor application, there is no escape from "bad" weather. Ultimately, computer vision systems must include mechanisms that enable them to function (even if somewhat less reliably) in the presence of haze, fog, rain, hail and snow. We begin by studying the visual manifestations of different weather conditions. For this, we draw on what is already known about atmospheric optics. Next, we identify effects caused by bad weather that can be turned to our advantage. Since the atmosphere modulates the information carried from a scene point to the observer, it can be viewed as a mechanism of visual information coding. Based on this observation, we develop models and methods for recovering pertinent scene properties, such as three-dimensional structure, from images taken under poor weather conditions.

1 Vision and the Atmosphere

Virtually all work in vision is based on the premise that the observer is immersed in a transparent medium (air). It is assumed that light rays reflected by scene objects travel to the observer without attenuation or alteration. Under this assumption, the brightness of an image point depends solely on the brightness of a single point in the scene. Quite simply, existing vision sensors and algorithms have been created only to function on "clear" days. A dependable vision system however must reckon with the entire spectrum of weather conditions, including, haze, fog, rain, hail and snow.

The study of the interaction of light with the atmosphere (and hence weather) is widely known as atmospheric optics. Atmospheric optics lies at the heart of the most magnificent visual experiences known to man, including, the colors of sunrise and sunset, the blueness of the clear sky, and the rainbow (see [Minnaert, 1954]). The literature on this topic has been written over the past two centuries. A summary of where the subject as a whole stands would be too ambitious a pursuit. Instead, our objective will be to sieve out of this vast body of work, models of atmospheric optics that are of direct relevance to computational vision. Our most prominent sources of background material will be the works of McCartney [McCartney, 1976] and Middleton [Middleton, 1952] whose books, though dated, serve as excellent reviews of prior work.

The key characteristics of light, such as its intensity and color, are altered by its interactions with the atmosphere. These interactions can be broadly classified into three categories, namely, *scattering*, *absorption* and *emission*. Of these, scattering due to suspended particles is the most pertinent to us. As can be expected, this phenomenon leads to complex visual effects. So, at first glance, atmospheric scattering may be viewed as no more than a hindrance to an observer. However, it turns out that bad weather can be put to good use. The farther light has to travel from its source (say, a surface) to its destination (say, a camera), the greater it will be effected by the weather. Hence, bad weather could serve as a powerful means for coding and conveying scene structure. This observation lies at the core of our investigation; we wish to understand not only what bad weather does *to* vision but also what it can do *for* vision.

Surprisingly little work has been done in computer vision on weather related issues. An exception is the work of Cozman and Krotkov [Cozman and Krotkov, 1997] which uses the scattering models in [McCartney, 1976] to compute depth cues. Their algorithm assumes that all scene points used for depth estimation have the same intensity on a clear day. Since scene points can have their own reflectances and illuminations, this assumption is hard to satisfy in practice.

In this paper, we develop algorithms that recover complete depth maps of scenes without making assumptions about the properties of the scene points or the atmospheric conditions. How do such scene recovery methods compare with existing ones? Unlike binocular stereo, they do not suffer from the problems of correspondence and discontinuities. Nor do they require tracking of image features as in structure from motion. Furthermore, they are particularly useful for scenes with distant objects (even miles away) which pose problems for stereo and motion. The techniques we present here only require changes in weather conditions and accurate measurement of image irradiance.

2 Bad Weather: Particles in Space

Weather conditions differ mainly in the types and sizes of the particles involved and their concentrations in space. A great deal of effort has gone into measuring particle sizes and con-

---

*This work was supported by the DARPA/ONR MURI Program under Grant N00014-95-1-0601 and the David and Lucile Packard Foundation. The authors thank Jan Koenderink of Utrecht University for pointers to early work on atmospheric optics.

CONDITION	PARTICLE TYPE	RADIUS (μm)	CONCENTRATION (cm^{-3})
AIR	Molecule	10^{-4}	10^{19}
HAZE	Aerosol	10^{-2} - 1	10^3 - 10
FOG	Water Droplet	1 - 10	100 - 10
CLOUD	Water Droplet	1 - 10	300 - 10
RAIN	Water Drop	10^2 - 10^4	10^{-2} - 10^{-5}

Table 1: Weather conditions and associated particle types, sizes and concentrations (adapted from McCartney[1976]).

centrations for a variety of conditions (see Table 1). Given the small size of air molecules, relative to the wavelength of visible light, scattering due to air is rather minimal. We will refer to the event of pure air scattering as a *clear* day (or night). Larger particles produce a variety of weather conditions which we will briefly describe below.

Haze: Haze is constituted of *aerosol* which is a dispersed system of small particles suspended in gas. Haze has a diverse set of sources including volcanic ashes, foliage exudations, combustion products, and sea salt (see [Hidy, 1972]). The particles produced by these sources respond quickly to changes in relative humidity and act as nuclei (centers) of small water droplets when the humidity is high. Haze particles are larger than air molecules but smaller than fog droplets. Haze tends to produce a distinctive gray hue and is certain to effect visibility.

Fog: Fog evolves when the relative humidity of an air parcel approaches a saturation level. Then, some of the nuclei grow by condensation into water droplets. Hence, fog and haze have similar origins and an increase in humidity is sufficient to turn haze into fog. This transition is quite gradual and an intermediate state is referred to as *mist*. While perceptible haze extends to an altitude of several miles, fog is typically just a few hundred feet thick. A practical distinction between fog and haze lies in the greatly reduced visibility induced by the former. There are many types of fog which differ from each other in their formation processes [Myers, 1968].

Cloud: A cloud differs from fog only in existing at high altitudes (troposphere) rather than sitting at ground level. While most clouds are made of water droplets like fog, some are composed of long ice crystals and ice-coated dust grains. Details on the physics of clouds and precipitation can be found in [Mason, 1975]. For now, clouds are of less relevance to us as we restrict ourselves to vision at ground level rather than high altitudes.

Rain and Snow: The process by which cloud droplets turn to rain is a complex one [Mason, 1975]. When viewed up close, rain causes random spatial and temporal variations in images and hence must be dealt with differently from the more stable weather conditions mentioned above. Similar arguments apply to snow, which, at a simple level may be

viewed as frozen rain where the drops are solid, rougher and have more complex shapes and optical properties [Koenderink and Richards, 1992] [Ohtake, 1970]. Snow too, we will set aside for now.

3 Mechanisms of Atmospheric Scattering

The manner in which a particle scatters incident light depends on its material properties, shape and size. The exact form and intensity of the scattering pattern varies dramatically with particle size [Minnaert, 1954]. As seen in Figure 1, a small particle (about $1/10 \lambda$, where λ is the wavelength of light) scatters almost equally in the forward (incidence) and backward directions, a medium size particle (about $1/4 \lambda$) scatters more in the forward direction, and a large particle (larger than λ) scatters almost entirely in the forward direction. Substantial theory has been developed to derive scattering functions [Mie, 1908] (see [Nieto-Vesperinas and Dainty, 1990] for more recent advances).

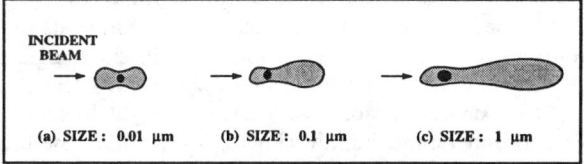

Figure 1: A particle in the path of an incident light wave abstracts and reradiates incident energy. It therefore behaves like a point source of light. The exact scattering function is closely related to the ratio of particle size to wavelength of incident light. (Adapted from [Minnaert, 1954]).

Figure 1 illustrates scattering by a single particle. Clearly, particles are accompanied in close proximity by numerous other particles. However, the average separation between weather particles is several times the particle size. Hence, the particles can be viewed as *independent* scatterers whose scattered intensities do not interfere with each other. This does not imply that the incident light is scattered only by a single particle. *Multiple* scatterings take place and any given particle is exposed not only to the incident light but also light scattered by other particles. In effect, this causes the single scattering functions in Figure 1 to get smoother and less directional.

Now, consider the simple illumination and detection geometry shown in Figure 2. A unit volume of scattering medium with suspended particles is illuminated with spectral irradiance $E(\lambda)$. The radiant intensity $I(\theta, \lambda)$ of the unit volume in the direction θ of the observer is:

$$I(\theta, \lambda) = \beta(\theta, \lambda) E(\lambda) , \qquad (1)$$

where, $\beta(\theta, \lambda)$ is the *angular scattering coefficient*. The radiant intensity $I(\theta, \lambda)$ is the flux radiated per unit solid angle, per unit volume of the medium. The irradiance $E(\lambda)$ is, as always, the flux incident on the volume per unit cross-section area.

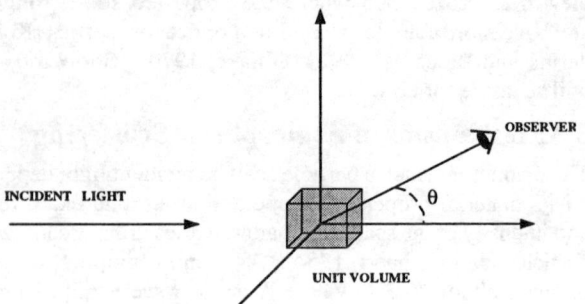

Figure 2: A unit volume of randomly oriented suspended particles illuminated and observed.

3.1 Attenuation

The first mechanism that is relevant to us is the attenuation of a beam of light as it travels through the atmosphere. This causes the radiance of a scene point to fall as its depth from the observer increases. Here, we will summarize the derivation of the attenuation model given in [McCartney, 1976]. Consider a collimated beam of light incident on the atmospheric medium, as shown in Figure 3. The beam is assumed to have unit cross-sectional area. Consider the beam passing through an infinitesimally small sheet (lamina) of thickness dx. The intensity scattered by the lamina is $I(\theta, \lambda) = \beta(\theta, \lambda) E(\lambda) dx$. The total flux scattered (in all directions) by this lamina is obtained by integrating over the entire sphere:

$$\phi(\lambda) = \beta(\lambda) E(\lambda) dx , \qquad (2)$$

where, $\beta(\lambda)$ is the *total scattering coefficient*. It represents the ability of the volume to scatter flux of a given wavelength in all directions. Hence, the fractional change in irradiance at location x can be written as:

$$\frac{dE(x, \lambda)}{E(x, \lambda)} = -\beta(\lambda) dx . \qquad (3)$$

By integrating both sides between the limits $x = 0$ and $x = d$ we get: $E(d, \lambda) = E_o(\lambda) e^{-\beta(\lambda) d}$, where, $E_o(\lambda)$ is the irradiance at the source ($x = 0$). This is Bouguer's exponential law of attenuation, derived in 1729. Its utility is somewhat limited as it assumes a collimated source of incident energy. This is easily remedied by incorporating the inverse-square law for diverging beams from point sources:

$$E(d, \lambda) = \frac{I_o(\lambda) e^{-\beta(\lambda) d}}{d^2} , \qquad (4)$$

where, $I_o(\lambda)$ is the radiant intensity of the point source. This is Allard's law developed in 1876.

At times, attenuation due to scattering is expressed in terms of *optical thickness* which is $T = \beta(\lambda) d$. It is generally

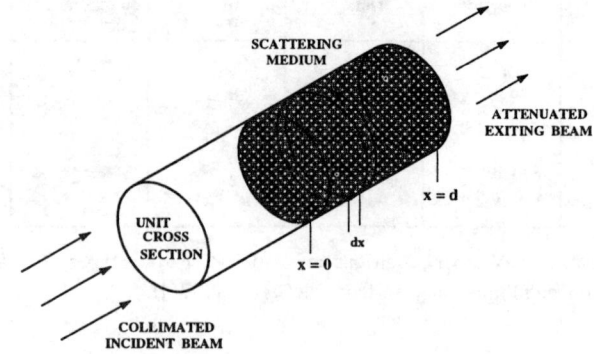

Figure 3: Attenuation of a collimated beam of light by suspended particles. The attenuation can be derived by viewing the medium as a collection of thin sheets (laminae).

assumed that the coefficient $\beta(\lambda)$ is constant (homogeneous medium) over horizontal paths. To satisfy this constraint, we will restrict ourselves to the case where the observer is at (or close to) ground level and is interested not in the sky but other objects on (or close to) ground level. Finally, we have assumed that all scattered flux is removed from the incident energy. The fraction of energy that remains is called *direct transmission* and is given by expression (4). We have ignored the flux scattered in the forward direction (towards the observer) by each particle. Fortunately, this component is small in vision applications since the solid angles subtended by the source and the observer with respect to each other are small (see [Middleton, 1949]).

3.2 Airlight

A second mechanism causes the atmosphere to behave like a source of light. This phenomenon is called airlight [Koschmieder, 1924] and it is caused by the scattering of environmental illumination by particles in the atmosphere. The environmental illumination can have several sources, including, direct sunlight, diffuse skylight and light reflected by the ground. While attenuation causes scene radiance to decrease with pathlength, airlight increases with pathlength. It therefore causes the apparent brightness of a scene point to increase with depth. We now build upon McCartney's [McCartney, 1976] derivation of airlight as a function of pathlength.

Consider the illumination and observation geometry shown in Figure 4. The environmental illumination along the observer's line of sight is assumed to be constant but unknown in direction, intensity and spectrum. In effect, the cone of solid angle $d\omega$ subtended by a single receptor at the observer's end, and truncated by a physical object at distance d, can be viewed as a source of airlight. The infinitesimal volume dV at distance x from the observer may be written as $dV = d\omega x^2 dx$. Irrespective of the exact type of envi-

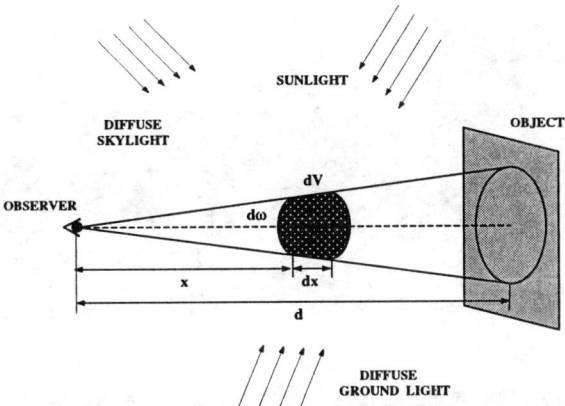

Figure 4: The cone of atmosphere between an observer and an object scatters environmental illumination in the direction of the observer. It therefore acts like a source of light, called airlight, whose brightness increases with pathlength.

ronmental illumination incident upon dV, its intensity due to scattering in the direction of the observer is:

$$dI(x, \lambda) = dV\, k\, \beta(\lambda) = d\omega\, x^2\, dx\, k\, \beta(\lambda), \quad (5)$$

where, $\beta(\lambda)$ is the total scattering coefficient and the proportionality constant k accounts for the exact nature of the illumination and the form of the scattering function.

If we view element dV as a source with intensity $dI(x, \lambda)$, the irradiance it produces at the observer's end, after attenuation due to the medium, is given by (4):

$$dE(x, \lambda) = \frac{dI(x, \lambda)\, e^{-\beta(\lambda)\, x}}{x^2}. \quad (6)$$

We can find the radiance of dV from its irradiance as:

$$dL(x, \lambda) = \frac{dE(x, \lambda)}{d\omega} = \frac{dI(x, \lambda)\, e^{-\beta(\lambda)\, x}}{d\omega\, x^2}. \quad (7)$$

By substituting (5) we get $dL(x, \lambda) = k\, \beta(\lambda)\, e^{-\beta(\lambda)\, x}\, dx$. Now, the total radiance of the pathlength d from the observer to the object is found by integrating this expression between $x = 0$ and $x = d$:

$$L(d, \lambda) = k\, (1 - e^{-\beta(\lambda)\, d}). \quad (8)$$

If the object is at an infinite distance (at the *horizon*), the radiance of airlight is maximum and is found by setting $d = \infty$ to get $L_h(\infty, \lambda) = k$. Therefore, the radiance of airlight for any given pathlength d is:

$$L(d, \lambda) = L_h(\infty, \lambda)\, (1 - e^{-\beta(\lambda)\, d}). \quad (9)$$

As expected, the radiance of airlight for an object right in front of the observer ($d = 0$) equals zero. Of great significance to us is the fact that the above expression no longer includes the unknown angular factor k. Instead, we have the airlight radiance $L_h(\infty, \lambda)$ at the horizon, which is an observable.

4 Depths of Light Sources from Attenuation

Consider the image of an urban setting taken at *night* (see Figure 5). Environmental illumination of the scene due to sunlight, skylight and reflected ground light are minimal and hence airlight can be safely ignored. The bright points in the image are mainly sources of light such as street lamps and windows of lit rooms. On a clear night, these sources are visible to a distant observer in their brightest and clearest forms. As haze or fog sets in, the radiant intensities of the sources diminish due to attenuation. Our goal here is to recover the relative depths of the sources in the scene from two images taken under different (unknown) atmospheric conditions.

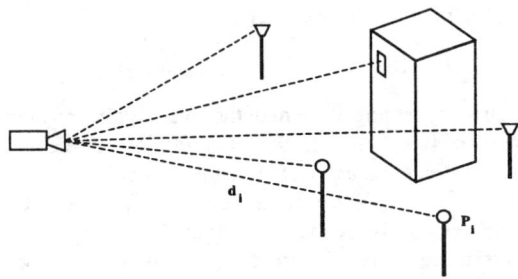

Figure 5: The relative depths of sources of unknown intensities can be recovered from two images taken under different but unknown atmospheric conditions.

Since environmental illumination is negligible at night, the image irradiance of a light source in the scene can be expressed using the attenuation model (4) as:

$$E(d, \lambda) = g\, \frac{I(\lambda)\, e^{-\beta(\lambda)\, d}}{d^2}, \quad (10)$$

where, $I(\lambda)$ is the radiant intensity of the source, d is the distance between the source and the camera and the constant gain g accounts for the optical parameters (aperture, for instance) of the camera. It is important to note that $\beta(\lambda)$ is the total scattering coefficient and not the angular one. We are assuming here that the lines of sight are not too inclined and hence all lines of sight pass through the same atmospheric conditions. This removes all dependence on the exact form of the scattering function; the attenuation is determined by a single coefficient $\beta(\lambda)$ which is independent of viewing direction.

If the detector of the camera has spectral response $s(\lambda)$, the final image brightness value recorded is determined as:

$$E' = \int s(\lambda)\, E(d, \lambda)\, d\lambda = \int g\, s(\lambda)\, \frac{I(\lambda)\, e^{-\beta(\lambda)\, d}}{d^2}\, d\lambda. \quad (11)$$

Since the spectral bandwidth of the camera is rather limited (visible light range when camera is black and white, and even narrower spectral bands when the camera is color), we will assume the total scattering coefficient $\beta(\lambda)$ to be constant over this bandwidth. Then, we have:

$$E' = g \frac{e^{-\beta d}}{d^2} \int s(\lambda) I(\lambda) \, d\lambda = g \frac{e^{-\beta d}}{d^2} I'. \quad (12)$$

Now consider two different weather conditions, say, mild and dense fog. Or, one of the conditions could be clear with $\beta = 0$. In either case we have two different attenuation coefficients, β_1 and β_2. If we take the ratio of the two resulting image brightness values, we get:

$$R = \frac{E'_1}{E'_2} = e^{-(\beta_1 - \beta_2) \, d}. \quad (13)$$

Using the natural log, we obtain:

$$R' = \ln R = -(\beta_1 - \beta_2) \, d. \quad (14)$$

This quantity is independent of the sensor gain and the radiant intensity of the source. In fact, it is nothing but the *difference in optical thicknesses* (DOT) of the source for two weather conditions. Now, if we compute the DOTs of two different light sources in the scene (see Figure 5) and take their ratio, we determine the relative depths of the two source locations:

$$\frac{R'_i}{R'_j} = \frac{d_i}{d_j} \quad (15)$$

Hence, the relative depths of all sources (with unknown radiant intensities) in the scene can be computed from two images taken under unknown but different haze or fog conditions. Since we may not entirely trust the DOT computed for any single source, the above calculation may be made more robust by using:

$$\frac{R'_i}{\sum_{j=0}^{j=N} R'_j} = \frac{d_i}{\sum_{j=0}^{j=N} d_j} \quad (16)$$

By setting the denominator on the right hand side to an arbitrary constant we have computed the depths of all sources in the scene up to a scale factor.

Figure 6 shows experimental results on the recovery of light sources from night images. This experiment and all subsequent ones are based on images acquired using a Nikon N90s SLR camera and a Nikon LS-2000 slide scanner. All images are linearized using the radiometric response curve of the imaging system that is computed off-line using a color chart. Figure 6(a) shows a clear day image of a scene with five lamps. This image is provided only to give the reader an idea of where the lamps are located in the scene. Figures 6(b) and (c) are clear night and foggy night images of the same scene. The above algorithm for depth estimation was used to recover the locations of all five light sources up to a scale factor. Figure 6(d) shows different perspectives of the recovered coordinates of the lamps in three-dimensional space. The poles and the ground plane are added only to aid visualization of the results.

(a)

(b)

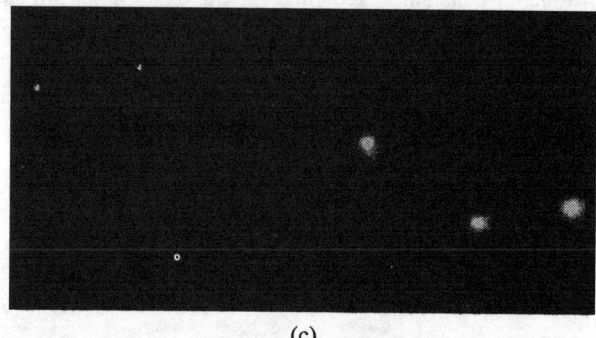

(c)

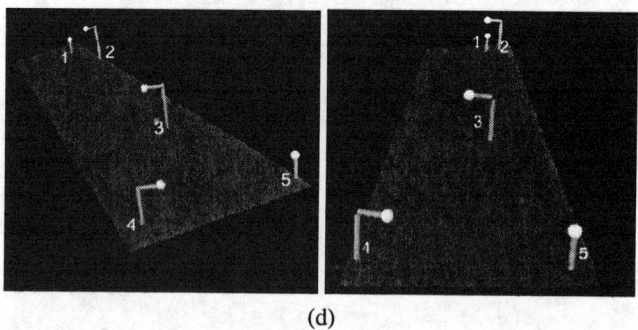

(d)

Figure 6: (a) A scene with five light sources (street lamps). This image is shown only to convey the relative locations of the sources to the reader. (b) An image of the scene taken on a clear night. (c) An image of the scene taken on a foggy night. The three-dimensional coordinates of the five sources were computed from images (b) and (c). (d) Rotated graphical illustrations used to demonstrate the accuracy of the computed lamp coordinates (small bright spheres). The lamp poles and the ground plane are added only to aid visualization.

5 Structure from Airlight

When we have dense fog and close by objects or mild fog and distant objects, attenuation of object brightness is severe and airlight is the main cause of image irradiance. Also, in the case of dense haze around noon, most visible scene points are not illuminated and airlight dominates. In both cases, airlight causes object brightness to increase with distance from the observer. Here, we present a simple method for computing scene structure from a single airlight image. A different but related method for computing depth cues was proposed by Cozman and Krotkov (see [Cozman and Krotkov, 1997]).

Let a scene point with depth d produce airlight radiance $L(d, \lambda)$. If our camera has a spectral response $s(\lambda)$, the final brightness value recorded for the scene point is:

$$E'(d) = \int g \, s(\lambda) \, L(d, \lambda) \, d\lambda, \qquad (17)$$

where, g accounts for the constant of proportionality between scene radiance and image irradiance. Substituting the model for airlight given by (9) we get:

$$E'(d) = \int g \, s(\lambda) \, L_h(\infty, \lambda) \, (1 - e^{-\beta(\lambda) d}) \, d\lambda \qquad (18)$$

where, $L_h(\infty, \lambda)$ is again the radiance of airlight at the horizon. As before, we will assume that the scattering coefficient $\beta(\lambda)$ is more or less constant over the spectral band of the camera. This allows us to write:

$$E'(d) = E_h'(\infty) (1 - e^{-\beta d}). \qquad (19)$$

Let us define:

$$S = \frac{E_h'(\infty) - E'(d)}{E_h'(\infty)}. \qquad (20)$$

By substituting (19) in the above expression and taking the natural logarithm, we get:

$$S' = \ln S = -\beta d. \qquad (21)$$

Hence, the three-dimensional structure of the scene can be recovered up to a scale factor (the scattering coefficient β) from a single image. Clearly, at least a small part of the horizon must be visible to obtain $E_h'(\infty)$. If so, this part is easily identified as the brightest region of the image. If there is a strong (directional) sunlight component to the illumination, scattering would be greater in some directions and airlight could be dependent on viewing direction. This problem can be alleviated by using the horizon brightness $E_h'(\infty)$ that lies closest to the scene point under consideration. Figure 7 shows the structure of an urban setting computed from a hazy image taken around noon, and the structure of a mountain range computed using a foggy image. Given that some of the objects are miles away from the camera, such scenes are hard to compute using stereo or structure from motion.

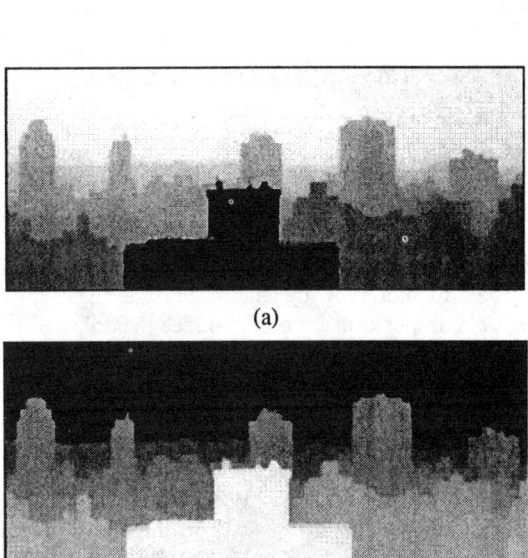

(a)

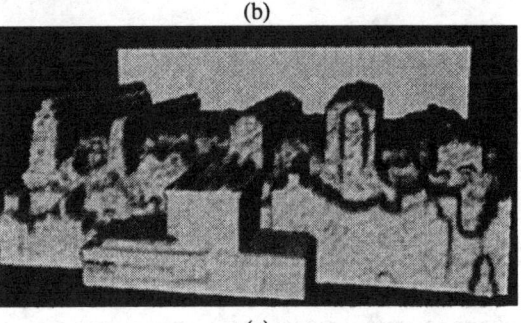

(b)

(c)

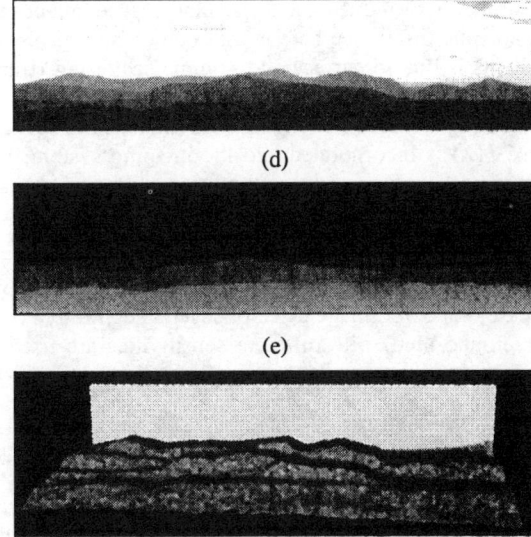

(d)

(e)

(f)

Figure 7: (a) Image of an urban scene taken under noon haze. (b) Depth map of the scene computed using the image in (a). (c) A three-dimensional (rotated) rendering of the scene. (d) Image of a mountain range taken under foggy conditions. (e) Depth map computed from the image in (d). (f) A three-dimensional (rotated) rendering of the scene. Some of the objects in these scenes are several miles away from the camera.

6 Dichromatic Atmospheric Scattering

Thus far, we have not exploited the chromatic effects of atmospheric scattering. As we know, attenuation causes the radiance of the surface to decay as it travels to the observer. In addition, if the particle sizes are comparable to the wavelengths of the reflected light, the spectral composition of the reflected light can be expected to vary as it passes through the medium. Fortunately, for fog and dense haze, these shifts in the spectral composition are minimal (see [Middleton, 1952] and [Nayar and Narasimhan, 1999] for details), and hence we may assume the hue of direct transmission to be independent of the depth of the reflecting surface. The hue of airlight depends on the particle size distribution and tends to be gray or light blue in the case of haze and fog. Therefore, the final spectral distribution $E(d, \lambda)$ received by the observer is a sum of the distributions $E_{dt}(d, \lambda)$ of directly transmitted light and $E_a(d, \lambda)$ of airlight, which are determined by the attenuation model (10) and the airlight model (9):

$$
\begin{aligned}
E(d, \lambda) &= E_{dt}(d, \lambda) + E_a(d, \lambda), \quad (22)\\
E_{dt}(d, \lambda) &= g \, \frac{e^{-\beta(\lambda)\, d}}{d^2} \, L_r(\lambda),\\
E_a(d, \lambda) &= g \, (1 - e^{-\beta(\lambda)\, d}) \, L_h(\lambda).
\end{aligned}
$$

Here, $L_r(\lambda)$ is the surface radiance prior to attenuation, $L_h(\lambda)$ is the radiance of the horizon ($d = \infty$), and g is a constant that accounts for the optical settings of the imaging system. We refer to the above expression as the *dichromatic atmospheric scattering model*. It is similar in its spirit to the dichromatic reflectance model [Shafer, 1985] that describes the spectral effects of diffuse and specular surface reflections. A fundamental difference here is that one of our chromatic components is due to surface and volume scattering (transmission of reflected light) while the other is due to pure volume scattering (airlight). If a chromatic filter with a spectral response $f(\lambda)$ is incorporated into the imaging system, image irradiance is obtained by multiplying (22) by $f(\lambda)$ and integrating over λ:

$$
E^{(f)}(d) = E_{dt}^{(f)}(d) + E_a^{(f)}(d). \quad (23)
$$

In the case of a color image detector several such filters (say, red, green and blue) with different sensitivities are used to obtain a color measurement vector. The dichromatic model can then be written as (see Figure 8):

$$
\mathbf{E}(d) = \mathbf{E_{dt}}(d) + \mathbf{E_a}(d) \quad (24)
$$

where, $\mathbf{E} = [E^{(f_1)}, E^{(f_2)}, \ldots E^{(f_n)}]^T$. As we mentioned earlier, the dependence of the scattering coefficient $\beta(\lambda)$ on the wavelength of light tends to be rather small. Therefore, except in the case of certain types of metropolitan haze, we may assume scattering to be constant with respect to wavelength ($\beta(\lambda) = \beta$). Then, expression (23) may be simplified as:

$$
E^{(f)}(d) = p(d) E_r^{(f)} + q(d) E_h^{(f)}, \quad (25)
$$

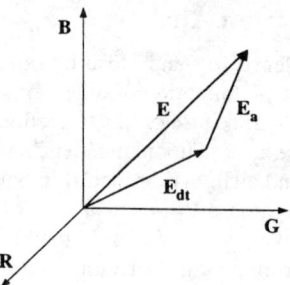

Figure 8: The color at an image point is the sum of two vectors, namely, the color due to transmission of light reflected by the scene point and the color due to airlight.

$$
E_r^{(f)} = \int g f(\lambda) L_r(\lambda) \, d\lambda \, , \quad E_h^{(f)} = \int g f(\lambda) L_h(\lambda) \, d\lambda \, ,
$$

$$
p(d) = \frac{e^{-\beta d}}{d^2} \, , \quad q(d) = (1 - e^{-\beta d}). \quad (26)
$$

Here, $E_r^{(f)}$ is the image irradiance due to the scene point *without* atmospheric attenuation and $E_h^{(f)}$ is the image irradiance at the horizon in the presence of bad weather. We are assuming here that the clear and bad weather have illuminations with similar spectral distributions. Hence, the final color measurement given by (24) can be rewritten as: $\mathbf{E}(d) = p(d) \mathbf{E_r} + q(d) \mathbf{E_h}$. Since the intensity of illumination at a scene point is expected to vary between clear and bad weather, it is more convenient to write:

$$
\mathbf{E}(d) = r \, p(d) \, \hat{\mathbf{E}}_\mathbf{r} + s \, q(d) \, \hat{\mathbf{E}}_\mathbf{h} \quad (27)
$$

where $\hat{\mathbf{E}}_\mathbf{r}$ and $\hat{\mathbf{E}}_\mathbf{h}$ are unit vectors and r and s are scalars.

7 Structure from Chromatic Decomposition

Consider color images of a scene taken under clear weather and foggy or hazy weather. Assume that the clear day image is taken under environmental illumination with similar spectral characteristics as the bad weather image. If not, a white patch in the scene may be used to apply the needed color corrections. The horizon in the bad weather image reveals the *direction* of the airlight color $\hat{\mathbf{E}}_\mathbf{h}$. The *direction* of the color $\hat{\mathbf{E}}_\mathbf{r}$ of each scene point is revealed by the clear weather image. Therefore, equation (27) can be used to decompose the bad weather color $\mathbf{E}(d)$ at each pixel into its two components and determine the scaled airlight magnitude $s q(d)$. The resulting airlight image is then used to compute a depth map as in section 5. Figure 9 shows experimental results obtained using the above decomposition method. In computing depth from the airlight component, we have assumed that the atmosphere itself is uniformly illuminated. Consider a pathlength that extends from a point on a building to an observer. Clearly, atmospheric points closer to the building see less of the sky due to occlusion by the building. This effect increases towards the foot of the building. Some of the errors in our computed depth maps can be attributed to this effect (see [Nayar and Narasimhan, 1999] for details).

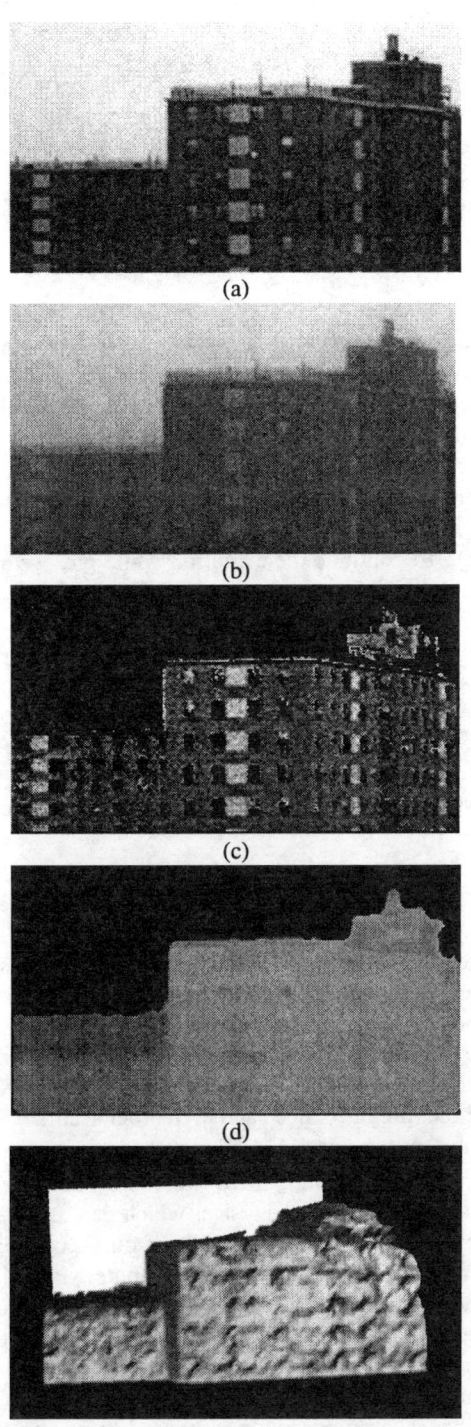

8 Conclusion

Ultimately, vision systems must be able to handle problems posed by bad weather. This article is no more than an initial attempt at understanding and exploiting the manifestations of weather. We summarized existing models in atmospheric optics and proposed new ones, keeping in mind the constraints faced by most vision applications. In addition, we presented three simple algorithms for recovering scene structure from one or two images, without requiring prior knowledge of atmospheric conditions. We intend to use these results as building blocks for developing more advanced weather-tolerant vision techniques.

References

[Cozman and Krotkov, 1997] F. Cozman and E. Krotkov. Depth from scattering. *Proc. of IEEE Conf. on Comp. Vision and Pattern Recog.*, 31:801–806, 1997.

[Hidy, 1972] ed. G. M. Hidy. *Aerosols and Atmospheric Chemistry*. Academic Press, New York, 1972.

[Koenderink and Richards, 1992] J. J. Koenderink and W. A. Richards. Why is snow so bright? *Journal of Optical Society of America*, 9(5):643–648, 1992.

[Koschmieder, 1924] H. Koschmieder. Theorie der horizontalen sichtweite. *Beitr. Phys. freien Atm.*, 12:33–53,171–181, 1924.

[Mason, 1975] B. J. Mason. *Clouds, Rain, and Rainmaking*. Cambridge University Press, Cambridge, 1975.

[McCartney, 1976] E. J. McCartney. *Optics of the Atmosphere: Scattering by Molecules and Particles*. John Wiley and Sons, New York, 1976.

[Middleton, 1949] W. E. K. Middleton. The effect of the angular aperture of a telephotometer on the telephotometry of collimated and non-collimated beams. *Journal of Optical Society of America*, 39:576–581, 1949.

[Middleton, 1952] W. E. K. Middleton. *Vision through the atmosphere*. University of Toronto Press, 1952.

[Mie, 1908] G. Mie. A contribution to the optics of turbid media, especially colloidal metallic suspensions. *Ann. of Physics*, 25(4):377–445, 1908.

[Minnaert, 1954] M. Minnaert. *The Nature of Light and Color in the Open Air*. Dover, New York, 1954.

[Myers, 1968] J. N. Myers. Fog. *Scientific American*, pages 75–82, December 1968.

[Nayar and Narasimhan, 1999] S. K. Nayar and S. G. Narasimhan. Computer Vision in Bad Weather. Technical report, Dept. of Computer Science, Columbia University, New York, (in prep.), July 1999.

[Nieto-Vesperinas and Dainty, 1990] M. Nieto-Vesperinas and J. C. Dainty. *Scattering in volumes and surfaces*. North-Holland, New York, 1990.

[Ohtake, 1970] T. Ohtake. Factors affecting the size distribution of raindrops and snowflakes. *Journal of Atmospheric Science*, 27:804–813, 1970.

[Shafer, 1985] S. Shafer. Using color to separate reflection components. *Color Research and Applications*, pages 210–218, 1985.

Figure 9: Removal of fog and depth estimation using the dichromatic atmospheric scattering model. (a) Clear day image of buildings. (b) Foggy day image of the same scene. (c) The direct transmission component (brightened) estimated by the chromatic decomposition algorithm. Black and gray points (windows) are discarded due to lack of color. (d) Depth map of the scene computed from the airlight component (depths of window areas are interpolated). (e) A three-dimensional rendering of the computed depth map. (**See CDROM version of the proceedings for color images.**)

The Hamilton-Jacobi Skeleton

Kaleem Siddiqi[*] Sylvain Bouix[†] Allen Tannenbaum[‡] Steven W. Zucker[§]

Abstract

The eikonal equation and variants of it are of significant interest for problems in computer vision and image processing. It is the basis for continuous versions of mathematical morphology, stereo, shape-from-shading and for recent dynamic theories of shape. Its numerical simulation can be delicate, owing to the formation of singularities in the evolving front, and is typically based on level set methods. However, there are more classical approaches rooted in Hamiltonian physics, which have received little consideration in computer vision. In this paper we first introduce a new algorithm for simulating the eikonal equation, which offers a number of computational and conceptual advantages over the earlier methods when it comes to shock tracking. Next, we introduce a very efficient algorithm for shock detection, where the key idea is to measure the net outward flux of a vector field per unit volume, and to detect locations where a conservation of energy principle is violated. We illustrate the approach with several numerical examples including skeletons of complex 2D and 3D shapes.

1. Introduction

Variational principles emerged naturally from considerations of energy minimization in mechanics [11]. We consider these in the context of the eikonal equation, which arises in geometrical optics and, recently, which has become of great interest for problems in computer vision [4]. It is the basis for continuous versions of mathematical morphology [3, 18, 25], as well as for Blum's grassfire transform [2] and new dynamic theories of shape representation including [9, 23]. It has also been widely used for applications in image processing and analysis [19, 5], shape-from-shading [10] and stereo [8].

The numerical simulation of this equation is non-trivial,

because it is a hyperbolic partial differential equation for which a smooth initial front may develop singularities or *shocks* as it propagates. At such points, classical concepts such as the normal to a curve, and its curvature, are not defined. Nevertheless, it is precisely these points that are important for the above applications in computer vision since, e.g., it is they which denote the skeleton (see Figure 3). To continue the evolution while preserving shocks, the technology of level set methods introduced by Osher and Sethian [15], has proved to be extremely powerful. The approach relies on the notion of a weak solution, developed in viscosity theory [6], and the introduction of an appropriate entropy condition to select it. The representation of the evolving front as a level set of a hypersurface allows topological changes to be handled in a natural way, and robust, efficient implementations have recently been developed [20].

Level set methods are Eulerian in nature because computations are restricted to grid points whose locations are fixed. For such methods, the question of computing the locus of shocks for dynamically changing systems remains of crucial importance, i.e., the methods are shock *preserving* but do not explicitly *detect* shocks. Shock detection methods which rely on interpolation of the underlying hypersurface are computationally very expensive. Numerical thresholds are introduced and high order accurate numerical schemes must be used [14, 22].

On the other hand, there are more classical methods rooted in Hamiltonian physics, which can also be used to study shock theory. To the best of our knowledge, these have not been considered in the computer vision literature. The purpose of this paper is twofold. First, we introduce the above methods and a straightforward algorithm for simulating the eikonal equation, which offers a number of computational and conceptual advantages when it comes to shock tracking. The proposed algorithm is Lagrangian in nature, i.e., the front is explicitly represented as a sequence of marker particles. The motion of these particles is then governed by an underlying Hamiltonian system. Such systems are of course fundamental in classical physics, and have a natural physical interpretation based on elementary Hamiltonian and Lagrangian mechanics. Second, we introduce a very efficient algorithm for shock detection based on the net

---

[*]School of Computer Science & Center for Intelligent Machines McGill University, Montréal, PQ, Canada H3A 2A7

[†]School of Computer Science & Center for Intelligent Machines McGill University, Montréal, PQ, Canada H3A 2A7

[‡]Department of Electrical and Computer Engineering, University of Minnesota, 200 Union Street S. E. Minneapolis, MN 55455

[§]Department of Computer Science & Department of Electrical Engineering, Yale University, New Haven, CT 06520-8285

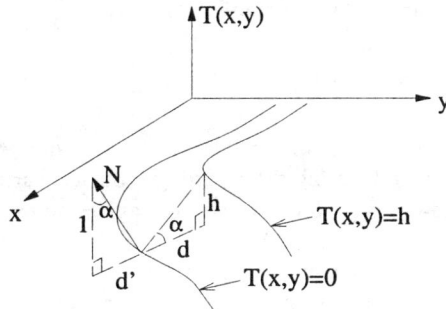

Figure 1: A geometric view of a monotonically advancing front (Eq. 1). $T(x,y)$ is a graph of the 'solution' surface, the level sets of which are the evolved curves.

outward flux per unit volume of the vector field underlying the Hamiltonian system.

2. The Eikonal Equation

We begin by showing the connection between a monotonically advancing front, and the well known eikonal equation. Consider the curve evolution equation

$$\frac{\partial \mathcal{C}}{\partial t} = F\mathcal{N}, \qquad (1)$$

where $\mathcal{C}$ is the vector of curve coordinates, $\mathcal{N}$ is the unit inward normal, and $F = F(x,y)$ is the speed of the front at each point in the plane, with $F \geq 0$ (the case $F \leq 0$ is also allowed). Let $T(x,y)$ be a graph of the solution surface, obtained by superimposing all the evolved curves in time (see Figure 1). In other words, $T(x,y)$ is the time at which the curve crosses a point (x,y) in the plane. Referring to the figure, the speed of the front is given by

$$F(x,y) = \frac{d}{h} = \frac{1}{\tan(\alpha)} = \frac{1}{d'} = \frac{1}{\|\nabla T\|}.$$

Hence, $T(x,y)$ satisfies the *eikonal equation*

$$\|\nabla T\| \, F = 1. \qquad (2)$$

A number of algorithms have been recently developed to solve a quadratic form of this equation, i.e., $\|\nabla T\|^2 = \frac{1}{F^2}$. These include Sethian's fast marching method [20], which relies on an interpretation of Huygens's principle to efficiently propagate the solution from the initial curve, and Rouy and Tourin's viscosity solutions approach [17]. However, neither of these methods address the issue of shock detection explicitly, and more work has to be done to track shocks.

A different approach, which is related to the solution surface $T(x,y)$ viewed as a graph, has been proposed by Shah *et al* [21, 23]. Here the key idea is to use an edge strength

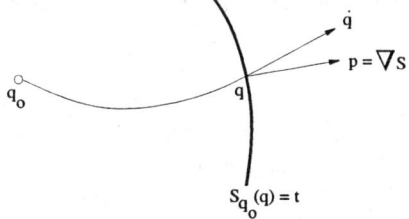

Figure 2: Direction of a ray $\dot{q}$ and the direction of motion of the wave front p. From [1].

functional v in place of the surface $T(x,y)$, computed by a linear diffusion equation. The equation can be efficiently implemented, and the framework extends to greyscale images as well as curves with triple point junctions. It provides an approximation to the reaction-diffusion space introduced in [9], but does not extend to the extreme cases, i.e., morphological erosion by a disc structuring element (reaction) or motion by curvature (diffusion). Hence, points of maximum (local) curvature are interpreted as skeletal points. This regularized skeleton is typically not connected, and its relation to the classical skeleton, obtained from the eikonal equation with $F = 1$, is as yet unclear.

In the next section, we shall consider an alternate framework for solving the eikonal equation, which is based on the canonical equations of Hamilton. The technique is widely used in classical mechanics, and rests on the use of a Legendre transformation (see [1] for the precise definition) which takes a system of n second-order differential equations to a (mathematically equivalent) system of $2n$ first-order differential equations. We believe that for a number of vision problems involving shock tracking and skeletonization, this represents a natural way of implementing the eikonal equation.

3. Hamilton's Canonical Equations

Following Arnold [1, pp. 248–258], we shall use Huygens' principle to show the connection between the eikonal equation and the Hamilton-Jacobi equation. For every point q_0, define the function $S_{q_0}(q)$ as the optical length of the path from q_0 to q (see Figure 2). The wave front at time t is given by $\{q : S_{q_0}(q) = t\}$. The vector $p = \frac{\partial S}{\partial q}$ is called the *vector of normal slowness of the front*. By Huygens' principle the direction of the ray $\dot{q}$ is conjugate to the direction of motion of the front, i.e., $p \cdot \dot{q} = 1$. Note that these directions do not coincide in an anisotropic medium.

Let us specialize to the case of a monotonically advancing front in an inhomogeneous but isotropic medium (Eq. 1). Here the speed $F(x,y)$ depends only on position (not on direction), and the directions of p and $\dot{q}$ coincide.

The action function minimized, $S(\mathbf{q}, t)$, is defined as

$$S_{\mathbf{q}_0, t_0}(\mathbf{q}, t) = \int_\gamma L dt,$$

along the extremal curve γ connecting the points $(\mathbf{q}_0, t_0)$ and $(\mathbf{q}, t)$. Here the Lagrangian

$$L = \frac{1}{F(x, y)} \|\partial \gamma / \partial t\|$$

is a conformal (infinitesimal) length element, and we have assumed that the extremals emanating from the point $(\mathbf{q}_0, t_0)$ do not intersect elsewhere, i.e., they form a *central field of extremals*. Note that for an isotropic medium the extremals are straight lines, and that for the special case $F(x, y) = 1$, the action function becomes Euclidean length.

It can be shown that the vector of normal slowness, $\mathbf{p} = \frac{\partial S}{\partial \mathbf{q}}$, is not arbitrary but satisfies the Hamilton-Jacobi equation

$$\frac{\partial S}{\partial t} = -H\left(\frac{\partial S}{\partial \mathbf{q}}, \mathbf{q}\right), \tag{3}$$

where the Hamiltonian function $H(\mathbf{p}, \mathbf{q})$ is the Legendre transformation with respect to $\dot{\mathbf{q}}$ of the Lagrangian function $L(\mathbf{q}, \dot{\mathbf{q}})$. Rather than solve the nonlinear Hamilton-Jacobi equation for the action function S (which will give the solution surface $T(x, y)$ to Eq. 2), it is much more convenient to look at the evolution of the phase space $(\mathbf{p}, \mathbf{q})$ under the equivalent Hamiltonian system

$$\dot{\mathbf{p}} = -\frac{\partial H}{\partial \mathbf{q}}, \qquad \dot{\mathbf{q}} = \frac{\partial H}{\partial \mathbf{p}}.$$

This offers a number of advantages, the most significant being that the equations become linear, and hence trivial to simulate numerically. In the following we shall derive this system of equations for the special case of a front advancing with speed $F(x, y) = 1$.

4. The Hamilton-Jacobi Skeleton Flow

For the case of a front moving with constant speed, recall that the action function being minimized is Euclidean length, and hence S can be viewed as a Euclidean distance function from the initial curve C_0. Furthermore, the magnitude of its gradient, $\|\nabla S\|$, is identical to 1 in its smooth regime, which is precisely where the assumption of a central field of extremals is valid.

With $\mathbf{q} = (x, y)$, $\mathbf{p} = (S_x, S_y)$, associate to the evolving plane curve $C \subset \mathbf{R}^2$ the surface $\tilde{C} \subset \mathbf{R}^4$ given by

$$\tilde{C} := \{(x, y, S_x, S_y) : (x, y) \in C, \ S_x^2 + S_y^2 = 1, \ \mathbf{p} \cdot \dot{\mathbf{q}} = 1\}.$$

The Hamiltonian function obtained by applying a Legendre transformation to the Lagrangian $L = \|\dot{\mathbf{q}}\|$ is given by

$$H = \mathbf{p} \cdot \dot{\mathbf{q}} - L = 1 - (S_x^2 + S_y^2)^{\frac{1}{2}}.$$

The associated Hamiltonian system is:

$$\dot{\mathbf{p}} = -\frac{\partial H}{\partial \mathbf{q}} = (0, 0), \qquad \dot{\mathbf{q}} = \frac{\partial H}{\partial \mathbf{p}} = -(S_x, S_y). \tag{4}$$

$\tilde{C}$ can be evolved under this system of equations, with $\tilde{C}(t) \subset \mathbf{R}^4$ denoting the resulting (contact) surface. The projection of $\tilde{C}(t)$ onto $\mathbf{R}^2$ will then give the parallel evolution of C at time t, $C(t)$.

We shall now make use of the fact that all Hamiltonian systems are conservative [16, p. 172]. In particular:

Theorem 1 *The total energy $H(\mathbf{p}, \mathbf{q})$ of the Hamiltonian system (4) remains constant along trajectories of (4).*

Proof. The total derivative of $H(\mathbf{p}, \mathbf{q})$ along a trajectory $\mathbf{p}(t), \mathbf{q}(t)$ of (4) is given by

$$\frac{dH}{dt} = \frac{\partial H}{\partial \mathbf{p}} \cdot \dot{\mathbf{p}} + \frac{\partial H}{\partial \mathbf{q}} \cdot \dot{\mathbf{q}} = \frac{\partial H}{\partial \mathbf{p}} \cdot \frac{\partial H}{\partial \mathbf{q}} - \frac{\partial H}{\partial \mathbf{p}} \cdot \frac{\partial H}{\partial \mathbf{q}} = 0.$$

Thus $H(\mathbf{p}, \mathbf{q})$ is constant along any trajectory of (4).

5. Flux and Divergence

The analysis carried out thus far applies under the assumption of a central field of extremals, see Section 3, such that trajectories of the Hamiltonian system do not intersect. Conversely, when shocks form due to the intersection of trajectories, the conservation of energy principle will be violated (energy will be absorbed). As we shall now show, this loss of energy can be used to formulate a robust and very efficient algorithm for shock detection, based on an application of the divergence theorem.

The key is to measure the flux of the vector field $\dot{\mathbf{q}}$, which is analogous to the flow of an incompressible fluid such as water. Note that for a volume with an enclosed surface, an excess of outward or inward flow through the surface indicates the presence of a *source*, or a *sink*, respectively, in the volume. The latter case is the one we are interested in, and we shall use the divergence of the vector field to provide a measure proportional to the net outward flux. More specifically, in physics the divergence of a vector field at a point, $\text{div}(\dot{\mathbf{q}})$, is defined as the net outward flux per unit volume, as the volume about the point shrinks to zero:

$$\text{div}(\dot{\mathbf{q}}) \equiv \lim_{\Delta v \to 0} \frac{\int_S <\dot{\mathbf{q}}, \mathcal{N}> ds}{\Delta v} \tag{5}$$

Here Δv is the volume, S is its surface and $\mathcal{N}$ is the outward normal at each point on its surface. This definition can be shown to be equivalent to the more common definition of the divergence as the sum of the partial derivatives with respect to each of the vector field's component directions:

$$\text{div}(\dot{\mathbf{q}}) = \frac{\partial \mathbf{q}_{x_1}}{\partial x_1} + \ldots + \frac{\partial \mathbf{q}_{x_n}}{\partial x_n} \tag{6}$$

However, Eq. 6 cannot be used at points where the vector field is singular, and hence is not differentiable. These are precisely the points we are interested in, and Eq. 5 offers significant advantages for shock detection. In particular, the numerator, which represents the net outward flux of the vector field through the surface which bounds the volume, is an index computation on the vector field. As we shall see, this is numerically much more stable than the estimation of derivatives in the vicinity of singularities. Further, via the divergence theorem,

$$\int_v \text{div}(\dot{\mathbf{q}})\text{dv} \equiv \int_S < \dot{\mathbf{q}}, \mathcal{N} > \text{ds}. \quad (7)$$

Hence, the net outward flux through the surface which bounds a finite volume is just the volume integral of the divergence of the vector field within that volume. Locations where the flux is negative, and hence energy is lost, correspond to sink points or shocks.

6. Numerical Simulations

We now apply the above theory to formulate an efficient algorithm for simulating the eikonal equation, while tracking the shocks which form. We shall later discretize the flux computation of Eq. 7 to formulate a very efficient algorithm for shock detection. This can be used to provide an explicit stopping condition for the eikonal evolution.

Recall that since the approach is a Lagrangian one, marker particles will have to first be placed along the initial curve, which in our simulations is assumed to be a simple closed curve in the plane.[1] The evolution of marker particles is then governed by Eq. 4. With $\mathbf{q} = (x, y)$, $\mathbf{p} = (S_x, S_y) = \nabla S$, the system of equations $\{\dot{S}_x = 0, \dot{S}_y = 0; \quad \dot{x} = -S_x, \dot{y} = -S_y\}$ gives a gradient dynamical system. The second equation indicates that the trajectory of the marker particles will be governed by the vector field obtained from the gradient of the Euclidean distance function S, and the first indicates that this vector field does not change with time, and can be computed once at the beginning of the simulation. Projecting this 4D system onto the (x, y) plane for each instance of time t will give the evolved curve $\mathcal{C}(t)$.

In order to obtain accurate results, three numerical issues need to be addressed. First, in order to obtain a dense sequence of marker particles, a continuous representation of the initial shape's boundary ($T(x, y) = 0$, see Figure 1) is needed. Second, it is possible for marker particles to drift apart in rarefaction regions, i.e., concave portions of the curve may fan out. Hence, new marker particles must be interpolated when necessary. Third, whereas finite central differences are adequate for estimating the gradient of the

---

[1]The method would also extend naturally to open curves, where an outward distance function would have to be defined.

Figure 3: The evolution of marker particles under the Hamiltonian system. The initial particles are placed on the boundary, and iterations of the process are superimposed. These correspond to level sets of the solution surface $T(x, y)$ in Figure 1. Individual marker particles are more clearly visible in the zoom-in on the fingers of the hand (top right).

Euclidean distance function in its smooth regime, such estimates will lead to errors near singularities, where S is not differentiable. Hence, we use ENO interpolants for estimating derivatives [14]; the key idea is to obtain information from the "smooth" side, in the vicinity of a singularity. The algorithm may now be stated as follows:

1. Take as the initial curve $T(x(s), y(s)) = 0$, the given boundary of an object, assumed to be a simple closed curve in the plane.

2. Create an ordered sequence of marker particles at positions Δs apart along the boundary.

3. Compute a Euclidean distance transform, where each grid point in the interior of the boundary is assigned its Euclidean distance to the closest marker particle.

4. For each grid point in the interior of the boundary compute and store the components of the vector field ∇S, using ENO interpolants.

5. Do for **step** from **0** to **TOTALSTEPS** {
    Do for **particle** from **0** to **NPARTICLES** {
      • Update the particle's position based on ∇S at the closest grid point:
$$x(step + 1) = x(step) - \Delta t \times S_x,$$
$$y(step + 1) = y(step) - \Delta t \times S_y$$
      • **if** (Distance(particle,next_particle) $> a\Delta s$){
        interpolate a new particle in between.
      }
    }
}

In our experiments, we have used a piecewise circular arc representation of the boundary, obtained using the contour tracer developed in [22], on the signed distance transform of the original binary shape. The distance transform is blurred very slightly to combat discretization. The birth of new marker particles (step 5) is also based on circular arc interpolation. Figure 3 depicts the evolution of marker particles, with speed $F = 1$, for several different shapes. For all simulations, the spacing Δs of initial marker particles is 0.25 pixels, the spacing criterion for interpolating a new particle in the course of the evolution is $a\Delta s = 0.75$ pixels, and the resolution of the Euclidean distance transform S is the same as that of the original binary image. The timestep Δt is 0.5 pixels, and results for every second iteration are saved. The superposition of all the level curves gives the solution surface $T(x, y)$ in Figure 1. It is important to note that in principle higher order interpolants can be used for the placement of marker particles, and the resolution of the exact distance transform is not limited by that of the original (binary) shape.

The results are comparable to those obtained using higher order ENO implementations, although the algorithm is computationally more efficient (linear in the number of marker particles). Informal timing experiments indicate

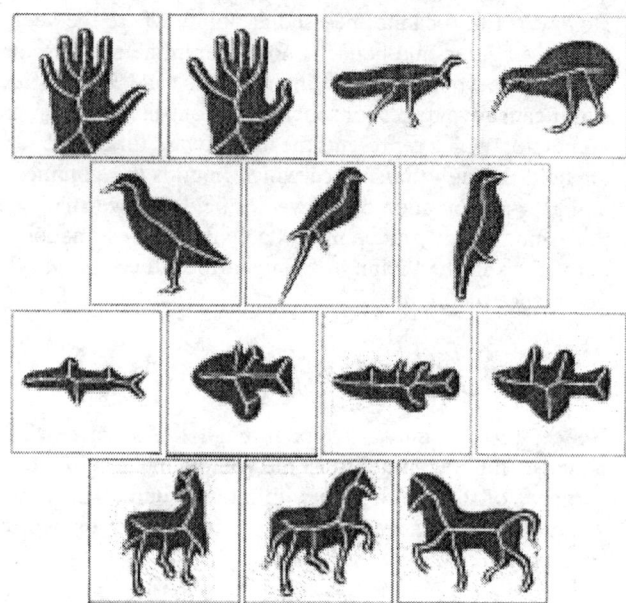

Figure 4: A divergence-based skeleton, superimposed in white on the original binary shapes (shown in grey). Comparing with the Hamiltonian system based flows in Figure 3, these maps can be used to formulate an explicit stopping condition for the individual marker particles.

that the efficiency of the algorithm exceeds that of level set methods, except under the "fast marching" implementation, with which it compares favorably. However, when shock detection is included, the Hamiltonian approach has important conceptual and computational advantages. In particular, in contrast with level set approaches, topological splits are not explicitly handled, but shocks (collisions of marker particles) are. In effect, the marker particles are jittered back and forth along the crest lines of the distance function S, leading to the thick traces in Figure 3.

We now turn to the implementation of the flux computation (Eq. 7) detailed in Section 5. This turns out to be extremely straightforward and efficient to implement, because the computations are local and hence parallelizable. For each grid point consider a small disc in 2D (or a sphere in 3D) centered at the point, such that it passes through its nearest neighboring grid points, i.e., its radius is equal to the grid point spacing Δd. Now, over all neighboring grid points, compute the sum of the inner products of the outward normals to the disc and the vector field $(-S_x, -S_y)$ (in 2D), or the sphere and the vector field $(-S_x, -S_y, -S_z)$ (in 3D). Finally, mark those points where the net outward flux (the volume integral of the divergence) is negative, as sink points or shocks.

Figure 4 illustrates this computation in 2D, using a 3x3 neighborhood, for the same shapes as before. Note that these computations use the same signed distance function

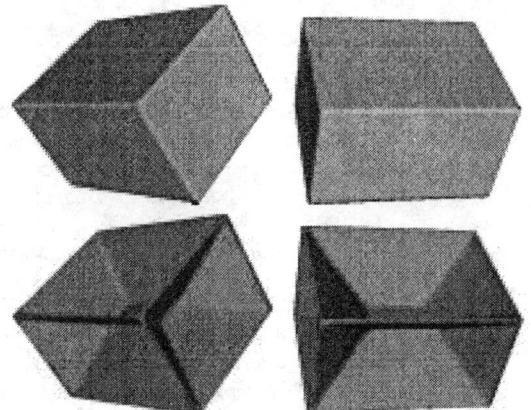

Figure 5: FIRST ROW: Two views of a 3D box. SECOND ROW: The corresponding divergence-based 3D skeletons.

as the earlier marker particle evolutions, but are otherwise entirely independent. Hence, they can be used to provide an explicit stopping condition for the marker particles, should this be desired. Figures 5, 6 and 7 illustrate the divergence-based computation in 3D, using a 3x3x3 neighborhood, on volumetric data of increasing complexity. The box data is synthetic; the brain ventricles and the outer surface of the brain were obtained using surface evolution based segmentation techniques on volumetric MR data. Whereas alternate approaches based on Voronoi techniques provide a topologically organized set of skeletal branches or faces [13, 12], their complexity increases with the number of points on the bounding curve or surface. More significantly, heuristic measures of significance are used for pruning, in order to obtain reasonable results. In contrast, the notion of divergence provides a very natural measure of significance. Furthermore, since the computation is purely local, the 2D or 3D implementations are linear in the number of pixels or voxels in the array; the 3D version takes less than 20 seconds on a 400 MHz Pentium. Whereas naive thresholding can, in principle, yield skeletons which are disconnected or have holes, it is straightforward to extend the method to yield skeletons which are homotopic with the original object. The basic idea is to use the divergence to guide a 2D or 3D thinning process. This extension will be described in future work.

7. Conclusions

This paper makes two main contributions. First, a new algorithm for simulating the eikonal equation has been introduced. The method is rooted in Hamiltonian physics and offers a number of computational advantages when it comes to shock tracking. Second, based on the violation of a conservation of energy principle at singular points of the Hamiltonian system, we have introduced a very efficient

and robust algorithm for shock detection. Here the key idea is to measure the net outward flux of a vector field per unit volume, and to detect locations where energy is lost.

In future work we plan to further develop the eikonal equation simulation in 3D, as well as the divergence implementation. The current implementation of divergence is purely local, and involves fixed size discs, which suffices to demonstrate a proof of concept. In closing, we note that in related recent work, a wave propagation framework on a discrete grid has been proposed for curve evolution and mathematical morphology [24], and that vector fields rooted in magneto-statics have also been used for extracting symmetry and edge lines in greyscale images [7].

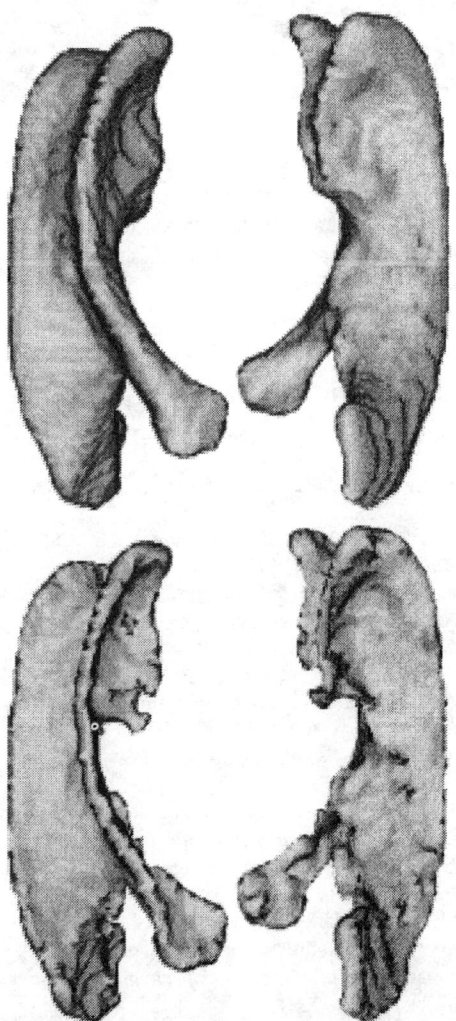

Figure 6: FIRST ROW: Two views of the ventricles of a brain, obtained using surface evolution based segmentation techniques on volumetric MR data. SECOND ROW: The corresponding divergence-based 3D skeletons.

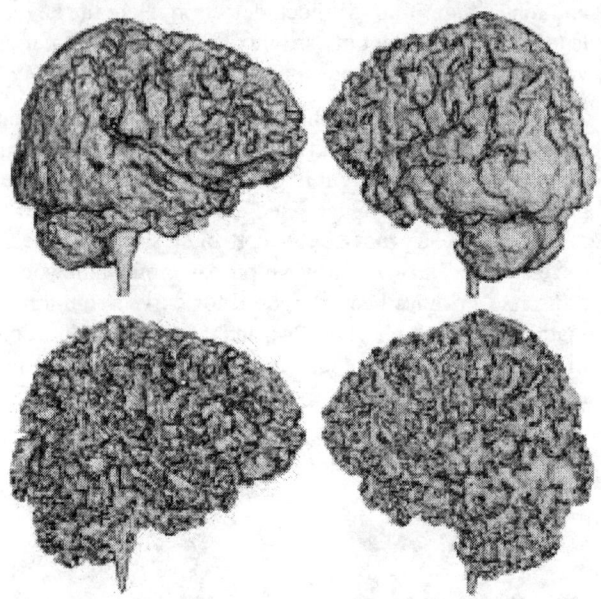

Figure 7: FIRST ROW: Two views of the outer surface of a brain, obtained using surface evolution based segmentation techniques on volumetric MR data. SECOND ROW: The corresponding divergence-based 3D skeletons.

Acknowledgements This work was supported by NSERC, FCAR, NSF, AFOSR, ARO, and a Multi University Research Initiative grant.

References

[1] V. Arnold. *Mathematical Methods of Classical Mechanics, Second Edition.* Springer-Verlag, 1989.

[2] H. Blum. Biological shape and visual science. *J. Theor. Biol.,* 38:205–287, 1973.

[3] R. Brockett and P. Maragos. Evolution equations for continuous-scale morphology. In *Proceedings of the IEEE Conference on Acoustics, Speech and Signal Processing,* San Francisco, CA, March 1992.

[4] A. R. Bruss. The eikonal equation: Some results applicable to computer vision. In B. K. P. Horn and M. J. Brooks, editors, *Shape From Shading,* pages 69–87, Cambridge, MA, 1989. MIT Press.

[5] V. Caselles, J.-M. Morel, G. Sapiro, and A. Tannenbaum, editors. *IEEE Transactions on Image Processing, Special Issue on PDEs and and Geometry-Driven Diffusion in Image Processing and Analysis,* 1998.

[6] M. G. Crandall, H. Ishii, and P.-L. Lions. User's guide to viscosity solutions of second order partial differential equations. *Bulletin of the American Mathematical Society,* 27(1):1–67, 1992.

[7] A. D. J. Cross and E. R. Hancock. Scale-space vector fields for feature analysis. In *Conference on Computer Vision and Pattern Recognition,* pages 738–743, June 1997.

[8] O. Faugeras and R. Keriven. Complete dense stereovision using level set methods. In *Fifth European Conference on Computer Vision,* volume 1, pages 379–393, 1998.

[9] B. B. Kimia, A. Tannenbaum, and S. W. Zucker. Shape, shocks, and deformations I: The components of two-dimensional shape and the reaction-diffusion space. *International Journal of Computer Vision,* 15:189–224, 1995.

[10] R. Kimmel, K. Siddiqi, B. B. Kimia, and A. Bruckstein. Shape from shading: Level set propagation and viscosity solutions. *International Journal of Computer Vision,* 16(2):107–133, 1995.

[11] C. Lanczos. *The Variational Principles of Mechanics.* Dover, 1986.

[12] M. Näf, O. Kübler, R. Kikinis, M. E. Shenton, and G. Székely. Characterization and recognition of 3d organ shape in medical image analysis using skeletonization. In *IEEE Workshop on Mathematical Methods in Biomedical Image Analysis,* 1996.

[13] R. L. Ogniewicz and O. Kübler. Hierarchic voronoi skeletons. *Pattern Recognition,* 28:343–359, 1995.

[14] S. Osher and C.-W. Shu. High-order essentially non-oscillatory schemes for Hamilton-Jacobi equations. *SIAM Journal of Numerical Analysis,* 28:907–922, 1991.

[15] S. J. Osher and J. A. Sethian. Fronts propagating with curvature dependent speed: Algorithms based on hamilton-jacobi formulations. *Journal of Computational Physics,* 79:12–49, 1988.

[16] L. Perko. *Differential Equations and Dynamical Systems.* Springer-Verlag, 1986.

[17] E. Rouy and A. Tourin. A viscosity solutions approach to shape-from-shading. *SIAM. J. Numer. Analy.,* 29(3):867–884, June 1992.

[18] G. Sapiro, B. B. Kimia, R. Kimmel, D. Shaked, and A. Bruckstein. Implementing continuous-scale morphology. *Pattern Recognition,* 26(9), 1992.

[19] J. Sethian. *Level Set Methods: evolving interfaces in geometry, fluid mechanics, computer vision, and materials science.* Cambridge University Press, Cambridge, 1996.

[20] J. A. Sethian. A fast marching level set method for monotonically advancing fronts. *Proc. Natl. Acad. Sci. USA,* 93:1591–1595, February 1996.

[21] J. Shah. A common framework for curve evolution, segmentation and anisotropic diffusion. In *Conference on Computer Vision and Pattern Recognition,* pages 136–142, June 1996.

[22] K. Siddiqi, B. B. Kimia, and C. Shu. Geometric shock-capturing eno schemes for subpixel interpolation, computation and curve evolution. *Graphical Models and Image Processing,* 59(5):278–301, September 1997.

[23] Z. S. G. Tari, J. Shah, and H. Pien. Extraction of shape skeletons from grayscale images. *Computer Vision and Image Understanding,* 66:133–146, May 1997.

[24] H. Tek and B. B. Kimia. Curve evolution, wave propagation and mathematical morphology. In *Fourth International Symposium on Mathematical Morphology,* June 1998.

[25] R. van den Boomgaard and A. Smeulders. The morphological structure of images: The differential equations of morphological scale-space. *IEEE Transactions on Pattern Analysis and Machine Intelligence,* 16(11):1101–1113, November 1994.

Colour by Correlation: A Simple, Unifying Approach to Colour Constancy

G. D. Finlayson and S. D. Hordley*
School of Information Systems
University of East Anglia
Norwich, NR4 7TJ

P. M. Hubel
Hewlett-Packard Labs.
Hewlett Packard Inc.
Palo Alto, CA 94306

Abstract

In this paper we consider the problem of colour constancy; how given an image of a scene under an unknown illuminant can we recover an estimate of that light? Rather than recovering a single estimate of the illuminant as many previous authors have done, in the first instance we recover a measure of the likelihood that each possible illuminant was the scene illuminant. We do this by correlating image colours with the colours that can occur under each of a set of possible lights. We then recover an estimate of the scene illuminant based on these likelihoods. Computation is expressed and performed in a generic correlation framework which we develop in this paper. We develop a new probabilistic instantiation of this framework which delivers very good colour constancy on synthetic and real images. We show that the proposed framework is rich enough to allow many existing algorithms to be expressed within it; e.g. the grey-world and gamut mapping algorithms. We explore too the relationship of these algorithms to other probabilistic and neural network approaches.

1 Introduction

In this paper we consider the colour constancy problem; that is, given an image of a scene under an unknown illumination how we can recover an estimate of the unknown illuminant? This is an important problem to solve since various applications (e.g. object recognition, digital photography) require that we be able to disambiguate factors in an image; for example, the surface reflectance properties of the imaged objects, and the spectral power distribution of the incident illumination.

Over many years a number of authors [17, 19, 4, 5, 2, 3, 19, 22, 10, 6] have proposed computational theories and algorithms for colour constancy but to date only limited success has been achieved. At the heart of almost all approaches is the simple Lambertian model of image formation:

$$p_k^x = \int_\omega E(\lambda) S^x(\lambda) R_k(\lambda) d\lambda \qquad (1)$$

where p_k^x is the response of the imaging device's k^{th} sensor at pixel x. It is clear from Equation (1) that changing either the surface reflectance function, $S(\lambda)$, or the illuminant spectral power distribution $E(\lambda)$, will change the values recorded by the imaging device. The task for a colour constancy algorithm is then to transform p_k^x to values which are independent of $E(\lambda)$, and hence which correlate with $S(\lambda)$, or equivalently, to recover an estimate of $E(\lambda)$ (since the transform that discounts $E(\lambda)$ depends only on $E(\lambda)$).

The problem is difficult to solve; $E(\lambda)$ and $S(\lambda)$ are continuous functions, yet to estimate them we typically have only 3 measurements: the camera RGB. Even if we define the colour of lights and surfaces by their respective RGBs there are still more unknowns to solve for than there are knowns (with n surfaces in a scene, we have $3n$ knowns and $3n + 3$ unknowns). It follows that the problem is intrinsically ill-posed.

Many authors [17, 3, 14, 19, 4] have tried to deal with the under-constrained nature of the problem by making additional assumptions about the world. For example Land [17] implicitly assumes that every image contains a white patch, hence there are now only $3n$ unknowns and $3n$ equations. A similar assumption employed by a number of authors [3, 14], is to assume that the average reflectance of all surfaces in a scene is achromatic, so that the average colour of the light leaving the surfaces in a scene will be the colour of the incident illumination. Another approach often adopted [19, 4] has been to model lights and surfaces using low-dimensional linear models and to develop recovery schemes which exploit the features of these models. Other authors have used features such as specularities [18, 22], shadows [7] or mutual illumination [11], to recover information about the scene illuminant. Unfortunately, the assumptions made by all these algorithms are quite often violated in real images, and it has been shown [12] that none of these schemes is capable of delivering adequate colour constancy.

[1]This work was carried out at the Colour & Imaging Institute, University of Derby. The authors wish to thank that institute for their support of this work.

The fact that the problem is under-constrained implies that in general the combination of surfaces and illuminant giving rise to a particular image is not unique. So setting out to solve for a unique answer (the goal of most colour constancy algorithms) is not the best way to proceed. This point of view has only been considered in more recent algorithms. For example, the gamut mapping algorithms developed by Forsyth [10], and later by Finlayson [6] and others [8], do not, in the first instance, attempt to find a unique solution to the problem. Rather, the set of all possible solutions are found and from this set "the best" solution is chosen. Other authors [2, 21, 5], recognising that the problem does not have a unique solution, have tried to exploit information in the image to recover "the most likely" solution. Several authors [2, 5] have posed the problem in a probabilistic framework, and more recently Sapiro [21] has developed an algorithm based on the Probabilistic Hough Transform. The neural network approach [13] can similarly be seen as a method of dealing with the inherent uncertainty in the problem.

The first contribution of this paper is to present a new general correlation framework for colour constancy. In this new framework colour constancy is posed as a correlation of the colours in an image and our prior knowledge about which colours can appear under which lights. Intuitively, this correlation idea has merit; if the colours in an image "look" more yellow than they ought to then one might assume that this yellowness correlated with a yellow illuminant. We develop a particular instantiation of this framework, a new correlation algorithm, which has a number of attractive properties. It enforces the physical realizeability of lights and surfaces, it is insensitive to spurious image colours, it is fast to compute and it calculates the most likely answer. Perhaps more important than all this is that it delivers good colour constancy.

The second contribution of this paper is to show that the correlation framework we have developed is general and can be used to describe many existing colour constancy algorithms. This leads to a deep understanding of the colour constancy problem, the proposed solutions and their interrelations. Furthermore, solving for colour constancy with any of these algorithms in our framework is always computationally very simple. Yet in comparison algorithms like gamut mapping have previously been criticised for their inherent complexity. Here we see that they are in fact no more complex than the simplest type of colour constancy computation.

In Section 2 of this paper we present our framework (for which a patent has been applied [16]) for solving colour constancy and instantiate a new algorithm within it. We then show, in Section 3, that a number of existing algorithms can be precisely formulated in the same framework. Section 4 details the experiments we performed to test the new algorithm and gives a quantitative and qualitative assessment of its performance. Finally we draw some conclusions from this work in Section 5.

2 Colour by Correlation

We pose the colour constancy problem as that of recovering an estimate of the scene illumination from an image of a scene taken under an unknown illuminant since given this estimate it is relatively straightforward to transform image colours to illuminant independent descriptors [15]. We restrict attention here to the case of an imaging system with three classes of sensors. In such a case it is not possible to recover the full spectral power distribution of the illuminant, so instead an illuminant with spectral power distribution $E(\lambda)$ is characterised by $\underline{p}^E$; the response of the imaging device to an achromatic surface under $E(\lambda)$. An estimate of the illuminant will accordingly be a 3-vector sensor response, $\underline{\hat{p}}^E$, or since we cannot recover the overall intensity of the illuminant, but only its orientation, a 2-d chromaticity vector $\underline{\hat{c}}^E$.

Characterising illuminants in this way we can define the set of all distinguishable illuminants. For example, for a digital camera which gives 8-bit data, the sensor responses will be in the range 0 to 255, and the set of illuminants which can be recovered are the set of all possible sensor responses, $\underline{p}^E$ whose elements are in this range. For the purpose of our algorithm we represent illuminants by their chromaticity vectors and define an $N_{ill} \times 2$ matrix C_{ill} whose i^{th} row is the chromaticity of the ith illuminant. Similarly we use the notation C_{im} to denote the $N_{pix} \times 2$ matrix of image chromaticities (the N_{pix} pixels in an image stretched out). As for illuminants and RGBs we will assume that chromaticity space is discretised. Specifically, we assume chromaticity space is split into $N \times N$ uniform regions i.e. there are at most N^2 distinct chromaticities in an image.

We solve for colour constancy in three stages. First we build a correlation matrix to correlate image colours with the set of possible scene illuminants. Then, given a set of image data we determine the relative likelihood that each of the possible illuminants was the scene illuminant. That is, we determine for each illuminant E a measure of the likelihood that the illuminant was E, given the image data C_{im}. Finally, we use these likelihoods to recover an estimate of the scene illuminant.

Given a set of image data C_{im} we would like to recover $Pr(E|C_{im})$ - the probability that E was the scene illuminant given C_{im}. Now, if we know the probability of observing a certain chromaticity $\underline{c}$ under illuminant E; $Pr(\underline{c}|E)$, then Bayes' rule tells us how to calculate the corresponding probability $Pr(E|\underline{c})$:

$$Pr(E|\underline{c}) = \frac{Pr(\underline{c}|E)Pr(E)}{Pr(\underline{c})} \quad (2)$$

It follows that the probability that the illuminant was E given the image data C_{im} is given by:

$$Pr(E|C_{im}) = \frac{Pr(C_{im}|E)Pr(E)}{Pr(C_{im})} \quad (3)$$

For a given image $Pr(C_{im})$ is constant, and if furthermore we assume that all illuminants are equally likely, and that image chromaticities are independent then we can re-write Equation (3) as:

$$Pr(E|C_{im}) = k \prod_{\underline{c} \in C_{im}} Pr(\underline{c}|E) \quad (4)$$

where k is a constant. Now, we define a likelihood function:

$$l(E|C_{im}) = \sum_{\underline{c} \in C_{im}} \log(Pr(\underline{c}|E)) \quad (5)$$

and note that the illuminant which maximises $Pr(E|C_{im})$ will also maximise $l(E|C_{im})$. The log-probabilities effectively measure the *correlation* between a particular chromaticity and a particular illumination. Maximising l in Equation (5) finds the illuminant that correlates most strongly with the image chromaticities. We talk here about correlation rather than just likelihoods since correlation is a more general term. As we shall see in the next section many other algorithms can be cast in the language of correlation.

Usually we think about correlation in terms of a vector dot-product. For example if $\underline{a}$ and $\underline{b}$ are vectors then they are strongly correlated if $\underline{a}.\underline{b}$ is large. A similar dot-product definition is used here in order to implement Equation (5). We define a correlation matrix M_{Bayes} whose ij^{th} entry is: $\log(Pr(\text{image chromaticity } i|\text{illuminant } j))$ and a vector $\underline{h}$ whose i^{th} entry is one if chromaticity i occurs in the image and zero otherwise. It then follows that the log likelihood function $l(E|C_{im})$ is given by $\underline{h}^t M_{Bayes}$; the correlation of $\underline{h}$ with each column (i.e. illuminant) in M_{Bayes}. Alternatively, we can write this as:

$$l(E|C_{im}) = thr(chist(C_{im}))^t M_{Bayes} \quad (6)$$

where the operation $chist()$ is a histogramming operation returning an $N^2 \times 1$ vector $\underline{h}$, the ith element of which holds the number of times a chromaticity corresponding to the ith row of C_{ill} occurs in the image, normalised by N_{pix}, the total number of pixels in the image and $thr(\underline{h})$ returns a vector whose i^{th} element is one if $h(i) > 0$ and is zero otherwise.

Based on this log likelihood function we want to recover an estimate of the chromaticity, $\underline{\hat{c}}^E$ of the unknown illuminant. In this algorithm we choose the illuminant which maximises $l(E|C_{im})$, that is:

$$\underline{\hat{c}}^E = thr2(thr(chist(C_{im}))^t M_{Bayes})C_{ill} \quad (7)$$

where $thr2()$ returns a vector with entries corresponding to:

$$thr2(\underline{h}) = \underline{h}' \quad h_i' = \begin{cases} 1, & \text{if } h_i = max(\underline{h}) \\ 0, & \text{otherwise} \end{cases} \quad (8)$$

Equation (7) defines a well founded maximum likelihood solution to colour constancy. It is important to note that since we have computed likelihoods for all illuminants we can augment the illuminant calculated in (7) with error bars. That is we can inform the user that the illuminant was probably yellow Tungsten but it could have been cool white fluorescent but it was definitely not Blue sky daylight. We believe that this is a major strength inherent in our method and will be of significant value in other computer vision applications.

3 Other algorithms in this framework

Our framework for solving colour constancy is encapsulated in Equation (7). At the heart of this framework is a correlation matrix which encodes our knowledge about the interaction between lights and image colours. To solve for colour constancy we simply have to correlate the image data with this matrix to recover a measure of the likelihood that each illuminant was the scene illuminant and then use these likelihoods to estimate the scene illuminant. We show in this section that many existing algorithms can be re-formulated in the framework set out above. To do this we simply have to change the entries of the correlation matrix so as to reflect the assumptions about the interactions between lights and image colours made (at least implicitly) by these algorithms.

3.1 Grey-World

We begin with the so called *grey-world* algorithm which as well as being one of the simplest is still widely used (despite the fact that it often fails). This algorithm has been proposed in a variety of forms by a number of different authors [3, 14] and is based on the assumption that the spatial average of surface reflectances in a scene is achromatic. Since the light reflected from an achromatic surface is changed equally at all wavelengths, it follows that the spatial average of the light leaving the scene will be the colour of the incident illumination. To recover an estimate of the scene illuminant in the form we require; that is in terms of the sensor response of a device to the illuminant, is trivial; we simply need to take the average of all sensor responses in the image: $\underline{p}^E = mean(RGB_{im})$. Equivalently, this can be written in our framework as:

$$\underline{\hat{p}}^E = hist(RGB_{im})^t \mathcal{I} RGB_{ill} \quad (9)$$

where RGB_{ill} characterises the set of all possible illuminants in camera RGB space, the operation $hist()$ is $chist()$ modified to work on RGBs rather than chromaticities, and the matrix $\mathcal{I}$ is the identity matrix. In this formulation $\mathcal{I}$ replaces the correlation matrix M_{Bayes} and, as before, can be interpreted as representing our knowledge about the interaction between image colours and surfaces. In this interpretation the columns and rows of $\mathcal{I}$ represent possible illuminants and possible image colours respectively. Hence, $\mathcal{I}$ tells us that given a sensor response $\underline{p}$ in an image, the only illuminant consistent with it is the illuminant characterised by the same sensor response.

3.2 Gamut Mapping

Clearly $\mathcal{I}$ does not accurately represent our knowledge about lights and surfaces; for example a reddish RGB is consistent with both a red surface under a white light and a white surface under a red light. Forsyth [10] developed an algorithm, called CRULE to exploit this fact. CRULE is founded on the idea of colour gamuts: the set of all possible sensor responses observable under different illuminants. He showed that colour gamuts are closed, convex, bounded, and most importantly that each is a strict subset of the set of possible image colours. The gamut of possible image colours for a light is determined by imaging all possible surfaces (or a representative subset thereof) under that light. We can similarly determine gamuts for each of our possible illuminants, i.e. for each row of RGB_{ill} and can code them in a matrix M_{For} such that, if image colour i can be observed under illuminant j then we put a one in the ij^{th} entry of M_{For}, otherwise we put a zero. The matrix M_{For} more accurately represents our knowledge about the world and can be used to replace $\mathcal{I}$ in Equation (9).

Forsyth used the colours present in an image to determine a set of feasible illuminants. An illuminant is taken to be feasible if all image colours fall within the gamut defined by that illuminant. In our framework, the number of image colours consistent with each illuminant can be calculated:

$$\underline{l} = thr(hist(RGB_{im})^t)M_{For} \qquad (10)$$

where $thr()$ and $hist$ are as defined previously and ensure that each distinct image colour is counted only once.

Once the set of feasible illuminants has been determined, the final step in CRULE is to select a single illuminant from this set as an estimate of the unknown illuminant. Previous work has shown [1] that the best way to do this is to take the mean of the feasible illuminants. In our framework this can be achieved by:

$$\hat{\underline{p}}^E = thr2(thr(hist(RGB_{im}))^t M_{For})RGB_{ill} \qquad (11)$$

where $thr2()$ is defined as before. In CRULE the notion of which image colours can appear under which lights was modelled analytically as closed continuous convex regions of RGB space which leads to a very expensive computation. Equation (11), though equivalent to CRULE (with mean selection) is a much simpler implementation of it.

Computation aside, our new formulation has another significant advantage over CRULE; rather than saying that an illuminant is possible if and only if it is consistent with all image colours we can instead look for illuminants that are consistent with *most* image colours. This subtle change cannot be incorporated easily into the CRULE algorithm yet it is important to do so. In CRULE, if no illuminant is globally consistent then a null set of mappings is returned. That is, there is no solution to colour constancy. What we really are looking for is majority consistency and this is in fact implemented in our new computational framework. The function $thr2$ depends on the maximum count in the histogram. Of course we may wish to make the threshold a little less than the maximum so as not to exclude illuminants that have more or less the same likelihood. We define $thr3()$ operating on the vector $\underline{l}$ such that:

$$\begin{aligned} thr3(x) &= 1, && \text{if } x \geq m, \\ thr3(x) &= 0, && (otherwise) \end{aligned} \qquad (12)$$

Where m is chosen in an adaptive fashion such that $m \leq max(\underline{h})$. Thus, we rewrite (11) as:

$$\hat{\underline{p}}^E = thr3(thr(hist(RGB_{im}))^t M_{For})RGB_{ill} \qquad (13)$$

3.3 Colour In Perspective

While the formulation of Forsyth's CRULE algorithm given above addresses some of its limitations there are other problems with CRULE which this formulation doesn't resolve. First, Finlayson recognised that features such as shape and shading, affect the magnitude of the recovered light but significantly, not its colour. To avoid calculating calculating the intensity of the illuminant (which cannot be recovered) Finlayson carried out computation in a 2-d chromaticity space. If we once again characterise image colours and illuminants by their chromaticities we can define a new matrix, M_{Fin} whose ij^{th} element will be set to one when chromaticity i can be seen under illuminant j and to zero otherwise. We can then substitute M_{Fin} in Equation (7)

$$\hat{\underline{c}}_E = thr2(thr(chist(C_{im}))^t M_{Fin})C_{ill} \qquad (14)$$

Assuming the thresholding operations, $thr()$ and $thr2()$ are chosen as for Forsyth's algorithm (we could of course use $thr3()$ instead of $thr2()$ if we wished to implement majority consistency), then the illuminant estimate $\hat{\underline{c}}^E$ is the averaged chromaticity of all illuminants consistent with all image colours. Previous work [8] has shown however, that this is not the best estimate of the illuminant, and that the chromaticity transform should be reversed before the averaging operation is performed. This can be achieved here by defining a matrix RGB_{ill}^N, whose i^{th} row is the ith row of RGB_{ill} normalised to unit length. The illuminant estimate is now calculated:

$$\underline{p}^E = thr2(thr(chist(C_{im}))^t M_{Fin})RGB_{ill}^N \qquad (15)$$

Another problem with gamut mapping is that not all illuminants in C_{ill} are plausible (for example purple lights do not occur in practice). This observation is also simple to implement. Suppose the kth row of C_{ill} denotes the chromaticity of an illuminant that does not occur in practice. By setting all the entries in the kth column of M_{Fin} to 0 we record the fact that no image colours are consistent with the kth illuminant and so guard against the possibility of ever choosing illuminant k (which, by assumption, is impossible). Equivalently we can completely remove the kth row of C_{ill} and the kth column of M_{Fin}.

3.4 Illuminant Color by Voting

Sapiro [21] has recently proposed an algorithm for estimating scene illumination which is based on the Probabilistic Hough Transform. In this work lights and surfaces are represented as low-dimensional linear models and probability distributions are defined from which surfaces are drawn. Given a sensor response from an image, a surface is selected according to the defined distribution. This surface, together with the sensor response is used to recover an illuminant. If the recovered illuminant is a feasible illuminant (in Sapiro's case an illuminant on the daylight locus) a vote is cast for that light. For each sensor response many surfaces are selected and so many votes are cast. To get an estimate of the illuminant the cumulative votes for each illuminant are calculated by summing the votes from all sensor responses in the image. The illuminant with maximum votes is selected as the scene illuminant.

The votes for all illuminants for a single sensor response, p, represent an approximation to the probability distribution: $Pr(E|\underline{p})$ - the conditional probability of the illuminant given the observed sensor response. Sapiro chooses the illuminant which maximises the function: $\sum_{p \in RGB_{im}} Pr(E|\underline{p})$ Since we know the range of possible image colours, rather than compute the probability distributions $Pr(E|\underline{p})$ on a per image basis, we could instead, using Bayes rule, compute them once for all combinations of sensor responses and illuminants. We can then define a matrix M_{Sapiro} whose ij^{th} entry is $Pr(\text{illuminant } j|\text{image colour } I)$ - which, by Bayes rule, is proportional to the probability of observing image colour i under illuminant j. It then follows that Sapiro's estimate of the illuminant can be found in our framework by:

$$\underline{p}^E = thr3(thr(hist(RGB_{im})^t M_{Sapiro})RGB_{ill}) \quad (16)$$

and we note that the matrix M_{Sapiro} is equal to $ke^{M_{Bayes}}$.

3.5 Probabilistic Algorithms

Brainard *et al* [2] have recently given a Bayesian formulation of the colour constancy problem. Their approach is again founded on a linear models representation of lights and surfaces so that lights and surfaces are characterised by low-dimensional vectors of weights. They used principal component analyses of collections of surfaces and illuminants to define probability distributions for these weights and then used Bayesian decision theory to recover estimates of the weights for the surfaces and illuminant in an image. If $\underline{x}$ represents the combined vector of weights for surfaces and lights, the problem is to find an estimate $\hat{\underline{x}}$, of $\underline{x}$.

If there are N surfaces in the image then the vector to be recovered is $(3N + 3)$-dimensional. Finding $\hat{\underline{x}}$ is therefore computationally extremely complex. The authors have implemented the algorithm as a numerical search problem and shown results for the case $n = 8$. However, since typical images contain many more surfaces than eight, as a practical solution for colour constancy this approach is far too complex. A precise formulation of their algorithm is not possible within our framework, however we can use their prior distributions on surfaces and illuminants when constructing our correlation matrix. If we then restrict the problem to that of recovering an estimate of the unknown illuminant, then the two approaches should produce similar results.

An approach which is closer to the algorithm we have presented was proposed by D'Zmura *et al* [5]. They also adopted a linear models representation of surfaces, but they used these models to derive a likelihood distribution $Pr((x,y)|E(\lambda))$ that is the probability of observing a given CIE-xy chromaticity [24] co-ordinate, under an illuminant $E(\lambda)$. This is done by first defining distribution functions for the weights of their linear model of surfaces. They then generated a large number of surfaces by selecting weights according to these distributions and calculated the corresponding chromaticity co-ordinates for these surfaces. By selecting a large number of surfaces, a good approximation to $Pr((x,y)|E(\lambda))$ can be found. If we put likelihoods corresponding to these probabilities in a correlation matrix, then this algorithm can be formulated in the framework we have developed. We point out that this algorithm like grey-world takes no account of the relative frequency of individual chromaticities: the function thr is not used. As such, the algorithm is highly sensitive to large image areas of uniform colour and so can suffer serious failures (similar to grey-world).

3.6 Neural Networks

The final algorithm we consider here is the neural network approach of Funt *et al* [13]. Computation proceeds in three stages and is summarised below:

$$\begin{aligned} output_1 &= thr4(thr(hist(C_{im})^t)M_{Funt}) \\ output_2 &= thr4(output_1^t M_{Funt,1}) \\ output_3 &= output_2^t M_{Funt,2} \end{aligned} \quad (17)$$

where $thr4$ is similar to $thr3$ but exactly what it is has not been specified[13]. In the parlance of Neural Nets $output_1$ is the first stage in a 3 layer perceptron calculation. The 2nd, hidden layer computation, is modelled by the second equation and the final output of the Neural net is $output_3$. The correlation matrix $M_{Funt,1}$ typically has many fewer columns than M_{Funt}. Moreover, $M_{Funt,2}$ only has two columns and so the whole network only outputs two numbers. These two numbers are trained to be the chromaticity of the actual scene illuminant. As such we can replace $M_{Funt,2}$ by C_{ill} (though it is important to realise that here C_{ill} is discovered as a result of training and does not bear a one to one correspondence with actual illuminants).

In the context of this paper $output_1$ is very similar to Equation (7) albeit with a different correlation matrix and slightly different threshold functions. The other two stages address the question of how a range of possible illuminants is translated into a single illuminant chromaticity estimate. As one might imagine the Neural net approach, which basically fits a parametric equation to model image data, has been shown to deliver reasonably good estimates. However, unlike the approach advocated here, it is not possible to give certainty measures with the estimate nor is it possible to really understand the nature of the computation that is taking place.

4 Results

We conducted a number of experiments to assess the performance of our new correlation algorithm and to compare it to existing algorithms. We present the results of two experiments here. To get some of idea of the algorithm's performance over a large data set we tested it first on synthetically generated images. In a second experiment we tested the algorithm on a number of real images captured with a digital camera. We show exemplar results of these tests for a small number of images here.

Before running the algorithm we must make the correlation matrix; this could be M_{Fin}, M_{Bayes}, or some other matrix M depending on the algorithm we wish to test. In the case of M_{Fin} we want to determine which image chromaticities are possible under each of the illuminants between which we wish to distinguish. For these experiments we chose a set of 37 illuminants, representing a wide range of commonly occurring indoor and outdoor lights; this set includes a number of daylights of different correlated colour temperatures, Tungsten lights, and a variety of fluorescent sources. To determine the range of possible chromaticities we used Equation (1) to calculate the responses of a digital camera to a large set of surface reflectance functions (a combination of the Munsell chip set [24] and a collection of object surface reflectances measured by Vrhel et al [23] were used in this experiment) under a given light. From these sensor responses we calculated the corresponding chromaticity co-ordinates, and considered any chromaticity within the convex hull of this set to be a possible chromaticity. The columns of the matrix M_{Fin} were formed by repeating this process for all of the 37 illuminants. Rows of M_{Fin} were formed by dividing the chromaticity space

into a grid of discrete bins. A one in the ij^{th} entry of M_{Fin} implies that a chromaticity in the ith bin of the chromaticity space is observable under illuminant j.

The entries of the matrix M_{Bayes} are found in a similar manner, except now, rather than recording only whether a chromaticity is possible or not, we want to record the relative frequency with which it occurs. To do this we took the same set of surface reflectances and calculated chromaticity co-ordinates as before, then, when we discretised the chromaticity space we simply counted the number of chromaticities falling in each bin. The entries of M_{Bayes} are the log of these raw counts normalised by the total number of chromaticities. The matrix M_{Sapiro} is similarly created except that we put actual probabilities rather than log probabilities in the matrix.

To create the synthetic images on which we tested the algorithms we randomly selected between 2 and 64 surfaces from a set of surface reflectances, and a single illuminant, drawn from the set of 37. To make the test more realistic we used reflectances from a set of natural surface reflectances measured by Parkkinen et al [20] rather than using the same reflectances on which the correlation matrices were created. We calculated the sensor response for a surface and then weighted each surface by a random factor chosen to ensure that the number of pixels in each image was 512×512.

To run the algorithm, we simply built an image histogram, and calculated the likelihood for each illuminant, by multiplying this histogram by the correlation matrix. These likelihoods were then used to select a single illuminant from the set as an estimate of the scene illuminant. For matrix M_{Fin} we used the mean selection method [8], whereas for M_{Bayes} and M_{Sapiro} we chose the illuminant with maximum likelihood.

In total we tested 4 algorithms; grey-world, colour in perspective (with mean selection), Sapiro's algorithm, and our new algorithm. Each of these algorithms was used to generate an estimate of the unknown scene illuminant. We used this estimate to re-render the image as it would have appeared under standard daylight D65 illumination by mapping the image data by a 3×3 diagonal matrix whose entries map an algorithm's estimate of the scene white to white under D65 illumination. We also corrected the image using the actual (measured) scene illuminant. We then calculated the root mean square error in chromaticity space between these two images. Figure 1 shows the relative performance of these four algorithms. This figure shows the average root mean square error in chromaticity for images containing between 2 and 64 surfaces. In each case the average was taken over 500 synthetic images. We can draw a number of conclusions from these results. First, accurately encoding information about the world leads to improved colour constancy performance; the gamut mapping algorithm, and the two algorithms exploiting probability information all per-

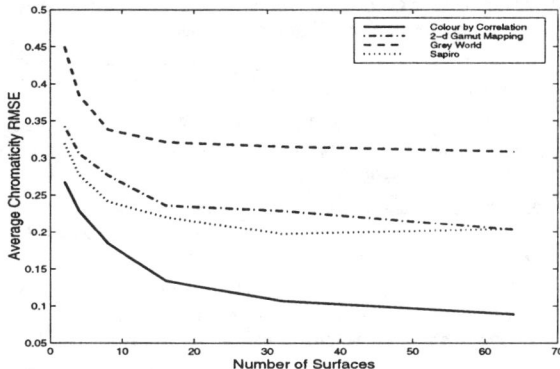

Figure 1. Average RMSE Chromaticity Error. For: grey word (dashed line), 2-d gamut mapping (dotted line), Sapiro's algorithm (dash-dot line), and Colour by Correlation (solid line).

form considerably better than grey-world. Further, we can see that adding information about the probabilities of image colours under different illuminants significantly improves performance. It is important though, that this information is encoded correctly. Our new algorithm, which correctly employ Bayes's rule, gives significantly lower average RMSE than the second best algorithm. However, Sapiro's algorithm which does not correctly encode probability information performs only slightly better than the gamut mapping algorithm.

Previous work [8] has demonstrated that 2-d gamut mapping produces better results than most other algorithms [9, 8]. So, it is significant that our new approach delivers much better constancy. Moreover, the Neural Net approach (for which there insufficient information for us to implement) has also been shown to perform similarly to 2-d gamut mapping. Thus, to our knowledge, our new algorithm significantly outperforms all other algorithms.

The second experiment we ran was to test the performance of the algorithm on real images. To this end we captured a number of images with a digital camera under a variety of different lights. We then used our algorithm to find an estimate of the scene illuminant. As before, we then used this estimate to re-render the captured image under D65 illumination. Figure (2) gives typical examples of the algorithm's performance for two images[1]. While two images do not represent an exhaustive test of the algorithm they do illustrate its typical performance. The figure also shows that the new algorithm works well even on images on which other commonly used algorithms, such as grey-

---

[1]A colour version of this paper is provided on the CDROM supplied with the conference proceedings.

Figure 2. Top to bottom: raw camera image, correction based on measured illuminant, grey-world, and colour by correlation.

world, perform badly.

5 Conclusions

In this paper we have considered the colour constancy problem; that is how we can find an estimate of the unknown illuminant in a captured scene. We have seen that existing constancy algorithms are inadequate for a variety of reasons. For example, many of them make unrealistic assumptions about images, or their computational complexity is such that they are unsuitable as practical solutions to the problem. We have presented here a correlation framework in which to solve for colour constancy. The simplicity, flexibility and robustness of this framework makes solving for colour constancy easy (in a complexity sense). Moreover, we have shown how a particular Bayesian instantiation of the framework leads to excellent colour constancy (and which is significantly better than other algorithms tested). Many other previously proposed algorithms are also placed within the correlation framework.

Acknowledgements

This work was supported by Hewlett-Packard Incorporated and the EPSRC.

References

[1] K. Barnard. Computational Color Constancy: Taking Theory Into Practice. Master's thesis, Simon Fraser Univ., School of Computing Science, 1995.

[2] David H. Brainard and William T. Freeman. Bayesian color constancy. *Journal of the Optical Society of America, A*, 14(7):1393–1411, 1997.

[3] G. Buchsbaum. A spatial processor model for object colour perception. *Journal of the Franklin Institute*, 310:1–26, 1980.

[4] M. M. D'Zmura and G. Iverson. Color constancy. I. basic theory of two-stage linear recovery of spectral descriptions for lights and surfaces. *Journal of the Optical Society of America, A*, 10(10):2148–2165, 1987.

[5] M. M. D'Zmura and G. Iverson. Probabilistic Color Constancy. In M. M. D'Zmura, D. Hoffman, G. Iverson, and K. Romney, editors, *Geometric Representations of Perceptual Phenomena: Papers in Honor of Tarow Indow's 70th Birthday*. Laurence Erlbaum Associates, 1994.

[6] G. D. Finlayson. Color in Perspective. *IEEE Transactions on Pattern Analysis and Machine Intelligence*, 18(10):1034–1038, 1996.

[7] G. D. Finlayson and B. V. Funt. Color constancy with shadows. *Perception*, 23:89–90, 1994. Special Issue on the 17th European Conference on Visual Perception, Eindhoven.

[8] Graham Finlayson and Steven Hordley. A theory of selection for gamut mapping colour constancy. In *Computer Vision and Pattern Recognition '98*, pages 60–65. IEEE, June 1998.

[9] Graham D. Finlayson, Paul M. Hubel, and Steven Hordley. Color by Correlation. In *Fifth Colour Imaging Conference*, pages 6–11. IS&T/SID, November 1997.

[10] D. A. Forsyth. A Novel Algorithm for Colour Constancy. *International Journal of Computer Vision*, 5(1):5–36, 1990.

[11] B. V. Funt, M.S. Drew, and J.Ho. Color constancy from mutual reflection. *International Journal on Computer Vision*, 6:5–24, 1991.

[12] Brian Funt, Kobus Barnard, and Lindsay Martin. Is machine colour constancy good enough? In *5th European Conference on Computer Vision*, pages 455–459. Springer, June 1998.

[13] Brian V. Funt, Vlad Cardei, and Kobus Barnard. Learning color constancy. In *Proceedings of the Fourth Color Imaging Conference*, pages 58–60, November 1996.

[14] Ron Gershon, Allan D. Jepson, and John K. Tsotsos. From [R,G,B] to Surface Reflectance: Computing Color Constant Descriptors in Images. *Perception*, pages 755–758, 1988.

[15] Paul M. Hubel, Jack Holm, Graham D. Finlayson, and Mark S. Drew. Matrix calculations for digital photography. In *Proceedings of the Fifth Color Imaging Conference*, pages 105–111. IS&T/SID, November 1997.

[16] P.M. Hubel and G.D. Finlayson. Whitepoint determination using correlation matrix memory. U.S. Patent Application, Submitted.

[17] Edwin H. Land. The Retinex Theory of Color Constancy. *Scientific American*, pages 108–129, 1977.

[18] Hsien-Che Lee, Edwin J. Breneman, and Carl P. Schulte. Modeling Light Reflection for Computer Color Vision. *IEEE Transactions on Pattern Analysis and Machine Intelligence*, 12(4):402–409, 1986.

[19] Laurence T. Maloney and Brian A. Wandell. Color constancy: a method for recovering surface spectral reflectance. *Journal of the Optical Society of America, A*, 3(1):29–33, 1986.

[20] J. Parkkinen, T. Jaaskelainen, and M. Kuittinen. Spectral representation of color images,. In *IEEE 9th International Conference on Pattern Recognition*, volume 2, pages 933–935, November 1998.

[21] Guillermo Sapiro. Bilinear voting. In *ICCV98*, pages 178–183, November 1998.

[22] S. A. Shafer. Using color to separate reflection components. *Color Research and Application*, 10:210–218, 1985.

[23] M.J. Vrhel, R. Gershon, and L.S. Iwan. Measurement and analysis of object reflectance spectra. *Color Research and Application*, 19(1):4–9, 1994.

[24] G. Wyszecki and W.S. Stiles. *Color Science: Concepts and Methods, Quantitative Data and Formulas*. New York:Wiley, 2nd edition, 1982.

The Optimal Axial Interval in Estimating Depth from Defocus

Yoav Y. Schechner
Department of Electrical Engineering
Technion - Israel Institute of Technology
Haifa, Israel 32000
yoavs@tx.technion.ac.il

Nahum Kiryati
Dept. of Electrical Engineering - Systems
Faculty of Engineering, Tel-Aviv University
Ramat Aviv, Israel 69978
nk@eng.tau.ac.il

Abstract

We analyze the effect of perturbations on the estimation of Depth from Defocus (DFD) implemented by changing the focus setting (e.g., axially moving the sensor). The analysis yields the optimal change of focus setting, and the spatial frequencies for which estimation is most robust. For stable estimation at all spatial frequencies, the change in focus setting should be less than twice the depth of field. For the most robust estimation in the highest spatial frequencies the axial interval should be equal to the depth of field.

1. Introduction

In recent years, range imaging based on the limited depth of field (DOF) of lenses has been gaining popularity. Depth from Defocus (DFD) is an elegant method since it enables depth estimation based on only two images of the scene, taken from the same viewpoint. The defocus blur is made different in the two images by changing the internal settings of the imaging system. The effect of those changes on the defocus blur can be modeled either empirically or by analysis. This model provides the necessary a-priori knowledge for the estimation of the defocus blur and consequently the distance of the object from the imaging system. One way to change the defocus blur between images is to change the aperture size. Another approach is to change the focus setting of the system. For example, the sensor array can be moved axially between image acquisitions. The latter implementation is considered in this paper.

It has been shown [16] that DFD is a manifestation of the principle of geometric triangulation. However, the two-dimensionality of the lens aperture (in contrast to the one-dimensional stereo or motion baseline), makes depth estimation based on two images potentially more robust in DFD than in stereo [16]. Our general goal is to exploit this potential advantage. This requires the robustness of DFD to be studied in detail. Optimizing the change of internal settings

in the imaging system was investigated in [15]. In that work the optimal ratio between the effective blur-diameters in the images was derived. However, the result was dependent on the image contents. The issue of estimation stability was also considered in [21]. Stability at all spatial frequencies was required. This guided the choice of axial movement of the sensor between the image acquisitions, regardless of the image content. The numeric derivation of the axial interval in [21] was oriented towards a specific estimation algorithm (rational operators).

In this paper, we study the robustness of DFD in a general framework by analyzing the influence of perturbations in each spatial frequency of which the image is composed. We show that certain frequency components are most useful for range estimation, while others do not provide stable contributions. It is possible to accomplish stable depth estimation in frequency (or defocus) bands that contain some unstable frequency components, by filtering out the problematic components. This extends the results of [21].

Our analysis also reveals a new property of depth of field (DOF): it is the optimal interval between focus-settings in depth-from-*defocus* in terms of robustness. We also show that if the interval used is larger than the DOF by a factor of 2 or higher, the estimation process can be unstable. This sets limits on the interval between focus settings that ensures robust operation of DFD.

2. Error propagation

Consider the imaging system sketched in Fig. 1. The sensor at distance $\tilde{v}$ behind the lens (of focal length F) can image in-focus a point at distance $\tilde{u}$ in front of the lens. An object point at distance u is defocused, and its image is a blur-circle of radius r in the sensor plane. For simplicity we adopt the common assumption that the imaging system is invariant to transversal shift. This is approximately true for paraxial systems, where the angles between light rays and the optical axis are small. The diameter of the blur-circle

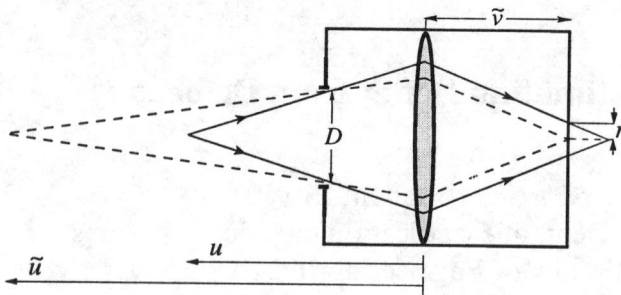

Figure 1. The imaging system is tuned to view in focus object points at distance $\tilde{u}$. The image of an object point at distance u is a blur circle of radius r in the sensor plane.

$d = 2r$ is a function of the distance u,

$$d = f(u) \ . \qquad (1)$$

For example, in a telecentric system [11, 21], as sketched in Fig. 1, with the aperture stop at distance F from the lens,

$$f(u) = \frac{D}{F} \left| \tilde{v} - \frac{Fu}{u - F} \right| \ , \qquad (2)$$

where D is the diameter of the aperture stop [18]. For other systems the relation $f(u)$ may be different. In a simple-lens system $f(u) = D|uF - \tilde{v}u + F\tilde{v}|/(Fu)$. To maintain generality, we will not use a specific form of this function throughout this paper. In DFD, at least two images of the scene are acquired and compared. The comparison yields an estimate of the diameter d of the blur-circle in one of the images, which through the inversion of Eq. (1) leads to an estimate of the distance u.

We now analyze the response of DFD to perturbations by concentrating on the effect of a perturbation in some spatial frequency component of the image, as we suggested in [17]. The perturbation affects the estimated transfer function between the images, which in turn causes an error in the estimated blur-diameter. This leads to an error in the depth estimation. We note that studying the behavior of each spectral component has an algorithmic ground in DFD: there are several methods [2, 6, 13, 14, 21] which rely directly on the frequency components or on frequency bands [14], fitting a curve or a model to data obtained in several frequencies. Thus, even though the analysis refers to a single spatial frequency component, its results are relevant to general images.

Suppose that the pinhole image of the scene (in which everything is in focus) is g_0. Let the two finite-aperture (thus defocus blurred) images be $g_1 = g_0 \star h_d$ and $g_2 = g_0 \star h_{d+\Delta d}$. Δd is the change in the blur-diameter due to the known axial shift in sensor position. We assume that geometric changes in magnification are compensated or do not take place (e.g. by the use of a telecentric system [11, 21]). Moreover, in telecentric systems Δd is invariant to the focus settings and the object depth u [11, 18]. Therefore, the results presented here are best applicable to telecentric systems. In the frequency domain, let one image be

$$G_1(\nu) = G_0(\nu)H_d(\nu) + N_1(\nu) \ , \qquad (3)$$

where ν denotes a spatial frequency component and $N_1(\nu)$ is a perturbation. The other image is

$$G_2(\nu) = G_0(\nu)H_{d+\Delta d}(\nu) \ . \qquad (4)$$

If there is no perturbation, the two images satisfy

$$G_2(\nu)H_d(\nu) - G_1(\nu)H_{d+\Delta d}(\nu) = 0 \ . \qquad (5)$$

We wish to estimate $\hat{d}$ by searching for the value that satisfies

$$G_2(\nu)H_{\hat{d}}(\nu) - G_1(\nu)H_{\hat{d}+\Delta d}(\nu) = 0 \ . \qquad (6)$$

Assume for a moment that $H_d(\nu) \neq 0$, and define

$$H(\nu) = \frac{H_{d+\Delta d}(\nu)}{H_d(\nu)} \quad , \quad \hat{H}(\nu) = \frac{H_{\hat{d}+\Delta d}(\nu)}{H_{\hat{d}}(\nu)} \ . \qquad (7)$$

Usually constraint (6) cannot be satisfied by the same $\hat{d}$ at all frequencies, hence a common method [4] is to minimize a MSE criterion such as

$$E^2 = \int_\nu |G_2(\nu) - \hat{H}(\nu)G_1(\nu)|^2 \mathrm{d}\nu =$$

$$= \int_\nu |G_0(\nu)H_d|^2 \left| H(\nu) - \hat{H}(\nu)\left[1 + \frac{N_1}{G_0 H_d}\right] \right|^2 \mathrm{d}\nu. \qquad (8)$$

This is achieved by looking for the extremum points

$$0 = -\frac{\partial(E^2)}{\partial\hat{d}} = 2\mathrm{Re}\int_\nu |G_0(\nu)H_d(\nu)|^2 \left[1 + \frac{N_1^*(\nu)}{G_0^* H_d^*}\right] \cdot$$

$$\cdot \left\{ H(\nu) - \hat{H}(\nu)\left[1 + \frac{N_1}{G_0 H_d}\right] \right\} \frac{\partial\hat{H}^*(\nu)}{\partial\hat{d}} \mathrm{d}\nu \ . \qquad (9)$$

The locations of minima of E^2 depend on the spectral composition of the signal and noise. Consider a signal made of a single frequency ν

$$G_0(\nu') = G(\nu)\delta(\nu - \nu') \ . \qquad (10)$$

If at that frequency $\partial\hat{H}^*(\nu)/\partial\hat{d} = 0$, the estimation of $\hat{d}$ is ill posed. Otherwise, nulling the integrand yields

$$H_{\hat{d}+\Delta d}(\nu)H_d(\nu) = H_{\hat{d}}(\nu)H_{d+\Delta d}(\nu) - \frac{N_1(\nu)}{G_0(\nu)}H_{\hat{d}+\Delta d}(\nu) \qquad (11)$$

Eq. (11) can be written as

$$\hat{H}(\nu) = H(\nu) \left[1 + \frac{N_1(\nu)}{G_0(\nu)H_d(\nu)}\right]^{-1} \quad . \quad (12)$$

The true blur-diameter d controls the transfer function $H(\nu)$ between the images. Basically, the estimate $\hat{d}$ is deduced from measurements of $H(\nu)$. However, due to the perturbation, a different $\hat{H}(\nu)$ is measured.

$$\frac{\partial \hat{H}(\nu)}{\partial |N_1(\nu)|} = -\frac{1}{\left[1 + \frac{N_1(\nu)}{G_0(\nu)H_d(\nu)}\right]^2} \frac{e^{j\theta(\nu)}}{|G_0(\nu)|} \frac{H_{d+\Delta d}(\nu)}{H_d^2(\nu)}$$

$$\approx -\frac{e^{j\theta(\nu)}}{|G_0(\nu)|} \frac{H_{d+\Delta d}(\nu)}{H_d^2(\nu)} \quad (13)$$

where $\theta(\nu)$ is the phase of the perturbation relative to the signal component $G_0(\nu)$. The approximation in the right hand side of Eq. (13) is for the case that $|N_1(\nu)|$ is small compared to $|G_0(\nu)H_d(\nu)|$.

From $\hat{H}(\nu)$ the parameter $\hat{d}$ is derived, leading (Eq. 1) to the depth estimate $\hat{u}$. Therefore, the error due to the perturbation propagates to $\hat{d}$ and consequently to $\hat{u}$. Note that

$$\frac{\partial \hat{u}(\nu)}{\partial |N_1(\nu)|} = \frac{\partial \hat{u}}{\partial f(\hat{u})} \frac{\partial f(\hat{u})}{\partial |N_1(\nu)|} \quad . \quad (14)$$

In the following analysis we use $\partial f(u)/\partial |N_1|$ as a measure for the response to perturbations. We make do with analyzing the influence of the perturbations on the estimation of $f(u)$ since it is simpler and it is easily related to depth by Eq. (1). Since the estimation will be frequency-dependent, we write

$$\frac{\partial f(\hat{u},\nu)}{\partial |N_1(\nu)|} = \frac{\partial \hat{H}(\nu)}{\partial |N_1(\nu)|} \cdot \left[\frac{\partial \hat{H}(\nu)}{\partial f(\hat{u})}\right]^{-1} \quad . \quad (15)$$

For small perturbations we assume that $\hat{H}(\nu) \approx H(\nu)$, so Eq. (15) becomes

$$\frac{\partial f(\hat{u},\nu)}{\partial |N_1(\nu)|} \approx C \frac{H_{d+\Delta d}(\nu)}{\frac{\partial H_{d+\Delta d}(\nu)}{\partial d}H_d(\nu) - \frac{\partial H_d(\nu)}{\partial d}H_{d+\Delta d}(\nu)} \quad , \quad (16)$$

where

$$C \equiv -\frac{e^{j\theta(\nu)}}{|G_0(\nu)|} \quad . \quad (17)$$

According to Eqs. (13) and (16), if $H_{d+\Delta d}(\nu) = 0$ for some frequency ν, a perturbation $N_1(\nu)$ does not affect the estimation.

If $|H_d(\nu)| \ll |H_{d+\Delta d}(\nu)|$ we define the transfer function between the images as the reciprocal of Eq. (7):

$$H^{-1}(\nu) = \frac{H_d(\nu)}{H_{d+\Delta d}(\nu)} \quad , \quad \widehat{H^{-1}}(\nu) = \frac{H_{\hat{d}}(\nu)}{H_{\hat{d}+\Delta d}(\nu)} . \quad (18)$$

This takes care of the cases in which $H_d(\nu) = 0$ but $H_{d+\Delta d}(\nu) \neq 0$. Eq. (11) can then be written as

$$\widehat{H^{-1}}(\nu) = H^{-1}(\nu) + \frac{N_1(\nu)}{G_0(\nu)H_{d+\Delta d}(\nu)} \quad . \quad (19)$$

The perturbation causes the estimated transfer function to change:

$$\frac{\partial \widehat{H^{-1}}(\nu)}{\partial |N_1(\nu)|} = \frac{e^{j\theta(\nu)}}{|G_0(\nu)|H_{d+\Delta d}(\nu)} \quad . \quad (20)$$

Calculating the influence on the depth estimation based on this form of the transfer function, we arrive at the same relation as Eq. (16) without assuming the perturbation $|N_1(\nu)|$ to be small relative to $|G_0(\nu)H_d(\nu)|$.

We use the pillbox point spread function (PSF) model [11, 12, 21], since it is valid for aberration-free geometric optics, and has been shown to be a good approximation for large defocus [7, 10, 20]. In this model

$$H_d(\nu) = 2\frac{D^2}{D_0^{\,2}} \frac{J_1(\pi\nu d)}{\pi\nu d} \quad , \quad (21)$$

where D_0 is the diameter of the arbitrarily small aperture being used to mimic the pinhole in the conceptual generation of G_0. We note that when the sensor is axially moved, the light gathered by the system remains unchanged since D is the same for all the images acquired. Using the relation

$$\frac{\partial[J_1(\xi)/\xi]}{\partial \xi} = -\frac{J_2(\xi)}{\xi} \quad (22)$$

Eq. (16) takes a relatively simple form,

$$\frac{\partial f(\hat{u},\nu)}{\partial |N_1(\nu)|} \approx -C\frac{D_0^{\,2}}{D^2}\frac{d}{2} \cdot$$

$$\cdot \frac{J_1[\pi\nu(d+\Delta d)]}{J_2[\pi\nu(d+\Delta d)]J_1(\pi\nu d) - J_2(\pi\nu d)J_1[\pi\nu(d+\Delta d)]} \quad . \quad (23)$$

At high frequencies ν (or at large blur-diameters d), Eq. (23) becomes

$$\frac{\partial f(\hat{u},\nu)}{\partial |N_1(\nu)|} \approx -C\frac{D_0^{\,2}}{D^2}\frac{\pi d\sqrt{\nu d}}{2\sqrt{2}} \cdot$$

$$\cdot \frac{\sin[\pi\nu(d+\Delta d) - (\pi/4)]}{\sin(\pi\nu\Delta d)} \quad (24)$$

where we used the relation

$$J_\mu(\xi) \overset{\xi \to \infty}{\longrightarrow} \sqrt{2/(\pi\xi)}\cos[\xi - \mu(\pi/2) - (\pi/4)] \quad . \quad (25)$$

A similar relation is obtained in case a perturbation N_2 is present in G_2 rather than in G_1:

$$\frac{\partial f(\hat{u},\nu)}{\partial |N_2(\nu)|} \approx C\frac{D_0^2}{D^2}\frac{\pi(d+\Delta d)\sqrt{\nu(d+\Delta d)}}{2\sqrt{2}} \cdot$$

$$\cdot \frac{\sin[\pi\nu d - (\pi/4)]}{\sin(\pi\nu\Delta d)} \quad . \quad (26)$$

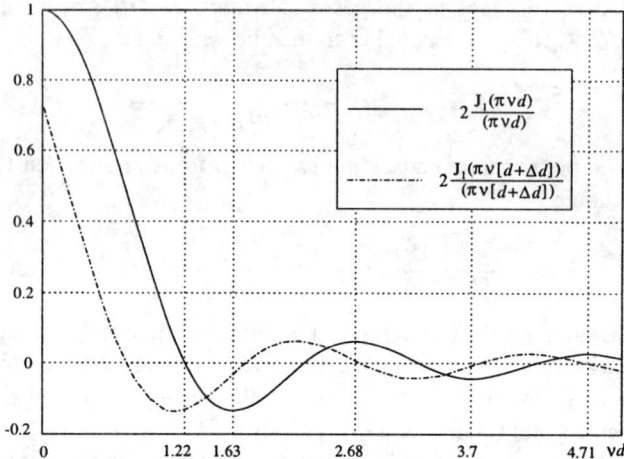

Figure 2. [Solid line] The attenuation of a frequency component ν between a focused and a defocused image as a function of the diameter of the blur kernel d. The horizontal axis is scaled by ν. [Dashed line] The attenuation of the same frequency component when the focus settings are changed so that the blur diameter is $d + \Delta d$, for the case $\Delta d = 1/(2\nu)$.

3. Optimal axial interval

To appreciate the significance of Eqs. (24,26), observe that the reliability of the defocus estimation at high frequencies is optimized (for unknown u hence for unknown d) if

$$|\nu \Delta d| = 0.5, \quad 1.5, \quad 2.5 \ldots. \tag{27}$$

There, the magnitude of the term $\sin(\pi \nu \Delta d)$ in the denominator is maximal, minimizing the effect of the perturbation on the estimation $\hat{d} = f(\hat{u}, \nu)$. Thus, if DFD is implemented by changing the focus settings, the change (e.g. the axial movement of the sensor) is optimized if it causes the blur-diameter to change according to Eq. (27), where ν is the high frequency component used. Alternatively, *if Δd is given, Eq. (27) indicates the optimal frequency components for depth estimation.* The optimal Δd was used in Fig. 2, that shows the normalized $H_d(\nu)$ (21) of the pill-box model, at a specific frequency ν, as a function of the blur-diameter d. Fig. 2 also shows $H_{d+\Delta d}(\nu)$. Note that at high frequencies or defocus, the Bessel function resembles a cosine function (25), and the two functions are out of phase by $\pi/2$. Hence, in this situation extrema of H_d are at zero-crossings of $H_{d+\Delta d}$ and vice-versa. Thus, these values of $\nu \Delta d$ maximize the ratio between these functions (or its reciprocal).

On the other hand, if

$$|\nu \Delta d| = 1, \quad 2, \quad 3 \ldots. \tag{28}$$

the denominator of Eqs. (24,26) is zero. In this situation the estimation is highly ill-conditioned. Note that as the axial interval is increased, hence Δd is increased, for a given scene, the number of useful frequency components that satisfy Eq. (27) and the number of problematic components that satisfy Eq. (28) both increase.

Suppose that the highest frequency in the image is ν_{max}. Then Eq. (28) dictates that for stable estimation of all frequency components, Δd must satisfy

$$\Delta d < \frac{1}{\nu} \leq \frac{1}{\nu_{max}} = 2\Delta x \ , \tag{29}$$

where Δx is the inter-pixel period of the sensor and we assumed that $\nu_{max} = 1/(2\Delta x)$ (the Nyquist rate). However, according to Eq. (27), in order to obtain reliable results, one should use an axial interval leading to a change in the blur-diameter that is at least half that written in Eq. (29), that is, one inter-pixel spacing. Thus *the change of the focus settings that leads to robust and accurate estimation corresponds to a change in the blur diameter that is bounded by*

$$\Delta x \leq \Delta d < 2\Delta x \ . \tag{30}$$

Eq. (30) can be interpreted to reveal a new property of depth of field (DOF). The depth of field of the system is the range of distances u around the focused distance $\tilde{u}$ in which the defocus blur is undetectable. This depends on the inter-pixel distance Δx [1, 3] and on the blur-diameter d: the blur can be sensed when $d \sim \Delta x$ or larger. d depends on $\tilde{u} - u$ and the system dimensions. When using the threshold value $\Delta d = \Delta x$, if one of the images is in focus (having $d = 0$), the blur kernel in the other image will have a diameter $d_{\text{th}} = 0 + \Delta d = \Delta x$. Thus, using $\Delta d < \Delta x$ is an attempt to sense defocus (generally, change of defocus) for changes in distance that are smaller than the DOF. Hence, *sampling the axial position in DOF intervals (for which $\Delta d = \Delta x$) is optimal with respect to robustness to perturbations at the Nyquist frequency.* Changing the focus setting by a smaller axial interval means that no frequency in the image will satisfy the optimality condition (27). Changing the focus setting by a larger axial interval will be sub-optimal for the Nyquist frequency, but will be optimal for some lower frequency. If the interval of the axial position is twice than the DOF or more, there will be some frequency components in the image, for which estimation will be unstable (28). We note that sampling depth at DOF intervals is known to be efficient [9], particularly in depth from *focus* algorithms [1, 18]. Here we showed that DOF sampling is also a meaningful threshold for robust operation of DFD algorithms.

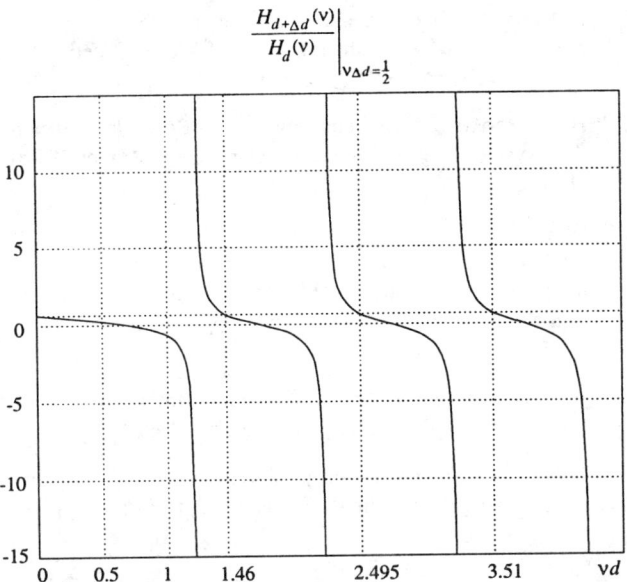

Figure 3. Two images are acquired with different focus settings. The transfer function between the images is the ratio between their individual frequency responses (relative to the focused state), plotted in Fig. 2. In the DOF threshold $\Delta d = 1/(2\nu)$, the width of the band without ambiguities satisfies $\nu d \approx 1.46$. For infinitesimal Δd this width satisfies $\nu d \approx 1.63$.

4. Uniqueness and stability

DFD infers depth by the comparison of images taken with different defocus blurring. If the defocus change is achieved by change of the focus settings, then basically, DFD estimates d from measurement of the ratio H (Eq. (7)). From $\hat{d}$, the depth u is derived. Implicitly, DFD algorithms fuse information from several frequency bands.

To have a unique solution, we should check the uniqueness of the estimation of d. Fig. 3 plots H for the case $\Delta d = 1/(2\nu)$, that is, the ratio of the two functions plotted in Fig. 2. Each ratio between these responses can be yielded by many diameters d, as it is not one-to-one. The lowest band for which the ratio is one-to-one in this figure is $0 < \nu d < 1.46$. However, if the axial increments of the sensor position are smaller, this bandwidth broadens. As Δd is decreased, the responses shown in Fig. 2 converge. Convergence is fastest near the local extrema of $H_d(\nu)$. Hence, as $\Delta d \to 0$ the lowest band in which the matching (correspondence) ambiguity is avoided is between the two first local extrema, i.e.,

$$0 < \nu d < 1.63 \ . \tag{31}$$

However, according to Eqs. (24,26), if $\Delta d \to 0$ the estimation becomes unstable. If we use the guideline (27) Fig. 3

(where $\nu \Delta d = 0.5$) shows that for unambiguous *and* stable estimation

$$0 < \nu d < 1.46 \ . \tag{32}$$

If a coarse estimate of the depth is available (e.g., by using only the band of Eq. (32)), higher frequencies may be used without ambiguity problems, as suggested in [16]. Then, unstable frequency components exist (Eq. 28) and filtering them out improves the estimation.

Simulation and experimental results reported in [21] support the results of our analysis. In the DFD method suggested in [21], the defocus change between acquired images was obtained by changing the focus settings. The images were then filtered by several band pass operators, and the ratios of their outputs were used to fit a model. The ratios are actually a function of the transfer function defined in Eq. (7) between the images. The authors of [21] noticed that the solution may be ambiguous due to the unmonotonicity of the ratios, as a function of the frequency and the blur diameter. They thus limited the band used to the first zero crossing of the pillbox model (21) which occurs at $\nu d = 1.22$ ($\nu r = 0.61$). However, their tests revealed that the frequency band can be extended by about 30%, i.e., to $\nu d \approx 1.6$. This is in agreement with the bound for unique solution set by Eq. (31), i.e. $\nu d = 1.63$.

For reasons of numerical stability (measured by the behavior of the Newton-Raphson algorithm for estimation), the frequency band limit was actually set in [21] to $\nu d = 1.46$ (i.e., $\nu r = 0.73$). Within this band the results came out to be stable, while beyond it the range estimation became unstable. Note that this is in excellent agreement with Eq. (32).

5. Discussion

We analyzed the effect of perturbations on DFD estimation, by examining their influence in each spatial frequency component of the images. Estimation that relies on certain frequency components is most robust, while the contribution of other frequencies is very sensitive to perturbations. A possible application of this theoretical framework would be an algorithm that relies on a coarse estimate of the blur-diameter to select the optimal spatial frequencies (for which the response to perturbations is minimal) to obtain a fine estimate.

In DFD estimation based on a spectral component with frequency ν, the axial movement of the sensor is optimal if it causes the change Δd in the blur diameter to satisfy $|\nu \Delta d| = 0.5, 1.5, 2.5 \ldots$. Using the DOF as the axial interval is optimal with respect to robustness to perturbations at the Nyquist frequency. Using an axial interval which is twice or more than that, can lead to unstable results at some frequency components.

In telecentric systems, Δd is independent of the depth and invariant on axial shifts of the plane of best focus. Thus Δd has a linear and constant relation to the axial interval of the sensor position: $\Delta v = F\Delta d/D$. Therefore the results obtained in this work can be easily applied to such systems. Generally, if the system is not telecentric, Δd (and thus the preferable frequencies) depends on the depth we wish to estimate, and which may not be spatially constant. In these cases, axial shift invariance of Δd may be initially assumed, and a coarse depth estimate will indicate the deviation from this assumption. Consequent estimation of the true Δd may serve as a guideline for improving the depth estimate using the corresponding optimal frequencies.

The presence of unstable frequency components, in which the denominator of Eq. (16) is zero, is related to local extrema of the defocus transfer function. Unmonotonic transfer functions are theoretically predicted in [5, 10, 20] and measured in [8]. Thus our analysis provides guidelines for determining the optimal intervals and frequencies in a broad range of defocus PSF's.

The analysis in this paper is essentially deterministic. However, the presence of independent noise in both of the acquired images simultaneously, at all spatial frequencies, may be better analyzed in a stochastic framework that is based on the deterministic analysis presented here. In [15] stochastic methods have been used. Comparison and integration of the two approaches is an interesting topic for future research.

This research was carried out in the Ollendorff Center of the Department of Electrical Engineering, Technion, and in the Department of Electrical Engineering - Systems, Faculty of Engineering, Tel-Aviv University. It was funded in part by the Israeli Ministry of Science.

References

[1] A. L. Abbott and N. Ahuja, "Active stereo: integrating disparity, vergence, focus, aperture and calibration for surface estimation," IEEE Trans. PAMI 15 pp. 1007-1029 [1993].

[2] V. M. Bove Jr., "Discrete fourier transform based depth-from-focus," Image Understanding and Machine Vision 1989. Technical Digest Series 14, Conference ed., pp. 118-121 [1989].

[3] K. Engelhardt and G. Hausler, "Acquisition of 3-D data by focus sensing," App. Opt. 27, pp. 4684-4689 [1988].

[4] J. Ens and P. Lawrence, "An investigation of methods for determining depth from focus," IEEE Trans. PAMI 15, pp. 97-108 [1993].

[5] A. R. FitzGerrell, E. R. Dowski, Jr. and T. Cathey, "Defocus transfer function for circularly symmetric pupils" App. Opt. 36, pp. 5796-5804 [1997].

[6] S. Hiura, G. Takemura and T. Matsuyama, "Depth measurement by multi-focus camera," Proc. of Model-Based 3D Image Analysis, pp. 35-44 [Mumbai 1998].

[7] H. H. Hopkins, "The frequency response of a defocused optical system," Proc. R. Soc. London Ser. A 231 pp. 91-103 [1955].

[8] W. N. Klarquist, W. S. Geisler and A. C. Bovic, "Maximum-likelihood depth-from-defocus for active vision," Proc. Inter. Conf. Intell. Robots and Systems: Human Robot Interaction and Cooperative Robots, vol. 3, pp. 374-379 [Pittsburgh 1995].

[9] A. Krishnan and N. Ahuja, "Panoramic image acquisition," Proc. CVPR, pp. 379-384 [San-Francisco 1996].

[10] H. C. Lee, "Review of image-blur models in a photographic system using the principles of optics," Opt. Eng. 29, pp. 405-421 [1990].

[11] S. K. Nayar, M. Watanabe and M. Nogouchi, "Real time focus range sensor," Proc. ICCV, pp. 995-1001 [Cambridge 1995].

[12] M. Noguchi and S. K. Nayar, "Microscopic shape from focus using active illumination," Proc. ICPR-A, pp. 147-152 [Jerusalem 1994].

[13] A. P. Pentland, "A new sense for depth of field," IEEE Trans. PAMI 9, pp. 523-531 [1987].

[14] A. Pentland, S. Scherock, T. Darrell and B. Girod, "Simple range camera based on focal error," J. Opt. Soc. Amer. A 11, pp. 2925-2934 [1994].

[15] A. N. Rajagopalan and S. Chaudhuri, "Optimal selection of camera parameters for recovery of depth from defocused images," Proc. CVPR, pp. 219-224 [San Juan 1997].

[16] Y. Y. Schechner and N. Kiryati, "Depth from Defocus vs. Stereo: How Different Really are They?" Proc. ICPR, pp. 1784-1786 [Brisbane 1998].

[17] Y. Y. Schechner and N. Kiryati, "Depth from Defocus vs. Stereo: How Different Really are They?" EE-PUB-1155, Technion - Israel Institute of Technology. Accepted to the IJCV.

[18] Y. Y. Schechner, N. Kiryati and R. Basri, "Separation of transparent layers using focus," Proc. ICCV, pp. 1061-1066 [Mumbai 1998].

[19] S. Scherock, "Depth from defocus of structured light," TR-167, Media-Lab, MIT [1991].

[20] G. Schneider, B. Heit, J. Honig and J. Bremont, "Monocular depth perception by evaluation of the blur in defocused images," Proc. ICIP, vol. 2, pp. 116-119 [Austin 1994].

[21] M. Watanabe and S. K. Nayar, "Minimal operator set for passive depth from defocus," Proc. CVPR pp. 431-438 [San Francisco 1996].

A Representation of Specular Appearance

Stephen Lin and Sang W. Lee
University of Michigan, Ann Arbor, MI 48109, USA
{stevelin, swlee}@eecs.umich.edu

Abstract

The appearance of an object can vary considerably with changes in illumination conditions. Methods have been developed to describe these differences for diffuse reflection using the Lambertian model, but little work has been done in characterizing specular appearance. Towards a more comprehensive global reflectance descriptor, this paper focuses on a representation of specular appearance based on an approximate specular reflection model derived from Torrance-Sparrow. We propose that under certain illumination and surface conditions local specular structure can be expressed by the logarithms of three intensity-normalized photometric images. The total number of photometric images needed for representing global specular appearance depends on the object surface roughness, and we suggest an illumination planning method for determining the number of images. Experimental results demonstrate the effectiveness of this logarithmic model as a specular descriptor.

1. Introduction

Variability in object appearance from changes in illumination conditions is a problem that has plagued a broad range of computer vision applications. Seemingly minor changes in lighting directions may produce significant differences in appearance. Photometric stereo methods have been developed to utilize these resultant intensity changes for shape recovery [17] [7], and recently there has been increasing attention focused upon representing the set of possible lighting appearances for a given scene. Toward a physical understanding of these illumination effects, reflectance models have been developed to characterize image radiance with respect to illumination environment, viewing angles and material properties [14] [11] [16] [5]. These models provide a local description of reflection mechanisms from which global appearance representations may be derived.

Because of its simplicity and effectiveness, the Lambertian reflectance model has widely been used to describe diffuse appearance. Shashua [12] derived an illumination model for Lambertian reflectance, showing that the shading appearance of an object under arbitrary illumination can be expressed as a linear combination of three photometric images. Belhumuer and Kriegman [1] expanded the Lambertian appearance description to include attached shadows in their illumination cone approach. The assumption that reflection adheres to the Lambertian property is intrinsic to these methods, and specular reflections are disregarded.

A different approach for describing illumination appearance does not make explicit use of reflectance models. These *appearance-based* methods instead represent illumination effects with a large set of images which sample a range of lighting configurations. Turk and Pentland [15] introduced this approach with faces using a few illumination conditions. Nayar and Murase [8] later employed this method to demonstrate that three images taken with linearly independent light sources adequately describe the illumination appearance of an ideal diffuse surface. Although these approaches have demonstrated utility for diffuse reflection, the enumeration of possible lighting appearances can be a prohibitive task for specular reflections, whose effects on appearance must be considered for general application of reflectance-based methods.

In comparison to diffuse reflection, specular reflections transform more significantly in location and shape from changes in the light direction. This behavior has been utilized for obtaining surface shape information [6] [2] [10], but for an appearance-based structure, a larger set of images would consequently be needed to capture these variations. Epstein *et al.* [4] present an empirical investigation of the number of eigenimages needed to represent lighting appearance that includes both diffuse and specular reflections. They concluded that 5 ± 2 eigenimages are sufficient for representing a range of objects that are not highly specular, where the eigenimages are computed from a larger set of training images.

Rather than data-driven modeling from an extensive collection of images, we analyze in this paper local and global specular appearance with respect to accepted physical reflectance models. Our presented representation deals specifically with specular, and not diffuse, reflection. Although most objects reflect both specularly and diffusely, there exists a range of materials that exhibit primarily specular reflectance, such as metals and dark-colored dielectrics. We propose that under certain typical illumination and object surface conditions the specular appearance of such objects can be concisely represented in a manner analogous to models for Lambertian appearance. The restrictions on illumination and surfaces are similar to those that have been used previously to reduce the variability of specular appearance to a manageable degree [6] [13].

In this paper, we present our approximate local specularity model that is based on three photometric measurements. For global specular appearance, the number of photometric images required for adequate characterization depends upon the lower-bound surface roughness of the examined object, and we suggest an illumination planning method for determining the number of needed images.

2. Reflection Models

The directional distribution of reflected light is dependent upon surface properties and the configuration of illumination sources. The geometric relationship among these factors and the camera position may be described by the incident illumination direction L, the normal N of the surface patch under consideration, the viewing direction V, and the unit angular bisector H of L and V.

Reflection from a dielectric surface can be divided into two physically different components. One is diffuse reflection, characterized by subsurface scattering and by disperse re-emittance that is commonly modelled as having the Lambertian property:

$$I(x) = \rho(x)N(x) \cdot \sigma L$$

where $I(x)$ is the reflection intensity at surface point x, $\rho(x)$ is the surface albedo at x, and σ is the light intensity. A property of diffuse images derived from this Lambertian model is that an image $I(x)$ of an object taken under any arbitrary lighting configuration can be expressed as a linear combination

$$I(x) = \alpha_1 I_1(x) + \alpha_2 I_2(x) + \alpha_3 I_3(x)$$

of three photometric images I_1, I_2, I_3 with respective noncoplanar illumination directions L_1, L_2, L_3 and coefficients $\alpha_1, \alpha_2, \alpha_3$. This property allows representation of diffuse appearance by three images [12].

The second reflection component is specular reflection, the intensity of which is highly viewpoint dependent. The Torrance-Sparrow model is utilized for describing the structure of this reflection. One factor of this model is the gaussian probability distribution of the microfacets that compose the surface:

$$P(\alpha) = b \, e^{-\alpha^2/g^2} \tag{1}$$

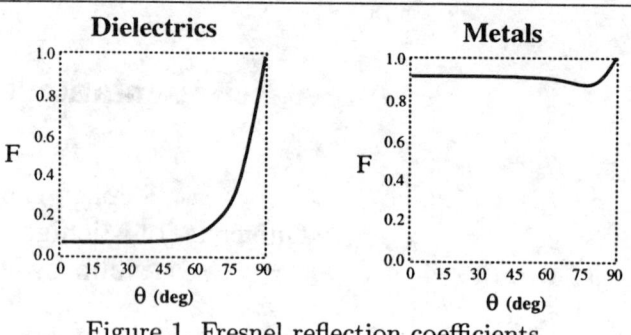

Figure 1. Fresnel reflection coefficients

where $\alpha = \cos^{-1}(N \cdot H)$, b is a constant, and g is the surface roughness parameter, defined as the RMS slope of the microfacet normals. Another factor of the model is the geometric attenuation

$$G = min\{1, \frac{2(N \cdot H)(N \cdot V)}{(V \cdot H)}, \frac{2(N \cdot H)(N \cdot L)}{(V \cdot H)}\} \tag{2}$$

attributed to masking and shadowing of microfacets by neighboring facets. The third factor is the Fresnel reflectance $F(\theta, \eta, \lambda)$ which describes the attenuation of reflected radiance that characterizes surface material of complex refractive index η for incidence angle $\theta = \cos^{-1}(N \cdot L)$ and wavelength λ. Fresnel reflectance coefficients typical of dielectrics and metals are graphed in Figure 1 and are discussed in greater detail in Born and Wolf [3]. These factors together form the Torrance-Sparrow equation:

$$R(N, V, L, g, \eta, \lambda) = \frac{F(N, L, \eta, \lambda)P(N, V, L, g)G(N, V, L)}{N \cdot V}. \tag{3}$$

In the following section, we utilize this reflection model to derive our proposed specular representation.

3. Representation of Specular Appearance

Photometric methods for representing diffuse appearance generally regard specular reflections as noise and assume that its effect on object appearance is minimal. This neglect of specularities largely results from the intricacy of the Torrance-Sparrow model. Although the incorporation of this specular reflection model in a recognition scheme may be cumbersome, there exist conditions where this model simplifies, thereby facilitating its use. In this section, we describe a context and method where the specularity model may be approximated to allow a representation of specular appearance analogous to that of Lambertian appearance, using a linear combination of images taken under a small number of illumination directions.

In the Lambertian photometric method, the linear combination property of three photometric images arises from the representation of an arbitrary illumination direction in

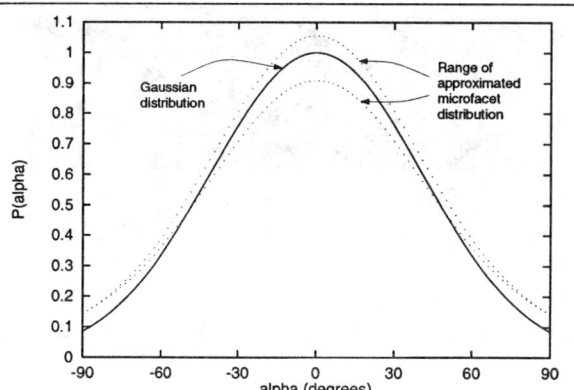

Figure 2. Approximated microfacet distribution

terms of the three spanning photometric light directions. We will likewise describe an arbitrary lighting direction $L' = c_1 L_1 + c_2 L_2 + c_3 L_3$ as a linear combination of three basis directions L_1, L_2, L_3 with constants c_1, c_2, c_3 in the Torrance-Sparrow model of Equation 3.

In recognition applications, assumptions on viewing conditions may be used to reduce the complexity of this equation. One condition is to consider only surface patches with normals N within 45° of the viewing direction V. These frontal surfaces generally provide the most prominent information for object distinction and are less affected by foreshortening. Another bound constrains lighting vectors L to within 45° of the optical axis. Since object recognition typically presupposes full visibility, anterior illumination can reasonably be assumed. Viewing conditions similar to these are also assumed and further justified by Healey and Binford [6]. From these two conditions, we can presume that angles between light direction and surface normal generally lie below 45° for specular reflections.

With these viewing parameters, two factors of the Torrance-Sparrow model are tightly restricted in value. The Fresnel coefficient $F(N, L, \eta, \lambda)$ is nearly constant for incidence angles below 45°, as exhibited for both dielectrics and metals in Figure 1. Likewise, the geometric attenuation coefficient $G(N, V, L)$ of Equation 2 is generally 1 with the given angle constraints. This simplification of the Torrance-Sparrow model was also utilized by Solomon and Ikeuchi [13] for surface roughness determination.

Besides the simplifications that result from angle constraints, the gaussian probability distribution function for microfacet orientations $P(N, V, L)$ given in Equation 1 can be approximated by a more employable expression:

$$P(N, V, L) = k_1 e^{\frac{k_2}{g} N \cdot (V+L)}.$$

Since this microfacet distribution function is dependent on the angle subtending the illumination and viewing directions, it varies according to the light direction. The bounds of variation for this approximation of the gaussian distribution are displayed in Figure 2 for $k_1 = 0.15$, $k_2 = 1$, and surface roughness $g = 0.3$. The shape of the distribution function remains reasonably consistent with that of a gaussian, and because of the previously-mentioned constraints on illumination angles, the range of variation is not major.

With the given approximations and defining $k_3 = k_2/g$, the Torrance-Sparrow model of Equation 3 simplifies to

$$R(N, V, L', g, \eta, \lambda) = k e^{k_3 N \cdot (V+L')} \quad (4)$$

where k represents the constant $(F \cdot G)/(N \cdot V)$. Since the object and camera are fixed, $N \cdot V$ is constant for each pixel. The natural logarithm of this equation yields the expression

$$\ln(R) = \ln(k) + k_3 N \cdot V + k_3 N \cdot (c_1 L_1 + c_2 L_2 + c_3 L_3).$$

A restatement of this equation reveals that the logarithm of an arbitrary intensity-normalized specularity image is a linear combination of three intensity-normalized photometric log images:

$$\ln(R) = c_1 \ln(R_1) + c_2 \ln(R_2) + c_3 \ln(R_3) + E$$

where the term $E = (1 - c_1 - c_2 - c_3)(lnk + k_3 N \cdot V)$ is small and negligible when $c_1 + c_2 + c_3 \approx 1$, which exists for the given constraints on illumination angles. Despite these approximations, it will be shown that the presented illumination model provides suitable basis functions for specular appearance.

Similar to the Lambertian photometric method, this linear combination property is valid for a given pixel only when there exists at least three photometric images that contain a specular component for the pixel. In the Lambertian case, each photometric light source essentially illuminates the entire image, so a total of three lights is sufficient for all pixels in a scene. But for specular reflection, merely a subset of the surface is observable in the image for each light source. Consequently, more than three illumination directions are generally needed to produce specular reflection for each scene pixel in three of the photometric images. If n illumination sources are required to satisfy this photometric constraint, then our global specularity equation becomes:

$$\ln(R) = \sum_{i=1}^{n} c_i \ln(R_i)$$

where R denotes an image vector of pixels. For locations where $R = 0$, we let $ln(R) = 0$ for computational convenience. Since a single set of linear coefficients c_i is used for representing all pixels of a specular image, knowledge of surface normals is unnecessary for determining which photometric images are used to represent a given pixel.

To determine the placement of a given number of photometric light sources, we maximize the minimum number of

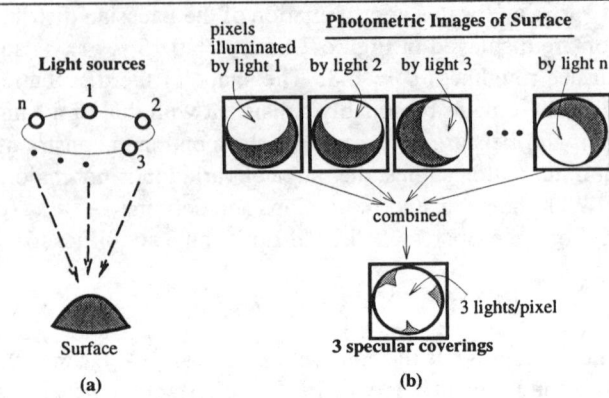

Figure 3. Light distribution: (a) source placement; (b) specular coverings

specular coverings over the scene pixels, where a scene is considered to be specularly covered by m lights if at least 90% of its pixels exhibit specular reflection in at least m of the photometric images. In Figure 3(a), we show a potential distribution of n light sources, and Figure 3(b) illustrates how the resulting n photometric specularity images yields three specular coverings. With this method of light arrangement, we can compute the minimum number of photometric illumination sources that provides three specular covers over the pixels and therefore satisfies our conditions for specular representation. The number and positions of lights depend upon the surface roughness of the examined object and are simple to compute numerically.

4. Experimental Results

In this section, we employ a simulation to support the photometric log image property, and then continue with experimentation on real objects to demonstrate the effectiveness of this specular representation.

4.1 Simulation

This simulation provides results that corroborate the use of three logarithmic images for specular characterization, and moreover, demonstrates the relative descriptive power of logarithmic images and raw images in representing specular appearance. We perform this simulation on a partial sphere, depicted in Figure 4(a), whose range of surface normals extends up to 45° from the viewing direction. For this object with surface roughness of $g = 0.45$, it is computed that six photometric images provide the requisite three specular coverings. To support our specular appearance representation, we measure the reconstruction accuracy for different numbers of photometric log images.

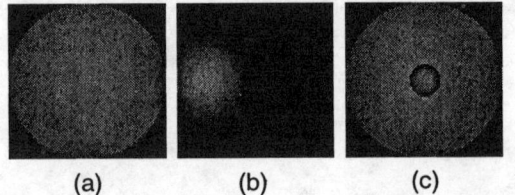

Figure 4. Partial sphere: (a) Lambertian image; (b) specular image; (c) Lambertian image of sphere with bump

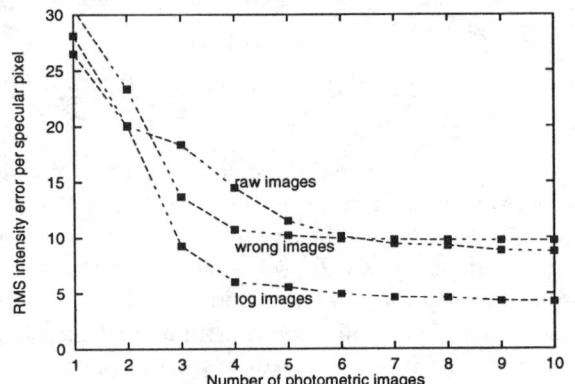

Figure 5. Basis function graph of logarithmic, raw, and wrong (sphere with bump) images

The graph of Figure 5 displays the results of this simulation, charting the RMS error between reconstructed and actual specular intensities for 25 test images that sample light directions up to 45° from the viewing direction. It is seen that having more than the six required photometric log images does not appreciably enhance the reconstruction of the test images, thus suggesting that three logarithmic images can adequately represent specular appearance. The reconstruction error associated with six logarithmic images stem from the approximations within our model. The graph additionally illustrates the difference in performance between logarithmic images and their associated raw images.

To indicate a capacity of this representation for recognition, the graph also includes an error curve for a different object with the same photometric light directions. The large error of this partial sphere with a bump, depicted in Figure 4(c), in relation to that of the correct object reflects the unsuitability of noncorresponding objects and basis images. The object distinguishability of the photometric log representation is examined for actual objects in the following experimental results.

4.2 Black Masks

Experiments were performed on twelve black masks, displayed consecutively in the rows of Figure 6. The masks

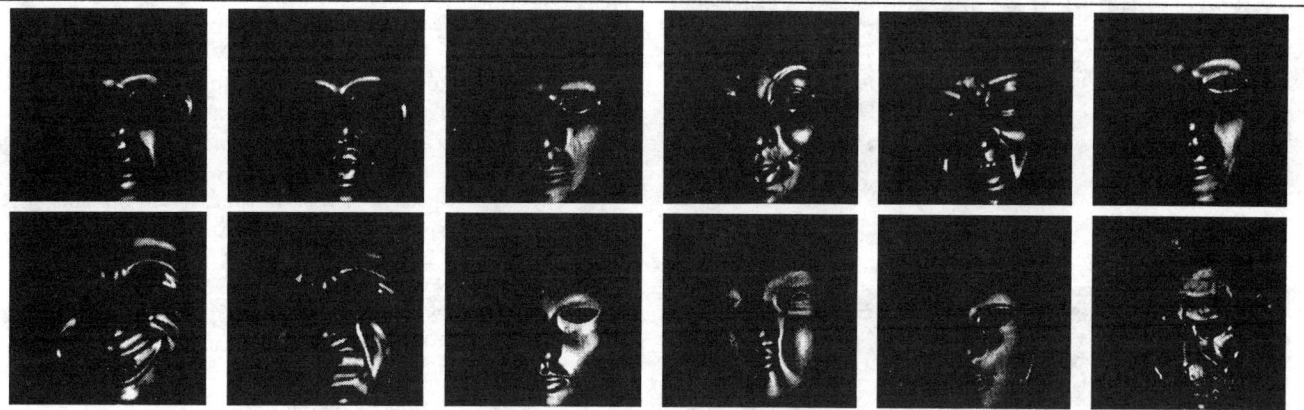

Figure 6. Database masks

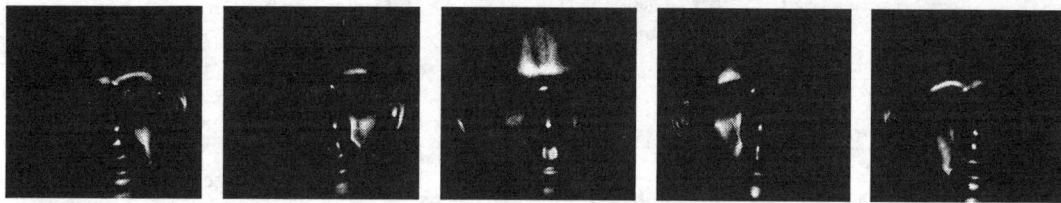

Figure 7. Photometric images

have surface roughness of approximately $g = 0.5$ and have surface normal directions that do not entirely lie within our assumed range. Our representation consisted of five photometric images per mask, as displayed for Mask 1 in Figure 7, where the illumination directions were 72° apart on a circle 45° from the optical axis. Three test images for recognition were taken with each mask and are shown for Mask 1 in Figure 8. The three light source directions for the test images were: (a) on the circle 45° from the optical axis and halfway between two representational light sources, (b) nearly along the optical axis, and (c) 20° from the optical axis opposite from test light (a).

Figure 9 exhibits the relative representation quality between logarithmic images and raw images for test image 1a. As seen on areas such as the cheek, forehead, and the tip of the nose, the raw image reconstruction appears to be a sum of two photometric images that does not interpolate the illumination appearance as well as logarithmic images. This is further demonstrated in Table 1, which lists the average RMS reconstruction errors of specular intensity for test images of the twelve masks, where the errors are normalized by the smaller of the two errors. For this experiment, a linear combination of logarithmic images also more closely describes the test images than a combination of raw images. In Table 2, we similarly display reconstruction errors for each of the 36 test images using the logarithmic descriptors for each database mask. These errors may be utilized for recognition, and for this experiment, all test images are correctly recognized with a fair margin for error.

These experimental results suggest that specular reflections provide significant information for distinguishing objects and that photometric log images can more effectively describe specular appearance than the raw images themselves. In these results, we tested only instances with single light sources, but multiple light source scenes clearly can be described by a superposition of single light source scenes. For cases when the surface roughness is unknown or variable, an estimate of its lower bound may be used for determining the number of photometric lights.

5. Conclusion

In this paper, we examine global specular appearance using physical models of reflectance and have proposed that specular reflections of each surface point measured under three illumination directions sufficiently encompass specular appearance under certain typical conditions. Since more than three photometric images are generally required to provide three instances of specular reflection for each pixel, we present a method that can determine the number of photometric images needed. Experimental results demonstrate the validity of specularities as a recognition cue and support the use of the logarithmic representation. Although the proposed method is framed for purely specular objects, this specular characterization may provide a step towards a more comprehensive illumination model of appearance.

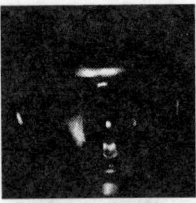

Figure 8. Test images

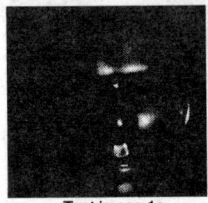

Test image 1a   Logarithmic reconstruction   Raw reconstruction

Figure 9. Reconstructed images

Table 1: Logarithmic vs. Raw Error Table

Mask	1	2	3	4	5	6	7	8	9	10	11	12
Log	**1.00**	**1.00**	**1.00**	**1.00**	**1.00**	**1.00**	**1.00**	**1.00**	**1.00**	**1.00**	**1.00**	**1.00**
Raw	1.32	1.31	1.39	1.48	1.60	1.40	1.29	1.30	1.45	1.48	1.32	1.28

Table 2: Mask Recognition Error Table

Mask	1	2	3	4	5	6	7	8	9	10	11	12
T1a	**1.00**	2.55	2.40	2.46	2.39	2.58	2.94	2.85	2.66	2.58	2.51	2.76
T1b	**1.00**	1.27	1.46	1.47	1.40	1.57	1.60	1.59	1.42	1.50	1.48	1.50
T1c	**1.00**	1.56	1.75	1.84	1.77	1.90	1.88	1.89	1.68	1.81	1.80	1.85
T2a	2.26	**1.00**	2.49	2.42	2.39	2.62	2.68	2.65	2.45	2.49	2.48	2.57
T2b	1.51	**1.00**	1.69	1.67	1.70	1.78	1.81	1.80	1.66	1.71	1.67	1.74
T2c	1.75	**1.00**	1.95	1.99	2.02	2.09	2.13	2.13	1.98	2.03	2.00	2.07
T3a	2.88	3.14	**1.00**	2.38	2.38	2.86	3.19	3.02	2.77	2.37	2.65	3.20
T3b	1.73	2.12	**1.00**	1.79	1.62	2.00	2.40	2.28	1.51	1.76	1.66	2.09
T3c	2.04	2.25	**1.00**	1.78	1.95	2.14	2.47	2.38	1.56	1.81	1.80	2.01
T4a	3.46	3.73	2.69	**1.00**	2.78	3.14	3.46	3.20	3.72	2.52	3.34	3.56
T4b	2.06	2.26	1.65	**1.00**	1.69	1.86	2.27	2.09	2.01	1.66	1.74	2.02
T4c	2.32	2.55	1.96	**1.00**	1.98	2.17	2.61	2.48	1.99	1.91	1.91	2.18
T5a	4.42	4.82	3.48	4.04	**1.00**	4.63	5.01	4.91	4.76	4.11	4.19	5.08
T5b	2.52	3.02	2.28	2.70	**1.00**	2.70	3.19	3.09	2.43	2.66	2.37	2.98
T5c	2.57	2.87	2.43	2.48	**1.00**	2.54	2.95	2.93	2.37	2.43	2.48	2.70
T6a	3.46	3.58	3.23	2.97	3.24	**1.00**	3.15	3.07	3.44	2.87	3.35	3.26
T6b	1.81	1.92	1.59	1.56	1.58	**1.00**	1.74	1.62	1.74	1.50	1.62	1.64
T6c	2.17	2.23	1.94	1.92	1.91	**1.00**	2.21	2.07	2.04	1.88	2.09	2.12
T7a	2.91	3.04	2.83	2.72	2.83	2.70	**1.00**	2.49	2.97	2.64	2.87	2.85
T7b	2.25	2.34	2.02	1.80	1.80	1.80	**1.00**	1.73	2.35	1.73	2.02	2.19
T7c	2.25	2.32	2.20	2.06	2.05	1.94	**1.00**	1.86	2.35	2.04	2.18	2.27
T8a	3.65	3.73	3.38	3.19	3.47	3.39	3.01	**1.00**	3.80	3.03	3.65	3.62
T8b	1.77	1.84	1.48	1.39	1.39	1.35	1.44	**1.00**	1.84	1.27	1.50	1.62
T8c	1.90	1.98	1.74	1.60	1.59	1.49	1.64	**1.00**	1.93	1.55	1.57	1.83
T9a	2.86	2.87	2.39	2.76	2.73	2.86	3.27	3.19	**1.00**	2.62	2.21	2.87
T9b	1.84	1.96	1.49	1.62	1.74	1.99	2.22	2.15	**1.00**	1.69	1.61	1.75
T9c	2.08	2.18	1.56	1.90	2.16	2.22	2.46	2.38	**1.00**	1.97	1.75	2.10
T10a	3.64	3.87	2.67	2.55	2.88	3.28	3.30	3.08	3.80	**1.00**	3.48	3.62
T10b	2.06	2.33	1.47	1.58	1.68	1.76	2.19	2.06	2.04	**1.00**	1.77	2.12
T10c	2.26	2.50	1.78	1.81	1.89	1.92	2.45	2.35	1.97	**1.00**	1.96	2.22
T11a	2.76	2.92	2.44	2.65	2.62	3.02	3.34	3.21	2.46	2.73	**1.00**	2.88
T11b	2.24	2.47	2.04	1.90	2.06	2.37	2.69	2.57	1.91	2.07	**1.00**	2.05
T11c	2.37	2.46	2.05	1.93	2.25	2.40	2.67	2.57	1.90	2.11	**1.00**	2.11
T12a	2.91	2.98	2.85	2.72	2.83	2.80	2.94	2.80	2.84	2.76	2.74	**1.00**
T12b	1.94	2.07	1.90	1.81	1.88	1.91	2.09	1.99	1.85	1.91	1.75	**1.00**
T12c	2.37	2.51	2.23	2.15	2.25	2.33	2.54	2.46	2.15	2.27	2.02	**1.00**

References

[1] P. N. Belhumeur and D. J. Kriegman. What is the set of images of an object under all possible lighting conditions. In *Proc. IEEE Conf. Compt. Vision and Pattern Recog.*, pages 270–277, 1996.

[2] A. Blake. Specular stereo. In *Proc. of 9th Int. Joint Conf. Artif. Intell.*, pages 973–976, Los Angeles, CA, 1985.

[3] M. Born and E. Wolf. *Principles of Optics*. Pergamon Press, New York, NY, 1959.

[4] R. Epstein, P. Hallinan, and A. Yuille. 5 ± 2 eigenimages suffice: An empirical investigation of low-dimensional lighting models. In *Proc. IEEE Workshop on Physics-based Modeling for Compt. Vision*, 1995.

[5] G. H. Healey. Using color for geometry-insensitive segmentation. *Journal of the Optical Society of America A*, 6, 1989.

[6] G. H. Healey and T. O. Binford. Local shape from specularity. *Computer Vision, Graphics and Image Processing*, 42, 1988.

[7] K. Ikeuchi. Determining surface orientation of specular surface by using the photometric stereo method. *IEEE Trans. PAMI*, 3:661–669, 1981.

[8] S. Nayar and H. Murase. Dimensionality of illumination in appearance matching. In *Proc. IEEE Conf. Robotics and Automation*, 1996.

[9] S. K. Nayar, K. Ikeuchi, and T. Kanade. Surface reflection: Physical and geometrical perspective. *IEEE Trans. PAMI*, 13:611–634, 1991.

[10] M. Oren and S. K. Nayar. A theory of specular surface geometry. In *Proc. of IEEE Int. Conf. on Computer Vision*, pages 740–747, Cambridge, MA, 1995.

[11] M. O. Oren and S. K. Nayar. Generalization of the lambertian model. In *Proceedings of the DARPA Image Understanding Workshop*, pages 1037–1048, Washington, DC, 1993.

[12] A. Shashua. *Geometry and Photometry in 3D Visual Recognition*. PhD thesis, MIT, 1992.

[13] F. Solomon and K. Ikeuchi. Extracting the shape and roughness of specular lobe objects using four light photometric stereo. In *Proc. IEEE Conf. Compt. Vision and Pattern Recog.*, pages 466–471, 1992.

[14] K. E. Torrance and E. M. Sparrow. Theory for off-specular relfection from roughened surfaces. *Journal of the Optical Society of America*, 57:1105–1114, 1967.

[15] M. A. Turk and A. Pentland. Face recognition using eigenfaces. In *Proc. IEEE Conf. Compt. Vision and Pattern Recog.*, pages 586–591, 1991.

[16] L. B. Wolff. Diffuse and specular reflection from dielectric surfaces. In *Proceedings of the DARPA Image Understanding Workshop*, pages 1025–1030, Washington, DC, 1993.

[17] R. J. Woodham. Photometric stereo: A reflectance map technique for determining surface orientation from image intensity. In *Proc. SPIE*, pages 136–143, San Diego, CA, 1978.

Estimation of Diffuse and Specular Appearance

Stephen Lin and Sang W. Lee
University of Michigan, Ann Arbor, MI 48109, USA
{stevelin, swlee}@eecs.umich.edu

Abstract

To account for the variability of object appearance due to differences in illumination, attention has recently been focused on representing the set of images for all possible lighting conditions. Approaches that address this problem have primarily focused on lighting differences for diffuse reflection using the Lambertian model; however, specular reflections can additionally present considerable disparity in appearance. We present a method for representing illumination appearance for both diffuse and specular reflections for objects of uniform surface roughness using four photometric images. This approach uses separation of reflection components, extracts surface reflectances and roughness, and produces arbitrary lighting images without explicit computation of surface shape. Experimental results demonstrate the validity of the proposed method for constructing diffuse and specular appearances.

1. Introduction

The photometric appearance of an object in an image results from the amalgamated effects of illumination, surface shape and reflectance. In an effort to manage the results of these effects, various approaches have been introduced in computer vision to account for the variability of photometric appearance. Reflectance models have been developed to characterize image radiance with respect to illumination environment, viewing angles and material properties [16] [13] [18] [8]. These basic physical models provide a local description of reflection mechanisms that can serve as a foundation for appearance representations. Photometric stereo approaches utilize reflection models for estimating surface shape and reflectance from transformations of image intensities that arise from illumination changes [19] [10]. These photometric stereo methods, which are simple and elegant for Lambertian diffuse models, require complex models and algorithms for accurately estimating multiple reflectance and shape parameters when specular reflections are involved.

Without explicitly estimating object shape and reflectance, "appearance-based" approaches represent illumination effects using a large set of images which sample a range of lighting or viewing configurations [17] [11]. This technique has been extended by recent illumination models that account for appearance variations due to shading and attached shadows [14] [2]. These illumination models show that the shading appearance of an object under arbitrary illumination can be expressed as a linear combination of three photometric images.

In the various appearance-based approaches, the assumption that reflection adheres to the Lambertian property is essential, and specular reflections are simply disregarded as noise. In comparison to diffuse reflections, specular reflections transform more significantly in location and shape from changes in the light direction. This behavior has been utilized for obtaining surface shape information [9] [12], but for an appearance-based framework, a larger set of images would consequently be needed to capture these variations. Since the number of images required for this approach can be prohibitively large, it is desirable to develop more concise representations. Epstein *et al.* [6] present an empirical investigation of the number of eigenimages needed to represent lighting appearance that includes both diffuse and specular reflections. They concluded that 5 ± 2 eigenimages are sufficient for representing a range of objects that are not highly specular, where the eigenimages are computed from a larger set of training images.

Although diffuse appearance can be compactly represented using physical models of reflection, the complexity of specular reflections cannot be captured using a small number of images. In this paper, we present an approach that represents diffuse appearance using an accepted illumination model and describes specular appearance using an illumination condition that provides accessibility to implicit information about the specular structure of an object. Having uniform lighting intensities and an illumination source along the optical axis allows us to estimate albedo and specularity appearance parameters without requiring computation of surface shape and illumination directions.

Using physical models of reflectance, our method con-

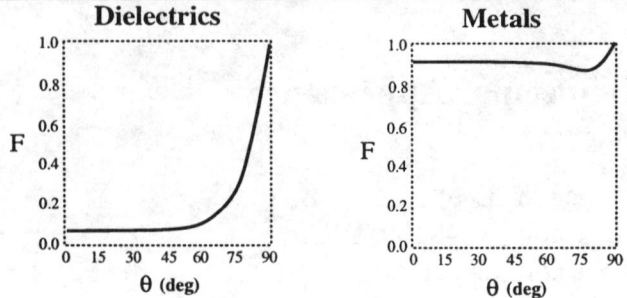

Figure 1. Fresnel reflection coefficients

sists of separation of diffuse and specular components, determination and normalization of surface reflectances, estimation of surface roughness, and construction of illumination appearances. By including specularity in appearance models, increased reliability for recognition and tracking methods, as well as greater realism of camera images within a graphics environment, may be achieved. Before elaborating on the proposed approach, we briefly outline the underlying reflection models.

2. Reflection Models

The directional distribution of reflected light is dependent upon surface properties and the configuration of illumination sources. The geometric relationship among these factors and the camera position may be described by the incident illumination direction L, the normal N of the surface patch under consideration, the viewing direction V, and H, defined to be the unit angular bisector of L and V.

Reflection from a dielectric surface can be divided into two physically different components. One is diffuse reflection, characterized by subsurface scattering and by disperse re-emittance that is commonly modelled as having the Lambertian property. The other reflection mechanism, which occurs at the air/material interface and exhibits a low amount of dispersion, is referred to as specular reflection. This type of reflection also typifies metals and is commonly described using the Torrance-Sparrow model. These two reflection components together comprise the reflectance function:

$$R(L, N, V, \lambda) = R_d(L, N, \lambda) + R_s(L, N, V, \lambda) \quad (1)$$

where λ is the illumination wavelength, R_d is the diffuse component and R_s is the specular component. In this section, we briefly describe the two reflectance models.

2.1 Diffuse Model

Diffuse reflection under the Lambertian model appears uniformly bright from all viewing directions and can be rep-

resented at a surface point x as the inner product

$$I(x) = \rho(x) N(x) \cdot \sigma L \quad (2)$$

where $I(x)$ is the reflection intensity at x, $\rho(x)$ is the surface albedo at x, and σ is the light intensity. A property of diffuse images derived from this Lambertian model is that an image $I(x)$ of an object taken under any arbitrary lighting configuration can be expressed as a linear combination

$$I(x) = \beta_1 I_1(x) + \beta_2 I_2(x) + \beta_3 I_3(x) \quad (3)$$

of three photometric images I_1, I_2, I_3 with respective non-coplanar illumination directions L_1, L_2, L_3 and coefficients $\beta_1, \beta_2, \beta_3$. This property allows representation of diffuse appearance by three images [14]. The set of all Lambertian images can be generated from this representation by enumerating all the values of $\beta_1, \beta_2, \beta_3$. In our proposed method, these linear coefficients lead not only to construction of diffuse appearance, but specular appearance as well.

2.2 Specular Model

In contrast to Lambertian reflection, the intensity of specular reflection is highly viewpoint dependent. The Torrance-Sparrow model details the structure of this reflection by first assuming that a surface is composed of mirror-like microfacets oriented randomly. The distribution of these facets can be modelled by the Beckmann distribution as described by Cook and Torrance [5]:

$$P(\alpha, m) = \frac{1}{m^2 \cos^4 \alpha} \exp(-\frac{\tan^2 \alpha}{m^2}) \quad (4)$$

where $\alpha = \cos^{-1}(N \cdot H)$ and m is the surface roughness parameter, defined as the RMS slope of the microfacet normals. Another factor of the model is the geometric attenuation

$$G = min\{1, \frac{2(N \cdot H)(N \cdot V)}{(V \cdot H)}, \frac{2(N \cdot H)(N \cdot L)}{(V \cdot H)}\} \quad (5)$$

attributed to masking and shadowing of microfacets by neighboring facets. The third factor is the Fresnel reflectance $F(\theta, \eta, \lambda)$ which describes the attenuation of reflected radiance that characterizes surface material of complex refractive index η for incidence angle $\theta = \cos^{-1}(N \cdot L)$ and wavelength λ. Fresnel reflectance coefficients typical of dielectrics and metals are graphed in Figure 1 and are discussed in greater detail in Born and Wolf [3].

These factors together form the Torrance-Sparrow equation:

$$R(N, V, L, m, \eta, \lambda) = \frac{F(N, L, \eta, \lambda) P(N, V, L, m) G(N, V, L)}{N \cdot V}. \quad (6)$$

In the following section, we employ the Torrance-Sparrow reflection model for surface roughness estimation and for generation of specular appearance.

3. Illumination Appearance

Our proposed method utilizes the described physical reflection models for constructing novel illumination appearances. In contrast to photometric stereo, we do not require the estimation of parameters such as surface normals and lighting directions which are difficult to accurately compute without a fair amount of *a priori* information about the illuminations and/or surface. Under the simplifying conditions that the photometric light intensities are uniform and that one light direction is collinear with the camera axis, we show that photometric stereo methods can be circumvented for constructing diffuse and specular appearance.

These described illumination conditions are chosen to facilitate the use of the intricate Torrance-Sparrow model for describing specular appearance. From the four photometric images I_0, I_1, I_2, I_3, we select I_0 to have an illumination source located approximately along the optical axis. This constraint provides us with a means for inferring information related to the viewing vector V. By assuming that the illumination intensities are uniform among the photometric sources, the recovery of reflectance values becomes achievable without *a priori* information about the viewed surface.

From this set of photometric images, we begin our algorithm for constructing illumination appearance by separating the diffuse and specular image components using the Lambertian property. With the computed diffuse images, we describe a technique for recovering surface reflectances in order to dissociate shading from albedo. From the resulting albedo-normalized images, surface roughness is estimated for describing specular structure, and we present our method of image construction that directly uses shading patterns derived from the photometric images.

3.1. Separation of Reflection Components

In order to obtain shading information, we need to separate specular reflection from diffuse reflection in the images. Since our image construction approach already requires four photometric images, separation using the Lambertian property can be applied without gathering additional data. Since three images uniquely determine the Lambertian component of the fourth image according to Equation 3, intensity deviations in the fourth image from what is predicted by the Lambertian property represent the magnitude of specular reflection. This separation technique is described by Shashua [14] and is similar to a specularity detection method by Coleman and Jain [4]. An assumption of this approach is that specular reflections among the photometric images do not spatially overlap, as this would cause some pixels to have purely diffuse reflection in fewer than three images and consequently prohibit full Lambertian characterization of the viewed object. Although this separation method is convenient for our overall approach, other techniques may be substituted in its place.

3.2. Normalization of Surface Reflectance

In the computed diffuse reflection images, our method isolates shading information from surface reflectance, or albedo. Albedo represents the degree of light reflection from a surface point. Areas of high albedo on an object reflect most of the incident illumination and is intrinsically brighter than regions of low albedo, where much of the incident light energy is absorbed by the surface. From the determination of surface reflectances on the viewed object, the four Lambertian photometric images can then be depicted as though the object had uniform albedo. This process of albedo normalization removes the influence of surface reflectance from the images, yielding image intensities that result only from object shape and illumination. Angelopoulou *et al.* [1] introduced a three-light photometric method for albedo normalization that does not assume uniform light intensity but requires a constant-albedo reference object to obtain partial illumination information. Solomon and Ikeuchi [15] described a method using four-source photometric stereo with calibrated lighting for determining albedo in the presence of specularity. In this subsection, we present an approach for recovering surface reflectances without the use of a reference object or calibrated lighting, given four uniform-intensity light sources.

Since the illumination strengths are equal for the four images, we designate their lighting vectors as unit length, thus eliminating σ from Equation 2. From the resulting equation, it is seen that when $L = N(x)$, the image intensity at surface point x reaches its highest value and is equal to the albedo $\rho(x)$. To utilize this property for estimating the reflectance at each surface point, we determine the illumination direction that maximizes the diffuse intensity of each pixel. For pixel x, this can be formulated as

$$\max_{\alpha_1, \alpha_2, \alpha_3} I(x) = \alpha_1 I_1(x) + \alpha_2 I_2(x) + \alpha_3 I_3(x). \quad (7)$$

Since the lighting vector $L = \alpha_1 L_1 + \alpha_2 L_2 + \alpha_3 L_3$ associated with this function must be unit length in order for the maximum value to equal the albedo, this maximization is constrained by the equation

$$\alpha_1^2 + \alpha_2^2 + \alpha_3^2 + 2\alpha_1\alpha_2\langle L_1, L_2\rangle + 2\alpha_1\alpha_3\langle L_1, L_3\rangle + 2\alpha_2\alpha_3\langle L_2, L_3\rangle = 1 \quad (8)$$

where the inner products of the light vectors can be calculated as shown in Appendix A. The computed intensity $I(x)$ is then taken as the estimated albedo $\rho(x)$ at point x. This function for albedo determination can be maximized analytically using the method briefly outlined in Appendix B.

Each Lambertian photometric image I_l is subsequently divided by the computed reflectance values to produce an albedo-normalized image $\hat{I}_l(x) = I_l(x)/\rho(x)$. This normalization converts the photometric images into a form that facilitates our process for image construction.

3.3. Surface Roughness Estimation

In addition to directional quantities, specular appearance depends on the surface roughness and Fresnel reflectance parameters, which can be determined from the specular structure of the photometric images. Solomon and Ikeuchi [15] detailed a method for recovering surface roughness using specular reflections and surface normals, but in this presented approach, no explicit shape information is assumed to be available. Using the albedo-normalized image $\hat{I}_0$, we can estimate surface roughness according to the Torrance-Sparrow model. Since the illumination direction for this image is collinear with the optical axis, the point of maximum intensity in the corresponding specularity image, which we will refer to as pixel c, has a surface normal that approximates the illumination and viewing direction. The unit-length illumination vector L is equivalent to V for image $\hat{I}_0$, and consequently the intensities in $\hat{I}_0$ represent the quantity $N \cdot V$ according to Equation 2. Moreover, the $\hat{I}_0$ intensities also represent the values of $N \cdot H$ since H is the unit angular bisector of L and V. This allows the Torrance-Sparrow model of Equation 6 to express the specular intensity of image I_0 in terms of $\hat{I}_0$:

$$I_s(x) = \frac{F}{m^2 \hat{I}_0(x)^5} \exp(-\frac{\tan^2(cos^{-1}\hat{I}_0(x))}{m^2}).$$

The pixels that surround the specular maximum at c can then be used to estimate the surface roughness m and Fresnel coefficient F with this equation. Since the illumination and viewing directions are the same and the surface normals of the examined pixels are generally close to the viewing direction, the geometric attenuation coefficient G is equal to 1 and can be disregarded. Within an $n \times n$ neighborhood N around pixel c, we compute the values of m and F from the actual separated specular intensities R_s and the diffuse intensities $\hat{I}_0$ by minimizing the mean squared error of I_s:

$$MSE = \frac{1}{n^2} \sum_{x \in N} \left[R_s(x) - \frac{F}{m^2 \hat{I}_0(x)^5} \exp(-\frac{\tan^2(\cos^{-1}\hat{I}_0(x))}{m^2}) \right]^2.$$

Uniform surface roughness of the object is assumed, since m is computed at a single location. Determination of these parameters yields a specularity model for the viewed object.

3.4. Image Construction

With the computed specularity parameters and albedo-normalized Lambertian images, we show that the set of dif-fuse/specular illumination appearances for an object can be constructed from the same coefficients that generate Lambertian appearance as described in Equation 3. The diffuse image component is computed from the Lambertian equation, but avoids the use of identified specular regions in each photometric image. Since it is assumed that specular reflections among the photometric images do not overlap, there exist three images that exhibit purely diffuse reflection for each pixel, and the constructed diffuse reflection appearance R_d is produced from these three images. If pixel x were purely diffuse in images I_1, I_2, I_3, then the constructed diffuse component at that point would be

$$R_d(x) = \beta_1 \hat{I}_1 + \beta_2 \hat{I}_2 + \beta_3 \hat{I}_3$$

Generation of the specular reflection component R_s uses the albedo-normalized photometric images in conjunction with the Torrance-Sparrow model. Since the surface roughness m and Fresnel reflectance coefficient F have been computed, Equations 4 - 6 show that the quantities $N \cdot V$, $N \cdot H$ and $V \cdot H$ need to be determined for each pixel in order to construct specular appearance. As described in the previous subsection, the intensities of image $\hat{I}_0$ provide the values of $N \cdot V$. From Equation 2, $N \cdot L$ is equal to R_d/ρ, so we compute the quantity $N \cdot H$ as

$$N \cdot H = N \cdot \frac{V + L}{\|V + L\|} = \frac{\hat{I}_0 + R_d/\rho}{\|V + L\|}.$$

The magnitude of $V + L$ is determined using the angle ψ between V and L. Since $N = V$ at pixel c,

$$\cos\psi = V \cdot L = N(c) \cdot L = R_d(c)/\rho(c).$$

Consequently,

$$\|V + L\| = \sqrt{(1 + \cos\psi)^2 + \sin^2\psi}.$$

Finally, we compute $V \cdot H$ as

$$V \cdot H = V \cdot \frac{V + L}{\|V + L\|} = \frac{1 + \cos\psi}{\|V + L\|}.$$

With these quantities that are computed directly from image intensities, specular appearance can be estimated. By adding the two reflection components R_d and R_s, we obtain a constructed illumination image. Although the Torrance-Sparrow model describes specular reflection in terms of surface orientation and reflectance angles, our approach nevertheless applies this model by utilizing image intensities that implicitly contain this information.

4. Experimental Results

In this section, we demonstrate the use of our image construction method for estimating the diffuse and specular appearance of a real object. Our experimental setup

Figure 2. Experimental photometric images

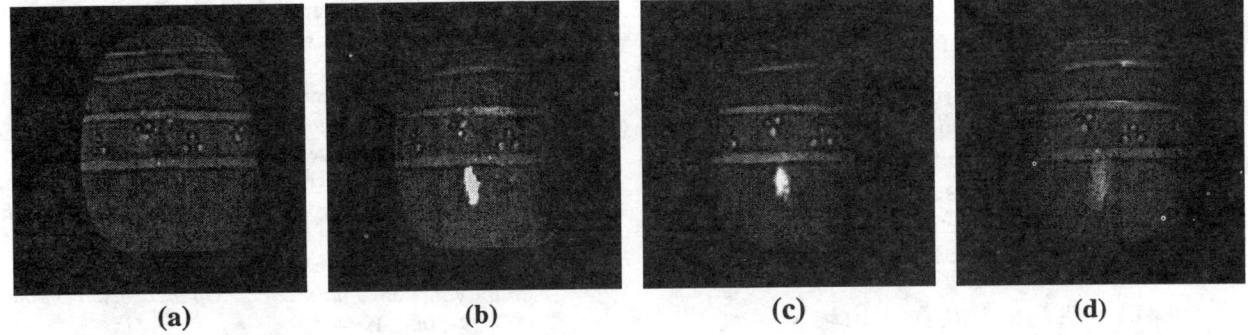

| (a) | (b) | (c) | (d) |

Figure 3. Experimental image results: (a) albedo; (b) constructed; (c) actual; (d) comparison

includes a Sony XC-77 camera with a 50mm lens. The viewed object is located about 1.5m from the camera and the illuminants. Directions of the photometric light sources from the camera axis are approximately $(\theta, \phi) = (0^o, 0^o), (30^o, 10^o), (25^o, 210^o), (20^o, 115^o)$.

Experiments were performed on a painted wooden egg whose photometric images are shown in Figure 2. Figure 3 displays from left to right the computed surface reflectances, an image constructed using the proposed method, a real image with a light direction that approximates that of the constructed image, and an image computed from the comparison method described in the preceding section. As seen in the albedo and constructed images, areas where the separation of reflection components is inaccurate will result in some problems in image construction.

In the literature, there is no mention of a procedure for obtaining surface orientations given only the information provided in our experiments, so we designed such a method for comparison with the proposed algorithm. Because the focus of this paper is not on this comparison method, we summarize it briefly. Relative surface normals are computed by first performing singular-value decomposition on a matrix of photometric images [7]. Since this factorization produces a surface normal matrix that is affine-transformed, additional constraints are needed for estimation of relative surface normals. These constraints are obtained from a devised technique for albedo computation, which yields reli-

able results. From the estimated surface normals, illumination appearance can be computed from reflection models.

The comparison algorithm generates an image, Figure 3(d), whose diffuse and specular components are incongruous. Edges of the egg are clipped due to insufficient information for surface normal computation, and the structure of the specularity is distorted. These problems may partially be explained by inaccurate lighting matrix computation and the encoding of image noise within surface normals from singular-value decomposition.

Perturbations in image intensities, both from the imaging system and from poor separation of reflection components, impairs the proposed method as it does for photometric stereo. Although the impact of camera noise can be reduced by averaging multiple images and smoothing, errors in separation are difficult to improve. Consequently, specularity construction on regions of inaccurate separation will likewise be inexact. Our image construction method does not specifically require the particular separation technique that was employed, so other separation algorithms may be substituted in its place.

5. Conclusion

In this paper we develop a method for constructing diffuse and specular appearance for arbitrary illumination conditions. Generation of diffuse reflection is similar to previous approaches, but we moreover utilize diffuse intensity information for producing specular appearance. Rather than attempting to extract surface shape information from the photometric images, we utilize shading patterns to obtain surface reflectances, to estimate surface roughness, and to create novel illumination appearances. By generalizing illumination appearance models to include the effects of specularity, vision algorithms in areas such as recognition and tracking can identify objects with increased reliability, and camera images incorporated into a graphics environment can exhibit greater realism.

Appendix A

Let $\beta_1, \beta_2, \beta_3$ be the Lambertian coefficients computed from the separation of reflection components, and let ψ_1, ψ_2, ψ_3 be the angles between V and L_1, L_2, L_3 respectively. For each surface point, its surface normal and albedo are constant among the photometric images. So from Equations 2 and 3, we can derive the following equality:

$$\|L_0 - \beta_1 L_1\| = \|\beta_2 L_2 + \beta_3 L_3\|.$$

Let θ_{23} be the angle between L_2 and L_3. Then these magnitudes can be expressed as

$$\|L_0 - \beta_1 L_1\| = \sqrt{(1 - \beta_1 \cos \psi_1)^2 + (\beta_1 \sin \psi_1)^2},$$

$$\|\beta_2 L_2 + \beta_3 L_3\| = \sqrt{(\beta_2 + \beta_3 \cos \theta_{23})^2 + (\beta_3 \sin \theta_{23})^2}.$$

Similar to the computation of ψ in Section 3.4, ψ_1 can be calculated as

$$\psi_1 = \cos^{-1} \frac{\hat{I}_1(c)}{\rho(c)}.$$

Equating the above magnitudes, we can solve for the inner product

$$\langle L_2, L_3 \rangle = \cos \theta_{23} = \frac{1 + \beta_1^2 - \beta_2^2 - \beta_3^2 - 2\beta_1 \cos \psi_1}{2\beta_2 \beta_3}.$$

The other inner products can be computed in a similar manner.

Appendix B

Setting the function $f(\alpha_1, \alpha_2, \alpha_3)$ to be the right-hand side of Equation 7 and the function $g(\alpha_1, \alpha_2, \alpha_3)$ to be the left-hand side of Equation 8 minus one, we can utilize the method of Lagrange multipliers to maximize the albedo determination function. The critical points of the expression $f(\alpha_1, \alpha_2, \alpha_3) - \lambda g(\alpha_1, \alpha_2, \alpha_3)$ for Lagrange multiplier λ yield two sets of $\alpha_1, \alpha_2, \alpha_3$ values, of which one set maximizes Equation 7.

References

[1] E. Angelopoulou, J. P. Williams, and L. B. Wolff. A curvature based descriptor invariant to pose and albedo derived from photometric data. In *Proc. IEEE Conf. Compt. Vision and Pattern Recog.*, pages 165–171, 1997.

[2] P. Belhumeur and D. Kriegman. What is the set of images of an object under all possible lighting conditions. In *Proc. IEEE Conf. Compt. Vision and Pattern Recog.*, pages 270–277, 1996.

[3] M. Born and E. Wolf. *Principles of Optics*. Pergamon Press, New York, NY, 1959.

[4] E. N. Coleman and R. Jain. Obtaining 3-dimensional shape of textured and specular surface using four-source photometry. *Computer Graphics and Image Processing*, 18:308–328, 1982.

[5] R. Cook and K. E. Torrance. A relfectance model for computer graphics. *Computer Graphics*, 15:307–316, 1981.

[6] R. Epstein, P. Hallinan, and A. Yuille. 5 ± 2 eigenimages suffice: An empirical investigation of low-dimensional lighting models. In *Proc. IEEE Workshop on Physics-based Modeling for Compt. Vision*, 1995.

[7] H. Hayakawa. Photometric stereo under a light source with arbitrary motion. *Journal of the Optical Society of America*, 11:3079–3089, 1994.

[8] G. Healey. Using color for geometry-insensitive segmentation. *Journal of the Optical Society of America A*, 6, 1989.

[9] G. Healey and T. Binford. Local shape from specularity. *Computer Vision, Graphics and Image Processing*, 42, 1988.

[10] K. Ikeuchi. Determining surface orientation of specular surface by using the photometric stereo method. *IEEE Trans. PAMI*, 3:661–669, 1981.

[11] S. Nayar and H. Murase. Dimensionality of illumination in appearance matching. In *Proc. IEEE Conf. Robotics and Automation*, 1996.

[12] M. Oren and S. Nayar. A theory of specular surface geometry. In *Proc. of IEEE Int. Conf. on Computer Vision*, pages 740–747, 1995.

[13] M. O. Oren and S. K. Nayar. Generalization of the lambertian model. In *Proceedings of the DARPA Image Understanding Workshop*, pages 1037–1048, 1993.

[14] A. Shashua. *Geometry and Photometry in 3D Visual Recognition*. PhD thesis, MIT, 1992.

[15] F. Solomon and K. Ikeuchi. Extracting the shape and roughness of specular lobe objects using four light photometric stereo. In *Proc. IEEE Conf. Compt. Vision and Pattern Recog.*, pages 466–471, 1992.

[16] K. E. Torrance and E. M. Sparrow. Theory for off-specular relfection from roughened surfaces. *Journal of the Optical Society of America*, 57:1105–1114, 1967.

[17] M. Turk and A. Pentland. Face recognition using eigenfaces. In *Proc. IEEE Conf. Compt. Vision and Pattern Recog.*, pages 586–591, 1991.

[18] L. B. Wolff. Diffuse and specular reflection from dielectric surfaces. In *Proceedings of the DARPA Image Understanding Workshop*, pages 1025–1030, 1993.

[19] R. J. Woodham. Photometric stereo: A reflectance map technique for determining surface orientation from image intensity. In *Proc. SPIE*, pages 136–143, 1978.

Spectral Gradient: A Material Descriptor Invariant to Geometry and Incident Illumination[1]

Elli Angelopoulou[*†], Sang W. Lee[❖] and Ruzena Bajcsy[*]

[*]University of Pennsylvania   [†]Stevens Institute of Technology   [❖]University of Michigan
GRASP Laboratory   Computer Science Department   Computer Vision Laboratory
Philadelphia, PA 19104   Hoboken, NJ 07030   Ann Arbor, MI 48109
elli@cs.stevens-tech.edu,   swlee@eecs.umich.edu,   {elli, bajcsy}@grip.cis.upenn.edu

Abstract

The light reflected from a surface depends on the scene geometry, the incident illumination and the surface material. A novel methodology is presented which extracts reflectivity information of the various materials in the scene independent of incident light and scene geometry. A scene is captured under different narrow-band color filters and the spectral derivatives of the scene are computed. The resulting spectral derivatives form a spectral gradient at each pixel. This spectral gradient is a material descriptor which is invariant to scene geometry and incident illumination for smooth diffuse surfaces. Spectral gradients can discriminate among smooth dielectrics with different reflectance properties independent of viewing conditions.

1. Introduction

The starting point of most computer vision techniques is the light intensity reflected from an imaged scene. The reflected light is directly related to the geometry of the scene, the reflectance properties of the materials in the scene and the lighting conditions under which the scene was captured. One of the complications which have troubled computer vision algorithms is the variability of an object's appearance as illumination and scene geometry change. Slight variations in viewing conditions often cause large changes in an object's appearance. Consider, for example a yellow car seen in a sunny day, at night, or in dense fog.

Many areas of computer vision are affected by variations in an object's appearance. Among the most well-known problems is color constancy, the task of consistently identifying colors, despite changes in lighting conditions. Maloney and Wandell[17] were the first to develop a tractable color constancy algorithm by modeling both the surface reflectance and the incident illumination as a finite dimensional linear model. This idea was further explored by Forsyth[6], Ho et al.[12], Finlayson et al.[5, 7, 4, 1] and Healey and Slater[10]. Color is a very important cue in object identification. Swain and Ballard[24] showed that objects can be recognized by using color information alone. Combing color cues with color constancy[10, 22, 7, 4] generated even more powerful color-guided object recognition systems.

At the same time, Nayar and Bolle[18], Slater and Healey[20, 21], Lin and Lee[16] and Jacobs et al.[15], among others, concentrated their object identification techniques on identifying reflectance-based object properties that are invariant to illumination. In texture recognition, Healey and Wang[11] developed an illumination invariant distance function for comparing color textures. In real-time tracking Hager and Belheumer[9] adapted the sum of squared differences (SSD) algorithm to handle variations in illumination.

All these systems in order to handle the variations in viewing conditions had to introduce some additional constraints that are often limiting their applicability. For example, most color techniques assume that the spectral reflectance functions have the same degrees of freedom as the number of photoreceptor classes (typically three.) Thus, none of these methods can be used in greyscale images for extracting illumination invariant color information. Furthermore, a considerable body of work on color assumes that the incident illumination has two or three degrees of freedom. However, Slater and Healey[23] showed that for outdoor scenes, the illumination functions have seven degrees of freedom.

We propose a novel method for cancelling variations in geometry and incident illumination by examining the rate of change in reflected intensity with respect to wavelength. The only assumption that we make is that incident illumination remains stable over small intervals in the visible spectrum. It will be demonstrated that this is a reasonable assumption.

We take a greyscale image of a scene under three different color filters and compute the spectral derivatives of the scene. Unlike many color constancy methods, our color filters are narrow bandpass filters (10nm wide as opposed to the typical 75nm). The use of narrow filters increases the

---

1. This work was supported in part by the Army Research Office Multidisciplinary University Research Initiative (MURI), ARO grant DAAH04-96-1-0007.

discriminatory power of our method (see section 6.3.) An additional advantage of our technique over the more traditional band-ratios is that spectral derivatives are used on a per pixel basis. They do not depend on neighboring regions, an assumption that is common in other photometric methods, which use logarithms and/or narrow-band filters[7, 18].

The collection of spectral derivatives evaluated at different wavelengths forms a spectral gradient. This gradient is a surface reflectance descriptor, invariant to scene geometry and incident illumination for smooth diffuse surfaces. Spectral gradients go a step beyond color constancy. They can differentiate materials of the same apparent color, if their reflectance behavior is distinct.

Experiments on surfaces of different colors and materials demonstrate the accuracy of our method in both: a) identifying materials with the same reflectance under variable viewing conditions and b) discriminating materials with distinct reflectance functions.

2. Spectral derivative

The intensity images that we process in computer vision are formed when light from a scene falls on a photosensitive sensor. The amount of light reflected from each point $p = (x, y, z)$ in the scene depends on the light illuminating the scene, E and the surface reflectance S of the materials composing the scene:

$$I(p, \lambda) = E(p, \lambda)S(p, \lambda)$$

where λ, the wavelength, shows the dependence of incident and reflected light on wavelength. The reflectance function $S(p, \lambda)$ depends on the surface material, the scene geometry scene and the viewing and incidence angles.

When the spectral distribution of the incident light does not vary with the direction of the light, the geometric and spectral components of the incident illumination are separable:

$$E(\theta_i, \varphi_i, \lambda) = e(\lambda)E(\theta_i, \varphi_i)$$

where (θ_i, φ_i) are the spherical coordinates of the unit-length light-direction vector and $e(\lambda)$ is the illumination spectrum. Note that, the incident light intensity is included in $E(\theta_i, \varphi_i)$ and may vary as the position of the illumination source changes. The scene brightness then becomes:

$$I(p, \lambda) = e(p, \lambda)E(p, \theta_i, \varphi_i)S(p, \lambda) \qquad (1)$$

By taking the logarithm of the image irradiance equation we alter the multiplicative effect into an additive effect:

$$\mathcal{L}(p, \lambda) = \ln e(p, \lambda) + \ln E(p, \theta_i, \varphi_i) + \ln S(p, \lambda) \qquad (2)$$

We are interested in investigating the behavior of the natural logarithm of an image as we vary the wavelength in the visible range, i.e., 400nm to 700nm. Thus, we compute the partial derivative of the logarithmic image with respect to wavelength λ:

$$\mathcal{L}_\lambda(p, \lambda) = \frac{e_\lambda(p, \lambda)}{e(p, \lambda)} + \frac{S_\lambda(p, \lambda)}{S(p, \lambda)} \qquad (3)$$

where $e_\lambda(p, \lambda) = \partial e(p, \lambda)/\partial\lambda$ is the partial derivative of the spectrum of the incident light with respect to wavelength and $S_\lambda(p, \lambda) = \partial S(p, \lambda)/\partial\lambda$ is the partial derivative of the surface reflectance with respect to wavelength. Ho, Funt and Drew[12] have shown, that for natural objects the surface spectral reflectance curves, i.e. the plots of $S(p, \lambda)$ versus λ, are usually reasonably smooth and continuous over the visible spectrum, 400nm to 700nm.

3. Invariance to incident illumination

Although the spectral distribution of the most commonly used indoor-scene illuminations sources (i.e., tungsten and fluorescent light) is not constant, one can assume that e changes slowly over small increments of λ. This means that its derivative with respect to wavelength is approximately zero.

$$e_\lambda(p, \lambda) \approx 0$$

In implementing the differentiation, we must compute the partial derivative over small increments of λ. The typical red, green and blue filters used in color cameras are approximately 100nm apart. At such large increments approximating e_λ with zero no longer holds.

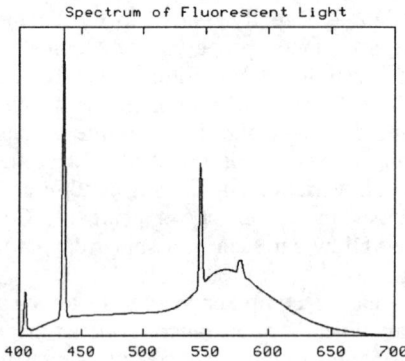

Figure 1. Spectrum of fluorescent light.

In general, the assumption of a slowly changing e is valid over most of the visible range. As seen in fig. 1, the four discontinuities of the spectral distribution of fluorescent light, (at approximately 405nm, 436nm, 545nm, and

578nm) are localized and the spectrum remains smoothly varying over the remaining visible range. Thus, one can safely assume that in general the partial derivative of the logarithmic image depends only on the surface reflectance:

$$\mathcal{L}_\lambda(p, \lambda) \approx \frac{S_\lambda(p, \lambda)}{S(p, \lambda)} \qquad (4)$$

4. Invariance to geometry and viewpoint

4.1. Lambertian model

A very simple model that is often used by both the computer vision community and the graphics community is the Lambertian reflectance model. Lambert's law describes the behavior of a perfectly diffuse surface, where the reflected light is independent of viewpoint. For a homogeneous surface, the reflected light changes only when the angle of incidence $\theta(p)$ between the surface normal at point p and the incident illumination changes.

$$S(p, \lambda) = \cos\theta(p)\rho(p, \lambda)$$

where $\rho(p, \lambda)$ is the albedo or diffuse reflection coefficient at point p.

Since, by definition, Lambertian reflectance is independent of viewpoint, the spectral gradient is also independent of viewpoint. Furthermore, the scene geometry, including the angle of incidence, is independent of wavelength. Therefore, when we take the partial derivative with respect to wavelength, the geometry term vanishes:

$$\mathcal{L}_\lambda(p, \lambda) \approx \frac{S_\lambda(p, \lambda)}{S(p, \lambda)} = \frac{\rho_\lambda(p, \lambda)}{\rho(p, \lambda)} \qquad (5)$$

where $\rho_\lambda(p, \lambda) = \partial\rho(p, \lambda)/\partial\lambda$ is the partial derivative of the surface albedo with respect to wavelength.

One of the advantages of spectral derivatives is that since the dependence on the angle of incidence gets cancelled out, there is no need for assuming an infinitely distant light source. The incident illumination can vary from one point to another, without affecting the resulting spectral gradient.

4.2. Smooth diffuse reflectance model

In reality there are very few objects that exhibit perfectly Lambertian reflectance. The light that is reflected from a smooth diffuse object varies with respect to viewpoint. Wolff[25] introduced a new smooth diffuse reflectance model that incorporates the dependence on viewpoint:

$$S(p, \lambda) = \cos\theta(p)\rho(p, \lambda)(1 - F(\theta(p), n(p)))$$

$$\left(\left(1 - F\left(\sin^{-1}\left(\frac{\sin\varphi(p)}{n(p)}\right), \frac{1}{n(p)}\right)\right)\right)$$

where $\theta(p)$ and $\varphi(p)$ are the incidence and viewing angles respectively, $F()$ is the Fresnel reflection coefficient, and $n(p)$ is the index of refraction. The index of refraction depends theoretically on wavelength. However, in dielectrics the refractive index changes by a very small amount over the visible range[2, 3, 8]. Thus, for dielectrics n is commonly treated as a material constant under visible light.

By taking the logarithm of the surface reflectance function, we simplify the underlying model, by altering multiplicative terms into additive terms:

$$\begin{aligned}\ln S(p, \lambda) &= \ln\cos\theta(p) + \ln\rho(p, \lambda) \\ &+ \ln(1 - F(\theta(p), n(p))) \\ &+ \ln\left(1 - F\left(\sin^{-1}\left(\frac{\sin\varphi(p)}{n(p)}\right), \frac{1}{n(p)}\right)\right)\end{aligned}$$

The next step is to compute the partial derivative with respect to wavelength. Once again, all the terms except the albedo are set to zero. The dependence on the viewing and incidence angles have been cancelled out (invalidating the need for distant light sources). The spectral derivative becomes:

$$\mathcal{L}_\lambda(p, \lambda) \approx \frac{S_\lambda(p, \lambda)}{S(p, \lambda)} = \frac{\rho_\lambda(p, \lambda)}{\rho(p, \lambda)} \qquad (6)$$

5. Spectral gradient

For smooth diffuse surfaces the partial derivative with respect to wavelength of the logarithmic image $\mathcal{L}_\lambda(p, \lambda)$ is a function of only the surface albedo. Consider now a collection of spectral derivatives of a logarithmic image at various spectral locations λ_k, $k = 1, 2, 3, ..., M$. The resulting *spectral gradient* is an M-dimensional vector $(\mathcal{L}_{\lambda_1}, \mathcal{L}_{\lambda_2}, ..., \mathcal{L}_{\lambda_M})$ which is invariant to illumination, surface geometry and viewpoint. All it encodes is information at discrete spectral locations about how fast the surface albedo changes as the spectrum changes. It is a profile of the rate of change of albedo with respect to wavelength over a range of wavelengths.

6. Experiments

In order to compute the spectral derivatives we took images of each scene under three different narrow-band filters: a Corion S10-570-F, a Corion S10-600-F and a Corion S10-630-F. Each of these filters has a bandwidth of approximately 10nm and a transmittance of about 50%. The central wavelengths are at 570nm, 600nm and 630nm respectively. These filters avoid sampling the spectrum at wavelengths where the incident light may be discontinuous (see section 3.) The images were captured with a Sony XC-77 camera using a 25mm lens (fig. 2.)

Figure 2. Camera and filter setup.

The only source of illumination was a single tungsten light bulb mounted in a reflected scoop. For each scene we used four different illumination setups, generated by the combination of two distinct light bulbs, a 100W bulb and a 200W bulb and two different light positions. One illumination position was to the left of the camera and at about the same height as the camera. Its direction vector formed approximately a 20° angle with the optic axis. The other light-bulb position was to the right of the camera and about 25cm above it. Its direction vector formed roughly a 55° angle with the optic axis. Both locations were 55cm away from the scene.

The imaged objects were positioned 75cm from the camera/filter setup. We tried four different types of materials: foam, paper, ceramic and plastic. Foam and paper came in a variety of colors. In foam we had green, magenta, orange, pink, red, white and yellow samples. Our pieces of paper came in brown, green, orange, pink, red white and yellow. We used two ceramic objects, a pink plate and a white mug, and one white plastic polyhedron.

Figure 3. A sample of the colors, materials and shapes used in the experiments.

Fig. 3 shows in the top left the different colors of foam and in the top right the different colors of paper used in the experiments. In the bottom of fig. 3 are a ceramic pink plate, a white ceramic mug and a white plastic container that were also used in our experiments.

Figure 4. Images used in the experiments.

Fig. 4 shows in the top row and from left to right small samples of green foam, yellow foam and red paper. On the bottom row are images of the ceramic and plastic objects. These images were taken using the Corion S10-600-F filter.

6.1. Computing the spectral gradient

Once a filtered image was captured, its logarithmic image was generated. In a logarithmic image the value stored at each pixel was the natural logarithm of the original image intensity. For example, $\mathcal{L}_{570} = \ln(I_{570})$, where I_{570} was the image of a scene taken with the S10-570-F filter and $\mathcal{L}_{570}$ was its logarithmic image.

Figure 5. Sample logarithmic images.

As fig. 5 shows, the logarithmic images preserved the overall appearance of the original image. However, the intensity values were scaled down significantly. From a maximum of 255 in an 8-bit image we went down to a maximum of 5.54. The images shown in fig. 5 were linearly scaled for display purposes.

The last step was the computation of the spectral derivatives of the logarithmic images. Differentiation was approximated via finite-differencing. Thus, $\mathcal{L}_\lambda$ was computed over the wavelength interval $\delta\lambda = 30nm$ by subtracting two logarithmic images taken under two different color filters which were 30nm apart:

$$\mathcal{L}_{\lambda_1} = \mathcal{L}_{600} - \mathcal{L}_{570} \qquad \mathcal{L}_{\lambda_2} = \mathcal{L}_{630} - \mathcal{L}_{600} \qquad (7)$$

Figure 6. Sample derivative images.

Typically, the resulting derivative images have a median value around 0.2 with minimal variation on smooth materials like glossy ceramic and plastic. The best way to depict this minimal variation was to show the reverse video of the derivative image. Again, this was done for display purposes only. Fig. 6 shows the derivative images of a piece of green foam and the ceramic and plastic objects.

For each scene taken under the three narrow-band color filters we had two derivative images, $\mathcal{L}_{\lambda_1}$ and $\mathcal{L}_{\lambda_2}$. The spectral gradient at a pixel was the vector $(\mathcal{L}_{\lambda_1}, \mathcal{L}_{\lambda_2})$. This vector was expected to remain constant for materials with the same reflectance function, independent of variations in viewing conditions. At the same time, it should differ significantly for materials that exhibit distinct surface reflectance functions.

6.2. Comparing spectral gradients

The desired goal was to determine whether two regions (in the same or different scenes) are depicting objects with the similar or distinct reflectance functions. We performed a pixel by pixel comparison. Let p and p' be two pixels belonging to these two regions and let $(\mathcal{L}_{\lambda_1}, \mathcal{L}_{\lambda_2})$ and $(\mathcal{L}_{\lambda_1}', \mathcal{L}_{\lambda_2}')$ be their respective spectral gradients. The metric we used was the absolute difference vector, after it was normalized for variations in intensity level:

$$(d_1, d_2) = (|\mathcal{L}_{\lambda_1} - \mathcal{L}_{\lambda_1}'|, |\mathcal{L}_{\lambda_2} - \mathcal{L}_{\lambda_2}'|)/I_{avg} \qquad (8)$$

where $I_{avg} = (i_{570} + i_{600} + i_{630} + i'_{570} + i'_{600} + i'_{630})/6$ was the average value of the intensities registered in these two pixels in the original filtered images.

The pixel metric of equation (8) was the basis for comparing regions. The (d_1, d_2) metric was computed for all the corresponding pixels in the two regions, i.e. pixels which had the same coordinates (for instance, both in position x_0, y_0) in the local coordinate system of each region. The median of all the pixel measurements became the region distance metric:

$$(D_1, D_2) = (median \forall d_1, median \forall d_2) \qquad (9)$$

Typically, the values of D_1 and D_2 were very small, mainly because the spectral gradients themselves were small. Hence, subtraction and normalization of such derivative values resulted in values for D_1 and D_2 that ranged in our experiments from 0.001 to 3.898.

6.2.1. Same material and color. According to our theory, materials with the same reflectance function should generate the same spectral gradient resulting in a (D_1, D_2) tuple that is almost equal zero. Indeed, we observed that when we were comparing the same material and the same color, independent of illumination conditions and surface orientation, the average of D_1 and D_2 was consistently small. More precisely, out of 28 such comparisons, 27 times both $D_1 < 0.2$ and $D_2 < 0.2$. There was a single case, when we compared two regions of orange foam illuminated under two different light intensities (same light position), where $D_1 = 0.2564$ and $D_2 = 0.0057$, but their average was still very small.

We compared different regions of the ceramic mug, with distinct viewing and incidence angles. The resulting spectral gradients differed by less than 0.1. A similar behavior was observed around the smooth corners of the plastic container. The specular region on the white mug did not affect the stability of spectral gradients. For example, comparing the shiny region in the center of the mug with a region in the right side of the mug generated the following tuple $(D_1, D_2) = (0.0288, 0.0402)$. In general, same color and same material comparisons generated very stable spectral gradients. Sample comparisons can be found in Table 1.

Table 1: Same material and color

Material	(D_1, D_2)
magenta foam	(0.0126, 0.0333)
yellow foam	(0.0010, 0.0036)
red paper	(0.1472, 0.0209)
green paper	(0.0788, 0.0519)
white mug	(0.0262, 0.0558)

6.2.2. Same material but different colors. Surfaces made out of different colors of the same material follow the same reflectance model, but have distinct spectral responses. Thus, their spectral gradients should be distinguishable, at least over some part of the visible spectrum.

We performed 35 comparisons between distinct colors of the same material under similar or different illumination conditions. The spectral gradients were distinguishable 34 out of the 35 times. The average of both D_1 and D_2 was distinctly larger in these cases.

The two times that the spectral gradients were very similar were when we compared a piece of pink foam with a piece of magenta foam under 200W illumination. These two materials have very similar reflectance spectra that vary the most around 550nm (see fig. 7), a wavelength that we are not sampling at the current set-up.

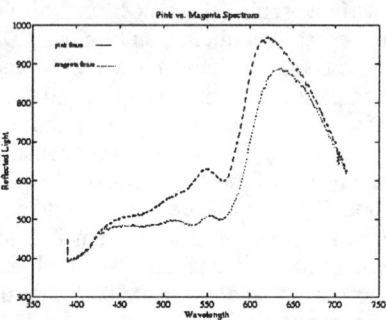

Figure 7. The spectrum of pink foam versus magenta foam.

Examples of (D_1, D_2) for different colors of the same material under possibly varying illumination are shown in Table 2.

Table 2: Same material but different colors

Color 1	Color 2	(D_1, D_2)
magenta foam	red foam	(0.7976, 1.0465)
green foam	orange foam	(0.6755, 0.2663)
red paper	yellow paper	(0.1703, 1.1402)
green paper	orange paper	(0.3806, 1.075)
white ceramic	pink ceramic	(0.2759, 0.5555)

6.2.3. Different materials but same color. Spectral gradients are a measurement of the surface reflectance function, independent of viewing conditions. As such, if two distinct materials have similar reflectance, the respective spectral gradients would be similar too. Out of the four materials we tested, the foam and the paper, had very similar reflectance behavior. The ceramic and the plastic samples were also very similar in terms of reflectance behavior. Our paper was a bit smoother than foam resulting in a reflectance function that was close to that of the ceramic reflectance. There was also a hue discrepancy between the red paper and the red foam, as well as between the green paper and the green foam.

Overall, when the materials exhibited clearly distinct reflectance functions, the average of both D_1 and D_2 was large. Look for example at pink ceramic versus pink foam

in Table 3. Differentiating between foam and paper of very similar color was very difficult. Both materials exhibit an approximately Lambertian reflectance. It was interesting to note that small color variations, like different shades of dark green, were distinguishable across different materials of the same reflectance behavior.

Table 3: Different materials but same color

Color 1	Color 2	(D_1, D_2)
green foam	green paper	(0.2365, 0.6161)
orange foam	orange paper	(0.0120, 0.0765)
pink foam	pink paper	(0.0767, 0.2968)
pink ceramic	pink paper	(0.1359, 0.1243)
pink ceramic	pink foam	(0.0331, 0.4527)

6.3. Error analysis

Our experimentations showed that spectral gradients achieved a 100% correct identification when it was comparing the same material, independent of the variations in illumination conditions. The success of spectral gradients in discriminating between different colors of the same material was good, about 97%, but it clearly depended on the wavelengths at which we were sampling the partial derivatives. Higher dimensional spectral gradients should provide better discriminatory power. Finally, spectral gradients can discriminate between different materials of the same color, only if their surface reflectance behavior differs.

We have tried a variety of filters with different bandwidths, including the more traditional red, green and blue filters. Since we were approximating a sampling function (Dirac delta function), the narrower filters gave more consistent results. We also experimented with various $\delta\lambda$ over which to perform the finite differencing approximation to partial derivatives. Again, as expected, the smaller $\delta\lambda$ performed better, as long as the two filters did not have overlapping bandwidths.

7. Conclusions and future work

We developed a surface reflectance measurement that is invariant to changes in illumination and scene geometry. We made no assumptions about the nature of incident light, other than that its spectrum does not change with its position. We showed that spectral gradients can be used on a pixel basis and do not depend on neighboring regions. The effectiveness of spectral gradients as a surface reflectance descriptor was demonstrated on various empirical data.

The invariant properties of spectral gradients together with their ease of implementation and the minimalism of assumptions, make this methodology a particularly appealing tool in many diverse areas of computer vision. They can be used in material classification, grey-scale color constancy, or in tracking different regions under variable illumination.

We believe that spectral gradients are a powerful tool that should be further investigated. This research is in its initial stages. We started out with only three filters. Our next step is to use additional narrow-band filters that span a bigger range of the visible spectrum. We would also like to test this methodology using tunable filters, adding thus more flexibility and portability to our system.

Further experimentation under different types and colors of light sources is under way. Simultaneous use of multiple lights is another issue that is being examined. It is also very important to study more extensively the behavior of spectral gradients in areas with specular highlights. Finally, we would like to study the behavior of spectral gradient on rough surfaces.

References

[1] Barnard, K., Finlayson, G. and Funt, B. "Color Constancy for Scenes with Varying Illumination," *Computer Vision and Image Understanding*, Vol. 65, No. 2, February 1997, pp. 311-321.

[2] Bass, Michael, ed., *Handbook of Optics: Fundamentals, Techniques and Design*, 2nd ed., Vol. I, McGraw-Hill, 1995.

[3] Born, Max and Wolf, Emil, *Principles of Optics: Electromagnetic Theory of Propagation, Interference and Diffraction of Light*, 5th ed., Pergamon Press, 1975

[4] Finlayson, G. D., "Color in Perspective," *IEEE Transactions on Pattern Analysis and Machine Intelligence*, Vol. 18, No. 10, October 1996, pp. 1034-1038.

[5] Finlayson, G. D., Drew, M. S. and Funt, B. V., "Color Constancy: Generalized Diagonal Transforms Suffice," *Journal of the Optical Society of America A*, Vol. 11, 1994, pp. 3011-3019.

[6] Forsyth, D., "A Novel Algorithm for Color Constancy," *International Journal of Computer Vision*, Vol. 5, No.1, 1990, pp. 5-36.

[7] Funt, B.V., and Finlayson, G. D, "Color Constant Color Indexing," *IEEE Transactions on Pattern Analysis and Machine Intelligence*, Vol. 17, 1995, pp. 522-529.

[8] Garbuny, Max, *Optical Physics*, Academic Press, 1965.

[9] Hager, G. D. and Belhumeur, P. N., "Real-Time Tracking Of Image Regions With Changes In Geometry And Illumination," *Proceedings IEEE Conference on Computer Vision and Pattern Recognition*, 1996, pp. 403-410.

[10] Healey, G. and Slater, D. "Global Color Constancy: Recognition of Objects by Use of Illumination-Invariant Properties of Color Distribution," *Journal of the Optical Society of America A*, Vol. 11, No. 11, November 1994, pp. 3003-3010.

[11] Healey, G. and Wang, L. "Illumination-Invariant Recognition of Texture in Color Images," *Journal of the Optical Society of America A*, Vol. 12, No. 9, September 1995, pp. 1877-1883.

[12] Ho, J., Funt, B. V. and Drew, M. S., "Separating A Color Signal Into Illumination And Surface Reflectance Components: Theory And Applications," *IEEE Transactions on Pattern Analysis and Machine Intelligence*, Vol. 12, No. 10, October 1990, pp. 966-977.

[13] Horn, B. K. P., "Understanding Image Intensities," *Artificial Intelligence*, Vol. 8, No. 2, 1977, pp. 1-31.

[14] Horn, B. K. P. and Brooks, M. J., *Shape from Shading*, MIT Press, 1989.

[15] Jacobs, D. W., Belheumer, P. N. and Basri, R. "Comparing Images Under Variable Illumination," *Proceedings IEEE Conference on Computer Vision and Pattern Recognition*, 1998, pp. 610-617.

[16] Lin, S. and Lee, S. W., "Using Chromaticity Distributions and Eigenspaces for Pose-, Illumination-, and Specularity Invariant 3D Object Recognition" *Proceedings IEEE Conference on Computer Vision and Pattern Recognition*, 1997, pp. 426-431.

[17] Maloney, L. T. and Wandell, B. A. "A Computational Model of Color Constancy," *Journal of the Optical Society of America A*, Vol. 3. No. 1, 1986, pp. 29-33.

[18] Nayar, S. K. and Bolle, R. "Reflectance Based Object Recognition," *International Journal of Computer Vision*, Vol. 17, No. 3, March 1996, pp. 219-240.

[19] Oren, M. and Nayar, S. K., "Generalization of the Lambertian Model," *Proceedings Image Understanding Workshop 1993*, Morgan Kaufmann Publishers, 1993, pp. 1037-1048.

[20] Slater, D. and Healey, G., "Using A Spectral Reflectance Model For The Illumination-Invariant Recognition Of Local Image Structure," *Proceedings IEEE Conference on Computer Vision and Pattern Recognition*, 1996, pp. 770-775.

[21] Slater, D. and Healey, G., "Object Recognition Using Invariant Profiles," *Proceedings IEEE Conference on Computer Vision and Pattern Recognition*, 1997, pp. 827-832.

[22] Slater, D. and Healey, G. "The Illumination-Invariant Recognition of 3D objects Using Local Color Invariants," *IEEE Transactions on Pattern Analysis and Machine Intelligence*, Vol. 18, No. 2, February 1996, pp. 206-210.

[23] Slater, D. and Healey, G., "What Is the Spectral Dimensionality of Illumination Functions in Outdoor Scenes?," *Proceedings IEEE Conference on Computer Vision and Pattern Recognition*, 1998, pp. 105-110.

[24] Swain, M. J. and Ballard, D. H. "Color Indexing," *International Journal of Computer Vision*, Vol. 7, No.1, 1991, pp. 11-32.

[25] Wolff, L. B. "Diffuse-Reflectance Model for Smooth Dielectric Surfaces," *Journal of the Optical Society of America A*, Vol. 11, No. 11, November 1994, pp. 2956-2968.

Coupled Lighting Direction and Shape Estimation from Single Images

Dimitrios Samaras and Dimitris Metaxas
Vision, Analysis and Simulation Technologies Laboratory
Department of Computer & Information Science
University of Pennsylvania
Philadelphia PA 19104-6389

Abstract

This paper presents a new method for the simultaneous estimation of lighting direction and shape from shading. The method estimates the shape and the lighting direction using a two step iterative process. We assume an initial (possibly incorrect) estimate of the lighting position. A stiff deformable model is then fitted to the image, assuming this lighting position. Next, a least-squares estimate of the lighting position is derived from the model using the Levenberg-Marquart method. The two steps — model fitting and lighting-position estimation — are iterated. Once the light direction has converged to a stable solution the deformable model stiffness is lowered and the model fits accurately given the lighting model. In addition, we show how the method can be used with either orthographic or perspective projection assumptions. In a variety of experiments on real and synthetic data, the method is robust to errors both to the initial light position and shape estimates.

1 Introduction

We present a new method for the simultaneous estimation of lighting direction and shape from shading. The difficulty of the problem stems from the nonlinear relationship between the lighting direction and the surface properties, regardless of the lighting model used. Most of the previous work in this area has focused on either shape from shading or on light direction estimation. There have been attempts to address both problems, but they are limited to either assuming a Lambertian lighting model or making local surface assumptions. In addition, they do not provide a tight coupling between shape from shading and the lighting direction estimation.

The method we present in this paper couples the shape from shading and the lighting direction estimation problems using a deformable model framework. Our approach requires the use of a lighting model that is differentiable with respect to both the surface parameters and the lighting direction. Hence, a Lambertian or a more sophisticated lighting model can be used. We use deformable models as shape primitives due to their wide coverage of shapes. A deformable grid is used, based on both global and local parameters.

The method estimates the shape and the lighting direction using a coupled two step iterative process. We first assume an initial (possibly incorrect) estimate of the lighting position. A stiff deformable model is then fitted to the image [19], assuming this lighting position. In the beginning of the fit, only gross-scale shape features will emerge. These features will be roughly correct under most light source configurations, so they will be an improved estimate for the correct light source as well. Next, a least-squares estimate of the lighting position is derived from the model using the Levenberg-Marquart method. The two steps — model fitting and lighting-position estimation — are iterated. Once the light direction has converged to a stable solution the deformable model stiffness is lowered and the model fits accurately given the lighting model.

We aim to solve two tightly coupled problems: a) to improve the fit of the model, and b) to gain a more accurate estimate of the light position. The quality of a model's fit to shading data strongly depends on knowledge of the lighting conditions. Fitting to an incorrect light will either cause the fitting process to not converge or will introduce additional error in the form of excessive wrinkling. Fig. 1 shows two fitted models. In (b), the model is fitted with fixed light position, as estimated by the method in [22]. While the method of [22] gives an approximate estimate of the light position, it is clearly not sufficient for accurate model fitting. In (c), the model is fitted using the method described in this paper; re-estimation of the light position gives a clear improvement, and the error of fit reduces by 11.2 percent. We performed multiple experiments of the method on two synthetic data sets, illuminated under three different lighting conditions. In all cases the lighting direction converged to within 10 degrees of the true direction; in five out of six cases the error was 5.6 degrees or less. In the two cases where the light direction estimate in [22] was rather poor, our method showed some striking improvements. These experiments showed improvements in the light direction estimation error from 42 degrees to 2.2 degrees and 83 degrees to 5.6 degrees. A number of experiments exploring the importance of the initial estimate of the light position demonstrated that the convergence of the light estimation method is almost independent from it. Convergence was within 5 degrees of the true light vector in all of the examples where the initial light estimate was within 30 degrees of the true position and for most of the examples where the light vector was initialized 45 to 90 degrees off. In an example performed on a real image of a face, the final estimate of the light was not affected by such violations of the lighting model as specularities, or varying albedo. Finally, we show how the method can be used with either orthographic or perspective projection assumptions.

The paper is organized as follows. Section 2 describes previous work, and the integration of SFS in deformable models. Section 3 describes the simultaneous estimation of light position and model shape. Section 4 describes two generalizations of the model: the incorporation of perspective projection, and the use of singular points information. Section 5 gives results and section 6 gives the conclusions.

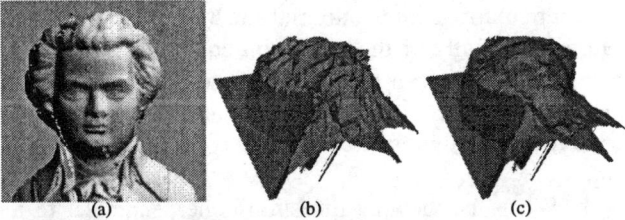

Figure 1: The effects of inaccurate light source position on shape estimation are evident in (b). (a) is the original image; (b) is the fitted model without light position re-estimation; (c) is the fitted model with the light position re-estimation method described in this paper.

2 Background
2.1 Previous work

This work is based on an approach that integrates shape from shading (SFS) within the deformable models framework. Most of the earlier work on SFS has been compiled in [7]; the first comprehensive comparative study of a number of SFS algorithms is [21]. Most of the methods use a regularization approach combined with some additional constraints [3, 8, 11, 9, 22, 12]. [9, 4] combine stereo and shading; [4] handles perspective projection in their stereo and shading mesh. Other approaches are described in [6, 16, 10, 20].

A useful discussion of the ambiguities involved in light source estimation can be found in [2]. A number of researchers have proposed methods for the estimation of the light source direction. [3] proposes an iterative method that updates both the shape and the illuminant direction at every iteration. To avoid local minima a good initial state is often necessary, and furthermore, the requirement for a light source vector of unit length is not enforced. [10] used a Gaussian sphere model for the surface normal distribution and local spherical patches, but did not take shadowing effects into account. [22] presents the most sophisticated of the image based methods, considering shadowing effects and using a uniform distribution of the tilt and slant angles of surface normals (instead of a Gaussian sphere). They

still assume local spherical patches and their algorithm suffers on surfaces that deviate significantly from this assumption. [9] derives accurate light source information from stereo data.

In our approach we use the method of [22] to obtain an initial estimate which we then refine using our two step iterative process within our deformable model framework. Our process makes no assumptions about the surface shape, instead it uses the already recovered shape information.

2.2 Deformable Models

In this section we review briefly the general formulation of deformable models [14, 15].

Geometrically, the models used in this paper are parameterized surfaces in space whose intrinsic parameters are $\mathbf{u} = (u, v)$, defined on a domain Ω. The positions $\mathbf{x}(\mathbf{u}, t)$ of points on the model relative to an inertial frame of reference Φ in space are given by $\mathbf{x} = \mathbf{c} + \mathbf{R}\mathbf{p}$, where $\mathbf{c}(t)$ is the origin of the model frame, ϕ, and $\mathbf{R}(t)$ is the rotation matrix expressing the orientation of ϕ. $\mathbf{p}(\mathbf{u}, t)$ denotes the positions of points on the model relative to the model frame. We introduce global and local deformations, by further expressing $\mathbf{p}$ as the sum of a reference shape $\mathbf{s}(\mathbf{u}, t)$ and a displacement function $\mathbf{d}(\mathbf{u}, t)$, i.e., $\mathbf{p} = \mathbf{s} + \mathbf{d}$.

For the applications in this paper, we define $\mathbf{s}$ as a geometric primitive parameterized in uv space (see [14, 15] for details and formulas). Local displacements $\mathbf{d}$ are computed based on the use of triangular finite elements [14, 15], which provide a tessellation of the deformable model's surface. Associated with every finite element node i is a nodal vector variable $\mathbf{q}_{d,i}$. We collect all the nodal variables into a vector of local degrees of freedom $\mathbf{q}_d = (\ldots, \mathbf{q}_{d,i}^\top, \ldots)^\top$, and we compute the local displacement $\mathbf{d}$ based on finite element theory as $\mathbf{d} = \mathbf{S}\mathbf{q}_d$. $\mathbf{S}$ is the shape matrix whose entries are the finite element shape functions.

$$\mathbf{q} = (\mathbf{q}_c^\top, \mathbf{q}_\theta^\top, \mathbf{q}_s^\top, \mathbf{q}_d^\top)^\top \qquad (1)$$

are the model parameters with $\mathbf{q}_c = \mathbf{c}$ and $\mathbf{q}_\theta$ is the model's rotational degrees of freedom expressed as a quaternion.

Our goal when fitting the model to visual data is to recover the vector $\mathbf{q}$ which expresses the model's degrees of freedom. Based on Lagrangian dynamics we make our model dynamic in $\mathbf{q}$, and we arrive at the motion equations:

$$\dot{\mathbf{q}} + \mathbf{K}\mathbf{q} = \mathbf{f}_q, \qquad (2)$$

where $\mathbf{K}$ is the stiffness matrix, (see [15] for definitions). $\mathbf{f}_q$ are the generalized external forces computed from the 3D forces which in our application will be computed from edge information.

2.3 Integration of Illumination Constraints in Deformable Models

We now briefly summarize the method for integration of lighting constraints in deformable models, as presented in [19], where it was applied to two lighting models; the simple Lambertian model, also briefly described below, and the more accurate and complex model proposed in [17].

In the Lambertian model, if we assume a point light source at infinity, the scene radiance is expressed as

$$I_L = B\frac{\rho}{\pi}\cos\theta = B\rho'\,\hat{\mathbf{s}}\cdot\hat{\mathbf{n}}, \qquad (3)$$

where θ is the angle between the surface unit normal vector, $\hat{\mathbf{n}} = \mathbf{n}/\|\mathbf{n}\|$, and the unit light source direction vector $\hat{\mathbf{s}}$. B is the strength of the light source and ρ the constant albedo of the surface. From (3) we get the brightness constraint: $C = \hat{\mathbf{s}}\cdot\mathbf{n} - I'_L\|\mathbf{n}\| = 0$, where $I'_L = I_L/(B\rho')$, and the values of I'_L range between 0 and 1. We want to recover the shape parameters based on the intensity information at n points and therefore we will have an n-component constraint vector $\mathbf{C}$.

We use Lagrange multipliers to incorporate the constraint vector $\mathbf{C}$ in a deformable model framework, as a *nonlinear holonomic constraint* $\mathbf{C}(\mathbf{q}, t) = 0$. (2) then becomes:

$$\dot{\mathbf{q}} = \mathbf{f} - \mathbf{K}_d\mathbf{q} - \mathbf{C}_{\mathbf{q}}^\top\boldsymbol{\lambda}, \qquad (4)$$

where $\boldsymbol{\lambda} = [\lambda_1, \lambda_2, \ldots, \lambda_n]^\top$ are the Lagrange multipliers, $\mathbf{f}$ are generalized edge based forces and $\mathbf{C}_{\mathbf{q}}$ is the Jacobian matrix of the constraints $\mathbf{C}$ w.r.t. the shape parameters. We can consider $-\mathbf{C}_{\mathbf{q}}^\top\boldsymbol{\lambda}$ to be the vector of generalized forces on the model parameters due to the lighting constraint.

To obtain the additional necessary equations we differentiate the constraint equation w.r.t. time $\dot{\mathbf{C}}(\mathbf{q}, t) = 0$ yielding $\mathbf{C}_{\mathbf{q}}\dot{\mathbf{q}} + \mathbf{C}_t = 0$. In our application $\mathbf{C}$ is not directly dependent on time, therefore $\mathbf{C}_t = 0$. Since we will be fitting a deformable model to the data, the constraints will be far from being satisfied initially, so we will use Baumgarte's [1] stabilization method [14], to replace $\dot{\mathbf{C}}(\mathbf{q}, t) = 0$ with the following constraint equation

$$\dot{\mathbf{C}} + \alpha\mathbf{C} = 0, \qquad (5)$$

where α is a stabilization factor. Combining (4), (5) we can solve for the generalized constraint forces $-\mathbf{C}_{\mathbf{q}}^\top\boldsymbol{\lambda}$ and obtain

$$\mathbf{C}_{\mathbf{q}}^\top\boldsymbol{\lambda} = \mathbf{C}_{\mathbf{q}}^+(\alpha\mathbf{C} + \mathbf{C}_{\mathbf{q}}(\mathbf{f} - \mathbf{K}_d\mathbf{q})). \qquad (6)$$

The matrix $\mathbf{C}_{\mathbf{q}}^+$ is the pseudo-inverse of the matrix $\mathbf{C}_{\mathbf{q}}$, and if we define the vector of all non-constraint (generalized) forces, as $\mathbf{b} = \mathbf{f} - \mathbf{K}_d\mathbf{q}$, (4) becomes

$$\dot{\mathbf{q}} = \mathbf{b} - \mathbf{C}_{\mathbf{q}}^+(\alpha\mathbf{C} + \mathbf{C}_{\mathbf{q}}\mathbf{b}) = -\mathbf{C}_{\mathbf{q}}^+\alpha\mathbf{C} + (\mathbf{I} - \mathbf{C}_{\mathbf{q}}^+\mathbf{C}_{\mathbf{q}})\mathbf{b}. \qquad (7)$$

The first term $-\mathbf{C}_{\mathbf{q}}^+\alpha\mathbf{C}$ in (7) is a model-based least-squares solution to the Baumgarte lighting constraint equations, while the second term $(\mathbf{I} - \mathbf{C}_{\mathbf{q}}^+\mathbf{C}_{\mathbf{q}})\mathbf{b}$ projects the forces $\mathbf{b}$ (in this case due to the smoothness of the model) to the space of the constraint forces, thus canceling the part that violates the lighting constraint.

3 Coupling Light and SFS Estimation

In this section we will describe our method that allows the simultaneous estimation of the light source direction and the object shape from shading information. This is done by iteratively improving the estimates of the shape and of the light vector.

3.1 Overview

In monocular orthographic images of Lambertian surfaces, there is inherent ambiguity in the configuration of light and surface shape for the generation of images; in the most general case there is an infinite number of combinations of surface shape and albedo on one hand and light position and intensity on the other [2]. However, considering only surfaces of constant and known albedo, it has been shown that for every image point there are two possible configurations for the normal and the light source [3, 2]. More specifically, if the constraint equations $\mathbf{C}$ are satisfied by shape A with normals $\hat{\mathbf{n}}_A$ under light source $\hat{\mathbf{s}}_A$, then they are also satisfied by a dual shape B with normals $\hat{\mathbf{n}}_B$ under light source $\hat{\mathbf{s}}_B$ with $\hat{\mathbf{n}}_B = 2\hat{\mathbf{v}}(\hat{\mathbf{n}}_A\hat{\mathbf{v}}) - \hat{\mathbf{n}}_A$ and $\hat{\mathbf{s}}_B = 2\hat{\mathbf{v}}(\hat{\mathbf{s}}_A\hat{\mathbf{v}}) - \hat{\mathbf{s}}_A$, where $\hat{\mathbf{v}}$ is the viewer direction. When the viewing direction is perpendicular to the image plane, this relation preserves unit lengths. This is the standard *in-out* ambiguity which apart from the case of the source being collinear with the viewer, can be easily resolved by taking shadow information into account. Our goal is to estimate either the pair $(\hat{\mathbf{n}}_A, \hat{\mathbf{s}}_A)$ or the pair $(\hat{\mathbf{n}}_B, \hat{\mathbf{s}}_B)$.

Our method is based on the following observation: The integrability constraint on the shape of the model surface, (i.e., the requirement for a physically plausible shape), which is implicitly imposed by our deformable model and the constant albedo assumption, make the image plausible under only one light vector (and its dual)[2]. Therefore, any fitting process, unless we use the correct light vector (or its dual), will not satisfy the constraint by modifying only the surface normals. This is due to the two sources of error: the incorrect normals and the incorrect light position.

In the beginning of the fitting process, while the model surface is still smooth and the model is stiff, only gross-scale shape features will emerge. These features (or their duals) will be roughly correct under most light source configurations (or their duals), so they will result into an improved estimate for the correct light source. That increases our hope that if we re-estimate the light at this point, we will move closer to the true light vector. We can then fit the model to the new light source, re-estimate the light position and iterate this process until convergence.

We therefore introduce the following process which consists of an initial step and an iterative two step procedure.

3.2 Initial light estimate

In the initial step we fit the model under a crude estimate of the light source which we obtain using the image based method described in [22]. This method estimates the light source based on image statistics, under certain assumptions on the probability distribution of the surface normals. These assumptions are general and do not take into account any already existing knowledge about the model shape. Therefore we cannot use it to take advantage of any improvement in the model shape estimates. However it is useful in the initial step given the absence of any shape information; in most of the images we tested it on, it estimated a light direction vector forming an angle of less than $\pi/4$ from the correct solution. As will be seen in the experiments section this is good enough for our algorithm. Since we want the light source vector to be of unit length, we only need to estimate the slant γ (the angle between the illuminant and the positive z axis) and the tilt τ (the angle between the illuminant and the $x-y$ plane). Therefore $\hat{s} = (\cos\tau\sin\gamma, \sin\tau\sin\gamma, \cos\gamma)$.

For the estimation of τ [22] uses the formulas

$$\tau = \arctan\left(\frac{E_{x,y}\left\{\frac{\tilde{y}_L}{\sqrt{\tilde{x}_L^2+\tilde{y}_L^2}}\right\}}{E_{x,y}\left\{\frac{\tilde{x}_L}{\sqrt{\tilde{x}_L^2+\tilde{y}_L^2}}\right\}}\right), \qquad (8)$$

where $E\{\}$ are ensemble averages over the local estimates $\tilde{x}_L, \tilde{y}_L$ are the x and y components of the local estimate of τ, which can be computed by:

$$\begin{bmatrix} \tilde{x}_L \\ \tilde{y}_L \end{bmatrix} = \mathbf{B}^+ \begin{bmatrix} \delta I_1 \\ \vdots \\ \delta I_N \end{bmatrix}, \text{ with } \mathbf{B} = \begin{bmatrix} \delta x_1 & \delta y_1 \\ \vdots & \vdots \\ \delta x_N & \delta y_N \end{bmatrix},$$
$$(9)$$

where $\mathbf{B}^+$ the pseudoinverse of $\mathbf{B}$. N is the number of local image derivatives δI.

The slant γ can be determined numerically from the monotonically decreasing function

$$f_3(\gamma) = \frac{E_{x,y}\{I\}}{E_{x,y}\{I^2\}} \qquad (10)$$

3.3   Two Step Iteration

In the first iteration of the iterative process we fit the model to the image data using the light source direction estimated in the above initial step. Using the method described in [19], with high stiffness coefficients ($w_0 = w_1 = 0.05$ in our experiments) we compute an initial fit of the shape. The model parameters are updated using (7).

Based on the fitted shape, we can now re-estimate the light direction. This time we want to estimate the source direction, taking into account the surface shape. We want the closest estimate to the source direction which, given the current shape would produce an image as close as possible to the original. We define "closeness" in a least squares sense, in the absence of any general knowledge of which

parts of the image are more conforming to the illumination model than others. However one could envision more powerful error metrics for applications where more information is available. We cannot use linear least squares to estimate the three components of the light source independently, because the resulting vector would not be of unit length. For this reason we need the non-linear (τ, γ) parameterization. We use the Levenberg-Marquart method [13, 18], a standard non-linear least-squares estimation technique, to update the values of τ and γ. Levenberg-Marquart smoothly combines an inverse-Hessian method and a steepest descent method, with the objective of minimizing all the jacobians of the error w.r.t. the model's parameters. The method approximates its solution rapidly, but then can wander around the true minimum. So we stop iterating when the error decreases minimally (less than 10^{-3}). In our experiments this typically happens within a few iterations.

Once we have re-estimated the model's parameters, we repeat the model fitting stage under the new light source. We continue iterating between these two steps until the light stabilizes. At that point we decrease (in decrements of 10 percent) the model's stiffness parameters, allowing it to minimize the lighting constraint error.

3.4   Another formulation

Another formulation of the light and state estimation problem is to include the light parameters in the deformable model framework. Although the light source is physically independent from changes in the deformable model's shape parameters, (they do not appear in the formalism of equations (1) and (2)) they can still be estimated using the parameter update rule of (4) through the constraint Jacobian matrix $\mathbf{C_q}$. We can include the illuminant direction parameters in the parameter vector $\mathbf{q}$ to obtain $\mathbf{q}\prime = (\mathbf{q}^\top, \tau, \gamma)^\top = (\mathbf{q}_c^\top, \mathbf{q}_\theta^\top, \mathbf{q}_s^\top, \mathbf{q}_d^\top, \tau, \gamma)^\top$ and proceed in the same manner as in section (2.3). Experiments show that the above two methods are equivalent in terms of results. However, the first approach is faster, since the light parameters are not updated at every step. An added advantage of the first approach is that this procedure can be used with any iterative shape estimation method.

4   Further Generalizations of the Approach

In this section we present two further generalizations of the approach to account for perspective projection and incorporate singular point information.

4.1   Perspective Projection

A common assumption in shape estimation from shading is that of orthographic projection. Perspective projection can be easily handled in the deformable model formulation since the reconstruction takes place in 3D space and so the mathematical treatment does not change. There are two differences which affect the reconstruction process.

(a) Original image   (b) Fitted model

Figure 2: A model fitted under perspective projection, with a low-resolution model

An image point $\mathbf{P} = (X, Y, -f)$, where f is the focal length of the projection will correspond to model point $\mathbf{p} = (x, y, z) = (-z * X/f, -z * Y/f, z)$. That means that as z changes the model point that corresponds to $\mathbf{P}$ changes too. Points that were visible might become occluded, and visibility checking would be required after every iteration. Furthermore, the surface cannot be canonically sampled in u, v anymore and the local deformation updates have to be computed simultaneously and not per element. That increases substantially the size of the pseudoinverse $\mathbf{C_q^+}$ that needs to be computed with SVD.

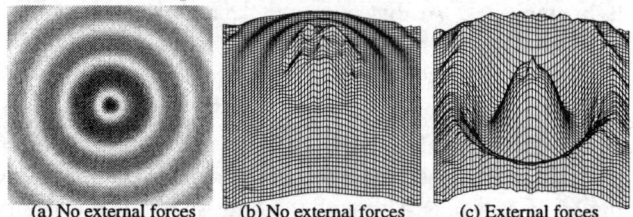

(a) No external forces   (b) No external forces   (c) External forces

Figure 3: In the case of the sombrero lit from the top, there is convex/concave ambiguity. Knowledge about how to resolve the ambiguity, (eg. singular points) can be applied to the model in the form of external forces. Here a few points in the inner lower circle were pulled down.

4.2 Singular Points Information

It has been shown [16], that the known ambiguities in shape from shading estimation can be resolved with the knowledge of singular points in the image. Here we show how we can incorporate such biases in the deformable model formulation. In the sombrero image viewed head-on in figure 3, there is a convex-concave ambiguity. Our deformable model fits the convex solution only. If we know that we want the inner lower circle to be lowered down, we can simply apply external forces $\mathbf{f}_e$ in (4) on a few of the points on that circle (in the example presented here just five). Then the whole model will converge to the desired solution, in order to satisfy the illumination constraint. Each shading ambiguity has to be resolved independently through the introduction of the proper forces; no forces were applied to the tip of the sombrero which still points upwards.

5 Results

We now present experiments of coupled estimation of light direction and SFS on real and synthetic data. We get substantially improved results in light estimation than previous methods, and consequently in the shape estimation.

(a) Original Image   (b) Fitted Model   (c) Dual of fitted model

Figure 5: In the case of the penny lit from [1,0,1], the correct shape (c) is the dual of the fitted model (b).

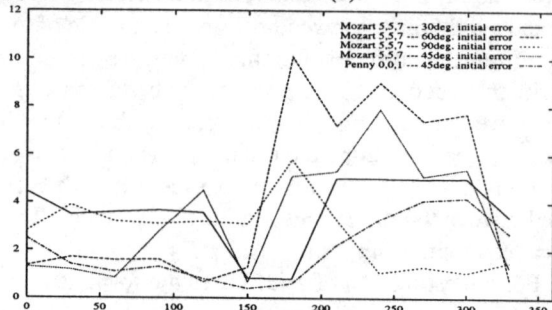

Figure 6: Light direction error analysis w.r.t. initial estimate. We plot the error in the final estimate when the direction of the initial estimate is 30,45,60 and 90 degrees off the true direction. Each initial lighting direction off the true light forms a cone w.r.t. the true light axis. We sample the cone at intervals of 30 degrees. Four sequences at different angles were generated for the Mozart image with true light direction (5,5,7) and one sequence for Penny illuminated from above (0,0,1).

5.1 Synthetic Data

We first present results of experiments on synthetic data sets where we had ground truth for the shape and the generating light source direction. Each data set was illuminated under three different light source directions. For each image we first estimated the light source directions using the method in [22]. This method gave accurate results for the images that were lit head-on (with direction (0,0,1)). In these cases our method obviously gave no improvement (although it did not decrease accuracy — the lighting position remained stable). In all other cases there was a marked im-

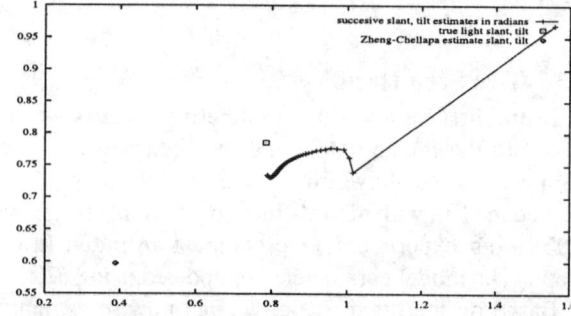

Figure 7: Light estimation results for Mozart lit from [5,5,7]. Initial estimate at top right was 45 degrees off the true light, denoted by a square. Crosses are the estimates of our algorithm connected by a line in the order that the algorithm successively generates them. The final estimate was 2 degrees off the truth. The circle at the bottom left is the estimate generated by the algorithm in [22] which was 23.7 degrees off the true light.

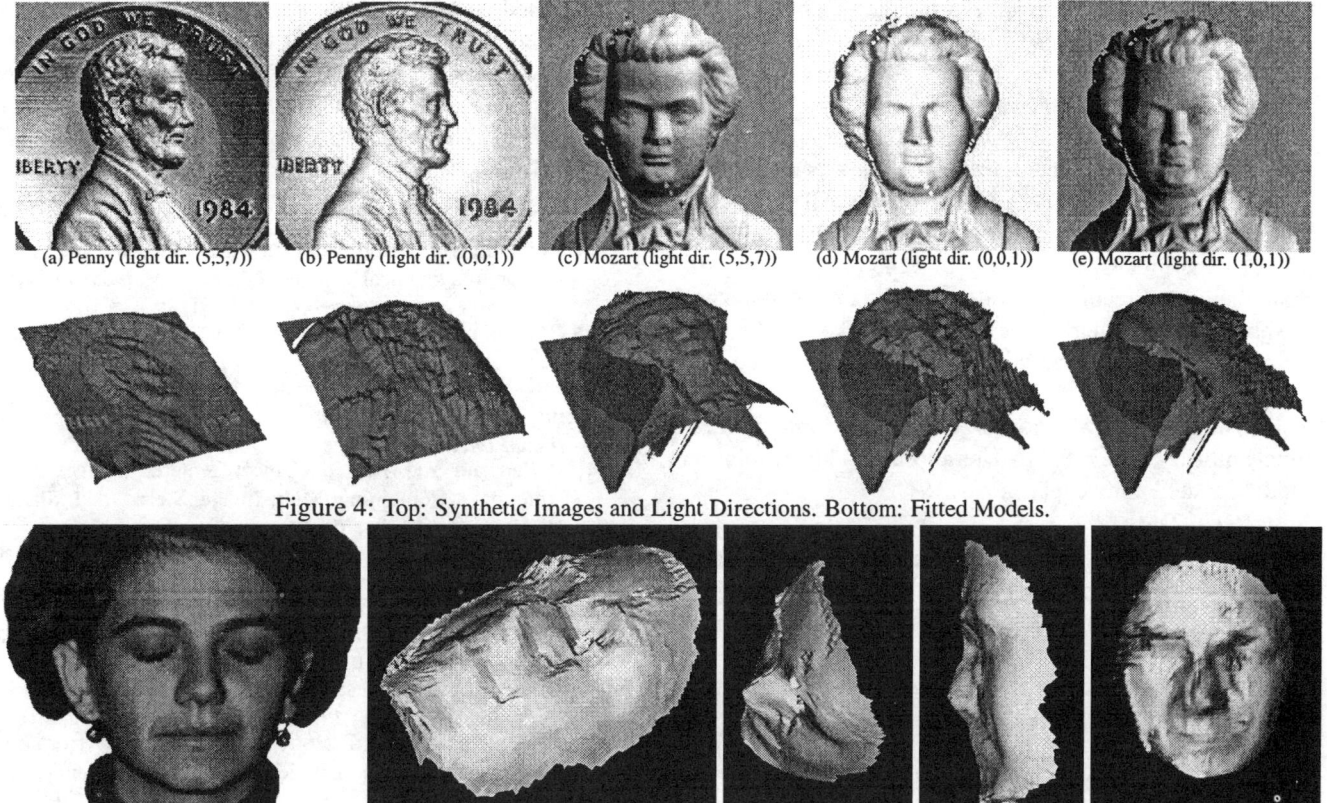

(a) Penny (light dir. (5,5,7))　(b) Penny (light dir. (0,0,1))　(c) Mozart (light dir. (5,5,7))　(d) Mozart (light dir. (0,0,1))　(e) Mozart (light dir. (1,0,1))

Figure 4: Top: Synthetic Images and Light Directions. Bottom: Fitted Models.

Figure 8: Experiments on real data. Initial image on the left and 4 views of the recovered model

provement over [22].

To test the robustness of our method to an initially poor lighting-direction estimate, we introduced to the images obtained with lighting direction (0,0,1) an initial lighting direction error of 45 degrees. In the mozart example the light estimate converged to 4.8 degrees from the true direction vector and the in the penny example it converged to 3.1 degrees. The recovered shapes can be seen in fig. 4.

The examples with light source direction (5,5,7) (or $\tau = \gamma = \pi/4$) gave the best results. The initial estimate from the [22] method for Mozart was 23.7 degrees off the true vector and our method recovered the illumination direction with a 2 degrees error. The initial estimate for the penny was 83 degrees off. Our model converged to 5.6 degrees of the true light vector.

The examples lit sideways (with $\tau = 0$, direction (1,0,1)) were the ones with the highest errors. The method in [22] gave an estimate for mozart that was 18.9 degrees off from the correct direction. Our method reduced the error to 9.7 degrees. Although a significant improvement, it still wasn't close enough to avoid visible errors in the reconstruction. As for the penny example, the initial estimate was 83 degrees off from the true light but only 7 from its dual (direction (-1,0,1)). As expected, our method converged to the dual with an error of 5 degrees. As can be seen in fig. 5 the fitting process gave us the dual shape, as described earlier.

We converted this to the correct fit by taking the complement of the normals w.r.t the viewing direction.

In fig. 2 we show the results of fitting to a perspective projection image. The focal length was assumed to be 2 and the distance from the focal point was assumed to be 4, so the perspective distortion effects on the image are quite noticeable. The light source direction was (5,5,7). Our light source estimate was 2.5 degrees off. We show the coarse model that we used while still estimating the light source. Once the light stabilizes we increase the model's resolution and fit it more closely to the lighting constraints.

In our experiments, we found the Levenberg-Marquart method typically to converge very quickly (within three to five iterations) for the estimates of τ and γ.

We analyzed how the choice of the initial lighting estimate affects the error of the recovered light direction. The initial estimates were chosen in the following way: We selected an initial estimate at 30, 45, 60, 90 degrees off the true vector. Then we rotated each estimate around the true vector and formed a cone. We sampled the cone at intervals of 30 degrees. This gave us 12 different estimates for each fixed angle off the true vector, which we used as initial estimates to our method. We see that for all the experiments where the initial estimate was no more than 30 degrees off the true vector, our algorithm gave a lighting position within 5 degrees from the correct answer (fig. 6).

The successive light estimates returned in one of those experiments (initial estimate is 45 degrees off from the truth) are shown in fig. 7, as they quickly converge towards the the true light source direction.

Furthermore, we tested how the initial shape affects the light estimation. The Mozart (5,5,7) image was fitted using a sphere, an ellipsoid and a planar mesh. All three converged to 2.2, 3.5 and 4.6 degrees, respectively. So, based on our experiments, we observe that the method can estimate the light direction, provided that the initial shape has the ability to deform to fit the data. It can take significantly longer to converge if the initial shape is far from the true data.

The method typically converges to the accurate light estimate quickly, in less than 20 iterations of a low resolution model for the Penny experiments.

5.2 Real Data

Fig 8 shows the fitting results to a real image of a face. We compare the reconstruction to data obtained by stereo using the method in [5]. The camera pose and the perspective projection parameters were supplied with the stereo data. We compared the recovered light vector, to the light vector that can be estimated from the stereo data, and the two estimates are 2.6 degrees off. The recovered depth is on average 1.34 percent off from the true data. There are visible errors in the reconstruction of the mouth and the eyes due to the albedo changes and at the tip of the nose due to specularities that violate the Lambertian assumption. These are typical shortcomings when SFS alone is used on real data. However, the light estimation was not adversely affected by the violations of the shading assumptions.

6 Conclusion

We have presented an approach for the simultaneous shape from shading and lighting direction estimation using a deformable model framework. As opposed to previous approaches the method only requires that the lighting constraint used is differentiable with respect to the lighting direction parameters and the deformable model parameters. We have shown that we can solve the above two nonlinearly coupled problems under both orthographic and perspective projections, based on a two step iterative process . Our experiments demonstrate that even if the initial estimate of the lighting direction is very crude, the correct shape and lighting direction are estimated at the end of our iterative approach. Future work includes integrating this methodology with other cues such as optical flow. We plan to experiment with other lighting models, but this is beyond the scope of this paper due to the higher number of parameters they have.

Acknowledgments

The test data sets and images were obtained from the University of Central Florida Computer Vision lab. Stereo data used as ground truth for the face image were supplied by Pascal Fua. Michael Collins and Doug De Carlo provided useful comments. This research has been partially supported by grants from NSF (IRI-97-01803, IRI-9624604, EIA98-09209), ARO and ONR-YIP N00014-97-1-0817.

References

[1] J. Baumgarte. Stabilization of constraints and integrals of motion in dynamical systems. *Computer Methods in Applied Mechanics and Engineering*, 1:1-16, 1972.

[2] P Belhumeur, D Kriegman, A Yuille. The Bas-Relief Ambiguity. In *CVPR 1997* (1060-1066)

[3] M.J. Brooks and B.K.P. Horn. Shape and source from shading. In *Proceedings of International Joint Conference on Artificial Intelligence*, pages 932-936, 1985.

[4] P. Fua and Y.G. Leclerc. Object-Centered Surface Reconstruction: Combining Multi-Image Stereo and Shading, IJCV(16), September 1995.

[5] , P. Fua and C. Miccio, From Regular Images to Animated Heads: A Least Squares Approach, ECCV 1998, (188-202)

[6] B.K.P Horn. 1970. Shape from Shading: A Method for Obtaining the Shape of a Smooth Opaque Object from One View. PhD thesis, MIT, 1970.

[7] B.K.P. Horn and M.J. Brooks. eds. Shape from Shading. Cambridge, MA: MIT Press, 1989

[8] K. Ikeuchi and B.K.P Horn. Numerical Shape from shading and occluding boundaries. *Artificial Intelligence*, 17(1-3):141-184, 1981.

[9] Y.G. Leclerc and A.F. Bobick. The Direct Computation of Height from Shading. In *CVPR 1991*, pages 552-558,1991.

[10] C.H. Lee and A. Rosenfeld. Improved methods of estimating shape from shading using the light source coordinate system. *Artificial Intelligence*, 26:125-143, 1985.

[11] K.M. Lee and C.C. Kuo. Shape from Shading with a Linear Triangular Element Surface Model. *PAMI* 15(8) Aug. 1993

[12] S.H. Lai and B.C. Vemuri. Physically-Based Adaptive Preconditioning for Early Vision, PAMI(19), June 1997.

[13] D.W. Marquart *SIAM* 11:431-441, 1963

[14] D. Metaxas and D. Terzopoulos. Shape and Nonrigid Motion Estimation Through Physics-based Synthesis. *PAMI-15*(6), pp. 580–591, June 1993.

[15] D. Metaxas, Physics-Based Deformable Models: Applications to Computer Vision, Graphics and Medical Imaging, Kluwer-Academic Publishers, November 1996.

[16] J. Oliensis and P. Dupois. A global algorithm for shape from shading. In *ICCV 1993*, pages 692-701, 1993.

[17] M. Oren and S.K. Nayar. Diffuse reflectance from rough surfaces. In *ICCV 1993* pages 763-764, 1993.

[18] W.H. Press, S.A. Teukolsky, W.T. Vettering and B.P. Flannery. *Numerical Recipes in C*, Cambridge University Press, 1992.

[19] D. Samaras and D. Metaxas Incorporating Illumination Constraints in Deformable Models In CVPR '98 (322-329)

[20] P.S. Tsai and M. Shah. A simple shape from shading algorithm. In *CVPR 1992* pages 734-736, 1992.

[21] R. Zhang, P. Tsai, J.E. Cryer, M. Shah. Analysis of shape from shading techniques. In *CVPR 1994* pages 377-384, 1994.

[22] Zheng, Chellappa Estimation of illumination direction, albedo, and shape from shading. *PAMI* 13(7):680-702, 1991.

Illumination Distribution from Brightness in Shadows: Adaptive Estimation of Illumination Distribution with Unknown Reflectance Properties in Shadow Regions

Imari Sato, Yoichi Sato, and Katsushi Ikeuchi
Institute of Industrial Science, University of Tokyo
7-22-1 Roppongi, Minato-ku, Tokyo 106-8558, Japan
{imarik, ysato, ki}@iis.u-tokyo.ac.jp

Abstract

This paper describes a new method for estimating the illumination distribution of a real scene from a radiance distribution inside shadows cast by an object in the scene. First, the illumination distribution of the scene is approximated by discrete sampling of an extended light source. Then the illumination distribution of the scene is estimated from a radiance distribution inside shadows cast by an object of known shape onto another object in the scene. Instead of assuming any particular reflectance properties of the surface inside the shadows, both the illumination distribution of the scene and the reflectance properties of the surface are estimated simultaneously, based on iterative optimization framework. In addition, this paper introduces an adaptive sampling of the illumination distribution of a scene. Rather than using a uniform discretization of the overall illumination distribution, we adaptively increase sampling directions of the illumination distribution based on the estimation at the previous iteration. Using the adaptive sampling framework, we are able to estimate overall illumination more efficiently by using fewer sampling directions. The proposed method is effective for estimating an illumination distribution even under a complex illumination environment.

1 Introduction

Image brightness is a function of shape, reflectance, and illumination [4]. The relationship among them has provided three major research areas in physics-based vision: shape-from-brightness (with a known reflectance and illumination) [6, 7, 8, 16], reflectance-from-brightness (with a known shape and illumination) [9, 1, 11, 12, 15, 17], and illumination-from-brightness (with a known shape and reflectance).

In the past, shape-from-brightness and reflectance-from-brightness have been extensively explored. In contrast, relatively limited amounts of research have been conducted in the third area, illumination-from-brightness [3, 14]. Some researchers attacked this problem as a related analysis of shape-from-shading. For example, Brooks and Horn determine shape as well as light sources from image brightness [7]. However, their analyses are conducted under very specific illumination conditions as in, for example, the case where there is only one direct light source in the scene; the analyses cannot be extended for more natural illumination conditions that include many types of direct and indirect illumination.

Recently, we proposed a method to recover an illumination distribution of a scene from image brightness with known shape and reflectance of an real object [19]. The method modeled illumination distribution of the scene with discrete sampling of the illumination radiance distribution, then formulated them as a simultaneous linear equation of unknown point sources. Then their brightness was determined by solving them from observed radiance changes inside shadows cast by an object of known shape onto another object surface of known shape and reflectance.[1] This method was effective and could estimate an illumination distribution even under a complex illumination environment such as an ordinary office, including reflections from the wall and other objects in the scene.

This method, however, has two limitations. First, it assumes that the reflectance properties of the surface inside shadows are given a priori. Otherwise, the method is applicable only if the surface is a Lambertian surface. Second, since the method uses a uniform discretization of the overall illumination for the estimation, the number of sampling

---

[1] In the past, shadows have been used for determining the 3D shapes and orientations of an object which cast shadows onto the scene [2, 10, 13, 20], while very few studies have focused on the the illumination information which shadows could provide.

directions of illumination tends to be exceedingly large in order to accurately approximate the illumination distribution.

This paper presents a method to overcome these limitations. The solution consists of two main aspects. First, we combine the illumination analysis with an estimation of the reflectance properties of a surface inside shadows. As a consequence, the proposed method becomes applicable to the case where reflectance properties of a surface are not known. This enlarges the variety of images to which the method can be applied. Second, we propose an adaptive sampling framework for efficient estimation of illumination distribution. Rather than using a uniform discretization of the overall illumination distribution, we adaptively increase the sampling directions of the illumination distribution based on the estimation at the previous iteration. Using this adaptive sampling framework, we can avoid unnecessarily dense sampling of the illumination and estimate the entire illumination distribution more efficiently with a smaller number of sampling directions of the illumination distribution.

Our method estimates the illumination distribution of a real scene by using a single color image of the scene with shadows cast by an object. The rest of the paper refers to the image with shadows as the *shadow image*, to the object which casts shadows onto the scene as the *occluding object*, and to the surface onto which the *occluding object* casts shadows as the *shadow surface*. In our experiments, we recovered the camera parameters and the shape of the *occluding object* by using a photo-modeling tool interactively.[2]

The rest of the paper is organized as follows. We first obtain a formula which relates an illumination distribution of a scene with the image irradiance of the *shadow image* in Section 2. In Section 3, we describe the basic steps of the proposed method for simultaneously estimating both an illumination distribution of a scene and reflectance properties of the *shadow surface*. In Section 4, we explain how to estimate an illumination radiance distribution from given reflectance parameters of the *shadow surface* and the observed image irradiance of a *shadow image*. In Section 5, we describe how to estimate the reflectance parameters of the *shadow surface* for a current estimation of the radiance distribution of the scene. In Section 6, we introduce an adaptive sampling framework for efficient approximation of the entire illumination. In Section 7, we show experimental results of the proposed method applied to real images. In Section 8, we present concluding remarks.

---

[2]In our examples shown in Section 7, we used a modeling tool called the 3D Builder from 3D Construction Company [22] for modeling the shape of an *occluding object* from a *shadow image*. At the same time, the plane of $z = 0$ is defined on the *shadow surface*.

2 Formula for Relating Illumination Radiance with Image Irradiance

In this section, we obtain a formula which relates an illumination distribution of a real scene with the image irradiance of a *shadow image*. The formula will later be used as a basis for estimating the illumination distribution of a real scene and reflectance properties of the *shadow surface*.

2.1 From Illumination Radiance to Scene Irradiance

First, we find a relationship between the illumination distribution of a real scene and the irradiance at a surface point in the scene. To take illumination from all directions into account, let us consider an infinitesimal patch of the extended light source, of a size $\delta\theta_i$ in polar angle and $\delta\phi_i$ in azimuth as shown in Figure 1.

Seen from the center point A, this patch subtends a solid angle $\delta\omega = sin\theta_i\delta\theta_i\delta\phi_i$. Let $L_0(\theta_i, \phi_i)$ be the illumination radiance per unit solid angle coming from the direction (θ_i, ϕ_i); then the radiance from the patch is $L_0(\theta_i, \phi_i)sin\theta_i\delta\theta_i\delta\phi_i$[5], and the total irradiance of the surface point A is

$$E = \int_{-\pi}^{\pi} \int_{0}^{\frac{\pi}{2}} L_0(\theta_i, \phi_i)cos\theta_i sin\theta_i d\theta_i d\phi_i \qquad (1)$$

Then occlusion of the incoming light by the *occluding object* is considered as

$$E = \int_{-\pi}^{\pi} \int_{0}^{\frac{\pi}{2}} L_0(\theta_i, \phi_i)S(\theta_i, \phi_i)cos\theta_i sin\theta_i d\theta_i d\phi_i \qquad (2)$$

where $S(\theta_i, \phi_i)$ are occlusion coefficients; $S(\theta_i, \phi_i) = 0$ if $L_0(\theta_i, \phi_i)$ is occluded by the occluding object; Otherwise $S(\theta_i, \phi_i) = 1$.

2.2 From Scene Irradiance to Scene Radiance

Some of the incoming light at point A is reflected toward the image plane. As a result, point A becomes a secondary light source with scene radiance.

The bidirectional reflectance distribution function (BRDF) $f(\theta_i, \phi_i; \theta_e, \phi_e)$ is defined as a ratio of the radiance of a surface as viewed from the direction (θ_e, ϕ_e) to the irradiance resulting from illumination from the direction (θ_i, ϕ_i). Thus, by integrating the product of the BRDF and the illumination radiance over the entire hemisphere, the scene radiance $Rs(\theta_e, \phi_e)$ viewed from the direction (θ_e, ϕ_e) is computed as

$$Rs(\theta_e, \phi_e) = \int_{-\pi}^{\pi} \int_{0}^{\frac{\pi}{2}} f(\theta_i, \phi_i; \theta_e, \phi_e)L_0(\theta_i, \phi_i)$$
$$S(\theta_i, \phi_i)cos\theta_i sin\theta_i d\theta_i d\phi_i \qquad (3)$$

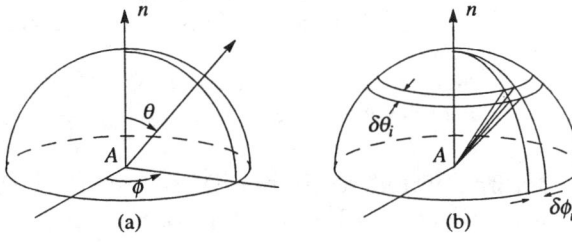

Figure 1. (a) the direction of incident and emitted light rays (b) infinitesimal patch of an extended light source

2.3 From Scene Radiance to Image Irradiance

Finally, the illumination radiance of the scene is related with image irradiance on the image plane. Since what we actually observe is not image irradiance on the image plane, but rather a recorded pixel value in a *shadow image*, it is also necessary to consider the conversion of the image irradiance into a pixel value of a corresponding point in the image. This conversion includes several factors such as D/A and A/D conversions in a CCD camera and a frame grabber.

Other studies concluded that image irradiance was proportional to scene radiance [5]. In our work, we calibrate a linearity of the CCD camera by using a Macbeth color chart with known reflectivity so that the recorded pixel values also become proportional to the scene radiance of the surface. From Equation 3 the pixel value of the *shadow image* $P(\theta_e, \phi_e)$ is thus computed as

$$P(\theta_e, \phi_e) = k \int_{-\pi}^{\pi} \int_{0}^{\frac{\pi}{2}} f(\theta_i, \phi_i; \theta_e, \phi_e) L_0(\theta_i, \phi_i)$$
$$S(\theta_i, \phi_i) cos\theta_i sin\theta_i d\theta_i d\phi_i \quad (4)$$

where k is a scaling factor between scene radiance and a pixel value. Due to the scaling factor k, we are able to estimate unknown $L_0(\theta_i, \phi_i)(i = 1, 2, .., n)$ up to scale. To obtain the scale factor k, we need to perform photometric calibration between pixel intensity and physical unit $(watt/m^2)$ for the irradiance.

2.4 Approximation of Illumination Distribution with Discrete Sampling

In an actual implementation of our method, the illumination distribution is approximated by discrete sampling of radiance over the entire surface of the extended light source. This can be considered as representing the illumination distribution of the scene by using a collection of imaginary

directional light sources. As a result, the double integral in Equation 4 is approximated as

$$P(\theta_e, \phi_e) = \sum_{i=0}^{n} f(\theta_i, \phi_i; \theta_e, \phi_e) L(\theta_i, \phi_i) \omega_i S(\theta_i, \phi_i) cos\theta_i$$
$$(5)$$

where n is the number of sampling directions, $L(\theta_i, \phi_i)$ is the illumination radiance per unit solid angle coming from the direction (θ_i, ϕ_i), which also includes the scaling factor k between scene radiance and a pixel value, and ω_i is a solid angle for the sampling direction (θ_i, ϕ_i).

For instance, node directions of a geodesic dome can be used for uniform sampling of the illumination distribution. By using n nodes of a geodesic dome in a northern hemisphere as a sampling direction, the illumination distribution of the scene is approximated as a collection of directional light sources distributed with an equal solid angle $\omega = 2\pi/n$.

In our method, BRDF $f(\theta_i, \phi_i; \theta_e, \phi_e)$ in Equation 5 is then parameterized using a simplified Torrance-Sparrow model [15, 21]. Using the model, the pixel value of the *shadow image* $P(\theta_e, \phi_e)$, is computed as

$$P(\theta_e, \phi_e) = \sum_{i=0}^{n} (K_d cos\theta_i + K_s \frac{1}{cos\theta_r} e^{\frac{-\gamma(\theta_i, \phi_i)^2}{2\sigma^2}})$$
$$S(\theta_i, \phi_i) L(\theta_i, \phi_i) \omega_i \quad (6)$$

where θ_r is the angle between the surface normal and the viewing direction, $\gamma(\theta_i, \phi_i)$ is the angle between the surface normal and the bisector of the light source direction and the viewing direction, K_d and K_s are constants for the diffuse and specular reflection components, and σ is the standard deviation of a facet slope of the Torrance-Sparrow reflection model.

Note that, since each pixel consists of 3 color bands (R, G, and B), each band of radiance $L(\theta_i, \phi_i)$ is also estimated from the corresponding color band of the image separately. Also, based on the dichromatic reflection model, five parameters $(K_{d,R}, K_{d,G}, K_{d,B}, K_s,$ and $\sigma)$ are considered as the reflectance parameters of the *shadow surface*. Accordingly, $L(\theta_i, \phi_i)$ is estimated using K_s, σ, and the corresponding color band of K_d. In this paper, we explain our method by using $L(\theta_i, \phi_i), K_d, K_s,$ and σ for the simplicity of our discussion.

3 Basic Steps of the Proposed Method

Based on the formula in Equation 6 which relates the illumination radiance of the scene with the pixel values of the *shadow image*, the illumination radiance distribution of the scene is estimated from image brightness inside shadows as described in the following steps.

1. Initialize the reflectance parameters of the *shadow surface*. Typically, we assume the *shadow surface* to be Lambertian, and the diffuse parameter K_d is set to be the pixel value of the brightest point on the *shadow surface*. The specular parameters are set to be zero $(K_s = 0, \sigma = 0)$. [3]

2. Estimate radiance values $L(\theta_i, \phi_i)$ of imaginary directional light sources which model the illumination distribution of a real scene. By using the reflectance parameters (K_d, K_s, σ) and image brightness inside shadows in the *shadow image*, the radiance distribution $L(\theta_i, \phi_i)$ is computed. (Section 4)

3. Estimate the reflectance parameters of the *shadow surface* (K_d, K_s, σ) from the obtained radiance distribution of the scene $L(\theta_i, \phi_i)$ by using an optimization technique. (Section 5)

4. Estimate the radiance distribution of the scene $L(\theta_i, \phi_i)$ from the obtained reflectance parameters (K_d, K_s, σ). (Section 4)

5. Proceed to the next step if there is no significant change in the estimated values $L(\theta_i, \phi_i), K_d, K_s,$ and σ. Otherwise, go back to Step 3. By estimating both the radiance distribution of the scene and the reflectance parameters of the *shadow surface* iteratively, we can obtain the best estimation of those values for a given set of sampling directions of the illumination radiance distribution of the scene.

6. Terminate the estimation process if the obtained illumination radiance distribution approximates the real radiance distribution with sufficient accuracy. Otherwise, proceed to the next step.

7. Increase the sampling directions of the illumination distribution adaptively based on the obtained illumination radiance distribution $L(\theta_i, \phi_i)$ (Section 6). Then go back to Step 2.

We should clarify the assumptions that we made for the proposed method. In our method, it is assumed that light sources in the scene are sufficiently distant from the objects, and thus all light sources project parallel rays onto the object surface. Also, the method does not take into account interreflection between a shadow region and an *occluding object* casting the shadow. We also assume that the *shadow surface* has uniform reflectance properties over the entire surface. Although these assumptions are not exactly true

---

[3]Note that the initial value of K_d is not so important since there is a scaling factor between the reflectance parameters and illumination radiance values in any case. To fix the scaling factor, we need to perform photometric calibration of our imaging system with a calibration target whose reflectance is given a priori.

in real situations, we find through experiments that these assumptions have little effect on estimated illumination distribution in most cases.

In the following sections, each step of the proposed method will be explained in more detail.

4 Estimation of Radiance Distribution based on Reflectance Parameters of Shadow Surface

In this section, we explain how to estimate the radiance distribution of the scene $L(\theta_i, \phi_i)$ for a given set of reflectance parameters (K_d, K_s, σ). In the following sections, we refer $L(\theta_i, \phi_i)$ as to L_i for simplicity.

Using Equation 6 which relates the illumination radiance of the scene with the pixel values of the *shadow image*, illumination radiance is estimated based on the recorded pixel values of the *shadow image*. From Equation 6, a linear equation is obtained for each image pixel of the *shadow image* as

$$a_1 L_1 + a_2 L_2 + a_3 L_3 + \cdots + a_{1n} L_n = P \qquad (7)$$

where $L_i \ (i = 1, 2, .., n)$ are n unknown illumination radiance specified by n sampling directions of the radiance distribution for the scene. The coefficients $a_i (i = 1, 2, .., n)$ represent $(K_d cos\theta_i + K_s \frac{1}{cos\theta_r} e^{\frac{-\gamma(\theta_i, \phi_i)^2}{2\sigma^2}}) S(\theta_i, \phi_i) \ (i = 1, 2, .., n)$; we compute $\theta_i, \theta_r, \gamma(\theta_i, \phi_i),$ and $S(\theta_i, \phi_i)$ based on 3D geometry of the surface point corresponding to the image pixel, the illumination direction, and the shape of the *occluding object*. P is the values of the image pixel $P(\theta_e, \phi_e)$.

If we select a number of pixels, say m pixels, a set of linear equations is obtained as

$$
\begin{aligned}
a_{11} L_1 + a_{12} L_2 + a_{13} L_3 + & \cdots + a_{1n} L_n & = P_1 \\
a_{21} L_1 + a_{22} L_2 + a_{23} L_3 + & \cdots + a_{2n} L_n & = P_2 \\
a_{31} L_1 + a_{32} L_2 + a_{33} L_3 + & \cdots + a_{3n} L_n & = P_3 \\
& \cdots & \cdots \\
a_{m1} L_1 + a_{m2} L_2 + a_{m3} L_3 + & \cdots + a_{mn} L_n & = P_m \quad (8)
\end{aligned}
$$

Therefore, by selecting a sufficiently large number of image pixels, we are able to solve for a unique solution set of unknown L_i's.

In general, the number of image pixels in shadows is far larger than the number of illumination radiance values to be estimated. Thus we need to select appropriate image pixels for better computational efficiency. In our method, image pixels are selected by considering their coefficients a_i so that the set of linear equations (Equation 8) becomes sufficiently over determined by a smaller number of image pixels.

5 Estimation of Reflectance Parameters of Shadow Surface based on Radiance Distribution

In this section, we describe how to estimate the reflectance parameters of the *shadow surface* (K_d, K_s, σ) by using the estimated radiance distribution of the scene L_i.

Unlike the estimation of the radiance distribution of the scene L_i which can be done by solving a set of linear equations (Equation 8), we estimate the reflectance parameters of the *shadow surface* by minimizing a sum of squared difference between the observed pixel intensities in the *shadow image* and pixel values for the corresponding surface points. Hence the function to be minimized is defined as

$$f = \sum_{j=0}^{m} (P_j' - P_j)^2 \qquad (9)$$

where P_j' is the observed pixel intensities in shadows cast by the *occluding object*, P_j is the pixel value of the corresponding surface points computed by using the given radiance distribution of the scene L_i in Equation 6, m is the number of pixels used for minimization. In our method, the error function in Equation 9 is minimized with respect to the reflectance parameters $K_d, K_s,$ and σ by the Powell method to obtain the best estimation of those reflectance parameters.

6 Adaptive Sampling of Radiance Distribution

If the estimated radiance distribution for a set of sampling directions does not approximate the illumination distribution of the scene with sufficient accuracy, we increase the sampling directions adaptively based on the current estimation of the illumination radiance distribution.

Radiance distribution changes very rapidly around a direct light source such as a fluorescent light. Therefore, the radiance distribution has to be approximated by using a large number of samplings so that the rapid change of radiance distribution around a direct light source is captured. Also, to correctly reproduce soft shadows cast by extended light sources, radiance distribution inside a direct light source has to be sampled densely.

On the other hand, coarse sampling of radiance distribution is enough for an indirect light source such as a wall whose radiance remains small. As a result, the number of sampling directions required for accurately estimating an illumination distribution of a real scene becomes exceedingly large.

To overcome this problem, we increase sampling directions adaptively based on the estimation at the previous iteration, rather than by using a uniform discretization of the overall illumination distribution. In particular, we increase sampling directions around and within direct light sources.

Based on the estimated radiance distribution L_i for the sampling directions at the previous step, additional sampling directions are determined as follows.

Suppose three sampling directions with radiance values $L_1, L_2,$ and L_3 are placed to form a triangle M_1 as illustrated in Figure 2. To determine whether a new sampling direction needs to be added between L_1 and L_2 or not, we consider the following cost function.

$$U(L_1, L_2) = diff(L_1, L_2) + \alpha min(L_1, L_2) angle(L_1, L_2) \qquad (10)$$

where $diff(L_1, L_2)$ is the radiance difference between L_1 and L_2, $min(L_1, L_2)$ gives the smaller radiance of L_1 and L_2, $angle(L_1, L_2)$ is the angle between directions to L_1 and L_2, and α is a manually specified parameter which determines the relative weights of those two factors. The first term is required to capture the rapid change of radiance distribution around direct light sources, while the second term leads to fine sampling of the radiance distribution inside direct light sources. The additional term $angle(L_1, L_2)$ is used for avoiding unnecessarily dense sampling inside direct light sources. In our experiments, α is set to 0.5.

If the cost U is large, a new sampling direction is added between L_1 and L_2. In our experiments, we computed the cost function values U for all pairs of neighboring sampling directions, then added additional sampling directions for the first 50% of all the pairs in order of the cost function values U.

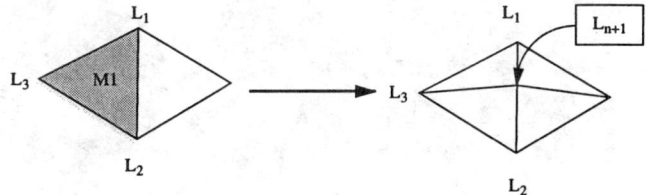

Figure 2. Subdivision of sampling directions

7 Experimental Results

We have tested the proposed method by using real images taken in both indoor and outdoor environments.

An image with an *occluding object*, i.e., *shadow image*, was taken under usual illumination environment in our office, including direct light sources such as fluorescent lamps, as well as indirect illumination such as reflections from a ceiling and a wall. The input image is shown in Figure 3 (a).

First, the shape of the *occluding object* and the camera parameters of the input image were obtained by using a

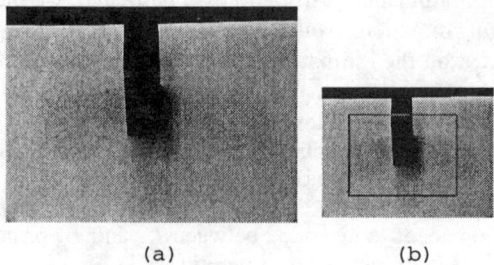

(a)   (b)

Figure 3. Input image : (a) *shadow image* taken in an indoor scene (b) the region where synthesized images with the estimated radiance distribution and reflectance parameters are superimposed in Figure 4

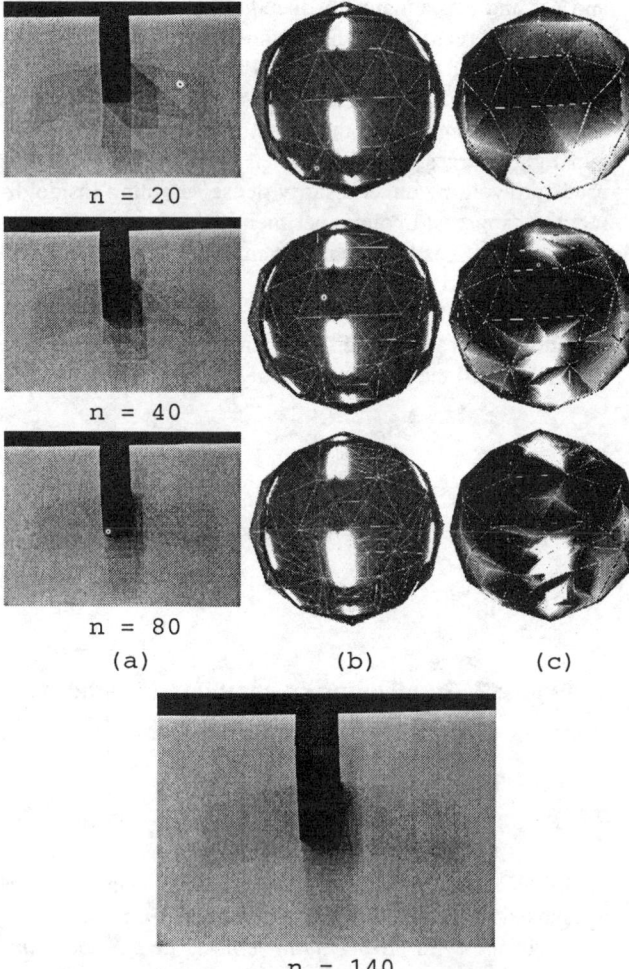

Figure 4. Adaptive refinement of illumination distribution estimation: (a) synthesized images with the estimated radiance distribution and reflectance parameters (b) adaptive refinement of sampling directions with a ground truth of an omni-directional image of the scene (c) the estimated radiance values visualized for comparison with the ground truth

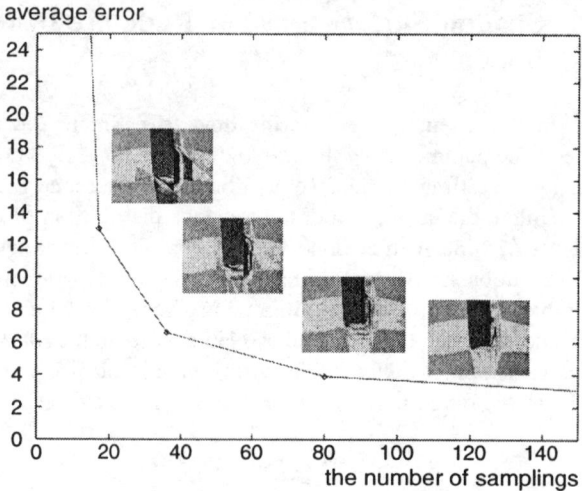

Figure 5. Error Analysis

photo-modeling tool [22]. Then, an illumination distribution of the scene was estimated using the image irradiance inside shadows in the *shadow image* as explained in Section 3. Starting from a small number of uniform sampling directions of the illumination distribution, the estimation of the radiance distribution of the scene was iteratively refined as described in Section 6. At the same time, the reflectance parameters (K_d, K_s, and σ) of the *shadow surface* were estimated as explained in Section 5.

Then an appearance of the *shadow surface* around the *occluding object* was synthesized by using the estimated radiance distribution of the scene and the estimated reflectance parameters of the *shadow surface*. To demonstrate how well the estimated radiance distribution and the reflectance parameters could represent the scene, we replaced the region inside the red rectangle in Figure 3 (b) with the synthesized appearances. The left column in Figure 4 shows the results synthesized by the estimated radiance distribution and the estimated reflectance parameters of the *shadow surface*. The number of sampling directions of the radiance distribution used for the estimation is shown under the resulting images.

We found through our experiments that, the larger number of sampling directions we used, the more the shadows of the synthetic object resembled those of the *occluding object* in the *shadow image*. Especially in the case of 140 sampling directions, we can see hardly any distinct boundaries in the shadows, and the synthesized shadow of the *occluding object* matches the real one in the input image very well: this shows that the estimated illumination distribution gives a good presentation of that of the real scene.

To see how well the adaptive sampling of radiance distribution works for real images, we took an omni-directional image of the office scene as a ground truth. The middle column of Figure 4 shows the omni-directional image of the scene taken by placing a camera with a fisheye lens looking upward on the *shadow surface* in Figure 3 (a). The omni-directional image shows both direct light sources, i.e., fluorescent lamps in our office, and indirect light sources such as a ceiling and walls. The right column of Figure 4 shows the estimated radiance values visualized for comparison with the ground truth. In those images in Figure 4 (b) and (c), we can see that sampling directions of the radiance distribution were nicely added only around the direct light sources at each step by the proposed adaptive sampling framework, starting from the coarse sampling directions at the top row.

Figure 5 numerically shows the improvement of the accuracy by adaptive refinement of sampling directions and the estimation of reflectance properties of the *shadow surface*. The vertical axis represents average error in pixel values inside the synthesized images in the region shown in Figure 3 (b) compared with that in the input image Figure 3 (a). Here, the initial average pixel values of shadow regions in the *shadow image* are set to 100 %. The horizontal axis represents the number of sampling directions used for the estimation. From the plot in the figure, we can clearly see that the accuracy improves rapidly as we adaptively increase sampling directions of the radiance distribution. Also the small pictures at the bottom show error distributions inside the region. Darker color represents larger error in a pixel value in the shadow regions compared with the real shadows of the *occluding object* in the *shadow image*.

To confirm the merit of the adaptive sampling framework and the estimation of the reflectance parameters of the *shadow surface*, we also estimated the illumination radiance distribution with uniform sampling and fixed reflectance parameters. In that case, even 300 uniformly sampled directions could not achieve the same level of accuracy as the estimation result obtained by 80 sampling directions with the method proposed in this work.

Figure 6 (a) shows another example image taken outside the entrance lobby of our building in the late afternoon. In this image, we used the rectangular pole with two colors as an *occluding object* casting shadows. In the same way as the previous example, the shape of the *occluding object* and the camera parameters of the input image were obtained by using a photo-modeling tool. Then, an illumination distribution of the scene was estimated using the image irradiance inside shadows in the input image as explained in Section 3.

Then an appearance of the *shadow surface* around the *occluding object*, illustrated with a red rectangle in Figure 7 (b), was synthesized by using the estimated radiance distribution of the scene and the estimated reflectance parameters of the *shadow surface* [18]. Figure 7 shows the result-

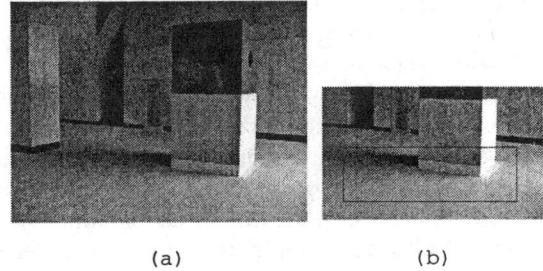

(a)   (b)

Figure 6. Input image : (a) *shadow image* taken in an outdoor scene (b) the region where synthesized images with the estimated radiance distribution and reflectance parameters are superimposed in Figure 7

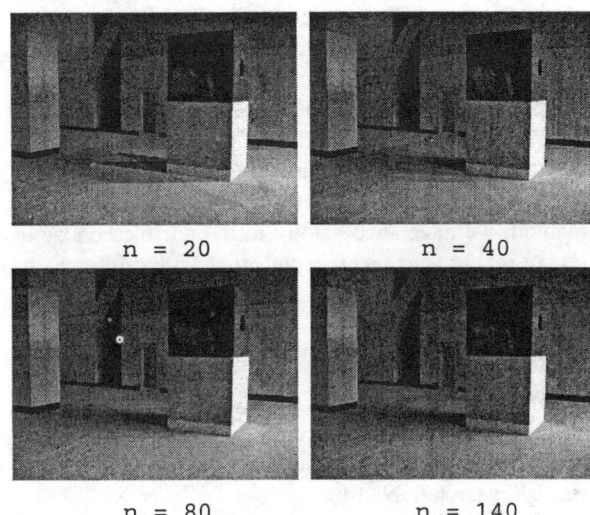

n = 20   n = 40

n = 80   n = 140

Figure 7. Adaptive refinement of illumination distribution estimation: synthesized images with the estimated radiance distribution and reflectance parameters

ing images by our method. Although the grid pattern on the *shadow surface* is missing in those synthesized images due to the assumption of uniform reflectance on the *shadow image*, the appearance of the shadow around the *occluding objects* is virtually indistinguishable in the case of 140 sampling directions. This shows that the estimated illumination distribution gives a good representation of the characteristics of the real scene.

8 Conclusions

In this paper, we have proposed a new method for estimating an illumination distribution of a real scene from a radiance distribution inside shadows cast by a real object of known shape onto other object surfaces of known shape and known reflectance. By using the occlusion information of the incoming light, we were able to estimate an illumination distribution of a real scene reliably, even for the images taken in a complex illumination environment.

In particular, the proposed method has been significantly extended from our previous approach in two main aspects. First, we combine the illumination analysis with an estimation of the reflectance properties of a shadow surface. As a consequence, the proposed method becomes applicable to the case where reflectance properties of a surface are not known. Second, we propose an adaptive sampling framework for efficient estimation of illumination distribution. Rather than using a uniform discretization of the overall illumination distribution, we adaptively increase the sampling directions of the illumination distribution based on the estimation at the previous iteration. Using this adaptive sampling framework, we can avoid unnecessarily dense sampling of the illumination and estimate the entire illumination distribution more efficiently with a smaller number of sampling directions of the illumination distribution.

To demonstrate the effectiveness of the proposed method, we have successfully tested our method by using sets of real images taken in our office with different surface materials of shadow regions.

Acknowledgments

This research was supported by the Ministry of Education, Science, Sports and Culture grant-in-Aid for Creative Basis Research 09NP1401.

References

[1] R. Baribeau, M. Rioux, and G. Godin, "Color Reflectance Modeling Using a Polychromatic Laser Range Sensor," *IEEE Trans. PAMI*, vol. 14, no. 2, pp. 263-269, 1992.

[2] J. Bouguet and P. Perona, "3D Photography on Your Desk," *Proc. IEEE Intl. Conference on Computer Vision 98*, pp.43-50, 1998.

[3] A. Fournier, A. Gunawan and C. Romanzin, "Common Illumination between Real and Computer Generated Scenes,"*Proc. Graphics Interface '93*, pp.254-262, 1993.

[4] B. K. P. Horn,"Understanding Image Intensities," *Artificial Intelligence, 8(2)*, pp.201-231, 1977.

[5] B. K. P. Horn, *Robot Vision*, The MIT Press, Cambridge, MA., 1986.

[6] B. K. P. Horn, "Obtaining Shape from Shading Information," *The psychology of Computer Vision*, McGraw-Hill Book Co., New York, N.Y., 1975.

[7] B. K. P. Horn and M. J. Brooks, "The Variational Approach to Shape from Shading," *Computer Vision, Graphics, and Image Processing*, 33(2), pp.174-208, 1986.

[8] K. Ikeuchi and B. K. P. Horn, "Numerical Shape from Shading and Occluding Boundaries," *Artificial Intelligence 17(1-3)*, pp.141-184, 1981.

[9] K. Ikeuchi and K. Sato, "Determining Reflectance using Range and Brightness Images," *Proc. IEEE Intl. Conference on Computer Vision 90*, pp.12-20, 1990.

[10] J. R. Kender and E. M. Smith, "Shape from Darkness: Deriving Surface Information from Dynamic Shadows," *Proc. IEEE Intl. Conference on Computer Vision 87*, pp.539-546, 1987.

[11] G. Kay and T. Caelli, "Estimating the Parameters of an Illumination Model using Photometric Stereo,"*Graphical Models and Image Processing*, vol. 57, no. 5, pp. 365-388, 1995.

[12] J. Lu and J. Little, "Reflectance Function Estimation and Shape Recovery from Image Sequence of a Rotating Object,"*Proc. IEEE Intl. Conference on Computer Vision '95*, pp. 80-86, 1995.

[13] A. K. Markworth, "On the Interpretation of Drawings as Three-Dimensional Scenes," *PhD thesis, University of Sussex*, 1974.

[14] S. R. Marschner and D. P. Greenberg, "Inverse Lighting for Photography," *Proc. IS&T/SID Fifth Color Imaging Conference*, pp.262-265, 1997.

[15] S. K. Nayar, K. Ikeuchi, and T. Kanade, "Surface reflection: physical and geometrical perspectives," *IEEE Trans. PAMI*, vol. 13, no. 7, pp. 611-634, 1991.

[16] A. P. Pentland, "linear Shape From Shading," *Intl. J. Computer Vision*, 4(2), pp153-162, 1990.

[17] Y. Sato, M. D. Wheeler, and K. Ikeuchi, "Object shape and reflectance modeling from observation," *Proc. SIGGRAPH 97*, pp. 379-387, 1997.

[18] I. Sato, Y. Sato, and K. Ikeuchi, "Acquiring a Radiance Distribution to Superimpose Virtual Objects onto a Real Scene", *IEEE Trans. Visualization and Computer Graphics*, vol. 5, no. 1, pp. 1-12, 1999.

[19] I. Sato, Y. Sato, and K. Ikeuchi, "Illumination from Shadows", *Proc. IEEE Conference on Computer Vision and Pattern Recognition 99*, pp.306-312, 1999.

[20] S. A. Shafer and T. Kanade, "Using Shadows in Finding Surface Orientations," *Computer Vision, Graphics, and Image Processing*, 22(1), pp. 145-176, 1983.

[21] K. E. Torrance and E. M. Sparrow, "Theory for off-specular reflection from roughened surface," *J. Optical Society of America*, vol.57, pp.1105-1114, 1967.

[22] 3D Construction Company, http://www.3dcomstruction.com

Segmentation, Grouping, and Feature Extraction

Subpixel-Precise Extraction of Watersheds

Carsten Steger

Forschungsgruppe Bildverstehen (FG BV), Informatik IX
Technische Universität München, Orleansstr. 34, 81667 München
Phone: +49 (89) 48095-211, Fax: +49 (89) 48095-203
E-mail: stegerc@informatik.tu-muenchen.de

Abstract

An approach to extract watersheds and watercourses, as well as their corresponding valleys and hills, from images with subpixel precision is proposed. The critical points of the terrain are essential as the starting points for the construction of these separatrices. They are extracted efficiently with subpixel precision using an approach based on derivatives of Gaussian filters. The separatrices are extracted by integrating their defining differential equation. Finally, the hills and valleys are constructed by an efficient graph search algorithm. Examples show the quality of the results that can be achieved with the proposed approach.

1 Introduction

Watersheds and watercourses are important geomorphological features, which play an important role in hydrological GIS applications. Intuitively, watersheds can be regarded as the lines that separate the area where water drains to different locations. The areas that are enclosed by the watersheds are precisely the regions where water drains to the same place, and are conventionally called basins or valleys. Likewise, watercourses can be regarded as the lines where water accumulates when it drains on the terrain. If water would only run on the surface, the watercourses would be the location of the river beds.

Watersheds also play an important role for the segmentation of images, because the gray value of an image can be regarded as the height of the terrain, and many interesting features, e.g., cell walls in microscopic images, can be described by watersheds.

One of the major categories of approaches to extract watersheds are the ridge detectors, which were first proposed in the early part of the 19th century (see [2, 8] for a historical overview). [1] gives a good overview over the existing classes of ridge detectors. However, it is well known that they do not model the way water runs downhill [2], and can therefore not be used to extract watersheds.

Another theory was proposed in the second half of the 19th century by Maxwell, Jordan, and Cayley (see [4, 6] and references therein). It is based on the observation that for generic surfaces there is a unique slope line through every non-critical point of the surface. Each slope line is the solution of a first-order ordinary differential equation (ODE). Loosely speaking, all slope lines converging at the same maximum are said to form a hill, while all slope lines converging at the same minimum comprise a valley. The lines that separate the hills and valleys are called watercourses and watersheds, respectively. An important aspect of this definition is that these separatrices are given by special slope lines emanating from saddle points, and running to a maximum or minimum, respectively. An implementation roughly following this theory has been described in [7]. However, it suffers from some poor implementation choices that lead to inaccurate results and some surprising cases, in which, for example, slope lines can cross each other.

A different characterization is given in [8]. This definition basically replaces the gradient vector field in the above ODE by its dual 1-form, to obtain another differential equation, which is inexact, i.e., does not have a general integral. To integrate the DE, an integrating divisor must be found, which obeys a first-order partial differential equation (PDE) [8, 2]. The level crossings of the integrating surface of the PDE are the slope lines. Among them, some are singled out as singular solutions, which contain the watersheds and watercourses. Unfortunately, this definition is almost impossible to implement as a computer algorithm. The defining equation of the integrating divisor is a first-order PDE, which could be solved by the method of characteristic strips. However, no boundary conditions can be given. Therefore, no true implementations of this theory have been given, although some erroneously claim to be one [3].

A third way to extract watersheds from the image is to use the fact that water will accumulate at the minima of the landscape. This means that each minimum in the image defines a valley or water catchment basin. Watersheds are the boundaries between different basins. This can be implemented by flooding the landscape from the minima [11].

Since all of the approaches to extract watersheds return the result only with pixel resolution, a subpixel accurate watershed and watercourse extraction algorithm is desirable. This means that either the definition of Maxwell, Jordan, and Cayley, or the definition of Rothe must be used. Since the latter definition can be implemented only with great difficulties, if it can be implemented at all, only the first definition seems to be viable.

2 Theory

As mentioned above, the definition of watersheds and watercourses given by Maxwell, Jordan, and Cayley is the definition that is most suitable for an implementation as a computer program. This section will describe the theory in detail, so that its implementation can be easily understood.

The definition of watersheds and watercourses, collectively called separatrices, regards the terrain as a surface $f(x)$, where $x \in \mathbb{R}^2$. This means that overhanging walls in mountains cannot be modeled, but since water falls down vertically at such places, this poses no restrictions on the approach. Each generic surface possesses isolated critical points, i.e., points where the gradient $\nabla f = 0$ [4, 6]. These are the maxima (peaks), minima (pits), and saddle points (passes) of the terrain.

Every non-critical point p of the terrain lies on exactly one slope line. The point p divides the corresponding slope line into an ascending and a descending part. These two parts of the slope line are the solutions of the ODE

$$\dot{x}(t) = \pm \nabla f(x(t)) \qquad (1)$$

with the initial condition $x(0) = p$. The ascending part of the slope line corresponds to the positive gradient. Critical points do not lie on any slope lines, but we can say that a slope line reaches a critical point c if

$$\lim_{t \to \infty} x(t) = c \ . \qquad (2)$$

With this, we can define the terms "hill" and "valley" quite intuitively. All points, from which the ascending slope line reaches the same maximum, form the *hill* that corresponds to the maximum, while all points, from which the descending slope line reaches the same minimum, form the *valley* that corresponds to the minimum. Furthermore, we can define that all points, from which the slope line reaches the same minimum and maximum, form the *slope district* of the minimum and maximum. It follows that all hills are disjunct and cover the plane $\mathbb{R}^2$, and likewise for valleys. Therefore, there must be curves that separate the hills and the valleys. We can define that curves that separate adjacent valleys are called *ridge lines*, while curves that separate adjacent hills are called *valley lines*. Note that the term ridge

line is defined differently from most ridge detectors. The ridge lines are, as we will see below, very close to what we would intuitively call *watersheds*, i.e., lines that separate regions where water drains to different locations, while the valley lines are very close to what we would call *watercourses*, i.e., possible locations of rivers.

While the above definition of the ridge and valley lines is quite intuitive, it cannot be used for an efficient implementation, since we would have to construct the slope lines for every point of the image. However, the following observation will lead to an efficient algorithm, as we will see below. In every saddle point, four special slope lines "emanate" in the following sense: Every saddle point possesses two preferred directions, its directions of principal curvature, i.e., the directions in which the second directional derivative at the critical point obtains its minimum and maximum value, respectively. The principal directions are perpendicular to each other. The corresponding principal curvatures are of opposite sign, indicating an upward and downward curved direction. Although no slope line leaves the saddle point, since the gradient there vanishes, we can take an infinitesimally small step in the four directions defined by the two principal directions. This will lead to two ascending and two descending slope lines. The ascending slope lines necessarily reach a maximum or another saddle point, while the descending slope lines reach a minimum or another saddle point. The key observation is that the valley lines are exactly the descending slope lines emanating from the saddle points, while the ridge lines are exactly the ascending slope lines emanating from the saddle points.

The above definitions lead to the fact that for generic surfaces, every maximum is surrounded by a "ring" of valley lines, on which only minima and saddle points occur as critical points. Likewise, every minimum is surrounded by a ring of ridge lines, on which only maxima and saddle points occur as critical points.

If we regard valley and ridge lines together, it can be seen that these lines partition the plane $\mathbb{R}^2$ completely into the slope districts. The critical points, along with the ridge and valley lines, from a graph that describes the borders of the slope districts. Here, the vertices of the graph are the critical points, while the edges are the ridge and valley lines.

It is interesting to note that all slope district boundaries are equivalent to one of the four types of slope districts shown in Figure 1 [4]. The equivalence relation is defined by inserting an arbitrary number of saddle points into the graph, where the slope district boundary makes a right angle turn at each of the inserted saddle points. The slope district type in the upper left part of Figure 1, where there are two paths from a minimum to a maximum via two different saddle points, occurs most frequently for real data. The configuration in the lower left corresponds to a crater, whereas the configuration in the upper right corresponds to

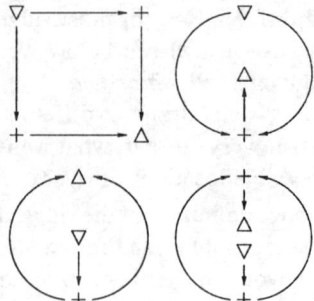

Figure 1. The four generic types of slope district boundaries. Maxima are indicated by $\triangle$, minima by $\triangledown$, and saddle points by $+$. Edges are drawn in the upward direction of the underlying terrain.

an isolated mountain (imagine a crater that has been turned upside-down). The final configuration has no good real-world interpretation, and was argued to be unstable in [7].

Figure 1 gives a good example why not every ridge line is a watershed and not every valley line is a watercourse. Consider, for example, the ridge line that runs from the saddle point to the maximum in the upper right configuration. There, all water that falls onto this slope district accumulates at the minimum. Hence, the ridge line does not separate two regions where water accumulates at different places, and therefore it cannot be a watershed. The same line of reasoning shows that the valley line in the lower left configuration is not a watercourse, since water will run down the crater walls more or less equally, and hence the water does not really accumulate at a watercourse.

3 Extraction of Critical Points

Based on the above discussion, it is clear that the critical points of the terrain play a crucial role for the extraction of separatrices. If the saddle points of the terrain are known, one can start constructing the four special slope lines that emanate from each saddle point by integrating the ODE (1). To know when to stop integrating, one has to know the minima, maxima, and saddle points of the terrain.

Because the slope lines eventually reach the critical points, the location of these points has to be known with high accuracy in order to be able to stop the integration of the slope lines at the right time and place. More importantly, the saddle points and their principal directions have to be known with high accuracy to enable the starting of the integration. These requirements rule out pixel-based approaches to the extraction of the critical points, because the principal directions of the critical points cannot be determined accurately.

A method for the extraction of minima and maxima with subpixel accuracy was presented in [10]. It can easily be modified to extract saddle points as well. The method works by constructing a second-order Taylor polynomial for every image point. The necessary partial derivatives of the image are obtained by convolving the image with the appropriate partial derivatives of a Gaussian kernel [10, 9]. Smoothing the input data is necessary to remove noise and plateaus. If we denote the Hessian matrix, i.e., the matrix of the second partial derivatives, of the Gaussian-smoothed terrain by $\mathbf{H}_g f$, and the gradient of the smoothed terrain by $\nabla_g f$, we can extract the critical points by solving the following linear equation for every image pixel:

$$\mathbf{H}_g f \cdot x = -\nabla_g f \ . \tag{3}$$

To ensure that the critical point lies within the current pixel, $x \in [-\frac{1}{2}, \frac{1}{2}] \times [-\frac{1}{2}, \frac{1}{2}]$ must be required.

The above procedure returns the critical points with subpixel resolution. In addition, a classification into maxima, minima, and saddle points, as well as the principal directions at the critical points are needed. Both can be obtained from the Hessian matrix $\mathbf{H}_g f$. The eigenvalues λ_1 and λ_2 $(\lambda_1 < \lambda_2)$ of the Hessian give the required classification: A critical point is a maximum if $\lambda_1, \lambda_2 < 0$, a minimum if $\lambda_1, \lambda_2 > 0$, and a saddle point if $\lambda_1 < 0$ and $\lambda_2 > 0$. Note that because we assume the surface f to be generic, the case $\lambda_{1,2} = 0$ occurs with probability zero. Additionally, the eigenvectors e_1 and e_2 corresponding to the two eigenvalues give the two principal directions at each saddle point, and hence the four starting directions $\pm e_{1,2}$ for the integration of the separatrices. Figure 2 shows the result of extracting the critical points from a digital terrain model (DTM) with 20 m pixel size of the Vernagtferner glacier. The critical points are visualized by crosses which point in their principal directions. One important point to note is that because the image is mirrored at the borders during smoothing and subsequent processing, critical points are created in the correct places for further processing at the border of the DTM automatically.

While the locations of the extracted critical points are quite good, they can be refined even further. The reason for this is that the critical points are *extrapolated* from the Taylor polynomial at each pixel's center. Because terms of order 3 and higher are neglected, the locations can contain extrapolation errors of up to about 1/10 of a pixel, especially of the critical point lies near the pixel's borders. Furthermore, because of this the Taylor polynomials do not agree at the pixel's boundaries, and can therefore not be used for interpolation purposes. However, the construction of the separatrices discussed in the next section requires a consistently interpolated surface. By consistent we mean that the gradient $\nabla_g f = (g_x, g_y)$ of the ODE (1) must fulfill the

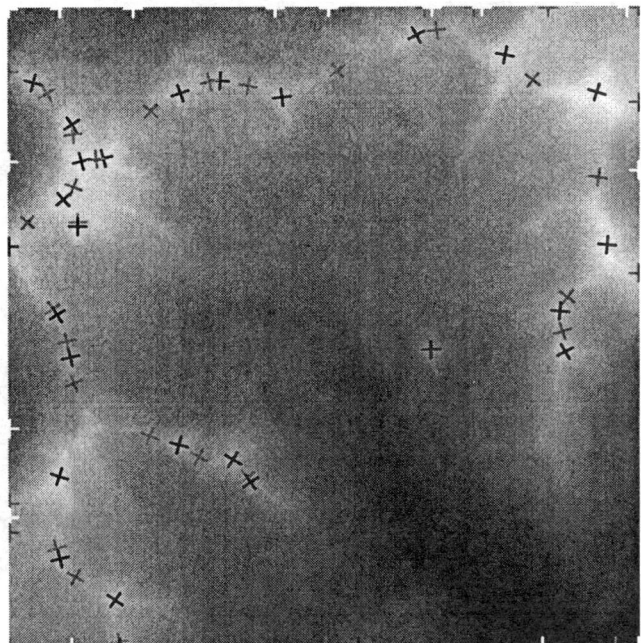

Figure 2. Critical points extracted from a DTM of the Vernagtferner glacier. The left image shows the DTM visualized by gray levels, while the right image shows the DTM shaded from the north east. Maxima are displayed as black crosses in the left image and as dashed crosses in the right image, respectively, minima as white and dotted crosses, and saddle points as medium gray and solid crosses. The axes of the crosses point to their principal directions.

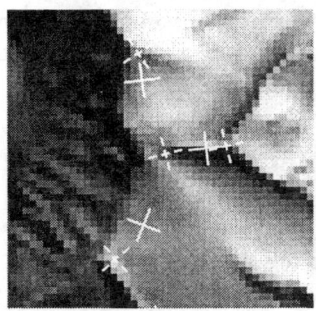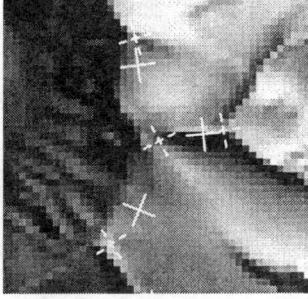

Figure 3. Comparison between the extrapolated and refined locations of the critical points in the vicinity of the peak in the north west corner of Figure 2.

integrability condition

$$\frac{\partial g_x}{\partial y} = \frac{\partial g_y}{\partial x} . \tag{4}$$

Note that this implies that the terrain must have continuous derivatives up to second order. A bicubical interpolation of the terrain fulfills all these requirements, and hence is used from now on to interpolate the partial derivatives of the DTM or image at subpixel positions.

With this, the extrapolated critical points can be regarded as initial guesses for a root finding algorithm that calculates the critical points (recall that their location is given by $\nabla_g f = 0$). A Newton-Raphson-type root finding algorithm [5] will locate the critical points with sufficient accuracy with few iterations. Of course, the principal directions have to be recalculated at the refined locations of the critical points. Figure 3 shows a comparison between the extrapolated and refined locations of the critical points. As can be seen, the location changes are relatively minor, but the changed principal directions indicate that the refinement step is important to get good results.

4 Extraction of Separatrices

With the critical points extracted, the construction of the separatrices can be done in a straightforward manner by integrating their defining ODE 1, i.e., $\dot{x}(t) = \nabla f(x(t))$ for ridge lines and $\dot{x}(t) = -\nabla f(x(t))$ for valley lines. The initial condition $x(0) = p$ needed to start the integration can be obtained by taking a small step away from the saddle points in their principal direction, i.e., $\pm e_1$ ($\lambda_1 < 0$) for valley lines and $\pm e_2$ ($\lambda_2 > 0$) for ridge lines, as discussed in Section 2. In the current implementation, this step is 1/4 pixel. Of course, to get a topologically complete result,

Figure 4. Separatrices extracted from the DTM in Figure 2.

Figure 5. 3d visualization of the separatrices extracted from the DTM in Figure 2. Watersheds are displayed in white. The view is along the ridge from the east to south of the center of the image.

the saddle point itself has to be added to each separatrix as well. The integration of the ODE stops if the separatrix gets close enough to another critical point (recall that it cannot get to the critical point itself). To perform the integration, a Runge-Kutta algorithm with adaptive step size control is both robust and efficient enough [5].

With this procedure, all separatrices in the interior of the DTM or image are extracted correctly. At the border of the DTM, some special treatment is necessary since it might happen that a maximum and a minimum are adjacent on the border. In such cases, no separatrix will be constructed between the two critical points. However, to ensure a complete segmentation of the DTM into regions, it is essential that in such cases a separatrix is constructed artificially. Hence, the algorithm examines all adjacent pairs of critical points and inserts a separatrix on the border wherever necessary to ensure that there is a closed ring of ridge and valley lines around the image border.

The results of applying the algorithm described above to the DTM of Figure 2 can be seen in Figure 4, which displays all the extracted separatrices. Figure 5 displays the extracted separatrices on a 3d visualization of the DTM to give an impression of the excellent subpixel accuracy of the algorithm. The keen observer will note that all of the slope districts are of the two types in the upper row of Figure 1, where the right type occurs three times. One surprising fact is that in the south west corner two separatrices approach each other very closely, but then separate again, before con-

verging in the main valley in the south east. This result can only be explained by the fact that polynomial interpolation sometimes introduces oscillations, which might lead to a "phantom ridge" between the two "valleys" in this case.

5   Extraction of Hills and Valleys

The separatrices are often useful by themselves. However, most of the times the regions defined by the separatrices, i.e., the hills, valleys, and, to a limited extent, the slope districts, are the objects that need to be returned by the algorithm. Especially the valleys are of great importance, since their borders are exactly the watersheds of the processed DTM or image.

As discussed in Section 2, the critical points form the vertices of a graph, whose edges are the separatrices. From this graph, we can extract the slope districts by extracting the regions of the plane that are enclosed by the separatrices. Conceptually, the regions are given by "minimal" cycles in the graph, i.e., cycles that do not contain edges, which intersect the region enclosed by the cycle such that several smaller regions could be produced. The same can be said for hills and valleys. Here, we only need to insert a subset of the separatrices into the graph. For valleys, the ridge lines and the corresponding vertices need to be inserted, while for hills the valley lines are required.

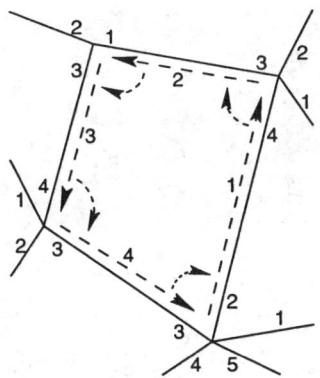

Figure 6. Algorithm to construct the regions enclosed by the edges of a graph. The solid lines are the edges of the graph. The numbers on the edges indicate the counterclockwise sorting order of the edges in each vertex. The dashed lines are the edges that enclose the region in counterclockwise direction. The numbers on the dashed lines, along with the dotted arrows indicate the order in which the region is constructed.

Thus, in order to extract the regions defined by the separatrices, a bidirectional graph, i.e., a graph that for every separatrix contains the edge from the saddle point to the critical point it reaches as well as the corresponding back edge, needs to be constructed. To see how the regions enclosed by the graph can be computed, assume for the moment that all edges, i.e., separatrices, are straight line segments. Then, we could easily sort the edges of the graph in each vertex according to the edge direction, i.e., we could order the edges counterclockwise (see Figure 6).

With this, the algorithm to construct the regions is relatively straightforward. To construct a region, take the first unprocessed edge of the graph, and look up the vertex to which it leads, i.e., the tip of the edge. From the edges that leave the vertex, select the one that precedes the incoming edge in the ordering. Mark the incoming as processed, and continue in the same manner until the edge selected at the current vertex is already marked as processed, i.e., until you have formed a cycle. It is easy to see that, by construction, the cycles computed by this algorithm are minimal in the above sense. Obviously, all regions have been constructed if there are no more unprocessed edges.

As can be seen, the crucial part of the algorithm is the counterclockwise ordering of the edges in each vertex. While this is easy to define for straight lines, unfortunately for separatrices this is a rather complicated problem since often several separatrices reach a critical point in the same direction, i.e., are tangential to each other, as shown in Figure 7. Therefore, the ordering cannot be determined locally

Figure 7. Often the separatrices reach a critical point tangential to each other. Therefore, the ordering of the separatrices in the vertices is non-trivial.

at each vertex, e.g., based on angles. An angle-based ordering can only be used for separatrices that enter the critical point non-tangentially. For tangential separatrices, the ordering must be done based on the criterion that a vertex "eventually lies to the left" of another vertex. Based on Figure 7, the meaning of this criterion is fairly obvious for a human. In the computer implementation, this criterion can be defined based on the directions of the separatrices at the point at which they move apart by a sufficient distance.

Figure 8 shows the valleys and hills that are extracted from the DTM in Figure 2 with the proposed approach. As can be seen, all regions have been computed correctly. Note that the ridge lines that are no watersheds and the valley lines that are no watercourses have been removed from the result. This was done by successively removing the adjacent edge pairs on the cycles that correspond to the same separatrices.

Another example of the results obtainable with the proposed approach is given in Figure 9. Here, watersheds were extracted from an image of human skin cells. Note again the accuracy and completeness of the segmentation.

6 Conclusions

This paper proposes an approach to extract watersheds and watercourses from grid DTMs and digital images with subpixel accuracy. The approach is based on the theory put forward by Maxwell, Caley, and Jordan. For the first time, a consistent and efficient implementation of this theory is developed. It rests on the fact that the critical points of the terrain, most importantly the saddle points, and their principal directions can be found efficiently with subpixel accuracy. The separatrices are then constructed with subpixel accuracy by interpolating the terrain appropriately so that a standard ODE integration algorithm can be used. Finally, the hills, valleys, and slope districts are constructed by an efficient graph search algorithm.

One of the consequences of the algorithm and of the morphology of the earth is that often separatrices, especially

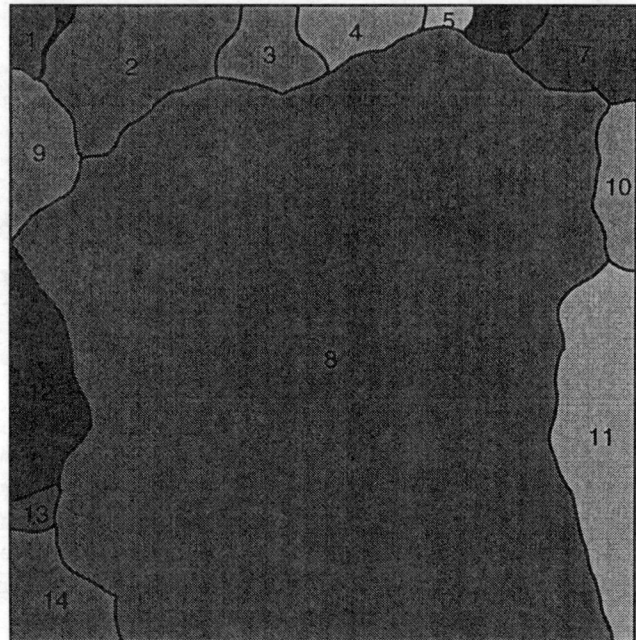
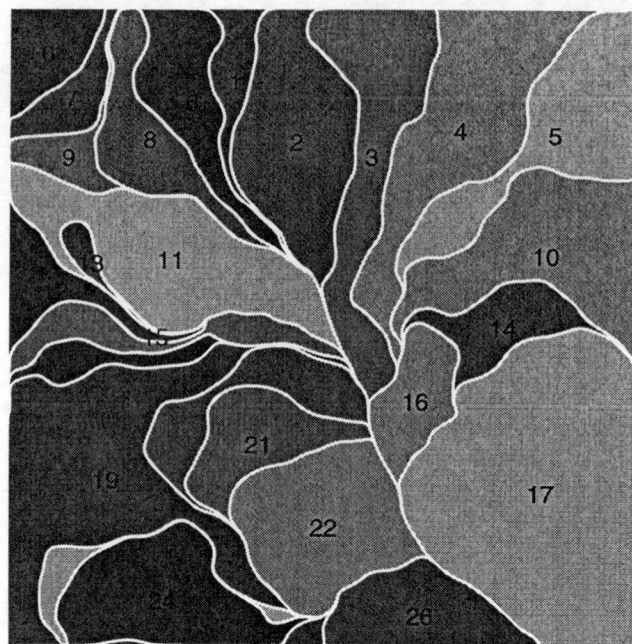

Figure 8. Valleys and hills extracted from the DTM in Figure 2.

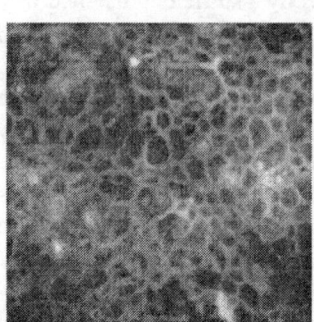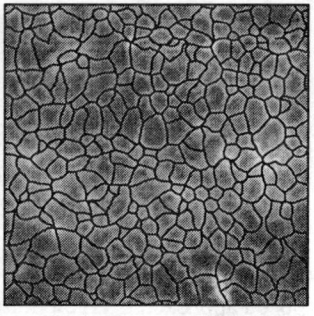

Figure 9. Watersheds extracted from an image of human skin cells.

watercourses, join tangentially long before the corresponding critical point is reached. This leads to elongated region with line-like appendages of nearly zero area. Although this results from the definitions of the separatrices, it is not intuitive from a user's standpoint. Therefore, it might be useful to insert "confluence points" at the appropriate locations into the graph. However, this is a quite complicated problem since it has to be done in a topologically sound manner.

References

[1] D. Eberly, R. Gardner, B. Morse, S. Pizer, and C. Scharlach. Ridges for image analysis. *Journal of Mathematical Imaging and Vision*, 4:353–373, 1994.

[2] J. J. Koenderink and A. J. van Doorn. Two-plus-one-dimensional differential geometry. *Pattern Recognition Letters*, 15(5):439–443, May 1994.

[3] A. M. López and J. Serrat. Tracing crease curves by solving a system of differential equations. In B. Buxton and R. Cipolla, editors, *Fourth European Conference on Computer Vision*, volume 1064 of *Lecture Notes in Computer Science*, pages 241–250, Berlin, 1996. Springer-Verlag.

[4] L. R. Nackman. Two-dimensional critical point configuration graphs. *IEEE Transactions on Pattern Analysis and Machine Intelligence*, 6(4):442–450, Apr. 1984.

[5] W. H. Press, S. A. Teukolsky, W. T. Vetterling, and B. P. Flannery. *Numerical Recipes in C: The Art of Scientific Computing*. Cambridge University Press, Cambridge, 2nd edition, 1992.

[6] J. H. Rieger. Topographical properties of generic images. *International Journal of Computer Vision*, 23(1):79–92, Jan. 1997.

[7] P. L. Rosin, A. C. F. Colchester, and D. J. Hawkes. Early image representation using regions defined by maximum gradient paths between singular points. *Pattern Recognition*, 25(7):695–711, 1992.

[8] R. Rothe. Zum Problem des Talwegs. In *Sitzungsberichte der Berliner Mathematischen Gesellschaft*, volume XIV, pages 51–68, Leipzig, 1915. B. G. Teubner Verlag.

[9] C. Steger. An unbiased detector of curvilinear structures. *IEEE Transactions on Pattern Analysis and Machine Intelligence*, 20(2):113–125, Feb. 1998.

[10] C. Steger. *Unbiased Extraction of Curvilinear Structures from 2D and 3D Images*. Dissertation, Fakultät für Informatik, Technische Universität München, 1998. Herbert Utz Verlag, München.

[11] L. Vincent and P. Soille. Watersheds in digital spaces: An efficient algorithm based on immersion simulations. *IEEE Transactions on Pattern Analysis and Machine Intelligence*, 13(6):583–598, June 1991.

Segmentation of Salient Closed Contours from Real Images

Shyjan Mahamud
Dept. of Computer Science
Carnegie Mellon University
Pittsburgh, PA 15213

Karvel K. Thornber
NEC Research Institute, Inc.
4 Independence Way
Princeton, NJ 08540

Lance R. Williams
Dept. of Computer Science
University of New Mexico
Albuquerque, NM 87131

Abstract

Using a saliency measure based on the global property of contour closure, we have developed a method that reliably segments out salient contours bounding unknown objects from real edge images. The measure also incorporates the Gestalt principles of proximity and smooth continuity that previous methods have exploited. Unlike previous measures, we incorporate contour closure by finding the eigen-solution associated with a stochastic process that models the distribution of contours passing through edges in the scene. The segmentation algorithm utilizes the saliency measure to identify multiple closed contours by finding strongly-connected components on an induced graph. The determination of strongly-connected components is a direct consequence of the property of closure. We report for the first time, results on large real images for which segmentation takes an average of about 10 secs per object on a general-purpose workstation. The segmentation is made efficient for such large images by exploiting the inherent symmetry in the task.

1 Introduction

Visual perception evolved in a world of objects many of which are bounded by smooth closed contours. We hypothesize that these contours obey a stochastic distribution which is utilized by perceptual processes in finding contours bounding objects. In prior work [10, 12, 13] this distribution has been modeled and used to derive a saliency measure that exploits the closure of contours bounding objects. It was found that this measure provides a significant improvement over previous approaches in highlighting edges lying on contours bounding objects in small synthetic scenes created from contours of real objects and natural background texture [13]. However, no method was presented for actually segmenting out the salient object contours. Despite the effectiveness of the saliency measure, it will be shown later that a simple threshold on the saliency measure is not sufficient for segmentation, escpecially in cases where two or more object contours have similar saliencies. In this paper, we present a method for segmenting out multiple contours bounding salient objects. Moreover, previously [13] the determination of the saliencies was computationally infeasible for large real images. We have developed an efficient technique that exploits the symmetry inherent in the task, using which, we report for the first time, results on large real images.

Given an edge image as in Fig. 1 (a), we would like to extract out separately the individual contours bounding the two pears. We wish to achieve such a segmentation with no *a-priori* knowledge of the specific objects that generate these contours. Such a task is one of the goals of *perceptual grouping*. In lieu of any specific knowledge about the objects generating the contours, we impose a subset of the Gestalt principles for perceptual organization. Most previous approaches to perceptual grouping of edges have incorporated the local principles of proximity of edges and smooth-continuation of contours in some form or other (e.g., [4, 8]). These methods assume that successive edges are in close proximity and that contours bounding objects are smooth. In addition to these two local properties, we exploit the global property that contours bounding objects must be closed. Unlike proximity and smooth-continuation, closure cannot be reduced to any local property of the contour.

Previous approaches [2, 3] have used graph based search techniques to find closed contours. A graph of affinities between edges is constructed where the affinities model proximity and smooth-continuation. The affinity between two edges is a purely local measure that is proportional to the likelihood that a smooth contour (open or closed) passes through the given edges. Closure is imposed by searching the graph for closed contours while minimizing a global cost function that is related to how salient the closed contours are. Our approach differs from these previous approaches because we first use the local affinity measure (which as noted above does not differentiate between open and closed contours) to compute a global saliency measure, which is proportional to the relative number of closed contours which join a pair of edges. Such a measure for closed contours was first proposed and compared extensively with previous approaches (including [7, 8, 12]) that do not incorporate closure in [13]. It is only after the computation of this global saliency that we employ a graph search to identify individual closed contours. We will show that in our case, the incorporation of closure in the saliency measure leads naturally to a specific type of graph search, namely, the determination of strongly connected components. This dependency of the specific graph search used on the saliency measure is a distinguishing feature of our work as compared with previous approaches where generic search techniques have been employed that are not dependent on the properties of the specific saliency measures that were used. To illustrate the crucial role played by the global property of closure, we show that a method based on a purely local affinity measure produces poor segmentations.

The determination of the saliency measure requires the solution of an eigen-problem of a matrix that exhibits a special kind of symmetry. Ordinary techniques for the solution of the eigen-problem are infeasible for large real images. We have developed efficient techniques that exploit the special symmetry of the matrix to significantly reduce the time required to compute the eigen-solution. In this paper, we report the first results on real images with a large number of edges. Our technique reduces the time taken to compute the segmentation for each object contour from an average of around 2 1/2 hrs. to around 10 seconds.

2 Problem Formulation

Since the Gestalt principles of proximity and smooth-continuation arise from local properties of the positions and orientations of two edges, we can model them using only local information. Following [10, 12], both of these local properties can be modeled by the distribution of smooth curves that join two given edges. The distribution of curves is modeled by a particle with motion determined by a stochastic process favoring short, smooth, trajectories. Given two directed edges i and j, they determine the probability that a particle starts with the position and direction of edge i and ends with the position and direction of edge j. The particles leave or arrive at an edge at a constant speed γ independent of the edge. The "affinity" from edge i to edge j is denoted by P_{ji} and is the sum of the probabilities of all paths that a particle can take between the two edges (see [10] for details). Essentially, two parameters control the motion of the

particle and embody the principles of proximity and smooth-continuation. Each particle has a half-life (τ) which models the principle of proximity. The variance (T) of the directional change of the particle model the principle of smooth-continuation. The speed γ determines the effective scale at which the scene is analyzed, since the affinity between a pair of edges varies with the speed of the particle. At larger speeds, a pair of edges are effectively closer to each other, whereas at slower speeds the same pair are effectively farther apart. In our application we choose a fixed speed that we judge to give a good effective scale for all images.

Because particles need not reach any another edge due to the half-life, in general $\sum_j P_{ji} < 1$. Hence P is not a stochastic (Markov) matrix, and methods based on Markov chains are not applicable. While closed contours do form a Markov chain, the corresponding Markov matrix for the edge saliencies is not known until the edge and link saliencies have been determined.

Smooth-continuity of a curve between two edges implies that the tangent at any point along the curve is continuous. Such tangent-continuity for curves passing between a pair of edges is modeled by the smooth stochastic motion of the particle going from one edge to the other. If we wish to extend the curves to include additional edges then tangent continuity must be enforced at the edges themselves. A contour coming in along a given direction must continue along that direction to satisfy tangent-continuity. This requirement can be ensured by replacing each edge of a given orientation with two oppositely directed edges. A contour can come into and leave a directed edge only along a single direction. If we do not impose tangent-continuity at the edges, we could get contours with cusps (i.e., reversals in direction) at the edges, which are not judged to be salient in practice. For more details see [13]. Since every directed edge i has a sibling edge at the same position but pointing in the opposite direction, it will be convenient to denote the sibling edge by $\bar{i}$.

Imposing tangent-continuity through directed edges has an important implication for the structure of the matrix of affinities P. From symmetry, the probability that any particle travels along a curve starting from edge i and ending in edge j is the same as the probability of a particle traveling the same curve along the reverse direction from edge $\bar{j}$ to edge $\bar{i}$. Hence $P_{ji} = P_{\bar{i}\bar{j}}$. We call this special symmetry of the affinity matrix *reversal-symmetry* which is distinct from the usual symmetry $P_{ji} = P_{ij}$ which need not hold in general. Reversal-symmetry has important implications for both the form of the expressions which define the saliencies and for efficiently computing them.

In the rest of the paper we will have occasion to associate a vector s with the set of *directed* edges (e.g. the vector of saliencies for each directed edge), one component for each directed edge. Analogous with the case for edges, a component of such a vector s_i associated with edge i will have a sibling component denoted by $\bar{s}_i = s_{\bar{i}}$ associated with edge $\bar{i}$.

3 Saliency measure

In this section, we first motivate the expression for the saliency measure [13]. We then show that the saliency measure can be determined by the solution to an eigen-problem associated with the affinity matrix P. Given an edge image, we define a closed contour as a finite closed sequence of edges. By a closed sequence we mean that if we start from any edge in the sequence and trace out the contour we will return to the same edge. Each closed contour α has a likelihood (or probability) associated with it, which we denote by $p(\alpha)$ and is the product of the transition probabilities (given by the affinity matrix P) between successive edges in the contour.

3.1 Edge Saliency

We would like to define our saliency measure for an edge to be related to the likelihoods of the various closed contours that thread through that edge. Rather than derive the contribution of each individual closed contour to the saliency for an edge, it is simpler to consider the contribution of the ensemble of all closed contours through that edge by considering the set of infinite closed contours passing through that edge. Each infinite closed contour can be decomposed into a sequence of finite closed contours, and hence the relative likelihood of different infinite closed contours passing through an edge depends on the relative likelihood of the individual finite closed contours that they are composed of. In order to calculate the relative saliencies of infinite contours, we start by considering the relative saliencies of closed contours of finite but large length and take the limit as the length goes to infinity. Restricting ourselves to finite contours for now, the saliency of an edge should be proportional to the expected number of closed contours that pass through that edge. The expected number of closed contours of length n that thread through edge i is simply the sum of the probabilities of all such closed contours :

$$E_i^n = \sum_\alpha p(\alpha \mid i \in \alpha, |\alpha| = n) \qquad (1)$$

Since we are interested in the relative saliencies of the various infinite contours that thread through different edges, we take the limit $n \to \infty$ for the expected number of closed contours through a given edge i relative to the expected number through all edges and obtain the formal definition for the saliency of edge i :

$$C_i = \lim_{n \to \infty} \frac{E_i^n}{\sum_j E_j^n}$$

With this definition, it turns out that there is a simple relationship between edge saliencies and the eigenvector corresponding to the largest eigenvalue of the affinity matrix P.

Theorem 1 (First Saliency Theorem) *The saliency for edge i is given by :*

$$C_i = s_i \, \bar{s}_i \qquad (2)$$

where the s_i's are the components of the eigenvector (normalized such that $\sum_i s_i \bar{s}_i = 1$) corresponding to the largest eigenvalue λ in magnitude of the affinity matrix $\mathbf{P}$*, i.e.* $\mathbf{Ps} = \lambda \mathbf{s}$*.*

Proof. See [5] and also [13] for an earlier proof.

Note that due to reversal-symmetry, we would expect $C_i = C_{\bar{i}}$ as can be verified from the expression above.

3.2 Link Saliency

For the purpose of segmentation, in addition to the edge saliencies, we will also need information that will help us trace out contours given a starting edge. Specifically, given two edges j and i we would like to know the relative likelihood that closed contours pass through edges j and i successively. We define the *link saliency* C_{ij} to be the relative saliencies of the closed contours that pass through edges j and i successively. Analogous to the definition for the edge saliencies, we have :

$$C_{ij} = \lim_{n \to \infty} \frac{E_{ij}^n}{\sum_l E_l^n}$$

where E_{ij}^n is the expected number of closed contours of length n that go through edges j and i successively, and E_l^n is as defined before in (1). The link saliencies also turn out to have a simple relationship with the eigenvector corresponding to the largest eigenvalue of P.

Theorem 2 (Second Saliency Theorem) *The link-saliencies between any two edges j and i are given by :*

$$C_{ij} = \frac{\bar{s}_i P_{ij} s_j}{\lambda} \qquad (3)$$

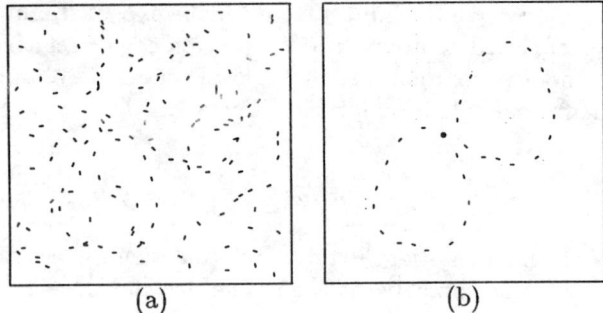

(a)   (b)

Figure 1: (a) An example edge image created from two copies of a real pear contour superimposed on a background texture (b) Saliency plot.

where the s_i's are the components of the eigenvector (normalized such that $\sum_i s_i \bar{s}_i = 1$) corresponding to the largest eigenvalue λ of the affinity matrix P.

Proof. See [5]. It should be noted that the notion of the edge saliencies C_i's was first introduced in [13]. However, the notion of link saliencies and the above theorem is new and has not been presented before.

Again, as in the case of the edge saliencies, due to reversal-symmetry we would expect $C_{ij} = C_{\bar{j}\bar{i}}$ as can be verified from the expression above (recall, $P_{ij} = P_{\bar{j}\bar{i}}$ and $\bar{\bar{s}}_i = s_i$).

Since we are concerned with closed contours, an important conservation property holds for all edges. Any *closed* contour that goes from some edge k into a second edge i must continue onto some third edge j. This is not necessarily true in the case of open contours. We confirm this conservation property and at the same time use it as a consistency check on the expressions for the C_{ij}'s and C_i's :

$$\sum_k C_{ik} = \sum_k \frac{\bar{s}_i(P_{ik}s_k)}{\lambda} = \frac{\bar{s}_i(\lambda s_i)}{\lambda} = \bar{s}_i s_i = C_i$$

Doing a similar calculation for $\sum_j C_{ji}$, we find

$$\sum_k C_{ik} = C_i = \sum_j C_{ji}$$

We conclude this section by demonstrating how well our saliency measure performs for the two-pear example of Fig. 1. The saliency measure for each edge in the figure was determined through the expressions for C_i in equation (2) after solving for the largest eigenvalue of P and its corresponding eigenvector. The saliency plot is shown in Fig. 1 (b). The length of an edge in the plot is proportional to its saliency. As can be seen,

the edges bounding both pears have high (and comparable) saliencies. The saliencies of all other edges have been suppressed (numerically, their saliencies are 20 orders of magnitude smaller than those of the pears).

In order to separately identify the two contours bounding the pears, we might think of simply thresholding the saliencies. However, as illustrated in this example (and in general), it is possible for such a simple thresholding scheme to group together edges bounding distinct objects. In the next section, we develop a more robust approach that uses the link saliencies C_{ij}'s to group together the set of edges that belong to distinct objects.

4 Segmentation

The goal of segmentation is to group together in distinct sets, edges bounding distinct objects in the scene. To motivate our segmentation algorithm, consider the hypothetical case where some oracle provided us with a set S of closed contours in the scene whose saliencies are above some threshold. We can construct a graph whose vertices correspond to the edges in our scene. We create a directed link in this graph from edge i to edge j if i and j are successive edges in some salient contour in S. It is proved in [5] that such a construction induces a partition of the graph into a set of isolated *strongly-connected* components. A strongly-connected component [1] is a set of edges in which any pair of edges i and j have a path from one to the other, i.e., $i \rightsquigarrow j$ as well as $j \rightsquigarrow i$. In general each strongly-connected component will contain multiple salient contours that share common edges. It is shown in [5] that the partition into a set of strongly-connected components is a direct consequence of the property of closure of the contours in S. As noted in the introduction, the strong dependence between the nature of the partition and the property of closure is a distinguishing feature of our approach, as compared with other approaches [2, 3] that employ generic graph search techniques that are not dependent on any specific property of the saliency measures used. More precisely, in our approach, the determination of strongly-connected components makes sense only in the context of using a saliency measure that incorporates closure.

In practice, of course, we do not know the salient contours beforehand. Nevertheless, since the links in the salient contours become the links in the graph, all we need to know is which of the links are salient, i.e. the likelihood that some salient contour passes through a given link. The *link-saliencies* (C_{ij}'s) provide precisely an encoding of such information.

Ideally, the set of edges will be partitioned into

isolated components. However, in practice not all of the components provide reliable segmentations. The dominant contours tend to suppress the saliencies of all other contours to such an extent that the saliencies of these non-dominant contours are not sufficient to induce components that can be isolated reliably. Hence in practice, we begin by extracting the most salient contours. Since such contours will normally pass through the most salient edge, we first identify the contours corresponding to the strongly-connected component containing the most salient edge. Having identified the most salient contours, we suppress their link saliencies in order to reveal the next set of dominant contours. We suppress the current set of dominant contours by deflating the affinities of *all* links among the edges in the strongly-connected component. Specifically, if i and j are edges in the component, then the link $i \rightarrow j$ is deflated by setting $P_{ji} = 0$ (as well as setting the reversal-symmetric "sibling" $P_{\bar{i}\bar{j}} = 0$). We then iterate this process to reveal multiple salient contours.

Again considering the ideal case, the strongly-connected component containing the most salient edge will be isolated from the other components. In practice, due to noise, some of the C_{ij}'s might wrongly indicate that the strongly-connected component containing the most salient edge is connected to one or more of the other strongly-connected components. Nevertheless, we can extract the component of interest by utilizing an important property of strongly-connected components–the set of edges in a strongly-connected component containing a given edge is the intersection of the set of edges reachable from the given edge and the set of edges reachable from the same edge when all the links have their directions reversed [1]. In our case, due to reversal-symmetry, the above property reduces to a particularly simple form. In order to identify the strongly-connected component containing the most salient edge i, we find the intersection of the set of undirected edges reachable from edge i and the set of undirected edges reachable from $\bar{i}$ (note that both i and $\bar{i}$ have the same saliency as discussed in section 3).

5 Results

We show results of our segmentation algorithm on a few real images. All the images were taken using a Kodak DC50 480x480 pixel digital color camera. The Canny edge detector was run on the images after converting them to greyscale, with the parameters $\sigma = 3.0$, low hysteresis threshold = 0.2 and high hysteresis threshold = 0.8. The set of edges returned by the Canny edge detector were found to be quite re-

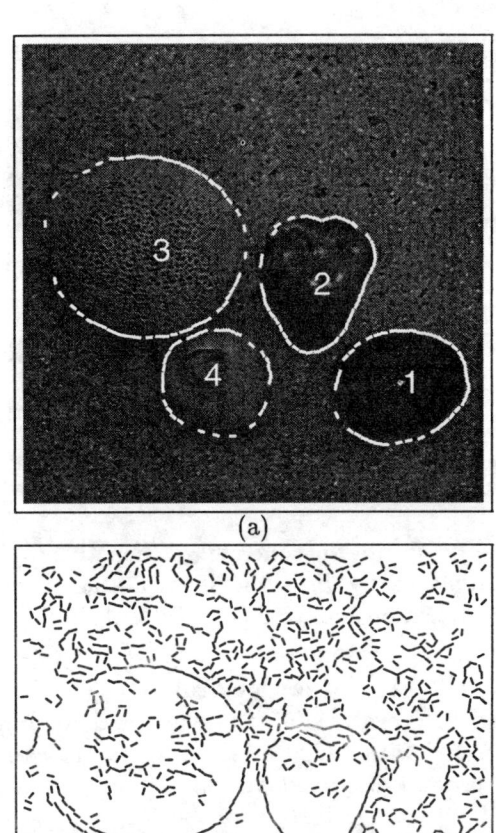

(a)

(b)

Figure 2: Fruits on concrete. (a) Greyscale image with the segmented contours numbered in the order they are extracted (b) Canny edge output.

dundant. The edges are sampled to improve running times with almost no sacrifice in performance. In our experiments we sample the edges such that no two edges are closer than 5 pixels apart.

The entries of the affinity matrix $\mathbf{P}$ were calculated with parameter settings (see § 2 for their descriptions and also [10]) $\gamma = 0.15$, $T = 0.004$ and $\tau = 5.0$. All edge images are remapped to a 64×64 image size. Since the affinity matrix $\mathbf{P}$ has a special symmetry (the reversal symmetry), we had previously developed an algorithm that finds the eigenvector corresponding to the largest eigenvalue of $\mathbf{P}$ (required for the computation of our saliency measures) by exploiting the reversal symmetry. See [11] for details. In our first example we chose a simple scene where non-occluding objects (fruits) were placed on a textured background

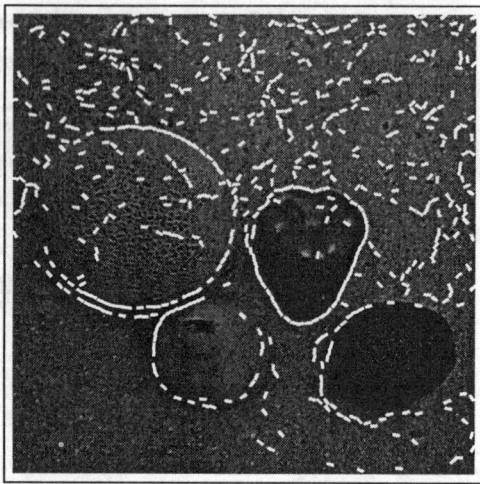

Figure 3: Fruits on concrete. When the C_{ij}'s have been replaced by P_{ij}'s the segmentation during the second iteration breaks down (see text)

Figure 4: Fruits on grass. Greyscale image with segmentations superimposed.

(concrete). Fig. 2 shows four fruits on a concrete background in greyscale (a) and the corresponding edge image (b) (with 2800 directed edges after the sampling process described above). Notice that the contrast between the texture of the fruit on the top-left (a cantelope) and that of the background is quite low. As a result, few edges are detected along some parts of the boundary of the cantelope. Superimposed on Fig. 2 (a) are the contours which are identified during the successive iterations of the segmentation algorithm. It is interesting to note that the contour bounding the cantelope has been extracted despite the fact that there are large gaps in some parts of the contour. We next show the importance of the global information encoded by our link saliencies C_{ij}'s for segmentation by replacing them with the P_{ij}'s that encode only local information. The edge saliencies C_i's are left unchanged. With this replacement, the segmentation algorithm extracts out the same contour in the first iteration as the original algorithm with the C_{ij}'s. Note that this contour is easy to trace out since there are no large gaps present between successive edges of the contour. However, the hard part is to get a starting edge (i.e., the most salient edge in the current iteration) which (for this demonstration) is still being provided by the C_i's. Fig. 3 shows the segmentation after the second iteration. As can be seen, the segmentation completely breaks down. The P_{ij}'s are sufficient as long as we start off from the most salient edge in each iteration and there are no large gaps in the contours being traced. The breakdown in the second iteration shows the need for the more global information encoded in the C_{ij}'s in cases where there are large gaps

in the contours being traced.

The eigen-solver for the matrix $\mathbf{P}$ described above (see [11] for details) is adaptive, the time roughly varying according to the complexity of the contours extracted and the number of edges in it. As expected the first iteration took the least time of 3 sec since the contour extracted is relatively simple. The third iteration took the longest time of 20 sec possibly because of the large gaps in the contour being extracted (bounding the cantelope). The average time for the 4 iterations is 9.9 sec. Fig. 4 shows the same four fruits with grass as the background and with one of the fruits occluding another. Due to poor contrast between the two dark fruits and the background the Canny edge detector does not reliably detect the edges bounding the two fruits. The fruits are hardly salient in the edge image (not shown) even for human observers. Our algorithm can be expected to extract out contours only when provided with reliable edge information. In this case the algorithm picks out only the other two fruits in the image. Of the two fruits that it does pick out, one partly occludes the other. Due to the poor contrast between the two fruits, the edge information (especially the orientation) is quite poor in the region around the occlusion. However, despite this fact, and the fact that the contour bounding the occluded fruit contains a large gap at the occlusion, the algorithm segments out both fruits individually. Finally, Fig. 5 shows an example where there are significant shadows (around the stones) which produce strong smooth contours. However, since they are open contours, they are not as salient as the closed contours bounding the stones and hence do not confuse the algorithm.

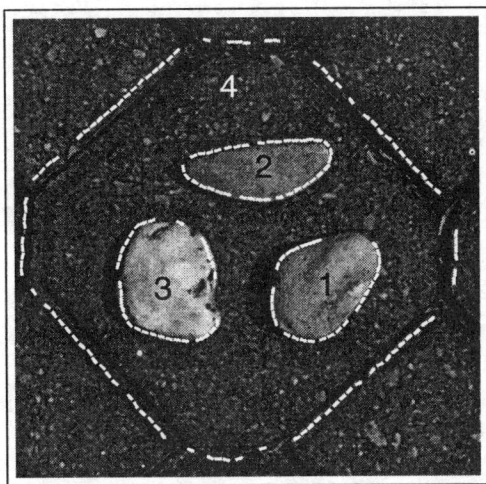

Figure 5: Stones on pavement. Greyscale image with segmentations superimposed.

6 Conclusion

We have demonstrated the usefulness of a saliency measure based on the global property of contour closure in segmenting out multiple closed contours from real images. We have shown the importance of the global information encoded by our link saliencies C_{ij}'s for segmentation as opposed to using just the P_{ij}'s that encode only local information.

Our approach to grouping edges into salient contours involves the solution of an eigen-problem. Recently, other approaches [6, 9, 7] have also proposed grouping image features by solving a corresponding eigen-problem. The normalized minimum-cut approach proposed in [9] can group more general image features than our approach can. However, since we restrict ourselves to grouping edges into salient closed contours, we are able to impose the important constraint of edge-directionality that is not applicable for other features like pixel intensities. Also, imposing edge-directionality results in a non-symmetric affinity matrix $\mathbf{P}$ for which the min-cut approach proposed in [9] does not apply. As noted in § 2, we can get a symmetric affinity matrix if we do not impose edge-directionality, in which case the min-cut approach would apply. However, the symmetric affinity matrix permits contours with cusps at the edges to be salient (see the discussion in § 2). Hence, we would expect poor performance with a min-cut approach when edge-directionality is not imposed. The dominant eigenvector approach that was proposed in [6, 7], while applicable to more general features than edges, also applies only to symmetric matrices and hence cannot exploit edge-directionality. Summarizing, since in this paper, we are interested in finding out how much can be ac-

complished using only edge information, methods that exploit constraints from the specific domain, such as ours, are expected to give better results compared with more general-purpose methods.

The segmentation algorithm assumes a fixed value for the speed γ of the particle modeling the distribution of curves between two given edges. Equivalently, this fixes the effective scale or size for the input image (see § 2). A more principled approach would be able to extract out a contour regardless of the rate at which its edges are sampled. A straightforward approach would be to sweep the scale (by varying the speed γ) in each iteration and find the most salient contour across all scales (see [11]). Contours with different samplings would become dominant at different scales. We are currently investigating this approach and expect it to result in improved, scale-invariant segmentations.

References

[1] Cormen, T.H., Leiserson, C.E. and Rivest, R.L. 1989. *Introduction to Algorithms*, Chapter 23, MIT Press.

[2] Elder, J.H. and Zucker, S.W. 1996. Computing contour closure. In *ECCV '96*, Cambridge, UK. **Vol. I**:14–18.

[3] Jacobs, D. 1993. Robust and Efficient Detection of Convex Groups. In *CVPR*, 770–771.

[4] Lowe, D.G. 1985. *Perceptual Organization and Visual Recognition*, Kluwer, Boston.

[5] Mahamud, S., Thornber, K.K. and Williams, L.R. 1998. Extracting Multiple Salient Closed Contours from Real Images. *NEC Tech. Report 98-120*

[6] Perona, P. and Freeman, W. 1998. A Factorization Approach to Grouping. In *ECCV*, Freiburg, Germany.

[7] Sarkar, S. and Boyer, K. 1996. Quantitative Measures for Change based on Feature Organization: Eigenvalues and Eigenvectors, In *CVPR '96*, San Fransisco, CA.

[8] Shashua, A. and Ullman, S. 1988. "Structural Saliency : The Detection of Globally Salient Structures Using a Locally Connected Network", In *ICCV*, FL.

[9] Shi, J. and Malik, J. 1997. Normalized Cuts and Image Segmentation. In *CVPR '97*, Puerto Rico, USA.

[10] Thornber, K.K. and Williams, L.R. 1996. Analytic Solution of Stochastic Completion Fields. *Biol. Cybern.* **75**:141–151.

[11] Thornber, K.K., Mahamud, S. and Williams, L.R. 1998. The Eigenvalue Problem for Reversal Matrices. *NEC Tech. Report 97-162*

[12] Williams, L.R. and Jacobs, D.W. 1997. Local Parallel Computation of Stochastic Completion Fields. *Neural Computation* **9**:859–881.

[13] Williams, L.R. and Thornber, K.K. 1998. A Comparison of Measures for Detecting Natural Shapes in Cluttered Backgrounds. In *ECCV*, Freiburg, Germany.

A Statistical Approach to Snakes for Bimodal and Trimodal Imagery *

Anthony Yezzi, Jr.   Andy Tsai   Alan Willsky

Department of Electrical Engineering and Computer Science

Massachusetts Institute of Technology

Cambridge, MA 02139

Abstract

In this paper, we describe a new region-based approach to active contours for segmenting images composed of two or three types of regions characterizable by a given statistic. The essential idea is to derive curve evolutions which separate two or more values of a predetermined set of statistics computed over geometrically determined subsets of the image. Both global and local image information is used to evolve the active contour. Image derivatives, however, are avoided, thereby giving rise to a further degree of noise robustness compared to most edge-based snake algorithms.

1 Introduction

A number of region-based approaches to snakes have been proposed in recent years [1, 2, 8, 9, 12, 13] with the tremendous appeal over edge-based approaches of avoiding computations to explicitly detect edges. Such computations typically require derivative information which is extremely sensitive to noise in the image. These approaches also tend to use both local and global image information whereas most edge-based approaches rely primarily on local information around the active contours.

This paper presents a new class of region-based active contour models that assume an image consists of a finite number of regions, characterizable by a predetermined set of features (e.g. means, variances, textures) which may be inferred or estimated from the image data. Curve evolution equations are derived by computing the gradient directions of energy functionals which favor a maximal separation of these features. Introducing a penalty on the length of the active contours gives rise to a class of geometrically constrained clustering algorithms in which data elements are grouped both by value and by mutual proximity. We should point out that the approach presented here

shares common aspects with the region competition approach of Zhu-Yuille [12, 13]. The relationship between the two approaches is discussed in detail in [11].

In contrast to [12, 13] and most other region based approaches to segmentation, we operate on a set of independent curves and use these curves to define a set of regions as opposed to operating on a set of regions and using their boundaries to define a set of curves. The difference may sound subtle at first, but the key benefits of working directly with curves come at the implementation level. In particular, we are able to utilize level set techniques (see Osher and Sethian [7, 10] and the references therein) to implement the flows presented in this paper.

The remainder of this paper is a shortened version of [11], to which we refer the interested reader for all of the details (including the level set implementations) and a much more complete set of references to other curve evolution techniques for segmentation.

2 Binary Flows

In this section, we present gradient flows designed to segment bimodal images via an evolving curve. The flow presented in the first part of this section for simple binary intensity images is offered for the purpose of illustration (since such images are already segmented) and to develop an intuition for more general flows designed for less trivial forms of bimodal imagery.

2.1 Flows for binary images

We begin with the assumption that the domain of an image $I(x, y)$ consists of a foreground region R of intensity I^r and a complementary background region R^c of intensity $I^c \neq I^r$. We wish to determine an evolution that will continuously attract any initial closed curve $\vec{C}$ toward the boundary ∂R of R.

Since an arbitrary closed curve over the domain of I will enclose some portion of R and some portion of R^c, the average intensities u and v inside and outside the curve respectively are bounded above and below by I^r and I^c. Consequently, using the distance between u and v to measure how well $\vec{C}$ has sepa-

---

*This work was supported by ONR grant N00014-91-J-1004, by subcontract GC123919NGD from Boston University under the AFOSR Multidisciplinary Research Program on Reduced Signature Target Recognition, and by ARO grant DAAH04-96-1-0494 through Washington University.

rated the foreground from the background will ensure an upper-bound of $|I^r - I^c|$ that is uniquely attained when $\vec{C} = \partial R$. A related strategy, which also assumes no previous previous knowledge of I^r or I^c, would be to descend along the following quadratic energy functional:

$$E = -\frac{1}{2}(u - v)^2. \qquad (1)$$

Letting $S_u = \int_{R^u} I dA$ and $A_u = \int_{R^u} dA$, where R^u denotes the interior of $\vec{C}$, and expressing their first variations as $\nabla S_u = I\vec{N}$ and $\nabla A_u = \vec{N}$ (see [11] for details), where $\vec{N}$ denotes the outward unit normal of $\vec{C}$, allows us to compute the first variation of $u = S_u / A_u$ as follows:

$$\nabla u = \frac{A_u \nabla S_u - S_u \nabla A_u}{A_u^2} = \frac{A_u I - S_u}{A_u^2}\vec{N} = \frac{I - u}{A_u}\vec{N}.$$

We may use this expression (and a similar expression for ∇v) to compute the following gradient descent curve evolution

$$\frac{d\vec{C}}{dt} = -\nabla E = (u - v)(\frac{I - u}{A_u} + \frac{I - v}{A_v})\vec{N}, \qquad (2)$$

yielding a flow that pulls apart the mean intensities inside and outside the curve as fast as possible.

2.2 Binary images with additive noise

Our previous model may be easily modified to handle greyscale images which are well-approximated by binary images plus additive white noise so long as the the contaminating noise is zero-mean. Clearly, since our cost functional is based on *average* intensity values inside and outside the evolving contour, zero-mean noise away from the contour will not have a significant effect on its evolution. This is not the case for noise in the vicinity of the contour. The contour may end up weaving around or encircling extremely small regions due to noise in order to gain tiny decreases in the cost functional, causing the contour to appear fractal. To counter these effects, we follow the philosophy of Mumford and Shah [5, 6] by incorporating a geometric constraint on the evolving contour via an additional term in the energy functional (1) which penalizes its arclength (analogous to the internal energy term of the original snake formulation in [3]). Doing so yields the following new energy

$$E = -\frac{1}{2}(u - v)^2 + \alpha \int_{\vec{C}} ds, \qquad (3)$$

where $\alpha \geq 0$ and s represents the arclength parameter of $\vec{C}$. Since the gradient direction for length is given

by $\kappa\vec{N}$, where κ denotes the signed curvature of $\vec{C}$, the corresponding gradient descent on E is given by

$$\frac{d\vec{C}}{dt} = (u - v)(\frac{I - u}{A_u} + \frac{I - v}{A_v})\vec{N} - \alpha\kappa\vec{N}. \qquad (4)$$

The influence of the second term in this flow is most strongly felt where the magnitude of the curvature is very large. This helps prevent the contour from wrapping around tiny pieces of noise, with the tradeoff that sharp corners in the underlying binary image may be rounded off by the final contour.

2.3 More general binary flows

Until now we have used the term binary to suggest two separate scalar intensities (greylevels). We may readily generalize our results to the vector-valued case by employing the following more general energy functional:

$$E = -\frac{1}{2}\|u - v\|^2 + \alpha \int_{\vec{C}} ds, \qquad (5)$$

where $u = (u_1, \dots, u_n)$ and $v = (v_1, \dots, v_n)$ now denote average values of some vector-valued measurement $I(x, y) = (I_1(x, y), \dots, I_n(x, y))$ inside and outside the curve respectively. The corresponding gradient flow is given by

$$\frac{d\vec{C}}{dt} = \sum_{i=1}^n (u_i - v_i)(\frac{I_i - u_i}{A_u} + \frac{I_i - v_i}{A_v})\vec{N} - \alpha\kappa\vec{N}. \qquad (6)$$

The measurements $I_1, \dots, I_n$ do not necessarily have to represent image intensities (as in a color image) but may represent wavelet coefficients from a greyscale image or other forms of multi-spectral measurements. With this observation, one could segment an image consisting of two different textures using (6) so long as a distinguishing "texture vector" can be derived.

Finally, the binary approach may be further generalized by considering statistics other than means. The basic idea is to formulate a set of statistics which distinguish the foreground and background regions from each other and then derive curve evolutions to "pull them apart".

Suppose, for example, that an image consists of two regions with identical means but different variances. In this case, one could descend along the following energy functional

$$E = -\frac{1}{2}(\sigma_u^2 - \sigma_v^2)^2 + \alpha \int_{\vec{C}} ds, \qquad (7)$$

where σ_u^2 and σ_v^2 denote the sample variances inside and outside $\vec{C}$, using the corresponding gradient flow:

$$\frac{d\vec{C}}{dt} = \left\{ (\sigma_u^2 - \sigma_v^2)\left(\frac{(I - u)^2 - \sigma_u^2}{A_u} + \frac{(I - v)^2 - \sigma_v^2}{A_v}\right) - \alpha\kappa \right\}\vec{N}. \qquad (8)$$

3 Generalization

In this section, we generalize the methodology of Section 2 to develop flows for segmenting trimodal or more general forms of multimodal imagery. The *binary flows* (2), (4), (6), and (8) of Section 2 partition an image domain into exactly two regions. These regions may be multiply connected, consisting of many individual *subregions*; however, the evolving contour distinguishes just two *classes* of regions at any given time.

In the first part of this section, we present a framework for handling *ternary flows*, which partition an image domain into three different region classes. Later, the approach is generalized for an arbitrary number of classes.

3.1 Ternary flows

We begin our discussion of ternary flows by assuming (for now) that the domain of an image $I(x,y)$ consists of two disjoint, simply connected, foreground regions R^a and R^b and a background region R^c (the complement of $R^a \cup R^b$) with mutually distinct intensities I^a, I^b, and I^c, respectively. A closed curve $\vec{C}_u$ in the domain of I will generally enclose some portion of each region; thus, the average intensity u inside $\vec{C}_u$ can be written as a convex combination of I^a, I^b, I^c (i.e. $u = \alpha I^a + \beta I^b + \gamma I^c$ where $0 \leq \alpha, \beta, \gamma \leq 1$ and $\alpha + \beta + \gamma = 1$). Unfortunately, if I takes its values in $\mathbf{R}$, there is no unique convex combination since any three points in $\mathbf{R}$ are obviously collinear. This poses a problem since the algorithm we are about to present relies upon geometrically independent[1] statistics to distinguish the regions R^a, R^b, and R^c.

To be geometrically independent I^a, I^b, and I^c must belong to $\mathbf{R}^2$ or a higher dimensional space. Accordingly, assume that I is a vector-valued image with vectors in $\mathbf{R}^2$ and that $I^a = (I_1^a, I_2^a)$, $I^b = (I_1^b, I_2^b)$, and $I^c = (I_1^c, I_2^c)$ are geometrically independent. We may now represent $u = (u_1, u_2)$ as a unique convex combination of these three values. The same situation applies to the average intensity v within the interior of a second curve $\vec{C}_v$ and to the average intensity w within the mutual exterior of $\vec{C}_u$ and $\vec{C}_v$. Our segmentation goal is to construct coupled flows that will continuously attract $\vec{C}_u$ toward one of the boundaries ∂R^a or ∂R^b (of R^a and R^b respectively) while simultaneously attracting $\vec{C}_v$ toward the other.

By virtue of their geometric independence, I^a, I^b, and I^c form the vertices of a triangle T_{abc}. As convex combinations of these three values, u, v, and w lie within this triangle, forming another triangle T_{uvw} completely contained in T_{abc}. (This is true even if the

---

interiors of $\vec{C}_u$ and $\vec{C}_v$ overlap, providing a flexibility to our approach that is not provided by region competition in which evolving regions must be disjoint.) As such, the area of the triangle T_{uvw} will always be less than or equal to the area of the triangle T_{abc}, with equality holding if and only if $\vec{C}_u = \partial R^a$ and $\vec{C}_v = \partial R^b$ or vice-versa. We may therefore attract $\vec{C}_u$ and $\vec{C}_v$ toward the desired boundaries without any prior knowledge of I^a, I^b, or I^c by trying to maximize the area of T_{uvw} using the following tri-quadratic energy functional:

$$E = -\frac{1}{2}\det^2(u - w, v - w) = -2\,\text{area}^2(T_{uvw}). \quad (9)$$

If u, v, and w are geometrically independent, then $u - w$ and $v - w$ are linearly independent and therefore yield a nonzero determinant.

By computing the partial variations $\nabla_{\vec{C}_u} E$ and $\nabla_{\vec{C}_v} E$ of this energy functional with respect to $\vec{C}_u$ and $\vec{C}_v$, we may derive the following pair of coupled gradient descent equations (a detailed derivation appears in [11]).

$$\frac{d\vec{C}_u}{dt} = (u_1 v_2 - u_1 w_2 + v_1 w_2 - v_1 u_2 + w_1 u_2 - w_1 v_2) \times$$
$$\left\{ (v_2 - w_2)\frac{I_1 - u_1}{A_u} - (v_1 - w_1)\frac{I_2 - u_2}{A_u} - \right. \quad (10)$$
$$\left. (u_2 - v_2)\frac{I_1 - w_1}{A_w}(1 - \chi_v) + (u_1 - v_1)\frac{I_2 - w_2}{A_w}(1 - \chi_v) \right\} \vec{N}_u$$

$$\frac{d\vec{C}_v}{dt} = (u_1 v_2 - u_1 w_2 + v_1 w_2 - v_1 u_2 + w_1 u_2 - w_1 v_2) \times$$
$$\left\{ (w_2 - u_2)\frac{I_1 - v_1}{A_v} - (w_1 - u_1)\frac{I_2 - v_2}{A_v} - \right. \quad (11)$$
$$\left. (u_2 - v_2)\frac{I_1 - w_1}{A_w}(1 - \chi_u) + (u_1 - v_1)\frac{I_2 - w_2}{A_w}(1 - \chi_u) \right\} \vec{N}_v$$

where $\vec{N}_u$ and $\vec{N}_v$ denote the outward unit normals of $\vec{C}_u$ and $\vec{C}_v$ and χ_u and χ_v denote the characteristic functions over R^u and R^v (the interiors of $\vec{C}_u$ and $\vec{C}_v$ respectively)

When R^u and R^v are disjoint, the evolution of each curve is not directly tied to the other curve. The coupling, arising from the common set of parameters u, v, and w, is indirect. The characteristic functions χ_u and χ_v yield a more direct coupling when the curves overlap. Nevertheless, in both cases, each curve evolves as a separate entity, enabling the use of curve evolution rather than region-based methods. Level set implementations in particular allow automatic merging and splitting of initial contours (see [11] for a discussion of these implementations and their advantages).

Note that the evolution of each curve depends upon statistics computed over every region in the image. In this sense, (10) and (11) comprise a truly global model for segmentation. On the other hand, the need for vector-valued statistics imposes a restriction on the types of data acceptable to our algorithm, The need for a vector-valued statisitic, however, does not necessarily require vector-valued data. Ternary flows may be applied to greyscale images, for example, by considering both means and variances.

3.2 More general ternary flows

We now modify the flows (10) and (11) and their associated energy functional (9) to handle more general forms of trimodal imagery.

First, we allow the vector-valued data I to take its values in $\mathbf{R}^n$ where $n \geq 2$ as opposed to just $\mathbf{R}^2$. Unfortunately, the determinant in (9) no longer makes sense when $n > 2$. However, three noncollinear points, $I^a, I^b, I^c \in \mathbf{R}^n$ still comprise a triangle in $\mathbf{R}^n$, and $u, v, w \in \mathbf{R}^n$, as convex combinations of these values, will always lie inside this triangle (within the context of its two-dimensional plane). We may therefore generalized the ternary energy functional with the same goal of maximizing the area of the triangle T_{uvw}:

$$|\text{area}(T_{uvw})| = \frac{1}{2}\|u - w\|\|v - w\|\sin\theta$$

$$4\,\text{area}^2(T_{uvw}) = \|u - w\|^2\|v - w\|^2 - ((u - w)\cdot(v - w))^2$$

where θ denotes the angle between $u - w$ and $v - w$.

Next, we attach a geometric penalty on the lengths of $\vec{C}_u$ and $\vec{C}_v$ (as in Section 2.2) to handle the presence of zero-mean noise in the image. In general one may penalize the two lengths differently; here we consider an equal penalty and rewrite (9) more generally as

$$E = -2\,\text{area}^2(T_{uvw}) + \alpha\left(\int_{\vec{C}_u} ds + \int_{\vec{C}_v} ds\right) \quad (12)$$

where $\alpha \geq 0$. We now use the previous expression to compute the variation of the first term

$$\nabla(2\,\text{area}^2(T_{uvw})) = \{\bar{w}\cdot\nabla u + \bar{u}\cdot\nabla v + \bar{v}\cdot\nabla w\}\,\vec{N}$$

with the following definitions:

$$\nabla u = (\nabla u_1 \cdot \vec{N}, \dots, \nabla u_n \cdot \vec{N})$$

(likewise for ∇v and ∇w)

$\bar{u}$	$=$	$\tilde{u} - \tilde{v}$,	$\tilde{u}$	$=$	$\hat{u}(\hat{v}\cdot\hat{w})$,	$\hat{u}$	$=$	$u - v$
$\bar{v}$	$=$	$\tilde{v} - \tilde{w}$,	$\tilde{v}$	$=$	$\hat{v}(\hat{w}\cdot\hat{u})$,	$\hat{v}$	$=$	$v - w$
$\bar{w}$	$=$	$\tilde{w} - \tilde{u}$,	$\tilde{w}$	$=$	$\hat{w}(\hat{u}\cdot\hat{v})$,	$\hat{w}$	$=$	$w - u$

Since $\nabla_{\vec{C}_u} v = \nabla_{\vec{C}_v} u = 0$ the gradient descent equations for E become

$$\frac{d\vec{C}_u}{dt} = \left\{\sum_{i=1}^{n}\left(\bar{w}_i\frac{I_i - u_i}{A_u} - \bar{v}_i(1 - \chi_v)\frac{I_i - w_i}{A_w}\right) - \alpha\kappa_u\right\}\vec{N}_u \quad (13)$$

$$\frac{d\vec{C}_v}{dt} = \left\{\sum_{i=1}^{n}\left(\bar{u}_i\frac{I_i - v_i}{A_v} - \bar{v}_i(1 - \chi_u)\frac{I_i - w_i}{A_w}\right) - \alpha\kappa_v\right\}\vec{N}_v \quad (14)$$

where κ_u and κ_v denote the signed curvatures of $\vec{C}_u$ and $\vec{C}_v$ respectively.

3.3 Segmenting more than three regions

In general one may wish to partition an image domain into m different types of regions, where m is an arbitrarily large number. By adhering to the same philosophy of associating the preferred segmentation with a maximal separation of some statistic over each region, a vector-valued statistic, U, with at least $m - 1$ components would be required. If the m distinct values, $U^1, \dots, U^m$, of this statistic constitute a set of geometrically independent points in the preferred segmentation of the image, and if the statistic is chosen such that an arbitrary segmentation yields values $u^1, \dots, u^m$, which are convex combinations of $U^1, \dots, U^m$ (which is the case if we are considering means of a vector-valued image) then the natural energy functional will relate to the volume of the $m-1$ dimensional simplex whose vertices are given by $u^1, \dots, u^m$. The corresponding gradient flow equations will yield a coupled evolution of $m - 1$ curves which tend to maximize the volume of this simplex, with the interiors of each curve representing $m - 1$ regions and their mutual exteriors representing the m'th region.

4 Simulations

In this section, we demonstrate the performance of binary and ternary flows on real data.

Flow (4) is used in Fig. 1, to segment a microscopic image of red blood cells, providing a compelling demonstration of the topological transitions allowed by its level set implementation (see [7, 10, 4, 11] for details). A single initial contour appears in the first frame; the multiple steady state contours and the resulting segmentation, showing the steady state mean intensity values, appear in the last two frames.

The synthetic aperture radar (SAR) image of a forrest's tree line in Fig. 2 constitutes a bimodal image of a rather different nature. Means cannot be used here to distinguish one region from the other. The forrest region in the lower left half of the image and the grassy region in the upper right half of the image give rise to two different textures with approximately the same greyscale mean, but with different variances. Flow

(8), therefore, is able to segment the image quite successfully by separating variances rather than means.

Means and variances may also be used together in this methodology as components of a two-dimensional vector which must be chosen to minimize the energy functional (5). However, due to the dissimilarity between these two statistics, their first variations have different forms. Thus the gradient flow equation is not given by (6) but by a hybrid flow using the sum of the image-driven terms of (4) and (8). Such a flow was used to capture the tadpole dermal cells in the optical coherence tomography (OCT) image of Fig. 3.

The coupled ternary flows (13) and (14) were used to segment the clouds, the sky, and the B-2 bomber from the color image shown in Fig. 4. The final segmentation, showing the steady state mean color intensity values, appears in the last frame.

5 Conclusions

We have presented a novel statistical approach to snakes for the segmentation of images which are known *a priori* to consist of a given number of regions distinguishable by a given set of statistics. The resulting gradient flows, derived from *deterministic* considerations, were designed to essentially pull the values of these statistics as far apart as the data in a given image would allow, subject to geometric constraints on the length of the active contour(s).

Two key attractions of the flows in this paper were a natural use of both local and global information in the image and a deliberate avoidance of differential operators for detecting edges. In addition, our adherence to separate (although coupled) curve evolution equations enabled the use of level set techniques in the implementation of our flows.

To summarize, we have outlined a very general curve evolution approach to segmentation that clusters pixels in an image based upon both geometric and statistical considerations. The performance of our algorithm depends upon how well the chosen set of statistics is able to distinguish the various regions within a given image. Specifically, we have demonstrated the use of means, and variances as the discriminating statistics.

References

[1] A. Chakraborty and J. Duncan, "Game-Theoretic Integration for Image Segmentation," *IEEE Trans. Pattern Anal. Machine Intell.*, vol. 21, no. 1, pp. 12–30, Jan. 1999.

[2] A. Chakraborty, L. Staib, and J. Duncan, "Deformable Boundary Finding in Medical Images by Integrating Gradient and Region Information," *IEEE Trans. Medical Imaging*, vol. 15, no. 6, pp. 859–870, Dec. 1996.

[3] M. Kass, A. Witkin, and D. Terzopoulos, "Snakes: active contour models," *Int. Journal of Computer Vision*, vol. 1, pp. 321–331, 1987.

[4] R. Malladi, J. Sethian, and B. Vemuri, "Shape modeling with front propagation: a level set approach," *IEEE Trans. Pattern Anal. Machine Intell.*, vol. 17, pp. 158–175, 1995.

[5] D. Mumford and J. Shah, "Optimal approximations by piecewise smooth functions and associated variational problems," *Communications in Pure and Applied Mathematics*, vol. 42, no. 4, 1989.

[6] D. Mumford and J. Shah, "Boundary detection by minimizing functonals," *Proceedings of IEEE Conference on Computer Vision and Pattern Recognition*, San Francisco, 1985.

[7] S. Osher and J. Sethian, "Fronts propagation with curvature dependent speed: Algorithms based on Hamilton-Jacobi formulations," *Journal of Computational Physics*, vol. 79, pp. 12–49, 1988.

[8] N. Paragios and R. Deriche, "Geodesic Active Regions for Texture Segmentation," Research Report 3440, INRIA, France, 1998.

[9] R. Ronfard, "Region-Based Strategies for Active Contour Models," *Int. J. Comuter Vision*, vol. 13, no. 2, pp. 229–251, 1994.

[10] J. Sethian, *Level Set Methods: Evolving Interfaces in Geometry, Fluid Mechanics, Computer Vision, and Material Science*, Cambridge University Press, 1996.

[11] A. Yezzi, A. Tsai, and A. Willsky, "A Statistical Approach to Curve Evolution for Image Segmentation," LIDS Technical Report, January, 1999 (submitted to *IEEE Trans. on Pattern Analysis and Machine Intelligence*).

[12] S. C. Zhu, T. S. Lee, and A. L. Yuille, "Region Competition: Unifying snakes, Region Growing, and Bayes/MDL for Multiband Image Segmentation," *Proc. of ICCV*, pp. 416–423, 1995.

[13] S. Zhu and A. Yuille, "Region Competition: Unifying snakes, Region Growing, and Bayes/MDL for Multiband Image Segmentation," *IEEE Trans. on Pattern Anal. Machine Intell.*, vol. 18, no. 9, pp. 884–900, Sep. 1996.

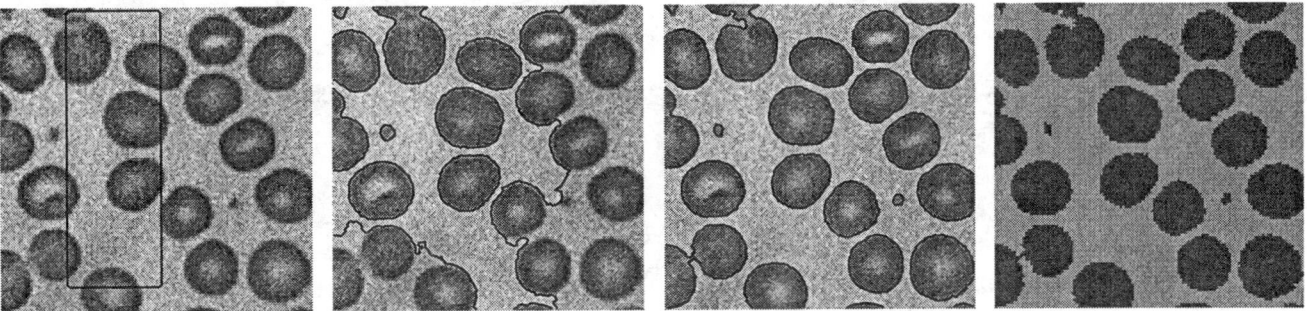

Figure 1: Multiple red blood cells are captured by a single contour using flow (4).

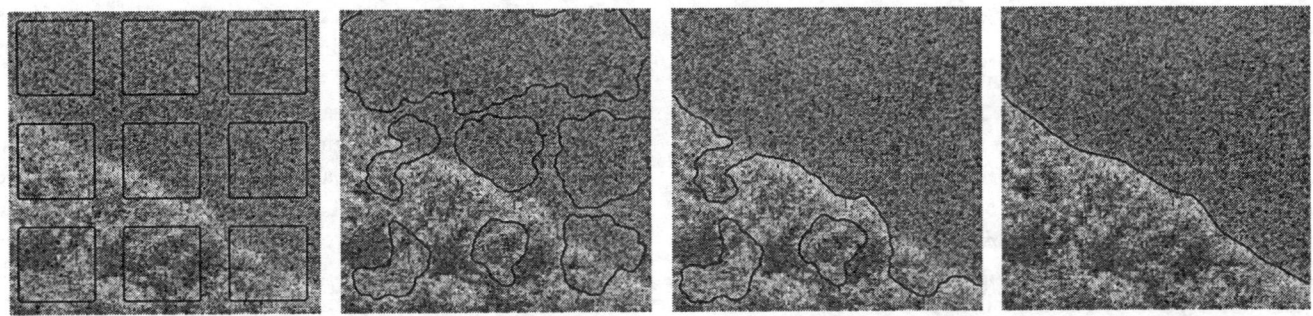

Figure 2: The tree line shown here is captured using flow (8) to separate variances.

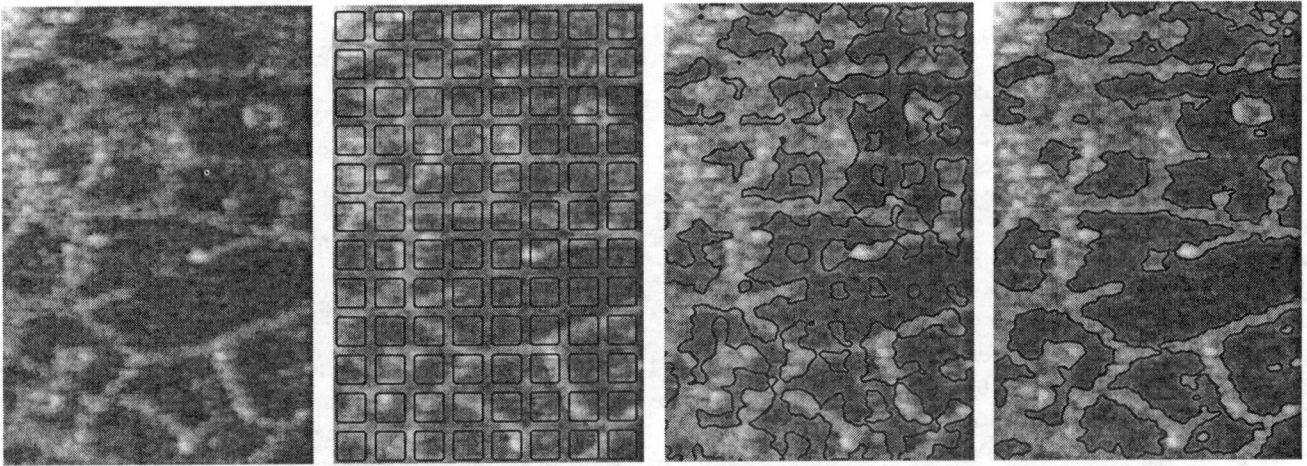

Figure 3: Both means and variances are used to segment this OCT image of tadpole cells (image courtesy of S. Boppart and J. Fujimoto of MIT, and appears in *Nature Medicine*, vol. 4, pp. 861–865, July 1998).

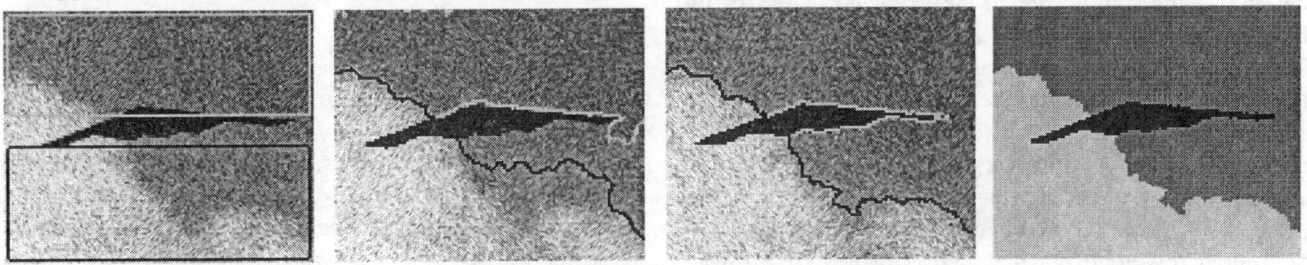

Figure 4: The B-2 bomber, clouds, and sky are captured by coupled flows (13) and (14).

Globally Optimal Regions and Boundaries

Ian H. Jermyn and Hiroshi Ishikawa
Courant Institute of Mathematical Science
New York University, New York, NY, U.S.A.
jermyn@cs.nyu.edu, ishikawa@cs.nyu.edu

Abstract

We propose a new form of energy functional for the segmentation of regions in images, and an efficient method for finding its global optima. The energy can have contributions from both the region and its boundary, thus combining the best features of region- and boundary-based approaches to segmentation. By transforming the region energy into a boundary energy, we can treat both contributions on an equal footing, and solve the global optimization problem as a minimum mean weight cycle problem on a directed graph. The simple, polynomial-time algorithm requires no initialization and is highly parallelizable.

1. Introduction

Image segmentation methods generally fall into two classes, being either region-based or boundary-based. The former class uses properties of areas of the image to choose among possible segmentations, while the latter looks at the properties of the image only on the boundary of the proposed segmented regions.

Both methods have their advantages and drawbacks. Region-based methods tend to be global, optimizing a functional of the image segmentation. On the other hand, they often ignore important boundary properties such as smoothness. Boundary-based approaches can treat such properties very naturally, but suffer from their own difficulties. First, most algorithms find only local minima, and thus have no measure of the significance of the extracted boundary for the image as a whole. Second, although there do exist algorithms guaranteed to find global minima, using graph techniques such as dynamic programming and Dijkstra's algorithm, these do not adapt easily to closed contours. Unfortunately, open contours do not segment regions in the image, so that further processing is needed to group the contours into proto-surfaces. Third, boundary-based methods cannot incorporate region information such as texture easily. In addition, many of the extant algorithms require initialization by the user in some way, by specifying the end-points of the contour, or by defining an initial contour that then evolves to a solution.

In this paper we propose a new form of energy functional for the segmentation of regions in images, and an efficient method for finding its global optima in energy order. The energy is of a very general form (equation (1)), being the modulus of the integral over the region of any integrable function, divided by a measure of the length of the boundary of the region. The solution to the optimization problem is the global maximum of this energy over all regions. The region integral can be transformed to a boundary integral, and then combined with boundary-dependent terms. In this way the energy can have contributions from both the region and its boundary, allowing region information such as texture and homogeneity to be combined with boundary information such as intensity gradients. Once expressed as a boundary integral, we can cast the global optimization problem into the form of a minimum mean weight cycle problem in a digraph. This problem has a simple, polynomial-time algorithm that requires no initialization, and is highly parallelizable, with each pixel able to perform its computations independently, reading from, but never writing to, its neighbours.

The paper is laid out as follows. In the next section, we discuss related work. In section 3, we describe the general form of the energy functional and its properties, and give some examples of possible uses. We discuss the algorithm that globally optimizes such energies and its relation to our problem in section 4. In section 5 we describe some specific models of regions, and show the results of experiments with these models.

2. Related work

Image segmentation has a huge literature, and here we only touch on some of the work more closely related to ours.

Contour-based grouping methods include Parent and Zucker's [20] work using relaxation methods, Sha'ashua and Ullman's [21] work on saliency networks, and Guy and Medioni's [10] work using voting schemes. There is also the work of Cox et al. on a Bayesian sequential tracking scheme [4]. Elder and Zucker [8] have developed a method for finding closed contours using chains of tangent vectors. Williams and Thornber [25, 23] and Williams and Jacobs [24] discuss contour closure using stochastic completion fields. Closest to our work however, because it starts from an energy optimization criterion, is the work on active contours. The seminal works in this area are Kass et al. [14] and Blake and Zisserman [2], and much subsequent work follows this both in the form of the energy functionals used, and in algorithmic techniques. Another body of work applies dynamic programming techniques to minimize the contour energy. Amini et al. [1] use dynamic programming as part of a gradient descent procedure. Montanari [19] uses dynamic programming to find the minimum energy path between given end-points. Geiger et al. [9] use initialization with a series of points, and a choice of window around those points, to delineate the space of contours considered. Much of this work uses initialization and restricted regions of the image to limit the space of contours over which the optimization proceeds, and most algorithms find local minima, or approximations to global minima over a limited set of contours. Globally minimum closed contours are not found.

The paper by Cox, Rao, and Zhong [3] is particularly related to our work. They use a graph algorithm known as the pinned ratio algorithm to find closed contours in an image. The method can be made initialization-free, and finds a global minimum under some weak constraints. Their method is not as general as ours however, as they cannot combine region and boundary information, and the region information they use must be positive everywhere in the image.

Related work in the area of region-based segmentation is that of Shi and Malik [22]. They use a generalized eigenvalue method to find normalized cuts. The denominator in our equation (1) plays a similar role to the cut normalization. Leung and Malik [17] extend their work by incorporating weak contour continuity information into the region-based model.

Psychological work has emphasized the importance of closure in perception since the Gestalt movement. Work in illusory contours has also shown the importance of the Gestalt concept of closure to the perceptual organization involved in these phenomena [11, 12]. More recent work by Kovács and Julesz, and Elder and Zucker has demonstrated that closure is a very important determinant of contour saliency [15, 6, 7].

3. Theoretical framework

An image is a real-valued function I on a domain in $\mathbb{R}^2$. A simple region is denoted $\mathcal{R}$ and its boundary $\partial \mathcal{R}$.

A Gaussian is denoted G, and convolution $*$.

3.1. Combining regions and boundaries

The form of energy functional with which we deal is

$$E(I, \mathcal{R}) = \frac{\left| \int_{\mathcal{R}} f \, dx \, dy \right|}{\int_{\partial \mathcal{R}} g \, ds} \quad (1)$$

where s is the arc length parameter, f is any real-valued function on $\mathbb{R}^2$, and g is any positive real-valued function on $\partial \mathcal{R}$. We define the solution to the optimization problem as the global maximum of E over all regions $\mathcal{R}$. For reasons that will become clear, we note that by assigning two energies to each region, $\pm E(I, \mathcal{R})$, and then minimizing over all such energies, we achieve the same solution. This can be viewed as an assignment of two orientations to each region, and then a minimization over all oriented regions. The denominator is a (possibly weighted) measure of the length of the boundary, and has the effect of damping the scaling behaviour of the energy, which would otherwise have a strong preference for large regions. It also functions as a boundary smoothing term, as follows. If f and g were unity we would be maximizing the area over the length, and fixing the length of the boundary would produce a disc as the solution to the optimization problem. This is also the solution to an active contour model with a fixed length and a smoothing term that is the square of the curvature. In general, the effect of the dependence on area divided by that on length will be to produce smoother boundaries.

The numerator of equation (1) can always be rewritten as an integral over the boundary $\partial \mathcal{R}$ of the region $\mathcal{R}$:

$$E(I, \partial \mathcal{R}) = \frac{\left| \int_{\partial \mathcal{R}} \hat{n} \cdot \vec{A} \, ds \right|}{\int_{\partial \mathcal{R}} g \, ds} \quad (2)$$

where $\hat{n}$ is the normal vector to the boundary, and $\vec{A}$ is defined by the equation $\vec{\nabla} \cdot \vec{A} = f$. Such an $\vec{A}$ always exists. It can for instance be given by the following integrals:

$$\vec{A}_x(x, y) = \frac{1}{2} \int_0^x f(x', y) dx'$$

$$\vec{A}_y(x, y) = \frac{1}{2} \int_0^y f(x, y') dy'$$

There is a choice of constant functions that can be added to this vector field, but the choice does not affect the value of the boundary integral in equation (2). Indeed, we can add any divergence-free vector field and still have the same boundary integral.

Similarly to equation (1), we can view the boundary as having two possible orientations corresponding to the bounding curve running in the two possible directions. Removing the modulus signs and minimizing over all oriented boundaries is then equivalent to the original maximization problem over un-oriented regions.

Remarks

- As advertized, the form of equation (2) allows us elegantly to include boundary as well as region information in our model. Indeed the present work shows that they are essentially the same, although one description may be more appropriate than the other. We can add to $\vec{A}$ any other vector field $\vec{B}$ and still compute the global optimum.

- Averaging the weight of the boundary over a measure of its length has at least two important advantages over unaveraged contour models. First, it removes the uncontrollable dependence on contour length that such models inevitably exhibit. This is most noticeable if the energy has a gradient term and a length term for example. The length term is normally positive, while the gradient term is negative. Depending on the parameters, the global solution could be trivial in one of two ways: infinitely long or infinitely short. These are extreme examples, but the implicit dependence on length is always present. Second, a simple polynomial-time algorithm exists for the minimum mean weight cycle problem, whereas the minimum weight cycle problem is NP-hard.

3.2. Forms of region function

The function f in equation (1) can be any integrable function. In particular, it can be the convolution of the image with any filter F: $f(p) = I * F(p)$. In this case, equation (2) also takes the form of a convolution:

$$E(I, \mathcal{R}) = \frac{\int_{\mathcal{R}} (I * F) \, dx \, dy}{\int_{\partial \mathcal{R}} g \, ds}$$

$$E(I, \partial \mathcal{R}) = \frac{\int_{\partial \mathcal{R}} \hat{n} \cdot (I * \vec{v}) \, ds}{\int_{\partial \mathcal{R}} g \, ds}$$

where $\vec{\nabla} \cdot \vec{v} = F$.

The function f need not be a linear filter however. Some choices of f and their meaning in our model are given below. Throughout we include the possibility of a Gaussian smoothing of the image, or in other words the possibility of examining the image at various scales. The examples are intended to include the case of zero variance, when G is a delta function.

$I * G$. In this case the model is looking for globally maximum intensity regions. It will find bright spots such as specular reflections, as well as large regions of high intensity.

$I * \vec{\nabla}^2 G$. Viewed as a region integral, this function finds the region with the largest absolute value of the integrated Laplacian of the smoothed intensity. Such regions correspond to "lumps" or "dips" in the intensity

function, since regions with undulations in the intensity will make both positive and negative contributions to the region integral, reducing its absolute value. Converted to the form of equation (2), $\vec{A} = I * \vec{\nabla} G$. $\vec{A}$ is thus the vector field of wavelet coefficients. Viewed in this way, the model finds regions whose boundaries pass through points with high smoothed intensity gradient, in a direction perpendicular to the gradient. The model averages over length, thus removing the dependence on scale, and our algorithm finds the globally optimal region and boundary. We investigate such a model in section 5.

$|I * \vec{\nabla}^2 G|$. The previous function does not deal well with the case of contrast-reversing boundaries, which introduce both positive and negative contributions to the region integral. We can deal with the case of general boundaries (including contrast-reversing) using the absolute value of the Laplacian, at the expense of losing a simple boundary interpretation. This region function is a better way to deal with contrast-reversing boundaries than the normal method of taking the magnitude of the gradient, since it preserves the notion that intensity change should be normal to the boundary.

$|I * \vec{\nabla} G|^{-1}$. f is a positive, monotonically decreasing function of the magnitude of the wavelet coefficients $|I * \vec{\nabla} G|$, such as $1/|I * \vec{\nabla} G|$ or $M - |I * \vec{\nabla} G|$ (M is an upper bound on the magnitude of the wavelet coefficients in the image). The integral of such a term over a region will be large if the gradient has small magnitude everywhere. It will thus seek out the region with globally most homogeneous intensity.

$I * T$. A filter T (or linear combination of filters) that responds strongly to a particular class of textures can be used to segment globally optimal regions of that texture.

Most interestingly, the function can be a combination of these examples, so that we could search for the region with the best response to a given texture and that had a high intensity gradient boundary for example, or that had a homogeneous intensity surrounded by a high intensity gradient boundary.

Before passing to a description of the algorithm that we use to solve the global optimization problem, we make two observations about the form of energy functional.

As mentioned, equation (2) has an interesting invariance. If we add to $\vec{A}$ any vector field with zero divergence, we can see by transforming to the form of equation (1) that the energy will not change. When $f = I * \vec{\nabla}^2 G$, this corresponds to adding a harmonic function to the intensity.

Equation (1) is the most general form of energy that we can optimize globally at present (although see section 6). In the experiments we use a slightly restricted form, in which the function g is unity and the length is approximated by an edge count. The algorithms to find the global maximum of the more general case [16, 5, 18] are more complex than the one we describe in section 4. For the sake of clarity, we restrict ourselves to this case.

4. Algorithmic solution

To find the global maximum of the energy in equation (2) (or equivalently equation (1)) we use a graph algorithm due to Richard Karp [13]. This algorithm finds the minimum mean weight cycle in a directed graph.

The algorithm requires no initialization by the user. It is also highly parallelizable, with each pixel able to perform its computations independently, reading from, but never writing to, its neighbours. In the experiment, we iteratively apply the algorithm. After each iteration, we remove from the graph those vertices through which the previous solution passed. We thus find a series of regions of increasing energy, which can be viewed as a series of hypotheses about regions in the image of gradually decreasing probability.

We first describe the algorithm and then clarify its relation to our problem.

4.1. Algorithm

We begin with a weighted directed graph G, with weight function w. We wish to find the minimum mean weight simple cycle, where the mean weight of an edge progression composed of edges $\{e_i : i \in \mathcal{I}\}$ is defined as $\frac{\sum_{i \in \mathcal{I}} w(e_i)}{|\mathcal{I}|}$.

First, define the function $F_k(v)$ taking each vertex $v \in V$ (V is the vertex set) to the weight of the minimum weight path of length $k \geq 0$ to v from an arbitrary start vertex s, and define it to be ∞ if no path exists of length k. Then it can be shown (proof is given in [13]) that the weight λ^* of the minimum mean weight cycle is given by

$$\lambda^* = \min_{v \in V} \max_{k \in [0..(n-1)]} \left\{ \frac{F_n(v) - F_k(v)}{n - k} \right\} \qquad (3)$$

where $n = |V|$.

$F_k(v)$ can be computed using the recurrence

$$F_k(v) = \min_{(u,v) \in E} F_{k-1}(u) + w((u,v))$$

$$F_0(s) = 0$$

$$F_0(v) = \infty , \; \forall v \neq s$$

where E is the edge set of G. With in

The computation of F for all $k \in [0..(n-1)]$ can be performed using dynamic programming in time $O(n|E|)$. The minimum weight paths can be computed simultaneously. Using a further $O(n^2)$ time we can compute λ^* from

$F_k(v)$, leading to an overall computation time of $O(n|E|)$. The cycle itself can be extracted by selecting the minimizing v and k in equation (3), and finding a cycle of length $n - k$ in the minimum weight path from s to v.

4.2. Application

We recall that, as discussed in section 3, if we remove the modulus signs from equations (1) and (2) and view the region and boundary as having two possible orientations, minimizing over all oriented regions or boundaries is equivalent to maximizing equations (1) and (2) over all un-oriented regions or boundaries.

To cast our problem in the form of a minimum mean weight cycle problem, we embed a directed graph in the image, with the property that for every two vertices, u and v, if (u, v) is an edge then (v, u) is also. Thus each cycle can have two possible orientations. The embedding η takes each vertex v to a point $\eta(v)$, and each edge $e = (s, t)$ to a tangent vector $\eta(e)$ located at the median point of $\eta(s)$ and $\eta(t)$, and directed from $\eta(s)$ to $\eta(t)$. The unit normal vectors $\hat{n}(e)$ required by equation (2) can then be defined from the tangent vectors by a fixed rotation. A region boundary is then by definition a simple cycle in this graph.

The weight of an edge $e = (u, v)$ is defined as $\Delta s \{\hat{n}(e) \cdot \vec{A}\}$, where the vector field $\vec{A}$ is evaluated at the midpoint of the edge, and so lies in the same tangent space as $\hat{n}(e)$. Δs is the Euclidean distance between $\eta(u)$ and $\eta(v)$, and plays the role of the measure ds in equation (2). Note that because $\hat{n}(e)$ is defined using a fixed orientation from the tangent vectors, the weights of edges between the same two points but in opposite directions will have the same absolute value but opposite sign. This ensures that the weights of cycles that differ only in orientation will have the same absolute value but opposite sign, as required when we remove the modulus signs and minimize over oriented boundaries in equation (2). Summing the edge weights so defined over a cycle in the graph then gives a discrete version of the numerator in equation (2).

We can now apply the minimum mean weight cycle algorithm to find the solution to our problem on this discrete domain. If the graph is dense enough in the image plane, we will have a good solution to the continuous problem.

5. Experiments

For the bulk of the experiments, we chose $f = I * \vec{\nabla}^2 G$ in equation (1). Thus we are finding regions over which the absolute value of the integral of the Laplacian is as large as possible. These correspond to "lumps" or "dips" in the intensity function, since regions with undulations in the intensity will make both positive and negative contributions to the region integral, reducing its absolute value. With

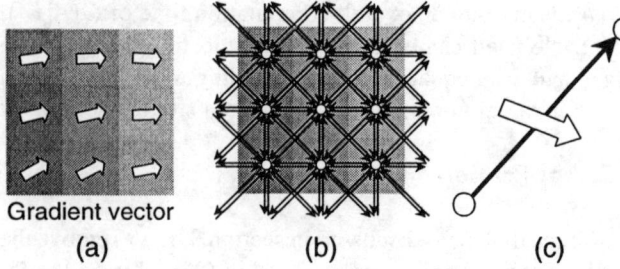

Gradient vector

(a)   (b)   (c)

Figure 1. (a) For each pixel we compute the gradient vector. (b) The graph has a node for each pixel and eight outgoing edges for each node (except at the boundary.) (c) The edge weight is calculated by taking a cross product of the gradient vector and the edge vector.

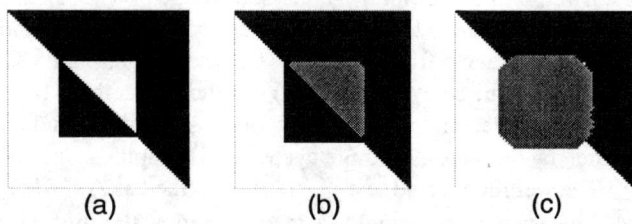

(a)   (b)   (c)

Figure 2. (a) A synthetic contrast-reversing boundary. (b) The result of applying the region energy $I * \vec{\nabla}^2 G$. (c) The result of applying the region energy $|I * \vec{\nabla}^2 G|$. The region found is shown in grey.

this choice of f, the vector field $\vec{A}$ in equation (2) becomes $I * \vec{\nabla} G$, the wavelet coefficients of the image at a scale dictated by the width of G. (We took the width to be small, of the order of a few pixels, so that we are dealing with a very slightly blurred estimate of the gradient at pixel scale.) As a boundary integral, the energy becomes

$$E(I, \partial \mathcal{R}) = \frac{\int_{\partial \mathcal{R}} \hat{n} \cdot (I * \vec{\nabla} G) \, ds}{\int_{\partial \mathcal{R}} ds} \qquad (4)$$

The integrand in equation (4) is minimal when the boundary tangent vector is perpendicular to the intensity gradient.

To apply the algorithm of section 4, we used a directed graph with an eight-valent node for each pixel (Figure 1). For each node, we computed the gradient vector at the pixel

by taking a wavelet coefficient:

$$\vec{A} = (I * \vec{\psi}_s)(\vec{x})$$
$$\vec{\psi}_s(\vec{x}) = s^{-1} \vec{\psi}(s^{-1} \vec{x})$$
$$\vec{\psi}(\vec{x}) = \pi^{-1} e^{-|\vec{x}|^2} \vec{x},$$

where "$*$" denotes a convolution and $\vec{\psi}$ is the derivative of a Gaussian. For an edge going from node $n_{\vec{u}}$ to node $n_{\vec{v}}$ corresponding to pixels $\vec{u}$ and $\vec{v}$, the edge weight is computed as

$$(\vec{v} - \vec{u}) \times \frac{\vec{A}(\vec{u}) + \vec{A}(\vec{v})}{2}.$$

This is the cross product of the tangent vector with length equal to the Euclidean distance between the nodes with the wavelet coefficients. This is the same as taking the dot product of the coefficients with the appropriately oriented normal vector, and weighting by the Euclidean distance between the nodes.

We iteratively applied the algorithm explained in section 4. After each iteration, we removed from the graph those vertices through which the previous solution passed. In this way a series of regions of increasing energy was extracted. This can be viewed as a series of hypotheses about regions in the image of gradually decreasing probability. Results are shown in Figure 3. The numbers indicate the order in which the regions were found. The finding of specularities (and their reverse - dark spots) by the method is to be expected as these are isolated peaks or troughs in the image. Although potentially interesting, these tiny regions can be eliminated by the addition of a term that favors larger areas (for example homogeneity).

In order to illustrate that the method can also deal with the case of contrast-reversing boundaries, we took a synthetic image and used the region function $|I * \vec{\nabla}^2 G|$. The results are shown in Figure 2. They illustrate that replacing the Laplacian by its absolute value finds contrast-reversing boundaries. The expansion of the region found beyond the contrast-reversing boundary is a consequence of using an edge count instead of the geometrical length. It results in multiple degenerate solutions, one of which is illustrated. Use of the more sophisticated algorithm mentioned at the end of section 3.2 would break the degeneracy and pick out the (correct) solution of minimum length.

We note that the region functions used in the experiments have no parameters. The scale at which we compute the gradient is variable, but we chose a small pixel-size scale beforehand, and stayed with it throughout the experiments.

6. Conclusion

In this paper we proposed a new form of energy functional for the segmentation of regions in images, and an

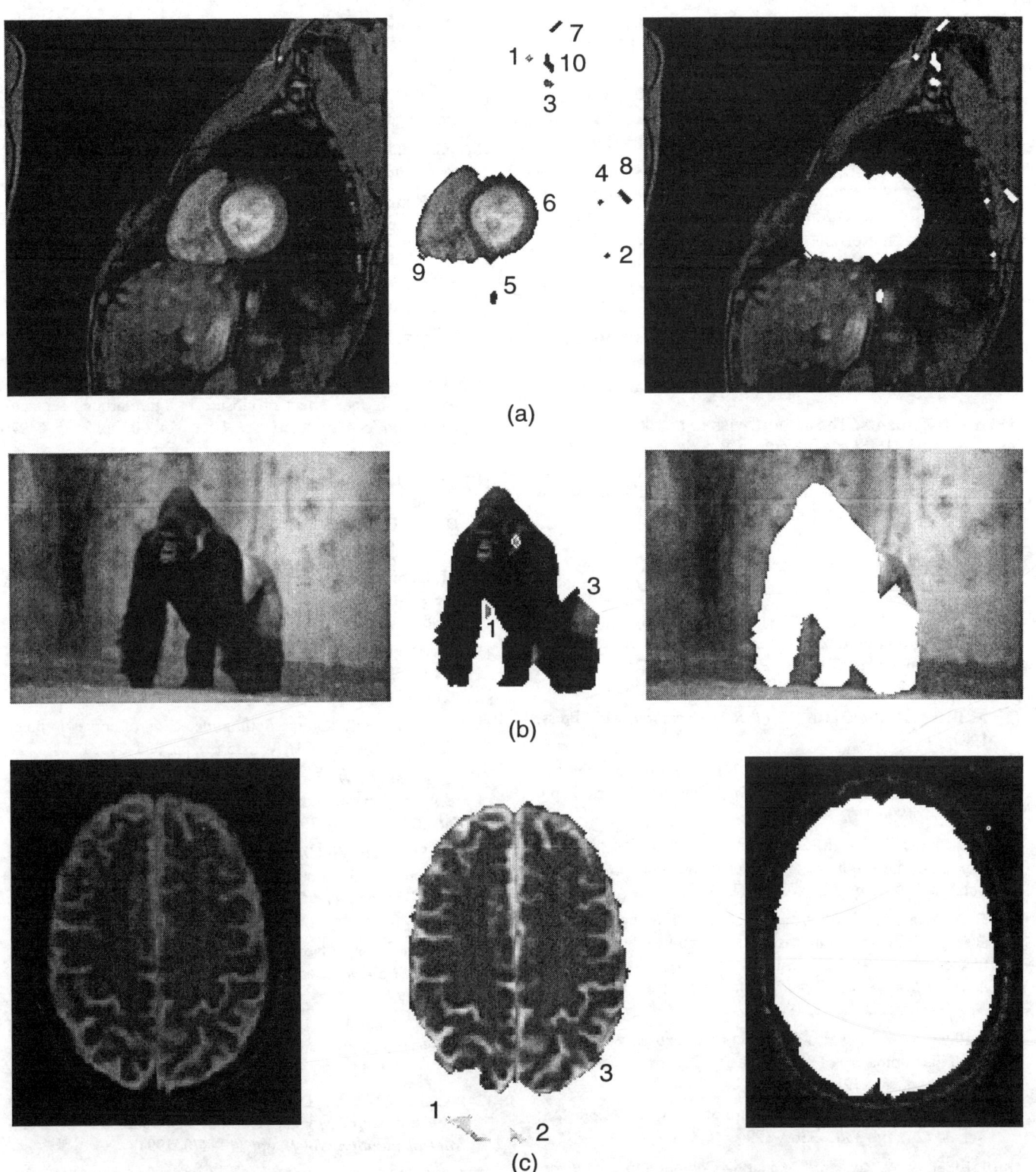

Figure 3. (a) A 256 × 256 pixel image. Ten regions are shown. (b) A 200 × 134 pixel image. Shown are three least energy regions (the left ear, under the right arm, and the gorilla.) (c) A 124 × 166 pixel image. Three regions are shown. The numbers indicate the order in which the regions were found.

efficient method for finding its global optima in energy order. The energy can have contributions from both the region and its boundary, thus allowing typical region information such as texture and homogeneity to be combined with typical boundary information such as intensity gradients. The two types of energy are transformable into each other however, and by transforming the region energy into a boundary energy we can cast the global optimization problem into the form of a minimum mean weight cycle problem in a digraph. This problem has a simple, polynomial-time algorithm that requires no initialization, and is highly parallelizable. We described experiments using combinations of region and boundary information that illustrate the strength of the method. The energy is of a very general form, although always globally optimizable by the same algorithm, and offers many other possibilities for further modeling.

Acknowledgments. The authors wish to thank the Instituto de Matemática Pura e Aplicada in Rio de Janeiro for their generous hospitality, and Professor Davi Geiger for his advice and encouragement. This work was partially supported by grant number MURI-AFOSR 25-74100-F1837.

References

[1] A. Amini, S. Tehrani, T. Weymouth, "Using dynamical programming for minimizing the energy of active contours in the presence of hard constraints," *Proc. Int'l Conf. Comp. Vis.*, pp. 95–99, 1988.

[2] A. Blake, A. Zisserman, *Visual Reconstruction*, MIT Press, 1987.

[3] I. J. Cox, S. B. Rao, Y. Zhong, "Ratio regions: a technique for image segmentation," *Proc. Int'l Conf. Patt. Rec.*, 2, pp. 557–564, 1996.

[4] I. J. Cox, J. M. Regh, S. Hingorani, "A bayesian mulitple-hypothesis approach to edge grouping and contour segmentation," *Int'l J. Comp. Vis.*, Vol. 11 (1), 1996.

[5] G. B. Dantzig, W. Blatner, M. R. Rao, "Finding a cycle in a graph with minimum cost to time ratio with application to the ship routing problem," in *Theory of Graphs: International Symposium*, Dunod, Paris, and Gordon and Breach, New York, pp. 209–213, 1966.

[6] J. Elder, S. W. Zucker, "The effect of contour closure on the rapid discrimination of two-dimensional shapes," *Vision Res.*, Vol. 33, pp. 981–991, 1993.

[7] J. Elder, S. W. Zucker, "A Measure of Closure," *Vision Res.*, Vol. 34 (24), pp. 3361–3369, 1994.

[8] J. Elder, S. W. Zucker, "Computing Contour Closure," *Proc. Euro. Conf. Comp. Vis.*, pp. 399–412, June, 1996.

[9] D. Geiger, A. Gupta, L. Costa, J. Vlontzos, "Dynamic progra-

[10] G. Guy, G. Medioni, "Inferring global perceptual contours from local features," *Int'l J. Comp. Vis.*, Vol. 20 (1-2), 1996.

[11] G. Kaniza, "Contours without gradients or cognitive contours," *Italian Jour. Psych.*, Vol. 1, pp. 93–112, 1971.

[12] G. Kaniza, *Organization in Vision: essays on gestalt perception*, Praeger, New York, p. 150, 1979.

[13] R. Karp, "A characterization of the minimum cycle mean in a digraph," *Dis. Math.*, Vol. 23, pp. 309–311, 1978.

[14] M. Kass, A. Witkin, and D. Terzopoulos, "Snakes: Active Contour Models," *Int. J. Comp. Vis.*, Vol. 1 (4), pp. 321–331, 1988.

[15] I. Kovács, B. Julesz, "A closed curve is much more than an incomplete one: effect of closure in figure-ground segmentation," *Proc. Natl. Acad. Sci. USA*, Vol. 90, pp. 7495–7497, 1993.

[16] E. L. Lawler, "Optimal cycles in doubly weighted linear graphs," in *Theory of Graphs: International Symposium*, Dunod, Paris, and Gordon and Breach, New York, pp. 209–213, 1966.

[17] T. Leung, J. Malik, "Contour continuity in region based image segmentation," *Proc. Euro. Conf. Comp. Vis.*, Germany, 1998.

[18] N. Meggido, "Combinatorial optimization with rational objective functions," *Mathematics of Operations Research*, Vol. 4, pp. 414–424, 1979.

[19] U. Montanari, "On the optimal detection of curves in noisy pictures," *Comm. ACM*, Vol. 15 (5), pp. 335–345, 1971.

[20] P. Parent, S. W. Zucker, "Trace inference, curvature consistency, and curve detection ," *IEEE Trans. Patt. Anal. Mach. Intell.*, Vol. 11 (8), 1989.

[21] A. Sha'ashua, S. Ullman, "Structural saliency: the detection of globally salient structures using a locally connected network," *Proc. Second. Int'l Conf. Comp. Vis.*, Florida, USA, 1988.

[22] J. Shi, J. Malik, "Normalized Cuts and Image Segmentation," *Proc. IEEE Conf. Comp. Vis. Patt. Rec.*, Puerto Rico, pp. 731–737, 1997.

[23] K. K. Thornber, L. R. Williams, "Analytic Solution of Stochastic Completion Fields," *Biological Cybernetics*, Vol. 75, pp. 141–151, 1996.

[24] L. R. Williams, D. W. Jacobs, "Stochastic Completion Fields: A Neural Model of Contour Shape and Salience," *Neural Computation*, Vol. 9, pp. 849–870, 1997.

[25] L. R. Williams, K. K. Thornber, "A Comparison of Measures for Detecting Natural Shapes in Cluttered Backgrounds," *Proc. Euro. Conf. Comp. Vis.*, pp. 432–448, June, 1998.

mming for detecting, tracking, and matching deformable contours," *IEEE Trans. Patt. Anal. Mach. Intell.*, Vol. 17 (3), pp. 294–302, 1993.

3D Surface Topography from Intensity Images

Philip L. Worthington   Edwin R. Hancock

Department of Computer Science, University of York, UK.

{plw,erh}@cs.york.ac.uk

Abstract

This paper demonstrates how a new shape from shading scheme can be used to extract topographic information from 2D intensity imagery. The shape-from-shading scheme has two novel ingredients. Firstly, it uses a geometric update procedure which allows the image irradiance equation to be satisfied as a hard-constraint. This not only improves the data-closeness of the recovered needle-map, but also removes the necessity for extensive parameter tuning. Secondly, we use curvature information to impose topographic constraints on the recovered needle-map. The topographic information is captured using the shape-index of Koenderink and VanDoorn [12] and consistency is imposed using a robust error function. We show that the new shape-from-shading scheme leads to a meaningful topographic labelling of 3D surface structures.

1 Introduction

Shape-from-shading (SFS) provides an appealing yet elusive route to understanding 3D surface structure via the $2\frac{1}{2}$D sketch [16, 6]. The process has been been an active area of research for over two decades, and has been tackled in a variety of ways since the pioneering work of Horn and his co-worker's in the 1970's [6, 7, 9, 2, 11].

The classical approach to shape-from-shading is couched as an energy minimisation process using the apparatus of variational calculus [7, 8]. Here the aim is to iteratively recover a needle-map representing local surface orientation by minimising an error-functional. The functional contains a data-closeness term, and a regularizing term that controls the smoothness of the recovered needle-map. Since the recovery of the needle-map is under-constrained, the variational equations must be augmented with boundary constraints.

Despite considerable progress in the recovery of needle-maps using SFS [2, 11, 17], there are few examples of the use of the method for 3D surface analysis and recognition from 2D imagery [1]. This is a disappointing omission since

there is strong psychophysical evidence that shading information is a useful shape cue [13, 14], albeit in providing qualitative shape information rather than a quantitatively accurate measure. This leads us to take a pragmatic approach to SFS in this paper, in which we are more concerned with recovering a rich, qualitatively correct and stable representation than attempting to recover quantitatively accurate surfaces. This is a novel departure based upon the evidence of what the human visual system can, and more significantly, can't do with shading information alone [13, 14].

In traditional SFS, the failure to recover surface detail has led to few attempts at using the needle-map for high-level goals such as object recognition. We have recently embarked on a programme to use SFS as a source of information for 3D surface analysis and recognition. We have commenced by bringing the apparatus of robust statistics to bear on the problem of needle-map recovery [19]. By using robust error kernels to model the smoothness of the needle map, we have limited some of the problems of over-smoothing of surface detail. We have also shown how the needle-map can be used for view-based object recognition [20]. Here SFS has been shown to deliver usable information for a simple histogram-based recognition scheme.

Encouraged by these first results, we are currently investigating how more sophisticated surface representations can be elicited from 2D intensity imagery using SFS. In particular, we would like to capture the differential or topographic structure of surfaces. Although this is a routine procedure in range imagery, there has been little effort directed at extracting topographic structure using shape-from-shading. One notable exception is the work of Lagarde and Ferrie [4], in which the curvature consistency process of Sander and Zucker [18] is applied to the needle map as a post-processing step to improve the organisation of the field of principal curvature directions.

To meet the goal of recovering topographic information, we present a new SFS algorithm. The algorithm is based on a geometric interpretation of the ambiguity structure of the IIR in the under-constrained conditions that apply in SFS. At each image location, the brightness is taken to constrain the corresponding normal to a cone of possible directions.

The axis of the cone points in the light source direction. We can impose organisation on neighbouring surface normals by allowing them to rotate on their respective cones so as to satisfy consistency constraints. Here we impose the neighbourhood organisation constraints in such a way as to encourage curvature consistency. Our modelling of curvature consistency uses Koenderink and Van Doorn's shape index [12]. This is a scale-invariant measure which captures the different topographic classes using a continuous angular variable. Using the shape index allows surfaces to be segmented into meaningful topographic structures such as ridges or valleys, saddle points or lines, and, domes or cups. These structures can be further organised into simply connected elliptical or hyperbolic regions which are separated from one-another by parabolic lines. Our consistency model uses robust error kernels to model acceptable local variations in the shape-index. The model encourages parabolic structures (i.e. ridges and ruts) to be thin and contour-like. Hyperbolic and elliptical structures (domes, cups etc.) are encouraged to form contiguous regions.

2 A Novel Framework for SFS

Central to SFS is the idea that local regions in an image $E(x, y)$ correspond to illuminated patches of a piecewise continuous surface, $z(x, y)$. The measured brightness $E(x, y)$ will vary depending on the material properties of the surface (whether matte or specular), the orientation of the surface at the co-ordinates (x, y), and the direction of illumination.

The *reflectance map*, $R(p, q)$ characterizes these properties, and provides an explicit connection between the image and the surface orientation. The surface orientation is characterised by the components of the surface gradient in the x and y direction, i.e. $p = \frac{\partial z}{\partial x}$ and $q = \frac{\partial z}{\partial y}$. SFS aims to recover the surface $z(x, y)$ from the image $E(x, y)$, or alternatively the set of surface normals or *needle-map*, may be the goal.

To simplify the problem, most research has concentrated on recovering ideal Lambertian surfaces illuminated by a single point source located at infinity [3]. A Lambertian surface has a matte appearance and reflects incident light uniformly in all directions. Hence, the light reflected by a surface patch in the direction of the viewer is simply proportional to the orientation of the patch relative to the light source direction. If $\mathbf{n} = (-p, -q, 1)^T$ is the local unit surface normal, and $\mathbf{s} = (-p_l, -q_l, 1)^T$ the global light source direction, then the normalized reflectance function is given by $R(p, q) = \mathbf{n} \cdot \mathbf{s}$.

The IIR states that the measured brightness of the image is proportional to the radiance at the corresponding point on the surface, which is $R(p, q)$. Normalising both image intensity and reflectance map, the constant of proportionality becomes unity, and the IIR is simply $E(x, y) = R(p, q)$.

Since the recovery of both p and q is underconstrained by the IIR, the traditional approach of iterative, global SFS has been to cast the problem in a regularization framework using some form of smoothness constraint. However, the principal criticism of the Horn and Brooks algorithm [3] and similar approaches, is the tendency to over-smooth the recovered needle-map. Specifically, the smoothness term dominates the data term. Since the smoothness constraint is formulated in terms of the directional derivatives of the needle-map, it is trivially minimised by a flat surface. Thus, the conflict between the data and the model leads to a strongly smoothed needle-map and the loss of fine-detail. The problem is exacerbated by the need to select a conservative value for the regularization Lagrange multiplier in order to ensure numerical stability [9].

Horn [9] attempts to reduce the model dominance problem by annealing the Lagrange multiplier to reduce the influence of the smoothness constraint as a final solution is approached. Meanwhile, we have used the apparatus of robust statistics to moderate the penalization of discontinuities [19].

The idea underpinning our new framework for shape-from-shading is to guarantee data-closeness by treating the IIR as a hard constraint. In other words, we aim to recover a valid needle-map which satisfies the IIR at every iteration. Subject to this data-closeness constraint, the task of SFS becomes that of iteratively improving the needle-map estimate. Here, we do this using curvature consistency constraints.

Our approach is a geometric one. We view the IIR as defining a cone of ambiguity about the light source direction for each surface normal. The individual surface normals which constitute the needle-map can only assume directions which fall on this cone. At each iteration the updated normal is free to move away from the cone under the action of the local consistency constraints. However, it is subsequently mapped back onto the closest normal residing on the cone. By applying this constraint, we gain dual advantages in terms of both numerical stability and obviating the need for a Lagrange multiplier.

2.1 Hard Constraints

The new framework requires us to minimize the constraint functional

$$I_C = \int \int \psi\left(\mathbf{n}(x, y), \mathbf{N}(x, y)\right) dx dy \qquad (1)$$

whilst satisfying the hard constraint, imposed by the image irradiance equation

$$\int \int (E - \mathbf{n} \cdot \mathbf{s}) \, dx dy = 0 \qquad (2)$$

Here, $\mathbf{N}(x,y)$ is the set of local neighbourhood vectors about location (x,y). The function $\psi\left(\mathbf{n}(x,y),\mathbf{N}(x,y)\right)$ is a localized function of the current surface normal estimates. The size of the neighbourhood may be varied according to the nature of ψ. Clearly, it is possible to incorporate the hard data-closeness constraint directly into ψ, but this needlessly complicates the mathematics. Instead, we choose to impose the constraint after each iteration by mapping the updated normals back to the most similar normal lying on the cone. The resulting update equation for the surface normals can be written as

$$\mathbf{n}_{i,j}^{k+1} = \Theta \hat{\mathbf{n}}_{i,j}^k \qquad (3)$$

where $\hat{\mathbf{n}}_{i,j}^k$ is the surface normal that minimises the constraint functional I_C. The hard image irradiance constraint is imposed by a rotation matrix, Θ, which maps the updated normal to the closest normal lying on the cone of ambiguity. Another way to look at this is that we allow the smoothness constraint to select the direction of the normal estimate in the image plane only, whilst fixing the angle between the normal estimate and the light source direction.

To achieve the rotation, we define an axis perpendicular to the intermediate update normal, $\bar{\mathbf{n}}_{i,j}^k$, and the light source direction. The axis of rotation is found by taking the cross-product of the intermediate update normal with the light source direction

$$(u,v,w)^T = \bar{\mathbf{n}}_{i,j}^k \times \mathbf{s} \qquad (4)$$

The angle of rotation is the difference between the angle subtended by the intermediate update and the light source, and the apex angle of the cone of ambiguity. Since the image is normalized, the latter angle is simply $\cos^{-1} E$, giving a rotation angle of

$$\theta = -\cos^{-1}\left(\frac{\bar{\mathbf{n}}_{i,j}^k \cdot \mathbf{s}}{\|\bar{\mathbf{n}}_{i,j}^k\| \, \|\mathbf{s}\|}\right) + \cos^{-1} E \qquad (5)$$

Hence, the rotation matrix is given by

$$\Theta = \begin{pmatrix} c + u^2 c' & -ws + uvc' & vs + uwc' \\ ws + uvc' & c + v^2 c' & -us + vwc' \\ -vs + uwc' & us + vwc' & c + w^2 c' \end{pmatrix}$$

where $c = \cos(\theta)$, $c' = 1 - c$, and $s = \sin(\theta)$.

2.2 Initialization

The new framework requires an initialization which ensures that the IIR is satisfied. This differs from the Horn and Brooks algorithm, which is usually initialized by estimating the occluding boundary normals, with all other normals set to point in the light source direction.

We choose to initialize each normal such that its projection onto the image plane lies in the opposite direction to the image gradient direction. This results in an initialization with an implicit bias towards convex rather than concave surfaces. We have also applied this initialization to the Horn and Brooks algorithm in place of the traditional occluding boundary initialization, and find that it produces significantly better and faster results.

3 Needle Map Smoothness

Before we describe our modelling of curvature consistency, we pause to consider how needle-map smoothness can be incorporated into our new framework for shape-from-shading. In a recent paper [19], we showed how needle-map smoothness could be modelled using robust error kernels. Here the adopted framework was based on a regularised energy-function similar to that underpinning the Horn and Brooks algorithm. However, rather than using a quadratic smoothness prior, we used a continuous variant of the Huber robust error kernel. In this section we show how this smoothness model can be used in conjunction with our geometric needle-map update process In essence, we consider that the recovered surface should be smooth, except where there is a high probability that a discontinuity is present, in which case the smoothing is reduced.

We define the robust regularizer constraint function as

$$\psi\left(\mathbf{n},\mathbf{N}\right) = \rho_\sigma\left(\left\|\frac{\partial \mathbf{n}}{\partial x}\right\|\right) + \rho_\sigma\left(\left\|\frac{\partial \mathbf{n}}{\partial y}\right\|\right) \qquad (6)$$

where $\rho_\sigma(\eta)$ is a robust kernel defined on the residual η and with width parameter σ. Applying the calculus of variations to the resulting constraint function I_C yields the general update equation

$$\mathbf{n}_{i,j}^{(k+1)} = \Theta\left(\frac{\partial}{\partial x}\rho_\sigma'\left(\left\|\frac{\partial \mathbf{n}}{\partial x}\right\|\right) + \frac{\partial}{\partial y}\rho_\sigma'\left(\left\|\frac{\partial \mathbf{n}}{\partial y}\right\|\right)\right) \qquad (7)$$

where

$$\rho_\sigma'\left(\left\|\frac{\partial \mathbf{n}}{\partial x}\right\|\right) = \frac{\partial}{\partial \mathbf{n}_x}\left(\rho_\sigma\left(\left\|\frac{\partial \mathbf{n}}{\partial x}\right\|\right)\right) \qquad (8)$$

and similarly for $\rho_\sigma'\left(\left\|\frac{\partial \mathbf{n}}{\partial y}\right\|\right)$.

In [19] we experiment with several robust error kernels, including Li's Adaptive Potential Functions [15], and the Tukey [5] and Huber [10] estimators. However, the sigmoidal-derivative M-estimator, a continuous version of Huber's estimator, proved to possess the best properties for handling surface discontinuities, and is defined to be

$$\rho_\sigma(\eta) = \frac{\sigma}{\pi}\log\cosh\left(\frac{\pi\eta}{\sigma}\right) \qquad (9)$$

The robust regularizer approach provides significantly improved results over the simple Horn and Brooks smoothness constraint, but at the expense of introducing the parameter, σ.

4 Curvature Consistency

Needle-map smoothness appears to be an over-strong and inappropriate constraint for shape from shading. This is primarily because real surfaces are more likely to be *piecewise* smooth; in other words, formed of smooth regions separated by sharp discontinuities in depth or orientation. Here we take a different tack by using curvature consistency. Although the curvature classes either side of a depth discontinuity may be completely unrelated, this is not the case for an orientation discontinuity. Orientation discontinuities usually correspond to surface ruts or ridges. Furthermore, the curvature classes for locations either side of a rut or a ridge should be the most similar classes, either trough or saddle rut for a rut, or dome or saddle ridge for a ridge. This property of smooth variation in class suggests that curvature consistency may be a more appropriate constraint for SFS than smoothness, which strongly penalises legitimate orientation discontinuities.

The use of a curvature consistency measure was introduced to SFS by Ferrie and Lagarde [4]. They use global consistency of principal curvatures [18] to refine the surface estimate returned by local shading analysis. An alternative method of representing curvature information is to use $H - K$ (Mean and Gaussian curvature) labels, but these require us to set 4 thresholds to define the classes in terms of the mean and Gaussian curvatures. However, here we propose to use curvature consistency based upon the shape index of Koenderink and van Doorn [12]. This is a continuous measure which encodes the same curvature class information as $H - K$ labels in a single, angular representation.

4.1 The Shape Index

We reformulate the definition of the shape index in terms of the needle-map. This allows us to use the needle-map directly, rather than needing to reconstruct the surface.

The differential structure of a surface is captured by the Hessian matrix, which may be approximated in terms of surface normals by

$$\mathcal{H} = \begin{pmatrix} \left(\frac{\partial \mathbf{n}}{\partial x}\right)_x & \left(\frac{\partial \mathbf{n}}{\partial x}\right)_y \\ \left(\frac{\partial \mathbf{n}}{\partial y}\right)_x & \left(\frac{\partial \mathbf{n}}{\partial y}\right)_y \end{pmatrix} \qquad (10)$$

where $(\cdots)_x$ and $(\cdots)_y$ denote the x and y components of the parenthesized vector respectively.

The eigenvalues of the Hessian matrix, found by solving the eigenvector equation $|\mathcal{H} - \kappa \mathbf{I}| = 0$, are the principal curvatures of the surface.

Koenderink and van Doorn [12] defined the shape index

$$\phi = \frac{2}{\pi} \arctan \frac{\kappa_2 + \kappa_1}{\kappa_2 - \kappa_1} \qquad \kappa_1 \geq \kappa_2 \qquad (11)$$

By approximating the principal curvatures in terms of surface normals, we obtain the shape index in terms of normal estimates

$$\phi = \frac{2}{\pi} \arctan \frac{\left(\frac{\partial \mathbf{n}}{\partial x}\right)_x + \left(\frac{\partial \mathbf{n}}{\partial y}\right)_y}{\sqrt{\left(\left(\frac{\partial \mathbf{n}}{\partial x}\right)_x - \left(\frac{\partial \mathbf{n}}{\partial y}\right)_y\right)^2 + 4\left(\frac{\partial \mathbf{n}}{\partial x}\right)_y \left(\frac{\partial \mathbf{n}}{\partial y}\right)_x}} \qquad (12)$$

Figure 1 shows the range of shape index values, the type of curvature which they represent, and the grey-levels used to display different shape-index values.

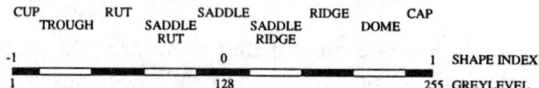

Figure 1. The shape index scale ranges from -1 to 1 as shown. The shape index values are encoded as a continuous range of grey-level values between 1 and 255.

4.2 Adaptive Robust Regularizer Using Curvature Consistency

As stated above, since the shape index is an angular, physical measure, we expect it to vary gradually over a smooth surface. For instance, with reference to Figure 1, we would not expect the shape index at adjacent pixels to differ by more than one curvature class unless they lie on opposite sides of a surface discontinuity. Since the over-smoothing effect of the quadratic smoothness constraint stems directly from the indiscriminate averaging of normals lying across a discontinuity, we anticipate that weighting according to curvature consistency will reduce the problem in a physically-principled manner.

To meet these goals we use curvature consistency to control the robust weighting kernel applied to the variation in the needle-map direction. The idea is a simple one. We use the variance of the shape-index in the neighbourhood $\mathbf{N}$ to control the width σ of the robust error-kernel applied to the directional derivatives of the needle map. The kernel width determines the level of smoothing applied to the surface normals in the neighbourhood. If the variance of the shape index is large i.e. the neighbourhood contains a lot of topographic structure, then we choose a small kernel width. This rejects outliers and allows significant local variation in the local needle-map direction. From a topographic viewpoint, we can see the rationale for this choice by considering the behaviour of the needle-map and the shape-index at ridges and ravines. For such features, the direction of the needle-map changes rapidly in a particular direction. These two structures are parabolic lines which intercede between elliptic and hyperbolic regions. As a result there is a rapid local variation in shape index. Turning our attention to the case where the shape-index variance is small, then the kernel width is large. This is the case when we are situated in a hyperbolic or elliptic region. Here the shape-index is locally uniform and the needle-map direction varies slowly.

Once again, we use the robust error-kernel to model needle-map smoothness. As a result, we have

$$\psi\left(\mathbf{n}, \mathbf{N}\right) = \rho_\sigma \left(\left\| \frac{\partial \mathbf{n}}{\partial x} \right\| \right) + \rho_\sigma \left(\left\| \frac{\partial \mathbf{n}}{\partial y} \right\| \right) \quad (13)$$

where again $\mathbf{N}$ is the set of local neighbourhood normals used to calculate the finite difference approximations to $\frac{\partial \mathbf{n}}{\partial x}$ and $\frac{\partial \mathbf{n}}{\partial y}$. However, instead of using a fixed kernel of width, σ, we adapt the width. The variance dependance of the kernel is controlled using the exponential function

$$\sigma = \sigma_0 \exp \left(- \left(\frac{1}{N} \sum_{l \in \mathbf{N}} \frac{(\phi_l - \phi_c)^2}{\Delta \phi_d^2} \right)^{\frac{1}{2}} \right) \quad (14)$$

Here ϕ_c is the shape index associated with the central normal of the neighbourhood, $\mathbf{n}_{i,j}$, ϕ_l is one of the neighbouring shape-index values and $\Delta \phi_d$ is the difference in shape index between the centre values of adjacent curvature classes. The number of neighbourhood normals used in calculating the finite difference approximations to $\frac{\partial \mathbf{n}}{\partial x}$ and $\frac{\partial \mathbf{n}}{\partial y}$ is denoted N, and σ_0 is a reference kernel width which we set to unity. Using the scale of Figure 1, $\Delta \phi_d = \frac{1}{8}$.

The update is identical to Equation 7, but with locally adaptive kernel width.

5 Experiments

In this section we provide some experimental evaluation of the new shape-from-shading technique. The evaluation focuses on the quality of the shape-index information extracted from the intensity images used in our experiments. The images used in our study are taken from the Columbia University COIL data-base. We furnish some comparison between the use of curvature consistency constraints and the simple needle-map smoothness constraint.

We commence in Figure 2 by showing comparing the shape index labels recovered using curvature consistency compared to the new framework used in conjunction with quadratic smoothness. Note that the Horn and Brooks algorithm yields considerably worse labelling than the latter.

Using the curvature consistency scheme, the elliptic and hyperbolic region classes become more connected while the parabolic lines (i.e. ridges and ravines) become thinner and more continuous. In contrast, using the smoothness constraint leads to loss of the ridge and ravine structure. The regions are noisy and exhibit poor connectivity.

The shape index images generated using curvature consistency contain some features which merit special mention. In particular the ruts defining the boundaries of the wing of the duck are well segmented. In addition, the slot in the top of the piggy-bank is correctly identified as rut. Whilst the scheme is not absolutely accurate in its labelling, it does represent a good approximation from a single image. In subsequent experiment, we consider questions of stability and robustness, which we would argue are at least as important as accuracy for the purpose of object recognition.

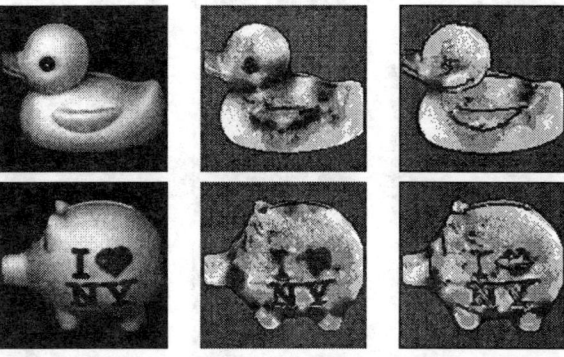

Figure 2. Shape index labelling of images. Left column: input images. Middle column: shape index labelling using the new framework with a quadratic smoothness constraint. Right column: shape index labels recovered using curvature consistency.

Figure 3 demonstrates that the curvature classes recovered using shape-from-shading are relatively stable to viewpoint changes. Here we show six views of a toy-duck. Notice how the valley lines around the beak and the wing are well recovered at each viewing angle. Also notice how the shape of the saddle structure below the wing is maintained.

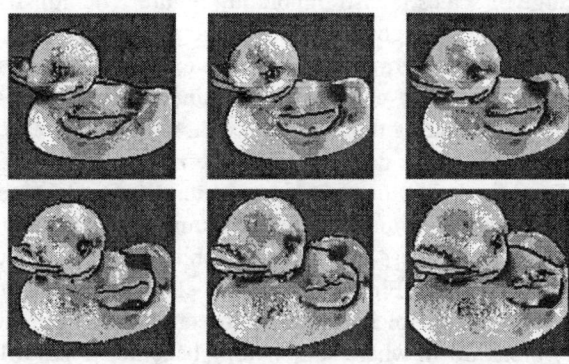

Figure 3. As the duck rotates by 10° intervals, left to right and top to bottom, the labelling remains consistent

Another important property of our scheme is its relative stability to occlusion, in the sense that the effects of an occluding object remain localized. This is also important in situations where segmentation is difficult, since we wish to recover a labelling independent of background clutter. In Figure 4 we demonstrate qualitatively that the topographic labelling is not significantly disrupted by the presence of an occluding object, and that any disruption is localized.

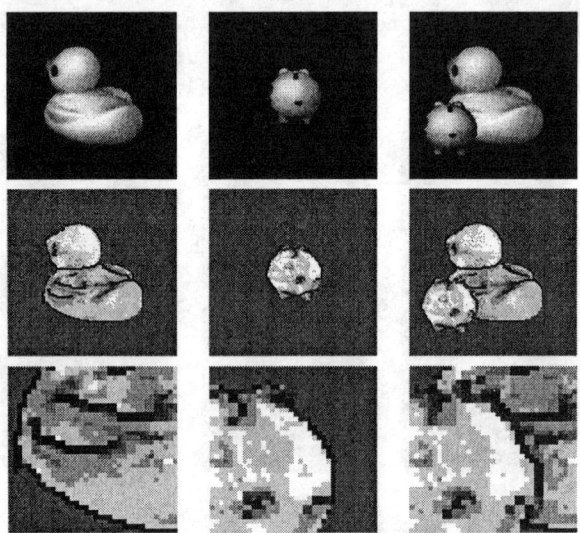

Figure 4. Effects of occlusion. Top row: duck image,piggy-bank image and the piggy-bank occluding the duck. 2nd row: corresponding shape index labels. Bottom row: zoom of details of the duck, the piggy-bank, and the occlusion region. Note that the labels away from the occlusion boundary are relatively un-affected, and even those at the boundary are only changed by around one curvature class at most by the disruption.

The capability to provide consistency of labelling over a range of scales is also important. Figure 5 demonstrates that the curvature consistency scheme provides good scale invariance. Furthermore, the scheme exhibits considerable robustness to both changes in illumination direction, and errors in estimating the light source direction (Figure 6).

Since the COIL database does not include images taken under variable illumination, we use images of a plaster dolphin model taken under different illuminations to demonstrate the robustness of the topographic labelling to actual lighting changes (Figure 7). The labels remain consistent over a 60° range of illumination direction, and in practice only break down where self-shading becomes a major factor.

6 Conclusions

This paper has presented a new shape-from-shading algorithm which uses curvature consistency to extract topo-

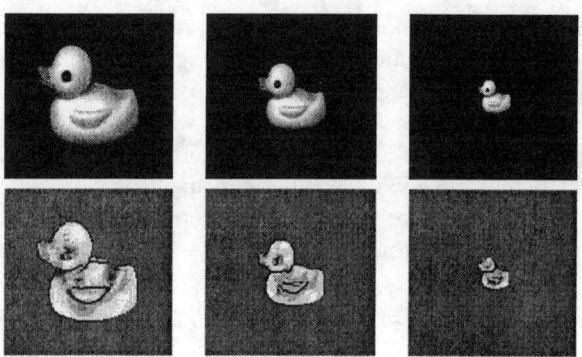

Figure 5. Effect of scale on labelling. Top row: images of duck reduced to 60%, 40% and 20% of original size. 2nd row: corresponding shape index labels. Note that the labelling remains consistent throughout, allowing for sampling effects.

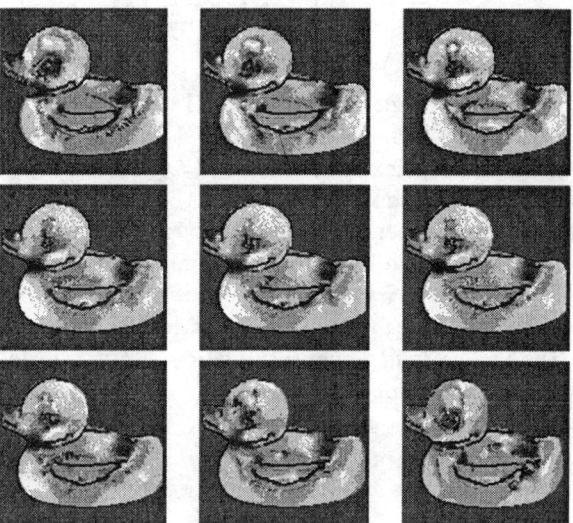

Figure 6. Results of mis-estimation of light source direction. The middle image shows the labelling resulting from the correct estimate of light source direction (0,0,1). Top row, left to right: illumination "estimated" at −30° to (0,0,1) in the x-direction, −20° and −10°. 2nd row: −5°, 0° (correct) and 5°. Bottom row: 10°, 20° and 30°. The labelling is relatively consistent over most of the object for even large errors in light source direction estimation.

graphic information from 2D intensity images. The approach has two novel ingredients. Firstly, we provide a geometric framework for needle-map recovery. This process iterates between two steps. Firstly, we modify the local surface normal direction to satisfy local consistency constraints. Secondly, we back-project the updated normals onto a cone of shading ambiguity so as to satisfy the image

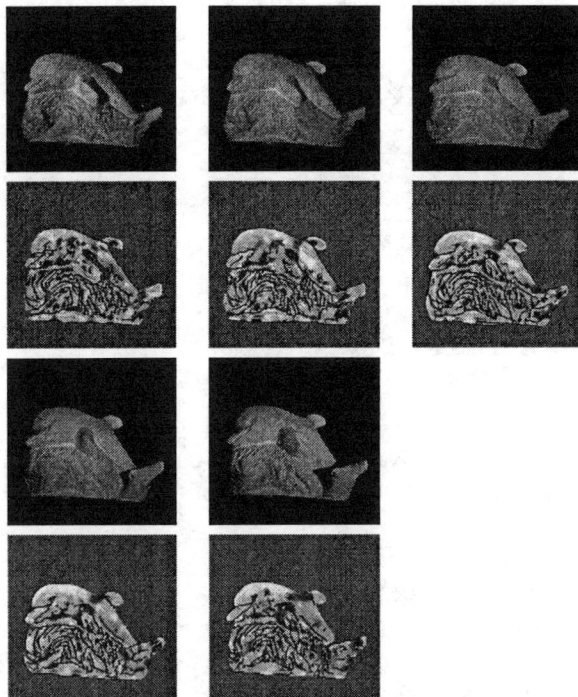

Figure 7. Labelling an object under variable illumination. Top row, left to right: images of object illuminated from $-30°$, $-15°$ and $0°$ to perpendicular in the x-direction. Second row, corresponding labelings. Third row: illumination $15°$ and $30°$. Bottom row: corresponding labelings.

irradiance equation as a hard constraint. The second novel contribution resides in the modelling of curvature consistency. Here we use the Koenderink and Van Doorn shape-index as a measure of surface topography. We use the variance of the shape-index to control the width of a robust error kernel which controls needle-map smoothness errors. In this way we ensure that the local smoothness of the needle-map responds to the variability of the local surface topography. We illustrate the comparative advantages of the new method on real-world imagery from the COIL object databas. Here it proves to be reliable in delivering both smooth elliptic and hyperbolic regions together with thin and continuous parabolic lines. Moreover, we have demonstrated that the labelling generated by our scheme posessesses excellent properties which make it potentially useful for object recognition. These properties include scale invariance, robustness to light-source estimation erros, stability to variable illumination and localization of occlusion effects.

Our future plans revolve around exploiting the topographic information delivered by the new shape-from-shading scheme for 3D object recognition from 2D imagery.

References

[1] Belhumeur, P.N. and Kriegman, D.J. (1996) What is the Set of Images of an Object Under All Possible Lighting Conditions? *Proc. CVPR*, pp. 270-277.

[2] Bichsel, M. and Pentland, A.P. (1992) A Simple Algorithm for Shape from Shading, *Proc. CVPR*, pp. 459-465.

[3] Brooks, M.J. and Horn, B.K.P. (1986) Shape and Source from Shading, *IJCAI*, pp. 932-936, 1985.

[4] Ferrie, F.P. and Lagarde, J. (1990)Curvature Consistency Improves Local Shading Analysis, *Proc. ICPR*, Vol. I, pp. 70-76.

[5] Hoaglin, D.C., Mosteller, F. and Tukey, J.W. (eds.) (1983) *Understanding robust and exploratory data analysis,* Wiley, New York.

[6] Horn, B.K.P. (1975) Obtaining Shape from Shading Information. In Winston, P.H. (ed.), *The Psychology of Computer Vision,* McGraw Hill, NY, pp.115-155.

[7] Horn, B.K.P. and Brooks, M.J. (1986) The Variational Approach to Shape from Shading, *CVGIP*, Vol. 33, No. 2, pp. 174-208.

[8] Horn, B.K.P. and Brooks, M.J. (eds.), *Shape from Shading,* MIT Press, Cambridge, MA, 1989.

[9] Horn, B.K.P. (1990) Height and Gradient from Shading, *IJCV,* Vol. 5, No. 1, pp. 37-75.

[10] Huber, P. (1981) *Robust Statistics,* Wiley, Chichester.

[11] Kimmel, R. and Bruckstein, A.M. (1995) Tracking Level Sets by Level Sets: A Method for Solving the Shape from Shading Problem, *CVIU*, Vol. 62, No. 1, pp. 47-58.

[12] Koenderink, J.J. and van Doorn, A.J. (1992) Surface Shape and Curvature Scales, *IVC*, Vol. 10, pp. 557-565.

[13] Koenderink, J.J. and van Doorn, A.J. (1995) Relief - Pictorial and Otherwise, *IVC*, Vol. 13, No. 5, pp. 321-334.

[14] Koenderink, J.J., van Doorn, A.J., Christou, C. and Lappin, J.S. (1996) Perturbation study of shading in pictures, *Perception,* Vol. 25, No. 9, pp. 1009-1026.

[15] Li, S.Z. (1995) Discontinuous MRF Prior and Robust Statistics: a Comparative Study, *IVC*, Vol.13, No.3, pp. 227-233.

[16] Marr, D.C. (1982), *Vision,* Freeman, San Francisco.

[17] Pentland, A.P. (1984) Local Shading Analysis, *IEEE PAMI,* Vol. 6, pp. 170-187.

[18] Sander P. and Zucker S.W., "Inferring Surface Structure and Differential Structure from 3D Images", *IEEE PAMI*, **12**, 833-854, 1990.

[19] Worthington, P.L. and Hancock, E.R. (1998) Needle Map Recovery using Robust Regularizers, *IVC*, Vol. 17, No. 8, pp.545-558.

[20] Worthington P.L., Huet B. and Hancock E.R., "Appearance based object recognition using shape-from-shading", Proc. Int. Conf. Pattern Recognition, pp. 412–416, 1998.

[21] Worthington, P.L. and Hancock, E.R. (1999) Data-driven Shape-from-Shading using Curvature Consistency, *Proc. CVPR*, Vol. I, pp. 287-293.

Textons, Contours and Regions: Cue Integration in Image Segmentation

Jitendra Malik, Serge Belongie, Jianbo Shi and Thomas Leung
Computer Science Division
University of California at Berkeley
Berkeley, CA 94720
{malik,sjb,jshi,leungt}@cs.berkeley.edu

Abstract

This paper makes two contributions. It provides (1) an operational definition of textons, the putative elementary units of texture perception, and (2) an algorithm for partitioning the image into disjoint regions of coherent brightness and texture, where boundaries of regions are defined by peaks in contour orientation energy and differences in texton densities across the contour.

Julesz introduced the term texton, analogous to a phoneme in speech recognition, but did not provide an operational definition for gray-level images. Here we re-invent textons as frequently co-occurring combinations of oriented linear filter outputs. These can be learned using a K-means approach. By mapping each pixel to its nearest texton, the image can be analyzed into texton channels, each of which is a point set where discrete techniques such as Voronoi diagrams become applicable.

Local histograms of texton frequencies can be used with a χ^2 test for significant differences to find texture boundaries. Natural images contain both textured and untextured regions, so we combine this cue with that of the presence of peaks of contour energy derived from outputs of odd- and even-symmetric oriented Gaussian derivative filters. Each of these cues has a domain of applicability, so to facilitate cue combination we introduce a gating operator based on a statistical test for isotropy of Delaunay neighbors. Having obtained a local measure of how likely two nearby pixels are to belong to the same region, we use the spectral graph theoretic framework of normalized cuts to find partitions of the image into regions of coherent texture and brightness. Experimental results on a wide range of images are shown.

1 Introduction

This paper has twin objectives. It provides (1) an operational definition of textons, the putative elementary units of image analysis, and (2) an algorithm for partitioning the image into disjoint regions based on both brightness and texture. These objectives are coupled—cue integration relies on, and thus reveals, the advantages of the texton representation.

1.1 Introducing Textons

Julesz introduced the term *texton*, analogous to a phoneme in speech recognition, more than 20 years ago [9] as the putative units of preattentive human texture perception. He described them qualitatively for simple binary line segment stimuli—oriented segments, crossings and terminators—but did not provide an operational definition for gray-level images. Subsequently, texton theory fell into disfavor as a model of human texture discrimination as accounts based on spatial filtering with orientation and scale-selective mechanisms which could be applied to arbitrary gray-level images became popular.

There is a fundamental, well recognized, problem with linear filters. Generically, they respond to any stimulus. Just because you have a response to an oriented odd-symmetric filter doesn't mean there is an edge at that location. It could be that there is a higher contrast bar at some other location in a different orientation which has caused this response. Tokens such as edges or bars or corners can not be associated with the output of a single filter. Rather it is the signature of the outputs over scales, orientations and order of the filter that is more revealing.

Here we introduce a further step by focussing on the *outputs* of these filters considered as points in a high dimensional space (typically on the order of 36 filters are used). We perform vector quantization, or clustering, in this high-dimensional space to find prototypes. Call these prototypes *textons*—we will find empirically that these do tend to correspond to oriented bars, terminators and so on. One can construct a universal texton vocabulary by processing a large number of natural images, or we could find them adaptively in windows of images. In each case the *k*-means technique can be used. By mapping each pixel to the texton nearest to its vector of filter responses, the image can be analyzed into texton channels, each of which is a point set.

It is our opinion that the analysis of an image into textons will prove useful for a wide variety of visual processing tasks. For instance, in [13] we use the related notion of 3D textons for recognition of textured materials. In the present paper, our objective is to develop an algorithm for the segmentation of an image into regions of coherent brightness and texture–we will find that the texton representation will enable us to address the key problems in a very natural fashion. Let's begin with a review of the outstanding issues in low level image segmentation.

1.2   Challenges in image segmentation

Scale selection in textured regions continues to be a fundamental problem–whatever one's choice of textured descriptor, it has to be computed over a local window whose size and shape need to be determined adaptively. What makes scale selection a challenge is that the technique must deal with the wide range of textures–regular such as the polka dots in Figure 8(b), stochastic in Figure 8(a), or intermediate cases such as the stripes of the tiger in Figure 8(c)–in a seamless way. Furthermore it would be desirable if in the neighborhood of boundaries, the windows over which texture descriptors are computed could be shaped to lie largely on the correct side of the boundary.

The other major issue is dealing with images which have both textured and untextured regions. Here boundaries must be found using *both* contour and texture analysis. However what we find in the literature are approaches which concentrate on one or the other.

Contour analysis (e.g. edge detection) may be adequate for untextured images, but in a textured region it results in a meaningless tangled web of contours. Think for instance of what an edge detector would return on the snow region in Figure 8(a). The traditional "solution" for this problem in edge detection is to use a high threshold so as to minimize the number of edges found in the texture area. This is obviously a non-solution–such an approach means that low-contrast extended contours will be missed as well. There is no recognition of the fact that extended contours, even weak in contrast, are perceptually significant.

While the perils of using edge detection in textured regions have been noted before (see eg. [2]), a complementary problem of contours constituting a problem for texture analysis does not seem to have been recognized before. Typical approaches are based on measuring texture descriptors over local windows, and then computing differences between window descriptors centered at different locations. Boundaries can then give rise to thin strip-like regions, as in Figure 1. For specificity, assume that the texture descriptor is a histogram of linear filter outputs computed over a window. Any histogram window near the boundary of the two regions will contain large filter responses from filters oriented along the direction of the edge. However, on both

sides of the boundary, the histogram will indicate a featureless region. A segmentation algorithm based on, say, χ^2 distances between histograms, will inevitably partition the boundary as a group of its own. As is evident, the problem is not confined to the use of a histogram of filter outputs as texture descriptor. Figure 1 (b) shows the actual groups found by an EM style algorithm using an alternative color/texture descriptor [1].

(a)   (b)

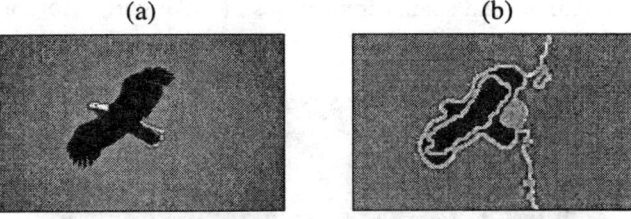

Figure 1. Demonstration of the "contour-as-a-texture" problem using a real image. (a) Original image of a bald eagle. (b) The groups found by an EM style algorithm [1].

1.3   Our approach

We pursue image segmentation in the framework of Normalized Cuts introduced by Shi and Malik [18]. The image is considered to be a weighted graph where the nodes are pixels and arc weights denote a local measure of similarity between the two pixels. Grouping is performed by finding eigenvectors of the Normalized Laplacian of this graph. The fundamental issue then is that of specifying the arc weights W_{ij}; we rely on normalized cuts to go from these local measures to a globally optimal partition of the image.

The algorithm begins by analyzing the image into textons (§2). In the next stage (§3), we determine for every pixel a suitable local neighborhood, the appropriate window for computing the local texture descriptor, and a measure of the anisotropy of this neighborhood. A histogram of texton densities is used as the texture descriptor. We use a gating operator based on a statistical test for isotropy of Delaunay neighbors. These computations critically rely on the spatial analysis of individual texton channels. The fact that each texton channel is a point set is very convenient, because it enables one to use discrete techniques such as Voronoi diagrams and Delaunay triangulations.

We are now ready (§4) to specify the arc weights W_{ij} combining both brightness and texture information. The texture cue is coded by making the arc weight dependent on χ^2 differences between local texton histograms; and the brightness cue is treated in the *intervening contour* framework of Leung and Malik [12] using peaks in contour orientation energy. The anisotropy of the local descriptor window at a pixel serves to gate between these cues so as to circumvent the problems listed in §1.2.

Results from the algorithm are presented in §5.

2 Filters and Textons

Since the early 1980s, many approaches have been proposed in the computer vision literature that employ *filter-based* descriptions of images [6, 10, 14]. By the term *filter-based* we mean that the fundamental representation for a pixel in an image includes not only its brightness or color information, but also the inner product of the neighborhood centered on that pixel with a set of filters tuned to various orientations and spatial frequencies. (See Figure 2 for an example of such a filter set.)

Figure 2. Gaussian derivative filter set consisting of 2 phases (even and odd), 3 scales (spaced by half-octaves), and 6 orientations (equally spaced from 0 to π). The basic filter is a difference-of-Gaussian quadrature pair with 3 : 1 elongation. Each filter is divided by its L_1 norm for scale invariance.

As discussed for example in [8, 11], vectors of filter responses have many appealing properties, including relationships to physiological findings in the primate visual system [3] and to the basic mathematical notion of a Taylor series expansion.

Though the representation of textures using filter responses is extremely versatile, one might say that it is overly redundant (each pixel values is represented by N_{fil} filter responses, where N_{fil} is usually around 36). Moreover, it should be noted that we are characterizing textures, entities with some spatially repeating properties by definition. Therefore, we do not expect the filter responses to be totally different at each pixel over the texture. Thus, there should be several distinct filter response vectors and all others are noisy variations of them.

This observation leads to our proposal of clustering the filter responses into a small set of prototype response vectors. We call these prototypes *textons*. Algorithmically, each texture is analyzed using the filter bank shown in Figure 2. There are a total of 36 filters. Each pixel is now transformed to a $N_{fil} = 36$ dimensional vector of filter response These vectors are clustered using a K-means algorithm. The criterion for this algorithm is to find K "centers" such that after assigning each data vector to the nearest center, the sum of the squared distance from the centers is minimized. K-means is a greedy algorithm that finds a local minimum of this criterion[1]. In this paper, we use the

---

[1]For more discussions and variations of the K-means algorithm, the reader is referred to [4, 7].

kmeans function in the NETLAB toolbox [15].

It is useful to visualize the resulting cluster centers in terms of the original filter kernels. To do this, recall that each cluster center represents a set of projections of each filter onto a particular image patch. We can solve for the image patch corresponding to each cluster center in a least squares sense by premultiplying the vectors representing the cluster centers by the pseudoinverse of the filterbank [8]. The matrix representing the filterbank is formed by concatenating the filter kernels into columns and placing these columns side by side. The set of synthesized image patches for two test images are shown in Figures 3(b) and 4(b). These are our textons. The textons represent assemblies of filter outputs that are characteristic of the local image structure present in the image.

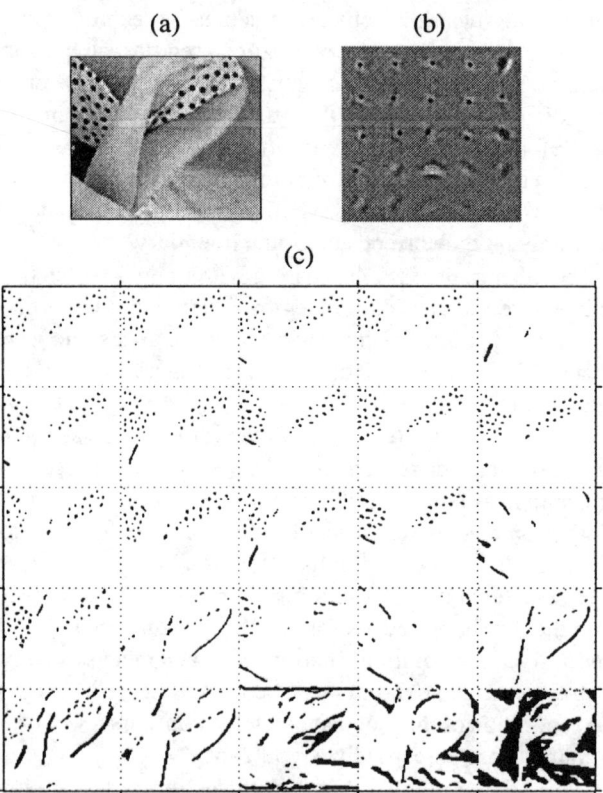

(a) (b)

(c)

Figure 3. (a) Polka-dot image. (b) Textons found via K-means with $K = 25$, sorted in decreasing order by norm. (c) Mapping of pixels to the texton channels. The dominant structures captured by the textons are translated versions of the dark spots. We also see textons corresponding to faint oriented edge and bar elements. Notice that some channels contain activity inside a textured region or along an oriented contour and nowhere else.

Looking at the polka-dot example, we find that many of

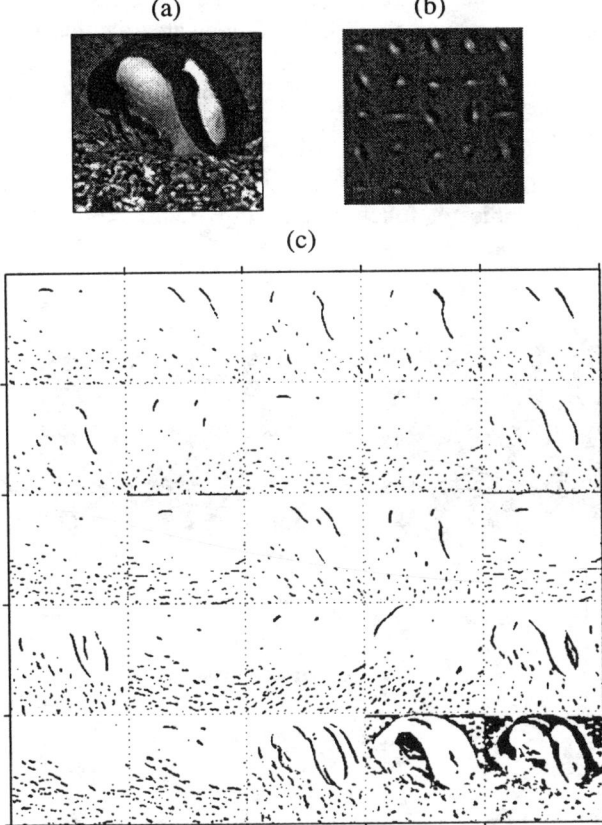

(a) (b)

(c)

Figure 4. (a) Penguin image. (b) Textons found via K-means with $K = 25$, sorted in decreasing order by norm. (c) Mapping of pixels to the texton channels. Among the textons we see edge elements of varying orientation and contrast along with elements of the stochastic texture in the rocks.

the textons correspond to translated versions of dark spots[2]. Also included are a number of oriented edge elements of low contrast and two textons representing nearly uniform brightness. The pixel-to-texton mapping is shown in Figure 3(c). Each subimage shows the pixels in the image that are mapped to the corresponding texton in Figure 3(b). We refer to this collection of discrete point sets as the texton *channels*. Since each pixel is mapped to exactly one texton, the texton channels constitute a partition of the image.

Textons and texton channels are also shown for the penguin image in Figure 4. Notice in the two examples how much the texton set can change from one image to the next. The spatial characteristics of both the deterministic

polka dot texture and the stochastic rocks texture are captured across several texton channels. In general, the texture boundaries emerge as point density changes across the different texton channels. In some cases, a texton channel contains activity inside a particular textured region and nowhere else. By comparison, vectors of filter outputs generically respond with some value at every pixel – a considerably less clean alternative.

3 Texton Channel Analysis

As discussed in the preceding section, the mapping from pixel to texton channel provides us with a number of discrete point sets where before we had continuous-valued filter vectors. Such a representation is well suited to the application of techniques from computational geometry and point process statistics. With these tools, one can approach questions such as, "what is the neighborhood of a texture element?" and "how similar are two pixels inside a textured region?"

3.1 Defining Local Scale Selection

The texton channel representation provides us a natural way to define texture scale. If the texture is composed of texels, we might want to define a notion of texel neighbors and consider the mean distance between them to be a measure of scale. Of course, many textures are stochastic and detecting texels reliably may be hard even for regular textures.

With textons we have a "soft" way to define neighbors. For a given pixel in a texton channel, first consider it as a "thickened point"— a disk centered at it. The idea is that while textons are being associated with pixels, since they correspond to assemblies of filter outputs, it is better to think of them as corresponding to a small image disk defined by the scale used in the Gaussian derivative filters. Recall Koenderink's aphorism about a point in image analysis being a Gaussian blob of small σ !

Now consider the Delaunay neighbors of all the pixels in the thickened point of a pixel i which lie closer than some outer scale.[3] The statistics of Delaunay edge lengths provides a natural measure of scale. In passing, we note that this neighborhood tends to be in the same image region as pixel i, since all the nodes in it belong to the same texton channel and are proximal.

In Figure 5a, the Delaunay triangulation of a zoomed-in portion of one of the texton channels in the rocky region of Figure 4 is shown atop a brightened version of the image. Here the nodes represent points that are similar in the image while the edges provide proximity information.

---

[2]It is straightforward to develop a method for merging translated versions of the same basic texton, though we have not found it necessary. Merging in this manner decreases the number of channels needed but necessitates the use of phase-shift information.

[3]This is set to 13 pixels in our experiments.

3.2 Characterizing Isotropy

We will find it necessary later in this paper when we examine cue integration to have a statistical test for whether a pixel is in the interior of a textured region or on its boundary. The notion of Delaunay neighborhood for a thickened point defined previously can be used. We consider the orientations of the vector from pixel i to each of these points. [4]

We obtain the local estimate of isotropy by performing a simple statistical test for randomness on the neighborhood the pixels inside each texton channel. The following description will use Figure 5 to illustrate this by example; here we consider two sample pixels in the penguin image, the first on the wing boundary, the second inside the rocky ground.

The neighborhood for a point on the wing boundary is shown in Figure 5c; the filled circle marks pixel i and the open circles mark its neighbors. For this pixel, the neighborhood is clearly not isotropic. This is quantified by computing the modified Kuiper statistic V [5] from the angles of the vectors connecting pixel i to its neighbors. Denoting the sorted angles by $\theta_1, \ldots, \theta_n$, the test proceeds as follows. Let

$$x_1 = \theta_1/2\pi, \ldots, x_n = \theta_n/2\pi$$

and compute the statistics

$$D_n^+ = \text{maximum of} \quad \frac{1}{n} - x_1, \frac{2}{n} - x_2, \ldots, 1 - x_n$$

$$D_n^- = \text{maximum of} \quad x_1, x_2 - \frac{1}{n}, x_3 - \frac{2}{n}, \ldots, x_n - \frac{n-1}{n}$$

$$V_n = D_n^+ + D_n^-, \quad \text{and} \quad V = V_n(n^{\frac{1}{2}} + 0.155 + 0.24/n^{\frac{1}{2}})$$

Intuitively, this is like a Kolmogorov-Smirnov test for uniformity where the data points are angles. Tabulated values for this test are given in [5]; from this we find that when $V > 2$ the neighborhood fails the isotropy test at an upper percentage point of 0.01. The value of V for the pixel on the wing boundary is 2.3; hence it is labelled "not isotropic." By contrast, a pixel chosen in the rocky ground area gives us $V = 0.8$, and is therefore labelled "isotropic."

3.3 Computing windowed texton histogram

Pairwise texture similarities can be computed by comparing windowed texton histograms, where the windows are centered around the two pixels being compared. Each histogram has K bins, one for each texton channel. The value of the kth histogram bin for a pixel i is found by counting how many pixels fall inside a box[5] centered around pixel i

---

[4]We exclude immediate 8 grid neighbors of i as they definitely do not constitute samples independent from i.

[5]At this stage we have not implemented scale selection and just use boxes of size 11×11 pixels.

in texton channel k. Thus the histogram represents texton frequencies in a local neighborhood. We can write this as

$$h_i(k) = \sum_{j \in \mathcal{W}(i)} I[T(j) = k]$$

where $\mathcal{W}(i)$ is the set of pixels in the box centered on i, $I[\cdot]$ is the indicator function, and $T(j)$ returns the texton assigned to pixel j.

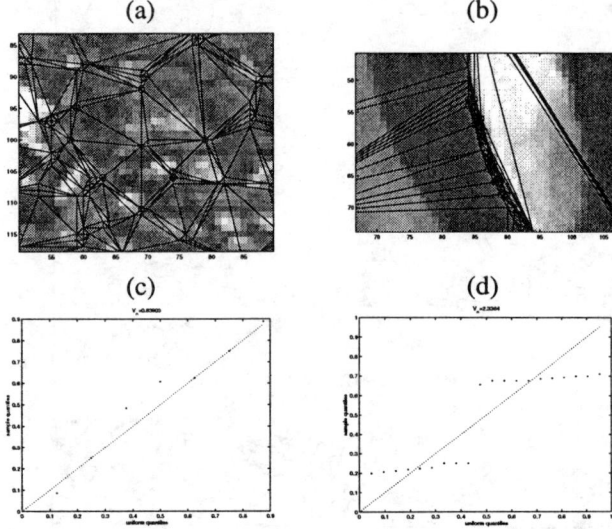

Figure 5. (a,b) Illustration of the Delaunay neighbors in zoomed in regions of two different texton channels on the penguin image. The filled circle marks pixel i and the open circles mark its neighbors. (c,d) Visualization of the computation of the statistical test for isotropy. The test value for (a) is $V = 0.8$ while that of (b) is $V = 2.3$. Using a significance level of 0.01, the isotropy hypothesis is rejected when $V > 2$.

4 Cue combination strategy

The obvious approach to cue integration (integrating information from both contours and textures) is to define the weight between pixels i and j as the product of the contribution from texture and that from contour: $W_{ij} = W_{ij}^{IC} \times W_{ij}^{TX}$. We have to be careful to avoid the problems listed in the Introduction (§1.2) by suitably gating the cues. The spirit of the gating method is to make each cue "harmless" in the vicinity of regions where one or the other cue should not be operating. This will manifest itself as suppression of oriented energy inside regions when computing the contour weights, and suppression of textons along boundaries when computing the texture weights.

Here is our way of defining the individual components and combining them:

4.1 Contour

The definition of W_{ij}^{IC} is adopted from that defined in [12]. Contour information in an image is computed "softly" through orientation energies (OE) from elongated quadrature filter pairs. We introduce a slight modification here to allow for exact sub-pixel localization of the contour by finding the local maxima in the orientation energy perpendicular to the contour orientation [16]. The confidence of this contour is given by the orientation energy. W_{ij}^{IC} is then defined as follows:

$$W_{ij}^{IC} = \exp(-\max_{x \in M_{ij}} OE(x)/\sigma_{IC})$$

where M_{ij} is the set of local maxima along the line joining pixels i and j. In words, two pixels will have a weak link between them if there is a strong local maximum of orientation energy along the line joining the two pixels. On the contrary, if there is little energy, for example in a constant brightness region, the link between the two pixels will be strong.

4.2 Measuring Texture Similarity

Pairwise texture similarities can be computed by comparing windowed texton histograms computed using the technique described previously (§3.3). A number of methods are available for comparing histograms; among them a simple and effective choice is the χ^2 test, defined as

$$\chi^2(h_i, h_j) = \frac{1}{2} \sum_{k=1}^{K} \frac{[h_i(k) - h_j(k)]^2}{h_i(k) + h_j(k)}$$

where h_i and h_j are the two histograms. For a comparison of the χ^2 test versus other texture similarity measures, the readers are referred to [17].

W_{ij}^{TX} is defined using the χ^2 distance between texton histograms at pixels i and j:

$$W_{ij}^{TX} = \exp(-\chi^2(h_i, h_j)/\sigma_{TX})$$

4.3 Cue Combination

Cue combination is accomplished in the following steps.

1. We first compute the isotropic measure $\alpha(i)$ and unisotropic measure $\beta(i)$ at each point, i, in the image. One can think of $\alpha(i)$ as the 1D-ness measure, while $\beta(i)$ as the texture-ness measure. Define

$$\alpha(i) = \text{sigmoid}(V(i), threshold)$$
$$\beta(i) = 1 - \text{sigmoid}(V(i), threshold)$$

To simplify the computaton, a discrete version of the sigmoid is used in our experiments. We select the threshold V at 2.0 at each pixel as discussed in §3.2. Figure 6 shows one such computed α and β map on a tiger image.

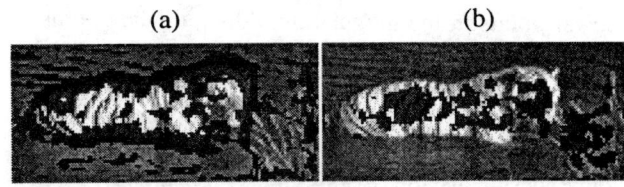

Figure 6. Subplot (a) and (b) shows the computed α and β measure in a tiger image. The α and β values are thresholded at 2.0, and masked on the original image.

2. We then compute the texture feature descriptor at each pixel of the image, gated by the function $\alpha(i)$. The main idea is to ignore any neighboring pixels which are near a region boundary in the histogram computation. Define the gated histogram as:

$$h_i^\alpha(k) = \frac{1}{Z(i)} \sum_{j \in \mathcal{W}(i)} [1 - \alpha(j)]I[T(j) = k]$$

where $Z(i) = \sum_{j \in \mathcal{W}(i)} (1 - \alpha(j))$. This definition of texture histogram avoids the problem of texture comparison near object boundaries. At intensity boundaries, the boundaries themselves can no longer be used as features, and therefore will not form groups on their own. This definition of the gated histogram also has a desirable behavior near texture boundaries: it tends to pool information from the correct side of the region. Figure 7 illustrates this point. From the gated texture

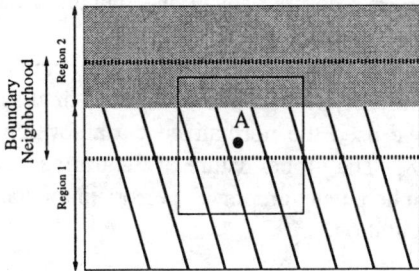

Figure 7. At the texture boundary, the proposed gated histogram tends to pool information from the "correct region". Take the point marked "A" in the boundary region between the dashed lines as an example. By masking out all features in the boundary neighborhood, the texture histogram computed for "A" will contain only the information from region 1. This avoids the problem of having corrupted texture histogram information as we get closer to the region boundary.

histogram, we can compute the pair-wise texture similarity, $W^{TX}(i, j)$ as :

$$W^{TX}(i, j) = \exp(-\chi^2(h_i^\alpha, h_j^\alpha)/\sigma_{TX})$$

As we move deeper into the boundary region, we have

fewer points in the neighborhood to compute the histogram. In that case, the histogram difference becomes less reliable, and therefore should be discounted. We define the reliability measure for each histogram measure at pixel $p(i) = \text{sigmoid}(Z(i), threshold_p)$. In our experiments, the $threshold_p$ is set to $0.05*|\mathcal{W}(i)|$.

3. In parallel to the texture computation, the intervening contour cue gated by the texture-ness can be used to group/segment pixels. The computation is same as in §4.1, except the filter energy is suppressed by texture-ness measure $\beta(i)$.

$$W^{IC}(i,j) = \exp(- \max_{x \in l_{ij}, \beta(x) < 1.0} OE(x)/\sigma_{IC})$$

4. Let the two pair-wise feature distance functions computed in the two previous steps be $W^{tex}(i,j)$ and $W^{IC}(i,j)$, from the texture cue and intervening contour cue respectively. Since the test for isotropy is purely a local one, one expects the α and β function to misfire sometimes. By combining the two cues, and applying global grouping algorithm to this data, we hope to "smooth out" these errors in the α and β estimates. The rule we have for combining two cues is:

$$W(i,j) = [W^{TX}(i,j)]^{p(i,j)}[W^{IC}(i,j)]$$

where $p(i,j) = \min(p(i), p(j))$ is the significance of the histogram comparison between pixels i and j.

5. Applying grouping algorithm to the combined pairwise similarity measure to obtain the final segmentation. We used the normalized cut algorithm for this step [18]. The global nature of the normalized cut algorithm help us overcome the errors in the local α and β computation.

5 Results

We have run our algorithm on a variety of natural images. Figures 8 and 9 show typical segmentation results. In all the cases, the regions are cleanly separated from each other using combined texture and contour cues.

Grouping based on each of the cues alone would result in severe artifacts: In Figure 8a, the contours on the penguin would form isolated groups using the texture cue. Similar problems would occur at the intensity boundaries in 8b and 8c. Grouping based on contour information alone would result in over-fragmentation of the pebbles in 8a and 9a, and the tiger body in 8c. On the other hand, in Figure 8b the lower arm can not be separated from the upper arm without using contour information.

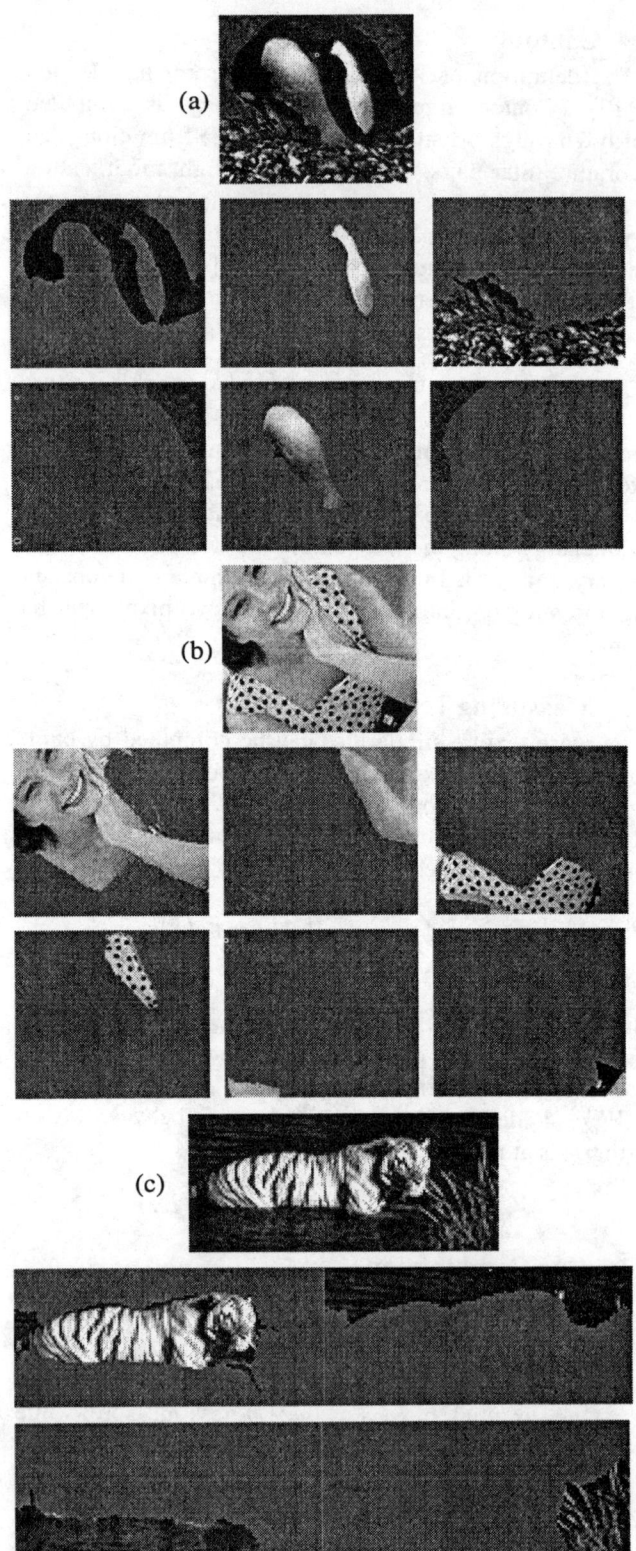

Figure 8. Segmentation results of three images using combined texture and intervening contour cue. The image regions are cleanly segmented from each other using the combined cues. In all three cases, grouping by each of the cues alone will not produce the right results.

Acknowledgement

This research was supported by (ARO) DAAH04-96-1-0341, the Digital Library Grant IRI-9411334, NSF Graduate Fellowships to SB and JS and a Berkeley Fellowship to TL.

References

[1] S. Belongie, C. Carson, H. Greenspan, and J. Malik. Color- and texture-based image segmentation using em and its application to content-based image retrieval. In *Proc. 6th Int. Conf. Computer Vision*, pages 675–82, Bombay, India, Jan. 1998.

[2] T. Binford. Inferring surfaces from images. *Artificial Intelligence*, 17(1-3):205–44, Aug. 1981.

[3] R. DeValois and K. DeValois. *Spatial Vision*. Oxford University Press, 1988.

[4] R. Duda and P. Hart. *Pattern Classification and Scene Analysis*. John Wiley & Sons, 1973.

[5] N. Fisher. *Statistical Analysis of Circular Data*. John Wiley & Sons, 1973.

[6] I. Fogel and D. Sagi. Gabor filters as texture discriminator. *Biological Cybernetics*, 61:103–13, 1989.

[7] A. Gersho and R. Gray. *Vector quantization and signal compression*. Kluwer Academic Publishers, 1992.

[8] D. Jones and J. Malik. Computational framework to determining stereo correspondence from a set of linear spatial filters. *Image and Vision Computing*, 10(10):699–708, Dec. 1992.

[9] B. Julesz. Textons, the elements of texture perception, and their interactions. *Nature*, 290(5802):91–7, March 1981.

[10] H. Knutsson and G. Granlund. Texture analysis using two-dimensional quadrature filters. In *Workshop on Computer Architecture for Pattern Analysis and Image Database Management*, pages 206–13, Oct. 1983.

[11] J. Koenderink and A. van Doorn. Representation of local geometry in the visual system. *Biological Cybernetics*, 55(6):367–75, 1987.

[12] T. Leung and J. Malik. Contour continuity in region-based image segmentation. In H. Burkhardt and B. Neumann, editors, *Proc. Euro. Conf. Computer Vision*, volume 1, pages 544–59, Freiburg, Germany, June 1998. Springer-Verlag.

[13] T. Leung and J. Malik. Recognizing surfaces using three-dimensional textons. In *Proc. Int. Conf. Computer Vision*, Corfu, Greece, Sep. 1999.

[14] J. Malik and P. Perona. Preattentive texture discrimination with early vision mechanisms. *J. Opt. Soc. America A*, 7(5):923–32, May 1990.

[15] I. Nabney and C. Bishop. Netlab neural network software. http://www.ncrg.aston.ac.uk/netlab/.

[16] P. Perona and J. Malik. Detecting and localizing edges composed of steps, peaks and roofs. In *Proc. 3rd Int. Conf. Computer Vision*, pages 52–7, Osaka, Japan, Dec 1990.

[17] J. Puzicha, T. Hofmann, and J. Buhmann. Non-parametric similarity measures for unsupervised texture segmentation and image retrieval. In *Proc. IEEE Conf. Comp. Vis. and Pat. Rec.*, pages 267–72, Jun. 1997.

[18] J. Shi and J. Malik. Normalized cuts and image segmentation. In *Proc. IEEE Conf. Computer Vision and Pattern Recognition*, pages 731–7, June 1997.

(a)

(b)

(c)

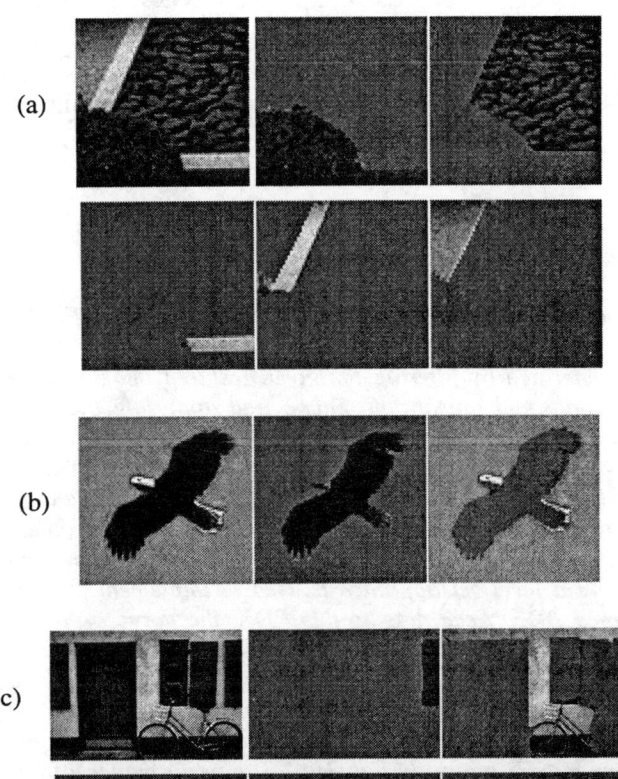

Figure 9. Segmentation results of three images using combined texture and intervening contour cue. Image (a) has regions defined by texture and contour, while images (b) and (c) only have regions defined by contour information alone. The proposed cue combination behaves correctly in both cases.

Geodesic Active Regions for Supervised Texture Segmentation*

Nikos Paragios   Rachid Deriche

I.N.R.I.A

BP. 93, 2004, Route des Lucioles

06902 Sophia Antipolis Cedex, France

e-mail: {nparagio,der}@sophia.inria.fr

Abstract

This paper presents a novel variational method for supervised texture segmentation. The textured feature space is generated by filtering the given textured images using isotropic and anisotropic filters, and analyzing their responses as multi-component conditional probability density functions. The texture segmentation is obtained by unifying region and boundary-based information as an improved Geodesic Active Contour Model. The defined objective function is minimized using a gradient-descent method where a level set approach is used to implement the obtained PDE. According to this PDE, the curve propagation towards the final solution is guided by boundary and region-based segmentation forces, and is constrained by a regularity force. The level set implementation is performed using a fast front propagation algorithm where topological changes are naturally handled. The performance of our method is demonstrated on a variety of synthetic and real textured frames.

1 Introduction

Texture segmentation, the problem considered in this paper, is one of the most important techniques for image analysis, understanding and interpretation.

The task of texture segmentation is to partition the image into a number of regions such that each region has the same textural properties [7]. Alternatively, this task can be viewed as the problem of accurately extracting the borders between different texture regions in an image [12]. If *a priory* knowledge regarding the textural properties in a given image is available, the problem is called supervised texture segmentation; otherwise it is called un-supervised.

Supervised texture segmentation requires texture analysis and modeling which is usually performed using two well-known techniques; **statistical modeling** [5, 20] and **filtering theory** [2, 11]. Additionally, feature-based image segmentation is performed using either **boundary-based methods** [12, 21] or **region-based methods** [1, 13].

*This work was funded in part under the VIRGO research network (EC Contract No ERBFMRX-CT96-0049) of the TMR Program.

During the last years, there is a significant effort to integrate boundary with region-based segmentation approaches [6, 4, 23]. The difficulty lies on the fact that even though the two modules yield complementary information, they involve conflicting and incommensurate objectives. The region-based methods attempt to capitalize on homogeneity properties, whereas boundary-based ones use the non-homogeneity of the same data as a guide. The most closely related work with this paper can be found in [23], where a two-step variational approach is proposed that combines the geometrical features of a snake/balloon model and the statistical techniques of region growing.

The present work has two main objectives: the first is to propose a complete framework for texture analysis and modeling that combines the filtering theory with the statistical modeling. The second objective is to combine the boundary and the region-based texture segmentation framework into a coupled model, that is derived from the geodesic active contour model. The observation set of this framework is composed of

1. A given set of texture pattern images,
2. A given input frame composed from these patterns.

Following our previous work [18] for supervised texture segmentation using geodesic active contours, we propose a considerable extension that incorporates region-based information to the existing boundary-based information under a coupled framework that can deal with the following problems:

1. The **segmentation of the input frame**, given the background pattern [**fig.** (5.1,5.4)],
2. The extraction of **regions of interest** from the input frame, given the corresponding patterns [**fig.** (5.2,5.3)].

The proposed algorithm is depicted in [**fig.** 1]. Initially, an off-line step is performed that creates multi-component probabilistic texture descriptors for the given set of texture patterns, where the multi-modal data is derived using a set of filter operators [**fig.** 1: *Learning Phase*]. Then, given the input frame, we apply the same operators and derive an observation set that is coherent with the texture descriptors. Then, for each pixel we estimate the probability of being on

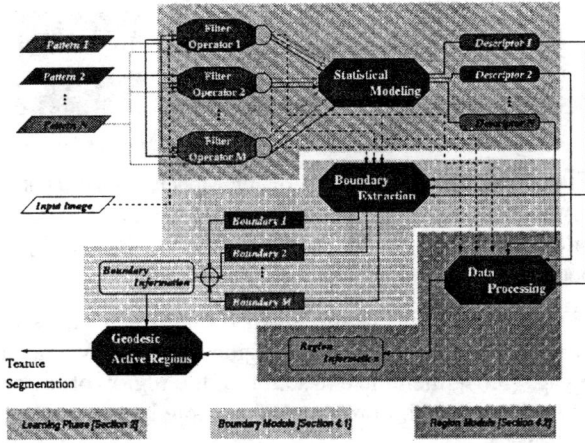

Figure 1. Geodesic Active Regions for supervised texture segmentation

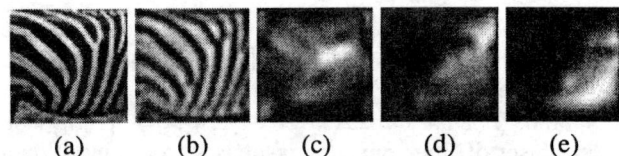

$$(a) \qquad (b) \qquad (c) \qquad (d) \qquad (e)$$

Figure 2. Filter Operator Responses (a) g(0.5), (b) LoG(0.5), (c) $A\left(1, \frac{\pi}{6}, 0\right)$, (d) $A\left(1, \frac{\pi}{3}, 0\right)$, (e) $A\left(1, \frac{\pi}{3}, \frac{\pi}{6}\right)$.

- The Gaussian operator $\{g(|\sigma)\}$ [**fig.** (2.a)]

$$\left[g(x, y|\sigma) = \frac{1}{\sqrt{2\pi}\sigma} e^{-\frac{x^2 + y^2}{2\sigma^2}} \right]$$

- The isotropic center-surround operator (Laplacian of Gaussian) $\{\mathbf{LoG}(|\sigma)\}$ [**fig.** 2(b)],

$$\left[f(x, y|\sigma) = S\left(1 - \frac{x^2 + y^2}{2\sigma^2}\right) e^{-\frac{x^2 + y^2}{2\sigma^2}} \right]$$

where S is a constant scale factor. Besides, the (x, y) anisotropic directional derivatives operators are also considered.

- The 2D Gabor operators analyze the image simultaneously in both space $[\sigma]$, and frequency domains $[\theta, \phi]$.

$$\left[G(x, y|\sigma, \theta, \phi) = \frac{1}{2\pi\sigma^2} e^{-\frac{x^2 + y^2}{2\sigma^2}} e^{-j2\pi(\theta x + \phi y)} \right]$$

These Gabor functions can be decomposed into two components; the real part $[G_R(x, y|\sigma, \theta, \phi)]$ and the imaginary part $[G_I(x, y|\sigma, \theta, \phi)]$. The texture features are captured by the spectrum analyzer $\{\mathbf{A}(|\sigma, \theta, \phi)\}$ of the Gabor components,

$$S(x, y|\sigma, \theta, \phi) = \sqrt{(G_R * I)(x, y)^2 + (G_I * I)(x, y)^2}$$

smoothed by a Gaussian function [**fig.**(2.[c,d,e])], where $(G_R * I)$ denotes the convolution operation between the image I and the filter G_R.

2.2 Modeling Features

The texture modeling phase aims at finding an appropriate model that can be expressed using a limited set of parameters and preserves strong discrimination power. The most common model related with filtering theory is the use of histograms, where the filter response is discretized using a limited number of values, that affects significantly the extracted model and requires a large set of parameters (histogram cells). We confront these problems, by adopting a statistical framework where the different filter responses (observed histograms) are modeled using continuous probabilities density functions that are Gaussian mixtures [**fig.** 1: *Statistical Modeling*].

In order to facilitate the notation, let us now make some definitions:

- Let $F = \{f_j : j \in [1, \mathrm{M}]\}$ be the set of M preselected filter operators.

---

the boundaries between two different texture regions. Since we deal with multi-modal data, a probability vector is obtained. The components of this vector (*e.g.* boundary probabilities) are combined to a single frame using some reliability measurements and provide the **boundary-based** texture information [**fig.** 1: *Boundary Module*]. Besides, using the texture descriptors and the observation set we determine the **region-based** information that is derived from the most probable temporal texture assignment [**fig.** 1: *Region Module*]. Then, the segmentation problem is stated under an improved Geodesic Active Contour model that aims at finding the best minimal length geodesic curve that preserves high boundary probabilities, and creates regions with maximum *a posteriori* segmentation probability with respect to the associated texture hypothesis. We call this model **Geodesic Active Region** model, since boundary and region information are cooperating in a coupled active contour model. The defined objective function is minimized using a gradient-descent method where a level set approach [14] is used to implement the obtained PDE. Finally, the curve propagation problem is implemented using a fast front propagation scheme, the *Hermes Algorithm* [17].

The remainder of this paper is organized as follows. Section 2 deals with the texture analysis and modeling problem while in Section 3, we introduce the main contribution of this paper, the **Geodesic Active Region Model** which is applied to the supervised texture segmentation problem in Section 4. Finally, experimental results and discussion appear in Section 5.

2 Texture Analysis and Modeling

2.1 Extracting Features

In many different applications the use of linear and nonlinear filter operators has been applied for feature extraction with quite satisfactory results. Following this example, we adopt a general filter bank composed of:

- Let $T = \{t_i : i \in [1, \mathbb{N}]\}$ be the set of $\mathbb{N}$ texture patterns, and $D = \{\mathbf{D}_i : i \in [1, \mathbb{N}]\}$ be the associated data set.
- And, let $\mathcal{D}(\mathbf{A}) = \{\mathbf{A}_{ij} : i \in [1, \mathbb{N}], j \in [1, \mathbb{M}]\}\}$ be the set of filter operator responses to the input data set, where $\mathbf{A}_{ij}$ is the response of f_j to $\mathbf{D}_i$.

We assume that each filter response can be modeled using low-level statistics, where its observed density function is assumed to be conditional probability. Let $p_{ij}(.)$ be the conditional probability density of the data component $\mathbf{A}_{ij}$. If we assume that this probability density function is homogeneous, *i.e.* independent of the pixel location, then it can be decomposed into many different Gaussian components;

$$p_{ij}(x|\Theta_{ij}) = \sum_{k=1}^{C_{ij}} P_{ij}^k p_{ij}^k(x|\mu_{ij}^k, \sigma_{ij}^k)$$

where C_{ij} is the number of mixture components, P_{ij}^k be the *a priori* probability of the component k, and Θ_{ij} is the vector of the unknown mixture parameters: $\Theta_{ij} = \{(P_{ij}^k, \mu_{ij}^k, \sigma_{ij}^k) : k \in [1, ..., C_{ij}]\}$. The component number is derived automatically form the observed data [18], while the estimation of the unknown parameters is done using the Maximum Likelihood Principle.

The output of this operation is a powerful probabilistic texture description model where each pattern is associated with a vector of probability density functions

- $\mathbf{p}_i(\mathbf{x}) = (p_{i1}(x_1), ..., p_{i\mathbb{M}}(x_\mathbb{M}))$

that characterizes its behavior with respect to the different filter operators [**fig.** 1: *Texture Descriptors*].

3 Geodesic Active Regions

The Geodesic Active Contour model has been initially proposed in [3, 8, 10] and successfully applied to a wide variety of computer vision applications. These methods are based on boundary-based information, and aim at finding the best minimal-length smooth curve for a measure derived from the properties of the image.

Besides, motivated by the work proposed in [4, 23], the Geodesic Active Region model has been initially introduced in [16] to deal with the problem of supervised texture segmentation and has been successfully exploited in [19] to deal with the tracking problem. This model is a considerable extension to the geodesic active contour model since it incorporates region-based information and aims at finding a partition where the interior as well as the exterior region preserves the desired image properties.

We are going to introduce this model for a simple segmentation case with two possible decisions. In order to facilitate the notation, let us make some definitions:

- Let $\mathbf{I} : \mathcal{R} \to \mathbf{R}$ be the input frame.
- Let $\mathcal{P}(\mathcal{R}) = \{\mathcal{R}_A, \mathcal{R}_B\}$ be a partition of the frame domain into two non-overlapping regions $\{\mathcal{R}_A \cap \mathcal{R}_B = \emptyset\}$, where $\mathcal{R}_A$ is the region of interest (hypothesis h_A).
- And, let $\{\partial\mathcal{R}_A\}$ be the $\mathcal{R}_A$ region boundaries.

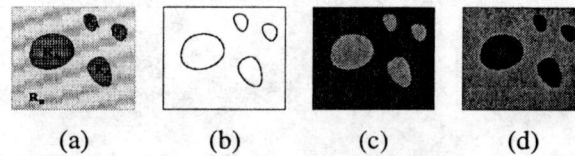

(a)   (b)   (c)   (d)

Figure 3. Geodesic Active Region Model: (a) the input, (b) the boundary-based information,(c,d) the region-based information [proportional to the frame intensity] for hypothesis h_A [c] and for hypothesis h_B [d].

If we assume that for the given frame [**fig.** (3.a)] some information regarding the real region boundaries is available [**fig.** (3.b)], then the extraction of the region of interest can be viewed as the problem of accurately extracting its boundaries.

Let $[\mathbf{p}(\mathbf{I}(s)|\mathbf{B})]$ be the **conditional boundary density function** that measures the probability of a given point being at the real boundaries of $\mathcal{R}_A$. Then, the region of interest can be obtained using the geodesic active contour framework, thus minimizing

$$E(\partial\mathcal{R}_A) = \int_0^1 g(p(\mathbf{I}(\partial\mathcal{R}_A(p)))|B) \left|\dot{\mathcal{R}}_A(p)\right| dp$$

where $\partial\mathcal{R}_A(p) : [0, 1] \to \mathbf{R}^2$ is a parameterization of the region boundaries in a planar form, and $g()$ is a positive monotonically decreasing function, such that $g(0) = 1$ and $g(x) \to 0$ as $x \to \infty$. The solution of the segmentation problem is equivalent with finding the geodesic curve of minimal length that best takes into account the desired image characteristics (important boundary probabilities)[9].

Let us now assume that **an a priori knowledge about the desired intensity properties of the different regions is available**; the conditional probability density functions $[p_A(\mathbf{I}(s)), p_B(\mathbf{I}(s))]$ with respect to the hypothesis h_A and h_B [**fig.** (3.c,3.d)].

Then, the extraction of the region of interest is equivalent to creating a consistent frame partition between *the observed data, the associated hypothesis and their expected properties*. This partition can be viewed as an optimization problem with respect to the *a posteriori* segmentation probability, given the observation set.

Let $[p(\mathcal{P}(\mathcal{R})|\mathbf{I})]$ be the *a posteriori* segmentation density function with respect to the different partitions $\mathcal{P}(\mathcal{R})$ given the input data $\mathbf{I}$. This density function is given by the Bayes rule as:

$$p(\mathcal{P}(\mathcal{R})|\mathbf{I}) = \frac{p(\mathbf{I}|\mathcal{P}(\mathcal{R}))}{p(\mathbf{I})} p(\mathcal{P}(\mathcal{R}))$$

If we assume that all the partitions are *a priori* equally possible then we can ignore the constant terms $p(\mathbf{I})$, $p(\mathcal{P}(\mathcal{R}))$ and we can rewrite the density function as:

$$p(\mathcal{P}(\mathcal{R})|\mathbf{I}) = p(\mathbf{I}|\{\mathcal{R}_A, \mathcal{R}_B\}) =$$
$$p([\mathbf{I}_A \mid \mathcal{R}_A] \cap [\mathbf{I}_B \mid \mathcal{R}_B]) = p(\mathbf{I}_A \mid \mathcal{R}_A)\, p(\mathbf{I}_B \mid \mathcal{R}_B)$$

Besides, if we assume that the points within each region are independent, we can replace the region probability with:

$$p(\mathbf{I}_X \mid \mathcal{R}_X) = \prod_{s \in \mathcal{R}_X} p_X(\mathbf{I}(s))$$

The maximization of *a posteriori* probability is equivalent with the minimization of the [**-log**()] function of this probability,

$$E(\partial\mathcal{P}(\mathcal{R})) = -\log\left[\prod_{s\in\mathcal{R}_A} p_A(\mathbf{I}(s)) \prod_{s\in\mathcal{R}_B} p_B(\mathbf{I}(s)\right]$$

$$= -\iint_{\mathcal{R}_A} \log\left[p_A(\mathbf{I}(x,y))\right] dxdy - \iint_{\mathcal{R}_B} \log\left[p_B(\mathbf{I}(x,y))\right] dxdy$$

We **fuse the two different segmentation models** by defining the Geodesic Active Region objective function as

$$E(\partial\mathcal{R}_A) = (1-\alpha)\int_0^1 g(p(\mathbf{I}(\partial\mathcal{R}_A(p))))|\partial\dot{\mathcal{R}}_A(p)|dp -$$

$$\alpha\left\{\iint_{\mathcal{R}_A} \log\left[p_A(\mathbf{I}(x,y))\right] dxdy + \iint_{\mathcal{R}_B} \log\left[p_B(\mathbf{I}(x,y))\right] dxdy\right\}$$

The minimization of this function is performed using a gradient descent method. If $u = (x,y)$ is a point of the initial curve (that can belong either to $\mathcal{R}_A$ or to $\mathcal{R}_B$) and we compute the Euler-Lagrange equations [23], then we should deform the curve to this point using the following equation:

$$\frac{du}{dt} = \left[\underbrace{\alpha\log\left(\frac{p_B(\mathbf{I}(u))}{p_A(\mathbf{I}(u))}\right)}_{region\ term} + \underbrace{(1-\alpha)\left(g(u)\mathcal{K}(u) - \nabla g(u)\cdot\mathcal{N}(u)\right)}_{boundary\ term}\right]\mathcal{N}(u)$$

where $\mathcal{K}$ is the Euclidean curvature of ∂R_A and $\mathcal{N}$ is the unit inward normal to ∂R_A.

The obtained PDE motion equation has two kind of *forces* acting on the curve, both in the direction of the normal. The **region force** aims at shrink or to expand the curve in the direction that maximizes the *a posteriori* segmentation probability. Thus, if u is a point of h_B $[p_B(\mathbf{I}(u)) > p_A(\mathbf{I}(u))]$ then this force acts to shrink the curve $\left[\alpha\log\left(\frac{p_B(\mathbf{I}(u))}{p_A(\mathbf{I}(u))}\right) > 0\right]$ otherwise acts to expand it. Besides, the **boundary force** contains two sub-terms; one that moves the curve towards the region boundaries constrained by the curvature effect and one that attracts these boundaries (refinement term).

4 Texture Segmentation

We view the segmentation as a frame partition problem [defined by a curve] into non-overlapping regions that preserve *homogeneous textural properties* and *characteristics*. Some complementary definitions are required:

- Let $\mathbf{I}$ be the textured input frame and let $D(\mathbf{I}) = \{\mathbf{I}_j : j \in [1, \mathbb{M}]\}$ be the set of filter responses to this frame.
- Let $\mathcal{P}(R) = \{\mathbf{R}_i : i \in [0, \mathbb{R}_\mathbb{N}]\}$ be a partition of frame domain into $\{\mathbb{R}_\mathbb{N}+1\}$ non-overlapping regions, where $\mathbf{R}_0$ is the region that corresponds to the *background* pattern.
- Let $\partial\mathcal{P}(R) = \{\partial\mathbf{R}_i : i \in [1, \mathbb{R}_\mathbb{N}]\}$ be the region boundaries of the partition $\mathcal{P}(R)$.
- And, let t_{R_i} be the texture pattern that corresponds to the region $\mathbf{R}_i$.

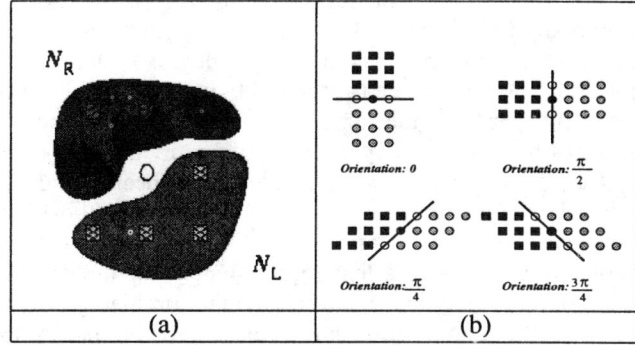

Figure 4. (a) Neighborhood partition that indicates a boundary point, (b) Possible partitions.

4.1 Defining the Boundary Information

It is well known that the extraction of boundary information for textured images is a very tougher task. We propose a probabilistic method to determine this information [18, 22].

Let $N_R(s)$ and $N_L(s)$ be the regions associated with a neighborhood partition, and let $\mathcal{D}(N(s))$ be the corresponding data. Under these assumptions and using the Bayes rule, the probability that s lies on the boundaries between two regions $p(B|\mathcal{D}(N(s)))$ is given by:

$$p(B|D(N(s))) = \frac{p(\mathcal{D}(N(s))|B)}{p(\mathcal{D}(N(s))|B\cup NB)}p(B)$$

where $p(\mathcal{D}(N(s))|B)$ (*resp.* $p(\mathcal{D}(N(s))|NB)$) is the conditional boundary (*resp.* non-boundary) probability and $p(B)$ is the *a priori* boundary probability which is a constant scale factor and can be ignored.

The conditional boundary and (*resp.* non-boundary) probability can be estimated directly from known quantities since *if s is a boundary point*, then there is a partition $[N_L(s), N_R(s)]$ where the most probable texture assignment for $N_L(s)$ is the *background* pattern $\{t_{R_0}\}$ and for $N_R(s)$ is a different pattern $\{t_{R_r}\}$ or the opposite. Besides, if s is not a boundary point, then the most probable texture assignment for $N_L(s)$ as well as for $N_R(s)$ is either $\{t_{R_0}\}$ or $\{t_{R_r}\}$. These probabilities are given by [16],

$$\begin{aligned}
p(\mathbf{I}(N(s))|B) &= p_{t_{R_0}}(\mathbf{I}(N_R(s)))p_{t_{R_r}}(\mathbf{I}(N_L(s))) \\
&\quad + p_{t_{R_r}}(\mathbf{I}(N_R(s)))p_{t_{R_0}}(\mathbf{I}(N_L(s))) \\
p(\mathbf{I}(N(s))|NB) &= p_{t_{R_0}}(\mathbf{I}(N_R(s)))p_{t_{R_0}}(\mathbf{I}(N_L(s))) \\
&\quad + p_{t_{R_r}}(\mathbf{I}(N_R(s)))p_{t_{R_r}}(\mathbf{I}(N_L(s)))
\end{aligned} \quad (1)$$

Since we deal with multi-modal data, each data component can provide boundary-based measurements for a given pixel s. Assuming that the neighborhood partition is known, the boundary probability $p_{jB}(s|\{\mathbf{I}_j, N, t_{R_r}\})$ for s with respect to the data component $\mathbf{I}_j$ is given by

$$p_{j\mathbf{B}}(s|\{\mathbf{I}_j, N, t_{R_r}\}) = \frac{p_j(\mathbf{I}(N(s))|B)}{p_j(\mathbf{I}(N(s))|B) + p_j(\mathbf{I}(N(s))|NB)}$$

where $p_j(\mathbf{I}(N(s))|B)$ (resp. $p_j(\mathbf{I}(N(s))|NB)$) is derived from [**eq.** (1)]. This probability is defined given a neighborhood partition as well as a texture assignment for the second local region, thus the next problem is to define this partition. We consider four possible neighborhood partitions (the vertical, the horizontal and the two diagonals) [**fig.** (4.b)], obtained by assuming four orientations $\theta = \left\{0:0, \frac{\pi}{4}:1, \frac{\pi}{2}:2, \frac{3\pi}{4}:3\right\}$; besides, it has been found experimentally that the illustrated in [**fig.** (4.b)] neighborhood size gives very satisfactory results. Finally, to estimate this probability, we need a texture assignment for the second neighborhood region. To overcome this problem, we estimate the boundary probability for all possible partitions and for all possible assignment by generating the matrix

$$
P_{\mathrm{B}}(s) =
\begin{bmatrix}
p_{j\mathrm{B}}(s|0,t_1) & p_{j\mathrm{B}}(s|1,t_1) & p_{j\mathrm{B}}(s|2,t_1) & p_{j\mathrm{B}}(s|3,t_1) \\
\vdots & \vdots & \vdots & \vdots \\
p_{j\mathrm{B}}(s|0,t_k) & p_{j\mathrm{B}}(s|1,t_k) & p_{j\mathrm{B}}(s|2,t_k) & p_{j\mathrm{B}}(s|3,t_k) \\
\vdots & \vdots & \vdots & \vdots \\
p_{j\mathrm{B}}(s|0,t_{\mathtt{N}}) & p_{j\mathrm{B}}(s|1,t_{\mathtt{N}}) & p_{j\mathrm{B}}(s|2,t_{\mathtt{N}}) & p_{j\mathrm{B}}(s|3,t_{\mathtt{N}})
\end{bmatrix}
$$

where the lines correspond to the possible texture assignments $\{t_1, ..., t_{t_{R_0}-1}, t_{t_{R_0}+1}, ..., t_{\mathtt{N}}\}$ and the columns to the different neighborhood partitions $\{0, 1, 2, 3\}$. The element (m, n) of this matrix, corresponds to the boundary probability of partition n if the second local region is assigned to the texture hypothesis t_m.

This operation provides $\{\mathtt{M}\}$ boundary probability frames (one for each data component $\{\mathbf{I}_j\}$) that have to be combined to a single frame. This can be done using the mean value between the different frames, but it is not the most proper solution since the quality of the boundary maps differs from data component to data component. We introduce a reliability measurement for each boundary map, which is associated with the discrimination power of the corresponding filter with respect to the *background* pattern.

At the end of the analysis and modeling phase, we have associated to each pattern, a descriptor, which given a value and its nature (data component) returns the probability of being part of this descriptor. A filter operator has strong discrimination power, if all the observed values of the corresponding *background* data component are being correctly classified, (*e.g.* the probability with respect to the *background* pattern is superior to the probability with respect to any other pattern). The probability of being correct $P_j(C)$ with respect to the filter f_j is equivalent to an observation x being classified as the *background* texture pattern t_{R_0}, where the true state of nature is t_{R_0}. As a consequence, for each filter operator f_j we have

$$
P_j(C) = P\left(x \in \mathbf{D}_{t_{R_0}j} \cap \left[p_{t_{R_0}j}(x) \geq p_{ij}(x) : \forall j \in [0, \mathtt{M}]\right]\right)
$$
$$
\iint_{\mathbf{D}_{t_{R_0}j}} p_{t_{R_0}j}(\mathbf{D}_{t_{R_0}j}(x,y)) H\left(\mathbf{D}_{t_{R_0}j}(x,y)\right) dx dy
$$

where $H(x,j) : R \times [0, \mathtt{N}], \rightarrow R$ is a binary function given by,

$$
H(a, j) = \begin{cases} 1 & , \quad \text{if } p_{t_{R_0}j}(a) \geq p_{ij}(a); \forall i \in [0, \mathtt{N}] \\ 0 & , \quad \text{otherwise} \end{cases}
$$

We normalize the reliability measurements $[P_j(C)]$ with respect to the different filter operators $\left[\mathbf{w}_j = \frac{P_j(C)}{\sum_{k=1}^{\mathtt{M}} P_k(C)}\right]$ and we use them to generate a global boundary matrix that combines the different filter responses:

$$
P_{\mathrm{B}}(s) =
\begin{bmatrix}
\sum_j^{\mathtt{M}} w_j\, p_j(s|0, t_1) & \sum_j^{\mathtt{M}} w_j\, p_i(s|3, t_1) \\
& \vdots & \\
\sum_j^{\mathtt{M}} w_j\, p_j(s|0, t_{\mathtt{N}}) & \sum_j^{\mathtt{M}} w_j\, p_j(s|3, t_{\mathtt{N}})
\end{bmatrix}
$$

The **boundary probability** $p_{\mathrm{B}}(s)$ for the pixel s is then provided by the highest element of the matrix $P_{\mathrm{B}}(s)$.

4.2 Defining the Region Information

Let $p(\mathcal{P}(R)|D(R))$ be the *a posteriori* segmentation probability with respect to the partition $\mathcal{P}(R)$. Since the *a posterior* region probabilities $p(D(\mathbf{R}_i)|t_{R_i})$ are independent, the global *a posteriori* segmentation probability is given by,

$$
p(\mathcal{P}(R)|D(\mathbf{I})) = p\left(\cap_{i=0}^{\mathtt{R}_{\mathtt{N}}} [D(\mathbf{R}_i)|t_{R_i}]\right) = \prod_{i=0}^{\mathtt{R}_{\mathtt{N}}} p(D(\mathbf{R}_i)|t_{R_i})
$$

where $D(\mathbf{R}_i)$ is the multi-modal data associated with the region R_i. The use of multi-modal data drives to multi-variate conditional probabilities. If we assume independence between the different filter responses, then the *a posteriori* segmentation probability is given by

$$
p(\mathcal{P}(R)|D(\mathbf{I})) = \prod_{i=0}^{\mathtt{R}_{\mathtt{N}}} \prod_{j=1}^{\mathtt{M}} p(\mathbf{I}_j(\mathbf{R}_i)|t_{R_i})
$$

where $p(\mathbf{I}_j(\mathbf{R}_i)|t_{R_i})$ is the *a posterior* segmentation probability for the region $\{\mathbf{R}_i\}$ with the respect to the data component $\{\mathbf{I}_j\}$.

4.3 Setting the Energy

Although we made the assumption that the different filter responses are independent, they have some uncertainty measurements, since we use a global statistical model to describe their behavior. These uncertainties are expressed from the discrimination power of the corresponding filters $\{w_j\}$.

The geodesic active region functional for supervised texture segmentation consists of minimizing

$$
E(\partial\mathcal{P}(R)) = (1-\alpha) \sum_{i=1}^{\mathtt{R}_{\mathtt{N}}} \int_0^1 g(p_{\mathrm{B}}(\partial\mathbf{R}_i(p_i))) |\partial\dot{\mathbf{R}}_i(p_i)| dp
$$
$$
- \alpha \sum_{i=0}^{\mathtt{R}_{\mathtt{N}}} \iint_{\mathcal{R}_i} \sum_{j=1}^{\mathtt{M}} w_j \log\left[p_{t_{R_i}j}(\mathbf{I}_j(x,y))\right] dx dy
$$

where $g()$ is a Gaussian function.

4.4 Minimizing the Energy

Let $u = (x, y)$ be a point of the initial curve. This point can either be at region R_0 or at region R_k. Based on this hypothesis, we compute the Euler-Lagrange equations [3, 23] (Section 2), and we derive the following motion equation for u:

$$\frac{du}{dt} = \left[\alpha \sum_{j=1}^{M} w_j \log\left(\frac{p_{t_{R_0}}j(\mathbf{I}_j(u))}{p_{t_{R_k}}j(\mathbf{I}_j(u))} \right) + (1 - \alpha)\left(g(p_{\mathbf{B}}(u))\mathcal{K}(u) - \nabla g(p_{\mathbf{B}}(u)) \cdot \mathcal{N}(u) \right) \right] \mathcal{N}(u)$$

The interpretation of the above PDE is obvious. Given a initial curve, it creates a partition of the image [determined by a curve that attracts the region boundaries] where the exterior curve region corresponds to the *background* pattern while the interior regions correspond to the other patterns.

The obtained PDE can be implemented using a Lagrangian approach, that is limited since it cannot deal with topological changes of the moving front and suffers from instability in the domain of numerical approximations.

This can be avoided by introducing the work of Osher and Sethian [14] in our scheme. The central idea is to represent the moving front $\partial R(t)$ as the zero-level set $\{\Phi = 0\}$ of a function Φ. This representation of $\partial R(t)$ is implicit, parameter-free and intrinsic. Additionally, it is topology-free.It is easy to show, that if the embedding function Φ deforms according to

$$\frac{d}{dt}\Phi(p, t) = \mathcal{F}(p) |\nabla\Phi(p, t)|$$

then the corresponding moving front evolves according to:

$$\frac{d}{dt}C(p, t) = \mathcal{F}(p)\mathcal{N}$$

Thus, the minimization of the proposed geodesic active region objective function is equivalent to searching for a steady-state solution of the following equation:

$$\frac{d}{dt}\Phi(u) = \left[\alpha \sum_{j=1}^{M} w_j \log\left(\frac{p_{t_{R_0}}j(\mathbf{I}_j(u))}{p_{t_{R_k}}j(\mathbf{I}_j(u))} \right) + (1 - \alpha) \right.$$
$$\left. \left(g(p_{\mathbf{B}}(u))\mathcal{K}(u) + \nabla g(p_{\mathbf{B}}(u)) \cdot \frac{\nabla\Phi(u)}{|\nabla\Phi(u)|} \right) \right] |\nabla\Phi(u)|$$

where the geometric properties are estimated directly from the level set frame.

The Level Set Equation is implemented using the **Hermes** algorithm [17, 15] that proposes a fast way to deform the initial curve locally towards the minimum of the objective function.

4.5 Implementation Issues

The proposed method can be used to segment a given texture frame, in the case where the *background* texture pattern is known [**fig.** (5.1,5.4)]. This method can be easily extend to extract some specific regions of interest determined by the corresponding *preferable* patterns [**fig.** (5.2,5.3)]. In both cases, the curve propagation requires a texture assignment for the given point that has to be compared with the

preferable assignments. This issue is confronted by assuming that the temporal segmentation map is derived by the most probable texture assignments. Thus for a given curve point, we assume that it is located between the *preferable* region and the region that corresponds to the most probable assignment (which is derived from the observed data).

5 Conclusions, Results

Synthetic data [**fig.** (5.1)], as well as real-word data [**fig.** (5.2, 5.3, 5.4)] have been used to test and validate the proposed approach [1].

Summarizing, we have considered a curve propagation approach for supervised texture segmentation. The main contribution of our approach is the proposition of **a coupled variational energy framework which integrates boundary-based and region-based information modules and connects the minimization of the objective function with the curve propagation theory**, namely the **Geodesic Active Region** framework. This framework was successfully applied to the supervised texture segmentation problem, where the boundary information is determined using a probabilistic framework, while the region-based information is expressed directly via conditional probabilities. The quality of this information is ensured by the use of powerful probabilistic texture descriptors (learning phase) that combine filtering theory and statistical modeling. The proposed model preserves robustness, and is *independent* from the initialization step thanks to the level set implementation and to the region-based term which creates data-dependent positive and negative propagation forces.

The proposed model is not limited to texture segmentation, but it can be used to deal with a wide variety of computer vision applications that can be reformulated as frame partition problems. The future direction of this work is to validate the proposed model to other computer vision domains.

An extended version of this paper can be found in [16]. Various experimental results (in MPEG format), including the ones shown in this article, can be found at:
http://www.inria.fr/robotvis/personnel/nparagio/demos/
http://www.inria.fr/robotvis/personnel/der/der-eng.html

---

[1] The segmentation performance of our method is demonstrated in [**fig.** (5.1, 5.4)]. Additionally, the performance with respect to the extraction of region of interest is demonstrated in [**fig.** (5.2, 5.3)] where the patterns of interest are given (zebra, chita). Each demonstration contains information about the modeling phase (patterns and filter operators). The filter operators are selected manually, and their size is either 7x7, or 9x9, or 11x11.

The independence of our method with respect to the initialization step is clearly demonstrated. As it concerns the curve propagation, in the case of the absence of curvature, it follows the normal direction (the boundary force is not valid, and the region force is not affected by the curvature), while the presence of curvature aims at creating a smooth curve propagation sequence.

Finally, the computational cost of our approach is related with the initialization step, and varies between 2 and 5 seconds using an ULTRA 10, 299 MHz (the learning phase is not included).

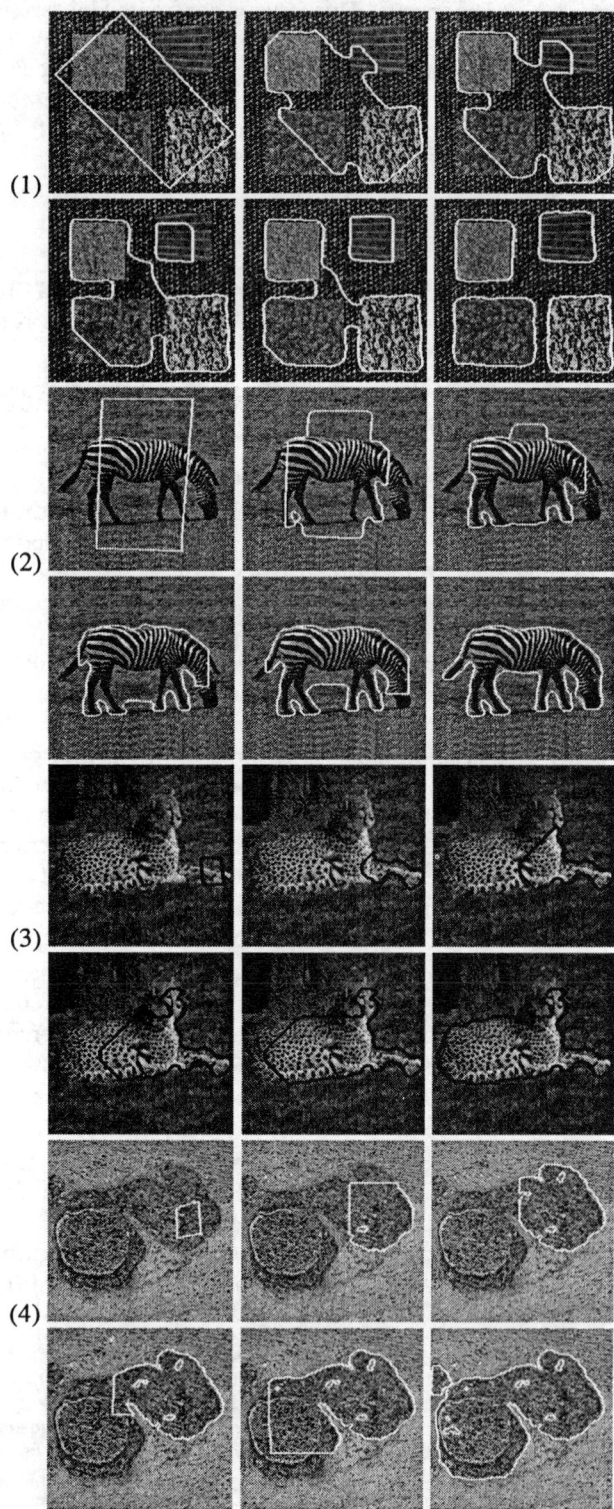

Figure 5. (1) Patterns: *5*, filters: *5* S(1), LoG(1), A[(1, 2π, 2π), A(1, $\frac{\pi}{6}$, 0), A(1, $\frac{\pi}{2}$, $\frac{\pi}{2}$). (2) Patterns: *3*, filters: *6* S(1), derivatives, A[(1, 2π, 2π), A(1, $\frac{\pi}{6}$, 0), A(1, $\frac{\pi}{3}$, 0), A(1, 0, $\frac{\pi}{3}$)]. (3) Patterns: *3*, filters: *8* S(1), GsA[(1, 2π, 2π, 0), A(1, $\frac{\pi}{6}$, 0), A(1, $\frac{\pi}{3}$, 0), A(1, 0, $\frac{\pi}{3}$), A(1, 0, $\frac{\pi}{6}$), A(1, $\frac{\pi}{6}$, $\frac{\pi}{3}$), A(1, $\frac{\pi}{3}$, $\frac{\pi}{6}$)]. (4) Patterns: *3*, filters: *9* S(1), LoG(1), A[(1, 2π, 2π, 0), A(1, $\frac{\pi}{6}$, 0), A(1, $\frac{\pi}{3}$, 0), A(1, 0, $\frac{\pi}{3}$), A(1, 0, $\frac{\pi}{6}$), A(1, $\frac{\pi}{3}$, $\frac{\pi}{3}$), A(1, $\frac{\pi}{6}$, $\frac{\pi}{6}$)].

References

[1] R. Adams and L. Bischof. Seeded Region Growing. *IEEE PAMI*, 16:641–647, 1994.

[2] A. Bovik, M. Clark, and W. Geister. Multichannel texture analysis using localized spatial filters. *IEEE PAMI*, 12:55–73, 1990.

[3] V. Caselles, R. Kimmel, and G. Sapiro. Geodesic active contours. *IJCV*, 22:61–79, 1997.

[4] A. Chakraborty, H. Staib, and J. Duncan. Deformable Boundary Finding in Medical Images by Integrating Gradient and Region Information. *IEEE Transactions on Medical Imaging*, 15(6):859–870, 1996.

[5] P. Chen and T. Pavlidis. Segmentation by texture using correlation. *IEEE PAMI*, 5:64–69, 1983.

[6] J. Haddon and J. Boyce. Inage Segmentation by Unifying Region and Boundary Information. *IEEE PAMI*, 12:929–948, 1990.

[7] A. Jain and F. Farrokhnia. Unsupervised texture segmentation using Gabor filters. *Pattern Recognition*, 24:1167–1186, 1991.

[8] S. Kichenassamy, A. Kumar, P. Olver, A. Tannenbaum, and A. Yezzi. Gradient flows and geometric active contour models. In *IEEE ICCV*, pages 810–815, Boston, USA, 1995.

[9] S. Kichenassamy, A. Kumar, P. Olver, A. Tannenbaum, and A. Yezzi. Conformal curvature flows: from phase transitions to active vision. *Archive of Rational Mechanics and Analysis*, 134:275–301, 1996.

[10] R. Malladi, J. Sethian, and B. Vemuri. Shape modeling with front propagation: A level set approach. *IEEE PAMI*, 17:158–175, 1995.

[11] S. Mallat. Multiresolution approximations and wavelet orthonormal bases of $L^2(R)$. *Trans. Amer. Math. Soc.*, 315:69–87, 1989.

[12] B. Manjunath and R. Chellapa. A Computational Approach to boundary detection. In *IEEE CVPR*, pages 358–362, 1991.

[13] B. Manjunath and R. Chellapa. Unsupervised texture segmentation using Markov Random Field models. *IEEE PAMI*, 13:478–482, 1991.

[14] S. Osher and J. Sethian. Fronts propagating with curvature-dependent speed : algorithms based on the hamilton-jacobi formulation. *Journal of Computational Physics*, 79:12–49, 1988.

[15] N. Paragios. *Geodesic Active Regions and Level Sets: Contributions and Applications in Artificial Vision*. PhD thesis, University of Nice/Sophia Antipolis, France, November 1999. http://www-sop.inria.fr/robotvis/personnel/nparagio/thesis.

[16] N. Paragios and R. Deriche. Geodesic Active Regions for Texture Segmentation. Research Report 3440, INRIA, France, 1998. http://www.inria.fr/rapports/sophia/RR-3440.html.

[17] N. Paragios and R. Deriche. A PDE-based Level Set approach for Detection and Tracking of moving objects. In *IEEE ICCV*, pages 1139–1145, Bombay, India, 1998.

[18] N. Paragios and R. Deriche. Geodesic Active Contours for Supervised Texture Segmentation. In *IEEE CVPR*, Colorado, USA, 1999.

[19] N. Paragios and R. Deriche. Unifying Boundary and Region-based Information for Geodesic Active Tracking. In *IEEE CVPR*, Colorado, USA, 1999.

[20] M. Unser. Local linear transforms for texture measurements. *Signal Processing*, 11:61–79, 1986.

[21] S. Yhann and T. Young. Boundary localization in texture segmentation. *IEEE IP*, 4:849–856, 1995.

[22] X. Zeng, L. Staib, R. Schukz, and J. Duncan. Volumetric Layer Segmentation Using Coupled Surfaces Propagation. In *IEEE CVPR*, pages 708–715, Santa Barbara, USA, 1998.

[23] S. Zhu and A. Yuille. Region Competition: Unifying Snakes, Region Growing, and Bayes/MDL for Multiband Image Segmentation. *IEEE PAMI*, 18:884–900, 1996.

United Snakes

Jianming Liang[1,2], Tim McInerney[2,3], and Demetri Terzopoulos[2]

[1] Turku Centre for Computer Science, DataCity, Lemminkäisenkatu 14 A, 20520 Turku, Finland
[2] Department of Computer Science, University of Toronto, 6 King's College Road, Toronto, ON M5S 3H5, Canada
[3] Department of Math, Physics and Computer Science, Ryerson Polytechnic University, 80 Gould St., Toronto, ON M5B 2K3, Canada
Email: liang@cs.utu.fi, tim@cs.toronto.edu, dt@cs.toronto.edu

Abstract

Since their debut in 1987, snakes (active contour models) have become a standard image analysis technique with several variants now in common use. We present a portable, reusable, software package called "United Snakes". The package unites the most popular snake variants, including finite difference, B-spline, and Hermite polynomial snakes within the mathematical framework of a general finite element formulation with a choice of shape functions. The package furthermore incorporates a recently proposed snake-like technique known as "livewire". We integrate snakes and livewire by introducing an effective method for imposing hard constraints on snakes. Our experiments demonstrate that snakes and livewire have complementary strengths and that their union offers a more powerful tool for interactive image analysis, especially for medical imaging applications. United Snakes is implemented in Java as a JavaBean so that it can easily be integrated in end-user application systems.

1. Introduction

Snakes (active contour models) quickly gained popularity following their debut in 1987 [7]. They have proven especially useful in medical image analysis [10, 14] and for tracking moving objects in video [17, 3], among other applications. Variants such as finite element snakes [4], B-snakes [11, 3], and Fourier snakes [15], have been proposed in an effort to improve aspects of the original finite difference implementation (e.g., to decrease initialization sensitivity, increase robustness against noise, improve selectivity for certain classes of objects, etc.). No formulation has yet emerged as a "gold standard". Rather, the variants seem well-suited to different applications with particular image modalities and processing scenarios.

Given the confusing array of choices for the user, there is a need for a portable and reusable snakes implementation which unites the best features of the variants while maintaining the simplicity and elegance of the original formulation. To this end, our first contribution in this paper is to unify the most important snakes variants, including finite difference, B-spline, and Hermite polynomial snakes, in a comprehensive finite element framework where a particular type of snake can be derived by simply changing the finite

element shape functions.

A technique, known as "livewire" or "intelligent scissors" [12, 2, 13, 5], has recently emerged as an effective interactive boundary tracing tool. Based on dynamic programming [5] or Dijkstra's graph search algorithm [13], it was originally developed as an interactive 2D extension to earlier optimal boundary tracking methods. Livewire features several similarities with snakes, but it is generally considered in the literature as a competing technique. Our second contribution in this paper is the idea that livewire and snakes are in fact complementary techniques that can advantageously be combined via a simple yet effective method to impose hard constraints on snakes.

We call our software implementation *United Snakes*, because it unites several snake variants with livewire to offer a general purpose tool for interactive image segmentation that provides more flexible control while reducing user interactions. We have implemented United Snakes in Java as a JavaBean (reusable Java software component), so that it may easily be integrated into any end-user application system.

We describe our finite element framework in Section 2 and show how several snake variants can be integrated within it. Section 3 describes the livewire technique. We justify the idea of combining snakes with livewire in Section 4 and develop a hard constraint mechanism in Section 5 that makes this combination possible. Section 6 presents results utilizing the United Snakes system in a medical image segmentation scenario. We conclude in Section 7 and propose future extensions of United Snakes.

2. Finite Element Unification of Snakes

A snake is a time-varying parametric contour $\mathbf{v}(s, t) = (x(s, t), y(s, t))^\top$ in the image plane $(x, y) \in \Re^2$, where x and y are coordinate functions of the parameter $s \in [0, L]$ and t is time. The shape of the contour subject to an image $I(x, y)$ is dictated by an energy functional $\mathcal{E}(\mathbf{v}) = \mathcal{S}(\mathbf{v}) + \mathcal{P}(\mathbf{v})$. The first term is the internal deformation energy defined as

$$\mathcal{S}(\mathbf{v}) = \frac{1}{2} \int_0^L \alpha(s) \left| \frac{\partial \mathbf{v}}{\partial s} \right|^2 + \beta(s) \left| \frac{\partial^2 \mathbf{v}}{\partial s^2} \right|^2 ds, \quad (1)$$

where $\alpha(s)$ controls the "tension" of the contour and $\beta(s)$ regulates its "rigidity". The second term is an external image energy

$$\mathcal{P}(\mathbf{v}) = \int_0^L P_I(\mathbf{v})\,ds, \qquad (2)$$

which couples the snake to the image via a scalar potential function $P_I(x, y)$ typically computed from $I(x, y)$ through image processing. The Lagrange equations of motion for a dynamic snake are

$$\mu\frac{\partial^2 \mathbf{v}}{\partial t^2} + \gamma\frac{\partial \mathbf{v}}{\partial t} - \frac{\partial}{\partial s}\left(\alpha\frac{\partial \mathbf{v}}{\partial s}\right) + \frac{\partial^2}{\partial s^2}\left(\beta\frac{\partial^2 \mathbf{v}}{\partial s^2}\right) = \mathbf{q}(\mathbf{v}). \quad (3)$$

The first two terms represent inertial forces due to the mass density $\mu(s)$ and damping forces due to the dissipation density $\gamma(s)$. The next two terms represent the internal stretching and bending deformation forces. On the right hand side are the external forces $\mathbf{q}(\mathbf{v}) = -\nabla P_I(\mathbf{v}) + \mathbf{f}$, where the image forces are the negative gradient of the image potential function. The user may guide the dynamic snake via time-varying interaction forces $\mathbf{f}(s, t)$ (usually applied through a mouse), driving the snake out of one energy minimizing equilibrium and into another. Viewed as a dynamical system, the snake may also be used to track moving objects in a time-varying (video) image $I(x, y, t)$.

2.1. Finite Element Formulation

In a finite element formulation, the parametric domain $0 \leq s \leq L$ is partitioned into finite sub-domains, so that the snake contour is divided into "snake elements". Each element e is represented geometrically with shape functions $\mathbf{N}(s)$ involving shape parameters $\mathbf{u}^e(t)$. The shape parameters of all the elements are collected together into the snake parameter vector $\mathbf{u}(t)$. This leads to a discrete form of the equations of motion (3) as a system of second order ordinary differential equations in $\mathbf{u}(t)$:

$$\mathbf{M\ddot{u}} + \mathbf{C\dot{u}} + \mathbf{Ku} = \mathbf{g}, \qquad (4)$$

where $\mathbf{M}$ is the mass matrix, $\mathbf{C}$ is the damping matrix, $\mathbf{K}$ is the stiffness matrix, and $\mathbf{g}$ is the external force vector. Appendix A details the finite element formulation.

The stiffness matrix $\mathbf{K}$ is assembled from element stiffness sub-matrices $\mathbf{K}^e$ which depend on the shape functions $\mathbf{N}$ (the matrices $\mathbf{M}$, $\mathbf{C}$, and the vector of nodal external forces $\mathbf{g}$ are assembled in a similar way and also depend on $\mathbf{N}$). The shape functions generate different stiffness matrices and, in turn, yield different snake behaviors suitable for different tasks. For example, snakes that use B-spline shape functions are typically characterized by a low number of degrees of freedom, typically use polynomial basis functions of degree 2 or higher, and are inherently very smooth. Therefore, these "B-snakes" [11, 3] can be effective in segmentation or tracking tasks involving noisy images where the target object boundaries may exhibit significant gaps in the images. On the other hand, object boundaries with many fine details or rapid curvature variations may best be segmented by a snake that uses simpler shape functions and more degrees of freedom, such as a finite difference snake [7]. The unification of these different shape functions in a single framework enhances the range of object modeling capabilities.

The following sections address Hermitian shape functions, B-spline shape functions, and "shape functions" for finite difference

snakes. Since the two coordinate functions $x(s)$ and $y(s)$ of the snake $\mathbf{v}(s)$ are independent, we shall discuss the shape functions in terms of only one component $x(s)$; the shape functions for $y(s)$ assume an identical form.

2.2. Hermitian Shape Functions

In the case of Hermitian snakes, $x(s)$ ($0 \leq s \leq l$, where l is the element parametric length) is approximated with a cubic polynomial function, parameterized by position x and slope θ at the endpoints $s = 0$ and $s = l$ of an element. We can show that $x(s) = \mathbf{N}_h\mathbf{u}^{e_i}$, where $\mathbf{u}^{e_i} = [x_i\ \theta_i\ x_{i+1}\ \theta_{i+1}]^\top$ are the shape parameters of element e_i and $\mathbf{N}_h = \mathbf{sH}$ are the Hermitian shape functions, with $\mathbf{s} = [1\ s\ s^2\ s^3]$ and the *Hermitian shape matrix*

$$\mathbf{H} = \begin{bmatrix} 1 & 0 & 0 & 0 \\ 0 & 1 & 0 & 0 \\ -3/l^2 & -2/l & 3/l^2 & -1/l \\ 2/l^3 & 1/l^2 & -2/l^3 & 1/l^2 \end{bmatrix}. \qquad (5)$$

It is reasonable to assume that the tension function $\alpha(s)$ and rigidity function $\beta(s)$ are constant within the element. Hence, the stiffness matrices associated with the tension and rigidity components for element e_i are respectively

$$\mathbf{K}_\alpha^{e_i} = \frac{\alpha_i}{30l}\begin{bmatrix} 36 & 3l & -36 & 3l \\ 3l & 4l^2 & -3l & -l^2 \\ -36 & -3l & 36 & -3l \\ 3l & -l^2 & -3l & 4l^2 \end{bmatrix}, \qquad (6)$$

$$\mathbf{K}_\beta^{e_i} = \frac{\beta_i}{l^3}\begin{bmatrix} 12 & 6l & -12 & 6l \\ 6l & 4l^2 & -6l & 2l^2 \\ -12 & -6l & 12 & -6l \\ 6l & 2l^2 & -6l & 4l^2 \end{bmatrix}. \qquad (7)$$

An analytic form of the external forces $\mathbf{q}(\mathbf{v})$ in (3) is generally not available. Therefore, Gauss-Legendre quadrature may be employed to approximate the value of the integral for the element external force vector $\mathbf{F}^e$. For element e_i we have

$$\begin{aligned} \mathbf{F}_x^{e_i} &= \int_0^l \mathbf{N}_h{}^\top \mathbf{q}_x(\mathbf{v}(s))\,ds \\ &= l\sum_j \rho_j \mathbf{N}_h(\xi_j)^\top \mathbf{q}_x(\mathbf{v}(\xi_j)), \end{aligned} \qquad (8)$$

where the subscript x indicates the association with coordinate function $x(s)$, and where ξ_j and ρ_j are the jth Gaussian integration point and its corresponding weighting coefficient, respectively. $\mathbf{F}_y^{e_i}$ is derived in a similar fashion.

To make the global matrix assembly process identical for all shape functions, we introduce *assembling matrices*. Suppose that we have a snake with n elements and N nodes ($N = n$ if the snake is closed and $N = n + 1$ if it is open). For the ith element e_i of the snake ($0 \leq i \leq n - 1$), the assembling matrices are $\mathbf{G}_\alpha^{e_i} = \mathbf{G}_\beta^{e_i} = \mathbf{G}_\mathbf{F}^{e_i} = \mathbf{G}^{e_i}$, where

$$(\mathbf{G}^{e_i})_{jk} = \begin{cases} 1 & \text{if } (j + di)\bmod(dN) = k \\ 0 & \text{otherwise,} \end{cases} \qquad (9)$$

are $(2 \cdot d) \times (d \cdot N)$ matrices, with d the number of degrees of freedom of each node in an element (here $d = 2$). Hence, $\mathbf{K}_\alpha$, $\mathbf{K}_\beta$ and $\mathbf{F}$ may be assembled as follows:

$$\mathbf{K}_\alpha = \sum_{i=0}^{n-1} (\mathbf{G}_\alpha^{e_i})^\top \mathbf{K}_\alpha^{e_i} (\mathbf{G}_\alpha^{e_i}), \qquad (10)$$

$$\mathbf{K}_\beta = \sum_{i=0}^{n-1} (\mathbf{G}_\beta^{e_i})^\top \mathbf{K}_\beta^{e_i} (\mathbf{G}_\beta^{e_i}), \qquad (11)$$

$$\mathbf{F} = \sum_{i=0}^{n-1} (\mathbf{G}_\mathbf{F}^{e_i})^\top \mathbf{F}^{e_i}. \qquad (12)$$

Only the shape matrix and the assembling matrices are determined by specific polynomial shape functions. Therefore, in the following section we shall focus only on the derivation of the shape matrix and the assembling matrices for B-spline shape functions, and briefly mention other kinds of shape functions which are suitable for snakes.

2.3. B-Spline Shape Functions

For B-spline shape functions, the $x(s)$ coordinate function of $\mathbf{v}(s)$ is constructed as a weighted sum of N_B basis functions $B_n(s)$, $n = 0, ..., N_B - 1$ as follows: $x(s) = \mathbf{B}(s)^\top \mathbf{Q}^x$, where $\mathbf{B}(s) = [\mathbf{B}_0(s), ..., \mathbf{B}_{N_B-1}(s)]^\top$, $\mathbf{Q}^x = [x_0, ..., x_{N_B-1}]^\top$ and x_i are the weights applied to the respective basis functions $B_n(s)$.

A B-spline span serves as an element in our finite element formulation (hence "span" and "element" are interchangeable terms). Consequently, we shall determine the nodal variables (*i.e.* snake shape parameters), the shape matrix, and the assembling matrix associated with a span. When all spans are unit length, the knot multiplicities at the breakpoints are $m_0, ..., m_L$ (L is the number of spans and the total number of knots $N_B = \sum_{i=0}^{L} m_i$), the knot values k_i are determined by $k_i = l$, such that $0 \leq (i - \sum_{j=0}^{l} m_j) < m_{l+1}$. Furthermore, the nth polynomial $B_{n,d}^\sigma$ in span σ can be computed as follows:

$$B_{n,1}^\sigma(s) = \begin{cases} 1 & \text{if } k_n \leq \sigma < k_{n+1} \\ 0 & \text{otherwise} \end{cases} \qquad (13)$$

$$B_{n,d}^\sigma(s) = \frac{(s + \sigma - k_n)B_{n,d-1}^\sigma(s)}{k_{n+d-1} - k_n} + \frac{(k_{n+d} - s - \sigma)B_{n+1,d-1}^\sigma(s)}{k_{n+d} - k_{n+1}} \qquad (14)$$

For span σ, the index b_σ for the first basis function whose support includes the span can be determined as $b_\sigma = [(\sum_{i=0}^{\sigma} m_i) - d] \bmod N_B$. Therefore, $I = [b_\sigma, (b_\sigma + 1) \bmod N_B, ..., (b_\sigma + d - 1) \bmod N_B]$ are the indices of the nodal variables and also those of the d polynomials $B_{n,d}^\sigma$.[1] Now, the shape matrix for span σ can be constructed by collecting the coefficients of each of the d polynomials $B_{n,d}^\sigma$ as its columns. For example, the shape matrix of a regular cubic B-

---

[1]In an open B-spline snake, d knots are introduced at the two ends. As a result, the index for the first basis function in the first span is zero (*i.e.* $b_0 = 0$) and the index of the last basis function in the last span is $N_B - 1$. For a closed B-spline snake, the index needs to be wrapped properly.

spline is

$$\mathbf{H} = \begin{bmatrix} 1/6 & 2/3 & 1/6 & 0 \\ -1/2 & 0 & 1/2 & 0 \\ 1/2 & -1 & 1/2 & 0 \\ -1/6 & 1/2 & -1/2 & 1/6 \end{bmatrix} \qquad (15)$$

and the element stiffness matrices for element e_i are

$$\mathbf{K}_\alpha^{e_i} = \alpha_i \begin{bmatrix} 0.0500 & 0.0583 & -0.1000 & -0.0083 \\ 0.0583 & 0.2833 & -0.2417 & -0.1000 \\ -0.1000 & -0.2417 & 0.2833 & 0.0583 \\ -0.0083 & -0.1000 & 0.0583 & 0.0500 \end{bmatrix}, \qquad (16)$$

$$\mathbf{K}_\beta^{e_i} = \beta_i \begin{bmatrix} 0.3333 & -0.5000 & 0 & 0.1667 \\ -0.5000 & 1.0000 & -0.5000 & 0 \\ 0 & -0.5000 & 1.0000 & -0.5000 \\ 0.1667 & 0 & -0.5000 & 0.3333 \end{bmatrix}. \qquad (17)$$

The assembling matrix $\mathbf{G}^{e_i}$ can be defined as

$$(\mathbf{G}^{e_i})_{jk} = \begin{cases} 1 & \text{if } (j + b_\sigma) \bmod N_B = k \\ 0 & \text{otherwise.} \end{cases} \qquad (18)$$

In a similar fashion as above, we may construct other kinds of shape functions; for instance, NURBS shape functions [16], Catmull-Rom shape functions, Bézier shape functions and Fourier shape functions. The latter are global shape functions over the whole snake [15], thus the associated assembling matrix becomes an identity matrix.

2.4. Finite Difference Snakes in Element Form

Despite the differences between finite element snakes and finite difference snakes, the finite difference snakes can also be constructed in the finite element fashion, using the Dirac delta function $\delta(s)$ as the shape function. The construction primitives are as follows: For a snake with n nodes, $\mathbf{K}_\alpha^{e_i}$ is a 2×2 matrix and its corresponding assembling matrix $\mathbf{G}_\alpha^{e_i}$ is a $2 \times n$ matrix as follows:

$$\mathbf{K}_\alpha^{e_i} = \alpha_i \begin{bmatrix} -1 & 1 \end{bmatrix}^\top \begin{bmatrix} -1 & 1 \end{bmatrix}$$
$$= \alpha_i \begin{bmatrix} 1 & -1 \\ -1 & 1 \end{bmatrix}, \qquad (19)$$

$$(\mathbf{G}_\alpha^{e_i})_{jk} = \begin{cases} 1 & \text{if } (j + i) \bmod n = k \\ 0 & \text{otherwise,} \end{cases} \qquad (20)$$

where $0 \leq i \leq n - 2$ for an open snake and $0 \leq i \leq n - 1$ for a closed snake. $\mathbf{K}_\beta^{e_i}$ is a 3×3 matrix and with it is associated a $3 \times n$ assembling matrix $\mathbf{G}_\beta^{e_i}$ as follows:

$$\mathbf{K}_\beta^{e_i} = \beta_i \begin{bmatrix} 1 & -2 & 1 \end{bmatrix}^\top \begin{bmatrix} 1 & -2 & 1 \end{bmatrix}$$
$$= \beta_i \begin{bmatrix} 1 & -2 & 1 \\ -2 & 4 & -2 \\ 1 & -2 & 1 \end{bmatrix}, \qquad (21)$$

$$(\mathbf{G}_\beta^{e_i})_{jk} = \begin{cases} 1 & \text{if } (j + i) \bmod n = k \\ 0 & \text{otherwise,} \end{cases} \qquad (22)$$

where $0 \leq i \leq n - 3$ for an open snake and $0 \leq i \leq n - 1$ for a closed snake. The $1 \times n$ assembling matrix $\mathbf{G}_\mathbf{F}^{e_i}$ is defined as

$$(\mathbf{G}_\mathbf{F}^{e_i})_{0,k} = \begin{cases} 1 & \text{if } i = k \\ 0 & \text{otherwise,} \end{cases} \tag{23}$$

where $0 \leq i \leq n - 1$ for both open and closed snakes.

With the above formulation of finite difference snakes, we have a uniform finite element construction for a variety of snake representations, which leads to a relatively straightforward United Snakes implementation in an object-oriented programming language, such as Java.

3. Livewire

Livewire is a recently proposed interactive boundary tracing technique [12, 2, 13, 5]. It has two essential components, a local cost function that assigns lower cost to image features of interest, such as edges, and an expansion process that forms optimal boundaries for objects of interest based on the cost function and seed points provided interactively by the user.

3.1. Trace Formation

Boundary finding in livewire can be formulated as a directed graph search for an optimal (minimum cost) path using Dijkstra's algorithm. First, nodes in the graph are initialized with the local costs as described in the next section. Once the user selects a seed point, it will be used as the starting point for a recursive expansion process. In the expansion process, the local cost at the seed point is summed into its neighboring nodes. The neighboring node with the minimum cumulative cost is then further expanded and the process produces a dynamic "wavefront". The wavefront expands in order of minimum cumulative cost. Consequently, it propagates preferentially in directions of highest interest (*i.e.* along edges). This process requires only n iterations over the wavefront for paths of length n. Furthermore, since the wavefront is maintained in a sorted list, the expansion happens at interactive rates.

Therefore, for any dynamically selected goal node (*i.e.*, the free point) within the wavefront, the optimal path back to the seed point which forms a livewire (trace) can be displayed in real time. When the cursor (the free point) moves, the old livewire trace is erased and a new one computed and displayed in real time. The expansion process aims to compute an optimal path from a selected seed point to *every* other point in the image and lets the user choose among paths interactively, based on the current cursor position.

Livewire may be implemented very efficiently in multithreaded programming languages, such as Java, because the expansion process and the user interface can execute in separate, parallel threads. Since the free point is generally near the target object boundary, the expansion process will most likely have already advanced beyond that point and the livewire trace can be displayed immediately. That is, the livewire trace can typically be displayed before the expansion process has finished sweeping over the entire image.

3.2. Local Cost Function

There are different ways to define the local cost function. We follow the definition given by Mortensen and Barrett [12]. The local cost $\mathsf{l}(\mathbf{p}, \mathbf{q})$ on the directed link from $\mathbf{p}$ to a neighboring pixel $\mathbf{q}$ is defined as a weighted sum of three local component costs created from various edge features:

$$\mathsf{l}(\mathbf{p}, \mathbf{q}) = \omega_Z \mathsf{f}_Z(\mathbf{q}) + \omega_D \mathsf{f}_D(\mathbf{p}, \mathbf{q}) + \omega_G \mathsf{f}_G(\mathbf{q}), \tag{24}$$

where $\mathsf{f}_Z(\mathbf{q})$ is the Laplacian zero-crossing function at $\mathbf{q}$, $\mathsf{f}_D(\mathbf{p}, \mathbf{q})$ is the gradient direction from $\mathbf{p}$ to $\mathbf{q}$, $\mathsf{f}_G(\mathbf{q})$ is the gradient magnitude at $\mathbf{q}$, and ω_Z, ω_D and ω_G are their corresponding weights. The Laplacian zero-crossing function $\mathsf{f}_Z(\mathbf{q})$ is a binary function defined as

$$\mathsf{f}_Z(\mathbf{q}) = \begin{cases} 0 & \text{if } I_L(\mathbf{q}) = 0 \\ 1 & \text{otherwise,} \end{cases} \tag{25}$$

where $I_L(\mathbf{q})$ is the Laplacian of the image I at pixel $\mathbf{q}$. The gradient magnitude serves to establish a direct connection between edge strength and cost. The function f_G is defined as an inverse linear ramp function of the gradient magnitude G

$$\mathsf{f}_G = \frac{\max(G') - G'}{\max(G')} = 1 - \frac{G'}{\max(G')} \tag{26}$$

where $G' = G - \min(G)$. When calculating $\mathsf{l}(\mathbf{p}, \mathbf{q})$, the function $\mathsf{f}_G(\mathbf{q})$ is further scaled by 1 if $\mathbf{q}$ is a diagonal neighbor to $\mathbf{p}$ and by $1/\sqrt{2}$ if $\mathbf{q}$ is a horizontal or vertical neighbor. The gradient direction $\mathsf{f}_D(\mathbf{p}, \mathbf{q})$ adds a smoothness constraint to the boundary by associating a higher cost for sharp changes in boundary direction. With $\mathbf{D}(\mathbf{p})$ defined as the unit vector normal to the gradient direction at pixel $\mathbf{p}$ (*i.e.*, $\mathbf{D}(\mathbf{p}) = [I_y(\mathbf{p}), -I_x(\mathbf{p})]$), the formulation of the gradient direction cost is

$$\mathsf{f}_D(\mathbf{p}, \mathbf{q}) = \frac{2}{3\pi} \left\{ \arccos[d_\mathbf{p}(\mathbf{p}, \mathbf{q})] + \arccos[d_\mathbf{q}(\mathbf{p}, \mathbf{q})] \right\}, \tag{27}$$

where $d_\mathbf{p}(\mathbf{p}, \mathbf{q}) = \mathbf{D}(\mathbf{p}) \cdot \mathbf{L}(\mathbf{p}, \mathbf{q})$ and $d_\mathbf{q}(\mathbf{p}, \mathbf{q}) = \mathbf{L}(\mathbf{p}, \mathbf{q}) \cdot \mathbf{D}(\mathbf{q})$ are vector dot products and

$$\mathbf{L}(\mathbf{p}, \mathbf{q}) = \frac{1}{\|\mathbf{p} - \mathbf{q}\|} \begin{cases} \mathbf{q} - \mathbf{p} & \text{if } \mathbf{D}(\mathbf{p}) \cdot (\mathbf{q} - \mathbf{p}) \geq 0 \\ \mathbf{p} - \mathbf{q} & \text{if } \mathbf{D}(\mathbf{p}) \cdot (\mathbf{q} - \mathbf{p}) < 0 \end{cases} \tag{28}$$

is the normalized bidirectional link or unit edge vector between pixels $\mathbf{p}$ and $\mathbf{q}$.

4. Combining Snakes and Livewire

With livewire, the user has no control of traces between seed points. When the shape of the object boundary is complex, or when it is near other strong but uninteresting object boundaries, many seed points are needed in order to generate an acceptable result. Furthermore, when a section of the desired object boundary has a weak edge relative to a nearby strong edge, the livewire snaps to the strong edge rather than the desired weaker boundary. In order to mitigate this problem, Mortensen and Barrett proposed *on-the-fly training* [13]. However, this method relies on the assumption that the edge property is relatively consistent along the object boundary. For example, in the lung image of Figure 1(a), the

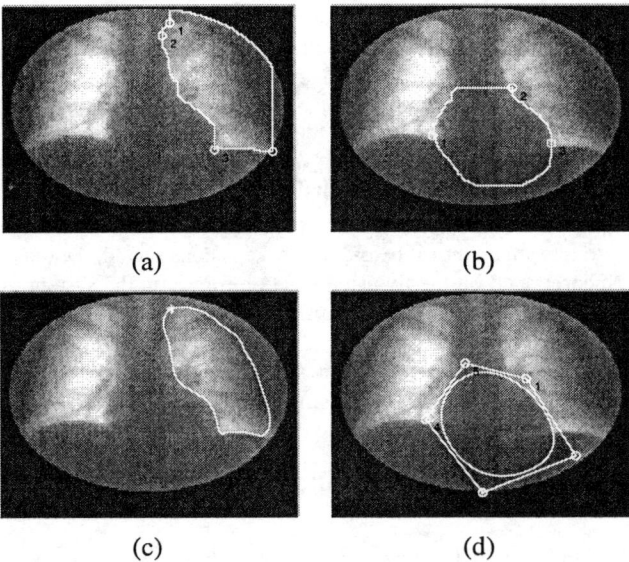

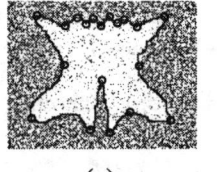 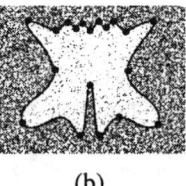 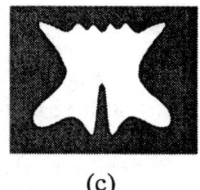

(a)   (b)   (c)

Figure 2. Performance of United Snakes demonstrated using a noisy synthetic image. (a) A livewire is sensitive to noise (the required seed points are shown). (b) The United Snake is robust against noise. (c) The segmented boundary accurately conforms to the ideal boundary.

(a)   (b)

(c)   (d)

Figure 1. Delineation of the lung (a) and heart (b) in X-ray fluoroscopy images using livewire (seed points are shown). (c) Delination with Hermite snake constructed from livewire trace using first seed point as a hard constraint. (d) Result using B-snake (and control polygon) constructed from livewire trace.

livewire snaps to the strong edges of the elliptical viewport rather than the desired lung boundary. In this case, on-the-fly training is ineffective since the edge property of the lung boundary varies considerably over it extent.

Livewire is fundamentally image-based. Thus, it cannot effectively bridge gaps where the desired object boundaries are missing, and the smoothness of the traces can hardly be guaranteed. For instance, in Figure 1(b), part of the livewire trace from seed point 1 to seed point 2 is a straight line where the cardiac boundary is missing. The livewire technique does not generate an acceptable cardiac boundary from seed point 3 to seed point 1, and we have manually drawn a rough curve between the points.

Therefore, it is desirable to allow the user to exercise control over the livewire traces between seed points, impose smoothness on livewire traces, and bridge gaps along object boundaries. This is what snakes are very good at doing. Snakes adhere to edges with sub-pixel accuracy and they may also be adjusted interactively as parametric curves with intuitively familiar physical behaviors. Furthermore, snakes have the power to track moving objects, while livewire does not.

In most cases, however, livewire can quickly give much better results than casual manual tracing. Hence, the resulting livewire boundary can serve to initialize a snake. The livewire seed points reflect the user's prior knowledge of the object boundary. They can therefore serve as either hard or soft point constraints for the snake, depending on the user's confidence in the accuracies of these seed points.

Because a livewire-traced initial object boundary is more accurate than a hand-drawn boundary, and with the further incorpo-

ration of the seed points as snake constraints, the snake will very quickly lock onto the desired object boundary. If necessary, the user may correct mistakes inherited from the livewire-generated boundary by applying mouse-controlled spring forces to the snake. Because the user still has the opportunity to correct the mistakes on the traces as the snake is deforming, the number of seed points needed by livewire to generate the object boundary can be further reduced. Consequently, a coarse object boundary can be generated very quickly using livewire.

Other hard or soft constraints may be added during the snake deformation process as well. Because constrained values may be changed dynamically, the user may adjust the seed points to further refine object boundaries as the snake deforms. In the lung segmentation example, a Hermite snake constructed from the livewire traces with the first seed as a hard constraint can firmly adhere to the lung apex, and it can easily be pulled out of the strong edge and lock onto the lung boundary as shown in Figure 1(c) without on-the-fly training. For the heart, a least squares approximation to the initial livewire curve with a 5-knot cubic B-spline is used to initialize a B-snake. A hard constraint may be further imposed on the control polygon node 3 to effectively bridge the gap along the heart boundary. The result is shown in Figure 1(d) after only a few iterations. The user may move the control polygon node 3 to refine that segment of the heart boundary if necessary.

As further evidence that United Snakes improves upon the robustness and accuracy of its component techniques, Fig. 2 shows a synthetic image of a known curve degraded by strong Gaussian white noise (variance 0.25). Given its image-based nature, the livewire is sensitive to noise as shown in Fig. 2(a). A snake initialized with the livewire gives a better result (Fig. 2(b)). Fig. 2(c) shows that the United Snakes result is very close to the boundary in the ideal image, despite the strong noise. This performance is a consequence of the imposed hard constraints, without which the snake would slip away from high curvature points.

5. Hard Constraints

The combination of snakes and livewire relies on an efficient constraint mechanism. A constraint on a snake may be either soft or hard. Hard constraints generally compel the snake to pass through certain positions or take certain shapes (generic hard constraints are discussed in [6]), while soft constraints merely encourage a snake to do so. Two kinds of soft constraints, springs and volcanos, were described in the original snakes paper [7] and they are incorporated into our finite element formulation. Hard constraints have been used to prevent snake nodes from clustering in dynamic programming snakes [1]. In this section, we propose a convenient mechanism, called *pins*, as a simple yet effective way to impose hard constraints on snakes for the integration of snakes and livewire.

Suppose that we wish to guarantee that the snake node i sticks at position (x_i^c, y_i^c) in the Hermitian parameterization. Recall that in the Hermitian parameterization, the polynomial shape of each element is parameterized by the position and slope of $x(s)$ and $y(s)$ at the two nodes (position and slope variables occupy alternating positions in the nodal variable vector $\mathbf{u}$). Therefore, the snake stiffness matrix $\mathbf{K}$ may be updated with

$$\mathbf{K}_{2 \cdot i, j} = \begin{cases} 1 & \text{if } 2i = j \\ 0 & \text{otherwise} \end{cases} \quad (29)$$

where $0 \leq j \leq 2(N-1)$ and N is the number of snake nodes, and the system force vector $\mathbf{F}$ is updated as

$$\mathbf{F}_{2 \cdot i}^x = x_i^c, \qquad \mathbf{F}_{2 \cdot i}^y = y_i^c, \quad (30)$$

where x and y indicate coordinate function $x(s)$ and $y(s)$, respectively. It is then guaranteed that the snake node i is always at position (x_i^c, y_i^c).

A drawback of this simple technique, however, is that the updated system stiffness matrix is no longer symmetric. Consequently, we are unable to economically save the stiffness matrix using skyline storage, nor factorize it in LDL^T form (see Appendix A). Nevertheless, since the position of node i is given, a constant force may be derived from the stiffness matrix for each degree of freedom and subtracted from its corresponding position in the system force vector so that we can restore the symmetry of the stiffness matrix while keeping the system in balance. That is, the system force vector $\mathbf{F}$ and the stiffness matrix are further updated with

$$\mathbf{F}_j^x = \mathbf{F}_j^x - \mathbf{K}_{j,2i} \times x_i^c \quad \text{if } j \neq 2i \quad (31)$$

$$\mathbf{F}_j^y = \mathbf{F}_j^y - \mathbf{K}_{j,2i} \times y_i^c \quad \text{if } j \neq 2i \quad (32)$$

$$\mathbf{K}_{j,2i} = \begin{cases} 1 & \text{if } 2i = j \\ 0 & \text{otherwise} \end{cases} \quad (33)$$

We can constrain the slope in the same way. If we constrain two node variables of an element in both position and slope, this element will be frozen. Its two neighboring elements will also be influenced by the constraint. The constraints on a B-snake are imposed on the nodes of its control polygon. Imposing hard constraints in this manner also lessens computational cost, in terms of both memory and time, since the number of entries in the skyline storage of the stiffness matrix is reduced. Consequently, the LDL^T factorization and forward/backward substitutions can be performed more efficiently (see Appendix A). It is also possible to apply more general constraints to any point on the snake as is described in [16].

In the formulation above, the updated stiffness matrix only indicates which degrees of freedom of the snake are constrained, it does not contain any constraint values. These are recorded in the system force vector. As a result, the constraint values may be updated dynamically during snake deformation. In other words, the user has the ability to move the constraint points around the image plane to refine the object boundary as the snake is deforming. This property is very useful when integrating snakes with livewire. While a snake is deforming, additional hard constraints may be imposed on the snake to restrict its deformation. Because these constraints are unknown before the snake is constructed, they may be incorporated on-the-fly using reaction forces on the system force vector without changing the stiffness matrix. However, small time steps are required to ensure the stability of the snake. In our implementation, we create a new snake from the current snake plus the hard constraints, since the LDL^T factorization is fast.

6. Applying United Snakes

In the United Snakes system, the user begins an image segmentation task using a livewire. An initial seed point is placed near the boundary of the object of interest. As the cursor, or free point, is moved around, the livewire or trace, is interactively displayed from the seed point to the free point. If the displayed trace is acceptable, the free point is collected as an additional seed point. For example, we can roughly capture a cell boundary in Figure 3(a) with just three seeds.

The livewire tends to stick to the object boundary using the seed points as a guide. The trace between the two adjacent seeds is frozen. The user has no further control over these traces other than backtracking. In order to generate a more accurate result in the area indicated by a rectangle, more seed points may be placed as in Figure 3(b). Although the livewire boundary is somewhat jagged and exhibits small errors, it is in general as accurate as manual tracing, but more efficient and reproducible.

Next we construct a snake using the livewire-generated boundary to initialize the snake and the seed points to constrain it. The user may select a shape function for the snake which is suitable for the object boundary. In our cell segmentation example, if the livewire result with five seed points is used to construct a finite difference snake, it is able to tolerate the livewire errors and very quickly and accurately lock onto the cell boundary (Figure 3(c)) without any need for further user interaction (the asterisks indicate the pins—imposed hard constraints). Using the livewire result with three seed points, the snake becomes "stuck" in the problematic area (Figure 3(d)) due to the livewire-generated boundary errors. However, this situation can be easily remedied using the mouse spring (Fig. 3(e)). Furthermore, as the snake is deforming, the hard constraints may be adjusted to refine the snake boundary. In Fig. 3(f) for example, constraint point 2 is moved to illustrate this snake boundary adjustment capability. By contrast, it is not nearly as easy to adjust a seed point in the livewire algorithm.

This form of livewire-snake integration is referred to as *static* integration—once the livewire result is used to initialize a snake, the segmentation process continues using only the constrained, user-controlled snake. The user may also set the United Snakes system to a more *dynamic* integration "mode": Once the livewire trace between the last seed point and the free point is formed, a corresponding open snake with constraints at the seed point and the

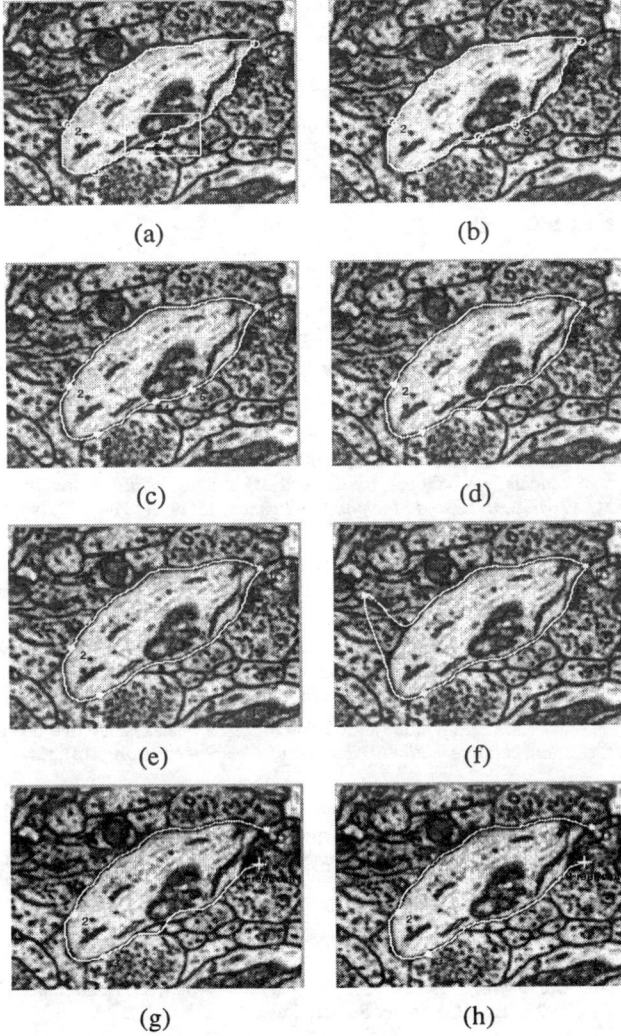

(a)   (b)

(c)   (d)

(e)   (f)

(g)   (h)

Figure 3. Using United Snakes to segment neuronal EM images (see text).

free point is constructed and automatically activated. When the free point is collected as a seed point, this open snake is merged with the snake constructed from the previous livewire traces (if they exist). All seed points are automatically applied as constraints. Fig. 3(g–h) illustrates this process, where "+" indicates the current free point. Since the snake is automatically set in motion, the user may use the mouse spring to correct it in any problematic areas along the snake (Fig. 3(h)).

In summary, the information from livewire including the user guidance and expert prior knowledge is fully utilized by the snake; the snake very quickly locks onto the image features of interest with reasonable tolerance to mistakes in the livewire traces. Thus, the integration of snakes and livewire creates an efficient, reproducible, accurate, semiautomatic segmentation tool which combines the power and flexibility of both techniques. We have applied United Snakes to several different medical image analysis projects in [8], demonstrating the generality, accuracy, robustness,

and ease of use of the tool.

7. Conclusion

We have unified several snake variants in a finite element framework, argued that snakes and livewire are complementary to one another, and through an effective hard constraint mechanism, demonstrated that a snakes/livewire union enhances the power of snakes for interactive image segmentation. Furthermore, to meet the demand for a portable, reusable, comprehensive snake software package, we have implemented our work as a JavaBean which may easily be integrated into application systems.

We the creators of the United Snakes, in order to form a more perfect union of snake technologies, plan to incorporate within our framework, affine cell image decomposition methods for snake topological adaptability [9], advanced snake motion tracking mechanisms [17, 3], and other snake techniques. We anticipate that such efforts will further enhance the effectiveness of this image segmentation tool.

Acknowledgments

JL gratefully acknowledges the valuable comments and suggestions of Prof. Timo Järvi as well as the support of the Turku Centre for Computer Science and the Instrumentarium Foundation. The chest image was collected by Dr. Raimo Virkki and provided by Dr. Aaro Kiuru. The cell image was obtained from Dr. Kristen Harris of the Harvard Medical School.

A. Finite Element Snakes Formulation

To develop the finite element formulation and the corresponding matrix equations, we apply Galerkin's method to the Euler-Lagrange equation

$$-\frac{\partial}{\partial s}\left(\alpha\frac{\partial \mathbf{v}}{\partial s}\right) + \frac{\partial^2}{\partial s^2}\left(\beta\frac{\partial^2 \mathbf{v}}{\partial s^2}\right) - \mathbf{q}(\mathbf{v}) = 0, \qquad (34)$$

which expresses the necessary condition for the snake at equilibrium. The average weighted residual is

$$I = \int_0^L \left(-\frac{\partial}{\partial s}\left(\alpha\frac{\partial \mathbf{v}}{\partial s}\right) + \frac{\partial^2}{\partial s^2}\left(\beta\frac{\partial^2 \mathbf{v}}{\partial s^2}\right) - \mathbf{q}(\mathbf{v})\right) w(s)\, ds = 0, \qquad (35)$$

where $w(s)$ is an arbitrary test function. By performing integrations by parts once for the first term and twice for the second term of equation (35), we arrive at the weak formulation of the snake model:

$$\int_0^L \left(\alpha\frac{\partial \mathbf{v}}{\partial s}\frac{\partial w}{\partial s}\right) ds + \int_0^L \left(\beta\frac{\partial^2 \mathbf{v}}{\partial s^2}\frac{\partial^2 w}{\partial s^2}\right) ds - \int_0^L \mathbf{q}w\,ds + \mathbf{B} = 0, \qquad (36)$$

where

$$\mathbf{B} = \left[-w\alpha\frac{\partial \mathbf{v}}{\partial s} + w\frac{\partial}{\partial s}\left(\beta\frac{\partial^2 \mathbf{v}}{\partial s^2}\right) - \frac{\partial w}{\partial s}\beta\frac{\partial^2 \mathbf{v}}{\partial s^2}\right]_0^L, \qquad (37)$$

are the boundary conditions at the two boundary points, $s = 0$ and $s = L$. We approximate $\mathbf{v}$ as

$$\mathbf{v} = \mathbf{N}\mathbf{u}, \tag{38}$$

where $\mathbf{N} = [N_1(s), N_2(s), ..., N_n(s)]$ are the shape functions, $\mathbf{u} = [u_1, u_2, ..., u_n]^{\top}$ the n nodal variables (degrees of freedom) of the snake model. In Galerkin's method, the arbitrary test function w takes the form

$$w = \mathbf{N}\mathbf{c}, \tag{39}$$

where $\mathbf{N}$ are the same shape functions as in equation (38), and $\mathbf{c}$ is an arbitrary vector. As w is a scalar, we have

$$w = w^{\top} = \mathbf{c}^{\top}\mathbf{N}^{\top}. \tag{40}$$

Substituting (38) through (40) into (36) yields

$$\mathbf{K}\mathbf{u} - \mathbf{F} + \mathbf{P} = 0, \tag{41}$$

where $\mathbf{K}$ is the stiffness matrix, $\mathbf{F}$ the force vector, and $\mathbf{P}$ the boundary forces, defined as follows:

$$\mathbf{K} = \mathbf{K}_\alpha + \mathbf{K}_\beta \tag{42}$$

$$\mathbf{K}_\alpha = \int_0^L \left(\frac{\partial \mathbf{N}}{\partial s}\right)^{\top} \alpha \left(\frac{\partial \mathbf{N}}{\partial s}\right) ds \tag{43}$$

$$\mathbf{K}_\beta = \int_0^L \left(\frac{\partial^2 \mathbf{N}}{\partial s^2}\right)^{\top} \beta \left(\frac{\partial^2 \mathbf{N}}{\partial s^2}\right) ds \tag{44}$$

$$\mathbf{F} = \int_0^L \mathbf{N}^{\top} \mathbf{q} ds \tag{45}$$

$$\mathbf{P} = \left[-\mathbf{N}^{\top}\alpha\frac{\partial \mathbf{N}}{\partial s} + \mathbf{N}^{\top}\frac{\partial}{\partial s}\left(\beta\frac{\partial^2 \mathbf{N}}{\partial s^2}\right) - \left(\frac{\partial \mathbf{N}}{\partial s}\right)^{\top}\beta\frac{\partial^2 \mathbf{N}}{\partial s^2} \right]_0^L \mathbf{u}. \tag{46}$$

Equation (41) gives the finite element formulation for the whole snake. To achieve acceptable accuracy in the finite element approximation, the integration domain should be discretized into a number of small subdomains resulting in the finite element mesh. That is, the snake contour is divided into small segments (elements), each of which can still be considered a snake. Applying equation (41) to an element, we have $\mathbf{K}^e\mathbf{u}^e - \mathbf{F}^e + \mathbf{P}^e = 0$, where $\mathbf{K}^e$ is the element stiffness matrix, $\mathbf{F}^e$ the element force vector, and $\mathbf{P}^e$ the element boundary forces applied to the boundary points of the element. Assembling the element matrices results in the system matrix equation

$$\mathbf{K}\mathbf{u} = \mathbf{F}, \tag{47}$$

where $\mathbf{F}$ is the generalized system force vector.

To solve the discrete form of the equations of motion (4), we replace the time derivatives of $\mathbf{u}$ with the backward finite differences $\ddot{\mathbf{u}} = (\mathbf{u}^{(t+\Delta t)} - 2\mathbf{u}^{(t)} + \mathbf{u}^{(t-\Delta t)})/(\Delta t)^2$, $\dot{\mathbf{u}} = (\mathbf{u}^{(t+\Delta t)} - \mathbf{u}^{(t)})/\Delta t$, where the superscripts denote the quantity evaluated at the time given in the parentheses and the time step is Δt. This yields the update formula

$$\mathbf{A}\mathbf{u}^{(t+\Delta t)} = \mathbf{b}\mathbf{u}^{(t)} + \mathbf{c}\mathbf{u}^{(t-\Delta t)}, \tag{48}$$

where $\mathbf{A} = \mathbf{M}/(\Delta t)^2 + \mathbf{C}/\Delta t + \mathbf{K}$ and $\mathbf{b} = 2\mathbf{M}/(\Delta t)^2 + \mathbf{C}/\Delta t$ and $\mathbf{c} = -\mathbf{M}/(\Delta t)^2$. Because $\mathbf{A}$ is symmetric and banded, it can be economically saved in skyline storage, and efficiently factorized uniquely into the form $\mathbf{A} = \mathbf{L}\mathbf{D}\mathbf{L}^{\top}$, where $\mathbf{L}$ is a lower triangular matrix and $\mathbf{D}$ is a diagonal matrix. The solution $\mathbf{u}^{(t+\Delta t)}$ to

equation (48) is obtained by first solving $\mathbf{L}\mathbf{s} = \mathbf{b}\mathbf{u}^{(t)} + \mathbf{c}\mathbf{u}^{(t-\Delta t)}$ with forward substitution, then $\mathbf{L}^{\top}\mathbf{u} = \mathbf{D}^{-1}\mathbf{s}$ with backward substitution. Since $\mathbf{A}$ is constant, only a single factorization is necessary. Therefore, at each time step only the forward/backward substitutions are performed to integrate the snake forward through time.

References

[1] A. Amini, T. Weymouth, and R. Jain. Using dynamic programming for solving variational problems in vision. *IEEE Trans. on Pattern Analysis and Machine Intelligence*, 12(9):855–867, 1990.

[2] W. Barrett and E. Mortensen. Interactive live-wire boundary extraction. *Medical Image Analysis*, 1(4):331–341, 1997.

[3] A. Blake and M. Isard. *Active Contours*. Springer-Verlag, 1998.

[4] L. Cohen and I. Cohen. Finite element methods for active contour models and balloons for 2D and 3D images. *IEEE Trans. on Pattern Analysis and Machine Intelligence*, 15(11):1131–1147, November 1993.

[5] A. X. Falão, J. K. Udupa, S. Samarasekera, and S. Sharma. User-steered image segmentation paradigms: Live wire and live lane. *Graphical Models and Image Processing*, 60:233–260, 1998.

[6] P. Fua and C. Brechbühler. Imposing hard constraints on deformable models through optimization in orthogonal subspaces. *Computer Vision and Image Understanding*, 65:148–162, 1997.

[7] M. Kass, A. Witkin, and D. Terzopoulos. Snakes: Active contour models. *International Journal of Computer Vision*, 1(4):321–331, 1988.

[8] J. Liang, T. McInerney, and D. Terzopoulos. Interactive medical image segmentation with united snakes. In *Proc. Second International Conf. on Medical Image Computing and Computer-Assisted Intervention (MICCAI 99)*, Cambridge, England, September 1999. Springer.

[9] T. McInerney and D. Terzopoulos. Topologically adaptable snakes. In *Proc. Fifth International Conf. on Computer Vision (ICCV'95)*, Cambridge, MA, June, 1995, pages 840–845, Los Alamitos, CA, 1995. IEEE Computer Society Press.

[10] T. McInerney and D. Terzopoulos. Deformable models in medical image analysis: A survey. *Medical Image Analysis*, 1(2):91–108, 1996.

[11] S. Menet, P. Saint-Marc, and G. Medioni. B-snakes: Implementation and application to stereo. In *Proceedings DARPA*, pages 720–726, 1990.

[12] E. N. Mortensen and W. A. Barrett. Intelligent scissors for image composition. In *Proceedings of Computer Graphics (SIGGRAPH'95)*, pages 191–198, Los Angeles, CA, August 1995.

[13] E. N. Mortensen and W. A. Barrett. Interactive segmentation with intelligent scissors. *Graphical Models and Image Processing*, 60:349–384, 1998.

[14] A. Singh, D. Goldof, and D. Terzopoulos, editors. *Deformable Models in Medical Image Analysis*. IEEE Computer Society Press, 1998.

[15] L. Staib and J. Duncan. Boundary finding with parametrically deformable models. *IEEE Trans. on Pattern Analysis and Machine Intelligence*, 14(11):1061–1075, November 1992.

[16] D. Terzopoulos and H. Qin. Dynamic NURBS with geometric constraints for interactive sculpting. *ACM Transactions on Graphics*, 13(2):103–136, 1994.

[17] D. Terzopoulos and R. Szeliski. Tracking with Kalman snakes. In A. Blake and A. Yuille, editors, *Active Vision*, pages 3–20. MIT Press, Cambridge, MA, 1992.

Manhattan World: Compass Direction from a Single Image by Bayesian Inference

James M. Coughlan   A.L. Yuille

Smith-Kettlewell Eye Research Institute
2318 Fillmore St.
San Francisco, CA 94115

Abstract

When designing computer vision systems for the blind and visually impaired it is important to determine the orientation of the user relative to the scene. We observe that most indoor and outdoor (city) scenes are designed on a Manhattan three-dimensional grid. This Manhattan grid structure puts strong constraints on the intensity gradients in the image. We demonstrate an algorithm for detecting the orientation of the user in such scenes based on Bayesian inference using statistics which we have learnt in this domain. Our algorithm requires a single input image and does not involve pre-processing stages such as edge detection and Hough grouping. We demonstrate strong experimental results on a range of indoor and outdoor images. We also show that estimating the grid structure makes it significantly easier to detect target objects which are not aligned with the grid.

1 Introduction

Recently there has been growing interest in building computer vision navigational systems for the blind [9], [10]. These systems can be used, for example, for navigation and for the detection and reading of informational signs. The goal of this paper is to determine the orientation of the viewer in the scene (indoor or outdoor) from a single image. A useful spin-off is the ability to detect target objects which are not aligned with the Manhattan grid.

Most indoor and outdoor city scenes are based on a cartesian coordinate system [3, 6] which we can refer to as a Manhattan grid. This grid defines an $\vec{i}, \vec{j}, \vec{k}$ coordinate system. This gives a natural reference frame for the viewer. If the viewer can determine his/her position relative to this frame – in other words, estimate the $\vec{i}, \vec{j}$ or $\vec{k}$ directions – then it becomes significantly easier to interpret the scene. In particular, it will be a lot easier to determine the most important lines in the scene (corridor boundaries and doors, street boundaries and traffic lights) because they will typically lie in either the $\vec{i}, \vec{j}$ or $\vec{k}$ directions. Knowledge of this reference frame will make it significantly easier and faster to detect informational signs. We will assume that the camera direction lies approximately in the horizontal plane and so lines in the $\vec{k}$ direction map to approximately vertical lines in the image. There is, of course, an ambiguity in the orientations of $\vec{i}$ and $\vec{j}$ so the compass heading can only be obtained modulo 90°.

2 Previous Work and Three- Dimensional Geometry

There has been an enormous amount of work in projective geometry [3, 6]. Techniques from projective geometry have been applied to finding the vanishing points [1], [5]. For a recent application to vision systems for the blind see [9] for the detection of pedestrian crossings using projection geometry. This work, however, has typically proceeded through the stages of edge detection, Hough transforms, and finally the calculation of the geometry. Alternatively, a sequence of images over time can be used to estimate the geometry, see for example [8]. In this paper, we demonstrate that accurate results can be obtained from a single image directly without the need for techniques such as edge detection and Hough transforms.

For completeness, we give the basic geometry. We assume that the camera is oriented in the horizontal plane. This is a reasonable assumption and it turned out to be approximately correct for the images in our datasets (all of which were photographed without taking this into account). (In our current work we are relaxing this constraint to allow for any camera configuration.)

We define Ψ to be the compass angle. This defines the orientation of the camera with respect to

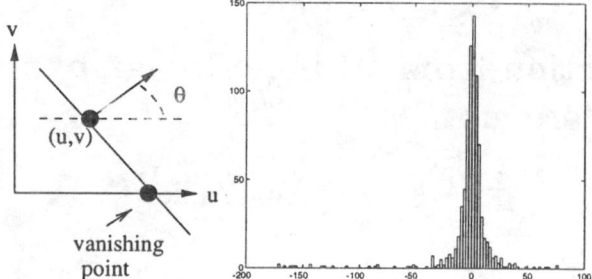

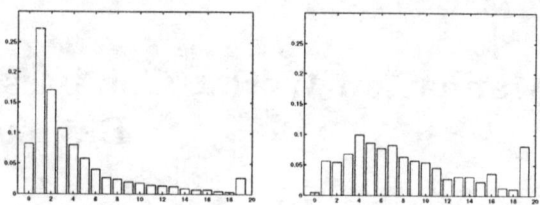

Figure 1: (Left). Geometry of an $\vec{i}$ line projected onto (u, v) image plane. θ is the normal orientation of the line in the image. Because our camera is assumed to point in a horizontal direction, the vanishing point lies on the u axis. (Right) Histogram of edge orientation error (displayed modulo 180°). Observe the strong peak at 0°, indicating that the image gradient direction at an edge is usually very close to the true normal orientation of the edge. We modelled this distribution using a simple box function.

Figure 2: $P_{off}(y)$ (left) and $P_{on}(y)$ (right), the empirical histograms of edge responses off and on edges, respectively. Here the response $y = \left| \vec{\nabla} I \right|$ is quantized to take 20 values and is shown on the horizontal axis. Note that the peak of $P_{off}(y)$ occurs at a lower edge response than the peak of $P_{on}(y)$. These distributions were very consistent for a range of images.

the Manhattan grid: the camera points in direction $\cos \Psi \vec{i} - \sin \Psi \vec{j}$. Camera coordinates $\vec{u} = (u, v)$ are related to the Cartesian scene coordinates (x, y, z) by the equations:

$$u = \frac{f\{-x \sin \Psi - y \cos \Psi\}}{x \cos \Psi - y \sin \Psi}, \quad v = \frac{fz}{x \cos \Psi - y \sin \Psi},$$
(1)

where f is the focal length of the camera (which we determined to be 797 pixel units for our images).

By standard geometry, the vanishing points of lines in the $\vec{i}$ and $\vec{j}$ directions lie at $(-f \tan \Psi, 0)$ and $(f \cot \Psi, 0)$ respectively in the (u, v) plane. (Lines in the $\vec{k}$ direction are all vertical in the image given our compass-world assumption.)

It is a straightforward calculation to show that a point in the image at $\vec{u} = (u, v)$ with intensity gradient at $(\cos \theta, \sin \theta)$ is *consistent with an $\vec{i}$ line in the sense that it points to the vanishing point* if $-v \tan \theta = u + f \tan \Psi$ (observe that this equation is unaffected by adding $\pm \pi$ to θ and so it does not depend on the polarity of the edge). We get a similar expression $v \tan \theta = -u + f \cot \Psi$ for lines in the $\vec{j}$ direction. (See Figure 1 (left) for an illustration of this geometry.)

3 P_{on} and P_{off}: Characterizing Edges Statistically

A key element of our approach is that we do not use a binary edge map. Such edge maps make premature decisions based on too little information. (The poor quality of some of the images – underexposed

and overexposed – makes edge detection particularly difficult).

Instead we use the power of statistics. Following work by Konishi *et al.* [4], we determine probabilities $P_{on}(E_{\vec{u}})$ and $P_{off}(E_{\vec{u}})$ for the probabilities of the response $E_{\vec{u}}$ of an edge filter at position $\vec{u}$ in the image *conditioned on whether we are on or off an edge.* These distributions were learnt by Konishi *et al* for the Sowerby image database which contain one hundred presegmented images. The more different P_{on} is from P_{off} then the easier edge detection becomes, see Figure 2. A suitable measure of difference is the Chernoff Information [2] $C(P_{on}, P_{off}) = - \min_{0 \leq \lambda \leq 1} \log \sum_y P_{on}^\lambda(y) P_{off}^{1-\lambda}(y)$. Konishi *et al* tested a variety of different edge filters and ranked them by their effectiveness based on their Chernoff information. For this project, we chose a very simple edge detector $\left| \vec{\nabla} G_{\sigma=1} * I \right|$ – the magnitude of the gradient of the grayscale image I filtered by a Gaussian $G_{\sigma=1}$ with standard deviation $\sigma = 1$ pixel units – which has a Chernoff of 0.26 nats. More effective edge detectors are available – for example, the gradient at multiple scales using colour has a Chernoff of 0.51 nats. But we do not need these more sophisticated detectors.

We extend the work of Konishi *et al* by putting probability distributions on how accurately the edge filter gradient estimates the true perpendicular direction of the edge. These were learnt for this dataset by measuring the true orientations of the edges and comparing them to those estimated from the image gradients.

This gives us distributions on the magnitude and direction of the intensity gradient $P_{on}(\vec{E}_{\vec{u}} | \beta)$, $P_{off}(\vec{E}_{\vec{u}})$, where $\vec{E}_{\vec{u}} = (E_{\vec{u}}, \phi_{\vec{u}})$, β is the true normal orientation of the edge, and $\phi_{\vec{u}}$ is the gradient direction measured at point $\vec{u}$. We make a *factorization assumption* that $P_{on}(\vec{E}_{\vec{u}}|\beta) = P_{on}(E_{\vec{u}})P_{ang}(\phi_{\vec{u}} - \beta)$ and $P_{off}(\vec{E}_{\vec{u}}) = P_{off}(E_{\vec{u}})U(\phi_{\vec{u}})$. $P_{ang}(.)$ (with argument evaluated modulo 2π and normalized to 1 over the range 0 to 2π) is based on experimental data, see Figure 1 (right), and is peaked about 0 and π. In practice, we use a simple box function model: $P_{ang}(\delta\theta) = (1 - \epsilon)/4\tau$ if $\delta\theta$ is within angle τ of 0 or π, and $\epsilon/(2\pi - 4\tau)$ otherwise (i.e. the chance of an angular error greater than $\pm\tau$ is ϵ). In our experiments $\epsilon = 0.1$ and $\tau = 4°$ for indoors and $6°$ outdoors. By contrast, $U(.) = 1/2\pi$ is the uniform distribution.

4 Bayesian Model

We devised a Bayesian model which combines knowledge of the three-dimensional geometry of the Manhattan world with statistical knowledge of edges in images. The model assumes that, while the majority of pixels in the image convey no information about camera orientation, most of the pixels with high edge responses arise from the presence of $\vec{i}, \vec{j}, \vec{k}$ lines in the three-dimensional scene. The edge orientations measured at these pixels provide constraints on the camera angle, and although the constraining evidence from any single pixel is weak, the Bayesian model allows us to pool the evidence over all pixels (both on and off edges), yielding a sharp posterior distribution on the camera angle. An important feature of the Bayesian model is that *it does not force us to decide prematurely which pixels are on and off* (or whether an on pixel is due to $\vec{i}, \vec{j},$ or $\vec{k}$), *but allows us to sum over all possible interpretations of each pixel.*

4.1 Evidence at one pixel

The image data $\vec{E}_{\vec{u}}$ at pixel $\vec{u}$ is explained by one of five models $m_{\vec{u}}$: $m_{\vec{u}} = 1, 2, 3$ mean the data is generated by an edge due to an $\vec{i}, \vec{j}, \vec{k}$ line, respectively, in the scene; $m_{\vec{u}} = 4$ means the data is generated by a random edge (not due to an $\vec{i}, \vec{j}, \vec{k}$ line); and $m_{\vec{u}} = 5$ means the pixel is off-edge. The prior probability $P(m_{\vec{u}})$ of each of the edge models was estimated empirically to be $0.02, 0.02, 0.02, 0.04, 0.9$ for $m_{\vec{u}} = 1, 2, \dots, 5$.

Using the factorization assumption mentioned before, we assume the probability of the image data $\vec{E}_{\vec{u}}$ has two factors, one for the magnitude of the edge strength and another for the edge direction:

$$P(\vec{E}_{\vec{u}}|m_{\vec{u}}, \Psi, \vec{u}) = P(E_{\vec{u}}|m_{\vec{u}})P(\phi_{\vec{u}}|m_{\vec{u}}, \Psi, \vec{u}) \quad (2)$$

where $P(E_{\vec{u}}|m_{\vec{u}})$ equals $P_{off}(E_{\vec{u}})$ if $m_{\vec{u}} = 5$ or $P_{on}(E_{\vec{u}})$ if $m_{\vec{u}} \neq 5$. Also, $P(\phi_{\vec{u}}|m_{\vec{u}}, \Psi, \vec{u})$ equals $P_{ang}(\phi_{\vec{u}} - \theta(\Psi, m_{\vec{u}}, \vec{u}))$ if $m_{\vec{u}} = 1, 2, 3$ or $U(\phi_{\vec{u}})$ if $m_{\vec{u}} = 4, 5$. Here $\theta(\Psi, m_{\vec{u}}, \vec{u}))$ is the predicted normal orientation of lines determined by the equation $-v\tan\theta =$

$u + f\tan\Psi$ for $\vec{i}$ lines, $v\tan\theta = -u + f\cot\Psi$ for $\vec{j}$ lines, and $\theta = 0$ for $\vec{k}$ lines.

In summary, the edge strength probability is modeled by P_{on} for models 1 through 4 and by P_{off} for model 5. For models 1,2 and 3 the edge orientation is modeled by a distribution which is peaked about the appropriate orientation of an $\vec{i}, \vec{j}, \vec{k}$ line predicted by the compass angle at pixel location $\vec{u}$; for models 4 and 5 the edge orientation is assumed to be uniformly distributed from 0 through 2π.

Rather than decide on a particular model at each pixel, we marginalize over all five possible models (i.e. creating a mixture model):

$$P(\vec{E}_{\vec{u}}|\Psi, \vec{u}) = \sum_{m_{\vec{u}}=1}^{5} P(\vec{E}_{\vec{u}}|m_{\vec{u}}, \Psi, \vec{u})P(m_{\vec{u}}) \quad (3)$$

In this way we can determine evidence about the camera angle Ψ at each pixel without knowing which of the five model categories the pixel belongs to.

4.2 Evidence over all pixels

To combine evidence over all pixels in the image, denoted by $\{\vec{E}_{\vec{u}}\}$, we assume that the image data is conditionally independent across all pixels, given the compass direction Ψ:

$$P(\{\vec{E}_{\vec{u}}\}|\Psi) = \prod_{\vec{u}} P(\vec{E}_{\vec{u}}|\Psi, \vec{u}) \quad (4)$$

Thus the posterior distribution on the compass direction is given by $\prod_{\vec{u}} P(\vec{E}_{\vec{u}}|\Psi, \vec{u})P(\Psi)/Z$ where Z is a normalization factor and $P(\Psi)$ is a uniform prior on the compass angle.

To find the MAP (maximum a posterior) estimate, we need to maximize the log posterior term (ignoring Z, which is independent of Ψ) $\log[P(\{\vec{E}_{\vec{u}}\}|\Psi)P(\Psi)] = \log P(\Psi) + \sum_{\vec{u}} \log[\sum_{m_{\vec{u}}} P(\vec{E}_{\vec{u}}|m_{\vec{u}}, \Psi, \vec{u})P(m_{\vec{u}})]$. Our algorithm evaluates the log posterior numerically for the compass direction Ψ in the range $-45°$ to $+45°$, in increments of $1°$.

5 Experimental Results

We tested our model on two datasets of indoor and outdoor scenes. These images were taken by an unskilled photographer unfamiliar with the goals of the study. No special attempt was made to hold the camera horizontal. The camera was set on automatic so some images are over- or under- exposed. Experiments performed by a blind user (W. Gerrey) at the Smith-Kettlewell Institute demonstrate that similar quality images can be attained by a camera mounted on the chest of a blind user (personal communication – Dr. J. Brabyn, Director of the Rehabilitation, Engineering,

Figure 3: Estimates of the compass angle and geometry obtained by our algorithm. The estimated orientations of the $\vec{i}, \vec{j}$ lines are indicated by the black line segments drawn on the input image. At each point on a subgrid two such segments are drawn – one for $\vec{i}$ and one for $\vec{j}$. Observe how the $\vec{i}$ directions align with the wall on the right hand side and with features parallel to this wall. The $\vec{j}$ lines align with the wall on the left (and objects parallel to it). (Indoor 17).

Figure 4: Another indoor scene. Standard conventions for display of $\vec{i}, \vec{j}$ directions. Observe that the $\vec{i}, \vec{j}$ directions align with the appropriate walls despite the poor quality of the image (i.e. under-exposed). (Indoor 15).

and Research Center, Smith-Kettlewell Eye Research Institute, San Francisco, CA 94115. 1998).

Our results show strong success of our approach in both domains.

5.1 Indoor Scenes

A total of twenty-five images were tested. On twenty-three images, the estimated angle was accurate to within $5°$. On two images, the orientation of the camera was far from horizontal and the estimation was poor. Examples of successes, demonstrating the range of images used, are shown in Figures 3,4,5, 6. The log posteriors for typical images, plotted as a function of Ψ, are shown in Figure 7.

5.2 Outdoor Scenes

We next tested the accuracy of estimation on outdoor scenes. Again we used twenty-five test images (taken by a naive photographer). In these scenes the vast majority of the results (twenty-two) were accurate up to $10°$. On three of the images the angles were worse than $10°$, see Figure 8. Inspection of these images showed that the log posterior had multiple peaks, see Figure 10. There was always a peak corresponding to the true compass angle (to within $10°$), however, there were false peaks which were higher in these cases. What causes these errors? Observe in Figure (8) that the vanishing point of the $\vec{i}$ lines occurs near a car *whose edges are aligned only approximately to the Manhattan grid*. The car's edges may therefore cause a small distortion in the vanishing point esti-

mate. The correct alignment for this image can be obtained, see Figure (9), by ignoring the image data within a circle of radius 100 pixels centered around the vanishing point for each compass angle considered (this means the car will no longer contribute when evaluating the likelihood of the compass angle corresponding to the false vanishing point). Observe the difference, see Figure (10), between the log posteriors for the compass angle with and without this procedure (i.e. ignoring, or not ignoring, the circle). This new procedure, however, is intended only to show proof of concept and a thorough stability analysis is required (this is current work).

On twenty-two of the twenty-five images, however, the algorithm gave estimates accurate to $10°$ which is sufficient for the task (observe that a blind user will typically have access to a sequence of images which can be used to improve the compass estimate). See Figure 11 for a representative set of images on which the algorithm was successful.

6 Detecting Objects in Manhattan world

We now consider applying the Manhattan assumption to the alternative problem of detecting target objects in background clutter. To perform such a task effectively requires modelling the properties of the background clutter in addition to those of the target object. It has recently been appreciated [7] that simple models of background clutter based on Gaussian probability

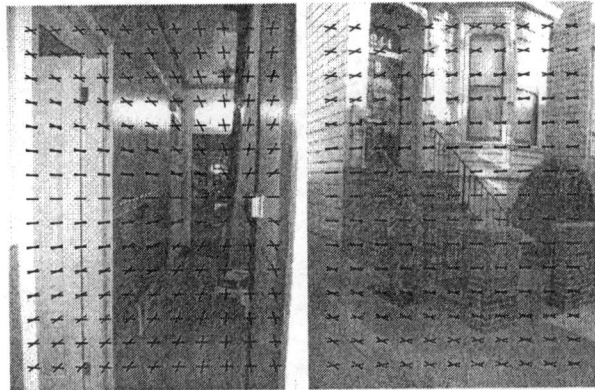

Figure 5: Another indoor scene and its exterior. Same conventions as above. The vanishing points are estimated to within 5° (perfectly adequate for our purposes). Note poor quality of the indoor image (i.e. over-exposed). (Indoor 23 and Outdoor 12).

Figure 6: Another indoor scene. Same conventions as above. (Indoor 8).

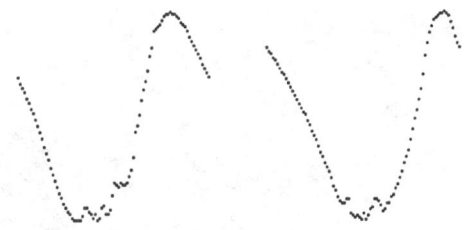

Figure 7: The log posteriors as a function of compass angle (from −45° to 45° along the horizontal axis) for images Indoor 17 (left) and Indoor 15 (right). These results are typical for both the indoor and outdoor dataset. See Figure 10 for an exception where there are multiple peaks.

Figure 8: Incorrect estimation of compass angle for outdoor scene. The algorithm computes the vanishing point to be more than 10° to the right of the true vanishing point. (Outdoor 35).

distributions are often inadequate and that better performance can be obtained using alternative probability models [11].

The Manhattan world assumption gives an alternative way of probabilistically modelling background clutter. The background clutter will correspond to the regular structure of buildings and roads and its edges will be aligned to the Manhattan grid. The target object, however, is assumed to be unaligned (at least, in part) to this grid. *Therefore many of the edges of the target object will be assigned to model 4 by the algorithm.* (Note the algorithm first finds the MAP estimate Ψ^* of the compass angle, see section (4), and then estimates the model by doing MAP of $P(m_{\vec{u}}|\vec{E}_{\vec{u}}, \Psi^*, \vec{u})$ to estimate $m_{\vec{u}}$ for each pixel $\vec{u}$.) This enables us to significantly simplify the detection task by removing all edges in the images except those

assigned to model 4.

This idea is demonstrated in Figure (12) where the target is a bike and a robot respectively. Observe how most of the edges in the image are eliminated as target object candidates because of their alignment to the Manhattan grid. The bike and the robot stand out as outliers to the grid.

This simple example illustrates a method of modelling background clutter which we refer to as *scene clutter* because it is effectively the same as defining a probability model for the entire scene. Observe that scene clutter models require external variables – in this case the Ψ angle – to determine the orientation of the viewer relative to the scene axes. These variables must be estimated to help distinguish between target and clutter. This differs from standard models used for background clutter [7],[11] where no external variable is used.

Figure 9: A correct estimate of the compass angle for the previous figure can be obtained by ignoring data from image points within a circle of radius 100 pixels centered about the vanishing point for each compass angle considered.

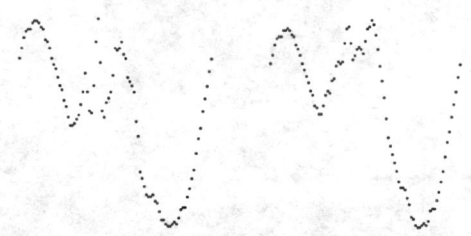

Figure 10: Log posterior as a function of compass angle for the previous two figures. Observe that for these images the log posterior has multiple peaks. For the original algorithm, the false peak had higher probability (left). For the modified algorithm which ignores the central circle of data (right) the true peak is higher.

7 Summary and Conclusions

Our work has demonstrated proof of concept and shows the potential of our approach. The system, however, needs to be tested more extensively before it will be suited for blind users.

One obvious limitation is that we have assumed that the only unknown variable is the compass angle. This is only correct if the camera is held approximately horizontal although our results have shown robustness to this condition. It is straightforward to adjust our theory to extend the theory to estimate all three orientation angles simultaneously.

Other improvements would come from using better filters. As demonstrated by Konishi *et al* [4] the use of colour and multi-scale can give quantifiably better measures of edgeness (improving the Chernoff information from 0.26 nats to 0.51 nats). We anticipate that such filters will give more accurate angle esti-

Figure 11: Results on four outdoor images. Same conventions as before. Observe the accuracy of the $\vec{i}, \vec{j}$ projections in these varied scenes despite the poor quality of some of the images.

mates.

Further statistical analysis of the domains is also required. We should quantify the amount of outliers, particularly in the outdoor scenes. In particular, we should investigate the number of structured outliers and determine techniques to detect them. In addition, we should use error analysis to improve our estimates of the probability distributions and, in particular, to see how the angle errors change as a function of distance from a vanishing point. This will enable us to do performance analysis such as estimating Cramer-Rao lower bounds for the accuracy of the estimates.

We should mention the issues of algorithmic speed. At present the algorithm takes a minute which is too slow for practical use. However, this is for unoptimized code when it is run on images of size 640×480. Optimizing the code (e.g. by using look-up tables to pre-compute trigonometric functions) and subsampling the image will allow the algorithm to work significantly faster. Other techniques involve rejecting image pixels where the edge detector response is so low that there is no realistic chance of an edge being present. This would mean that at least 70% of the image pixels could be removed from the computation. We observe that the algorithm is entirely parallelizable. Overall, there seems little difficulty in getting this algorithm to work in a few seconds –which is perfectly adequate for blind users.

Acknowledgments

We want to acknowledge funding from NSF with award number IRI-9700446, support from the Smith-

Figure 12: Detecting bikes (left column) and robots (right column) in urban scenes. The original image (top row) and the edge maps (centre row) computed as $\log P_{on}(E_{\vec{u}})/P_{off}(E_{\vec{u}})$ – see Konishi *et al* 1999 – displayed as a grey-scale image where black is high and white is low. In the bottom row we show the edges assigned to model 4 (i.e. the outliers) in black. Observe that the edges of the bike and the robot are now highly salient (and make detection straightforward) because most of them are unaligned to the Manhattan grid.

Kettlewell core grant, and from the Center for Imaging Sciences with Army grant ARO DAAH049510494. It is a pleasure to acknowledge email conversations with Song Chun Zhu about scene clutter.

References

[1] B. Brillault-O'Mahony. "New Method for Vanishing Point Detection". *Computer Vision, Graphics, and Image Processing.* 54(2). pp 289-300. 1991.

[2] T. M. Cover and J. A. Thomas. *Elements of Information Theory.* Wiley Interscience Press. New York. 1991.

[3] O.D. Faugeras. **Three-Dimensional Computer Vision.** MIT Press. 1993.

[4] S. Konishi, A. L. Yuille, J. M. Coughlan, and S. C. Zhu. "Fundamental Bounds on Edge Detection: An Information Theoretic Evaluation of Different Edge Cues." *Proc. Int'l conf. on Computer Vision and Pattern Recognition,* 1999.

[5] E. Lutton, H. Maître, and J. Lopez-Krahe. "Contribution to the determination of vanishing points using Hough transform". *IEEE Trans. on Pattern Analysis and Machine Intelligence.* 16(4). pp 430-438. 1994.

[6] J.L. Mundy and A. Zisserman. (Eds). **Geometric Invariants in Computer Vision.** MIT Press. 1992.

[7] J. A. Ratches, C. P. Walters, R. G. Buser and B. D. Guenther. "Aided and Automatic Target Recognition Based upon Sensory Inputs from Image Forming Systems". *IEEE Trans. on PAMI,* vol. 19, No. 9, Sept. 1997.

[8] P. Torr and A. Zisserman. "Robust Computation and Parameterization of Multiple View Relations". In *Proceedings of the International Conference on Computer Vision.* ICCV'98. Bombay, India. pp 727-732. 1998.

[9] S. Utcke. "Grouping based on Projective Geometry Constraints and Uncertainty". In *Proceedings of the International Conference on Computer Vision.* ICCV'98. Bombay, India. pp 739-746. 1998.

[10] A.L. Yuille, D. Snow, and M. Nitzberg. "Signfinder". In *Proceedings of the International Conference of Computer Vision.* (ICCV'98). Bombay. India. January 1998.

[11] S. C. Zhu, A. Lanterman, and M. I. Miller. "Clutter Modeling and Performance Analysis in Automatic Target Recognition". In *Proceedings Workshop on Detection and Classification of Difficult Targets.* Redstone Arsenal, Alabama. 1998.

Measuring Convexity for Figure/Ground Separation *

Hsing-Kuo Pao
Courant Institute
New York University
New York, NY 10012
hsingkuo@cs.nyu.edu

Davi Geiger
Courant Institute
New York University
New York, NY 10012
geiger@cs.nyu.edu

Nava Rubin
Center for Neural Science
New York University
New York, NY 10012
nava@cns.nyu.edu

Abstract

In human perception, convex surfaces have a strong tendency to be perceived as the "figure". Convexity has a stronger influence on figural organization than other global shape properties, such as symmetry ([9]). And yet, there has been very little work on convexity properties in computer vision.

We present a model for figure/ground segregatation which exhibits a preference for convex regions as the figure (i.e., the foreground). The model also shows a preference for smaller regions to be selected as figures, which is also known to hold for human visual perception (e.g., Koffka [11]). The model is based on the machinery of Markov random fields/random walks/diffusion processes, so that the global shape properties are obtained via local and stochastic computations. Experimental results demonstrate that our model performs well on ambiguous figure/ground displays which were not captured before. In particular, in ambiguous displays where neither region is strictly convex, the model shows preference to the "more convex" region, thus offering a continuous measure of convexity in agreement with human perception.

1. Introduction

The selection of salient surfaces in ambiguous figure/ground displays such as those shown in Figure 1 ([9]) reveals important properties of the human visual system. For these figures, the detection of closed boundaries is a straightforward problem, as exact and complete surface boundaries can be obtained by computing the level sets (the location of change from black to white colors).

And yet, these figures present a challenging image segmentation problem, since a decision needs to be made as to

which of the regions is seen as the foreground and which as the background. Thus, we consider figure/ground separation to be an integral part of the process of image segmentation. One can formulate the figure-ground problem as a *border ownership* problem ([17], [18], [14]): given the complete description of the boundary contours, how does a system decide on which side of the boundary is the surface that gives rise to that border? The resolution of the border-ownership ambiguity and the determination of the salient regions in the image are thus two interrelated problems. Consider, for example, Figure 1(a): most observers report that the white regions are seen as figures, with the black regions completing behind them in the background. Equivalently we may say that white/black boundaries belong (perceptually) to the white shapes, and the black regions (perceived as background) terminate along the boundaries merely because of occlusion.

1.1. A Continuous Measure of Convexity

The factors that determine which regions are perceived as figure (or foreground) in Figures 1(a-d) must be related to the *shape* of the regions, and not by their contrast polarity, or any other lightness or texture property [1].

What, then, determines the figural organization in Figures 1(a-d)? These figures were developed by Kanizsa ([9]), to illustrate the role of *convexity* in determining border ownership and figure/ground organization: the regions perceived as foreground are more convex than those assigned as background. More specifically, Figures 1(a-d) set off two different global shape properties against each other: convexity vs. symmetry. Note that the regions perceived here as background are perfectly mirror symmetric – a global shape property which was suggested by several Gestalt researchers to strongly bias a surface to be perceived as foreground (e.g., Koffka [11]). The fact that those regions were nevertheless judged as background in Figure 1

---

*This work was supported by NSF CAREER award and the Sloan Foundation

[1]Contrast polarity and/or other surface-quality factors can play larger role in figure/ground assignment, but not in the cases discussed here.

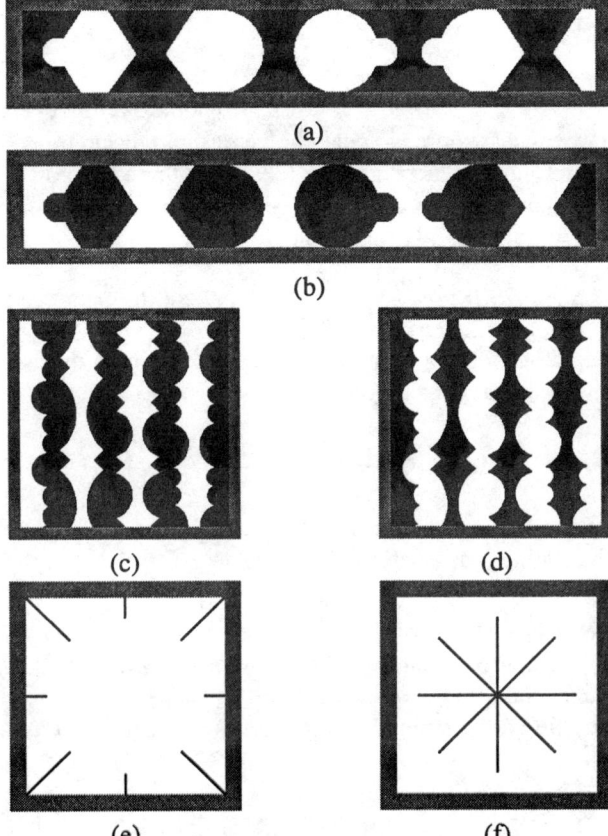

(a)

(b)

(c)   (d)

(e)   (f)

Figure 1. Convexity as a determinant of perceptual saliency (adapted from Kanizsa [9]), observers report perceiving the white regions as the figures in (a) and (d), whereas in (b) and (c) the black regions are the ones perceived as figures. This suggests convexity plays a much larger role in determining figural organization than other factors, such as contrast polarity and symmetry. The effect is also present on illusory figures, where in (e), the convex illusory circle is strongly perceived as foreground, but on (f), the illusory white flat plane with a concave circular hole is hardly perceived as foreground. Here each figure and ground regions are designed to own the same size.

suggests convexity played a larger role than symmetry in determining figural organization. Note, however, that most of the perceptually salient regions in Figure 1 are not convex in the strict mathematical sense, which is an all-or-none definition. Instead, *perceptual* convexity behaves in a continuous manner, where regions can be "more or less convex".

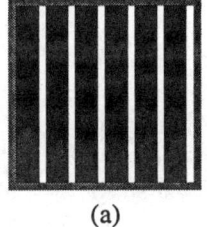   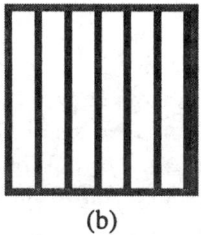

(a)   (b)

Figure 2. Without convexity, small size objects tend to be perceived as foreground and large size objects as background, regardless of the polarity (adapted from Koffka [11].)

We presents a segmentation model which exhibits a similar preference to select convex regions as foreground. Moreover, the model detects boundaries when they are not readily available (see Figure 1(e)–(f).)

The model is based on local (pixel-to-pixel) computations in a stochastic two-dimensional network. The preference for global shape properties (specifically, convexity) is obtained by propagation of the local interactions, given by the diffusion-like processes. The model, like human perception, selects regions which are intuitively (or perceptually) more convex even in cases when neither region obeys the exact mathematical definition of convexity. The model therefore provides a continuous measure of convexity. Effectively, the diffusion process groups intensity edges to produce closed regions, without any restriction on the number of regions and with topological freedom for admitting any number of holes in each region.

There has been few previous work on using convexity for recognition, so they need to be pointed out ([8], [7] and [20]). Our effort differs from them in that we are extending the notion to a continuous measure of convexity used in studying vision perception. Moreover, our stochastic formulation is unique in this context.

Finally, our model also shows a preference for *smaller* regions to be selected as figures, which is known to hold for human visual perception as well (especially when all other factors are held equal; see Figure 2, adapted from Koffka [11]).

2. Figure-Ground and Entropy Criteria

We start by thinking a shape-figure as a "two dimensional cave" and the shape-figure-boundary as a source of "heat", diffusing inwardly while the background has the source of "heat" diffusing outwardly. In many cases, the partition of the image in regions is not known (Figure 1 (e)-(f)), the source of "heat" are then sparse, at the so called *inducers* such as corners, T-junctions, end lines, and possibly all available intensity edges. After the diffusion process is done, an "entropy" criteria is used to select the best figure-ground configuration. This framework is inspired by Kumaran et al. [12], However, (i) their work concentrated more on the illusory figures. When the figure/ground boundary detection become trivial (Figure 1 (a)-(d)), the closed door diffusion give no difference for each totally blocked region. We, on the other hand, use "leaking energy diffusion process" to overcome this minor (Section 3); (ii) Their sources/inducers must be special intensity change places, such as junctions or corners, while we consider any intensity change as a potential source. Our approach will work even if a curved edge is not detected as a corner. Thus, we put no extra burdens on the feature detection process.

We emphasize here, that we do not address the problem of the combinatorial explosion of multiple hypothesis. Rather, we focus on formulating a criteria to select the best hypothesis.

2.1. Naming the Variables

The input image is defined on a discrete lattice of size N by N,

$$\mathbf{I}^2 \equiv \{k = 1, ..., N^2\}. \qquad \langle \text{ set of pixels }\rangle$$

Let us indicate a shape-figure $\mathbf{S}$ of size S pixels in the image either by

$$\mathbf{S} \equiv \{k_s : s = 1, ..., S\} \qquad \langle \text{ shape representation }\rangle$$

with area $\mathcal{A}(\mathbf{S}) = \#\mathbf{S} = S$ pixels, or simply by

$$C(\mathbf{S}). \qquad \langle \text{ shape boundary }\rangle$$

Image wise, closed boundary like to "sit" on intensity edges, but boundary points may not have an intensity edge. We then define the edge-perimeter of $\mathbf{S}$ as the size of the boundary set weighted by the normalized intensity edges, i.e.,

$$\mathcal{P}(\mathbf{S}, I) = \sum_{k \in C(\mathbf{S})} e(k), \qquad \langle \text{ edge-perimeter }\rangle$$

where $e(k) \in [0, 1]$ is the intensity edge (magnitude of intensity gradient) at pixel k, normalized by the largest intensity edge on a given image I. All pixels k of the perimeter belong to $\mathbf{S}$ and since $0 \leq e(k) \leq 1$, we have

$$S = \mathcal{A}(\mathbf{S}) > \#C(\mathbf{S}) \geq \mathcal{P}(\mathbf{S}, I).$$

Let us assign the ("heat") source value at the *inducer* regions as (see Figure 3b.)

$$\sigma_0(k) = \begin{cases} e(k) & \text{if } k \text{ is figure} \\ -e(k) & \text{if } k \text{ is background}. \end{cases}$$

$$\langle \text{ hypothesis at inducers }\rangle$$

At every heat source a local choice of figure/background is thus required. These are the local hypotheses and an entropy measure will select the best hypothesis (best set of local hypotheses). Let us also define

$$P(k) : \mathbf{I}^2 \to \mathbf{R}, \qquad \langle \text{ diffusion field }\rangle$$

a function to be evaluated, at every pixel k, by a diffusion network of the local hypotheses.

2.2. Variational Model

We create a diffusion process model for the field $P(k)$ by formulating it as a variational problem.

Local Hypotheses and Data Fitting: We prefer the field $P(k)$ fitting the local hypotheses, where they are available. In our model they are available at all intensity edge pixels according to its strength ($e(k)$), i.e., we want $P(k)$ to minimize

$$E(P|\sigma_0) = \sum_{k=1}^{N^2} e(k) (P(k) - \sigma_0(k))^2.$$

Smoothness: In order to obtain a diffusion process, from a minimization standing point, we insert a smoothness constraint on $P(k)$. A simple one minimizes the square of the length of the gradient vector $(\frac{\partial P(x,y)}{\partial x}, \frac{\partial P(x,y)}{\partial y})$, or in the discrete setting we write

$$Smooth(\{P\}) = \mu \sum_{k=1}^{N^2} \sum_{k' \in N_k} (1 - e(k, k')) (P(k) - P(k'))^2,$$

where μ is the smoothness coefficient, $N_k = \{k+1, k-1, k-N, k+N\}$ are the four neighbors of pixel k, and $e(k, k')$ is the magnitude of the intensity change from pixel k to pixel k', normalized to the largest $e(k, k')$. Note that we can define $e(k) = \max_{k' \in N_k} e(k, k')$.

Energy Model and Level Set: With the smoothing criteria, the total cost function becomes

$$E(P) = \sum_{k=1}^{N^2} \Big[e(k) (P(k) - \sigma_0(k))^2 \\ + \sum_{k' \in N_k} \mu (1 - e(k, k')) (P(k) - P(k'))^2 \Big]. \text{(1)}$$

Thus, the optimal solution $P^*(k)$ balances fitting the local hypothesis and smoothing. It is clear (e.g., [12]) that $P^*(k)$ is bounded by the maximum and minimum values of σ_0, i.e., ± 1. This gives a diffusion property to this process.

2.3. Shape-Figure and Entropy

In order to select the set of hypotheses that produce the "best figure" (best shape), we consider an entropy measure. After all, given a source, we do not know which side takes $\sigma_0(k) = e(k)$ or $-e(k)$. At junctions the multiplicity of hypotheses grows (see [12], [3]). We first, for simplicity, convert $-1 \leq P^*(k) \leq 1$ into a probability distribution at each pixel, via the linear mapping

$$p^*(k) = \frac{1}{2}(1 + P^*(k)).$$

Thus, the entropy criteria becomes

$$S(p^*) = \\ -\frac{1}{S} \sum_{k \in S} p^*(k) \log p^*(k) + (1 - p^*(k)) \log(1 - p^*(k)),$$

where $\mathbf{S}$ is defined as the set of pixels k such that $p^*(k) \geq 0.5$ (that means $P^*(k) \geq 0$). For the background entropy (that needs to be compared against), one can also compute

$$\overline{S}(p^*) = \\ -\frac{1}{\overline{S}} \sum_{k \notin S} p^*(k) \log p^*(k) + (1 - p^*(k)) \log(1 - p^*(k)),$$

where $\overline{S} = N^2 - S$. The sharper is the diffusion, the closer to 1 is $P^*(k)$ inside $\mathbf{S}$, the better is the figure perception, i.e., the lower the entropy the more salient is the region. Note that the entropy is a per pixel entropy or the total entropy normalized by the number of pixels.

Problem: This criteria favors closed contour that "track" the intensity edges, e.g., the black-and-white four pack men on Figure 3. In this case, with all $e(k, j) = 0, 1$ (edges or non-edges), the four pack man solution gives $P^*(k) = \pm 1$ everywhere, i.e., $S(p^*) = 0$. This is the best solution one can hope. Moreover, with this criteria we can not distinguish between the black and white regions of Figures 1(a)-(d) as both regions will give zero entropy. Thus, we need to devise a criteria that would favor geometric properties as well as intensity edges, that would favor the Kanizsa square solution and convex regions. We now address the trust of our work: How can we fully characterize a desired shape via an entropy criteria and how can we measure convexity?

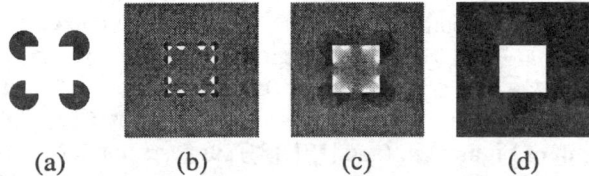

(a)   (b)   (c)   (d)

Figure 3. (a) the Kanizsa square. (b) local hypothesis where $\sigma_0 = 1$ is white (figure) and $\sigma_0 = -1$ is black (background). (c) $P^*(k)$-diffusion of all the local hypotheses. (d) threshold (level set) at $P = 0$. The entropy of the diffusion is $S = 0.75$.

3. Decay Process and Convexity

In order to balance intensity edges (number of inducers) and shape we introduce a "decay" process outside the inducers (sources). We require non-source pixels k to be a non-commitment between figure and ground, i.e., we require $P(k)$ to be zero ("neutral"). This idea can be implemented in the variational approach by adding an energy term $E_{decay} = \sum_{k=1}^{N^2} \nu(1 - e(k))P^2(k)$. The energy(1) becomes

$$E(P) = \sum_{k=1}^{N^2} \left[\lambda_k (P(k) - \sigma_0(k))^2 \\ + \sum_{k' \in N_k} \mu_{k,k'} (P(k) - P(k'))^2 \right], \quad (2)$$

where $\mu_{k,k'} = \mu(1 - e(k, k'))$ and now

$$\lambda_k = \max(e(k), \nu(1 - e(k))) \quad \text{and} \quad \sigma_0(k) = \pm e(k),$$

where $e(k) \in [0, 1]$ and ν is the decay coefficient. In Appendix A, we show that adding this energy term is equivalent to adding a decay to the random process associated to the previous energy.

The solution to equation (2) can be written (e.g., [12]) as

$$\mathbf{P}^* = \mathbf{D}^{-1}(\mu, \nu) \lambda \sigma_0. \quad (3)$$

where the symmetric and band limited matrix $\mathbf{D}(\mu, \nu)$ have the following structure

(i) The diagonal element $D_{k,k} = \lambda_k + \mu b(k, N_k)$,

(ii) The non-zero off-diagonal elements are $D_{k,k'} = -\mu(1 - e(k, k'))$ for $k' \in N_k$,

where $b(k, N_k) = \sum_{k' \in N_k}(1 - e(k, k'))$. Results of this minimization are shown in Figure 3.

In order to obtain the figure **S**, we consider all pixels $k \in \mathbf{I}$ such that $P^*(k) \geq 0$. The background pixels are obtained as pixels $k \in \mathbf{I}$ such that $P^*(k) < 0$. The level sets $k \in \mathbf{I}$ such that $P^*(k) = 0$, represent the closed contours $C(\mathbf{S})$. The result of Figure 3 d. (and [12], [3]) suggests that the shapes obtained are "roughly" in agreement to perception. Finally in the Appendix A, we derive the solution $P^*(k)$ and show that it indicates an "average" over the number of random walks starting at the sources and passing through pixel k.

We can now examine and discriminate closed intensity regions, since the associated entropies are no longer zero. We note that "clearly" convex regions have lower entropy than concave ones (see figure 4).

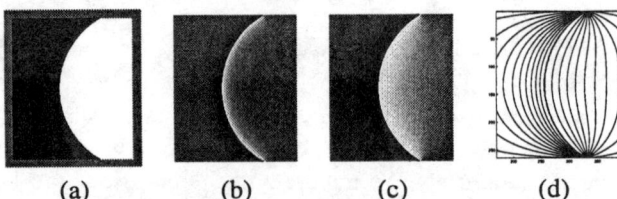

(a)　　　　(b)　　　　(c)　　　　(d)

Figure 4. (a) is an image with two regions, one is convex and concave is another. Both of them own the same area and inducers. (b), (c) are the maps according to the typical hypothesis that assumes the white region is salient. We set $\nu = 5 \times 10^{-4}, 1 \times 10^{-5}$ with (b) & (c) respectively. The maps show decay when it is away from the arc. The entropy (convex / concave or $S / \overline{S}$) for them are (b) 0.972 / 0.974 and (c) 0.880 / 0.916. (d) the isocontour (iso-$P^*(k)$) for the map (c). It shows how the diffusion expand larger distance on the convex side.

3.1. Convexity Measurement

Let us show how the entropy measure is capturing convexity (and capturing, simultaneously, size). Let us start with the definition of convexity for a given shape **S**.

Convexity: *A shape* **S** *is convex if and only if for any pair of points inside* **S** *the line segment connecting this pair of points is completely inside* **S**.

Let us represent $\overline{kj}$ to be the Euclidean distance between pixels k and j. Let us denote the shortest legal path between k and j **within** the shape **S** by $d(k, j)$. The distinction between convex and concave regions is that for convex regions, $d(k, j) = \overline{kj}$ $\forall k, j \in \mathbf{S}$ (by definition) while for concave ones there are $k, j \in \mathbf{S}$ such that $d(k, j) > \overline{kj}$.

Consider Figure 5 where two regions, one convex and the other concave, have the same area and same inducers. Given a source pixel p (along the boundary) and given a pixel q at the convex side of the figure, there is a pixel q' equally

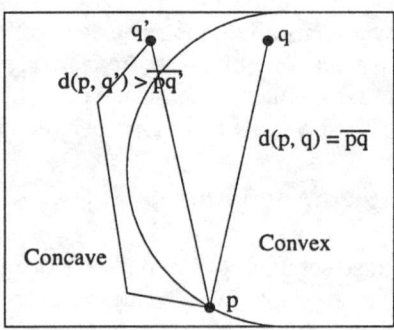

Figure 5. We examine how convexity is captured by the model. Consider all the path starting at the boundary pixel p. In the concave region the shortest random walk from p to q is given by $d(p, q') > \overline{pq'}$ while the shortest random walk to q' is $d(p, q) = \overline{pq} = \overline{pq'}$. The shorter are the random walks the more support is obtained by the source, otherwise the random walk tend to decay. Thus, concave regions get weaker response. The reflectivity makes random walks even longer at concave regions.

distant to p (Euclidean distance) in the concave side. There are many pixels q' with such property. In the concave region the shortest legal walk between p and q' traverse a distance $d(p, q') > \overline{pq'}$ while in the convex region, the shortest legal walk between p and q traverse a distance $d(p, q) = \overline{pq} = \overline{pq'}$.

We now invoke the theory of random walks (see Appendix A) to suggest that the entropy is lower for convex regions than for concave ones.

The contribution to the the final solution $P^*(q)$ and $P^*(q')$ of the source p to q and q' is directly dependent on $d(p, q)$ and $d(p, q')$ respectively. This is because with the decay term, only the pixels with shorter distance can be reached by the random walk. The longer is the path to reach a pixel the more likely it will die (yielding the decay). More precisely, from the Markov theory the probability of a particle dying when going in the shortest path from p to q is exactly $\sum_{s=1}^{d(p,q)} (Q^s_{pa(s)} R_a)$, where the sum is over all pixels a in the shortest path from p to q, parameterized by $s = 1, ..., d(p, q)$. Thus, the longer is the path, the more terms in the sum over a, and the smaller is the probability to reach q. Thus, a point q in a convex side will be reached by more random walks than a point q' in the concave side. This implies that $P^*(q)$ will be more defined to 1 or -1 (to figure or ground) than $P^*(q')$ and the entropy will satisfy $S^*(q) < S^*(q')$. Thus, convexity is encouraged by the entropy criteria.

3.2. Size

The entropy is lower for smaller size objects. Indeed, neglecting the smoothing in (3), and for shapes with inducers on all edges ($e(k) = 1$), we have $P^*(k) = \sigma_0(k)$ and $S(P^*) = log2\,\frac{(\mathcal{A}(\mathbf{S}) - \mathcal{P}(\mathbf{S},\mathbf{I}))}{\mathcal{A}(\mathbf{S})} = log2\left(1 - \frac{Perimeter}{Area}\right)$. Note, that the perimeter is adapted to the number of inducers. The more inducers the smaller is our "size" criteria.

3.3. Reflectivity

In order to enhance the convexity effect, we studied a "reflectivity" term that bounces the random walk perpendicular to the tangent to the boundary shape once it reaches the boundary. Thus, the diffusion tends to go along perpendicular directions to the tangent of the boundary contour.

Let us consider a pixel k at the boundary $C(\mathbf{S})$. The reflective can be considered by increasing the probability of a jump from k to the neighbor pixel, $f(k)$, in the direction perpendicular to the tangent to the curve. In a corner there may be two such directions, $f1(k)$ and $f2(k)$, so, we consider the set $F_k = \{f1(k), f2(k)\}$ to contain both directions.

Within the theory of random walks, these modifications are simple to implement. More precisely, we modify Q to

$$Q_{k,k'} = \begin{cases} \frac{2\mu}{\lambda_k + \mu(b(k,F_k) + b(k,N_k))} & \forall k' \in F_k \\ \frac{\mu}{\lambda_k + \mu(b(k,F_k) + b(k,N_k))} & \forall k' \in N_k - F_k \\ 0 & \text{otherwise} \end{cases}$$

We are also forced to modify $R_k = \frac{\lambda_k}{\lambda_k + \mu(b(k,F_k) + b(k,N_k))}$ so that M is always stochastic ($\sum_{j=0}^{N^2} M_{k,j} = 1$). This modification of Q only affects pixels near the boundary, where the set $F(k)$ is not empty (where $b(k,F_k) \neq 0$). We note that there is an associated energy to this process

$$E_{reflectivity}(P) = \mu \sum_{k=1}^{N^2} \sum_{k' \in F_k} \mu_{k,k'}(P(k) - P(k'))^2.$$

In order to keep the symmetry of the process we request that if $k' \in F_k$ then $k \in F_{k'}$.

In Figure 5 the reflectivity enhances $d(p,q')$ making the difference $d(p,q') - d(p,q)$ larger.

4. Experiments

The first series (see Figure 6) is set for examining the convexity effect. We test our model on a series of images where black and white regions own the same size. The degree of the angle θ in those images are $n\pi/36$, where $n = 6,7,...,36$. The difference in entropy decreases as the angle becomes wider (Figure 6). We then test other images (see Figure 7,8).

We set the smoothness coefficient $\mu = 10^{-1}$ and the decay coefficient $\nu = 5 \times 10^{-4}$ through all our experiments (Except in Figure 4). The numerical method we apply here for the optimization process is conjugate gradient descent method.

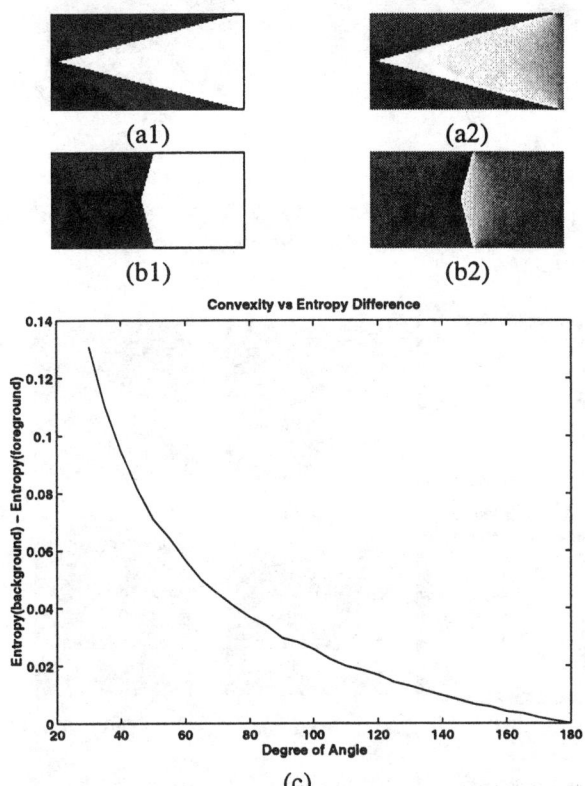

Figure 6. (a1), (b1), The parallel pentagon image with angle of $\pi/6$ and $5\pi/6$ degree, (a2), (b2) the saliency map of them. The entropy values for (a2) and (b2) are (convex/concave or $S / \bar{S}$) 0.721 / 0.870 and 0.944 / 0.950 respectively, with $\nu = 1 \times 10^{-5}$. (c) The difference between the entropy for the convex and concave region as a function of the angle ("inverse of convexity").

A. Random Walk Formulation

Let us now bring the theory of Markov chains to understand our approach as "an average over random walks" or as a diffusion. This view will allow us to modify the model and construct a measure of convexity and size.

The matrix $\mathbf{D}$ from equation (3) can be written as

$$\mathbf{D} = \mathcal{D}(\mathbf{I} - \mathbf{Q}),$$

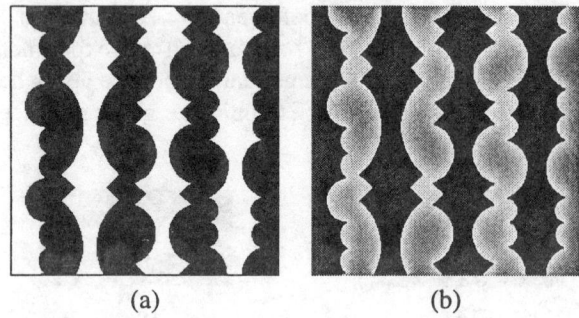

(a)　　　　　　　(b)

Figure 7. Inducers are placed along all the perimeter. The entropy values are $S = 0.521$ / $\overline{S} = 0.534$ **for the black/white regions.**

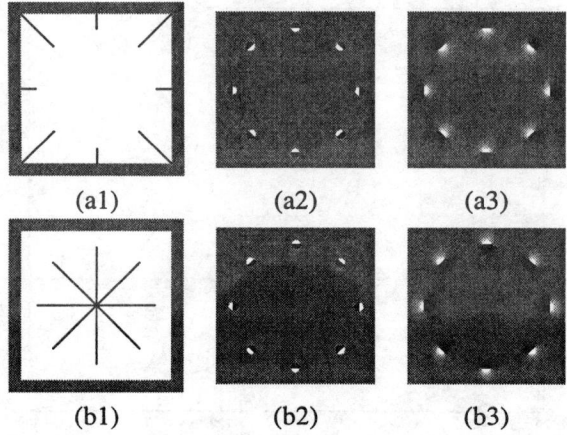

(a1)　　　　(a2)　　　　(a3)

(b1)　　　　(b2)　　　　(b3)

Figure 8. (a1), (b1), initial figures, (a2), (b2), sparse data and (a3), (b3), the diffusion results. The figure entropy values ($P^*(k) > 0$) **are (a3)**$S = 0.968$, **(b3)**$S = 0.975$.

with $\mathcal{D}$ being the diagonal matrix with elements $\mathcal{D}_{k,k} = \lambda_k + \mu b(k, N_k)$ ($\mathcal{D}_{k,k'} = 0$ for $k \neq k'$.) Therefore $\mathbf{Q}$ must have four off-diagonals non-zero and positive i.e.,

$$Q_{k,k'} = \begin{cases} \frac{\mu}{\lambda_k + \mu b(k, N_k)} & \forall k' \in N_k \\ 0 & \text{otherwise} \end{cases} \quad (4)$$

The inverse of $\mathbf{D}$ is

$$\mathbf{D}^{-1} = (\sum_{n=1}^{\infty} \mathbf{Q}^n) \mathcal{D}^{-1},$$

and so,

$$P^* = (\sum_{n=1}^{\infty} \mathbf{Q}^n) g, \quad (5)$$

with $g = \mathcal{D}^{-1} \lambda \sigma_0$, i.e., $g_k = \frac{\lambda_k}{\mathcal{D}_{kk}} \sigma_0(k)$. We can think g as our "new" input data. The matrix $\mathbf{Q}$ is the "transient" part of an "absorbing Markov chain" $\mathbf{M}$, where $\mathbf{M}$ is

$$\mathbf{M} = \begin{pmatrix} 1 & 000... \\ R & Q \end{pmatrix}, \quad (6)$$

with R being a $N \times 1$ matrix with elements

$$R_k = 1 - \sum_j Q_{kj} = \frac{\lambda_k}{\lambda_k + \mu b(k, N_k)}, \quad (7)$$

so that $\sum_{j=0}^{N} M_{ij} = 1 \quad \forall i$. The stochastic matrix $\mathbf{M}$ is of size $N + 1$ by $N + 1$. It is clear that

$$\mathbf{M}^n = \begin{pmatrix} 1 & 000... \\ R' & Q^n \end{pmatrix},$$

where $R' = \sum_{\alpha=0}^{n} \mathbf{Q}^{\alpha} R$. $\mathbf{M}$ is an absorbing Markov chain in the sense that if one starts with any state s_0, by successively applying $\mathbf{M}$, one ends up in the state $s_{final} = (1, 0, 0, ..., 0)$, i.e., $s_{final} = \lim_{n \to \infty} s_0 \mathbf{M}^n$ (we are applying the matrix to the vector to the "left") This is clear from the fact that $\lim_{n \to \infty} Q^n = 0$, since all the elements of Q are less than 1 and sum less than 1 for each row. This is why Q is the transient part of $\mathbf{M}$. The interpretation of the state $s = (\pm 1, 0, ..., 0)$, is of "death" of the random walk, since the random walk jumped to the zero-th coordinate that is not a pixel in the lattice. Moreover, once it reaches the zero-th coordinate it never leaves, i.e., $s = (\pm 1, 0, 0, ..., 0)$ is an eigenstate of $\mathbf{M}$ or $s \mathbf{M} = s$ (or equivalently, to the "right" $s^{\dagger}$ is an eigenstate of $\mathbf{M}^{\dagger}$, with $\mathbf{M}^{\dagger} s^{\dagger} = s^{\dagger}$. This is the absorbing state.

Random Walk View: Let us clarify the random walk interpretation of the matrices.

$(Q^n)_{k,j}$- probability that a random walk that started at pixel k will reach pixel j in n steps.

R_k- probability that a random walk starting at pixel k will die (move to the zero-th state coordinate.)

$R' = \sum_{\alpha=0}^{n} \mathbf{Q}^{\alpha} R$ - probability that the random walk of n+1 steps has died at any stage before reaching pixel k.

$(\sum_{k=1}^{n} \mathbf{Q}^n)_{k,j}$-probability that the random walk started at pixel k and reached pixel j in any number of steps.

In one step, for example, the random walk starting at k has probability non-zero, $Q_{k,j} = \frac{\mu}{\lambda_k + \mu b(k, N_k)}$, to move to one of its $j \in N_k$ neighbors and probability $R_k = \frac{\lambda_k}{\lambda_k + \mu b(k, N_k)}$ to die. Note that inside the shape $\mathbf{S}$ we have $\lambda_k = 0$ and therefore the random walk can not die there. It will only die, possibly, when reaching back the boundary.

The initial state $g = \mathcal{D}^{-1} \lambda \sigma_0$ can be written as

$$g(j) = \sum_{k \in C(\mathbf{S})} \frac{1}{1 + \mu b(k, N_k)} e_k(j),$$

where $e_k(j) = \delta_{jk}$, with $\delta_{jk} = 1, 0$ and is 1 only if $j = k$. Thus, we conclude this section with the random walk view interpretation of the solution P^* (equation 3) :

The solution P^* correspond to the average of multiple source averaged over the random walks, where each random walk starts at a boundary pixel $k \in C(\mathbf{S})$ and carry the weight $g(k) = \frac{1}{1+\mu b(k, N_k)}$ (i.e., corners tend to weight more).

So far, we had $R_k = \frac{\lambda_k}{\lambda_k + \mu b(k, N_k)} = 0$ inside the shape, since $\lambda_k = 0$. We now modify it to $R_k = \frac{v}{v + \mu b(k, N_k)}$ where $1 > v > 0$, so that the probability of jumping to the zero-th coordinate (and dying) is small, depending how small v is, but not zero.

References

[1] M. Brady and W. E. L. Grimson. The perception of subjective surfaces. A.I. Memo No. 666, AI Lab., MIT, Nov. 1982.

[2] J. Elder and S. W. Zucker. A measure of Closure. *Vision Research*, Vol. 34 (24), pp.3361-3369, 1994.

[3] D. Geiger, H. Pao and N. Rubin. Salient and multiple illusory surfaces. *Computer Vision and Pattern recognition.*, June. 1998.

[4] G.Guy and G. Medioni. Inferring global perceptual contours from local features. In *Proc. IU Workshop DARPA*, Sept. 1992.

[5] S. Grossberg and E. Mingolla. Neural dynamics of perceptual grouping: textures, boundaries and emergent segmentations. *Perception & Psychophysics*, 38(2):141–170, 1985.

[6] F. Heitger and R. von der Heydt. A computational model of neural contour processing: Figure-ground segregation and illusory contours. *Proceedings of the IEEE*, 1993

[7] D. Huttenlocher and P. Wayner, P., "Finding Convex Edge Groupings in an Image," *International Journal of Computer Vision*, **8**(1):7-29, 1992.

[8] D. Jacobs. Robust and efficient detection of convex groups" *IEEE Trans. PAMI* 1995.

[9] G. Kanizsa. *Organization in Vision*. Praeger, New York, 1979.

[10] B. Kimia, A. Tannenbaum, S. Zucker. "Shapes, Shocks, and Deformations I: The components of two-dimensional shape and the reaction-diffusion space", *Int. J. Comp. Vis.* **1**: 189-224, 1995.

[11] K. Koffka. *Principles of Gestalt Psychology*. New York: Harcourst. 1935.

[12] K. Kumaran, D. Geiger, and L. Gurvits. Illusory surfaces and visual organization. *Network: Comput. in Neural Syst.*, 7(1), Feb. 1996.

[13] D. Mumford. Elastica and computer vision. In C. L. Bajaj, editor, *Algebraic Geometry and Its Applications*. Springer-Verlag, New York, 1993.

[14] K. Nakayama, Z. J. He, S. Shimojo, "Visual surface representation: a critical link between lower-level and higher-level vision", in *Visual Cognition Eds S M Kosslyn and D N Osherson* (Cambridge, MA: Cambridge, MA), pp. 1-70, 1995.

[15] M. Nitzberg and D. Mumford. The 2.1-d sketch. In *ICCV*, pages 138–144. 1990.

[16] S. Parent and S. W. Zucker, "Trace inference, curvature consistency and curve detection", *IEEE PAMI*, Vol. 11, No. 8, pp. 823-839, 1989.

[17] E. Rubin, *Visuell wahrgenommene Figuren*, (Copenhagen: Gyldendals), 1921.

[18] N. Rubin, K. Nakayama, R. Shapley, "Enhanced perception of illusory contours in the lower versus upper visual hemifields", *Science*, 271, pp.651-653, 1996

[19] S. Ullman. Filling in the gaps: The shape of subjective contours and a model for their generation. *Biological Cybernetics*, 25:1–6, 1976.

[20] Y. Weiss. Interpreting images by propagating Bayesian beliefs. In M. Mozer, M. Jordan and T. Petsche, editors, *Advances in Neural Information Processing System 9*, 1996.

Bayesian Fusion of Color and Texture Segmentations

Roberto Manduchi

Jet Propulsion Laboratory
California Institute of Technology
Pasadena, CA 91109
manduchi@jpl.nasa.gov

Abstract

In many applications one would like to use information from both color and texture features in order to segment an image. We propose a novel technique to combine "soft" segmentations computed for two or more features independently. Our algorithm merges models according to a maximum descriptiveness criterion, and allows to choose any number of classes for the final grouping. This technique also allows to improve the quality of supervised classification based on one feature (e.g. color) by merging information from unsupervised segmentation based on another feature (e.g., texture.)

1 Introduction

Image segmentation is a fundamental task in Computer Vision. Color and texture provide powerful cues for segmenting a still image, and much work has been devoted to developing grouping algorithms based on these two features [1],[3],[5]. In fact, most of the literature deals with segmentation based on either color or texture; this work was originated by the intuition that using information provided by *both* features, one should be able to obtain more robust and meaningful results.

Underlying our approach is the hypothesis that in typical images color and texture features are not statistically independent. Perhaps the simplest way to exploit this dependency is to concatenate the color and texture feature vectors together, and then run the grouping algorithm of choice on such super–vectors. This approach, however, may give the feeling of "comparing apples with oranges". Indeed, color and texture features often have very different statistical behaviors; one may prefer to use the most suitable grouping algorithm for each feature separately, and then somehow combine the results of the two segmentations together.

This work introduces a strategy to merge together in a Bayesian framework segmentations computed on color and texture features independently. The only requirement is that the segmentations are expressed in terms of posterior probabilities [2]. Note that most clustering algorithms explicitly compute estimates of the posterior distributions, and do the final assignment by Bayesian classification (i.e., they assign a feature to the class that most likely generated it.)

For example, in Figure 2 (b) and (c) we show instances of color and texture segmentation of the image in Figure 2 (a). The texture features are vectors formed by the absolute values of the outputs of a bank of Gabor filters, after smoothing by a gaussian filter [3]. The posterior distributions in both cases have been estimated by Expectation Maximization [2]; the "hard" segmentation shown in the figures is the result of Bayesian classification based on such distributions. Both models have four classes, although our algorithm can accept any combination of classes. The scene in figure 2(a) is composed by a small number of homogeneous parts: two bushes, a paved road on the right, dirt soil on the left, a shadow area near a bush and piece of dark background. The color segmenter (figure 2(b)) successfully separates the "bush", the "background" and the "road" areas, but is unable to discriminate the "road" from "soil" parts, which have very similar color. The texture segmenter does separate the "road" and "soil" areas, but cannot discriminate the "road" from the "background" parts; in addition, it assigns the "soil" area to two distinct classes.

Our technique for model fusion involves two steps. First, the two models are merged by a "Cartesian product" operator, discussed in section 2. This operation preserves all the information about the models, but has the disadvantage of creating a large number of classes, equal to the product of the number of classes of the two original models. Then, the number of classes of the combined model is reduced by a technique, presented in section 3, that "clips together" sets of classes

956

based on a maximum descriptiveness criterion. This procedure may be extended straightforwardly to any number K of segmentations. An intriguing application of our algorithm is discussed in section 4, and involves information fusion from supervised classification (e.g., based on color) and unsupervised segmentation (e.g., based on texture.) The unsupervised segmentation is used to leverage the estimates provided by the trained model, resulting in a more accurate classification.

2 Cartesian product of mixture models

Our merging technique starts from K given mixture models [2] (called "models" in the following.) The i-th model, $\mathcal{M}_i$, is composed by N_i classes, and defines a probability density function $p_i(z_i)$:

$$p_i(z_i) = \sum_{j_i=1}^{N_i} p_i(z_i|j_i)P_i(j_i) \qquad (1)$$

where z_i, the observed feature, lives in a space Z_i. For example, z_i may be a color vector, or a texture feature in a multiscale/multiorientation space. The conditional likelihood functions $p_i(z_i|j_i)$ and the priors $P_i(j_i)$ specify the model completely. The posterior distributions are given by Bayes' rule:

$$P_i(j_i|z_i) = \frac{p_i(z_i|j_i)P_i(j_i)}{p_i(z_i)} \qquad (2)$$

$P_i(j_i|z_i)$ is the probability that the observed feature z_i was generated by the class of index j_i. The Bayesian classifier for $\mathcal{M}_i$ assigns a feature z_i to the class indexed by the location of the maximum of $P_i(j_i|z_i)$. To simplify our presentation, we will assume in the following that all priors are strictly positive: if a prior $P_i(j_i)$ is null, we can safely remove the class with index j_i from the model. Note that

$$P_i(j_i) = \int P_i(j_i|z_i)p_i(z_i)dz_i = E[P_i(j_i|z_i)] \qquad (3)$$

where the expectation is computed with respect to the density $p_i(z_i)$.

The *Cartesian product* $\mathcal{M}$ of the models $\mathcal{M}_i$ is a new model with probability distribution $Z_1 \times \ldots \times Z_N$. $\mathcal{M}$ is completely specified by the following axioms:

1. $\mathcal{M}$ has $N = \prod_{i=1}^{K} N_i$ classes, corresponding to the Cartesian product of the classes of the models $\mathcal{M}_i$: $j \leftrightarrow (j_1, \ldots, j_K)$.

2. The conditional likelihood of the feature $z = (z_1, \ldots, z_K)$ given the class of index j is equal to $p(z|j) = \prod_{i=1}^{K} p_i(z_i|j_i)$.

3. The priors factorize as $P(j) = \prod_{i=1}^{K} P_i(j_i)$.

It follows straightforwardly that the likelihood and the posteriors of the Cartesian product of models factorize as well:

$$p(z) = \prod_{i=1}^{K} p_i(z_i), \; P(j|z) = \prod_{i=1}^{K} P_i(j_i|z_i) \qquad (4)$$

Note that all the information about the K original models is preserved in their Cartesian product $\mathcal{M}$. The Bayesian classifier for $\mathcal{M}$ assigns a feature z to the model $j \leftrightarrow (j_1, \ldots, j_N)$ such that j_i is the class assigned to z_i by the Bayesian classifier for $\mathcal{M}_i$. Figure 2 (d) shows the Bayesian segmentation relative to the Cartesian product of the color and texture models of figure 2 (b) and (c). The new model has 16 classes. In the next section we describe a procedure to reduce the dimensionality (i.e., the number of classes) of a model, in such a way that the loss of "descriptiveness" of the model is minimized.

3 Dimensionality reduction

Assume we are given a model $\mathcal{M}$ with N classes. We introduce here a technique to build a new model that has fewer classes than $\mathcal{M}$ but explains the data exactly as $\mathcal{M}$, i.e., it defines the same likelihood $p(z)$ as $\mathcal{M}$. Suppose for example that we want to reduce the dimensionality of the model to $N - M$. Our strategy is very simple: we just "clip together" $M + 1$ classes of $\mathcal{M}$ into a new super-class, leaving the other classes untouched. We may decide, for instance, to clip together the classes of index $N - M, \ldots, N$ into a new class of index $N - M$. The probability that a feature z was generated by the union of such classes according to $\mathcal{M}$ is equal to the sum of the corresponding posteriors. This is the value that we assign to the posterior $P^{new}(N - M|z)$ for the new model; the posteriors for the other classes are the same as in $\mathcal{M}$:

$$P^{new}(j|z) = P(j|z), \; 1 \leq j < N - M$$
$$P^{new}(N - M|z) = \sum_{j=N-M}^{N} P(j|z)$$

If in addition we impose that the likelihood function $p(z)$ is the same in both models, the new model is completely specified.

In general, to reduce the model dimension from N to $N - M$, we may choose any $L \leq M$ disjoint groups of classes with L_l components each, such that $\sum_{l=1}^{L} L_l = L + M$, and clip together the classes in each group. A criterion for the selection of the most appropriate clipping scheme is presented in the next section.

3.1 Maximum descriptiveness criterion

Dimensionality reduction via class–clipping involves some loss of descriptiveness of the model, where by "descriptiveness" we mean the information that the model provides about the image. If for example two classes that "explain" well two different portions of the image are clipped together, the new, less informative model will probably assign both portions of the image to the same class. In this section we give a formal definition of descriptiveness, and present an algorithm for selecting a class–clipping scheme that minimizes the loss of descriptiveness for a given model.

Loosely speaking, we will say that a model is highly descriptive if its classes "explain well" the features that are assigned to them. More precisely, we define the descriptiveness $D(j)$ of class j as follows:

$$D(j) = \int P(j|z)p(z|j)dz \qquad (5)$$

while the descriptiveness of the model, D, is the sum of the class descriptivenesses:

$$D = \sum_{j=1}^{N} D(j) \qquad (6)$$

Thus, the class descriptiveness $D(j)$ is the integral of the conditional likelihood weighted by the posterior distribution. It is clear from (5) that $0 < D(j) \leq 1$ (since $\int p(z|j)dz = 1$, $p(z|j) \geq 0$ and $0 \leq P(j|z) \leq 1$) and therefore $D \leq N$. A single–class model has $D = 1$, which is the smallest value of descriptiveness attainable by a model (this property derives straightforwardly from Fact 1, presented later in this section.)

To justify our choice for the descriptiveness, let us consider two diametrically different examples of models with two classes. In the first model, the two posterior probabilities have disjoint supports in feature space. Each class thus completely describes (by means of the corresponding conditional likelihood) the set of features that are assigned to it. It is easily seen that $D(j) = 1$ for both classes, and therefore the model descriptiveness D is equal to 2, the highest attainable value for a two–class model. It is intuitive that clipping together these two classes would result in a major loss of information (descriptiveness) of the model. The corresponding variation of descriptiveness is actually $\Delta D = -1$. In the second model, the two classes have exactly the same conditional likelihood and priors (and therefore the same posteriors $P(j|z) = 0.5$.) This model is "redundant": there is really no need to use two classes to describe the data! No information is lost if such two classes are clipped together. This

notion is captured by our definition of descriptiveness, that assigns $D = 1$ to the model. Class–clipping thus gives $\Delta D = 0$ in this case.

In both previous examples the model descriptiveness did not increase as a consequence of class clipping. This is actually a general property of descriptiveness, as stated by the following result (whose proof can be found in the Appendix):

Fact 1 *Class–clipping never increases the descriptiveness of a model.*

We thus propose the following criterion for dimensionality reduction: choose the clipping scheme that minimizes the decrement of the model descriptiveness.

Unfortunately, the number of possible clipping schemes may be very high even for small model dimensions. For example, in order to reduce the number of classes from 16 to 13 we may choose among 165,620 different combinations of class clipping. Measuring the decrement of model descriptiveness for each one of those schemes may require a prohibitive computational cost. A suboptimal solution can be found using a fast greedy algorithm that builds a sequence of clippings involving only two classes at a time. At each step, the two classes that minimize the decrement of model descriptiveness are selected. To compute the model descriptiveness, we make use of the following identity (from (5) and using Bayes' rule):

$$\begin{aligned} D(j) &= \int P(j|z)\frac{P(j|z)p(z)}{P(j)}dz \qquad (7)\\ &= \frac{E[P(j|z)^2]}{P(j)} \end{aligned}$$

where the expectation is computed with respect to $p(z)$. In practice, the expectations in (7) are estimated by averaging $P(j|z)^2$ over the image. Our greedy algorithm for class–clipping is described in detail in figure 1.

Figure 2 (e)–(i) shows the results of Bayesian segmentation after dimensionality reduction from 16 to 7, 6, 5, 4 and 3 classes respectively, based on our maximum descriptiveness criterion. Each class of the reduced dimension models now correctly represents a characteristic area of the image (compare for example figure 2 (h) with (b) and (c) for the 4-class model). The computation of the optimal clipping scheme for reducing the model dimension from 16 to 4, using a Matlab implementation of our greedy algorithm, requires about 15 seconds of execution time on a Power Mac G3 266 Mhz (the image size is 256×380 pixels.)

In figure 2 (k) we plotted the variation of model descriptiveness during the class–clipping process for

Greedy algorithm for
dimensionality reduction: $N \to N - M$

Given the set of posteriors $P(j|z)$ and of priors $P(j)$, $1 \leq j \leq N$:

Build auxiliary vector $\mathbf{D}$ and matrix $\mathbf{\Delta}$:
$\mathbf{D}[j] = \frac{E[P(j|x)^2]}{P(j)}$, $1 \leq j \leq N$:

$$\mathbf{\Delta}[j, k] = \begin{cases} \mathbf{D}[j] + \mathbf{D}[k] - \\ \quad - \frac{E[(P(j|x)+P(k|x))^2]}{P(j)+P(k)} & , 1 \leq k < j \leq N \\ \infty & , \text{otherwise} \end{cases}$$

Initialize an empty list L;
Repeat M times:
  $(\bar{j}, \bar{k}) = \arg \min \mathbf{\Delta}[j, k]$;
  Add $\bar{k}$ to the list L;
  Update $P(\bar{j}|z) \leftarrow P(\bar{j}|z) + P(\bar{k}|z), P(\bar{k}|z) \leftarrow 0$;
  Update $P(\bar{j}) \leftarrow P(\bar{j}) + P(\bar{k})$;
  Update $\mathbf{D}[\bar{j}]$;
  Update $\mathbf{\Delta}[\bar{j}, k]$ for $k < \bar{j}$, $k \notin L$;
  Update $\mathbf{\Delta}[k, \bar{j}]$ for $k > \bar{j}$, $k \notin L$;
  Set $\mathbf{\Delta}[j, \bar{k}] = \infty$ for $j > \bar{k}$;
  Set $\mathbf{\Delta}[\bar{k}, j] = \infty$ for $j < \bar{k}$;
Remove the classes indexed by the elements of L.

Figure 1: The greedy algorithm to select a class–clipping scheme that minimizes the decrement of model descriptiveness (see section 3.1.)

our example (for each model dimension we plotted the (negative) increment ΔD consequent to the 2-class clipping that generated that model.) Note that the algorithm for the greedy selection of classes, which reduces the dimension by one at a time, allows us to easily compute these values as a by-product. From figure 2 (k) we notice that the decrement of descriptiveness ($-\Delta D$) usually increases as the dimension of the model decreases (remember that our algorithm chooses for each dimension the class–clipping that gives the smallest value of $-\Delta D$.) Future work will be devoted to studying the possibility of selecting the "most appropriate" number of classes for the final segmentation based on the analysis of the model descriptiveness behavior.

3.2 Equalization

In the previous sections we have described a strategy for model fusion that first builds the Cartesian product of two models, and then performs dimensionality reduction via class–clipping. An implicit assumptions was that the two original models should give the

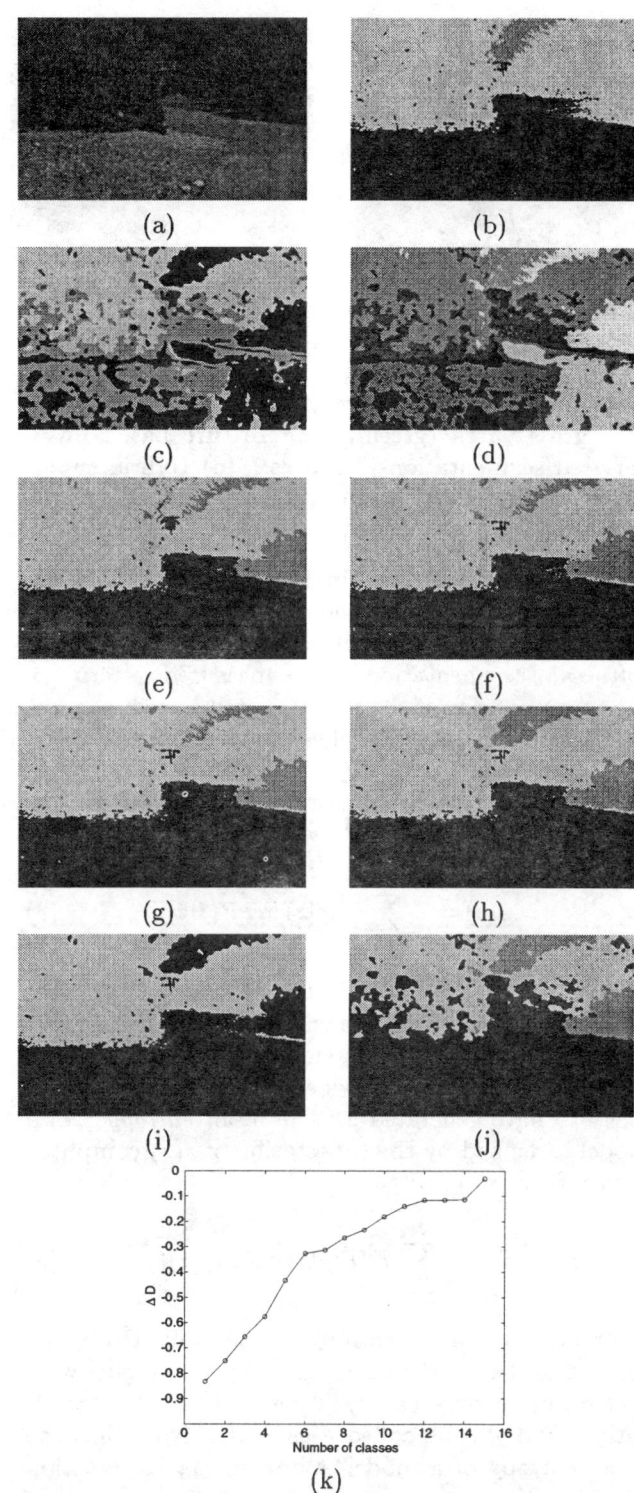

Figure 2: (a): Test image. (b) Color–based segmentation (4 classes.) (c) Texture–based segmentation (4 classes.) (d) Segmentation after Cartesian product (16 classes.) (e)–(i): Segmentation after model merging ((e): 7 classes, (f): 6 classes, (g): 5 classes, (h): 4 classes, (i): 3 classes.) (j): Segmentation after model merging (4 classes), with mean entropy of the color–based model set to a value 3 times larger than the mean entropy of the texture–based model. (k) Variation ΔD of model descriptiveness as a function of the number of classes.

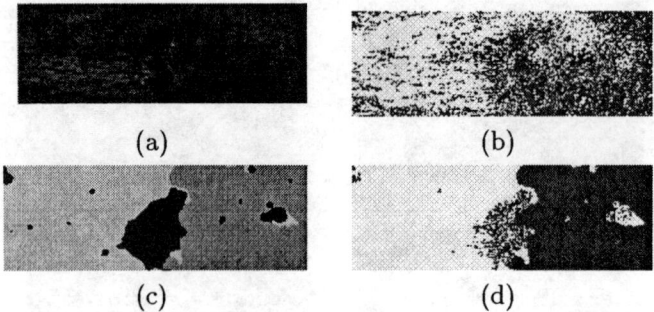

(a)   (b)

(c)   (d)

Figure 3: (a): Test image. (b) Color–based supervised classification into the "road" class (yellow) and the "grass" area (green.) (c) Texture–based unsupervised segmentation (3 classes.) (d) Hybrid supervised/unsupervised classification.

same contribution to the final segmentation. This hypothesis does not hold true if the "softness" of segmentation is very different in the two models. The softness of segmentation can be measured in terms of the *mean entropy* of the model, a well-known concept in the fields of statistical physics and mixture estimation [4],[6].

Given a feature z, the entropy of the posterior distribution $P(j|z)$ is defined by [2]

$$s(z) = -\sum_{j=1}^{N} P(j|z) \log P(j|z) \qquad (8)$$

The entropy $s(z)$ measures the softness of the class assignment. A distribution with null entropy assigns z to exactly one class; the maximum value of the entropy is $\log N$, and is attained when all classes are equally likely to have generated z. The *mean entropy S* of a model is defined by the expectation of $s(z)$ computed with respect to $p(z)$:

$$S = -\sum_{j=1}^{N} E\left[P(j|z) \log P(j|z)\right] \qquad (9)$$

In practice, the mean entropy can be estimated by averaging $s(z)$ over the observed image. A model with null mean entropy can only perform "hard" classification, and will be called *degenerate*. Note that the mean entropy of a model estimated via Expectation Maximization is a function of the "temperature" of the algorithm [6].

It is easy to see that if two models to be merged have very different values of the mean entropy, the model with the smallest entropy will "dominate" the combined model. This undesirable effect may be corrected by applying to one of the two models the simple

entropy equalization procedure proposed in the following.

Our equalization operator starts from a model $\mathcal{M}$ and produces a new model with the same number of classes N. The entropy of this new model can be tuned to match any desired value $S_0 < \log N$, and the associated Bayesian classifier yields the same results as the Bayesian classifier for $\mathcal{M}$. The equalization operator simply replaces each posterior distribution $P(j|z)$ with the new distribution $P^{eq}(j|z)$ defined as follows:

$$P^{eq}(j|z) = c(z)P(j|z)^{\alpha} , \ \alpha \geq 0 \qquad (10)$$

where c is a normalizing coefficient:

$$c(z) = \frac{1}{\sum_{j=1}^{N} P(j|z)^{\alpha}} \qquad (11)$$

The mean entropy properties of the equalization operator are summarized by the following result:

Fact 2 *Equalization decreases the mean entropy of a non–degenerate model if $\alpha > 1$, and increases it if $\alpha < 1$.*

The proof can be found in the Appendix. Note that $\alpha = 0$ implies that the mean entropy of $P^{eq}(j|z)$ is equal to $\log N$; the mean entropy of $P^{eq}(j|z)$ can be made as small as desired by a suitably large value of α. Also note that for each feature z the location of the maximum of the posterior distribution is not changed by the equalization, so that the Bayesian classifier will yield the same segmentation for the two models.

Now, suppose that the two models to be merged have different mean entropies. We may modify one of the models via the equalization operator, so that its mean entropy matches the mean entropy of the other model. The appropriate value of the parameter α may be found using any non–linear one–dimensional minimization technique.

In some cases, equalization may also be used to make either of the two models dominant, i.e. to assign different "weights" to the models to be merged. For example, figure 2 (j) shows the results of Bayesian segmentation after equalizing the color–based model to a value of the mean entropy 3 times larger than the mean entropy of the texture–based model (the combined model dimension was reduced to 4 by class–clipping.) By comparing figure 2 (j) with (h) and (c) it results clear that the final segmentation is dominated by the texture–based model. We should point out, however, that while this and other experimental results are very encouraging, we still lack a complete understanding of the relation between mean entropy and model dominance, which will be the object of future research.

4 Hybrid classification

The main differences between supervised classification and unsupervised clustering can be summarized as follows:

1. The classes ("labels") of a supervised classifier usually represent "physical" causes, and therefore are not logically interchangeable;

2. The statistical model of a supervised classifier is usually learned from training data, while unsupervised clustering does not require training in principle.

The Bayesian classifier assigns a feature z to the maximizer of the posterior distribution [2]. In many instances, only the conditional likelihoods $p(x|j)$ are learned; however, reasonable assumptions about the class priors $P(j)$ are often available, and the posterior distributions can be computed using Bayes' rule.

In this section we propose to merge a model $\mathcal{M}^s$ for supervised classification with a model $\mathcal{M}^u$ for unsupervised segmentation (based on a different feature space,) to create a "hybrid" classifier which assigns each image point to some label of $\mathcal{M}^s$. The intuition is that information from the "unsupervised model" (which identifies clusters in the feature space based on the current image) may be used to leverage the classification performed by the "supervised model", which is learned from a large training data set and may not be optimal for the current instance.

The merging algorithm discussed in the previous sections defines a model $\mathcal{M}$ with classes that are the union of elements of the Cartesian product of $\mathcal{M}^s$ and $\mathcal{M}^u$. If $\mathcal{C}$ represents a generic class of $\mathcal{M}$, we may write

$$\mathcal{C} = \bigcup_{v \in V} \bigcup_{w(v)} (\mathcal{C}_v^s, \mathcal{C}_{w(v)}^u) \qquad (12)$$

where $\mathcal{C}^s$ and $\mathcal{C}^u$ are classes of $\mathcal{M}^s$ and $\mathcal{M}^u$ respectively, indexed by the corresponding subscripts. To complete the definition of the hybrid classification model, we need to be able to assign labels from $\mathcal{M}^s$ to the image using the new super-model. In other words, we need to identify each class $\mathcal{C}$ with some class of $\mathcal{C}^s$. If the set V of classes of $\mathcal{M}^s$ that form the super-class $\mathcal{C}$ is composed by just one element v, than we simply identify $\mathcal{C}$ with $\mathcal{C}_v^s$. In general, however, V may have more than one element; in this case, we identify $\mathcal{C}$ with the class $\mathcal{C}_v^s$ that maximizes the *contribution* to $\mathcal{C}$, defined by

$$E[P(\bigcup_{w(v)} (\mathcal{C}_v^s, \mathcal{C}_{w(v)}^u)|z)] = \qquad (13)$$

$$= E[P_s(v|z_s) \sum_{w(v)} P_u(w(v)|z_u)]$$

where the expectation is computed with respect to $p(z)$ (with $z = (z_s, z_u)$.) $P_s(\cdot|\cdot)$, $P_u(\cdot|\cdot)$ and $P(\cdot|\cdot)$ represent the posteriors of the models $\mathcal{M}_s$, $\mathcal{M}_u$ and $\mathcal{M}$ respectively.

We present an example of hybrid classification in Figure 3. Figure 3(a) shows a scene with a dirt road on the left and dry grass on the right. Supervised color-based classification (figure 3(b)) is performed using a trained gaussian model. The "road" class and the "grass" class have very similar colors; this is the reason why pixels in the top–right quadrant are misclassified as belonging to the "road" class. Figure 3(c) shows the results of unsupervised texture segmentation with three classes, computed via Expectation Maximization. The segmenter isolates uniform regions corresponding to the road and to the grass areas, plus a region corresponding to the border of the road. After mean entropy equalization, the two models are merged into a new model with four classes; the final hybrid classification is shown in Figure 3(d). The hybrid classifier has correctly labeled each one of the four classes of the merged model as either "road" or "grass". The information from the texture model has helped to correctly classify most pixels that were misclassified in figure 3(b).

5 Conclusions

We have presented a technique for merging together two segmentations computed independently over color and texture. Our technique is very general, and in principle can be applied also to other classes of features, such as motion; it only requires that the posterior distributions that originated the segmentations are available. The results show the effectiveness of the maximum descriptiveness criterion for reducing the dimensionality of the Cartesian product of the two mixture models. We have also introduced a technique for hybrid supervised/unsupervised classification, based on our merging algorithm, that can improve the performance of supervised classification using consensus from different features.

Acknowledgments

The research described in this paper was carried out by the Jet Propulsion Laboratory, California Institute of Technology, under a contract with the National Aeronautics and Space Administration. This work was supported in part by the NASA Telerobotics program and by the NASA Remote Exploration and Experimentation task. Reference herein to any specific commercial product, process, or service by trade name, trademark, manufacturer, or otherwise, does not constitute or imply its endorsement by the United States Government or the Jet Propulsion Laboratory, California Institute of Technology.

This work was originated by discussions with Eric Mjolsness and Becky Castano. Matt Klimesh is kindly acknowledged for fruitful feedback.

Appendix

Proof of Fact 1. A class–clipping operation can always be implemented by a sequence of class–clippings involving two classes at a time. We show in the following that the model descriptiveness can never increase with any such step. Assume classes j and k are clipped together; using (7) and (6), and remembering that the likelihood $p(z)$ does not change after class–clipping, we maintain that the variation ΔD of the model descriptiveness is

$$
\begin{aligned}
\Delta D &= \frac{\int (P(j|z)+P(k|z))^2 p(z)dz}{P(j)+P(k)} - \\
&\quad - \frac{\int P(j|z)^2 p(z)dz}{P(j)} - \frac{\int P(k|z)^2 p(z)dz}{P(k)} \\
&= \int \left(\frac{(P(j|z)+P(k|z))^2}{P(j)+P(k)} - \frac{P(j|z)^2}{P(j)} - \frac{P(k|z)^2}{P(k)} \right) p(z)dz
\end{aligned}
$$
(14)

Now, it is easy to prove that, for any z, term $\frac{(P(j|z)+P(k|z))^2}{P(j)+P(k)} - \frac{P(j|z)^2}{P(j)} - \frac{P(k|z)^2}{P(k)}$ is always non–positive. Thus, since $p(z)$ is always non–negative, $\Delta D \leq 0$, and the claim is proved.

Proof of Fact 2. We just need to prove the claim for the case $\alpha < 1$. The proof is based on the following two results.

Lemma 1. The entropy of a probability distribution increases if two values of the distribution are moved closer to each other, while the other values are left untouched.
Proof. The claim is a direct consequence of the convexity of the function $-x \log x$.

Lemma 2. Let $P(j), 1 \leq j \leq N$ be a probability distribution and, for a given $K < N$, let J_1 and J_2 be the sets of the indices of the K smallest values and of the $N - K$ largest values of $P(j)$ respectively. Now form a new distribution $\bar{P}(j)$ from $P(j)$ by increasing some of the values with index in J_1 while at the same time decreasing some of the values with index in J_2, with the requirement that

$$
\max\{\bar{P}(j), j \in J_1\} \leq \min\{\bar{P}(i), i \in J_2\}
$$

Then the entropy of $\bar{P}(j)$ is higher than the entropy of $P(j)$.

Proof. The transformation from $P(j)$ to $\bar{P}(j)$ can be decomposed into a sequence of steps, each one involving just one value with index in J_1 and just one value with index in J_2. Therefore, by Lemma 1, the entropy is increased at each such step.

Now, it is easy to prove that the function $c(z)x^\alpha - x$, with $c(z)$ defined in (11), vanishes in correspondence of the value $x = c(z)^{\alpha-1}$, which is located between the smallest and the largest values of $P(j|z)$. Therefore, if $P(j|z)$ has non-null entropy, the equalization operator (10) with $\alpha < 1$ falls into the class of transformations considered in Lemma 2: the set J_1 is composed by all the j such that $P(j|z) \leq c(z)^{\alpha-1}$, the set J_2 is composed by all the other indices. This proves that for any z the entropy of $P(j|z)$ increases as a consequence of equalization with $\alpha < 1$.

References

[1] S. Belongie, C. Carson. H. Greenspan, J. Malik. Color- and texture-based image segmentation using EM and its application to content-based image retrieval. 675–682, *6th ICCV*, New Delhi, India, January 1998.

[2] C.M. Bishop. *Neural networks for pattern recognition.* Clarendon Press, Oxford, U.K., 1995.

[3] B.S. Manjunath and W.Y. Ma. Texture features for browsing and retrieval of image data. *IEEE Trans. Pattern Anal. Mach. Intell.*, 18(8):837–842, August 1996.

[4] R.M. Neal and G.E. Hinton. A new view of the EM algorithm that justifies incremental and other variants. Submitted to *Biometrika*.

[5] Y. Rubner, L. Guibas, and C. Tomasi. The earth mover's distance, multi-dimensional scaling, and color-based image retrieval. *Proc. ARPA Image Understanding Workshop*, May 1997.

[6] Y. Weiss and E.H. Adelson. A unified mixture framework for motion segmentation: incorporating spatial coherence and estimating the number of models. *Proc. IEEE CVPR'96*, 321–326, San Francisco, 1996.

A Level Line Selection Approach for Object Boundary Estimation

Charles Kervrann, Mark Hoebeke and Alain Trubuil
INRA - Biométrie
Domaine de Vilvert, 78352 Jouy-en-Josas, France
{Charles.Kervrann,Mark.Hoebeke,Alain.Trubuil} @jouy.inra.fr

Abstract

An energy model-based approach for estimating object boundaries is presented. We study a particular energy, which minimizer can be determined. The method estimates the unknown number of objects and draws object boundaries by selecting the "best" level lines computed from level sets of the original image. Unlike previous standard methods, the proposed method does not require iteration for minimizing the energy. In addition, our segmentation algorithm combines anisotropic diffusion-based regularization with level line selection to extract smooth object boundaries. Experimental results on 2D biomedical and meteorological images are reported.

1. Introduction

Image segmentation consists in partitioning the image into homogeneous regions ideally corresponding to physical objects. Several different methods have already been proposed in the literature: local filtering methods [8], region growing techniques [20] or global optimization techniques [5, 19, 14, 10]. Many of them rely on the design and minimization of an energy function which captures the interaction between models and image data. They can be roughly classified into two main categories according to features. The first category of approaches relies on gradient features near object boundaries whereas the other one examines the features homogeneity inside object boundaries. Nevertheless, several methods combine both approaches [24].

Among the boundary-based approaches, filtering techniques (edge detectors [8]) and energy-based active contours (snakes [12] and variants) have been used to detect discontinuities or to extract continuous contour lines. *Geodesic active contours* [13, 7] based on the theory of surfaces evolution and geometric flows have been introduced to detect an arbitrary number of objects in the image. These models precisely delineate object boundaries but can rely on unreliable local information to make a decision.

In region-based approaches, the segmentation model aims at splitting or merging the image into zones the most homogeneous as possible. Homogeneity is traditionally measured by a given cost functional [17] or a Bayesian criterion [18, 10, 24]. In that case, the boundaries are the set of curves that minimizes a global energy function. Some energy models are based on a discrete model of the image, such as Markov random fields ([9, 1, 14, 10] whereas variational models are based on a continuous model of the image [5, 19, 18]. Specific *a priori* constraints generally encourage the emergence of few regions which boundaries are regular [19, 14]. High-level constraints [10] can be introduced to detect specific complex objects. All these methods are generally robust to noise but computationally demanding if stochastic iterative procedures are used to conduct the minimization [5, 14, 10]. This motivates the search for energy models allowing non-iterative inference.

The aim of this paper is to provide energy models, which minimizers can be determined in advance. Accordingly, energy minimization methods and iterative algorithms are not necessary to solve the optimization problem. We have modified a particular segmentation energy first introduced in a discrete setting by Beaulieu and Goldberg [2]. The original model tends to obtain a partition with a few number of regions and small variances without *a priori* knowledge on the image. However, the energy which is efficiently minimized using a split-and-merge algorithm [2], has the drawback of giving no control on the smoothness of the object boundaries [17]. Here, our approach is completely different to determine its minimizer. Indeed, we prove in Section 3 that the set of curves that minimizes the modified energy is a family of level lines defined from level sets of the image. In that case, the method is deterministic and equivalent to a procedure that selects the "best" level lines delimiting object boundaries. Additionally, we combine anisotropic diffusion-based regularization with level line selection to estimate smooth object boundaries. For the completeness of the paper, a description of this segmentation algorithm is included in section 4. In section 5, experiments on several examples demonstrate the effectiveness of the approach.

2. Preliminaries

Our theoretical setting is the following. One assumes the existence of an unknown function f, i.e. the true image, from our image domain $S : [0,a] \times [0,b]$ to $\mathbb{R}$. The minimization of the energy on f defines the true segmentation. One observes a regular discretization of a corrupted image $y = f + \varepsilon$, where ε is a gaussian white noise (variance σ_ε^2). The observations are therefore

$$y(s) = f(s) + \varepsilon(s), \qquad 0 \leq s \leq N \qquad (1)$$

with $s = (x,y) \in S$ is on one of N pixels. A nonparametric estimator of f is built and plugged in the defined energy. We assume that the minimization with respect to f leads to an image partition into regions.

Let $\Omega_i \subset S$, $i = 1, \ldots, P$ an non-empty image domain or object. We associate with the unknown domains Ω_i the following energy, inspired from [2, 11]:

$$E(f, \Omega_1, \ldots, \Omega_P) =$$
$$\sum_{i=1}^{P} \int_{\Omega_i} (f(x,y) - \overline{f_{\Omega_i}})^2 \, dx dy + \lambda \, J(P, \Omega_i) \qquad (2)$$

where $\overline{f_{\Omega_i}}$ denotes the maximum likelihood estimate of the mean of f over Ω_i

$$\overline{f_{\Omega_i}} = \frac{1}{|\Omega_i|} \int_{\Omega_i} f(x,y) \, dx dy \,, \quad |\Omega_i| = \int_{\Omega_i} dx dy, \qquad (3)$$

λ is a given positive weight and $J(P, \Omega_i)$ is a *a priori* functional corresponding to a loose constraint to be defined. Note that (2) can be interpreted as a *maximum a posteriori* estimator when we assume all sites are independent and all sites belonging to a given object Ω_i have identical distributions characterized by parameters $\{\overline{f_{\Omega_i}}, \sigma_\varepsilon^2\}$.

Our aim is now to define objects in f. Therefore, we define the following class C_P, $P \geq 1$ of admissible objects

$$C_P = \{(\Omega_1, \ldots, \Omega_P) \subset S \text{ are regular, closed and connected};$$
$$1 \leq i, j \leq P-1, \, i \neq j \implies \Omega_i \cap \Omega_j = \emptyset;$$
$$\Omega_i \cap \Omega_P = \emptyset; \quad \cup_{i=1}^{P} \Omega_i = S\},$$

the subsets $(\Omega_1, \ldots, \Omega_{P-1})$ are the objects of the image and Ω_P is the background. When $P = 1$, no object is on the image. An optimal segmentation of image f over C_P is by definition a global minimum of the energy (when exists)

$$(\Omega_1^\star, \ldots, \Omega_{P\star}^\star) =$$
$$\text{argmin}_{P \geq 1} \, \text{argmin}_{(\Omega_1, \ldots, \Omega_P) \in C_P} E(f, \Omega_1, \ldots, \Omega_P) \,. \qquad (4)$$

A direct minimization with respect to all unknown domains Ω_i and parameters $\overline{f_{\Omega_i}}$ is a very intricate problem. In the next section, we prove that the object boundaries are level

lines of the nonparametric estimator of f if we choose $J(P, \Omega_i) = P$ or $J(P, \Omega_i) = \sum_{i=1}^{P-1} |\Omega_i|$. In that case, $J(P, \Omega_i)$ gives no control on the smoothness of boundaries and λ can be interpreted as a scale parameter that only tunes the number of regions [2, 17].

3. Estimator

Our plug-in estimator is defined by (when exists)

$$(\widehat{\Omega}_1, \ldots, \widehat{\Omega}_{\widehat{P}}) =$$
$$\text{argmin}_{P \geq 1} \, \text{argmin}_{(\Omega_1, \ldots, \Omega_P) \in C_P} E(\widehat{f}, \Omega_1, \ldots, \Omega_P) \,. \qquad (5)$$

The question of the existence of an admissible global minimum for energies like Beaulieu and Goldberg's energy [2] or Mumford and Shah's energy [19] is a difficult problem (see [17] for more details). Here, our aim is not to investigate conditions for having an admissible global minimum.

3.1. Minimizer description

In what follows, we make an *ad-hoc* assumption ensuring the existence of an unique minimum of the energy taken for functions in an neighborhood of the true image f [11]. In that case, we propose the following lemma

Lemma *If there exists an unique admissible global minimum for each function of a small neighborhood of f and that no pathological minimum exists [11], then*

$$\widehat{f}_{|\partial \Omega_i} \equiv \mu_i, \quad i = 1, \ldots, \widehat{P} - 1 \,.$$

i.e. the border of each Ω_i is a boundary of a level set of $\widehat{f}$.

Proof of lemma Without loss of generality, we prove this lemma for one object Ω and a background Ω^c, where Ω^c denotes the closure of the complementary set of Ω. For two sets A and B, denote $\int_{A-B} \widehat{f} \equiv \int_A \widehat{f} - \int_B \widehat{f}$. Let Ω_δ be a small perturbation of Ω, i.e. the Hausdorff distance $d_\infty(\Omega_\delta, \Omega) \leq \delta$. Then, we define

$$\int_{\Omega_\delta - \Omega} \mathbb{I} \triangleq |\Omega_\delta| - |\Omega| \,, \qquad (6)$$

$$\left(\int_{\Omega_\delta} \widehat{f}\right)^2 - \left(\int_\Omega \widehat{f}\right)^2 = 2 \int_\Omega \widehat{f} \int_{\Omega_\delta - \Omega} \widehat{f} + \left(\int_{\Omega_\delta - \Omega} \widehat{f}\right)^2 .$$

The difference between the involved energies is equal to
$$E(f, \Omega_\delta, \Omega_\delta^c) - E(f, \Omega, \Omega^c) = T_1 + T_2 + T_3 + T_4, \text{ with}$$

$$T_1 = \int_{\Omega_\delta} \widehat{f}^2 - \int_\Omega \widehat{f}^2, \quad T_2 = -\frac{1}{|\Omega_\delta|} \left(\int_{\Omega_\delta} \widehat{f}\right)^2 + \frac{1}{|\Omega|} \left(\int_\Omega \widehat{f}\right)^2,$$

$$T_3 = \int_{S - \Omega_\delta} \widehat{f}^2 - \int_{S - \Omega} \widehat{f}^2, \qquad (7)$$

$$T_4 = -\frac{1}{1-|\Omega_\delta|}\left(\oint_{S-\Omega_\delta}\widehat{f}\right)^2 + \frac{1}{1-|\Omega|}\left(\oint_{S-\Omega}\widehat{f}\right)^2.$$

Using (6)

$$T_1 = \int_{\Omega_\delta-\Omega}\widehat{f}^2, \tag{8}$$

$$T_2 = -\frac{2}{|\Omega|}\int_{\Omega_\delta-\Omega}\widehat{f}\int_\Omega\widehat{f} - \frac{1}{|\Omega|}\left(\int_{\Omega_\delta-\Omega}\widehat{f}\right)^2$$

$$+\frac{1}{|\Omega|^2}\int_{\Omega_\delta-\Omega}\mathbb{I}\left(\int_\Omega\widehat{f}\right)^2 + O\left(\int_{\Omega_\delta\Delta\Omega}\mathbb{I}\right)^2$$

and similar expression for T_3 and T_4. Define

$$m_0 = \int_\Omega\mathbb{I}, \quad m_1 = \int_\Omega\widehat{f}, \quad K_1 = \int_S\widehat{f}, \tag{9}$$

$$P_0 = -\frac{2m_1}{m_0} + \frac{2(K_1-m_1)}{1-m_0}, \quad P_1 = \frac{m_1^2}{m_0^2} - \frac{(K_1-m_1)^2}{(1-m_0)^2}.$$

Let M be a fixed point of the border $\partial\Omega$. Choose Ω_δ such that $\partial\Omega_\delta = \partial\Omega$ except on a small neighborhood of M. The energy having a minimum for Ω, $\widehat{f}(M)$ needs to be solution of the following equation

$$P_0\,\widehat{f}(M) + P_1 = 0. \tag{10}$$

Equation (10) has an unique solution. P_0 and P_1 do not depend on M and $\widehat{f}(M)$ and $P_0 \neq 0$. $\widehat{f}$ is continuous and $\partial\Omega$ is a connected curve. Therefore $\widehat{f}(M)$ is constant when M covers $\partial\Omega$. □

In conclusion, we proved that the minimizer is a family of iso-intensity curves of the image. They can be determined by boundaries of level sets defined in Section 3.2.

3.2. Image representation by level sets

As argued by the *Mathematical Morphology* [15, 23], it follows that the basic information of an image is contained in the family of its binary shadows or *level sets*, that is, in the family of sets $\mathcal{S}_\eta$ defined by

$$\mathcal{S}_\eta = \{s \in S : f(s) \geq \eta\} \tag{11}$$

for all values of η in the range of f. Level sets provide a complete, contrast invariant image representation unlike representation by "edges" or "luminance" [16].

A recent variant of this representation is proposed in [6] by considering the boundary of level sets, that is the level lines. This representation does not differ with respect to the set of level sets. Level sets can be computed from all possible connected components which are based both on the image gray levels and spatial relations between pixels. To extract a connected component of a level set $\mathcal{S}_\eta$, we threshold the image at the gray level η and extract the components

of the binary image we obtain. In the following, we basically consider that the level lines are built from connected components Ω_i extracted at each level set. They are just a set of η-isovalue pixels at the borders $\partial\Omega_i$ of connected components. More precise concepts about level lines, level sets and connected components can be found in [16]. Nevertheless level lines, i.e. object boundaries, are not generally regular curves in the image. Therefore, anisotropic diffusion is introduced to remove noise and fine-scale details and preserve well-localized smooth level lines.

3.3. Regularization of level lines

Anisotropic diffusion aims at smoothing original image while preserving brightness discontinuities [21]. Black *et al.* showed that anisotropic diffusion can be interpreted as a robust procedure that estimates a piecewise constant image from noisy input image [4]. They derived a relationship between anisotropic diffusion and the error norm and influence function in the robust estimation framework, yielding to new anisotropic diffusion equations.

In [4] it is established that the *Tukey's biweight* robust error norm produces sharper discontinuities than the original "stopping-edge" function introduced by Perona and Malik [21]. The corresponding anisotropic diffusion equations are

$$f_{t+1}(s) = f_t(s) + \frac{\tau}{|\mathcal{G}_s|}\sum_{p \in \mathcal{G}_s} z_{sp}\left(f_t(p) - f_t(s)\right) \tag{12}$$

$$z_{sp} = \begin{cases} \left[1 - ((f_t(p)-f_t(s))/\sigma)^2\right]^2 & |f_t(p)-f_t(s)| \leq \sigma \\ 0 & \text{otherwise} \end{cases}$$

where $f_t(s)$ is a filtered image of $f(s)$, t denotes iterations, τ is a strictly positive constant that determines the rate of diffusion, $\mathcal{G}_s$ represents the first-order spatial neighborhood of s, $|\mathcal{G}_s|$ is the number of neighbors, σ is a "robust scale" parameter [3] and $z_{sp} \in [0,1]$ is analog to a line process. The line process indicates the presence (z close to 0) or absence (z close to 1) of discontinuities or outliers.

Scale parameter σ can be estimated in a robust way (see [22]). Here, we adaptively estimate a scale parameter $\sigma_i = k\,\tilde{\sigma}_i$ for each object Ω_i where k is a positive constant,

$$\tilde{\sigma}_i = 2,6477\sqrt{\frac{2}{|\Omega_i|}\sum_{l=0}^{|\Omega_i|/2} r_{O(l)}^2}, \tag{13}$$

and $r_{O(1)}^2 \leq r_{O(2)}^2 \leq \cdots \leq r_{O(|\Omega_i|/2)}^2$ are the $|\Omega_i|/2$ ordered squared residuals. The constant factor makes $\tilde{\sigma}_i$ roughly unbiased at gaussian error distributions [22]. Only the first ranked half of data belonging to Ω_i is used to estimate σ_i and $r_{O(\cdot)}^2$ is computed from the image gradient magnitude approximation (in a particular direction) as $f_t(p) - f_t(s)$, $p \in \mathcal{G}_s$. This filter creates consistent results with the level line selection approach.

The connection between anisotropic diffusion and extraction of objects Ω_i is then established. At each iteration t, data are smoothed in each region Ω_i using (12) where σ_i is substituted to σ. In that case, the number of iterations to converge can be easily controlled. The same level lines are invariably selected if the restored image is a piecewise smooth image. Usually this can be accomplished with less than 10 iterations in sufficient precision. Note that the two tasks would be independent in the original formulation in [21], for which the diffusion stopping rule is not well defined. This relationship is more underlined through a practical segmentation algorithm described in the next section.

4. Numerical implementation

To implement our level set image segmentation, a four step method is used. Given a smoothed image f_t obtained using (12), the first step completes a mapping of each image pixel on a given level set. It is followed by an object extraction stage in which sets of simply connected pixels are extracted from the level sets. The connected components are then combined during the third step to form object configurations. Objects Ω_i are defined by connected components and $\partial\Omega_i$ are boundaries of connected components. In the final stage, calculations are performed on all object combinations. The configuration with the lowest energy is then selected as the best segmentation.

LEVEL SET CONSTRUCTION Let $f_t(s) \in [f_{min}, f_{max}]$ the image partitioned in $K = 4$, 8 or 16 equal-sized and non-overlapping intervals $\{[l_1, h_1[, \ldots, [l_K, h_K]]\}$. A pixel s will then belong to the interval $[l_j, h_j[$ if $l_j \leq f_t(s) < h_j$.

OBJECT EXTRACTION A crude way to build pixels sets corresponding to objects is to proceed to a connected components labeling and to associate each label with an object Ω_i. The background Ω_P corresponds to the closure of the complementary set of objects Ω_i. This amounts to building K images g_t^j, $j = 1, \ldots, K$ in which $g_t^j(s) = \eta$, $\forall s \in \mathcal{S}_\eta$ and $g_t^j(s) = 0$, $\forall s \notin \mathcal{S}_\eta$. The list of connected components of each of these then forms the list of objects $\{\Omega_1, \ldots \Omega_{P-1}\}$.

CONFIGURATION DETERMINATION Having the final object list, configurations are combinations of objects of the C_p class. These configurations can be built by enumeration of all possible object combinations, i.e. 2^{P-1} configurations. Nevertheless, we decide to discard objects which areas are under a predetermined threshold. Each possible configuration can then be represented by a binary number b_i which is the binary expansion of i ($0 \leq i \leq 2^{P-1} - 1$). The value of each bit in b_i determines the presence or absence of a given object in the configuration.

ENERGY COMPUTATION Each configuration represents a set of objects which in turn is a set of pixels. Energy calculations take the image intensities at each of these pixels to establish mean (3) and approximation error (2). Note that only energies corresponding to each object are computed once and stored, and energies corresponding to the background are efficiently updated for each configuration. The configuration that minimizes the global energy corresponds to the optimal segmentation. The time necessary to perform image segmentation essentially depends on the length of the object list, i.e. the number of connected components P. Nevertheless, all configurations are independent and could be potentially evaluated on suitable parallel architectures.

The steps of the algorithm are the following:

- INITIALIZATION: Let f_{t_0} the original image data. Set parameters K, λ, τ and k.

- WHILE $f_{t+1}(s) \neq f_t(s)$, $\forall s \in S$ REPEAT

    - *Image segmentation:*
        1. Level set construction
        2. Object extraction
        3. 2^{P-1} configurations determination
        4. Energy computation and configuration selection with the lowest energy.

    - *Anisotropic diffusion:* see (12).

    - Updating of σ_i and $k \leftarrow 0.9\,k$ and increment t;

END WHILE.

5. Experimental results

We demonstrate segmentation results on synthetic images as well as on 2D confocal microscopy, medical and meteorological images. The algorithm parameters were set as follows: $K = 8$, $J(P, \Omega_i) = \sum_{i=1}^{P-1} |\Omega_i|$ and regions which areas $|\Omega_i| < 0.01 \times N$ are discarded, $\tau = 1$ and the value of k is initially set to 5 and linearly lowered by a factor of 0.9 at each iteration. The segmentation was terminated if the convergence criterion was met. Most segmentations required less than 10 iterations for convergence, according to image contents and noise, and took approximately 5s per iteration on a 296MHz workstation.

To see the effect of adaptive estimation of σ_i on segmentation results consider the simple example in Figure 1. The corrupted version with a white gaussian noise (s.d. 10) of a 256×256 image coming from the GdR ISIS is shown on the left. This image is composed of six objected against a background. The next column shows the segmentation results when $\sigma_i = \sigma$, $\forall \Omega_i$ and σ is computed in a robust way for

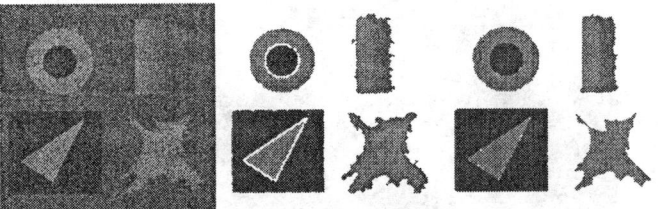

Figure 1. Segmentation results ($\lambda = 650$) after 5 iterations. Left: corrupted image. Middle: segmentation with $\sigma_i = \sigma$, $\forall \Omega_i$. Right: segmentation with $\sigma_i \neq \sigma_j$, $\forall (\Omega_i, \Omega_j)$.

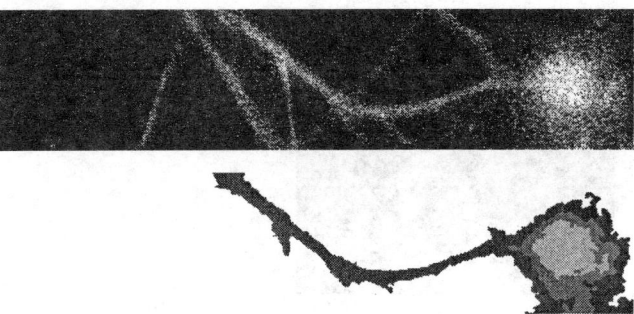

Figure 2. Segmentation in 2D confocal microscopy after $61s$ and 10 iterations ($\lambda = 650$).

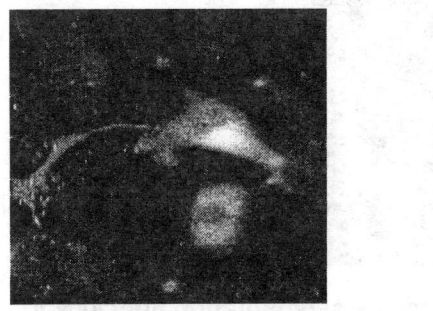

Figure 3. Segmentation in 2D confocal microscopy after $51s$ and 8 iterations ($\lambda = 3250$).

the whole image. Background is labeled in "white" and undesirable regions are visible close to edges. The column on the right of Fig. 1 shows better results when σ_i is adaptively computed for each Ω_i using (13). This modeling prevents oversmoothing of edges.

We have tested the proposed algorithm on 2D confocal microscopy images (Figs. 2-3), courtesy of INSERM 413 IFRMP n^o23 (Rouen, France). Confocal fluorescence microscopy is a non-invasive technology for visualizing specimens in their natural tissue context. A 3D representation of the fluorescence-stained specimen and unstained background is built up from a stack of 2D image slices, referred to as optical sections. The first 115×512 image depicts a neurite in cultured cerebellar granule cells. This study aims at estimating calcium concentration in neurites. Figure 2 shows regions corresponding to three different calcium densities. The segment boundaries are correctly located and smooth. The second 256×239 confocal image depicts motility of two splitting neural cells. In this study, real-time changes in the shape of granule cells are examined. Figure 3 shows the detection of two objects of interest made up connected regions.

Figures 4-5 illustrate how our method selects the number of segments in a 2D medical MR image (256×228). in this application, background is previously eliminated by thresholding. The aim is to segment the corpus callosum (Fig. 4) or both the corpus callosum and brain (Fig. 5) by increasing λ. Semantic segmentations are obtained.

An example of cloud detection is provided in Fig. 6. The algorithm labeled seas and small clouds as "background". The significant clouds and continents are crudely extracted from the 383×260 image. Here, our approach can potentially provide an insight on the analyzed weather situation.

6. Conclusion and perspectives

In this paper, we have presented a level line selection approach for extracting structures in images. We proved that the minimizer of our segmentation energy can be directly determined. We introduced a robust anisotropic diffusion framework to preserve sharper boundaries of objects and regularize level lines in the image. A total CPU time of a few seconds for segmenting a 256×256 image on a workstation makes the method attractive for many time-critical applications. The contribution of this approach has been illustrated on synthetic as well as real-world images. Several promising directions may be explored for continued research. First, we plan to examine new energy functions which minimizers can be determined as well. An other direction for future work is to extend the proposed approach to operate on multi-spectral 3D images.

References

[1] R. Azencott. Image analysis and markov fields. In *Proc. of ICIAM SIAM Congress*, Paris, France, 1987.

[2] J. Beaulieu and M. Goldberg. Hierarchy in picture segmentation: a stepwise optimization approach. *IEEE Trans. Pattern Anal. and Machine Intell.*, 11(2):150–163, 1989.

[3] M. Black and A. Rangarajan. On the unification of line processes, outlier rejection, and robust statistics with applications in early vision. *Int. J. Computer Vision*, 19(1):57–92, 1996.

[4] M. Black, G. Sapiro, D. Marimont, and D. Heeger. Robust anisotropic diffusion. *IEEE Trans. Image Processing*, 7(3):421–432, 1998.

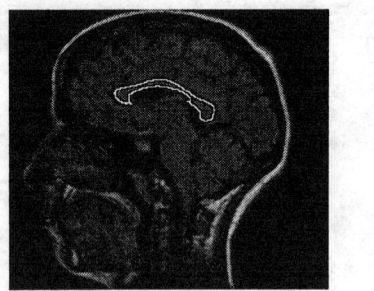

Figure 4. MR image segmentation after $4s$ **and only one iteration** ($\lambda = 32500$).

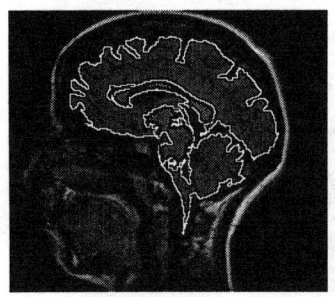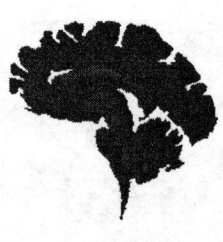

Figure 5. MR image segmentation after $4s$ **and only one iteration** ($\lambda = 6500$).

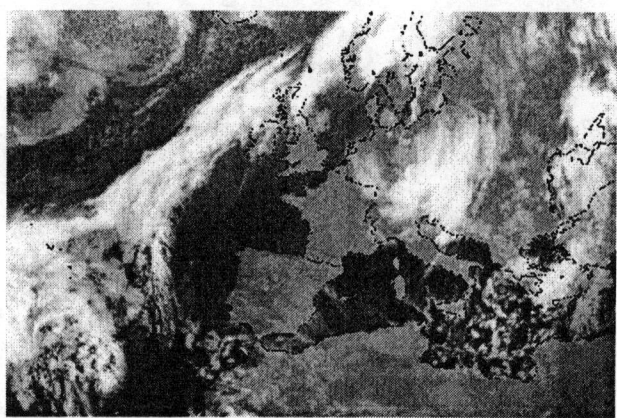

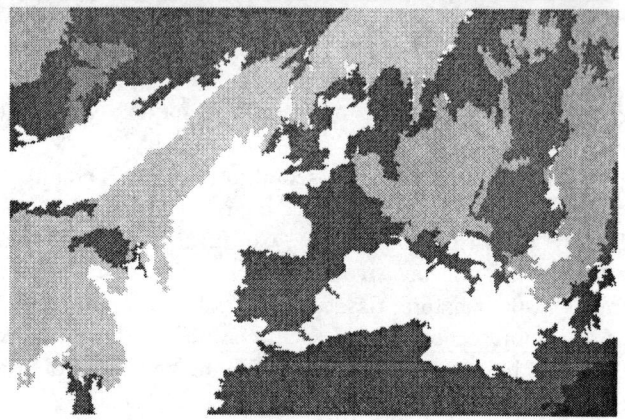

Figure 6. meteorological image segmentation after $18s$ **and only one iteration** ($\lambda = 2000$).

[5] A. Blake and A. Zisserman. *Visual reconstruction.* MIT Press, Cambridge, Mass, 1987.

[6] V. Caselles, B. Coll, and J. Morel. Topographic maps. *preprint CEREMADE*, 1997.

[7] V. Caselles, R. Kimmel, and G. Sapiro. Geodesic active contours. *Int J. Computer Vision*, 22(1):61–79, 1997.

[8] R. Deriche. Using canny's criteria to derive a recursively implemented optimal edge detector. *Int J. Computer Vision*, 2(1):167–187, 1987.

[9] S. Geman and D. Geman. Stochastic relaxation, gibbs distributions, and the bayesian restoration of images. *IEEE Trans. Pattern Anal. and Machine Intell.*, 6(6):721–741, 1984.

[10] U. Grenander and M. Miller. Representations of knowledge in complex systems. *J. Royal Statistical Society, series B*, 56(4):549–603, April 1994.

[11] J. Istas. *Statistics of processes and signal-image segmentation.* University of Paris VII, 1997.

[12] M. Kass, A. Witkin, and D. Terzopoulos. Snakes: active contour models. *Int J. Computer Vision*, 12(1):321–331, 1987.

[13] S. Kichenesamy, A. Kumar, P. Olver, and A. Yezzi. Conformal curvature flows: from transition to active contours. *Archive for Rational Mechanics and Anal.*, 134:275–301, 1996.

[14] Y. Leclerc. Constructing simple stable descriptions for image partitioning. *Int J. Computer Vision*, 3:73–102, 1989.

[15] G. Matheron. *Random sets and integral morphology.* John Wiley, New York, 1975.

[16] P. Monasse and F. Guichard. Fast computation of a contrast-invariant image representation. *IEEE Trans. Image Processing*, 1999.

[17] J. Morel and S. Solimini. *Variational methods in image segmentation.* Birkhauser, Boston, 1994.

[18] D. Mumford. The bayesian rationale for energy functionals. *Geometry-driven diffusion in computer vision*, pages 141–153, Bart Romeny ed., Kluwer Academic, 1994.

[19] D. Mumford and J. Shah. Optimal approximations by piecewise smooth functions and variational problems. *Communication on Pure and applied Mathematics*, 42(5):577–685, 1989.

[20] T. Pavlidis and Y. Liow. Integrating region growing and edge detection. *IEEE Trans. Pattern Anal. and Machine Intell.*, 12:225–233, 1990.

[21] P. Perona and J. Malik. Scale-space and edge detection using anisotropic diffusion. *IEEE Trans. Pattern Anal. and Machine Intell.*, 12(7):629–639, 1990.

[22] P. Rousseeuw and A. Leroy. *Robust regression and outlier detection.* Wiley Series in Probability and Mathematical Statistics, Wiley, 1987.

[23] J. Serra. *Image Anal. and mathematical morphology.* Academic Press, 1982.

[24] S. Zhu and A. Yuille. Region competition: unifying snakes, region growing, and bayes/mdl for multiband image segmentation. *IEEE Trans. Pattern Anal. and Machine Intell.*, 18(9):884–900, 1996.

Unsupervised Image Classification with a Hierarchical EM Algorithm

Annabelle Chardin and Patrick Pérez
IRISA-INRIA Rennes
Campus Universitaire de Beaulieu
35042 Rennes Cedex, France
Annabelle.Chardin@irisa.fr, Patrick.Perez@irisa.fr

Abstract

This work takes place in the context of hierarchical stochastic models for the resolution of discrete inverse problems from low level vision. Some of these models lie on the nodes of a quad-tree which leads to non-iterative inference procedures. Nevertheless, if they circumvent the algorithmic drawbacks of grid-based models (computational load and/or great dependance on the initialization), they admit modeling shortcomings (cumbersome and somehow artificial). We investigate a new hierarchical stochastic model which takes benefit from both the spatial and the hierarchical prior modelings. The independance graph is based on a tree which has been pollarded with the nodes at the coarsest resolution exhibiting a grid-based interaction structure. For this class of models, we address the critical problem of parameter estimation. To this end, we derive an EM algorithm on the hybrid structure which mixes an exact EM algorithm on each subtrees and a low cost Gibbsian EM algorithm on the coarse spatial grid. Experiments on a synthetic image and on multispectral satellite images are reported.

1. Introduction and background

Many inverse problems from image analysis can be managed by designing an *energy* function $U(x, y)$ which captures the interaction between a large number of unknown variables $x = (x_i)_i$ to be estimated, and the observed variables –the measurements or data–, $y = (y_j)_j$. The manipulation of this function is made tractable by its usual decomposition as a sum of *local* terms involving just a few variables at a time. This kind of problem is encountered in Markov random field(MRF)-based approaches as well as in partial differential equation (PDE)-based approaches. Within the framework of MRF, x and y are random vectors and we have the following relation between the joint distribution and the energy function: $P(x, y) \propto \exp\{\ U(x, y)\}$.

The decomposition property makes the models very flexible, but implies a parameterization of the posterior distribution which has to be known to perform the inference of

x. The crucial point here is the estimation of parameters, since it will strongly condition the quality of the inference. Supervised and unsupervised inference methods have been proposed in the literature. In the supervised approaches, the image and the noise model parameters are assumed to be known, whereas in the unsupervised approaches the parameter estimation and the inference of x are conducted at the same time without any human interaction.

1.1. Hierarchical energy-based models

It turns out that for most energy-based models suitable for image analysis problems, one has to devise deterministic or stochastic iterative algorithms exploiting the locality of the model in order to conduct the inference of x. While permitting tractable single-step computations, the locality results in a very slow propagation of information. As a consequence, these iterative procedures may converge very slowly. This motivates the search for specific models allowing non-iterative or more efficient inference.

So far, the more fruitful approaches in both cases have relied on some notion of *hierarchy*. Hierarchical models or algorithms allow the information to be integrated in a progressive and efficient way (especially in the case of multiresolution data, when images come into a hierarchy of scales) providing gains in terms of both computational efficiency and quality of results.

Model-based hierarchical approaches aim at defining a new global hierarchical model which has nothing to do with any original (spatial) model. It has to be manipulated as a whole, but according to procedures of reduced complexity. These models usually lie on the nodes of a quad-tree (e.g., see Fig. 1(a)) whose leaves fit the pixels of (maximum resolution) images [2, 6, 10, 11, 12]. In this case, the peculiar dependency structure, like in case of Markov chains, allows *non-iterative* inference procedures made of two sweeps: a bottom-up sweep propagating all information to the root, and a top-down one which in turn allows optimal estimate to be obtained at each node given *all the data*.

One of the drawbacks of these tree-based approaches lies in the structural constraints they impose: first of all they might appear artificial for certain types of problems or data; in any case the relevance of the inferred variables at coarsest levels is not obvious (especially at the root). Second, the complete tree-structure is cumbersome in case of large images. To circumvent this, a hierarchical model based on a "hybrid" structure which combines a spatial grid of reduced size at a coarser level with "sub-trees" appended below it, down to the finest level has been proposed [4].

1.2. EM algorithm

The so-called EM algorithm is the most used method for parameter estimation. This algorithm [7] considers the observed variables y as the "incomplete data" and the couple (x, y) as the "complete data" characterized by the joint distribution $P(x, y | \theta)$ where θ is a parameter vector to be estimated. The purpose is to find $\hat{\theta}$ which maximizes the likelihood of observed data $P(y|\theta)$.

The EM procedure is iterative and repeats the two following steps until convergence: the E-step computes the expectation of log joint likelihood, conditionned on observed data and current parameter fit: $Q(\theta|\theta^{(k)}) \triangleq \mathbb{E}[\log P(X, Y|\theta)|y, \theta^{(k)}]$; the Maximization step then defines the new parameter values as those that maximize this expectation: $\theta^{(k+1)} \triangleq \arg\max_\theta Q(\theta|\theta^{(k)})$. The convergence is guaranteed, but toward an estimate $\hat{\theta}$ that depends very much on the initial guess $\theta^{(0)}$ [13]. As a consequence $\theta^{(0)}$ must be chosen carefully.

This paper investigates an EM-type algorithm on the hybrid structure introduced in [4] and is organized as follows. The section 2 first describes the hybrid hierarchical model and its associated energy function and secondly the EM algorithm derived from it. The section 3 illustrates this procedure for an unsupervised image classification with synthetic and real images.

2. Hierarchical EM algorithm

2.1. Hybrid hierarchical models

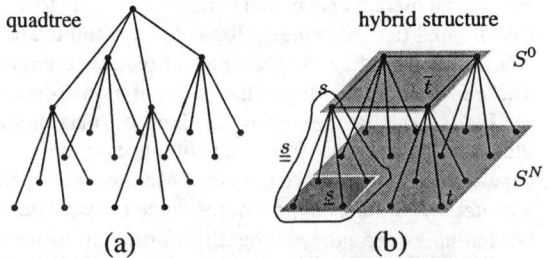

Figure 1. Two hierarchical structures: (a) quadtree with three levels; (b) truncated tree with two levels.

The hierarchical model we use is based on a hybrid structure for which one example is shown in Fig. 1(b) for a single level below the coarsest grid. To describe this graph, we shall introduce some notations.

First, we define the coarsest level S^0 as a rectangular grid with a 1st-order neighborhood. Then each site of S^0 initiates a quadtree, so that the set S^n ($0 < n \leq N$) made up by the nodes at the level n is $2^n \times 2^n$ times larger than S^0. Now each site s of S^n has four natural correspondents in S^{n+1} (provided that s does not belong to the finest level S^N), its children, forming site set $\underline{s}$, and one natural correspondent in S^{n-1} (provided that s does not belong to the coarsest level S^0), its parent, denoted as $\bar{s}$. Finally, the site set forming the tree rooted at s is denoted $\underline{s}$ (Fig. 1(b)). Vectors x and y are now indexed by the nodes of $S \triangleq \bigcup_{n=0}^{N} S^n$.

Given this graphical structure consider an energy function of the following form:

$$U(x,y) \triangleq \sum_{<s,t> \in S^0} v_{st}(x_s, x_t) + \sum_{s \in S \setminus S^0} w_s(x_s, x_{\bar{s}}) + \sum_{s \in S} l_s(x_s, y_s),$$

where $< s, t >$ designates pairs of neighbors in S^0, v_{st} and w_s are local functions capturing respectively the spatial prior and the hierarchical prior (they will usually encourage identity between neighbors and between parents and children, resp.), and l_s expresses the point-wise relation between the observed variable y_s and the unknown one x_s. From a probabilistic point of view, the associated joint distribution of (x, y) is: (with Z a normalizing constant)

$$P(x,y) \triangleq \frac{1}{Z} \prod_{<s,t> \in S^0} \underbrace{\exp\{ v_{st}(x_s, x_t)\}}_{\triangleq g_{st}(x_s, x_t)}$$
$$\times \prod_{s \in S \setminus S^0} \underbrace{\exp\{ w_s(x_s, x_{\bar{s}})\}}_{\triangleq f_s(x_s, x_{\bar{s}})} \prod_{s \in S} \underbrace{\exp\{ l_s(x_s, y_s)\}}_{\triangleq h_s(x_s, y_s)}. \quad (1)$$

2.2. EM algorithm on the hybrid structure

In the case of a spatial grid ($N = 0$), the computation of $Q(\theta|\theta^{(k)})$ is untractable due to the normalizing constant which depends on θ. Some authors [3, 15] attempt to overcome this difficulty by using the pseudo-likelihood (PL) function $\mathbb{P}(x, y|\theta)$ instead of the likelihood function. It is defined as:

$$\mathbb{P}(x,y|\theta) \triangleq P(y|x, \theta)\mathbb{P}(x|\theta)$$
$$= \prod_s P(y_s|x_s, \theta)P(x_s|x_{\mathcal{V}_s}, \theta),$$

where $\mathcal{V}_s$ represents the set of the neighbors of s and local prior conditionnal distributions can be exactly deduced from (1), according to

$$P(x_s|x_{\mathcal{V}_s}) = \frac{\prod_{t \in \mathcal{V}_s} g_{st}(x_s, x_t)}{\sum_\lambda \prod_{t \in \mathcal{V}_s} g_{st}(\lambda, x_t)}.$$

Despite the elimination of the normalizing constant problem, the maximization of $Q(\theta|\theta^{(k)})$ still requires the computation of an untractable expectation. This expectation is approximated by using a Gibbs sampler in the case of the Gibbsian EM algorithm [3].

In the case of a complete tree where S^0 reduces to a single site, a non-iterative two-sweep procedure, similar to Baum-Welch algorithm on a chain [1], can be designed to compute exactly all sitewise and pairwise posterior marginals. Then the EM algorithm can be conducted without any PL and Monte Carlo approximation ([10, 14] for discrete cases, [8, 9] for continuous Gaussian models).

With our hybrid structure, we deal both with non-causal interactions (on S^0) and tree-based interactions on subtrees $\underline{s}$, $s \in S^0$. We thus have to introduce a PL function for the non-causal spatial part of the hybrid structure, to avoid the problem of Z. Assuming without loss of generality, that $f_s(i, j) = \mathrm{P}(X_s = i | X_{\overline{s}} = j)$, and $h_s(i, l) = \mathrm{P}(Y_s = l | X_s = i)$, the PL we deal with is:

$$\mathbb{P}(x, y | \theta) \triangleq \prod_{s \in S^0} \mathrm{P}(x_s | x_{\nu_s}, \theta) \prod_{s \in S \setminus S^0} f_s(x_s, x_{\overline{s}}, \theta)$$
$$\times \prod_{s \in S} h_s(x_s, y_s, \theta).$$

We further assume that f_s is independant from s whereas h_s only depends on the level n to which s belongs (these two assumptions can easily be softened or tightened in the following). We then denote: $f(i, j) \triangleq \mathrm{P}(X_s = i | X_{\overline{s}} = j)$, $\forall s \in S \setminus S^0$, and $h^n(i, l) \triangleq \mathrm{P}(Y_s = l | X_s = i)$, $\forall s \in S^n$. Each X_s taking its values in discrete state space Λ, the neighborhood configuration set Λ^{ν_s} can always be partitionned in J parts such that $\mathrm{P}(x_s | x_{\nu_s}, \theta)$ only depends on the "type" $\nu \in \{1 \dots J\}$ to which x_{ν_s} belongs. Then we denote $\mathrm{P}(X_s = i | X_{\nu_s} \text{ of type } \nu) \triangleq a(i, \nu)$, $\forall s \in S^0$.

The more general parameterization is given by $\theta \triangleq \{a(i, \nu), f(i, j), h^n(i, l)\}$ under constraints $\sum_i a(i, \nu) = 1$, $\sum_i f(i, j) = 1$ and $\sum_l h^n(i, l) = 1$. The maximization is readily solved by using a Lagrangian based on:

$$Q(\theta | \theta^{(k)}) =$$
$$\sum_{i, \nu} [\log a(i, \nu) \sum_{s \in S^0} \underbrace{\mathrm{P}(X_s = i, X_{\nu_s} \text{ of type } \nu | y, \theta^{(k)})}_{=\mathbb{E}[n_{i\nu}(X_{S^0}) | y, \theta^{(k)}]}]$$
$$+ \sum_{i, j} [\log f(i, j) \sum_{s \in S \setminus S^0} \zeta_s^{(k)}(i, j)]$$
$$+ \sum_{n, i, l} [\log h^n(i, l) \sum_{s \in S^n : y_s = l} \gamma_s^{(k)}(i)],$$

where $n_{i\nu}(x_{S^0}) \triangleq \#\{s \in S^0 : x_s = i, x_{\nu_s} \text{ of type } \nu\}$, $\gamma_s^{(k)}(i) \triangleq \mathrm{P}(X_s = i | y, \theta^{(k)})$ and $\zeta_s^{(k)}(i, j) \triangleq \mathrm{P}(X_s = i, X_{\overline{s}} = j | y, \theta^{(k)})$, the updating formulae of the parameters are:

$$a^{(k+1)}(i, \nu) = \frac{\mathbb{E}[n_{i\nu}(X_{S^0}) | y, \theta^{(k)}]}{\sum_i \mathbb{E}[n_{i\nu}(X_{S^0}) | y, \theta^{(k)}]} \quad (2)$$

$$f^{(k+1)}(i, j) = \frac{\sum_{s \in S \setminus S^0} \zeta_s^{(k)}(i, j)}{\sum_{s \in S \setminus S^0} \gamma_{\overline{s}}^{(k)}(j)} \quad (3)$$

$$h^{n\,(k+1)}(i, l) = \frac{\sum_{s \in S^n : y_s = l} \gamma_s^{(k)}(i)}{\sum_{s \in S^n} \gamma_s^{(k)}(i)} \quad (4)$$

In the case of Gaussian data likelihoods with the parameters (μ_i, σ_i), the equation (4) is replaced by:

$$\mu_i^{n(k+1)} = \frac{\sum_{s \in S^n} \gamma_s^{(k)}(i) y_s}{\sum_{s \in S^n} \gamma_s^{(k)}(i)} \quad (5)$$

$$\sigma_i^{n(k+1)} = \left[\frac{\sum_{s \in S^n} \gamma_s^{(k)}(i)(y_s - \mu_i^{n(k+1)})^2}{\sum_{s \in S^n} \gamma_s^{(k)}(i)} \right]^{1/2} \quad (6)$$

The use of these re-estimation equations requires the computation of the expectation $\mathbb{E}[n_{i\nu}(X_{S^0}) | y, \theta^{(k)}]$ on the coarse grid, and the computation of the local posterior marginals $\gamma_s^{(k)}(i)$ and of $\zeta_s^{(k)}(i, j)$ on the sub-trees below. The computation of the local posterior marginals is exactly achieved on each node of a complete tree through a non-iterative procedure made of two sweeps [10]. This procedure can be easily extended to the truncated tree [5]. The dowward recursion is now based on $\mathrm{P}(x_s | y) = \sum_{x_{\overline{s}}} \mathrm{P}(x_s | x_{\overline{s}}, y) \mathrm{P}(x_{\overline{s}} | y)$, $\forall s \notin S^0$, where $\mathrm{P}(x_s | x_{\overline{s}}, y) = \mathrm{P}(x_s | x_{\overline{s}}, y_{\underline{s}})$ due to separation property. The use of this recursion requires that a previous upward sweep provides $\mathrm{P}(x_s | x_{\overline{s}}, y_{\underline{s}})$ for $s \notin S^0$ and $\mathrm{P}(x_s | y)$ for $s \in S^0$. The former is achieved by successively summing out the x_s's for all $s \notin S^0$. The recursion is based on:

$$\mathrm{P}(x_s | x_{\overline{s}}, y_{\underline{s}})$$
$$\propto f_s(x_s, x_{\overline{s}}) h_s(x_s, y_s) \times \sum_{x_{\underline{s} \setminus \{s\}}} \prod_{t \in \underline{s} \setminus \{s\}} f_t(x_t, x_{\overline{t}}) h_t(x_t, y_t)$$
$$\propto f_s(x_s, x_{\overline{s}}) h_s(x_s, y_s) \times \prod_{t \in \underline{s}} \underbrace{\sum_{x_t} \prod_{k \in \underline{t}} f_k(x_k, x_{\overline{k}}) h_k(x_k, y_k)}_{\triangleq \mathbb{F}_t(x_s)},$$

with $\mathbb{F}_t(x_s) = \sum_{x_t} f_t(x_t, x_{\overline{t}}) h_t(x_t, y_t) \prod_{k \in \underline{t}} \mathbb{F}_k(x_t)$. Functions $\mathbb{F}_t(x_s)$ being computed in a bottom-up way, one can then derive:

$$\mathrm{P}(x_s | x_{\overline{s}}, y_{\underline{s}}) = \frac{f_s(x_s, x_{\overline{s}}) h_s(x_s, y_s) \prod_{t \in \underline{s}} \mathbb{F}_t(x_s)}{\sum_\lambda f_s(\lambda, x_{\overline{s}}) h_s(\lambda, y_s) \prod_{t \in \underline{s}} \mathbb{F}_t(\lambda)}.$$

Note that the functions $\mathbb{F}_s(x_{\overline{s}})$ depend on $y_{\underline{s}}$, even though this is not made explicit by abuse of notation. The upward sweep also provides eventually the probability $\mathrm{P}(x_{S^0} | y) = \sum_{x_{S \setminus S^0}} \mathrm{P}(x | y)$. Because of the non-causal structure on S^0, $\mathrm{P}(x_s | y)$ for $s \in S^0$ has to be approximated with the help of a Gibbs sampling of distribution $\mathrm{P}(x_{S^0} | y)$. This sampling also allows the approximation of the expectation in (2). Now the laws $\gamma_s^{(k)}(i)$ are available as well as $\mathrm{P}(x_s | x_{\overline{s}}, y_{\underline{s}})$. The computation of $\zeta_s^{(k)}(i, j)$ can be done thanks to the relation: $\mathrm{P}(x_s, x_{\overline{s}} | y, \theta^{(k)}) = \mathrm{P}(x_s | x_{\overline{s}}, y, \theta^{(k)}) \mathrm{P}(x_{\overline{s}} | y, \theta^{(k)})$.

The whole procedure is shown in Tab. 1. At convergence, an estimate of x is provided by the estimator of the Mode of Posterior Marginals (MPM), as a by-product of the posterior marginal computation: $\forall s$, $\hat{x}_s = \arg\max_{x_s} \mathrm{P}(x_s | y)$.

EM algorithm on the hybrid structure

Repeat until convergence

▲ upward sweep

    Leaves ($s \in S^N$): $\mathbb{F}_s(x_{\bar{s}}) = \sum_{x_s} f_s(x_s, x_{\bar{s}}) h_s(x_s, y_s)$

    Recursion (for $n = N-1 \dots 1, s \in S^n$): $\mathbb{F}_s(x_{\bar{s}}) = \sum_{x_s} f_s(x_s, x_{\bar{s}}) h_s(x_s, y_s) \prod_{t \in \underline{s}} \mathbb{F}_t(x_s)$

◄► coarse Gibbsian EM:

    Repeat until convergence:

        draw samples $x_{S^0}(1), \dots, x_{S^0}(m)$ from $\mathrm{P}(x_{S^0}|y)$

        approximations of $\begin{cases} \gamma_s^{(k)}(i) &= \frac{1}{m-r} \sum_{q=r+1}^{m} \delta[x_s(q), i] \\ a^{(k+1)}(i, \nu) &= \frac{\sum_{q=r+1}^{m} n_{i\nu}(x_{S^0}(q))}{\sum_i \sum_{q=r+1}^{m} n_{i\nu}(x_{S^0}(q))} \end{cases}$

        computation of $h^{0(k+1)}(i, l)$ according to (4), or of $\mu_i^{0(k+1)}$ and $\sigma_i^{0(k+1)}$ according to (5-6)

▼ downward sweep

    Recursion (for $n = 1 \dots N, s \in S^n$): $\begin{cases} \zeta_s^{(k)}(i, j) &= \gamma_{\bar{s}}^{(k)}(j) \frac{f_s(i,j) h_s(i, y_s)}{\mathbb{F}_s(j)} \prod_{t \in \underline{s}} \mathbb{F}_t(i) \\ \gamma_s^{(k)}(i) &= \sum_j \zeta_s^{(k)}(i, j) \end{cases}$

Computation of $f^{(k+1)}(i, j)$ according to (3)

Computation of $h^{n(k+1)}(i, l)$ according to (4), or of $\mu_i^{n(k+1)}$ and $\sigma_i^{n(k+1)}$ according to (5-6)

Table 1. Synopsis of the EM algorithm on the hybrid structure

3. Unsupervised classification comparisons

To demonstrate the practicability and the relevance of the approach for discrete low-level image analysis, we first reported comparative experiments for unsupervised classification led for $N \in \{0, 3, 4, p\}$. For $N = 0$ the algorithm corresponds to the Gibbsian EM of Chalmond [3], while $N = p$, when the size of S^N is $2^p \times 2^p$, corresponds to the complete tree ($|S^0| = 1$). $N = 3, 4$ correspond to the hybrid structure with four and five levels.

In section 1.1, we mentioned that the initialization of the EM algorithm determined the quality of the results. As a consequence, we had to pay a great attention to it and use the same for all algorithms. To this end, a simple analysis of the finest resolution data histogram was carried out to get starting values for the class parameters which were used in a standard Maximum Likelihood inference procedure. The class parameters were then re-estimated with this classification. In addition, for the Gibbsian EM, the spatial prior parameters were initialized by $\frac{n_{i\nu}(x_{S^0}^0)}{\sum_i n_{i\nu}(x_{S^0}^0)}$. As for the model parameters on the truncated tree, we initialized the hierarchical prior with the parameterization of Bouman [2]: $f(i, j) \triangleq \alpha\delta(i, j) + \frac{1}{M-1}\alpha[1-\delta(i, j)]$, where M was the number of classes and with α close to 1. At each node s of S^0, we searched for the label that maximized the contribution of the subtree rooted at s, i.e., the term $\prod_{t \in \underline{s}} \mathbb{F}_t(x_s)$. From this configuration, a first estimate of the spatial prior parameters $a^{(0)}(i, \nu)$ for the coarse Gibbsian EM algorithm could be computed as for the Gibbsian EM algorithm on the lattice.

The EM algorithms were stopped when the variations of the class parameters from an iteration to another became non-significant. In our experiments, data were only available on the finest resolution level, consequently the stopping criterion was the following: $\frac{1}{M}\{\sum_{i=1}^{M}[(\mu_i^{(k+1)}-\mu_i^{(k)})^2 +$

$(\sigma_i^{(k+1)}-\sigma_i^{(k)})^2]\}^{1/2} < \epsilon$, with $\epsilon = 0.1$ in our experiments.

First, the experiments were carried out on a 256×256 synthetic image involving 5 classes (Fig. 2). We applied an additive Gaussian white noise with a different standard deviation for each class, thus the gray level means and variances $(\mu_i, \sigma_i^2)_{i=1}^5$ were known and could be compared to the ones estimated by the different EM procedures in Tab. 2(a). We reported here the results obtained by the four methods with the number of classes forced to five. The obtained MPM classifications are shown in Fig. 2 and the respective percentages of good classification and computational loads, including cpu times (on a 360 MHz Ultra 60 Sun workstation), can be found in Tab. 2(b).

As can be seen from the results, the hierarchical models provided much better results than the plain spatial Gibbsian EM algorithm and took less cpu time. Increasing the number of retained samples ($m-r$, see Tab. 1) in the plain Gibbsian EM algorithm improved slightly the classification but implied a redhibitory computational load. It should be noticed that the hierarchical algorithms provided almost same results both in terms of quality of the classification and in terms of accuracy of the parameter estimates. The coarse Gibbsian EM took no more than five iterations with 20 retained samples within each iteration. If we computed cpu time needed for one iteration of each hierarchical method, we found 4.3s for the complete-tree-based and the five-level-based algorithms and 4.5s for the last one. Thus the use of a sampling procedure in the hybrid EM algorithm did not seem to imply a significant extra computational load.

The previous algorithms were applied to SPOT satellite images provided by Costel (geography laboratory of the University of Rennes 2) in the context of remote sensing researches within a research project called GSTB ("Groupe-

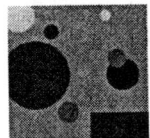  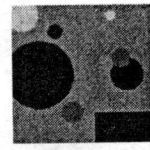 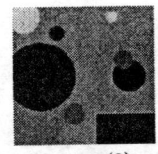  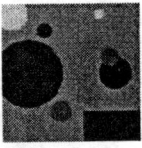 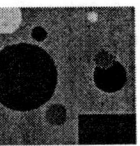

Ground-truth Noisy image $N = 0^{(1)}$ $N = 0^{(2)}$ $N = 3$ $N = 4$ $N = 8$

Figure 2. Unsupervised classifications with a synthetic image. ((1)=5 samples (2)=100 samples)

	Categories				
	1	2	3	4	5
GT	**20** (15)	**50** (30)	**100** (20)	**150** (30)	**210** (25)
$0^{(1)}$	**16.5** (12.8)	**55.2** (24.2)	**105.3** (19.0)	**152.5** (25.1)	**207.3** (22.0)
$0^{(2)}$	**14.9** (11.8)	**53.6** (23.5)	**103.0** (18.5)	**151.9** (26.1)	**208.0** (22.4)
3	**18.8** (13.1)	**50.2** (28.6)	**99.0** (20.4)	**149.3** (29.8)	**209.2** (23.7)
4	**14.3** (10.3)	**49.1** (28.4)	**99.1** (20.4)	**149.4** (29.7)	**209.1** (23.7)
8	**19.7** (13.9)	**49.9** (27.9)	**98.8** (20.2)	**149.0** (29.6)	**208.7** (23.8)

(a) Estimated class means and standard deviations. (GT=Ground truth)
(The bold-faced number corresponds to the mean and the one in parentheses to the variance.)

Model	good class.	nb iter.	nb samples	cpu time
$0^{(1)}$	88%	29	5	120s
$0^{(2)}$	91%	35	100	25min
3	99%	19	5×20	87s
4	98%	11	5×20	48s
8	99%	12	none	52s

(b) Performances of the different EM algorithms.

Table 2. Comparative results for the different EM algorithms with the synthetic image in Fig. 2. ($0^{(1)}$=Gibbsian EM with 5 samples, $0^{(2)}$=Gibbsian EM with 100 samples, 3=four-level hybrid structure-based EM, 4=five-level hybrid structure-based EM, 8=quad-tree-based EM)

ment Scientifique de Télédétection en Bretagne"). The extracted scene (Fig. 3) was composed of three 512×512 images with different wavelenghts and represented the Bay of Lannion, located in the north-west of France, during December 1996. The goal of this study was to determine the land cover of this area. To reach this aim, the geographers of Costel built a list of eight classification categories: (1) Sea and water, (2) Sand and bare soils, (3) Urban areas, (4) Forests and heath, (5) Temporary meadows, (6) Permanent meadows, (7) Colza, (8) Vegetables. Thanks to both tests on the lands and photointerpretations, they were also able to extract small image portions which are samples of the eight categories on the three SPOT images of the scene. We used them to assess the accuracy of the classifications and compared the parameters (gray level means, variances and possibly correlation coefficients) of each category for each image learned from the samples, to the ones given by the EM algorithms (see Tab. 3(a)). In fact, we fixed the parameters of the last four categories, because they were undistinguishable with automatic process but they were essential for the addressed application.

The model can be easily extended to the case of multi-spectral data by taking into account the correlation between the three spectral bands. We experimented both uncorrelated and correlated data likelihoods. However, even if the SPOT bands are known to be correlated, considering correlated channels in our example did not improve the classification results significantly. Thus we here only presented results considering the channels as independent.

The algorithms provided quite similar results of a good quality (see Tab. 3 and Fig. 4). About 89% of the pixels of

the samples were well classified.

4. Conclusion and extensions

In this paper, we presented an EM algorithm built on a hybrid hierarchical structure which is an interesting compromise between standard spatial models and hierarchical models based on a complete quad-tree. To study this algorithm thoroughly, we should concentrate on how it deals with different initializations of the class parameters, especially when they become very far from the right parameters.

With this structure we now plan to address the issue of automatically estimating the optimal number of levels in the struture. Moreover, we would like to investigate the possibility to truncate the tree in a heterogeneous manner, so that we could obtain pieces of coarse grids at different resolution depending on the available data.

References

[1] L. Baum, T. Petrie, G. Soules, and N. Weiss. A maximization technique occuring in the statistical analysis of probabilistic functions of Markov chains. *Ann. Math. Stat.*, 41:164–171, 1970.

[2] C. Bouman and M. Shapiro. A multiscale random field model for Bayesian image segmentation. *IEEE Trans.Im.Proc.*, 3(2):162–177, 1994.

[3] B. Chalmond. An iterative Gibbsian technique for reconstruction of m-ary images. *Pat. Recogn.*, 22(6):747–761, 1989.

[4] A. Chardin and P. Pérez. Semi-iterative inference with hierarchical models. In *ICIP'98*, pages 630–634, Chicago, USA, October 1998.

[5] A. Chardin and P. Pérez. Mode of posterior marginals with hierarchical models. In *ICIP'99*, Kobe, Japan, October 1999.

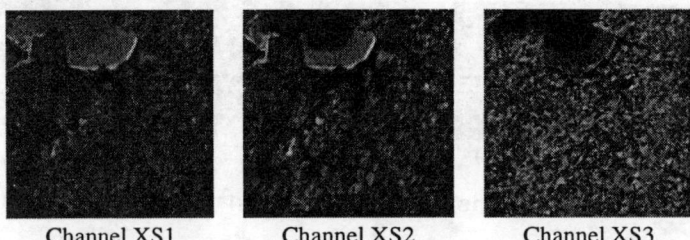

Channel XS1   Channel XS2   Channel XS3

Figure 3. 512×512 **SPOT images (courtesy of Costel, University of Rennes 2, and GSTB).**

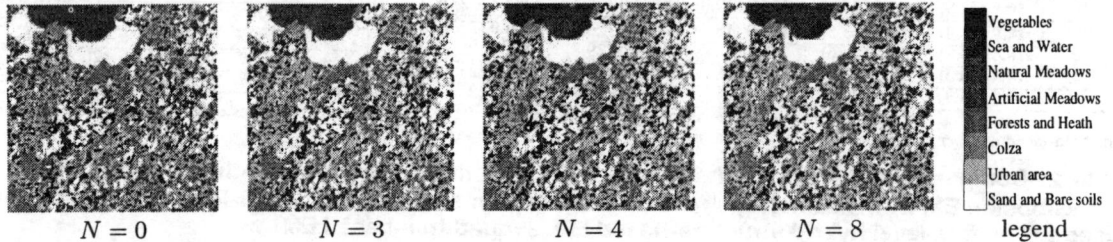

$N = 0$ $N = 3$ $N = 4$ $N = 8$ legend

Vegetables
Sea and Water
Natural Meadows
Artificial Meadows
Forests and Heath
Colza
Urban area
Sand and Bare soils

Figure 4. Unsupervised classifications with the multispectral satellite in Fig. 3.

[6] K. Chou, S. Golden, and A. Willsky. Multiresolution stochastic models, data fusion and wavelet transforms. *Sig. Proc.*, 34(3):257–282, 1993.

[7] A. Dempster, L. N.M., and D. Rubin. Mixtures densities, maximum likelihood from incomplete data via the EM algorithm. *Journal of the Royal Stat. Society*, 39(1):1–38, 1977.

[8] V. Digalakis, J. Rohlicek, and M. Ostendorf. ML estimation of a stochastic linear system with the EM algorithm and its application to speech recognition. *IEEE Trans. Speech and Audio Proc.*, 1(4):431–442, 1993.

[9] A. Kannan, M. Ostendorf, W. Karl, D. Castanon, and R. Fish. ML parameter estimation of a multiscale stochastic process using the EM algorithm. Technical Report ECE-96-009, Boston University, Nov. 1996.

[10] J.-M. Laferté, P. Pérez, and F. Heitz. Discrete Markov image modeling and inference on the quad-tree. *IEEE Trans.Im.Proc.*, Accepted for publication, 1999.

[11] M. Luettgen, W. Karl, and A. Willsky. Efficient multiscale regularization with applications to the computation of optical flow. *IEEE Trans.Im.Proc.*, 3(1):41–64, 1994.

[12] P. Pérez, A. Chardin, and J.-M. Laferté. Noniterative manipulation of discrete energy-based models for image analysis. *under press, Pat. Recogn.*, 1999.

[13] R. Redner and H. F. Walker. Mixtures densities, maximum likelihood and the EM algorithm. *SIAM Review*, 26(2):195–239, 1984.

[14] D. Tretter, C. Bouman, K. Khawaja, and A. Maciejewski. A multiscale stochastic image model for automated inspection. *IEEE Trans.Im.Proc.*, 4(12):1641–1654, 1995.

[15] J. Zhang, J. Modestino, and D. Langan. Maximum-likelihood parameter estimation for unsupervised stochastic model-based image segmentation. *IEEE Trans.Im.Proc.*, 3(4):404–420, 1994.

		water	bare soils	urban areas	forests
GT	XS1	**32.4** (1.4)	**40.2** (3.6)	**34.1** (1.4)	**28.1** (1.4)
	XS2	**12.2** (0.6)	**24.8** (2.9)	**17.5** (1.1)	**13.6** (1.0)
	XS3	**6.5** (0.6)	**23.9** (4.3)	**26.6** (3.5)	**22.8** (7.3)
N=0	XS1	**34.9** (2.2)	**40.6** (4.1)	**34.1** (1.4)	**30.4** (1.4)
	XS2	**13.7** (1.6)	**25.0** (3.8)	**19.7** (1.5)	**15.6** (1.4)
	XS3	**6.5** (0.6)	**26.7** (8.9)	**28.9** (5.5)	**26.3** (6.3)
N=3	XS1	**35.0** (2.2)	**39.6** (4.2)	**33.9** (1.2)	**30.6** (1.5)
	XS2	**13.8** (1.7)	**24.4** (3.7)	**19.2** (1.3)	**15.8** (1.4)
	XS3	**6.6** (0.6)	**27.3** (8.2)	**31.9** (7.2)	**26.9** (6.6)
N=4	XS1	**35.0** (2.2)	**39.1** (4.2)	**33.8** (1.1)	**30.6** (1.5)
	XS2	**13.8** (1.7)	**23.9** (3.7)	**19.1** (1.2)	**15.8** (1.4)
	XS3	**6.6** (0.6)	**27.5** (8.2)	**31.9** (7.1)	**26.9** (6.5)
N=9	XS1	**35.1** (2.2)	**40.0** (4.2)	**33.9** (1.3)	**30.5** (1.4)
	XS2	**13.8** (1.7)	**24.7** (3.7)	**19.2** (1.4)	**15.7** (1.4)
	XS3	**6.6** (0.6)	**27.0** (8.4)	**31.9** (7.2)	**26.8** (6.6)

(a) Estimated class parameters. (GT=Ground truth)
(means in bold-faced type and variances in parentheses.)

Model	good class.	nb iter.	nb samples	cpu time
$N = 0$	89%	15	5	880s
$N = 3$	89.2%	9	5×20	670s
$N = 4$	89.8%	10	5×20	700s
$N = 9$	89.3%	9	none	660s

(b) Performances of the different EM algorithms

Table 3. Comparative results for the different EM algorithms with the multispectral satellite images in Fig. 3.

Segmentation using eigenvectors: a unifying view

Yair Weiss
CS Division
UC Berkeley
Berkeley, CA 94720 - 1776
yweiss@cs.berkeley.edu

Abstract

Automatic grouping and segmentation of images remains a challenging problem in computer vision. Recently, a number of authors have demonstrated good performance on this task using methods that are based on eigenvectors of the affinity matrix. These approaches are extremely attractive in that they are based on simple eigendecomposition algorithms whose stability is well understood. Nevertheless, the use of eigendecompositions in the context of segmentation is far from well understood. In this paper we give a unified treatment of these algorithms, and show the close connections between them while highlighting their distinguishing features. We then prove results on eigenvectors of block matrices that allow us to analyze the performance of these algorithms in simple grouping settings. Finally, we use our analysis to motivate a variation on the existing methods that combines aspects from different eigenvector segmentation algorithms. We illustrate our analysis with results on real and synthetic images.

Human perceiving a scene can often easily segment it into coherent segments or groups. There has been a tremendous amount of effort devoted to achieving the same level of performance in computer vision. In many cases, this is done by associating with each pixel a feature vector (e.g. color, motion, texture, position) and using a clustering or grouping algorithm on these feature vectors.

Perhaps the cleanest approach to segmenting points in feature space is based on mixture models in which one assumes the data were generated by multiple processes and estimates the parameters of the processes and the number of components in the mixture. The assignment of points to clusters can then be easily performed by calculating the posterior probability of a point belonging to a cluster. Despite the elegance of this approach, the estimation process leads to a notoriously difficult optimization. The frequently used EM algorithm [3] often converges to a local maximum that depends on the initial conditions.

Recently, a number of authors [11, 10, 8, 9, 2] have suggested alternative segmentation methods that are based on eigenvectors of the (possibly normalized) "affinity matrix". Figure 1a shows two clusters of points and figure 1b shows the affinity matrix defined by:

$$W(i,j) = e^{-d(x_i, x_j)/2\sigma^2} \qquad (1)$$

with σ a free parameter. In this case we have used $d(x_i, x_j) = \|x_i - x_j\|^2$ but different definition of affinities are possible. The affinities do not even have to obey the metric axioms (e.g. [7]), we will only assume that $d(x_i, x_j) = d(x_j, x_i)$. Note that we have ordered the points so that all points belonging to the first cluster appear first and the points in the second cluster. This helps the visualization of the matrices but does not change the algorithms — eigenvectors of permuted matrices are the permutations of the eigenvectors of the original matrix.

From visual inspection, the affinity matrix contains information about the correct segmentation. In the next section we review four algorithms that look at eigenvectors of affinity matrices. We show that while seemingly quite different, these algorithms are closely related and all use dominant eigenvectors of matrices to perform segmentation. However, these approaches use different matrices, focus on different eigenvectors and use a different method of going from the continuous eigenvectors to the discrete segmentation. In section 2 we prove results on eigendecompositions of block matrices and use these results to analyze the behavior of these algorithms and motivate a new hybrid algorithm. Finally, in section 3 we discuss the application of these algorithms to affinity matrices derived from images.

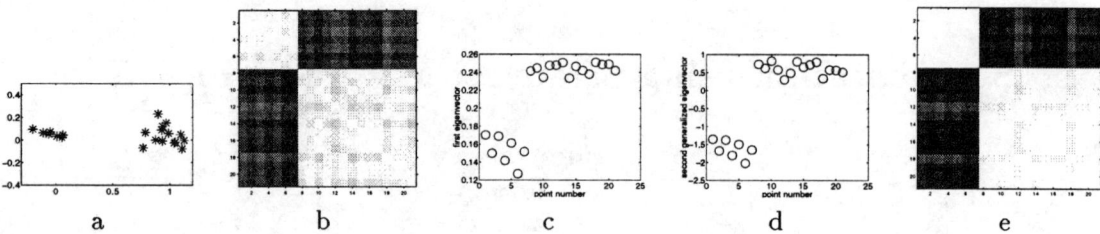

Figure 1: **a.** A simple clustering problem. **b.** The affinity matrix. **c.** The first eigenvector. **d.** The second generalized eigenvector. **e.** The Q matrix.

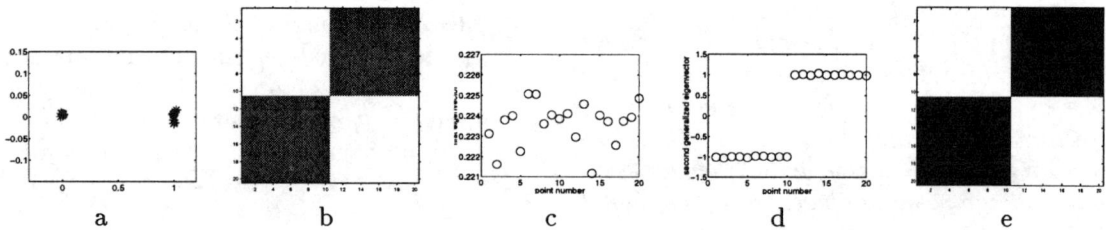

Figure 2: **a.** Another simple clustering problem. **b.** The affinity matrix. **c.** The first eigenvector. **d.** The second generalized eigenvector. **e.** The Q matrix.

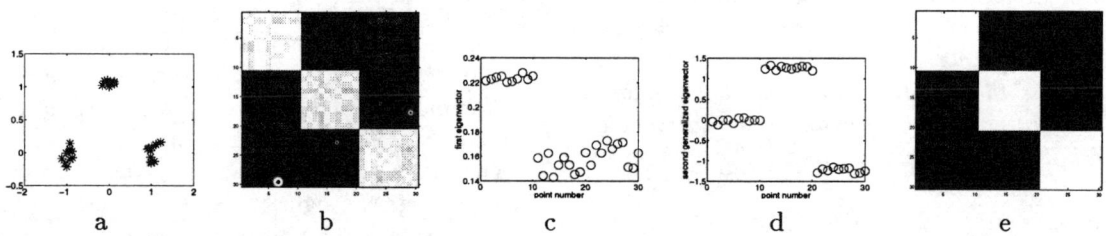

Figure 3: **a.** Another simple clustering problem. **b.** The affinity matrix. **c.** The first eigenvector. **d.** The second generalized eigenvector. **e.** The Q matrix.

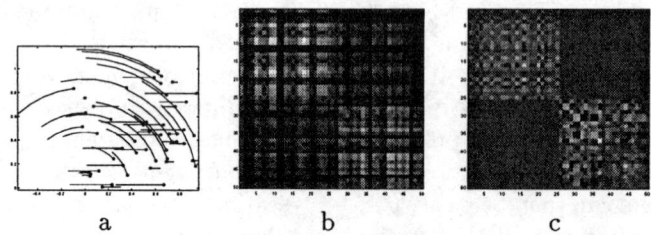

Figure 4: **a.** A single frame from a scene with two rigidly moving objects. **b.** The affinity matrix. **c.** The Q matrix.

1 The algorithms

1.1 The Perona and Freeman (1998) algorithm

Perona and Freeman [8] suggested a clustering algorithm based on thresholding the first eigenvector of the affinity matrix (throughout this paper we refer to the "first" eigenvector as the one whose corresponding eigenvalue is largest in magnitude). This is closely related to an approach suggested by Sarkar and Boyer [9] in the context of change detection.

Figure 1c shows the first eigenvector of the affinity matrix in figure 1b. Indeed, the eigenvector can be used to easily separate the two clusters.

Why does this method work? Perona and Freeman have shown that for block diagonal affinity matrices, the first eigenvector will have nonzero components corresponding to points in the dominant cluster and zeros in components corresponding to points outside the dominant cluster. Figure 2 shows that when the non-diagonal blocks are nonzero, the picture is a bit more complicated. Figure 2a shows two very tight clusters where we have constrained both clusters to have exactly the same number of points. Figure 2b shows the affinity matrix with the evident block structure. Figure 2c shows the first eigenvector. Note that there is no correlation between the components of the eigenvalues and the correct segmentation. Figure 3 shows another example where the Perona and Freeman (PF) algorithm works successfully.

1.2 The Shi and Malik (1997) algorithm.

Shi and Malik have argued for using a quite different eigenvector for solving these type of segmentation problems. Rather than examining the first eigenvector of W they look at generalized eigenvectors. Let D be the degree matrix of W:

$$D(i,i) = \sum_j W(i,j) \qquad (2)$$

Define the generalized eigenvector y_i as a solution to:

$$(D - W)y_i = \lambda_i D y_i \qquad (3)$$

and define the second generalized eigenvector as the y_i corresponding to the second *smallest* λ_i. Shi and Malik suggested thresholding this second generalized eigenvector of W in order to cut the image into two parts. Figure 1c and figure 2c show the second generalized eigenvector of W for the two cases. Indeed these vectors can be easily thresholded to give the correct segmentation.

Why does this method work? Shi and Malik have shown that the second generalized eigenvector is a solution to a continuous version of a *discrete* problem in which the goal is to minimize:

$$\frac{y^T(D-W)y}{y^T D y} \qquad (4)$$

subject to the constraint that $y_i \in \{1, -b\}$ and $y^T D1 = 0$ (where 1 is the vector of all ones).

The significance of the discrete problem is that its solution can be shown to give you the segmentation that minimizes the *normalized cut*:

$$Ncut(A, B) = \frac{cut(A, B)}{asso(A, V)} + \frac{cut(A, B)}{asso(B, V)} \qquad (5)$$

where $cut(A,B) = \sum_{i \in A, j \in B} W(i,j)$ and $asso(A, V) = \sum_j \sum_{i \in A} W(i,j)$. Thus the solution to the discrete problem finds a segmentation that minimizes the affinity between groups normalized by the affinity within each group.

As Shi and Malik noted, there is no guarantee that the solution obtained by ignoring the constraints and optimizing equation 4 will bear any relationship to the correct discrete solution. Indeed, they show that the discrete optimization of equation 4 is NP-complete.

Thus the connection to the discrete optimization problem does not rigorously answer the question of why the second generalized eigenvector should give us a good segmentation. Nevertheless, in cases when the solution to the unconstrained problem happens to satisfy the constraints (as in the first two examples), we can infer that it is close to the constrained problems. But what of cases when the second generalized eigenvector doesn't satisfy the constraints? Figure 3a shows an example. The second generalized eigenvector does not have two values but it obviously gives very good information on the correct segmentation (as does the first eigenvector). Why is that?

Note that while Perona and Freeman use the *largest* eigenvector, Shi and Malik use the second *smallest* generalized eigenvector. Thus the two approaches appear quite different. There is, however, a closer connection. Define the normalized affinity matrix:

$$N = D^{-1/2} W D^{-1/2} \qquad (6)$$

We call this a *normalized* affinity matrix following [1]. Note that $N(i,j) = W(i,j)/\sqrt{D(i,i)}\sqrt{D(j,j)}$. Given N the following normalization lemma is easily shown:

Normalization Lemma: 1. Let v be an eigenvector of N with eigenvalue λ then $D^{-1/2}v$ is a generalized eigenvector of W with eigenvalue $1 - \lambda$. 2. The vector $D^{1/2}1$ is an eigenvector of N with eigenvalue 1.

Thus the second smallest generalized eigenvector of W can be obtained by a componentwise ratio of the second and first *largest* eigenvectors of N. The Shi and Malik (SM) algorithm thus differs from PF in that (1) it uses a *normalized* W matrix and (2) it uses the first two eigenvectors rather than just the first one.

1.3 The Scott and Longuet-Higgins (1990) algorithm.

The Scott and Longuet-Higgins [10] relocalisation algorithm gets as input an affinity matrix W and a number k and outputs a new matrix Q calculated by:

- Constructing the matrix V whose columns are the first k eigenvectors of W.

- normalizing the *rows* of V so that they have unit Euclidean norm. $V(i, \rightarrow) = V(i, \rightarrow)/\|V(i, \rightarrow)\|$.

- Constructing the matrix $Q = VV^T$.

- Segmenting the points by looking at the elements of Q. Ideally, $Q(i,j) = 1$ if points belong to the same group and $Q(i,j) = 0$ if points belong to different groups.

Figures 1d–3d show the Q matrix computed by the Scott and Longuet-Higgins (SLH) algorithm for the cases surveyed above. Note that in all cases, the $Q(i,j)$ entries for points belonging to the same group are close to 1 and those belonging to different groups are close to 0.

1.4 The Costeira and Kanade (1995) algorithm

Independently of the recent work on using eigenvectors of affinity matrices to segment points in feature space, there has been interest in using singular values of the measurement matrix to segment the points into rigidly moving bodies in 3D [2, 4]. Although these algorithms seem quite different from the ones discussed so far, they are in fact very closely related.

To see the connection, we review the Costeira and Kanade algorithm. Suppose we track n points in f frames. The measurement matrix is a $nx(2f)$ matrix:

$$M = (XY) \tag{7}$$

where $X(i,j), Y(i,j)$ give the x, y coordinate of point i in frame j. The method of Costeira and Kanade segments these points by taking the first k singular vectors of M (where k is the rank of the matrix) and putting them into a matrix V whose columns are the singular vectors. Then constructing the matrix Q by:

$$Q = VV^T \tag{8}$$

Q is a nxn matrix and $Q_{ij} = 0$ for any two points that belong to different objects.

What does this have to do with eigenvectors of affinity matrices? Recall that the singular values of M are by definition the eigenvectors of $W = M^T M$. W is a nxn by matrix that can be thought of as an affinity matrix. The affinity of point i and j is simply the inner product between their traces $(X(i, \rightarrow)Y(i, \rightarrow))$ and $(X(j, \rightarrow)Y(j, \rightarrow))$. Given this definition of affinity, the Costeira and Kanade algorithm is nearly identical to the SLH algorithm. Figure 4 illustrates the Costeira and Kanade algorithm.

2 Analysis of the algorithms in simple grouping settings

In this section we use properties of block matrices to analyze the algorithms. To simplify notation, we assume the data has two clusters. We partition the matrix W into the following form:

$$W = \begin{pmatrix} A & C \\ C^T & B \end{pmatrix} \tag{9}$$

where A and B represent the affinities within the two clusters and C represents the between cluster affinity.

Our strategy in this section is to prove results on idealized block matrices and then appeal to perturbation theorems on eigenvectors [6] to generalize the results to cases where the matrices are only approximately of this form.

2.1 Approximately constant blocks

We begin by assuming the matrices A, B, C are constant. As can be seen from equation 1, this will be the case when the variation of the within and between cluster dissimilarities is significantly smaller than σ. Thus $W(i,j)$ depends only on the membership of points i and j. Note that we do not assume that the between cluster affinity B is zero, or even that it is smaller than the within cluster affinity.

Under these assumptions we can analyze the behavior of the three algorithms exactly:

Claim 1: Assume $W(i,j)$ depends only on the memberships of points i, j. Let v_1 be the indicator vector of the PF algorithm (i.e. the first eigenvector of W) . If point i and point j belong to the same cluster then $v_1(i) = v_1(j)$.

Claim 2: Assume $W(i,j)$ depends only on the memberships of points i, j. Let v be the indicator vector of the SM algorithm (the second generalized eigenvector of W). If point i and point j belong to the same clusters then $v(i) = v(j)$.

Claim 3: Assume $W(i,j)$ depends only on the memberships of points i, j. Let v be the indicator vector of the SM algorithm (the second $Q(i,j)$ in the SLH algorithm with $k = 2$ eigenvectors is equal to

1 if points i and j belong to the same group and 0 otherwise.

The proof of these claims follows from the following decomposition of W:

$$W = OSO^T \tag{10}$$

with O a binary matrix indicating whose columns are membership vectors for the clusters:

$$O = \begin{pmatrix} 1 & 0 \\ 1 & 0 \\ \cdots & \cdots \\ 0 & 1 \\ 0 & 1 \end{pmatrix} \tag{11}$$

and S a small $2x2$ matrix that contains the constant values of W:

$$S = \begin{pmatrix} a & c \\ c & b \end{pmatrix} \tag{12}$$

Obviously, if we had an algorithm that given W gave us O then segmentation would be trivial. Unfortunately, the decomposition in equation 10 is not an eigendecomposition so standard linear algebra algorithms will not recover it. However, eigendecomposition algorithms will recover a rotation of a suitably normalized O. It can be shown that if V is a matrix whose two columns are the first two eigenvectors of W then $V = OD_2R$ where D_2 is a $2x2$ diagonal matrix and R is a $2x2$ rotation matrix. Hence the claims.

Note that for the PF and SM algorithms we cannot prove that points belonging to different clusters will have different indicator values. We can only prove that points belonging to same clusters will have the same value. Thus in figure 2c the first eigenvector of W has roughly equal values for all points — both those belonging to the same cluster and those belonging to different clusters. Any visible variation is due to noise. It is only for the SLH algorithm that we can guarantee that points belonging to different clusters will be separated.

2.2   Non-constant block diagonal matrices

Here we assume that the within-cluster affinities, i.e. the matrices A, B are arbitrary matrices with positive elements. The between-cluster affinities, i.e. the matrix C is assumed to be zero. We denote by λ_i^A, λ_i^B the eigenvalues of matrices A and B respectively, ordered by decreasing magnitude.

Claim 4: Assume between cluster affinities are zero and within cluster affinities are positive. Let v_1 be the PF indicator vector. If $\lambda_1^A > \lambda_1^B$ then $v_1(i) > 0$ for all points belonging to the first cluster and $v_1(i) = 0$ for all points belonging to the second cluster.

Claim 5: Assume between cluster affinities are zero and within cluster affinities are positive. Let v be the SM indicator vector then $v(i) = v(j)$ if points i, j belong to the same cluster.

Claim 6: Assume between cluster affinities are zero and within cluster affinities are positive. Let Q be the SLH matrix constructed from W. If $\lambda_1^B > |\lambda_2^A|$ and $\lambda_1^A > |\lambda_2^B|$ then $Q(i,j) = 1$ if i, j belong to the same cluster and zero otherwise.

Claim 4 was proven in [8] and the proof of claim 6 is analogous: if v^a is an eigenvector of A then $v = (v^a; 0)$ is an eigenvector of W with the same eigenvalue. Thus the conditions of claim 6 guarantee that the first two eigenvectors of W will be $(v^a; 0), (0; v^b)$. Claim 5 follows from the normalization lemma proven in the previous section. The vectors $(D_A^{1/2}1; 0)$ and $(0; D_B^{1/2}1)$ are both eigenvectors of N with eigenvalue 1 where D_A, D_B are the degree matrices of A and B. Thus the second generalized eigenvector of W will be some linear combination of these two vectors multiplied by $D^{-1/2}$ so it will be constant for points belonging to the same cluster.

Note that as in the case for constant block matrices, for the PF and SM algorithms we cannot guarantee that points belonging to different clusters can be easily segmented. In the PF algorithm $v(i)$ is guaranteed to be positive for all points in the first cluster, but there is no guarantee of how positive. Figure 5c illustrates this. Many points in the "foreground" cluster have components that are positive yet close to zero. In the SM algorithm, since N has two identical first eigenvalues, v_2 may be any linear combination of the eigenvectors, so the difference between values for the first and second cluster is arbitrary and depends on the implementation details of the eigendecomposition algorithm. In the SLH algorithm, we can again guarantee that different clusters will be segmented but we require an additional constraint on the eigenvalues of the blocks. Figure 5d shows what happens when this additional constraint does not hold. In this case the first two eigenvectors of W are $(0; v_1^b), (0; v_2^b)$ and the Q matrix does not find the correct segmentation.

To summarize, when the matrix has constant blocks then all three algorithms will work, although extracting the discrete segmentation is probably easiest in the SLH algorithm. In this case, normalizing the W matrix does not make any difference. When the blocks are not constant, however, and the between cluster affinities are zeros, the normalization makes a big difference in that it reorders the eigenvectors.

This analysis suggests a combined (SM+SLH) algorithm in which the SLH algorithm is applied to the

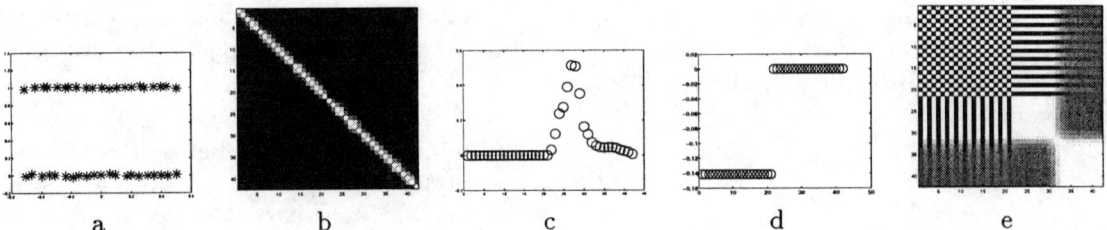

a   b   c   d   e

Figure 5: **a.** Another simple clustering problem. **b.** The affinity matrix. **c.** The first eigenvector. **d.** The second generalized eigenvector. **e.** The Q matrix of the SLH algorithm.

normalized W matrix, N, rather than to the raw affinity matrix. Indeed, when we run this combined algorithm on the data in figure 5a the correct segmentation is found.

We summarize the properties of the combined (SM+SLH) algorithm:

Claim 7: Assume affinities are only a function of point membership or assume that the between cluster affinities are zero and within cluster affinities are positive. Under both assumptions $Q(i,j)$ in the combined (SM+SLH) algorithm is one if points i and j belong to the same cluster and zero otherwise.

Note that in the idealized cases we have been analyzing, where between cluster affinities are zero and within cluster affinities are positive, then a simple connected-components algorithm will find the correct segmentation. However the perturbation theorems of eigenvectors guarantee that that our claims still hold with small perturbations around these idealized matrices, even when the between cluster affinities are nonzero. In the following section, we show that our analysis for idealized matrices also predicts the behavior on affinity matrices derived from images.

3 Affinity matrices of images

Perona and Freeman conducted a comparison between the first eigenvector of W and the second generalized eigenvector of W when W is constructed by representing each pixel with a (position,intensity) feature vector. In their comparison, the eigenvector of W had a much less crisp representation of the correct segmentation. We have found this to be the case generally for W matrices constructed in this way from images.

Figures 6–9 show examples. Figure 6a shows the baseball player figure from [11]. We constructed a W matrix using the same constants. Figure 6b-e show the first four eigenvectors of W. Note that there is very little information in these eigenvectors regarding the correct segmentation (the pictures do not change when we show log intensities). Figure 6f-i show the

first four eigenvectors of the normalized affinity matrix N. Note that at least visually all eigenvectors appear to be correlated with the correct segmentation.

How should this information be recovered? Figure 7a shows the SM indicator vector displayed as an image. Although it contains the information, it is not at all clear how to extract the correct segments from this image — the pixels belonging to the same object do not have constant value but rather have smooth variation. Furthermore, there is obviously additional information in the other eigenvectors.

Figure 7b shows a single column from the matrix Q constructed by the combined (SM+SLH) method with 6 eigenvectors displayed as an image. Ideally, if we had the correct k this column should be all ones for a single object and zeros for points not belonging to the object. Even for k that is too small, this column should have all ones for a single object (but not necessarily zeros for the other pixels). Indeed, we find that the value is nearly one for points belonging to the same object. Figure 7c shows a cross-section. Note that all points corresponding to the baseball player are essentially at 1. It is trivial to extract the baseball player from this representation. Figure 7d show a second column. Again, all pixels corresponding to the second baseball player are very close to 1.

Exactly the same behavior is observed in the dancer image. The information in figure 9a is sufficient to give a segmentation but it is not trivial. In the cross-section (figure 9b) the variation between groups is similar to the variation within groups. Figure 9c-d show the row of the $Q(i,j)$ matrix in the combined (SM+SLH) algorithm and the same cross-section. Extracting the discrete segmentation is trivial.

4 Discussion

Why do eigendecomposition methods for segmentation work? In this paper we have presented a unified view of three of these methods — Perona and Freeman [8], Shi and Malik [11] and Scott and Longuet-Higgins [10]. We showed the similarities and the dif-

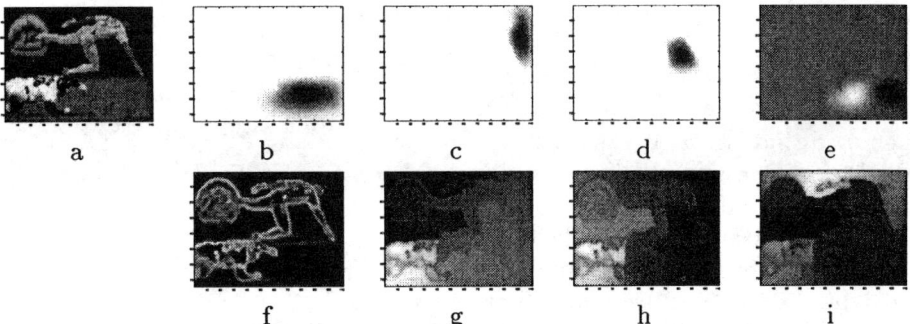

Figure 6: **a.** The baseball image from [11] **b-e.** The eigenvectors of the affinity matrix W. Note there is very little correlation with the desired segmentation. **f-i.** The eigenvectors of the normalized affinity matrix N. Note that all eigenvectors are correlated with the desired segmentation.

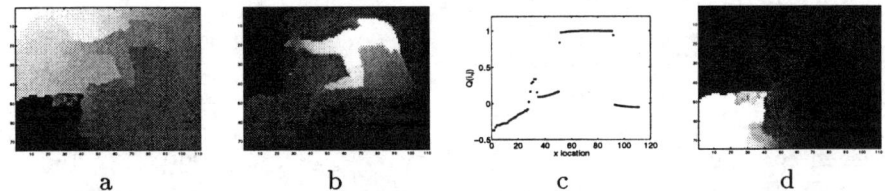

Figure 7: **a.** The second generalized eigenvector of W for the baseball image. Although there is information here regarding the correct segmentation, its extraction is nontrivial. **b.** A row of the Q matrix in the combined (SM+SLH) algorithm for the baseball image. Ideally all pixels corresponding to the same object should have value 1. **c.** A cross section through the pixels in **b**. Note that pixels corresponding to the first baseball player are nearly all 1. **d.** A different row of the Q matrix. All pixels corresponding to the second baseball player are 1.

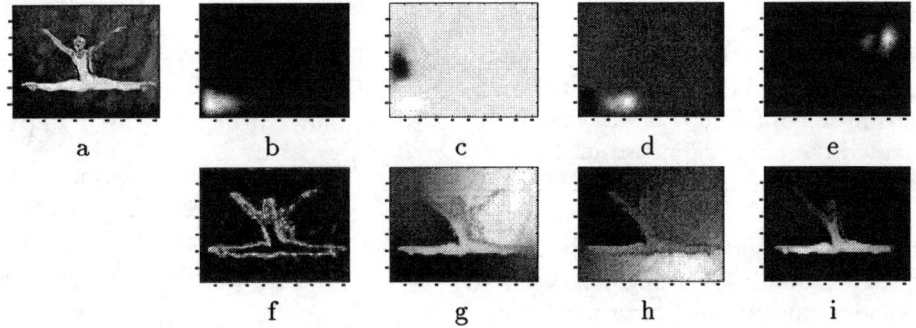

Figure 8: **a.** A gray level image of a ballet dancer. **b-e.** The eigenvectors of the affinity matrix W. Note there is very little correlation with the desired segmentation. **f-i.** The eigenvectors of the normalized affinity matrix N. Note that all eigenvectors are correlated with the desired segmentation.

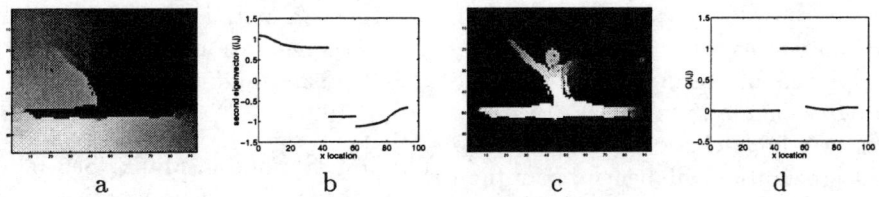

Figure 9: **a.** The second generalized eigenvector of W for the dancer image. Although there is information here regarding the correct segmentation, its extraction is nontrivial. **b.** A horizontal cross section through **a**. Note that the variation between groups is of similar order of magnitude as the variation within groups. **c.** A row of the Q matrix in the combined (SM+SLH) algorithm for the dancer image. Ideally all pixels corresponding to the same object should have value 1. **d.** A cross section through the pixels in **c**. Note that pixels corresponding to the dancer are nearly all 1.

ferences. The similarities are that they all use the top eigenvectors of a matrix. They differ in two ways — which eigenvectors to look at and whether to normalize the W matrix in advance. Using properties of block matrices we showed that when W has constant block structure, all three of these methods will yield eigenvectors that carry some information. We also showed analytically the importance of normalization when the matrix is block diagonal with non-constant blocks. As suggested by the analysis, we found that for real images, unless the W matrix is normalized in the form suggested by Shi and Malik [11] it is nearly impossible to extract segmentation information from the eigenvectors.

In all our analysis and experiments, we never found an example where using normalized W rather than raw W degraded performance. This suggested a scheme that combines the SM algorithm with the SLH algorithm — work with eigenvectors of normalized W but use the first k eigenvectors rather than just the first two. This is similar in spirit to the approach of [12] where the first k eigenvectors of W were used to define a new affinity matrix between the points. Our experimental results on real images are encouraging — by using the first k eigenvectors and combining them into the SLH Q matrix we extract a representation that leads trivially to a discrete segmentation.

We have also discussed a seemingly unrelated rigid body segmentation algorithm — Costeira and Kanade [2] and shown that it is nearly identical to SLH with a particular definition of affinity. It was this connection that motivated the analysis in section 2. We wanted to generalize that type of analysis for arbitrary affinity matrices.

In the case of multibody rigid grouping, there has been additional progress made by using algorithms that do not use eigendecompositions but rather other, more stable matrix decompositions such as the reduced echelon form [4, 5]. Given the close connection between the two problems, we are currently experimenting with using these alternative decompositions in the general grouping context.

The main goal of presenting these algorithms in a unified framework is to enable future work to build on the collective progress made by many researchers in different subfields. We hope that research into the difficult problem of segmentation will benefit from the connections we have pointed out between the different algorithms.

Acknowledgements

I thank W. Freeman, J. Shi, J. Malik and T. Leung for helpful comments and discussions. Supported by MURI-ARO-DAAH04-96-1-0341.

References

[1] F.R.K. Chung. *Spectral Graph Theory*. American Mathematical Society, 1997.

[2] J. Costeira and T. Kanade. A multibody factorization method for motion analysis. In *Proc. International Conf. Computer Vision*, pages 1071–1076, 1995.

[3] A. P. Dempster, N. M. Laird, and D. B. Rubin. Maximum likelihood from incomplete data via the EM algorithm. *J. R. Statist. Soc. B*, 39:1–38, 1977.

[4] C.W. Gear. feature grouping in moving images. In *Proc IEEE workshop on motion of non-rigid and articulated objects*, pages 214–219, 1994.

[5] C.W. Gear. multibody grouping from motion images. *IJCV*, 29(2):133–150, 1998.

[6] G.H. Golub and C.F. Van-Loan. *Matrix Computations*. Johns Hopkins Press, 1989.

[7] D. W. Jacobs, D. Weinshall, and Y. Gdalyahu. Class representation and image retrieval with non-metric distances. In *Proc. International Conference Computer Vision*, 1998.

[8] P. Perona and W. T. Freeman. A factorization approach to grouping. In H. Burkardt and B. Neumann, editors, *Proc ECCV*, pages 655–670, 1998.

[9] S. Sarkar and K.L. Boyer. quantitative measures of change based on feature organization: eigenvalues and eigenvectors. In *Proc. IEEE Conf. Computer Vision and Pattern Recognition*, 1996.

[10] G.L. Scott and H. C. Longuet-Higgins. Feature grouping by relocalisation of eigenvectors of the proxmity matrix. In *Proc. British Machine Vision Conference*, pages 103–108, 1990.

[11] J. Shi and J. Malik. Normalized cuts and image segmentation. In *Proc. IEEE Conf. Computer Vision and Pattern Recognition*, pages 731–737, 1997.

[12] J. Shi and J. Malik. Self inducing relational distance and its application to image segmentation. In *Proc. European Conf. Computer Vision*, pages 538–543, 1998.

An Integrated Bayesian Approach to Layer Extraction from Image Sequences

P. H. S. Torr, R. Szeliski, P. Anandan

Microsoft Research, One Microsoft Way, Redmond

WA 98052, USA

philtorr—szeliski—anandan@microsoft.com

Abstract

This paper describes a Bayesian approach for modeling 3D scenes as a collection of approximately planar layers that are arbitrarily positioned and oriented in the scene. In contrast to much of the previous work on layer based motion modeling, which compute layered descriptions of 2D image motion, our work leads to a 3D description of the scene. We focus on the key problem of automatically segmenting the scene into layers as a precursor to recovery of stereo disparity data. The prior assumptions about the scene are formulated within a Bayesian decision making framework, and are then used to automatically determine the number of layers and the assignment of individual pixels to layers. Although using a collection of 3D layers has been previously proposed as an efficient and effective representation for multimedia applications, results to date have relied on hand segmentation. In contrast, the work described here aims at getting a fully automatic segmentation.

1 Introduction

The classical approach to 3D scene modeling from multiple images is to break the problem into two subproblems: creating a 3D geometric model of the scene, and creating a texture map that captures the visual appearance of the scene. A more recent emerging paradigm is Image-Based Modeling and Rendering (IBMR) in which the representation of appearance and geometry are more tightly coupled. Examples include plenoptic modeling such as the Lumigraph, characteristic views etc. These representations are used as the basis for compression, new view rendering, and video editing. IBMR methods are tailored to this class of "image-in, image-out" functions which are important in multi media applications.

Since motion and stereo have been the dominant methods for recovering 3D scene structure from multiple images, there is a direct mapping between motion (or stereo disparity) recovery and 3D scene modeling. A recent trend in image motion modeling is the use of *layers* (e.g., [1, 9, 10]) which are 2D sub-images, such that pixels within a layer

move in a manner consistent with a 2D parametric transformation (e.g., affine). These 2D layers, however, are usually not intended to capture 3D scene structure. In contrast, it was proposed in [2] that the scene should be decomposed into a collection of *3D layers* (or *sprites*), each of which consists of a plane equation, a colour image that captures the appearance of the sprite, a per-pixel opacity map, and a per-pixel depth-offset relative to the nominal plane of the layer. The emphasis in this paper is at getting the first two of these. This approach to layered representation can be viewed as an extension of the plane+parallax decomposition of image disparities across multiple views. Although [2] proposed a generative model for images based on layers, the algorithm described in that paper for recovering the layers from a given set of input images is incomplete. Layer initialization was based *solely* on manual user input and as the paper confesses, the final assignment of pixels to layers was not fully developed.

In fact, the central problem of layer-based scene modeling is the determination of the number of layers and the assignment of pixels to layers. An infinite number of decompositions are equally consistent with the generative model proposed in [2], ranging from assigning one layer plane to every pixel (with no depth offset) to modeling the entire scene with a single layer plane (with lots of depth offset). Apart from object and scene level semantic information (which is important, but outside the scope of this paper), the natural criterion to use is compactness or *parsimony* of description. But computing a parsimonious description is implicitly and tightly tied to our prior assumptions about the scene and the imaging process that generated the input images. Bayesian decision theory provides a foundation for accurately and formally stating our prior assumptions and then developing algorithms for applying these priors during reconstruction.

2 The Bayesian Method

The approach that follows is unashamedly Bayesian, to quote E. T. Jaynes "Vision is inference from incomplete data". As set out in his internet book [6] (which every vision postgraduate would be well advised to read), the Bayesian method provides a consistent way of reasoning about the world that can be viewed as an extension of the Aristotelian calculus of logic to uncertainty. Some will complain that to use Bayesian methods one must introduce arbitrary priors on the parameters. However, far from being a disadvantage, this a tremendous advantage as it forces open acknowledgement of what assumptions were used in designing the algorithm, which all too often are hidden away beneath the veneer of equations. Furthermore there is nothing wrong with injecting our prior information into the design of vision algorithms – all vision researchers do it when ever they choose the probability distribution of their error. As will be seen, the validity of the prior assumptions can be tested by altering the priors and seeing whether this leads to radically different results.

In addition to the utilization of prior information, Bayesian methods are further distinguished from orthodox statistical methods by their use of full probability distributions rather than the mode to describe parameters. This difference can be illustrated by how to compare two competing models for the data. This will be useful later when we need to determine the number of layers used to describe the image.

Given a closed set[1] of k models $\mathbf{M}_1 \ldots \mathbf{M}_k$ that can explain the data $\mathbf{D}$ Bayes rule leads us to

$$\Pr(\mathbf{M}_i|\mathbf{DI}) = \frac{\Pr(\mathbf{D}|\mathbf{M}_i\mathbf{I})\Pr(\mathbf{M}_i|\mathbf{I})}{\Pr(\mathbf{D}|\mathbf{I})} \, , \qquad (1)$$

where $\mathbf{I}$ is the prior information assumed about the world. In this paper the set of models are: $\mathbf{M}_1$ that the data can be explained by one layer, $\mathbf{M}_2$ that the data can be explained by two layers, and so on. The posterior probability that a given model $\mathbf{M}_i$ is the correct one is

$$\Pr(\mathbf{M}_i|\mathbf{DI}) = \frac{\Pr(\mathbf{D}|\mathbf{M}_i\mathbf{I})\Pr(\mathbf{M}_i|\mathbf{I})}{\sum_{j=1}^{j=k}\Pr(\mathbf{D}|\mathbf{M}_j\mathbf{I})\Pr(\mathbf{M}_j|\mathbf{I})} \, . \qquad (2)$$

Note that by construction, $\sum_{j=1}^{j=k}\Pr(\mathbf{M}_j|\mathbf{D}) = 1$. The key to this equation is the evaluation of $\Pr(\mathbf{D}|\mathbf{M}_j\mathbf{I})$, which is called the evidence. In contrast to non-Bayesian techniques, the evidence for a model is in fact the integral of the likelihood over all possible values of the model's parameters:

$$\Pr(\mathbf{D}|\mathbf{M}_j\mathbf{I}) = \int \Pr(\mathbf{D}|\mathbf{M}_j\boldsymbol{\theta}_j\mathbf{I})\Pr(\boldsymbol{\theta}_j|\mathbf{M}_j\mathbf{I})d\boldsymbol{\theta}_j \quad (3)$$

$$\text{Evidence} = \int \text{likelihood} \times \text{prior}\, d\boldsymbol{\theta}_j \, , \qquad (4)$$

where $\boldsymbol{\theta}_j$ are the kth model's parameters, and $\Pr(\boldsymbol{\theta}_j|\mathbf{M}_j\mathbf{I})$ is the prior distribution of parameters of the model. How

---

[1]This is an important prerequisite, and the burden is on us to explore the most likely models.

does this relate to the principle of parsimony so prevalent in model selection (AIC, MDL etc.)? Not as it commonly believed, i.e., by penalizing more complex models *a priori* [2]. In the absence of any prior preference between the two models, $(\Pr(\mathbf{M}_i) = \Pr(\mathbf{M}_j))$, all the models are equally likely a priori. Rather, more complex models have the probability of the prior dispersed over a greater region of parameter space. Note by definition $\int \Pr(\boldsymbol{\theta}_j|\mathbf{M}_j\mathbf{I})d\boldsymbol{\theta}_j = 1$. Thus a more complex model will only be supported if there is a corresponding increase in the likelihood of the data given that model. This is a subtle point and worthy of some reflection. Equation (4) representing the evidence for a given model is a crucial equation and is worthy of close scrutiny. **If one accepts Bayes rule then logic dictates that this is the only way to calculate the posterior probability of each model [6].**

Another useful Bayesian technique is that of marginalization, which allows us to dispose of parameters that are not directly useful to us at any given time by integrating them out. This is effected by the following identity:

$$\int_{-\infty}^{\infty} \Pr(\mathbf{X}, \mathbf{Y}|\mathbf{I})d\mathbf{Y} = \Pr(\mathbf{X}|\mathbf{I}) \qquad (5)$$

As it turns out, the Bayesian technique of marginalization allows us to finesse a problem that has plagued motion algorithms for decades, namely the correspondence problem.

3 First Stage—preprocessing

The input to the algorithm is a sequence of images. These are the (raw) data $\mathbf{D}$. The first stage of the algorithm uses a coarse to fine algorithm to obtain initial disparity estimates for each pixel [3]. Then, calibration and camera matrices are recovered [8]. Each image is then transformed in such a way that the plane at infinity is stabilized. In other words the images are rectified to the first one by transforming under $\mathbf{H}_\infty^{1j}$ the homography of the plane at infinity between image 1 and the jth image to remove the effects of rotation. Registering each image to the plane at infinity has the effect that the disparity (motion) of each pixel now depends purely on depth. Here, the disparity $\delta(x, y)$ at pixel (x, y) in image 1 is taken to mean the motion along the epipolar line between image 1 and image 2. Because the images are rectified to the plane at infinity, it is a bijective function of the depth of that pixel, $\delta(x, y) = \rho(Z(x, y))$. The transformation ρ is purely a function of the calibration and camera matrices The notation $\mathbf{Z}$ is adopted for the set of depths, and $Z(x, y)$ for the depth of a pixel (x, y) in the first image.

4 Parametric Formulation of Problem

The set of input images is denoted by $\mathbf{D}$ (the data), the model $\mathbf{M}$ consists of a set of m planes $\boldsymbol{\Theta}$ with parameters

---

[2]Although there is nothing to stop us doing this it is not necessary.

θ_j, $j = 1 \ldots m$, and a set $\mathbf{L}$ of per pixel labels $l(x, y)$ for the first image. Nothing is known about the number of layers m – this must also be recovered. One image (image 1) is used to initialize the segmentation and from hereon the segmentation and labeling is done in the coordinate system of image 1. Because inter image motions are small it is more natural to do the segmentation in the image rather than in some 3D based coordinate system. Hence the aim is simply to extract $\mathbf{M}$ from $\mathbf{D}$. The information $\mathbf{I}$ that everything is conditioned on includes the camera pose for each image, the camera calibration, and our assumptions about the underlying noise distributions.

The parameters of each plane are $\boldsymbol{\theta} = (a, b, c)$ such that $aX + bY + cZ = 1$, where X, Y, Z are the Euclidean coordinates. This parametrization is chosen as it excludes all planes passing through the origin of the coordinate system (the optic centre of the first camera) i.e. planes of the form $aX + bY + cZ = 0$. These project to a line in the first image (and subsequent images if the baseline is small) and thus correspondence cannot be recovered for them. Note that $\boldsymbol{\theta} = (a, b, c)$ lies along the normal of the plane. The coordinate system is chosen such that the origin is at the first camera's optic centre. In image 1, $x = X/Z$ and $y = Y/Z$, leading to $ax + by + c = 1/Z$. Thus, given the plane and the (x, y) coordinate of any pixel, its depth may be found (and hence its corresponding pixel in any other image). For the case when the direction of motion along the optic access is small relative to the distance to the 3D point, $1/Z$ is roughly proportional to the disparity between images. The coefficients a and b give the disparity gradients in the x, y directions and c, the inverse depth of the plane at the principal point

One plane is privileged in that it is always represented by a layer and has fixed parameters $\boldsymbol{\theta}_\infty = (a, b, c) = (0, 0, 0)$: this is the plane at infinity. Although this ideal cannot truly exist in a Euclidean representation, it serves a useful purpose. All pixels that are so distant that their disparity is swamped by noise (e.g. sky) have very ill conditioned depths, and cannot be easily segmented. These are all grouped together into the plane at infinity.

5 Probabilistic Formulation

This section introduces the mixture model used to describe the layers. Although some will consider this standard fare, we consider it worth looking under the bonnet[3] to show the logical implications of our formulation. We will show how Bayesian reasoning can be used to describe two vision heuristics of long standing: the *disparity gradient limit* and *plane plus parallax*. We will also show how the layers can be recovered without estimating correspondence. It transpires that this is very useful for segmentation, as it finesses the problem of mismatches.

---

[3]hood

Posterior Probability of the Model The model parameters $m, \boldsymbol{\Theta}, \mathbf{L}$ are chosen so as to maximize the posterior probability:

$$\max_{m \boldsymbol{\Theta} \mathbf{L}} \Pr(m \boldsymbol{\Theta} \mathbf{L} | \mathbf{D} \mathbf{I}) = \frac{\Pr(\mathbf{D} | m \boldsymbol{\Theta} \mathbf{L} \mathbf{I}) \Pr(m \boldsymbol{\Theta} \mathbf{L} | \mathbf{I})}{\Pr(\mathbf{D} | \mathbf{I})}. \tag{6}$$

The denominator can be discounted for the purposes of parameter estimation, (but not for the purposes of model comparison as will be seen later), as it is constant for all values of the parameters. So far, the estimation of depth (or disparity) has not been mentioned, although it would apparently have a direct bearing on the likelihood.

Recovering the plane parameters without correspondence We can use the Bayesian method of marginalization to remove the depth parameter from the posterior probability of the plane

$$\Pr(m \boldsymbol{\Theta} \mathbf{L} | \mathbf{D} \mathbf{I}) = \Pr \int_{\mathbf{Z}} (m \boldsymbol{\Theta} \mathbf{L} \mathbf{Z} | \mathbf{D} \mathbf{I}) \, d\mathbf{Z} \tag{7}$$

Later it will be seen that this is most convenient when trying to determine what label a pixel should have, or when re-estimating the planes using ECM, described below. The advantage of marginalization is that it allows us to use a plane to capture the motion of a region of an image, but also allows for relief (or parallax) out of that plane. By marginalization of the depths rather than MAP estimation, we avoid a strong commitment to depth estimation. Typically, too early a commitment to a depth estimate in convergence to a local (rather than global) maximum of the posterior likelihood (especially in homogeneous regions of the image). By marginalization, we are in effect "hedging our bets" and not committing to a single depth estimate. Rather, the distribution of depth at a pixel is specified by the mixture model. Next the posterior likelihood will be decomposed into its component parts and it will be explained how it can be optimized using the ECM algorithm.

Decomposition. Assuming that the number of layers m has been determined (techniques to do this are set out below) and the noise across the image is not spatially correlated, this can be evaluated as the product of the MAP likelihoods at each individual pixel.

$$\int_{\mathbf{Z}} \Pr(\boldsymbol{\Theta} \mathbf{Z} \mathbf{L} | \mathbf{D} \mathbf{I}) \, d\mathbf{Z} \propto$$

$$\int_{\mathbf{Z}} \prod_{xy} \Pr(\mathbf{D} | \boldsymbol{\Theta} z(x, y) l(x, y) \mathbf{I}) \Pr(\boldsymbol{\Theta} \mathbf{L} \mathbf{Z} | \mathbf{I}) \, d\mathbf{Z}$$

Considering each pixel individually, dropping the (x, y) index, adopting the notation $l_j(x, y)$ for $l(x, y) = j$ and let $\tilde{\mathbf{L}}$

be the set of labels excluding the label for pixel (x, y). Then

$$\Pr(\mathbf{D}|\mathbf{\Theta}lz\mathbf{I})\Pr(\mathbf{\Theta}\mathbf{L}\mathbf{Z}|\mathbf{I}) =$$

$$\sum_{j=1}^{j=m} \Pr(\mathbf{D}|z\mathbf{I})\Pr(l_j|\mathbf{I})\Pr(z|\boldsymbol{\theta}_j\mathbf{I})\Pr(\boldsymbol{\theta}_j|\mathbf{I})\Pr\left(l_j|\tilde{\mathbf{L}}\mathbf{I}\right)$$

which is a mixture model [5] between the layers, with spatial correlation between the label parameters.

The Likelihood. The term $\Pr(\mathbf{D}|z\boldsymbol{\theta}_j\mathbf{I})$ is the likelihood of the pixel having a particular depth (or disparity) hypothesis z. It can be evaluated from the cross correlation between the pixel in question and its correspondences in each other image of the sequence. As such, it only depends directly on the depth, and fixing z, can be written $\Pr(\mathbf{D}|\boldsymbol{\theta}_j z\mathbf{I}) = \Pr(\mathbf{D}|z\mathbf{I})$ (This is logically correct; the likelihood purely depends on the estimated disparity, it cannot depend on anything else. How z is influenced by $\boldsymbol{\theta}_j$ is explained below). Suppose that the variation in intensity between images can be modeled as Gaussian with mean μ_i and standard deviation σ_i. Let $\Delta i_j(x, y)$ be the difference in (colour) intensity between the pixel in image 1 and its corresponding pixel in image j. Then

$$\Pr(\mathbf{D}|z\mathbf{I}) = \prod_{j \neq 1}((1 - p_o)\Phi(\Delta i_j(x, y)|\mu_i\sigma_i) + \alpha p_o) \quad (8)$$

where $\Phi(\Delta i_j(x, y)|\mu_i\sigma_i)$ is the Gaussian likelihood

$$\Phi(\Delta i_j(x, y)|\mu_i\sigma_i) = \left(\frac{1}{\sqrt{2\pi}\sigma_i}\right)\exp{-\frac{\Delta i_j(x, y)}{2\sigma_i^2}} \quad (9)$$

and p_o is the probability of occlusion, or that the pixel is in some other way radically different (for instance due to the interpolation error when working out the cross correlation), and α is a constant being the probability of the intensity difference given an occlusion (uniform over the range of intensity). Equation (8) is a form of contaminated Gaussian with parameters $\mu_i, \sigma_i, \alpha, p_o$ and distribution denoted by $\Upsilon(\Delta i_j|\mu_i, \sigma_i, \alpha, p_o)$. It provides a robust error metric: the effect of any one observation is bounded. In our work $p_o = 0.05$ (although there is a switch in the code to switch this up between $0.05 - 0.1$ depending on how far away the pixel is, encoding the fact that more distant pixels tend to be occluded more), and $\alpha = (1/256)^3$ the range of pixel intensities for RGB.

As mentioned earlier, the depth is integrated out. To do this, the likelihood must be discretized and convolved with the prior. To discretize the likelihood given for each pixel the likelihood Equation (8) is estimated over a set of disparity hypotheses. Typically the scenes that we are dealing with are from video sequences, the inter-frame motion is 0-4 pixels, thus 20 disparity hypotheses increasing in steps of 0.2 can be used to sample the 0-4 pixel disparity range. Next, the form of the priors are explained.

The priors. Using the product rule, the prior can be decomposed as follows,

$$\Pr(\mathbf{Z}\mathbf{\Theta}\mathbf{L}|\mathbf{I}) = \Pr(\mathbf{Z}|\mathbf{\Theta}\mathbf{L}\mathbf{I})\Pr(\mathbf{\Theta}\mathbf{L}|\mathbf{I}). \quad (10)$$

There is no reason to assume a prior correlation between the parameters and shape of the projection of a plane[4] thus $\Pr(\mathbf{\Theta}\mathbf{L}|\mathbf{I}) = \Pr(\mathbf{L}|\mathbf{I})\Pr(\mathbf{\Theta}|\mathbf{I})$. The prior $\Pr(\boldsymbol{\theta}|\mathbf{I})$ on a given plane's parameters is assumed to be Gaussian on the parameters a, b, c with zero mean and standard deviations σ_a, σ_b and σ_c. This has a very interesting physical interpretation. If a and b represent the disparity gradients, σ_a, σ_b can be chosen to favour fronto-parallel planes, and to control the disparity gradient limit of the plane. This elegantly combines Bayesian reasoning with an old vision heuristic. The parameter σ is a weak prior favouring more distant planes, and penalizes ones that are too close to the camera. These are weak priors and will be over-ruled by observed data. They serve as a regularization that helps finesse the effects of outliers and ambiguity.

The prior $\Pr(\mathbf{Z}|\mathbf{\Theta}\mathbf{L}\mathbf{I})$ controls the amount of parallax favoured. In real situations points will not always lie exactly on a plane. Yet many surfaces can be modeled as a plane together with some relief leading to the much vaunted plane plus parallax algorithms. However, this idea is typically used as a heuristic without concrete definition. Bayesian methods allow the idea to be made concrete, by defining the distribution of $\Pr(\mathbf{Z}|\mathbf{\Theta}\mathbf{L}\mathbf{I})$ in terms of a distribution of the parallax from the plane. This allows the plane to be recovered without knowing the disparities. The distribution $\Pr(\mathbf{Z}|\mathbf{\Theta}\mathbf{L}\mathbf{I})$ is specified in terms of the amount of parallax, as a mean zero Gaussian with $\sigma_p = 0.5$. This may then be convolved with the discretized likelihood specified above. To recover the likelihood that any given pixel belongs to a given layer j, given the plane parameters $\boldsymbol{\theta}_j$, the integrated likelihood may be used: $\Pr(\mathbf{D}|l_j\mathbf{I}) =$

$$\int_z \Pr(\mathbf{D}|z\mathbf{I})\Pr(l_j|\mathbf{I})\Pr(z|\boldsymbol{\theta}_j\mathbf{I})\Pr(\boldsymbol{\theta}_j|\mathbf{I})\Pr\left(l_j|\tilde{\mathbf{L}}\mathbf{I}\right)dz \quad (11)$$

A uniform prior distribution is taken on z. This is easier than it looks to evaluate, since the integration merely involves 20 multiplications, one for each putative disparity.

The prior $\Pr(\mathbf{L}|\mathbf{I})$ represents our belief about the likelihood of the spatial disposition of the world. In the general case, it is not known how to evaluate this. However, what can be evaluated is the probability that pixel (x, y) has a label k given $\mathbf{L}$. Let $l_k(x, y)$ be an indicator variable such that $l_k(x, y) = 1$ if pixel (x, y) is in the k layer, or 0 otherwise. Then

$$\Pr\left(l_k(x, y)|\tilde{\mathbf{L}}\mathbf{I}\right) = \frac{\Pr\left(\tilde{\mathbf{L}}|l_k(x, y)\mathbf{I}\right)\Pr(l_k(x, y)|\mathbf{I})}{\Pr\left(\tilde{\mathbf{L}}|\mathbf{I}\right)} \quad (12)$$

---

[4]This is not entirely true as one would expect distant objects to be smaller in extent, but we do not consider that here.

the normalizing constant is just

$$\Pr\left(\tilde{\mathbf{L}}|\mathbf{I}\right) = \sum_{j=1}^{j=m} \Pr\left(\tilde{\mathbf{L}}|l_j(x,y)\mathbf{I}\right) \Pr\left(l_j(x,y)|\mathbf{I}\right) . \quad (13)$$

The prior $\Pr\left(l_k(x,y)|\mathbf{I}\right)$ is simply the probability that a given pixel lies in a given layer. In the absence of other information, it seems reasonable that this should be uniform, except however for layer of the plane at infinity l_∞, which is deemed more likely *a priori*. Given points with low disparity (and hence high variance in Z) it is reasonable to assign them to the plane at infinity rather than some arbitrary and ill conditioned plane. Using a factored approximation

$$\Pr\left(\tilde{\mathbf{L}}|l_k(x,y)\mathbf{I}\right) \approx \prod_{uv} \Pr\left(l(u,v)|l_k(x,y)\mathbf{I}\right) . \quad (14)$$

As $l(u,v)$ is not known, only its distribution, the above quantity is replaced by its expectation when using EM:

$$\Pr\left(\tilde{\mathbf{L}}|l_k(x,y)\mathbf{I}\right) \approx \prod_{uv} \sum_{j=1}^{j=m} \Pr\left(l_j(u,v)|l_k(x,y)\mathbf{I}\right) \Pr\left(l_j(u,v)|\mathbf{I}\right)$$

$$(15)$$

The question then is how to evaluate $p_{jk} = \Pr\left(l_j(u,v)|l_k(x,y)\mathbf{I}\right)$. What information do we have that might affect this distribution? All that we have *a prior* is the distance between the points Δd, and the difference in their colour values Δc. We would like the following properties for this distribution. If $l(u,v) = k$, we would p_{jk} to be high. If the two pixels are close and or of the similar colour, they are more likely to have the same label, falling off to a probability $1/m$ (where m is the number of layers), if the pixels are far apart or dissimilar in colour. We would like the converse to also be true: if $l(u,v) \neq k$, we would like p_{jk} to be low if the pixels have the same colour or are near, rising to $m-1/m$ if they are distant.

There is not a clear answer for what this distribution should be. In the future, we hope to try and learn it from the data. In the results section, we shall try several forms for the distribution. Here is one suggestion: the probability that the two pixels belong to the same layer $p_{jk}, j = k$ could be modeled by a contaminated Gaussian (defined above) $\Upsilon(\Delta c|\mu_c, \sigma_c, \alpha_c, p_c)$ where $p_c = 1/m$. The mixing parameter α_c controls the amount of homogeneity expected in the layer, the mean $\mu_c = 0$ and the standard deviation is set to be a function of the distance $\sigma_c = \beta_c/\Delta x$. This function satisfies all the desiderata given above, as well as possessing some interesting properties. Consider the log probability that a given pixel has label k

$$\log \Pr\left(l_k(x,y)|\tilde{\mathbf{L}}\mathbf{I}\right) = \sum_{uv} \log(m \Pr\left(l(u,v)|l_k(x,y)\mathbf{I}\right)) +$$

$$\log \Pr\left(l_k(x,y)|\mathbf{I}\right) + \text{constant}. \quad (16)$$

For each pixel nearby that is expected to have label k there will be a positive addition to this log likelihood proportionate to the colour similarity and inverse distance of that pixel.

In addition, if neighbouring pixels have a similar colour but are likely to have a label other than k, there is a negative contribution to the log likelihood. Thus if a pixel takes on a particular interpretation it not only excites its neighbours to have a similar interpretation, it also inhibits its neighbours of a similar colour from having a different interpretation.

6 Generalized EM

With the priors specified, the next problem is how to optimize the posterior likelihood of the interpretation. One method of estimation that has been used successfully for estimation of mixtures is the EM algorithm [4] in which the labels are treated as missing data. It is a useful procedure to find the mode of a posterior distribution $\Pr(\Theta|\mathbf{D})$ in which it is hard to maximize $\Pr(\Theta|\mathbf{D})$ directly but easy to work with $\Pr(\Theta|\mathbf{LD})$ and $\Pr(\mathbf{L}|\Theta\mathbf{D})$. The EM algorithm proceeds as follows: (i) Estimate the number of layers m, and the parameters of their associated planes using the algorithm described in Section 7; (ii) Replace missing data values $\mathbf{L}$ by their expectations given the parameters Θ (iii); Estimate parameters Θ assuming the missing data are given by their expected values; (iv) Re-estimate the missing values assuming the new parameters are correct, (v) Re-estimate the parameters, and so forth, iterating until convergence. The EM algorithm has the very desirable property that each of its cycles will increase the posterior likelihood.

E-Step The expectation step proceeds as follows: For a given label $l_k(x,y)$, dropping terms that are independent,

$$\Pr\left(\hat{l}_k|\mathbf{D}\theta_k\tilde{\mathbf{L}}\mathbf{I}\right) = \frac{\Pr\left(\mathbf{D}|l_k\mathbf{I}\right)\Pr\left(\tilde{\mathbf{L}}|l_k\mathbf{I}\right)\Pr\left(l_k|\mathbf{I}\right)}{\sum_{j=1}^{j=k}\Pr\left(\mathbf{D}|l_j\mathbf{I}\right)\Pr\left(\tilde{\mathbf{L}}|l_j\mathbf{I}\right)\Pr\left(l_j|\mathbf{I}\right)},$$

$$(17)$$

where the quantities on the right hand side are those estimated at the previous iteration, and $\hat{l}_k$ is to be estimated. This can be evaluated using equation (11) and (13).

M-Step The maximization step involves finding the set of plane parameters Θ that maximize (6). This is computationally difficult if all of the plane parameters are to be maximized simultaneously as in traditional EM, as there are $3m$ parameters to be determined, where m is the number of layers. Fortunately we can use the ECM algorithm [5], one of the generalized EM algorithms, in which the posterior likelihood still increases at each iteration. Rather than maximize all the parameters simultaneously each plane is maximized in turn using a gradient descent technique whilst the others are held constant. The covariance matrix of each plane is approximated by the Hessian of the error function at the minimum.

Extension The parameters of the noise may also be estimated if desired using the ECM algorithm. This is not done here however.

7 Initialization

'One forms provisional theories and waits for time or fuller knowledge to explode them. A bad habit, Mr. Ferguson, but human nature is weak' [5].

The ECM algorithm described in the last section is provable convergent to a maximum of the posterior distribution, which is all well and good, except that typically it will (a) take a very long time to converge (b) converge to a local maximum. **The most important thing in a segmentation algorithm is the initialization.** The ECM algorithm is no panacea for poor initialization, and for something as complicated as image segmentation, it will get trapped in local minima unless started with a good solution. Careful examination of Bayesian methods and the effects of data on the cost function lead to a more insightful approach.

Choosing the number of layers to maximize the posterior likelihood. The Bayesian method for model selection is encapsulated by (2) and the evaluation of the evidence for each model (one layer, two layers, three layers etc.). Evaluation of the evidence involves integrating the posterior probability (6) over the prior range of the parameters. At present, this is simply not computationally feasible, so we must think of a good approximation to the evidence. Examination of the posterior probability (6) reveals that only pixels that have a high entropy distribution for $\Pr(\mathbf{D}|z\mathbf{I})$ (entropy is simply $\sum p \log p$, with normalization $\sum p = 1$) will affect the posterior distribution of Θ. This is simply the intuition that pixels for which there is great uncertainty about a correspondence (e.g. those within homogeneous regions) contribute little to the accuracy of the estimation of the plane parameters. Thus, computational effort is concentrated on those pixels with high entropy.

To detect these, a feature extractor is run on the first image, and features with high entropy used as input to the algorithm. Next, for each model $\mathbf{M}_i$, with i layers, $i = 1 \ldots k$ the $3i$ parameters of the plane Θ_i are robustly estimated from the high entropy points. To do the robust estimation, a RANSAC like algorithm is used (which shall be referred to as PILLAGE), but with a vast improvement. Rather than maximize the number of inliers the posterior (6) itself is estimated for each sample.

The PILLAGE algorithm proceeds as follows: (1) simultaneously sample 3 spatial close points for each plane, (2) estimate the parameters of each plane $\theta_i, i = 1 \ldots k$, (3) estimate label probabilities (one step of EM), (4) calculate the posterior for this set of plane parameters. The sampling is repeated a fixed number of times, the best result stored, and then ECM is used to improve the result.

In this way we can get initializations of the plane parameters for each $\mathbf{M}_i$. The evidence can then be approximated assuming that each of the estimated plane parameters

---

[5] Sherlock Holmes, The Adventure of the Sussex Vampire.

is approximately normally distributed around its mode, discounting the effect of spatial correlation (this is not so bad as it sounds, as there is less spatial correlation between a sparse set of features, and this is only an approximation to get a rough idea as to how many layers we should use). The details of this calculation using Laplace's approximation are not given here due to space consideration and the reader is referred to a detailed explanation given in Sivia [7] page 88. Figure 1 shows the graphs of the approximated unnormalized posterior likelihood given models $\mathbf{M}$ comprising different numbers of layers.

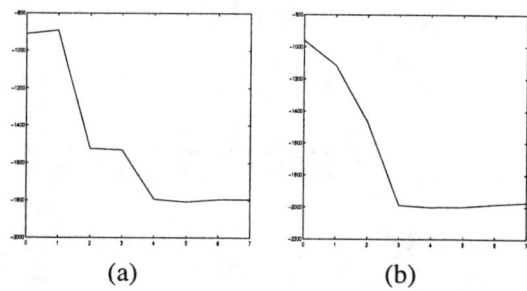

(a)   (b)

Figure 1. *The unnormalized approximation to the (negative log) posterior likelihood of the number of layers for (a) the garden (b) the Dayton sequences. For the garden sequence it can be seen that after four layers are selected the graph begins to increase with further layers being less likely. For three layers in the Dayton example.*

Initializing the Pixel Labeling Once the number of layers has been estimated, a labelling is assigned to the high entropy points. This is done by running the ECM algorithm *just on the high entropy points* at until convergence. This optimizes the segmentation of the points in which we have high confidence disparities prior to running ECM on every pixel.

8 Results

Figure 2 shows results on two sequences of six images: the MPEG garden sequence, and the Dayton Taylor symposium sequence. As the amount of support for the plane gets smaller, the parameters of the plane normal become increasing ill conditioned. Note for instance that the layer in 2 (o) is largely determined by the white haired fellow in the red shirt, and was fairly ill conditioned. It can be likened to a door on a hinge looking for something to latch on to–in this case it latched onto the jolly man on the left waving his arms in the air. This has happened for the layer shown in (r) to a lesser extent which is anchored by the large lady and the tree.

In the garden sequence (v) it is very difficult to segment the sky from the trees, as in this sequence the sky provides

Figure 2. *(a)-(d) four images of the garden sequence, (e)-(h) four images of the symposium sequence (provided by kind permission of Dayton Taylor) (i)-(k) top three layers with high entropy features superimposed on them. (l) Label image, cyan represents uncertain regions that have low confidence. (m)-(o) top three layers with high entropy features superimposed on them for Dayton Taylor sequence. (p) label image. (q)-(w) top four layers for each example sequence.*

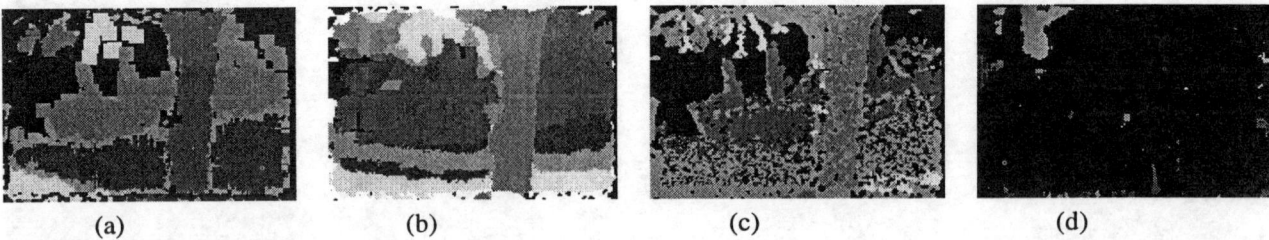

(a)   (b)   (c)   (d)

Figure 3. *(a)-(c) Effects of changing the prior by large amounts: (a) increased smoothness prior, (b) fronto parallel, (c) decreased smoothness prior (note that the twigs and branches are detected as seperate from the background) (d) Ambiguous piece of sky in the Dayton Taylor sequence.*

very little motion information being largely homogeneous, unless the prior on continuity for colour is turned up. But there is always a danger in choosing our prior that we see what we want to see. The effects of changing the prior on the Garden sequence segmentation are shown in 3 (a) for a prior with the smoothness (the probability two neighbouring pixels have the same label controlled by β_c) turned up, (b) for a prior favouring fronto-parallel planes (lower σ_a and σ_b), and (c) with smoothness turned down. In keeping with the Bayesian approach one should not only report the mode of the posterior but also solutions that might be "nearly as good". In Figure 3 (d) show another possible layer for the Dayton Taylor sequence that could also be part of any of the other layers with little change in the posterior likelihood as it is contains relatively little information (low entropy).

9 Summary and Conclusions

In this paper, we have developed a novel Bayesian framework for segmenting a 3D scene into plane+parallax layers. To initialize our ECM algorithm, we select high-confidence locations where the disparities are more likely to be known. From these the number of planes can be estimated, and the labelings of the rest of the pixels initialized from the initial labeling of the high entropy points. Several pieces of evidence are aggregated within a Generalized Expectation Maximization algorithm: the original votes from the image data as to the likelihood of a given disparity; the deviation from the plane equation of a particular layer; and the spatial and colour support of nearby pixels lying on the same layer. Because we use a Bayesian formulation, we can *integrate* all of the evidence for a particular layer (e.g., using an integral over all disparities weighted by the distance of a disparity to the plane), rather than relying on the most likely estimate (*mode*) provided by a traditional stereo algorithm. This approach is appropriate if we are primarily interested in the segmentation (e.g. for recognition). Otherwise a further step must be entered to estimate all the disparities. Although these can be obtained as MAP estimates in this scheme a more accurate modeling of occlusion may

be necessary for some scenes. This is the subject of future work.

A potential problem with the algorithm is that it segments purely based on the first image. This was done to get preliminary results as it was easy to implement. However the logical progression would be to model the planar layers in 3D as in [2], and use this generative model together with the methods outlined here for automatic segmentation.

We believe that the Bayesian framework developed in this paper provides a more principled approach to estimating layers than previous approaches. Instead of relying on heuristic assumptions such as smoothness or planarity, we are able to express our prior assumptions about the scene and the imaging process explicitly. The number of layers as well as the assignment of individual pixels to layers is automatically determined.

References

[1] S. Ayer and H. Sawhney. Layered representation of motion video using robust maximum-likelihood estimation of mixture models and mdl encoding. In *Proc. 5th Int'l Conf. on Computer Vision, Boston*, pages 777–784, 1995.

[2] S. Baker, R. Szeliski, and P. Anandan. A layered approach to stereo reconstruction. In *IEEE Computer Society Conference on Computer Vision and Pattern Recognition (CVPR'98)*, pages 434–441, Santa Barbara, June 1998.

[3] J. R. Bergen, P. Anandan, K. Hanna, and R. Hingorani. Hierarchical model-based motion estimation. In *Proc. 2nd European Conference on Computer Vision, LNCS 588, Santa Margherita Ligure*, pages 237–252, 1992.

[4] A. P. Dempster, N. M. Laird, and D. B. Rubin. Maximum likelihood from incomplete data via the EM algorithm (with discussion). *Journal of the Royal Statistical Society series B*, 39:1–38, 1977.

[5] A. Gelman, J. B. Carlin, H. S. Stern, and D. B. Rubin. *Bayesian Data Analysis*. Chapman & Hall, New York, 1995.

[6] E. T. Jaynes. Probability theory as extended logic. Not yet published a postscript version of this excellent book is available at ftp://bayes.wustl.edu/pub/Jaynes/, 1999.

[7] D. S. Sivia. *Data Analysis, A Bayesian Tutorial*. Clarendon, Clarendon, Oxford, 1996.

[8] R. Szeliski. A multi-view approach to motion and stereo. In *IEEE Computer Society Conference on Computer Vision and Pattern Recognition (CVPR'99)*, Fort Collins, June 1999.

[9] J. Y. A. Wang and E. H. Adelson. Layered representation for motion analysis. In *IEEE Computer Society Conference on Computer Vision and Pattern Recognition (CVPR'93)*, pages 361–366, New York, New York, June 1993.

[10] Y. Weiss. Smoothness in layers: Motion segmentation using nonparametric mixture estimation. In *Proceedings of IEEE conference on Computer Vision and Pattern Recognition*, pages 520–526, Puerto Rico, June 1997.

Modeling Bayesian Estimation for Deformable Contours

Stan. Z. Li   Juwei Lu

School of Electrical and Electronic Engineering

Nanyang Technological University, Singapore 639798

szli@szli.eee.ntu.edu.sg   http://markov.eee.ntu.edu.sg:8000/~szli/

Abstract

A novel trainable snake model, called EigenSnake, is presented in the Bayesian framework. In the EigenSnake, prior knowledge of a specific object shape, such as that of face outlines and facial features, is derived from a training set of the shape and incorporated into a Bayesian snake model in the form of the prior distribution. Further, a "shape space", which is constructed on the basis of a set of eigenvectors obtained from principle component analysis, is used to restrict and stabilize the search for the optimal solution. The effectiveness is demonstrated by experiments, which shows that the EigenSnake produces more reliable and accurate results than existing models.

1 Introduction

Correct location and extraction of objects of interest is an important step in many applications such as industrial inspection, medical image analysis, and object recognition. Deformable models, such as snake [7], G-Snake [8], Active Shape Model (ASM) [2] and deformable templates [6], are able to fit objects more closely and have proven to be more effective in detecting shapes subject to local deformation. Such models can be classified into two classes [6, 5]: (i) free-form, and (ii) parametric. In the free-form class, such as the snakes [13, 14], there is no global structure of the template; the template is constrained by only local continuity and smoothness constraints. Such models can be deformed to any arbitrary shapes deviating greatly from the shape of interest.

In the parametric class, a global shape model is designed and encoded by a small number of parameters [16, 4, 12, 8, 2, 11, 6, 1]. *Prior* knowledge about the structural properties is incorporated into the shape models, assuming that prior information of the geometrical shape or a set of training samples is available. Compared with the free-form class, the parametric class is more robust against to irrelevant structures, occlusion and bad initialization. A quite successful and versatile scheme in this class is that using statistical shape models in the Bayesian framework [3, 12, 11, 8, 6, 1]. In these models, both the prior knowledge and observation statistics are used to define the optimal, Bayesian estimate.

In this paper, a novel snake model, called EigenSnake, is presented in the Bayesian framework (Section 2). Three strategies are combined into the EigenSnake to make the object seeking more robust and accurate: (i) The prior knowledge of a specific object shape is derived from a training set of shape samples, and expressed as a prior distribution for defining a Bayesian estimate as the optimal solution for the object contour. The prior distribution can explain and represent the global and local variation in the training set. (ii) Constraints on object shapes are imposed in a "soft" manner, following the derived prior distribution. The shape encoding can adjust itself dynamically based on the up-to-date knowledge learned during the solution finding process. This adjustment allows the solution to fit more closely to the object shape. (iii) A shape space is constructed based on a set of eigenvectors derived by principle component analysis (PCA) performed on the training set. It is used to restrict and stabilize the search for the Bayesian optimum.

The affine invariant *shape matrix* method in the G-Snake [8] is used for encoding the global shape information. However, we noticed a drawback of the original method: It encodes the shape information in a "hard" manner in that the shape matrix is fixed. This actually assumes that the considered object shape undergoes only *rigid* (such as affine) transformation. So, only a small amount of local deformation is tolerated, and an incorrect solution results when the shape deformation is large, which is often a problem in many applications such as face detection. Because of this, a better solution, which is a contour fitting more closely to the object in the image, can have a higher energy value than an inferior solution. In contrast, in the Eigen-Snake, the shape matrix is dynamically modifiable based on the up-to-date information gathered from the solution finding process. This helps produce a more accurate result.

The shape space constraint used in the ASM [2, 9] is applied onto the solution finding process. The shape space, which is a subspace of the whole arbitrary contour space, explains and represents most of the non-rigid variance in the training set, based on the eigenvectors derived through PCA performed on the training contours. Every intermediate solutions (energy minima) is projected into the subspace and thus the solution is always restricted to be within the subspace. This proves to be effective in stabilizing the solution. However, in the ASM, no priori distribution accounting for global rigid motion is incorporated; therefore, the original ASM is unable to handle large scale and orientational shape-changes. This is amended in the Eigen-Snake.

Experiments are performed in the application domain of face extraction (Section 3). Four methods based on the G-Snake and the EigenSnake are compared to evaluate how various constraints and different prior knowledges have affected the results. Results demonstrate that the Eigen-Snake, as compared to the other three methods, is more stable to changes in scale and rotation and more robust to spurious structures and occlusions. It is also shown that the EigenSnake effectively overcomes problems due to initialization, occlusion and noise and produces much more accurate results.

2 Formulation of EigenSnake

The EigenSnake incorporates the prior knowledge about the distribution of training contours. The global and local variations in the training set are well represented by the resulting prior distribution. Moreover, a shape space is constructed to further constrain the solution.

2.1 Joint Prior Distribution

Let $\mathbb{E} = \left\{ (x, y) \in \mathbb{R}^2 \right\}$ be the image plane. An arbitrary contour can be represented by a vector of m points in $\mathbb{E}$, $f = [f_1^T, f_2^T, \cdots, f_m^T]$ (a $2 \times m$ matrix) where $f_i \in \mathbb{E}$ is a point. Given a prototype contour $\overline{f}$, a shape matrix $A = A(\overline{f})$ can be determined by $A(\overline{f})\overline{f}^T = 0$. The shape matrix is under affine transformation: If f^{aff} is an affine-transformed version of $\overline{f}$, then $A(\overline{f})f^{aff^T} = 0$ [8].

For the convenience of the following description, we express any contour as a $2m \times 1$ vector $f = [f_1, f_2, \cdots, f_m]^T \in \mathbb{R}^{2m}$. Given a prototype contour $\overline{f}$ and the corresponding shape matrix $A(\overline{f})$, the prior distribution of f is given as

$$p(f \mid \overline{f}) \propto \exp \left\{ -E(f \mid \overline{f}) \right\} \tag{1}$$

where $E(f \mid \overline{f}) = \sum_{i=1}^{m} \frac{E(f_i \mid \overline{f})}{\sigma_i^2}$ is the internal energy [8].

In the G-Snake, $\overline{f}$ is chosen to be the mean of the training contours and is fixed. This actually assumes that the

considered object shape (that of $\overline{f}$) is subject to *rigid* (such as affine) transformation only. However, it ignores prior knowledge about the fact that local variations exist among the training contours. This is equivalent to the assumption that f is a distribution with zero variance, which is obviously invalid with the training set. Since $\overline{f}$, and hence $A(\overline{f})$, is fixed, it is difficult for the solution f to converge closely to the object contour in the image when the local shape deformation is large (this is often the case for many applications such as face detection). Because of this, a better solution, which is a contour fitting more closely to the object in the image, can have a higher energy value than an inferior solution, as will be illustrated by experimental results. This is referred to as the incorrectness of an energy model.

The EigenSnake amends this problem by allowing $\overline{f}$ to deform according to a prior distribution derived from the training contour. In this case, the following joint prior is considered

$$P(f, \overline{f}) = p(f \mid \overline{f}) \cdot p(\overline{f}) \propto \exp\{-E(f, \overline{f})\} \tag{2}$$

Hence, the shape information is encoded in a "soft" manner, and $\overline{f}$ and hence $A(\overline{f})$ can be modified dynamically during the computation. The prior $p(\overline{f})$ is derived from a set of training contours in the following.

2.2 Learning Prior from Training Set

Let a set of L face contours $\{f^1, f^2, \ldots, f^L\}$ be given as the training set where each contour f^i is represented by a sequence of m evenly placed (done manually) points in $\mathbb{E}$ (i.e. $f_k^i \in \mathbb{E}$ and $f^i \in \mathbb{R}^{2m}$). The training contours are aligned at the centers of their gravities, and then scaled and rotated by using an iterative alignment algorithm so as to remove the rigid variation in the training samples as much as possible. Thus pre-processed contours constitute a random distribution. The mean contour $\overline{f}_{mean}$ is computed by averaging the corresponding contour points. See Fig.1.

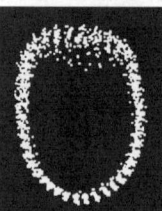

Figure 1. Left: A sample of face contour with $m = 44$ points. Middle: Scatter of points from normalized and aligned set of face boundary shapes. Right: The mean (average) of the training face contours.

Assume that the training samples obey a Gaussian distribution with the mean vector $\overline{f}_{mean}$ and the covariance matrix C:

$$p(f) \propto \exp\left\{ -\frac{1}{2} \left(f - \overline{f}_{mean}\right)^T C^{-1} \left(f - \overline{f}_{mean}\right) \right\}$$

(3)

The distribution represents the prior knowledge about local variation derived from the training contours. However, the covariance matrix C is often singular, thus C^{-1} non-existing, because the dimensionality of the samples is high and the number of available training contours is often small. The distribution has to be approximated by some means.

2.3 Approximation of Prior Using PCA

We adopt an optimal method proposed by Moghaddam and Pentland [10] to approximate the Gaussian density $p(f)$ by applying a PCA to the training samples to capture the main modes of the variation in the directionally elongated (*i.e.* elliptical) Gaussian distribution.

Let Ψ be the eigenvector matrix of C, and Λ be the corresponding diagonal matrix of eigenvalues. We have $\Lambda = \Psi^T C \Psi$. The first $M (\ll 2m)$ eigenvectors are selected: $\Phi = [\phi_1, \phi_2, \cdots, \phi_M]$. They are used as the basis vectors to constitute a specific *shape space* (*i.e.* the M-dimensional space spanned by the M orthonormal vectors). The shape space efficiently explains most of the local variation within the training set. Any contour $f \in \mathbb{R}^{2m}$ can be approximated by a linear combination of the M eigenvectors [15]

$$\hat{f} = \overline{f}_{mean} + \Phi\omega$$

(4)

where $\omega = \Phi^T (f - \overline{f}_{mean})$ is the vector of weights. $\hat{f}$ is the projection of f into the shape space, and ω is the coordinate of the projection point in the shape space. It provides an optimum approximation for f in the sense of least squares error. It discards the variation of f which is inconsistent with those reflected by training contours, while retaining most of the variation that the shape space can explain. The projection $\hat{f}$ has the following distribution [10]

$$p(\hat{f}) = p(\omega) = \frac{\exp\left\{ -\frac{1}{2} \sum_{k=1}^{M} \frac{\omega_k^2}{e_k} \right\}}{(2\pi)^{M/2} \prod_{k=1}^{M} e_k^{1/2}}$$

(5)

where e_k is the k-th largest eigenvalue of C, $\omega_k = \omega_k(f) = \phi_k^T (f - \overline{f}_{mean})$, $\varepsilon^2(f) = \left\| f - \overline{f}_{mean} \right\|^2 - \sum_{k=1}^{M} \omega_k^2$ is the residual error.

2.4 Prior Distribution of Prototype Contour

During solution finding process, the prototype contour $\overline{f}$ is modified dynamically according to the up to date MAP solution, and is confined in the shape space. The method is described below.

Denote the MAP solution currently found at iteration t by $f' = \arg\min_{f \in \mathcal{N}(f^{(t-1)})} E(f, \overline{f} \mid d)$ where $E(f, \overline{f} \mid d)$ is the posterior energy (to be defined later) and $\mathcal{N}(f^{(t-1)})$ is the neighborhood of previously found $f^{(t-1)}$. The MAP estimate f' is aligned with $\overline{f}_{mean}$ by minimizing $\left\| u + s \cdot R_\theta(f') - \overline{f}_{mean} \right\|$ where u (translation), s (scaling) and θ (rotation) are the rigid transformation parameters and $R_\theta(f)$ is a function that rotates the contour f by θ. The translation vector can be found as $u = (x_u, y_u) = \frac{1}{m} \sum_{i=1}^{m} [\overline{f}_{mean,i} - f'_i]$. The other two parameters can be calculated using a simple alignment algorithm. The aligned contour is given as $f'' = u + s \cdot R_\theta(f')$.

The aligned contour f'' is then projected into the shape space using Equ.(4), resulting in the projected version $\hat{f}''$. The prototype contour $\overline{f}$ is set to

$$\overline{f} = \hat{f}'' = \overline{f}_{mean} + \Phi\omega$$

(6)

where $\omega = \Phi^T(f'' - \overline{f}_{mean})$ is the coordinates of f'' in the shape space.

Therefore, $\overline{f}$ obtained in such a way follows the same distribution as that of $\hat{f}''$

$$p(\overline{f}) = p(\hat{f}'') = p(\omega)$$

(7)

as in Equ.(5). The corresponding prototype contour energy is

$$E(\overline{f}) = \frac{1}{2} \sum_{i=1}^{M} \frac{\omega_i^2}{e_i}$$

(8)

Note that $p(f \mid \overline{f})$ is scale and rotation invariant, and $p(\overline{f})$ depends only on the local deformation parameter vector ω and is independent of the global deformation parameter such as u, s, θ. As a consequence, $p(f, \overline{f})$ is also scale and rotation invariant, retaining the advantage of the prior distribution of the G-Snake.

To take the advantage of the shape space constraint, the solution found in iteration t is correspondingly revised into

$$f^{(t)} = -u + \frac{1}{s} \cdot R_{-\theta}(\hat{f}'')$$

(9)

The revised solution $f^{(t)}$ is in the shape space. It retains the rigid variation of f' (w.r.t. $\overline{f}_{mean}$), and has the local deformation consistent with the samples in the training set.

Two remarks about the imposition of the shape space constraints follow: (i) The imposition of the shape space constraint makes the EigenSnake more robust against spurious structures and occlusion. The effect will be demonstrated later in the experiments section. (ii) Because $\omega = 0$ when $f'' = \overline{f}_{mean}$, ω can be considered as the local deformation parameters of f'' or f'. Hence, the rigid transformation parameters (u, s and θ) and the non-rigid deformation parameters (ω) are separated. Therefore, the prior distribution $p(f, \overline{f})$ explains not only the global variation but also the local variation, derived from a training set.

2.5 Likelihood Distribution

Edges are detected from the image $d = \{d(x, y)\}$. The normalized edge direction at each pixel location (x, y), denoted $d^e(x, y) = (d_x^e(x, y), d_y^e(x, y))$, is used to provide constraints on the data, with $\|d^e(x, y)\| \in (0, 1]$ if an edge is detected at (x, y) or a zero vector $d^e(x, y) = 0$ if an edge is not detected there.

Denote the unit tangent directions of f by $f^e = [f_1^e, \ldots, f_m^e]$. The direction at a point $f_i = (x_i, y_i)$ can be estimated by using a finite difference formula: $\frac{f_{i+1} - f_i}{|f_{i+1} - f_i|} + \frac{f_i - f_{i-1}}{|f_i - f_{i-1}|}$. It is normalized into a unit-length vector: $f_i^e = (f_{x_i}^e, f_{y_i}^e)$, with $\|f_i^e(x, y)\| = 1$.

Constraints on the image d are imposed through the differences $\|f_i^e - d_i^e\|$. Assuming the differences have the same variance σ_e^2 for all i, we define the likelihood energy function as

$$E(d \mid f) = \frac{1}{\sigma_e^2} \sum_{i=1}^m \|f_i^e - d_i^e\|^2 \qquad (10)$$

where $d_i^e = d^e(x_i + x_u, y_i + y_u)$. The likelihood distribution can be defined as

$$p(d \mid f) = \frac{1}{Z'} \exp\{-E(d \mid f)\} \qquad (11)$$

where Z' is the normalizing constant

2.6 Bayesian Estimates

In the Bayesian framework, the problem of extracting a contour with unknown deformation from a given image can be posed as a problem of maximum a posterior (MAP) estimation. The posterior distribution of the EigenSnake is then defined as

$$p(f, \overline{f} \mid d) = \frac{p(d \mid f) \cdot p(f, \overline{f})}{p(d)} \qquad (12)$$

where $p(d \mid f) = p(d \mid f, \overline{f})$. The corresponding energy is

$$E(f, \overline{f} \mid d) = E(d \mid f) + E(f \mid \overline{f}) + E(\overline{f}) \qquad (13)$$

The MAP estimates f_{MAP} and $\overline{f}_{MAP}$ are then defined as

$$\{f_{MAP}, \overline{f}_{MAP}\} = \arg\min_{f, \overline{f}}\{E(f, \overline{f} \mid d)\} \qquad (14)$$

2.7 MultiEigenSnake

The EigenSnake is expanded into the MultiEigenSnake for detecting a compound object with multiple separate sub-objects. Suppose a compound object consists of L simple sub-objects. The shape of each sub-object is represented by a simple contour, and their combination is represented by a compound contour. Therefore, the MultiEigenSnake consists of $L + 1$ contours. For example, a

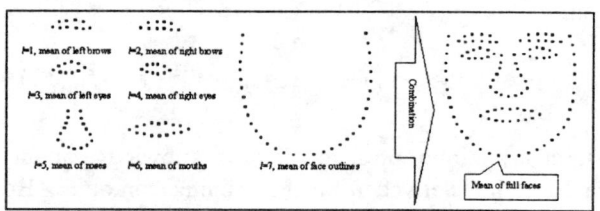

Figure 2. Means of training contours for MultiEigenSnake.

face, is considered as composed of $L = 7$ sub-objects: a face outline, a pair of brows, a pair of eyes, a nose and a mouth. Fig.2 shows the means of training contours and their combination for the representation of a full face.

Let $\overline{f^{ME}}$ denotes the prototype contours of the compound object, and $\overline{f}_\ell$ denotes the prototype contour of the ℓ-th sub-object. Corresponding to Equ.(13), we define the following posterior energy for the MultiEigenSnake

$$E(\overline{f^{ME}}, f^{ME}, f^1, \cdots, f^L, \overline{f^1}, \cdots, \overline{f^L} \mid d) = $$
$$E(\overline{f^{ME}}) + \sum_{\ell=1}^L [E(d \mid f^\ell) + E(f^\ell \mid \overline{f^\ell})] \quad (15)$$

The prior energy $E(\overline{f^{ME}})$ accounts for prior knowledge about local deformation of the compound object and the spatial configuration of its L sub-objects.

3 Experiments

Two sets of experiments are presented. The first examines the effects of using the specific prior knowledge and the shape space constraint by comparing the EigenSnake and other methods in extracting face outlines. The second set demonstrates the efficacy of the MultiEigenSnake in the extraction of the full facial features.

3.1 Comparison EigenSnake with Other Methods

Here, four methods are compared: the original G-Snake (GS), enhanced G-Snake with the shape space constraint imposed (GS+), EigenSnake without the imposition of the shape space (ES-), and the full EigenSnake (ES). Their respective performances will tell us how the incorporation of the specific prior knowledge (by comparing ES- vs GS, and ES vs GS+) and the imposition of the shape space constraint help improve the extraction of face outline (ES vs ES-, and GS+ vs GS).

The experiment data set contains 60 frontal face images of size 512×342 from the face database of Bern university. $m = 44$ landmark points are manually and evenly placed on the face outline of each training image as accurately as possible. A subset of 40 images are used as the *training set* and all the 60 images are used as the *testing set*.

The mean contours, which was shown in Fig.1:Right, is calculated from the training set. 8 eigenvectors are used to form the shape space. $M = 35$ eigenvectors are used to estimate the prior energy $E(\overline{f})$.

Contour initialization is done manually, as a common practice for snakes. It has the same shape as the mean contour but it is re-scaled randomly to between 70% and 120% of the true mean scale, shifted away randomly from the true position by between ± 20 pixels, and rotated randomly from the true orientation in the range of $\pm 15°$. All the methods have the same initial contour for each test image.

Table 1. Accuracy of the four methods.

Method	Init	GS	GS+	ES-	ES
D(method)	23.8	17.1	12.7	7.7	4.8

Table 1 compares the accuracy of face outlines detected by the four methods (plus that of the initial outline), where the accuracy is measured in terms of the average Euclidean distance (in pixels), denoted by D(method), between corresponding points in the extracted outline and the manual marked outline. The compared results illustrate that both the prior energy $E(\overline{f})$ and the shape space constraint can improve the accuracy. The improvement in accuracy made by the use of the shape space constraint may be calculated as $[(D(\text{GS}) - D(\text{GS}+)) + (D(\text{ES}-) - D(\text{ES}))]/2 = 3.65$ (the average of the two improvements, one from GS to GS+, the other from ES- to ES). The improvement in accuracy made by the use of the prior energy $E(\overline{f})$ may be calculated as $[(D(\text{GS}) - D(\text{ES}-)) + (D(\text{GS}+) - D(\text{ES}))]/2 = 8.65$ (the average of the two improvements, one from GS to ES-, the other from GS+ to ES). The two figures suggest that the contribution of the prior energy $E(\overline{f})$ is greater than that of the shape space constraint; in other words, more job was done by the imposition of the specific prior knowledge than by the use of the shape space constraint.

Fig.3 shows an example of face outline extraction. It can been seen that the GS often fails to localize objects. Although GS+ can modify the results of GS so that it looks more like "face outline", the improvement is less than that produced by ES- and ES. The two ES methods, which use the new energy functions with abundant prior knowledges incorporated, can effectively resist the disturbance from spurious structures, noisy edge map and improper initial scales.

The final energy values tell us the "correctness" of the four energy-minimization based models (for a correct energy model, a better solution should have a lower energy). The GS+ produced better results than the GS; however, the

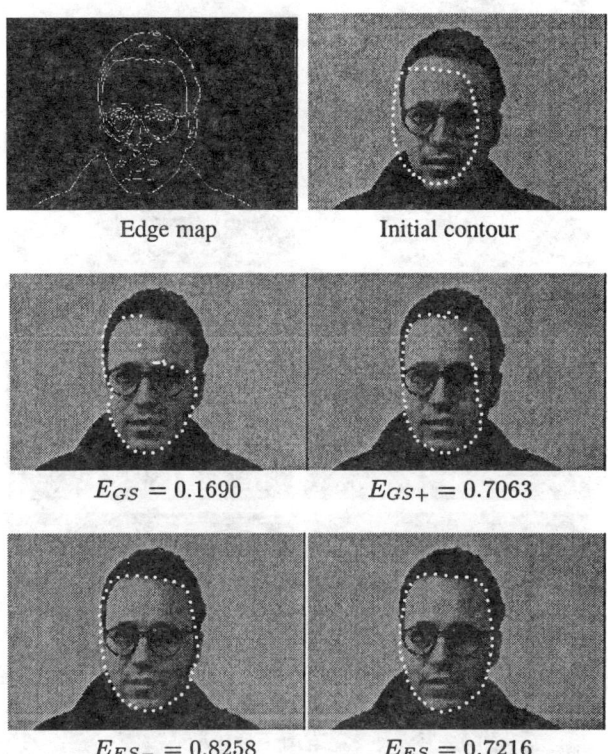

Edge map   Initial contour

$E_{GS} = 0.1690$ $E_{GS+} = 0.7063$

$E_{ES-} = 0.8258$ $E_{ES} = 0.7216$

Figure 3. Comparison of the four methods.

final GS+ energies are higher than corresponding GS energies. This means that the GS energy does not really define the optimal solution in its minimum and is therefore "incorrect". This is due to lack of constraint on the optimal solution. In contrast, the ES model has a proper energy function because a better solution is always associated with a lower energy.

3.2 Extracting Full Face Using MultiEigenSnake

This experiment demonstrates the MultiEigenSnake applied to extract a full face with $L = 7$ facial features. The training set consists of 120 frontal face images from the face database of Bern university. The testing set is chosen from the face database of Carnegie Mellon University.

A total of 108 landmark points is used to represent a full face, among which 10 for left brow, 10 for right brow, 10 for left eye, 10 for right eye, 17 for nose, 16 for mouth and 35 for the face boundary. The means of the training contours (shown as Fig.2) are used as initial prototype contours of L sub-models and the compound model respectively.

Some experimental results (initial (left) and final contours)are shown in Fig.4. Basically, the MultiEigenSnake can successfully extract the full face contours if the initial distance between the initial prototype contour and the target object is less than one fourth of the initial prototype

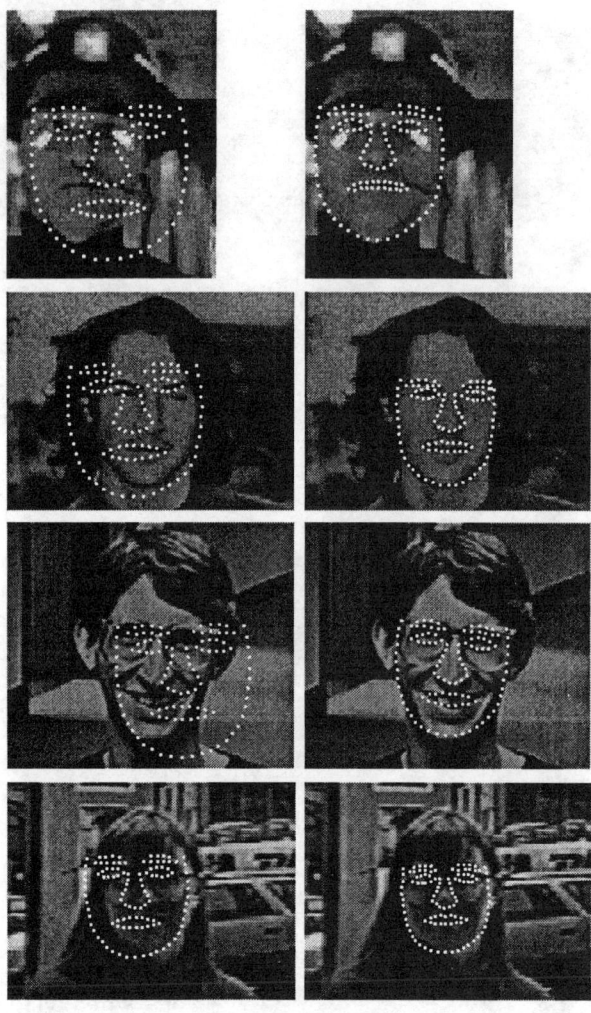

Figure 4. MultiEigenSnake results.

contour size. The MultiEigenSnake has certain scale insensitive and rotation insensitive; for example, it allows up to $\pm 20°$ rotation of initial prototype contour from orientation of the true object, as shown in Fig.4.

4 Conclusion

In this paper, we have presented a novel Bayesian model, EigenSnake, for extraction of deformable contours. The EigenSnake is trainable, general and capable of representing an arbitrary shape. It incorporates prior knowledge about both rigid and non-rigid deformations of expected shapes, and deforms to fit the contour in a way which reflects variations in the training set. The EigenSnake has the ability not only to account for global changes due to rigid motions, but also to learn local deformation of contours from examples. Experimental results show that the EigenSnake is more robust to initialization, spurious features, and occlusion, and can produce more accurate con-

tours than existing methods. The EigenSnake may be applied to other applications such as motion tracking. A more comprehensive report of this work can be found at http://markov.eee.ntu.edu.sg:8000/˜szli/papers/iccv99.ext.ps.

Acknowledgement This work was supported by NTU-AcRF RG 43/95 and RG 51/97.

References

[1] A. Blake, B. Bascle, M. Isard, and J. MacCormick. "Statistical models of visual shape and motion". *Phil. Trans. R. Soc. Lond. A*, 356:1283–1302, 1998.

[2] T. F. Cootes, C. J. Taylor, D. H. Cooper, and J. Graham. "Active shape models: Their training and application". *CVGIP: Image Understanding*, 61:38–59, 1995.

[3] U. Grenander. *Pattern synthesis: Lectures in pattern theory*. Springer-Verlag, 1976.

[4] U. Grenander and D. M. K. Y. Chow. *Hands : a pattern theoretic study of biological shapes*. Springer-Verlag, New York, 1991.

[5] A. K. Jain, Y. Zhong, and M.-P. Dubuisson-Jolly. "Deformable template models: A review". *Signal Processing*, 71:109–129, 1998.

[6] A. K. Jain, Y. Zhong, and S. Lakshmanan. "Object matching using deformable templates". *IEEE Transactions on Pattern Analysis and Machine Intelligence*, 18(3):267–278, March 1996.

[7] M. Kass, A. Witkin, and D. Terzopoulos. "Snakes: Active contour models". *International Journal of Computer Vision*, 1:321–331, 1988.

[8] K. F. Lai and R. T. Chin. "Deformable contour: modeling and extraction". *IEEE Transactions on Pattern Analysis and Machine Intelligence*, 17:1084–1090, 1995.

[9] A. Lanitis, C. J. Taylor, and T. F. Cootes. "Automatic interpretation and coding of face images using flexible models". *IEEE Transactions on Pattern Analysis and Machine Intelligence*, 19:743–756, 1997.

[10] B. Moghaddam and A. P. Pentland. "Probabilistic visual learning for object representation". *IEEE Transactions on Pattern Analysis and Machine Intelligence*, 19:696–710, 1997.

[11] D. Mumford. "Pattern theory: a unified perspective". In D. Knill and W. Richard, editors, *Perception as Bayesian Inference*, pages 25–62. Cambridge University Press, 1996.

[12] L. Staib and J. Duncan. "Boundary finding with parametrically deformable medels". *IEEE Transactions on Pattern Analysis and Machine Intelligence*, 14:1061–1075, 1992.

[13] D. Terzopolous, J. Platt, A. Barr, and K. Fleischer. "Elastically deformable models". *Comput. Graphic*, 21(4):205–214, 1987.

[14] D. Terzopolous, A. Witkin, and M. Kass. "Constraints on deformable models: Recovering 3d shape and nonrigid motion". *AI*, 36:91–123, 1988.

[15] M. A. Turk and A. P. Pentland. "Eigenfaces for recognition". *Journal of Cognitive Neuroscience*, 3(1):71–86, March 1991.

[16] A. L. Yuille, D. Cohen, and P. W. Hallinan. "Feature extraction from faces using deformable templates". In *Proc. CVPR*, pages 104–109, 1989.

Cluster-Based Segmentation of Natural Scenes

Eric J. Pauwels*

ESAT-PSI
K.U.Leuven
K. Mercierlaan 94
B-3001 Leuven, BELGIUM

Greet Frederix

Dept. of Mathematics
K.U.Leuven
Celestijnenlaan 200 B
B-3001 Leuven, BELGIUM

Abstract

In cluster-based segmentation pixels are mapped into various feature-spaces whereupon they are subjected to a grouping-algorithm. In this paper we develop a robust and versatile non-parametric clustering algorithm that is able to handle the unbalanced and irregular clusters encountered in such segmentation-applications. The strength of our approach lies in the definition and use of two cluster-validity indices that are independent of the cluster-topology. By combining them, an excellent clustering can be identified, and experiments confirm that the associated clusters do indeed correspond to perceptually salient image-regions.

Keywords: Segmentation, clustering, non-parametric, content-based image retrieval, grouping, density-estimation, regions.

1 Introduction

Segmentation has always played a central role in computer vision and recent years have witnessed marked resurgence in interest, due in part to the growing importance of *content-based image access and retrieval* (CBIR) for multi-media libraries. Here the aim is to retrieve images that are similar to a query-image. Extensive experimentation has shown that matching natural images solely on that basis of global similarities is often too crude an approach to produce satisfactory results. What is required is some form of *perceptually relevant* segmentation that allows one to identify a (small) number of salient and semantically meaningful image-regions. Once a number of such regions have been identified, it becomes possible to quantify their visual characteristics, location and spatial organisation with respect to each other, all crucial factors in the interpretation-process.

Clearly, as a first step towards tackling this problem, we need to agree what sort of image-regions are interesting or perceptually salient. *Saliency* is here defined in terms of *features* that capture essential visual or perceptual qualities such as colour, texture, shape-characteristics such as linearity or circularity, etc. ... Put differently, this means that when an image is mapped into the appropriate feature-space, salient regions (by their very definition) will stand out from the rest of the data and can more readily be identified. By the same token, pixels from disconnected parts in the image that have perceptually similar characteristics, will be mapped onto the same region in the appropriate feature-space and as a consequence can be grouped together.

Therefore, from an abstract point of view, segmentation and perceptual organization can be interpreted as a problem of *selecting appropriate features*, followed by *cluster-detection in feature-space*. In fact, we can tighten up this argument even further since both steps are but two aspects of the same problem, as a particular feature-space is deemed appropriate whenever it shows pronounced clusters. Indeed, if mapping the pixels into the feature-space lumps them all together, this particular set of features is obviously of little use in defining perceptual saliency.

This approach goes back at least to Coleman and Andrews [2], but a viable implementation of such a strategy has been severely hampered by the lack of reliable clustering-algorithms able to meet the challenges set by the highly unbalanced and convoluted clusters that are rife in image-processing applications. Indeed, clustering problems commonly encountered in low and intermediate level processing are particularly challenging as mapping the images to feature-spaces often produces very irregular data-clouds, a far cry from the Gaussian-like clusters seen in most textbook applications. Furthermore, given the fact that segmentation and region-extraction should proceed au-

*Postdoctoral Research Fellow, FWO Vlaanderen. Corresponding author; Email: eric.pauwels@esat.kuleuven.ac.be; http://www.esat.kuleuven.ac.be/~frederix/segmentation.html

tomatically, we cannot assume that prior knowledge about the number of clusters or their shape is available. This open-ended problem-formulation strongly suggests to adopt *non-parametric clustering methods,* and we will base our clustering-algorithm on *non-parametric density-estimation.*

2 Proposed non-parametric clustering-algorithm

2.1 Clustering based on non-parametric density-estimation

Clustering based on non-parametric density-estimation starts from the construction of a data-density obtained by convolving the dataset by a density-kernel. More precisely, given an n-dimensional dataset $\{x_i \in I\!R^n; i = 1 \dots N\}$, a density $f(x)$ is obtained by convolving the dataset with a unimodal density-kernel $K_\sigma(x)$ (typically a Gaussian):

$$f(x) = \frac{1}{N} \sum_{i=1}^{N} K_\sigma(x - x_i), \qquad (1)$$

where σ is the size-parameter for the kernel, measuring its width. After convolution we identify candidate-clusters by using *gradient ascent* (hill-climbing) to pinpoint local maxima of the density f. Specifically, the k nearest neighbours of every point are determined, whereupon each point is linked to the point of highest density among these neighbours (possibly itself). Upon iteration, this procedure ends up assigning each point to a nearby density-maximum, thus carving up the data-set in compact and dense clumps.

However, it is obvious that unless the clustering parameters (such as the width σ of the convolution kernel K_σ or the number of neighbours k) are preset within a fairly narrow range, this procedure will result in either too many (if σ is chosen too small) or too few clusters (if σ is set too large). A major part of the work on density-estimation concerns itself with this problem of choosing an "optimal" value for σ, but it is fair to say that it remains extremely tricky to try and estimate optimal (or even acceptable) clustering parameters.

For this reason *we have taken a different route.* We pick a value for σ which is small (with respect to the range of the dataset, see sect. 3) and, as before, proceed to identify candidate clusters by locating local maxima of the density f. As mentioned above, this choice of σ will result in an over-estimation of the number of clusters, carving up the dataset in a collection of relatively small "clumps" centered around local maxima. Next, we construct a hierarchical family of derived clusterings by using the data-density to systematically merge neighbouring clumps. More precisely, we establish an order of merging by comparing the density-values at neighbouring maxima with respect to the density at the "saddlepoint" in-between, which is defined as being the point of maximal density among the boundary points (i.e. points having neighbours in both clusters). Working systematically through this list of mergers produces the hierachically ordered family of clusterings. (Notice how this is very similar to the tree constructed in the case of hierarchical clustering, but with the crucial difference that the merging is based on the *density*, rather than on the *distance*, thus eliminating the unwelcome chaining-effect that vexes hierarchical clustering.) Now, in order to pick out the most satisfactory clustering we will concentrate on the development of *indices of cluster-validity* that directly assign a performance-score to every proposed clustering of the data.

2.2 Non-parametric measures for cluster-validity

A cursory glance at the clustering-literature reveals that there is no shortage of indices that measure some sort of grouping-quality. Some of the most successful are the silhouette coefficient (introduced by Kaufman and Rousseeuw), the (modified) Hubert-coefficient, the intra- over inter-variation quotient and the BD-index, introduced by Bailey and Dubes (see e.g. [3]). However, all of these coefficients are basically variations on the same theme in that they compare inter- versus intra-cluster variability and tend to favour configurations with ellipsoidally shaped well-separated clusters. Irregularly shaped clusters are problematic. It is for this reason that we have opted to restrict our attention to non-parametric indices which don't suffer the above-mentioned drawbacks.

Although an exact definition is difficult to come by, a "cluster" is understood to be a relatively *well-connected* region of high data-density that is *isolated,* in the sense that it is separated from other clusters by regions of low data-density (voids). We therefore introduce two non-parametric measures that quantify these qualitative descriptions for a given clustering of the dataset.

1. **Isolation** is measured in our algorithms by the *k-nearest neighbour norm* (NN-norm). More precisely, for fixed k (the precise value of which is not very critical), the k-nearest neighbour norm $\nu_k(x)$ of a data-point x is defined to be the fraction of the k nearest neighbours of x that have the same cluster-label as x. Obviously, if we have a satisfactory clustering and x is taken well within a cluster, then it is completely surrounded by points

with identical labels and therefore $\nu_k(x) \approx 1$. However, even nearby the boundary of a well-defined cluster we can still expect $\nu_k(x) \approx 1$, since most of the nearest neighbours will be located well within the interior of the cluster (see Fig. 1). Only when a bad clustering has artificially broken a densely populated region into two or more parts, we'll see that for points along the "faultline" $\nu_k(x)$ is significantly smaller than 1 (e.g. $\nu_k(x) \approx 0.5$). We get an measure of the homogeneity of the total clustering by averaging over all N points in the dataset:

$$\underline{\text{NN-norm:}} \qquad \mathcal{N}^{(k)} = \frac{1}{N} \sum_x \nu_k(x). \qquad (2)$$

In many regards, this is an extremely attractive quality-measure for clustering as it captures the fact that a cluster should be *isolated* with respect to the rest of the data. Furthermore, unlike most of the other criteria discussed above, it does not favour a particular cluster-structure, and is therefore very robust with respect to variations in the geometry of the cluster. This is most welcome, as most other criteria are biased towards compact sphere-like clusters.

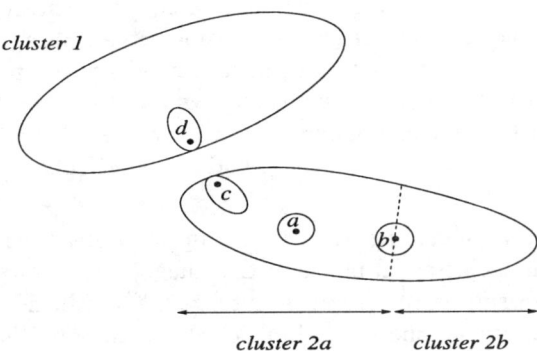

Figure 1: *Schematic representation of the so-called "nearest neighbour norm"; the neighbours of the point a obviously all have the same label. This is also the case for "boundary-points" such as c and d, since, unless k is very large, their neighbourhood of k nearest neighbours will be asymmetric and biased towards the high-density regions of their respective clusters. However, at the point b where the cluster is erroneously split in two different parts, only about half of the points have the same label as b.*

However, the major drawback of this index is that it doesn't notice whenever two clusters are merged, even if they are well-separated. In fact, lumping all points together in one big cluster, will

result in an optimal score for this criterion. For this reason we need an additional criterion that measures *connectivity*, i.e. that penalizes clusterings that erroneoulsy lump together widely separated clusters.

2. **Connectivity** relates to the fact that for any two points in the same cluster, there always is a path connecting both along which the data-density remains relatively high. In our algorithm we quantify this by choosing at random two points (say a and b) in the same cluster and connecting them by a straight line (see Fig. 2). We then pick a testpoint t halfway along this connecting line and subject it to gradient ascent to seek out its local density maximum. However, the constraint is that during its evolution the distance of this testpoint to either of the two "anchor-points" should remain roughly equal (to avoid that the testpoint converges to one of the anchor-points). In case the cluster has a curved shape, this allows the testpoint to position itself along the high-density crescent connecting the anchor-points. If the cluster-label at the repositioned testpoint coincides with the clusterlabels at the anchor-points a and b, the data-density $f(t)$ at this final position (averaged over a number of random choices for the anchor-points) can be used as a connectivity-indicator C (the so-called C-norm):

$$\underline{\text{C-norm:}} \qquad C = \frac{1}{K} \sum_{i=1}^{K} f(t_i) \qquad (3)$$

where t_i is the testpoint for K randomly chosen pairs of anchor-points (a_i, b_i). Notice how this dependence on a randomly chosen testset of anchorpoints makes the C-norm a *stochastic* measure. This has the advantage that we can easily quantify the confidence in the measure by generating several randomly chosen sets of anchorpoints.

Clearly, if the proposed clustering lumps together two well-separated clusters, many of these testpoints will get stuck in the void between the high-density regions, thus significantly lowering the value of this non-parametric connectivity-index.

2.3 Combining cluster-validity indices to select a clustering

¿From the previous considerations it transpires that in order to get a satisfactory clustering-result one has to try and maximise both indices simultaneously. However, as they are inversely correlated, any choice

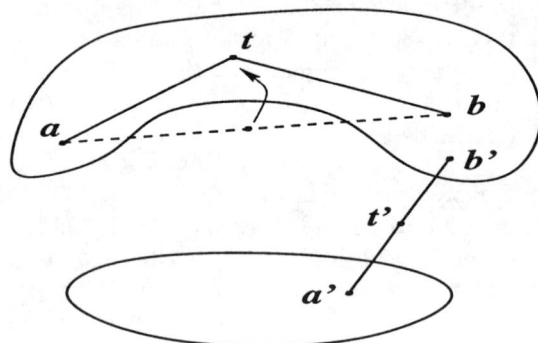

Figure 2: *Schematic representation of the (stochastic) connectivity index: the testpoint t is chosen halfway between the anchor-points a and b, and migrates towards the high density region without violating its "midpoint"-constraint. After convergence, the density at t is a measure of connectivity.*

will involve a trade-off between connectivity and isolation. The problem is further compounded by the fact that the relevant information is captured primarily by the way these indices change, rather than by their specific values. Typically, the NN-norm will decrease as the number of clusters grows, while the connectivity-index tends to increase, but both trends will usually exhibit a sudden transition whereafter they more or less level off. Localising such jump-events is the key to identifying important qualitative changes in the clustering.

However, as it is tricky to reliably identify such a "knee" in a graph, we go about it in a slightly different way. First of all, in order to make the indices directly comparable, we compute their Z-scores. Recall that the Z-score of an observation ξ_i in a sample $\xi_1, \ldots, \xi_\ell$ with mean $\overline{\xi}$ and standard deviation σ_ξ, is defined to be the standardised deviation:

$$Z(\xi_i) = \frac{\xi_i - \overline{\xi}}{\sigma_\xi}.$$

In fact, because the jumps cause the index-values for different clusterings to be rather irregularly spaced, additional sensitivity can be obtained by using $Z(\xi_i) = (\xi_i - \text{median}(\xi))/\text{MAD}(\xi)$, the robust version of the Z-score (MAD stands for *median absolute deviation*).

Since the NN-norm decreases as the number of clusters increases, large values for the Z-score will typically occur *before* the major downward jump of this graph, favouring well-isolated clusters. By the same token, high Z-scores for the connectivity-index C will be associated with clusterings following the ma-

jor up-jump in this graph, thus drawing attention to clusterings for which the individual clusters are well-connected.

To bring this to bear on the problem at hand, let L_p be the labeling for the pth clustering in the above-defined hierarchical tree, i.e. L_p maps each datapoint x to its corresponding cluster-label $L_p(x)$, (in most cases, p is equal to the total number of clusters in the clustering). Let $\mathcal{N}_p$ and C_p be the corresponding NN-norm and C-norm respectively, as defined by eqs.(2) and (3). The (robust) Z-score for the pth clustering is then defined to be

$$Z_p = Z(\mathcal{N}_p) + Z(C_p) \qquad (4)$$

and among the possible clusterings listed in the tree, we pick the one which maximises this robust Z-score.

3   Applications and discussion

Our original reason for embarking on this project was strongly motivated by the difficulties encountered in automatic segmentation of images for content-based image retrieval (CBIR). We therefore report in this paper on experimental results related to applications of the above-expounded clustering-algorithm to segmentation problems (mainly based on colour and texture). Although the underlying methodology is basically very simple and versatile, we consider it encouraging to find that the segmentations obtained are comparable to the state-of-the-art results, as can be found in recently published papers by, among others, Ma [4], Zhu *et.al.* [6], Carson *et.al.* [1], and Shi *et.al.* [5].

Pre-processing   To speed up computations, we didn't cluster all pixels in the image, but drew a random subsample (typically of size 2000) which we use as input for the algorithm. The remaining pixels were classified by computing the Mahalanobis-distance to the identified clusters. An additional bonus of subsampling is the fact that it is easy to draw a new and independent sample offering the possibility to check the stability of the first clustering.

Since the clustering-algorithm does not depend on the dimensionality of the space, it is easy to incorporate spatial information by including the pixel-coordinates as features (as has been suggested by a number of authors). This however turns out to be not a good idea as it often destroys cluster-information by spreading data-points over a extended region in feature-space. A far better way to include spatial information is by slightly averaging pixel-values (using convolution with a small mask) *before* mapping them into feature-space.

Choice of parameters We recall that there are basically two free parameters in our algorithm that needs to be preset. The first is k, the number of nearest neighbours that is used when computing the NN-norm (2). We fixed k to be *one percent* of N, the total number of datapoints, but with a minimum of $k = 10$. The second is the width σ of the convolution kernel K_σ that is used to generate the nonparametric density f. This is taken proportional to the average radius of the (smallest) ball that encloses the k nearest neighbours of a point. Hence the parameters are completely determined by the data and scale with the size and range of the dataset. Moreover, it is worth stressing the following two points. First, their specific value is not critical at all; all we need to make sure is that σ is "small" with respect to the range of the data (otherwise, the density will be over-smoothed), and that k is "small" compared to the total number of datapoints N. Secondly, we fixed the recipes for the determination of the parameter-values at the beginning of our experiments and then used *identical parameter-settings* for *all* datasets (both real and artificial)! So, this clustering proceeds truly *unsupervised*.

Experimental results We tested our algorithm on both artificial and real data. Our algorithm successfully partitioned a number of artificial datasets with complicated structures (such as banana- or ring-shaped clouds) that tend to trip up the more conventional clustering-algorithms (we refer the reader to our website[1]).

To generate real data we took a number of challenging natural images and mapped them into different colour- and texture-spaces whereupon we proceeded to cluster them. Some of the results are shown in Fig 3. The images in the first four rows are segmented by clustering in colour-space (in casu, *opponent colours* defined by $Y_1 = R - G$, $Y_2 = 2B - R - G$, and $W = R + G + B$). In the last row we show segmentation results based on texture-features. More precisely, in a window about each point we measured a small number of simple variability-coefficients, such as local variance and correlation-length. Clustering points with respect to these measures and mapping the identified clusters back into the image produced very acceptable segmentations.

We stress that *in all cases the number of regions in which the images were segmented was determined by the algorithm itself, on the basis of the number of clusters that were identified*. The fact that these clusters obviously correspond to perceptually meaningful regions underscores our contention that saliency is the result of datapoints clustering in appropriate feature-spaces!

Conclusion We have developed a generic and robust clustering-algorithm that determines both the shape and number of clusters. Segmentation based on the application of this algorithm in different feature-spaces, is able to extract perceptually salient regions from the image. Compared to classical clustering-algorithms such as K-means or Gaussian Mixture Models, our approach has the distinct advantage that *(i)* it determines the number of clusters automatically, and *(ii)* that it recognizes irregular (non-Gaussian) and unbalanced (large differences in cluster-size) clusters. Furthermore, being density-based it has none of the chaining-effects that vex hierarchical methods (which are distance-based).

We have illustrated the potential of the proposed algorithm on both artificial and real datasets. The latter were generated by mapping natural scenes in colour- or texture-spaces, but since the clustering-methodology is generic nothing prevents us from looking at other feature-spaces such as disparity, optical flow or edge-characteristics.

References

[1] C. Carson, S. Belongie, H. Greenspan, and J. Malik: *Region-Based Image Querying*. Proc. of CVPR'97 Workshop on Content-Based Access of Image and Video Libraries.

[2] G. Coleman and H.C. Andrews: *Image segmentation by clustering*. Proc. IEEE 67, 1979, pp. 773-785.

[3] A.K. Jain and R.C. Dubes: *Algorithms for Clustering Data*. Prentice Hall, 1988.

[4] W-Y Ma: *Netra: A Toolbox for Navigating Large Image Databases*. Ph.D.-thesis, Dept. of Electrical and Computer Engineering, University of California at Santa Barbara, June 1997.

[5] J. Shi and J. Malik: *Normalized Cuts and Image Segmentation*. Proc. IEEE Conf. oon Comp. Vision and Pattern Recognition, San Juan, Puerto Rico, June 1997.

[6] S.C. Zhu and A. Yuille: *Region Competition: Unifying Snake/balloon, Region Growing, and Bayes/MDL/Energy for multi-band Image Segmentation*. IEEE Trans. on PAMI, Vol. 18, No. 9, Sept. 1996.

[1] http://www.esat.kuleuven.ac.be/~frederix/segmentation.html

Figure 3: *Segmentation based on clustering in colour- (top 4 rows) and texture-space (bottom row). Scanning from left to right, top to bottom, the number of regions (for colour-segmentation in mean or false colours) identified by clustering was: stork and flamingo, 2 regions each; monkey-scene, 3; butterfly, 3 (notice the small yellow region); trees, 4; deer-scenes, both 3; antilope, 2; and 3 regions in each of the textured scenes.*

Curve Finder Combining Perceptual Grouping and a Kalman Like Fitting

Frédéric Guichard   Jean-Philippe Tarel
INRETS
2, ave. du Gen. Malleret-Joinville
BP 34-94114 Arcueil-Cedex, France

Abstract

We present an algorithm that extracts curves from a set of edgels within a specific class in a decreasing order of their "length". The algorithm inherits the perceptual grouping approaches. But, instead of using only local cues, a global constraint is imposed to each extracted subset of edgels, that the underlying curve belongs to a specific class. In order to reduce the complexity of the solution, we work with a linearly parameterized class of curves, function of one image coordinate. This allows, first, to use a recursive Kalman based fitting and, second, to cast the problem as an optimal path search in an directed graph. Experiments on finding lane-markings on roads demonstrate that real-time processing is achievable.

1 Introduction

Our study is motivated by the detection - via on-board camera - of road lane markings for automatic vehicle guidance. The difficulty of finding road markings and boundaries stems from two main facts. First, such "features" often suffer from low image contrast. They may also be masked by shadows, light spots, be partially occluded, or even be physically fragmented. Second, the extraction of markings must be performed in a reasonable time on a standard on-board computer.

To alleviate these adverse conditions, we assume that markings are ideally embedded into a family of smooth curves, S. A direct consequence of this modeling, is that we can now select edges based on their curve fitting performance, rather than a more traditional - and blind - gradient magnitude thresholding.

We favor the longest curves that belongs to S as characteristic of the features we seek to retrieve. Indeed, the existence of such curves in a typical image of a road, has a high probability to correspond to road boundaries or lane-markings.

When the family of curves S is of dimension 2 or 3, the Hough transform can be used to find the longest elements of that family. Nowadays, the most widely used curve finder involves, first, linking edgels via connectivity properties and, second, partitioning the result into line segments [7]. After such a partitioning the problem remains to aggregate such segments into curves [13]. In [4, 5] are proposed methods that follow the edgels and recursively fits a curve until the fitting error is large. But, important difficulties remain: the extracted curves are highly dependent on the selected starting points, as well as the order of the edgel linking. The approach we have explored tackles such problem.

Other approaches have been motivated by the idea of perceptual grouping. The edgels are organized as nodes of a graph, and linked to each other through arcs. The grouping relies on evaluating "perceptual cues", which are stored in each arc. Generally such cues correspond to some intuitive measure of the local geometrical consistency as evaluated for each pair of nodes. Measures such as alignment, co-circularity, and saliency have been proposed [14]. In [2] the grouping is modulated through statistical properties. Different algorithms have been proposed to find curves from such graphs, for instance: dynamic programming and relaxation (see [2, 1]). All such methods propose cues based on pair-wise interactions between edgels, and seem difficult to extend when a more global constraint on the curve is needed.

In [10], the author proposes a method that finds the longest convex subgraph. Convexity proves to be a strong enough constraint such that the computation can be performed by an exhaustive search.

We propose here to combine the above approaches tuned to the particular case of our road following application. The main difficulties are in designing (i) a global grouping technique that may result in a high combinatorial complexity, and (ii) a fitting technique (for the family S) that involves a large amount of computations. However, the problem can be drastically simplified thanks to two strong assumptions made on S. (1) We consider only parametric curves $x = f(y)$, where x is the horizontal coordinate, and y the vertical one. This is an acceptable assumption in the case of a vehicle well-aligned with the road. In turn this implies finding directed arcs between edgels, leading to a connected acyclic directed graph (i.e., a network). (2) We assume that S is a linear subspace of finite dimension, which allows us to use a recursive curve fitting.

The paper is organized as follow. First, we describe the variational statement of our problem. Second, we define a simple edgel detector based on level-lines. Third, we describe an efficient recursive implementation of the curve fitting using Kalman filtering. We then we show, how we can use it for finding curves described by $x = f(y)$ in an edgel set. Finally, we apply the designed technique to the retrieval of lane-markings on road images.

2 Geometric "Best-First Segmentation" of Edges

We want to select edges based on geometrical aspects. More precisely, we want to select a set of edgels corresponding to a shape approximatively in S. We define the fitting error e^{fit} of a set of edgels, $\{E_0, \ldots, E_m\}$, as the sum of the Least-Squared distances between the edgels and the best fitting shape s in S:

$$e^{fit}(E_0, \ldots, E_m) = \min_{s \in S} \sum_{i=0}^{m} d^2(E_i, s)$$

A large error indicates that the edgel set cannot be well represented by a curve in S. We obviously have

$$e^{fit}(E_0, \ldots, E_m) \leq e^{fit}(E_0, \ldots, E_m, E_{m+1})$$

which means that adding an edgel to a set of edgels will increase the fitting error. Therefore, in order to perform a grouping of edgels, we need to balance this increase of error. Hence we introduce a measure $e^{over}(\{E_0, \ldots, E_m\})$ based on the sum of the edgel lengths and on their density within the fitted curve. To balance the fitting error, it is sufficient that e^{over} satisfies:

$$e^{over}(E_0, \ldots, E_{m+1}) \geq e^{over}(E_0, \ldots, E_m) + e^{over}(E_{m+1})$$

A simple example of such a measure is the squared sum of the edgel lengths.

An "energy", that indicates how consistent the edgels are with respect to the best curve in S, can be defined by the weighted differences of e^{over} and e^{fit}:

$$G(E_0, \ldots, E_m) = \lambda e^{over}(E_0, \ldots, E_m) - e^{fit}(E_0, \ldots, E_m),$$

where λ controls the tradeoff between e^{fit} and e^{over}. We then derive the energy gain of grouping an edgel E_{m+1} with a set of edgels $\{E_0, \ldots, E_m\}$ by:

$$\Delta G = G(E_0, \ldots, E_m, E_{m+1}) - G(E_0, \ldots, E_m) - G(E_{m+1})$$

A positive ΔG represent a likely good grouping of edgels. A set of edgels having a large G is then clearly an important geometrical structure. Keeping only subsets, of the edgel set, that have a large enough G becomes a valid alternative over selecting edgels with respect to their contrast amplitudes. The problem is now how to find such subsets. Ideally, this involves finding the partition $\mathcal{P}$, of the edgel sets, that maximizes a "Mumford and Shah" like energy [12]:

$$E(\mathcal{P}) = \sum_{P \in \mathcal{P}} \left(\lambda e^{over}(\{E_i\} \in P) - e^{fit}(\{E_i\} \in P) \right)$$

(1)

Unfortunately, this problem is computationally difficult to solve for two reasons. First, the maximization is not local and its complexity is similar to the "salesman" problem. Second, this maximization of (1) requires the computation of e^{fit} for all subsets of the edgel set, which is highly computationally expensive. With respect to perceptual grouping techniques, the difference implied in our formulation is that global constraints are computed. Therefore, it is not obvious to directly apply one of the proposed algorithm that would computes an approximate solution. In addition, any iteration, with such algorithms, involves many fits of edgel subsets, which might not be computationally tractable.

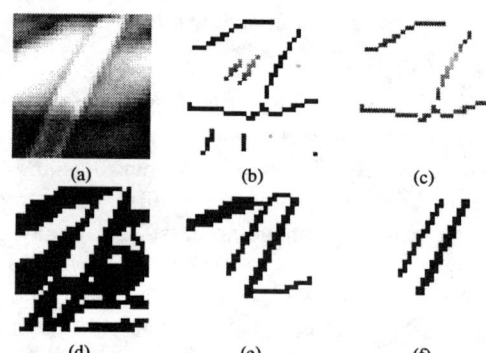

Figure 1. *(a) original image of a white lane perturbed by a spot light, results of Canny-Deriche edge detector with a 1 pixel size smoothing: (b) no threshold on the gradient magnitude and (c) 40 gray levels threshold. On the second line, results of the line segment detector for different values of the minimal length: (d) 4 pixels, (e) 15 pixels and (f) 20 pixels.*

Nevertheless, an approximative solution of (1) can be obtained in reasonable time under the following assumptions:

- Connected straight line edgels can be grouped together. Thus, edgels can be defined as straight line segments.

- The family of the shapes $\mathcal{S}$ is a linearly parameterizable subset of curves.

- The edgel set can be ordered. Therefore, the edgel graph is a connected acyclic directed graph.

Under these assumptions, we propose a new approach for an efficient partitioning which approximates the best solution $\mathcal{P}$ maximizing (1). Our approach consists in finding the longest edgel subset first. Then, to remove the found subset of the edgel set, and to iterate the optimal search for the next longest edgel subsets. With this partitioning approach, that we named *Best-First Segmentation*, the resulting subsets are ordered in decreasing energy.

3 Straight Line Segment Detector

3.1 Edgels as Straight Line Segments

Most of edge-detector algorithms involve (at least) a smoothing and a threshold steps [9]. Both steps decrease the number of resulting edgels, and in fact may remove useful information, as we explain below.

Smoothing. It removes from the image "small" details created by noise. Since, the chosen filtering is often linear, "small" detail means a "small" mix of spatial size and gray-level amplitude. Therefore the selection is harder on low-contrast zone. As example, we show in Fig. 1 (b) or (c), a Canny-Deriche edge detector applied on an image of a light spot on a white lane-markings. The magnitude of the gradient along the light spot is so strong that the smoothing removes the edge of the white lane-markings we want to detect.

Thresholding. It usually discards low contrast candidate edgels.

If we reduce as much as possible the effects of the smoothing and threshold steps, edgels in images are numerous, and a criterion for selecting these becomes mandatory. We believe that a selection based on geometrical considerations is a better alternative than one based on intensity contrast, as illustrated in Fig. 1.

3.2 Extracting Edgels

We start with an edge map defined as the set of all the *level lines* of the image. (As defined in [8], we call "level line" the boundary of a level set L_μ, i.e., the set of pixels having an intensity larger or equal to μ). Note that, at this point, no selection is performed. Of course, others edge map definitions could work (e.g. lines given by the zero crossings of the Laplacian). The important point here, is to reduce as much as possible the use of contrast-based selections, given the problems outlined above.

We then define an edgel as a straight segment embedded in the edge map, or equivalently, as part of a level line. Due to the use of an image grid, there exists only 8 possible local directions for any pixel. These directions are coded by

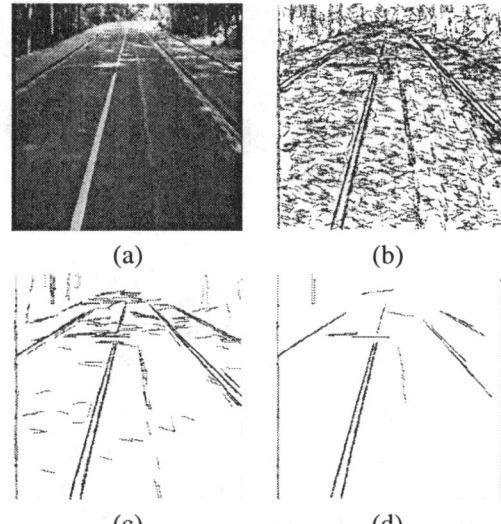

Figure 2. *(a) the original image and the result of the line segment detector for different values of the minimal length (b) 8 pixels, (c) 16 pixels and (d) 32 pixels.*

a number between 0 and 7, alike the well known Freeman codes. The list of directions on these connected edgels is thus equivalent to the chain-code of an edge.

Different algorithms have been proposed for recognizing when a chain code of a list of connected edgels is a straight line or not [11, 16]. Using such algorithms allows us to construct a complete tree of possible straight line chain-codes given a pre-specified target length. Due to the $\frac{\pi}{4}$ symmetry of the process, Freeman [16] proves that at most two basic directions are present in the chain code and these can differ only by unity, modulo 8. Therefore, this tree is a *binary tree*. Note that the size of such a tree remains relatively small.

Once the tree has been constructed, a fast algorithm for following connected straight segments of the edge map is used. Given a starting edgel, the tree of chain codes is traversed until a leaf is reached, i.e., until an end-point feature pixel is reached. We end up with a list of straight segments, denoted in the following by "edgels".

4 Curve Detector

In this section we explain how to group edgels lying on a certain shape and how to then find the principal curves from an image. As specified in Section 2, we first restrict our attention to a linearly parameterizable subset of underlying curves $\mathcal{S}$. Indeed as pointed out by [4], linear subspaces of curves allow recursive estimates of the curve parameters when a new edgel is provided. Noticeably, this is also the main property upon which Kalman filtering is based. Most common subsets such as straight lines, conics, cubics are examples of subspaces of curves. More complex curves may be approximated by higher degree algebraic curves [15].

We then consider the underlying curves explicitly described as a function of one of the image coordinates:

$$x = \sum_{i=0}^{d} f_i(y) a_i = F(y)^t A \qquad (2)$$

where (x, y) are the image coordinates of a point on the curve, $A = (a_i)_{0 \le i \le d}$ is the coefficient vector of the curve parameters, and $F(y) = (f_i(y))_{0 \le i \le d}$ is a vector of functions of the vertical coordinate y.

4.1 Recursive Fitting of a Curve in $\mathcal{S}$

As explained in Section 3, the used edgels are straight line segments with pixels as extrema. Thus, an edgel may be described by two pixel positions, i.e, by two points. Keeping in mind that we are still working on edgels, we will consider from now-on that the dataset comprises points only, for the sake of clarity.

The simplest way to fit a curve to data is to minimize distance over the set of given data points $(x_j, y_j)_{1 \le j \le m}$ with the least-squares criterion:

$$e_m^{fit} = \sum_{1 \le j \le m} (F(y_j)^t A_m - x_j)^2 \qquad (3)$$

The minimization of the previous fitting error gives the well-known normal equations:

$$M M^t A_m = M X_m \qquad (4)$$

where $X_m = (x_j)_{1 \le j \le m}$ is the vector of x coordinates, the matrix $M = (F(y_j))_{1 \le j \le m}$ is the *design matrix*, and $S_m = MM^t$ is the *scatter matrix*. Let $G_m = MX_m$, thus (4) is rewritten as $S_m A_m = G_m$. The computation of the best fit consists in solving the previous linear system.

Since the tasks of edgel grouping and curve fitting are not separable, a recursive algorithm is required. Given a new data point (x_{m+1}, y_{m+1}), we need to update the solution A_m to A_{m+1}. Therefore, an updated inverse of S_m is needed. We first compute the vector $F_{m+1} = F(y_{m+1})$. The updated scatter matrix is then given by $S_{m+1} = S_m + F_{m+1} F_{m+1}^t$, and we have $G_{m+1} = G_m + x_{m+1} F_{m+1}$.

In comparison to [4], where the recursive fitting is based on a QR decomposition of the design matrix M, we recast the curve fitting in the framework of Kalman filtering because less computer memory and power are then required. Kalman filtering is based on the following property for the updating:

$$(S + FF^t)^{-1} = S^{-1} - \gamma s^{-1} S^{-1} FF^t S^{-1} \qquad (5)$$

with $\gamma = (1 + F^t S^{-1} F)^{-1}$. Equation (5) assumes that the $p \times p$ matrix S can be inverted and is further based on the

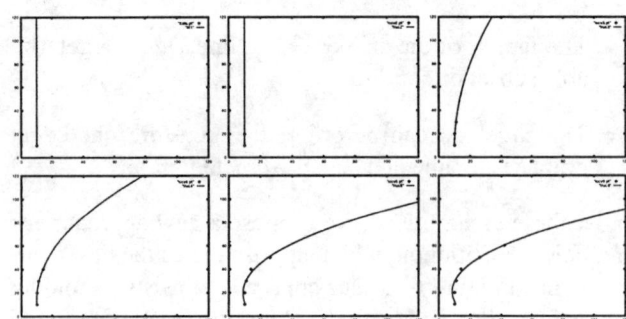

Figure 3. *Recursive fit with an increasing number of points (from 1 to 6) by a polynomial of degree 4. There is 5 parameters for this kind of curve. When the number of point is lower than 5, the recursive fitting algorithm gives curves of lower degree.*

fact that F is a vector of size p. From (5), we deduce the recursive computation of $K_{m+1} = S_{m+1}^{-1}$:

$$K_{m+1} = K_m - \gamma_{m+1} K_m F_{m+1} F_{m+1}^t K_m \qquad (6)$$

with $\gamma_{m+1} = (1 + F_{m+1}^t K_m F_{m+1})^{-1}$. The previous equation gives the so-called *covariance* matrix K_{m+1} of A_{m+1} as a function of the previous covariance matrix K_m and the vector F_{m+1}.

The updated curve parameters are then obtained via:

$$A_{m+1} = A_m + K_{m+1} F_{m+1} (x_{m+1} - A_m^t F_{m+1}) \qquad (7)$$

The recursive fitting algorithm consists in:

- Select an edgel and initialize the recursive fitting by setting K_0 to k times the identity matrix, and A_0 to zero. Then compute the covariance matrix K_1 using (6) and the curve parameters A_1 using (7).

- Given a new data point (x_{m+1}, y_{m+1}), the covariance matrix K_m is updated using (6) and the curve parameter vector A_m is updated using (7).

The previous choice of K_0 insures that (5) can be applied at each step without any problem, even if the number of points is not sufficient for constraining well-enough the least-squares minimization of (3). This is equivalent to the *Ridge Regression* regularization investigated in the context of non-recursive fitting of algebraic curves [15]. As shown in Fig. 3, when the data does not contain enough information for the accurate estimation of curves of degree d, the algorithm fits the data set by a lower degree curve.

The fitting error can be recursively updated, without requiring the updated curve parameters A_{m+1} and the updated covariance parameters K_{m+1}, using:

$$e_{m+1}^{fit} = e_m^{fit} + \frac{(x_{m+1} - A_m^t F(y_{m+1}))^2}{1 + F^t(y_{m+1}) K_m F(y_{m+1})} \qquad (8)$$

which is obtained by substituting (6) and (7) in (3). This is of practical importance for optimizing the speed of the curve finder described in the next section.

4.2 Search for the Best Curve

As explained in Section 2, our algorithm is not finding the curves in the image in a random order, but, rather, it first find the longest, and then the others ones by decreasing energy G.

Figure 4. *Main curves detected. Both longest curves are numbered. All curves have 3 parameters.*

The assumption of explicit curves allows us to order the edgels, e.g. in a decreasing order of the explicit coordinate (here y). Then, starting from the bottom of a curve (in the image), that curve is always grown upward toward smaller y.

We organize the edgels as nodes in an acyclic directed graph, where every edgel is linked to all other consistent edgels with smaller y coordinates. Let E_1 and E_2 be two edgels, we say that $E_1 \rightarrow E_2$ if there is a direct link in the graph, from E_1 to E_2. We associate to each edgel E: $E.c$ its coordinates, and the b best curves arriving at E. Each curve is specified by its energy $E.e$ (i.e G), its parameters $E.A$, its covariance matrix $E.K$, and its length $E.L$.

The Moore-Dijkstra algorithm performs optimal search when arc weights are fixed. Contrary to the use of local cues, these weights are unknown with fitted curves. Therefore, we propose a variation of the classical Moore-Dijkstra algorithm to find the longest path in the graph with positive but unknown arc weights:

For each ordered node E:

1. Compute the edgel energy $G(\emptyset, E) = \lambda e^{over}(E.c)$.

2. For the b best curves of every nodes E' such that $E' \rightarrow E$ compute:
$G(E', E) = E'.e + \lambda e^{over}(E'.L, E.c) - e^{fit}(E'.\{A, K\}, E.c)$.

3. Let $E_i.e$ be the $1 \leq i \leq b$ best G in step 2 and 1. Then compute the b best curves associated to the best energies: $E_i.\{A, K, L\} = RecFit(E_i'.\{A, K, L\}, E.c)$.

Figure 5. *Examples of main curves detected in images with complicated lightening conditions or with holes in the white lane-markings.*

At the end of the loop, the edgel with the curve of largest energy is the lowest coordinate edgel of the best curve. Finding the best curve is then straightforward. Let us described the ingredients of the algorithm:

e^{fit} is recursively computed as the distance of the extrema points of E to the chosen b best curve E_i' of E'. It uses (8) replacing x_{m+1}, y_{m+1} by the coordinates in $E.c$, and A_m, K_m by $E_i'.A, E_i'.K$.

e^{over} is the squared length, so that $e^{over}(E_i', E) = (E_i'.L + E.L)^2 = e^{over}(E_i') + e^{over}(E) + 2E.L \, E_i'.L$.

$RecFit$ denotes the recursive fitting where the edgel E is added to the fitted curve stored in E_i'. It follows formula (6) and (7), replacing A_{m+1}, K_{m+1} by $E.A$, $E.K$, and A_m, K_m by $E_i'.A, E_i'.K$. $RecFit$ may be reduced to initialize the fitting for the single edgel E to the straight line passing through it, as described in Section 4.1.

As we see, the algorithm involves two related loops on the edgels. Without, the proposed recursive process, a fitting step would have been needed *within* these two loops. Denoting by n the number of edgels, and considering an average of $n^{\frac{1}{2}}$ of edgels per curve, such a process would have yielded an average complexity of $bn^{\frac{5}{2}}$ (worse case is bn^3). The recursive fitting allows us to bring the fitting out of one loop as well as reducing its associated complexity. Inside the loops, it remains to estimate errors, which is a simple computation with fixed and small cost. The resulting complexity is therefore at worse bn^2.

The proposed algorithm represents a trade-off between optimality and efficiency. When b, the number of considered fitted curves for each node increases to the maximum path number, our search algorithm becomes optimal, to the detriment of processing speed.

5 Application to Real-time Video Analysis

Figure 6. *Left: Example of longest curves finding using cues based on only pair of edgels. (A fitting is performed afterwards on the found edgel subsets). We see that since no global geometrical constraints is asked, the edgels of the white marks are linked to a telegraphic post located out of the road. Right: two longest lines found by the algorithm.*

In this section we present experiments for curve detection in the context of lane-markings recognition for automatic control of vehicles [3, 6]. We assume here that the road is planar and that its shape may be approximated by a polynomial: $x^* = \sum_{i=0}^{d} a_i \, y^{*i}$. The transformation between the road plane (x^*, y^*) and the image plane (x, y) is: $x = l_x \frac{x^*}{y^*}$ and $y = l_y \frac{1}{y^*}$, where l_x and l_y are only functions of the camera calibration parameters. We set the origin of coordinate system to a point on the *line of horizon* - the position of this line can be computed from the camera calibration. We can then compute how the road is projected in the image as the curve:

$$x = \sum_{i=0}^{d} a_i y^{1-i} \qquad (9)$$

We have found experimentally that in most cases, $d = 2$ or 3 is sufficient for a correct approximation of the road shape. In Fig. 6, we compute the two best curves using only local cues (a), and the two best curves that stands in S (b). The first algorithm links the white lane markings to a telegraphic post, which constitutes the best curve having a small mean curvature. Whereas the second follows the lane markings which is better represented by a function of S. Figures 4 and 5 show the best found curves where d is respectively 2 and 3. Size of the images is 256×256. Typical computation time (in seconds) on a Pentium 200Mhz, 32Mo are: edgels set computation (keeping only those that are at least 8 pixels long): $0.04s$, and for best curve finding, when based on local cues: $0.06s$, when embedded in a family: between 0.1 and 0.5 second depending on d and on

the image complexity (only the best fitted curve is saved $b = 1$).

6 Conclusion

We have described an algorithm for finding subsets of edgels that are embedded in a specific family of curves. Thanks to two assumptions made on the family of curves - i.e., linear parameterization, and functions of one coordinate - we derived a process based on a classical graph algorithm combined with a Kalman based recursive fitting. This allows the process to run in a reasonable time. We are currently working on optimizing this algorithm, and extending the technique for finding more generic curves.

References

[1] T. Alter and R. Basri. Extracting salient curves from images: An analysis of the saliency network. *IJCV*, 27(1):51–69, March 1998.

[2] A. Amir and M. Lindenbaum. A generic grouping algorithm and its quantitative analysis. *PAMI*, 20(2):168–185, February 1998.

[3] T. K. C. Thorpe, M. Herbert and S. Shafer. Vision an navigation for the canegie-mellon navlab. *PAMI*, 10(3), 1988.

[4] D. Chen. A data-driven intermediate level feature extraction algorithm. *PAMI*, 11(7):749–758, July 1989.

[5] I. Cox, J. Rehg, and S. Hingorani. A bayesian multiple-hypothesis approach to edge grouping and contour segmentation. *IJCV*, 11(1):5–24, August 1993.

[6] E. Dickmanns and A. Zapp. A curvature-based scheme for improving road vehicle guidance by computer vision. In *Proceedings of SPIE Conference on Mobile Robots S.161-16*, volume 727, 1986.

[7] M. Fischler and R. Bolles. Perceptual organization and curve partitioning. *PAMI*, 8(1):100–105, January 1986.

[8] F. Guichard. *Axiomatization of images and movies scale-space*. PhD thesis, University of Paris IX-Dauphine, 1994.

[9] M. Heath, S. Sarkar, T. Sanocki, and K. Bowyer. A robust visual method for assessing the relative performance of edge detection algorithms. *PAMI*, 19(12):1338–1359, December 1997.

[10] D. Jacobs. Robust and efficient detection of salient convex groups. *PAMI*, 18(1):23–37, January 1996.

[11] W. G. Kropatsch and H. Tockner. Detecting the straightness of digital curves in O(N) steps. *Computer Vision, Graphics, and Image Processing*, 45(1):1–21, Jan. 1989.

[12] D. Mumford and J. Shah. Boundary detection by minimizing functionals. In *CVPR*, pages 22–26, 1985.

[13] P. Rosin and G. West. Nonparametric segmentation of curves into various representations. *PAMI*, 17(12):1140–1153, December 1995.

[14] A. Shashua and S. Ullman. Grouping contours by iterated pairing network. *Neural Info*, 3:335–341, 1991.

[15] T. Tasdizen, J.-P. Tarel, and D. Cooper. Improving the stability of algebraic curves for applications. *accepted in IEEE Transactions on Image Processing*, 1999. also as LEMS Tech. Report 176, Brown University.

[16] L. Wu. On the chain code of a line. *PAMI*, 4(3):347–353, May 1982.

Texture

Recognizing surfaces using three-dimensional textons

Thomas Leung and Jitendra Malik
Computer Science Division
University of California at Berkeley
Berkeley, CA 94720
{leungt,malik}@cs.berkeley.edu

Abstract

We study the recognition of surfaces made from different materials such as concrete, rug, marble or leather on the basis of their textural appearance. Such natural textures arise from spatial variation of two surface attributes: (1) reflectance and (2) surface normal. In this paper, we provide a unified model to address both these aspects of natural texture. The main idea is to construct a vocabulary of prototype tiny surface patches with associated local geometric and photometric properties. We call these 3D textons. Examples might be ridges, grooves, spots or stripes or combinations thereof. Associated with each texton is an appearance vector, *which characterizes the local irradiance distribution, represented as a set of linear Gaussian derivative filter outputs, under different lighting and viewing conditions.*

Given a large collection of images of different materials, a clustering approach is used to acquire a small (on the order of 100) 3D texton vocabulary. Given a few (1 to 4) images of any *material, it can be characterized using these textons. We demonstrate the application of this representation for recognition of the material viewed under novel lighting and viewing conditions.*

1 Introduction

We study the recognition of surfaces made from different materials such as concrete, rug, marble or leather on the basis of their textural appearance. Such natural textures arise from spatial variation of two surface attributes: (1) reflectance; and (2) surface normal. In this paper, we provide a unified model to address both of these aspects of natural texture.

In the past, texture recognition/discrimination has been posed primarily as a 2D problem. Viewpoint and illumination are assumed constant. Some representative techniques include Markov random fields [2] and filter responses [6, 16]. In all these work, surface normal variations are ignored. However, nature shows an abundance of such

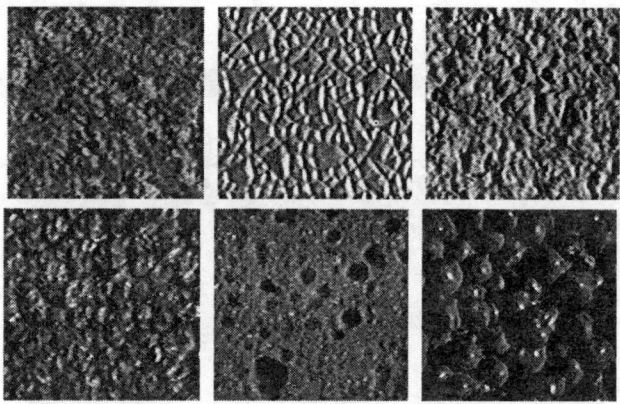

Figure 1. Some natural 3D textures from the Columbia-Utrecht database [4]. Left to right: "Terrycloth", "Rough Plastic", "Plaster-b", "Rug-a", "Sponge", "Painted Spheres". These textures illustrate the problems caused by the 3D nature of the material: *specularities*, *shadows* and *occlusions*.

relief textures. Examples are shown in Figure 1. Notice in particular the effect of surface normal variations: *specularities*, *shadows* and *occlusions*. Figure 2 shows samples of the same material under different viewpoint/lighting settings. The appearance looks drastically different in the 3 views. Recognizing that they belong to the same material is a challenging task.

Variations due to surface relief cannot be dealt with by simple brightness normalization or intensity transforms. For example, if the surface structure is a ridge, a dark-light transition in one image under one illumination will become a light-dark transition when the light source is moved to the other side of the ridge. Shadows also cause significant problems: two regions will have the same intensity under one illumination; while the shadowed region will be darker in another.

The complexity in the relationship between the image intensity values to the viewing/lighting settings and the properties of 3D textures led to recent interest in building ex-

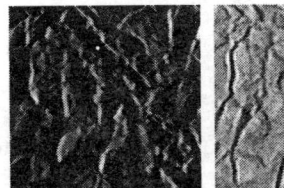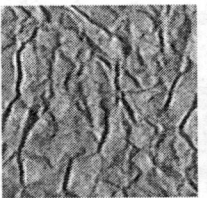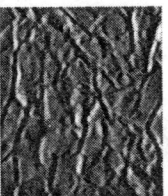

Figure 2. The same patch of the material "Crumpled Paper" imaged under three different lighting and viewing conditions. The aspect ratio of the figure is determined by the slant of the surface. Even though the three images are corresponding patches from the same material, the appearances are drastically different.

plicit models of 3D textures [3, 4, 13, 14, 20]. However, the problem of texture recognition under varying lighting and viewing conditions has not yet been addressed.

The main idea of this paper is the following — at the local scale, there are only a small number of perceptually distinguishable micro-structures on the surface. For example, the local surface relief $\hat{n}(x, y)$ might correspond to ridges, grooves, bumps, hollows, etc. These could occur at a continuum of orientations and heights, but perceptually we can only distinguish them up to an equivalence class. Similarly, reflectance variations fall into prototypes like stripes, spots, etc. Of course one can have the product of these two sources of variation.

Our goal is to build a small, finite vocabulary of microstructures, which we call 3D textons. This term is by analogy to 2D textons, the putative units of preattentive human texture perception proposed by Julesz more than 20 years ago. Julesz's textons [12] — orientation elements, crossings and terminators — fell into disuse as they did not have a precise definition for gray level images. In this paper, we re-invent the concept and operationalize it in terms of learned co-occurences of outputs of linear oriented Gaussian derivative filters. In the case of 3D textons, we look at the concatenation of filter response vectors corresponding to different lighting and viewing directions.

Once we have built such a universal vocabulary of 3D textons, the surface of any material such as marble, concrete, leather or rug can be represented as a spatial arrangement (perhaps stochastic) of symbols from this vocabulary. Only a small number of views are needed for this. Suppose we have learned these representations for some materials, and then we are presented with a single image of a patch from one of these materials, the objective is to recognize which one. We have developed a recognition algorithm using a Markov Chain Monte Carlo (MCMC) sampling method.

The structure of this paper is as follows. In Section 2, we show an operationalization of finding 2D textons from images. We analyze images of different viewing and light-

ing conditions together and extend the notion of textons to 3D textons in Section 3. The algorithm for computing a 3D texton vocabulary is given in Section 4. How a material is represented in terms of the learned textons is discussed in Section 5. The problem of 3D texture recognition is presented in Section 6 and results are shown for classifying materials under novel viewing and lighting conditions. In Section 7, we present an application of the 3D texton vocabulary to predict the appearance of textures under novel viewing and lighting conditions. We conclude in Section 8.

2 2D Textons

We will characterize a texture by its responses to a set of orientation and spatial-frequency selective linear filters (a filter bank). This approach has proved to be useful for segmentation [6, 16], synthesis [10], as well as recognition [18].

Though the representation of textures using filter responses is extremely versatile, one might say that it is overly redundant (each pixel values is represented by N_{fil} filter responses, where N_{fil} is usually around 50). Moreover, it should be noted that we are characterizing textures, entities with some spatially repeating properties by definition. Therefore, we do not expect the filter responses to be totally different at each pixel over the texture. Thus, there should be several distinct filter response vectors and all others are noisy variations of them.

This intuition leads to our proposal of clustering the filter responses into a small set of prototype response vectors. We call these prototypes *textons*. Algorithmically, each texture is analyzed using the filter bank shown in Figure 3. There are a total of 48 filters. Each pixel is now transformed to a $N_{fil} = 48$ dimensional vector. These vectors are clustered using a K-means algorithm [5]. The criterion for this algorithm is to find K *centers* such that after assigning each data vector to the nearest center, the sum of the squared distance from the centers are minimized. K-means is a greedy algorithm which will achieve a local minimum of this criterion.

K-means is a vector quantization algorithm [8]. A useful way to evaluate such algorithms is to compare the original image with the quantized image. Figure 4 shows such comparisons. The original image is shown in (a). The cluster centers are visualized in terms of the original filter kernels in (b). This is done by premultiplying the vectors representing the cluster centers by the pseudoinverse of the filterbank [11]. The reconstructed image after quantization is shown in (c). The close resemblance between (a) and (c) suggests that the quantization does not introduce much error perceptually.

In the next section, we will extend the texton theory to 3D textures — texture with significant local surface relief. For more discussions on 2D textons, the readers are referred

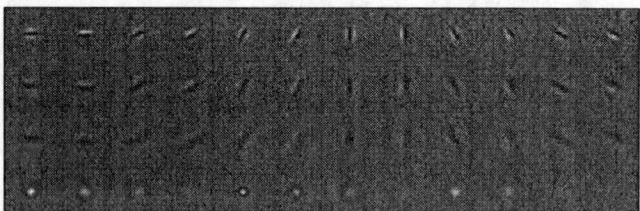

Figure 3. The filter bank used in our analysis. Total of 48 filters: 36 oriented filters, with 6 orientations, 3 scales and 2 phases; 8 center surround derivative filters and 4 low-pass Gaussian filters.

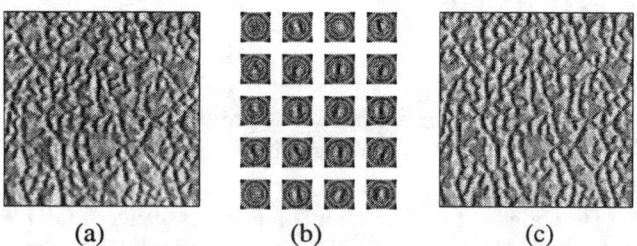

(a) (b) (c)

Figure 4. Illustration of K-means clustering and reconstruction from filter responses with $K = 20$. (a) Original image. (b) the K-means centers reconstructed as a local filter. These centers mainly correspond to the dominant features in the image: bars and edges at various orientations and phases; (c) Reconstruction of the quantized image. Close resemblance between (a) and (c) suggests that quantization does not introduce much error perceptually.

to [15], where we applied the idea of textons to the problem of image segmentation using multiple cues.

3 3D Textons

For painted textures with lambertian material, characterizing one image is equivalent to characterizing all the images under all lighting and viewing directions. However, for 3D textures, this is not the case. The effects of masking, shadowing, specularity and mutual illumination will make the appearance of the texture look drastically different according to the lighting and viewing directions (Figure 2). The presence of albedo variations on a lot of natural textures only makes the problem more difficult.

Let us first consider what the problems are if we try to characterize a 3D texture with only 1 image using the K-means clustering algorithm on filter outputs described in Section 2. Suppose the image of the texture consists of thin dark-light bars arising from 3 causes: (1) albedo change; (2) shadows; and (3) a deep groove. Despite the different underlying causes, all these events produce the same appearance in this particular lighting and viewing setting. Quite naturally, the K-means algorithm will cluster them together. What this means is that pixels with the same label

will look different under different lighting and viewing conditions: (1) the albedo change varies according to the cosine of the lighting angle (assuming a lambertian surface); (2) the location of the shadow boundary changes according to the direction of the light; and (3) the deep groove remains the same for a wide range of lighting and viewing conditions. Thus, we will pay a significant price for quantizing these events to the same texton.

To characterize 3D textures, many images at different lighting and viewing directions will be needed. Let the number of images be N_{vl}, with $N_{vl} \gg 1$[1]. The argument is that if any two local texture structures are equivalent under N_{vl} different lighting and viewing conditions, we can safely assume that the two structures will look the same under all lighting and viewing conditions. Notice that work in the literature have attempted to show that $3 - 6$ images will be able to completely characterize a structure in all lighting and viewing conditions [1, 19]. These results are not applicable because of the very restrictive assumptions they made: lambertian surface model and the absence of occlusion, shadows, mutual illumination and specularity. Indeed, deviations from these assumptions are the defining properties of most, if not all, natural 3D textures.

What this means is that the co-occurrence of filter responses across different light and viewing conditions specifies the local geometric and photometric properties of the surface. If we concatenate the filter responses of the N_{vl} images together and cluster these long $N_{fil}N_{vl}$ data vectors, the resulting textons will encode the appearances of dominant features in all the images. Let us first understand what these textons correspond to. Consider the following two geometric features: a groove and a ridge. In one image, they may look the same, however, at many lighting and viewing angles, their appearances are going to differ considerably. With the filter response vectors from all the images, we can tell the difference between these two features. In other words, each of the K-means centers encodes geometric features such as ridges at particular orientations, bumps of certain sizes, grooves of some width, etc.. Similarly, the K-means centers will also encode albedo change vs. geometric 3D features, as well as materials of different reflectance properties (e.g. shiny vs. dull). The appearances of different features and different materials at various lighting and viewing angles are captured by the filter responses. Thus, we call these K-means centers 3D textons, and the corresponding filter response vector, the appearance vector.

4 Constructing the Vocabulary of 3D Textons

Our goal in this paper is to use images from a set of materials (the training materials) to learn a vocabulary which characterizes all materials. This is a realistic goal because,

---

[1] $N_{vl} = 20$ in our experiments.

as we have noted, the textons in the vocabulary are going to encode the appearances of local geometric and photometric features, e.g. grooves, ridges, bumps, reflectance boundaries etc. All natural materials are made up of these features. In this section, we will describe the exact steps taken to construct this universal 3D texton vocabulary.

All the images used in this paper are taken from the Columbia-Utrecht dataset [4][2]. There are 60 different materials, each with 205 images at different viewing and lighting angles[3]. 20 materials are taken randomly as the training set. For each material, 20 images of different lighting and viewing directions are used to build the texton vocabulary. The 20 images for each material are registered using the standard area-based sum-of-square-differences (SSD) algorithm.

To compute the universal vocabulary, the following steps are taken:

1. For each of the 20 training materials, the filter bank is applied to each of the $N_{vl} = 20$ images under different viewing and lighting conditions. The response vectors at every pixel are concatenated together to form a $N_{fil}N_{vl}$ vector[4].

2. For each of the 20 materials individually, the K-means clustering algorithm is applied to the data vectors. The number of centers, denoted as K, for this step is 400. The K-means algorithm is initialized by random samples from the image.

3. The centers for all the materials are merged together to produce a universal alphabet of size $K = 8000$.

4. The codebook is pruned down to $K = 100$ by merging centers too close together or those centers with too few data assigned to them[5].

5. The K-means algorithm is applied again on samples from all the images to achieve a local minimum.

Steps 2 to 4 can be viewed as finding an initialization for the final K-means step in 5.

A comparison of the texton vocabularies of different sizes are shown in Figure 5. The filter responses from a frontal-parallel image of each material is quantized into the 3D texton vocabulary. Filter responses at each pixel are replaced by the appearance vector of the 3D texton labeled at the pixel. The SSD error between the reconstructed image and the original image is plotted in the figure[6]. The first diagram is the error for new samples of the training

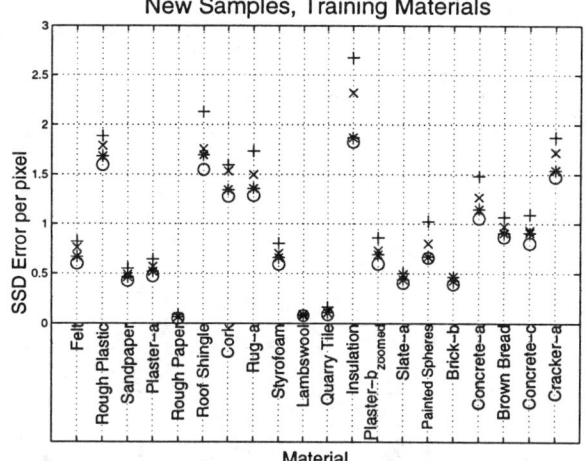

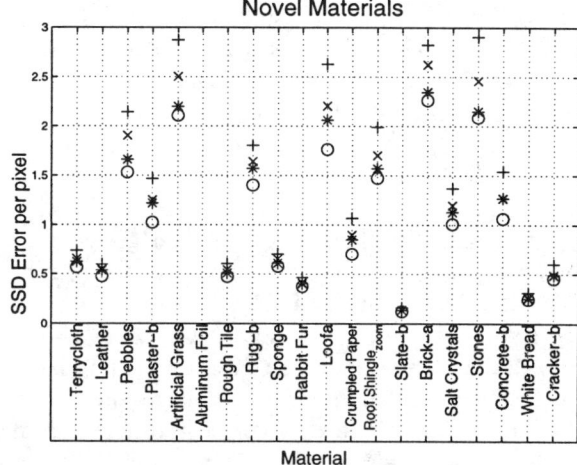

Figure 5. SSD reconstruction error for different materials. Top: the 20 materials used to create the texton vocabulary. Bottom: 20 novel materials. Several vocabularies of different sizes are created: "o" for $K = 800$; "*" for $K = 400$; "+" for $K = 200$ and "+" for $K = 100$.

materials[7]. The lower diagram is for novel materials. Notice three points: (1) there is no significant difference in the reconstruction error between training materials and novel materials. In other words, our texton vocabulary is encoding generic features, rather than material-specific properties. This is due to the small number of 3D textons allowed in our vocabulary. (2) The SSD errors are small for almost all materials. The 3D texton vocabulary is doing a very good job encoding the properties of the materials. This reconfirms our intuition that textures are made of a small set of features. (3) The differences between reconstruction errors from vocabularies of different sizes are not significant. In all the texture recognition results in this paper, the same texton vocabulary of size 100 is used.

---

[2] http://www.cs.columbia.edu/CAVE/curet/

[3] More images if the material is anisotropic.

[4] In our experiments, $N_{fil} = 48$.

[5] For the comparisons in Figure 5, $K = 800, 400$ and 200 as well.

[6] We recognize that the SSD error is by no means perceptually correct, but it is a convenient way of comparing two images.

[7] Note that these pixels are not in the training set, though they are from the materials used to construct the texton vocabulary.

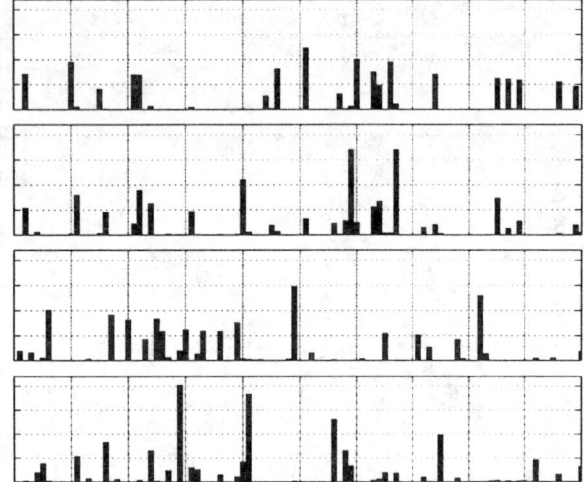

Figure 6. Top to bottom: the histograms of labels for the materials: "Rough Plastic", "Plaster-a", "Pebbles" and "Terrycloth" respectively. These histograms are the representation for recognizing the different textures.

In our studies here, only 20 ($N_{vl} = 20$) different viewing and lighting directions are used. 20 images form a very sparse sampling of the viewing and illumination spheres. When more images are available, we should take advantage of them. However, this does not mean that we need to run the clustering algorithm on a formidably large dimensional space. We argue that 20 images are enough to make sure that each 3D texton represents different local geometric/photometric structures. Therefore, to enlarge the appearance vector of each texton, we can simply append to the vectors the average of filter responses at pixels with the corresponding label.

5 Model Acquisition

Once we have built such a vocabulary of 3D textons, we can acquire a model for each material to be classified. Using all the images (under different viewing and lighting conditions) available for each material, each point on the surface is assigned one of the 100 texton labels by finding the minimum distance between the texton appearance vectors to the filter responses at the point. The surface of any material such as marble, concrete, leather or rug can now be represented as a spatial arrangement of symbols from this vocabulary. In this paper, we ignore the precise spatial relationship of the symbols and use a histogram representation for each material. Sample histograms for 4 materials are shown in Figure 6. Notice that these histograms are very different from each other, thus allowing good discrimination. The chi-square significance test is used to provide a measure between the similarity of two histograms (h_1 and h_2):

$$\chi^2(h_1, h_2) = \sum_{n=1}^{\#bins} \frac{(h_1(n) - h_2(n))^2}{h_1(n) + h_2(n)} \quad (1)$$

The significance for a certain chi-square distance is given by the chi-square probability function: $P(\chi^2|\nu)$. $P(\chi^2|\nu)$ is the probability that two histograms from the same model will have a distance larger than χ^2 by chance; and $\nu = \#bins - 1$. $P(\chi^2|\nu)$ is given by the incomplete gamma function [17]:

$$P(\chi^2|\nu) = Q(\nu/2, \chi^2/2) \quad (2)$$
$$\text{and} \quad Q(a, x) = \frac{1}{\Gamma(a)} \int_0^x e^{-t} t^{a-1} dt$$

where $\Gamma(a)$ is the gamma function.

6 Texture recognition

In this section, we will demonstrate algorithms and results on texture recognition.

6.1 3D Texture Recognition from Multiple Viewpoint/Lighting Images

We first investigate 3D texture recognition when multiple images of each sample are given. Every time we get a sample of the material, 20 images of different lighting and viewing directions are provided. From these images, a texton labeling is computed. Then the sample is classified to be the material with the smallest chi-square distance between the sample histogram and the model histogram. For each material, 4 disjoint samples of size 100×100 are to be classified. The overall recognition rate is 95.6%[8].

Another way to demonstrate the result is to use the classification matrix in Figure 7. Each element in the matrix e_{ij} is given by the chi-square probability function (Equation 2) that samples of material j will be classified as material i. Here, we only show the probability for 14 materials because of space limitations.

"Receiver Operation Characteristics" (ROC) curves are also good indications of the preformance . The ROC curve is a plot of the probability of detection versus the probability of false alarms. It is parametrized by a *detection threshold*. In our case, it is a threshold on the chi-square distance (τ). For any incoming sample, we declare that it is the same as material n if the chi-square distance between their histograms is smaller than τ. If the sample is indeed material

---

[8]Recognition rate is 95.0% for new samples of materials used to create the texton vocabulary and 96.3% for novel materials. There is no significant difference between the performance for the training materials and that of the novel materials in all our experiments. Therefore, we will report only the overall recognition performance. The main reason for this indifference in performance is that the texton vocabulary is encoding generic local features, rather than retaining material-specific information.

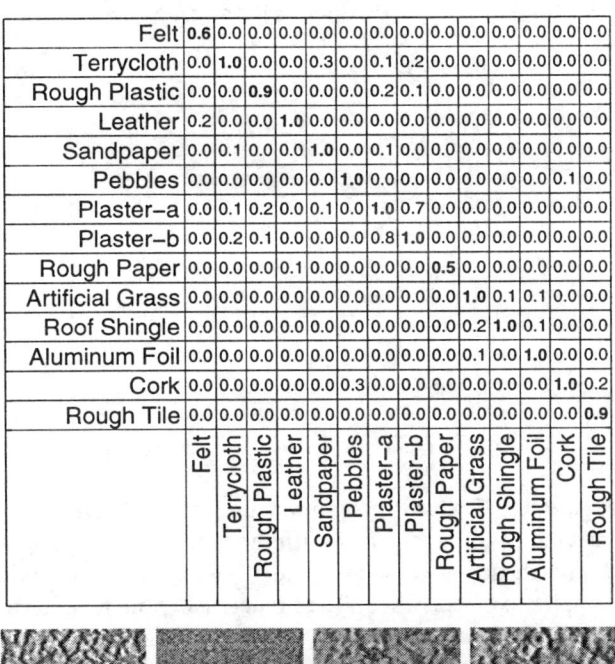

	Felt	Terrycloth	Rough Plastic	Leather	Sandpaper	Pebbles	Plaster-a	Plaster-b	Rough Paper	Artificial Grass	Roof Shingle	Aluminum Foil	Cork	Rough Tile
Felt	**0.6**	0.0	0.0	0.0	0.0	0.0	0.0	0.0	0.0	0.0	0.0	0.0	0.0	0.0
Terrycloth	0.0	**1.0**	0.0	0.0	0.3	0.0	0.1	0.2	0.0	0.0	0.0	0.0	0.0	0.0
Rough Plastic	0.0	0.0	**0.9**	0.0	0.0	0.0	0.2	0.1	0.0	0.0	0.0	0.0	0.0	0.0
Leather	0.2	0.0	0.0	**1.0**	0.0	0.0	0.0	0.0	0.0	0.0	0.0	0.0	0.0	0.0
Sandpaper	0.0	0.1	0.0	0.0	**1.0**	0.0	0.1	0.0	0.0	0.0	0.0	0.0	0.0	0.0
Pebbles	0.0	0.0	0.0	0.0	0.0	**1.0**	0.0	0.0	0.0	0.0	0.0	0.0	0.1	0.0
Plaster–a	0.0	0.1	0.2	0.0	0.1	0.0	**1.0**	0.7	0.0	0.0	0.0	0.0	0.0	0.0
Plaster–b	0.0	0.2	0.1	0.0	0.0	0.0	0.8	**1.0**	0.0	0.0	0.0	0.0	0.0	0.0
Rough Paper	0.0	0.0	0.0	0.1	0.0	0.0	0.0	0.0	**0.5**	0.0	0.0	0.0	0.0	0.0
Artificial Grass	0.0	0.0	0.0	0.0	0.0	0.0	0.0	0.0	0.0	**1.0**	0.1	0.1	0.0	0.0
Roof Shingle	0.0	0.0	0.0	0.0	0.0	0.0	0.0	0.0	0.0	0.2	**1.0**	0.1	0.0	0.0
Aluminum Foil	0.0	0.0	0.0	0.0	0.0	0.0	0.0	0.0	0.0	0.1	0.0	**1.0**	0.0	0.0
Cork	0.0	0.0	0.0	0.0	0.0	0.0	0.3	0.0	0.0	0.0	0.0	0.0	**1.0**	0.2
Rough Tile	0.0	0.0	0.0	0.0	0.0	0.0	0.0	0.0	0.0	0.0	0.0	0.0	0.0	**0.9**

Rough Plastic   Leather   Plaster-a   Plaster-b

Figure 7. Classification matrix for 14 materials. Each entry e_{ij} is given by the chi-square probability function (Equation 2) that samples of material j will be classified as material i. As shown in this figure, for example, "Leather" and "Rough Plastic" are likely to be classified correctly; while "Plaster-a" and "Plaster-b" are likely to be mistaken between them. Sample images from these four materials are shown as well.

n, we have a detection, otherwise, it is a false alarm. Figure 8 shows the ROC curve for our recognition problem. The top-left corner represents perfect recognition. Our algorithm performs very well.

6.2 3D Texture Recognition from a Single Image

Let us now consider the much more difficult problem of 3D texture recognition: for each material, the histogram model is built from 4 different light/view conditions; and for each sample to be classified, we only have a single image under *any* light/view condition. This problem is very similar to the problem formulation of object recognition — given a small number of instances of the object, try to recognize it under all poses and illumination. However, in the context of texture recognition, this problem is rarely studied.

A problem now arises in the fact that given only 1 image, finding the texton label for each pixel is very difficult. As

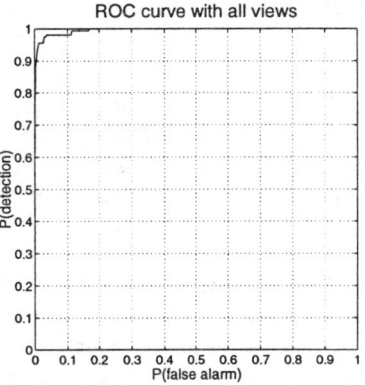

Figure 8. Receiver operation characteristics (ROC) curve for a very simple texture recognition problem. The top-left corner represents perfect recognition performance. The diagonal line refers to chance. The performance for our algorithm is very good.

noted before, in just one single viewing and lighting condition, physically different features may have the same appearance. Thus, trying to assign a texton label to the pixels from just one image is ambiguous. Doing it by simply assigning to the label with the smallest distance can result in a texton histogram that has no resemblance to that of the target material.

We solve this problem of finding a labelling using a Markov chain Monte Carlo (MCMC) algorithm. Instead of giving each pixel a single label in the texton vocabulary, we allow each pixel i to have N_i possibilities at first. The MCMC algorithm will try to find the best labelling given the possibilties and the material type.

An MCMC algorithm with metropolis sampling for finding texton labelling is shown below. For each material n and the corresponding model histogram h_n, do:

1. Randomly assign a label to each pixel i among the N_i possibilities. Call this assignment the initial state $x^{(t)}$ with $t = 0$;

2. Compute the probability of the current state $P(x^{(t)})$ using Equation 2 with h_n as the model histogram;

3. Obtain a tentative new state x' by randomly changing M labels of the current state;

4. Compute $P(x')$ with Equation 2;

5. Compute $\alpha = \frac{P(x')}{P(x^{(t)})}$;

6. If $\alpha \geq 1$, the new state is accepted, otherwise, accept the new state with probability α;

7. Goto step 2 until the states converge to a stable distribution.

What the MCMC algorithm does is to draw samples from the following distribution: $P(\text{labelling}|\text{material } n)$ or

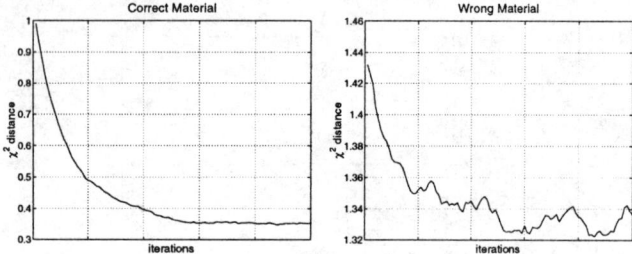

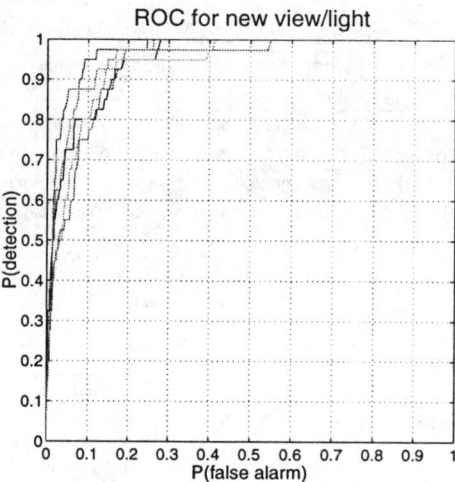

Figure 9. Left: the decay of the χ^2 distance between the histogram of the state $x^{(t)}$ and the histogram of the correct material. Right: same for a wrong material. For the correct material, the decay of the distance is much faster and the minimum distance is much smaller. Notice that the y-axes are at different ranges.

$P(x|h_n)$ where x is in the space of possible labellings. $P(x|h_n)$ is given by the chi-square probability function in Equation 2. Once the states settle in a stable distribution, we can compute the probability that the incoming image sample is drawn from material n by computing $\max_t P(x^{(t)}|h_n)$.

MCMC algorithms have been applied to computer vision for a long time, most well-known in the paper by Geman and Geman [7], where the problem of image restoration is studied. For details about variations in MCMC algorithms, convergence properties and methods to speed up convergence, please consult [9].

In our experiments, each pixel is allowed to have 5 possible labels, chosen from the closest 5 textons. In other words, $N_i = 5 \; \forall i$. Each iteration, we are allowed to change 5% of the size of the image (M in step 3)[9]. Figure 9 shows typical behavior of the MCMC algorithm. Shown on the left is the chi-square distance between the histogram of the state $x^{(t)}$ and h_n where material n is the correct material, while that for a wrong material is shown on the right. For the correct material, the decay of the distance is much faster and the minimum distance is much smaller (the y-axes are at different ranges).

The recognition performance is shown in the ROC curves in Figure 10. The 5 different curves represent 5 randomly chosen novel viewing and lighting directions for the samples to be classified. The model histogram for each material is obtained using images from 4 different view/light settings. The top-left corner of the plot stands for perfect performance. The performance of our algorithm is excellent. Given the difficulty of the task, one interesting comparison to make will be to contrast the performance of our algorithm and that of a human.

---

[9]A cooling schedule can definitely be employed here. At first, more sites are allowed to change to speed up exploration of the space. When the distribution is close to convergence, fewer sites are allowed to alter to "fine-tune" the distribution.

Figure 10. Texture recognition under novel lighting and viewing conditions. The 5 different curves represent 5 randomly chosen novel viewing and lighting directions for the samples to be classified. The model histogram for each material is obtained using images from 4 different view/light settings. The performance of our algorithm is excellent.

7 Novel View/Light Prediction

The universal 3D texton vocabulary can also be used to predict the appearance of materials at a novel viewing and lighting conditions. This application is of primary interest in computer graphics.

Consider one image of a novel texture at a particular lighting and viewing angle. We label the filter response vector at each pixel to one of the K elements in the texton vocabulary. In other words, each pixel in the input texture is labelled as being one of the K textons. Since we know exactly how each texton changes its appearance under a new lighting and viewing direction through the appearance vector, the appearance of the input image at a different viewing and lighting arrangement can be computed readily. If we have more images of the incoming texture (say 4), the labels can be computed using all these images.

Results for novel view/light prediction are shown in Figure 11. In these examples, 4 images of the material under different light/view arrangements are given. We then predict the appearance of the material at other lighting and viewing conditions using the texton vocabulary. The results shown are for novel materials—those not used to construct the texton vocabulary. The first column shows images obtained using traditional texture mapping; middle column shows the ground truth and the last column displays our results. Because traditional texture mapping assumes the surface is painted and lambertian, it produces images that look "flat". Our method, on the other hand, correctly captures the 3D nature of the surface — highlights, shadows and occlusions.

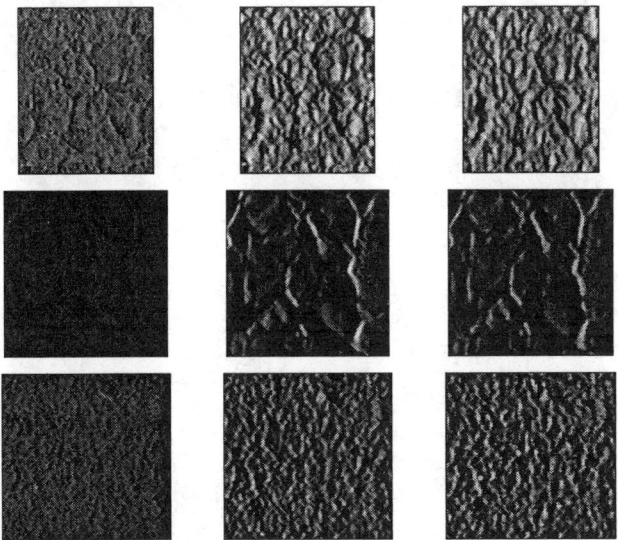

Figure 11. Predicting appearance of novel materials at various lighting and viewing conditions. First column: traditional texture mapping; middle column: ground truth; last column: results using texton vocabulary. Our algorithm correctly captures the highlights, shadows and occlusions while traditional texture mapping produces images that look "flat".

8 Discussion

In this paper, we have presented a framework for recognizing textures made up of both reflectance and surface normal variations. The basic idea is to build a universal texton vocabulary that decribes generic local features of texture surfaces. Using the texton vocabulary and an MCMC algorithm, we have demonstrated excellent results for recognizing 3D textures from a single image under any lighting and viewing directions.

Our model also enables us to recognize curved texture surfaces. The curved surface essentially provide multiple views and light directions in one image. Since our model for each material is invariant to light source direction or viewpoint, such curved surfaces can be handled the same way.

Acknowledgement

This research was supported by (ARO) DAAH04-96-1-0341, the Digital Library Grant IRI-9411334, and a Berkeley Fellowship to TL.

References

[1] P. Belhumeur and D. Kriegman. What is the set of images of an object under all possible illumination conditions? *Int. J. Computer Vision*, 28(3), 1998.

[2] R. Chellappa and S. Chatterjee. Classification of textures using gaussian markov random fields. *IEEE Trans. Acoust., Speech, Signal Processing*, ASSP-33, 1985.

[3] K. Dana and S. Nayar. Histogram model for 3d textures. In *IEEE Conf. Computer Vision and Pattern Recognition*, pages 618–24, Santa Barbara, CA, June 1998.

[4] K. Dana, B. van Ginneken, S. Nayar, and J. Koenderink. Reflectance and texture of real-world surfaces. *ACM Trans. Graphics*, 18(1):1–34, 1999.

[5] R. Duda and P. Hart. *Pattern Classification and Scene Analysis*. John Wiley & Sons, 1973.

[6] I. Fogel and D. Sagi. Gabor filters as texture discriminator. *Biological Cybernetics*, 61:103–13, 1989.

[7] S. Geman and D. Geman. Stochastic relaxation, gibbs distributions, and the bayesian restoration of images. *IEEE Trans. Pat. Ana. Mach. Int.*, 6:721–41, 1984.

[8] A. Gersho and R. Gray. *Vector quantization and signal compression*. Kluwer Academic Publishers, 1992.

[9] W. Gilks, S. Richardson, and D. Spiegelhalter. *Markov Chain Monte Carlo in Practice*. Chapman and Hall, 1996.

[10] D. Heeger and J. Bergen. Pyramid-based texture analysis/synthesis. In *Computer Graphics Proceedings, SIGGRAPH 95*, pages 229–38, Los Angeles, CA, Aug. 1995.

[11] D. Jones and J. Malik. Computational framework to determining stereo correspondence from a set of linear spatial filters. *Image and Vision Computing*, 10(10):699–708, Dec. 1992.

[12] B. Julesz. Textons, the elements of texture perception, and their interactions. *Nature*, 290(5802):91–7, March 1981.

[13] J. Koenderink and A. van Doorn. Illuminance texture due to surface mesostructure. *J. Optical Soc. Am. A*, 13(3):452–63, March 1996.

[14] T. Leung and J. Malik. On perpendicular texture or: Why do we see more flowers in the distance? In *IEEE Conf. Computer Vision and Pattern Recognition*, pages 807–13, San Juan, Puerto Rico, June 1997.

[15] J. Malik, S. Belongie, J. Shi, and T. Leung. Textons, contours and regions: cue integration in image segmentation. In *Proc. IEEE Intl. Conf. Computer Vision*, Corfu, Greece, Sept. 1999.

[16] J. Malik and P. Perona. Preattentive texture discrimination with early vision mechanisms. *J. Opt. Soc. America A*, 7(5):923–32, 1990.

[17] W. Press, B. Flannery, S. Teukolsky, and W. Vetterling. *Numerical Recipes in C*. Cambridge University Press, 1988.

[18] J. Puzicha, T. Hofmann, and J. Buhmann. Non-parametric similarity measures for unsupervised texture segmentation and image retrieval. In *Proc. IEEE Conf. Comp. Vis. and Pat. Rec.*, pages 267–72, San Juan, Puerto Rico, 1997.

[19] A. Shashua. On photometric issues in 3d visual recognition from a single 2d image. *Int. J. Computer Vision*, 21(1-2), 1997.

[20] B. van Ginneken, M. Stavridi, and J. Koenderink. Diffuse and specular reflectance from rough surfaces. *Applied Optics*, 37(1):130–9, January 1998.

Texture-Based Image Retrieval Without Segmentation

Yossi Rubner and Carlo Tomasi
Computer Science Department
Stanford University
Stanford, CA 94305
[rubner,tomasi]@@cs.stanford.edu

Abstract

Image segmentation is not only hard and unnecessary for texture-based image retrieval, but can even be harmful. Images of either individual or multiple textures are best described by distributions of spatial frequency descriptors, rather than single descriptor vectors over presegmented regions. A retrieval method based on the Earth Movers Distance with an appropriate ground distance is shown to handle both complete and partial multi-textured queries. As an illustration, different images of the same type of animal are easily retrieved together. At the same time, animals with subtly different coats, like cheetahs and leopards, are properly distinguished.

1. Introduction

Perceptually adequate descriptors of image texture are important cues for image retrieval [14, 15, 8, 13, 2, 21] when used in combination with other descriptors like color and shape. Gabor filters [9] where shown to be perceptually plausible texture descriptors [6], and, for individual textures, the Earth Movers distance (EMD) [19, 17] was shown to both match perceptual similarity well and tolerate variations in orientation, scale, illumination, and other sources of changes in texture appearance.

In image retrieval, however, multi-texture queries are to be compared to multi-texture images. How can individual texture descriptors and distances for texture comparison be lifted, so to speak, to the level of distances between entire *distributions* of textures descriptors? To make this task even harder, queries usually specify *partial* image content: one looks, say, for a cheetah chasing a zebra (multiple textures) without regard for the background (partial query). The standard answer [14, 8, 13, 11, 3] to these questions relies on texture segmentation. The images are first split into regions of uniform textures, and a similarity measure that compares individual textures is then applied between pairs of such re-gions. Thus, the similarity of two images will be determined by some combination of the similarities between pairs of regions in the two images. Two major problems with this approach are the following:

• Texture segmentation is hard, and the notion of "uniform texture" that it implies is not well defined. In addition, different segmentations may be plausible at different scales of resolution. For example, each leaf in a tree might be segmented out at one scale, while the whole tree-top or the whole forest might be considered to be individual regions at coarser scales. A mismatch between query and image descriptors in terms of resolution scales may lead to retrieval errors.

• Retrieval based on comparing texture segments is usually sensitive to over- and under-segmentation. On one hand, spatial changes in texture appearance can cause single textures to be split into smaller segments (over-segmentation). On the other hand, the segmentation algorithm can mistakenly combine together small regions of different textures (under-segmentation). In addition, problems may occur when some texture in the image, although significant in size when combined together, is scattered over the image and therefore lost. An example of this phenomenon is an aerial view of a town in a richly vegetated area, in which both buildings and vegetation are made up of numerous but small texture patches.

In this paper, we show that the EMD, which worked well for individual texture descriptors, can be used once more, at a higher level, to address all these difficulties at once, and that partial and multi-texture queries can be answered well on a database of complex, natural images without performing any segmentation. This is possible because of the EMD's built-in ability to find appropriate correspondences in texture space between the elements that comprise the query's texture distribution on one hand, and the image's distribution on the other.

1018

2. Distributions in Texture Space

Texture involves a strong notion of spatial extent: a single point has no texture. If texture is defined in the frequency domain, the texture information of a point in the image is carried by the frequency content of a neighborhood of it. Gabor functions are commonly used in texture analysis to capture this information (e.g. [4, 7, 13]). There is also evidence that simple cells in the primary visual cortex can be modeled by Gabor functions tuned to detect different orientations and scales on a log-polar grid [6].

In this paper we used a similar dictionary of Gabor filters as the one derived in [13][1]. Applying these Gabor filters to an image results for every image location in a texture vector

$$\mathbf{t} = [t_1, \ldots, t_d]^T , \qquad (1)$$

where d is the number of scales times the number of orientations that are used in the filter dictionary. We used four scales and six orientations so that $d = 24$.

These *texture features* reflect the components of the texture in terms of scales and orientations. Figure 1 shows an example of a texture feature. Part (b) shows the spatial average of each of the 24 filter responses over the image in part (a) of the figure. Darker squares represent stronger responses. Notice the two strong responses that correspond to the vertical and horizontal texture components at an intermediate scale.

The texture content of an entire image is represented by a distribution of texture features, a cloud of points in a space of 24 dimensions. This distribution accounts for four sources of variation in the filter responses:

1. The size of the basic texture element ("texton") is often larger than the support of at least the finest scale Gabor filters. This causes a variation in the filter responses even within textures that a human would perceive as homogeneous in the image. To address this variation, many texture analysis methods (see for instance [1, 22, 12]) integrate filter responses over areas that are larger than the largest filter support.

2. Texture regions that a human would perceive as being homogeneous *in the world* can produce inhomogeneous regions *in the image* because of foreshortening and variations in illumination. This spreads the distribution in texture space and increases its variability.

3. Textures exhibit spatial variation even in the world. For instance, most natural textures are regular only in a statistical sense, so filter responses will vary regardless of viewing conditions.

4. Images with multiple textures result in a combination of the distributions of the constituent textures.

Because of all these sources of variation, a single image can produce nearly as many 24-dimensional texture vectors

[1] The full derivation of our Gabor filters can be found in [17]

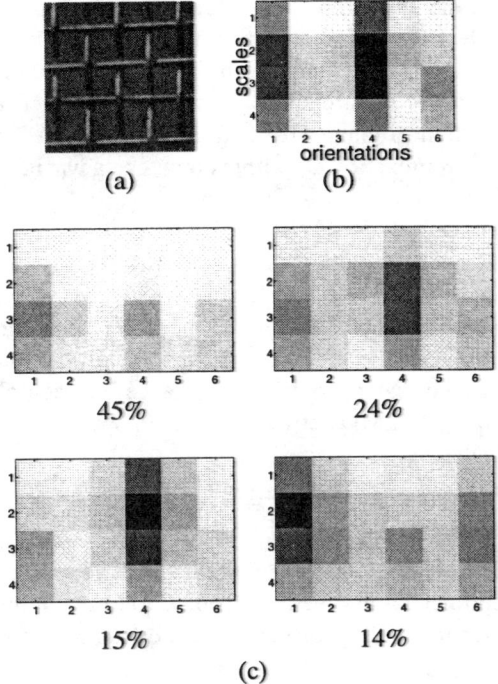

Figure 1. (a) Texture patch from [5]. (b) Average over all texture features. The Gabor filter bank consists of four scales and six orientations. (c) The four clusters in the texture signature together with their weights (in percentage of the number of pixels).

as it has pixels. To represent the full distribution of image texture in a compact way, we first find the dominant clusters in the 24 dimensional texture space by using a similar clustering algorithm as the one used for color in [18]. This algorithm returns a variable number of clusters depending of the complexity of the distribution. While this method is simple and fast, so that large number of images can be processed quickly, more sophisticated clustering algorithms (e.g., see [3]) may further improve our texture similarity methods. The resulting set of cluster centers together with the fractional cluster weights is the *texture signature* of the image. An example of a texture signature with four clusters is shown in Figure 1(c).

3. Texture Distance

In [19] the *Earth Mover's Distance* (EMD) is introduced as a flexible similarity measure between multidimensional distributions, and is described in detail in [17]. Intuitively, given two distributions represented by signatures, one can be seen as a mass of earth properly spread in space, the other as a collection of holes in that same space. Then, the EMD measures the least amount of work needed to fill the holes with earth. Here, a unit of work corresponds to transporting a unit of earth by a unit of *ground distance*, which is a distance in the feature space. The EMD is based on the transportation problem [10] and can be solved efficiently by linear optimization algorithms that take advantage of its special structure.

Formally, let $P = \{(\mathbf{p}_1, w_{\mathbf{p}_1}), \ldots, (\mathbf{p}_m, w_{\mathbf{p}_m})\}$ be the first signature with m clusters, where $\mathbf{p}_i$ is the cluster representative and $w_{\mathbf{p}_i}$ is the weight of the cluster; $Q = \{(\mathbf{q}_1, w_{\mathbf{q}_1}), \ldots, (\mathbf{q}_n, w_{\mathbf{q}_n})\}$ the second signature with n clusters; and $\mathbf{DIST} = [\text{dist}(\mathbf{p}_i, \mathbf{q}_j)]$ the ground distance matrix where $\text{dist}(\mathbf{p}_i, \mathbf{q}_j)$ is the distance between clusters $\mathbf{p}_i$ and $\mathbf{q}_j$. The EMD between signatures P and Q is then

$$\text{EMD}(P, Q) = \frac{\sum_{i=1}^m \sum_{j=1}^n f_{ij}\text{dist}(\mathbf{p}_i, \mathbf{q}_j)}{\sum_{i=1}^m \sum_{j=1}^n f_{ij}} . \quad (2)$$

where $\mathbf{F} = [f_{ij}]$, with $f_{ij} \geq 0$ the flow between $\mathbf{p}_i$ and $\mathbf{q}_j$, is the optimal admissible flow from P to Q that minimizes the numerator of (2) subject to the following constraints:

$$\sum_{j=1}^n f_{ij} \leq w_{\mathbf{p}_i}, \qquad \sum_{i=1}^m f_{ij} \leq w_{\mathbf{q}_j}$$
$$\sum_{i=1}^m \sum_{j=1}^n f_{ij} = \min(\sum_{i=1}^m w_{\mathbf{p}_i}, \sum_{j=1}^n w_{\mathbf{q}_j}) .$$

In this work we take advantage of the following properties of the EMD:
• Adaptive representation of high-dimensional distributions of features for each image independently (in contrast to other methods that either use one global adaptive representation based on the combined distributions of all the images together, or represent only the one-dimensional marginals of the full distribution [13, 16]).
• Robustness to small variations of feature values.
• No need for explicit segmentation. The representation by a finite number of clusters does not suffer from over- and under-clustering. Also, splitting a cluster into few sub-clusters will not significantly change the EMD results as long as the sub-clusters are mutually close in the feature space.
• Partial matches can be done in a very natural way. This is important, for instance, for image retrieval and in order to deal with occlusions and clutter, and is illustrated in section 4 below.

More details on the EMD can be found in [17].

For our texture signatures, we use the following ground distance:

$$\text{dist}(\mathbf{p}, \mathbf{q}) = 1 - e^{-\frac{\|\mathbf{p} - \mathbf{q}\|_1}{D}}, \quad (3)$$

where $\mathbf{p}$ and $\mathbf{q}$ are two texture vectors as in (1), $\|\cdot\|_1$ is the L_1 norm, and D is a constant that distinguishes between "close" and "far" distances in the feature space. In this paper we use

$$D = d(0, \frac{1}{2}\sigma),$$

where $\mathbf{0}$ is the zero vector, $\boldsymbol{\sigma} = [\sigma_1 \ldots \sigma_d]^T$ is a vector of standard deviations of the components of the features in each dimension from the overall distribution of all images in the database, and d is the dimensionality of the feature space. Assuming that the distribution of the features is unimodal, D is a measure of the spread of the distribution. The bigger the spread, the larger the distances are, in general. This saturated ground distance agrees with results from psychophysics. In [20] it is argued that the similarity between stimuli of any type can be expressed as *generalization data* by $g(\delta(S_i, S_j))$, where δ is a perceptual distance between two stimuli, the L_1 norm in our case, and g is a generalization function such as $g(\delta) = \exp(-\delta^\tau)$. This is equivalent to our dissimilarity measure which can be expressed in term of the similarity $g(\delta)$ by $1 - g(\delta)$. The rationale for this distance measure is that only texture descriptors that closely agree in several of their components are deemed to be close to each other. In a space with 24 dimensions, any metric that increases with point separation as fast as the L_2 norm (Euclidean distance) or even as fast as the L_1 norm (Manhattan distance) is bound to give poor retrieval results. This is because with such metrics distances between unrelated features are very large. As a consequence, if a distribution of descriptors from a single texture is marred by a few outliers, the EMD between similar textures will be dominated by a small number of large flow values. With our definition, ground distances are saturated to 1, and numerous agreements between individual elements in two similar distributions can still cause the EMD to be relatively small. In addition, since the constant D in (3) is based on a statistical parameter of the database at hand, our ground distance adapts naturally to the range of variation within the database itself.

4. Partial Matches

Having defined texture signatures and a ground distance between them, we can now use the EMD to retrieve images with textures. Here we demonstrate the ability to handle images that contain more than one texture without first segmenting the images.

In the first experiment we constructed a database of 1792 texture patches, by dividing each of 112 textures from the Brodatz album [5], into 4 by 4 non-overlapping 128 by 128 pixel patches. To this database we added images that were composed by mosaicing together several texture patches from the database. After the clustering process, the average size of the texture signatures was 12 clusters per patch.

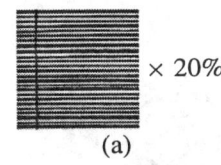

(a)

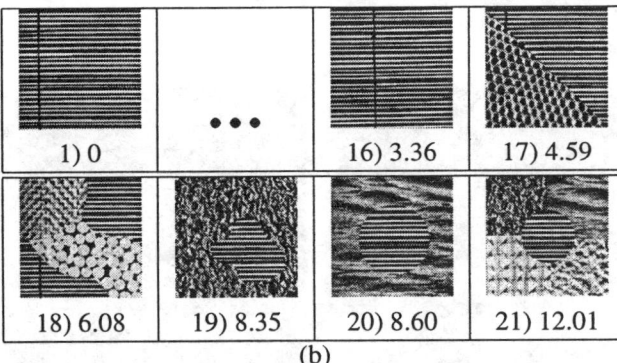

| 1) 0 | ••• | 16) 3.36 | 17) 4.59 |
| 18) 6.08 | 19) 8.35 | 20) 8.60 | 21) 12.01 |

(b)

Figure 2. Partial texture query: 20% of the texture in part (a) and 80% "don't care." (b) The 21 best matches: 16 patches from the same texture (only the first and last are shown), followed by all the compositions that contain some part of the queried texture.

Figure 2 shows an example of a partial query. The query was 20% of the texture in part (a) and 80% "don't care." The best matches are shown in part (b) with the 16 patches from the same texture at the beginning followed by all the compositions with some part of the queried texture. We emphasize that no segmentation was performed. Since the total weight of the signature is only 20%, the EMD will return as good matches also images with relatively small amount of the queried texture. Figure 3 demonstrates a partial query where the query has more than one texture.

5. Retrieving Natural Images

In the next experiment we created a database of 500 grayscale images of animals from the Corel Stock Photo Library[2] with image sizes of 768-by-512 pixels. We preprocessed the images by our clustering procedure, and obtained an average signature size of 32 clusters. Since most of the queries consists of a single, or a few textures, their signatures are significantly smaller and the EMD computation is more efficient.

---

[2] The Corel Stock Photo Library consists of 20,000 images organized into sets of 100 images each. We used the following sets: 123000 (Backyard Wildlife), 134000 (Cheetahs, Leopards & Jaguars), 130000 (African Specialty Animals), 173000 (Alaskan Wildlife), and 66000 (Barnyard Animals).

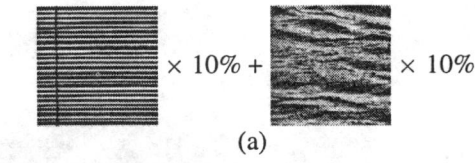

(a)

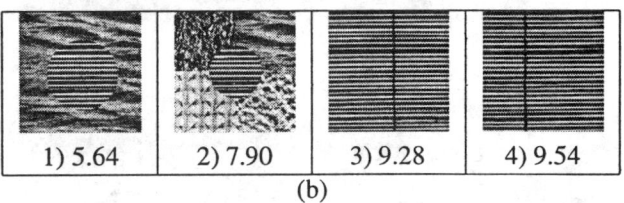

| 1) 5.64 | 2) 7.90 | 3) 9.28 | 4) 9.54 |

(b)

Figure 3. Another partial query. The query now contains 10% of each of the two patches in part (a) and 80% "don't care." (b) The two best matches are the two compositions that contain the textures in the query, followed by the patches that contain only one of the queried textures.

Figure 4(a) shows an example of a query that used a rectangular patch from an image of a zebra. We asked for images with at least 20% of this texture. The 16 best matches (Figure 4(b) shows the 12 most similar to the query) are all images of zebras, out of a total of 34 images of zebras in the database. The various backgrounds in the retrieved images were ignored by the system because of the EMD's ability to handle partial queries. Notice also that in some of the retrieved images there are a few small zebras, which provide a significant amount of "zebra texture" only when combined together. Methods based on segmentation are likely to have problems with such images.

Next we searched for images of cheetahs. The database has 33 images of cheetahs, and 64 more images of leopards and jaguars that have similar texture as cheetahs. Figure 5 shows the query and the 12 best matches. The first eight images are indeed cheetahs. The other four matches are images of leopards and jaguars.

To check if our method can distinguish between the different families of wild cats, we looked for images of jaguars. Figure 6 shows the query results. From the best twelve matches, eleven are jaguars and leopards, which are almost indistinguishable. Only the sixth match was an image of a cheetah.

6. Conclusions

The main point of this paper is that segmentation is not only unnecessary for texture-based image retrieval, but can even be harmful. Because of variations of appearance both within the same texture and across different textures in an

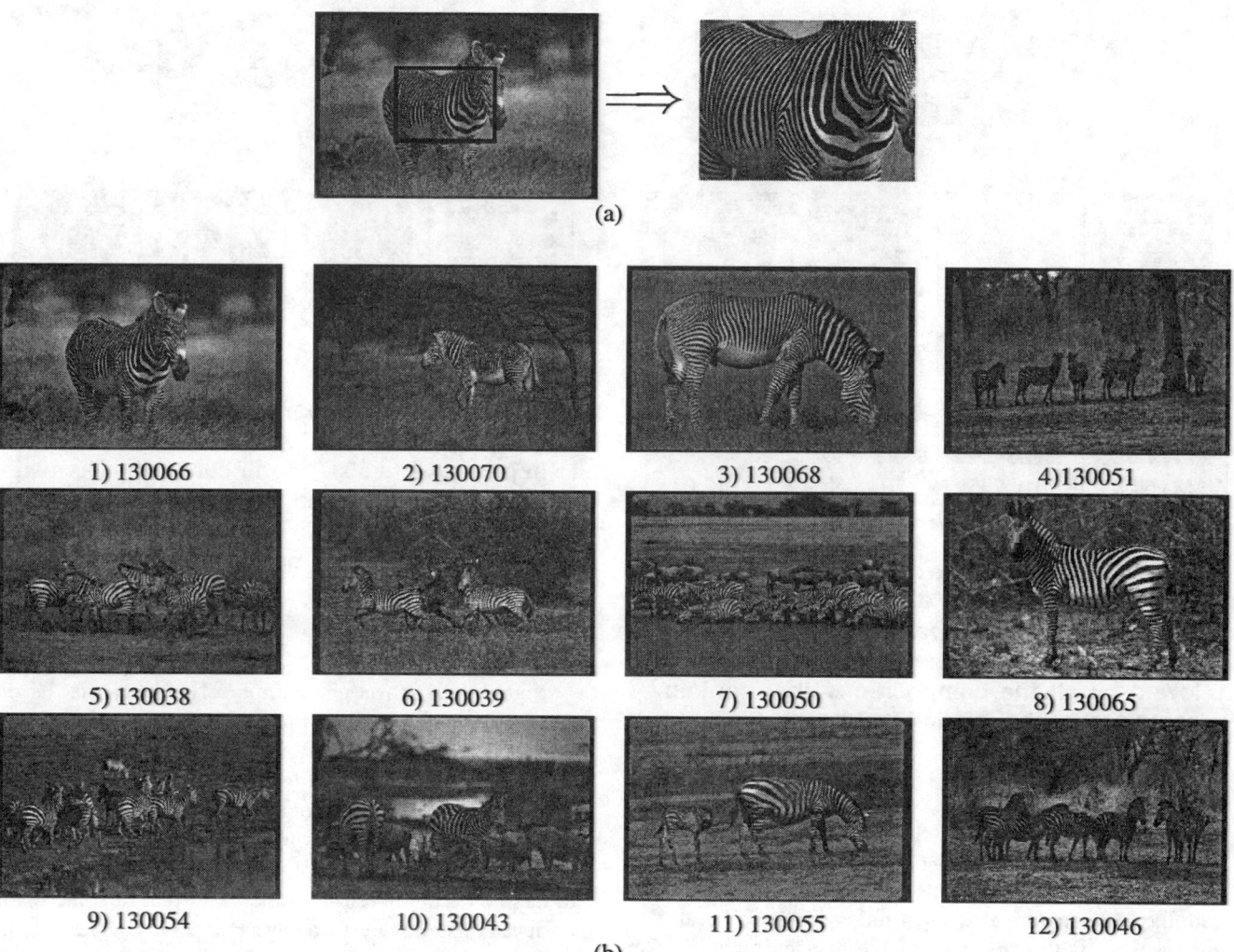

Figure 4. Looking for zebras. (a) An image of a zebra and a block of zebra stripes extracted from it. (b) The best matches to a query asking for images with at least 10% of the texture in (a). The numbers in the thumbnail captions are indices into Corel CDs.

image, both individual textures and multi-textured images are best described by distributions of descriptors, rather than by individual descriptors. We have proposed an effective implementation of this principle by replacing image segmentation with clustering of similar texture descriptors into compact, but detailed and versatile texture *signatures*. The Earth Movers Distance, together with an appropriate ground distance, has proven effective in handling queries, both complete and partial, in a small but difficult test database. Retrieval based on these ideas can handle the wide variations between very different images of related subjects, and can for instance retrieve images of zebras regardless of their number, sizes, backgrounds, or viewing conditions. At the same time, the proposed retrieval techniques can distinguish between rather subtly different images, and can for instance

tell cheetahs apart from leopards and jaguars.

Of course, more quantitative experiments with larger databases are in order. However, we believe that we have provided a new and effective approach to a difficult problem in image retrieval.

References

[1] E. H. Adelson and J. R. Bergen. Spatiotemporal energy models for the perception of motion. *JOSA A* , 2(2):284–299, 1985.

[2] J. R. Bach, C. Fuller, A. Gupta, A. Hampapur, B. Horowitz, R. Humphrey, R. Jain, and C. Shu. Virage image search engine: an open framework for image management. In

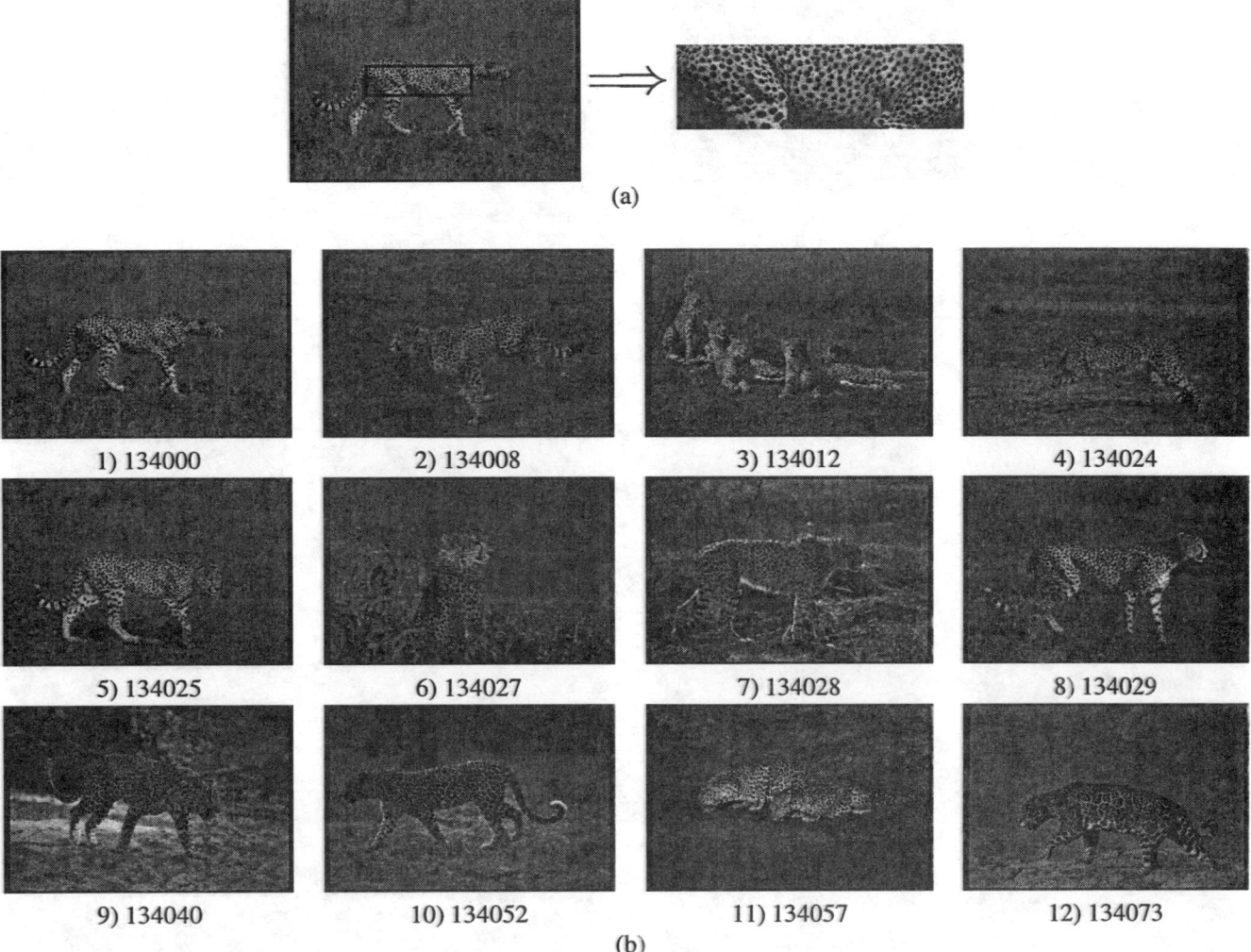

Figure 5. Looking for cheetahs. (a) The query. (b) The best matches with at least 10% of the query texture. The last four images are leopards and jaguars which have similar texture as cheetahs. However, cheetahs come first.

SPIE Conf. on Storage and Retrieval for Image and Video Databases IV, 2670: 76–87, 1996.

[3] S. Belongie, C. Carson, H. Greenspan, and J. Malik. Color- and texture-based image segmentation using EM and its application to content-based image retrieval. In *ICCV*, pages 675–682, 1998.

[4] A. C. Bovik, M. Clark, and W. S. Geisler. Multichannel texture analysis using localized spatial filters. *IEEE PAMI*, 12(12):55–73, 1990.

[5] P. Brodatz. *Textures: A Photographic Album for Artists and Designers*. Dover, New York, NY, 1966.

[6] J. D. Daugman. Complete discrete 2-d Gabor transforms by neural networks for image analysis and compression. *IEEE ASSP*, 36:1169–1179, 1988.

[7] F. Farrokhnia and A. K. Jain. A multi-channel filtering approach to texture segmentation. In *CVPR*, pages 364–370, 1991.

[8] D. Forsyth, J. Malik, M. Fleck, H. Greenspan, and T. Leung. Finding pictures of objects in large collections of images. In *Int'l Workshop on Object Recognition for Computer Vision*, Cambridge, UK, 1996.

[9] D. Gabor. Theory of communication. *The Journal of the IEE, Part III*, 93(21):429–457, 1946.

[10] F. L. Hitchcock. The distribution of a product from several sources to numerous localities. *J. Math. Phys.*, 20:224–230, 1941.

[11] W. Y. Ma. *NETRA: A Toolbox for Navigating Large Image Databases*. PhD thesis, University of California at Santa Barbara, 1997.

[12] J. Malik and P. Perona. Preattentive texture discrimination with early vision mechanisms. *JOSA A*, 7(5):923–932, 1990.

[13] B. S. Manjunath and W. Y. Ma. Texture features for browsing and retrieval of image data. *IEEE PAMI*, 18(8):837–842, 1996.

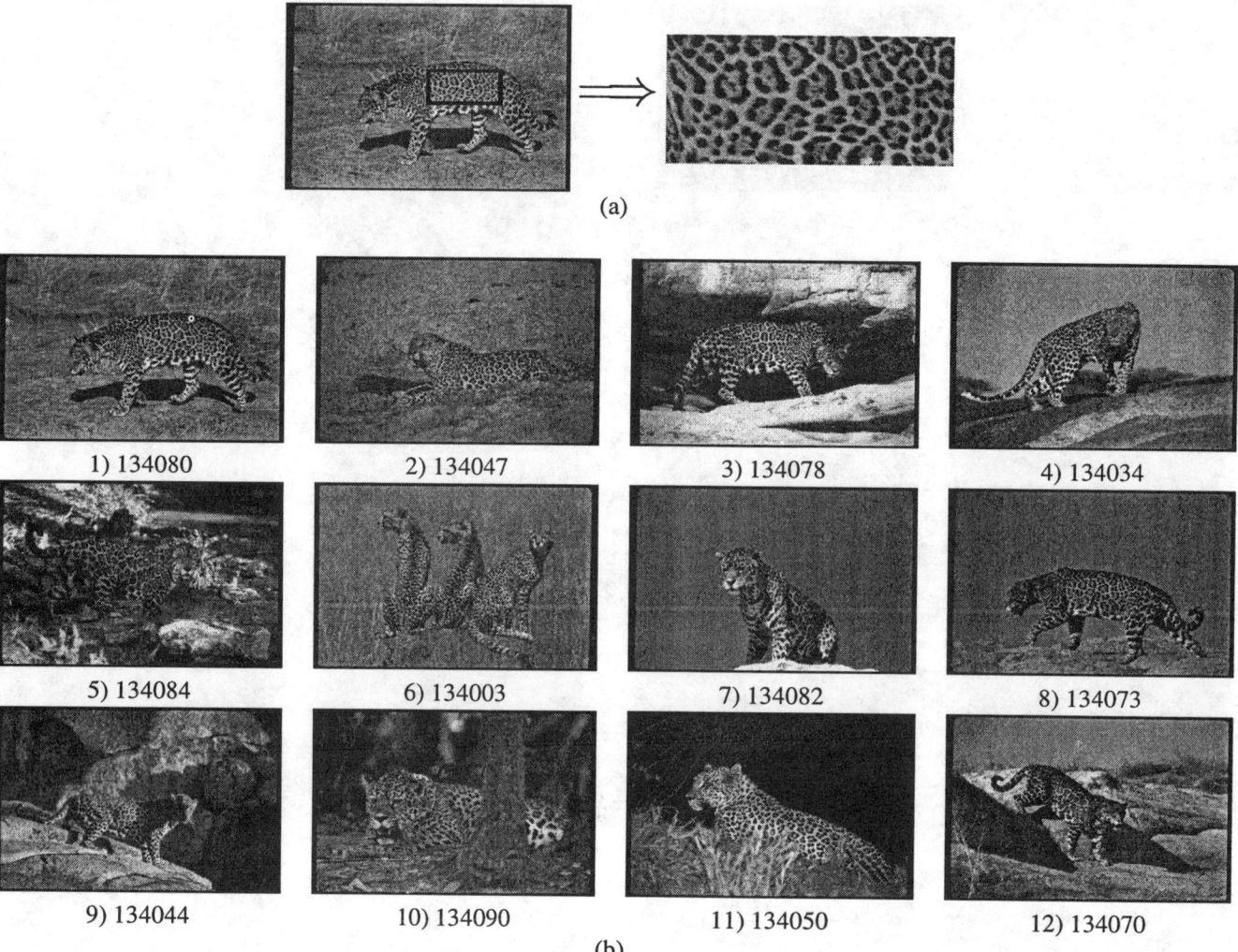

Figure 6. Looking for leopards and jaguars. (a) The query. (b) The best matches with at least 10% of the query texture. All but the sixth image are leopards and jaguars. The sixth image is of cheetahs.

[14] W. Niblack, R. Barber, W. Equitz, M. D. Flickner, E. H. Glasman, D. Petkovic, P. Yanker, C. Faloutsos, G. Taubin, and Y. Heights. Querying images by content, using color, texture, and shape. In *SPIE Conf. on Storage and Retrieval for Image and Video Databases*, 1908:173–187, 1993.

[15] A. Pentland, R. W. Picard, and S. Sclaroff. Photobook: content-based manipulation of image databases. *IJCV*, 18(3):233–254, 1996.

[16] J. Puzicha, T. Hofmann, and J. Buhmann. Non-parametric similarity measures for unsupervised texture segmentation and image retrieval. In *CVPR*, pages 267–272, 1997.

[17] Y. Rubner. *Perceptual Metrics for Image Database Navigation*. PhD thesis, Stanford University, 1999.

[18] Y. Rubner, L. J. Guibas, and C. Tomasi. The earth mover's distance, multidimensional scaling, and color-based image retrieval. In *ARPA IU Workshop*, pages 661–668, 1997.

[19] Y. Rubner, C. Tomasi, and L. J. Guibas. A metric for distributions with applications to image databases. In *ICCV*, pages 59–66, 1998.

[20] R. N. Shepard. Toward a universal law of generalization for psychological science. *Science*, 237:1317–1323, 1987.

[21] J. R. Smith. *Integrated Spatial and Feature Image Systems: Retrieval, Analysis and Compression*. PhD thesis, Columbia University, 1997.

[22] H. Voorhees and T. Poggio. Detecting textons and texture boundaries in natural images. In *ICCV*, pages 250–258, 1987.

Equivalence of Julesz and Gibbs Texture Ensembles

Ying Nian Wu[1], Song Chun Zhu[2], and Xiuwen Liu[2]
[1]Dept. of Statistics, Univ. of Michigan, Ann Arbor, MI 48109
[2]Dept. of Computer and Info. Science, Ohio State Univ., Columbus, OH 43210

Abstract

Research on texture has been pursued along two different lines. The first line of research, pioneered by Julesz (1962), seeks the essential ingredients in terms of *features and statistics* in human texture perception. This leads us to a mathematical definition of texture as a *Julesz ensemble*. A Julesz ensemble is the maximum set of images that share the same value of some basic feature statistics as the image lattice $\Lambda \to Z^2$, or equivalently it is a uniform distribution on this set. The second line of research studies *statistical models*, in particular, Markov random field (MRF) and FRAME models (Zhu, Wu, and Mumford 1997), to characterize texture patterns locally. In this article, we bridge the two lines by the fundamental principle of *equivalence of ensembles* in statistical mechanics (Gibbs, 1902). We prove that 1). The conditional probability of a arbitrary image patch given its environment, under the Julesz ensemble or the uniform model, is inevitably a FRAME (MRF) model, and 2). The limit of the FRAME (MRF) model, which we called the Gibbs ensemble, is equivalent to a Julesz ensemble as $\Lambda \to Z^2$. Thus the advantages of the two methodologies can be fully utilized.

1 Introduction

Texture modeling and synthesis has been intensively studied in computer vision and psychophysics in the past three decades. From a global view, the research has been pursued along two different lines.

Research along the first line, pioneered by Julesz (1962), studies the basic feature statistics that lead to human texture impression, so that images sharing the same values of feature statistics cannot be told apart in pre-attentive vision. Examples of feature statistics include co-occurrence matrices, clique statistics, and more recently, histograms of linear filter responses. For a set of feature statistics, as the image lattice $\Lambda \to Z^2$, we call the set of images sharing the same value of feature statistics, or more precisely, the uniform distribution over this set, the *Julesz ensembles* (Zhu, et al., 1999). Markov chain Monte Carlo (MCMC) can be used to synthesize texture images by sampling from the Julesz ensemble (Zhu, et al., 1999), and thus we can verify the sufficiency of the feature statistics. The Julesz ensemble is globally defined on Z^2, in the literature, it was unclear what local statistical properties the Julesz ensembles have when they are applied to tasks like texture segmentation and discrimination.

Research along the second line builds statistical models to characterize texture patterns. Among them, Markov random fields (MRF), or equivalently the Gibbs distributions are the most successful models (e.g., Besag, 1974; Cross and Jain, 1983; Geman and Geman, 1984). Recently, Zhu, Wu, and Mumford (1997) have shown that these models can be unified under a minimax entropy learning principle, and that MRF models incorporating statistics of filter responses (called FRAME) can model a wide variety of natural textures. We call the limit of the FRAME model as $\Lambda \to Z^2$ the *Gibbs ensemble*. The Markov property makes the Gibbs distributions suitable for image reconstruction and image segmentation, but it is necessary to know its global statistical property of the Gibbs ensembles for model verification and model selection purposes.

For a comparison between the Julesz ensemble and the Gibbs ensemble, the former is more fundamental scientifically and is defined by global hard constraints, whereas the latter is more elegant mathematically and is defined by local interactions or a "soft" constraint through maximum entropy (see Zhu, Wu and Mumford 1997). In this article, we unify the two research lines by showing the equivalence between the Julesz ensemble and the Gibbs ensemble, borrowing the fundamental principle of equivalence of ensembles in statistical mechanics. The equivalence of ensembles reveals two significant facts in texture modeling. 1). Locally, under the Julesz ensemble, the conditional distribution of an image patch of arbitrary shape given its environment is exactly the FRAME model. 2). Globally, on Z^2 (or large enough lattice) the Gibbs ensemble concentrates its probability mass uniformly over a set of images sharing the same value of feature statistics – the Julesz ensemble. Therefore, a Gibbs ensemble is also a Julesz ensemble.

The key to the equivalence of ensembles is the *probability rate function* in the large deviation theory (e.g., Lewis, Pfister, and Sullivan, 1995). The probability rate function describes the asymptotic behavior of the probabilities of different image sets, and sheds light on concepts like "typical" and "modeling". An important conclusion is that when we sample from the Julesz ensemble or the Gibbs ensemble, we will always get images with the same statistical property (and therefore, the same appearance).

2 Julesz ensemble and Gibbs ensemble

2.1 A simple example

In this subsection, we will use a simple example to demonstrate the important fact that *a statistical model defined on a large image lattice concentrates its probability mass uniformly on a set of images*. The key is the probability rate function in the large deviation theory, which is built on the simple fact that *the term with the largest exponential order dominates the sum, and the order of the sum is the largest order in the individual terms*. One can see this easily from the following simple example. Consider two terms, one is e^{5n}, and the other is e^{3n}. As $n \to \infty$, the sum $e^{5n}+e^{3n}$ is dominated by e^{5n}, and the order of this sum is still 5, i.e., $\log(e^{5n} + e^{3n})/n \to 5$.

Let $\mathbf{I}$ be an image defined on a finite lattice $\Lambda \subset \mathbf{Z}^2$, and the intensity at pixel $v \in \Lambda$ is denoted by $\mathbf{I}(v) \in \mathcal{L} = \{1, 2, ..., L\}$. Thus $\Omega_\Lambda = \mathcal{L}^{|\Lambda|}$ is the space of images on Λ, with $|\Lambda|$ being the number of pixels in Λ.

let's consider a simple statistical model where the image intensities are independent and identically distributed (i.i.d.) with $P(\mathbf{I}) = \prod_{v \in \Lambda} P(\mathbf{I}(v))$, and $P(\mathbf{I}(v) = l) = p_l$ for $l = 1, ..., L$, and $\sum_l p_l = 1$. We write $p = (p_1, ..., p_L)$.

For each image $\mathbf{I} \in \Omega_\Lambda$, let the histogram of $\mathbf{I}$ be $h(\mathbf{I}) = (h_1(\mathbf{I}), ..., h_L(\mathbf{I}))$, where $h_l(\mathbf{I})$ is the proportion of pixels with level l in the image $\mathbf{I}$. Then $h(\mathbf{I})$ is the sufficient statistics for model P, i.e., if we denote by $\Omega_\Lambda(h)$ the set of images with $h(\mathbf{I}) = h$, then $P(\mathbf{I})$ assigns equal probabilities to images in $\Omega_\Lambda(h)$. Thus the image space is partitioned into equivalence classes

$$\Omega_\Lambda = \cup_h \Omega_\Lambda(h).$$

As shown in figure 1, each equivalence class $\Omega_\Lambda(h)$ is mapped into one point h on a *simplex* – a plane defined by $h_1 + \cdots + h_L = 1$ and $h_l \geq 0, \forall l$ in an L-dimensional space. We call images in $\Omega_\Lambda(h)$ as images of *type h*.

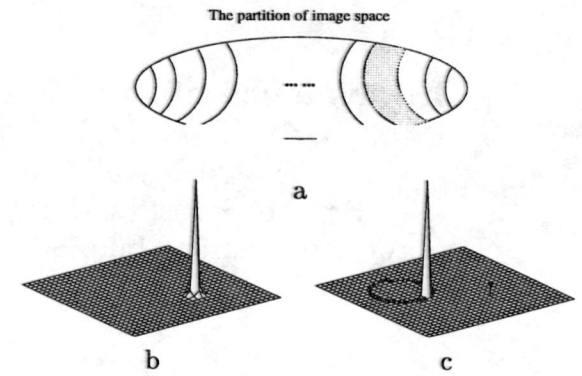

Figure 1: a). The partition of image space into equivalence classes, and each class corresponds to an h on the probability simplex in b). b). A function on the simplex with exponential fall-off, and it approaches a Dirac delta function as $\Lambda \to \mathbf{Z}^2$. c). Zoom-in view at a disk area in b). The function at one point on the border of the circle dominates the entire integration.

For an image $\mathbf{I}$ of type h, the log-likelihood is

$$\log P(\mathbf{I}) = \log \prod_{l=1}^{L} p_l^{|\Lambda| h_l} = |\Lambda| \sum_l h_l \log p_l. \quad (1)$$

The number of images of type h, or the volume of the set $\Omega_\Lambda(h)$ is

$$|\Omega_\Lambda(h)| = \frac{|\Lambda|!}{(|\Lambda| h_1)! \cdots (|\Lambda| h_L)!}, \quad (2)$$

for which it is easy to prove that

$$\lim_{\Lambda \to \mathbf{Z}^2} \frac{1}{|\Lambda|} \log |\Omega_\Lambda(h)| = -\sum_{l=1}^{L} h_l \log h_l = \text{entropy}(h). \quad (3)$$

Combining equations (3) and (1), the probability mass for the entire set $\Omega_\Lambda(h)$ of images of type h has an exponential rate,

$$\lim_{\Lambda \to \mathbf{Z}^2} \frac{1}{|\Lambda|} \log p(\mathbf{I} \in \Omega_\Lambda(h)) = -D(h\|p), \quad (4)$$

where

$$D(h\|p) = \sum_{l=1}^{L} h_l \log \frac{h_l}{p_l} \geq 0,$$

is the Kullback-Leibler divergence from h to p.

Equation (4) tells us that the probability mass for each equivalence class $\Omega_\Lambda(h)$ is distributed in the order of $\exp\{-|\Lambda| D(h\|p)\}$, i.e., the distribution of $h(\mathbf{I})$ under model P is in the order of $\exp\{-|\Lambda| D(h\|p)\}$.

So we call $s_p(h) = -D(h\|p)$ the probability rate function of $h(\mathbf{I})$ under model P. Clearly, $s_p(h)$ achieves its unique maximum 0 at $h = p$, and for $h \neq p$, the probability mass the model P assigns to $\Omega_\Lambda(h)$ becomes exponentially small as the image lattice Λ gets large. Therefore, when the image lattice is large, model P concentrates its probability mass on $\Omega_\Lambda(p)$. Because model P assigns equal probabilities to all images in $\Omega_\Lambda(p)$, model P on a large image lattice is essentially a uniform distribution over $\Omega_\Lambda(p)$. So $h = p$ is the typical value of histogram $h(\mathbf{I})$ under model P, i.e., if we randomly draw an image from model P defined on a large lattice, then essentially we will always get an image of type $h = p$. Thus, although locally the pixel intensities are randomly distributed, globally, we always observe the same value for the statistics $h(\mathbf{I})$. Figure 1.b) illustrates the intuitive interpretation of the exponential fall-off in the probability simplex. As $\Lambda \to \mathbf{Z}^2$, the probability $P(\mathbf{I} \in \Omega_\Lambda(h))$ converges to a Dirac delta function centered at $h = p$.

Furthermore, as shown in Figure 1.c), for any set $\mathcal{H}$ on the simplex, let $\Omega_\Lambda(\mathcal{H}) = \{\mathbf{I} : h(\mathbf{I}) \in \mathcal{H}\}$. Then the probability

$$P(\mathbf{I} \in \Omega_\Lambda(\mathcal{H})) = \int_{h \in \mathcal{H}} P(\mathbf{I} \in \Omega_\Lambda(h)) dh.$$

In the above integral (which is a continuous version of sum), $P(\mathbf{I} \in \Omega_\Lambda(h))$ is of the order $\exp\{|\Lambda| s_p(h)\}$. Therefore, the integral is dominated by the $h_\star$ with the largest $s_p(h)$ in $\mathcal{H}$, and the order of the whole integral is still $s_p(h_\star)$. To be more specific, let

$$h_\star = \arg\max_{h \in \mathcal{H}} s_p(h) = \arg\min_{h \in \mathcal{H}} D(h\|p),$$

then

$$\lim_{\Lambda \to \mathbf{Z}^2} \frac{1}{|\Lambda|} \log p(\mathbf{I} \in \Omega_\Lambda(\mathcal{H}))$$
$$= \lim_{\Lambda \to \mathbf{Z}^2} \frac{1}{|\Lambda|} \log p(\mathbf{I} \in \Omega_\Lambda(h_\star))$$
$$= s_p(h_\star) = -D(h_\star\|p).$$

2.2 Features and statistics

Recent approaches to texture modeling begin with introducing a set of features/filters $\{F^{(\alpha)}, \alpha = 1, 2, ..., A\}$, and computing the sub-band images $\mathbf{I}^{(\alpha)}$, with $\mathbf{I}^{(\alpha)}(v) = F^{(\alpha)} * \mathbf{I}(v)$ for linear filters. A general feature statistics can be computed as follows. First, choose a G-polygon whose G vertices lie on various sub-bands in the pyramid as displayed in Figure 2. So we can index the G-polygon by $\{(\alpha_g, u_g), g = 1, ..., G\}$, with α_g indexes the pyramid level, and u_g the displacement of the vertex. Because texture is a statistical

property of local spatial structures, the u_g's should be close to each other. Then we can move this G-polygon over the image lattice, and collect a set of G-tuples of filter responses, $\{(\mathbf{I}^{(\alpha_1)}(v + u_1), ..., \mathbf{I}^{(\alpha_G)}(v + u_G)), v \in \Lambda\}$. Finally, the feature statistics for this polygon can be computed as the G-dimensional histogram of these G tuples,

$$H(\mathbf{I}) = \sum_{(h_1, ..., h_G)} \prod_{g=1}^{G} 1_{\mathbf{I}^{(\alpha_g)}(v + u_g) = h_g},$$

where $(h_1, ..., h_G)$ runs through all possible values of the G-tuple, which are assumed to be suitably quantitized.

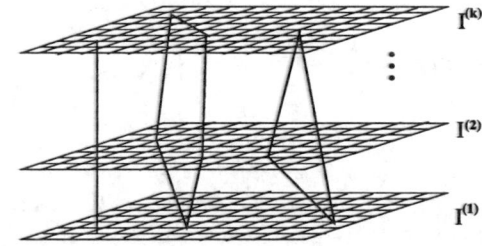

Figure 2: The general feature statistics are multi-dimensional histograms for polygons in the image pyramid.

If the pyramid has only one layer, i.e., the raw image $\mathbf{I}$, then the feature statistics reduce to co-occurrence matrices (Julesz, 1962; Gagalowicz and Ma, 1986). For a polygon with only one vertex, the feature statistics become the marginal histogram used in Heeger (1996) and Zhu et al. (1997). If the polygon is a straight line (see figure 2), the feature statistics become the joint histogram used by De Bonet and Viola (1999). The histograms can be further reduced to moments, rectified moments, or other more parsimonious statistics.

2.3 The Julesz ensemble

Our definition of the Julesz ensemble is motivated by Julesz's quest for a general "texton theory". In his seminal paper (Julesz, 1962), Julesz asked the following fundamental question:

> what features and statistics are characteristic of a texture pattern, so that texture pairs that share the same features and statistics cannot be told apart by pre-attentive human visual perception?

Suppose on the image pyramid, K polygons are used for texture modeling, which give K unnormalized histograms $H_1(\mathbf{I}), ..., H_K(\mathbf{I})$. We let $\mathbf{H}(\mathbf{I}) =$

$(H_1(\mathbf{I}), ..., H_K(\mathbf{I}))$, and $\mathbf{h}(\mathbf{I}) = \mathbf{H}(\mathbf{I})/|\Lambda|$ be the normalized histograms. Let

$$\Omega_\Lambda(\mathbf{h}) = \{\mathbf{I} : \mathbf{h}(\mathbf{I}) = \mathbf{h}\} \qquad (5)$$

be the set of images sharing the same value $\mathbf{h}$ of feature statistics. The value $\mathbf{h}$ is often extracted from some observed images. For finite lattice Λ, the exact constraint $\mathbf{h}(\mathbf{I}) = \mathbf{h}$ may not be satisfied. So we relax this constraint a little bit, and replace $\Omega_\Lambda(\mathbf{h})$ by

$$\Omega_\Lambda(\mathcal{H}) = \{\mathbf{I} : \mathbf{h}(\mathbf{I}) \in \mathcal{H}\}$$

with $\mathcal{H}$ being an open neighborhood around $\mathbf{h}$. Then the associate uniform distribution is

$$q(\mathbf{I}; \mathcal{H}) = \begin{cases} 1/|\Omega_\Lambda(\mathcal{H})|, & \text{if } \mathbf{I} \in \Omega_\Lambda(\mathcal{H}), \\ 0, & \text{otherwise,} \end{cases} \qquad (6)$$

where $|\Omega_\Lambda(\mathcal{H})|$ is the volume of $\Omega_\Lambda(\mathcal{H})$.

Definition *Given a set of feature statistics* $\mathbf{h}(\mathbf{I}) = (h_1(\mathbf{I}), ..., h_K(\mathbf{I}))$, *a Julesz ensemble with parameter* $\mathbf{h}$ *is a limit of* $q(\mathbf{I}; \mathcal{H})$ *as* $\Lambda \to \mathbf{Z}^2$ *and* $\mathcal{H} \to \mathbf{h}$ *with some boundary condition.*

A Julesz ensemble is a mathematical idealization of $q(\mathbf{I}; \mathcal{H})$ for a large Λ with some boundary condition and with $\mathcal{H}$ close to $\mathbf{h}$. We assume $\Lambda \to \mathbf{Z}^2$ in the sense of van Hove, i.e., the ratio between the boundary and the size of Λ goes to 0.

Then, we are ready to give a *mathematical definition* for texture.

Definition *A texture is the Julesz ensemble for the set of feature statistics* $\mathbf{h}(\mathbf{I})$ *employed by human vision in forming texture impression.*

Then, texture modeling can be posed as an inverse problem, i.e., given a set of observed images sampled by natural stochastic precesses (physical or chemical), find the largest Julesz ensemble, or more specifically, the minimal set of feature statistics, such that images sampled from this Julesz ensemble have the same texture appearance as the observed ones.

The verification of the sufficiency of feature statistics $\mathbf{h}(\mathbf{I})$ can be accomplished by first computing $\mathbf{h}_{\text{obs}}$ from observed texture images, and then sampling from the Julesz ensemble with parameter $\mathbf{h}_{\text{obs}}$, or more practically from $q(\mathbf{I}; \mathcal{H})$ on a large lattice with $\mathcal{H}$ close to $\mathbf{h}_{\text{obs}}$, to see if the sampled images resemble the visual appearance of the observed ones. The necessity of feature statistics is a much more delicate issue as there are infinitely many ways to reduce $\mathbf{h}(\mathbf{I})$, and some reduction of $\mathbf{h}(\mathbf{I})$ may still be judged by human vision as being sufficient. For texture synthesis in computer graphics, the necessity is not an important issue. For

texture modeling in computer vision, however, the necessity or the parsimony of feature statistics is very important.

The $q(\mathbf{I}; \mathcal{H})$ can be sampled by simulated annealing. We first define an energy function

$$\mathcal{E}(\mathbf{I}) = \begin{cases} 0, & \text{if } \mathbf{h}(\mathbf{I}) \in \mathcal{H}, \\ D(\mathbf{h}(\mathbf{I}), \mathbf{h}_{\text{obs}}(\mathbf{I})), & \text{otherwise,} \end{cases}$$

where D is a suitably chosen distance (e.g., L_1 distance). Then the distribution

$$q(\mathbf{I}) = \frac{1}{Z_T} \exp(-\frac{\mathcal{E}(\mathbf{I})}{T}) \qquad (7)$$

goes to $q(\mathbf{I}; \mathcal{H})$, i.e. the uniform distribution over the minima of $\mathcal{E}(\mathbf{I})$ as the temperature T goes to 0. We can sample $q(\mathbf{I})$ by the Gibbs sampler (Geman and Geman, 1984) or a generalized version of the Gibbs sampler (see Zhu, et al. 1999 and references therein).

In our experiments, we select all the 56 filters (Gabor filters at various scales and orientations and small Laplacian of Gaussian filters) used by Zhu, et al. (1997). We match the *marginal histograms* of the 56 filters all together. Some of the results are displayed in Figures 4 and 5. See Zhu, et al. (1999) for more details and discussions of the results. For simplicity, for the rest of the paper, we assume that the feature statistics are marginal statistics of filter responses, although our results apply to more general situations.

2.4 MRF models and the Gibbs ensemble

Statistical modeling of texture is motivated by vision problems such as texture clustering, discrimination and segmentation. Among all statistical models, the MRF models (e.g., Besag, 1974; Cross and Jain, 1983) are the most successful and the most elegant.

Recently, Zhu, et al. (1997) discovered the following general MRF model. Given statistics $\mathbf{H}(\mathbf{I}) = (H_1(\mathbf{I}), ..., H_K(\mathbf{I}))$, the MRF model for $\mathbf{I}$ is

$$\begin{aligned} p(\mathbf{I}; \beta) &= \frac{1}{Z_\Lambda(\beta)} \exp\{-\sum_{k=1}^{K} < \beta_k, H_k(\mathbf{I}) >\} \\ &= \frac{1}{Z_\Lambda(\beta)} \exp\{-|\Lambda| < \beta, \mathbf{h}(\mathbf{I}) >\}, \end{aligned}$$

where $Z_\Lambda(\beta)$ is the normalizing constant. This model is specified by the parameter $\beta = (\beta_1, ..., \beta_K)$, whose value is determined by the constraint

$$E_{p(\mathbf{I}; \beta)}[\mathbf{h}(\mathbf{I})] = \mathbf{h}_{\text{obs}},$$

where $\mathbf{h}_{\text{obs}}$ is computed from observed images. We call the above constraint a soft constraint because it only requires that the statistics are matched on ensemble average. Among all the distributions $p(\mathbf{I})$ satisfying $E_p[\mathbf{h}(\mathbf{I})] = \mathbf{h}_{\text{obs}}$, $p(\mathbf{I}; \beta)$ has the maximum entropy, so it integrates the observed statistics $\mathbf{h}_{\text{obs}}$ in the most unbiased way.

The $p(\mathbf{I}; \beta)$ unifies all the MRF texture models, which are different only in their definitions of feature statistics $\mathbf{H}(\mathbf{I})$. Although the MRF models are less straightforward than the Julesz ensembles, they are much more analytically tractable due to the Markov property. More specifically, for any patch $\Lambda_0 \subset \Lambda$, the conditional distribution of $\mathbf{I}_{\Lambda_0}$ given the rest of the image $\mathbf{I}_{\Lambda/\Lambda_0}$ only depends on the pixels that can share the same filters with pixels in Λ_0. We call the set of such pixels the neighborhood of Λ_0, and denote it by $\partial\Lambda_0$. The condition distribution is

$$p(\mathbf{I}_{\Lambda_0} \mid \mathbf{I}_{\Lambda/\Lambda_0}; \beta) = p(\mathbf{I}_{\Lambda_0} \mid \mathbf{I}_{\partial\Lambda_0}; \beta)$$
$$= \frac{1}{Z_{\Lambda_0}(\beta)} \exp\{- < \beta, \mathbf{H}(\mathbf{I}_{\Lambda_0}|\mathbf{I}_{\partial\Lambda_0}) >\},$$

where $\mathbf{H}(\mathbf{I}_{\Lambda_0}|\mathbf{I}_{\partial\Lambda_0})$ is the statistics computed by filtering within $\Lambda_0 \cup \partial\Lambda_0$. Similar to the definition of the Julesz ensemble, we have

Definition *Given a set of feature statistics* $\mathbf{h}(\mathbf{I}) = (h_1(\mathbf{I}), ..., h_K(\mathbf{I}))$*, a Gibbs ensemble with parameter* β *is a limit of* $p(\mathbf{I}; \beta)$ *as* $\Lambda \to \mathbf{Z}^2$ *with some boundary condition.*

The Gibbs ensemble is a mathematical idealization of $p(\mathbf{I}; \beta)$ on a large Λ with some boundary condition.

3 Equivalence of ensembles

3.1 Local Markov property of the Julesz ensemble

In this subsection, we derive the local Markov property of the Julesz ensemble, which is globally defined by $\mathbf{h}$. This derivation is adapted from the traditional argument in statistical mechanics (Gibbs, 1902), where the Julesz ensemble can be identified with the micro-canonical ensemble (an isolated system with fixed energy), and the Gibbs ensemble with the canonical ensemble (a system in equilibrium with a heat reservoir). To do this, we need to first derive the probability rate function of $\mathbf{h}(\mathbf{I})$ under the uniform distribution.

Let μ_Λ be the uniform distribution over the entire image space Ω_Λ, and let $\mu_\Lambda(\mathcal{H})$ be the probability that μ_Λ assigns to the image set $\Omega_\Lambda(\mathcal{H})$. Then the volume of $\Omega_\Lambda(\mathcal{H})$ is $L^{|\Lambda|}\mu_\Lambda(\mathcal{H})$. For μ_Λ, we have

Proposition 1 *The limit*

$$\lim_{\Lambda \to \mathbf{Z}^2} \frac{1}{|\Lambda|} \log \mu_\Lambda(\mathcal{H}) = s(\mathcal{H})$$

exists. Let $s(\mathbf{h}) = \lim_{\mathcal{H} \to \mathbf{h}} s(\mathcal{H})$*, then* $s(\mathbf{h})$ *is strictly concave, and* $s(\mathcal{H}) = \sup_{\mathbf{h} \in \mathcal{H}} s(\mathbf{h})$*.*

The probability rate function $s(\mathbf{h})$ tells us that the distribution $\mu_\Lambda(\mathbf{h})$ behaves like $\exp\{|\Lambda|s(\mathbf{h})\}$. The equation $s(\mathcal{H}) = \sup_{\mathbf{h} \in \mathcal{H}} s(\mathbf{h})$ can be understood in the same way as in the simple i.i.d. example we discussed, i.e., the term with the largest order dominates. See Lanford (1973) for a detailed analysis of the above result.

With $s(\mathbf{h})$, we are ready to derive the Markov property of the Julesz ensemble. Consider the model $q(\mathbf{I}; \mathcal{H})$. For simplicity, we shall just take $\mathcal{H}$ to be $\mathbf{h}$, and assume that Λ is large, so $q(\mathbf{I}; \mathbf{h})$ is uniform over $\Omega_\Lambda(\mathbf{h})$. First, we fix $\Lambda_1 \subset \Lambda$, and then fix $\Lambda_0 \subset \Lambda_1$. We are interested in the conditional distribution of the local patch $\mathbf{I}_{\Lambda_0}$ given its local environment $\mathbf{I}_{\Lambda_1/\Lambda_0}$ under the model $q(\mathbf{I}; \mathbf{h})$ with a large Λ. We denote this distribution by $q(\mathbf{I}_{\Lambda_0} \mid \mathbf{I}_{\Lambda_1/\Lambda_0}, \mathbf{h})$. We assume that Λ_0 is sufficiently smaller than Λ_1 so that the neighborhood of Λ_0, $\partial\Lambda_0$, is contained in Λ_1.

Let $\mathbf{H}_0 = \mathbf{H}(\mathbf{I}_{\Lambda_0}|\mathbf{I}_{\partial\Lambda_0})$ be the statistics computed for $\mathbf{I}_{\Lambda_0}$ where filtering takes place within $\Lambda_0 \cup \partial\Lambda_0$. Let $\mathbf{H}_{01}$ be the statistics computed by filtering inside the fixed environment Λ_1/Λ_0. Let $\Lambda_{-1} = \Lambda/\Lambda_1$ be the big patch outside of Λ_1. Then the statistics computed for Λ_{-1} is $\mathbf{h}|\Lambda| - \mathbf{H}_0 - \mathbf{H}_{01}$. Let $\mathbf{h}' = (\mathbf{h}|\Lambda| - \mathbf{H}_{01})/|\Lambda_{-1}|$, then the normalized statistics for Λ_{-1} is $\mathbf{h}' - \mathbf{H}_0/|\Lambda_{-1}|$.

For a certain image patch $\mathbf{I}_{\Lambda_0}$, the number of images in $\Omega_\Lambda(\mathbf{h})$ with such a patch $\mathbf{I}_{\Lambda_0}$ and its local environment $\mathbf{I}_{\Lambda_1/\Lambda_0}$ is $|\Omega_{\Lambda_{-1}}(\mathbf{h}' - \mathbf{H}_0/|\Lambda_{-1}|)|$. So if we sample an image from $\Omega_\Lambda(\mathbf{h})$ randomly, then the probability we observe $\mathbf{I}_{\Lambda_0}$ on Λ_0 with an environment $\mathbf{I}_{\Lambda_1/\Lambda_0}$ is

$$q(\mathbf{I}_{\Lambda_0} \mid \mathbf{I}_{\Lambda_1/\Lambda_0}, \mathbf{h}) \propto 1/|\Omega_{\Lambda_{-1}}(\mathbf{h}' - \frac{\mathbf{H}_0}{|\Lambda_{-1}|})|.$$

Note that as a distribution of $\mathbf{I}_{\Lambda_0}$, $q(\mathbf{I}_{\Lambda_0} \mid \mathbf{I}_{\Lambda_1/\Lambda_0}, \mathbf{h})$ is decided by $\mathbf{H}_0$, which is the sufficient statistics. Therefore, we only need to trace $\mathbf{H}_0$ while leaving other terms as constants. For large Λ,

$$\log q(\mathbf{I}_{\Lambda_0} \mid \mathbf{I}_{\Lambda_1/\Lambda_0}, \mathbf{h}) = \text{const} + |\Lambda_{-1}|s(\mathbf{h}' - \frac{\mathbf{H}_0}{|\Lambda_{-1}|})$$
$$= \text{const} - < s'(\mathbf{h}'), \mathbf{H}_0 > + o(\frac{1}{|\Lambda|}),$$

where the first equation follows from Proposition 1, and the second equation follows from a Taylor expansion at $\mathbf{h}'$. Letting $\beta = s'(\mathbf{h})$, then, as $\Lambda \to \mathbf{Z}^2$, $\mathbf{h}' \to \mathbf{h}$, and

$$\log q(\mathbf{I}_{\Lambda_0} \mid \mathbf{I}_{\Lambda_1/\Lambda_0}, \mathbf{h}) \quad \to \quad \text{const} - < s'(\mathbf{h}), \mathbf{H}_0 >$$
$$= \text{const} - < \beta, \mathbf{H}_0 >,$$

so

$$q(\mathbf{I}_{\Lambda_0} \mid \mathbf{I}_{\Lambda_1/\Lambda_0}, \mathbf{h}) \to \frac{1}{Z_{\Lambda_0}(\beta)} \exp\{- <\beta, \mathbf{H}(\mathbf{I}_{\Lambda_0} \mid \mathbf{I}_{\partial\Lambda_0}) >\},$$

which is exactly the Markov property that governs the Gibbs ensemble. This derivation shows that local computation using the MRF model is justified under the Julesz ensemble. It also reveals an important relationship, i.e., the parameter β can be identified as the derivative of the probability rate $s(\mathbf{h})$.

3.2 Global statistical property of the Gibbs ensemble

In this subsection, we shall start with the Gibbs ensemble defined by β, and show that it is essentially a Julesz ensemble.

Clearly, the MRF model $p(\mathbf{I}; \beta)$ assigns equal probabilities to images in $\Omega_\Lambda(\mathbf{h})$ for any $\mathbf{h}$, because $\mathbf{h}(\mathbf{I})$ is the sufficient statistics. If we can show that $p(\mathbf{I}; \beta)$ eventually focuses on a certain value of $\mathbf{h}(\mathbf{I})$, say, $\mathbf{h}_\star$, then for large lattice, $p(\mathbf{I}; \beta)$ is essentially a uniform distribution over $\Omega_\Lambda(\mathbf{h}_\star)$, which leads to the equivalence of ensembles. For this purpose, we need to compute the probability rate function of $\mathbf{h}(\mathbf{I})$ under $p(\mathbf{I}; \beta)$.

Because the number of images with $\mathbf{h}(\mathbf{I}) = \mathbf{h}$ is $|\Omega_\Lambda(\mathbf{h})| = L^{|\Lambda|}\mu_\Lambda(\mathbf{h})$, the probability distribution of $\mathbf{h}(\mathbf{I})$ under the MRF model $p(\mathbf{I}; \beta)$ is

$$p(\mathbf{h}; \beta) = \frac{1}{Z_\Lambda(\beta)} \exp\{-|\Lambda| <\beta, \mathbf{h} >\} L^{|\Lambda|}\mu_\Lambda(\mathbf{h}),$$

and the probability rate

$$
\begin{aligned}
s_\beta(\mathbf{h}) &= \lim_{\Lambda \to \mathbf{Z}^2} \frac{1}{|\Lambda|} \log p(\mathbf{h}; \beta) \\
&= - <\beta, \mathbf{h} > + \lim_{\Lambda \to \mathbf{Z}^2} \frac{1}{|\Lambda|} \log \mu_\Lambda(\mathbf{h}) \\
&\quad - (\lim_{\Lambda \to \mathbf{Z}^2} \frac{1}{|\Lambda|} \log Z_\Lambda(\beta) - \log L).
\end{aligned}
$$

We already know that

$$\lim_{\Lambda \to \mathbf{Z}^2} \frac{1}{|\Lambda|} \log \mu_\Lambda(\mathbf{h}) = s(\mathbf{h})$$

is the probability rate function of $\mathbf{h}(\mathbf{I})$ under the uniform model. For the last term in $s_\beta(\mathbf{h})$, we have

Proposition 2 *The limit*

$$\rho(\beta) = \lim_{\Lambda \to \mathbf{Z}^2} \frac{1}{|\Lambda|} \log Z_\Lambda(\beta) - \log L$$

exists and is independent of the boundary condition. ρ is strictly convex.

See Griffiths and Ruelle (1971) for a proof. Therefore, we have

Proposition 3 *The probability rate function $s_\beta(\mathbf{h})$ of the MRF model $p(\mathbf{I}; \beta)$ is $s_\beta(\mathbf{h}) = s(\mathbf{h}) - <\beta, \mathbf{h}> -\rho(\beta)$.*

So we have the following theorem.

Theorem 1 *If there is a unique $\mathbf{h}_\star$ where $s_\beta(\mathbf{h})$ achieves its maximum 0, then $p(\mathbf{I}; \beta)$ eventually concentrates on $\mathbf{h}_\star$, and therefore the Gibbs ensemble defined by β is equivalent to the Julesz ensemble defined by $h_\star$, and $s'(\mathbf{h}_\star) = \beta$.*

The uniqueness of $\mathbf{h}_\star$ holds under the condition that there is no phase transition at β. See the next subsection for a discussion.

When there is no phase transition, the Julesz ensemble or the corresponding Gibbs ensemble concentrates its probability mass on a set of typical images sharing the same statistical property. To see this fact, consider an arbitrary new statistics $h_0(\mathbf{I})$ not used for modeling. It can be shown that the Julesz (or Gibbs) ensemble concentrates on the unique $h_{0\star}$ that maximizes $s(\mathbf{h}_\star, h_0)$, where $s(\mathbf{h}, h_0)$ is the probability rate function for the enlarged statistics $(\mathbf{h}(\mathbf{I}), h_0(\mathbf{I}))$ under the uniform model. That means that almost all images in the Julesz (or Gibbs) ensemble produce $h_{0\star}$ for the statistics $h_0(\mathbf{I})$, i.e., if we sample from the Julesz (or Gibbs) ensemble, we will always observe $h_{0\star}$, which is the typical value of the statistics $h_0(\mathbf{I})$. Because $h_0(\mathbf{I})$ is arbitrary, if we sample from the Julesz (or Gibbs) ensemble, we will always get images with the same statistical property. Such images can be called typical images, which absorb all the probability mass of the Julesz (or Gibbs) ensemble.

The equivalence of ensembles also sheds new light on the minimax entropy principle Zhu, et al. (1997) introduced for texture modeling. The minimum entropy principle means that we should choose the feature statistics $\mathbf{h}_{\text{obs}}$ so that $s(\mathbf{h}_{\text{obs}})$ is the smallest, or the volume of $\Omega_\Lambda(\mathbf{h}_{\text{obs}})$ is the smallest, under constraint on model complexity. $s(\mathbf{h}_{\text{obs}})$ is a measure of entropy rate, or the randomness of the observed texture image. The maximum entropy principle means that we should put a uniform distribution over $\Omega_\Lambda(\mathbf{h}_{\text{obs}})$, so that sampling from this uniform distribution gives us typical images in $\Omega_\Lambda(\mathbf{h}_{\text{obs}})$, because almost all images in $\Omega_\Lambda(\mathbf{h}_{\text{obs}})$ are typical images.

3.3 Uniqueness of ensembles

Given a parameter β, $p(\mathbf{I}; \beta)$ may go to different limits as $\Lambda \to \mathbf{Z}^2$ under different boundary conditions.

Such a phenomenon is called phase transition in statistical physics, and it can manifest itself if we sample from $p(\mathbf{I}; \beta)$: we may get images of different statistical properties if we use different large Λ and different boundary conditions. It is also possible that a sampled image consists of large image patches of different statistical properties. Mathematically, phase transition reflects the fact that there is a cusp, and thus not differentiable in the function $\rho(\beta)$, or a flat top in the function $s_\beta(\mathbf{h})$. When there is no phase transition, there is only one Gibbs ensemble which is an ergodic random field.

For a given $\mathbf{h}$, it is also possible that the uniform distribution $q(\mathbf{I}; \mathcal{H})$ goes to different limits as $\Lambda \to \mathbf{Z}^2$ and $\mathcal{H} \to \mathbf{h}$. This can manifest itself in a similar way as described above. See Martin-Lof (1979) for more details. Again, we consider such a Julesz ensemble unsuitable for texture modeling.

4 Discussion

There are two important goals in texture modeling. 1). Search for the sufficient and necessary statistics that define the underlying texture pattern. 2). Search for conditional probability of an arbitrary image patch given its environment.

The first goal leads us to the Julesz ensemble, and the second goal leads us to the Gibbs ensemble. In this paper, we establish the equivalence between the two ensembles, therefore justify the FRAME model of Zhu, et al. (1997) as an inevitable description of texture. Figure 3 summarizes the global picture for texture modeling. The dashed line (path 2) represents the research line which pursues the Julesz ensembles. The solid line represents the research which build minimax entropy models. The two lines are connected by the equivalence of ensembles. The advantages of both lines can now be better utilized, with the Julesz ensemble is much more efficient for texture synthesis, model verification, and statistics pursuit, and the Gibbs models provide precise local probability measures for image segmentation and classification.

References

[1] J. Besag (1974) Spatial interaction and the statistical analysis of lattice systems (with discussion). *J. Royal Stat. Soc., B*, **36**, 192-236.

[2] G. R. Cross and A. K. Jain (1983) Markov random field texture models. *IEEE Trans. PAMI*, **5**, 25-39.

[3] J. S. De Bonet and P. Viola (1997) A non-parametric multi-scale statistical model for natural images. *Advances in Neural Information Processing*, **10**.

[4] S. Geman and D. Geman (1984) Stochastic relaxation, Gibbs distribution, and the Bayesian restoration of images. *IEEE Trans. PAMI*, **6**, 721-741.

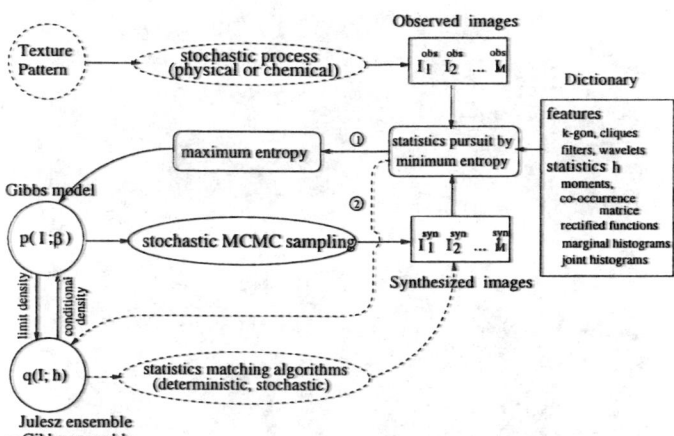

Figure 3: A global picture for texture modeling theories.

[5] A. Gagalowicz and S. D. Ma (1986) Model driven synthesis of natural textures for 3D scenes. *Computers and Graphics*. **10**, 161-170.

[6] J. W. Gibbs (1902) *Elementary Principles of Statistical Mechanics*. Yale University Press.

[7] R. Griffiths and D. Ruelle (1971) Strict convexity ("continuity") of the pressure in lattice system. *Comm. Math. Phys.,,* **23**, 169.

[8] D. J. Heeger and J. R. Bergen (1996) Pyramid-based texture analysis/synthesis. *SIGGRAPHS*.

[9] O. E. Lanford (1973) Entropy and equilibrium states in classical mechanics. In *Statistical Mechanics and Mathematical Problems*, A. Lenard ed. Springer.

[10] Lewis, J. T., Pfister, C.-E., and Sullivan, W. G. (1995) Entropy, concentration of probability and conditional limit theorems. *Markov Processes Relat. Fields*, **1**, 319-396.

[11] A. Martin-Lof (1979) The equivalence of ensembles and Gibbs' phase rule for classical lattice systems. *J. Stat. Phys.*, **20**, 557-569.

[12] Y. Wu and S. C. Zhu (1999) Equivalence of Image Ensembles and Fundamental Bounds — A unified theory of texture modeling and analysis, *Preprint* (available via www.cis.ohio-state.edu/~szhu/publication.html).

[13] S. C. Zhu, X. Liu, and Y. Wu (1999) Exploring Texture Enesmbles by Efiicient Markov Chain Monte Carlo, *Proc. of Workshop on Statistical and Computational Theories of Vision*, June 1999.

[14] S. C. Zhu, Y. Wu, and D. B. Mumford (1997). Minimax entropy principle and its application to texture modeling, *Neural Computation*, **9**, 1627-1660.

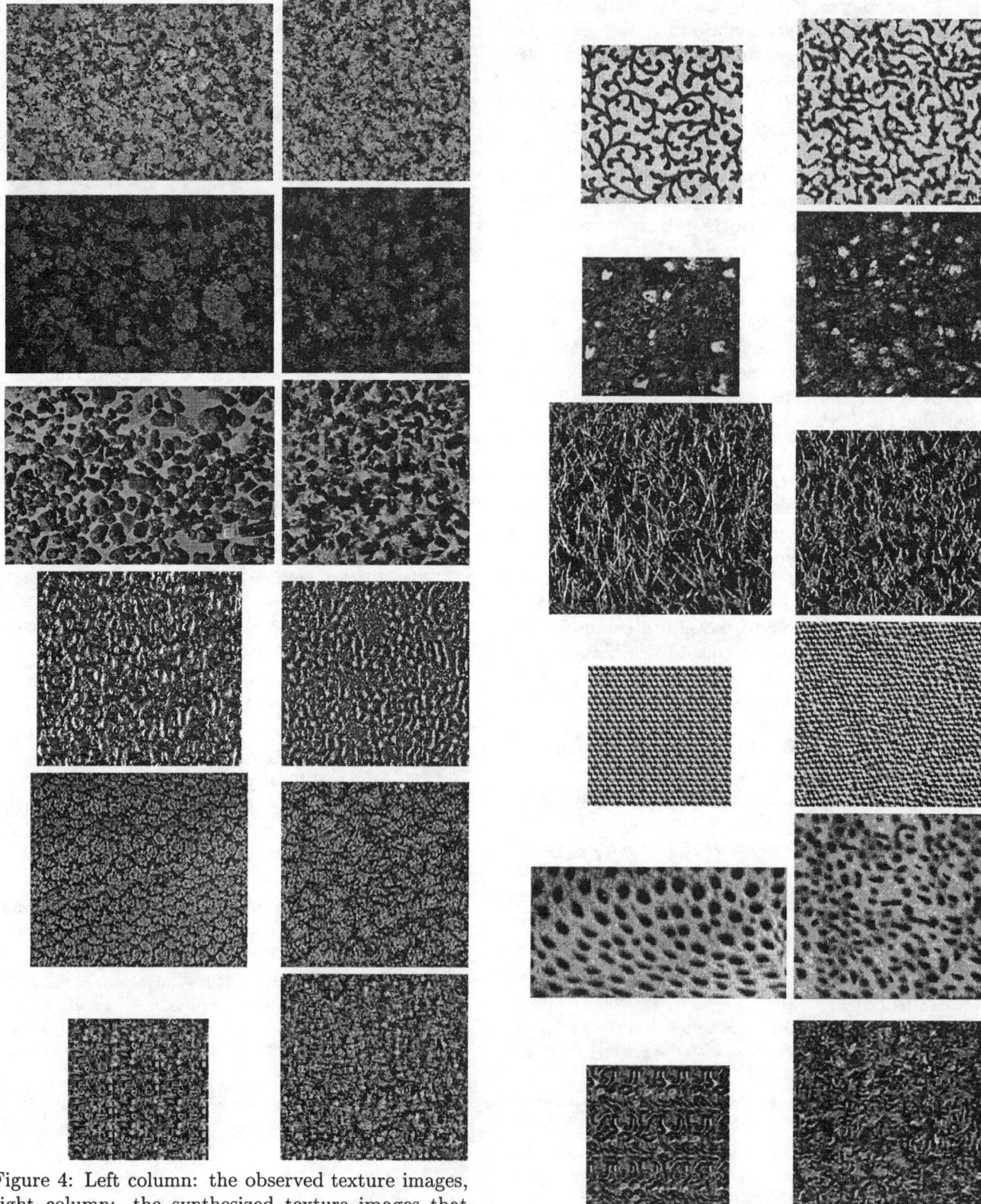

Figure 4: Left column: the observed texture images, right column: the synthesized texture images that share the exact histograms with the observed for 56 filters.

Figure 5: See caption of Figure 4.

Texture Synthesis by Non-parametric Sampling

Alexei A. Efros and Thomas K. Leung
Computer Science Division
University of California, Berkeley
Berkeley, CA 94720-1776, U.S.A.
{efros,leungt}@cs.berkeley.edu

Abstract

A non-parametric method for texture synthesis is proposed. The texture synthesis process grows a new image outward from an initial seed, one pixel at a time. A Markov random field model is assumed, and the conditional distribution of a pixel given all its neighbors synthesized so far is estimated by querying the sample image and finding all similar neighborhoods. The degree of randomness is controlled by a single perceptually intuitive parameter. The method aims at preserving as much local structure as possible and produces good results for a wide variety of synthetic and real-world textures.

1. Introduction

Texture synthesis has been an active research topic in computer vision both as a way to verify texture analysis methods, as well as in its own right. Potential applications of a successful texture synthesis algorithm are broad, including occlusion fill-in, lossy image and video compression, foreground removal, etc.

The problem of texture synthesis can be formulated as follows: let us define texture as some visual pattern on an infinite 2-D plane which, at some scale, has a stationary distribution. Given a finite sample from some texture (an image), the goal is to synthesize other samples from the same texture. Without additional assumptions this problem is clearly ill-posed since a given texture sample could have been drawn from an infinite number of different textures. The usual assumption is that the sample is large enough that it somehow captures the stationarity of the texture and that the (approximate) scale of the texture elements (*texels*) is known.

Textures have been traditionally classified as either regular (consisting of repeated texels) or stochastic (without explicit texels). However, almost all real-world textures lie somewhere in between these two extremes and should be captured with a single model. In this paper we have chosen a statistical non-parametric model based on the assumption of spatial locality. The result is a very simple texture synthesis algorithm that works well on a wide range of textures and is especially well-suited for constrained synthesis problems (hole-filling).

1.1. Previous work

Most recent approaches have posed texture synthesis in a statistical setting as a problem of sampling from a probability distribution. Zhu et. al. [12] model texture as a Markov Random Field and use Gibbs sampling for synthesis. Unfortunately, Gibbs sampling is notoriously slow and in fact it is not possible to assess when it has converged. Heeger and Bergen [6] try to coerce a random noise image into a texture sample by matching the filter response histograms at different spatial scales. While this technique works well on highly stochastic textures, the histograms are not powerful enough to represent more structured texture patterns such as bricks.

De Bonet [1] also uses a multi-resolution filter-based approach in which a texture patch at a finer scale is conditioned on its "parents" at the coarser scales. The algorithm works by taking the input texture sample and randomizing it in such a way as to preserve these inter-scale dependencies. This method can successfully synthesize a wide range of textures although the randomness parameter seems to exhibit perceptually correct behavior only on largely stochastic textures. Another drawback of this method is the way texture images larger than the input are generated. The input texture sample is simply replicated to fill the desired dimensions before the synthesis process, implicitly assuming that all textures are tilable which is clearly not correct.

The latest work in texture synthesis by Simoncelli and Portilla [9, 11] is based on first and second order properties of joint wavelet coefficients and provides impressive results. It can capture both stochastic and repeated textures quite well, but still fails to reproduce high frequency information on some highly structured patterns.

1.2. Our Approach

In his 1948 article, *A Mathematical Theory of Communication* [10], Claude Shannon mentioned an interesting way of producing English-sounding written text using n-grams. The idea is to model language as a generalized Markov chain: a set of n consecutive letters (or words) make up an n-gram and completely determine the probability distribution of the next letter (or word). Using a large sample of the language (e.g., a book) one can build probability tables for each n-gram. One can then repeatedly sample from this Markov chain to produce English-sounding text. This is the basis for an early computer program called MARK V. SHANEY, popularized by an article in *Scientific American* [4], and famous for such pearls as: *"I spent an interesting evening recently with a grain of salt"*.

This paper relates to an earlier work by Popat and Picard [8] in trying to extend this idea to two dimensions. The three main challenges in this endeavor are: 1) how to define a unit of synthesis (a letter) and its context (n-gram) for texture, 2) how to construct a probability distribution, and 3) how to linearize the synthesis process in 2D.

Our algorithm "grows" texture, pixel by pixel, outwards from an initial seed. We chose a single pixel p as our unit of synthesis so that our model could capture as much high frequency information as possible. All previously synthesized pixels in a square window around p (weighted to emphasize local structure) are used as the context. To proceed with synthesis we need probability tables for the distribution of p, given all possible contexts. However, while for text these tables are (usually) of manageable size, in our texture setting constructing them explicitly is out of the question. An approximation can be obtained using various clustering techniques, but we choose not to construct a model at all. Instead, for each new context, the sample image is queried and the distribution of p is constructed as a histogram of all possible values that occurred in the sample image as shown on Figure 1. The non-parametric sampling technique, although simple, is very powerful at capturing statistical processes for which a good model hasn't been found.

2. The Algorithm

In this work we model texture as a Markov Random Field (MRF). That is, we assume that the probability distribution of brightness values for a pixel given the brightness values of its spatial neighborhood is independent of the rest of the image. The neighborhood of a pixel is modeled as a square window around that pixel. The size of the window is a free parameter that specifies how stochastic the user believes this texture to be. More specifically, if the texture is presumed to be mainly regular at high spatial frequencies and mainly stochastic at low spatial frequencies, the size of

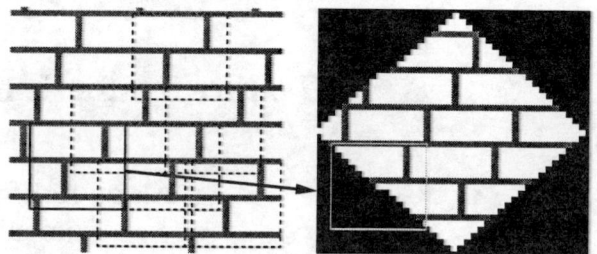

Figure 1. Algorithm Overview. Given a sample texture image (left), a new image is being synthesized one pixel at a time (right). To synthesize a pixel, the algorithm first finds all neighborhoods in the sample image (boxes on the left) that are similar to the pixel's neighborhood (box on the right) and then randomly chooses one neighborhood and takes its center to be the newly synthesized pixel.

the window should be on the scale of the biggest regular feature.

2.1. Synthesizing one pixel

Let I be an image that is being synthesized from a texture sample image $I_{smp} \subset I_{real}$ where I_{real} is the real infinite texture. Let $p \in I$ be a pixel and let $\omega(p) \subset I$ be a square image patch of width w centered at p. Let $d_{perc}(\omega_1, \omega_2)$ denote some perceptual distance between two patches. Let us assume for the moment that all pixels in I except for p are known. To synthesize the value of p we first construct an approximation to the conditional probability distribution $P(p|\omega(p))$ and then sample from it.

Based on our MRF model we assume that p is independent of $I \setminus \omega(p)$ given $\omega(p)$. If we define a set

$$\Omega(p) = \{\omega' \subset I_{real} : d_{perc}(\omega', \omega(p)) = 0\}$$

containing all occurrences of $\omega(p)$ in I_{real}, then the conditional pdf of p can be estimated with a histogram of all center pixel values in $\Omega(p)$.[1] Unfortunately, we are only given I_{smp}, a finite sample from I_{real}, which means there might not be any matches for $\omega(p)$ in I_{smp}. Thus we must use a heuristic which will let us find a plausible $\Omega'(p) \approx \Omega(p)$ to sample from. In our implementation, a variation of the k Nearest Neighbors technique is used: the closest match $\omega'_{best} = argmin_\omega d_{perc}(\omega(p), \omega) \subset I_{smp}$ is found, and all image patches ω' with $d_{perc}(\omega'_{best}, \omega') < \epsilon$ are included in Ω', where ϵ is a threshold. The center pixel values of patches in Ω' give us a histogram for p, which can then be sampled, either uniformly or weighted by d_{perc}.

Now it only remains to find a suitable d_{perc}. One choice is a normalized sum of squared differences metric d_{SSD}. However, this metric gives the same weight to any mismatched pixel, whether near the center or at the edge of the

---

[1] This is somewhat misleading, since if all pixels in $\Omega(p)$ except p are known, the pdf for p will simply be a delta function for all but highly stochastic textures, since a single pixel can rarely be a feature by itself.

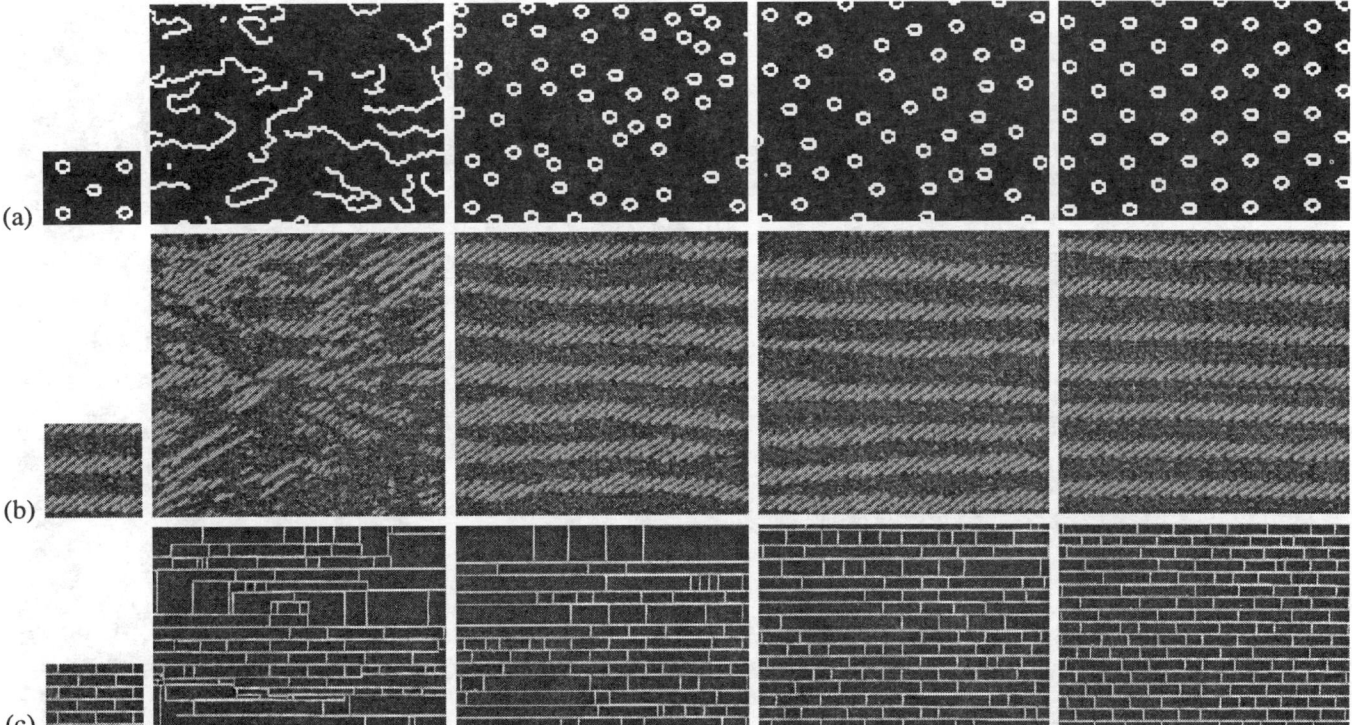

Figure 2. Results: given a sample image (left), the algorithm synthesized four new images with neighborhood windows of width 5, 11, 15, and 23 pixels respectively. Notice how perceptually intuitively the window size corresponds to the degree of randomness in the resulting textures. Input images are: (a) synthetic rings, (b) Brodatz texture D11, (c) brick wall.

window. Since we would like to preserve the local structure of the texture as much as possible, the error for nearby pixels should be greater than for pixels far away. To achieve this effect we set $d_{perc} = d_{SSD} * G$ where G is a two-dimensional Gaussian kernel.

2.2. Synthesizing texture

In the previous section we have discussed a method of synthesizing a pixel when its neighborhood pixels are already known. Unfortunately, this method cannot be used for synthesizing the entire texture or even for hole-filling (unless the hole is just one pixel) since for any pixel the values of only some of its neighborhood pixels will be known. The correct solution would be to consider the joint probability of all pixels together but this is intractable for images of realistic size.

Instead, a Shannon-inspired heuristic is proposed, where the texture is grown in layers outward from a 3-by-3 seed taken randomly from the sample image (in case of hole filling, the synthesis proceeds from the edges of the hole). Now for any point p to be synthesized only *some* of the pixel values in $\omega(p)$ are known (i.e. have already been synthesized). Thus the pixel synthesis algorithm must be modified to handle unknown neighborhood pixel values. This can be easily done by only matching on the known values in $\omega(p)$ and normalizing the error by the total number of known pixels

when computing the conditional pdf for p. This heuristic does not guarantee that the pdf for p will stay valid as the rest of $\omega(p)$ is filled in. However, it appears to be a good approximation in practice. One can also treat this as an initialization step for an iterative approach such as Gibbs sampling. However, our trials have shown that Gibbs sampling produced very little improvement for most textures. This lack of improvement indicates that the heuristic indeed provides a good approximation to the desired conditional pdf.

3. Results

Our algorithm produces good results for a wide range of textures. The only parameter set by the user is the width w of the context window. This parameter appears to intuitively correspond to the human perception of randomness for most textures. As an example, the image with rings on Figure 2a has been synthesized several times while increasing w. In the first synthesized image the context window is not big enough to capture the structure of the ring so only the notion of curved segments is preserved. In the next image, the context captures the whole ring, but knows nothing of inter-ring distances producing a Poisson process pattern. In the third image we see rings getting away from each other (so called Poisson process with repulsion), and finally in the last image the inter-ring structure is within the reach of the window as the pattern becomes almost purely structured.

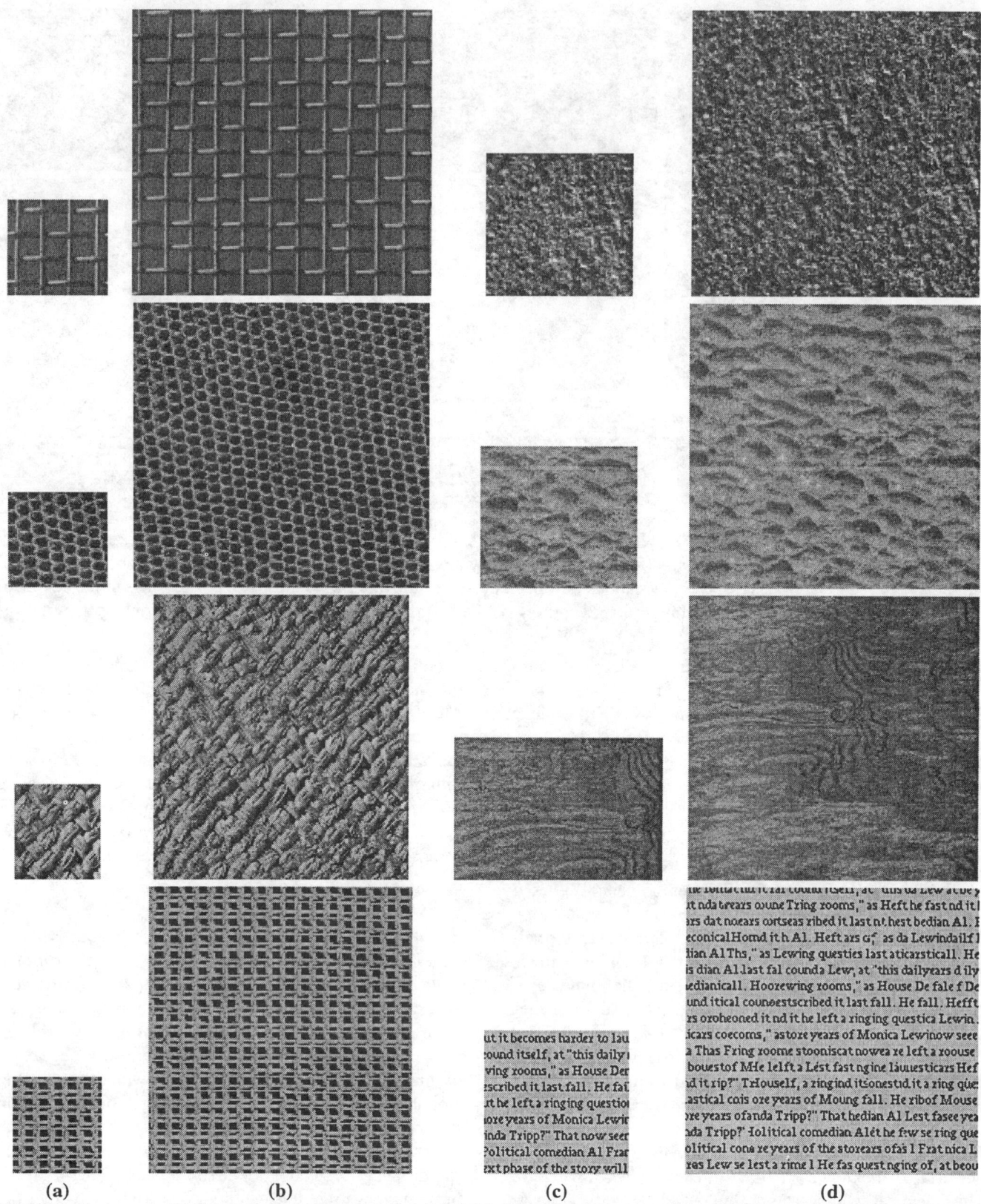

Figure 3. Texture synthesis on real-world textures: (a) and (c) are original images, (b) and (d) are synthesized. (a) images D1, D3, D18, and D20 from Brodatz collection [2], (c) granite, bread, wood, and text (a homage to Shannon) images.

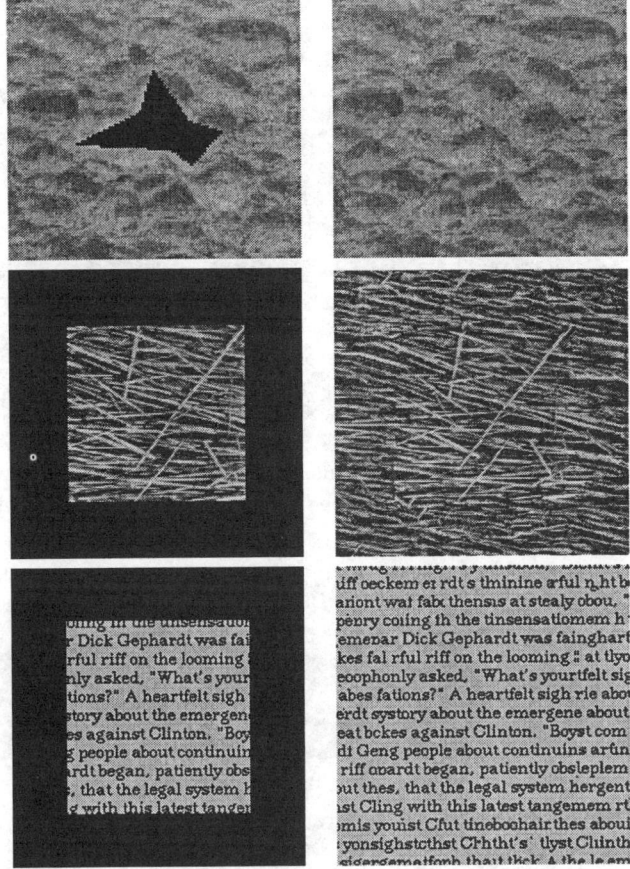

Figure 4. Examples of constrained texture synthesis. The synthesis process fills in the black regions.

(a)   (b)

Figure 5. Failure examples. Sometimes the growing algorithm "slips" into a wrong part of the search space and starts growing garbage (a), or gets stuck at a particular place in the sample image and starts verbatim copying (b).

Figure 3 shows synthesis examples done on real-world textures. Examples of constrained synthesis are shown on Figure 4. The black regions in each image are filled in by sampling from that same image. A comparison with De Bonet [1] at varying randomness settings is shown on Figure 7 using texture 161 from his web site.

4. Limitations and Future Work

As with most texture synthesis procedures, only frontal-parallel textures are handled. However, it is possible to use Shape-from-Texture techniques [5, 7] to pre-warp an image into frontal-parallel position before synthesis and post-warp afterwards.

One problem of our algorithm is its tendency for some textures to occasionally "slip" into a wrong part of the search space and start growing garbage (Figure 5a) or get locked onto one place in the sample image and produce verbatim copies of the original (Figure 5b). These problems occur when the texture sample contains too many different types of texels (or the same texels but differently illuminated) making it hard to find close matches for the neighborhood context window. These problems can usually be

eliminated by providing a bigger sample image. We have also used growing with limited backtracking as a solution.

In the future we plan to study automatic window-size selection, including non-square windows for elongated textures. We are also currently investigating the use of texels as opposed to pixels as the basic unit of synthesis (similar to moving from letters to words in Shannon's setting). This is akin to putting together a jigsaw puzzle where each piece has a different shape and only a few can fit together. Currently, the algorithm is quite slow but we are working on ways to make it more efficient.

5. Applications

Apart from letting us gain a better understanding of texture models, texture synthesis can also be used as a tool for solving several practical problems in computer vision, graphics, and image processing. Our method is particularly versatile because it does not place any constraints on the shape of the synthesis region or the sampling region, making it ideal for constrained texture synthesis such as hole-filling. Moreover, our method is designed to preserve local image structure, such as continuing straight lines, so there are no visual discontinuities between the original hole outline and the newly synthesized patch.

For example, capturing a 3D scene from several camera views will likely result in some regions being occluded from all cameras [3]. Instead of letting them appear as black holes in a reconstruction, a localized constrained texture synthesis can be performed to fill in the missing information from the surrounding region. As another example, consider the problem of boundary handling when performing a convolution on an image. Several methods exist, such as zero-fill, tiling and reflection, however all of them may in-

Figure 6. The texture synthesis algorithm is applied to a real image (left) extrapolating it using itself as a model, to result in a larger image (right) that, for this particular image, looks quite plausible. This technique can be used in convolutions to extend filter support at image boundaries.

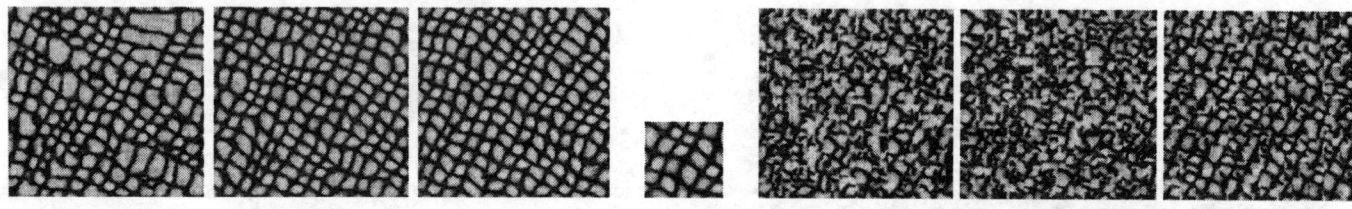

Our method   sample image   De Bonet's method

Figure 7. Texture synthesized from sample image with our method compared to [1] at decreasing degree of randomness.

troduce discontinuities not present in the original image. In many cases, texture synthesis can be used to extrapolate the image by sampling from itself as shown on Figure 6.

The constrained synthesis process can be further enhanced by using image segmentation to find the exact sampling region boundaries. A small patch of each region can then be stored together with region boundaries as a lossy compression technique, with texture synthesis being used to restore each region separately. If a figure/ground segmentation is possible and the background is texture-like, then foreground removal can be done by synthesizing the background into the foreground segment.

Our algorithm can also easily be applied to motion synthesis such as ocean waves, rolling clouds, or burning fire by a trivial extension to 3D.

Acknowledgments: We would like to thank Alex Berg, Elizaveta Levina, and Yair Weiss for many helpful discussions and comments. This work has been supported by NSF Graduate Fellowship to AE, Berkeley Fellowship to TL, ONR MURI grant FDN00014-96-1-1200, and the California MICRO grant 98-096.

References

[1] J. S. D. Bonet. Multiresolution sampling procedure for analysis and synthesis of texture images. In *SIGGRAPH '97*, pages 361–368, 1997.

[2] P. Brodatz. *Textures*. Dover, New York, 1966.

[3] P. E. Debevec, C. J. Taylor, and J. Malik. Modeling and rendering architecture from photographs: A hybrid geometry- and image-based approach. In *SIGGRAPH '96*, pages 11–20, August 1996.

[4] A. Dewdney. A potpourri of programmed prose and prosody. *Scientific American*, 122-TK, June 1989.

[5] J. Garding. Surface orientation and curvature from differential texture distortion. *ICCV*, pages 733–739, 1995.

[6] D. J. Heeger and J. R. Bergen. Pyramid-based texture analysis/synthesis. In *SIGGRAPH '95*, pages 229–238, 1995.

[7] J. Malik and R. Rosenholtz. Computing local surface orientation and shape from texture for curved surfaces. *International Journal of Computer Vision*, 23(2):149–168, 1997.

[8] K. Popat and R. W. Picard. Novel cluster-based probability model for texture synthesis, classification, and compression. In *Proc. SPIE Visual Comm. and Image Processing*, 1993.

[9] J. Portilla and E. P. Simoncelli. Texture representation and synthesis using correlation of complex wavelet coefficient magnitudes. TR 54, CSIC, Madrid, April 1999.

[10] C. E. Shannon. A mathematical theory of communication. *Bell Sys. Tech. Journal*, 27, 1948.

[11] E. P. Simoncelli and J. Portilla. Texture characterization via joint statistics of wavelet coefficient magnitudes. In *Proc. 5th Int'l Conf. on Image Processing Chicago, IL*, 1998.

[12] S. C. Zhu, Y. Wu, and D. Mumford. Filters, random fields and maximum entropy (frame). *International Journal of Computer Vision*, 27(2):1–20, March/April 1998.

Corner Detection in Textured Color Images

Mark A. Ruzon   Carlo Tomasi

Computer Science Department
Stanford University
Stanford, CA 94305

Abstract

Corner models in the literature have lagged behind edge models with respect to color and shading. We use both a region model, based on distributions of pixel colors, and an edge model, which removes false positives, to perform corner detection on color images whose regions contain texture. We show results on a variety of natural images at different scales that highlight the problems that occur when boundaries between regions have curvature.

1 Introduction

Corners and junctions (multiple corners at the same image location) are crucial for high-level vision tasks because they represent occlusions useful to stereo and motion algorithms, and they provide shape information for object recognition. They are arguably at least as important as edges, yet current edge models invoke fewer assumptions and are more robust than current corner models.

Specifically, edge models proposed in the literature are superior to existing corner models with respect to color and shading. Many color edge detectors have been proposed ([1], [5], and [11] form a representative sample), but corner detectors have been confined to greyscale images. Certain algorithms (e.g. [8]) appear to be easily extendable to color images. The effects of shading on the direction of the image gradient were modeled by Wang and Binford [12] to create an edge detector insensitive to shading, while most corner detectors assume that regions are of constant intensity (Alvarez and Morales [2] assumed level sets).

Many corner detectors start with an edge map rather than an image (e.g. [6] and [7]), which would appear to mitigate such effects. However, we argue against using these indirect methods for two reasons: (1) using the output of an algorithm whose goal is something other than corner detection causes unknown biases and errors to propagate into the corner detector, and (2) the analysis of Deriche and Giraudon [4] showed that edges found by first-derivative operators tend to "round off" corners. Without using the image itself, it is impossible to distinguish true corners from curved boundaries. Therefore, we opt for a direct approach.

At a conceptual level, corner and edge detection algorithms both compute the degree to which two adjacent regions are dissimilar. Corners do not bisect an operator's support, however, and the resulting asymmetry must be accounted for. Also, corners are point features, so only one response to the same part of the image can be accepted. Detecting junctions, though, requires accepting multiple responses of the corner detector in the same or nearly the same image location.

Our approach uses both a region model, from which we create a set of corner candidates, and an edge model, which decides whether to accept or reject a candidate. We model a corner as two adjacent regions that differ in their color distributions. The resulting operator generalizes edge detection to asymmetric regions with multiple colors per region. Multiple colors are represented by a set of point masses in a color space. The distance between two such sets is found using the Earth Mover's Distance, which measures the minimum amount of "work" required to transform one set into the other in that space.

The advantage of this model is that we can detect corners (and edges, see [10]) in textured regions where other detectors cannot. Two textures may have the same "mean color," for example, even though they have no color in common. Furthermore, the texture need not be homogeneous as long as its colors are sufficiently different from its neighbors.

An edge model is also necessary, because corners cannot exist independently of edges. Our model, inspired by Deriche and Giraudon's, presumes that at the two endpoints of the corner, there is a strong edge response in the same direction. Furthermore, the edge response between the two endpoints of the corner should be weaker than the corner response. We can

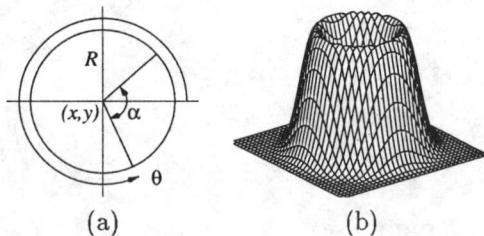

(a)   (b)

Figure 1: Parts of the region model. (a) Illustration of operator parameters. (b) The pixel weighting function, a surface of revolution of half of a Gaussian derivative function.

compare corner candidates with this model to exclude most false positives in the operator's response. If multiple candidates all respond well to the same corner, we group them and choose the "best" candidate.

The next two sections explain the region and edge models, respectively, after which we present the results and our conclusions.

2   The Region Model

In this section we develop a model of two adjacent regions and the perceptual distance between them. In Section 2.1 we summarize the representation of a region as a color signature; details are in [10]. Section 2.2 tackles the problem of asymmetry between the two regions, and Section 2.3 explains how initial corner candidates are selected.

2.1   Color Signatures

A *color signature* is a set of point masses that represents one of the two regions. There are five parameters that determine which pixels will belong to each region: (x, y), the location of the center of the window; $\theta \in [0, 360)$, the orientation of the corner (defined as the angle formed by the positive x-axis and the "clockwise" side of the corner); $\alpha \in (0, 180]$, the angle subtended by the corner; and R, the scale parameter (Figure 1(a)). Because it is natural to consider a corner as a wedge, the window is a circle of radius R.

Vector quantization applied to the circle determines the number and location of the point masses. Each pixel contributes a weight dependent only on its distance to the center. The polar function $f(r) = cre^{-\frac{r^2}{2\sigma^2}}$, where c is a normalizing constant and $\sigma = R/3$, is the positive half of a 1-D Gaussian derivative function revolved around the y-axis (Figure 1(b)). Isotropy simplifies computations over all combinations of θ and α because the mass that each pixel contributes remains constant. Sampling the ranges of θ and α

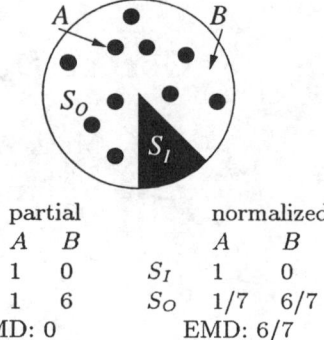

partial			normalized		
	A	B		A	B
S_I	1	0	S_I	1	0
S_O	1	6	S_O	1/7	6/7
EMD: 0			EMD: 6/7		

Figure 2: The normalized EMD can detect corners that the partial EMD cannot.

equally breaks the circle into wedges, allowing efficient updating of the signatures. We use 15° wedges.

We represent colors in the CIE-Lab color space [13], in which short, Euclidean distances are perceptually accurate. To account for the fact that long distances are not, we use a normalized measure that saturates:

$$d_{ij} = 1 - \exp(-E_{ij}/\gamma),$$

where E_{ij} is the Euclidean distance between color i and color j, and $\gamma = 14.0$ is a constant determining the steepness of the function.

The distance between two color signatures is found using the Earth Mover's Distance (EMD) [9]. The EMD measures the minimum amount of physical work needed to move the masses of one signature into correspondence with the other. In our formulation, the EMD lies in [0, 1] since the maximum amount of mass that can be moved and the maximum distance it can move are both 1.

2.2   Partial EMD vs. Normalized EMD

After creating two color signatures, S_I inside the corner and S_O outside it, we can use the EMD to measure the similarity between the two regions. An important issue in this computation that is not present when using this model for edge detection is that S_O always has more mass than S_I.

We normalize S_I to have a mass of 1, regardless of the value of α, to preserve the same output range. There are two ways to normalize S_O: we can use the same constant and find the EMD between signatures of unequal mass ("partial" EMD), or we can assign S_O a mass of 1 also ("normalized" EMD).

Each type of EMD has different advantages. In Figure 2 the normalized EMD detects a corner that the partial EMD does not. A 45° corner consists entirely of color A, while the outside region has amounts of colors A and B (a perceptual distance of 1 from A) in

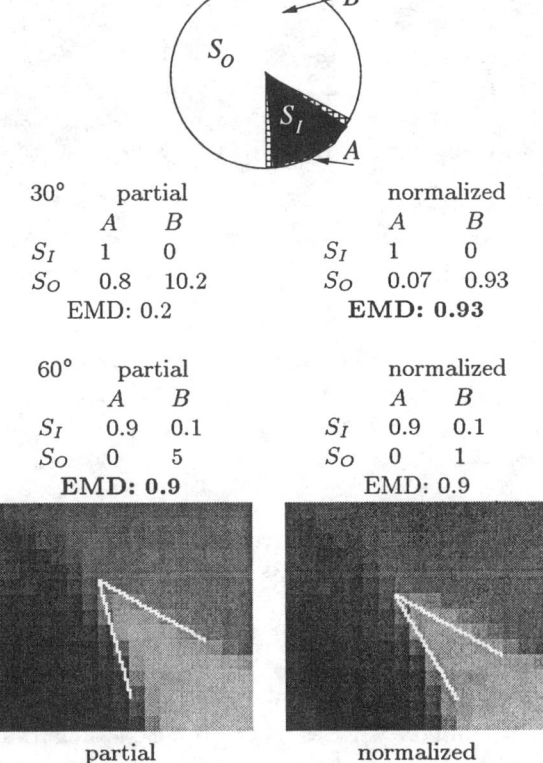

30°	partial		normalized	
	A	B		A	B
S_I	1	0	S_I	1	0
S_O	0.8	10.2	S_O	0.07	0.93
	EMD: 0.2		**EMD: 0.93**	

60°	partial		normalized	
	A	B		A	B
S_I	0.9	0.1	S_I	0.9	0.1
S_O	0	5	S_O	0	1
	EMD: 0.9		EMD: 0.9	

partial   normalized

Figure 3: The partial EMD can more accurately describe a corner.

a 1:6 ratio. We define the mass of S_I to be 1, and the mass of S_O can be either 1 or 7. If we choose the mass to be 7 (partial EMD), then S_I becomes a subset of S_O, and the distance is 0. If instead we choose the mass of S_O to be 1 (normalized EMD), the distance is 6/7, and a corner is likely to be found.

Figure 3 shows a situation where the partial EMD describes a corner more accurately than the normalized EMD. A 60° corner consists entirely of color A except for the two edges, which contain some pixels of color B. If 10% of the pixels inside the corner have color B, then the values of the EMD are those shown in the accompanying table. Both types of EMD detect a corner, but the normalized EMD estimates α to be 30° while the partial EMD correctly estimates α to be 60°. An example of the differences for real image data is shown below the table. The corner found by the partial EMD runs along the edges, while the other does not.

We have chosen the partial EMD for our experiments. Although we may have false negatives, the number is likely to be small because the frequency of the phenomenon illustrated in Figure 2 is inversely proportional to α, and such corners are less frequent

in natural images. For the corners that we do detect, it is best to describe them as accurately as possible.

2.3 Finding Corner Candidates

The process of corner detection begins by measuring the EMD over all circular windows and for all combinations of θ and α. The result is a list of three-dimensional tensors, one for each value of α. Corner candidates are maximum values over x, y, and θ that are above a threshold. Parabolic interpolation over θ gives the actual strength and orientation of a candidate.

Output for different values of α cannot be compared directly, however, even though the range of values is the same. From a purely statistical standpoint, it is less likely that a large EMD will result from a smaller value of α because of the greater imbalance in the amount of mass. The net effect is that we must vary our threshold linearly with α.

In addition, we must choose bounds on α because the output at small values is less reliable due to noise, and large corners are hard to distinguish from edges. We have chosen $\alpha_{min} = 30°$ and $\alpha_{max} = 150°$.

3 Corner Detection

In this section, we present our edge model (Section 3.1) and consider the problem of pruning multiple responses to the same corner that all satisfy this model (Section 3.2).

3.1 The Edge Model

In order for a true corner to exist, there must be evidence of strong edges that are consistent with the location, orientation, and angle of the corner. A basic schematic of our model is illustrated in Figure 4(a). Specifically, our model incorporates three ideas:

1. Edge direction at each end of a corner must match the orientation of the side of that corner.

2. Edge response at each end of a corner must be high.

3. Between the two ends of a corner, the edge response must be weaker than the corner response.

In theory, none of these conditions is satisfied when a corner candidate falsely responds to an edge (Figure 4(b)).

Before we can measure the degree to which a corner matches our model, we must have edge information. This is found by applying our operator with $\alpha = 180°$, and finding the orientation at each image location that maximizes the response (see [10] for details).

Once this is done, we find two angles: θ_C, the difference in orientation between the clockwise side of the

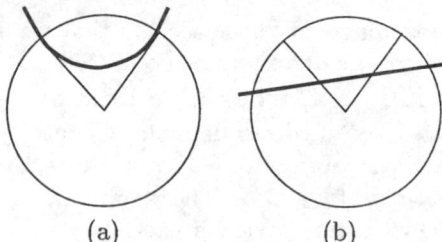

Figure 4: (a) A true corner. The edge is aligned with the corner at the endpoints and "rounded off" in the middle, where the response weakens. (b) A false positive due to inhomogeneities on one side of an edge.

corner and the edge response at the corner's endpoint, and θ_{CC}, the corresponding angle for the counterclockwise side. Because edges have two valid orientations (differing by 180°), we choose the one that yields the smaller angle. Our measurement P can be expressed as

$$P = \cos\theta_C + \cos\theta_{CC},$$

which lies between 0 and 2. We threshold P at 1.97.

Finally, where the edge crosses the line that bisects the corner, the projection of the edge response onto the line normal to the bisector must be weaker than the corner response. We check responses on a small interval along the bisector line centered at a point $R(\sec\frac{\alpha}{2} - \tan\frac{\alpha}{2})$ pixels away from the corner. This quantity is the distance from the corner point to the circumference of an imaginary circle tangent to the sides of the corner at its endpoints.

Applying all three parts of the model to the set of initial corner candidates greatly reduces their number. Figure 5(a) shows the candidates for an image patch consisting of cut stone against an ivy-covered wall. Though all the candidates are near the boundary between the two regions, most of them do not fit the boundary well. Figure 5(b) shows the results after applying the edge model.

3.2 Pruning Multiple Responses

Using edge data, however, does not completely solve our problem. Figure 5(b) contains two corners, each of which gives a strong corner response to the same area of the image and matches the edges well. Obviously, we would like to have only one.

The question of which corners to group together in this image is trivial, but the general question of when two or more corners are "close enough" to each other that one should be accepted and the rest rejected has no definitive answer in natural images.

We define two corners as being "close enough" if the corner points are within $3R/4$ pixels of each other

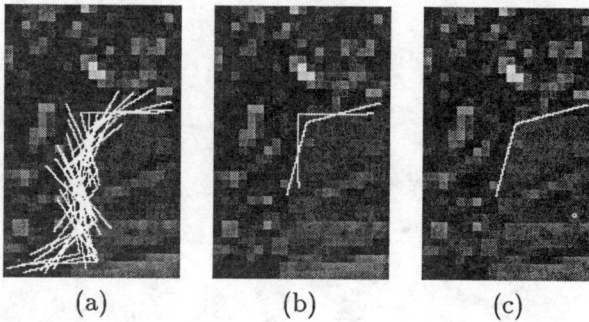

Figure 5: Corner detection steps applied to operator output of cut stone occluding an ivy-covered wall. (a) Initial corner candidates. (b) After applying the edge model. (c) Final result after pruning multiple responses.

and one of the following conditions is true: (1) the two clockwise orientations differ by no more than 10°, (2) the two counterclockwise orientations differ by no more than 10°, or (3) the sum the differences is no more than 40°. These conditions group "nested" corners while preserving multiple corners near junctions.

An ambiguity arises when corner X is close to corners Y and Z, but Y and Z are not close to each other. If our notion of "closeness" is global, then the order in which we examine corners affects the final output. Since this is unacceptable, we compute the transitive closure of "closeness," that is, X, Y, and Z will all become part of the same set. It is theoretically possible that corners in distant parts of the image could become part of the same set; in practice, however, the application of the edge model removes enough candidates that this does not happen often.

Once we have computed the transitive closure, we pick the member of each set that maximizes the expression $2C + P + E$, where C is the corner response, P is the degree of orientation match described earlier, and E is the sum of the edge responses at the endpoints of the two sides of the corner. C is doubled so that each term contributes equally. The final corner of our example is shown in Figure 5(c).

4 Results

In this section we present results on a variety of image patches in order to convey the versatility of the operator. All the results in this paper that use the partial EMD were computed with the same thresholds. The lengths of the sides of the corners in the images are equal to the chosen value of R. Color versions of the results are available from http://vision.stanford.edu/public/publication/.

Figure 6 shows one fabric occluding another. Al-

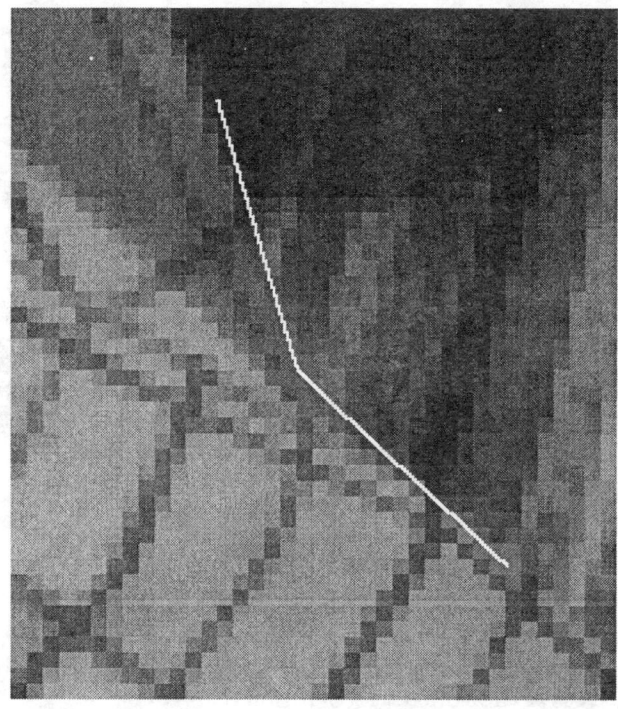

Figure 6: Two fabrics. Note the heterogeneity of each texture, as well as the existence of shadows.

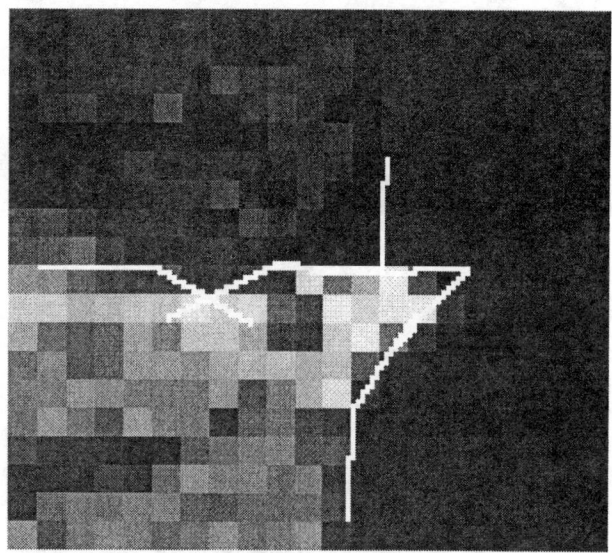

Figure 7: Corners found between three regions.

though each contains texture that varies greatly in color and has regions in partial shadow, the corner is correctly detected.

Figure 7 is more complicated because three textures are involved: trees (upper left), rock (lower left), and rock in deep shadow (right). Five corners are found that separate the regions and, incidentally, form most of the boundary of the illuminated rock.

In Figure 8 we show output at three different scales. The image contains a junction, but the textured region subtends an angle greater than α_{max}, and the region boundaries are not rays emanating from the junction. At all three scales we find the two smaller corners with compatible orienations and corner points near each other. We emphasize that corners are estimated independently; a true junction detector would combine these corners, perhaps with knowledge of the lack of symmetry near the junction [10], to estimate its location and parameters.

Other researchers have examined the evolution of corners across scales in more detail. Mokhtarian and Suomela [7] detected corners at a large scale and used smaller scales to localize them, an approach that might work well here. Alvarez and Morales' framework [2] caused corners to evolve along the line bisecting the corner. Their framework depends on the level set as-

sumption, which is violated here. Neither appears to have been tested on boundaries with continuously changing curvature or on corners as large as 150°, though.

Finally, we wish to mention the running time. The operator is implemented in C and can process image locations (each including all combinations of θ and α) at a rate on the order of 1500 per minute on an SGI Indigo 2, depending on R.

5 Conclusion

We have presented an operator that outputs high values when two regions inside and outside of a corner have different color distributions. Using color signatures and the Earth Mover's Distance allows us to detect corners in situations that others have not even considered because they are forced to assume that each region is constant.

The edge model eliminates those corners that are not supported by evidence of strong edges. This basic dependence of corners on edges is both conceptually important and practically effective.

The application of corner detection to natural images that are not composed mostly of polygons brings up many interesting issues, the most important of which is the definition of a corner. We have not specified an optimality condition from which our operator can be derived, because deciding that a corner exists is mostly a question of thresholding the curvature of an edge with respect to the chosen scale. By the same token, there is no ground truth in natural images to compare our results to. The results are best evaluated

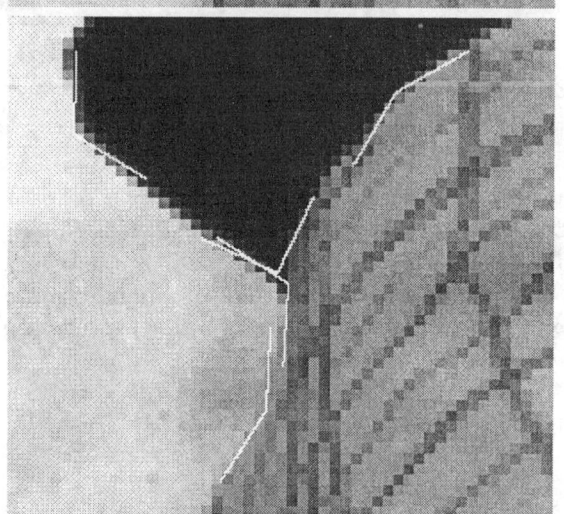

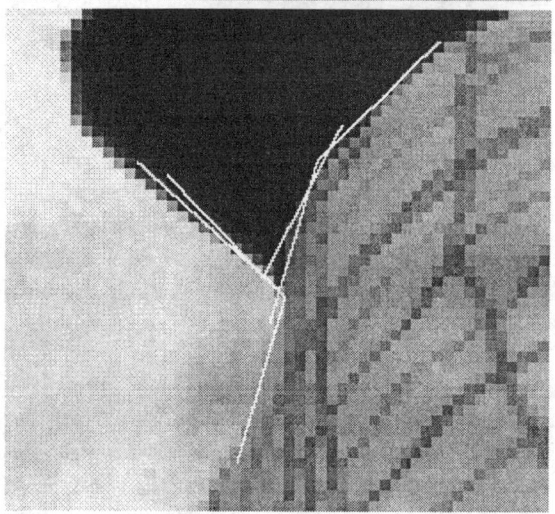

Figure 8: Comparison of output at three different scales near a junction. One corner of the junction is greater than 150° and cannot be recovered directly.

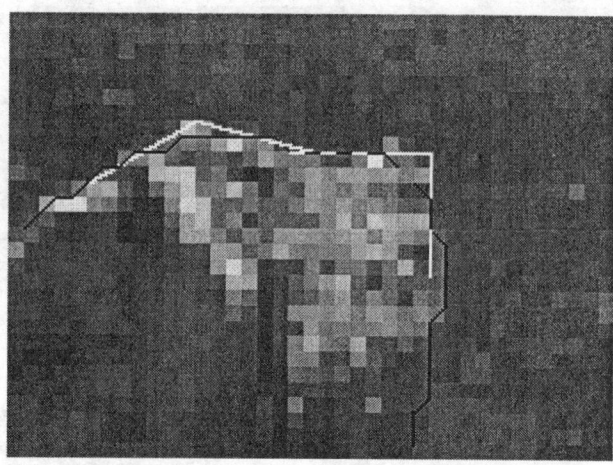

Figure 9: A rock with edges (black) and corners (white) drawn. The features are complementary.

in the context of an application, such as tracking landmarks for robotic navigation or, more generally, shape recovery for object recognition.

Another fundamental issue is the integration of corners and edges. One approach may be to detect them separately and use the corners to perturb the edges toward the true boundary. In Figure 9 we have drawn, in addition to the two corners, a set of edges found by thresholding and performing non-maximal suppression [3] on the operator's output at $\alpha = 180°$. Through a suitable process (e.g. energy minimization), it may be possible to conform the edges to the corners and produce a more accurate boundary.

However, the fact that we can compute edge and corner information in the same framework by changing the value of α begs the question of whether the two are fundamentally different at all. It is unsatisfactory that we must exclude corners between 150° and 180°. In Figure 10 we have drawn both edges and corners, including $\alpha = 165°$, on top of a natural image. The large amount of overlap indicates that the two different algorithms are producing nearly the same output, though they do complement each other in a few places. Future research will investigate a boundary model in which both edges and corners can be detected and related to each other without creating an artificial distinction between them.

Acknowledgment

We thank Yossi Rubner for the EMD code.

References

[1] R. Alberto Salinas, C. Richardson, M.A. Abidi, and R.C. Gonzalez. Data fusion: Color edge detection and

Figure 10: Canyon with corners (left) and edges (right). Note the high amount of overlap. 165° corners have been included.

surface reconstruction through regularization. *IEEE Trans. on Ind. Elec.*, 43(3):355–363, 1996.

[2] L. Alvarez and F. Morales. Affine morphological multiscale analysis of corners and junctions. *IJCV*, 25(2):95–107, 1997.

[3] J. Canny. A computational approach to edge detection. *PAMI*, 8(6):679–698, 1986.

[4] R. Deriche and G. Giraudon. A computational approach for corner and vertex detection. *IJCV*, 10(2):101–124, 1993.

[5] S. Di Zenzo. A note on the gradient of a multi-image. *CVGIP*, 33(1):116–125, 1986.

[6] Q. Ji and R. Haralick. Breakpoint detection using covariance propagation. *PAMI*, 20(8):845–851, 1998.

[7] F. Mokhtarian and R. Suomela. Robust image corner detection through curvature scale space. *PAMI*, 20(12):1376–1381, 1998.

[8] L. Parida, D. Geiger, and R. Hummel. Junctions: Detection, classification, and reconstruction. *PAMI*, 20(7):687–698, 1998.

[9] Y. Rubner, C. Tomasi, and L.J. Guibas. A metric for distributions with applications to image databases. In *ICCV98*, pages 59–66, 1998.

[10] M. Ruzon and C. Tomasi. Color edge detection with the compass operator. In *CVPR99*, volume 2, pages 160–167, 1999.

[11] P.E. Trahanias and A.N. Venetsanopoulos. Vector order-statistics operators as color edge detectors. *IEEE SMC-B*, 26(1):135–143, 1996.

[12] S.-J. Wang and T.O. Binford. Generic, model-based estimation and detection of discontinuities in image surfaces. In *ARPA IUW*, volume II, pages 113–116, 1994.

[13] G. Wyszecki and W.S. Stiles. *Color Science: Concepts and Methods, Quantitative Data and Formulae*. John Wiley and Sons, New York, NY, 1982.

A Cluster-Based Statistical Model for Object Detection

Thomas D. Rikert

Michael J. Jones

Paul Viola

Artificial Intelligence Lab
Mass. Inst. of Tech.
545 Technology Sq
Cambridge, MA 02139
tdrikert@ai.mit.edu

Cambridge Research Lab
Compaq Computer Corp.
One Kendall Sq., Bldg 700
Cambridge, MA 02139
mjones@crl.dec.com

Artificial Intelligence Lab
Mass. Inst. of Tech.
545 Technology Sq
Cambridge, MA 02139
viola@ai.mit.edu

Abstract

This paper presents an approach to object detection which is based on recent work in statistical models for texture synthesis and recognition [7, 4, 23, 17]. Our method follows the texture recognition work of De Bonet and Viola [4]. We use feature vectors which capture the joint occurrence of local features at multiple resolutions. The distribution of feature vectors for a set of training images of an object class is estimated by clustering the data and then forming a mixture of gaussian model. The mixture model is further refined by determining which clusters are the most discriminative for the class and retaining only those clusters. After the model is learned, test images are classified by computing the likelihood of their feature vectors with respect to the model. We present promising results in applying our technique to face detection and car detection.

1 Introduction

This paper is a response to a scientific question that has its root both in computational vision and visual psychology: "What underlies the human ability to recognize objects under *deformation* and changes in pose?" Take for example the recognition of a jacket casually tossed to the floor. Somehow the almost infinite variation in appearance is easily captured by the observer's model of the jacket. It seems unlikely that recognition of the jacket's image is based on purely geometric reasoning. It also seems unlikely that the observer has built a complex model of jacket deformation painstakingly acquired over many thousands of examples. The hypothesis addressed in this paper is that object recognition under these very difficult conditions relies on texture recognition.

Motivation for this experimental investigation has come from recent successes in texture representation and recognition [7, 4, 23, 17]. Each of these approaches

can be used both to recognize texture as well as generate novel images. Based on the quality of these generated textures, it is clear that these four approaches have gone far beyond the previous state of the art in texture modeling. Taken together these new results have destroyed classical distinctions between textons, noisy textures and highly structured patterns.

The Heeger and Bergen approach is perhaps the most efficient of the four, but it has some difficulty in modelling highly structured patterns. While Zhu, Wu and Mumford is the most formal and well grounded of the four, it currently lacks an efficient algorithm for learning and recognition. The De Bonet and Viola approach combines the efficiency and simplicity of the Bergen and Heeger model with the modeling power of Zhu, Wu and Mumford. In this paper we will extend the work of De Bonet and Viola in an effort to model object detection under challenging circumstances.

The main contribution of this paper is the investigation of a new framework for object class detection based on an extended texture model (e.g. face or car detection). The advantage of this approach is that it can handle larger variations in the appearance of the object class than previous techniques. Starting from the De Bonet and Viola texture model, we will extend it to allow learning from hundreds or thousands of images. In order to do this we must eliminate much of the complexity in the density model. Complexity is removed in two ways: i) using an unsupervised approach to cluster the features space; ii) using a supervised approach to maximize the discriminative ability of the density estimate.

2 Related Work

Recently there has been a surge in interest in statistical object recognition models as a means of handling, or perhaps ignoring, the wide variations that are observed in natural images. Many of the strongest results are in face detection and recognition: [20, 19, 13]. A statistical modelling approach can potentially provide a principled mechanism for learning which properties of images are important for recognition and which are not. One criticism of these approaches is that they attempt to model the entire image as a single rigid patch – making it difficult to model changes in pose and feature location. More recently these technique have been generalized to include schemes for modelling deformations in the image plane [1, 8, 5, 10]. These techniques not only learn a set of allowed variations in the image values, but also a set of allowed variations in pixel location. Nevertheless reliable detection and recognition of faces across a wide variety of faces is not yet a solved problem.

More recently a number of more general statistical models of recognition have been proposed: [21, 15, 2]. These attempt to model the appearance of localized features and then separately model feature location. While these are steps in the right direction, these approaches often require a great deal of computational time both for model learning and for image recognition.

Each of the above approaches attempts to model the distribution of images directly. Our approach instead attempts to model the distribution of multi-scale features. von der Malsburg and colleagues have shown excellent results on face recognition using a similar set of multi-scale features [9, 22]. Recently, Papageorgiou *et al.* have proposed multi-scale features for object class detection [11]. They use Haar wavelets computed at particular positions in the image to form feature vectors for a support vector machine classifier. Our approach is much more radical in its disregard for feature location.

Schiele and Crowley's work on multidimensional receptive field histograms [14] also has some similarities to our work. They also look at the distribution of feature vectors formed from filter responses at different scales. Their focus differs in that they are looking at building models of single objects as opposed to object classes. Also their feature vectors do not use the parent vector structure that we use. Furthermore, they use fairly low dimensional feature vectors which makes the use of histograms practical.

3   The Statistical Model

This paper proposes a general statistical model for learning an object class from a set of example images and correctly classifying new images according to their membership in the class. Our framework follows De Bonet and Viola [4] in that it models the distribution of "parent vectors" in each training image.

The parent vectors are a collection of filter responses at different scales of a steerable image pyramid [16]. Figure 1 illustrates the structure of a parent vector. We estimate the distribution of these parent vectors from many training images using a mixture of gaussian model. We show results using this framework for face detection and car detection.

De Bonet and Viola's texture recognition work modeled the distribution of parent vectors using a Parzen window density esimator. The Parzen density estimator, while quite flexible, requires time proportional to the quantity of training data. In our experiments we will use over a thousand training images. If evaluated in a naive fashion, the resulting density estimator would require many minutes to compute. Instead of the Parzen window model, we use a clustering algorithm to find a relatively small number of significant clusters of parent vectors from hundreds of training images. From these clusters a mixture of gaussian model is used to approximate this distribution of parent vectors.

The motivation for expecting parent vectors to make useful features for object detection comes from their use in texture synthesis [3, 4]. In that work, an example texture was first analyzed by finding its parent vectors. Then perceptually similar textures were synthesized by creating a new parent vector tree in which similar parent vectors were randomly interchanged. This representation captures the structure inherent in the example texture, but also allows for random variations which do not break the structure. What happens when we use face images as input to this texture synthesis framework? Figure 2 shows some examples. Each of these images was synthesized from a texture model built from many face images as described in [3]. Notice how features (such as eyes or nose) in one face are replaced by corresponding features from another face. From this figure it appears that the parent vector representation does capture some important structure even for face images.

4   Overview

The basis of our framework is using a mixture of gaussian model to estimate the distribution of parent vectors from a large set of example images of an object class. We present two datasets as examples: human faces and side views of cars.

Our method for building a model can be divided into four steps:

1. Apply multi-scale, multi-orientation filters to the training images to produce parent vectors.

2. Find clusters of similar parent vectors.

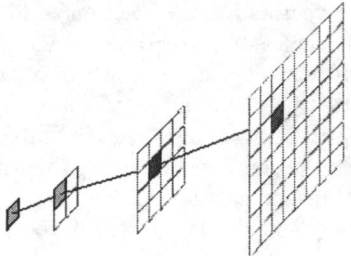

Figure 1: Illustration of parent vector structure. The grids represent an image pyramid. Each pixel is associated with a set of filter values capturing local features. The chain of line segments show the pixels whose filter values make up a single parent vector.

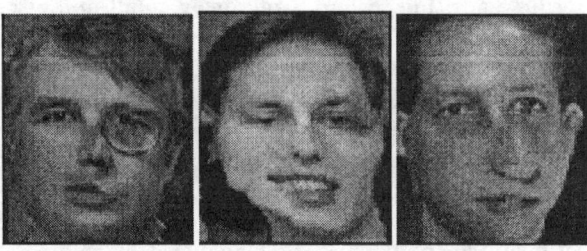

Figure 2: Texture synthesis examples using a set of face images as input textures. See text for an explanation.

3. Find an optimal subset of clusters for detection.

4. Build the final model as a mixture of multidimensional gaussian kernels centered on each cluster, with weight proportional to the population in the cluster and mean and variance proportional to the mean and variance of the cluster.

The same procedure is used to build an out-of-class (or background) model. The out-of-class model is combined with the in-class model using Bayes' rule to yield the probability of in-class given a parent vector.

To classify a test image, the parent vectors of the test image are computed. Then the average probability of the parent vectors from the test image is computed. If this percentage is above some threshold, the test image is classified as in-class.

Each of these steps is described in detail below.

5 Computing Parent Vectors

Parent vectors are computed from a multiresolution wavelet transform as described by De Bonet and Viola [4]. We will use the same notation as in [4]. First, a

gaussian pyramid is created from an input image I: $G_0 = I$, $G_1 = 2 \downarrow (g \otimes G_0)$ and $G_{i+1} = 2 \downarrow (g \otimes G_i)$, where $2 \downarrow$ downsamples an image by a factor of 2 in each dimension and g is a low pass filter. At each level of the pyramid, a series of filter functions are applied: $F_j^i = f_i \otimes G_j$, where the f_i's are oriented derivative filters. For every pixel in an image define the *parent vector* of that pixel:

$$\vec{V}(x,y) = \left[F_0^0(x,y), F_0^1(x,y), \dots, F_0^N(x,y), \right.$$
$$F_1^0(\lfloor \tfrac{x}{2} \rfloor, \lfloor \tfrac{y}{2} \rfloor), F_1^1(\lfloor \tfrac{x}{2} \rfloor, \lfloor \tfrac{y}{2} \rfloor), \dots, F_1^N(\lfloor \tfrac{x}{2} \rfloor, \lfloor \tfrac{y}{2} \rfloor), \dots$$
$$F_M^0(\lfloor \tfrac{x}{2M} \rfloor, \lfloor \tfrac{y}{2M} \rfloor), F_M^1(\lfloor \tfrac{x}{2M} \rfloor, \lfloor \tfrac{y}{2M} \rfloor), \dots,$$
$$\left. F_M^N(\lfloor \tfrac{x}{2M} \rfloor, \lfloor \tfrac{y}{2M} \rfloor) \right]$$

$$(1)$$

where M is the top level of the pyramid and N is the number of features.

As depicted in figure 1, each parent vector corresponds to exactly one pixel in the original image, and stores the wavelet coefficient for each scale and orientation at that pixel location. The high-pass and low-pass residual values are also included in the vector.

6 Estimating the distribution

The model we build to represent an object class is an estimate of the distribution of parent vectors from a set of example images of the object class. To estimate the distribution of parent vectors, a clustering algorithm is first run on the data and then the resulting clusters are used to build a mixture of gaussian model as in [12].

We have found the standard k-means algorithms [6] for clustering to be too computationally expensive for our purposes. The problem is we have very many data points and the data requires very many clusters to estimate it well. For example, we have a training set of over 1 million parent vectors in a 26 dimensional space that requires hundreds of thousands of clusters to represent it well. We can use our results from texture synthesis to give a good idea of the maximum distance that should be allowed between data points belonging to the same cluster. Using distance thresholds from synthesis, we can take a bottom-up approach to clustering which starts with every data point as its own cluster and then combine clusters which are close together according to our distance function. We use the function, **near()**, defined below to determine if two parent vectors are close.

```
near(v₁, v₂) {
    flag = 1
    for k=1 to d
        if D(v₁[k], v₂[k]) > Tₖ  then
            flag = 0
    return flag
}
```

where d is the dimension of the parent vectors, $\{T_k\}$ is a set of thresholds and

$$D(\mathbf{v}_1[k], \mathbf{v}_2[k]) = \frac{|\mathbf{v}_1[k] - \mathbf{v}_2[k]|}{|\mathbf{v}_1[k]| + |\mathbf{v}_1[k]| + 1}. \tag{2}$$

The intuition behind the distance function, $D()$, is that we want to look at the absolute difference between corresponding components of two parent vectors and scale that difference by the size of the components. We achieve the scaling by dividing by the sum of the magnitudes of the two components (plus one to avoid division by zero).

The following pseudo code describes our clustering algorithm:

```
N = number of parent vectors
M = number of clusters
Let v₁, v₂,..., vₙ be the list of N
d-dimensional parent vectors

M = N;

Make a cluster for each parent vector with
mean μᵢ = vᵢ and variance  σᵢ² = 0

do {
    for i=1 to M-1
        for j=i+1 to M
            if near(μᵢ, μⱼ) then {
                combine cluster i and j
                (keeping track of the
                mean, variance and
                population count)

                M = M - 1
            }
} until the decrease in M is insignificant
```

The resulting clusters are used to build a gaussian mixture model to generalize the distribution by placing a multidimensional gaussian kernel at the center of each cluster. Popat and Picard [12] use a similar procedure to model distributions obtained from images. The probability of vector $\mathbf{v}$ in the model for class C is given by

$$P_C(\mathbf{v}) = \sum_{m=1}^{M} w_m \prod_{i=1}^{d} k_{m,i}(\mathbf{v}[i]) \tag{3}$$

where the kernel k is the one-dimensional gaussian

$$k_{m,i}(\mathbf{v}[i]) = \frac{1}{\sqrt{2\pi\hat{\sigma}_{m,i}^2}} e^{-\frac{(\mathbf{v}[i] - \mu_{m,i})^2}{2\hat{\sigma}_{m,i}^2}} \tag{4}$$

and $w_m = N_m/N$ where N_m is the number of parent vectors in cluster m.

7 Using discriminative analysis to refine the distribution

The clustering algorithm eventually produces a set of feature clusters. If the number of parent vectors in the training set is large (say over one million) then the number of clusters will often also be large (sometimes hundreds of thousands). We wish to reduce the number of clusters for two reasons: 1) to improve the accuracy of the model by keeping only clusters which discriminate between in-class and out-of-class parent vectors and 2) to increase the speed of evaluating test images by having fewer gaussians to compute.

We use discriminative analysis to achieve this. The idea is to take a set of in-class and out-of-class training images and create two histograms showing how many times parent vectors from each set fall near an in-class cluster. Then we keep only those clusters which have a significantly larger count for in-class parent vectors than for out-of-class parent vectors. This reduces our in-class model to the most discriminative clusters. We can use the same method to reduce the number of clusters in the non-face model.

There are many possible tests to determine whether the count for in-class parent vectors is "significantly" more than the count for out-of-class vectors. The test we are currently using is as follows. Let $hist_C[i]$ be the count of in-class parent vectors which are near cluster i. Let $hist_{\bar{C}}[i]$ be the count of out-of-class parent vectors which are near cluster i. Then if

$$\frac{hist_C[i]}{hist_C[i] + hist_{\bar{C}}[i]} > \Theta \tag{5}$$

then cluster i is a discriminative cluster and therefore retained. The threshold Θ can be any real number between 0 and 1. We used a value of 0.8 in the experiments that follow.

8 Classifying a test image

The previous sections have described using parent vectors as features and building models of the distributions of parent vectors from example in-class and out-of-class images. The in-class and out-of-class mixture models for a class C give $P(\mathbf{v}|C) = P_C(\mathbf{v})$ and $P(\mathbf{v}|\bar{C}) = P_{\bar{C}}(\mathbf{v})$. We can use Bayes rule to yield

$$P(C|\mathbf{v}) = \frac{P(\mathbf{v}|C)P(C)}{P(\mathbf{v}|C)P(C) + P(\mathbf{v}|\bar{C})P(\bar{C})}. \quad (6)$$

This equation gives the probability of class C given a single parent vector $\mathbf{v}$.

The priors $P(C)$ and $P(\bar{C})$ can be chosen arbitrarily such that $P(C)+P(\bar{C}) = 1$. The choice does not effect the receiver operating characteristics curve which expresses the relationship between correct detections and false positives for classifying parent vectors [6].

The question remains of how to use this probability model to determine if a *set* of parent vectors from a test image are more likely to come from an in-class image than an out-of-class image. De Bonet and Viola [4] suggest comparing the distribution of parent vectors from a test image against the in-class model distribution using the Kullback-Liebler (KL) divergence. The problem with this idea in our case is that the distribution from a single test image will probably not look like the distribution from a large set of training images. The reason is the parent vectors from an image are not independent of each other. They form a tree structure. The model distribution is more like a collection of these trees than like a single tree. Thus, the two distributions will probably not be similar.

Instead of comparing distributions, we have used the simple idea of calculating the average probability of C given each of the parent vectors in a single test image and then thresholding this value to classify the image. Thus, if

$$\frac{\sum_{j=1}^{N} P(C|\mathbf{v}_j)}{N} > t \quad (7)$$

for some threshold t then the image is classified as belonging to C, otherwise it is classified as $\bar{C}$.

The average probability can be viewed as one of many possible statistics we could calculate. If we estimate the distribution of this statistic for the training data, we could then evaluate the likelihood of this statistic computed for a test image. Using multiple such statistics to evaluate test images could produce more accurate tests for a classifier. We leave this idea for future work.

9 Results

9.1 Face Detection

We have built a model of faces from a set of 1060 face images cropped from photographs found on the World Wide Web. The faces were chosen to be approximately frontal. There were small variations in scale as well as large variations in lighting and image quality. Each face image was scaled to be 32 by 32 pixels, converted to gray scale and then histogram equalized to reduce the variations from lighting. Some example face images are shown in figure 3 (shown before histogram equalization).

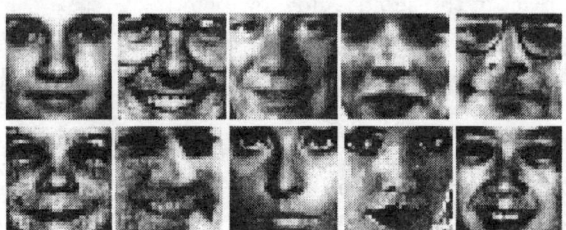

Figure 3: Example face images from the training set.

To build a background model of non-face images, we selected windows of random size and position from a set of Web images which did not contain people. The windows were then scaled to be 32 by 32 pixels and histogram equalized as with the faces. We used 1016 such non-face examples.

The parent vectors for each of the example faces and non-faces were computed as described in section 5. This yielded 1,085,440 ($= 1060 \times 32 \times 32$) face parent vectors and 1,040,384 ($= 1016 \times 32 \times 32$) non-face parent vectors. We used parent vectors with 4 scales and 6 oriented edge filters per scale. Including the high and low pass residuals, this resulted in parent vectors with 26 components.

To construct face and non-face models we first applied the clustering algorithm described in section 6 to the two sets of parent vectors separately. For the face model we used a threshold of 0.7 for all T_i in the function **near()**. For non-faces we used a threshold of 0.8 for all T_i. The clustering algorithm yielded 351,615 different clusters for the face parent vectors and 155,222 different clusters for the non-face parent vectors.

Next we applied discriminative analysis as discussed in section 7 to reduce the number of clusters and improve the models. This analysis yielded a face model with 1447 clusters and a non-face model with 483 clusters. A mixture of gaussian model was built from these clusters as described in section 6.

We can improve our intuition for the cluster-based model by verifying that some clusters correspond to particular perceptual features in a face. In other words, does a cluster encode a feature in the image such as an eye or lip that is useful for face detection? To test this hypothesis, we collected a new set of 266 face images and computed the parent vectors for these images. We then selected a parent vector cluster from the model and highlighted test image regions containing parent vectors from within this cluster. Cluster membership was determined using the distance function and thresholds defined before. Figure 4 shows the location where a "lip cluster" responds in several face images. While this cluster only responds to 6% of the *test* faces, in almost every case the response is localized near the lip region. In each of the remaining faces their is no response. Although this is a small percentage of faces, together the 1447 clusters provide enough coverage to detect most faces.

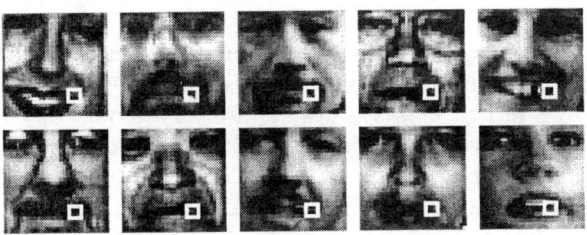

Figure 4: A cluster was chosen from the face model and compared to all parent vectors in each test image. The white boxes show the postion in each image where a parent vector was near the cluster. This cluster apparently represents a lip-corner feature.

To test the model we used the 266 face images mentioned before and a new set of 2500 non-face images. For each image, the parent vectors were computed and then the test in equation 7 was applied to classify the image.

The results are shown as a receiver operating characteristics curve (ROC curve) in figure 5. The ROC curve shows promising preliminary results. For example, we get 90% correct detection with a false positive rate of 1.2% or 70% correct detection with 0.28% false positives.

It is difficult to compare these results with those of Sung and Poggio or Rowley and Kanade. These systems process entire images; first decomposing them into a set of overlapping patches at multiple scales, and then classifying each patch. There are ten's of thousands of such patches in each image, most containing only background. While it is a daunting task to reject each and every background patch, it is im-

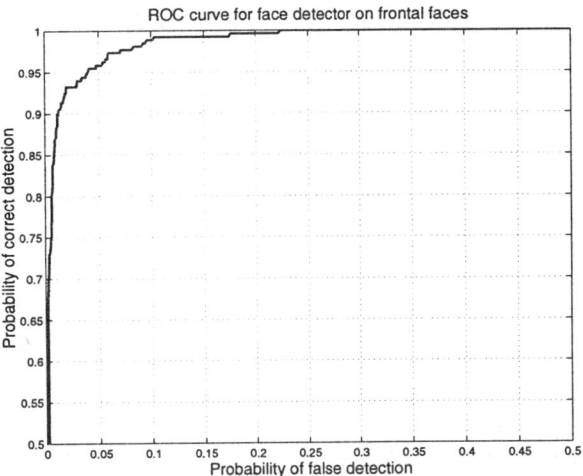

Figure 5: Receiver operating characteristics curve for a test set of 266 frontal faces and 2500 non-faces. Note that to focus on the interesting part of the graph, the correct detection rate axis begins at 50%.

portant to point out that since they overlap many of the patches are highly redundant. A patch that is correctly rejected because it does not contain a face is very likely to be rejected if it is shifted by a single pixel. A similar issue arises in the detection of faces. Since a single face will appear in many overlapping patches, there will be many opportunities to detect it.

The above ROC curve demonstrates performance on independently selected patches. There is no redundancy in this dataset. We believe that when placed in an end-to-end system this detector will demonstrate improved detection and rejection rates. One obvious refinement is to let the system bootstrap its non-face training set by adding false positive images into the non-face training set and relearning the model. This work is currently underway.

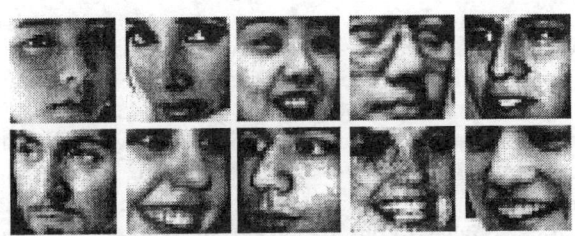

Figure 6: Example non-frontal face images which the face detector correctly classified.

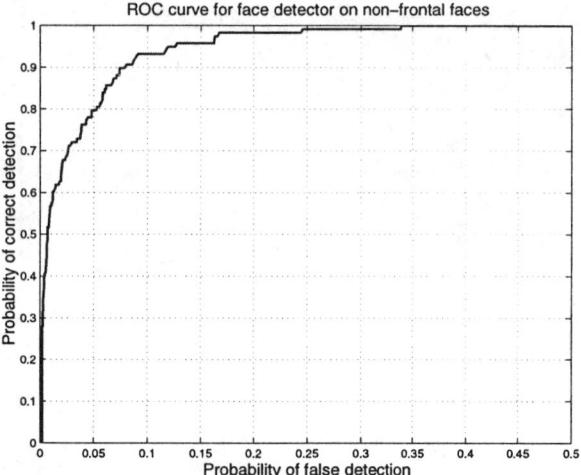

Figure 7: Receiver operating characteristics curve for a test set of 266 non-frontal faces and 2500 non-faces.

The main advantage of our framework for object detection is that it should be able to handle more variability than most other classifier-based methods. With faces this means that we expect parent vectors for frontal face images to be similar to parent vectors for non-frontal faces. To test this, we evaluated our face detector on a set of non-frontal faces, some of which are shown in figure 6. We used the same face detector just described which was trained on frontal faces. The preliminary results support the robustness of our framework. The ROC curve for a test set of 118 non-frontal faces and the same set of 2500 non-faces is shown in figure 7. The results are surprisingly good considering that non-frontal faces were not used in the training set. For example, we get a correct detection rate of 80% with a false positive rate of 5% or a correct detection rate of 60% with a false positive rate of 1.2%. These results should be improved by including non-frontal faces in the training set.

9.2 Car Detection

As a second example, we also learned a model for side views of cars. We only had a database of 48 car images available for this experiment. However, since all the cars were photographed under similar conditions, our intuition was that this should be sufficient to learn a model. We split the set into 24 training images and 24 test images. We also used a set of 1024 non-car images to build a background model. The image size used was 52 pixels in width by 16 pixels in height. Figure 8 shows a few example cars. All of the car images were acquired by taking photographs of toy cars.

The parent vectors consisted of the values from 6 oriented edge filters computed over 3 scales. Including the high and low resolution residuals, the parent vectors contained 20 components each. Initial clustering of the car parent vectors yielded 12,295 clusters using a threshold of $T_i = 0.5$ in the distance function of equation 2. Initial clustering of the parent vectors from the 1024 non-car images yielded 32,405 clusters using a threshold of $T_i = 0.8$. After discriminative analysis, the car model contained 1229 clusters and the non-car model contained 1001 clusters.

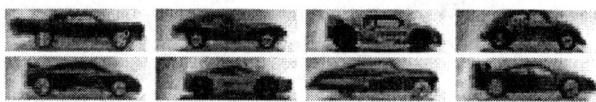

Figure 8: Eight of the 24 example cars used to train the car detector.

This model was then tested on a test set of 24 car and 200 non-car images. The resulting ROC curve is shown in figure 9. The results are very good. Only 1 false positive was made with 100% correct detections.

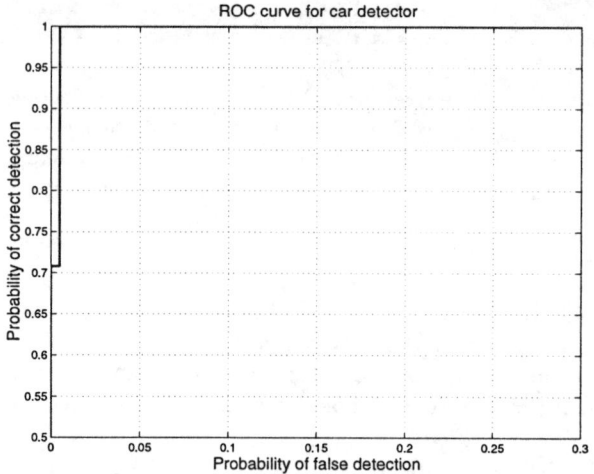

Figure 9: Receiver operating characteristics curve for a test set of 24 side views of cars and 200 non-cars.

10   Conclusions and future work

We have presented a new approach to detecting classes of objects which is based on De Bonet and Viola's recent technique for representing textures. The results we have obtained for face detection and car detection are very promising. They show that object detection for an object class with large variations can rely on texture recognition.

Our future work in this area will focus on implementing a face detector that searches over positions and scales. We also intend to improve the computational expense of the method to make it a practical solution for object detection.

Acknowledgments

This research was supported by Compaq Computer Corporation's Cambridge Research Laboratory. Thanks to L.J. Ruell and Gene Preble for collecting the face database used in this research.

References

[1] D. Beymer, A. Shashua and T. Poggio, "Example Based Image Analysis and Synthesis", *A.I. Memo 1431*, MIT, 1993.

[2] M.C. Burl, T.K. Leung, P. Perona, "Face Localization via Shape Statistics", in *Int'l Conf. on Automatic Face and Gesture Recognition*, IEEE, 1995, pp. 154-159.

[3] J. De Bonet, "Multiresolution sampling procedure for analysis and synthesis of texture images," in *Computer Graphics*. ACM SIGGRAPH, 1998.

[4] J. De Bonet and P. Viola, "Texture recognition using a non-parametric multi-scale statistical model," in *CVPR*, 1998.

[5] G.J. Edwards, C.J. Taylor and T.F. Cootes, "Interpreting Face Images using Active Appearance Models" in *Int'l Conf. on Automatic Face and Gesture Recognition*, IEEE, 1998, pp. 300-305.

[6] K. Fukunaga, *Introduction to Statistical Pattern Recognition*, Academic Press, Inc., San Diego, CA. 1990.

[7] D. Heeger and J. Bergen, "Pyramid-based texture analysis/synthesis," In *Proc. of ACM SIGGRAPH*, August 1995, pp 229-238.

[8] M. Jones and T. Poggio, "Multidimensional Morphable Models: A Framework for Representing and Matching Object Classes" in *IJCV*, Volume 29, No. 2, August 1998, pp. 107-131.

[9] M. Lades, *et al.*, "Distortion Invariant Object Recognition in the Dynamic Link Architecture", *IEEE Trans. on Computers*, Vol 42, No 3, March 1993, pp. 300-311.

[10] B. Moghaddam, C. Nastar and A. Pentland, "Bayesian Face Recognition using Deformable Intensity Surfaces" in *CVPR*, 1996.

[11] C. Papageorgiou, M. Oren and T. Poggio, "A General Framework for Object Detection," in *ICCV*, January 1998, pp 555-562.

[12] K. Popat and R. Picard, "Cluster-based probability model and its application to image and texture processing," *IEEE Trans. on Image Processing*, Vol. 6, No. 2, Feb 1997, pp. 268-284.

[13] H. Rowley, S. Baluja, T. Kanade, "Human Face Detection in Visual Scenes," *Technical Report CMU-CS-95-158R*, CMU, 1995.

[14] B. Schiele and J. Crowley, "Recognition without Correspondence using Multidimensional Receptive Field Histograms" *MIT Media Laboratory Perceptual Computing Section TR No. 453*, December 1997.

[15] H. Schneiderman and T. Kanade, "Probabilistic Modeling of Local Appearance and Spatial Relationships for Object Recognition", in *CVPR*, 1998, pp. 45-51.

[16] E. Simoncelli and W. Freeman, "The Steerable Pyramid: A flexible architecture for multi-scale derivative computation," In *IEEE Int'l Conf. on Image Processing*, pp. 444-447, Washington, D.C., October 1995.

[17] E. Simoncelli and J. Portilla, "Texture Characterization via Joint Statistics of Wavelet Coefficient Magnitudes," in *c. IEEE Int'l Conf. on Image Processing*, 1998.

[18] E. Simoncelli and R. Buccigrossi, "Embedded Wavelet Image Compression Based on a Joint Probability Model," in *IEEE Int'l Conf. on Image Processing*, 1997.

[19] K. Sung and T. Poggio, "Example-based learning for view-based human face detection", *A.I. Memo 1521*, MIT, December 1994.

[20] M. Turk and A. Pentland, "Face Recognition Using Eigenfaces" in *CVPR*, 1991, pp. 586-591.

[21] P. Viola, "Complex Feature Recognition: A Bayesian Approach for Learning to Recognize Objects", *A.I. Memo 1591*, MIT, November, 1996.

[22] L. Wiskott, *et al.*, "Face Recognition by Elastic Bunch Graph Matching", *IEEE Int'l Conf. on Image Processing*, Vol. I, 1997.

[23] S. Zhu, Y. Wu and D. Mumford, "Filters, Random Fields and Maximum Entropy (FRAME) - Towards A Unified Theory For Texture Modeling" in *IJCV*, Vol 27, No 2, March 1998, pp. 107-126.

Independent Component Analysis of Textures

Roberto Manduchi

Jet Propulsion Laboratory
California Institute of Technology
Pasadena, CA 91109
manduchi@jpl.nasa.gov

Javier Portilla

Instituto de Optica
Consejo Super. de Investig. Cientificas
Serrano 121, Madrid, Spain
iodpm79@pinar2.csic.es

Abstract

A common method for texture representation is to use the marginal probability densities over the outputs of a set of multi-orientation, multi-scale filters as a description of the texture. We propose a technique, based on Independent Components Analysis, for choosing the set of filters that yield the most informative marginals, meaning that the product over the marginals most closely approximates the joint probability density function of the filter outputs. The algorithm is implemented using a steerable filter space. Experiments involving both texture classification and synthesis show that compared to Principal Components Analysis, ICA provides superior performance for modeling of natural and synthetic textures.

1 Introduction

One of the main goals of computer vision is the compact representation of visual entities. Textures, the visual objects considered in this paper, are best represented by their statistical properties. We introduce an information-theoretic framework that provides a better understanding of filter-based approaches to texture analysis and leads to a technique for improving the quality of those texture representations that are based on marginal statistics over filter outputs.

Loosely speaking, textures are characterized by two basic properties: *homogeneity* and *locality of representation*. In other words, the "visual flavour" of a texture can be captured by its statistical behavior within a limited size window. Suitable statistical models for textures are stationary Markov Random Fields (MRF), which are completely characterized by their joint probability density function (pdf) within a suitable neighborhood. Estimating and representing even low-dimensional joint pdf's, however, can be an overwhelming task. The size of the representation grows exponentially with the model dimension, as does the minimum number of samples required to achieve a given estimation accuracy [10]. In fact, techniques that attempt to completely characterize joint distributions either consider very small neighborhoods [27], measure only pairwise dependency [17], or use specific MRF models [12],[8].

A different approach is based on the analysis of feature vectors formed by the output of a filter bank [20],[9],[21],[23]. With a suitable choice of the analysis filters, we can assume that the feature vectors capture the local visually significant texture character. In other words, the filters map the image values in each neighborhood onto a "perceptually relevant" subspace, thereby reducing the representation size while preserving structural information.

Barring a few exceptions [27],[13],[30], typical filter-based algorithms do not estimate the joint statistical description of the texture features. Instead, they build models based on the *marginal statistics* of the feature components, usually represented by the channel variances or their histograms. For example, by analyzing the directional characteristics of a texture along a dense (ideally continuous) set of orientations and scales, one obtains its "scale/orientation signature", which can be used for classification [23],[29].

Texture representation by marginal statistics is a simple and attractive approach. To make efficient use of it, though, we should understand how well a given set of marginals represents the joint statistical description of a texture feature. Zhu et al. [32] pointed out that, in general, one needs the marginal pdf's along every possible projection direction to completely characterize the joint feature vector pdf. Thus, one approach to improving the quality of representation is to use a large number of filters, perhaps exploiting steerable schemes [15],[26] for computational efficiency.

In this work we follow a different route, and devise a technique for finding the basis of a given filter space which generates the most informative marginals for a given texture, meaning that the product over the marginal densities most closely approximates the joint pdf. We show by experimental tests of classification and synthesis that by selecting such "optimal" filter basis the quality of the representation increases significantly.

Our basis selection algorithm is based on Independent Component Analysis (ICA) theory. ICA has been an area of intense research during the last decade, stimulated by problems of blind source separation and deconvolution. ICA can be regarded as a technique for statistical modeling that proves superior to Principal Component Analysis in the case of non-gaussian random vectors. It is an established notion that natural images do not behave like gaussian processes [22],[4]; our experiments show that ICA provides better models for natural and synthetic textures.

Other filter selection techniques have been proposed for texture analysis, usually based on energy [7] or class separability [14]. Perhaps closest to our approach is the entropy–based algorithm of Zhu et al. [32], which uses a greedy strategy to sequentially introduce one filter at a time.

This paper is organized as follows. Section 2 describes the filter spaces that we use for texture analysis, and introduces the filter basis selection problem. Section 3 provides some necessary background of ICA, and shows its application to texture modeling. Section 4 describes texture classification and synthesis experiments from which we were able to assess the performance of ICA modeling. Section 5 has the conclusions.

2 Steerable spaces for texture analysis

Given an image $l(x)$ and a set of N filters $\{h_i(x)\}$, we will say that the vector $f(x) = [f_1(x) = l * h_1(x), \ldots, f_N(x) = l * h_N(x)]$ is the *feature representation* of the image at point x. We will assume that a texture is completely represented by the joint pdf of its feature vector $f(x)$ (which, by stationariety, is independent of x.) By this we mean that two textures with the same joint distribution of their feature vectors are "perceptually" indistinguishable.

Which filters produce meaningful feature representations of textures? Several design criteria have been proposed. Basically, they all share the following characteristics: 1) zero-DC response, to enforce invariance to slow-varying illumination bias; 2) good spatial/spectral concentration, to ensure energy separation while preserving locality of description. Another useful property of analysis filter banks is *steerability* [15],[16] defined as follows. Let H be the linear space spanned by the N kernels $\{h_i(x)\}$, and let $\mathcal{G}$ be a suitable group of domain transformations (e.g., rotations

or isotropic scaling.) We will say that H is steerable over $\mathcal{G}$ if for every kernel $h(x)$ in H, and for every transformation $A(\cdot)$ in $\mathcal{G}$, the "transformed" kernel $h_A(x) = h(A(x))$ belongs to H. For example, assume the filter space is steerable over the group of rotations. Let $f(x)$ and $f^R(x)$ be the feature vector description of a texture and of the rotated version of the texture, respectively (R is the rotation matrix). Then, $f(x)$ and $f^R(R^{-1}x)$ are related by a linear transformation (a matrix), which is a function of the rotation angle only. Steerability, thus, ensures uniformity of representation for transformed versions of the same texture. Methods exist to design exact and approximate finite dimensional steerable filter spaces over rotations and isotropic scaling over a finite scale range of interest [26].

Joint spatial/spectral concentration is achieved, for example, using Gabor kernels or directional derivatives of gaussian kernels [21],[23]. Such filters effectively capture directional texture attributes. If a N-dimensional steerable analysis space is used, the texture signatures are completely characterized by the joint statistics of the output of N basis filters. Note that one can always find a set of basis filters which are scaled/rotated versions of a prototype kernel in the steerable space.

In this paper we study reduced representations formed by the marginal statistics of the feature vectors. Let us recall that the marginal density of the i-th component of a random vector z, $p_i(z_i)$, is the projection of the joint pdf $p(z)$ onto the i-th axis. The set of marginal statistics is represented by the outer product of the marginal pdf's: $\bar{p}(z) = \prod_i p_i(z_i)$, which is equal to $p(z)$ if and only if the components of the feature vector are statistically independent. In particular, we are concerned with the selection of the "optimal" basis in a steerable filter space. Note that the choice of the basis is irrelevant if the joint pdf of the feature vector is considered. Indeed, if f_1 and f_2 are the feature vectors at point x, computed using two different filter bases, then $f_2 = Af_1$, where A is a full-rank matrix. Thus, the joint pdf's of the feature vectors, $p_1(z)$ and $p_2(z)$, are related to one another as $p_2(z) = p_1(A^{-1}z)/|\det(A)|$ [25]. This one-to-one relation, however, holds for joint pdf's only. In general, the marginal pdf's of f_1 *cannot* be computed from the marginal pdf's of f_2. This somewhat paradoxical observation stems from the fact that marginal pdf's are projections of a joint pdf along different directions. A finite set of marginals does not carry enough information in general to allow reconstructing all the other projections.

Assume, however, that a particular choice of basis filters gives statistically independent feature components. Then, as noted above, the marginals completely characterize the joint pdf of the feature vector: from this set of marginals, all the other marginals can be reconstructed. The converse is not true: other filter bases will produce, in general, features with "less informative" marginal statistics.

Unfortunately, only very few textures can be represented by independent component features. Still, it is almost always the case that some filter bases produce "more informative" marginals than others. This intuitive notion can be made more rigorous using the theory of Independent Components Analysis (ICA); ICA also leads to an algorithm for selecting an "optimal" filter basis.

3 Independent Component Analysis

In this section we report some results of Independent Component Analysis theory that are instrumental to the development of the texture classification and synthesis algorithms discussed in later sections. We refer the reader to the excellent tutorial of Cardoso [5] for a general overview of the theory.

We first introduce the ICA problem as a statistical approximation tool, and then briefly outline Comon's ICA algorithm, which we have adopted in our experiments.

3.1 Problem formulation

The theory of Independent Component Analysis is traditionally associated with the Blind Source Separation (BSS) problem. In its simplest formulation, the BSS problem assumes that N independent causes (random variables) have been linearly combined by a full rank matrix A to produce N observed variables. The goal is to identify the mixing matrix from the observations, possibly using prior information about the statistics of the causes if available.

ICA, however, may also be regarded as a general estimation method [11], without explicit reference to the BSS model. If z is a random vector with joint pdf $p(z)$ and full-rank covariance matrix[1], ICA seeks a full rank matrix A such that the pdf of the vector $y = Az$ is "best represented" by the outer product of its marginal pdf's. The quality of the separable approximation is measured by the *contrast*, which is a deterministic function of a joint pdf. Let $e(z)$ be the "model error", defined as the difference between the logarithm of the density $p(z)$ and the log-likelihood of

---

[1] If the covariance matrix V is not full rank, we may consider the projection of z onto the range space of V [11].

the separable model:

$$e(z) = \log p(z) - \log \prod_i p_i(z_i) \qquad (1)$$

where $p_i(z_i)$ are the marginal pdf's of the components of z. The contrast [11] of $p(z)$ is defined as the expectation of the model error $e(z)$, which is equal to the Kullback-Leibler (KL) divergence between $p(z)$ and the separable model pdf:

$$E\left[e(z)\right] = \int_{-\infty}^{\infty} p(z) \log \frac{p(z)}{\prod_i p_i(z_i)} \, dz \qquad (2)$$

$$= \sum_i H_i(z_i) - H(z)$$

where $H(\cdot)$ represents the differential entropy of its argument: $H(z) = -\int_{-\infty}^{\infty} p(z) \log p(z)$ (terms $H_i(z_i)$ are called *marginal entropies* of z.) This contrast takes also the name of *mutual information* of z, and being a KL divergence it is always positive (it vanishes if and only if z has independent components). Intuitively, the mutual information tells us how much we lose in terms of average information if we neglect to consider the statistical dependence among the components of z.

Other contrast functions have been proposed for ICA. For example, if the distributions $g_i(z_i) = \int_{-\infty}^{z_i} p_i(\hat{z}) d\hat{z}$ of the original independent components in a BSS model are known, we may define the "infomax" contrast [1] of the vector z as $-H(g(z))$, where $g(z) = [g_1(z_1), \ldots, g_N(z_N)]$. However, in the case of texture descriptors we don't know the distributions $g_i(z_i)$, and mutual information is a more appropriate criterion. Thus, in this paper we will use the following definition of the ICA problem:

> **ICA problem:** find a full-rank matrix A such that $y = Az$ has minimal mutual information.

Note that the solution to the ICA problem is not unique: if A minimizes the mutual information of Az, so do all matrices obtained by permuting the rows of A or by pre-multiplying A by a diagonal matrix.

If z is jointly gaussian, its mutual information is null if and only if its covariance matrix is diagonal. Principal Component Analysis (PCA, also known as Karhunen-Loève transform) is a technique to diagonalize a vector covariance by an orthonormal matrix, and therefore solves the ICA problem for gaussian vectors. In the general non-gaussian case, however, diagonal covariance is not sufficient to ensure the minimal mutual information condition; hence, more work is needed.

It can be shown [11] that, if z has been "pre-whitened" to unit covariance (by PCA followed by axis rescaling), the ICA problem is solved by an orthonormal linear transformation that minimizes the sum of the marginal entropies of the transformed vector. This fact has a nice counterpart in the context of BSS. Since the gaussian distribution has the highest entropy for a given variance, we may argue that the demixing matrix is the one that produces marginals as "far from gaussian" as possible. This observation agrees with intuition: indeed, as suggested by the central limit theorem, linear mixing of independent causes produces gaussian-like distributions.

3.2 A high–order contrast algorithm

ICA algorithms try to minimize the contrast of a vector without explicitly computing its joint pdf. Comon [11] proposed an efficient technique based on high-order statistics[2]. In fact, Comon's algorithm minimizes a different contrast than mutual information; the relation between the two contrast functions can be highlighted using Edgeworth functional expansions [19]. An intuitive justification of high-order methods is based on the fact that all the cross-cumulants of an independent component vector are null [19]. Thus, one may try to minimize mutual information by actually minimizing the n-th order dependence among the vector components. For example, Comon's technique finds an orthonormal matrix A that minimizes the sum of the squared fourth-order cross-cumulants of $y = Az$, provided that z has been pre-whitened. It can be shown that this is equivalent to maximizing the sum of the squared marginal kurtosis (fourth-order cumulants) of y. It is a well known fact that gaussian distributions have zero kurtosis [19]: cumulant–based algorithms do push the vector components away from gaussianity. Leptokurtic, heavy tailed exponential-like distributions are characteristic of "sparse codes" [24], and are often used to model the output of wavelet filter banks for image coding [22]. Platykurtic distributions are also often observed in texture analysis.

Comon's design algorithm is based on Jacobi iterations. Its complexity is $\mathcal{O}(N^4)$ (including pre-whitening,) and it always converges to a (possibly local) minimum of the contrast. Due to these desirable properties, we have selected such a technique for our experiments. It should be noted that several other

---

[2]High–order statistics methods have often been neglected by neural network researchers involved in ICA. A recent paper by Cardoso [6] compares cumulant–based algorithms with gradient–descent techniques, and shows the practical effectiveness of the former from an algorithmic point of view, as well as on the ground of experimental results.

fast algorithms for ICA exist [5]; we plan to experiment with some of those in future work.

4 Experimental tests

4.1 Supervised classification

In this section we use ICA pdf modeling in a test of supervised texture discrimination. For the sake of simplicity, we perform training and classification on the same data set, formed by the $K = 8$ textures of Figure 1 (chosen from the MIT VisTex database). Each texture is modeled by the marginal pdf's over the selected channels in a fixed steerable space, together with the corresponding ICA matrix. The marginal densities are estimated and represented by 50-bins histograms.

An image formed by the mosaic of all textures is classified pixel-wise using a Bayesian technique [3]. Spatial coherence is enforced by using a "soft" version of Besag's Iterated Conditional Modes (ICM) algorithm [2], which uses MRF modeling to estimate the posterior class probabilities for each pixel from the conditional likelihoods (as produced by ICA modeling.) The experiment proceeds as follows:

- **Training:** for each texture model k,

  1. filter the training image with a fixed filter bank;
  2. compute the ICA matrix A_k from the output of the filters (we will assume, without loss of generality, that $|\det(A_k)| = 1$;)
  3. multiply the output vectors by the ICA matrix A_k and compute the channel histograms.

- **Classification:** apply the fixed filter bank to the test image. For each texture model k,

  1. multiply the filter output vectors by the model ICA matrix A_k, and use the corresponding channel histograms to compute the marginal conditional likelihoods $p_i(z_i|k)$;
  2. the conditional likelihood $p(z|k)$ of any pixel value z is equal to the product of the corresponding marginal conditional likelihoods:

$$p(z|k) = \prod_i p_i(z_i|k) \qquad (3)$$

From the conditional likelihoods, compute the posterior class probabilities using the ICM algorithm and perform pixel-wise Bayesian classification.

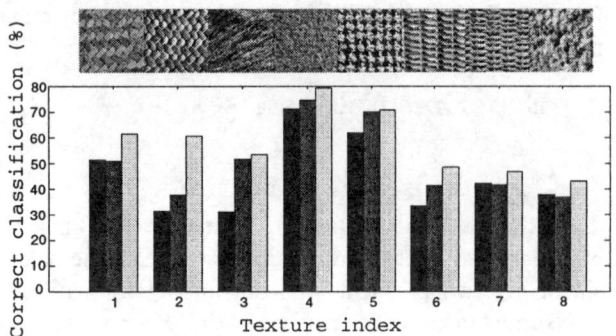

Figure 1: Supervised classification test (see text). The system is trained and tested on the eight textures shown above. The plots represent the percentage of correct classification for each texture. White bars: using ICA transformation. Gray bars: using PCA transformation. Black bars: without transformation.

For our experiment we have chosen a steerable pyramid filter bank [31] with just two orientations and three scales ($N = 6$ filters overall). For each training texture (size 256×256 pixels), Comon's Matlab implementation of ICA required 27 seconds of computation time on a Power Macintosh G3 266 MHz. The results, in terms of percentage of correctly classified pixels for each texture, are shown by the white bar plot of figure 1. If PCA is used instead of ICA, we obtain the correct classification rates shown by grey bars; the classification performances of the system without transformation (i.e., using the original filters) are shown by the black bars. ICA pdf modeling consistently yields the highest correct classification rates.

We have observed that the performance gain provided by PCA and ICA modeling relative to the nominal feature vector representation decreases if the number of orientations in the steerable filter bank is increased. This should not come as a surprise: many marginal statistics can provide sufficient information even if they are not statistically independent; however, the benefit comes at the price of increased representation size.

4.2 Texture synthesis

Synthesis-by-analysis algorithms [18],[28],[32],[30] create new textures which "look like" a given prototype. This is equivalent to sampling a random process whose statistical description has been estimated from a given sample.

A simple and effective synthesis technique has been proposed by Heeger and Bergen [18]. First, the prototype texture is analyzed by a filter bank which in-

cludes the "identity" filter, and the marginal channel histograms are recorded. Then, a random image is generated, and its channel histograms (computed by the same filter bank) are iteratively adjusted to match those of the prototype texture. The algorithm usually converges to a texture that has the same channel histograms as the prototype: the two textures are therefore identical on the grounds of marginal statistical description.

We have adopted such an algorithm as a testbed for our experiments because it represents the ideal "Turing test" to validate texture models based on marginal channel statistics. Our only addition to Heeger and Bergen's model is the multiplication of the channel vectors at the output of the filter bank by the ICA matrix computed for the prototype texture, as in the scheme of section 4.1. After the channel histograms have been adjusted to match those of the prototype texture, the channel vectors are multiplied by the inverse of the ICA matrix. Note that the presence of the ICA matrix requires that all the channels be kept to the same sampling rate.

Heeger and Bergen use steerable pyramid analysis filter banks [31], and synthesize samples that successfully reproduce some unstructured characteristics of the prototype texture. Such simple marginal statistics modeling, though, fails to capture more complex spatial structures, such as elongated patterns. A simple way to boost the performance of Heeger and Bergen's scheme is to enrich the filter space with the *shifted* versions of the filters. In other words, for each filter $h(x)$ we add the filters $h^n(x) = h(x + n)$ with n belonging to a suitable neighborhood of the origin. The feature representation thus "looks around" over a larger neighborhood of each point, and allows us to synthesize patterns with highly structured spatial dependency. This new information comes at no cost: the output of filter $h^n(x)$ at point x_0 is equal to the output of filter $h(n)$ at point $x_0 + n$. In particular, the shifting grid in our implementation is a function of the filter scale. For example, if for the smallest scale filters $h(x)$ (with scale $\sigma = \sigma_0$) we use the shifted kernels $h^n(x)$ with $n \in \{(0,0), (-1,0), (0,-1), (1,0), (0,1)\}$, for wider filters with scale $\sigma = \sigma_0 * k$ we will use $n \in \{(0,0), (-k,0), (0,-k), (k,0), (0,k)\}$.

Shifted filters, though, are useless if the marginals statistical description is built directly from their output, like in Heeger and Bergen's original algorithm: by stationariety, the marginal pdf of a filter output does not change if the filter is shifted. The contribution of the shifted filters becomes relevant if a different basis of the steerable space is chosen, that is, if the output

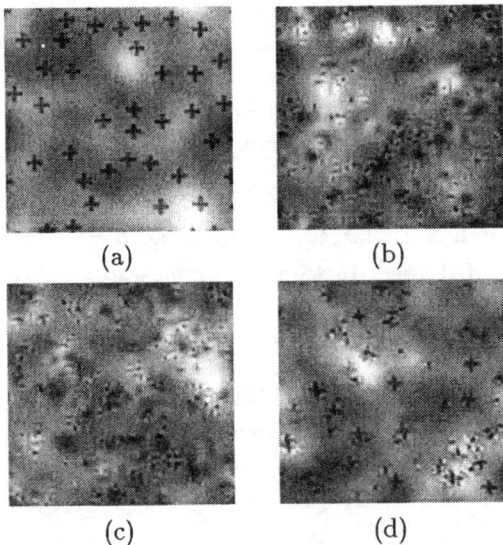

(a)　　　　　(b)

(c)　　　　　(d)

Figure 2: Examples of texture synthesis. (a) The prototype texture "Crosses on clouds" is synthesized using Heeger and Bergen's technique (b) with no channel transformation , (c) with PCA transformation and (d) with ICA transformation.

of the filters is multiplied by the PCA or ICA matrix.

We show in figures 2 and 3 examples of synthesis from the prototype textures "Crosses on clouds" and "Squares". For the "Crosses on clouds" texture we have used a steerable pyramid filter bank which comprised both odd-symmetric and even-symmetric kernels at two orientations and four scales (overall $N = 16$ filters). For the "Squares" texture we have used odd-symmetric kernels at two orientations and three scales, shifted over five different positions (overall $N = 30$ filters). These prototype textures are highly non-gaussian, which makes PCA modeling inadequate (see figure 2(c) and 3(c)). ICA modeling proves superior in both cases. In particular, for the "Crosses on clouds" texture, ICA does a good job at separating the low-pass, isotropic components (the "clouds") from the line-shaped, oriented ones (the "crosses".) In the case of the "Squares" texture, ICA is able to extract the local structure by correctly combining the shifted filters outputs.

5 Conclusions

We have presented an algorithm that chooses the basis filters in a steerable space in such a way as to yield the most informative marginals for texture representation. The method is based on the minimization of the mutual channel information via Independent Component Analysis. The experimental results show the

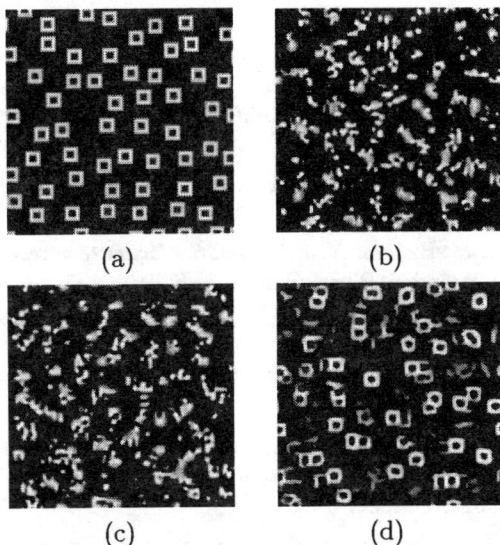

(a)　　　　　(b)

(c)　　　　　(d)

Figure 3: Examples of texture synthesis for the prototype texture "Squares" (see caption of figure (2)).

superiority of ICA modeling with respect to PCA for natural and synthetic textures and small dimensional filter spaces.

An interesting open problem, which we are currently investigating, is subspace selection based on information–theoretic criteria. We expect that by choosing a small number of highly informative channels, one should be able to obtain reduced size representations that maintain good discrimination properties.

Acknowledgments

The research described in this paper was carried out by the Jet Propulsion Laboratory, California Institute of Technology, under a contract with the National Aeronautics and Space Administration. RM was supported in part by the NASA Telerobotics program and by the NASA Remote Exploration and Experimentation task. JP was supported by the Consejo Superior de Investigaciones Cientificas (CSIC, Spain), and the Comision Interministerial de Ciencia y Tecnologia (CICYT, Spain), under grant TIC97-325. Reference herein to any specific commercial product, process, or service by trade name, trademark, manufacturer, or otherwise, does not constitute or imply its endorsement by the United States Government or the Jet Propulsion Laboratory, California Institute of Technology.

The authors would like to thank Dr. Michael Burl for his proofreading of the paper, which unquestionably improved the clarity of the presentation.

References

[1] A.J. Bell and T.J. Sejnowski. An information-maximization approach to blind separation and blind deconvolution. *Neural Computation*, 7:1129-1159, 1995.

[2] J. Besag. On the statistical analysis of dirty pictures. *J. R. Statist. Soc. B*, 48(3):259–302, 1986.

[3] C.M. Bishop. *Neural networks for pattern recognition*. Clarendon Press, Oxford, U.K., 1995.

[4] R.W. Buccigrossi and E. Simoncelli. Progressive wavelet image coding based on a conditional probability model. *Proc. IEEE ICASSP*, 4:2957–2960, Munich, 1997.

[5] J.-F. Cardoso. Blind signal separation: Statistical principles. *Proceedings of the IEEE*, 86(10):2009–2025, October 1998.

[6] J.-F. Cardoso. High–order contrasts for Independent Component Analysis. *Neural Computation*, 11:157–192, 1999.

[7] T. Chang and C.-C. J. Kuo. Texture analysis and classification with tree–structured wavelet transform. *IEEE Trans. Image Proc.*, 2(4):429–441, October 1993.

[8] R. Chellappa and S. Chatterjee. Classification of textures using Gaussian Markov Random Fields models. *IEEE Trans. Acoust., Speech, Signal Proc.*, 33(4):959–963, August 1985.

[9] J.M. Coggins and A.K. Jain. A spatial filtering approach to texture analysis. *Pattern Recognition Letters*, 3:195–203, May 1985.

[10] P. Comon. Supervised classification: A probabilistic approach. *Proc. ESANN*, 111–128, Verleysen, April 1995.

[11] P. Comon. Independent Component Analysis: A new concept? *Signal Processing*, 36(3):287–314, April 1994.

[12] G.C. Cross and A.K. Jain. Markov Random Field texture models. *IEEE Trans. Pattern Anal. Mach. Intell.*, 5:25–39,1983.

[13] J.S. De Bonet and P. Viola. Texture recognition using a non-parametric multi-scale statistical model. *Proc. IEEE CVPR*, 641–647, Santa Barbara, June 1998.

[14] K. Etemad and R. Chellappa. Separability–based multiscale basis selection and feature extraction for signal and image classification. *IEEE Trans. Image Proc.*, 7(10):1453–1465, October 1998.

[15] W. Freeman and E.H. Adelson. The design and use of steerable filters. *IEEE Trans. Pattern Anal. Mach. Intell.*, 13:891-906, 1991.

[16] H. Greenspan, S. Belongie, R. Goodman, P. Perona. Rotation invariant texture recognition using a steerable pyramid. *Proc. 12th IAPR*, 2:162-167, Jerusalem, Israel, 1994.

[17] R.M. Haralick. Statistical and structural approaches to texture. *Proceedings of the IEEE*, 67(5):786–804. May 1979.

[18] D. Heeger and J. Bergen. Pyramid-based texture analysis/synthesis. *Proc. ACM SIGGRAPH*, August 1995.

[19] M. Kendall and A. Stuart. *The advanced theory of statistics*. MacMillan Publishing, New York, 1977.

[20] K.I. Laws. Texture energy measures. *Proc. Image Underst. Workshop*, 47–51, November 1979.

[21] J. Malik and P. Perona. Preattentive texture discrimination with early vision mechanisms. *Journ. Optical Society of America*, 7(5):923–932, May 1990.

[22] S.G. Mallat. A theory for multiresolution signal decomposition: The wavelet representation. *IEEE Trans. Pattern Anal. Mach. Intell.*, 11:674–693, July 1989.

[23] B.S. Manjunath and W.Y. Ma. Texture features for browsing and retrieval of image data. *IEEE Trans. Pattern Anal. Mach. Intell.*, 18(8):837–842, August 1996.

[24] B.A. Olshausen and D.J. Field. Emergence of simple-cell receptive field properties by learning a sparse code for natural images. *Nature*, 381:607–609, June 1996.

[25] A. Papoulis. *Probability, random variables and stochastic processes*. McGraw-Hill, New York, 1965.

[26] P. Perona. Deformable kernels for early vision. *IEEE Trans. Pattern Anal. Mach. Intell.*, 17(5):488-499, May 1995.

[27] K. Popat and R. Picard. Cluster-based probability model and its application to image and texture processing. *IEEE Trans. Image Proc.*, 6(2):268–284, February 1997.

[28] J. Portilla, R. Navarro, O. Nestares and A. Tabernero. Texture synthesis-by-analysis based on a multiscale early-vision model. *Optical Engineering*, 35(8):2403-2417, 1996.

[29] Y. Rubner and C. Tomasi. A metric for distributions with applications to image databases. *Proc. 6th ICCV*, 59–66, Bombay, 1998.

[30] E.P. Simoncelli and J. Portilla. Texture characterization via second-order statistics of wavelet coefficient amplitudes. *Proc. IEEE ICIP'98*, 1998.

[31] E. Simoncelli and W.T. Freeeman. The steerable pyramid: A flexible architecture for multi-scale derivative computation. *Proc, of 2nd IEEE ICIP*, 444-447, Washington DC, October 1995.

[32] S.C. Zhu, Y. Wu and D. Mumford. Minimax entropy principle and its application to texture modeling. *Neural Computation*, 9(8), November 1997.

Correlation Model for 3D Texture

Kristin J. Dana and Shree K. Nayar
Department of Computer Science
Columbia University
New York, NY 10027

Abstract

While an exact definition of texture is somewhat elusive, texture can be qualitatively described as a distribution of color, albedo or local normal on a surface. In the literature, the word texture is often used to describe a color or albedo variation on a smooth surface. We refer to such texture as 2D texture. In real world scenes, texture is often due to surface height variations and can be termed 3D texture. Because of local foreshortening and masking, oblique views of 3D texture are not simple transformations of the frontal view. Consequently, texture representations such as the correlation function or power spectrum are also affected by local foreshortening and masking. This work presents a correlation model for a particular class of 3D textures. The model characterizes the spatial relationship among neighboring pixels in an image of 3D texture and the change of this spatial relationship with viewing direction.

1 Introduction

While an exact definition of texture is somewhat elusive, texture can be qualitatively described as a distribution of color, albedo or local normal on a surface. In the literature, the word texture is often used to describe a color or albedo variation on a smooth surface. We refer to such texture as *2D texture*. In real world scenes, texture is often due to surface height variations and can be termed *3D texture*. Only recently has the issue of 3D texture become a topic of interest in the literature [7][14][3][5][4][17][9][15]. Our prior work on 3D texture includes [3][5] which provides measurements of 3D texture as a starting point for the investigation of texture appearance as a function of illumination and viewing direction and [4] which presents a histogram model for the class of 3D texture that is randomly rough, Lambertian, monochrome and isotropic. This work continues the development by presenting a correlation model for the same class of 3D textures to characterize the spatial relationship among pixels and the change of the spatial relationship with viewing direction.

Many texture algorithms have been developed for 2D texture analysis such as shape from texture [11][16][10], texture recognition and texture segmentation [6][18][8][12]. Most of these algorithms are based implicitly or explicitly on the power spectrum or equivalently on the correlation of image texture. For 3D texture, the correlation function of image texture changes in a complicated manner with viewing direction because of local foreshortening ef-

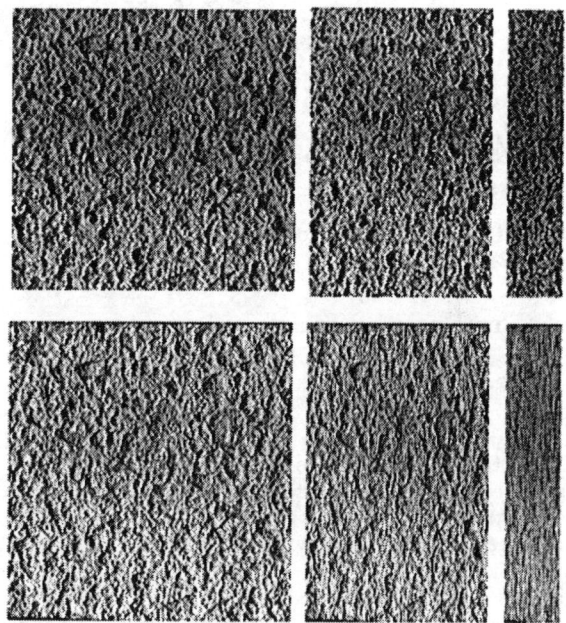

Figure 1. (Top Row) Oblique views of 3D texture. From left to right, the associated viewing angle θ_v is $33.75°$, $56.25°$ and $78.75°$. These images were obtained from a rough plaster sample of the texture database described in [5]. (Bottom Row) Oblique views of a 2D texture with θ_v varying as in top row. These views were generated by warping the frontal view of the same plaster surface. This contrived 2D texture has the same appearance in the frontal view as the rough plaster sample.

fects that depend on the varying local surface normal. In this work we present a model which uses surface statistical parameters to predict the change in the correlation length with viewing direction. Consider the texture images in Figure 1. This figure shows three oblique views of two surfaces at increasingly oblique viewing angles. The surfaces shown have the same image texture viewed frontally, but one surface is rough (3D texture) and the other surface is smooth (2D texture). The images of the smooth texture are simply warped versions of the frontally viewed 3D texture. Notice oblique views of the 2D and 3D texture are quite different. In particular, the oblique views of 2D texture show higher spatial frequencies and therefore a smaller correlation length than the oblique views of 3D texture. A computational model which quantifies the change in correlation length with viewing direction is

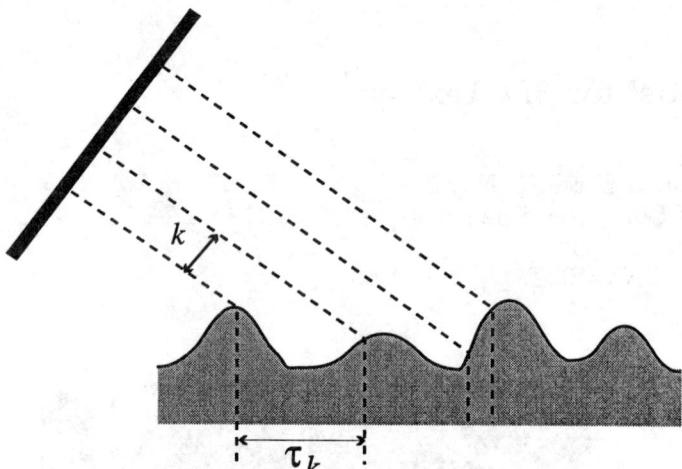

Figure 2. For a fixed distance k in the image, the corresponding surface distance is a random variable τ_k.

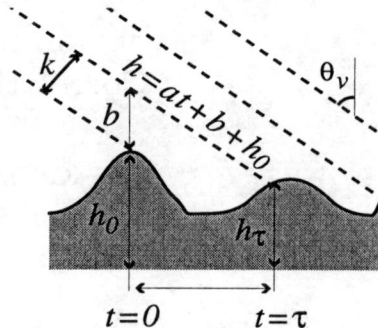

Figure 3. The probability $p_{\tau_k}(\tau)\,d\tau$ can be expressed as the probability the line $h = at + h_0 + b$ intersects the surface at $t = \tau$ and the surface point at $t = \tau$ is visible.

clearly important for algorithms which rely on spectral characteristics of texture.

2 Correlation Model

We assume that the 3D texture of interest is Lambertian and has a random height profile that can be modeled as a gaussian distribution with variance σ_h^2. We further assume that two surface points are jointly normal and the autocorrelation of the surface height process is gaussian with variance β^2. The image of this surface gives rise to an image texture. The details of the surface model are given in Appendix 5.1. In this work, we are interested in finding the correlation length of the image texture for an arbitrary illumination and viewing direction. A fixed distance k in the image corresponds to a random distance τ_k on the surface due to the varying surface profile as shown in Figure 2. Because τ_k is a random variable denoting the surface sampling, the correlation function can be written as

$$E(I[j], I[j-k]) = E\{E(I(t), I(t-\tau_k)|\tau_k)\}, \quad (1)$$

where E denotes the expected value, $I[j]$ is the intensity for image pixel j and $I(t)$ is the intensity for the surface point at t. Note that the image intensity is written as a one-dimensional quantity for notational simplicity. To further simplify the notation let $I(t)$ and $I(t-\tau)$ be denoted by I_0 and I_τ respectively. Then the expected value can be expressed as

$$E(I[j], I[j-k]) = \int_0^\infty E(I_0, I_\tau|\tau_k = \tau)\,p_{\tau_k}(\tau)\,d\tau, \quad (2)$$

where $p_{\tau_k}(\tau)$ is the probability density function (pdf) of the random variable τ_k.

2.1 PDF of Surface Sampling

To derive p_{τ_k} we have adapted and extended the rough surface analysis given in the acoustics literature [1][19][2]

several decades ago by researchers who modeled the acoustics of a rough ocean floor. Using the law of total probability,

$$p_{\tau_k}(\tau) = \int p(\tau|n_0 = n)\,p(n_0 = n)\,dn, \quad (3)$$

where n_0 is the surface normal at $t = 0$.

Let h_0 denote the surface height at $t = 0$, and let h_τ denote the height at $t = \tau$. Then,

$$\Pr[\tau_k = \tau]$$
$$= \Pr\left[\begin{array}{l} \text{surface point at } \tau \text{ is visible} \\ \text{AND } h_\tau = a\tau + h_0 + b|\ X_{v0} \end{array}\right], \quad (4)$$

where

$$a = \tan\theta_v,$$
$$b = \frac{k}{\sin\theta_v},$$

θ_v = polar angle of viewing direction,

X_{v0} = event that surface point at $t = 0$ is visible.

This situation is illustrated in Figure 3. The conditional expression is

$$\Pr[\tau_k = \tau|n_0] =$$
$$\Pr\left[\begin{array}{l} \text{surface point at } \tau \text{ is visible} \\ \text{AND } h_\tau = a\tau + h_0 + b|n_0, X_{v0} \end{array}\right]. \quad (5)$$

That is,

$$\Pr[\tau_k = \tau|n_0]$$
$$= \Pr[X_{v\tau} \text{ AND } h_\tau = a\tau + h_0 + b|n_0, X_{v0}].$$
$$= \int p(X_{v\tau}, h_0 = h, h_\tau = a\tau + h + b|n_0, X_{v0})\,dh$$
$$= \int p(X_{v\tau}|h_0 = h, h_\tau = a\tau + h + b, n_0, X_{v0}) \times$$
$$p(h_0 = h, h_\tau = a\tau + h + b|n_0, X_{v0})\,dh, \quad (6)$$

where $X_{v\tau}$ = event that surface point at $t = \tau$ is visible.

The term $p(X_{v\tau}|h_0 = h, h_\tau = a\tau + h + b, n_0, X_{v0})$ can be found by extending the analysis of [19] and [1] as in

Appendix 5.2. The result is,

$$p\left(X_{v\tau}|h_0 = h, h_\tau = a\tau + h + b, n_0, X_{v0}\right)$$
$$\approx \Pr\left(\text{surface doesn't cross the ray } a\tau + h + b \text{ in } (0, \tau)\right)$$

$$= \left(\int_{M_v} p(n)\, dn\right) \exp\left[-\kappa\left(\begin{array}{c}\text{erf}\left(\frac{h+b+a\tau}{\sqrt{2}\sigma_h}\right) - \\ \text{erf}\left(\frac{h+b}{\sqrt{2}\sigma_h}\right)\end{array}\right)\right], \quad (7)$$

where κ is a function of σ_h/β and the viewing direction and is derived in Appendix 5.2; M_v is the set of surface normals that have a positive dot product with the viewing direction.

The term $p\left(h_0, h_\tau|n_0, X_{v0}\right)$ can be expressed as

$$p\left(h_0, h_\tau|n_0, X_{v0}\right) = \frac{p\left(X_{v0}|h_0, h_\tau, n_0\right) p\left(h_0, h_\tau, n_0\right)}{p\left(n_0, X_{v0}\right)}$$

$$= \frac{p\left(X_{v0}|h_0, n_0\right) p\left(h_0, h_\tau, n_0\right)}{p\left(X_{v0}|n_0\right) p\left(n_0\right)}$$

$$= \frac{p\left(X_{v0}|h_0, n_0\right) p\left(h_0, h_\tau|n_0\right)}{p\left(X_{v0}|n_0\right)}$$

$$= \frac{\exp\left(\frac{-B(1-\text{erf}(h_0))}{\sqrt{2}\sigma_h}\right) p\left(h_0, h_\tau|n_0\right)}{q_v}, \quad (8)$$

for $n_0 \in M_v$, where we use the following results from [19]

$$p\left(X_{v0}|h_0, n_0\right) = \exp\left(\frac{-B\left(1 - \text{erf}\left(h_0\right)\right)}{\sqrt{2}\sigma_h}\right), \quad (9)$$

$$p\left(X_{v0}|n_0\right) = q_v. \quad (10)$$

The terms B and q_v are derived in [19] and are a function of the surface statistics and viewing direction. Putting it all together and letting

$$\nu = \left(\int_{M_v} p(n)\, dn\right) / q_v,$$

we have

$$p\left(\tau|n_0\right) =$$
$$\int p\left(X_{v\tau}|h_0 = h, h_\tau = a\tau + h + b, n_0, X_{v0}\right) \times$$
$$p\left(h_0 = h, h_\tau = a\tau + h + b|n_0, X_{v0}\right) dh$$

$$= \nu \int_0^\infty \exp\left[-\kappa\left(\begin{array}{c}\text{erf}\left(\frac{h+b+a\tau}{\sqrt{2}\sigma_h}\right) - \\ \text{erf}\left(\frac{h+b}{\sqrt{2}\sigma_h}\right)\end{array}\right)\right] \times$$
$$\exp\left(\frac{-B\left(1 - \text{erf}\left(h\right)\right)}{\sqrt{2}\sigma}\right) p\left(h_0, h_\tau|n_0\right) dh. \quad (11)$$

So,

$$p_{\tau_k}(\tau)\, d\tau = \int p(\tau|n_0 = n) p(n_0 = n)\, dn\, d\tau$$

$$= \nu \int \int_0^\infty \exp\left(\begin{array}{c}-\kappa\left(\begin{array}{c}\text{erf}\left(\frac{h+b+a\tau}{\sqrt{2}\sigma_h}\right) - \\ \text{erf}\left(\frac{h+b}{\sqrt{2}\sigma_h}\right)\end{array}\right) - \\ B\left(1 - \text{erf}\left(\frac{h+b+a\tau}{\sqrt{2}\sigma_h}\right)\right)\end{array}\right) \times$$
$$\exp\left(-\xi h^2 - \gamma h - \eta\right) dh\, dn\, d\tau, \quad (12)$$

where

$$\exp\left(-\xi h^2 - \chi h - \eta\right) = p\left(h_0 = h, h_\tau = h + b + a\tau, n_0 = n\right). \quad (13)$$

The parameters ξ, χ and η are readily derived from the multivariate normal surface model. The resulting integral is too complicated to solve analytically and is evaluated using numerical integration.

2.2 Examples of $p_{\tau_k}(\tau)$

The sampling on the surface varies with the local height variations on the surface. When the viewing ray intersects uphill (positive sloped) portions of the surface, the distance between samples is small. On the other hand, when the viewing ray intersects downhill (negative sloped) portions, the sampling distance is large. In addition, peaks on the surface cause neighboring surface points to be occluded and therefore the corresponding sampling distance is large. In this section we look at several examples of the predicted sampling distance pdf p_{τ_k} as derived in the previous section.

Figure 4 shows the simulated surface for four different combinations of σ_h and β. These simulated surfaces are provided only as a reference to interpret the sampling pdf examples and were not used in the calculations. Figure 5 shows the predicted values of p_{τ_k} for $k = 1, 2, 3$ and $\theta_v = 33.75°$. Consider the characteristics of each curve. In example A of Figure 5, where σ_h is low and β is low, the sampling distance has a mean value at $k/\cos\theta_v$ and has approximately equal distribution of sample values lower and heigher than this mean value. As k increases, p_{τ_k} shows very little change with the exception of its mean value. To see that this behavior is expected, consider the corresponding simulated surface shown in example A of Figure 4. For this viewing direction, there are very few occlusions and the area of uphill points projected to the image are approximately equal to the area of downhill points. Therefore we expect an equal distribution of the curve p_{τ_k} around the mean. The value of the mean is what we expect; it is the sampling distance that would occur in the limit as σ_h goes to zero or β goes to ∞ and the rough surface becomes smooth.

In example B of Figure 5, with its corresponding simulated surface shown in Figure 4, the value of σ_h is low but the value of β is large. Because of this relatively large correlation distance, the surface is smoother and there is less variation of τ_k, i.e. p_{τ_k} has a smaller variance than example A. Also, small values of k are likely to correspond to values of τ_k that are within the correlation length and therefore p_{τ_k} for smaller k values have a smaller variance.

Example C of Figure 5, corresponds to large σ_h and small β. In this case there are significant occlusions from tall surface points. The length of the occluding mask varies causing a large variation of τ. For smaller k values, there is more of a chance of intersecting an uphill portion of the surface so the curve has more weight at low τ values.

In example D, which corresponds to large σ_h and large β, the curves for p_{τ_k} are similar to those of example B with the exception of a large variation of τ around the means caused by a larger value of σ_h.

Figure 6 shows the same examples with a more oblique viewing direction, $\theta_v = 56.25°$. The plots are similar to

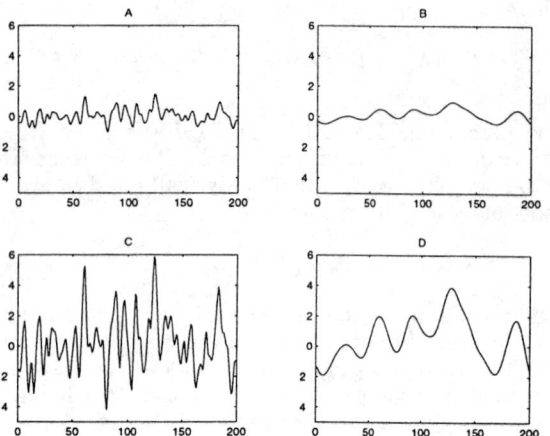

Figure 4. Four one dimensional surfaces provided for illustration purposes. A: $\sigma_h = 0.5, \beta = 1$. B: $\sigma_h = 0.5, \beta = 5$. C: $\sigma_h = 2, \beta = 1$. D: $\sigma_h = 2, \beta = 5$.

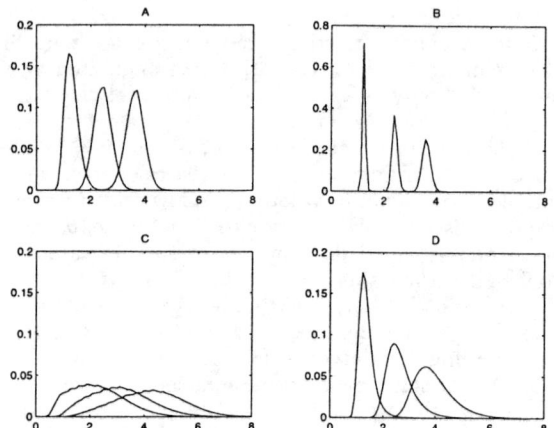

Figure 5. Four examples of p_{τ_k} obtained from the derived model with $\theta_v = 33.75°$ and $k = 1, 2, 3$. A: $\sigma_h = 0.5, \beta = 1$. B: $\sigma_h = 0.5, \beta = 5$. C: $\sigma_h = 2, \beta = 1$. D: $\sigma_h = 2, \beta = 5$.

those shown in Figure 5 with the exception that the occlusions from tall surface points are large at the oblique angles causing much larger τ values to be significantly probable.

These plots show the correct behavior by qualitative arguments. In addition, during model development the predicted pdf of τ_k was compared to a computed version obtained by ray-tracing simulated surfaces. There was a good correspondence between the model predictions and these simulations.

2.3 Correlation Length

Let the correlation length of the surface be τ', so that when $\tau_k > \tau'$,

$$E\left(I_0, I_\tau | \tau_k = \tau\right) = 0.$$

We see from Equation 2 that if

$$p_{\tau_k}\left(\tau\right) = 0 \text{ for } \tau < \tau',$$

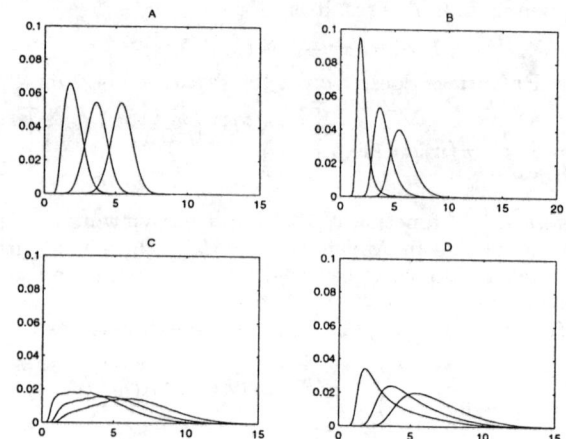

Figure 6. Four examples of p_{τ_k} obtained from the derived model with $\theta_v = 56.25°$ and $k = 1, 2, 3$. A: $\sigma_h = 0.5, \beta = 1$. B: $\sigma_h = 0.5, \beta = 5$. C: $\sigma_h = 2, \beta = 1$. D: $\sigma_h = 2, \beta = 5$.

then

$$E\left(I\left[j\right], I\left[j - k\right]\right) = 0.$$

Let L be the value such that

$$p_{\tau_k}\left(\tau\right) = 0 \text{ for } \tau < \tau' \text{ whenever } k > L. \quad (14)$$

This value of L is the correlation length in the image, i.e.

$$E\left(I_0, I_k\right) = 0 \text{ when } k > L. \quad (15)$$

We note that L is a function of the viewing direction and the surface statistics. The correlation length is not independent of illumination direction in the presence of cast shadows. However if cast shadows are not dominant and the correlation is computed using only non-shadowed pixels, the resulting correlation length is equal to L.

While the random variable τ_k is not directly observable from the image, $E\left(I_0, I_k\right)$ and therefore L can be estimated from the image. The estimated values of L can be used to estimate surface statistics from a set of images obtained with known viewing direction but unknown illumination direction. Conversely, if the surface statistics are known the viewing direction can be estimated using the value of L obtained from the image.

3 Results

We employ the texture images obtained from the publicly available database described in [5]. Figure 7 shows the images of rough plaster taken under 9 different illumination and viewing directions. From left to right, the columns correspond to $\theta_v = 33.75°, 56.25°$ and $78.75°$. From top to bottom the illumination polar angle is $\theta_s = 11.25°, 33.75°$ and $-11.35°$. For the images in each row the correlation length was computed and plotted as a function of θ_v in Figure 8 (dashed lines). Using the correlation lengths we estimated the value of σ_h and β for this surface as $\sigma_h = 0.57$ and $\beta = 1.16$. The corresponding model estimate of the correlation length L is shown in Figure 8. Also shown in this figure is the correlation length for a planar

Figure 7. Images of rough plaster (sample 11 in the texture database) taken under 9 different illumination and viewing directions. From left to right the columns correspond to $\theta_v = 33.75°, 56.25°$ and $78.75°$. From top to bottom the illumination polar angle is $\theta_s = 11.25°, 33.75°$ and $-11.35°$.

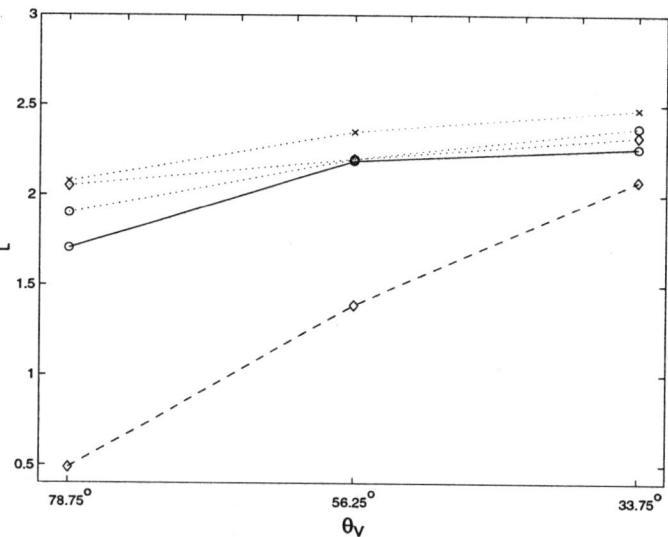

Figure 8. Measured and modeled correlation lengths. The dotted lines show the measured correlation length L as a function of $\theta_v = 33.75°, 56.25°$ and $78.75°$. Each dotted line corresponds to a different illumination direction $\theta_s = 11.25°, 33.75°, -11.25°$. The solid line corresponds to the model of the correlation length using the parameters that best match the measurements: $\sigma_h = 0.57$ and $\beta = 1.16$. The dashed line shows the correlation length that would be predicted if we assume the texture is a 2D texture.

surface (2D texture). There are two important things to notice here. First, the measured correlation length as a function of viewing direction is similar for all three illumination directions considered. Second, the model does a good job predicting the correct value of the correlation length especially when compared to the prediction obtained by assuming 2D texture.

4 Conclusion/Summary

For image understanding in real world scenes, algorithms and models which handle 3D texture are becoming increasingly important. In [4], we developed a histogram model for 3D texture that predicts the histogram of image intensities as a function of viewing and illumination direction. Using the histogram model, we estimated surface roughness from a series of images taken under different illumination and viewing directions. However, the histogram does not provide information on the spatial relationship of image pixels and the estimated surface roughness does not reveal the spatial relationship of surface points. The new model presented here allows the prediction of correlation length as a function of viewing direction. From a series of images we've estimated both surface roughness and surface correlation. Consequently, the model is used to determine the spatial relationship of image pixels and surface points.

5 Appendix

5.1 Surface Statistics

We assume the height of the surface is a gaussian random variable, i.e. the pdf of the height p_h has a standard deviation σ_h and is given by

$$p_h = \frac{1}{\sqrt{2\pi\sigma_h^2}} \exp\left(-\frac{(h - m_h)^2}{2\sigma_h^2}\right).$$

We assume the correlation function is gaussian with a standard deviation of β, i.e.

$$E\left(h\left(x_1, y_1\right), h\left(x_2, y_2\right)\right)$$
$$= \sigma_h^2 \exp\left(\frac{-\left(x_1 - x_2\right)^2 - \left(y_1 - y_2\right)^2}{2\beta^2}\right).$$

5.2 Ray Crossing PDF

In this section we've adapted our notation to be more consistent with [19]. According to the development in [19],

$$\Pr\left(\text{surface doesn't cross the ray } a\tau + \delta \text{ in } (0, \tau) \,|\, \delta, \delta'\right)$$
$$= C \exp\left[\begin{array}{c} -\int_0^\tau \frac{1}{2\pi\sigma_h\sigma} \times \\ \int_{\eta_0}^\infty (\eta - \eta_0) \exp\left(-\frac{(\delta + \eta_0\tau)^2}{2\sigma_h^2} - \frac{\eta^2}{2\sigma^2}\right) d\eta \end{array}\right],$$

where η_0 is the slope of the viewing ray, δ is the height of the surface, δ' is the slope of the surface, $\sigma = \sigma_h/\beta$, and C is the unit step function

$$C = u\left(\eta_0 - \delta'\right) = \begin{array}{c} 1 \text{ if } \delta' \geq \eta_0 \\ 0 \text{ otherwise.} \end{array}$$

Therefore,

$$\Pr\left(\text{surface doesn't cross the ray } a\tau + \delta \text{ in } (0, \tau) \,|\, \delta, \delta'\right)$$
$$= C \exp\left[\begin{array}{c} -\int_0^\tau \frac{1}{2\pi\sigma_h\sigma} \int_{\eta_0}^\infty (\eta - \eta_0) \times \\ \exp\left(-\frac{(\delta + \eta_0\tau)^2}{2\sigma_h^2} - \frac{\eta^2}{2\sigma^2}\right) d\eta d\tau \end{array}\right]$$
$$= C \exp\left[-\int_0^\tau \frac{1}{2\pi\sigma_h\sigma} A \exp\left(-\frac{(\delta + \eta_0\tau')^2}{2\sigma_h^2}\right) d\tau\right],$$

where

$$A = \begin{pmatrix} -\sqrt{2\pi}\sigma\eta_0 + \sigma\sqrt{2\pi}\,\mathrm{erf}\left(\frac{1}{\sqrt{2}\sigma}\eta_0\right)\eta_0 \\ +2\sigma^2\exp\left(-\frac{\eta_0^2}{2\sigma^2}\right) \end{pmatrix}.$$

Because

$$\int_{\eta_0}^{\infty}(\eta-\eta_0)\exp\left(-\frac{(\delta+\eta_0\tau)^2}{2\sigma_h^2}-\frac{\eta^2}{2\sigma^2}\right)d\eta =$$

$$= A\exp\left(-\frac{(\delta+\eta_0\tau')^2}{2\sigma_h^2}\right),$$

the integral can be evaluated as follows

$$-\frac{1}{2\pi\sigma_h\sigma}\int_0^{\tau}\left(A\exp\left(-\frac{(\delta+\eta_0\tau')^2}{2\sigma_h^2}\right)\right)d\tau'$$

$$= -\frac{1}{2}\sqrt{2\pi}\sigma_h A\frac{-\mathrm{erf}\left(\frac{\delta+\eta_0\tau}{\sqrt{2}\sigma_h}\right)+\mathrm{erf}\left(\frac{1}{\sqrt{2}\sigma_h}\delta\right)}{\eta_0}$$

$$= \left(\frac{1}{\sqrt{2\pi}}\frac{\sigma}{\eta_0}e^{-\frac{1}{2}\frac{\eta_0^2}{\sigma^2}}-\frac{1}{2}\left(1-\mathrm{erf}\left(\frac{\eta_0}{\sqrt{2\sigma^2}}\right)\right)\right)\times$$

$$\left(-\mathrm{erf}\left(\frac{\delta+\eta_0\tau}{\sqrt{2}\sigma_h}\right)+\mathrm{erf}\left(\frac{\delta}{\sqrt{2}\sigma_h}\right)\right).$$

So the result is

$$\Pr\left(\text{surface doesn't cross the ray } a\tau+\delta \text{ in } (0,\tau)\,|\,\delta,\delta'\right)$$

$$= C\exp\left[\begin{array}{c}\left(\frac{1}{\sqrt{2\pi}}\frac{\sigma}{\eta_0}e^{-\frac{1}{2}\frac{\eta_0^2}{\sigma^2}}-\frac{1}{2}\left(1-\mathrm{erf}\left(\frac{\eta_0}{\sqrt{2\sigma^2}}\right)\right)\right)\times \\ \left(-\mathrm{erf}\left(\frac{\delta+\eta_0\tau}{\sqrt{2}\sigma_h}\right)+\mathrm{erf}\left(\frac{\delta}{\sqrt{2}\sigma_h}\right)\right)\end{array}\right].$$

Now we integrate over δ',

$$\Pr\left(\text{surface doesn't cross the ray } a\tau+\delta \text{ in } (0,\tau)\,|\,\delta\right) =$$

$$\int\Pr\begin{pmatrix}\text{surface doesn't cross the ray}\\ a\tau+\delta \text{ in } (0,\tau)\,|\,\delta,\delta'\end{pmatrix}p(\delta')\,d\delta'$$

$$= \left(\int_{M_v}p(n)\,dn\right)\Pr\begin{pmatrix}\text{surface doesn't cross the ray}\\ a\tau+\delta \text{ in } (0,\tau)\,|\,\delta,\delta'\in M_v\end{pmatrix}$$

$$= \left(\int_{M_v}p(n)\,dn\right)\exp\left[\kappa(\sigma,\eta_0)\begin{pmatrix}-\mathrm{erf}\left(\frac{\delta+\eta_0\tau}{\sqrt{2}\sigma_h}\right)+\\ \mathrm{erf}\left(\frac{\delta}{\sqrt{2}\sigma_h}\right)\end{pmatrix}\right],$$

where M_v is the set of surface normals that have a positive dot product with the viewing direction. Therefore,

$$\kappa(\sigma,\eta_0) = \left(\frac{1}{\sqrt{2\pi}}\frac{\sigma}{\eta_0}e^{-\frac{1}{2}\frac{\eta_0^2}{\sigma^2}}-\frac{1}{2}\left(1-\mathrm{erf}\left(\frac{\eta_0}{\sqrt{2\sigma^2}}\right)\right)\right).$$

References

[1] P. Beckman, "Shadowing of random rough surfaces," *IEEE Trans. Antennas Propag.*, vol. 13, p. 384, 1965.

[2] R. Brockelman and T. Hagfors, "Note on the effect of shadowing on the backscattering of waves from a random rough surfaces," *IEEE Trans. Antennas Propag.*, vol. 14, p. 621, 1966.

[3] K. J. Dana, B. van Ginneken, S. K. Nayar and J. J. Koenderink, "Reflectance and texture of real-world surfaces," *IEEE Conference on Computer Vision and Pattern Recognition (CVPR)*, pp. 151-157, 1997.

[4] K. J. Dana and S. K. Nayar, "Histogram model for 3D textures," *IEEE Conference on CVPR*, pp. 618-624, 1998.

[5] K. J. Dana, B. van Ginneken, S. K. Nayar and J. J. Koenderink, "Reflectance and texture of real-world surfaces," *ACM Transactions on Graphics*, pp. 1-34, vol. 18, no. 1, January 1999.

[6] J. S. De Bonet and P. Viola, "Texture recognition using a non-parametric multi-scale statistical model," *IEEE Conference on CVPR*, pp. 641-647, 1998.

[7] J. J. Koenderink and A. J. van Doorn, "Illuminance texture due to surface mesostructure," *J. Optical Soc. Am. A*, vol. 13 pp. 452-463, 1996.

[8] J. Krumm and S. A. Shafer, "Texture segmentation and shape in the same image," *IEEE Conference on Computer Vision*, pp. 121-127, 1995.

[9] T. Leung and J. Malik, "On perpendicular texture or: Why do we see more flowers in the distance," *IEEE Conference on CVPR*, pp. 807-814, 1997.

[10] J. Malik and R. Rosenholtz, "Computing local surface orientation and shape from texture for curved surfaces," *International Journal of Computer Vision*, vol. 23, no.2, pp.149-168, 1997.

[11] M. A. S. Patel and F. S. Cohen, "Shape from texture using Markov random field models and stereo-windows," *IEEE Conference on CVPR*, pp. 290-305, 1992.

[12] R. W. Picard, T. Kabir and F. Liu, "Real-time recognition with the entire Brodatz texture database," *IEEE Conference on CVPR*, pp. 638-639, 1993.

[13] B. Smith, "Geometrical shadowing of randomly rough surfaces," *IEEE Trans. Antennas Propag.*, p. 668, vol. 15, 1967.

[14] M. Stavridi and J. J. Koenderink, "Surface bidirectional reflection distribution function and the texture of bricks and tiles," *Applied Optics*, vol. 36, no. 16, p. 3717, 1997.

[15] P. Suen and G. Healey, "Analyzing the bidirectional texture function," *IEEE Conference on CVPR*, pp. 753-758, 1998.

[16] B. J. Super and A. C. Bovik, "Shape from texture using local spectral moments," *IEEE Transactions on Pattern Analysis and Machine Intelligence*, vol. 17, pp. 333-343, 1995.

[17] B. van Ginneken, J. J. Koenderink, and K. J. Dana, "Texture histograms as a function of irradiation and viewing direction," *IJCV-to appear 1999*.

[18] L. Wang and G. Healey, "Illumination and geometry invariant recognition of texture in color images," *IEEE Conference on CVPR*, pp. 419-424, 1996.

[19] R. Wagner, "Shadowing of randomly rough surfaces," *Journal of the Acoustical Society of America*, p. 138, vol. 41, 1967.

[20] P. Welton, K. Hawker, and H. Frey, "Experimental shadowing measurements on randomly rough surfaces," *Journal of the Acoustical Society of America*, vol. 54, no. 2, p. 446, 1973.

Matching, Recognition, and Indexing

Object Localization by Bayesian Correlation

J. Sullivan, A. Blake, M. Isard and J. MacCormick
Department of Engineering Science, University of Oxford, Oxford OX1 3PJ, UK.
Web*— http://www.robots.ox.ac.uk/~vdg/

Abstract

Maximisation of cross-correlation is a commonly used principle for intensity-based object localization that gives a single estimate of location. However, to facilitate sequential inference (eg over time or scale) and to allow the representation of ambiguity, it is desirable to represent an entire probability distribution for object location. Although the cross-correlation itself (or some function of it) has sometimes been treated as a probability distribution, this is not generally justifiable.

*Bayesian correlation achieves a consistent probabilistic treatment by combining several developments. The first is the interpretation of correlation matching functions in probabilistic terms, as observation likelihoods. Second, probability distributions of filter-bank responses are learned from training examples. Inescapably, response-learning also demands statistical modelling of background intensities, and there are links here with image coding and Independent Component Analysis. Lastly, multi-scale processing is achieved, in a Bayesian context, by means of a new algorithm, **layered sampling**, for which asymptotic properties are derived.*

1 Introduction

Object localization in an image $I(\mathbf{x})$ can be viewed as the problem of recovering the warp $g_X(\mathbf{x})$ that transported a certain template $T(\mathbf{x})$ into the image. Here, the warp g_X is parameterised by $X \in \mathcal{X}$, where $\mathcal{X}$ is a configuration space for the warped template, for example, planar-affine space or some space of non-rigid deformations. Following the warp, it is assumed that random imperfections are introduced as a result of sensor-noise and unmodelled variations.

"Analysis by synthesis" [14] then consists of the Bayesian construction of a posterior distribution for X. Given a prior distribution $p_0(X)$ for the configuration X, and an observation likelihood $p(Z|X)$ where $Z \equiv Z(I)$ is some finite-dimensional representation of the image I, then the posterior density for X is given by

$$p(X|Z) \propto p_0(X)p(Z|X). \tag{1}$$

In more straightforward, Gaussian cases, (1) can be computed in closed form. In the non-Gaussian cases commonly

arising, for example in image clutter or with multiple models, sampling methods are needed [8], and random sampling underlies the development of Bayesian correlation here.

Relation to previous work Key elements of the work presented here are:

IB *Intensity Based* observations, not just edges.

FL *Foreground Learning* in terms of probability distributions estimated from one or more training examples.

MS *Multiple Scale* search is well known to be a sound basis for efficient searching of images.

PD *Posterior Distributions* for object location, rather than just a single estimate, supports sequential reasoning for multi-scale and image-sequence analysis, and potentially across sensory modalities.

BM *Background Modelling*: in a valid Bayesian analysis, image observations Z must not be a function $Z(X)$ of the hypothesis X. For example, sum-squared difference violates this principle by considering only the portion of an image directly under the template $T(\mathbf{x})$. A Bayesian approach must use evidence about where the object is *not*. That requires a probabilistic model of the image background.

SI *Statistical Independence* of observations must be ensured if constructed observation likelihoods are to be valid. For instance, assuming independence across adjacent pixels is unjustified, and leads to exaggerated variations in the likelihood $p(Z|X)$ for even minor perturbations of X.

There are three outstanding precursors to Bayesian correlation; one concerns random diffeomorphisms [8]; the second is an algorithm [17] for registration by maximisation of mutual information; third is localisation by foreground/background learning [7]. Attributes of these and other important prior work are summarised in table 1, in terms of elements of Bayesian correlation as listed above.

2 Probabilistic inference of shape

A natural choice for the set Z of image observations is a filter-bank consisting of inner-product elements z_k, $k = 1, \ldots, K$ applied to the image I. Each filter-element has the form

$$z_k = \int_{S_k} W_k(\mathbf{x})I(\mathbf{x})d\mathbf{x}, \tag{2}$$

---

*for a version of this paper with colour figures and a movie of figure 15

	IB	FL	MS	PD	BM	SI	Comments
Burt [5]	×		×				multi-scale pyramid
Witkin *et al.* [18], Scharstein & Szeliski [16]	×		×				scale-space matching
Grenander *et al.* [8]	×			×	×		random diffeomorphisms
Viola & Wells [17]	×	×					mutual information
Cootes *et al.* [6]	×	×	×				multi-scale active contours
Black & Yacoob [3], Bascle & Deriche [1], Hager & Toyama [9]	×	×					affine flow/warp
Isard & Blake [11]		×		×			random active contours
Olshausen & Field [15], Bell & Sejnowski [2]	×				×	×	independent components (ICA)
Geman & Jedynak [7]	×	×			×		response learning

Table 1: **Precursors to Bayesian correlation.**

computing an inner product of the image and the element function W_k, over a finite support S_k. Element functions may consist of copies of a single response-function $W(\mathbf{x})$, translated to the nodes of a regular grid, so that the world is effectively being viewed through a sieve, as in figure 1. In the familiar case that the space of warps $\mathcal{X}$ consists of

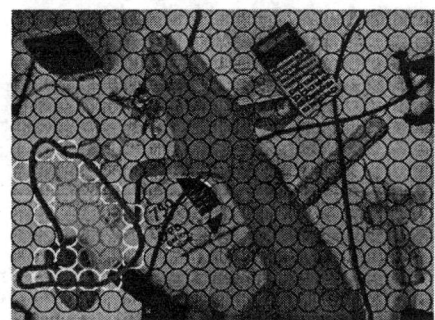

Figure 1: **The world through a filter bank** $Z = (z_1, \ldots, z_K)$, with circular supports $S_1, \ldots, S_K$ on a regular grid. Given some hypothesised X (thick hand-shaped outline), supports are labelled foreground (inside outline), background or mixed. (Note: example shows an X that is far from the true hand configuration.)

two-dimensional translations, the bank can be thought of as a discrete sampling of the cross-correlation of W with I. In that case, the response-function $W(\mathbf{x})$ could well be a translated copy of the object template $T(\mathbf{x})$, which would have the effect of tuning $z(X)$ to respond to object position. For the higher-dimensional warp-spaces $\mathcal{X}$ (e.g. planar affine) that we want to deal with here, systematic sampling of $z(X)$, $X \in \mathcal{X}$ is no longer feasible. Generalising the filter bank Z therefore has to take a different tack. The two-dimensional grid layout can remain, but the response-function W becomes something more general. The translated copies W_k generate a set of linear functionals to encode (partially) an image I, with the necessary statistical independence, but no longer tuned to any particular object. Of course, an important generalisation is that there may be more than one type of response-function (eg for various scales), each of which is replicated over the grid to form the components z_k of Z. The entire filter-bank scheme has the attraction that fixed, computationally efficient architectures can be used to compute Z, for instance wavelets [13], pyramids [5] or biological "hypercolumn" hardware [10].

Learning We have argued that $p(Z|X)$ contains both foreground and background components. Tackling image-texture modelling head-on would be complex. An oblique approach is to learn filter-likelihoods $p(z_k|X)$ directly from training images, as [7] but, crucially, also tackling the inescapable issue of *mixed* supports (figure 1). This side-steps any need for a complete model of foreground or background, modelling them *only as they appear in the sieve* of figure 1. Then, provided also that the W_k can be chosen to give the necessary statistical independence, the full observation likelihood can be constructed as a product:

$$p(Z|X) = \prod_{k=1}^{K} p(z_k|X). \tag{3}$$

Factored sampling For non-Gaussian problems, (1) can be simulated by generating random variates from a distribution that approximates the posterior $p(X|Z)$. In *factored sampling* [8], a weighted particle-set $\{(s_1, \pi_1), \ldots, (s_N, \pi_N)\}$, of size N, is generated from the prior density $p_0(X)$ and each particle s_i is associated with a likelihood weight $\pi_i = f(s_i)$ where $f(X) = p(Z|X)$. Then, an index $i \in \{1, \ldots, N\}$ is sampled with replacement, with a probability proportional to π_i; the associated s_i is effectively drawn from a distribution that converges (weakly) to the posterior, as $N \to \infty$. It will prove useful later to express the sampling scheme graphically, as a "particle diagram"

$$\boxed{p_0} \xrightarrow{\;\;N\;\;} \bigcirc \xrightarrow{\;\times f\;} \bigcirc \xrightarrow{\;\;N\;\;} \bigcirc. \tag{4}$$

It is interpreted as follows: the first arrow denotes drawing N particles from a known density p_0, with equal weights $\pi_i = 1/N$. (Particle sets are represented by open circles.) The $\times f$ operation denotes likelihood weighting of a particle set: $(s_i, \pi_i) \to (s_i, f(s_i)\pi_i)$, $i = 1, \ldots, N$. The final step denotes sampling with replacement, as described above, repeated N times, to form a new set of size N in which each particle is given equal weight, and which is drawn approximately from the posterior.

3 Probabilistic modelling of observations

The observation (ie output value) z from an individual filter is generated by integration over a support-set S (figure 2) and generally has both a background component $B(X)$ and a foreground component $F(X)$:

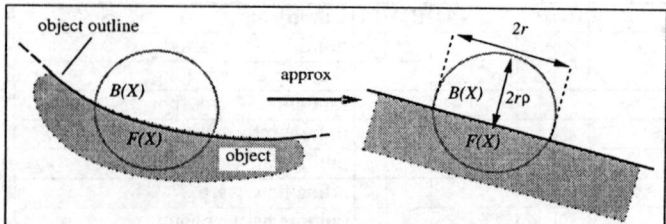

Figure 2: **The support of a filter** is split into subsets $F(X)$ — foreground and $B(X)$ — background. The boundary between subsets is approximated as a line, so $B(X)$ and $F(X)$ are segments of a circle with offsets $2r\rho$ and $2r(1-\rho)$ respectively.

$$z|X = \underbrace{\int_{B(X)} W(\mathbf{x})I_B(\mathbf{x})\,\mathrm{d}\mathbf{x}}_{\text{MAIN NOISE SOURCE}} + \int_{F(X)} W(\mathbf{x})I_F(\mathbf{x})\,\mathrm{d}\mathbf{x}.$$

(5)

Then, considering the output z_k of the kth filter at run-time, under a hypothesised configuration X, the Bayesian correlation algorithm needs to compare the measured z_k against the likelihood $p_k(z_k|X)$. Likelihood $p_k(z|.)$ represents a sum of background and foreground components, and is therefore constructed as a (numerically approximated) convolution $p_k(z|X) = p_k^B(z|X) * p_k^F(z|X)$ of learned background and foreground density functions.

The main source of variability in $z|X$ is expected to come from the background which is a sample from some class of scenes, assumed large and only generally known. In contrast, the foreground relates to a given object, relatively precisely known, though still subject to some ambient- and class-variability. This means that there should be a steady reduction in the variance of the distribution of $z|X$ as X changes from values in which the circular support is over foreground, via mixed foreground/background, to pure background. This is supported by experiments shown later. Distributions $p(z|X)$ are learned for fixed values of X and effectively assembled and sliced to give observation likelihoods (figure 3). For example, $z = 2$ in the figure depicts a relatively high value which, in the example, is more likely to be associated with a filter-support lying mainly over the foreground. The resulting likelihood is peaked around a value of X corresponding to predominant foreground support. Conversely, for $z = -1$, the mode of the likelihood shifts towards background values of X.

4 Learning the background likelihood

It proves efficient to approximate the curve dividing $F(X)$ and $B(X)$ as a straight line (figure 2). In that case, if each filter functional $W_k(\mathbf{x})$ is isotropic the background distribution p^B can be parameterised by a single offset parameter ρ, so that the background density $p_k^B(z_k|X)$ for the kth filter takes a simpler form as $p^B(z_k|\rho_k(X))$. Then, at run-time, the Bayesian correlation algorithm will repeatedly evaluate the *offset function* $\rho_k(X)$ in order to evaluate likelihood.

Now training examples must be constructed over circu-

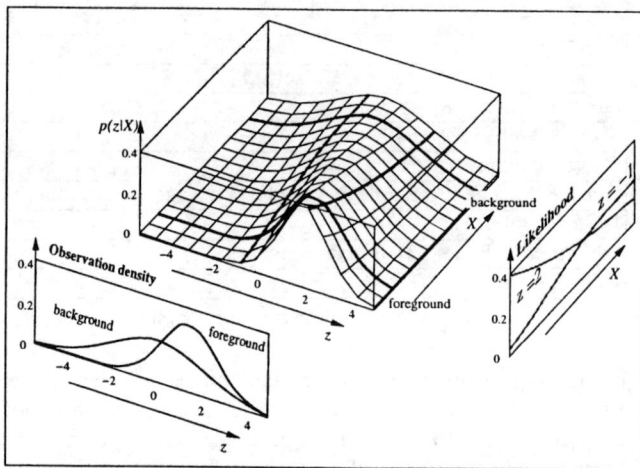

Figure 3: **Observation likelihood.** The density $p(z|X)$ is formally a function of z with X as a parameter, and is illustrated for foreground and background cases. Now $p(z|X)$ is "sliced" in the orthogonal direction, to generate likelihoods — functions of X for fixed z

lar segments with offsets throughout the range $0 \leq \rho \leq 1$, to learn the distributions $p^B(z|\rho)$. (In practice, ρ-values are sampled and interpolated.) The $p^B(z_k|\rho_k(X))$ should be independent so that a joint likelihood can be constructed, aggregating all observations z_k (3). Independence is an issue also in "neural coding" [15]: efficient codes that avoid redundancy need statistically independent components. Independent components of natural scenes are known to have "kurtotic" or "sparse" distributions — ones with extended tails compared with those of a normal distribution [2]. A necessary condition for independence is freedom from correlation, so autocorrelation was estimated, for four different scenes (desk-top, rooms, tree), by random sampling of pairs of supports, with varying separation. This was done for two filter functions $W(\mathbf{x})$: Gaussian $G(\mathbf{x})$ (positive mean) and Laplacian of Gaussian $\nabla^2 G(\mathbf{x})$ (zero mean), where $G(\mathbf{x}) = \frac{1}{\sigma^2}\exp{-\frac{|\mathbf{x}|^2}{2\sigma^2}}$, in a circular support of radius $r = 3\sigma$, as in figure 4. As expected, the $G(\mathbf{x})$ filter is correlated at a rea-

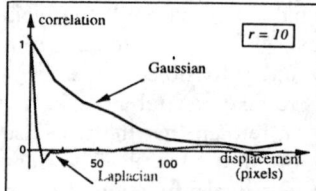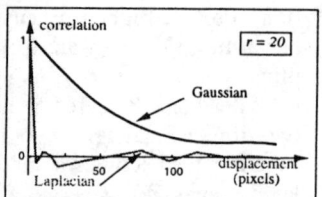

Figure 4: **Autocorrelation of filter output.** Results for the desk-top scene, at two spatial scales r. The Gaussian filter $G(\mathbf{x})$ shows substantial long-range correlation whereas, for $\nabla^2 G(\mathbf{x})$ correlation falls to zero for non-overlapping supports.

sonable displacement such as $2r$ and hence cannot be independent. The $\nabla^2 G(\mathbf{x})$ filter is uncorrelated at $2r$ and further experiments, looking at the entire joint distributions for responses z_k, z_l of two filters with variable separation, confirm statistical independence. The independence is at the cost of discarding information about mean response, but this can be beneficial in conferring some invariance to illumination variations. Experiments so far have been for complete, circular supports. With part-segments of a circle ($\rho < 1$), statistical independence of $\nabla^2 G(\mathbf{x})$ responses deteriorates. This is established by experiments like the ones in figure 4, but now with $\rho < 1$, that show correlation lengths increasing for $\rho < 1$, with $\rho = \frac{1}{4}$ the worst case. This means greater statistical dependence between mixed supports, and it is not clear how this could be improved, but note at least that it is typically a minority of filter supports that are mixed.

It is known that, for ∇G filters, the learned background distributions turn out to be strikingly constant across scenes [19]. Our own experimentation confirms that this holds also for $\nabla^2 G(\mathbf{x})$ filters and that the distribution is quite well modelled as a single-exponential distribution $p^B(z) \propto \exp -|z|/\lambda$, like those emerging in independent components of images [2] and from maximum entropy arguments [20]. The model fits experimental data quite well for $\rho = 1$, though not so well for mixed supports $\rho < 1$, and could be used directly to represent background density, rather than carrying entire histograms.

5 Learning the foreground likelihood

Learning distributions for foreground responses is similar to the background case. As before, $p^{\mathcal{F}}(z|\rho)$ is learned for some finite set of ρ-values, and interpolated. There are some important differences however.

Deformations and pooling: three-dimensional transformations and deformations of the foreground object must be taken into account. Tabulating $p^{\mathcal{F}}$ not only against ρ but also against transformation parameters is computationally infeasible. Variations that cannot be modelled parametrically can nonetheless be *pooled* into the general variability represented by $p^{\mathcal{F}}(z|\rho)$. This implies that $p^{\mathcal{F}}(z|\rho)$ should be learned not simply from one frame, but from a set of frames containing a succession of typical transformations of the object. These frames may either be separately captured images, or be generated by applying random deformations to one image.

Outline constraint: $p^B(z|\rho)$ for $0 < \rho \leq 1$ was learned from segments dropped down at random, anywhere on the background. Over the foreground, and for the case that $\rho = 0$, $p^{\mathcal{F}}(z|\rho)$ is similarly learned from a circular support, dropped now at any location wholly inside the training object. However, whenever $\rho > 0$, the foreground support $F(X)$ must touch the object outline; therefore $p^{\mathcal{F}}(z|\rho)$ is learned entirely from segments abutting the outline.

Foreground subdivision: Learning $p^{\mathcal{F}}(z|\rho)$ by pooling responses throughout the object interior is effective with distinctive object outlines (eg hand), but pooling does discard information concerning gross spatial layout. Gross layout can be captured by sub-dividing the

object (figure 5) and pooling separately over each subregion. This is especially beneficial with more nearly

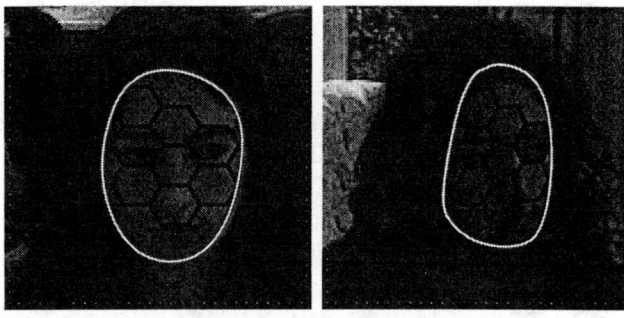

Figure 5: **Foreground subregions.** Object interior $\mathcal{F}$ is subdivided (left): $\mathcal{F} = \mathcal{F}_0 \cup \mathcal{F}_1 \cup \ldots \cup \mathcal{F}_{N_F}$, where sub-regions $\mathcal{F}_1, \ldots, \mathcal{F}_{N_F}$ here are hexagons, and $\mathcal{F}_0$ is the remainder of $\mathcal{F}$. Then sub-regions must be warped (right) onto any novel view.

circular objects (eg faces) for which, if isotropic filters are used, the observation likelihood is insensitive to 2D rotation of the object.

Sub-regions are defined for a standard configuration (figure 5a)); for a general configuration, warped forms of $\mathcal{F}_i$ are needed (figure 5b)). An affine approximation to the interior warp is obtained by projection in function-space [4, ch 6] and approximation error is dealt with simply by pooling it into the learned distributions $p^{\mathcal{F}_i}$.

Statistical independence: known behaviour for independence of natural scenes, which applied well to background modelling, could not necessarily be expected to apply for foreground models, given that the foreground is far less variable. Nonetheless, repeating the autocorrelation experiments has produced evidence of good independence for $\nabla^2 G$ filters over the foreground too.

Distribution model: whereas filter response z over (highly variable) background texture assumed the characteristic kurtotic form, the foreground is far less variable and therefore does not have extended tails (figure 6).

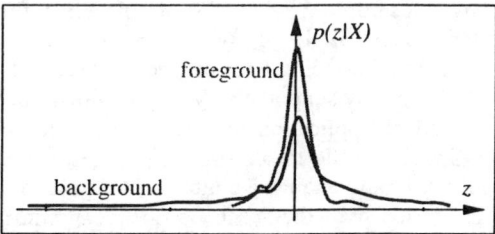

Figure 6: **Foreground and background distributions for $\nabla^2 G$ filter,** with support radius $r = 20$ pixels. As expected, the background distribution is more "kurtotic".

Results: learned observation likelihood First, for the hand scene of figure 1, $p(Z|X)$ — the joint likelihood composed of a product (3) of likelihoods $p(z_k|X)$ for individual filters — is exercised systematically, over a configuration space of Euclidean similarities (figure 7). The joint likelihood fuses information from individual supports effectively,

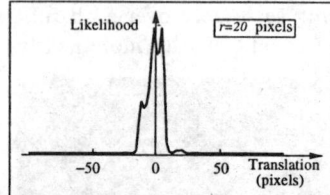 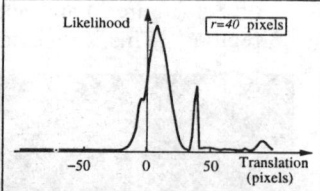 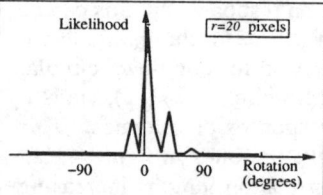 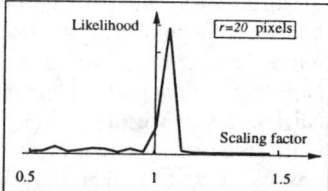

Figure 7: **Exercising the joint likelihood** $p(Z|X)$, as X ranges over coordinate translation (at 2 different scales), scaling and rotation.

with a maximal value, as expected, near the true solution (graph origin). The effect of changing the filter scale r is also demonstrated; as expected, the likelihood function is more broadly tuned, at a coarser scale, appearing to have a width of about $2r$ or (due to hyperacuity effects) rather less.

As a final check, it is interesting to consider the likelihood ratio for two configurations, one correctly positioned over the target, and one way out over background as in figure 1. In such cases, treating pixels as independent typically produces ridiculously large likelihood ratios. Even using Gaussian masks ($r = 20$), which we know not to be independent, gives a likelihood ratio of $1 : 10^{55}$ in this case — implausibly large. However, this falls considerably with $\nabla^2 G$ masks, as expected given the independence of their output over foreground and background, to a far more plausible $1 : 10^4$

Sampling from the posterior The full joint likelihood function $p(Z|X)$ is constructed as a product (3), in which the offset ρ for each support segment is obtained from its offset function $\rho_k(X)$:

$$p(Z|X) = \prod_{k=1}^{K} p_k(z_k|\rho_k(X)). \quad (6)$$

Evaluation of the offset function requires a geometrical calculation of the size of the circle-segment that approximates the intersection of the object (at configuration X) with the kth support. It is interesting to note that, although Bayesian analysis requires that Z should consist of the entire set of filters z_k in figure 1, some economies can legitimately be made. Given a sample $X_1, \ldots, X_N$ of object hypotheses, if some filter support S_k lies always in the background for *all* the X_n, the corresponding term can be factored out of (6), and similarly for any support always in the foreground.

The practical application of Bayesian correlation is to problems involving the localization of objects. For example, to locate a hand against a cluttered background, a prior $p_0(X)$ is chosen over the space of Euclidean similarities. Samples from the posterior, at several scales, are shown in figure 8. The broad prior is focused down to a posterior distribution which is narrower at finer scales. It is not clear from figure 8 that coarse scales actually have a useful role — the finest scale, after all, gives the most precise information. However, if the sampling process is "pressed" harder, by expanding the prior without increasing the size N of the particle-set, the finer scales break down, as figure 9 shows, while at coarse scale, sampling from the posterior continues to operate correctly. That suggests a role for coarser scales

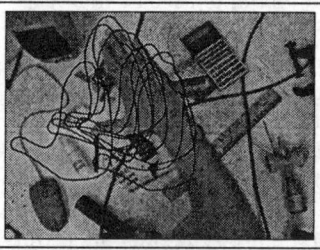 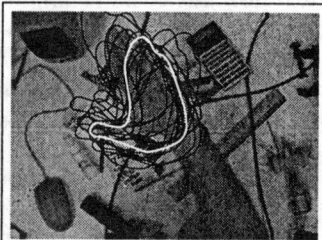
prior   posterior: $r = 40$ pixels

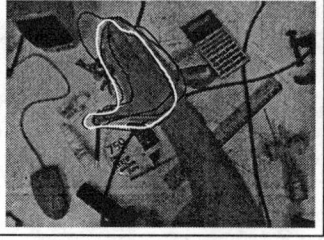 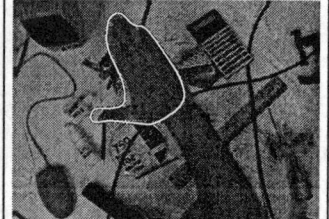
posterior: $r = 20$ pixels   posterior: $r = 10$ pixels

Figure 8: **Random samples from the posterior.** $p(X|Z)$. The prior $p_0(X)$ is a broad distribution of Euclidean similarities (planar rigid motion plus size-scaling). At each scale r, the posterior mean $\mathcal{E}[X|Z_r]$ (white outline) is close to the true configuration; $\mathrm{Var}[X|Z_r]$ decreases with r, as expected. Particle set size is $N = 240$ here. (For clarity, not all particles are shown.)

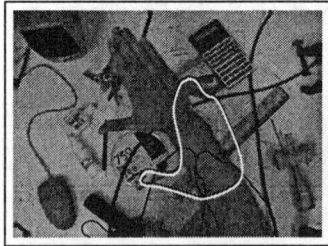 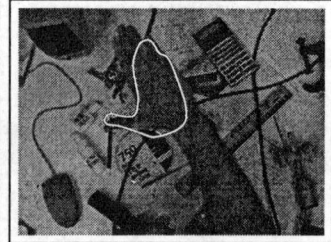
posterior: $r = 20$ pixels   posterior: $r = 10$ pixels

Figure 9: **A broader prior "overloads" factored sampling.** Now the experiment of figure 8 is repeated, but with a prior 1.5 times as broad, causing sampling at these finer scales to break down. (Again, $N = 240$.)

in guiding or constraining finer ones, if only a Bayesian sampling mechanism can be found to do it, and that is the subject of the next section.

6 Layered sampling

In section 5, the practical problem of "overloading" was demonstrated, that occurs when image observations are made at fine spatial scale, in Bayesian correlation. Layering, introduced here, is a powerful general strategy for reducing computational complexity of factored sampling when the observation likelihood function $f(X)$ is narrow. Layered sampling proves effective in dealing with the problem of multi-scale overloading.

Importance resampling   Layered sampling uses what we term "importance resampling", in which the particles representing some prior distribution $p_0(X)$ are replicated and re-weighted (but, unlike conventional importance sampling [12], none are generated in new configurations). Particles are replicated to a degree that is proportional to the value of some weighting function $g(X)$, denoted $\sim g$ in the top half of figure 10. Following the re-distribution, likelihood weights are

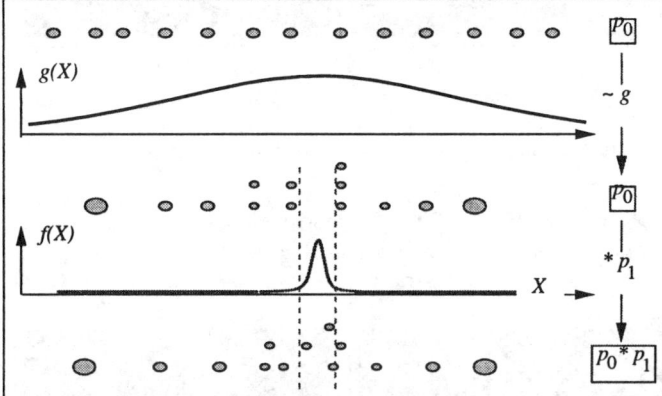

Figure 10: **Resampling followed by convolution.** A simplified example to illustrate that importance resampling ($\sim g$) on its own may not repopulate the sparsely sampled support of the likelihood f. A subsequent random step, with distribution p_1, is needed.

adjusted to compensate, so that the particle-set continues to represent the same underlying prior p_0. The re-sampling operation is denoted by a $\sim$ operator with a weighting function g, as in the following example of factored sampling (4) with an extra, intermediate, weighted resampling stage:

$$\boxed{p_0} \xrightarrow{N} \bigcirc \xrightarrow{\sim g}{N} \bigcirc \xrightarrow{\times f}{N} \bigcirc \xrightarrow{\sim}{N} \bigcirc.$$

In terms of particle-sets, the resampling operation $\sim g$ is defined as follows

$$\{(s_i, \pi_i),\ i = 1..M\} \to \{(s_{i(j)}, 1/g(s_{i(j)})),\ j = 1..N\}$$

where each $i(j)$ is sampled with replacement from $i = 1..M$ with probability proportional to $\pi_i g(s_i)$. (Note that in the original factored sampling example (4), we had $M = N$.)

A key property of the resampling operation $\sim g$ is that it is an *asymptotic identity*: random resampling from its input and output particle sets, respectively, produce random variables whose distributions converge to one another, weakly as $N \to \infty$.

Resampling with the $\sim g$ operation does not, on its own, deal with the problem of a narrow likelihood function. Although it does concentrate sampling to a narrower region of configuration space, the gaps between particles are not reduced (figure 10). Adding independent random variables

with density p_1 to each particle has the effect of diffusing apart identical copies of particles generated in the resampling step and filling the gaps. The combined operation is no longer an asymptotic identity — particles at the output are distributed asymptotically according to the density $p_0 * p_1$.

The layered sampling algorithm   Layered sampling is applicable when importance resampling functions $f_1, \ldots, f_M$ are available, in which $f_M = f$ the true likelihood, and each f_{m-1} is a coarse approximation to f_m. In addition, the prior p_0 must be decomposable as a series of convolutions

$$p_0 = p_0' * p_1' \ldots * p_{M-1}' \tag{7}$$

and this corresponds to expressing X *a priori* as a sum of random variables. Functional forms for the densities p_m' need not necessarily be known, provided only that a random sample generator can be constructed for each. For example, in processing motion sequences using the CONDENSATION algorithm [11], p_0' could be represented as a set of particles from the previous time $t - 1$, and $p_d = p_1' \ldots * p_{M-1}'$ is some decomposition of a Gaussian model $p_d(X(t)|X(t-1))$ for the likely displacement over one time-step. With this decomposition of the prior, the sampling process (4) can be replaced by a sequence of layers:

$$\boxed{p_0'} \xrightarrow{N} \bigcirc$$
$$\xrightarrow{\sim f_1}{N} \bigcirc \xrightarrow{* p_1'} \bigcirc \ldots \xrightarrow{\sim f_{M-1}}{N} \bigcirc \xrightarrow{* p_{M-1}'} \bigcirc \tag{8}$$
$$\xrightarrow{\times f_M} \bigcirc \xrightarrow{\sim}{N} \bigcirc,$$

where $* p$ denotes the particle-set operation $(s_i, \pi_i) \to (s_i + Y_i, \pi_i)$, $i = 1, \ldots, N$, and Y_i are random variables drawn independently from $p(.)$. Each layer includes an importance resampling step, with the observation likelihood f_i at the ith scale as the resampling function, until the Mth and final layer, at which the fine-scale f_M acts multiplicatively on likelihood weights, in the usual way.

Proof of asymptotic correctness   The diagrammatic form of specification of the particle filter facilitates the proof of asymptotic correctness — that each particle in the output set is drawn from a distribution that converges (weakly) to the posterior, as $N \to \infty$. Asymptotically (using the identity property of $\sim$), (8) can be rewritten, deleting resampling links, to give

$$\boxed{p_0'} \xrightarrow{N} \bigcirc \xrightarrow{* p_1'} \bigcirc \ldots \xrightarrow{* p_{M-1}'} \bigcirc$$
$$\xrightarrow{\times f_M} \bigcirc \xrightarrow{\sim}{N} \bigcirc$$

and now all the p_m' convolutions can be composed to give p_0, as in (7), and since $f_M = f$, the process reduces to the original factored sampling (4). There remains the issue of how to choose the decomposition of p_d. A good argument can be made (details omitted) that, in order to minimise N, successive spatial scales should be in fixed ratio; further work is needed to generalise this.

7 Results

Layered sampling is applied here to the problem of multi-scale localization and pose determination.

Sampling across scales The f_m from the layered sampling algorithm correspond to observation likelihoods from the coarsest scale $m = 1$ to the finest $m = M$. Operation of the algorithm is illustrated here, in figure 11, for the hand-finding problem that caused the overloading of single-scale sampling in section 5. The Gaussian prior p_0 is split, as a sum of Gaussian variables, into 3 factors $p_0 = p_0' * p_1' * p_2'$, each factor to be used before respective scales r_1, r_2, r_3 which diminish in fixed ratio for maximum efficiency, as mentioned earlier. The ith scale generates an observation likelihood function f_i, where $f_i(X) = p(Z_i|X)$. Note that the formal likelihood derives from observations only at the finest scale. Observations at other scales are cast by layered sampling in an "advisory" role, via importance resampling before the next finer scale. This avoids any need for a formal

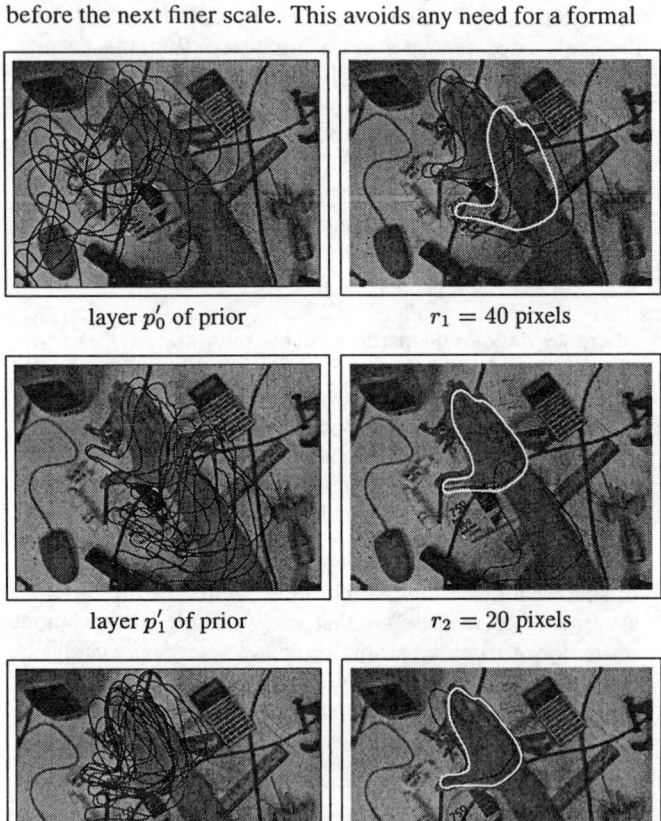

layer p_0' of prior $r_1 = 40$ pixels

layer p_1' of prior $r_2 = 20$ pixels

layer p_2' of prior $r_3 = 10$ pixels

Figure 11: **Layered sampling across spatial scales** The experiment of figure 9 is repeated, but now with layered sampling, from coarse to fine scale. The overload evident in figure 9 is rectified here, with similar computational effort ($N = 240$ particles, $N/3 = 80$ particles per layer).

assumption of independence across scales.

Occlusion One of the attractions of correlation is its robustness to disturbances in the image data, and a severe form of disturbance is presented by occlusion. Where occlusion is anticipated, this is dealt with in the Bayesian Correlation framework simply by treating the occluder as part of the background, and evaluating the appropriate observation-likelihood functions there. More challenging is occlusion that is not anticipated, as in figure 12.

prior $r_3 = 10$ pixels

Figure 12: **Layered sampling with occlusion** An experiment like the one in figure 11 but now with the object suffering unpredicted occlusion (intermediate scales not displayed).

Pose variations Bayesian correlation is capable of handling a configuration space $\mathcal{X}$ that incorporates varying 3D pose, as the demonstration of figure 13 shows. The fore-

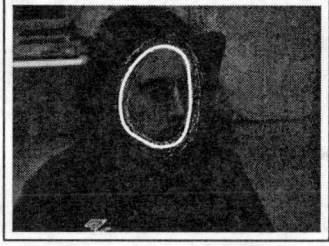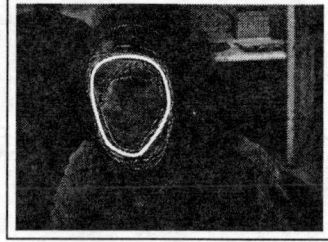

Figure 13: **Pose variations** A foreground distribution was trained on 3 training images. Test images here show the posterior from broadly distributed priors, under variation of pose.

ground distribution is learned using pooling over $\mathcal{X}$ and foreground subdivision, as discussed in section 5.

Motion tracking Random sampling lends itself to serial Bayesian inference, for example over multiple scales as above. Serial inference can also proceed over time, in order to analyse motion sequences. Edge-based temporal analysis [11] requires fairly precise initial alignment whereas, in Bayesian correlation, use of intensity information allows a degree of automatic initialisation, as in figure 14, even against camouflage, and despite the vigour of the motion. We are not yet sure, though, whether Bayesian correlation can align as precisely as edge-based analysis can.

Finally, an example is shown of motion analysis for deforming objects. A person walking across a room is tracked (figure 15) *without background subtraction*. Instead, distracting background clutter is dealt with by the learned foreground/background models embedded in the observation

Figure 14: Motion analysis: leaf blowing vigorously, in camouflage. A prior (a) is chosen that is too badly misaligned for edge-based tracking. Bayesian correlation nonetheless initialises correctly and, 1120 ms later, is still tracking (b) — trail of mean shapes shown. (Data and learned motion model as in [11]; $r = 10$ pixels and $N = 1500$ samples.)

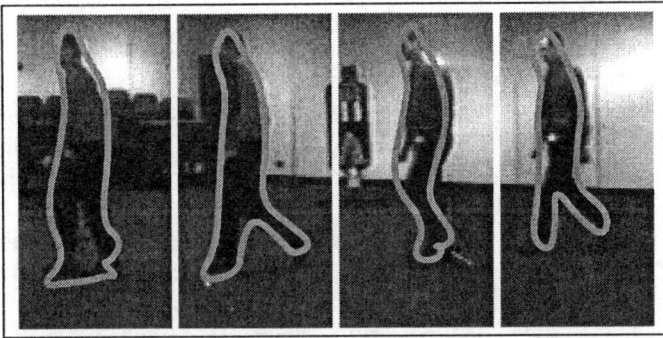

Figure 15: Deformable motion. A deformable contour model with 8 free parameters is used to track a walking person, over about 3 seconds. (Scale: $r = 15$ pixels with $N = 1500$ samples. See version of this paper on our web-site for a movie.)

likelihood. Consequently, the method is not limited to backgrounds that are stationary, or moving in some easily predictable fashion. The computational load consists principally of: evaluating the likelihood (6), of which offset functions $\rho_k(X)$ are the main burden; image processing to obtain the z_k. The image processing could be done using pyramid hardware [5]. The offset functions (at scale $r = 40$) can be evaluated, for $N = 500$, at frame-rate, on a desk-top workstation (SGI Octane). Bayesian correlation at video frame-rate should therefore be quite feasible.

8 Conclusions

Bayesian correlation is a synthesis of cross-correlation matching with probabilistic sampling. Its key, original elements are: the development of likelihood functions for correlation; learning of foreground and background distributions, with particular attention to statistical independence and "mixed" receptive fields; probabilistic multi-scale analysis by means of "layered sampling".

The approach has been widely tested on a variety of foregrounds and backgrounds. It is capable of planar object localisation, even with unpredicted occlusion, and versatile enough to work with 3D pose changes, and with image sequences of moving objects, including nonrigid ones. A number of issues are raised: the choice of partition for the prior in layered sampling; the use of spatio-temporal filters and associated independence arguments; temporal updating of the foreground distribution. These remain for future investigation.

Acknowledgements We are grateful for the support of the Royal Society of London (AB), EPSRC (AB,JS,MI) and the EU (JM). We have enjoyed discussions with D. Mumford, S. Mallat, G. Hinton, B. Buxton, A. Zisserman and P. Torr.

References

[1] Bascle, B., and Deriche, R. Region tracking through image sequences. In *Proc. 5th Int. Conf. on Computer Vision* (Boston, Jun 1995), 302–307.

[2] Bell, A., and Sejnowski, T. Edges are the independent components of natural scenes. In *Advances in Neural Information Processing Systems* (1997), vol. 9, MIT Press, 831–837.

[3] Black, M., and Yacoob, Y. Tracking and recognizing rigid and non-rigid facial motions using local parametric models of image motion. In *Proc. 5th Int. Conf. on Computer Vision* (1995), 374–381.

[4] Blake, A., and Isard, M. *Active contours.* Springer, 1998.

[5] Burt, P. Fast algorithms for estimating local image properties. *Computer Vision, Graphics and Image Processing 21* (1983), 368–382.

[6] Cootes, T., Taylor, C., Cooper, D., and Graham, J. Active shape models — their training and application. *Computer Vision and Image Understanding 61*, 1 (1995), 38–59.

[7] Geman, D., and Jedynak, B. An active testing model for tracking roads in satellite images. *IEEE Trans. Pattern Analysis and Machine Intell. 18*, 1 (1996), 1–14.

[8] Grenander, U., Chow, Y., and Keenan, D. *HANDS. A Pattern Theoretical Study of Biological Shapes.* Springer-Verlag. New York, 1991.

[9] Hager, G., and Toyama, K. Xvision: combining image warping and geometric constraints for fast tracking. In *Proc. 4th European Conf. Computer Vision* (1996), 507–517.

[10] Hubel, D., and Wiesel, T. Receptive fields and functional architecture of monkey striate cortex. *J. Physiol. Lond. 195* (1968), 215–244.

[11] Isard, M., and Blake, A. Visual tracking by stochastic propagation of conditional density. In *Proc. 4th European Conf. Computer Vision* (Cambridge, England, Apr 1996), 343–356.

[12] Isard, M., and Blake, A. ICondensation: Unifying low-level and high-level tracking in a stochastic framework. In *Proc. 5th European Conf. Computer Vision* (1998), 893–908.

[13] Mallat, S. A theory for multiresolution signal decomposition: the wavelet representation. *IEEE Trans. on Pattern Analysis and Machine Intelligence 11* (1989), 674–693.

[14] Mumford, D. Pattern theory: a unifying perspective. In *Perception as Bayesian inference*, D. Knill and W. Richard, Eds. Cambridge University Press, 1996, 25–62.

[15] Olshausen, B., and Field, D. Emergence of simple-cell receptive field properties by learning a sparse code for natural images. *Nature 381* (1996), 607–609.

[16] Scharstein, D., and Szeliski, R. Stereo matching with nonlinear diffusion. *Int. J. Computer Vision 28*, 2 (1998), 155–174.

[17] Viola, P., and Wells, W. Alignment by maximisation of mutual information. In *Proc. 5th Int. Conf. on Computer Vision* (1993), 16–23.

[18] Witkin, A., Terzopoulos, D., and Kass, M. Signal matching through scale space. In *5th National Conference on AI* (1986).

[19] Zhu, S., and Mumford, D. GRADE: Gibbs reaction and diffusion equation. *IEEE Trans. on Pattern Analysis and Machine Intelligence 19*, 11 (1997), 1236–1250.

[20] Zhu, S., Wu, Y., and Mumford, D. Filters, random fields and maximum entropy (FRAME). *Int. J. Computer Vision 27*, 2 (1998), 107–126.

The Earth Mover's Distance under Transformation Sets *

Scott Cohen   Leonidas Guibas
Computer Science Department
Stanford University, Stanford, CA 94305

Abstract

The Earth Mover's Distance (EMD) is a distance measure between distributions with applications in image retrieval and matching. We consider the problem of computing a transformation of one distribution which minimizes its EMD to another. The applications discussed here include estimation of the size at which a color pattern occurs in an image, lighting-invariant object recognition, and point feature matching in stereo image pairs. We present a monotonically convergent iteration which can be applied to a large class of EMD under transformation problems, although the iteration may converge to only a locally optimal transformation. We also provide algorithms that are guaranteed to compute a globally optimal transformation for a few specific problems, including some EMD under translation problems.

1. Introduction

A major challenge in image retrieval applications is that the images we desire to match can be visually quite different. This can happen even if these images are views of the same scene because of illumination changes, viewpoint motion, occlusions, etc.. Two common approaches to measure image similarity modulo some given factors are: (I) compare invariant image signatures (e.g. [4]), and (II) compare non-invariant signatures with a distance measure that allows for differences due to the given factors (e.g. [6, 12]).

The challenge in approach (I) is to compute invariants that still distinguish images with differences that should be penalized. Using invariants computed over entire images assumes that two images are similar only if all the information in one image matches all the information in the other. Such a complete matching measure is usually not appropriate in an image retrieval system because semantic image similarity often follows from only a partial match. Approach (II) is better in the partial matching case since invariance can be built on top of a distance function which allows for partial

matching. Of course, approach (I) can be modified to use invariants computed over parts of images, but this can require quite a lot of space because invariants must be computed for all image regions which might be matched at query time.

A very general distance measure with applications in content-based image retrieval is the Earth Mover's Distance (EMD) between distributions ([10]). The EMD allows for partial matching, and has been successfully used for measuring image similarity with respect to color and texture ([11]). For example, in [11] the color signature of an image is a collection of dominant image colors in CIE-Lab space ([16]), where each color is weighted by the fraction of image pixels classified as that color. Also in [11], the texture signature of a single texture image is a collection of spatial frequencies in log-polar coordinates, where each frequency is weighted by the amount of energy present at that frequency. Experiments in [10] show the superiority of the EMD for color-based image retrieval over many histogram dissimilarity measures, including a common quadratic form distance ([8]).

In this paper, we extend the EMD to allow unpenalized distribution transformations. The goal is to find a transformation of one distribution which minimizes its EMD to another, where a set of allowable transformations is given. Consider, for example, using the EMD to measure object similarity with respect to color. An EMD between color signatures does not account for lighting differences. In [4], the authors show that an illumination change results in a linear transformation of image pixel colors (under certain reasonable assumptions). For the texture signatures mentioned above, a change in texture scale and orientation results in a translation of signature points in log-polar spatial frequency space.

The EMD under transformation ($\text{EMD}_{\mathcal{G}}$) problem is to compute $\min_{g \in \mathcal{G}} \text{EMD}(\mathbf{x}, g(\mathbf{y}))$, where $\mathbf{x} = \{(x_i, w_i)\}_{i=1}^m$ and $\mathbf{y} = \{(y_j, u_j)\}_{j=1}^n$ are summary distributions (we also call them *signatures*) for the images being compared and $\mathcal{G}$ is a set of transformations. For example, the points x_i and y_j are points in CIE-Lab space and log-polar spatial frequency space in the color and texture cases, respectively. The weights w_i and u_j are the amounts of features x_i and y_j present in the images. The set of allowable transformations

*Authors' email: (scohen,guibas)@cs.stanford.edu. See
http://vision.stanford.edu/~scohen or the CD-ROM proceedings for a color version of this work.

is application-dependent. In the lighting-invariant object recognition application, $\mathcal{G}$ is the set of linear transformations $\{g_L\}$, and $g_L(\mathbf{y}) = \{(Ly_j, u_j)\}$. For texture comparison which is insensitive to differences in scale and orientation, $\mathcal{G}$ is the set of translations $\{g_t\}$, and $g_t(\mathbf{y}) = \{(y_j + t, u_j)\}$. In both these examples, the allowable transformations change the points of a distribution but leave its weights fixed. We shall also consider a set of transformations $\mathcal{G} = \{g_c\}$ in which g_c changes only the weights of a distribution as $g_c(\mathbf{y}) = \{(y_j, cu_j)\}$. This set arises in estimating the size at which color pattern occurs in a color image.

We begin in section 2 with a brief review of the EMD. In section 3, we consider the problem of computing the EMD under various transformation sets. We start in section 3.1 with a discussion of the scale estimation application and the corresponding $\mathrm{EMD}_\mathcal{G}$ problem in which $g \in \mathcal{G}$ changes only distribution weights. This $\mathrm{EMD}_\mathcal{G}$ problem has structure which we exploit to compute a globally optimal transformation. In section 3.2, we consider $\mathrm{EMD}_\mathcal{G}$ problems in which $g \in \mathcal{G}$ changes only distribution points. For such $\mathcal{G}$, we present in section 3.2.1 a very general, monotonically convergent iteration called the *FT iteration*. We apply the FT iteration to the applications of lighting-invariant object recognition and point feature matching in stereo images in sections 3.2.2 and 3.2.3, respectively. The main drawback of the FT iteration is that it may converge to only a locally optimal transformation. In sections 3.2.4 and 3.2.5, we discuss EMD under translation problems which can be solved directly for a globally optimal translation. Finally, section 4 contains some concluding remarks.

2. The Earth Mover's Distance (EMD)

We denote a discrete *distribution* as a set of weighted points $\mathbf{x} = \{(x_i, w_i)\}_{i=1}^m \equiv (X, w) \in \mathbf{D}^{K,m}$, where $X = [\, x_1 \cdots x_m \,]$, with each $x_i \in \mathbf{R}^K$, $w_i \geq 0$. Here K is the dimension of the ambient space of the points x_i, and m is the number of points. The weight of $\mathbf{x}$ is $w_\Sigma = \sum_{i=1}^m w_i$.

Given two distributions $\mathbf{x} = (X, w) \in \mathbf{D}^{K,m}$ and $\mathbf{y} = (Y, u) \in \mathbf{D}^{K,n}$, a *flow* between $\mathbf{x}$ and $\mathbf{y}$ is any matrix $F = (f_{ij}) \in \mathbf{R}^{m \times n}$. Intuitively, f_{ij} is the amount of weight at x_i which is matched to weight at y_j. F is a *feasible flow* between $\mathbf{x}$ and $\mathbf{y}$ iff (i) $f_{ij} \geq 0$, (ii) $\sum_{j=1}^n f_{ij} \leq w_i$, (iii) $\sum_{i=1}^m f_{ij} \leq u_j$, and (iv) $\sum_{i=1}^m \sum_{j=1}^n f_{ij} = \min(w_\Sigma, u_\Sigma)$. Constraint (ii) ensures that the weight in $\mathbf{y}$ matched to x_i does not exceed w_i. Similarly, (iii) ensures that the weight in $\mathbf{x}$ matched to y_j does not exceed u_j. Finally, constraint (iv) forces the total amount of weight matched to be equal to the weight of the lighter distribution. In the unequal-weight case $w_\Sigma \neq u_\Sigma$, some weight in the heavier distribution remains unmatched.

Let $\mathcal{F}(\mathbf{x}, \mathbf{y})$ denote the set of all feasible flows between $\mathbf{x}$ and $\mathbf{y}$. The work done by a feasible flow $F \in \mathcal{F}(\mathbf{x}, \mathbf{y})$

in matching $\mathbf{x}$ and $\mathbf{y}$ is given by $\mathrm{WORK}(F, \mathbf{x}, \mathbf{y}) = \sum_{i=1}^m \sum_{j=1}^n f_{ij} d(x_i, y_j)$, where $d(x_i, y_j)$ is the "ground distance" between x_i and y_j. The *Earth Mover's Distance* $\mathrm{EMD}(\mathbf{x}, \mathbf{y})$ is the minimum amount of work to match $\mathbf{x}$ and $\mathbf{y}$, normalized by the weight of the lighter distribution:

$$\mathrm{EMD}(\mathbf{x}, \mathbf{y}) = \frac{\min_{F \in \mathcal{F}(\mathbf{x}, \mathbf{y})} \mathrm{WORK}(F, \mathbf{x}, \mathbf{y})}{\min(w_\Sigma, u_\Sigma)}. \quad (1)$$

In other words, the EMD is the average ground distance that weights travels during an optimal flow. The work minimization problem in (1) is a special type of linear program called the *transportation problem*, and it can be solved efficiently by the transportation simplex algorithm ([5]).

The EMD matches all the weight in the lighter distribution. The *partial Earth Mover's Distance* EMD^γ matches only a given fraction $\gamma \in (0, 1]$ of the weight of the lighter distribution. The constraint (iv) is replaced by $\sum_{i=1}^m \sum_{j=1}^n f_{ij} = \gamma \min(w_\Sigma, u_\Sigma)$ to define $\mathcal{F}^\gamma(\mathbf{x}, \mathbf{y})$, and the minimum work is normalized by $\gamma \min(w_\Sigma, u_\Sigma)$.

3. The EMD under Transformation Sets

The *EMD under transformation set* $\mathcal{G}$ is defined as $\mathrm{EMD}_\mathcal{G}(\mathbf{x}, \mathbf{y}) = \min_{g \in \mathcal{G}} \mathrm{EMD}(\mathbf{x}, g(\mathbf{y}))$, where $g(\mathbf{y})$ is the result of applying the transformation $g \in \mathcal{G}$ to the distribution $\mathbf{y}$. In words, we seek a transformation of one distribution which minimizes its EMD to another.[1] The *partial EMD under transformation set* $\mathcal{G}$ is simply $\mathrm{EMD}_\mathcal{G}^\gamma(\mathbf{x}, \mathbf{y}) = \min_{g \in \mathcal{G}} \mathrm{EMD}^\gamma(\mathbf{x}, g(\mathbf{y}))$.

3.1. Example Use in Scale Estimation (only weights change)

In this section, the problem of estimating the size at which a color pattern occurs in an image is phrased and efficiently solved as an $\mathrm{EMD}_\mathcal{G}$ problem. Suppose that a pattern occurs in an image as a fraction $c^* \in (0, 1]$ of the total image area. An instance is shown in Figure 1(a). Let $\mathbf{x}$ and $\mathbf{y} = (Y, u)$ denote unit-weight color signatures of the image and pattern, respectively. A small set of dominant image colors $\{x_i\}_{i=1}^m$ in CIE-Lab space is computed via the color clustering algorithm in [9]. The weight w_i is the fraction of image pixels whose nearest color cluster is x_i. See Figure 1(b),(d). We use $d = L_2$.[2]

Since $(Y, c^* u)$ is lighter than $\mathbf{x}$, the computation $\mathrm{EMD}(\mathbf{x}, (Y, c^* u))$ finds an optimal matching between c^* of the image color weight and the color weight in $(Y, c^* u)$. Consider the ideal case of an exact pattern occurrence in

---

[1] In some situations, the symmetric definition $\mathrm{EMD}_\mathcal{G}(\mathbf{x}, \mathbf{y}) = \min(\min_{g \in \mathcal{G}} \mathrm{EMD}(\mathbf{x}, g(\mathbf{y})), \min_{g \in \mathcal{G}} \mathrm{EMD}(g(\mathbf{x}), \mathbf{y}))$ may be more appropriate.

[2] Euclidean distance in CIE-Lab space matches perceptual distance between two colors that are not very different ([16]).

the image, with the same color clusters used in $\mathbf{x}$ and $\mathbf{y}$ for the pattern colors. Then the c^* of $\mathbf{x}$'s color weight contributed by the pattern occurrence will match exactly the color weight in (Y, c^*u), and $\text{EMD}(\mathbf{x}, (Y, c^*u)) = 0$. Furthermore, $\text{EMD}(\mathbf{x}, (Y, cu)) = 0$ for $c \in (0, c^*]$ since there is still enough image weight of each pattern color to match all the weight in (Y, cu).

In general, we will prove that $\text{EMD}(\mathbf{x}, (Y, cu))$ decreases as c decreases and eventually becomes constant for $c \in (0, c^0]$, as shown in Figure 1(e). If the graph levels off at a small EMD, then the pattern might occur in the image, and we take c^0 to be the scale estimate. Consider the example in Figure 1. The scale estimate c^0 is such that the amounts of red and yellow in the scaled pattern signature (Y, c^0u) are roughly equal to the amounts of red and yellow in the image, as shown in Figure 1(c). At scale c^0, there is still plenty of image weight to match the other pattern colors in (Y, c^0u). If there were a bit more red and yellow in the image, then the scale estimate c^0 would be a bit too high ($> c^*$).

The main property of our scale estimation method is that in the ideal case it overestimates the scale by the *minimum* amount of background clutter over all pattern colors, where the amount of background clutter for a color is the amount of that color present in the image but not part of the pattern occurrence. In practice, we have observed scale estimates which are a little smaller than predicted by an ideal case analysis. Just one pattern color with a small amount of background clutter in the image is enough to obtain an accurate scale estimate. Note that an accurate scale estimate is computed in Figure 1 even though there is a lot of background clutter for the dark green in the Comet label.

Now consider the function $E(c) = \text{EMD}(\mathbf{x}, (Y, cu))$. The distribution (Y, cu) has total weight $c \le 1 = w_\Sigma$, so

$$E(c) = \frac{\min_{(f_{ij}) \in \mathcal{F}(\mathbf{x}, (Y, cu))} \sum_{i=1}^{m} \sum_{j=1}^{n} f_{ij} d(x_i, y_j)}{c},$$

where $(f_{ij}) \in \mathcal{F}(\mathbf{x}, (Y, cu))$ iff $f_{ij} \ge 0$, $\sum_{i=1}^{m} f_{ij} = cu_j$, and $\sum_{j=1}^{n} f_{ij} \le w_i$. Now set $h_{ij} = f_{ij}/c$. Then

$$E(c) = \min_{(h_{ij}) \in \mathcal{F}((X, w/c), \mathbf{y})} \sum_{i=1}^{m} \sum_{j=1}^{n} h_{ij} d(x_i, y_j),$$

where $(h_{ij}) \in \mathcal{F}((X, w/c), \mathbf{y})$ iff (A) $h_{ij} \ge 0$, (B) $\sum_{i=1}^{m} h_{ij} = u_j$, and (C) $\sum_{j=1}^{n} h_{ij} \le w_i/c$. Note that

$$\mathcal{F}((X, w/c_1), \mathbf{y}) \subseteq \mathcal{F}((X, w/c_2), \mathbf{y}) \iff c_2 \le c_1 \quad (2)$$

since the final constraints (C) get weaker (stronger) as c decreases (increases).

Since $E(c)$ is a minimum over $\mathcal{F}((X, w/c), \mathbf{y})$, it follows from (2) that $E(c_1) \ge E(c_2)$ iff $c_1 \ge c_2$. Now consider $Q \subseteq \mathbf{R}^{mn}$ defined by (A) and (B), and $P(c) \subseteq \mathbf{R}^{mn}$ defined by (C), so that $\mathcal{F}((X, w/c), \mathbf{y}) = Q \cap P(c)$. Q

is bounded since its constraints imply that $h_{ij} \in [0, u_j]$. The polytope $P(c)$ converges to $\mathbf{R}^{mn}$ as c decreases to zero since $1/c$ increases to ∞. Since Q is bounded, $\exists c^0$ for which $Q \subseteq P(c) \ \forall c \le c^0$. It follows that $\mathcal{F}((X, w/c), \mathbf{y}) = Q$ and $E(c) = E(c^0)$ for $c \le c^0$.

The scale estimation problem is the $\text{EMD}_\mathcal{G}$ problem $c^0 = \max \arg \min_{g_c, 0 < c \le 1} \text{EMD}(\mathbf{x}, g_c(\mathbf{y}))$, where $g_c(\mathbf{y}) = (Y, cu)$. In practice, we take as the scale estimate the largest c for which there is no real improvement in the EMD when c is decreased. The estimate c^0 can be found efficiently via binary search. See Figure 2. Initially, we assume $c^0 \in [c_{\min}, 1]$. At any step, we have localized $c^0 \in [c_{\text{low}}, c_{\text{high}}]$. Let $c_{\text{mid}} = (c_{\text{low}} + c_{\text{high}})/2$. If $E(c_{\text{mid}}) = E(c_{\text{low}})$, then $c^0 \in [c_{\text{mid}}, c_{\text{high}}]$. Here "=" is approximate with respect to a parameter ε_d. Otherwise, $E(c_{\text{mid}}) > E(c_{\text{low}})$ and $c^0 \in [c_{\text{low}}, c_{\text{mid}}]$. The search stops once $|c_{\text{high}} - c_{\text{low}}| \le \varepsilon_c$, the required accuracy. In the SEDL image retrieval system, the optimal flow when $c = c^0$ is used to find quickly image regions similar in color signature to the query pattern ([2], pp. 189–200).

Figure 3 shows some results of the scale estimation algorithm for the color pattern problem. The scale estimate is very accurate in the examples shown in Figure 3(a)-(c). In the example shown in Figure 3(d), the scale is overestimated because the pattern occurs twice within the image. Since our method does not use the positions of colors, it cannot tell the difference between one pattern occurrence at scale $c_1 + c_2$ and two pattern occurrences at scales c_1 and c_2. See pp. 85–96 in [2] for more details and examples.

3.2. Point Transformations

In contrast to the previous section, we now consider sets of transformations that modify the points of a distribution but leave its weights fixed. Since $g(\mathbf{y}) = (g(Y), u)$ has the same weights as $\mathbf{y}$, we have $\mathcal{F}(\mathbf{x}, \mathbf{y}) = \mathcal{F}(\mathbf{x}, g(\mathbf{y}))$ and

$$\text{EMD}_\mathcal{G}(\mathbf{x}, \mathbf{y}) = \frac{\min_{g \in \mathcal{G}, F \in \mathcal{F}(\mathbf{x}, \mathbf{y})} \text{WORK}(F, \mathbf{x}, g(\mathbf{y}))}{\min(w_\Sigma, u_\Sigma)}. \quad (3)$$

$W(F, g) = \text{WORK}(F, \mathbf{x}, g(\mathbf{y}))$ is linear in F, so the minimum value in (3) occurs at one of the vertices of the convex polytope $\mathcal{F}(\mathbf{x}, \mathbf{y})$. Therefore, we can compute $\text{EMD}_\mathcal{G}(\mathbf{x}, \mathbf{y})$ by solving $\min_{g \in \mathcal{G}} W(F, g)$ for each vertex F of $\mathcal{F}(\mathbf{x}, \mathbf{y})$. Although this strategy is guaranteed to find a globally optimal transformation, it is not practical because the number of vertices of $\mathcal{F}(\mathbf{x}, \mathbf{y})$ is usually very large even for relatively small values of m and n.

Given F or g, we can solve for an optimal value of the other. This leads to an iteration which alternates between finding the best flow for a given transformation, and the best transformation for a given flow. It generates a sequence of (F, g) pairs for which W decreases or remains constant at every step. The details are given in the next section.

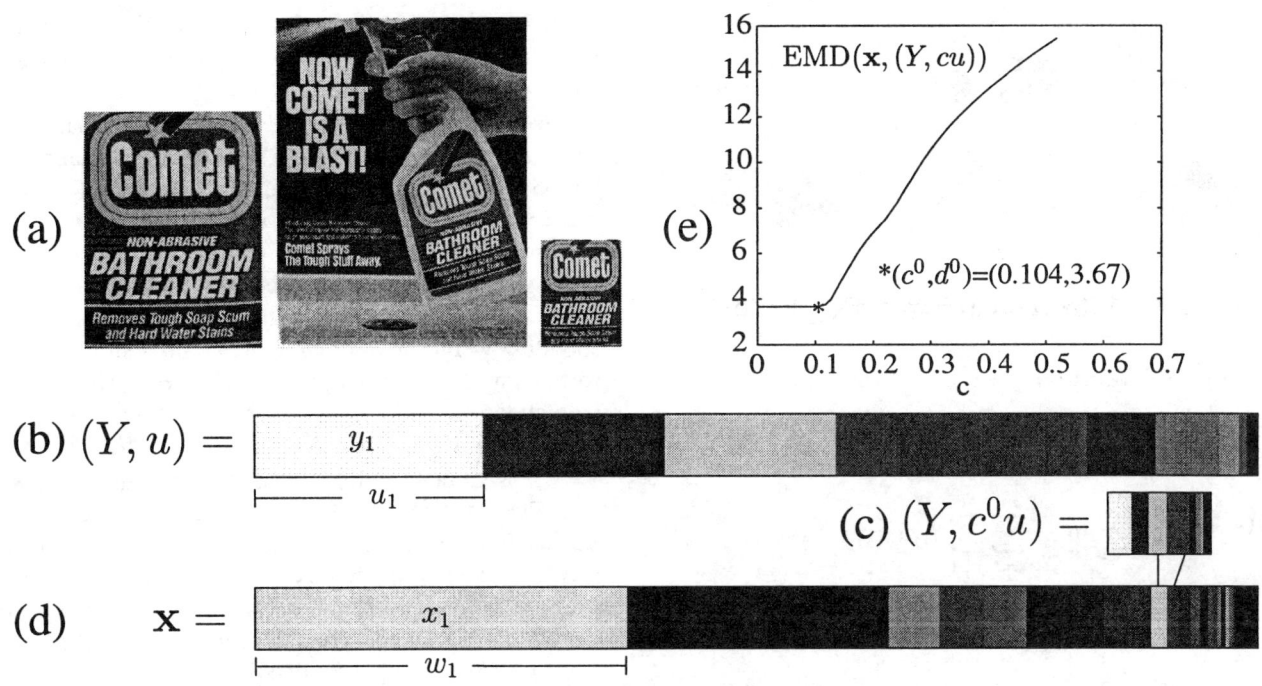

Figure 1. Scale Estimation. (a) pattern, image, and pattern scaled by the scale estimate c^0. (b),(d) pattern, image signatures. (c) pattern signature with weights scaled by c^0. (e) $\mathrm{EMD}(\mathbf{x}, (Y, cu))$ v. c.

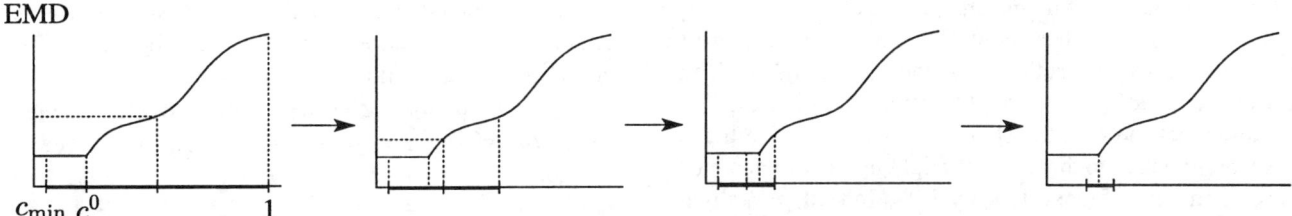

Figure 2. Scale Estimation Algorithm. Binary search narrows the interval in which c^0 must occur.

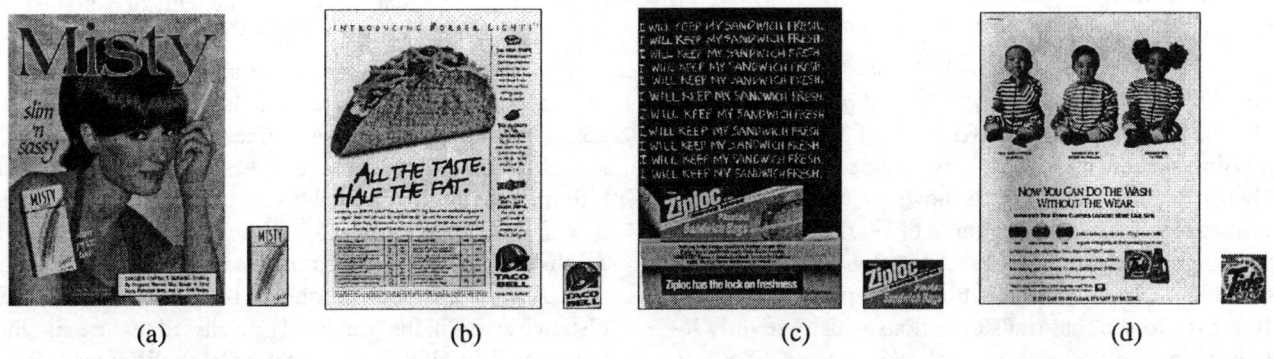

Figure 3. Scale Estimation Results. See the text for discussion.

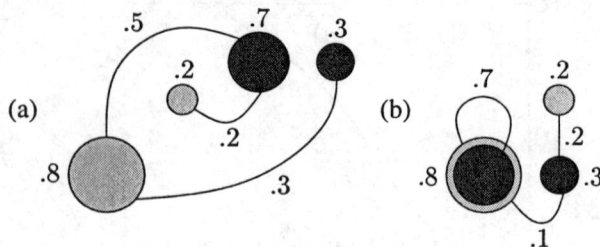

Figure 4. FT Iteration example. See the text.

3.2.1. The FT Iteration

Consider the following iteration that begins with an initial transformation $g^{(0)}$:

$$F^{(k)} = \arg \min_{F \in \mathcal{F}(\mathbf{x}, \mathbf{y})} \sum_{i=1}^{m} \sum_{j=1}^{n} f_{ij} d(x_i, g^{(k)}(y_j)), \qquad (4)$$

$$g^{(k+1)} = \arg \min_{g \in \mathcal{G}} \sum_{i=1}^{m} \sum_{j=1}^{n} f_{ij}^{(k)} d(x_i, g(y_j)). \qquad (5)$$

The minimization in (4) is the transportation problem. Since this iteration alternates between finding an optimal <u>F</u>low and an optimal <u>T</u>ransformation, we refer to (4) and (5) as the *FT iteration*. It can be applied to equal-weight and unequal-weight distributions.

Figure 4(a) shows an example with a dark and a light distribution that we will match under translation starting with $g^{(0)} = 0$. The best flow $F^{(0)}$ for $g^{(0)}$ is shown by the labelled arcs connecting dark and light weights. This flow matches half (.5) the weight over a large distance. We should expect the best translation for $F^{(0)}$ to move the .7 dark weight closer to the .8 light weight in order to decrease the total amount of work done by $F^{(0)}$. Indeed, $g^{(1)}$ aligns these two weights as shown in Figure 4(b). The best flow $F^{(1)}$ for $g^{(1)}$ matches all of the .7 dark weight to the .8 light weight. No further translation improves the work – $g^{(2)} = g^{(1)}$ and the FT iteration converges.

Define $\text{WORK}^{(k)} = W\left(F^{(k)}, g^{(k)}\right)$. Then (4) and (5) imply $W\left(F^{(k+1)}, g^{(k+1)}\right) \leq W\left(F^{(k)}, g^{(k+1)}\right)$ and $W\left(F^{(k)}, g^{(k+1)}\right) \leq W\left(F^{(k)}, g^{(k)}\right)$, respectively (by definition, $F^{(k+1)}$ is optimal for $g^{(k+1)}$, and $g^{(k+1)}$ is optimal for $F^{(k)}$). It follows that $\text{WORK}^{(k+1)} \leq \text{WORK}^{(k)}$. The decreasing sequence $\text{WORK}^{(k)}$ is bounded below by zero, and hence it converges. There is, however, no guarantee that it converges to the global minimum of $\text{WORK}(F, \mathbf{x}, g(\mathbf{y}))$. In general, the iteration must be repeated with different $g^{(0)}$s in search of a globally optimal transformation.

It is easy to see that transformations which are only locally optimal can occur in unequal-weight cases. If $\mathbf{x}$ is L copies $\mathbf{y} \oplus t_l$ of $\mathbf{y}$, then $\text{EMD}(\mathbf{x}, \mathbf{y} \oplus t_l) = 0$ for $l = 1, \ldots, L$. If the copies of $\mathbf{y}$ in $\mathbf{x}$ are well-separated, then we can produce $\geq L - 1$ only locally optimal translations by slightly

perturbing the points in each copy of $\mathbf{y}$. We have observed that only locally optimal transformations can also occur in equal-weight cases ([2], pp. 163–170).

The FT iteration can also be applied with the partial EMD since $\mathcal{F}^{\gamma}(\mathbf{x}, g(\mathbf{y})) = \mathcal{F}^{\gamma}(\mathbf{x}, \mathbf{y})$ if g does not change distribution weights. Furthermore, it can be modified to give a decreasing EMD sequence if a transformation changes points *and* modifies weights by a factor c. Such problems arise, for example, if a distribution point contains the position of an image region with some property, the corresponding weight is the region area, and a similarity transformation of the image plane is allowed. The basic idea is to choose $F^{(k)}$ from an increasing sequence of flow sets $\mathcal{F}^{(k)}$. Then $W\left(F^{(k+1)}, g^{(k+1)}\right) \leq W\left(F^{(k)}, g^{(k+1)}\right)$ since $F^{(k+1)}$ is an optimal flow for $g^{(k+1)}$ chosen from $\mathcal{F}^{(k+1)}$, and $F^{(k)} \in \mathcal{F}^{(k)} \subseteq \mathcal{F}^{(k+1)}$. The change of variables $h_{ij} = f_{ij}/c$ (as used in section 3.1) yields an equivalent EMD problem in which the weight of the lighter distribution is constant throughout the iteration, and hence a decreasing WORK sequence gives a decreasing EMD sequence. See pp. 148–151 in [2] for details.

The FT iteration is similar to the ICP (Iterative Closest Point) iteration ([1]) used to register 3D shapes. The computation of an optimal flow plays the same role as the computation of the closest "model shape" points to the "data shape" points in the ICP iteration. Both these steps determine matches used to compute a transformation that improves the EMD/registration. Another well-known application of the alternation idea is the EM algorithm ([7]) for computing mixture models in statistics.

The FT iteration can be applied whenever the *optimal transformation problem* (5) can be solved. If we let $[a_1 \cdots a_N] = [x_1 \cdots x_1 x_2 \cdots x_2 \cdots x_m \cdots x_m]$, $[b_1 \cdots b_N] = [y_1 \cdots y_n y_1 \cdots y_n \cdots y_1 \cdots y_n]$, and $[c_1 \cdots c_N] = [f_{11} \cdots f_{1n} f_{21} \cdots f_{2n} \cdots f_{m1} \cdots f_{mn}]$, where $N = mn$, then (5) can be rewritten as $\min_{g \in \mathcal{G}} \sum_{k=1}^{N} c_k d(a_k, g(b_k))$. Given a correspondence between point sets, the goal is to find a transformation of the points in one set that minimizes the sum of weighted distances to corresponding points in the other set.

The above problem has been solved with $d = L_2^2$ for translation (straightforward calculus), Euclidean and similarity transformations ([14]), linear transformations ([3]), and affine transformations (easy extension to the linear solution). The optimal translation problems with $d = L_2$ and $d = L_1$ are covered in [15], while the case $d = L_{1,T}$, the L_1 distance in a circular domain with period T (e.g. angles with $T = 2\pi$), is covered on pp. 142–146 in [2]. This last distance arises in the previously discussed texture similarity application in allowing for unpenalized differences in texture orientation (pp. 135–137 in [2], [11]). We show the generality of the FT iteration in the next two sections by applying it for a few different $\mathcal{G}$s and with the partial EMD.

| (B)alloon | (C)halk | (D)ragon | (L)emur | (P)lant | (T)iger | (W)aldo |

Figure 5. Object Database. For some objects, signatures are computed over only the outlined area.

3.2.2. Lighting-Invariant Object Recognition

For a linear, trichromatic color imaging system with a 3D linear model for the reflectance functions of object surfaces, Healey and Slater ([4]) showed that an illumination change results in a linear transformation of image pixel colors. The following experiment uses a subset of the images in [4]. There are four images of each object, one under nearly white illumination and the other three under yellow, green, and red illumination. See Figure 5 for images of the objects under white light.

Images are indexed by unit-weight color distributions in the RGB color space. Our experiment[3] uses each image as the query, where the desired distance is the EMD under a linear transformation with $d = L_2^2$. To compare a database signature $\mathbf{x}$ to a query signature $\mathbf{y}$, we applied the FT iteration twice: once to transform $\mathbf{y}$ so that it is as close as possible to $\mathbf{x}$, and once to transform $\mathbf{x}$ so that it is as close as possible to $\mathbf{y}$. Both trials were started with $g^{(0)}$ equal to the identity map. The smaller of the results of the two trials is used as the distance between $\mathbf{x}$ and $\mathbf{y}$. Ideally, the closest images to the image of an object are the other three images of the same object.

Figure 6 shows the results of our experiment. These results are excellent, but not perfect as in [4]. It is possible that we are not finding the globally optimal transformation in some comparisons.

3.2.3. Point Feature Matching in Stereo Images

In this section, we use the partial EMD under a transformation set $\text{EMD}_{\mathcal{G}}^{\gamma}$ to compute the best partial matching of two point feature sets extracted from stereo image pairs. The fraction parameter γ compensates for the fact that only some features appear in both images, and the set parameter $\mathcal{G}$ accounts for the appropriate transformation between corresponding features. In our experiments, we extract 50 features of an image using an algorithm due to Shi and Tomasi ([13]). See the first two columns of Figure 7. The points in the distribution summary of an image are its feature locations, and the weight of each point is one. The ground distance is $d = L_2^2$ between image coordinates. We set $\gamma = 0.5$, so only 25 of the 50 features per image will be matched, and use $g^{(0)} = I$, the identity map.

---

[3] All experiments in this work were done on a 250 MHz SGI Indigo[2].

In the first example, we match features in two images from a motion sequence in which the camera moves approximately horizontally and parallel to the image plane. Figure 7(a) shows the result of applying the FT iteration with $\mathcal{G} = \mathcal{T}$, the group of translations. For this camera motion, all image points translate along the same direction, but the amount of translation for an image point is inversely proportional to the depth of the corresponding scene point. The model of a single translation vector is accurate for a set of features that correspond to scene points with roughly the same depth. In this example, the FT iteration matched features on objects toward the back of the table.

The images in Figure 7(b) are from a motion sequence with a forward camera motion perpendicular to the image plane. Here we apply the FT iteration with $\mathcal{G} = \mathcal{S}$, the set of similarity transformations. In the final example, we match features in images of a toy hotel. The results of the FT iteration with $\mathcal{G} = \mathcal{A}$, the set of affine transformations, are shown in Figure 7(c). In all three cases, it appears that the FT iteration converged to a globally optimal transformation. In many examples, however, running the iteration once leads to only a locally optimal solution. In the next two sections, we consider two equal-weight EMD under translation problems which can be solved directly for a globally optimal translation.

3.2.4. Equal-Weight $\text{EMD}_{\mathcal{T}}$ with $d = L_2^2$

It is easily proven that $\min_t \sum_{i=1}^m \sum_{j=1}^n f_{ij} \|x_i - (y_j + t)\|_2^2$ occurs at $t^* = (\sum_{i=1}^m \sum_{j=1}^n f_{ij}(x_i - y_j)) / \sum_{i=1}^m \sum_{j=1}^n f_{ij}$. In the equal-weight case, $F \in \mathcal{F}(\mathbf{x}, \mathbf{y})$ requires $\sum_{i=1}^m f_{ij} = u_j$ and $\sum_{j=1}^n f_{ij} = w_i$ since all the weight in both distributions must be matched. Using these facts, $t^* = \overline{\mathbf{x}} - \overline{\mathbf{y}}$, where $\overline{x} = \sum_{i=1}^m w_i x_i / w_{\Sigma}$ and $\overline{y} = \sum_{j=1}^n u_j y_j / u_{\Sigma}$ are the centroids of $\mathbf{x}$ and $\mathbf{y}$. The translation that lines up the centroids is optimal for every feasible flow. To compute $\text{EMD}_{\mathcal{T}, L_2^2}(\mathbf{x}, \mathbf{y})$ for equal-weight $\mathbf{x}$ and $\mathbf{y}$, we simply compute $\text{EMD}(\mathbf{x}, \mathbf{y} \oplus (\overline{\mathbf{x}} - \overline{\mathbf{y}}))$.

3.2.5. Equal-Weight $\text{EMD}_{\mathcal{T}}$ in 1D with $d = L_1$

There is a simple solution to computing the EMD between equal-weight distributions in 1D with $d = L_1$ that involves the cumulative distribution functions (CDFs). See Figure 8(a). The CDF for $\mathbf{x}$ starts at 0, increases an amount w_i

	B_W	B_Y	B_G	B_R	C_W	C_Y	C_G	C_R	D_W	D_Y	D_G	D_R	L_W	L_Y	L_G	L_R	P_W	P_Y	P_G	P_R	T_W	T_Y	T_G	T_R	W_W	W_Y	W_G	W_R
W	1	3	2	3	1	4	2	3	1	2	3	2	1	4	6	2	1	4	2	3	1	3	2	2	1	4	3	3
Y	3	1	3	5	4	1	3	2	2	1	⬚2	4	4	1	4	4	4	1	3	2	3	1	3	3	2	1	2	2
G	2	2	1	2	2	3	1	4	3	3	1	3	3	2	1	3	2	3	1	5	2	2	1	4	4	2	1	4
R	5	5	4	1	3	2	4	1	4	4	4	1	2	3	2	1	3	2	5	1	4	4	7	1	3	3	4	1
Σ	11	11	10	11	10	10	10	10	10	10	13	10	10	10	13	10	10	10	11	11	10	10	13	10	10	10	10	10

Figure 6. Query Results. The column labels are the query images, and the row labels are the illuminants (W)hite, (Y)ellow, (G)reen, and (R)ed. The boxed entry, for example, indicates that the yellow (Y) dragon image is returned as the second closest image for the green dragon (D_G) query image. The number at the bottom of each column is the total of the ranks in that column, where 10 is the ideal value. The query precision is perfect for 21 of the 28 queries, and the average rank sum is 10.4. One run of the FT iteration required an average of 7.4 steps and 4.6 seconds to converge.

at each point x_i, and eventually becomes w_Σ at the largest point x_m. The CDFs for $\mathbf{x}$ and $\mathbf{y}$ are the bold and regular thickness staircase graphs, respectively. Since $\mathbf{x}$ and $\mathbf{y}$ are equal-weight distributions, the two CDFs become constant at the same value $w_\Sigma = u_\Sigma$. The EMD is equal to the area between the CDFs (shaded) divided by the total weight ([2], pp. 71–80). The corresponding optimal *CDF flow* is indicated with arrows.

The CDF flow is given by $f_{ij}^{\mathrm{CDF}} = |[W_{i-1}, W_i] \cap [U_{j-1}, U_j]|$, where $W_k = \sum_{i=1}^{k} w_i$, $U_l = \sum_{j=1}^{l} u_j$, and $W_0 = U_0 = 0$. Here the points and weights in a distribution are numbered according to increasing position along the real line. The partial sums $U_0, U_1, \ldots, U_n$ are the same for every translated version of $\mathbf{y}$, so the CDF flow is an optimal flow between $\mathbf{x}$ and $\mathbf{y} \oplus t$ for every translation t. See Figure 8(b), where we have re-used the labels y_j instead of using $y_j + t$ in order to save space. To compute the EMD under translation in this case, we simply solve the optimal translation problem for $d = L_1$ ([15]) with $F = F^{\mathrm{CDF}}$.

4. Conclusion

The $\mathrm{EMD}_\mathcal{G}$ problem is an example of the common computer vision problem of simultaneously estimating dependent sets of parameters (e.g. shape and motion in structure from motion, or motions and groups in motion mixture models). Avoiding local minima during iterative improvement of the estimation is a challenging problem in general, and the difficulty is magnified in the $\mathrm{EMD}_\mathcal{G}$ problem because partial matching is allowed. Some cases with special structure that allow direct computation of a globally optimal transformation were identified. In the absence of such structure, however, an important area for future work is to develop efficient and effective strategies for choosing initial transformations for the FT iteration which are close to a global optimum, particularly in partial matching cases where choosing $g^{(0)}$ based on global statistics such as centroids and principal components will not work.

Acknowledgements

This research was sponsored in part by DARPA under contract DAAH04-94-G-0284. We thank Madirakshi Das for the color ads, David Slater for the object database, Stan Birchfield for his feature extraction code, and Yossi Rubner for his EMD code.

References

[1] P. J. Besl and N. D. McKay. A method for registration of 3-d shapes. *PAMI*, 14(2):239–256, Feb. 1992.

[2] S. Cohen. Finding color and shape patterns in images. Technical Report STAN-CS-TR-99-1620, Stanford University, May 1999. Available online at http://vision.stanford.edu/~scohen.

[3] G. H. Golub and C. F. Van Loan. *Matrix Computations*. The Johns Hopkins University Press, 1989.

[4] G. Healey and D. Slater. Global color constancy: recognition of objects by use of illumination-invariant properties of color distributions. *JOSA A*, 11(11):3003–3010, 1994.

[5] F. S. Hillier and G. J. Lieberman. *Introduction to Mathematical Programming*. McGraw-Hill, 1990.

[6] D. P. Huttenlocher et al. Comparing images using the Hausdorff distance. *PAMI*, 15(9):850–863, Sept. 1993.

[7] G. McLachlan and K. Basford. *Mixture Models: Inference and Applications to Clustering*. Marcel Dekker, 1989.

[8] W. Niblack et al. The QBIC project: querying images by content using color, texture, and shape. In *Proceedings of the SPIE*, volume 1908, pages 173–187, 1993.

[9] Y. Rubner et al. The earth mover's distance, multi-dimensional scaling, and color-based image retrieval. In *ARPA IUW*, pages 661–668, May 1997.

[10] Y. Rubner et al. The earth mover's distance as a metric for image retrieval. Technical Report STAN-CS-TN-98-86, Stanford Computer Science Department, Sept. 1998.

[11] Y. Rubner et al. A metric for distributions with applications to image databases. In *ICCV*, pages 59–66, Jan. 1998.

[12] W. J. Rucklidge. Locating objects using the Hausdorff distance. In *ICCV*, pages 457–464, 1995.

[13] J. Shi and C. Tomasi. Good features to track. In *CVPR*, pages 593–600, June 1994.

[14] S. Umeyama. Least-squares estimation of transformation parameters between two point patterns. *PAMI*, 13(4):376–380, Apr. 1991.

[15] G. O. Wesolowsky. The Weber problem: History and perspectives. *Location Science*, 1(1):5–23, May 1993.

[16] G. Wyszecki and W. Styles. *Color Science: Concepts and Methods, Quantitative Data and Formulae*. Wiley, 1982.

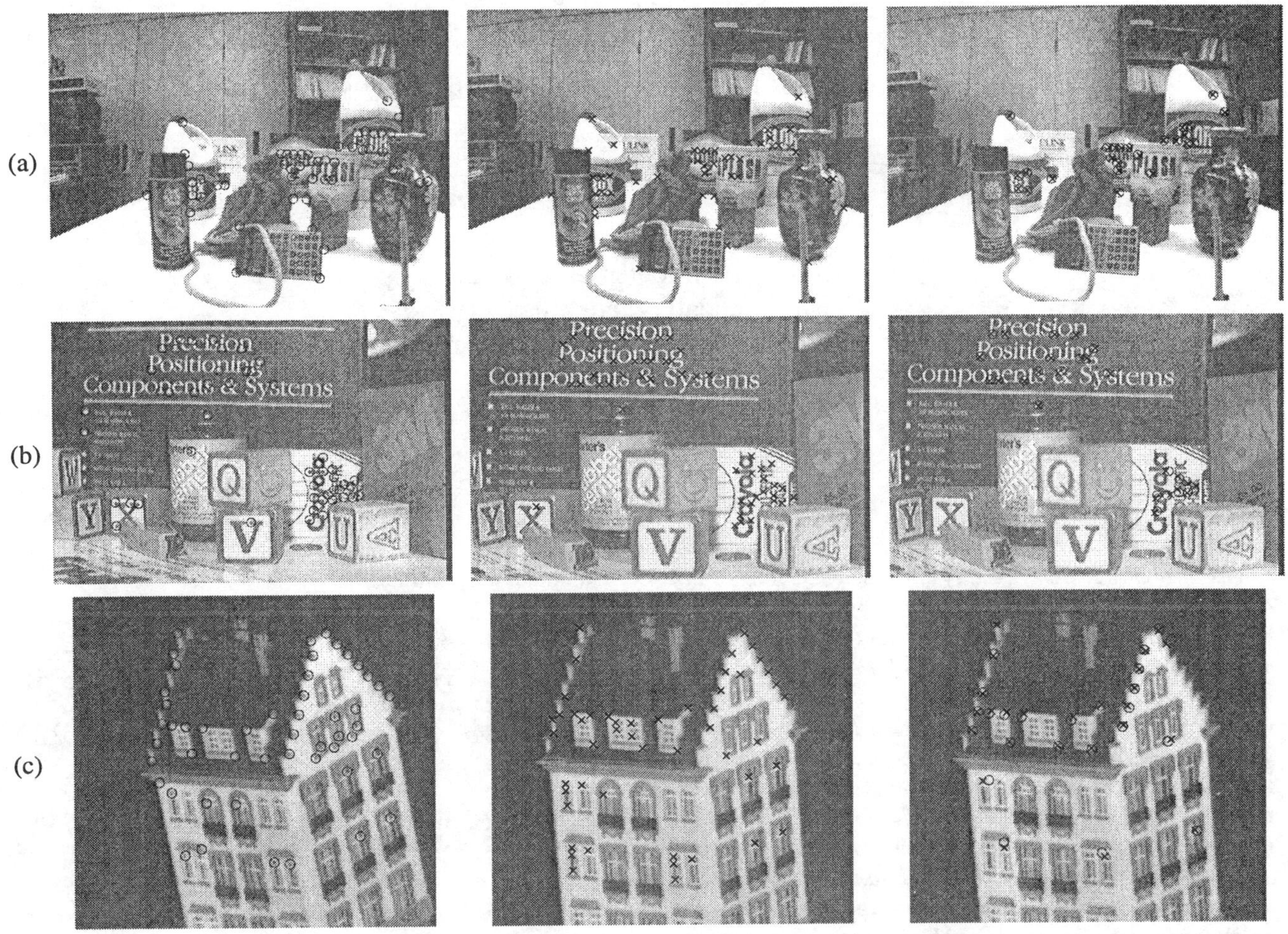

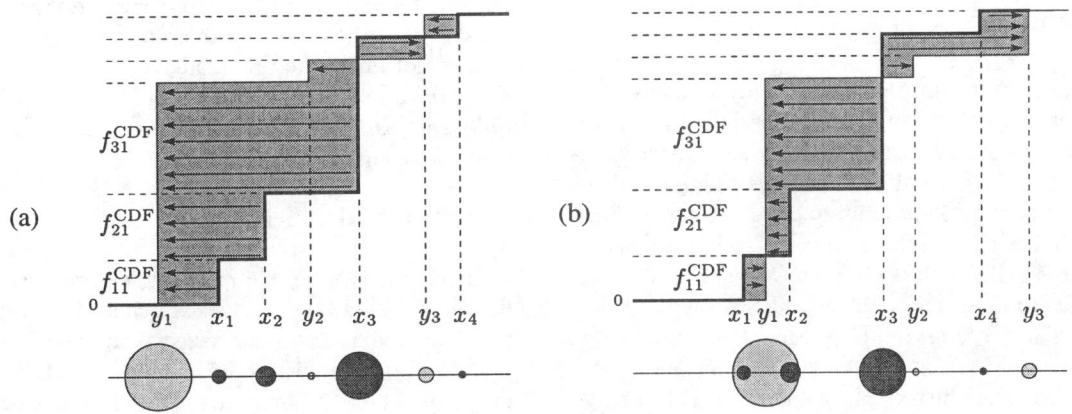

Figure 7. Point Set Matching. See the text. We report the number of steps S and the time T in seconds (s) for the FT iteration to converge. (a) $S = 11$, $T = 1.8$s. (b) $S = 4$, $T = 1.1$s. (c) $S = 8$, $T = 36.2$s.

Figure 8. The Equal-Weight EMD under Translation in 1D with $d = L_1$. The same flow F^{CDF} is optimal for (a) x and y, and (b) x and y $\oplus$ t. See the text for details.

Dynamic Feature Ordering for Efficient Registration

Tat-Jen Cham   James M. Rehg

Cambridge Research Laboratory
Compaq Computer Corporation
One Kendall Square, Ste 721
Cambridge, MA 02139
{tjc,rehg}@crl.dec.com

Abstract

Existing sequential feature-based registration algorithms involving search typically either select features randomly (eg. the RANSAC[8] approach) or assume a predefined, intuitive ordering for the features (eg. based on size or resolution). This paper presents a formal framework for computing an ordering for features which maximizes search efficiency. Features are ranked according to matching ambiguity measure, and an algorithm is proposed which couples the feature selection with the parameter estimation, resulting in a dynamic feature ordering. The analysis is extended to template features where the matching is non-discrete and a sample-refinement process is proposed. The framework is demonstrated effectively on the localization of a person in an image, using a kinematic model with template features. Different priors are used on the model parameters and the results demonstrate nontrivial variations in the optimal feature hierarchy.

1 Introduction

Spatial registration is a topic which concerns many areas of computer vision including image mosaicing, structure-from-motion, medical imaging, tracking and object localization. One of the most difficult and interesting problems is that of registering a kinematic structure to a person in an image. This has many difficult aspects, such as choice of features and handling self-occlusions. While these difficulties continue to exist, the problem which we will address in this paper is that of maximizing search efficiency in registering a high dof model with known features (eg. predefined appearance templates), but without prior knowledge of the model state (see figure 1). Scenarios which benefit directly from a solution to this problem include boostrapping a person tracker for individuals recorded in a image

database, or the re-initialization of trackers when tracking failure has been detected. A naive approach would be to search the entire kinematic state-space, which is however computationally intractable.

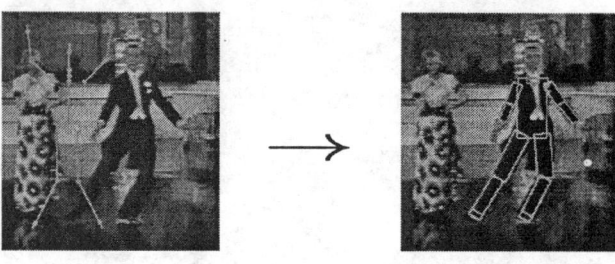

Figure 1. Registering a high dof kinematic model with known features, but without prior knowledge of the model state. Left image shows the initial state of the model, right image shows the desired state.

In this paper we will describe an approach to minimizing the amount of search in order to provide a tractable method of registration. Furthermore the analysis we provide is not limited to articulated structures but applies to *any form of spatial registration involving a model with multiple features*. Previous work on person localization is also summarized in section 7.

1.1 Minimizing Search

In situations when the prior knowledge is weak, registration almost always involves search as there will often be multiple candidates for the correct feature location. An important goal in the design of the algorithm is to minimize the amount of search required in order to maximize the efficiency of the registration process.

An existing approach to minimizing search would be to carry out the feature-matching in a *sequential* manner. The reason for this is to reduce the uncertainty in the states of subsequent features such that the amount of search required for matching these features is reduced [20, 18].

A probabilistic estimation framework for incrementally improving the model state and covariance estimates by incorporating features sequentially was proposed by Hel-Or and Werman [11]. The framework is based on Kalman filter estimation [2] except that a prediction step is not used. It treats each feature as a separate observation which updates the model state and covariance matrix using the standard Kalman update step. This is also the framework which we will adopt in our paper, and the relevant equations are given later in (5)-(7).

Although we adopt the same estimation framework as [11], we disagree with their search strategy of selecting features sequentially along the articulated chain. Although this is an intuitive idea, it is also a *sub-optimal* strategy – the optimal strategy which we will propose in this paper can choose features on an articulated structure *out of sequential order*. Figure 4 illustrates this quite clearly.

A number of methods involve selecting features in no specific order. The various RANSAC-derived methods [8, 17] select random minimal sets of feature pairs to compute an initial estimate for the model parameters, which are then validated or invalidated based on the number of subsequent pairings admitted by this estimate. These additional feature pairs are used to improve the previous model estimate.

Other techniques offer a predefined feature ordering. Methods which adopt a multi-resolution approach [5, 13, 19, 14, 12] order features according to their resolution level – an initial model estimate is obtained at a lower resolution before proceeding to higher resolutions in order to maximize search efficiency. Similarly, this is also the case for methods which select features according to a known hierarchical decomposition of components [10].

While some of these methods provide an intuitively search-efficient feature ordering, they implicitly assume some weak generic prior for the model parameters. For example, methods which are based on always registering coarse features first do not optimally handle cases when the positions some fine-scale features are accurately known in advanced.

In the following sections we will formalize a framework for optimal feature ordering and show that it evolves dynamically according to the estimated model state and covariance. Particularly in cases where the prior encodes specific spatial information, the optimal feature ordering differs significantly from the predefined intuitive ordering.

2 Spatial Registration Framework

In this paper, we express the general spatial registration framework as follows: We start with a set of known 'source' features $\mathcal{F}$ and a transformation model $\mathcal{M}$ which maps these features into an image. Then given a target image, the goal is to match these features to their correct locations in the image and also to recover the parameters of $\mathcal{M}$ denoted as a vector x. These features can either be prior knowledge as part of the model specification, or in the case of registering two images they represent extracted features.

Feature-based registration may be classified into two categories:

- *Feature-to-feature matching*. In this case a separate set of features is extracted from the target image. Matching is done in a discrete manner by attempting to match 'source' features to 'target' features. The features applicable for this form of matching are discrete features such as corners, edges and contours.

- *Feature-to-image matching*. Here the source features are projected into the image and compared directly. For example, template features can be matched to the image by minimizing a measure of pixel difference.

The amount of search required in the registration process depends significantly on the apriori knowledge of the model parameters. For example if x has a small prior covariance, such as in video-based tracking applications, discrete feature-matching may simply involve mapping the source features into the image and searching for the nearest target features. The model parameters may then be computed directly from these correspondences. Similarly if template features are used instead, registration may be carried out in the model state-space by locally minimizing the pixel residual error. Registration in these problems which have strong priors do not have significant search complexities and all features can be matched simultaneously.

In the case of registering a kinematic model of the figure to an image, F may be the set of template features associated with the links in the model, and M is parameterized by a vector of joint angles and link lengths. These features are not necessarily limited to a single class, as F can simultaneously include templates, corners and edges. It can also include features from different levels of resolution.

3 Analysis of Spatial Features

A feature $f \in \mathcal{F}$ is formally described by a number of attributes:

1. A function $G : x \mapsto u$ which maps the model state x to a feature state u in a common feature space.

2. A property vector ρ which allows a feature to be compared with another through a comparison function, or compared to the image.

3. Additionally for image-based features such as templates, we specify the dimensions for the **basin of attraction** in feature space. This specifies the maximum displacement between the true and predicted locations of the feature in feature space for which local optimization of the estimated location (via the maximization of a comparison function) will guarantee to converge on the true location.

In the case of discrete feature-matching, a feature comparison function $C_{ff}(\rho_i, \rho_j)$ generates a similarity measure for comparing feature pairs. In the case of feature to image matching, the comparison function $C_{fI}(\rho_i, u_i, I)$ measures the compatibility between the feature in its current feature state with the image I – it is through the maximization of this function by which the image-based features can be optimally localized.

In this paper, we assume that the correct feature pair or feature state maximizes the relevant comparison functions, ie. once all candidate features or states are tested, the correct solution will be obtained. Obviously this is not necessarily true in cases where the comparison functions generate noisy measures, and a framework for obtaining multiple-hypothesis solutions to the registration problem will be proposed in a future paper.

3.1 Matching Ambiguity of a Feature

Given the estimated model state μ and covariance Σ, we define the matching ambiguity of a feature as follows:

Definition 1 *(Matching Ambiguity)*
The matching ambiguity of feature f_i, denoted by α_i, is defined as the number of search operations required to find the true match with some specified minimum probability.

The idea proposed here applies the *validation gate* [3] used in extended Kalman filters. Linearizing the mapping $G_i(x)$ about μ, the covariance S_i in feature space is expressed as

$$S_i = J_i \, \Sigma \, J_i^T \qquad (1)$$

where

$$J_i = \nabla G_i|_{x=\mu} \qquad (2)$$

is the Jacobian. The validation gate is then the volume bounded by an equiprobability surface which may be specified as a factor ψ of standard deviations. In our experiments, the validation gates used span 2.5 standard deviations ($\psi = 2.5$).

For feature-to-feature matching, the matching ambiguity is then the number of target features which lie within the validation gate. This may be obtained by evaluating the Mahalanobis distances to potential target features and counting. Unfortunately, this is a potentially intensive computation because it would involve pairwise comparisons of features. A reasonable approximation which can be used when

target features are approximately uniformly distributed is that the matching ambiguity is proportional to the size of the validation gate, ie.

$$\alpha_i \propto (\|S_i\|)^{\frac{1}{2}} \qquad (3)$$

Since in the algorithm proposed later the matching ambiguities are used to sort the features, the exact values of the matching ambiguities need not be evaluated as long as they can be ranked in the right order.

For feature-to-image matching, the matching ambiguity is the number of minimally-overlapping regions which have the same dimensions as the basin of attraction that would fit into the validation gate. This can be approximately computed through the following steps:

1. obtain the eigenvalues e_j and eigenvectors v_j to the covariance matrix S_i;

2. calculate the span of the basin of attraction b_j along each of the v_j directions;

3. the matching ambiguity is then computed as

$$\alpha_i \approx \prod_j \mathrm{ceil}\left(\psi \frac{\sqrt{e_j}}{b_j}\right) \qquad (4)$$

where ceil($\cdot$) rounds fractional values up to the next integer.

Figure 2 illustrates the concept of matching ambiguity for the two separate cases.

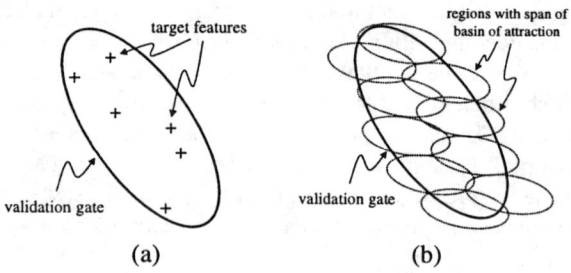

(a)   (b)

Figure 2. Matching ambiguity. Feature-to-feature matching: (a) shows the target features located within the validation gate of a source feature; the matching ambiguity in this case is the number of candidates to be search, which is 6. Feature-to-image matching: (b) shows minimally overlapping regions with the span of the basin of attraction covering the validation gate; the matching ambiguity here is the number of regions required, which is 10.

4 Sequential Registration with Dynamic Feature Ordering

As each feature is used in the estimation step during sequential search, the model state becomes increasingly more accurate and the state covariance decreases. This observation can be formalized using the standard Kalman filter covariance update step (6). Correspondingly based on (1), the size of the validation gates for each feature decreases, thereby leading to a reduction in the matching ambiguities α_i.

Assuming that the intention is to use all available features sequentially in the registration process[1], the total number of search operations involved can be minimized by selecting features and estimating the model parameters in the algorithm described below, which we call the *Coupled Dynamic Feature Ordering and Registration (2DYFOR)* algorithm.

The 2DYFOR Algorithm

1. Set the list of used features L as empty.

2. Compute the matching ambiguities α_i for all unused features.

3. Select the feature f_b for which α_b is the smallest matching ambiguity.

4. Carry out the necessary α_b search operations to recover the optimal feature state u_b. This is the minimum number of search operations which have to be performed to register a feature.

5. The optimal feature state u_b and the associated observation covariance S_b is used to improve the model state and covariance by applying the standard Kalman filter update steps:

$$\mu_k = \mu_{k-1} + K_k(u_b - J_k\mu_{k-1}) \quad (5)$$
$$\Sigma_k = \Sigma_{k-1} - K_k J_k \Sigma_{k-1} \quad (6)$$

where the subscript k denote the sequential update index and K_k is the Kalman gain given by

$$K_k = \Sigma_{k-1}J^T(J\Sigma_{k-1}J^T + S_b)^{-1} \quad (7)$$

6. Append f_b to the L.

7. If all features have been used, stop; otherwise return to step 2.

---

[1]This is not always true, as there may be formulations based on sampling of features [1] or *optimal stopping* strategies [7].

At the end of the registration process, the feature list L contains the *feature hierarchy*. The feature hierarchy represents the optimal sequential ordering of features and is dependent on the prior model state and covariance, as well as the accuracy of registering each feature. The feature hierarchy has to be formed dynamically as part of the estimation process. While the predefined feature orderings used in the algorithms may be reasonably efficient in typical situations, the optimal feature hierarchy can often be found at negligible cost using the 2DYFOR algorithm. Furthermore, the dynamic feature ordering copes even when the prior knowledge changes significantly – using the original predefined feature ordering may not take full advantage of the additional prior knowledge for increasing search efficiency.

5 Search Method for Feature-to-Image Matching

While it may be straightforward to carry out feature-to-feature matching based on the 2DYFOR algorithm described in section 4, implementing feature-to-image matching is more complex and will be discussed in further detail in the following section.

5.1 The Sample-Refinement Approach to Search

In feature-to-image matching problems an attempt to recover the optimal feature can be made by locally maximizing a similarity measure obtained from the comparison function C_{fI}, which is described by the term *refinement*. However the starting feature state must be within the basin of attraction of the correct solution for the refinement process to succeed. Hence it is necessary to generate a number of starting points (termed as *samples*) for the refinement step, spaced at intervals corresponding to the span of the basin of attraction, in order to guarantee that the optimal feature state will be found.

One issue which arises for this method is whether samples should be obtained as feature state-vectors or model state-vectors. It turns out that generating the samples in model state-space has two advantages:

- If the non-linearity between the feature and model state-spaces is significant with respect to the validation gate, and if the feature state-space is not mapped entirely by the model state-space, sampling in model state-space ensures the starting feature states are valid for the model, even if the spacing of the samples is inaccurate due to the nonlinearity.

- Often the refinement step can be improved by using previously registered features as well, especially when the comparison function generates noisy measures. Using the additional features improves the robustness to the noise.

Using notation from section 3.1, the desired displacement between samples in feature space along the eigenvector direction v_j is $b_k v_j$. The equivalent displacement in model state-space may be found by the following analysis:

$$S\, v_j = e_k\, v_j$$

$$\Longleftrightarrow$$

$$J\, \Sigma\, J^T\, v_j = e_k v_j$$

$$\Longleftrightarrow$$

$$J\left(\frac{b_k}{e_k}\, \Sigma\, J^T\, v_j\right) = b_k\, v_j \qquad (8)$$

Noting that J represents the linearized mapping between model and feature state-spaces, it may be observed that using the term in the parentheses on the LH side of (8) as the displacement in model state-space generates the desired displacement in feature space, given by the RH side of (8).

The samples in the model state-space are then generated by integral vector sum combinations of the displacement vectors associated with each eigenvector direction in feature space, such that the span of the validation gate in feature space is covered by these samples. Once the initial samples have been generated in the model state-space, each sample is then refined through the local maximization process. The optimal solution is then taken to be the refined sample which generates the maximum similarity measure from the comparison function.

6 Kinematic Model Registration

The model used in our experiments is the 2D Scaled-Prismatic Model (SPM) proposed by Morris and Rehg [15]. The kinematic model lies in the image plane, with each link having a degree-of-freedom (dof) in rotation and another dof in length. The model is parameterized by a state-space which encodes a global 2D translation, joint angles and link lengths. Each link is associated with an template which describes the apppearance of the link. The approach used to locally refine the state of the kinematic model is to minimize the SSD error between the templates and the image using the Gauss-Newton method. The model used for the Fred Astaire image has 19 states and 16 template features, while the model used for the walking figure has 8 states (arms are ignored and link lengths are fixed) and 10 template features.

In our experiments which involve localizing the figure with minimal prior knowledge, the model state is initialized as denoted by the pose of the stick figure in the leftmost images of figure 3. The prior covariance is set as a diagonal matrix with standard deviations of 50 pixels for global x

translation, 20 pixels for global y translation, 2 radians for joint angles and 10 pixels for link lengths. The only strong prior is that the torso is approximately upright as we wish to restrict our search to upright figures. For each template, the basin of attraction for the refinement step is set to be its minimum dimension at present, although a more formal analysis may be applied in the future based on the spatial frequency content of the templates.

The sequences shown from left to right in figure 3 illustrate the feature ordering which arises in the registration process. The feature ordering obtained in these instances is similar to a size-based ordering, except in our algorithm the ordering is done both automatically and dynamically. The registration localizes the figure well despite the high dimensionality of the figure model and the weak prior knowledge.

In figure 4, we show the results obtained when various forms of strong prior knowledge are available which is captured in the prior covariance. For the top test image, the feet template positions are accurately positioned, while for the bottom test image the front shin template position is accurately positioned. A 5-pixel standard deviation is used for these constraints. The feature ordering in these instances differs significantly from the ordering obtained in figure 3. Also notice from the third-from-left image in the top sequence, the optimal feature ordering does not propagate along the articulated chains which contradicts the proposed heuristic of Hel-Or and Werman [11].

The top test images generally took approximately one to two minutes for the localization, while the bottom test images took approximately twenty seconds because of the simpler model used. In both instances the number of samples used for initializing the search of individual templates appears to be significantly more than is necessary, which is due to the conservative estimates for the span of the basins of attraction in the refinement process. Hence there is still significant room to improve the efficiency of the registration.

7 Previous Work on Person Localization

While current systems are good at detecting humans as moving blobs, few solutions are available when the *full articulated pose* of a person including the position of the arms and legs is required. For example, the full-body tracking systems described in [6, 4] currently depend on manual initialization of a figure model in the first image frame. The method in [9] has automatic initialization but requires an accurate background model for segmentation and restrictive assumptions on limb positions. An interesting method for registering articulated structures based on EM motion segmentation is proposed in [16], but has only been applied to low dimensional models. Furthermore, many systems depend on independent motion of the figure for segmentation

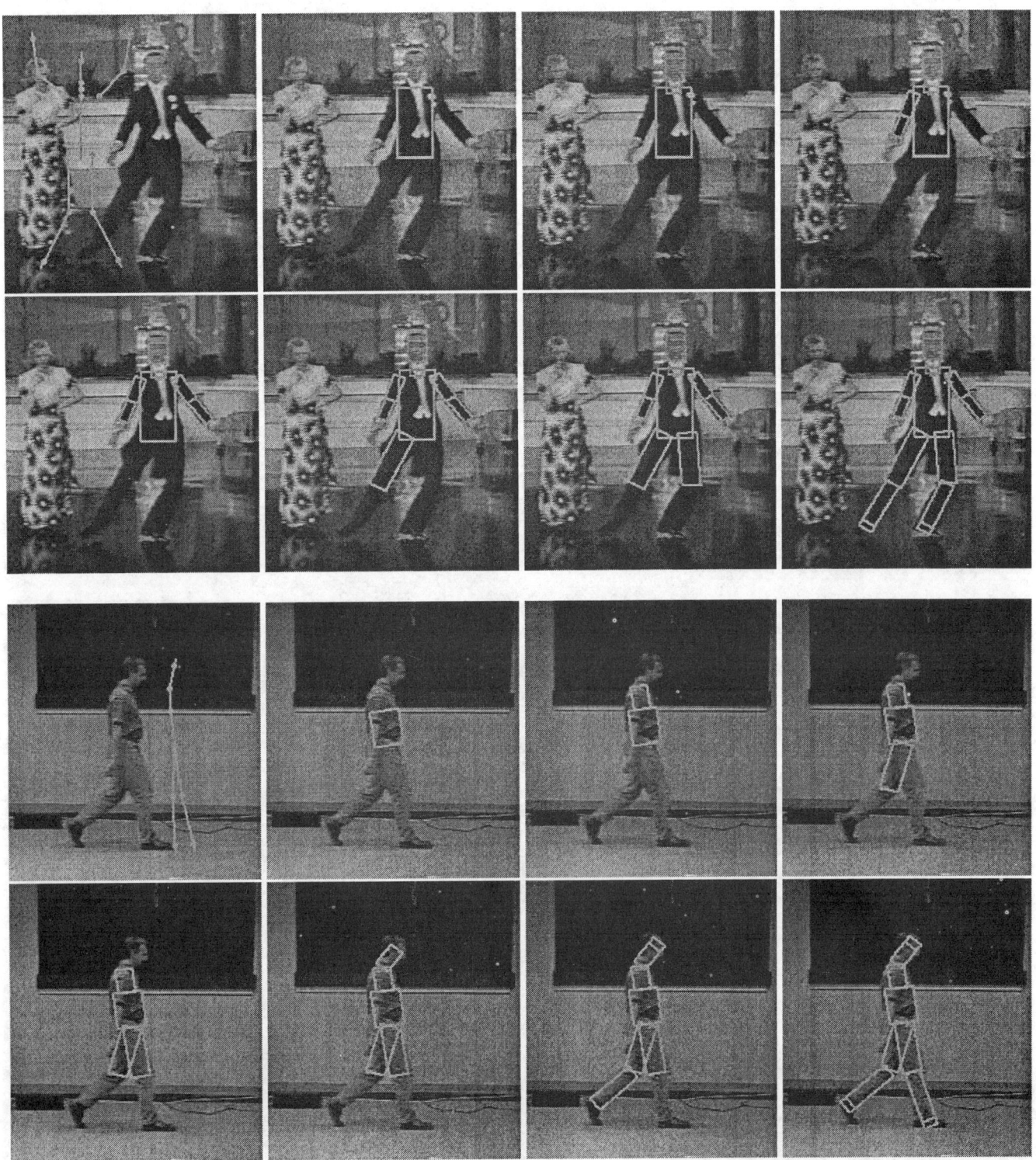

Figure 3. Results obtained using weak generic priors. The top-left image of each block show the prior state of the kinematic model which is represented by a stick figure. Weak generic priors are used in these two test cases. As the coupled dynamic feature ordering algorithm is iterated, the next template feature selected is the one requiring the least amount of search operations for registration. The left-to-right sequences show the feature ordering.

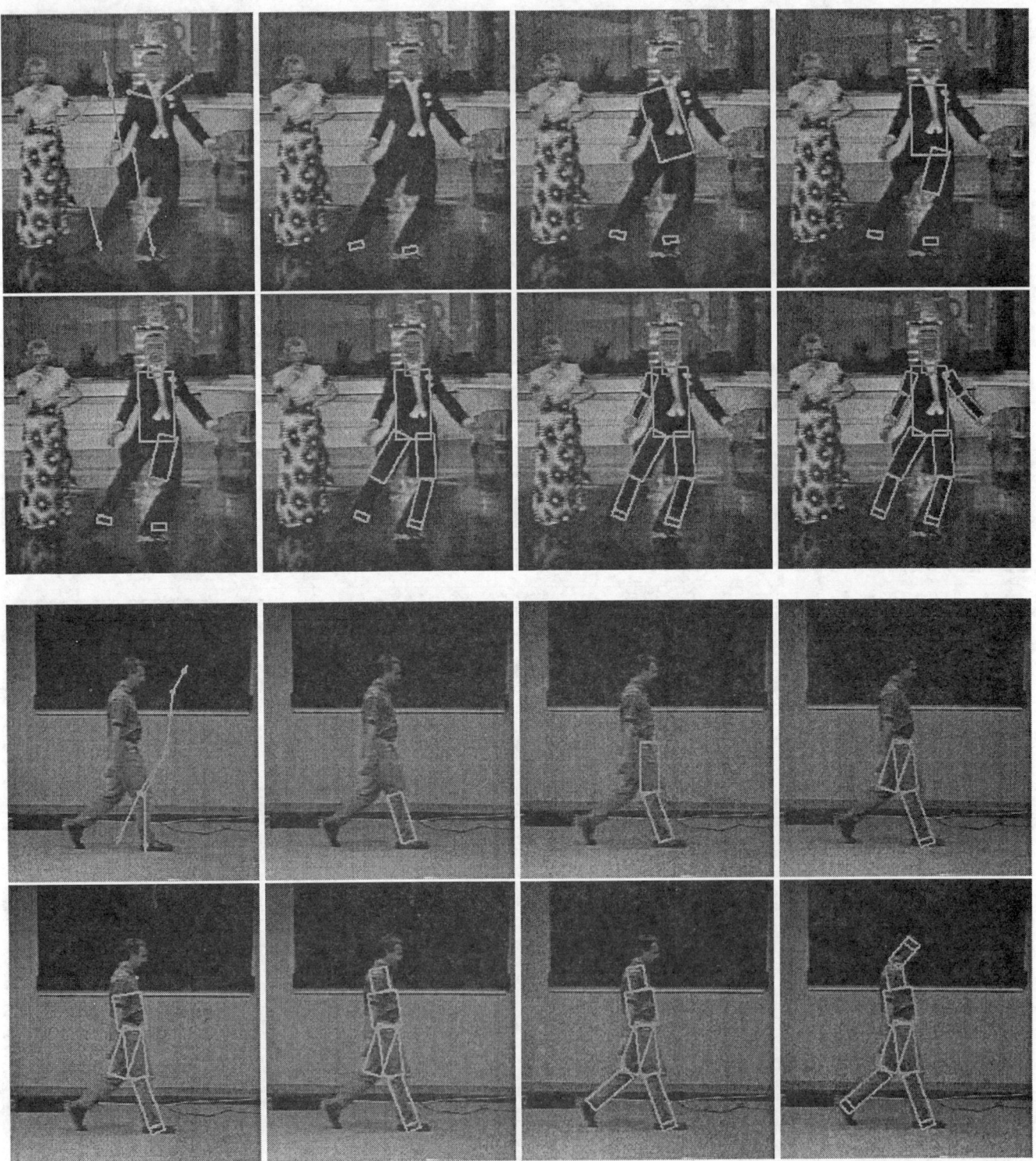

Figure 4. Results obtained using some strong prior knowledge. In the top test case, the position of the two feet templates as assumed to be known accurately. In the bottom test case, the position of the front shin template is known accurately. The feature ordering obtained when strong prior knowledge is available can be significantly different from the ordering with weak generic priors. Note the registration of the left leg in the top test case is *corrected* as more features are integrated into the estimation.

and registration (eg. those based on optic-flow), and cannot be applied to static images or to still figures.

8 Conclusions and Future Work

This paper presents a general algorithm for maximizing search efficiency for a sequential registration problem. At each iteration in the registration process, the feature with the minimum matching ambiguity is selected and used in the estimation. The means of computing the matching ambiguity is discussed separately for problems involving feature-to-feature matching and feature-to-image matching. Additionally for the latter cases, a search method is proposed which is based on generating samples in the model state-space such that at least one sample will fall into the basin of attraction for the correct solution. These samples are further refined to obtain the optimal feature state which is then used to improve the model state estimation.

The current application of this framework is registering kinematic models to human figures in images. Despite the high dimensional kinematic models used and the weak priors assumed, the framework is able to register the models accurately and efficiently. Furthermore, the optimal feature ordering is shown to be significantly different when additional strong prior knowledge can be used to constraint the searches.

There are a number of situations when the strong prior knowledge is available. For example, partial figure tracking failure may result from the occlusion of the torso by a shoulder-height object, although the person's head will still be well tracked; in this instance the smaller head feature will provide strong constraints on the location of the torso. Another example would be a semi-automated tracking system (eg. for video editing) where the user provides partial registration of a model in a video sequence. In both scenarios, our proposed method would efficiently obtain the remaining correspondences by utilizing the available prior knowledge.

Currently, our system is based on the assumption that the feature searches always return the correct registration. However, multiple registration candidates may arise as a result of clutter and self-occlusion. A future research direction would be to combine our registration approach with the multiple-hypothesis probabilistic framework proposed in [6] to cope with these problems.

References

[1] M. Akra, L. Bazzi, and S. Mitter. Sampling of images for efficient model-based vision. *IEEE Trans. Pattern Analysis and Machine Intelligence*, 21(1):4–11, 1999.

[2] B. D. Anderson and J. B. Moore. *Optimal Filtering*. Prentice-Hall, 1979.

[3] Y. Bar-Shalom and T. E. Fortmann. *Tracking and Data Association*. Academic Press, 1988.

[4] C. Bregler and J. Malik. Estimating and tracking kinematic chains. In *Proc. IEEE Conf. Computer Vision and Pattern Recognition*, pages 8–15, Santa Barbara, CA, 1998.

[5] T.-J. Cham and R. Cipolla. A statistical framework for long-range feature matching in uncalibrated image mosaicing. In *Proc. IEEE Conf. Computer Vision and Pattern Recognition*, pages 442–447, Santa Barbara, CA, 1998.

[6] T.-J. Cham and J. Rehg. A multiple hypothesis approach to figure tracking. In *Proc. IEEE Conf. Computer Vision and Pattern Recognition*, volume II, pages 239–245, Fort Collins, Colorado, 1999.

[7] M. H. DeGroot. *Optimal Statistical Decisions*. McGraw-Hill, 1970.

[8] M. Fischler and R. Bolles. Random sample consensus: A paradigm for model fitting with applications to image analysis and automated cartography. *Comm. ACM*, 24(6):381–395, June 1981.

[9] I. Haritaoglu, D. Harwood, and L. Davis. W^4: Who? When? Where? What? A real time system for detecting and tracking people. In *Proc. Intl. Conf. on Automatic Face and Gesture Recognition*, pages 222–227, Nara, Japan, 1998.

[10] A. Hauck, S. Lanser, and C. Zierl. Hierarchical recognition of articulated objects from single perspective views. In *Proc. IEEE Conf. Computer Vision and Pattern Recognition*, pages 870–876, San Juan, Puerto Rico, 1997.

[11] Y. Hel-Or and M. Werman. Constraint fusion for recognition and localization of articulated objects. *Int. Journal of Computer Vision*, 19(1):5–28, 1996.

[12] M. Luettgen, W. Karl, A. Willsky, and R. Tenney. Multiscale representations of markov random fields. *IEEE Trans. on Signal Processing*, 41(12):3377–3396, 1993.

[13] S. Marapane and M. Trivedi. Multi-primitive hierarchical (MPH) stereo analysis. *IEEE Trans. Pattern Analysis and Machine Intelligence*, 16(3):227–240, 1994.

[14] E. Mémin and P. Pérez. A multigrid approach for hierarchical motion estimation. In *Proc. Intl. Conf. on Computer Vision*, pages 933–938, Bombay, India, 1998.

[15] D. Morris and J. Rehg. Singularity analysis for articulated object tracking. In *Proc. IEEE Conf. Computer Vision and Pattern Recognition*, pages 289–296, Santa Barbara, CA, 1998.

[16] H. A. Rowley and J. M. Rehg. Analyzing articulated motion using expectation-maximization. In *Proc. IEEE Conf. Computer Vision and Pattern Recognition*, pages 935–941, San Juan, Puerto Rico, 1997.

[17] P. Torr. *Motion Segmentation and Outlier Detection*. PhD thesis, University of Oxford, 1995.

[18] K. Toyama and G. Hager. Incremental focus of attention for robust visual tracking. In *Proc. IEEE Conf. Computer Vision and Pattern Recognition*, pages 189–195, San Francisco, CA, 1996.

[19] J. Weng, N. Ahuja, and T. Huang. Matching two perspective views. *IEEE Trans. Pattern Analysis and Machine Intelligence*, 14(8):806–825, 1992.

[20] L. Wixson. *Gaze Selection for Visual Search*. PhD thesis, Department of Computer Science, University of Rochester, 1994.

Finding people by sampling

Sergey Ioffe
Computer Science Division
U.C. Berkeley
Berkeley, CA 94720
ioffe@cs.berkeley.edu

David Forsyth
Computer Science Division
U.C. Berkeley
Berkeley, CA 94720
daf@cs.berkeley.edu

Abstract

We show how to use a sampling method to find sparsely clad people in static images. People are modeled as an assembly of nine cylindrical segments. Segments are found using an EM algorithm, and then assembled into hypotheses incrementally, using a learned likelihood model. Each assembly step passes on a set of samples of its likelihood to the next; this yields effective pruning of the space of hypotheses. The collection of available nine-segment hypotheses is then represented by a set of equivalence classes, which yield an efficient pruning process. The posterior for the number of people is obtained from the class representatives. People are counted quite accurately in images of real scenes using an MAP estimate. We show the method allows top-down as well as bottom up reasoning. While the method can be overwhelmed by very large numbers of segments, we show that this problem can be avoided by quite simple pruning steps.
Keywords: *Object recognition, sampling, Probabilistic inference*

1. Introduction

Finding people in static images is difficult, because the number of internal degrees of freedom defeats simple correspondence reasoning. However, people can be quite accurately modeled as assemblies of cylinders, and these assemblies are constrained by the kinematics of human joints. There is a long tradition of using these constraints to find people (e.g. [1, 6, 8, 3]; pedestrians in a standard configuration can be found by template matching [7]). No existing work can count people, and serious difficulties with segmentation remain.

These segmentation difficulties can only be overcome by using object level knowledge as early as possible in the segmentation process. We represent people as collections of nine body segments, one for the torso and two for each limb (the face could be dealt with by current, very accurate, face-finding algorithms [10, 9]). In this strategy, we find individual body segments; these segments are then assembled into pairs that satisfy kinematic constraints; the pairs are assembled into triples, etc. The main advantage of this approach is that poor hypotheses can be pruned early (as in [5]). However, there is the danger of pruning a hypothesis that is locally poor but which is a component of a good global hypothesis. This is a common problem in recognition — false negatives are much harder to resolve than false positives — and is a version of the horizon problem in search.

We finesse this difficulty by using a probabilistic inference method. A standard method forms a posterior, and then represents possible inferences by drawing samples from this posterior [4]. Building a good sampler for finding people is tricky, because the posterior that a person is present given a single segment will be very small, so that it is difficult to start the assembly process. Instead, we *sample the likelihood*. We use the term "assembly" to refer to a group of segments, labeled with correspondence to human body segments. For any nine segment assembly A, define the likelihood $L(A) = \Pr[A$ will appear in the image|a person is present]. We now sample subassemblies from the available segments in the image according to marginalised versions of this distribution. This prunes the set of assemblies without denying any hypothesis a chance to grow. We show the results may be used to count people in the image, segment them from the background, and infer their configurations, and find body parts missed by the original segmentation.

1.1. Resampling

There are too many nine segment assemblies to compute the likelihood for each. However, we can build assemblies incrementally. For example, having generated a set of samples $\{s_T\}$ of potential `torso` segments and samples $\{s_{LUA}\}$ of `left upper arms`, we can form all combinations $\{s_T, s_{LUA}\}$ and then resample it, so that the resulting pairs (s_T, s_{LUA}) come from the appropriate marginal like-

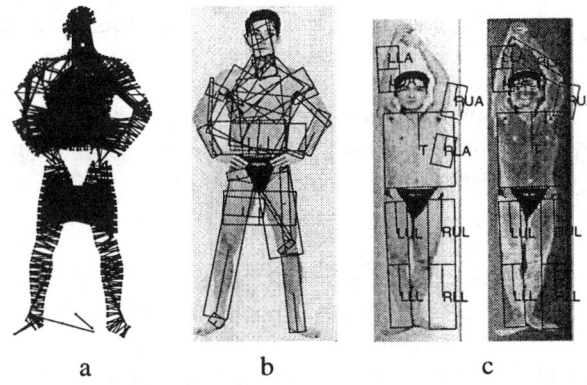

Figure 1. *Symmetries* (a) *and segments* (b) *produced for an image.* (c): *Assemblies corresponding to the same person often share* `torsos`

lihood. We can proceed by similarly sampling 3-, 4-, ..., 9-segment sub-assemblies, in such a way that the resulting set of 9-segment assemblies is sampled from $L(\cdot)$.

At each stage, we use *importance sampling*, which is a method for drawing samples from (possibly intractable) distributions (as used in [2]). In particular, to draw a sample from $g(x)$, we first draw a large number of independent samples $\{s_1, \ldots, s_n\}$ from a proposal distribution $f(x)$, and then set $s = s_i$ with probability proportional to $w_i = \frac{g(x)}{f(x)}$. As $n \to \infty$, the distribution for the sample s will approach $g(x)$. In our case, the proposal distributions are the marginal likelihoods for the subassemblies. Thus, we are more likely to propose a pair (s_{RUA}, s_{RLA}) if the two segments individually are more likely to be `upper right arm` and `lower right arm` of a person.

2. Implementation

Our system starts by finding *symmetries* (fig. 1(a)), which are pairs of edge elements that are approximately symmetric about some symmetry axis and whose tangents are approximately parallel to that axis. These symmetries are grouped into *segments* — extended groups of symmetries which approximately share the same axis — (fig. 1(b)) using an expectation-maximization algorithm that assumes a fixed number of segments. From the segments, we use a learned *likelihood model* to form *assemblies* by sampling (fig. 1(c)). Finally, the set of assemblies is replaced with a smaller set of *representatives*, which are used to count people in the image.

2.1. Finding Segments Using EM

Each segment is represented with a *symmetry axis* and a *width*. Each symmetry has a label showing which of at most one segment it belongs to. A symmetry fits a segment best when the midpoint of the symmetry lies on the segment's symmetry axis, the endpoints lie half a segment width away from the axis, and the symmetry is perpendicular to the axis (that is, the axes of symmetry of the symmetry and the segment coincide). This yields the conditional likelihood for a symmetry given a segment as a four-dimensional Gaussian (two numbers for each endpoint), and an EM algorithm can now fit a fixed number of segments to the symmetries. After that, we determine where each segment begins and ends by finding the range of symmetries for which this segment has the largest posterior. If there is a large gap between these symmetries (that is, symmetries from different image regions are attributed to the same segment), then the segment is broken into two or more pieces.

2.2. Representing Likelihoods for People

The likelihood for a nine segment assembly is computed from a set of 41 geometric features, invariant to translation, rotation and scale. These include angles and distances between segments, aspect ratios of segments, length ratios, etc. As nine rectangles have 41 degrees of freedom up to a rigid transformation, we choose the features so as to have a one-to-one correspondence between the feature space and the space of all assemblies. Each feature in our model depends on either one or two segments, and the two-segment features can be computed either from the two halves of the same limb (such as `right upper arm` and `right lower arm`), or from an upper limb and the torso.

This choice of features allows us to assume that features are independent with a relatively small error. The main errors will be due to interactions between kinematic constraints on the hips and shoulders, and viewing pose. This assumption is attractive because the likelihood has an especially simple form,

$$L(A) = \prod_{i=1}^{41} d_i(f_i), \qquad (1)$$

where f_i is the value of the ith feature, and $d_i(f_i)$ is the corresponding one-dimensional marginal likelihood. In our experiments, we chose for $d_i(\cdot)$ to be a histogram for the values f_i.

2.3. Building Assemblies Incrementally by Resampling

We fix a permutation $(l_1, \ldots, l_9)$ of labels $\{T, LUA, \ldots\}$, and generate a sequence $(S_1, \ldots, S_9)$

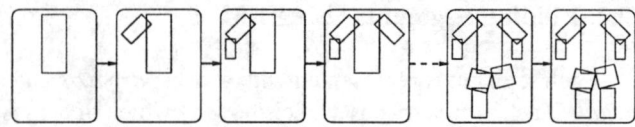

Figure 2. *We sample assemblies incrementally, by generating sets of samples of 1-, 2-, ..., 9-segment assemblies, so that the latter are drawn from the likelihood $L(\cdot)$*

of multisets of samples, where each S_k contains N (not necessarily distinct) assemblies of k segments labeled as $l_1, \ldots, l_k$ (fig. 2). For example, in our implementation, $(l_1 \ldots l_9) = (\text{T}, LUA, LLA, \ldots)$, and so S_1 will contain the samples (s_T) of `torso` segments, while S_3 will contain samples $(s_\text{T}, s_{LUA}, s_{LLA})$ of triples corresponding to the `torso`, the `left upper arm` and the `left lower arm`. The samples in S_k are drawn from the *marginal likelihood* $L_{l_1 \ldots l_k}(A) = \prod_i d_i(f_i)$, where the product is over all the features computable from segments labeled as $l_1, \ldots, l_k$. We write s_{l_i} for the segment of the sub-assembly whose label is l_i. For our feature set and the choice of $(l_1 \ldots l_9)$, each of the marginal likelihoods $L_{l_1 \ldots l_k}(s_{l_1}, \ldots, s_{l_k})$ models the probability that the sub-assembly $(s_{l_1}, \ldots, s_{l_k})$ is seen in a random view of a human.

We generate the set of samples S_{k+1} from S_k using importance sampling. First, we form the set of sub-assemblies $(s_{l_1}, \ldots, s_{l_k}, s_{l_{k+1}})$ for all groups $(s_{l_1}, \ldots, s_{l_k}) \in S_k$ and all choices of $s_{l_{k+1}}$. The first component is a sample from the relevant marginal distribution. We now *resample* this set of samples, by independently drawing N samples, with the probability of drawing $(s_{l_1}, \ldots, s_{l_{k+1}})$ proportional to $w(s_{l_1}, \ldots, s_{l_{k+1}}) = \frac{L_{l_1 \ldots l_{k+1}}(\cdot)}{L_{l_1 \ldots l_k}(\cdot)} = \prod_i d_i(f_i)$, where the product is over all features that depend on $s_{l_{k+1}}$ and, possibly, some of $s_{l_1}, \ldots, s_{l_k}$.

2.4. Directing the sampler

Our sampler is working in a discrete space of labels and image segments. It can be difficult to focus the activity of such samplers on components with large probability. For example, if there are two people in the image, and one results in a large group of segments and the other in a small group (due to mischief in the segment finder), the sampler may repeatedly draw samples from the large group corresponding to the one person, and never get to the other. A natural strategy is to break the domain into a set of equivalence classes, sample the classes, and then sample within the classes drawn by that sampler.

We define equivalent assemblies to be those that label the

same segment as a `torso`. This is a good choice, because different people in an image will tend to have their torsos in different places. We represent the class by the assembly that has the highest likelihood. This means that we have a tight upper bound for the likelihoods within the equivalence class, which means that classes that are omitted when we sample classes tend to be those which contain elements of relatively low likelihood. For an exact algorithm we would need elements within classes to have similar likelihoods; our results suggest that this is not particularly important.

The highest likelihood assembly is found by a simple greedy algorithm. As an example, suppose that all of the segments in an assembly, except the lower left arm, are fixed, and we are to choose the lower left arm that maximizes the likelihood of the resulting assembly. It is easy to see that, in our model, the lower left arm can be found by considering all the pairs of a lower left arm (which can be any segment) and the upper left arm (which is fixed), and choosing the one with the highest marginal likelihood $L_{LUA,LLA}$. Now, let us suppose that we have fixed a `torso` and, possibly, some limbs, and we want to add the left arm that would maximize the likelihood of the result. First, we will find the highest-likelihood left arm for each choice of the upper arm. Since no feature involves the left arm and any other limb, we can choose the best left arm by considering all the pairs of the `torso` (which is fixed) and a left arm, and choosing the one with the largest marginal likelihood.

Now we have a greedy algorithm which, for each choice of upper left arm, finds the lower left arm so as to maximize the marginal $L_{LUA,LLA}$, and similarly for the other limbs. Then, for each possible `torso` segment, the limbs are added in a sequence, maximizing the corresponding marginal likelihoods $L_{\text{T},LUA,LLA}$, $L_{\text{T},LUA,LLA,RUA,RLA}$, etc. At the end, we have the largest likelihood assembly for each `torso` segment. The algorithm is efficient: if there are n segments in the image, we never have more than n sub-assemblies of each type, thus the algorithm runs in $O(n^2)$ time (and much faster in practice, if we only try to pair up segments that are close).

Although the upper bounds provided by this algorithm are very effective for directing the sampler to relevant image regions, they may not be tight. For example, in the resulting assemblies the legs may coincide, since ensuring distinct legs would require a (binary) feature involving both legs. Such assemblies do not consist of 9 segments; they do, however provide upper bounds on the likelihoods of assemblies with a given segment as the `torso`.

3. Counting People

Our sampling algorithm allows to count people in images. To estimate the number of people, we begin by select-

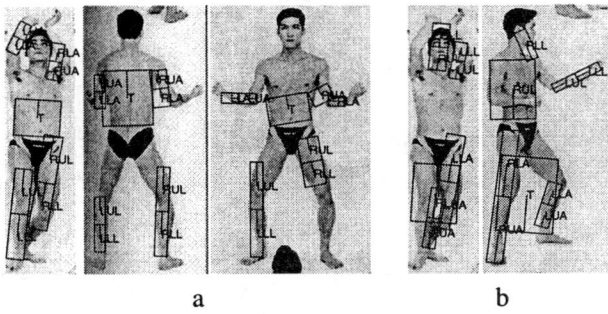

a   b

Figure 3. *The representatives that do* (a) *and do not* (b) *correspond to the configurations of people in the images.*

ing a small set of *representative assemblies* in the image, and then use them for counting.

3.1. Finding representative assemblies

We assume that distinct people have distinct torsos, accepting that occlusion of one torso by another will lead to a miscount. We break the set of all assemblies in the image into (not necessarily disjoint) *blocks* — sets of assemblies such that any two assemblies from the same block have overlapping `torsos`. Then, the *representative* is chosen from each block as the assembly with the highest likelihood, over all assemblies available from the block. Because we have assumed that any people in the image are spaced apart, we can use representatives to count people — by replacing the set of assemblies with that of representatives, we do not diminish the count. Indeed, any assembly that is not a representative must be overlapped by a higher-likelihood representative, and so if there was a human assembly in some region of the image, there will be a representative there as well. In fact, the configuration of a person can often be inferred from that of representatives (Fig. 3).

We can efficiently find representatives, since we can use the upper bounds on the likelihoods, computed in Section 2.4. In particular, if the algorithm of Sec. 2.4 produced a valid assembly (no coinciding segments) for some `torso` segment, then sampling need not be performed for that `torso` (since this assembly has a higher likelihood than any other we can obtain by sampling). If, however, the assembly obtained for the upper bound is not a valid one, we have to sample assemblies with the given `torso`, but only retain the one with the highest likelihood (since all of the assemblies share the `torso`). Furthermore, we need not sample for a given `torso` segment if there is already an overlapping assembly, whose likelihood is greater than the upper bound for the given `torso`.

3.2. Estimating the number of people

Once the representative set has been computed for an image, we want to obtain the estimate on the number of people in the image. We assume that assemblies corresponding to people do not overlap and have independent configurations. Let the set of representatives be $\{A_1, \ldots, A_m\}$, and let us consider any set $G \subseteq \{1 \ldots m\}$, such that no assemblies from $\{A_i | i \in G\}$ overlap. We will look at the *posterior probability* $\Pr[$each of A_i represents a person|image data$]$ that the representatives $\{A_i | i \in G\}$ are people while $\{A_j | j \notin G\}$ are not. To count people, we choose the set G for which the posterior is largest, and the size $|G|$ will give the MAP estimate of the number of people in the image. We could also represent this posterior as a set of samples to give some insight into the reliability of a particular count.

We assume that each assembly has the *a priori* probability β of being a person, independently of the others. Then, the prior for G is $\pi(G) = \beta^{|G|}(1-\beta)^{m-|G|}$, and the posterior is proportional to $\Pr[A_1, \ldots, A_m|G]\pi(G)$. Since the human assemblies do not overlap, $\Pr[A_1, \ldots, A_m|G] = 0$ if some of $\{A_i | i \in G\}$ overlap. Otherwise, we have $\Pr[A_1, \ldots, A_m|G] = \prod_{i \in G} L(A_i) \prod_{i \notin G} L_{\text{non}}(A_i)$, where we still use $L(A) = \Pr[$person in random configuration looks like $A]$, and define $L_{\text{non}}(A) = \Pr[A|$random view not containing a person$]$. Finally, we assume $L_{\text{non}}(\cdot)$ to be uniform. We get that, for non-overlapping $\{A_i | i \in G\}$, the posterior is proportional to $L_{\text{non}}^{m-|G|} \prod_{i \in G} L(A_i)\beta^{|G|}(1-\beta)^{m-|G|}$, or

$$c^{|G|} \prod_{i \in G} L(A_i), \qquad (2)$$

where the constant $c = \frac{\beta}{(1-\beta)L_{\text{non}}}$ is to be estimated so as to yield best classification.

4. Results

To learn the likelihood model $L(\cdot)$, we used a set of 193 training images, scanned from [11]. Each contained a photograph of a single person, standing against a uniform background. All the views were frontal and all limbs were visible, although the configurations varied. The models wore swimsuits or no clothes, since clothes make it hard to propose body segments. The symmetries produced for each image were used to determine sets of segments, although the segment finder was not the EM-based one used on the test data. We hand-labeled the segments by marking those corresponding to the 9 body segments. In fact, the training images were the part of a larger collection that resulted in complete assemblies (no segment finder misses). Since the likelihood should not favor an assembly over its mirror image, we expanded the training set by adding the mirror image of each assembly, thus resulting in 386 configurations. The likelihood $L(\cdot)$ was defined as in Eqn. (1), where $d_i(\cdot)$ were the histograms (with 20 bins) for each of the 41 geometric features for the training set.

4.1. Test data

The test data included 145 *control images* with no people, and 228, 72, and 65 images with 1, 2, and 3 people, respectively. The control images came from the COREL database, while those with people were obtained by combining single-person images from the same collection as, but distinct from, the training data.

The sets of symmetries were produced for each test image. The parts of the control images differing significantly in color from people's skin (no more than 1/2 of each image) were blanked out before finding symmetries; no such preprocessing was done for images with people. The EM-based segment finder was applied to each set of symmetries by fitting 50 mixture components to each control image, 20 and 40 (on separate runs) to the 1-person images, and 40 and 60 to both 2- and 3-person images. The actual number of segments produced varied, due to splitting of segments with gaps. The resulting collections of segments were then used for testing.

To be able to find both straight (1 segment) and bent (2 segments) limbs, we added both halves (lengthwise) of each segment to the segment sets. The halves of a segment, however, could only appear either together in the same limb, or as the `torso`.

4.2. People vs No people

We used sampling and representative selection to count people, as in Sec. 3.2. For each image, we found the MAP subset $\{A_i | i \in G\}$ of representatives classified as people, and classify the image as containing a person if $|G| \geq 1$, and no people if $G = \emptyset$. Fig. 4(a) shows how the success of this classification depends on the value of c, from Eqn. (2).

4.3. Counting people

Similarly to the above, we used the size $|G|$ of the MAP set G as the estimate of the number of people. Fig. 4(b) shows, for images with $k = 0 \ldots 3$ people, the fraction of segment sets that yielded the correct estimate $|G| = k$.

The 3-person images did not yield as good results as those with fewer people. This could be due either to the fact that with more people in the image the segment finder is more likely to miss a body segment, or to our choice of

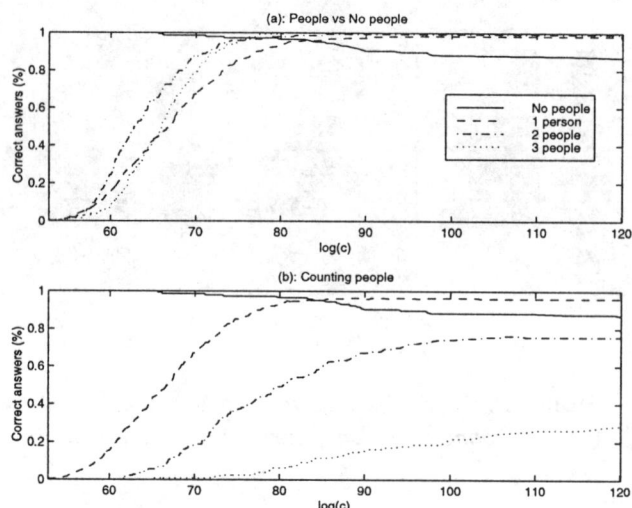

Figure 4. *Percentage of correct decisions for Person vs No person classification (a) and Counting (b), as a function of c. Each figure shows the percentages separately for images with 0,1,2, and 3 people*

representatives: it is possible that, while non-overlapping assemblies exist for each of the people in the image, the representatives do overlap, thus diminishing the people count. For many cases, the representatives give quite a good indication of the configuration of the people present (figure 6).

5. Discussion

The control set used in these results had been censored to remove regions of high texture and of a particular range of colours (censored regions in figure 5 are shown in white). This significantly reduces the number of segments reported. If one uses an uncensored control set, the program almost always finds one person because the number of available segments overwhelms the selectivity of our constraints. This suggests that segment finding is insufficient to segment people; other possible tests include using the characteristic contour shape of muscle or a more detailed shading test.

Seeing recognition as an inference problem has the advantage that top-down information flow can coexist with bottom up information flow quite reasonably. Often, the segments corresponding to one or more of a person's body parts are missing from the segment set of the image. This can be caused by either occlusion or a failure of the segment finder. For such *incomplete assemblies*, the likelihood $L(\cdot)$ is not available; nevertheless, we want to be able to find incomplete assemblies. Furthermore, having found one, we want to guess where the missing segments could be. Then, we could go back to the image and try and analyze the possi-

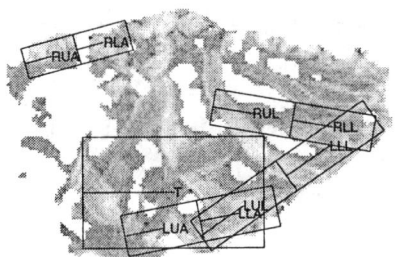

Figure 5. *A control image for which a human assembly was found*

bility of the occlusion, or re-run the segment finder, paying closer attention to the specified image regions, so as to find the missing segments. A method currently in development would solve the problem by first adding a large number of random "dummy segments" to the segment set, and then running our original sampling algorithm, limiting the number of dummy segments in an assembly. This would allow to obtain samples of incomplete assemblies from the corresponding marginal likelihoods, and those of missing segments (the dummy segments in assemblies) — from conditionals $\Pr[\text{missing segments}|A_{\text{inc}}]$, for each incomplete assembly A_{inc}.

Performance of our algorithm would be improved by a better likelihood model and by principled feature selection. Future work will involve incorporating the segment finder and the assembly builder in a single Markov Chain Monte-Carlo framework yielding a chain of probabilistic reasoning from pixel to person.

Acknowledgements

SI is supported by an NSF Graduate Fellowship. Thanks to Stuart Russell for pointing out the significance of MCMC as an inference technique.

References

[1] G. Agin. *Representation and description of curved objects.* PhD thesis, Stanford University, Stanford, CA, 1972.

[2] A. Blake and M. Isard. *Active Contours: The Application of Techniques from Graphics, Vision, Control Theory and Statistics to Visual Tracking of Shapes in Motion.* Springer Verlag, 1998.

[3] D. Forsyth, M. Fleck, and C. Bregler. Finding naked people. In *European Conference on Computer Vision*, 1996.

[4] W. Gilks, S. Richardson, and D. Spiegelhalter, editors. *Markov chain Monte Carlo in practice.* Chapman and Hall, 1996.

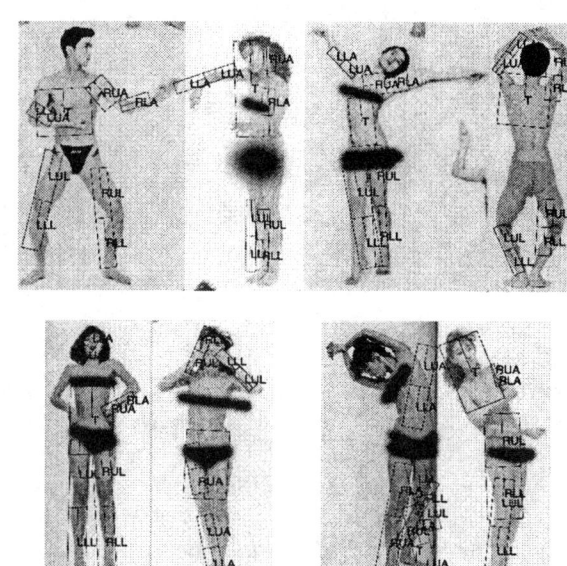

Figure 6. *Examples showing representatives for images with two people; these representatives give quite a good guide to the person's configuration (top row); the bottom row shows bad cases. Images have been airbrushed so they can be shown* salve pudore.

[5] W. Grimson and T. Lozano-Pérez. Model-based recognition and localization from sparse range or tactile data. *International Journal of Robotics Research*, 3(3), 1984.

[6] R. Nevatia and T. Binford. Description and recognition of complex curved objects. *Artificial Intelligence*, 8:77–98, 1977.

[7] M. Oren, C. Papageorgiou, P. Sinha, and E. Osuna. Pedestrian detection using wavelet templates. In *IEEE Conf. on Computer Vision and Pattern Recognition*, pages 193–9, 1997.

[8] J. O'Rourke and N. Badler. Model-based image analysis of human motion using constraint propagation. *IEEE T. Pattern Analysis and Machine Intelligence*, 2:522–546, 1980.

[9] T. Poggio and K.-K. Sung. Finding human faces with a gaussian mixture distribution-based face model. In *Asian Conf. on Computer Vision*, pages 435–440, 1995.

[10] H. Rowley, S. Baluja, and T. Kanade. Human face detection in visual scenes. In D. Touretzky, M. Mozer, and M. Hasselmo, editors, *Advances in Neural Information Processing 8*, pages 875–881, 1996.

[11] E. Shuppan. *Pose file*, volume 1-7. Books Nippan, 1993-1996. A collection of photographs of human models, annotated in Japanese.

Free-Form Surface Registration Using Surface Signatures

Sameh M. Yamany and Aly A. Farag

Computer Vision and Image Processing Lab, Electrical Engineering Dept.

University of Louisville, Louisville, KY 40292, USA

email: (yamany,farag)@cvip.uofl.edu

Abstract

This paper introduces a new free-form surface representation scheme for the purpose of fast and accurate registration and matching. Accurate registration of surfaces is a common task in computer vision. The proposed representation scheme captures the surface curvature information, seen from certain points and produces images, called surface signatures, at these points. Matching signatures of different surfaces enables the recovery of the transformation parameters between these surfaces. We propose to use template matching to compare the signature images. To enable partial matching, another criterion, the overlap ratio, is used. This representation scheme can be used as a global representation of the surface as well as a local one and performs near real-time registration. We show that the signature representation can be used to match objects in 3-D scenes in the presence of clutter and occlusion. Applications presented include free-form object matching, multimodal medical volumes registration and dental teeth reconstruction from intra-oral images.

I Introduction

The registration process is an integral part of computer and robot vision systems and still presents a topic of high interest in both fields. The importance of the registration problem in general comes from the fact that it is found in different applications including surface matching[1], 3-D medical imaging[2], [3], pose estimation[4], object recognition[5], [6], [7] and data fusion[8].

In order for any surface registration algorithm to perform accurately and efficiently, appropriate representation scheme for the surface is needed. Most of the surface representation schemes found in literature have adopted some form of shape parameterization especially for the purpose of object recognition. One benefit of the parametric representation is that the shape of the object is defined everywhere which enables high level tasks such as visualization, segmen-

This work was supported in part by grants from the NSF (ECS-9505674) and the DoD under contract: USNV N00014-97-11076.

tation and shape analysis to be performed. Moreover, such representation allows stable computation of geometric entities such as curvatures and normal directions. However, parametric representation are not suitable to present general shapes especially if the object is not of planar, cylindrical or toroidal topology. Free-form surfaces, in general, may not have simple volumetric shapes that can be expressed in terms of parametric primitives. Dorai and Jain[5] have defined a free-form surface to be *"a smooth surface, such that the surface normal is well defined and continuous almost everywhere, except at vertices, edges and cusps."* Discontinuities in the surface normal or curvature, and consequently in the surface depth, may be present anywhere in a free-form surface. Some representation schemes for free-form surfaces found in literature include the *splash* representation proposed by Stein and Medioni[9], the *point signature* by Chua and Jarvis[10] and *COSMOS* by Dorai and Jain[5]. Recently Johnson and Hebert[7] introduced the *spin image* representation. Their surface representation, comprises descriptive images associated with oriented points on the surface. Using a single point basis, the positions of the other points on the surface are described by two parameters. These parameters are accumulated for many points on the surface and result in an image at each oriented point which is invariant to rigid transformation.

This paper contributes in the development of a similar surface representation with the exception of using the curvature information rather than the point density to create the signature image. Furthermore, we apply a selection process to select feature points on the surface to be used in the matching process. This reduction process solves the long registration time reported in the literature, especially for large surfaces. Our technique starts by generating a signature image capturing the surface curvature information seen from each feature point. This image represents a signature of the surface at that point due to the fact that it is almost unique for each point location on the surface. Surface registration is then performed by matching signature images of different surfaces and hence finding corresponding points in each surface. For rigid registration, three point correspondences are enough to estimate the transformation parameters. This paper is organized as follows. The signature representation is described in section II. The points selection process is introduced in section III and the matching process in section IV. Results and discussions are given in section V and the paper concluded in section VI.

II Surface Signature Generation

Our approach for fast registration is to establish a "surface signature," for selected points on the surface, rather than just depending on the 3-D coordinates of the points. The idea of obtaining a "signature" at each surface point is not new [9], [10], [7]. The signature, computed at each point encodes the surface curvature seen from this point using all other points. This requires an accurate measure of the surface curvature at the point in focus.

For parametric curves or surfaces, curvature measures can be obtained using the *Frenet Frame* values for the case of a curve or the *Weingarten Map* for the case of surfaces[11]. This requires the calculation of curve or surface derivative which is a complex operation and may introduce computational errors to the representation scheme used. Moreover, such measures are hard to obtain for the case of unstructured free-form surfaces. Hebert[12] used a simplex angle to describe changes in a simplex mesh surface. We use the simplex angle to estimate the curvature value at points on a free-form surface.

A free-form surface, in its general form, is composed of unstructured triangular patches. There exists a dual form consisting of unstructured simplex mesh as shown in Fig. 1(a). A topological transformation is used to associate a k-simplex mesh to a k-triangulations or k-manifolds. This transformation works differently for vertices and edges located at the boundary of the triangulation from those located inside. The outcome of this transformation is a (k-p)-cell associated with a p-face of a k-triangulation [13]. In this work, a 2-simplex mesh form is considered in the curvature calculation. Let P be a vertex of a 2-simplex mesh and having three neighbors P_1, P_2, P_3. The three neighboring points define a plane with normal $\vec{U}_P$. They also lie on a circumscribe circle with radius r and the four points are circumscribed by a sphere with center O and radius R as shown in Fig. 1(b). The simplex angle θ shown in Fig. 1(c) is defined as [14]:

$$sin(\theta) = \frac{r}{R} sign(\vec{PP_1} \cdot \vec{U}_P) \qquad (1)$$

This definition is made with the assumption that the three neighbors are linearly independent, thus $r \neq 0$. The simplex angle is related to the mean curvature H

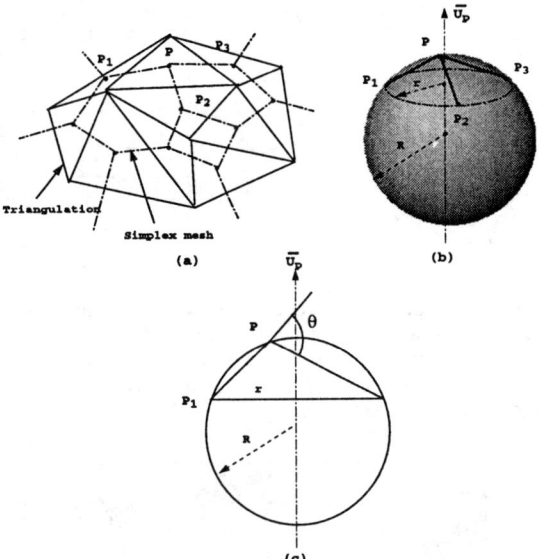

Fig. 1. (a) Duality between triangulation and simplex mesh. (b) The circumsphere of radius R that includes the four points. (c) Cross section of the sphere and the calculation of the simplex angle.

of the surface at the point P as follows:

$$H = \frac{sin(\theta)}{r} \qquad (2)$$

The idea is to use this curvature measure and create a reduced representation of the surface at certain points. This reduced representation encodes the curvature values at all other points and creates an image. This image is called a "signature image" for this point. This is because the change in curvature values with the distribution of all points forming the surface relative to the point in study is unique. This is not true for surfaces of revolution (SOR).

The signature image is generated as follows: As shown in Fig. 2, for each point P, defined by its 3-D coordinates and the normal $\vec{U}_P$, each other point P_i on the surface can be related to P by two parameters: (1) the distance $d_i = ||P - P_i||$ and (2) the angle $\alpha_i = cos^{-1}\left(\frac{\vec{U}_P \cdot (P - P_i)}{||P - P_i||}\right)$. This is a polar implementation of the signature image and it can be easily converted into cartesian form. Also we can notice that there is a missing degree of freedom in this representation which is the cylindrical angular parameter. This parameter depends on the surface orientation which defies the purpose of having an orientation independent representation scheme. The size of the image depends on the object size but for the sake of generalization, each object is normalized to its maximum

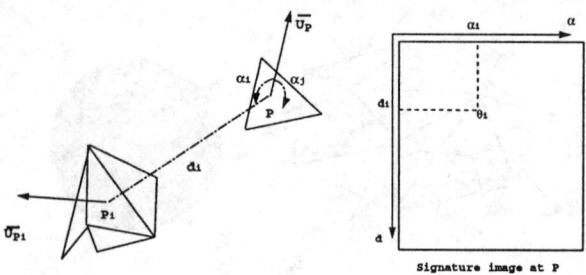

Fig. 2. For each point P we generate a signature image where the image axis are the distance d between P and each other point on the surface and the angle α between the normal at P, $\vec{U}_P$ and the vector from P to each other point. The image encodes the simplex angle θ.

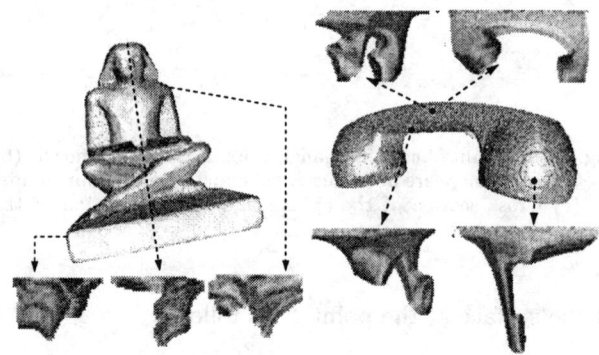

Fig. 3. Examples of signature images taken at different point locations. Notice how the image features the curvature information. The dark intensity in the image represents a high curvature seen from the point while the light intensity represents a low curvature.

length. At run-time matching, the scene-image is normalized to the maximum length of the object in study. At each location in the image the simplex angle θ_i is encoded. Ignoring the cylindrical angular degree results in the case where the same pixel in the image can represent more than one 3-D point on the surface. This usually occurs when the object have surfaces of revolution around the axis represented by the normal at the point P. These points have the same d_i and α_i and lie on the circle that has a radius $d_i cos(\alpha_i)$ and is distant by $d_i sin(\alpha_i)$ from the point P along the axis $\vec{U}_P$. The average of their simplex angles is encoded in the corresponding pixel location.

Figure 3 shows some signature images taken at different points on a statue and a phone handset. Each image uniquely defines the location of the point on the surface due to the encoded curvature information. In SOR, similar images can be obtained for different points. This can be expected as the registration of SOR objects is not unique and has infinite number of solutions.

TABLE I

A AT DIFFERENT λ, THEIR % FROM THE TOTAL M POINTS IN THE MODEL AND THE TIME TAKEN TO OBTAIN THEM ON AN SGI-O2

	statue	statue	speaker	speaker
λ	0.66	0.1	0.3	0.1
$|A|$	570	1200	280	1300
M	22541	22541	16150	16150
% $\frac{|A|}{M}$	3%	6%	2%	8%
Time	30sec	30sec	20sec	20sec

III Surface Points Selection

The concept of using special points for registration is not new. Thirion[2] used the same concept to register multimodal medical volumes, and he used "extremal" points on the volume edges (or ridges). Chua and Jarvis[10] used "seeds" points in their matching approach. Stein and Medioni[9] used only highly structured regions in their approach.

In many real life objects, the majority of points forming the surface are of low curvature value. These points are reduntant and do not serve as landmarks of the object. In this work, points of low curvature are eleminated and signature images are only generated for the set of remaing points. A test is also performed to eleminate spike points that have considerable higher curvature than its neighbors. These points are considered as noise.

The simplex angle is used as a criterion to reduce the surface points and use only a subset $A \subset S$ in the registration process, where S is the set of the simplex mesh points. The subset A is defined with respect to a threshold λ such that A contains the landmark regions of the surface.

$$A = \{P_i \in S|\ |sin(\theta_i)| \geq \lambda, \lambda \geq 0\} \quad (3)$$

Figure 4 shows two examples of objects and their scanned models. Figure 5 shows the reduced set of points A obtained for each model using different λ and table I summarizes the values obtained. With low threshold values, more details about the object model are considered with considerable reduction in the set cardinality. Even with higher threshold values, most of the landmarks of the object are still present in the set A.

There are two cases, however, where the above analysis will fail. The first is when the surface is a plane or is a piece-wise defined surface (e.g. a cube). In this case for any $\lambda > 0$ the set A will be empty. This can be deduced from Fig. 1(c) when P falls in the plane formed by its neighbors. In this case there exists no

Fig. 4. (Top) Two examples of real objects, a statue and a speaker. (Bottom) Rendered views of the scanned 3-D model of the objects. The statue 3-D model consists of 22541 patches and the speaker 3-D model consists of 16150 patches.

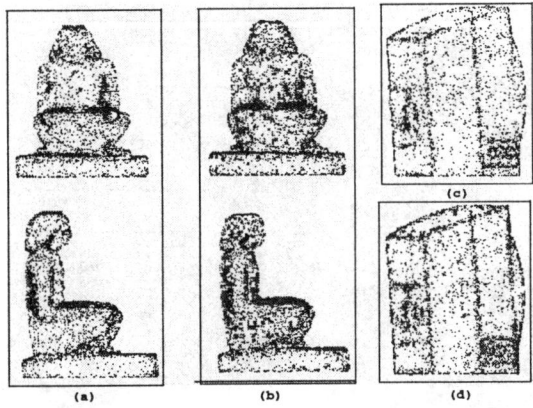

Fig. 5. The reduced set of points obtained for the statue and speaker models using (a) $\lambda = 0.66$, (b) $\lambda = 0.1$, (c) $\lambda = 0.3$ and (d) $\lambda = 0.1$.

sphere circumscribing the four points (i.e. $R = \infty$), thus $H = 0$. The second case is when the surface is part of a spherical, cylindrical or toroidal shape. In this case the curvature measure will be constant over the surface. Fortunalty, in either cases, these surfaces can be easily parameterized and the transformation parameters can be analytically recovered.

IV Signature Matching

The next step in the registration process is to match corresponding signature images of two surfaces/objects or between a 3-D scene and objects in a library. The ultimate goal of the matching process is to find at least three points correspondence to be able to calculate the transformation parameters. The benefit of using the signature images to find the correspondence is the use of image processing tools in the

matching, hence reducing the time taken to find accurate transformation. The developed matching engine should be simple based on the fact that the signature images of corresponding points should be identical in their content. Yet, due to the fact that 3-D scanning sensors are noisy in nature and that the 3-D scene may contain clutter or suffer from partial occlusion, a robust matching criteria is needed. One such criteria is *template matching* in which a measure defines how well a portion of an image matched a template. Let $g(i,j)$ be one of our scene signature images and $t(i,j)$ one of the library object (or original surface) signature templates and let D be the domain of definition of the template. Then a measure of how well a portion of the scene image matches the template can be defined as [15]:

$$M(m,n) = \sum_{(j,\ i),(i-m,j-n)\in D} |g(i,j) - t(i-m,j-n)|. \quad (4)$$

For surface signature matching, translation is not needed as the corresponding signature images have the same origin point at $(0,0)$ which means that only $M(0,0)$ is calculated. Another more discriminating measure, based on the standard Euclidean distance, can be:

$$E_n^2 = \frac{1}{N_D^2} \sum_{(j,\ i)\in D} \sum |g(i,j) - t(i,j)|^2. \quad (5)$$

where N_D is the total number of pixels in the domain D. The domain D is defined over the template size. To enable partial matching, the matching measure is augmented by adding the overlap ratio $O = \frac{D_o}{D}$, where D_o is the domain of the overlapping pixels. Figure 6 shows an example of two objects with known transformation parameters and another example where almost half of the object is missing. Table II shows that reducing the size of the signature image leads to a decrease in the number of correct points correspondence which means that more points are needed. Yet, the reduction in time with the smaller size is more suitable for real-time applications. It should be noticed that more reduction in the signature image size may lead to incorrect matching due to the averaging process. The end result of the matching process is a list of groups of likely three point correspondences that satisfy the geometric consistency constraint. The list is sorted such that correspondences that are far apart are at the top of the list. A rigid transformation is calculated for each group of correspondences and the verification is performed using a modified ICP technique[16]. Groups are ranked according to their verification scores, and the best group is refined using the modified ICP technique.

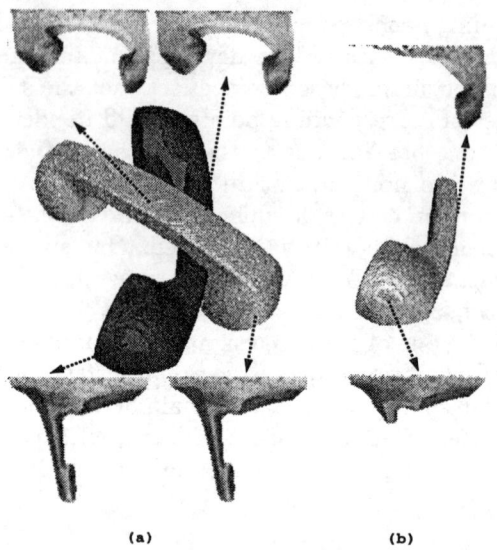

(a) (b)

Fig. 6. (a) case 1: Two telephone handsets with known transformation parameters. Notice how similar are the corresponding signature images. (b) case 2: Part of a telephone handset, almost 50% of the original model, and example of the corresponding signature images. Partial matching is needed to establish the correspondence.

TABLE II

COMPARISON IN MATCHING FOR DIFFERENT SIGNATURE IMAGE SIZES

	case 1		case 2	
$A_1 X A_2$	147X147		147X70	
image size	128X128	64X64	128X128	64X64
# of Correct matching	67	40	38	30
Reg. time	54sec	24sec	30sec	10sec

V Results and Discussions

We used the signature implementation in three applications. The first is object registration, an example of which is shown in Fig. 7 where two differently scanned objects are matched together. The signature registration was successful in recovering the transformation parameters. Also the signature representation was used in matching objects in a 3-D scene with their corresponding models in a library. The proximity of the objects in the scene creates large amounts of clutter and occlusion. These contribute to extra and/or missing parts in the signature images. Using the signature polar representation, the effect of clutter, for many points, is only found in the third and/or fourth quadrant of the image as shown in Fig. 8. Examples of such application is shown in Fig. 9. Using the signature matching criterion, all of the models in the scene are simultaneously matched and localized in their correct scene positions. The models in the library and

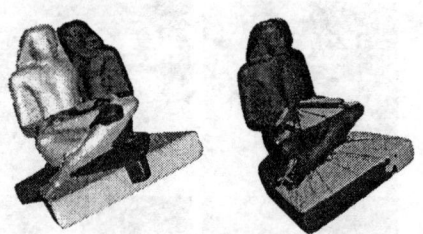

Fig. 7. The signature matching enabled fast recovery of the transformation parameter between these two models.

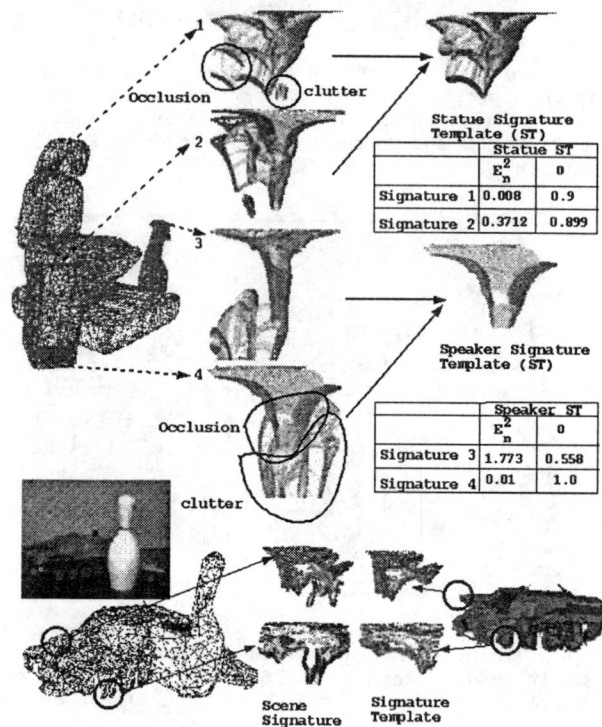

Statue Signature Template (ST)		
	Statue ST	
	E_n^2	0
Signature 1	0.008	0.9
Signature 2	0.3712	0.899

Speaker Signature Template (ST)		
	Speaker ST	
	E_n^2	0
Signature 3	1.773	0.558
Signature 4	0.01	1.0

Fig. 8. Illustration of the effect of scene clutter and occlusion on the signature matching.

the 3-D scenes are scanned using a Cyberware 3030 laser scanner with a resolution of 1mm. Some models (e.g. the duck, bell and cup) were obtained from a CAD/CAM library. Table III shows the time needed to match objects in a scene using their signature templates. We compared the performance of our approach with the ICP and the spin image approaches. For the case of matching the statue object, it took 650 seconds using the ICP and 415 seconds using the spin image. Applying the feature points selection process with the spin image, it took 120 seconds to match the object. This is due to the fact that we needed more feature points to match the spin image compared to the points needed to match the signature image.

Fig. 9. Examples of using the signature representation in object matching. A library of 10 objects is used. Some of these objects were scanned using a Cyberware 3030 laser scanner with a resolution of 1mm. Others are obtained from CAD libraries.

TABLE III

APPROX. MATCHING TIME IN RECOGNITION ON AN SGI-O2

model	# points	matching time (sec.)
Statue	22541	102
Speaker	16150	87
Bottle	15303	80
Duck	3807	30
Cup	7494	40
Bell	22800	80
Dino	35571	130
Tiger	21606	73
Tank	8619	48
Pin	2110	21

The second application is multimodal medical image registration as shown in Fig. 10(a). The dark surface represents the skin model reconstructed from the MR data and the light surface represents the skin model obtained from the CT. These models where obtained using a deformable contour algorithm that finds the outer contour in each slice and reconstructs a 3D mesh by connecting these contours. As the skin is modeled differently in the two image modalities, surface registration will only produce an initial registration. Other techniques like maximizing the mutual information (MI) [17] can be used to enhance the result. The registration using signature and MI was much faster than using MI alone [18]. The third application, shown in Fig. 10(b), is in the dental teeth reconsturction[19], [20]. The overall purpose of this system is to develop a model-based vision system for orthodontics to replace traditional approaches that can be used in diagnosis, treatment planning, surgical simulation and for implant purposes. Image acquisition is obtained using intra-oral video camera and range data are obtained using a 3D digitizer arm. A shape from shading technique is then applied to the intra-oral images. The required accurate orthodontic measurements cannot be deduced from the resulting shape, hence the need of some reference range data to be integrated with the shape from shading results. An neural network fusion algorithm[21] is used to integrate the shape from shading results and the range data. The output of the integration algorithm to each teeth segment image is a description of the teeth surface in this segment. The registration technique is then performed to register the surfaces from different views together.

VI Conclusions

This paper proposed a new surface representation of free-form surfaces and objects. The proposed representation reduces the complexity of the registration and matching problems from the 3-D space into the 2-D image space. This was done by capturing the surface

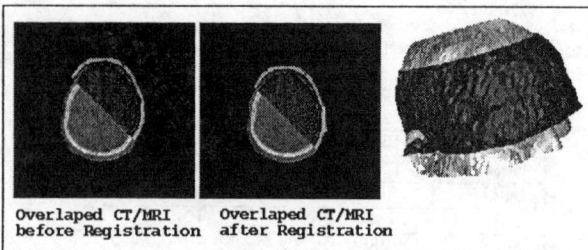

Overlaped CT/MRI before Registration   Overlaped CT/MRI after Registration

(a) Multimodal Volume Registration

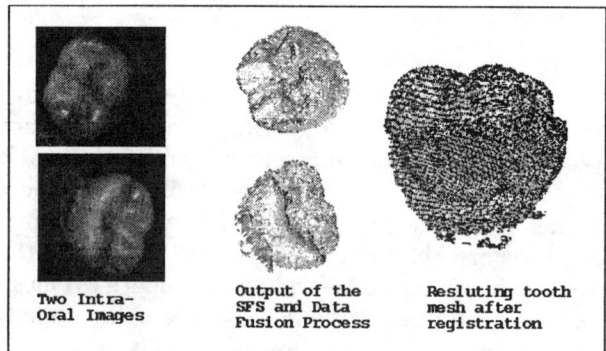

Two Intra-Oral Images   Output of the SFS and Data Fusion Process   Resluting tooth mesh after registration

(b) Registration in Dental Application

Fig. 10. Application of the signature representation for (a) Mutlimodal medical volume registration and (b) teeth reconstruction from intra-oral images

curvature information seen from feature points on the surface and encoding it into a signature image. Registration and matching were performed by matching corresponding signature images. The signature images were only generated for selected feature points. The results show a reduction in the registration and matching time compared to other known techniques, a major requirement for real-time applications. Applications included free-form object matching, multimodal medical volumes registration and dental teeth reconstruction from intra-oral images. Currently, we are exploiting the use of the signature representation in scale independent object matching. Regions of same curvature can be detected and segmented in the signature image and scale can be recovered by observing the inter-relationship between segmented curvature regions in different signature images. Future research includes studying the effect of shape deformation on the signature representation and modeling the change in the signature image with a deformation model. This will enable the signature representation to be used in non-rigid registration.

References

[1]   Z. Zhang, "Iterative point matching for registration of free-form curves and surfaces," *International Journal of Computer Vision* **13**(2), pp. 119–152, 1994.

[2]   J.-P. Thirion, "Extremal points: Definition and application to 3d image registration," *IEEE conf on Computer Vision and Pattern Recognition* , 1994. Seatle.

[3]   A. Gueziec and N. Ayache, "Smoothing and matching of 3-d space curves," *International Journal of Computer Vision* **12**(1), pp. 79–104, 1994.

[4]   S. Lavallee and R. Szeliski, "Recovering the position and orientation of free-form objects from image contours using 3d distance maps," *IEEE Transactions on Pattern Analysis and Machine Intelligence* **17**, pp. 378–390, April 1995.

[5]   C. Dorai and A. K. Jain, "Cosmos-a representation scheme for 3d free-form objects," *IEEE Transactions on Pattern Analysis and Machine Intelligence* **19**, pp. 1115–1130, October 1997.

[6]   C. S. Chua and R. Jarvis, "3d free-form surface registration and object recognition," *International Journal of Computer Vision* **17**, pp. 77–99, 1996.

[7]   A. Johnson and M. Hebert, "Surface matching for object recognition in complex three-dimensional scenes," *Image and Vision Computing* **16**, pp. 635–651, 1998.

[8]   R. Bergevin, D. Laurendeau, and D. Poussart, "Registering range views of multipart objects," *Computer Vision and Image Understanding* **61**, pp. 1–16, January 1995.

[9]   F. Stein and G. Medioni, "Structural indexing: Efficient 3-d object recognition," *IEEE Trans. Patt. Anal. Machine Intell.* **14**(2), pp. 125–145, 1992.

[10]   C. S. Chua and R. Jarvis, "Point signatures: A new representation for 3d object recognition," *Internation Journal of Computer Vision* **25**(1), pp. 63–85, 1997.

[11]   J. Opera, *Differential Geometry and its Applications*, Prentice Hall, 1997.

[12]   M. Hebert, K. Ikeuchi, and H. Delingette, "A spherical representation for recognition of free-form surfaces," *IEEE Trans. Patt. Anal. Machine Intell.* **17**(7), p. 681, 1995.

[13]   H. Delingette, "Simplex meshes: a general representation for 3d shape reconstruction," Tech. Rep. 2214, Unite de recherche INRIA Sophia-Antipolis, 2004 route des Luciols, BP93,06902 Sophia-Antipolis Cedex (France), Mars 1994.

[14]   H. Delingette, M. Hebert, and K. Ikeuchi, "Shape representation and image segmentation using deformable surfaces," *Image and Vision Computing* **10**, pp. 132–144, April 1992.

[15]   R. O. Duda and P. E. Hart, *Pattern Classification and Scene Analysis*, John Wiley and Sons, 1973.

[16]   S. M. Yamany, M. N. Ahmed, and A. A. Farag, "A new genetic-based technique for matching 3d curves and surfaces," *Pattern Recognition* **32**(10), p. 1817, 1999.

[17]   W. M. Wells, P. Viola, H. Atsumi, S. Nakajima, and R. Kikinis, "Multi-modal volume registration by maximization of mutual information," *Medical Image Analysis* **1**, pp. 35–54, March 1996.

[18]   A. Eldeib, S. M. Yamany, and A. A. Farag, "Multimodal medical volumes fusion by surface matching," *2nd International Conference on Medical Image Computing and Computer-Assisted Intervention (MICCAI'99)*, Cambridge, England , Sept 1999.

[19]   M. Ahmed, S. M. Yamany, E. E. Hemayed, S. Roberts, S. Ahmed, and A. A. Farag, "3d reconstruction of the human jaw from a sequence of images," *Proc. IEEE Comp. Vis. and Patt. Recog. (CVPR), Puerto Rico* , pp. 646–653, 1997.

[20]   S. M. Yamany, A. A. Farag, D. Tazman, and A. G. Farman, "A robust 3-d reconstruction system for human jaw modeling," *2nd International Conference on Medical Image Computing and Computer-Assisted Intervention (MICCAI'99), Cambridge, England* , Sept 1999.

[21]   M. G.-H. Mostafa, S. M. Yamany, and A. A. Farag, "Integrating shape from shading and range data using neural networks," *Proc. IEEE Int. Conf. Comp. Visi. Patt. Recog. (CVPR)* , June 1999. Fort Collins, Colorado.

A Bidirectional Matching Algorithm for Deformable Pattern Detection with Application to Handwritten Word Retrieval

Kwok-Wai Cheung, Dit-Yan Yeung and Roland T. Chin
Department of Computer Science
The Hong Kong University of Science and Technology
Clear Water Bay, Hong Kong
Tel: +852-23588771 Fax: +852-23581477
{william, dyyeung, roland}@cs.ust.hk

Abstract

A Bayesian framework for deformable pattern classification has been proposed in [1] with promising results for isolated handwritten character recognition. Its performance, however, degrades significantly when it is applied to detect deformable patterns in complex scenes, where the amount of outliers due to other neighboring objects or the background is usually large. Also, the fact that the associated evidence measure does not penalize models resting on white space results in a high false alarm rate. In this paper, another Bayesian framework for deformable pattern detection is proposed. The framework possesses the intrinsic property of matching with only part of an image (segmentation) and its associated evidence measure can penalize white space implicitly. However, limited data exploration capability is the major trade-off. By properly combining the two frameworks, a new matching algorithm called bidirectional matching is proposed. This combined approach possesses the advantages of the two frameworks and gives robust results for non-rigid shape extraction. To evaluate the performance of the proposed approach, we have applied it to shape-based handwritten word retrieval. Using a subset of the bb dataset in the CEDAR database, we can achieve a recall rate of 59% and a precision rate of 43%.

1. Introduction

An important advantage of model-based object recognition is its potential to achieve integrated segmentation and recognition in complex scenes. If the object of interest is non-rigid, the corresponding shape model is required to be deformable for more flexible matching. This leads to the need for distinguishing between the *inlier* data, which is important for controlling model deformation, and the *outlier* data, which should be suppressed because of the distraction

it causes to the model. For example, to extract a character from a handwritten word, the outliers may appear in the form of stroke anomalies, closely cluttered characters or the printed background.

The Bayesian framework proposed in [1] for deformable matching, though with promising results for isolated handwritten character recognition, does suffer from the outlier problem mentioned above. Besides, it has been pointed out that the evidence used for classification in the adopted framework does not penalize models resting on white space, which in turn leads to a high false alarm rate. These two intrinsic deficiencies have been addressed in [4], where the proposed solution for the outlier problem is to adopt a uniform noise model, which unfortunately has not been rigorously tested.[1] For the white space problem, the proposed solution in [4] is to model also the pixels of the white space, which as discussed in [4], will be too computationally expensive. In this paper, a new Bayesian framework for deformable pattern detection is proposed, which, when compared with the framework proposed in [1], is proved to have the nice implicit properties of a) localizing a model to match with only part of an image and b) penalizing white space. However, limited data exploration capability is the major trade-off. By combining the two frameworks in a way similar to the "forward-backward" idea of Hausdorff matching, we propose a new deformable matching algorithm called *bidirectional matching*. It possesses the advantages of the two Bayesian frameworks while its computational complexity is still of the same order as the two individual frameworks. To evaluate the effectiveness of the proposed bidirectional matching algorithm, we have applied it to the retrieval of handwritten word images based on input shape queries, using the *bb* dataset of the CEDAR database containing handwritten city name images as the test set.

---

[1]Our preliminary experimental results show that the noise modelling approach deteriorates quickly as the amount of outliers increases.

2. Bayesian Frameworks for Deformable Pattern Recognition

2.1. A Dual View of Generativity

In [4], there are some discussions about the perspective of generative models, on which the Bayesian framework for deformable pattern classification proposed in [1] is based. To summarize, an important assumption of the framework is that the input data (including both the inliers and outliers) is generated from the shape model. While lacking a good probabilistic model for the outliers, it is almost impossible for the shape model to generate back some data resembling its shape together with the outliers.

However, the roles of the model and the data can be interchanged and we then assume that the model shape is "generated" from the data. The question of interest now becomes whether the model can be generated from the data, or in order words, whether the model can be *detected* in the data. An input dataset, with an instance of the model embedded in it, normally contains a subset which resembles the model shape (except for the occlusion cases) and this makes the generation process possible. This changes the underlying assumption of the Bayesian framework proposed in [1] and suggests a new Bayesian framework for deformable pattern detection, which will be described in the rest of this section.

2.2. Analogy with the Forward and Reverse Distances in Hausdorff Matching

To cite from [5]: *"The Hausdorff distance is actually composed of two asymmetric distances: the forward distance, which is the distance from the model to the image, the reverse distance, the distance from the image to the model. The forward distance is small when every point in the model is close to some point in the image, and the reverse distance is small when every point in the image is close to some point in the model."* (cf. Helmholtz machine by Dayan *et al.* [3]).

From the above citation, one could see that the notion of model generating data is analogous to that of the reverse distance, while the notion of data generating model is analogous to that of the forward distance. Due to their similarity and for the sake of subsequent discussions, we denote the framework proposed in [1], which is restated here again for completeness, as the *reverse framework* while the newly proposed framework, to be described in the following section, as the *forward framework*.

2.3. Reverse Framework

Let H_i denote the shape model of the i-th character class, $\mathbf{D}$ the input image, $\mathbf{w}$ the model parameter vector describing character shape, α the regularization parameter, and β

the character stroke width. The parameters α and β are referred to as hyperparameters. Assuming equal prior probabilities for different character classes, the classified output is computed by finding the i-th class that maximizes $p(\mathbf{D}|H_i)$, which is approximated in [1] as

$$Pr(\mathbf{D}|H_i) \propto$$
$$\frac{p(\mathbf{D}|\mathbf{w}, \beta^*, H_i)p(\mathbf{w}|\alpha^*, H_i)}{p(\mathbf{w}|\mathbf{D}, \alpha^*, \beta^*, H_i)} p(\alpha^*, \beta^*|H_i) \Delta \log \alpha \Delta \log \beta \quad (1)$$

where $p(\mathbf{w}|\alpha, H_i)$ is the prior parameter distribution, $p(\mathbf{D}|\mathbf{w}, \beta, H_i)$ the likelihood function, $p(\mathbf{w}|\mathbf{D}, \alpha, \beta, H_i)$ the posterior parameter distribution given the data $\mathbf{D}$ and $\Delta \log \alpha$ and $\Delta \log \beta$ are the *effective* ranges of α and β, respectively. Parameters with the superscript "*" denote their MAP estimates.

2.3.1 Representation and Criterion Formulation

Handwritten digits are represented as cubic B-splines, each of which is parameterized by a small set of k control points $\mathbf{w}$ and affine transform parameters $\{\mathbf{A}, \mathbf{T}\}$. The distribution of the black pixels is represented by a mixture of Gaussians. The prior parameter distribution and the likelihood function are defined by two criterion functions - model deformation E_w and data mismatch E_D, respectively. They are given as

$$E_w(\mathbf{w}) = \frac{1}{2}(\mathbf{w} - \mathbf{h})^t \Sigma^{-1}(\mathbf{w} - \mathbf{h}) \quad (2)$$

$$p(\mathbf{w}|\alpha, H_i) = \frac{1}{Z_w(\alpha)} \exp(-\alpha E_w(\mathbf{w})) \quad (3)$$

$$E_D(\mathbf{w}, \mathbf{A}, \mathbf{T}; \mathbf{D}) =$$
$$-\sum_{l=1}^{N} \log \left[\frac{1}{N_g} \sum_{j=1}^{N_g} \exp \left(-\beta \frac{\|\mathbf{m}_j(\mathbf{w}, \mathbf{A}, \mathbf{T}) - \mathbf{y}_l\|^2}{2} \right) \right] \quad (4)$$

$$p(\mathbf{D}|\mathbf{w}, \mathbf{A}, \mathbf{T}, \beta, H_i) = \frac{1}{Z_D(\beta)} \exp(-E_D(\mathbf{w}, \mathbf{A}, \mathbf{T}; \mathbf{D})) \quad (5)$$

where $Z_w(\alpha) = \left(\frac{2\pi}{\alpha}\right)^k |\Sigma|^{1/2}$, $Z_D(\beta) = \left(\frac{2\pi}{\beta}\right)^N$, $\mathbf{h}$ is the mean control point, Σ is the covariance matrix of $\mathbf{w}$, $\mathbf{S}_j$ is a matrix containing cubic B-spline coefficients, $\mathcal{A}$ and $\mathcal{T}$ composed of $\mathbf{A}$ submatrices and $\mathbf{T}$ subvectors respectively, $\mathbf{m}_j(\mathbf{w}, \mathbf{A}, \mathbf{T}) = \mathbf{S}_j^t(\mathcal{A}\mathbf{w} + \mathcal{T})$ is the mean of the j-th Gaussian, N is the number of black pixels, N_g is the number of Gaussians along the spline, α is the regularization parameter, β is the inverse of the Gaussians' variance for modeling the character stroke width, $\mathbf{y}_l$ is the location vector of an individual black pixel and $\mathbf{D}$ denotes the set $\{\mathbf{y}_l | 1 \le l \le N\}$.

2.3.2 Matching

The matching is done by maximum a posteriori (MAP) estimation of $\{\mathbf{w}, \mathbf{A}, \mathbf{T}\}$, where the posterior distribution $p(\mathbf{w}, \mathbf{A}, \mathbf{T}|\mathbf{D}, \alpha, \beta, H_i)$ is defined as

$$p(\mathbf{w}, \mathbf{A}, \mathbf{T}|\mathbf{D}, \alpha, \beta, H_i) = \frac{1}{Z_M} \exp(-E_M(\mathbf{w}, \mathbf{A}, \mathbf{T}; \mathbf{D})) \quad (6)$$

where $E_M(\mathbf{w}, \mathbf{A}, \mathbf{T}; \mathbf{D}) = \alpha E_w(\mathbf{w}) + E_D(\mathbf{w}, \mathbf{A}, \mathbf{T}; \mathbf{D})$ and Z_M is the corresponding partition function. The expectation-maximization (EM) algorithm is used where an h-function is typically involved and is here defined as

$$h_j^l(\hat{\mathbf{w}}_n, \hat{\mathbf{A}}_n, \hat{\mathbf{T}}_n; \mathbf{y}_l) = \frac{\exp(-\beta \frac{\|\mathbf{m}_j(\hat{\mathbf{w}}_n)-\mathbf{y}_l\|^2}{2})}{\sum_p \exp(-\beta \frac{\|\mathbf{m}_p(\hat{\mathbf{w}}_n)-\mathbf{y}_l\|^2}{2})} \quad (7)$$

where $\hat{\mathbf{w}}_n$ and $\{\hat{\mathbf{A}}_n, \hat{\mathbf{T}}_n\}$ are the estimates of the control point vector and the affine transform obtained in the n-th EM iteration. The MAP estimates of α and β are also computed after each EM iteration using the formula given as,

$$\alpha^* = \frac{\gamma}{2E_w(\mathbf{w}^*)} \quad \beta^* = \frac{2N-\gamma}{2E_D'(\mathbf{w}^*, \mathbf{A}^*, \mathbf{T}^*; \hat{\mathbf{w}}, \hat{\mathbf{A}}, \hat{\mathbf{T}}, \mathbf{D})} \quad (8)$$

where γ can be intrepreted as the effective numbers of parameters and E_D' is derived from E_D in the E-step of the EM algorithm. Readers are referred to [1] for more details.

2.3.3 Classification

Referring to EQ.(1), the classification step is based on $p(\mathbf{D}|H_i)$, which requires the matching results together with the effective ranges of α and β, given by

$$\Delta \log \alpha = \sqrt{2/\gamma} \quad \Delta \log \beta = \sqrt{2/(2N-\gamma)}. \quad (9)$$

2.4. Forward Framework

Let H denote a shape model to be detected, $\mathcal{D}$ a set of images, and $\mathbf{D}_i$ the i-th image in $\mathcal{D}$. Given $\mathbf{D}_i$, a shape model H is said to be detected in it when $Pr(H|\mathbf{D}_i) > \phi$ where ϕ is a threshold parameter.

Expanding $Pr(H|\mathbf{D}_i)$ according to the Bayes rule and assuming that $\mathbf{w}$ is independent of α when $\mathbf{D}_i$ is given,[2] it gives

$$Pr(H|\mathbf{D}_i)$$
$$= \int Pr(H|\alpha, \beta, \mathbf{D}_i)p(\alpha, \beta|\mathbf{D}_i)d\alpha d\beta \quad (10)$$
$$= \int Pr(H|\alpha, \beta, \mathbf{w}, \mathbf{D}_i)p(\mathbf{w}|\beta, \mathbf{D}_i)d\mathbf{w} \; p(\alpha, \beta|\mathbf{D}_i)d\alpha d\beta.$$

We further assume that H is independent of $\mathbf{D}_i$ and β when $\mathbf{w}$ is given and $Pr(H|\mathbf{D}_i)$ becomes

$$Pr(H|\mathbf{D}_i) =$$
$$\int \frac{p(\mathbf{w}|\alpha, H)Pr(H|\alpha)}{p(\mathbf{w}|\alpha)} p(\mathbf{w}|\beta, \mathbf{D}_i) \; d\mathbf{w} p(\alpha, \beta|\mathbf{D}_i)d\alpha d\beta. (11)$$

Assuming that $Pr(H|\alpha)$ and $p(\mathbf{w}|\alpha)$ are constants and applying Laplacian approximation, $Pr(H|\mathbf{D}_i)$ becomes

$$Pr(H|\mathbf{D}_i) \propto$$
$$p(\mathbf{w}^*|\alpha^*, H)p(\mathbf{w}^*|\beta^*, \mathbf{D}_i)p(\alpha^*, \beta^*|\mathbf{D}_i)$$
$$\Delta \mathbf{w} \Delta \log \alpha \Delta \log \beta. \quad (12)$$

If we compare EQ.(12) of this forward framework with EQ.(1) of the reverse framework, it can be noted that the first factor, $p(\mathbf{w}^*|\alpha^*, H)$, is the prior distribution of $\mathbf{w}$ and remains unchanged. The second factor, $p(\mathbf{w}^*|\beta^*, \mathbf{D}_i)$, is now the probability distribution of the model parameters given the data, instead of the probability distribution of the data given the model parameters.

2.4.1 A New Mismatch Criterion

The mismatch criterion for the reverse framework is called a *data* mismatch criterion which measures the discrepancy of *all* the data from the model. To impose the data-generating-model notion, we define a new criterion for the forward framework called *sub-data* mismatch criterion E_{D_s}, defined as

$$E_{D_s}(\mathbf{w}, \mathbf{A}, \mathbf{T}; \beta, \mathbf{D}_i) =$$
$$-\sum_{j=1}^{N_g} \log \left[\frac{1}{N} \sum_{l=1}^{N} \exp \left(-\beta \frac{\|\mathbf{m}_j(\mathbf{w}, \mathbf{A}, \mathbf{T}) - \mathbf{y}_l\|^2}{2} \right) \right] \quad (13)$$

and we define

$$p(\mathbf{w}, \mathbf{A}, \mathbf{T}|\beta, \mathbf{D}_i) = \frac{1}{Z_{D_s}(\beta)} \exp(-E_{D_s}(\mathbf{w}, \mathbf{A}, \mathbf{T}; \mathbf{D}_i)) \quad (14)$$

where $Z_{D_s}(\beta) = \left(\frac{2\pi}{\beta} \right)^{N_g}$. According to EQ.(13) and EQ.(14), each point $\mathbf{m}_j$ along the spline is modeled by a uniformly weighted mixture of Gaussians with their means being the data $\mathbf{D}_i$. This coheres with the data-generating-model assumption. In the new definition, however, we lose the interpretation that β is related to the character stroke width as in [1]. Instead, it is related to the size of the localized search region to be controlled for each model point to explore.

3. Implementation Differences between the Forward and Reverse Frameworks

3.1. Matching

3.1.1 Estimation of Shape Parameters

The optimal shape parameters $\{\mathbf{w}^*, \mathbf{A}^*, T^*\}$ are estimated by maximizing $p(\mathbf{w}, \mathbf{A}, \mathbf{T} | \alpha, \beta, \mathbf{D}_i, H)$, which is equivalent to minimizing $\alpha E_w(\mathbf{w}) + E_{D_s}(\mathbf{w}, \mathbf{A}, \mathbf{T}; \beta, \mathbf{D}_i)$. The EM algorithm can be used again for the maximization problem, with just the h-function modified as follows

$$h_j^l(\hat{\mathbf{w}}_n, \hat{\mathbf{A}}_n, \hat{\mathbf{T}}_n; y_l) = \frac{\exp(-\beta \frac{\|\mathbf{m}_j(\hat{\mathbf{w}}_n) - \mathbf{y}_l\|^2}{2})}{\sum_{p=1}^N \exp(-\beta \frac{\|\mathbf{m}_j(\hat{\mathbf{w}}_n) - \mathbf{y}_p\|^2}{2})}. \quad (15)$$

3.1.2 Estimation of Hyperparameters

The optimal hyperparameters, according to EQ.(10), are estimated by maximizing $Pr(H | \alpha, \beta, \mathbf{D}_i) p(\alpha, \beta | \mathbf{D}_i)$ with respect to α and β. To derive the updating formula for α and β, assuming $p(\alpha, \beta | \mathbf{D}_i)$ to be constant, we can further expand $Pr(H | \alpha, \beta, \mathbf{D}_i)$ as

$$Pr(H | \alpha, \beta, \mathbf{D}_i) \propto$$
$$p(\mathbf{w}^* | \alpha, H) p(\mathbf{w}^*, \mathbf{A}^*, \mathbf{T}^* | \beta, \mathbf{D}_i) \Delta \mathbf{w}. \quad (16)$$

When compared with EQ.(8) of the reverse framework, the updating formula for α is unchanged but that for β has to be modified as

$$\beta^* = \frac{2N_g - \gamma}{2E'_{D_s}(\mathbf{w}^*, \mathbf{A}^*, \mathbf{T}^*; \hat{\mathbf{w}}, \hat{\mathbf{A}}, \hat{\mathbf{T}}, \mathbf{D}_i)}. \quad (17)$$

3.2. Detection

A shape model H is considered to be detected in the input data $\mathbf{D}_i$ if $Pr(H | \mathbf{D}_i)$ (which will later be referred to as the *evidence* of the forward framework) is found to be greater than a threshold ϕ. The value of $Pr(H | \mathbf{D}_i)$ can be computed by substituting the prior distribution of $\mathbf{w}$ of the reverse framework together with the new sub-data mismatch criteria (given by EQ.(13)) into EQ.(12). Also, the computation of $\Delta \mathbf{w}$ and $\Delta \log \alpha$ remains the same as that in the reverse framework, while that of $\Delta \log \beta$ is modified as

$$\Delta \log \beta = \sqrt{2/(2N_g - \gamma)}. \quad (18)$$

4. Comparison of the Two Frameworks

For the sake of further discussions, the matching processes of the reverse and forward frameworks are referred to as *reverse matching* and *forward matching* respectively.

Similarly, the evidences of the two frameworks are referred to as *reverse* and *forward evidences*. It can be theoretically shown that both frameworks have their own strengths and shortcomings [2]. Due to the page limit, we only summarize and discuss the result of the analysis.

4.1. Shape Discriminating Properties

Considering the shape discriminating properties of the two frameworks, it can be shown that:

Proposition 1 *The reverse evidence does not penalize models resting on white space.*

Proposition 2 *The forward evidence does penalize models resting on white space.*

These two properties provide a better understanding of the relationship between the two evidences and the reverse and forward distances in Hausdorff matching. The reverse distance is small when every point in the image is close to some point in the model, i.e., white space is allowed for the matched model. This corresponds closely to our reverse evidence. Similar analogy is also true for the forward distance and our forward evidence. From an application point of view, the reverse evidence, which does not incorporate white space penalty, is good for detecting patterns with broken lines or occluded patterns. However, it suffers from the sub-part problem described in [1]. The forward framework, which penalizes white space, is good for minimizing false alarms and solves the sub-part problem implicitly.

4.2. Shape Matching Properties

Considering the shape matching properties of the two frameworks, it can be shown that:

Proposition 3 *Reverse matching has good data exploration characteristics.*

Proposition 4 *Forward matching has good localization characteristics.*

These two propositions reveal the dilemma that forward matching is insensitive to outlier influence but lacks good data exploration capability, while reverse matching has good data exploration characterisitics but is heavily influenced by outliers. The dilemma is also discussed in Section 6.1.

5. Bidirectional Matching Algorithm and its Convergence Properties

The duality observed from the two frameworks suggests the idea of combining the two frameworks to get the best of both worlds. The success of Hausdorff matching gives the cue that taking the maximum of the two frameworks' data mismatch related criteria can be a good choice. Based on the idea, we propose an algorithm called *bidirectional matching* outlined in Figure 1, where the matching process switches between the two frameworks according to the values of E_D and E_{D_s} until some convergence criterion is satisfied. Figure 2 illustrates the limitation of the individual frameworks and the strength of the proposed *bidirectional matching*. The convergence proof of the algorithm can be found in [2].

---

1. Initialize an input model using chamfer-like matching.

2. Compute the data mismatch, E_D, and the sub-data mismatch, E_{D_s}, for the two frameworks.

3. do

   (a) If $E_D > E_{D_s}$,
      Perform reverse matching.
      else
      Perform forward matching.

   (b) $\beta := (1 + \epsilon)\beta$;

   (c) if $\beta > 4$, $\beta := 4$;
      /* equivalent to a Gaussian width = 0.5 */

4. until a convergence is reached with the difference in **w** for two consecutive iterations less than a threshold $\acute{e}$.

Figure 1. The matching algorithm.

6. Experimental Results

In order to evaluate the effectiveness of our bidirectional matching algorithm, we have applied it for recognizing handwritten word images. Our experiment contains two parts. The first part is concentrated on evaluating the matching performance of the bidirectional matching algorithm and the second part is concentrated on the performance of a retrieval application based on the algorithm, which tests both the shape matching and discriminating performance of the system. The *bb* subset[3] of the CEDAR database, which contains around 300 handwritten city name images, is used as the test set. For both experiments, we take the covariance matrix of the model parameter to be an identity matrix and thus no model training is adopted.

6.1. Handwritten Character Extraction

To test the matching performance of the algorithm, we applied it to extract the leftmost character from each binary

---

[3]This subset contains handwritten cursive scripts of city names and was created by the CEDAR group for testing character segmentation algorithms.

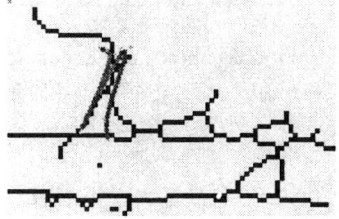

(a) Forward matching.

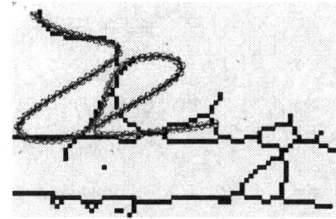

(b) Reverse matching.

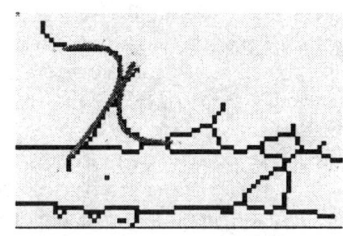

(c) Bidirectional matching.

Figure 2. Comparison of matching performance.

handwritten word image in the *bb* subset of the CEDAR database.[4] We assume that the identity of the leftmost character is known[5] but the goal is to locate it accurately through deformable matching. Being provided with a hand-drafted character model with an equivalent shape topology as the leftmost character, the algorithm first initializes the model and then starts matching. The matching performance is visually checked. While the reverse matching process fails for almost all the test cases (due to outliers), the success rate for bidirectional matching is found to be 85.5%. The error rates

---

[4]All the images in the CEDAR database are gray-level ones. So, they are preprocessed by first performing a simple intensity thresholding, and followed by thinning. The threshold for the thresholding is computed by detecting the valley in the image histogram.

[5]Note that the handwriting of a particular alphabet can have very different shapes or even topologies, e.g., "M" and "m" and their identities are considered to be different here.

due to bad initialization, bad matching and others are 9.7%, 3.4% and 1.4%, respectively. This shows the effectiveness of the bidirectional matching algorithm and the importance of good model initialization to good matching performance. Figure 3 depicts some of the matching results.

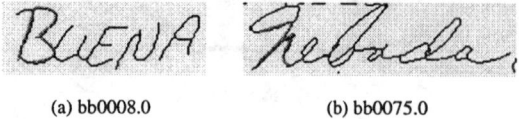

(a) bb0008.0   (b) bb0075.0

Figure 3. Some matching results.

6.2. Handwritten Word Retrieval based on Character Shape

To apply the algorithm to a non-rigid shape retrieval problem, we match a set of character shape models for the candidate characters, one by one, with the first 100 hand-written word images extracted from the *bb* dataset. We use the forward evidence as the final discriminating measure, which can penalize models resting on white space. Figure 4 shows the model set (7 models) we used for the input queries. To quantify the retrieval results, we first sort the list of word images according to their forward evidence values, cut off the list at a certain point to form the output list and compute the corresponding recall and precision rates. To determine the cut-off point, two different schemes are tested, one using the best-N approach and the other using the evidence thresholding approach. The overall precision rate and recall rate are found to be 43% and 59%, respectively, when the best 10 word images are selected for the output, and 45% and 65%, respectively, when the images with the negative logarithm of the forward evidence values larger than -5.5 are selected.[6]

To compare with the text retrieval problem where false alarms can be resulted from the fact that an input string is part of some other irrelevant strings, our retrieval system's false alarms are caused by the input shape being part of some other irrelevant portions of the handwritten cursive script. The irrelevant portion can be one single character (e.g., a "C" model can find a good match with part of an "O") or a composite of two adajacent characters (e.g., a "U" model can find a good match somewhere between the consecutive characters "dl").

7. Conclusion

A Bayesian framework for deformable pattern detection is proposed in this paper which can solve both the out-

[6]As a comparison, the average number of candidates is 12.7.

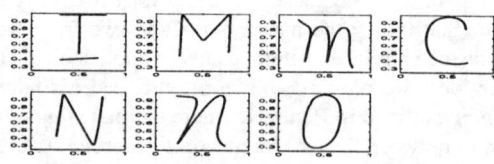

Figure 4. The input character shapes used for testing in our retrieval experiments.

lier and the white space problems implicitly. By comparing it with the framework proposed in [1] for deformable pattern classification, a reverse-and-forward duality is observed. Using only one of the two frameworks for extracting non-rigid shapes will suffer from being either too sensitive towards outliers or too poor in data exploration. By properly combining the two frameworks, a new matching algorithm called bidirectional matching is proposed. The combined framework bears a close theoretical analogy with Hausdorff matching and has been proved to converge. The proposed system has been applied to shape-based handwritten word retrieval. For the *bb* dataset in the CEDAR database with 300 handwritten city name images, we can achieve a correct matching rate of 85.5%. For a particular subset of the dataset containing 100 handwritten city name images, we achieve at best a 59% recall rate with a corresponding 43% precision rate based on the best 10 approach for selecting the candidates.

References

[1] K. W. Cheung, D. Y. Yeung, and R. T. Chin. A Bayesian framework for deformable pattern recognition with application to handwritten character recognition. *IEEE Transactions on Pattern Analysis and Machine Intelligence*, 20(12):1382–1388, Dec. 1998.

[2] K. W. Cheung. *Bayesian Frameworks for Deformable Pattern Classification and Retrieval: Application to Handwriting Recognition*. PhD thesis, The Hong Kong University of Science and Technology, Jan. 1999.

[3] P. Dayan, G. E. Hinton, R. M. Neal, and R. S. Zemel. Helmholtz machine. *Neural Computation*, 7(5):889–904, Sept. 1995.

[4] M. Revow, C. K. I. Williams, and G. E. Hinton. Using generative models for handwritten digit recognition. *IEEE Transactions on Pattern Analysis and Machine Intelligence*, 18(6):592–606, June 1996.

[5] W. Rucklidge. *Efficient Visual Recognition Using the Hausdorff Distance*. Springer, Berlin, 1996.

Utilizing Scatter for Pixel Subspace Selection

Haim Schweitzer (haim@utdallas.edu)

The University of Texas at Dallas, P.O Box 830688, Richardson, Texas 75083

Abstract

Measures of scatter are used in statistical pattern recognition to identify and select important features, computed as linear combinations of the given features. Examples include principal components and linear discriminants. The classic computational procedures require eigenvector decomposition of large matrices, and in the case of images they are only practical for identifying a low dimensional feature subspace. We investigate the case in which the selected features are required to be a subset of the given features. It is shown that the same scatter measures used in the general case can also be used in this discrete selection case, but the computational procedure no longer involves matrix eigenvector decomposition. Instead, the selection of pixels that optimize scatter measures can be accomplished by a very simple and efficient discrete optimization technique that runs in linear time regardless of the subspace size. Applications to clustering and content based indexing are discussed.

1 Introduction

Work on identifying and selecting features that optimize natural selection criteria can be traced back at least to the classic paper of Fisher [6]. The current theory is mature, and can be found in most standard textbooks on statistical pattern recognition (e.g., [4, 3, 7]).

The general statistical approach to (linear) feature selection is to define the "scatter" of data, and select features so that some combinations of these scatter measures are optimized in the feature subspace. Feature selection is the key to computer vision techniques that require indexing by content. See for example the use of "eigenfeatures" in [13, 11], and discriminant features in [12]. The algorithmic task of selecting these features is nontrivial, requiring eigenvector decomposition of large matrices. Recent research in data-mining [5, 1] points to a different problem with selecting eigenvectors as features. Since they are computed as linear combinations of the given features, projections on eigenvectors are hard to interpret. These references suggest the alternative of restricting the choice of selected features to subsets of the given features, and propose ad-hoc techniques for the selection.

In this paper we show that *the same scatter measures used to identify and select feature subspaces as "optimal" linear combinations of pixels can also be used to identify and select the "optimal" subsets of these pixels*. The algorithm for choosing these pixel subsets reduces to the selection of the largest k values out of n values, and this can be computed in linear time for any value of k.

In Section 2 we briefly review classic scatter measures and the way they are used in statistical pattern recognition. The key to our approach is the observation that for the purpose of discrete feature selection the large scatter matrices can be replaced by image size vectors. This is shown in Section 3. Applications to content-based-indexing are discussed in Section 4. Section 5 describes applications to automatic image clustering. Experimental results are described in Section 6.

2 Statistical scatter measures

The material in this section can be found in most pattern recognition texts (e.g., [3, 7]). Let $x_1, \ldots, x_m$ be m patterns. Let $G_1, \ldots, G_k$ be a partition of the patterns into k groups, and let $\mu_1, \ldots, \mu_k$ denote the means of these groups. The *within-class scatter matrix* is:

$$S_w = \sum_{j=1}^{k} \sum_{i \in G_j} (x_i - \mu_j)(x_i - \mu_j)'$$

The *between-class scatter matrix* is:

$$S_b = \sum_{j=1}^{k} m_j (\mu_j - \mu)(\mu_j - \mu)'$$

where $m_j = |G_j|$, and $\mu = \frac{1}{m} \sum_{j=1}^{k} m_j \mu_j$. The *mixture scatter matrix* is:

$$S_m = \sum_{i=1}^{m} (x_i - \mu)(x_i - \mu)'$$

Observe that $S_m = S_w + S_b$. To convert matrices into scalar scatter measures one can use either the trace or the determinant of a scatter matrix. For example, a measure of how "different" are the patterns $x_1, \ldots, x_m$ can be one of:

$$\mathsf{Trace}(S_m), \text{ or } \mathsf{Det}(S_m)$$

We consider only measures specified in terms of the trace function, since for images the scatter matrices are usually singular.

Cluster separability criteria require that within-class scatter is minimized while the between class scatter is maximized. The most natural criterion is:

$$\frac{\text{Trace}(S_b)}{\text{Trace}(S_w)}$$

It is common to normalize the patterns so that S_w becomes the identity matrix. It is easy to see that the normalized patterns $\tilde{x}_i$ are given by: $\tilde{x}_i = S_w^{-1/2}x_i$, so that:

$$\frac{\text{Trace}(\tilde{S}_b)}{\text{Trace}(\tilde{S}_w)} = \text{Trace}(S_w^{-1}S_b)$$

Let n be the length of a pattern. To select a subspace of dimension $r < n$ set $P_{n \times r} = (p_1, \ldots, p_r)$ to be an orthonormal matrix. Then an n-vector x_i is mapped to an r-vector y_i by:

$$y_i = P'x_i$$

The within, between, and mixture scatter matrices of the projected r-vectors are: $P'S_wP$, $P'S_bP$, and $P'S_mP$, respectively. Therefore, an optimal projection matrix P can be determined by computing P that maximizes one of the above criteria. Specifically, choosing P as the r dominant eigenvectors of S_m maximizes $\text{Trace}(P'S_mP)$. It is known [7, 3] that the matrix P which maximized both cluster separability criteria listed above is composed of the r dominant eigenvectors of the generalized eigenvalue problem $S_bp = \lambda S_wp$.

3 Scatter in discrete feature selection

In this section images are treated as n-coordinate vectors. Coordinate t of the image x_i (the t'th pixel) is written as $x_i(t)$. We analyze the case in which the matrix $P = (p_1, \ldots, p_r)$ of Section 2 represents a projection on r pixel locations. In our notation this means that $p'_t x_i = x_i(t)$ for $t = 1, \ldots, r$.

We observe that in order to compute scatter defined in terms of matrix traces there is no need to retain or process the scatter matrices S_w, S_b, S_m. Since a scatter matrix can be written as $S = \sum_i z_i z'_i$ it follows that:

$$p'_t S p_t = \sum_i (p'_t z_i)^2 = \sum_i (z_i(t))^2,$$

$$\text{Trace}(P'SP) = \sum_{t=1}^{r} p'_t S p_t = \sum_{t=1}^{r} q(t)$$

where $q(t) = \sum_i (z_i(t))^2$. With the same notation as in Section 2 for μ and μ_j we define the *between*, *within*, and *mixture scatter vectors*:

$$
\begin{aligned}
q_w(t) &= \sum_{j=1}^{k} \sum_{i \in G_j} (x_i(t) - \mu_j(t))^2 \\
q_b(t) &= \sum_{j=1}^{k} m_j (\mu_j(t) - \mu(t))^2 \\
q_m(t) &= \sum_{i=1}^{m} (x_i(t) - \mu(t))^2
\end{aligned}
$$

When the matrix P represents the selection of the r pixel locations in the set T, the scatter measures discussed in Section 2 can be expressed as:

$$\text{Trace}(P'S_mP) = \sum_{t \in T} q_m(t) \tag{1}$$

$$\frac{\text{Trace}(P'S_bP)}{\text{Trace}(P'S_wP)} = \frac{\sum_{t \in T} q_b(t)}{\sum_{t \in T} q_w(t)} \tag{2}$$

The normalization discussed in Section 2 is given by: $\tilde{x}_i(t) = x_i(t)/\sqrt{q_w(t)}$, and this gives: $\tilde{q}_w(t) = 1$, $\tilde{q}_b(t) = q_b(t)/q_w(t)$. Therefore, the related cluster separability criterion is:

$$\frac{\text{Trace}(P'\tilde{S}_bP)}{\text{Trace}(P'\tilde{S}_wP)} = \sum_{t \in T} \frac{q_b(t)}{q_w(t)} \tag{3}$$

When the vectors q_w, q_b, q_m are given, the selection of r pixel locations as the subset T that maximizes the criterion (1) or (3) amounts to the selection of r largest elements out of n elements. This is the well known *selection* problem for which algorithms of worst case linear time are known. See [2], and the available code and discussion in [10].

4 Content-based-indexing

Let $G_1, \ldots, G_k$ be groups of images, with m_j specifying the number of images in G_j. For each group we assume that the following statistics were computed: μ_j, the pixel by pixel mean of group G_j, and v_j, the pixel by pixel variance of group G_j. Specifically:

$$
\begin{aligned}
\mu_j(t) &= \frac{1}{m_j} \sum_{x \in G_j} x(t) \\
v_j(t) &= \frac{1}{m_j} \sum_{x \in G_j} (x(t) - \mu_j(t))^2
\end{aligned} \tag{4}
$$

Case 1: Compute a subset of r pixel locations that can be used to index the images in G_1.

Solution: maximize the mixture-class scatter as given in (1), using $q_m = v_1$.

Case 2: Compute a subset of r pixel locations that can be used to determine the class of an image, where the choice is between $G_1, \ldots, G_k$.

Solution: maximize (3) with the following scatter vectors:

$$
\begin{aligned}
q_w(t) &= \sum v_j(t) \\
q_b(t) &= \sum m_j (\mu_j(t) - \mu(t))^2
\end{aligned}
$$

where $m = \sum m_j$, and $\mu = \frac{1}{m} \sum m_j \mu_j$.

Case 1 is the discrete selection version of principal components. Case 2 is the discrete selection version of discriminant functions.

5 Applications to k-means clustering

In clustering one partitions a given set of m patterns into k disjoint groups specified by $G_1, \ldots, G_k$. Since the data may be well clustered only on some of the given features, the task of simultaneously identifying these features and computing the clustering was recently considered in the general data-mining context [14, 1]. In this section we describe a solution to this problem by augmenting the k-means clustering technique, which turns out to be a natural and immediate application of the scatter-based discrete feature selection ideas.

The k-means clustering algorithm [9, 7, 8] computes a partitioning that minimizes the following error:

$$s_w = \sum_{j=1}^{k} \sum_{i \in G_j} |x_i - \mu_j|^2 \qquad (5)$$

The minimization of s_w is achieved by iterating two steps. In the first step the partition is given, and each pivotal vector μ_j is computed as the mean of the patterns in group G_j. In the second step the pivotal vectors are given. Each group G_j is computed as the patterns closer to μ_j than to any other pivotal vector. The proof that both steps reduce the error s_w can be found in the above references.

5.1 k-means on a subspace

Suppose $P = (p_1, \ldots, p_r)$ is orthonormal. Then each n-vector x_i is mapped to an r-vector y_i by $y_i = P'x_i$. Our goal is to compute P and the clustering of the vectors y_i. Specifically, we are looking for a matrix P, a partition, and r-vectors $u_1, \ldots, u_k$ that minimize the error:

$$s_w(P) = \sum_{j=1}^{k} \sum_{i \in G_j} |y_i - u_j|^2 = \sum_{j=1}^{k} \sum_{i \in G_j} |P'(x_i - \mu_j)|^2$$

where μ_j is defined to be Pu_j. Expanding and changing the order of summation this error can also be expressed as:

$$s_w(P) = \sum_{t=1}^{r} p_t' S_w p_t = \mathsf{Trace}(P' S_w P)$$

where S_w is the within-class scatter matrix as defined in Section 2. Therefore, when P represents the selection of a subset T of r pixel locations $s_w(P)$ is precisely the within-class scatter on T, and can be written as:

$$s_w(T) = \sum_{t \in T} q_w(t), \quad \text{where } q_w = \sum_{j=1}^{k} v_j,$$

and the v_j are as defined in (4). The algorithm that computes the subset T and the clustering iterates the following three steps, each minimizing the same error $s_w(T)$:

Step A_1: $T, G_1, \ldots, G_k$ are unchanged. Set y_i to be the pixels of x_i that belong to T. Compute new $u_1, \ldots, u_k$.

For $j = 1, \ldots, k$, $u_j = \mathsf{Mean}\{y_i, i \in G_j\}$

Step A_2: $T, u_1, \ldots, u_k$ are unchanged. Set y_i to be the pixels of x_i that belong to T. Compute new $G_1, \ldots, G_k$.

For $i = 1, \ldots, m$ assign i to a class G_α that satisfies:

$$|y_i - u_\alpha|^2 = \min_j |y_i - u_j|^2$$

Step A_3: $G_1, \ldots, G_k$ are unchanged. Compute a new T as the r pixel locations that minimizes $s_w(T)$ given by:

$$s_w(T) = \sum_{t \in T} q_w(t), \quad \text{where } q_w = \sum_{j=1}^{k} v_j,$$

and the v_j are computed according to (4).

Steps A_1, A_2 are the standard k-means steps with the input restricted to the pixel locations in T, so they are guaranteed to reduce the error $s_w(T)$ that is explicitly minimized in Step A_3. Therefore, all three steps minimize the same

error, and the algorithm is guaranteed to converge to a local minimum, regardless of the initial condition or the order in which the above steps are applied.

6 Experimental results

We describe experiments on images taken from two datasets. The first is the Coil-20 image set, available from Columbia University. It contains pictures of several objects with 72 views of each object. Only the first two objects (144 images) were used. The second dataset is the ORL faces collection. It contains 10 facial images of 40 individuals, totaling 400 images.

6.1 Content based indexing

Pixel selection according to Case 1 in Section 4 was applied to the 144 images from the Coil-20 image set. The masks obtained for the selection of 2%, 10%, and 50% of the pixels are shown in Figure 1. The first row in Figure 2 shows 16 out of the 144 images that were used as input. Projections of these images on the 10% mask are shown in the second row of Figure 2. The area selected appears to be where most changes occur.

To quantitatively evaluate this indexing scheme we plot the Euclidean distance between the first frame (shown at the top left of Figure 2) and all 144 frames. (The frames are arranged according to the object rotation with the first 72 frames coming from the first object and frames 73-144 coming from the second object.) These plots are shown at the top row of Figure 3. The rightmost plot corresponds to the selection of all pixels. Observe the gradual change with approximately 0 distance for frames 1 and 72. Very similar results are evident in the plots that correspond to the partial pixel selections. If one attempts to select all frames that look the same as Frame 1, the answer would be frames 1,72 using the 100%, 50%, and 10% masks. Using the 2% mask the answer would be frames 1-13, 60-72, 80, 81, 131-133.

To experiment with pixel selection according to Case 2, the first 72 frames (the wooden duck) were taken as one class, and the other 72 frames were the second class. The masks computed for the selection of 2%, 10%, and 50% of the pixels are shown in Figure 1. Projection of the images on the 10% mask are shown in the third row in Figure 2. Observe that projections of frames from the same class look very similar, but the projections of frames from different classes look different.

Repeating the same quantitative measures of these projections as in Case 1 we plot the Euclidean distance between the first frame (shown at the top left of Figure 2) and all 144 frames. The plots are shown in the middle row of Figure 3. Clearly, for a 100% selection the results are identical to Case 1, but for smaller selections it is not. Instead, as expected distances between Frame 1 and other frames from its class are small, but distances to frames from the other class are much larger. In fact, for the selection of 2% and 10% masks all frames in the first group are closer Frame 1 than any frame from the second group.

The bottom row of Figure 3 is a plot of distances from the mean of Group 1 to all 144 frames. Here again it is clear that separation exists for all the selected subsets.

6.2 k-means on a subspace

The algorithm of Section 5.1 was implemented by repeating to convergence the specified steps in the order A_3, A_1, A_2. In most cases the introduction of pixel selection appears to yield a significant improvement in the resulting grouping, and to our opinion the results are more similar to the way a human observer groups the images. Some of these results are described below.

Applying standard k-means with $k = 4$ to the same 144 frames from the COIL dataset that were used in the previous section gives 4 clusters as shown at the top of Figure 4. The grouping found is not according to the objects, and seems to depend more on the object orientation. Running the algorithm of Section 5.1 with $k = 4$ while restricting the selection to 80% of the pixels gives the grouping shown at the bottom of Figure 4. (Very similar results were obtained for smaller mask sizes, up to a selection of 20%.) The images shown are the projections on the mask. It is clear that the mask blocks some changes that result from different orientations, and the grouping is according to both shape and orientation.

Another set of experiment was performed with the ORL dataset. Running the algorithm of Section 5.1 with $k = 20$, while restricting the selection to 50% gives the mask shown at the top right of Figure 5. The mask appears to block "irrelevant" facial variations such as lips motion, hair, and eyes. Two clusters out of the 20, and their projections on the mask are shown. Observe that in the projections the tongue and glasses are masked out. One cluster from the results obtained with $k = 10$ and a mask of 80% are shown at the bottom of Figure 5. It appears that the mask blocks differences in ears, lips motion, and small orientation, but leaves the hair as an important feature. The cluster appears to be mostly composed of "bald" faces.

We observed experimentally that the masks always have the appearance of a human face. This is not entirely surprising since they are computed (by the algorithm) to mask out features that can tell images apart. These turn out to be the important characteristics of the human face.

7 Concluding remarks

We have shown that the same scatter criteria used in statistical pattern recognition to select features expressed as linear combinations of given features can also be used to select a subset of the given features. It was argued that a selected subspace of pixels is easier to interpret than eigenfeatures and discriminant features. Another advantage of the proposed selection technique is that it runs in time linear in the number of pixels regardless of how many pixel locations are to be selected.

References

[1] R. Agrawal, J. Gehrke, D. Gunopulos, and P. Raghavan. Automatic subspace clustering of high dimensional data for data mining applications. In *Proc. ACM SIGMOD Int. Conf. Management of Data*, pages 94–105. ACM Press, June 1998.

[2] T. H. Cormen, C. E. Leiserson, and R. L. Rivest. *Introduction to algorithms*. MIT Press and McGraw-Hill Book Company, 6th edition, 1992.

[3] P. Devijver and J. Kittler. *Pattern Recognition: A Statistical Approach*. Prentice Hall, London, 1982.

[4] R. O. Duda and P. E. Hart. *Pattern Classification and Scene Analysis*. John Wiley & Sons, 1973.

[5] U. M. Fayyad, G. Piatetsky-Shapiro, P. Smyth, and R. Uthurusamy, editors. *Advances in Knowledge Discovery and Data Mining*. MIT Press, Menlo Park, 1996.

[6] R. A. Fisher. The use of multiple measurement in taxonomic problems. *Ann. Eugenics*, 7:111–132, 1936.

[7] K. Fukunaga. *Introduction to Statistical Pattern Recognition*. Academic Press, New York, second edition, 1990.

[8] A. K. Jain and R. C. Dubes. *Algorithms for Clustering Data*. Prentice-Hall, Englewood Cliffs, NJ, 1988.

[9] J. MacQueen. Some methods for classification and analysis of multivariate observations. In L. M. L. Cam and J. Neyman, editors, *Proceedings of the Fifth Berkeley Symposium on Mathematical Statistics and Probability*, volume 1, pages 281–297, Berkeley, CA, 1967. University of California Press.

[10] W. H. Press, S. A. Teukolsky, W. T. Vetterling, and B. P. Flannery. *Numerical Recipes in C: The Art of Scientific Computing*. Cambridge University Press, Cambridge, second edition, 1992.

[11] H. Schweitzer. A distributed algorithm for content based indexing of images by projections on Ritz primary images. *Data Mining and Knowledge Discovery*, 1(4):375–390, 1997.

[12] D. L. Swets and J. Weng. Using discriminant eigenfeatures for image retrieval. *IEEE Transactions on Pattern Analysis and Machine Intelligence*, 18(8):831–836, Aug. 1996.

[13] M. Turk and A. Pentland. Eigenfaces for recognition. *Journal of Cognitive Neuroscience*, 3(1):71–86, 1991.

[14] M. Zait and H. Messatfa. A comparative study of clustering methods. *Future Generation Computer Systems*, 13(2-3):149–59, 1997.

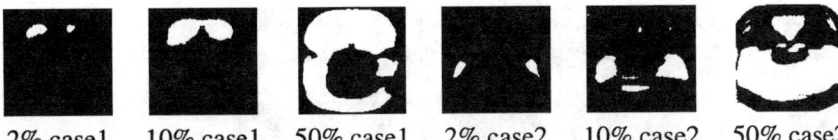

2% case1   10% case1   50% case1   2% case2   10% case2   50% case2

Figure 1: Content based pixel selection shown as image masks. The selected pixels are shown as white areas. In Case1 the pixels are selected to enable discrimination between all images. In Case2 the goal is discrimination between the two classes.

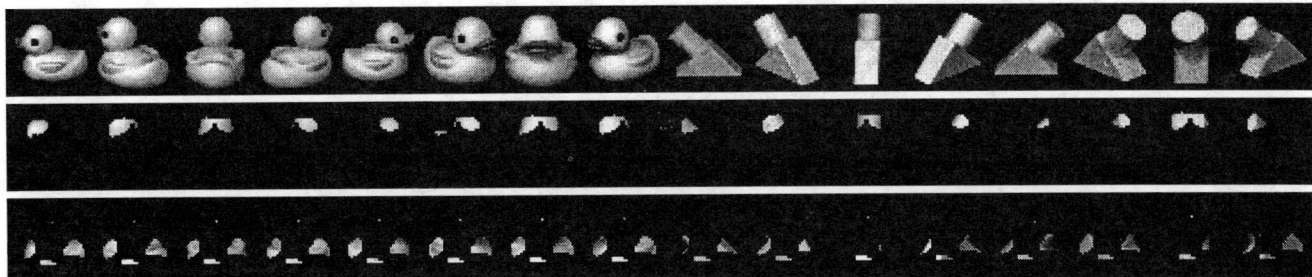

Figure 2. Row 1: 16 images out of the 144 images used in the experiments. The 8 on left are from first group; the 8 on right are from second group. Row 2: Projections on a mask of 10% computed in Case 1 (shown in Figure 1). Observe that the projections look different for different looking frames. Row 3: Projections on a mask of 10% computed in Case 2 (shown in Figure 1). Observe that for frames of the same class the projections look similar, but there is a clear difference between the classes.

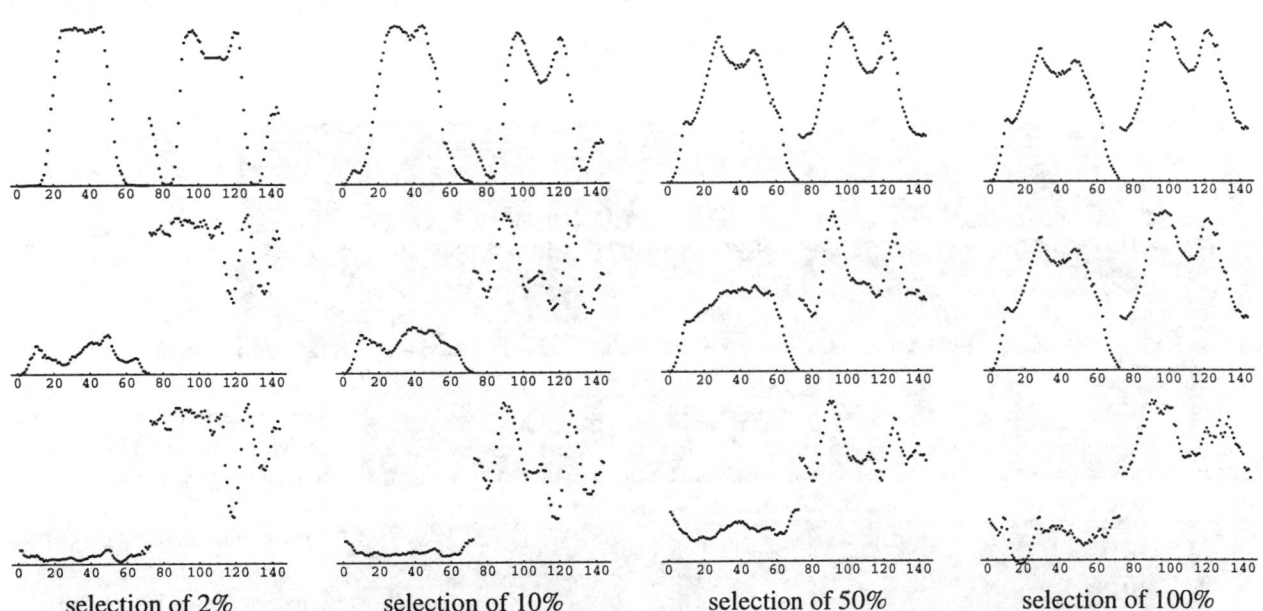

selection of 2%   selection of 10%   selection of 50%   selection of 100%

Figure 3. Plots of dissimilarity (distances) between images. The x axis is the frame number. The y axis is (normalized) Euclidean distances. Row 1: plots of distances of all 144 frames from Frame 1 restricted to the various pixel selections as computed in Case 1. Row 2: same as Row 1 for the pixel selections computed in Case 2. Row 3: distances from the mean of Group 1 for the various pixel selections computed in Case 2.

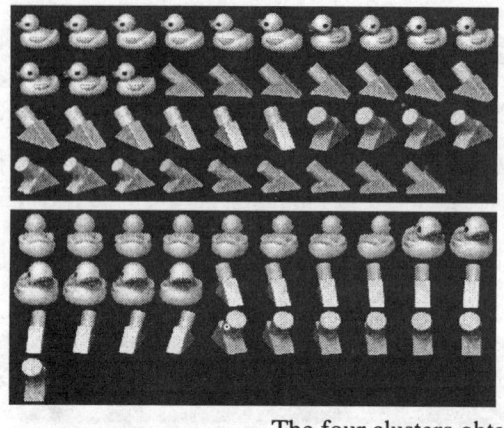
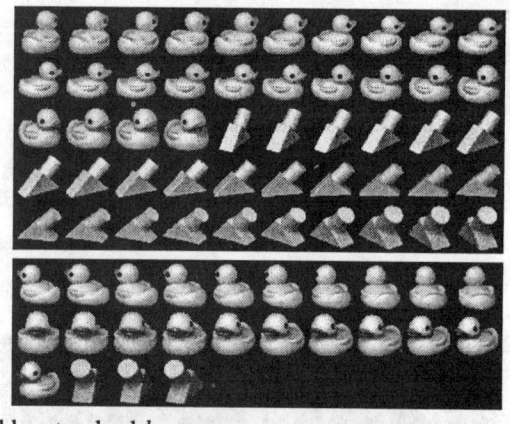

⇐ These 4 clusters are the result of applying standard k-means (with $k = 4$) to the 144 images.

The four clusters obtained by standard k-means

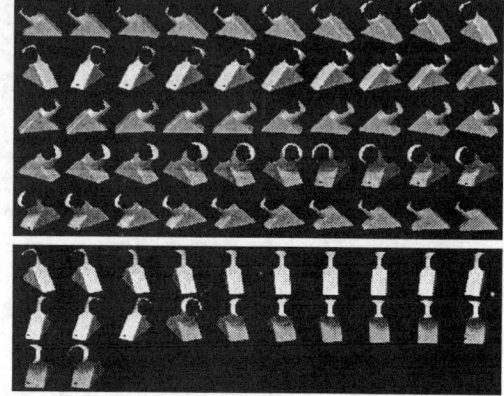

⇐ The 4 clusters computed by the algorithm of Section 5.1 applied to determine locations of 80% of the pixels where images are best clustered.

The four clusters obtained by k-means on 80% selection (masking out 20% of the pixels)

Figure 4.

the 80% mask

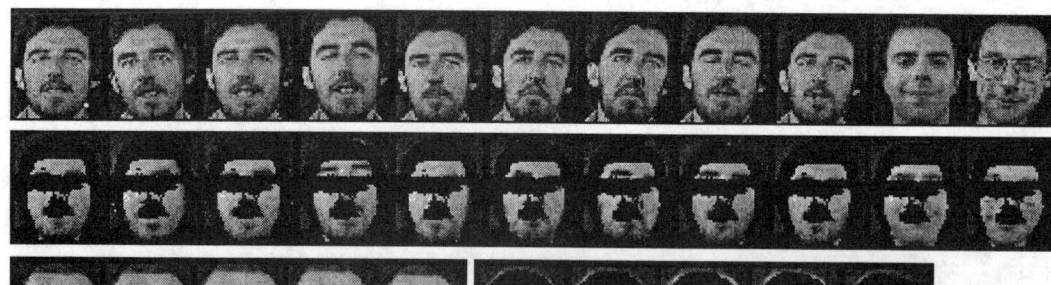

The ⇑ 50% mask

The images in two clusters, shown before and after projection on the 50% mask

The mask and two clusters (out of a total of 20) obtained with 50% pixel selection

Mask and one cluster (k=10) obtained with 80% selection. Images shown before and after projection on mask.

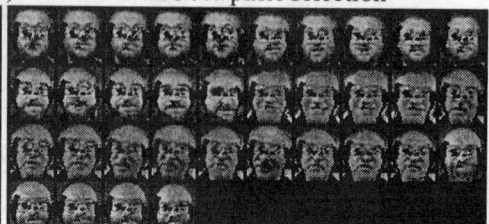

Figure 5.

1116

Finding Correspondences of Patches by Means of Affine Transformations*

R. Berthilsson
Centre for Mathematical Sciences
Lund University
P.O. Box 118, S-221 00 Lund, Sweden

Abstract

In this paper we present a novel method for finding the optimal affine transformation for matching of images. The method requires no feature points, does not rely on normalization of images and can be tuned to highlight interesting parts in the images. Furthermore, the method does not need any derivatives for obtaining the affine transformation and it has a computational cost proportional to $n^2 \log n$ for $n \times n$ images. The problem of finding the optimal affine transformation is solved by an iterative algorithm. In each step a global optimization is performed by the use of FFT. This global characteristic helps the algorithm from getting trapped in a local optimum. Novel theoretical results are presented that show under what restrictions the algorithm can be expected to work properly. Its intended primary use is for reconstruction problems in computer vision. These rely heavily on the establishment of point correspondences in the images. Since the method makes no assumptions on the images it can be used when feature points are difficult to detect. Experiments on real images are included and it is shown that the algorithm is robust and performs well even in difficult situations, with occlusions.

1 Introduction

Correlation techniques are important in computer vision, ranging from traditional correlation by translating one image relative the other, to the more complex problem of finding the best projective transformation for matching two images. A compromise in between is to use so called **affine correlation**, i.e. to find the best affine transformation, for matching two images. While maintaining a high degree flexibility it is shown in this paper that affine correlation is computational feasible.

The motivation for studying affine estimation in is that it is often an integral part in structure from motion problems. Here, the relative motion between viewer and scene induces distortions in the images. This distortion can not

usually be modeled by an affine transformation but for small patches of the images this is often a good approximation. For parallel projections of planar surfaces, the approximation is in fact exact.

Many methods have been proposed for the matching of images. Simple correlation techniques can be found in [10, 1]. A brief discussion, on matching images by using Euclidean transformations, is given in [13]. Transformation identification, based on centroid alignment and clustering techniques, can be found in [7]. Affine matching has been studied in [11, 2]. However, in [11] certain assumptions are made concerning the images. For example it is assumed that corresponding patches in two images have been determined beforehand. Special properties of the image textures are also assumed. In [2] the affine matching is only reliable for Euclidean matching. In the general case, these methods are not likely to work. In this paper, we propose a novel method that makes no assumptions about the images. It is fast with a computational cost proportional to $n^2 \log n$ for $n \times n$ images. Furthermore, the algorithm computes a global optimization in each iteration. Experiments on real images show that the algorithm performs very well.

Matching of images is also used for recognition. Knowledge of the best affine transformation can be used both to determine if an object is present in an image and for finding its position. Image normalization is often used in this context. There are many techniques for normalizing images. The use of moments is common, c.f. [4, 8, 12]. For detecting the orientation, it is possible to use principal axes [9], mirror symmetry [5], and lines through centroids [6].

We also present a thorough treatment of how transformations of the gray levels in images affect the affine correlation. If the sought affine transformation is known to be area preserving it is shown that the estimated affine transformation is in fact independent of gray level transformations.

2 Theory

The aim is to find an affine transformation that transforms one image into another such that they are as similar as possible. The degree of similarity is measured by the

---

*This work has been done within the VISIT program of Swedish Foundation for Strategic Research (SSF) and ESPRIT Reactive LTR project 21914, CUMULI.

affine correlation as defined below.

Assume that z_1 and z_2 are two images, each containing a patch that is image of a set of object points. If, for example, the scene is a human face and z_1 and z_2 are images thereof, then these patches could be the respective images of the right eye. If we neglect perspective effects, then these patches are affine transformations of each other, i.e. it is possible to obtain the image of the right eye in the first image by translating, rotating and stretching the second image in the right proportions. The errors that are introduced, by neglecting the perspective effects, are small if the patches are chosen small and they vanish for parallel projections of planar objects.

Below we will use integrals instead of sums when summing over an image. The reason for this is that it admits us to use the comprehensive theory for integration, e.g. change of variables, measure theory and so on.

Definition 2.1. Let μ be a positive Radon measure and let $\mathcal{A}$ be the set of affine transformation $\mathbb{R}^2 \to \mathbb{R}^2$. If $z \in L_\mu^2$ is a positive real valued function, such that $z \circ a \in L_\mu^2$ for all $a \in \mathcal{A}$, then z is called an **image**. Two images z_1 and z_2 are called **affinely related** if there exists an affine transformation $a : \mathbb{R}^2 \to \mathbb{R}^2$, such that

$$\frac{z_1}{\|z_1\|_2} = \frac{z_2 \circ a}{\|z_2 \circ a\|_2}, \quad \text{almost everywhere.} \qquad (1)$$

∎

The reason for introducing μ instead of the ordinary Lebesgue measure dx is that we need to cut out certain patches, or to pay more attention to some areas of an image. By the **support** of a function we mean the smallest closed set such that z is zero outside this set. It is denoted $\mathrm{supp}(z)$.

Equation (1) can be stated as

$$\frac{\langle z_1, z_2 \circ a \rangle}{\|z_1\|_2 \|z_2 \circ a\|_2} = 1,$$

with the scalar product

$$\langle z_1, z_2 \rangle = \int z_1 z_2 \, d\mu$$

and norm

$$\|z\|_2 = \left\{ \int |z|^2 d\mu \right\}^{1/2}.$$

Definition 2.2. Let $\mathcal{A}$ be the linear space of affine transformations $\mathbb{R}^2 \to \mathbb{R}^2$. Then the real valued function

$$C : \mathcal{A} \ni a \mapsto \frac{\langle z_1, z_2 \circ a \rangle}{\|z_1\|_2 \|z_2 \circ a\|_2},$$

is called the **affine correlation** between the images z_1 and z_2.

∎

Consider the maximization problem $\sup_{a \in \mathcal{A}} C(a)$. If z_1 and z_2 are affinely related, with an orientation preserving affine transformation, it is sufficient to maximize over the space $\mathcal{A}_+ = \{a \in \mathcal{A} \,|\, a(x) = Ax + b, \det(A) > 0\}$, i.e.

$$\sup_{a \in \mathcal{A}_+} C(a). \qquad (2)$$

A natural way of approaching this problem is to use a fixed step size for computing the derivatives of $C(a)$ numerically for all parameters of a, in order to obtain the gradient, and then to use some minimization method like, for example, the Gauss-Newton method. As $a(x) = Ax + b$, where A is a 2×2 matrix and b is a 2×1 matrix, six derivatives have to be computed numerically at a. This is of course feasible to do, but the method is of local character and thus highly dependent on start values for converging to a global maximum.

Here we propose a method that is more global and does not require any derivatives. This is achieved by maximizing along the axes of a certain coordinate system. First we do a global maximization from staring point a along the direction of the first axis. This gives a new point a. Then the same procedure is performed along the second axis from a, and so on. Finally, when the last axis has been maximized over, the first is considered again. Let us now describe this in more detail.

First note that if $A \in \mathcal{A}_+$, then $A = R(\theta_1) d R(\theta_2)^T$, where d is diagonal with $d_{j,j} \geq 0$, $j = 1, 2$, and

$$R(\theta) = \begin{pmatrix} \cos(\theta) & \sin(\theta) \\ -\sin(\theta) & \cos(\theta) \end{pmatrix}, \qquad (3)$$

is a matrix describing rotation by $-\theta$ radians. Denote the diagonal elements of d by σ_1 and σ_2. Then we can use the variables $(\theta_1, \theta_2, \sigma_1, \sigma_2, \beta_1, \beta_2)$, with $\sigma_1 > 0$ and $\sigma_2 > 0$ for defining any $a \in \mathcal{A}_+$, where a is given by $a(x) = Ax + b$, $b = (\beta_1, \beta_2)^T$ and $A = R(\theta_1) d R(\theta_2)^T$.

Let $R : [0, 2\pi) \ni \theta \mapsto R(\theta)$ be the rotation operator defined by (3), let $T(\beta) : x \to x - \beta$, $(\beta, x) \in \mathbb{R}^2 \times \mathbb{R}^2$, be the translation operator and let

$$D : \mathbb{R}_+^2 \ni \sigma \mapsto D(\sigma) = \begin{pmatrix} \sigma_1 & 0 \\ 0 & \sigma_2 \end{pmatrix}$$

be the dilation (scaling) operator. Instead of solving (2) consider the subproblems

$$\sup_{\beta \in \mathbb{R}^2} \frac{\langle z_1, z_2 \circ T(\beta) \rangle}{\|z_1\|_2 \|z_2 \circ T(\beta)\|_2} = \sup_{\beta \in \mathbb{R}^2} C_T(\beta), \qquad (4)$$

$$\sup_{\theta \in [0, 2\pi)} \frac{\langle z_1, z_2 \circ R(\theta) \rangle}{\|z_1\|_2 \|z_2 \circ R(\theta)\|_2} = \sup_{\theta \in [0, 2\pi)} C_R(\theta), \qquad (5)$$

and

$$\sup_{\sigma \in \mathbb{R}_+^2} \frac{\langle z_1, z_2 \circ D(\sigma) \rangle}{\|z_1\|_2 \|z_2 \circ D(\sigma)\|_2} = \sup_{\sigma \in \mathbb{R}_+^2} C_D(\sigma). \tag{6}$$

Dealing with digital images, assume that z_1 and z_2 and the indicator function ϕ are step functions. It is then possible to compute C_T by using the fast Fourier transformation (FFT) and noting that $\langle z_1, z_2 \circ T(\beta) \rangle$ and $\|z_2 \circ T(\beta)\|_2$ are almost convolutions.

Recall that if z_1 and z_2 are two images, then the convolution

$$h = (h_1, h_2) \to \int z_1(x) z_2(h-x) dx_1 dx_2$$
$$= \mathcal{F}^{-1}(\mathcal{F}(z_1)\mathcal{F}(z_2)),$$

where $\mathcal{F}$ is the discrete Fourier transformation and $\mathcal{F}^{-1}$ its inverse. The reason for using the Fourier transformation is that the computational cost of the right hand side is $O(N^2 \log(N))$, while the left hand side has a computational cost $O(N^4)$, where $N = 2^n$ is the side length of the images.

Let $z_\phi(x) = z_1(x)\phi(x)$. Then, for the rotation problem (5), it is seen that

$$\int\int z_1(x_1,x_2) z_2 \circ R(\theta)(x_1,x_2)\phi(x_1,x_2)dx_1 dx_2$$
$$= \int_{r=0}^{\infty}\int_{\alpha=0}^{2\pi} z_\phi(r\cos(\alpha), r\sin(\alpha))$$
$$z_2(r\cos(\alpha-\theta), r\sin(\alpha-\theta))rdrd\alpha. \tag{7}$$

By setting $f(r,\alpha) = z_\phi(r\cos(\alpha), r\sin(\alpha))r$, $g(r,\alpha) = z_2(r\cos(\alpha), r\sin(\alpha))$ and letting $\check{g}(r,\alpha) = g(r,-\alpha)$, it follows that

$$\langle z_1, z_2 \circ R(\theta)\rangle = \int_{r=0}^{\infty} f(r,\alpha) *_\alpha \check{g}(r,\alpha)dr,$$

where $*_\alpha$ denotes convolution in the α variable. This makes it possible to use FFT. The same idea applies for computing $\|z_2 \circ R(\theta)\|_2$ in the denominator of (5). Thus, the entire function $C_R(\theta)$ can be computed, hence also its maximum.

For the third subproblem (6), we just make another change of variables and use convolution by means of FFT again. It is assumed that $\text{supp}(z_1), \text{supp}(z_2) \subset \mathbb{R}_+^2$. If this is not the case, z_1, z_2 have to be treated on each quadrant separately. Then, by setting $y_j = \ln(x_j)$ and $\tilde{\sigma}_j = -\ln(\sigma_j)$, $j = 1,2$, and $z_\phi(x) = z_1(x)\phi(x)$, it is seen that

$$\int_{x \in \mathbb{R}_+^2} z_1(x_1,x_2) z_2(\sigma_1 x_1, \sigma_2 x_2)\phi(x_1,x_2)dx_1 dx_2 =$$
$$\int_{y \in \mathbb{R}^2} z_\phi(e^{y_1}, e^{y_1}) z_2(e^{y_1-\tilde{\sigma}_1}, e^{y_2-\tilde{\sigma}_2})e^{y_1+y_2}dy_1 dy_2. \tag{8}$$

Thus, by setting $f(y) = z_\phi(e^{y_1}, e^{y_1})e^{y_1+y_2}$, $g(y) = z_2(e^{y_1}, e^{y_1})$ and $\check{g}(y) = g(-y)$, it follows that $\langle z_1, z_2 \circ D(e^{\tilde{\sigma}_1}, e^{\tilde{\sigma}_2})\rangle = f * \check{g}$, where $*$ denotes convolution in both variables.

Instead of simply optimize along certain axes in a coordinate system, as in problems (4), (5) and (6), it is possible to use the same idea to solve more general subproblems. In fact, let A be an invertible 2×2 matrix that can be diagonalised as $s^{-1}As$, with s being a real matrix. Let b be a 2×1 matrix, and introduce the parametrised affine operator $h(t) : \mathbb{R}^2 \to \mathbb{R}^2$ defined by $h(t)x = (I+tA)x+tb$, where $t \in \mathbb{R}$. Then

$$\sup_{t \in \mathbb{R}} \frac{\langle z_1, z_2 \circ h(t)\rangle}{\|z_1\|_2 \|z_2 \circ h(t)\|_2} \tag{9}$$

can be solved by using FFT. However, we do not go into the details here.

A natural extension to the subproblems (4), (5) and (6), is given by letting A be an invertible matrix and optimizing over $\mathbb{R}_+^2 \ni \sigma \to C(AD(\sigma)A^{-1})$, where $D(\sigma)$ is the dilation operator, and $[0,2\pi] \ni \theta \to C(AR(\theta)A^{-1})$, where $R(\theta)$ is the rotation operator. In fact, by introducing the change of variables $\bar{x} = A^{-1}x$ and letting $\bar{f}(x) = f(Ax)$ the problems are reduced to (6) and (5), respectively.

Of course it is also possible to optimize $C(a)$ over rotations and dilations around another point than the origin by introducing the change of variables $\bar{x} = x - t_0$, where $t_0 \in \mathbb{R}^2$. It is also possible to optimize $C(a)$ over an isotropic dilation in (4) and to dilate over one axis while translating over the other.

A Gauss-Newton iteration method can also be included as a step in the algorithm, which will help for finding a more accurate local estimate. Instead of maximizing $C(a)$, we then minimize the left hand side of (1). The technique is standard and can be found in almost any book on optimization, e.g. [3].

The point about doing these extensions to the original subproblems (4), (5) and (6) is that they help to prevent the algorithm from getting stuck in local optima or saddle points. The values of A and t_0 can for example be realizations of some stochastic variables.

3 Transformation of gray levels
Let

$$z_2 = h \circ z_1, \qquad h : \mathbb{R} \to \mathbb{R} \tag{10}$$

define a transformation of the gray values in image z_1. Can we expect that the solution of (2) applied to z_1 and z_2 is given by a being the identity I? This is a relevant question, since it is a situation that occurs frequently when taking images, due to that the lightning conditions have changed between imaging instances or due to that different cameras

1119

have been used. This amounts to some change of the gray values in the second image compared to the first. Preferably, the correlation method should be insensitive to, at least, changes that can be expressed by an increasing function h in (10). This means that if the pixels in the images are ordered according to their gray values then this order is the same for both z_1 and z_2. Sometimes it is not possible to find a transformation h at all, and this occurs, for example, when $z_1(x_1) = z_1(x_2)$, $x_1 \neq x_2$, but $z_2(x_1) \neq z_2(x_2)$. The correlation method can not be expected to work properly under such conditions. The following theorem shows when we can expect to find the right solution.

Theorem 3.1. (i) Let $f \in L_\mu^2$ and let $O = \{\phi : \mathbb{R}^n \to \mathbb{R}^n \mid f \circ \phi \in L_\mu^2\}$. Then for any $c > 0$,

$$\sup_{\phi \in O} \frac{\langle f, (cf) \circ \phi \rangle}{\|f\|_2 \|(cf) \circ \phi\|_2} = 1$$

and the supremum is attained for $\phi = I$.

(ii) Let $\tilde{O} = \{\phi : \mathbb{R}^n \to \mathbb{R}^n \mid \phi, \phi^{-1} \in C^1, |\det \phi'| = 1\}$, $\mu = dx$ and let $f \in L^2 \cap L^\infty$. Then for any continuous and non decreasing $h : \mathbb{R} \to \mathbb{R}$, such that $h \circ f \in L^2$,

$$\sup_{\phi \in \tilde{O}} \frac{\langle f, h \circ f \circ \phi \rangle}{\|f\|_2 \|h \circ f \circ \phi\|_2} = \frac{\langle f, h \circ f \rangle}{\|f\|_2 \|h \circ f\|_2},$$

and the supremum is attained for $\phi = I$.

Thus, the affine correlation can be expected to yield the correct solution for a linear change of gray levels in the second image. However, in practice the affine correlation performs well for more general changes of gray levels than linear. This is shown in the last experiment in Section 6. If the optimum of $C(a)$ is solved by an area preserving affine transformation, then Theorem 3.1 (ii) shows that the solution is independent of the particular gray level transformation in the second image relative the first.

4   Algorithm

We propose the following basic algorithm, which can easily be enhanced, by the arguments in Section 2:

i: **Translation**: Find β from the solution of (4). Set $z_2 := z_2 \circ T(\beta)$.

ii: **Rotation**: Let $t_0 \in \mathbb{R}^2$ and set $\tilde{z}_i(x) = z_i(x - t_0)$, $i = 1, 2$. Find θ from the solution of (5) applied to $\tilde{z}_i(x)$, $i = 1, 2$. Set $z_2(x) := z_2(R(\theta)x - t_0)$.

iii: **Dilation**: Let A be a rotation matrix and set $\tilde{z}_i = z_i \circ A$, $i = 1, 2$. Find σ from the solution of (6) applied to $\tilde{z}_i(x)$, $i = 1, 2$. Set $z_2 := z_2 \circ AD(\sigma)A^{-1}$.

iv: Go to i.

The variables A and t_0 are preferably chosen to be realizations of stochastic variables, that are updated at each iteration of the algorithm.

5   Convergence of the algorithm

The algorithm can be viewed as iterated line search, with the line sometimes being a plane and where optimization is performed globally in each step. Thus, the algorithm is a descent method. As for all types of descent methods, e.g. the steepest descent method [3, p. 30], one can under some condition prove global convergence to a stationary point, but not guarantee that the global optimum is found. However, while ordinary descent methods tend to find a local minimum at the best, this algorithm has a more global character and is likely to find a better solution. This is also indicated by the experiments below. Furthermore, the result of the algorithm can be used as an initial point for a fast locally converging algorithm, e.g. Gauss-Newton iterations applied to the left hand side of (1).

As computations are performed numerically, care must be taken in choosing for example grid sizes for the integration, limits on variables, interpolation strategies when changing variables and so on. We do not go into the details here, but we caution that some care is needed.

Let z_1 and z_2 be the two images in the algorithm in Section 4, given by an $N_1 \times N_1$ matrix and an $N_2 \times N_2$ matrix, respectively. Then the computational cost for step ii, iii is $O(N_1^2 \log(N_1))$, and $O(N_2^2 \log(N_2))$ for step i, in the implementation at hand. The Gauss-Newton method has a computational cost of $O(N_1^2)$.

6   Experiments

We have performed the following experiments on real images. In the first two experiments the second image z_2 is obtained by selecting some $a \in \mathcal{A}_+$ and letting $z_2 = z_1 \circ a$, where z_1 is the first image. The measure $d\mu$ is chosen to be ϕdx, where dx is the Lebesgue measure and

$$\phi(x) = \begin{cases} 1, & x \in [0,1] \times [0,1] \\ 0, & \text{otherwise} \end{cases}$$

Furthermore, $\text{supp}(z_1) \subseteq \text{supp}(d\mu)$.

First let a be such that $ax = Rx + b$, where R is a rotation matrix with $\det(R) = 1$. Then a is a Euclidean transformation and it is sufficient to maximize over rotations and translations. Figure 1 shows how the algorithm performs under this assumption. The number of iterations that was used was three and the dilation step iii was not included.

In the second experiment, dilation of the image was allowed as well, i.e. $a \in \mathcal{A}_+$ was chosen so that $a(x) = Ax + b$ and $\det(A) \neq 1$. The singular values of A were $(1.3, 0.9)$, and the result is shown in Figure 2 after ten iterations. The result can be used as good initial point for Gauss-Newton iterations.

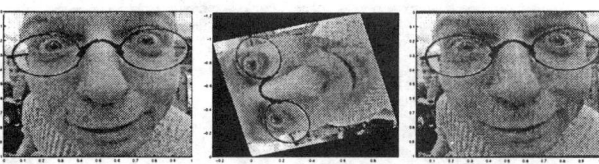

Figure 1. Original, Euclidean transformed and restored image.

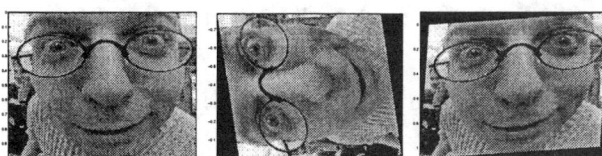

Figure 2. Original, affine transformed and restored image. (Singular values $(1.3, 0.9)$)

That z_2 not necessarily is an affine deformation of the entire image z_1 is seen in Figures 3 to 9. In these experiments a Gauss-Newton optimization was included as a fourth step. This helps for finding a more accurate solution.

For the third experiment z_1 is shown in Figure 4 left image and z_2 is shown in Figure 3 left image. z_2 can be transformed by a positive similarity transformation, i.e. scaling translation and rotation, with singular values $(1.5, 1.5)$ to match z_1. Figure 3 right shows the restored image $z_2 \circ a$, after optimizing $C(a)$. Figure 4 shows the patch that should be equal to z_1.

In the same way, the fourth experiment shows z_1 in Figure 6 left and z_2 in Figure 5 left image. Figure 5 right shows the restored image $z_2 \circ a$ and Figure 6 right shows the path that should be equal to z_1.

Finally we present an experiment on two real images taken from different view points. This brings in projective transformations, such that there does not in general exist an affine transformation that produces an exact match. Figure 7 shows image z_2 and Figure 9 left shows image z_1. Note that there are branches of some bushes present in z_1, that are not present in z_2. Figure 8 shows the restored image $z_2 \circ a$ obtained by optimizing $C(a)$ and Figure 9 right shows the patch of $z_2 \circ a$ that should be similar to z_1.

The overall number of iterations that are needed for convergence is about 10.

7 Conclusions

The proposed algorithm performs well on real images. It is shown that it is robust and that it can handle occlusions. Furthermore, the algorithm makes no assumptions

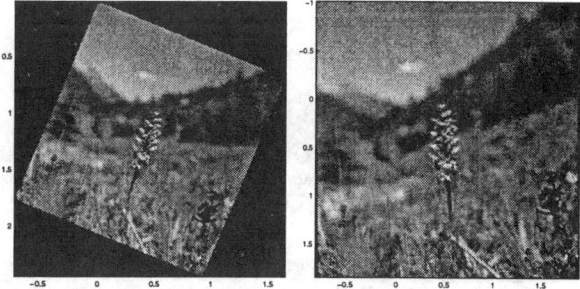

Figure 3. Original and restored image. sing. val. $(1.5, 1.5)$

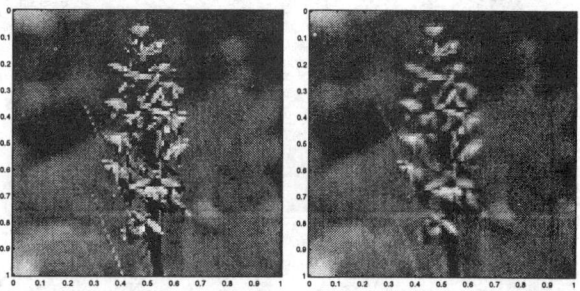

Figure 4. The mask and detail of restored image.

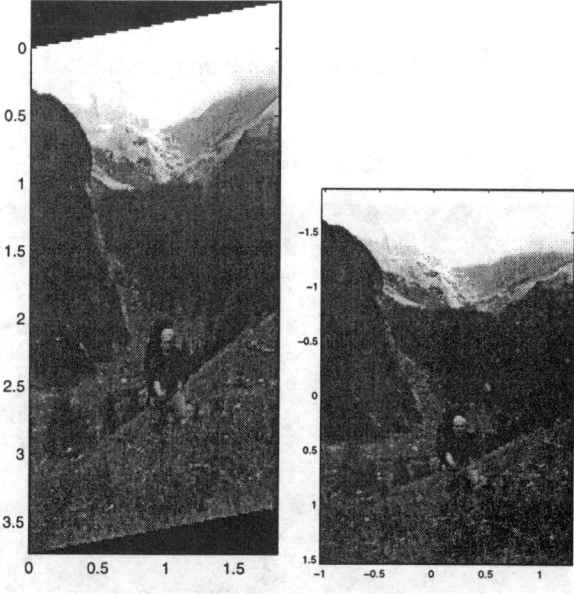

Figure 5. Original and restored image. sing. val. $(1.3, 0.9)$

Figure 6. The mask and detail of restored image.

Figure 9. The mask and detail of restored image.

on the images and does not rely on feature points or texture properties. It is also shown how gray level transformations may affect the estimate of affine transformation. The algorithm can be somewhat sensitive to the initial relative rotation between the images. If necessary this can be dealt with by rotating the second image an angle $0, \pi/2, \pi$ and $3\pi/2$ in turn before running the algorithm.

References

[1] D. H. Ballard and C. M. Brown. *Computer Vision*. Prentice-Hall, Englewood Cliffs, NJ, 1982.

[2] R. Berthilsson. Affine correlation. In *14th International Conference on Pattern Recognition*, volume 2, pages 1458–1460, Brisbane, Australia, 1998.

[3] R. Fletcher. *Practical Methods of Optimization*. John Wiley and Sons, 1987.

[4] J. Flusser. A moment based approach to registration of images with affine geometric distortion. *Transactions on Geoscience and Remote Sensing*, 32(2):382–387, 1994.

[5] G. Marola. On the detection of the axes of symmetry of the symmetric and almost symmetric planar image. *IEEE, Trans. Pattern Analysis and Machine Intelligence*, 11:104–108, 1989.

[6] A. Mitiche and J. Aggarwal. Contour registration by shape-specific points for shape matching. *Computer Vision Graphics Image Process*, 22:396–408, 1983.

[7] K. Nagao. Affine matching of planar sets. *CVIU*, 70(1):1–22, 1998.

[8] S. Pei and C. Lin. Image normalization for pattern-recognition. *Image and Vision Computing*, 13(10):711–723, 1995.

[9] A. Rosenfeld and A. Kak. *Digital Picture Processing*. Academic Press, 1982.

[10] A. Rosenfeld and A. C. Kak. *Digital Picture Processing*. Academic Press, New York, USA, 2nd edition, 1982.

[11] S. Sato and R. Cipolla. Extracting the affine transformation from texture moments. In J.-O. Eklundh, editor, *ECCV'94*, volume 2, pages 165–172. Springer Verlag, 1994.

[12] D. Shen and H. Horace. Generalized affine invariant image normalization. *Pattern Analysis and Machine Intelligence*, 19(5):431–440, 1997.

[13] M. Sonka, V. Hlavac, and R. Boyle. *Image Processing, Analysis and Machine Vision*. Chapman & Hall, 1993.

Figure 7. Original image.

Figure 8. Restored image.

Qualitative Probabilities for Image Interpretation

Allan Jepson*   Richard Mann[†‡]

*Department of Computer Science, University of Toronto, Toronto M5S 1A4 CANADA
[†]NEC Research Institute, Inc., 4 Independence Way, Princeton, NJ 08540 USA
[‡]Currently at: Dept. of Computer Science, Univ. of Waterloo, Waterloo, Ont. N2L 3G1 CANADA

Abstract

Two basic problems in image interpretation are: a) determining which interpretations are the most plausible amoungst many possibilities; and b) controlling the search for plausible interpretations. We address these issues using a Bayesian approach, with the plausibility ordering and search pruning based on the posterior probabilities of interpretations. However, due to the need for detailed quantitative prior probabilities and the need to evaluate complex integrals over various conditional distributions, a full Bayesian approach is currently impractical except in tightly constrained domains. To circumvent these difficulties we introduce the notion of qualitative probabilistic analysis. In particular, given spatial and contrast resolution parameters, we consider only the asymptotic order of the posterior probability for any interpretation as these resolutions are made finer. We introduce this approach for a simple card-world domain, and present computational results for blocks-world images.

1 Introduction

Two fundamental problems in image understanding are: a) choosing a plausible interpretation from many possible consistent interpretations for an image; and b) controlling the search for plausible interpretations. For example, consider the image segments shown in Fig. 1a. A human observer might infer that the corresponding scene is probably made up of three objects, namely a triangular card, a quadrilateral card, and a stick. Moreover, it is plausible that there were flaws in the image edge extraction process which caused "drop-outs" in the image data for both the stick and the quadrilateral. This interpretation is depicted in Fig. 1b. However, note that there are many other possible interpretations within such a "card-world" domain, such as the two depicted in Figs. 1c,d.

The standard explanation for why the interpretation in Fig. 1b is preferred is that it is nonaccidental [2, 10, 11]. That is, any other interpretation involves a careful (i.e. 'accidental') alignment of either the objects within the scene, or the viewer with respect to the scene, or both. In contrast, the scene model in the naturally selected interpretation involves only generic processes, namely a triangular card has been placed in front of a convex quadrilateral and a stick. Similarly, the imaging process for this interpretation is also nonaccidental, involving only two relatively common flaws (i.e. drop-out segments) in the feature extraction process.

A central contribution of this paper is that we formalize this type of nonaccidental reasoning, extend it, and ground

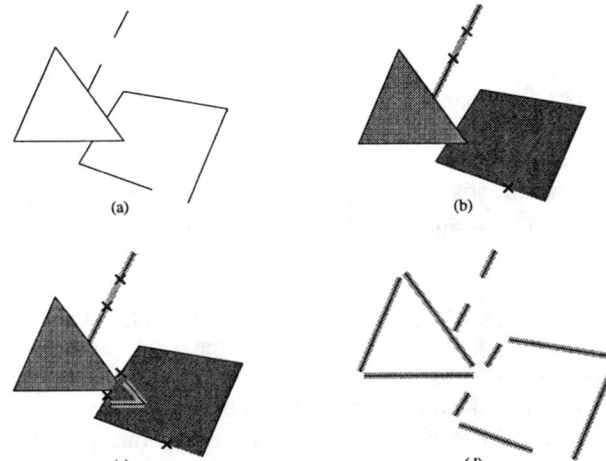

Figure 1: Multiple image interpretations in a "card-world" domain consisting of sticks and convex, opaque polygons. *Legend:* Image segments are shown as thin black lines. Thick grey lines depict sticks. Shaded grey regions depict (opaque) polygonal cards. Crosses depict breakpoints in the image segments for sticks and polygon edges. (a) Input image consisting of image segments. (b) The preferred interpretation consisting of a triangle in front of a quadrilateral and a stick. Drop-out segments arise in the image of the stick and the quadrilateral due to an imperfect image line-finder. (c) A less preferred interpretation with the triangle behind the quadrilateral. To explain the image two additional sticks and one more drop-out must be included in the interpretation, as compared to that in (b). (d) A trivial interpretation obtained by explaining every image segment with a stick.

it in Bayesian analysis through the use of 'qualitative probabilistic reasoning'. This provides a rigorous probabilistic framework for integrating information from nonaccidental features. We present computational results on blocks-world images. These results demonstrate that our approach forms a convenient basis for reasoning about images of scenes with multiple objects and occlusion. The implementation also indicates how this analysis can be used to significantly reduce the search complexity by pruning implausible search paths.

Our approach differs from current work in perceptual grouping [4, 6, 14, 16], image interpretation [1, 9], and object recognition [3, 5, 7, 10] in its use of the qualitative probabilistic framework. In particular, most work in perceptual grouping and object recognition has focussed on finding salient groups of image features based on

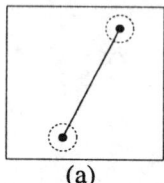 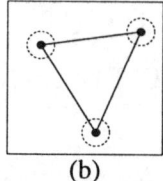 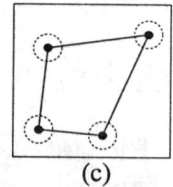

(a)　　　　　　(b)　　　　　　(c)

Figure 2: The resolution of endpoints and vertices for a stick (a), a triangle (b), and a quadrilateral (c).

some quantitative measures such as the fraction of model edges covered, energy functions which enforce consistency among features, and so on. Other researchers have presented Bayesian or minimum description length formulations for object recognition and scene interpretation. In contrast to both of these approaches, qualitative probabilities capture the structure available in nonaccidental features, but abstract away most of the information required for the quantitative prior distributions and likelihood functions.

Our approach is similar in spirit to ϵ-semantics [12] in knowledge representation, and to other approaches using defaults [4], but differs in that here the quantitative tools of probability theory are applied to weakly specified priors. In particular, the interaction of various defaults is cleanly and completely specified with our current approach.

2 Qualitative Probabilities

To begin, consider the prior probability for the occurrence of a single line segment in an image, as depicted in Fig. 2a. Let $p(L(\vec{x}_1, \vec{x}_2))$ denote the prior probability density for any particular line segment, $L(\vec{x}_1, \vec{x}_2)$, having endpoint positions $\vec{x}_1$ and $\vec{x}_2$. Instead of selecting a particular quantitative prior, $p(L)$, here we consider a wide equivalence class of such prior densities. The critical condition we impose on $p(L(\vec{x}_1, \vec{x}_2))$ is that

$$0 < d_0 \le p(L(\vec{x}_1, \vec{x}_2)) \le d_1 \qquad (1)$$

for some constants d_0 and d_1. That is, the prior probability density is bounded both from above and from below, away from zero.

To make use of this weak prior information, we consider an asymptotic analysis as a spatial resolution parameter becomes increasingly finer. In particular, suppose that the endpoints of a line segment can be resolved to within a radius of r pixels, and that the whole image is L pixels in either direction. Let $\epsilon = r/L$ denote the spatial resolution parameter. Consider the prior probability that one endpoint, say $\vec{x}_1$, of the line segment occurs within some disk of radius ϵ (see Fig. 2a). From equation (1) it follows that the prior probability of such an event is of order $\Theta(\epsilon^2)$ as $\epsilon \to 0$.[1] Similarly the prior probability of observing both

---

[1] Throughout this paper we use $\Theta(\epsilon^k)$ to denote the sharp order estimate, that is, $f(\epsilon) = \Theta(\epsilon^k)$ if and only if there exists constants $K_1, K_2 > 0$ such that $K_1\epsilon^k \le |f(\epsilon)| \le K_2\epsilon^k$, as $\epsilon \to 0$.

endpoints to be within a radius of ϵ of the predetermined points $\vec{x}_1$ and $\vec{x}_2$ is $\Theta(\epsilon^4)$. Both of these asymptotic results follow directly from equation (1) by integrating the density over the set of possible endpoint positions for a given resolution parameter ϵ.

Clearly such an asymptotic analysis can be extended to more general objects. For example, consider the prior density for any particular convex n-gon C_n, which can be taken to be a function of the n vertex positions $\{\vec{x}_i\}_{i=1}^n$. The critical condition on this prior density is again that it is both bounded above, and bounded away from zero from below. A similar asymptotic analysis now shows that the occurrence of any given n-gon, up to a resolution of ϵ for each of the $2n$ degrees of freedom in C_n, has prior probability $p(C_n) = \Theta(\epsilon^{2n})$. In particular, the prior for the triangle depicted in Fig. 2b is of order $\Theta(\epsilon^6)$, while the quadrilateral in Fig. 2c is of order $\Theta(\epsilon^8)$.

We also need to consider the arrangements of several objects within the scene. For card-world we take scene models to consist of 2D layered arrangement of sticks and convex, polygonal, opaque cards. Since the objects are opaque, the depth layering dictates the visibility of each point on any object. For example, the interpretation depicted in Fig. 1b involves a scene model consisting of a stick, a triangular card, and a quadrilateral card. The triangular card is in front of both the stick and the quadrilateral. For objects which do not intersect in the image, such as the stick and the quadrilateral, the depth relation is taken to be undefined (see [15] for a more general 2D layered scene model).

Qualitative priors can be derived for such scene models consisting of multiple objects. For the current paper we take the shape and position of any object to be independent of the shape and position of other objects. For example, the scene model depicted in Fig. 1b is a particular layered 2D arrangement of a triangle, a quadrilateral, and a stick, with the position of each endpoint and vertex resolved to within a disk of radius ϵ. Let $M_b(\vec{\alpha})$ denote this scene model, where the 'b' refers to panel b in Fig. 1, and the parameter vector $\vec{\alpha}$ denotes the 18 parameters needed to specify the locations of the endpoints and vertices of the three objects. By the independence assumption, the prior for $M_b(\vec{\alpha})$ is then simply the product of the prior for generating the triangle (which is $\Theta(\epsilon^6)$), the quadrilateral ($\Theta(\epsilon^8)$), and the stick ($\Theta(\epsilon^4)$). Note that, since the arrangement in depth layers only involves binary choices of which object of an overlapping pair is in front, there is no contribution to the order of the prior for arranging these objects in depth. As a result, we find the prior probability for the scene model depicted in Fig. 1b is $p(M_b) = \Theta(\epsilon^{18})$.

2.1 Posterior Probabilities

An interpretation of a set of image features, say I, involves a scene model and an imaging model which together account for I. Given the image data I, we wish to compute the posterior probability of any particular scene model,

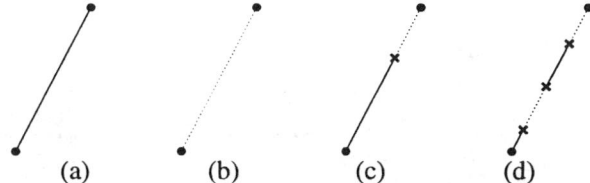

(a)   (b)   (c)   (d)

Figure 3: Possible image data for a scene model consisting of one stick. Here dotted lines denote line-finder drop-outs, and X's mark interior breakpoints. (a) Scene model. (b) Missing edge, $\Theta(\delta)$. (c) Missing end segment, $\Theta(\delta\epsilon)$. (d) Missing interior and end segments, $\Theta(\delta^2\epsilon^3)$

$\mathcal{M}$. According to Bayes theorem, the posterior probability of $\mathcal{M}$ satisfies,

$$p(\mathcal{M}|I) = \frac{p(I|\mathcal{M})p(\mathcal{M})}{p(I)}. \qquad (2)$$

Here $p(I|\mathcal{M})$ is the likelihood of observing the data I given the scene model $\mathcal{M}$, and $p(\mathcal{M})$ is the prior for $\mathcal{M}$. We refer to their product as the *unnormalized posterior*.

The likelihood term depends on the probability of the imaging model, which relates the scene model $\mathcal{M}$ to the observed image data I. To keep things simple in this introductory example, we take the imaging process to be almost veridical. We assume that the only error is that various subsegments (or all) of a visible scene edge may be missed by the image line-finder (see Fig. 3). The imaging model, then, must specify the occurrence and the endpoints of each of these 'drop-outs'.

The likelihood can now be defined in a similar way to the prior probability for a scene model. The occurrence of a drop-out is taken to appear with probability proportional to δ, where δ represents the resolution in image contrast necessary for the line-finder to detect an image edge. Moreover, the imaging model needs to account for the spatial positions of the endpoints of the drop-outs, which are determined to a spatial resolution of ϵ along the corresponding image segments.

In particular, consider the various ways that the single stick in Fig. 3a might be imaged. The likelihood of missing the stick entirely, as in Fig. 3b, is $\Theta(\delta)$, which depends only on the image contrast resolution δ. Similarly, a drop-out at one end of the stick (see Fig. 3c), requires one additional spatial parameter, and therefore has a likelihood of $\Theta(\epsilon\delta)$. (The other end of the drop-out in this case is dictated by the end of the stick, and is attributed to the scene model, not the imaging model). For Fig. 3d we require three drop-out endpoint parameters and there are two segments at which there is a loss of contrast. We take these separate drop-out segments to be independent, and therefore the likelihood is taken to be $\Theta(\epsilon^3\delta^2)$.

We can combine these likelihood computations with the previous asymptotic results for the priors to obtain expressions for the unnormalized posterior probability of various interpretations. For example, one interpretation for Fig. 1a

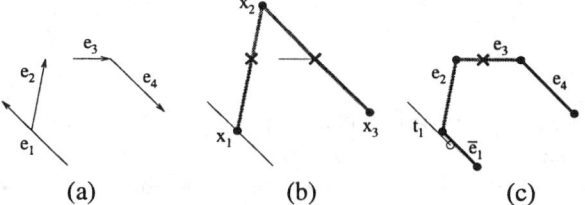

(a)   (b)   (c)

Figure 4: (a) Image edges. (b) Part of an example polygon in the set $C_n(\vec{x}_1, \vec{x}_2, \vec{x}_3)$. (c) Part of a polygon covering e_2, e_3, e_4 and the subsegment $\bar{e}_1$ of e_1. The remaining 'tail' t_1 has a free endpoint denoted by the circle on $\bar{e}_1$.

is given by the scene model $M_b(\vec{\alpha})$, discussed above, together with an imaging model which accounts for the drop-outs on the quadrilateral and the stick. These drop-outs have likelihoods of $\Theta(\epsilon\delta)$ and $\Theta(\epsilon^2\delta)$, respectively. Therefore we find the likelihood of generating the image I in Fig. 1a from the scene model $M_b(\vec{\alpha})$, is $p(I|M_b(\alpha)) = \Theta(\epsilon^3\delta^2)$. Since the prior for the scene model, $p(M_b(\vec{\alpha}))$, was shown above to be $\Theta(\epsilon^{18})$, the unnormalized posterior for this interpretation is then $\Theta(\epsilon^{18})\Theta(\epsilon^3\delta^2) = \Theta(\epsilon^{21}\delta^2)$.

Similarly, for the interpretations depicted in Figs. 1c,d, we find the unnormalized posteriors are of orders $\Theta(\epsilon^{31}\delta^3)$ and $\Theta(\epsilon^{40})$, respectively. Equation (2) then ensures that the posterior probabilities for these three interpretations are just the common factor $1/p(I)$ times these unnormalized posteriors.

2.2 Preferred Interpretations

In order to compare two unnormalized posteriors we may require information about the relative sizes of δ and ϵ. A simple form for this is to suppose that

$$\epsilon = \Theta(\delta^q), \qquad (3)$$

as $\epsilon \to 0$ for some constant $q \geq 0$. In the computational examples we find that the selection of the preferred interpretations are not sensitive to the precise choice of q. For convenience here we treat $\epsilon \ll \delta$ (i.e. $q = \infty$). This corresponds to the assumption that missing features are much more likely to occur than accidental alignments. As a result, an unnormalized posterior of order $\Theta(\epsilon^{n_1}\delta^{m_1})$ is preferred over one with order $\Theta(\epsilon^{n_2}\delta^{m_2})$ if and only if either $n_1 < n_2$, or $n_1 = n_2$ and $m_1 < m_2$.

This provides an intuitively plausible ordering for the three interpretations depicted in Fig. 1. In particular the posterior distribution for the interpretations depicted in Fig. 1b (with an unnormalized posterior of $\Theta(\epsilon^{21}\delta^2)$) is asymptotically much larger than that of Fig. 1c ($\Theta(\epsilon^{31}\delta^3)$), which in turn is much larger than that of Fig. 1d ($\Theta(\epsilon^{40})$). In fact, this same ordering remains valid so long as $q > 1/3$ in (3).

3   Hypothesis Generation and Search

It is critical that our qualitative probabilistic analysis can form the foundation for effective search heuristics. Even in the simple card-world domain the search space grows exponentially with the number of edges, so a brute-force search is impractical.

Here we show how qualitative probabilities can be used to determine the plausibility of partial interpretations, which can then be used to prune the search. For example, consider the image data in Fig. 4a along with the hypothesis depicted in Fig. 4b. In particular, the hypothesis is that the two image edges e_2 and e_4 are covered by consecutive edges of some convex n-gon for some $n \geq 3$. Let $C_n(\vec{x}_1, \vec{x}_2, \vec{x}_3)$ denote the set of all convex n-gons which have the points $\vec{x}_1$, $\vec{x}_2$, and $\vec{x}_3$ as three consecutive vertices (as shown in Fig. 4b). Since the three specified vertices are given to a spatial resolution of ϵ, the prior probability for the hypothesis $C_n(\vec{x}_1, \vec{x}_2, \vec{x}_3)$ is $\Theta(\epsilon^6)$.

Moreover, since there are two drop-outs each with a free endpoint (see Fig. 4b), the likelihood of generating e_2 and e_4 as a subset of the image data is $\Theta(\epsilon^2 \delta^2)$, Thus the unnormalized posterior for $C_n(\vec{x}_1, \vec{x}_2, \vec{x}_3)$ is of order $\Theta(\epsilon^8 \delta^2)$, for all $n \geq 3$.[2]

To determine the level of evidence for such a hypothesis, we use the odds of this hypothesis in comparison to one in which the same subset of image data is explained only by sticks. These odds are given by the ratio of posterior probabilities for the two hypotheses which, by Bayes rule (2), is just the ratio of the two unnormalized posteriors. Thus the odds for $C_n(\vec{x}_1, \vec{x}_2, \vec{x}_3)$ are $\Theta(\epsilon^8 \delta^2)/\Theta(\epsilon^8) = \Theta(\delta^2)$ (the denominator here is the unnormalized posterior for the hypothesis that e_2 and e_4 arise from two sticks). We see that, for sufficiently small δ, the odds actually favor the two sticks hypothesis. Similar calculations show that the odds for (e_2, e_3) being covered by consecutive edges of an n-gon are $\Theta(\epsilon^{-1} \delta)$, and the odds for edges (e_3, e_4) are $\Theta(\epsilon^{-2})$.

Finally, consider the hypothesis, say $H_v(e_1, e_2)$, that the pair of edges (e_1, e_2) arise from consecutive edges of an n-gon, such as the one depicted in Fig. 4c. This implies an under-segmentation error has occurred to form image edge e_1, and some other (independent) process must explain the 'tail' of edge e_1 extending outside of this polygon. Let $\bar{e}_1$ denote the subsegment of e_1 covered by the n-gon, and t_1 the tail segment, where t_1 can overlap $\bar{e}_1$, as long as its right endpoint (the open circle in Fig. 4c) is within $\bar{e}_1$.

The unnormalized posterior for $H_v(e_1, e_2)$ is then the product of the unnormalized posterior for the 'V' formed by $(\bar{e}_1, e_2)$, namely $\Theta(\epsilon^6)$, and the unnormalized posterior for the tail t_1. In the worst case, this latter term could be $\Theta(\epsilon^3)$, corresponding to the hypothesis that t_1 arose from a stick with an uncertain right endpoint. Alternatively, in the best case, the tail could be explained by a part of some other polygon. For a perfectly imaged n-gon the unnormalized posterior is $\Theta(\epsilon^{2n})$, and therefore the prorated value for each of the n edges is $\Theta(\epsilon^2)$. Using this best case, the

---

[2] Similar interpretations which have drop-outs on both ends of edges e_2 and/or e_4 are possible, but give smaller unnormalized posteriors.

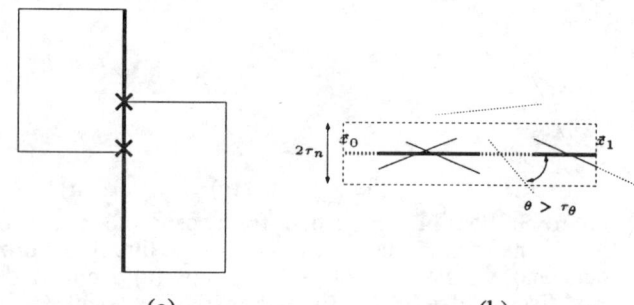

(a)   (b)

Figure 5: (a) Multiple scene edges (thin lines) can map to single image segment (thick line), as in abutment. Scene edges are merged whenever they project to nearly collinear image segments. We also predict the location of potential breakpoints (denoted "X") whenever there is a change in the surface on either side of an edge. (b) One visible scene edge, $[\vec{x}_0, \vec{x}_1]$ (thick line), can account for multiple image segments (thin lines). We use a fixed tolerance for perpendicular distance (τ_n) and angular error (τ_θ) between the observed image segments and the ideal edge. Unexplained parts of the scene edge ("drop outs") are shown as thick dotted lines. A scene edge may account for only a subsegment of an image edge, as for the rightmost image segment.

hypothesis $H_v(e_1, e_2)$ has an unnormalized posterior of order $\Theta(\epsilon^6)\Theta(\epsilon^2) = \Theta(\epsilon^8)$. And the odds for $H_v(e_1, e_2)$ are simply $O(1)$, in other words, there is no asymptotic evidence in favor of this hypothesis.

A detailed discussion of search using information provided by qualitative probabilities is beyond the scope of the current paper. Here we use a simple search heuristic based on the log of the odds for each hypothesis. These odds are compared to the maximal odds that can be obtained for any hypothesis in which m edges of an n-gon are partially covered by image edges (i.e. at least a subsegment of each of these scene edges is accounted for by an image edge, see Fig. 4b). For convex n-gons with $m < n$, we find that the maximal odds are $\Theta(\epsilon^{2m+2})/\Theta(\epsilon^{4m}) = \Theta(\epsilon^{-2m+2})$, as attained for convex open chains of m edges. We define $\tau(m)$ to be the log of these maximal odds, namely $\tau(m) = (2m - 2)|\log(\epsilon)|$ for $m < n$.

The 'plausible garden path' search heuristic involves pruning any hypothesis which consists of an n-gon with m partially covered scene edges and has log odds smaller than $\rho\tau(m)$ (for simplicity we ignore terms in δ). Here we use $\rho = 0.5$. From the odds computations above, we find that the only unpruned hypotheses involving pairs of edges from Fig. 4a are the ones which cover (e_2, e_3) and (e_3, e_4) with consecutive edges. Similarly, the only 3- and 4-edge plausible convex groups are (e_2, e_3, e_4), (e_1, e_3, e_4), or (e_1, e_2, e_3, e_4), which are intuitively reasonable. In Sec. 6.1 we discuss the results of applying this pruning heuristic to image data.

4 Detailed Imaging Model

To apply our system to real images it is critical that the imaging model accounts for typical imperfections in the feature extraction process. Here the only features we consider are image segments, as extracted by a typical line-finder. Therefore we need to model the different types of imperfections in the line-finder results, namely: 1) drop-outs; 2) false-targets; 3) over- and under-segmentation errors; 4) limited resolution; and 5) errors in the position and orientation estimates.

The first three of these types of imperfections can be dealt with using the approach described in Sec. 2.1. In particular, drop-out segments are explicitly accounted for by the imaging model within an interpretation. We use sticks in the scene model to represent false targets, which arise from unmodeled scene structure such as shadows, texture, or image noise. Over and under segmentation errors are dealt with by allowing several image segments to account for a single scene edge, and also several visible scene edges to account for a single image segment (see Fig. 5). The last two types of imperfections are discussed below.

4.1 Visible and Resolvable Edges

Visible scene edges are defined to be the set of visible points on the edges of the polygonal cards or sticks. (A point is visible if and only if that point is not within any other object which is deemed to be in front.) However, for a scene model in which two objects nearly abut, there can be two visible edges which are nearly colinear in the image (see Fig. 5a). The image line-finder will be unable to resolve such a pair if the perpendicular distance between them is too small.

To account for this limit in resolution we merge nearby visible scene edges into single visible edges. In addition, in order to predict the location of potential defects (such as drop-outs) in the observed image segments, we partition visible edges into collections of subedges that share common object boundaries (see Fig. 5a).

4.2 Position and Orientation Errors

The imaging model is conveniently described in terms of covering relationships between an image segment and a visible scene edge (see Fig. 5b). A visible scene edge can "cover" all or part of an image segment, and thereby provide an appropriate explanation for how that image segment (or part thereof) could have arisen. Conversely, an image segment can cover all or part of a visible scene edge, and thus provide data supporting the hypothesis of that scene edge's existence. We use a fixed perpendicular and angular tolerance to model the error in image segments (see Fig. 5b). In addition, we specify a minimum length for any drop-outs and false-targets.

5 Application to Blocks-World Scenes

We demonstrate our approach on blocks-world scenes (see Fig. 7). For simplicity we restrict the viewing conditions such that the image of any individual block is well-approximated by an orthographic view. The key to modeling blocks-world using layered arrangements of 2D cards

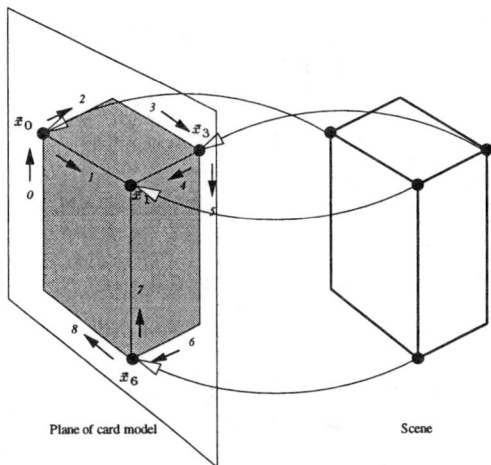

Figure 6: The card-world representation of a block is the orthographic projection of a block, depicted here in g. The arrows on the edges within the card indicate the ori on convention used.

is to depict the orthographic view of some 3D rectangular block on the cards themselves (see Fig. 6). Each of the visible edges of the corresponding 3D block is represented by an edge on this card, and the interior region of the card is considered to be opaque. The length of the sides can be varied, along with the particular viewpoint depicted on the card.

An orthographic view of a general 3D block is fully specified by four points in the image plane, as shown in Fig. 6. The coordinates of the three arrow junctions ($\vec{x}_0$, $\vec{x}_3$, and $\vec{x}_6$) and that of the Y-junction ($\vec{x}_1$) uniquely determine a block. Roberts [13] showed that a necessary and sufficient condition for such a parameterized 2D model to correspond to some orthographic view of a rectangular block is that each of the three interior edges (labelled 1, 4, and 7) must form an obtuse or right angle with both of the other two interior edges.

We use a qualitative prior for the scene models and a qualitative likelihood for the imaging models. Since the orthographic projection of a rectangular block is described by eight parameters, we take any particular block (up to a spatial resolution of ϵ) to have a prior probability of $\Theta(\epsilon^8)$. The likelihood of drop-outs are determined exactly as in Sec. 2.1. For example, the interpretation depicted Fig. 7c for image E involves 4 blocks, 2 sticks, and 10 drop-outs (four of which correspond to entirely missed edges) with a total of 7 free endpoints (marked by X's in the figure). The unnormalized posterior is then $\Theta(\epsilon^{4*8}\epsilon^{2*4}\epsilon^7\delta^{10}) = \Theta(\epsilon^{47}\delta^{10})$, as given by the 'score' in Fig. 7c.

6 Experiments

For our experiments we consider image data from images of simple blocks-world scenes. We used the line-finder in the *Khoros 1.2* package to generate the image data in Fig. 7a. Note that, even for human observers given this

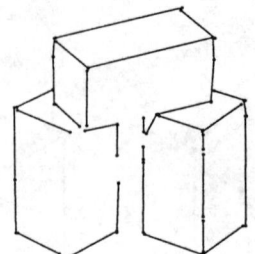

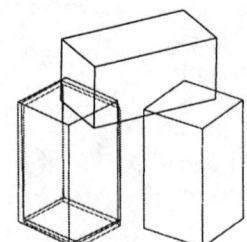

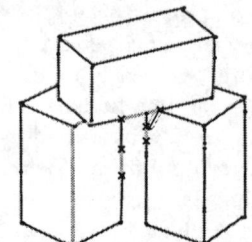

Image "9": 34 Segments

Individual blocks: 5

Score: $\epsilon^{34}\delta^5$ (next best $\epsilon^{42}\delta^7$)
Search (secs): 6, 10, 17, 20
Nodes: 29, 44, 69, 81

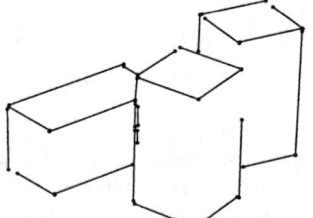

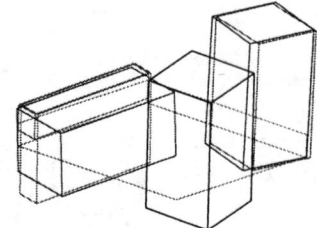

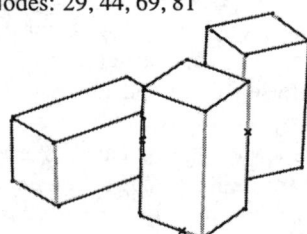

Image "5": 26 Segments

Individual blocks: 7

Score $\epsilon^{26}\delta^5$ (next best $\epsilon^{35}\delta^7$)
Search (secs): 12, 17, 31, 57
Nodes: 53, 67, 115, 188

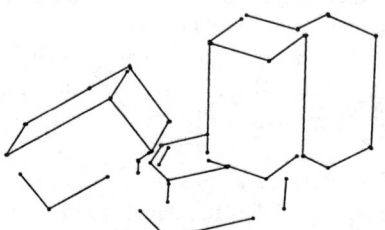

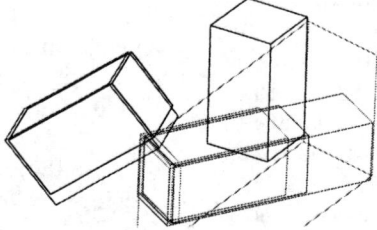

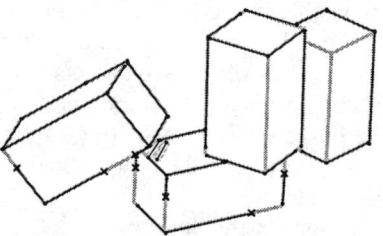

Image "E": 34 Segments

Individual blocks: 12
(Best 8 shown)

Score $\epsilon^{47}\delta^{10}$ (1 other within ϵ^2)
Search (secs): 56, 72, 192, 257
Nodes: 150, 210, 493, 671

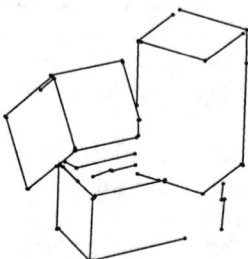

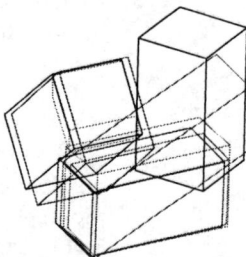

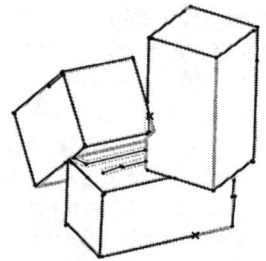

Image "D": 34 Segments

Individual blocks: 11
(Best 8 shown)

Score: $\epsilon^{42}\delta^7$ (1 other within ϵ^2)
Search (secs): 20, 37, 67, 142
Nodes: 80, 143, 241, 475

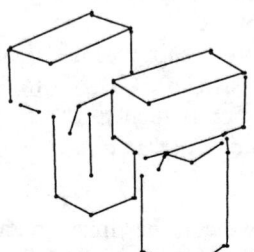

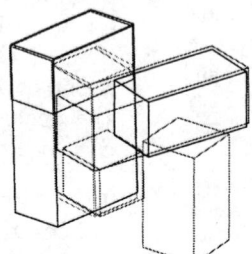

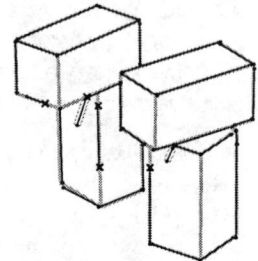

Image "7": 32 Segments

Individual blocks: 10
(Best 8 shown)

Score: $\epsilon^{45}\delta^8$ (1 other within ϵ^2)
Search (secs): 21*, 66, 132, 228
Nodes: 72*, 182, 351, 578

Continued from previous page.

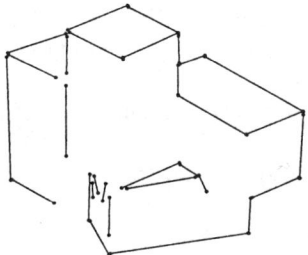 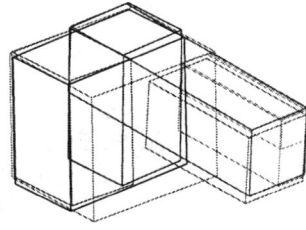 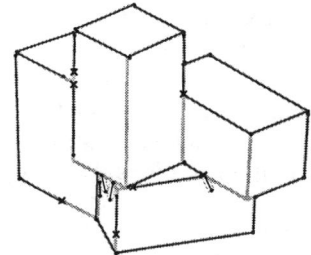

Image "4": 30 Segments	Individual blocks: 18 (Best 8 shown)	Score:$\epsilon^{51}\delta^9$ (7+ others within ϵ^2) Search (secs): 65*, 160*, 419, 518 Nodes: 221*, 479*, 1247, 1602
(a)	(b)	(c)

Figure 7: Experimental results for several blocks-world images. (a) Line-finder results. (b) The fully-instantiated blocks with the highest individual odds. For clarity, the individual blocks are shown with a slight random "jitter", and lighter greys indicate blocks with lower odds. (c) Preferred interpretation. *Legend:* Image segments are shown as thin black lines. Object edges are shown as thick grey lines. Breaks are denoted by crosses. Sticks are shown as thin grey boxes outlining one or more image segments. The unnormalized posterior (i.e. score) is shown below each preferred interpretation. The ambiguity of the preferred interpretation is indicated by either the score of the next best interpretation found, or by the number of other interpretations found with scores within ϵ^2 of this best one. The execution times (on a Pentium II 300MHz processor) and the number of unique interpretations visited for the band search algorithm are reported for $N = 1, 2, 4, 8$, respectively (here * denotes the search at this bandwidth failed to find the preferred interpretation). Note the preferred interpretations for images E and 4 involve individual blocks that are ranked 11th and 17th, respectively, and are therefore not displayed in column (b).

data, there are some minor ambiguities in the interpretations (eg. the bottom-left block in image "7", and the left-most block in image "4" are not completely resolved).

6.1 Individual Blocks

We first implemented a brute-force search similar to the IT search in [5]. The significant differences are that our imaging model is less restrictive (allowing subsegments of image edges to be matched to scene edges) and our scene model has more (i.e. 8) parameters. This search finds all maximal subsets of the image data that are consistent with the orthographic image of one block. In agreement with [5] this search proved to be impractical, taking 4 to 6 hours on a Pentium 133MHz processor. For the simple image data sets in Fig. 7a several thousand different individual block hypotheses were found. The majority of these were partially-instantiated blocks, that is, blocks for which the parameters are not completely specified by the covering set of image edges.

The odds for each block hypothesis, versus the hypothesis that the same subset of image edges come from sticks (see Sec. 3), was used as a plausibility measure to sort the list of blocks. The true blocks typically appeared in the top one percent of this sorted list. The only cases this failed was for the left block in image "4" and the bottom-left block in "7". Here the line-finder failed to detect enough edges to fully instantiate the block, and therefore the true block could not be found. Instead, in both of these cases the search algorithm grouped additional edges together with those from the true block (see Fig. 7b).

An order of magnitude speed-up in the search was obtained by using the plausible garden path heuristic dis-

cussed in Sec. 3. That is, we pruned any block hypothesis whose log odds fell below half the maximum possible log odds for any block hypothesis with the same number of covered edges. Another order of magnitude speed-up was obtained by first finding plausible local block fragments, and then grouping these fragments using the same odds measure to prune implausible hypotheses. The resulting search ran in under a minute on each of the examples in Fig. 7. The resulting search found every true block except for the two blocks missed by the full search.

6.2 Complete Interpretations

Here we consider the full 2D layered interpretations for the blocks-world image data in Fig. 7a. To simplify the implementation, we restrict our consideration to *fully instantiated* blocks. This restriction means the overlap between pairs of blocks is fully specified, which significantly simplifies the algorithm for determining the feasible depth layerings. A second simplification is that we restrict any sticks to be in front of all the blocks. The search space, then, consists of all subsets of the fully instantiated blocks (see Fig. 7b) arranged in all possible layered depth relations, plus zero or more sticks in the foreground.

To find plausible interpretations, we perform a greedy band-search. This is an iterative process which maintains a "band" of the best interpretations found so far. The ordering is prescribed by the power of ϵ in the unnormalized posterior; the term in δ is ignored. During the search the band is pruned by deleting all interpretations whose unnormalized posterior is asymptotically smaller than that of the Nth ranked interpretation. (Note that, in the case of ties for the Nth position, the band can contain more than N interpretations.) We refer to N as the search bandwidth.

The search proceeds by iteratively updating the interpretations in the band. Initially the band is set to contain only the trivial interpretation consisting of all sticks. To update the band at each iteration, new candidate interpretations are generated by adding one block to each interpretation in the band. These additional blocks are inserted at each feasible depth. Since the addition of a block could occlude much of an existing block, or even several blocks, single blocks are then greedily deleted from the candidate interpretations so long as the scores are increased by doing so. The union of current band and this resulting set of candidate interpretations is pruned at the Nth ranked score to form the band for the next iteration of the search. This process continues until the band does not change from one iteration to the next. Note that just one block can be added to any interpretation within the band during each iteration, and thus we again require a "garden path" to the preferred solution.

The results of this algorithm are presented in Fig. 7c, where the most preferred interpretations are displayed along with their unnormalized posteriors. The run-times for bandwidths $N = 1, 2, 4$, and 8 are observed to grow roughly linearly with N, as do the the number of unique interpretations visited. The search algorithm arrived at the most preferred solution in all cases except for Image 7 with bandwidth 1, and for Image 4 with bandwidths 1 and 2. Note that images 4 and 7 exhibit various accidental alignments which allow for edges from different blocks to be incorrectly grouped into larger blocks. These larger blocks are selected early in the search process and, for small bandwidths, cause it to be misled.

The ambiguity in the interpretation of the images is also represented in Fig. 7c. Images 5 and 9 are found to be strongly unambiguous, with the second best unnormalized posteriors 8 or 9 orders of ϵ smaller than the preferred one. For image E two interpretations differing only in a depth reversal of the rightmost block were found with the same maximal score. For Image D the ambiguity is between which of the top two blocks occludes a small part of the other. Finally, the ambiguities for images 7 and 4 arise because the image data is insufficient to resolve one of the blocks in each case, and several plausible choices exist. All these ambiguities seem natural given the image data.

Note that for imaging systems with finer resolution parameters (i.e. a finer image resolution and/or a better feature extraction process) one can expect that the odds used in the search will become more extreme. Thus the various decisions the search algorithm needs to make will be more clear cut and, if the representation is appropriate, we can expect the search to become easier for the same scenes. In comparison, note that the resolution of the images used for Fig. 7 was about the equivalent of the resolution the human fovea achieves on your thumbnail held at arms length (i.e. 2 degrees of arc).

7 Conclusion

Our results indicate that the qualitative probabilistic analysis provides a natural preference ordering on interpretations for simple card-world and blocks-world scenes. Moreover the analysis motivated the choice of effective search heuristics.

The same style of analysis can be applied to other domains, such as model-based object recognition [3, 5, 7, 10], curve and surface grouping [4, 14, 15], and simple motion interpretation [8]. These are important areas for further study.

An open question concerns how our approach based on qualitative probabilities performs compared to quantitative approaches for scene interpretation (eg., [1, 3, 7, 9]), and further if we can exploit quantitative probability information (such as the relative frequency of various types of objects) to obtain a stronger ordering on our interpretations and/or better search heuristics.

Acknowledgements

This research was supported by NSERC Canada. We would like to thank David Jacobs, Jacob Feldman, and Chakra Chennubhotla for helpful comments on an earlier version of this paper.

References

[1] E. Adelson and A. Pentland, The perception of shading and reflectance. In D. Knill and W. Richards, eds., *Perception as Bayesian Inference*, Cambridge University Press, 1996.

[2] T. Binford. Inferring surfaces from images. *AIJ*, 17:205–244, 1981.

[3] S. Dickinson, A. Pentland and A. Rosenfeld. From volumes to views: An approach to 3-D object recognition. *CVGIP*, 55(2):130–154, 1992.

[4] J. Feldman. Regularity-based perceptual grouping. *Computational Intelligence*, 13(4):582–623, 1997.

[5] W.E.L. Grimson and T. Lozano-Perez. Localizing overlapping parts by searching the interpretation tree. *IEEE PAMI* 9(4), 1997, pp.469-482.

[6] D. Jacobs. Robust and efficient detection of convex groups. *CVPR-93*, pp.770–771, 1993.

[7] D. Jacobs. Matching 3-D models to 2-D images. *IJCV*, (21)1/2:123–153 ,1997.

[8] A.D. Jepson, W. Richards, and D. Knill. Modal structure and reliable inference. In *Perception as Bayesian Inference*, pp. 63–92.

[9] Y. LeClerc, Constructing Simple Stable Descriptions for Image Partitioning. *IJCV*, (3):73–102, 1989.

[10] D. Lowe. *Perceptual Organization and Visual Recognition*. Kluwer Academic Publishers, Norwell, MA, 1985.

[11] K. Nakayama and S. Shimojo. Experiencing and perceiving visual surfaces. *Science*, 257:1357–1363, 1992.

[12] J. Pearl. *Probabilistic Reasoning in Intelligent Systems: Networks of Plausible Inference*. Morgan Kaufmann Pub., 1988.

[13] L.G. Roberts. Machine perception of three-dimensional solids. TR 315, Lincoln Lab, MIT, May 1963.

[14] E. Saund. Perceptual organization of occluding contours of opaque surfaces. CVPR-98 Workshop on Perceptual Organization, Santa Barbara, CA.

[15] L. Williams and A. Hanson. Perceptual completion of occluded surfaces. *CVIU*, 64(1):1–20, 1996.

[16] L. Williams and K. Thornber, A Comparison of Measures for Detecting Natural Shapes in Cluttered Backgrounds *ECCV-98*, p.432, 1998.

Principal Manifolds and Bayesian Subspaces
for Visual Recognition

Baback Moghaddam
Mitsubishi Electric Research Laboratory
201 Broadway, Cambridge MA 02139, USA
baback@merl.com

Abstract

We investigate the use of linear and nonlinear principal manifolds for learning low-dimensional representations for visual recognition. Three techniques: Principal Component Analysis (PCA), Independent Component Analysis (ICA) and Nonlinear PCA (NLPCA) are examined and tested in a visual recognition experiment using a large gallery of facial images from the "FERET" database. We compare the recognition performance of a nearest-neighbour matching rule with each principal manifold representation to that of a maximum a posteriori (MAP) matching rule using a Bayesian similarity measure derived from probabilistic subspaces and demonstrate the superiority of the latter.

1. Introduction

In recent years, computer vision research has witnessed a growing interest in subspace analysis techniques. In particular, eigenvector decomposition has been shown to be an effective tool for solving problems which use high-dimensional representations of phenomena which are intrinsically low-dimensional. This general analysis framework lends itself to several closely related formulations in object modeling and recognition which employ the *principal modes* or the characteristic *degrees-of-freedom* for description. The identification and parametric representation of data in terms of these "principal manifolds" is at the core of recent advances in parametric descriptions of shape [7], target detection [31, 4, 29], nonlinear image interpolation [3], visual learning [27, 28, 30, 25], automatic face recognition [34, 31, 24] as well as density estimation [25, 26].

Subspace methods also form the basis for exploratory data analysis and pattern recognition where they are used to extract low-dimensional manifolds comprised of statistically uncorrelated or independent variables which tend to simplify tasks such as classification. The Karhunen-Loève Transform (KLT) [17] and Principal Components Analysis (PCA) [14] are examples of eigenvector-based techniques which are commonly used for dimensionality reduction and feature extraction. Independent Component Analysis (ICA) [6] is yet another linear decomposition which seeks statistically *independent* and non-Gaussian components, modeling the observed data as a linear mixture of (unknown) independent sources. ICA's proficiency in "blind source separation" [15] has found a particular niche in the analysis of EEG [18] and fMRI [21] signals of the brain. Nonlinear PCA (NLPCA) [16, 8] and nonlinear Principal Surfaces [9, 10] are extensions of these linear techniques. In the following section we will briefly review these principal manifolds, their derivation and subsequent statistical properties. In Section 3, an alternative technique using subspace densities and Bayesian similarity is presented and in Section 4 its performance is compared to Euclidean similarity metrics on principal manifolds.

2. Subspace Representations

Spatiotopic visual data (*e.g.*, images, depth maps, flow fields, *etc.*) can be represented as vectors — *i.e.*, as points in a high-dimensional vector space. For example, a m-by-n pixel 2D image can be mapped to a vector $\mathbf{x} \in \mathcal{R}^{N=mn}$, by lexicographic ordering of the pixel elements.[1] Despite this high-dimensional embedding, the natural constraints of the physical world (and the imaging process) dictate that the data will in fact lie in a lower-dimensional manifold. The primary goal of subspace analysis is to identify, represent and parameterize this manifold in accordance with some optimality criteria. We will now review several leading approaches to obtaining both linear and nonlinear principal manifolds, and highlight their corresponding statistical properties.

---

[1] Without loss of generality we will hereafter assume that the mean image vector $\bar{\mathbf{x}}$ is always subtracted from the data.

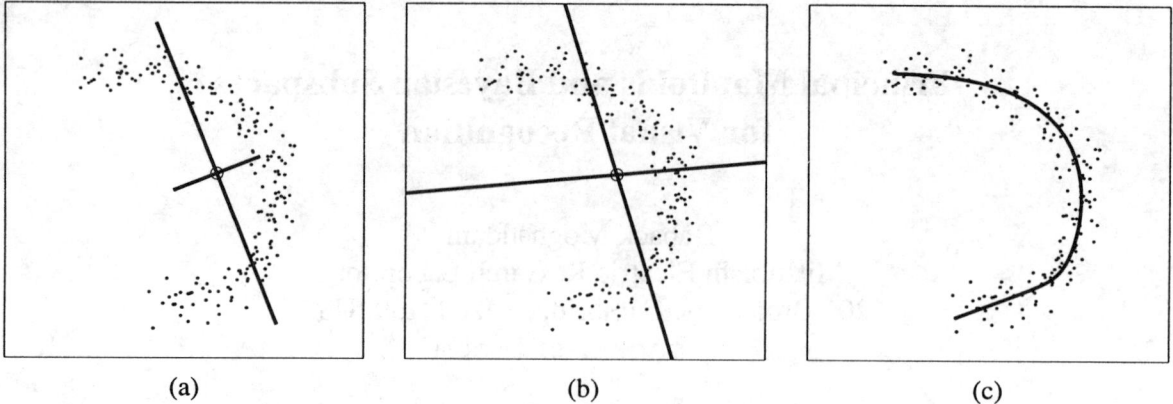

Figure 1. (a) PCA basis (linear, ordered and orthogonal) (b) ICA basis (linear, unordered and non-orthogonal) and (c) Principal Curve (parameterized nonlinear manifold)

2.1. Linear PCA Manifolds

In PCA [14] the basis functions in a discrete Karhunen-Loève Transform (KLT) [17] are obtained by solving the algebraic eigenvalue problem $\Lambda = \Phi^T \Sigma \Phi$ where Σ is the covariance matrix of the data, Φ is the eigenvector matrix of Σ and Λ is the corresponding diagonal matrix of eigenvalues. The unitary matrix Φ defines a coordinate transform (rotation) which *decorrelates* the data and makes explicit the *invariant subspace* of the matrix "operator" Σ. Most commonly, PCA is a partial KLT which identifies the largest (or principal) eigenvalue eigenvectors for projecting the data: $\mathbf{y} = \Phi_M^T \mathbf{x}$, where Φ_M is a submatrix of Φ containing the principal eigenvectors (from here on we will just use Φ to denote Φ_M). PCA can be seen as a linear projection $\mathcal{R}^N \to \mathcal{R}^M$ onto the lower-dimensional subspace corresponding to the maximal eigenvalues. The main properties of the PCA transform are summarized by the following:

$$\mathbf{x} \approx \Phi\mathbf{y} \;\to\; \Phi^T\Phi = \mathbf{I} \;\to\; E\{y_i y_j\}_{i \neq j} = 0 \quad (1)$$

corresponding to approximate reconstruction, orthonormality of the basis Φ and decorrelated principal components, respectively. Figure 1(a) illustrates the PC vectors (columns of Φ) obtained with a toy data set corresponding to an essentially one-dimensional (nonlinear) manifold. Projection of the data points onto the first PC would then correspond to a 1D linear manifold representation (the 2nd PC, shown as a smaller line segment in the figure, would be discarded in this low-dimensional example).

2.2. Linear ICA Manifolds

Independent Component Analysis (ICA) [15, 6] is similar to PCA except that the components are designed to be as non-Gaussian as possible (usually by minimizing/maximizing 4th-order cumulants such as kurtosis). ICA is also closely related to "projection pursuit" [12] where maximizing non-Gaussianity promotes statistical *independence*, which is the desired goal. Like PCA, ICA is also a linear projection $\mathcal{R}^N \to \mathcal{R}^M$ but with different properties:

$$\mathbf{x} \approx \mathbf{A}\mathbf{y} \;\to\; \mathbf{A}^T\mathbf{A} \neq \mathbf{I} \;\to\; P(\mathbf{y}) \approx \prod p(y_i) \quad (2)$$

corresponding to approximate reconstruction, *non-orthogonality* of the basis $\mathbf{A}$ and the near factorization of the joint distribution $P(\mathbf{y})$ into marginal distributions of the (non-Gaussian) ICs. An example of an ICA basis is shown in Figure 1(b) where we see two unordered non-orthogonal IC vectors one of which is roughly aligned with the first PC vector in Figure 1(a) — *i.e.*, the direction of maximum variance. We note that the actual non-Gaussianity and statistical independence achieved in this toy example are minimal at best.

2.3. Nonlinear Principal Manifolds

One of the simplest methods for computing nonlinear principal manifolds is the nonlinear PCA (NLPCA) auto-associative multi-layer neural network [16, 8] shown in Figure 2. Hinton [11] was first to point out that nonlinear networks form useful representations in their hidden layers and Ackley *et al.* [1] were the first to implement an "auto-encoder" trained to reproduce its inputs. The so-called "bottleneck" layer forms a lower-dimensional manifold representation by means of a (weighted-sum-of-sigmoids) nonlinear *projection* function $f(\mathbf{x})$. The resulting PCs $\mathbf{y}$ have an inverse mapping with a similar nonlinear *reconstruction* function $g(\mathbf{y})$, which reproduces the input data as accurately as possible. The defining property of principal

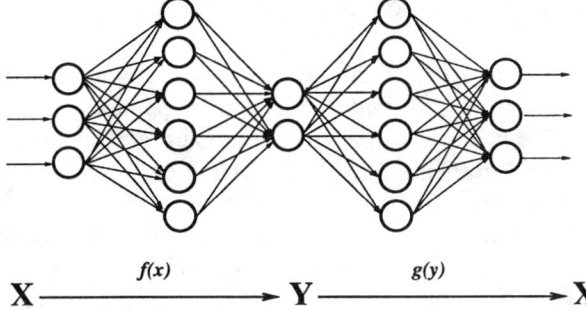

Figure 2. An auto-associative ("bottleneck") neural network for computing principal manifolds $y \in \mathcal{R}^M$ in the input space $x \in \mathcal{R}^N$

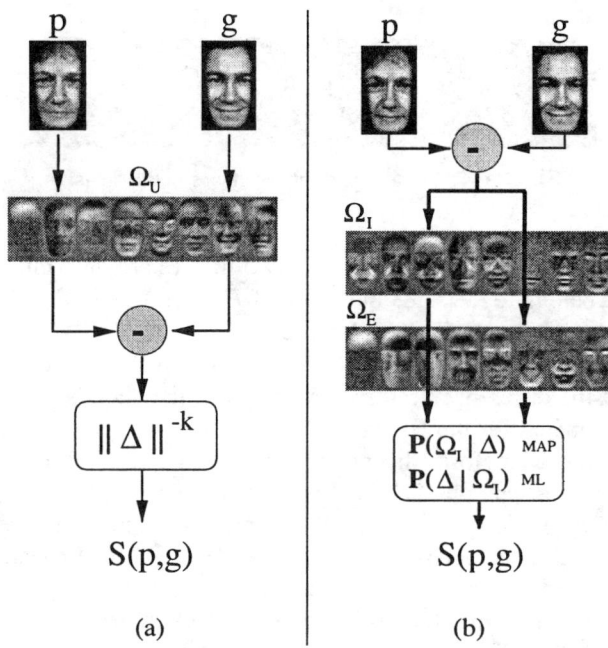

Figure 3. Signal flow diagrams for computing (a) Eigenface similarity and (b) Probabilistic similarity, between two images **p** and **g**.

manifolds is that the *inverse image* of the manifold in the original space $\mathcal{R}^N$ is (typically) a nonlinear (curved) lower-dimensional surface that "passes through the middle of the data" while minimizing the sum total distance between the data points and their projections on that surface [10]. Note that this is essentially a nonlinear regression on the data. Furthermore, the NLPCA computed by a multi-layer sigmoidal network is equivalent — with certain exceptions[2] — to a *principal surface* under the more general definition [9, 10]. To summarize, the main properties of NLPCA are:

$$y = f(x) \; \to \; x \approx g(y) \; \to \; P(y) = ? \qquad (3)$$

corresponding to nonlinear projection, approximate reconstruction and (almost always) no prior knowledge or certainty regarding the joint distribution of the components, respectively. An example of a principal curve is shown in Figure 1(c) which was obtained with a 2-4-1-4-2 layer neural network of the type shown in Figure 2. Note how the principal curve yields a compact and (relatively) accurate representation of the data.

3. Probabilistic Subspaces

The input visual data (or equivalently its manifold representation) can form the basis for simple recognition strategies using Euclidean metrics or normalized correlation. For example, in its simplest form, the similarity measure $S(I_1, I_2)$ between two images I_1 and I_2 (or their manifold projections) can be set to be inversely proportional to the norm $||I_1 - I_2||$. Such a simple formulation suffers from a major drawback: it does not exploit knowledge of which types of variation are critical (as opposed to incidental) in expressing similarity. However, one can formulate a

---

[2]The class of functions attainable by this type of neural network restricts the projection function $f(x)$ to be smooth and differentiable, hence suboptimal in some cases [19].

probabilistic similarity measure which is based on the probability that the image intensity differences, denoted by $\Delta = I_1 - I_2$, are characteristic of typical variations in appearance of the *same* object. For example, in face recognition, one can define two classes of facial image variations: *intrapersonal* variations Ω_I (corresponding, for example, to different facial expressions of the *same* individual) and *extrapersonal* variations Ω_E (corresponding to variations between *different* individuals). The similarity measure is then expressed in terms of the intrapersonal *a posteriori* probability $S(I_1, I_2) = P(\Omega_I | \Delta)$, by Bayes rule:

$$S = \frac{P(\Delta|\Omega_I)P(\Omega_I)}{P(\Delta|\Omega_I)P(\Omega_I) + P(\Delta|\Omega_E)P(\Omega_E)} \qquad (4)$$

The likelihoods $P(\Delta|\Omega_I)$ and $P(\Delta|\Omega_E)$ can be estimated by traditional means (given enough data) or alternatively by the subspace density estimation method [25] using Gaussians or Mixtures-of-Gaussians (for more details see [26]). Furthermore, the priors $P(\Omega)$ can be set to reflect specific operating conditions (*e.g.*, number of test images *vs.* the size of the database) or other sources of *a priori* knowledge regarding the two images being matched. Note that this particular Bayesian formulation casts the standard face recognition task (essentially an **m**-ary classification problem for **m** objects) into a *binary* pattern classification problem with Ω_I and Ω_E. This simpler problem is then solved using the maximum *a posteriori* (MAP) rule for

Figure 4. Some representative faces in the dataset.

classification. In other words, two images are determined to belong to the same individual if $P(\Omega_I|\Delta) > P(\Omega_E|\Delta)$, or equivalently, if $S(I_1, I_2) > 0.5$.

Note that this approach requires two linear projections of the difference vector Δ, from which likelihoods can be estimated for the Bayesian similarity measure $S(\Delta)$ as in [26]. Therefore, the projection step is linear while the posterior computation is nonlinear. Because of the double PCA projections required, this approach has been referred to as a "dual eigenspace" technique [23, 22]. This Bayesian method is contrasted to standard PCA or "eigenfaces" in Figure 3. Note the projection of the difference vector Δ onto the "dual subspaces" and the subsequent computation of the posterior in Equation 4. In contrast, the "eigenface" method projects images onto a common (universal) subspace wherein a Euclidean-based similarity is defined.

4. Experiments

Our experimental data consisted of a training "gallery" of 706 individual FERET faces and 1,123 test images or "probes" containing one or more images of every person in the gallery. All these images were aligned and normalized as described in [26]. The multiple probe images reflected different expressions, lighting, glasses on/off, *etc.*. In order to limit the fan-in of the NLPCA network (thus reducing its total number of free parameters) we downsampled the normalized images to 21-by-12 pixels, thus yielding input vectors in a $\mathcal{R}^{N=252}$ space. Examples from our dataset are shown in Figure 4. Note that with $N = 252$ we have nearly 3 times as many training samples than the data dimensionality, thus our parameter estimations (for PCA, ICA, NLPCA and Bayes) were properly over-constrained.

For our recognition experiments we selected a common manifold dimensionality of $M = 20$. This (somewhat arbitrary) choice of M was made for two reasons: it led to a reasonable PCA reconstruction error of MSE = 0.0012 (or 0.12% per pixel with a normalized intensity range of [0,1]) and a baseline PCA recognition rate of $\approx$ 80% which left a sizeable margin for improvement. To establish fairness in comparisons, all principal manifold projections (PCA, ICA and NLPCA) were required to have the *same* MSE of 0.0012, so that each of them could reconstruct the training set equally well. Naturally, this constraint does not necessarily result in equal recognition rates as we shall see.

4.1. PCA-based Recognition

The baseline algorithm for our face recognition experiments was the standard PCA-based "eigenfaces" [34, 31, 25]. The first 8 principal eigenvectors of our training data are shown in Figure 5 (top). Projection of the training/test set onto this 20-dimensional linear manifold (computed with PCA on the gallery only) and nearest-neighbor matching using a Euclidean metric yielded a 78.98% recognition accuracy with the 1,123 probe images. As a sanity check, we also did full image-vector nearest-neighbor matching (*i.e.*, on $\mathbf{x} \in \mathcal{R}^{252}$) yielding 86.46% (see Figure 6). Clearly, performance is degraded by the $252 \to 20$ dimensionality reduction, as expected.

4.2. ICA-based Recognition

For recognition experiments with ICA we used two different algorithms based on 4th-order cumulants: the "JADE" algorithm of Cardoso [5] and the fixed-point algorithm of Hyvärinen & Oja [13]. In both algorithms a PCA whitening step ("sphering") preceded the core ICA decomposition. The corresponding *non-orthogonal* JADE-derived ICA basis is shown in Figure 5 (bottom) — similar basis faces were obtained with Hyvärinen's method. These basis faces are the columns of the matrix $\mathbf{A}$ in the ICA equation $\mathbf{x} = \mathbf{A}\mathbf{y}$ and their linear combination (specified by the ICs) reconstructs the training data (and also preserves the MSE of the initial PCA step). The ICA manifold projection was obtained using $\mathbf{y} = \mathbf{A}^{-1}\mathbf{x}$ for both training and test images. Nearest-neighbour matching of the ICs, however, gave a recognition rate of 78.90% (with both ICA methods), providing no apparent advantage over PCA. This suggests that seeking non-Gaussian and independent components may not necessarily yield a better manifold representation for *recognition* purposes. We note that the experimental results of Bartlett *et al.* [2] with FERET faces did favor ICA over PCA, but mostly with more difficult time-separated images. Their ICA vs. PCA performance margin at the $\approx$ 80% recognition level was not as significant.[3]

4.3. NLPCA-based Recognition

The NLPCA recognition experiments used a fixed neural network architecture (252-64-20-64-252) with logistic sigmoid activation functions. This particular choice of the number of hidden units (64) was based on experimental trials (confirming network convergence) and also using information-theoretic arguments as in [16] such that the

---

[3]Compared to Bartlett *et al.* [2] our faces were cropped much tighter, leaving no information regarding hair and face shape and also were much lower in resolution; the combination of these factors makes the recognition task much more difficult.

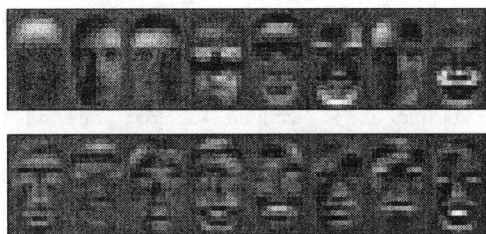

Figure 5. PCA faces (top) and ICA faces (bottom)

total number of free parameters (weights and biases) was roughly one-tenth the total number of data constraints. The nonlinear optimization (on the gallery set) used a conjugate gradient technique with line-search and Polak-Ribiere updates [32] until the MSE=0.0012 goal was reached.[4] Since more than one NLPCA manifold exists for a given MSE, we trained a total of 100 networks, after which both the training and test sets were projected onto the manifold using the projection $f(\mathbf{x})$ and then nearest-neighbour matching of the $\mathbf{y}$ components was performed. The mean recognition rate of the 100 experimental trials was found to be 60.14% with a standard deviation of 8.14% (see Figure 6) and the highest recognition rate obtained in the 100 trials was 74.89%.

4.4. Bayesian Recognition

Bayesian matching requires dual sets of training Δs for the Ω_I and Ω_E classes. But since we could not form Ω_I vectors from the gallery set (since it contained only one image per person) we divided the total dataset in half such that the new training set contained 353 gallery images (randomly selected) with their corresponding test images (594 probes) which were used to form training samples for both classes, $\{\Delta_i\}_{\Omega_I}$ and $\{\Delta_i\}_{\Omega_E}$. Single Gaussian density estimates were used for the corresponding likelihoods $P(\Delta|\Omega_I)$ and $P(\Delta|\Omega_E)$ using subspace dimensions of $M_I = 10$ and $M_E = 10$ (see [26] for details). Thus the total number of subspace projections required for Bayesian similarity ($M_I + M_E = 20$) was the same as in all the manifold experiments. Finally, using the other (unseen) half of the dataset, *maximum-posteriori* matching of the remaining 529 probes with their corresponding 353 gallery images yielded a 94.71% recognition rate (see Figure 6). Note that the dataset half used for training (density estimation) consisted of entirely different individuals than those used in testing. In contrast, the test set used in the manifold experiments consisted of individuals already represented in the training set. This demonstrates the Bayesian method's ability to

---

[4]Note that the usual neural network concerns regarding overfitting and generalization and the preventive use of methods such as "early-stopping" or "weight decay" do not apply here since the final MSE goal is preset.

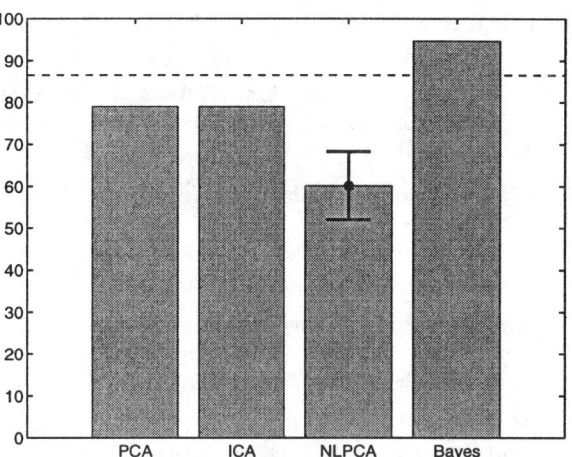

Figure 6. Recognition performance of PCA, ICA, and NLPCA manifolds vs. Bayesian similarity matching (dashed line is the performance of template-matching with the full-dimensional image vectors).

generalize to new data sets, a very desirable property made possible by the probabilistic representation of similarity.

5. Discussion

The relative performance of principal manifolds compared to Bayesian subspace matching is summarized in Figure 6. The advantage of probabilistic matching over Euclidean-based matching with principal manifolds is quite evident ($\approx 15\%$ increase). The NLPCA's poor performance can be attributed to the general difficulty of computing nonlinear manifolds and the complexity of cost functions riddled with local minima. More sophisticated nonlinear mapping techniques which preserve the local *topology* of the manifold such as [33, 20] are bound to yield better representations for recognition.

Note that both PCA and the dual eigenspaces are uniquely defined for a given training set (thus making experimental comparisons repeatable), whereas NLPCA and ICA are not unique due to the variety of different techniques used to compute them and the stochastic nature of the optimizations involved. Considering the relative computational complexity (of learning), NLPCA required many training epochs and the total number of floating-point operations was significantly large $O(10^{12})$ compared to PCA $O(10^8)$ and ICA $O(10^9)$. Since the Bayesian similarity method's learning stage requires two separate PCAs, its complexity is essentially twice that of PCA. Considering its significant performance gain and its relative simplicity, the Bayesian subspace method proves to be a very competitive alternative to Euclidean subspace matching methods.

References

[1] D. H. Ackley, G. E. Hinton, and T. J. Sejnowski. A learning algorithm for Boltzmann machines. *Cognitive Science*, 9(147), 1985.

[2] M. S. Bartlett, H. M. Lades, and T. J. Sejnowski. Independent component representations for face recognition. In *Proceedings of the SPIE, Vol. 2399: Conference on Human Vision and Electronic Imaging III*, pages 528–539, 1998.

[3] C. Bregler and S. M. Omohundro. Surface learning with applications to lip reading. In *Advances in Neural Information Processing Systems 6*, pages 43–50, 1994.

[4] M. C. Burl, U. M. Fayyad, P. Perona, P. Smyth, and M. P. Burl. Automating the hunt for volcanos on venus. In *Proc. IEEE Conf. on Computer Vision & Pattern Recognition*, Seattle, WA, June 1994.

[5] J-F. Cardoso. High-order contrasts for independent component analysis. *Neural Computation*, 11(1):157–192, 1999.

[6] P. Comon. Independent component analysis - a new concept? *Signal Processing*, 36:287–314, 1994.

[7] T. F. Cootes and C .J. Taylor. Active shape models: Smart snakes. In *Proc. British Machine Vision Conference*, pages 9–18. Springer-Verlag, 1992.

[8] D. DeMers and G. Cottrell. Nonlinear dimensionality reduction. In *Advances in Neural Information Processing Systems 5*, 1993.

[9] T. Hastie. *Principal Curves and Surfaces*. PhD thesis, Stanford University, 1984.

[10] T. Hastie and W. Stuetzle. Principal curves. *Journal of the American Statistical Association*, 84(406):502–516, 1989.

[11] G. E. Hinton. Learning distributed representations of concepts. In *Proc. Ann. Conf. of the Cognitive Science Society*, volume 1, 1986.

[12] P. J. Huber. Projection pursuit. *The Annals of Statistics*, 13:435–525, 1985.

[13] A. Hyvärinen and E. Oja. A family of fixed-point algorithms for independent component analysis. Technical Report A40, Helsinki University of Technology, 1996.

[14] I. T. Jolliffe. *Principal Component Analysis*. Springer-Verlag, New York, 1986.

[15] C. Jutten and J. Herault. Blind separation of sources. *Signal Processing*, 24:1–10, 1991.

[16] M. A. Kramer. Nonlinear principal components analysis using autoassociative neural networks. *AIChE Journal*, 32(2):233–243, 1991.

[17] M. M. Loève. *Probability Theory*. Van Nostrand, Princeton, 1955.

[18] S. Makeig, A. J. Bell, T. Jung, and T. J. Sejnowski. Independent component analysis of electroencephalographic data. In *Advances in Neural Information Processing Systems 8*, pages 145–151, 1996.

[19] E. C. Malthouse. Some theoretical results on nonlinear principal component analysis. Technical report, Northwestern University, 1998.

[20] T. Martinez and K. Schulten. Topology preserving networks. *Neural Computation*, 7(2), 1994.

[21] M. J. McKeown, S. Makeig, T Jung, A. J. Bell, and T. J. Sejnowski. Analysis of fMRI data by blind separation into spatial independent components. *Human Brain Mapping*, 6:160–188, 1998.

[22] B. Moghaddam, T. Jebara, and A. Pentland. Bayesian modeling of facial similarity. In *Advances in Neural Information Processing Systems 11*, 1998.

[23] B. Moghaddam, T. Jebara, and A. Pentland. Efficient MAP/ML similarity matching for face recognition. In *Proc. of Int'l Conf. Pattern Recognition*, Brisbane, Australia, August 1998.

[24] B. Moghaddam, C. Nastar, and A. Pentland. Bayesian face recognition using deformable intensity differences. In *Proc. of IEEE Conf. on Computer Vision and Pattern Recognition*, June 1996.

[25] B. Moghaddam and A. Pentland. Probabilistic visual learning for object detection. In *IEEE Proceedings of the Fifth International Conference on Computer Vision (ICCV'95)*, Cambridge, USA, June 1995.

[26] B. Moghaddam and A. Pentland. Probabilistic visual learning for object representation. *IEEE Transactions on Pattern Analysis and Machine Intelligence*, PAMI-19(7):696–710, July 1997.

[27] H. Murase and S. K. Nayar. Learning and recognition of 3D objects from appearance. In *Qualitative Vision Workshop*, New York, June 15-17 1993. CVPR '93.

[28] H. Murase and S. K. Nayar. Visual learning and recognition of 3D objects from appearance. *International Journal of Computer Vision*, 14(5), 1995.

[29] S. K. Nayar, S. Baker, and H. Murase. Parametric feature detection. In *Proc. of IEEE Conf. on Computer Vision & Pattern Recognition*, pages 471–477, San Francisco, CA, June 1996.

[30] S. K. Nayar, H. Murase, and S. A. Nene. General learning algorithm for robot vision. *Neural & Stochastic Methods in Image & Signal Processing*, 2304, 1994.

[31] A. Pentland, B. Moghaddam, and T. Starner. View-based and modular eigenspaces for face recognition. In *Proc. of IEEE Conf. on Computer Vision & Pattern Recognition*, Seattle, WA, June 1994.

[32] L. E. Scales. *Introduction to Non-Linear Optimization*. MacMillan Press, 1985.

[33] J. Tennenbaum. Mapping a manifold of perceptual observations. In *Advances in Neural Information Processing Systems 10*, 1998.

[34] M. Turk and A. Pentland. Eigenfaces for recognition. *Journal of Cognitive Neuroscience*, 3(1), 1991.

Sensitivity Analysis for Object Recognition
from Large Structural Libraries

Benoit Huet and Edwin R. Hancock
Department of Computer Science, University of York
York, YO10 5DD, UK
huetb@cs.york.ac.uk erh@cs.york.ac.uk

Abstract

This paper studies the structural sensitivity of line-pattern recognition using shape-graphs. We compare the recognition performance for four different algorithms. Each algorithm uses a set of pairwise geometric attributes and a neighbourhood graph to represent the structure of the line patterns. The first algorithm uses a pairwise geometric histogram, the second uses a relational histogram on the edges of the shape graph, the third compares the set of attributes on the edges of the shape graph and the final algorithm compares the arrangement of line correspondences using graph-matching. The different algorithms are compared under line deletion, line addition, line fragmentation and line end-point measurement errors. It is the graph-matching algorithm which proves to be the most effective.

1 Introduction

Graphs have proved to be seductive yet highly elusive as representations of shape in computer vision [2, 18, 22]. They are seductive since they convey the topological arrangements of features or object primitives in a manner which can be invariant to both viewing angle and shape deformation. On the other hand, they have proved to be very elusive since the process of eliciting a relational abstraction from poor image data is one of extreme fragility [22]. The idea of using graphs as representations of 2D scenes can be traced back to Barrow and Popplestone [2]. Over the past two and half decades, the topic has been the subject of sustained activity. However, the fact remains that inexact graph matching is a difficult problem and that there is no "free lunch" on offer. There is a stark choice of either accepting limited recognition performance or deploying considerable computational resources to get an acceptable answer. This trade-off has been highlighted by the interest in large image databases. If such databases are to be queried using high-level relational object descriptions rather than using low level feature characteristics, then a fast and reliable

means of graph-matching is required.

There are several recent examples of the use of graph-based representations for 2D shape recognition. For instance, the FORMS system of Zhu and Yuille [23] uses skeletal shape graphs to model articulated objects. Liu and Geiger [13] have taken these ideas further by developing a hierarchical model which achieves a degree of unification between the articulated shape graph and the detection of raw image features via the Mumford-Shah functional [14]. Amit and Kong [1] have a MAP framework for modelling 2D deformable shape using a decomposable graph representation. More recently, there have been several attempts to use graph retrieval as a means of recognising 2D shapes from databases. Much of this work can be viewed as providing a concrete realisation of the ideas introduced by Leyton's [12] process grammar for shape. For instance Siddiqi *et al* [20] have used the shock graph derived from the singularities of the reaction-diffusion equation to provide a skeletal representation of 2D binary shapes. Shape recognition is realised using the subtree matching algorithm of Reyner [16]. The matching process has been refined by Pelillo *et al* [15] who establish a mean of matching association trees using a relaxation algorithm to find the maximal clique.

The observation underpinning this paper is that although this work has done much to establish the representational expediency of shape graphs, there has been little effort directed at answering the question of how much structural corruption can be tolerated and how recognition accuracy is traded against the computational resources expended. It is these issues which are the focus of this paper. We aim to compare four different strategies for rapid graph-matching. The matching algorithms become increasingly complex by placing greater reliance on graph-structure in the shape recognition process. The application vehicle used in our recognition experiments is a demanding one. We aim to recognise large line-patterns segmented from grey-scale images. The simplest line-matching algorithm uses a histogram of pairwise geometric attributes on pairs of line-segments. The second algorithm uses the edge-set of a shape-graph to gate contributions to the histogram. The third method uses the similarity of features-sets defined on the graph-edges. The final algorithm uses an iterative process to recover an explicit arrangement of correspondences between graphs and retrieves the pattern from the database on the basis of maximum consistency.

Our study is conducted on a database of some 2500 line patterns. In order to investigate the structural and attribute sensitivity of our matching algorithms we subject the patterns in the database to four different kinds of segmentation error. These are line addition, line deletion, line-splitting and segment end-point measurement errors. We measure the recognition performance against each of these errors. Although the sensitivity pattern is quite subtle, the main conclusion of our study is that the iterative graph-matching algorithm offers the best overall performance.

2 Framework

Formally our recognition problem is posed as follows. We abstract the shapes to be recognised as attributed relational graphs (ARG's). Each ARG in the database is a triple, $G = (V_G, E_G, A_G)$, where V_G is the set of vertices (nodes), E_G is the edge set ($E_G \subset V_G \times V_G$), and A_G is the set of node attributes. In our experimental example, the nodes represent line-structures segmented from 2D images. The edges are established by computing the N-nearest neighbour graph for the line-centres. Each node $j \in V$ is characterised by a vector of attributes, $\underline{x}_j$ and hence $A_G = \{\underline{x}_j | j \in V\}$. In the work reported here the attribute-vector represents the contents of a normalised pairwise attribute histogram.

The database of line-patterns is represented by the set of ARG's $\mathcal{D} = \{G\}$. The goal is to retrieve from the database $\mathcal{D}$, the individual ARG that most closely resembles a query pattern $Q = (V_Q, E_Q, A_Q)$. We now furnish some details of the shape retrieval task used in our experimental evaluation of the recognition method. In particular, we focus on the problem of recognising 2D line patterns in a manner which is invariant to rotation, translation and scale. The raw

information available for each line segment are its orientation (angle with respect to the horizontal axis) and its length (see Figure 1). To illustrate how the Euclidean invariant pairwise feature attributes are computed, suppose that we denote the line segments associated with the nodes indexed a and b by the vectors $\underline{v}_a$ and $\underline{v}_b$ respectively. We use two pairwise attributes. The first is the relative angle given by

$$\theta_{a,b} = \arccos \left[\frac{\underline{v}_a \cdot \underline{v}_b}{|\underline{v}_a||\underline{v}_b|} \right]$$

The second is the normalised length ratio between the oriented baseline vector $\underline{v}_a$ and the vector $\underline{v}\prime$ joining the end (b) of the baseline segment (ab) to the intersection of the segment pair (cd).

$$\vartheta_{a,b} = \frac{1}{\frac{1}{2} + \frac{D_{ib}}{D_{ab}}}$$

The two attributes are used as a feature-vector $z_{a,b} = (\theta_{a,b}, \vartheta_{a,b})^T$ for the line-segment pair.

Each node in the shape graph, i.e. each line in the pattern, is represented by the histogram of its pairwise geometric attributes to the remaining lines in the pattern. This histogram can be thought of as a local estimate of the probability distribution for the pairwise attributes. Accordingly, the angle and position attributes $\theta_{a,b}$ and $\vartheta_{a,b}$ are binned in a histogram. Suppose that $S_a(\mu, \nu) = \{(a,b) | \theta_{a,b} \in A_\mu \wedge \vartheta_{a,b} \in R_\nu \wedge b \in V_D\}$ is the set of nodes whose pairwise geometric attributes with the node a are spanned by the range of directed relative angles A_μ and the relative position attribute range R_ν. The contents of the histogram bin spanning the two attribute ranges is given by $H_a(\mu, \nu) = |S_a(\mu, \nu)|$. Each histogram contains n_A relative angle bins and n_R length ratio bins. The normalised geometric histogram bin-entries are computed as follows

$$h_a(\mu, \nu) = \frac{H_a(\mu, \nu)}{\sum_{\mu'=1}^{n_A} \sum_{\nu'=1}^{n_R} H_a(\mu, \nu)}$$

In the remainder of this paper, we use the notation h^G to denote the normalised histogram for the graph G from the database and h^Q to denote the query histogram.

3 Graph Retrieval Algorithms

The aim in this paper is to compare four graph-based recognition algorithms for retrieving from the database the pattern that most closely resembles a query. The four algorithms use increasingly complex representations. The most straightforward uses a global histogram of pairwise geometric attributes [8]. The next method refines this idea by using only the attributes on the edges of a nearest neighbour graph [10]. The third algorithm uses the set of attributes

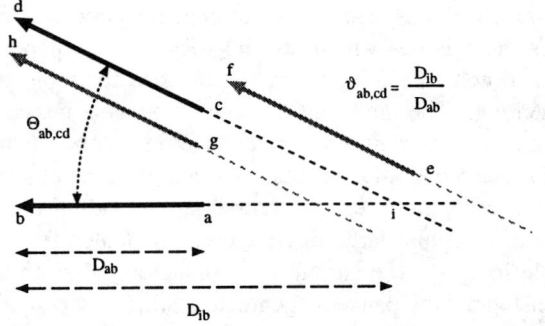

Figure 1. Geometry for shape representation

on the edges and realises comparison on an element-by-element basis using a robust error kernel [9]. Finally, we use a graph-matching algorithm. Here the similarity of the local attribute histograms is used to provide explicit node correspondences [7]. The matching algorithm iteratively modifies the pattern of correspondences to optimise the *a posteriori* probability of the library patterns given the query pattern. Retrieval is realised by identifying the line-pattern of largest matching probability.

3.1 Attribute Histograms

We commence by considering how pairwise geometric histograms can be used for the purposes of recognition [21]. The idea here is to conglomerate the node histograms into a global histogram [8]. This histogram provides a statistical summary for the pairwise attributes residing on the edges of a nearest neighbour graph. The normalised histogram bin-contents is given by

$$\hat{h}_T^G(\mu, nu) = \frac{\sum_{a \in V_G} H_a(\mu, \nu)}{\sum_{a \in V_G} \sum_{\mu'=1}^{n_A} \sum_{\nu'=1}^{n_R} H_a(\mu, \nu)}$$

The best-matching pattern is retrieved from the database on the basis of similarity with the query pattern histogram. Our similarity measure is the histogram correlation. The measure of pattern correlation is the Bhattacharyya distance. The class identity of the retrieved pattern is

$$\omega_Q = \arg\max_{G \in \mathcal{D}} \ln \sum_{\mu=1}^{n_A} \sum_{\nu=1}^{n_R} \sqrt{h_T^Q(\mu, \nu) \times h_T^G(\mu, \nu)}$$

This is the most efficient of our retrieval algorithms. Once the histograms have been pre-compiled and normalised, then the computational overheads are purely related to the number of bin comparisons that must be performed.

3.2 Relational Histograms

The next step is to consider how graph-structure can be used to compute a compact relational summary [6, 19, 3, 10]. This method represents a refinement of the global attribute histogram. Rather then binning the geometric attributes over all node-pairs, we restrict ourselfs to pairs of nodes that are connected by edges in the shape graph. To do this, we modify the set of attributes used to represent the node a to be those that belong to the first-order graph neighbourhood. In other words, we now have $S_a(\mu, \nu) = \{(a, b) | \theta_{a,b} \in A_\mu \wedge \vartheta_{a,b} \in R_\nu \wedge (a, b) \in E_D\}$. The normalised global histogram can now be computed in the way described in the previous subsection of this paper. The effect is to use the edges of the shape-graph to gate contributions to the histogram.

The run-time computation is identical to that for the attribute histogram. However, the amount of precompilation required can be less than that for the attribute histogram. The reason for this is that once the nearest neighbour graph is computed, then fewer angle and relative length attributes need to be computed.

3.3 Feature-sets

The next step is to consider how set-based representation can be used for the purposes of recognition [9]. Here we use a variant of Rucklidge's [17] idea of effecting object recognition by using a variant of the Hausdorff distance to compare a set of features. We aim to effect retrieval on the basis of the similarity of the set of attributes residing on the edges of the nearest neighbour graph. The Hausdorff distance provides a means of comparing a set of unordered observations without having to establish explicit correspondences between individual elements. However, this measure is notoriously susceptible to measurement outliers. For this reason, we choose instead to gauge similarity using a robust error kernel [9]. The class identity of the retrieved pattern is

$$\omega_Q = \arg\max_{G \in \mathcal{D}} \sum_{(i,j) \in E_G} \max_{(I,J) \in E_Q} \left(\Gamma_\sigma(\|z_{I,J}^Q - z_{i,j}^G\|) \right)$$

where $\Gamma_\sigma(\rho) = \exp\left(-\frac{\rho^2}{2\sigma^2}\right)$ is a robust weighting kernel, $z_{I,J}^Q$ is a pairwise feature-vector from the query graph and $z_{i,j}^G$ is a feature-vector from a target graph.

This recognition method is more computationally demanding than either of the histogram-based methods since it requires each of the set of attributes to be compared. When compared with the histogram-based methods, the computational effort required is increased by a factor which is proportional to the average bin contents of the histograms.

3.4 Graph Matching

The feature-based similarity measure does not utilise any information concerning the consistency of the arrangement of correspondences between the individual elements. In order to exploit the consistency of correspondences, we use a simplification of the graph-matching scheme developed by Finch, Wilson and Hancock [5]. This poses the retrieval process as one of associating with the query the graph from the database that has the largest *a posteriori* probability of match. In other words, the class identity of the graph which most closely corresponds to the query is

$$\omega_Q = \arg\max_{G' \in \mathcal{D}} P(G'|Q)$$

However, since we wish to make a detailed structural comparison of the graphs, rather than comparing their overall statistical properties, we must first establish a set of best-match correspondences between each ARG in the database and the query Q. At iteration n the set of correspondences between the query Q and the ARG G is a relation $f_G^n : V_G \mapsto V_Q$ over the vertex sets of the two graphs. The mapping function consists of a set of Cartesian pairings between the nodes of the two graphs, i.e. $f_G^n = \{(a, \alpha); a \in V_G, \alpha \in V_Q\} \subseteq V_G \times V_Q$. The retrieved pattern is the one which has the most consistent pattern of correspondences and satisfies the condition

$$\omega_Q = \arg \max_{G' \in \mathcal{D}} \max_{f_{G'}} P(f_{G'}|G', Q)$$

The pattern of correspondences is assigned to satisfy the following *maximum a posteriori* probability condition

$$f_G^n(a) = \arg \max_{\alpha \in V_Q} p(\underline{x}_a, \underline{x}_\alpha | f_G^n(a) = \alpha) P(f_G^n | E_G, E_Q)$$

Suppose that we use the notation

$$s_{a,\alpha}^n = \begin{cases} 1 & \text{if } f_G^n(a) = \alpha \\ 0 & \text{otherwise} \end{cases}$$

to represent the correspondence assignment. The consistency of global match against the query pattern can be improved by iterating the assignment condition

$$f_G^n(a) = \arg \max_{\alpha \in V_Q} \left[\ln p(\underline{x}_a, \underline{x}_\alpha | f_G^n(a) = \alpha) + \sum_{(a,b) \in E_G} \right.$$
$$\left. \sum_{(\alpha,\beta) \in E_Q} \left\{ \ln(1 - P_e) s_{a,\alpha}^{n-1} s_{b,\beta}^{n-1} + \ln P_e (1 - s_{a,\alpha}^{n-1} s_{b,\beta}^{n-1}) \right\} \right]$$

The probability of match between the pattern-vectors is computed using the Bhattacharyya coefficient between the normalised histograms.

$$P(f_G^n(a) = \alpha | \underline{x}_a, \underline{x}_\alpha) = \exp[-B_{a,\alpha}] =$$
$$\frac{\sum_{\mu=1}^{n_A} \sum_{\nu=1}^{n_R} \sqrt{h_a(\mu,\nu) h_\alpha(\mu,\nu)}}{\sum_{\alpha \in V_Q} \sum_{\mu'=1}^{n_A} \sum_{\nu'=1}^{n_R} \sqrt{h_a(\mu,\nu) h_\alpha(\mu,\nu)}}$$

With this modelling ingredient, and using the correspondence matches delivered by the graph-matching scheme, the condition for recognition is

$$\omega_Q = \arg \max_{G' \in \mathcal{D}} \sum_{(a,b) \in E'_G} \sum_{(\alpha,\beta) \in E_Q} \left\{ -B_{a,\alpha} - B_{b,\beta} + \right.$$
$$\left. \ln(1 - P_e) s_{a,\alpha}^n s_{b,\beta}^n + \ln P_e (1 - s_{a,\alpha}^n s_{b,\beta}^n) \right\}$$

This is the most computationally demanding of the methods. We have found it to be 10 times slower than the feature-set method and over a 1000 times slower than the histogram-based method.

4 Sensitivity Analysis

The aim in this section is to investigate the sensitivity of the four graph-based retrieval strategies to the systematics of the line-segmentation process. To this end we have simulated the segmentation errors that can occur when line-segments are extracted from realistic image data. Specifically, the different processes that we have investigated are listed below:

- **Extra lines:** Here we have added additional lines at random locations. The lengths and angles of the added lines have been generated by randomly sampling the distribution for the existing image-segments.

- **Missing lines:** Here we have deleted a known fraction of line-segments at random locations.

- **Split lines:** Here a predefined fraction of lines have been split into two segments. The splitting process is effected by deleting an internal fraction of each line-segment. The deleted segment is randomly positioned along the line. The fraction of the line deleted is uniformly sampled from the range $(0, 1)$.

- **Segment end-point errors:** Here we have introduced random displacements in the end-point positions for a predefined fraction of lines. The distribution of end-point errors is Gaussian. The degree of error is controlled by the variance of the Gaussian distribution.

- **Combined errors:** Here we have introduced the four different segment errors described above in equal proportion.

The performance measure used in our studies is computed as follows. We query the database with a sample of line patterns. For each pattern in turn we determine whether or not the correct retrieval occurs in the top-ranked position. By computing the fraction of queries that return a correctly recognised recall, we determine the average retrieval accuracy.

We have conducted our experiments with both exact and inexact queries. In the former case an exact match to the line pattern exists prior to the addition of noise. In the latter case, the query pattern is a distorted version of the target in the database. We commence by comparing the overall sensitivity pattern for each of the recognition schemes when exact and inexact queries are performed. Figure 2 shows the sensitivity plots for the case of exact query, while Figure 3 shows the plots for inexact query. Each plot shows the recognition accuracy for a particular matching scheme as a function of the fraction of pattern corruption. The different curves are for the different noise processes. The main feature to note is that in the case of inexact query the shoulder

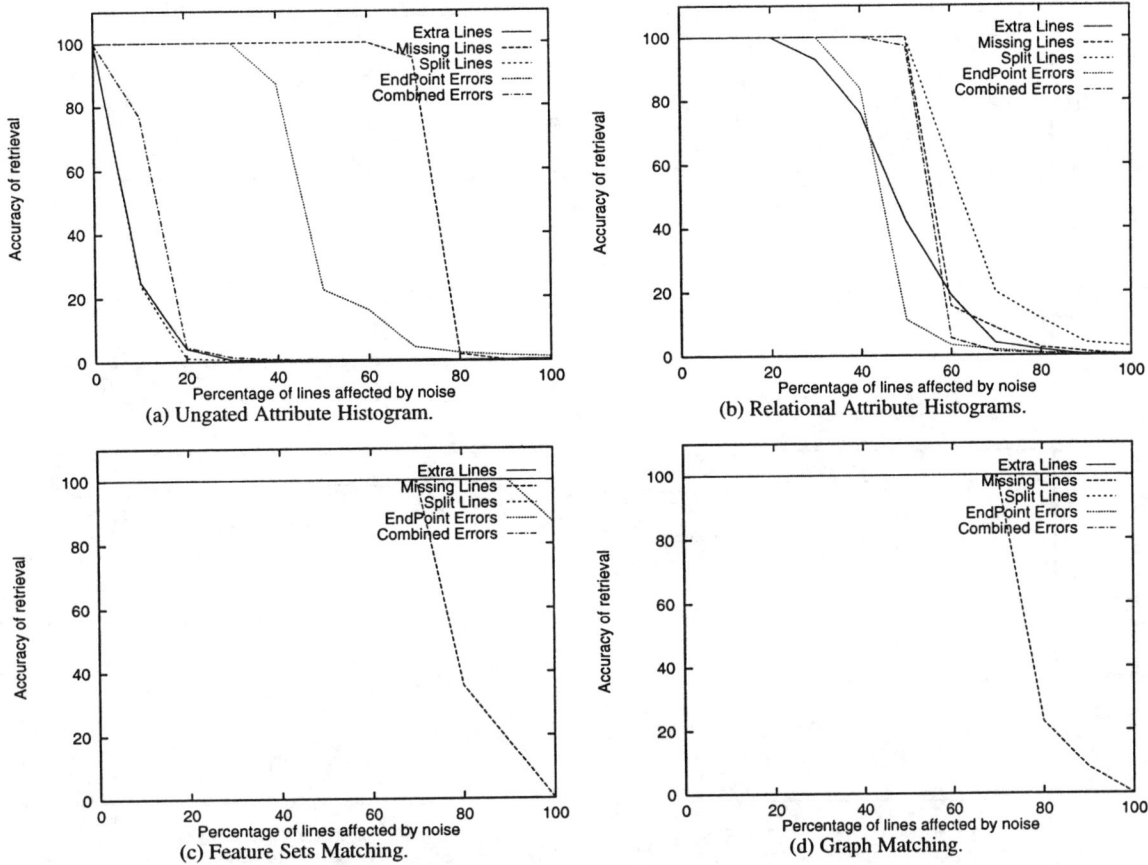

Figure 2. Effect of various kinds of noise for exact queries.

in the performance curves occurs at a lower noise level for each of the recognition strategies.

Turning our attention first to the sensitivity curves for exact query, we make the following observations. Firstly, the two histogram based methods (Figure 2(a) and (b)) are most susceptible to the addition of extra line-segments. By contrast, feature-set (Figure 2(c)) comparison and graph-matching (Figure 2(d)) are most susceptible to missing lines.

Since the process of inexact query is more typical of large-scale object recognition, we now focus on the associated sensitivity pattern in more detail in Figure 3.

When retrieval is attempted using graph-matching (Figure 3(d)), the following sensitivity pattern emerges. The most destructive noise process is the deletion of lines. Here, the onset of recognition errors occurs when 10% of lines are deleted. Line splitting results in the onset of recognition degradation when the error rate is 20%. The technique is most robust to the addition of extra lines. Here as many as 70% of the lines may be added clutter before any degradation in recognition performance results.

In the case of the feature-sets (Figure 3(c)) it is again line deletion that proves the most serious obstacle to accurate recognition. The onset of errors occurs when 40% of

the lines are deleted. The line-patterns are least sensitive to segment end-point errors. In the case of both line-addition and line-splitting there is an onset of errors when the fraction of segment errors is about 20%. However, at larger fractions of segmentation errors the overall effect is significantly less marked than in the case of line-deletions. The technique is considerably less robust to line additions than the graph-matching technique.

In the case of the gated or relational histogram (Figure 3(b)), segment end-point error, missing lines and line-splitting pose the most serious problems. This is attributable to the fact that the line-splitting introduces additional combinatorial background that swamps the query pattern. The line-patterns are least sensitive to segment end-point errors. In the case of both line-addition and line-splitting there is an onset of errors when the fraction of segment errors is about 20%. However, at larger fractions of segmentation errors the overall effect is significantly less marked than in the case of line-deletions. Moreover, in each case the recognition curves are consistently poorer than either graph-matching or feature-sets.

Finally, the recognition performance of the ungated histogram (Figure 3(a)) is poorest of all for inexact pattern matching and is effectively unuseable. Comparing Figures

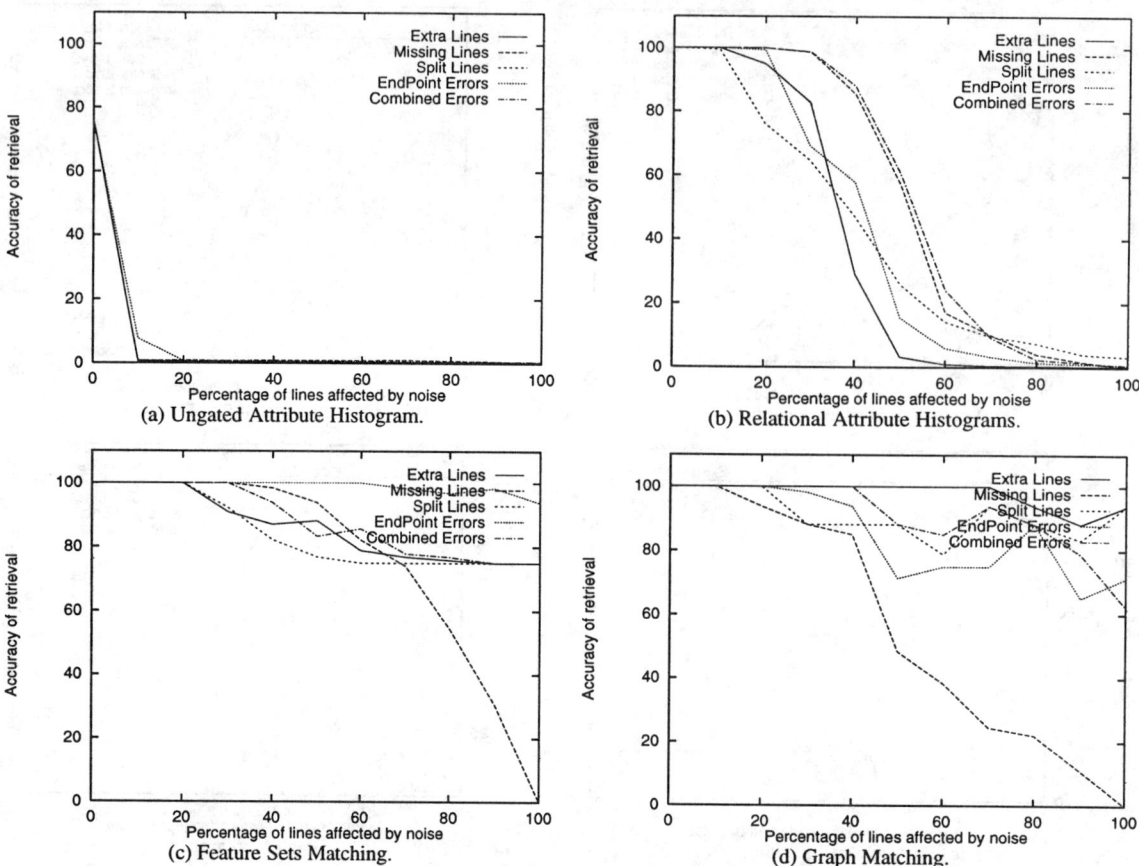

Figure 3. Effect of various kinds of noise for similarity queries.

2a and 3a it is clear that the transition from exact to inexact query has a significant effect on the matching performance.

To conclude the sensitivity study, we focus more closely on the role of segment end-point errors. The reason for this is that such errors will effect the accuracy of the relational measurements. Figure 4 shows the effect of line end-point position errors for inexact queries. The different curves in the plots correspond to different values of the standard deviation of the end-point position errors. They show the retrieval accuracy as a function of the fraction of lines affected by end-point errors. As the standard deviation of the position error increases, then so the fraction of corrupt lines for which perfect recall is possible decreases. The main point to note from these plots is that the graph-matching method degrades less rapidly under line end-point errors than the set-based method and the relational histogram.

5 Conclusions

We have compared three different strategies for recalling structural representations of line-patterns from a large database. The main conclusion to be drawn from the study is that the best recognition performance is realised when an iterative graph-matching scheme is used. This is an inter-

esting observation, since graph-structure is frequently perceived as too fragile to be used to noisy information retrieval. There are a number of ways in which the ideas presented in this paper can be extended. Firstly, we intend to explore more a perceptually meaningful representation of the line patterns, using grouping principal derived from Gestalt psychology. Secondly, we are exploring the possibility of using more complex relational entities as alternatives to edges. Examples include the triangular faces of Delaunay graphs [4]. Finally, we plan to investigate ways on combining the recognition strategies. This would offer the advantage that we could take advantage of the complementarity of the relational histogram and graph-matching. The relational histogram is most robust to missing lines while the graph-matching method is most robust to line-deletion. There are two ways in which combination might be achieved. The first is to use the different similarity measures to guide a heuristic search procedure such as the A-star algorithm. The second route is to treat each recognition strategy as a separate classifier and to combine the decisions in an information theoretic framework [11].

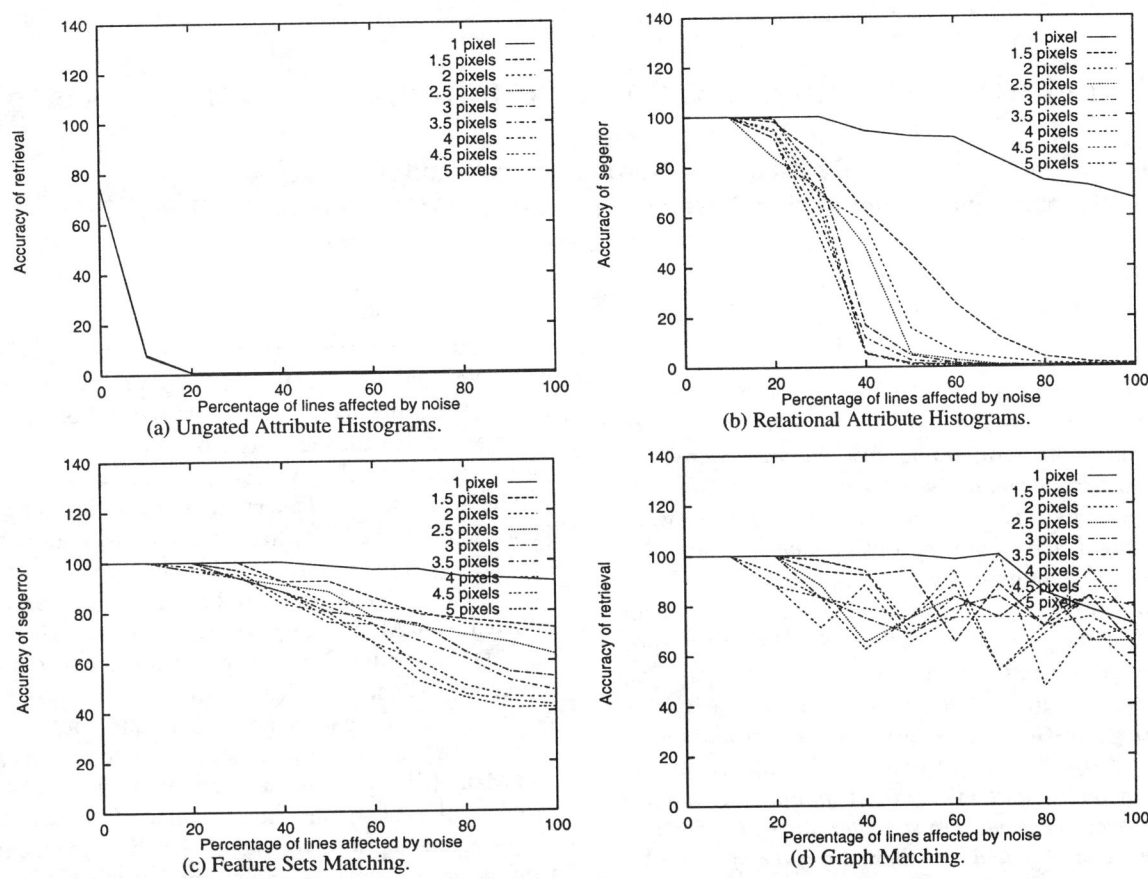

Figure 4. Effect of introducing segment end-point errors on retrieval performance.

References

[1] Y. Amit and A. Kong. Graphical templates for model registration. *IEEE PAMI*, 18(3):225–236, 1996.

[2] H. Barrow and R. Popplestone. Relational descriptions in picture processing. *Machine Intelligence*, 5:377–396, 1971.

[3] M. Costa and L. Shapiro. Scene analysis using appearance-based models and relational indexing. *ISCV95*, pages 103–108, 1995.

[4] A. M. Finch, R. C. Wilson, and E. R. Hancock. Matching Delaunay graphs. *Patern Recognition*, 30:123–140, 1997.

[5] A. M. Finch, R. C. Wilson, and E. R. Hancock. An energy function and continuous edit process for graph matching. *Neural Computation*, 10:1873–1894, 1998.

[6] J. Henikoff and L. Shapiro. Interesting patterns for model based machine vision. *ICCV90*, pages 535–538, 1990.

[7] B. Huet, A. D. J. Cross, and E. R. Hancock. Graph matching for shape retrieval. *NIPS98*, 1998.

[8] B. Huet and E. R. Hancock. Cartographic indexing into a database of remotely sensed images. *WACV96*, pages 8–14, 1996.

[9] B. Huet and E. R. Hancock. Fuzzy relational distance for large-scale object recognition. *CVPR98*, pages 138–143, 1998.

[10] B. Huet and E. R. Hancock. Relational histograms for shape indexing. *ICCV98*, pages 563–569, 1998.

[11] J. Kittler and S. Hojjatoleslami. A weighted combination of classifiers employing shared and distinct representation. *CVPR98*, pages 924–929, 1998.

[12] M. Leyton. A process grammar for shape. *Artificial Intelligence*, 34:213–247, 1988.

[13] T. Liu and D. Geiger. Visual deconstruction: recognizing articulated object. *EMMCVPR97*, pages 295–310, 1997.

[14] D. Mumford and J. Shah. Boundary detection by minimizing functionals. *CVPR85*, pages 22–26, 1985.

[15] M. Pelillo *et al.* Matching hierarchical structures using association graphs. *ECCV98*, pages 3–16, 1998.

[16] S. Reyner. An analysis of a good algorithm for the subtree problem. *SIAM J. Comput.*, vol. 6, pages 730–732, 1977.

[17] W. J. Rucklidge. Locating objects using the Hausdorff distance. *ICCV95*, pages 457–464, 1995.

[18] A. Sanfeliu and K. S. Fu. A distance measure between attributed relational graph. *IEEE SMC*, 13:353–362, 1983.

[19] L. Shapiro and R. Haralick. A metric for comparing relational descriptions. *IEEE PAMI*, 7(1):90–94, 1985.

[20] K. Siddiqi *et al.* Shock graphs and shape matching. *ICCV98*, pages 222–229, 1998.

[21] N. Thacker *et al.* Assessing the completeness properties of pairwise geometric histograms. *IVC*, 13(5):423–429, 1995.

[22] R. Wilson and E. R. Hancock. Structural matching by discrete relaxation. *IEEE PAMI*, 19(6):634–648, 1997.

[23] S. C. Zhu and A. L. Yuille. Forms: A flexible object recognition and modelling system. *IJCV*, 20(3):187–212, 1996.

Tracking through singularities and discontinuities by random sampling

J. Deutscher, B. North, B. Bascle and A. Blake

Department of Engineering Science, University of Oxford, Oxford OX1 3PJ, UK.

Web: http://www.robots.ox.ac.uk/~vdg/

Abstract

Some issues in markerless tracking of human body motion are addressed. Extended Kalman filters have commonly been applied to kinematic variables, to combine predictions consistent with plausible motion, with the incoming stream of visual measurements. Kalman filtering is applicable only when the underlying distribution is approximately Gaussian. Often, this assumption proves remarkably robust.

There are two pervasive circumstances under which the Gaussianity assumption can break down. The first is kinematic singularity, and the second is at joint endstops. Failure of Kalman filtering under these circumstance is illustrated. The non-Gaussian nature of the distributions is demonstrated experimentally by means of Monte-Carlo simulation. Random simulation — particle filtering or Condensation — proves to provide a robust alternative algorithm for tracking that can also deal with these difficult conditions.

1 Introduction

The study of human biometrics requires the measurement of limb motion for a variety of purposes, for instance gait-analysis, as used in medical diagnosis of orthopaedic conditions such as those arising from cerebral palsy. Existing commercial motion capture systems (eg. VICON[1]) use markers, either active or retro-reflective, attached to the skin. Their trajectories are tracked through time using stereovision, and used to infer the motion of the body skeleton. However, biometrics are now increasingly applied to sport biomechanics and computer graphics animation in which the use of markers is cumbersome. Therefore research is now aimed at capturing human motion from the body outline, with or without ad-hoc clothing.

There have been a variety of approaches to the problem. Perona *et al* [7] studied arm-tracking, using just one camera, by estimating the four line-segments forming the extremal contour of lower and upper arm. It uses Extended Kalman Filtering, following the pioneering work of Dickmanns and Graefe [5], to deal with the nonlinearities arising in the trigonometry of human body kinematics. In practice,

---

[1]Oxford Metrics Ltd marker tracking system — see http://www.metrics.co.uk/

it follows arm movements competently, albeit relatively slow ones. Wachter and Nagel *et al* [19] track people in monocular image sequences, using conic models of limbs, and a kinematic chain for the body, combining silhouette and region information. This works well tracking a person walking parallel to the image plane but deteriorates in a three-quarter view. Lerasle *et al* [14] tracked leg-motion during cycling. Special leggings with non repetitive texture were worn and a precise curved CAD model of the leg of the cyclist was constructed from MRI scans. Two cameras were used. for precise 3D localisation. Limitations include the cost of building a precise CAD model of each individual and the need to superimpose a deformation model to account for the change of limb-shape due to muscle and tissue deformation. Bregler and Malik [3] apply a linear parameterisation (twists) to the problem of tracking an articulated body from images, using elliptical shape primitives and observations from optic flow. Compared with [14], setting up models is more straightforward, but appears to be at the cost of some ability to handle agility. A final and remarkable example of articulated body motion tracking is Rehg's pioneering work [17] on the tracking of a fully articulated model of the hand with more than 20 degrees of freedom.

The aim of this paper is to put together some of the most effective ideas from the state of the art — conic models of limbs, silhouette-edge localisation and Kalman filtering — and study their limitations. In particular, Kalman filters propagate Gaussian probability distributions and the Extended Kalman filter applies only if the underlying distributions are approximately Gaussian. In this study we focus on the special cases where the Gaussianity assumption is stretched to the limit: kinematic singularities and discontinuities. A particle filter such as CONDENSATION can be used for Monte-Carlo simulation of the underlying distributions. We show that distributions take extreme, high-variance shapes at discontinuities and singularities, and may be non-Gaussian, with terminal results for the Kalman filter.

Particle filtering, as well as being a simulation tool, also constitutes an practical algorithm capable of tracking under these taxing conditions. Some might argue that discontinuities and singularities are rare events and the analysis presented here makes much of what are, after all, special cases.

1144

We believe that this is emphatically not the case. Discontinuities (end-stops and collisions) especially, occur generically along a trajectory, and a tracking algorithm that claims any kind of general competence must deal with them.

2 Kinematic model

Our experiments are carried out on a kinematic chain consisting of trunk, upper and lower arm. We consider a simplified model in which the shoulder is a ball joint and the elbow a planar hinge. Then the system has 11 degrees of freedom in its configuration vector — 6 for the pose of the trunk and five angles $\mathbf{X} = (\theta_1, \ldots, \theta_5)$ four of which are associated with the arm, as in figure 1, and the θ_5 is the angle of the collar bone. In experiments reported here, trunk pose was held roughly constant, so the configuration vector is effectively $\mathbf{X}$ as above.

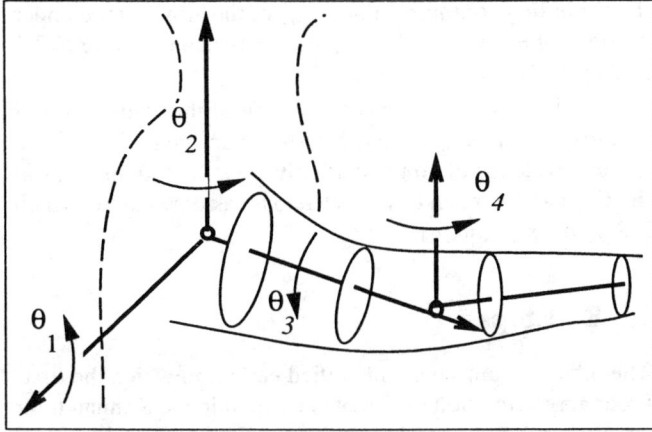

Figure 1: **Arm kinematics:** four angular variables $\theta_1, \ldots \theta_4$ are shown.

The upper and lower arm are each modelled as truncated cones and it is assumed that the silhouettes of the curved conical surfaces are visible as edges in any image of the arm. Normals $\mathbf{n}_i$, $i = 1, \ldots, M$ are cast from fixed locations along the silhouettes [15, 10] and the positions of each intersection with the nearest outward image edge are stored as image vectors $\mathbf{z}_1, \ldots, \mathbf{z}_M$. Then the entire set $\mathbf{Z} = (\mathbf{z}_1, \ldots, \mathbf{z}_M)$ is the joint image observation.

3 Visual observations

In order to assimilate measurements probabilistically into an estimate of the changing arm-configuration $X(t)$, it is necessary to model visual observations as a probability distribution $p(Z|X)$. When visual background clutter is dense, $p(Z|X)$ has to be taken as non-Gaussian [11], but for present purposes each of the $\mathbf{z}_i$ is taken to be distributed independently, along its normal, as a Gaussian with variance σ^2, so that

$$\mathbf{Z} = F(\mathbf{X}) + \mathbf{N} \tag{1}$$

where F is a (trigonometric) mapping from configuration space to image space.

Variance σ^2 can be estimated from just a single image as follows. An image is taken of a contour and observations $\mathbf{Z}$ are recorded. Then $\mathbf{X}$ is determined for that image by fitting manually (or by constrained least-squares fitting to $\mathbf{Z}$). Then the residual

$$R = \|\mathbf{Z} - F(\mathbf{X})\|^2$$

is computed, and observation variance can be estimated as $\sigma^2 = R/M$. It is worth pointing out that observed contours are not in fact projections of rigid, physical entities. Being silhouettes, they are projections of extremal contours, artefacts of surface and viewing geometry. However, it is known to be admissible (in first-order motion analysis) to treat silhouettes as if they were projections of rigid, physical shapes in three dimensions [10].

4 Kalman filtering

The core of the (extended) Kalman filter [6] is the computation of an updated configuration $\mathbf{X}$ as in response to new measurements Z. Suppose the configuration has a priori a Gaussian $\mathcal{N}(\hat{\mathbf{X}}(t-1), P(t-1))$ distribution, and the statistical information associated with the set of measurements along image normals [1] is S. Define the Jacobian J of the transformation F from kinematic variables to image plane to be

$$J(\mathbf{X}) = \frac{\partial F(\mathbf{X})}{\partial \mathbf{X}}. \tag{2}$$

Then after assimilating new measurements $Z(t)$, the new configuration $\mathbf{X}(t)$ is distributed approximately as a normal $\mathcal{N}(\hat{\mathbf{X}}(t), P(t))$ where

$$P(t)^{-1} = P(t-1)^{-1} + J(\hat{\mathbf{X}}(t-1))^\top S J(\hat{\mathbf{X}}(t-1)) \tag{3}$$

and

$$\hat{\mathbf{X}}(t) = \hat{\mathbf{X}}(t-1) + P(t)J(\hat{\mathbf{X}}(t-1))^\top \left(Z(t) - F(\hat{\mathbf{X}}(t-1)) \right). \tag{4}$$

Validity of the approximation depends on the first order Taylor series for F, with coefficients J, being a good approximation. This could break down under one of two conditions. One is when $J(\hat{\mathbf{X}})$ fails to exist because F is not differentiable. The other is when J is rank-deficient so that, at least for some directions $d\mathbf{X}$, the 1st differential $\nabla F(\mathbf{X}) \cdot d\mathbf{X}$ vanishes and the Taylor series approximation has to go to higher order than first. These two conditions correspond respectively to the endstop and kinematic singularities discussed below. Where the 1st order approximation breaks down, one of two things can happen to the true underlying distribution. Either it becomes non-Gaussian or, even if it remains approximately Gaussian, the EKF may generate the *wrong* Gaussian — one that is a poor approximation to the true distribution.

5 Simulation

In practice, away from such singularities and discontinuities, Kalman filtering is found to work well. This is tested, for example, on the earlier, non-singular, portion of the test sequence in the next section of the paper. At each time step, $F(X(t))$ is found to lie within the Gaussian distribution reported by the filter (with high statistical significance). One would expect that this is because the underlying distribution for $\mathbf{X}$ is indeed Gaussian. This is not a hypothesis that can be tested by looking at the Kalman filter itself which, being founded on an *assumption* of Gaussianity, begs the question. Approximate, non-parametric estimates of underlying distributions, can be formed by Monte-Carlo estimation. A general approach to Monte-Carlo simulation for temporal estimation problems was established some time ago [9] but has become practically feasible only recently with the development of time-recursive solutions [8, 13, 11].

The basic idea is to represent the posterior $p_t(\mathbf{X}(t)) \equiv p(\mathbf{X}(t)|Z(1), \ldots, Z(t))$ for $\mathbf{X}$ at time t, conditioned on the observations available up to time t, as a set

$$\{(\mathbf{X}_t^{(n)}, \pi_t^{(n)}), n = 1, \ldots, N\}$$

of "particles" $\mathbf{X}_t^{(n)}$. The $\pi_t^{(n)}$ are likelihood weights evaluated from the (Gaussian) observation density as

$$\pi_t^{(n)} = p(Z(t)|\mathbf{X}(t) = \mathbf{X}_t^{(n)}).$$

The interpretation of such a particle set is that if the set is *resampled*, meaning that an $\mathbf{X}$ is chosen to be one of $\mathbf{X}_t^{(n)}$, with probability proportional to its weight $\pi_t^{(n)}$, that $\mathbf{X}$ is distributed (approximately) according to the posterior p_t. Details of such algorithms, eg CONDENSATION, are omitted here as they are available elsewhere [11].

It should be noted, as a somewhat philosophical point, that any estimated distribution for $\mathbf{X}(t)$ is *necessarily* coloured by prior assumptions. Estimation is simply repeated application of Bayes' formula and as such demands prior assumptions, in the form of a distribution $p(\mathbf{X}(t)|\mathbf{X}(1), \ldots, \mathbf{X}(t-1))$, to be stated. Details of constructing such priors are well understood and practical methodologies are available [1]. Suffice it to say that here we have adopted a *critically damped* 2nd order linear-Gaussian model, with a time-constant of 1 second (commensurate with typical human time-scales for motion), and steady-state variances chosen to represent fairly the range of movement of the various joints (eg 1.5 radians for the shoulder).

Some simulations done by CONDENSATION, have used large numbers $N = 4000$ of particles at each time-step — large in the sense that N is about 100 times larger than the minimum value found experimentally to be sufficient for successful tracking. Choosing such a large N should allow accurate estimates of the $\mathbf{X}$ distribution and, indeed, comparing distributions obtained with a simulation with $N = 500$

showed little change, suggesting that $N = 500$ is large enough.

6 Singularity

For the kinematics of figure 1, coupled with image projection, $F(\mathbf{X})$ becomes singular in a variety of circumstances. A purely kinematic (or representational) singularity, like those familiar in robotic arms [4], arises when $\theta_2 = -\frac{\pi}{2}$, so that the θ_1 and θ_3 axes coincide.

A singularity that is more interesting, because it is not purely representational but indicates a genuine deficiency of visual information, arises at $\theta_4 = 0$, when the elbow joint is straight. In this case, a change in θ_3, representing axial rotation of the upper arm, is a rotation about an axis parallel to the image plane, and is unobservable. This is because the occluding contours (silhouette) of the arm is static under changes of θ_3, so that $\mathrm{d}F(\mathbf{X})/\mathrm{d}\theta_3 = 0$, and therefore $J(\mathbf{X})$ is singular — $\det J(\mathbf{X}) = 0$.

Results of Monte-Carlo simulation of the distribution of $\mathbf{X}$ through this singularity, are shown in figure 2. There is clear evidence of non-Gaussianity near the singularity, and the Kalman filter can be expected to break down there, which it duly does (figure 4).

7 Endstops

The other circumstance, identified earlier, in which the first-order approximation to F that is implicit in the Kalman filter should break down is where F is not differentiable. This happens in $F(X)$ for articulated bodies at hard limits. Clearly, representing hard limits is crucial for dynamical modelling, both for end-stops of joints and for freespace constraints such as walking on an impenetrable floor and collisions between limbs. Simulations under these circumstances have proved not to be possible with practical values of N, using the bland, critically damped motion prior from the previous experiments. This underlines still further, the notion that objective observation, uncoloured by prior knowledge cannot be attained.

In order for any practical simulation to work, we have had to adopt a more specific dynamical prior model for the experiments here on the hard-limits of the elbow joint (θ_4). This requires an explicit acknowledgement in the prior model that the straight configuration $\theta_4 = 0$ of the elbow is an end-stop and that motion may reverse there. The end-stop is represented by appending to the continuous state vector $\mathbf{X}(t)$, a discrete state component $y(t)$ as in [12] to make a "mixed" state. In these experiments, it takes one of two values $y(t) = 1, 2$, with 1 representing critically damped dynamics as before, and 2 representing an ephemeral velocity reversal state. State transitions are governed by a 1st order

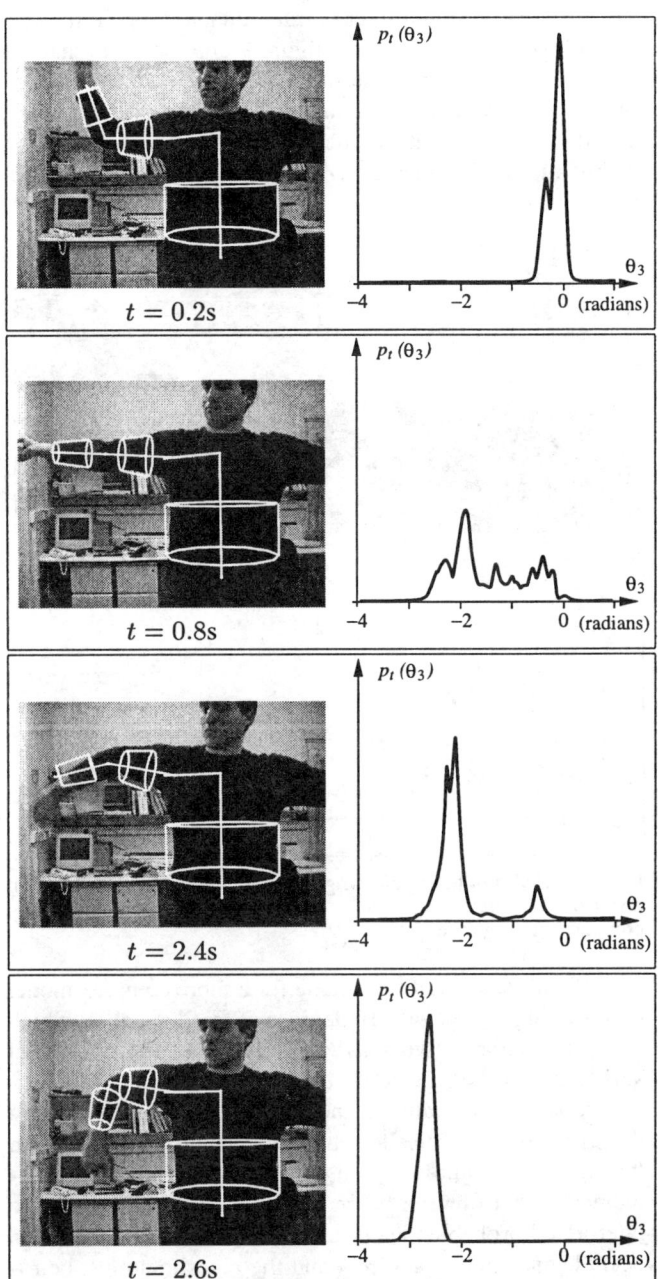

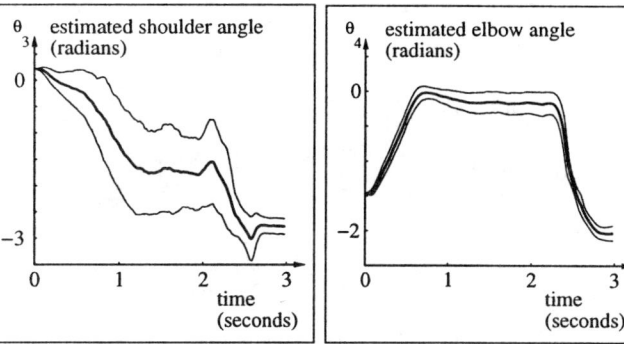

Figure 3: **Trajectory through a singularity — Monte-Carlo simulation.** Distributions for shoulder and elbow angles θ_3, θ_4 are displayed. Distribution mean is shown, with one standard deviation above and below, calculated from the simulation particle set. Shoulder angle variance grows markedly during the kinematic singularity, as expected, then collapses once the arm moves out of the singularity.

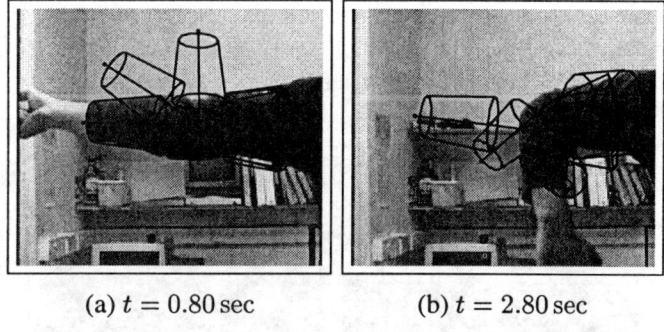

(a) $t = 0.80\,\mathrm{sec}$ (b) $t = 2.80\,\mathrm{sec}$

Figure 4: **Kalman filtering fails near a kinematic singularity.** Initially, when the arm is far from singularity, the Kalman filter tracks correctly (a) but fails as the singularity is approached. See also figure 5.

Figure 2: **Monte-Carlo simulation through a singularity** The axial rotation θ_3 of the upper arm is rendered unobservable by the singularity at $\theta_4 = 0$. Starting in a non-singular configuration, $p_t(\theta_3)$ is approximately Gaussian ($t = 0.2$s). It spreads by (non-linear) diffusion ($t = 0.8$s) close to the singularity, and becomes bimodal ($t = 2.4$s) and therefore decidedly non-Gaussian, reflecting growing ambiguity in the absence of observations. Its Gaussian form recovers ($t = 2.6$s) as the elbow (θ_4) moves away from singularity. See also figure 3. [Displayed configuration is the posterior mean. Simulation uses $N = 1000$ particles and endstops limiting θ_3 to π radians of travel.]

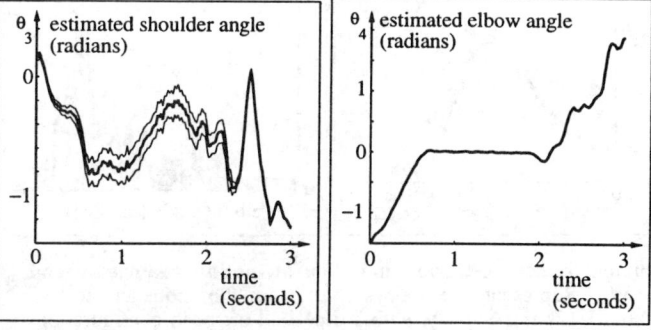

Figure 5: **Kalman filter trajectories.** Serious error sets in as the arm moves through the singularity, after about 2 seconds — compare with the simulation in figure 3.

Markov transition matrix

$$P(y(t) = y'|y(t-1) = y, \mathbf{X}(t-1)) = M(y,y')(\mathbf{X}(t-1)).$$

In our experiments we took

$$M = \begin{pmatrix} 1 - f(\mathbf{X}, \dot{\mathbf{X}}) & f(\mathbf{X}, \dot{\mathbf{X}}) \\ 1 & 0 \end{pmatrix}$$

where

$$f(\mathbf{X}, \dot{\mathbf{X}}) = \begin{cases} f_0(\mathbf{X}) & \text{if } \dot{\theta}_4 < 0 \\ 0 & \text{otherwise} \end{cases}$$

and $f_0(\mathbf{X}) = \exp -\frac{1}{2}\theta_4^2/\delta^2$, giving a "soft" onset of the probability of velocity reversal within about δ radians of the straight elbow configuration $\theta_4 = 0$. We took $\delta = 0.26$ radians (15°) in experiments here. The reversal itself is modelled as $\dot{\theta}_4 \to -\eta\dot{\theta}_4$ where the reflection coefficient η ranges from inelastic ($\eta = 0$), through elastic ($\eta = 1$) to superelastic ($\eta > 1$). In experiments here $\eta \in [0,4]$, drawn uniformly at random.

Simulating such a mixed state system can be done by standard forward filtering techniques [16, 2] *provided* observations are exact. Such filters cannot be used in the more general and practical case that observations are noisy, but particle filtering [12] is applicable, and results are shown in figure 6. The distribution of $\theta_4(t)$ is quite tight, without the

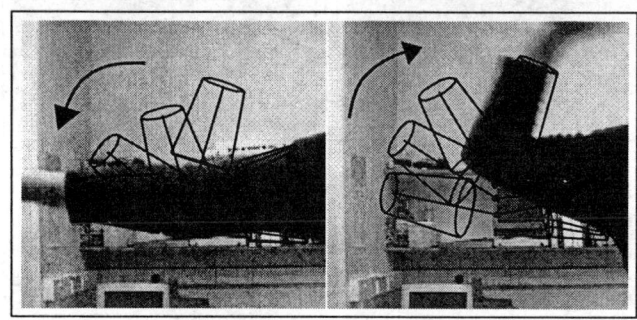

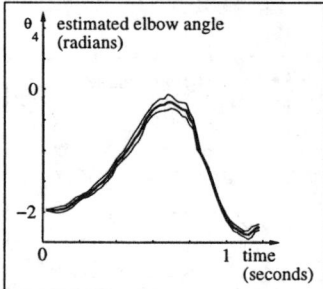
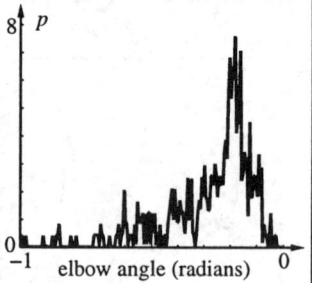

Figure 6: **Monte-Carlo simulation of motion against an end-stop.** Representative frames (top) from the sequence at $t = 0.60, 1.12s$ respectively, with a time-trail of mean configurations. The evolving distribution for $\mathbf{X}$ is shown (bottom left) in terms of mean and standard deviation as before. At the instant that the bounce against the elbow endstop occurs, the distribution for the elbow angle θ_4 is quite markedly non-Gaussian (bottom right).

increase of variance associated with singularities. This is because there is no loss of observability at an end-stop. As

expected, the Kalman filter is quite unable to track through an endstop configuration, as figure 7 shows. Note that the Kalman filter does not use the new dynamics with bounce. Such dynamics cannot be linearised, being discontinuous, and therefore fall outside the methodology of the extended Kalman filter. [Simulation with $N = 50$ particles per time-step.]

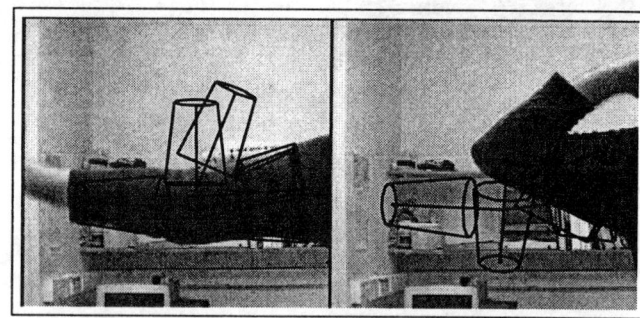

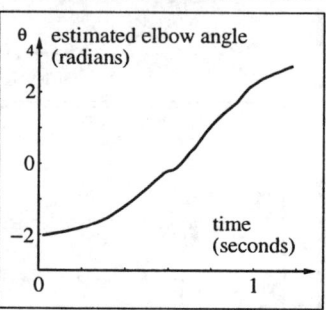

Figure 7: **Kalman filter tracking fails at an end-stop.** The sudden onset of rapid flexure cannot be followed by the Kalman filter — compare with figure 6.

A final demonstration is done for a more complex model of a walking figure, with 16 degrees of freedom, all of which vary considerably (whereas 6 of the 11 in the arm model varied very little, the torso being quite static). Discontinuities are incorporated in the form of endstops, built into the knee joints to disallow hyperextension. To deal with the additional complexity, edge-based observations are supplemented with region-based ones, using an SSD measure interpreted probabilistically as in [18]. Of course the legs occlude one another severely and the algorithm must be robust to this. Results in figure 8 show that hyperextension is dealt with effectively — see the version of this paper on http://www.robots.ox.ac.uk/~vdg/ for an mpeg video.

8 Conclusions

It has been confirmed experimentally that singularities and discontinuities (end-stops), where the linearisation on which the extended Kalman filter depends, breaks down, do indeed cause the filter to fail. Examination of the underlying distributions obtained by Monte-Carlo simulation reveal Gaussianity breaking down. The simulation tool itself — CON-

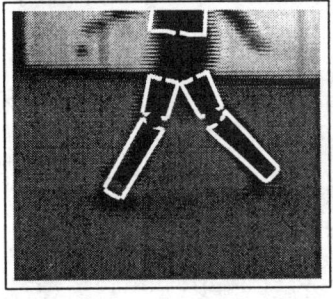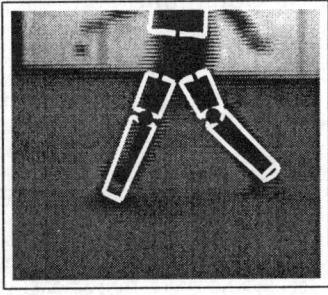

Figure 8: **Disallowing knee hyperextension.** A walker (top) is tracked over 3 seconds. Close-up snapshots shows that, without endstop constraints, hyperextension can occur in the tracked motion (left) which is effectively excluded using CONDENSATION with explicit endstops in the dynamical model (right).

DENSATION in these experiments — is a very interesting potential algorithm for body motion tracking.

With good prior models, relatively economical operation can be attained, for example $N = 50$ for the arm experiments, and excellent practical tracking performance. This may seem surprising given that the model has 5 (effective) degrees of freedom. However, it is not simply the *number* of parameters that determines the difficulty of a problem. What matters is the *breadth* of the probability distribution with respect to each parameter. For example, a straightforward tracking task, with reliable observations such as a Kalman filter could handle, may typically be filtered successfully using relatively few particles. In this problem, all variables are well constrained by data; even θ_3 which is subject to ambiguity near the endstop, is relatively tightly constrained, as figure 6 showed.

Progress on the details of coding have raised the speed of processing to approximately 10 Hz, for the arm experiments with $N = 50$. The rate limiting component is currently the calculation of occluding boundaries and occlusion prediction, and further work is needed there.

Acknowledgements We are grateful for the support of the Royal Society of London (AB), EPSRC (BN, BB) and Oxford Metrics (BN, JD). We have enjoyed numerous fruitful discussions with Dr J. Morris of Oxford Metrics.

References

[1] Blake, A., and Isard, M. *Active contours.* Springer, 1998.

[2] Bregler, C. Learning and recognising human dynamics in video sequences. In *Proc. Conf. Computer Vision and Pattern Recognition* (Jun 1997).

[3] Bregler, C., and Malik, J. Tracking people with twists and exponential maps. In *Proc. Conf. Computer Vision and Pattern Recognition* (1998).

[4] Craig, J. *Introduction to robotics: mechanics and control.* Addison-Wesley, 1986.

[5] Dickmanns, E., and Graefe, V. Dynamic monocular machine vision. *Machine Vision and Applications 1* (1988), 223–240.

[6] Gelb, A., Ed. *Applied Optimal Estimation.* MIT Press, Cambridge, MA, 1974.

[7] Goncalves, L., di Bernardo, E., Ursella, E., and Perona, P. Monocular tracking of the human arm in 3D. In *Proc. 5th Int. Conf. on Computer Vision* (1995), 764–770.

[8] Gordon, N., Salmond, D., and Smith, A. Novel approach to nonlinear/non-Gaussian Bayesian state estimation. *IEE Proc. F 140*, 2 (1993), 107–113.

[9] Handschin, J., and Mayne, D. Monte Carlo techniques to estimate the conditional expectation in multi-stage non-linear filtering. *Int. J. Control 9*, 5 (1969), 547–559.

[10] Harris, C. Tracking with rigid models. In *Active Vision*, A. Blake and A. Yuille, Eds. MIT, 1992, 59–74.

[11] Isard, M., and Blake, A. Visual tracking by stochastic propagation of conditional density. In *Proc. 4th European Conf. Computer Vision* (Cambridge, England, Apr 1996), 343–356.

[12] Isard, M., and Blake, A. A mixed-state Condensation tracker with automatic model switching. In *Proc. 6th Int. Conf. on Computer Vision* (1998), 107–112.

[13] Kitagawa, G. Monte Carlo filter and smoother for non-Gaussian nonlinear state space models. *Journal of Computational and Graphical Statistics 5*, 1 (1996), 1–25.

[14] Lerasle, F., Rives, G., Dhome, M., and Yassine, A. Human body tracking by monocular vision. In *Proc. 4th European Conf. Computer Vision (ECCV'96)* (1996), vol. II of *Lecture notes in computer science*, Springer-Verlag, 518–527.

[15] Lowe, D. Fitting parameterised 3D models to images. *IEEE Trans. on Pattern Analysis and Machine Intelligence 13*, 5 (1991), 441–450.

[16] Rabiner, L., and Bing-Hwang, J. *Fundamentals of speech recognition.* Prentice-Hall, 1993.

[17] Rehg, J. *Visual analysis of high dof articulated objects with application to hand tracking.* PhD thesis, Carnegie Mellon University, 1995.

[18] Szeliski, R. Bayesian modelling of uncertainty in low-level vision. *Int. J. Computer Vision 5*, 3 (1990), 271–301.

[19] Wachter, S., and Nagel, H. Tracking of persons in monocular image sequences. In *Proc. IEEE Non-Rigid and Articulated Motion Workshop (CVPR)* (1997).

Object Recognition from Local Scale-Invariant Features

David G. Lowe

Computer Science Department
University of British Columbia
Vancouver, B.C., V6T 1Z4, Canada
lowe@cs.ubc.ca

Abstract

An object recognition system has been developed that uses a new class of local image features. The features are invariant to image scaling, translation, and rotation, and partially invariant to illumination changes and affine or 3D projection. These features share similar properties with neurons in inferior temporal cortex that are used for object recognition in primate vision. Features are efficiently detected through a staged filtering approach that identifies stable points in scale space. Image keys are created that allow for local geometric deformations by representing blurred image gradients in multiple orientation planes and at multiple scales. The keys are used as input to a nearest-neighbor indexing method that identifies candidate object matches. Final verification of each match is achieved by finding a low-residual least-squares solution for the unknown model parameters. Experimental results show that robust object recognition can be achieved in cluttered partially-occluded images with a computation time of under 2 seconds.

1. Introduction

Object recognition in cluttered real-world scenes requires local image features that are unaffected by nearby clutter or partial occlusion. The features must be at least partially invariant to illumination, 3D projective transforms, and common object variations. On the other hand, the features must also be sufficiently distinctive to identify specific objects among many alternatives. The difficulty of the object recognition problem is due in large part to the lack of success in finding such image features. However, recent research on the use of dense local features (e.g., Schmid & Mohr [19]) has shown that efficient recognition can often be achieved by using local image descriptors sampled at a large number of repeatable locations.

This paper presents a new method for image feature generation called the Scale Invariant Feature Transform (SIFT). This approach transforms an image into a large collection of local feature vectors, each of which is invariant to image translation, scaling, and rotation, and partially invariant to illumination changes and affine or 3D projection. Previous approaches to local feature generation lacked invariance to scale and were more sensitive to projective distortion and illumination change. The SIFT features share a number of properties in common with the responses of neurons in inferior temporal (IT) cortex in primate vision. This paper also describes improved approaches to indexing and model verification.

The scale-invariant features are efficiently identified by using a staged filtering approach. The first stage identifies key locations in scale space by looking for locations that are maxima or minima of a difference-of-Gaussian function. Each point is used to generate a feature vector that describes the local image region sampled relative to its scale-space coordinate frame. The features achieve partial invariance to local variations, such as affine or 3D projections, by blurring image gradient locations. This approach is based on a model of the behavior of complex cells in the cerebral cortex of mammalian vision. The resulting feature vectors are called SIFT keys. In the current implementation, each image generates on the order of 1000 SIFT keys, a process that requires less than 1 second of computation time.

The SIFT keys derived from an image are used in a nearest-neighbour approach to indexing to identify candidate object models. Collections of keys that agree on a potential model pose are first identified through a Hough transform hash table, and then through a least-squares fit to a final estimate of model parameters. When at least 3 keys agree on the model parameters with low residual, there is strong evidence for the presence of the object. Since there may be dozens of SIFT keys in the image of a typical object, it is possible to have substantial levels of occlusion in the image and yet retain high levels of reliability.

The current object models are represented as 2D locations of SIFT keys that can undergo affine projection. Sufficient variation in feature location is allowed to recognize perspective projection of planar shapes at up to a 60 degree rotation away from the camera or to allow up to a 20 degree rotation of a 3D object.

2. Related research

Object recognition is widely used in the machine vision industry for the purposes of inspection, registration, and manipulation. However, current commercial systems for object recognition depend almost exclusively on correlation-based template matching. While very effective for certain engineered environments, where object pose and illumination are tightly controlled, template matching becomes computationally infeasible when object rotation, scale, illumination, and 3D pose are allowed to vary, and even more so when dealing with partial visibility and large model databases.

An alternative to searching all image locations for matches is to extract features from the image that are at least partially invariant to the image formation process and matching only to those features. Many candidate feature types have been proposed and explored, including line segments [6], groupings of edges [11, 14], and regions [2], among many other proposals. While these features have worked well for certain object classes, they are often not detected frequently enough or with sufficient stability to form a basis for reliable recognition.

There has been recent work on developing much denser collections of image features. One approach has been to use a corner detector (more accurately, a detector of peaks in local image variation) to identify repeatable image locations, around which local image properties can be measured. Zhang *et al.* [23] used the Harris corner detector to identify feature locations for epipolar alignment of images taken from differing viewpoints. Rather than attempting to correlate regions from one image against all possible regions in a second image, large savings in computation time were achieved by only matching regions centered at corner points in each image.

For the object recognition problem, Schmid & Mohr [19] also used the Harris corner detector to identify interest points, and then created a local image descriptor at each interest point from an orientation-invariant vector of derivative-of-Gaussian image measurements. These image descriptors were used for robust object recognition by looking for multiple matching descriptors that satisfied object-based orientation and location constraints. This work was impressive both for the speed of recognition in a large database and the ability to handle cluttered images.

The corner detectors used in these previous approaches have a major failing, which is that they examine an image at only a single scale. As the change in scale becomes significant, these detectors respond to different image points. Also, since the detector does not provide an indication of the object scale, it is necessary to create image descriptors and attempt matching at a large number of scales. This paper describes an efficient method to identify stable key locations in scale space. This means that different scalings of an image will have no effect on the set of key locations selected.

Furthermore, an explicit scale is determined for each point, which allows the image description vector for that point to be sampled at an equivalent scale in each image. A canonical orientation is determined at each location, so that matching can be performed relative to a consistent local 2D coordinate frame. This allows for the use of more distinctive image descriptors than the rotation-invariant ones used by Schmid and Mohr, and the descriptor is further modified to improve its stability to changes in affine projection and illumination.

Other approaches to appearance-based recognition include eigenspace matching [13], color histograms [20], and receptive field histograms [18]. These approaches have all been demonstrated successfully on isolated objects or pre-segmented images, but due to their more global features it has been difficult to extend them to cluttered and partially occluded images. Ohba & Ikeuchi [15] successfully apply the eigenspace approach to cluttered images by using many small local eigen-windows, but this then requires expensive search for each window in a new image, as with template matching.

3. Key localization

We wish to identify locations in image scale space that are invariant with respect to image translation, scaling, and rotation, and are minimally affected by noise and small distortions. Lindeberg [8] has shown that under some rather general assumptions on scale invariance, the Gaussian kernel and its derivatives are the only possible smoothing kernels for scale space analysis.

To achieve rotation invariance and a high level of efficiency, we have chosen to select key locations at maxima and minima of a difference of Gaussian function applied in scale space. This can be computed very efficiently by building an image pyramid with resampling between each level. Furthermore, it locates key points at regions and scales of high variation, making these locations particularly stable for characterizing the image. Crowley & Parker [4] and Lindeberg [9] have previously used the difference-of-Gaussian in scale space for other purposes. In the following, we describe a particularly efficient and stable method to detect and characterize the maxima and minima of this function.

As the 2D Gaussian function is separable, its convolution with the input image can be efficiently computed by applying two passes of the 1D Gaussian function in the horizontal and vertical directions:

$$g(x) = \frac{1}{\sqrt{2\pi}\sigma} e^{-x^2/2\sigma^2}$$

For key localization, all smoothing operations are done using $\sigma = \sqrt{2}$, which can be approximated with sufficient accuracy using a 1D kernel with 7 sample points.

The input image is first convolved with the Gaussian function using $\sigma = \sqrt{2}$ to give an image A. This is then repeated a second time with a further incremental smoothing of $\sigma = \sqrt{2}$ to give a new image, B, which now has an effective smoothing of $\sigma = 2$. The difference of Gaussian function is obtained by subtracting image B from A, resulting in a ratio of $2/\sqrt{2} = \sqrt{2}$ between the two Gaussians.

To generate the next pyramid level, we resample the already smoothed image B using bilinear interpolation with a pixel spacing of 1.5 in each direction. While it may seem more natural to resample with a relative scale of $\sqrt{2}$, the only constraint is that sampling be frequent enough to detect peaks. The 1.5 spacing means that each new sample will be a constant linear combination of 4 adjacent pixels. This is efficient to compute and minimizes aliasing artifacts that would arise from changing the resampling coefficients.

Maxima and minima of this scale-space function are determined by comparing each pixel in the pyramid to its neighbours. First, a pixel is compared to its 8 neighbours at the same level of the pyramid. If it is a maxima or minima at this level, then the closest pixel location is calculated at the next lowest level of the pyramid, taking account of the 1.5 times resampling. If the pixel remains higher (or lower) than this closest pixel and its 8 neighbours, then the test is repeated for the level above. Since most pixels will be eliminated within a few comparisons, the cost of this detection is small and much lower than that of building the pyramid.

If the first level of the pyramid is sampled at the same rate as the input image, the highest spatial frequencies will be ignored. This is due to the initial smoothing, which is needed to provide separation of peaks for robust detection. Therefore, we expand the input image by a factor of 2, using bilinear interpolation, prior to building the pyramid. This gives on the order of 1000 key points for a typical 512×512 pixel image, compared to only a quarter as many without the initial expansion.

3.1. SIFT key stability

To characterize the image at each key location, the smoothed image A at each level of the pyramid is processed to extract image gradients and orientations. At each pixel, A_{ij}, the image gradient magnitude, M_{ij}, and orientation, R_{ij}, are computed using pixel differences:

$$M_{ij} = \sqrt{(A_{ij} - A_{i+1,j})^2 + (A_{ij} - A_{i,j+1})^2}$$

$$R_{ij} = \text{atan2}\left(A_{ij} - A_{i+1,j}, A_{i,j+1} - A_{ij}\right)$$

The pixel differences are efficient to compute and provide sufficient accuracy due to the substantial level of previous smoothing. The effective half-pixel shift in position is compensated for when determining key location.

Robustness to illumination change is enhanced by thresholding the gradient magnitudes at a value of 0.1 times the

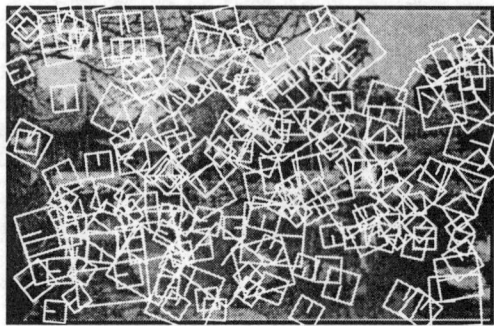
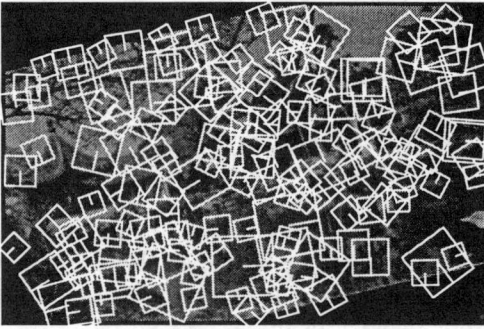

Figure 1: The second image was generated from the first by rotation, scaling, stretching, change of brightness and contrast, and addition of pixel noise. In spite of these changes, 78% of the keys from the first image have a closely matching key in the second image. These examples show only a subset of the keys to reduce clutter.

maximum possible gradient value. This reduces the effect of a change in illumination direction for a surface with 3D relief, as an illumination change may result in large changes to gradient magnitude but is likely to have less influence on gradient orientation.

Each key location is assigned a canonical orientation so that the image descriptors are invariant to rotation. In order to make this as stable as possible against lighting or contrast changes, the orientation is determined by the peak in a histogram of local image gradient orientations. The orientation histogram is created using a Gaussian-weighted window with σ of 3 times that of the current smoothing scale. These weights are multiplied by the thresholded gradient values and accumulated in the histogram at locations corresponding to the orientation, R_{ij}. The histogram has 36 bins covering the 360 degree range of rotations, and is smoothed prior to peak selection.

The stability of the resulting keys can be tested by subjecting natural images to affine projection, contrast and brightness changes, and addition of noise. The location of each key detected in the first image can be predicted in the transformed image from knowledge of the transform parameters. This framework was used to select the various sampling and smoothing parameters given above, so that max-

Image transformation	Match %	Ori %
A. Increase contrast by 1.2	89.0	86.6
B. Decrease intensity by 0.2	88.5	85.9
C. Rotate by 20 degrees	85.4	81.0
D. Scale by 0.7	85.1	80.3
E. Stretch by 1.2	83.5	76.1
F. Stretch by 1.5	77.7	65.0
G. Add 10% pixel noise	90.3	88.4
H. All of A,B,C,D,E,G.	78.6	71.8

Figure 2: For various image transformations applied to a sample of 20 images, this table gives the percent of keys that are found at matching locations and scales (Match %) and that also match in orientation (Ori %).

imum efficiency could be obtained while retaining stability to changes.

Figure 1 shows a relatively small number of keys detected over a 2 octave range of only the larger scales (to avoid excessive clutter). Each key is shown as a square, with a line from the center to one side of the square indicating orientation. In the second half of this figure, the image is rotated by 15 degrees, scaled by a factor of 0.9, and stretched by a factor of 1.1 in the horizontal direction. The pixel intensities, in the range of 0 to 1, have 0.1 subtracted from their brightness values and the contrast reduced by multiplication by 0.9. Random pixel noise is then added to give less than 5 bits/pixel of signal. In spite of these transformations, 78% of the keys in the first image had closely matching keys in the second image at the predicted locations, scales, and orientations

The overall stability of the keys to image transformations can be judged from Table 2. Each entry in this table is generated from combining the results of 20 diverse test images and summarizes the matching of about 15,000 keys. Each line of the table shows a particular image transformation. The first figure gives the percent of keys that have a matching key in the transformed image within σ in location (relative to scale for that key) and a factor of 1.5 in scale. The second column gives the percent that match these criteria as well as having an orientation within 20 degrees of the prediction.

4. Local image description

Given a stable location, scale, and orientation for each key, it is now possible to describe the local image region in a manner invariant to these transformations. In addition, it is desirable to make this representation robust against small shifts in local geometry, such as arise from affine or 3D projection.

One approach to this is suggested by the response properties of complex neurons in the visual cortex, in which a feature position is allowed to vary over a small region while orientation and spatial frequency specificity are maintained. Edelman, Intrator & Poggio [5] have performed experiments that simulated the responses of complex neurons to different 3D views of computer graphic models, and found that the complex cell outputs provided much better discrimination than simple correlation-based matching. This can be seen, for example, if an affine projection stretches an image in one direction relative to another, which changes the relative locations of gradient features while having a smaller effect on their orientations and spatial frequencies.

This robustness to local geometric distortion can be obtained by representing the local image region with multiple images representing each of a number of orientations (referred to as orientation planes). Each orientation plane contains only the gradients corresponding to that orientation, with linear interpolation used for intermediate orientations. Each orientation plane is blurred and resampled to allow for larger shifts in positions of the gradients.

This approach can be efficiently implemented by using the same precomputed gradients and orientations for each level of the pyramid that were used for orientation selection. For each keypoint, we use the pixel sampling from the pyramid level at which the key was detected. The pixels that fall in a circle of radius 8 pixels around the key location are inserted into the orientation planes. The orientation is measured relative to that of the key by subtracting the key's orientation. For our experiments we used 8 orientation planes, each sampled over a 4×4 grid of locations, with a sample spacing 4 times that of the pixel spacing used for gradient detection. The blurring is achieved by allocating the gradient of each pixel among its 8 closest neighbors in the sample grid, using linear interpolation in orientation and the two spatial dimensions. This implementation is much more efficient than performing explicit blurring and resampling, yet gives almost equivalent results.

In order to sample the image at a larger scale, the same process is repeated for a second level of the pyramid one octave higher. However, this time a 2×2 rather than a 4×4 sample region is used. This means that approximately the same image region will be examined at both scales, so that any nearby occlusions will not affect one scale more than the other. Therefore, the total number of samples in the SIFT key vector, from both scales, is $8 \times 4 \times 4 + 8 \times 2 \times 2$ or 160 elements, giving enough measurements for high specificity.

5. Indexing and matching

For indexing, we need to store the SIFT keys for sample images and then identify matching keys from new images. The problem of identifying the most similar keys for high dimensional vectors is known to have high complexity if an exact solution is required. However, a modification of the k-d tree algorithm called the best-bin-first search method (Beis & Lowe [3]) can identify the nearest neighbors with high probability using only a limited amount of computation. To further improve the efficiency of the best-bin-first algorithm, the SIFT key samples generated at the larger scale are given twice the weight of those at the smaller scale. This means that the larger scale is in effect able to filter the most likely neighbours for checking at the smaller scale. This also improves recognition performance by giving more weight to the least-noisy scale. In our experiments, it is possible to have a cut-off for examining at most 200 neighbors in a probabilistic best-bin-first search of 30,000 key vectors with almost no loss of performance compared to finding an exact solution.

An efficient way to cluster reliable model hypotheses is to use the Hough transform [1] to search for keys that agree upon a particular model pose. Each model key in the database contains a record of the key's parameters relative to the model coordinate system. Therefore, we can create an entry in a hash table predicting the model location, orientation, and scale from the match hypothesis. We use a bin size of 30 degrees for orientation, a factor of 2 for scale, and 0.25 times the maximum model dimension for location. These rather broad bin sizes allow for clustering even in the presence of substantial geometric distortion, such as due to a change in 3D viewpoint. To avoid the problem of boundary effects in hashing, each hypothesis is hashed into the 2 closest bins in each dimension, giving a total of 16 hash table entries for each hypothesis.

6. Solution for affine parameters

The hash table is searched to identify all clusters of at least 3 entries in a bin, and the bins are sorted into decreasing order of size. Each such cluster is then subject to a verification procedure in which a least-squares solution is performed for the affine projection parameters relating the model to the image.

The affine transformation of a model point $[x\ y]^T$ to an image point $[u\ v]^T$ can be written as

$$\begin{bmatrix} u \\ v \end{bmatrix} = \begin{bmatrix} m_1 & m_2 \\ m_3 & m_4 \end{bmatrix} \begin{bmatrix} x \\ y \end{bmatrix} + \begin{bmatrix} t_x \\ t_y \end{bmatrix}$$

where the model translation is $[t_x\ t_y]^T$ and the affine rotation, scale, and stretch are represented by the m_i parameters.

We wish to solve for the transformation parameters, so

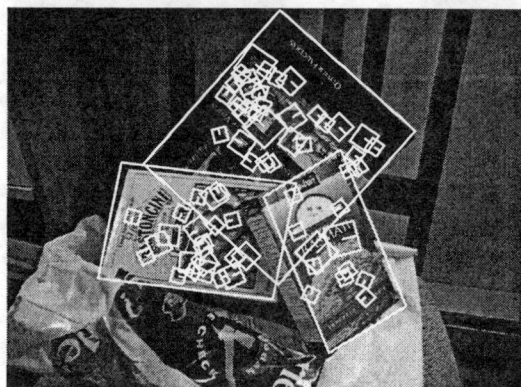

Figure 3: Model images of planar objects are shown in the top row. Recognition results below show model outlines and image keys used for matching.

the equation above can be rewritten as

$$\begin{bmatrix} x & y & 0 & 0 & 1 & 0 \\ 0 & 0 & x & y & 0 & 1 \\ & & \cdots & & & \\ & & \cdots & & & \end{bmatrix} \begin{bmatrix} m_1 \\ m_2 \\ m_3 \\ m_4 \\ t_x \\ t_y \end{bmatrix} = \begin{bmatrix} u \\ v \\ \vdots \end{bmatrix}$$

This equation shows a single match, but any number of further matches can be added, with each match contributing two more rows to the first and last matrix. At least 3 matches are needed to provide a solution.

We can write this linear system as

$$\mathbf{Ax = b}$$

The least-squares solution for the parameters $\mathbf{x}$ can be deter-

Figure 4: Top row shows model images for 3D objects with outlines found by background segmentation. Bottom image shows recognition results for 3D objects with model outlines and image keys used for matching.

mined by solving the corresponding normal equations,

$$x = [A^T A]^{-1} A^T b$$

which minimizes the sum of the squares of the distances from the projected model locations to the corresponding image locations. This least-squares approach could readily be extended to solving for 3D pose and internal parameters of articulated and flexible objects [12].

Outliers can now be removed by checking for agreement between each image feature and the model, given the parameter solution. Each match must agree within 15 degrees orientation, $\sqrt{2}$ change in scale, and 0.2 times maximum model size in terms of location. If fewer than 3 points remain after discarding outliers, then the match is rejected. If any outliers are discarded, the least-squares solution is re-solved with the remaining points.

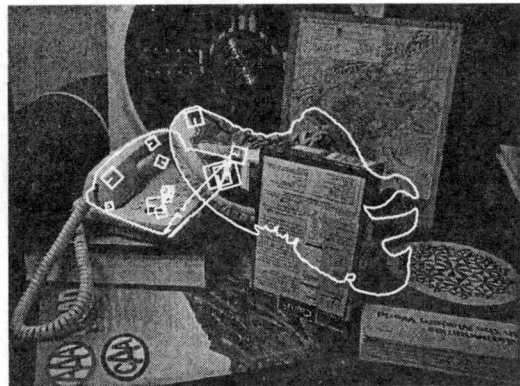

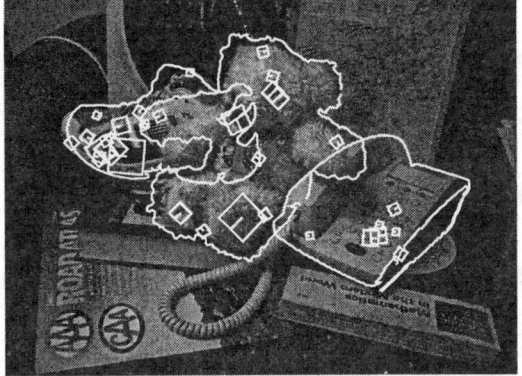

Figure 5: Examples of 3D object recognition with occlusion.

7. Experiments

The affine solution provides a good approximation to perspective projection of planar objects, so planar models provide a good initial test of the approach. The top row of Figure 3 shows three model images of rectangular planar faces of objects. The figure also shows a cluttered image containing the planar objects, and the same image is shown overlayed with the models following recognition. The model keys that are displayed are the ones used for recognition and final least-squares solution. Since only 3 keys are needed for robust recognition, it can be seen that the solutions are highly redundant and would survive substantial occlusion. Also shown are the rectangular borders of the model images, projected using the affine transform from the least-square solution. These closely agree with the true borders of the planar regions in the image, except for small errors introduced by the perspective projection. Similar experiments have been performed for many images of planar objects, and the recognition has proven to be robust to at least a 60 degree rotation of the object in any direction away from the camera.

Although the model images and affine parameters do not account for rotation in depth of 3D objects, they are still sufficient to perform robust recognition of 3D objects over about a 20 degree range of rotation in depth away from each model view. An example of three model images is shown in

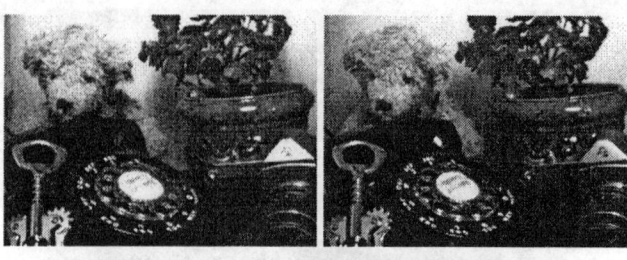

Figure 6: Stability of image keys is tested under differing illumination. The first image is illuminated from upper left and the second from center right. Keys shown in the bottom image were those used to match second image to first.

the top row of Figure 4. The models were photographed on a black background, and object outlines extracted by segmenting out the background region. An example of recognition is shown in the same figure, again showing the SIFT keys used for recognition. The object outlines are projected using the affine parameter solution, but this time the agreement is not as close because the solution does not account for rotation in depth. Figure 5 shows more examples in which there is significant partial occlusion.

The images in these examples are of size 384×512 pixels. The computation times for recognition of all objects in each image are about 1.5 seconds on a Sun Sparc 10 processor, with about 0.9 seconds required to build the scale-space pyramid and identify the SIFT keys, and about 0.6 seconds to perform indexing and least-squares verification. This does not include time to pre-process each model image, which would be about 1 second per image, but would only need to be done once for initial entry into a model database.

The illumination invariance of the SIFT keys is demonstrated in Figure 6. The two images are of the same scene from the same viewpoint, except that the first image is illuminated from the upper left and the second from the center right. The full recognition system is run to identify the second image using the first image as the model, and the second image is correctly recognized as matching the first. Only SIFT keys that were part of the recognition are shown. There were 273 keys that were verified as part of the final match, which means that in each case not only was the same key detected at the same location, but it also was the clos-

est match to the correct corresponding key in the second image. Any 3 of these keys would be sufficient for recognition. While matching keys are not found in some regions where highlights or shadows change (for example on the shiny top of the camera) in general the keys show good invariance to illumination change.

8. Connections to biological vision

The performance of human vision is obviously far superior to that of current computer vision systems, so there is potentially much to be gained by emulating biological processes. Fortunately, there have been dramatic improvements within the past few years in understanding how object recognition is accomplished in animals and humans.

Recent research in neuroscience has shown that object recognition in primates makes use of features of intermediate complexity that are largely invariant to changes in scale, location, and illumination (Tanaka [21], Perrett & Oram [16]). Some examples of such intermediate features found in inferior temporal cortex (IT) are neurons that respond to a dark five-sided star shape, a circle with a thin protruding element, or a horizontal textured region within a triangular boundary. These neurons maintain highly specific responses to shape features that appear anywhere within a large portion of the visual field and over a several octave range of scales (Ito *et. al* [7]). The complexity of many of these features appears to be roughly the same as for the current SIFT features, although there are also some neurons that respond to more complex shapes, such as faces. Many of the neurons respond to color and texture properties in addition to shape. The feature responses have been shown to depend on previous visual learning from exposure to specific objects containing the features (Logothetis, Pauls & Poggio [10]). These features appear to be derived in the brain by a highly computation-intensive parallel process, which is quite different from the staged filtering approach given in this paper. However, the results are much the same: an image is transformed into a large set of local features that each match a small fraction of potential objects yet are largely invariant to common viewing transformations.

It is also known that object recognition in the brain depends on a serial process of attention to bind features to object interpretations, determine pose, and segment an object from a cluttered background [22]. This process is presumably playing the same role in verification as the parameter solving and outlier detection used in this paper, since the accuracy of interpretations can often depend on enforcing a single viewpoint constraint [11].

9. Conclusions and comments

The SIFT features improve on previous approaches by being largely invariant to changes in scale, illumination, and local affine distortions. The large number of features in a typical image allow for robust recognition under partial occlusion in cluttered images. A final stage that solves for affine model parameters allows for more accurate verification and pose determination than in approaches that rely only on indexing.

An important area for further research is to build models from multiple views that represent the 3D structure of objects. This would have the further advantage that keys from multiple viewing conditions could be combined into a single model, thereby increasing the probability of finding matches in new views. The models could be true 3D representations based on structure-from-motion solutions, or could represent the space of appearance in terms of automated clustering and interpolation (Pope & Lowe [17]). An advantage of the latter approach is that it could also model non-rigid deformations.

The recognition performance could be further improved by adding new SIFT feature types to incorporate color, texture, and edge groupings, as well as varying feature sizes and offsets. Scale-invariant edge groupings that make local figure-ground discriminations would be particularly useful at object boundaries where background clutter can interfere with other features. The indexing and verification framework allows for all types of scale and rotation invariant features to be incorporated into a single model representation. Maximum robustness would be achieved by detecting many different feature types and relying on the indexing and clustering to select those that are most useful in a particular image.

References

[1] Ballard, D.H., "Generalizing the Hough transform to detect arbitrary patterns," *Pattern Recognition,* **13,** 2 (1981), pp. 111-122.

[2] Basri, Ronen, and David. W. Jacobs, "Recognition using region correspondences," *International Journal of Computer Vision,* **25,** 2 (1996), pp. 141–162.

[3] Beis, Jeff, and David G. Lowe, "Shape indexing using approximate nearest-neighbour search in high-dimensional spaces," *Conference on Computer Vision and Pattern Recognition,* Puerto Rico (1997), pp. 1000–1006.

[4] Crowley, James L., and Alice C. Parker, "A representation for shape based on peaks and ridges in the difference of low-pass transform," *IEEE Trans. on Pattern Analysis and Machine Intelligence,* **6,** 2 (1984), pp. 156–170.

[5] Edelman, Shimon, Nathan Intrator, and Tomaso Poggio, "Complex cells and object recognition," Unpublished Manuscript, preprint at http://www.ai.mit.edu/~edelman/mirror/nips97.ps.Z

[6] Grimson, Eric, and Thomás Lozano-Pérez, "Localizing overlapping parts by searching the interpretation tree," *IEEE Trans. on Pattern Analysis and Machine Intelligence,* **9** (1987), pp. 469–482.

[7] Ito, Minami, Hiroshi Tamura, Ichiro Fujita, and Keiji Tanaka, "Size and position invariance of neuronal responses in monkey inferotemporal cortex," *Journal of Neurophysiology,* **73,** 1 (1995), pp. 218–226.

[8] Lindeberg, Tony, "Scale-space theory: A basic tool for analysing structures at different scales", *Journal of Applied Statistics,* **21,** 2 (1994), pp. 224–270.

[9] Lindeberg, Tony, "Detecting salient blob-like image structures and their scales with a scale-space primal sketch: a method for focus-of-attention," *International Journal of Computer Vision,* **11,** 3 (1993), pp. 283–318.

[10] Logothetis, Nikos K., Jon Pauls, and Tomaso Poggio, "Shape representation in the inferior temporal cortex of monkeys," *Current Biology,* **5,** 5 (1995), pp. 552–563.

[11] Lowe, David G., "Three-dimensional object recognition from single two-dimensional images," *Artificial Intelligence,* **31,** 3 (1987), pp. 355–395.

[12] Lowe, David G., "Fitting parameterized three-dimensional models to images," *IEEE Trans. on Pattern Analysis and Machine Intelligence,* **13,** 5 (1991), pp. 441–450.

[13] Murase, Hiroshi, and Shree K. Nayar, "Visual learning and recognition of 3-D objects from appearance," *International Journal of Computer Vision,* **14,** 1 (1995), pp. 5–24.

[14] Nelson, Randal C., and Andrea Selinger, "Large-scale tests of a keyed, appearance-based 3-D object recognition system," *Vision Research,* **38,** 15 (1998), pp. 2469–88.

[15] Ohba, Kohtaro, and Katsushi Ikeuchi, "Detectability, uniqueness, and reliability of eigen windows for stable verification of partially occluded objects," *IEEE Trans. on Pattern Analysis and Machine Intelligence,* **19,** 9 (1997), pp. 1043–48.

[16] Perrett, David I., and Mike W. Oram, "Visual recognition based on temporal cortex cells: viewer-centered processing of pattern configuration," *Zeitschrift für Naturforschung C,* **53c** (1998), pp. 518–541.

[17] Pope, Arthur R. and David G. Lowe, "Learning probabilistic appearance models for object recognition," in *Early Visual Learning,* eds. Shree Nayar and Tomaso Poggio (Oxford University Press, 1996), pp. 67–97.

[18] Schiele, Bernt, and James L. Crowley, "Object recognition using multidimensional receptive field histograms," *Fourth European Conference on Computer Vision,* Cambridge, UK (1996), pp. 610–619.

[19] Schmid, C., and R. Mohr, "Local grayvalue invariants for image retrieval," *IEEE PAMI,* **19,** 5 (1997), pp. 530–534.

[20] Swain, M., and D. Ballard, "Color indexing," *International Journal of Computer Vision,* **7,** 1 (1991), pp. 11–32.

[21] Tanaka, Keiji, "Mechanisms of visual object recognition: monkey and human studies," *Current Opinion in Neurobiology,* **7** (1997), pp. 523–529.

[22] Treisman, Anne M., and Nancy G. Kanwisher, "Perceiving visually presented objects: recognition, awareness, and modularity," *Current Opinion in Neurobiology,* **8** (1998), pp. 218–226.

[23] Zhang, Z., R. Deriche, O. Faugeras, Q.T. Luong, "A robust technique for matching two uncalibrated images through the recovery of the unknown epipolar geometry," *Artificial Intelligence,* **78,** (1995), pp. 87-119.

Projective Alignment with Regions

Ronen Basri*
Department of Applied Math.
The Weizmann Inst. of Science
Rehovot, 76100, Israel

David Jacobs
NEC Research Institute
4 Independence Way
Princeton, NJ 08540

Abstract

We consider a recent approach to recognition that uses regions to determine the pose of objects while allowing for partial occlusion of the regions. In this paper we further analyze properties of the method for planar objects undergoing projective transformations. We prove that three visible regions are sufficient to determine the transformation uniquely, and that for a large class of objects two regions are insufficient. However, we show that when several regions are available the pose of the object can generally be recovered even when all but two regions are significantly occluded. Our analysis is based on investigating the flow patterns of points under projective transformations in the presence of fixed points.

1 Introduction

Estimating the pose of objects is important both for manipulating the objects and as a step in their recognition. In this paper we analyze the behavior of a region-based method of determining the pose of planar objects under projective transformations. Planar object recognition is potentially useful for flat objects, for polyhedral objects with markings on their flat surfaces, and for mobile robots to localize their position relative to flat indoor surfaces. By allowing projective transformations to represent pose we allow an object model to be acquired with an uncalibrated camera of unknown pose, and to be matched to an image taken with an uncalibrated camera.

A basic question is how to represent objects in order to estimate their pose accurately and efficiently. Recently, we proposed a method for pose estimation that uses regions ([1, 10]). This method expands the repertoire of possible representational primitives, using direct representation of region information. It does not require an exact localization of features. It handles objects with smooth curved boundaries, but does not require an algebraic description of such objects. Moreover, the method can recognize planar objects when the image regions are occluded, without needing to derive information about the extent of this occlusion. Also, region information can be seamlessly combined with local features, when they are available. Finally, this method computes the pose of objects efficiently using linear programming.

*The research of Ronen Basri was supported in part by the Israeli Ministry of Science, Grant No. 6281 and by the Unites States-Israel Binational Science Foundation, Grant No. 94-100. The vision group at the Weizmann Inst. is supported in part by the Israeli Ministry of Science, Grant No. 8504. Ronen Basri is an incumbent of Arye Dissentshik Career Development Chair at the Weizmann Institute.

In [1] we introduced the method and explored its properties for planar objects undergoing similarity and affine transformations. We now consider the case of aligning an image to a model of a planar object undergoing a projective transformation. We focus on the most basic problem of determining when there is enough region information to determine object pose. We prove that three regions generally determine a solution uniquely. In addition, we show that for a large class of objects two regions are insufficient for this purpose. This complements our previous results showing that two regions determine a unique solution under affine transformations. At the same time, we show that when several regions are available the pose of the object can generally be recovered even when all but two regions are significantly occluded.

We should compare these results to corresponding ones for other pose determination methods. First, a projective transformation relating a model with an image can be determined using four or more corresponding simple local features, such as points or lines (such methods are discussed, eg., in [8]). Our algorithm addresses the problem of pose determination when such local features are difficult to find or match. For example, in smooth convex shapes, there may not be local features that can be reliably computed and matched for arbitrary perspective views.

Second, one can determine the pose of two regions using their second moments or algebraic descriptions of conics (e.g., [7, 11]). We show that our method generally requires more than two regions. However, methods based on moments or algebraic descriptions require regions that have no occlusion. Our method correctly uses information derived from partially occluded image regions without any prior knowledge of which regions are occluded or the locus of occlusions. We show theoretically that our method produces correct results when several regions are matched and at least two are unoccluded, while others are arbitrarily occluded. We demonstrate experimentally that our method can correctly determine pose even when all regions are partially occluded. By handling arbitrarily occluded, arbitrarily shaped regions, our method handles some problems that cannot be solved by other existing methods.

The paper is divided as follows. In Section 2 we review the method of recognition with regions. In Section 3 we explore uniqueness under projective transformations. Experimental results are shown in Section 4.

2 Recognition with regions

In this section we briefly review the scheme for recognition using region correspondences. A more detailed de-

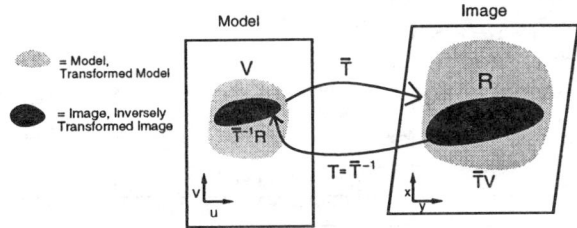

Model | Image

= Model,
Transformed Model

= Image, Inversely
Transformed Image

Figure 1: The backward constraints require that a feasible transformation satisfies $\bar{T}V \supseteq R_i$. Equivalently, $V \supseteq \bar{T}^{-1}(R_i) \equiv T(R_i)$.

scription can be found in [1]. We restrict our discussion to planar objects undergoing projective transformations.

We model an object with convex regions $(V_1, ..., V_k \subset \mathcal{R}^2)$. An image of the object contains corresponding regions $(R_1, ..., R_k \subset \mathcal{R}^2)$. Our task is to determine the transformation $\bar{T} \in \mathcal{T}$ that maps every model region V_i to its corresponding image region R_i ($1 \leq i \leq k$), where $\mathcal{T}$ denotes the set of projective transformations. [1, 10] extends the method to non-convex regions, using their convex hulls.

Determining a transformation that perfectly maps a set of model regions to their corresponding image regions is generally a non-convex optimization problem, since we can have multiple, locally optimal solutions. Moreover, such a transformation would not allow for partial occlusion of the image regions. For these reasons we divide the constraints that finding a perfect match would place on the transformation into two sets, one of which is unaffected by occlusion.

Forward constraints: every model point $\vec{p} \in V_i$ should project inside the region R_i (that is, $\bar{T}V_i \subseteq R_i$).

Backward constraints: every image point $\vec{q} \in R_i$ is the projection of some model point $\vec{p} \in V_i$ (that is, $\bar{T}V_i \supseteq R_i$, or equivalently, $V_i \supseteq \bar{T}^{-1}R_i$).

Each set of constraints produces a convex set of feasible transformations. Thus, each set of constraints can be solved efficiently by computing a linear discriminant function.

We proceed by defining the backward constraints under a projective transformation (see Fig. 1). The forward constraints can be defined in the same way. Solving for the transformation using the backward constraints alone is particularly useful in the case of occlusion. Image regions that are partly occluded lie inside the corresponding model regions (after the model and the image are brought into alignment), but the inclusion may be strict due to the occlusion.

We solve the backward constraints by formulating constraints on $T = \bar{T}^{-1}$, the inverse of the transformation we seek. Let $\vec{q} = (u, v, 1)^T \in V$ be a model point written in homogenuous coordinates. Then, since V is convex, every line $\vec{l} = (A, B, C)^T$ which does not intersect the interior of V satisfies $\vec{l}^T \vec{q} \geq 0$. Let $\vec{p} = (x, y, 1)^T \in R$ be an image point. The backward constraints imply that the appropriate transformation T maps $\vec{p}$ inside V. This implies that there exists some point $\vec{q} \in V$ such that $\vec{q} = \alpha T \vec{p}$, where T is 3×3 non-singular and α is a scalar factor. In actual images since the object is constrained to appear in front of the camera α must be positive. Combining these equations we

obtain that $\alpha \vec{l}^T T \vec{p} \geq 0$, with $\alpha > 0$. Since α is positive it can be eliminated from the equation, yielding

$$\vec{l}^T T \vec{p} \geq 0. \tag{1}$$

This equation is linear in the unknown transformation parameters, which are the components of T.

The backward problem introduces such a constraint for every pair of a point in the image regions and a tangent line to the model regions. In the forward problem the model and image change roles. The number of constraints for a curved object is therefore infinite. For such objects we obtain a finite system of inequalities by sampling the set of constraints. For polygonal regions the number of independent constraints is finite. These constraints are defined by the vertices of the image regions and the sides of the model regions.

The one-way problem, therefore, can be expressed as follows. We seek T that is consistent with the constraints

$$\vec{l}_i^T T \vec{p}_i \geq 0, \quad i = 1, ..., n. \tag{2}$$

Solving the one-way problem (2) involves finding a linear discriminant function. We can do this using linear programming. To generate a linear program a linear objective function should be specified. A common method is to introduce an additional unknown, λ, in the following way.

$$\max \lambda \quad s.t. \quad \vec{l}_i^T T \vec{p}_i \geq \lambda, \quad i = 1, ..., n \tag{3}$$

A solution to (2) exists if and only if a solution to (3) with $\lambda \geq 0$ exists. (Note that other objective functions, e.g., the perceptron function, can be used for recovering T, [6].)

2.1 Uniqueness

Whenever an error-free image contains an instance of the model, perhaps with occlusion, the backward constraints (2) are satisfied by the correct alignment transformation. However, other transformations may also satisfy (2). We are likely in such cases to find one of these incorrect transformations, typically by allowing the image regions to contract inside the corresponding model regions. It is therefore important to determine when the backward constraints specify a unique solution.

We define the uniqueness problem as follows. Assume $TR_i = V_i$ ($1 \leq i \leq k$). Does there exist another transformation $T' \neq T \in \mathcal{T}$ that satisfies the backward constraints? We focus first on the case where all k image regions are unoccluded. However, our method derives only valid constraints from arbitrarily occluded regions. So if k unoccluded regions produce a unique result, so do any set of regions with k of them unoccluded.

[1] proved a basic lemma that establishes that the uniqueness of a one-way matching problem depends on the model alone. The lemma states the following claim. The solution to a one-way matching problem under a group of transformations (similarity, affine, or projective) is unique if and only if there exists no transformation of that group (other than the identity) which projects the model regions entirely inside themselves. The transformation that produced an image does not affect whether it leads to a unique pose. Thus, we can modify the problem to: Does there exist a transformation $T \neq I$ (where I denotes the identity transformation) such that $TR_i \subseteq R_i$ for all $1 \leq i \leq k$?

Another property that is used below (and was used already in [1]) is that transformations that project the model regions entirely inside themselves introduce fixed points inside the model regions. That is, if $T(R_i) \subseteq R_i$, there exists $\vec{p} \in R_i$ such that $T(\vec{p}) = \vec{p}$. The presence of fixed points, and their particular nature, will play a key role in our proofs.

3 Projective transformations

[1] showed that two distinct regions generally determine the pose of a planar object undergoing similarity or affine transformations. In this section we extend the uniqueness results to the projective case. This depends on a further analysis of the fixed points, which is given in Section 3.1. Previous researchers ([3, 14]) have analyzed the fixed points of optical flow fields as dynamical systems, obtaining characterizations of the possible local properties of fixed points. We extend that work by presenting a taxonomy of the possible combinations of fixed points that can occur in a planar projective flow field. [3] pointed out that these fixed points are the eigenvalues of a transformation matrix, and we use that fact as the basis of our analysis. This analysis is relevant to our uniqueness questions because we also show that any projective transformation mapping a region inside itself must have a sink point inside that region. Our analysis shows that either there is just one sink point in planar projective flow, or there is a line on which all points are sink points. This implies that if three regions have no single line intersecting them all, they must lead to a unique transformation. It also allows us to derive necessary and sufficient conditions for collinear regions to produce non-unique solutions.

We use these conditions in Section 3.2, however, to show that every pair of distinct triangles or ellipses is degenerate. Finally, in Section 3.3 we explore, given three regions, to what extent one of the regions can be occluded and still maintain uniqueness.

3.1 Conditions for Uniqueness

We begin with a general discussion of the fixed points that may occur in planar projective flow. First, we note that a planar projective transformation can be written as a 3×3 matrix. Points in the projective plane can be written in homogenous coordinates as 3-D vectors, (x, y, w). The image coordinates of this point are then $(x/w, y/w)$. So, if $p = \lambda q$ for some scalar λ, then p and q represent the same point in the plane. p is a fixed point if $Tp = \lambda p$. Therefore, if p is a fixed point of T, p is an eigenvector of T, with λ being the associated eigenvalue.

Next, we consider a basic property of the fixed points that belong to regions obeying the one-way constraints under projective transformations. As stated above, to determine whether a model gives rise to unique solutions, without loss of generality we may assume that the identity transformation maps the model to the image, and ask whether $T \neq I$ exists such that $p \in V_i \Rightarrow Tp \in V_i$. Note that if T obeys this constraint, it must also be the case that $T(Tp)) \in V_i$, and in general that $T^n p \in V_i$, for all n. We are therefore especially interested in characterizing the limit points of $T^n p$.

There are several possible cases that can occur in the limit as n goes to infinity for $T^n p$. First, $T^n p$ can fail to converge (eg., by forming a cycle) when T has complex eigenvalues. T can have either zero or two complex eigenvalues. When it has two complex eigenvalues it can have only one fixed point (only one eigenvector associated with a real eigenvalue). When $T^n p$ converges to a point this point will be

# eigenvectors associated with largest eigenvalue	# linearly independent eigenvectors	# real eigenvalues	Max. # regions obeying constraints
0	1	1	1
1	1,2 or 3	1,2 or 3	1
2	2	1	1
2	3	2	2
3	3	1	All, $T = I$

Table 1: Topologically distinct cases involving fixed points.

an eigenvector of T. In general, this will be an eigenvector associated with T's largest eigenvalue. This is well known, and is the basis of the power method of computing eigenvalues. $T^n p$ will only converge to a different eigenvector in special cases. If p is an eigenvector to start with, then obviously $T^n p$ always remains at p. Or, if p is a linear combination of two eigenvectors associated with non-maximal eigenvalues of T, then $T^n p$ will remain a linear combination of these two eigenvectors, and will generically converge to the one that is associated with the second largest eigenvalue.

Geometrically, this means that there may be a line in the image such that for points on this line $T^n p$ does not converge to a fixed point associated with the largest eigenvalue. However, all other points in the plane do converge to such fixed points. We will now analyze topologically distinct cases involving these fixed points. Table 1 summarizes the results of this analysis.

First, consider the case in which T has three linearly independent eigenvectors associated with its largest eigenvalue. This case occurs only when T has a single real eigenvalue of multiplicity three. In this case, all linear combinations of these eigenvectors are also eigenvectors, implying that all points in the plane are fixed points, and $T = I$. Therefore, T cannot be distinct from I and have three linearly independent eigenvectors associated with one eigenvalue.

Second, we consider the case in which there is no eigenvector associated with a real eigenvalue of greatest magnitude. This can only occur when a complex eigenvalue is the eigenvalue of greatest magnitude. In this case, there are two complex eigenvalues, and one real one. So there is only one fixed point of the transformation, and there can only be one region that obeys the one-way constraints.

Third, consider the case in which there is one eigenvector associated with a real eigenvalue of greatest magnitude. In this case, for any point p that is not a linear combination of the other two eigenvectors, $T^n p$ converges to this *sink* eigenvector. Any region of non-zero area that obeys the backward constraints must contain this sink point, since for any point in the region, $T^n p$ is also in this region. Therefore, only one region can obey the backward constraints.

Finally, we consider the case in which the largest eigenvalue, λ, is real and has two linearly independent eigenvectors, p_1 and p_2. In this case, from elementary linear algebra, we know that since $Tp_1 = \lambda p_1$ and $Tp_2 = \lambda p_2$, $T(ap_1 + bp_2) = \lambda(ap_1 + bp_2)$, and $ap_1 + bp_2$ is a fixed point of T, for any choice of a and b. That is, all points on the line formed by p_1 and p_2 are fixed points, and we say this line is *pointwise fixed*. For any p, if p is not the third eigenvector of T, $T^n p$ converges to some point on this line. Therefore, every region that is not a point and obeys the backward constraints must contain a point on this line, and we have proven:

Theorem 1: Let $V_1, V_2, V_3 \subseteq \mathcal{R}^2$ be three regions, each containing more that a single point, such that there exists no straight line passing through all three regions. Then, the solution to the one-way matching problem with these regions as a model under a projective transformation is unique.

We have also shown that if two or more regions do obey the one-way constraints, then there must be a transformation T mapping the regions inside themselves such that T has exactly two linearly independent eigenvectors associated with its largest real eigenvalue. We now describe the form T must have more precisely.

First, we show that if T obeys the one-way constraints on two distinct regions, T must have a third eigenvector. Suppose this were not the case. WLOG we may assume that the pointwise fixed line is the x axis, in which case we have:

$$T = \begin{pmatrix} 1 & b & 0 \\ 0 & 1 & 0 \\ 0 & d & 1 \end{pmatrix}$$

(since we can scale the matrix without changing the projective transformation it produces, we may assume WLOG that $\lambda = 1$). Note that such a T has only two eigenvectors, unless $T = I$. Then we have:

$$T^n = \begin{pmatrix} 1 & nb & 0 \\ 0 & 1 & 0 \\ 0 & nd & 1 \end{pmatrix}$$

For $p = (x, y, 1)$, $T^n p = (x + nby, y, ndy + 1)$. In the limit as n goes to infinity, $T^n p$ therefore converges to the point $(\frac{b}{d}, 0)$. Therefore, in this case, any region with non-zero area that obeys the backward constraints must contain the point $(\frac{b}{d}, 0)$. This cannot be the case for two distinct regions. This proves that T must have a third eigenvector.

In summary T can obey the backward constraints with two or more distinct regions of non-zero area if and only if T has three eigenvectors, two of which are associated with the largest eigenvalue. These two eigenvectors imply that T has a pointwise fixed line, l. If we call the third eigenvector q, it follows that all lines through q are mapped by T onto themselves, since T maps lines to lines, and all lines through q intersect l also, and so have two fixed points. These are called *fixed lines*. If, WLOG, we choose our coordinate system so that l is the x axis, and $q = (0, 1, 1)$, then:

$$T = \begin{pmatrix} 1 & 0 & 0 \\ 0 & 1-a & 0 \\ 0 & a & 1 \end{pmatrix}$$

for $0 < a < 1$. T maps all points that are not fixed away from q and towards l, as shown in Figure 2.

We can derive one further useful condition if T obeys the one-way constraints with respect to a region R_i. Consider any point p that is on the boundary of R_i, so that the line through p and q is tangent to R_i. Then p must also lie on l.

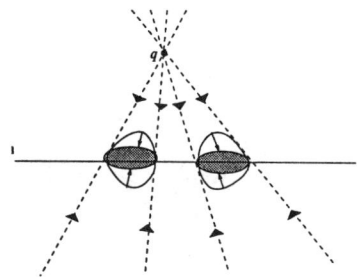

Figure 2: Two model regions lead to non-unique projective transformations when a line l, exists such that the tangents at all intersection points meet at a single point q. In this case, the regions can contract towards l in the directions emanating from q.

Otherwise, Tp also lies on the line tangent to R_i, but $Tp \neq p$, and so Tp is not in R_i, violating the one-way constraints. (It is also possible that a tangent line to R_i contains more than one point, if part of the boundary of R_i is a straight line. In this case, similar reasoining shows that at least one point on R_i on this tangent line must also lie on l). Alternately, we can say that if we draw lines through q tangent to all the regions, then the tangent points on the boundaries of these regions must all be collinear. This is also depicted in Figure 2. It is easy to see that this is not only a necessary but also a sufficient condition for T to obey the one-way constraints.

We have therefore shown (see Figure 2):

Theorem 2: Let $V_1, V_2 ... V_k \subseteq \mathcal{R}^2$ be distinct regions with non-zero areas. Then, the solution to the one-way matching problem with these regions as a model under a projective transformation is non-unique if and only if there exists a line l through the regions and a point q outside l such that contracting V_i in directions emanating from q toward l (denoted by $T_{l,q}$) implies

$$T_{l,q}(V_i) \subset V_i \qquad i = 1, 2 ... k.$$

This theorem is the natural generalization of the two region case under affine transformations. In that case, a degeneracy occurs when the tangent lines are parallel (i.e., intersect at a point at infinity). In the projective case, a degeneracy occurs when the tangent lines intersect at any point in the plane. Note also that the contracting transformation, which keeps a line pointwise fixed and has an additional fixed point, is known as a *projective homology*. Homologies were used recently to detect repeated structures and coincident sets of parallel lines in images [12, 13].

Using this result, we can show that generically, even when three smooth regions are intersected by a single line segment, they will give rise to a unique solution. This is because there are at most three degrees of freedom in placing a line that intersects all three regions. However, the condition that all six points where this line intersects the regions will have tangents that intersect at a single point provides five constraints on the location of the line. Simple equation counting shows that generically, we will not be able to satisfy these constraints.

3.2 Non-uniqueness of two regions

Similar reasoning shows that two regions will not give rise to a unique solution when one can use three degrees of

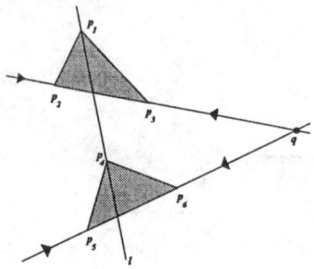

Figure 3: Two model regions lead to non-unique projective transformations when a line l, exists such that the tangents at all intersection points meet at a single point q. In this case, the regions can contract towards l in the directions emanating from q.

freedom to satisfy three constraints. The resulting equations are nonlinear so we are not guaranteed that a solution will exist, but it is plausible that often two regions provide insufficient constraint to determine the solution uniquely. To test this we examine two types of shapes, triangles and ellipses. Below we show that both objects composed of two triangles and objects composed of two ellipses give rise to non-unique solutions.

We now turn to showing that the solution for the projective one-way matching problem with a model consisting of two distinct triangles is always non-unique. To show this we have to find a line l through the two triangles and a point $\vec{q}$ outside the two triangles such that contracting the two triangles toward l in directions emanating from $\vec{q}$ will contract the triangles inside themselves. Given two distinct triangles notice that one can construct a line that enters each triangle at a vertex and exits the triangle at an edge or vice versa (see, e.g., Figure 3). Denote this line by l; l will be the fixed line. Now continue the two edges from which l exits until they intersect (which if they are parallel will be at infinity). Denote the point of intersection by $\vec{q}$. It can be readily verified that contracting the triangles toward l in directions emanating from $\vec{q}$ will keep the triangles inside their original regions. Consequently, under projective transformation any model consisting of two distinct triangles is degenerate.

Next we show that the solution for the projective one-way matching problem with a model consisting of two distinct ellipses is always non-unique. An ellipse in the projective plane is defined by a quadratic form $\vec{x}^T A \vec{x} = 0$, where A is a 3×3 symmetric matrix with negative determinant. Given an ellipse (or a general non-degenerate conic), two points $\vec{x}$ and $\vec{y}$ are called *conjugate* with respect to the conic if they satisfy the bi-linear equation $\vec{x}^T A \vec{y} = 0$. For a given point $\vec{x}$ the set of conjugate points to $\vec{x}$ forms a straight line. This line, l, called the *polar line* of $\vec{x}$, is given simply by $\vec{x}^T A \vec{y} = 0$, since the quadratic form is linear in $\vec{y}$. Similarly, $\vec{x}$ is called the *pole* of l.

Here are a few examples of conjugate points and polarities. A point is *self-conjugate* if and only if it lies on the conic. The polar line of a point on the conic is the tangent to the conic through that point. The polar line of a point $\vec{u}$ outside a conic is given by the following construction. Connect $\vec{u}$ to the conic by two tangent lines. Each tangent meets the conic at a single point. The polar line of $\vec{u}$ is the line connecting the two intersections of the tangents with

the conic.

The following lemma establishes that when two ellipses are contracted to inside themselves the fixed line is in fact the polar line of the fixed point, $\vec{u}$, from which contraction is emerging. This polarity relationship is used in Lemma 3 to relate the uniqueness of two ellipses with the generalized eigenvalue problem.

Lemma 3: *The solution to the projective one-way problem for two distinct ellipses $\vec{x}^T A \vec{x} \leq 0$ and $\vec{x}^T B \vec{x} \leq 0$ is non-unique if and only if the matrix $A^{-1}B$ has a positive eigenvalue.*

Proof: According to Theorem 2 two regions V_1 and V_2 give rise to a non-unique solution if and only if there exists a line l through the regions and a point $\vec{u}$ outside the regions such that contracting the regions in directions emerging from $\vec{u}$ toward l will map V_1 and V_2 to inside themselves. Notice that for smooth bounded regions the directions of contraction at the points of intersection of l with the boundaries of V_1 and V_2 must be tangential to the boundaries, or else the regions will not contract within themselves. Consequently, suppose that now V_1 and V_2 are two ellipses, $\vec{x}^T A \vec{x} \leq 0$ and $\vec{x}^T B \vec{x} \leq 0$ respectively, then l must be the polar line of $\vec{u}$ with respect to both A and B.

Since l is the polar line of $\vec{u}$ with respect to both A and B it is given by both $\vec{x}^T A \vec{u} = 0$ and $\vec{x}^T B \vec{u} = 0$. These two equations represent the same line if and only if $\lambda A \vec{u} = B \vec{u}$ for some $\lambda \neq 0$. λ and $\vec{u}$ respectively are called the generalized eigenvalue and eigenvector of B with respect to A. Alternatively, if we multiply the last equation by A^{-1} we obtain $A^{-1}B\vec{u} = \lambda \vec{u}$. We have proven so far that contraction is possible if and only if there exists a point $\vec{u}$ outside the two ellipses which is an eigenvector of $A^{-1}B$.

Next, we show that $\vec{u}$ lies outside the two ellipses if and only if $\lambda > 0$. Multiplying the two sides of $\lambda A \vec{u} = B \vec{u}$ by $\vec{u}^T$ from the left we obtain that $\lambda \vec{u}^T A \vec{u} = \vec{u}^T B \vec{u}$. Suppose that $\vec{u}$ lies outside the two ellipses, then $\vec{u}^T A \vec{u} > 0$ and $\vec{u}^T B \vec{u} > 0$, and consequently $\lambda > 0$. Conversely, suppose $\lambda > 0$, then $\vec{u}^T A \vec{u}$ and $\vec{u}^T B \vec{u}$ share the same sign. If $\vec{u}^T A \vec{u} < 0$ and $\vec{u}^T B \vec{u} < 0$ then $\vec{u}$ must be contained in both ellipses, but this is impossible because the two ellipses are distinct. Therefore, both $\vec{u}^T A \vec{u}$ and $\vec{u}^T B \vec{u}$ must be positive. $\square$

Using Lemma 3 we can now show:

Theorem 4: *The solution to the one-way projective problem with a model consisting of two ellipses is always non-unique.*

Proof: According to Lemma 3 the solution to the one-way projective problem with a model consisting of two distinct ellipses $\vec{x}^T A \vec{x} \leq 0$ and $\vec{x}^T B \vec{x} \leq 0$ is non-unique if and only if the matrix $A^{-1}B$ has a positive eigenvalue. Note that both $\det(A)$ and $\det(B)$ are negative. Therefore, $\det(A^{-1}B)$ must be positive. This implies that $A^{-1}B$ has a positive eigenvalue. To see this, note that the eigenvalues of C are the roots of the characteristic polynomial of C, which is a third order polynomial. Every third order polynomial has either three real roots, or two complex conjugate roots and one real root. In case all three roots are real they cannot all be

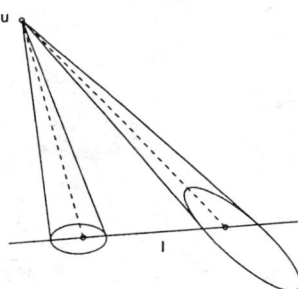

Figure 4: Contraction directions with two ellipses. The generalized eigenvalues of the ellipses are 13.14, -31.10, and -0.04. The eigenvector corresponding to the only positive eigenvalue determines the fixed point (denoted by u) and its polar line with respect to either of the ellipses is the pointwise fixed line (denoted by l). The two eigenvectors that correspond to the negative eigenvalues determine two points that lie on the fixed line and are located inside the two ellipses. (The points are denoted by circles and their respective polar lines are denoted by the dashed lines.)

negative since their product must be equal to $\det(C)$, which is positive. In case only one of the three roots is real this root still must be positive because the two other roots are conjugate and so their product is positive. Consequently, $A^{-1}B$ must have at least one positive eigenvalue, and so the solution to the one-way projective problem for any two ellipses is non-unique. □

An example of two ellipses and the fixed point and line that they produce is shown in Figure 4. One eigenvector produces the fixed point; the other two eigenvectors, which correspond to negative eigenvalues, lie on the fixed line and are located inside the two ellipses. Note that it is known that given two pairs of ellipses related by a projective transformation the transformation that aligns the two pairs of ellipses exactly is determined uniquely. Theorem 4 above shows that this transformation is not determined uniquely by the backward constraints alone. However, by considering the backward constraints we can align more than two convex shapes even in the presence of unknown occlusion.

3.3 Uniqueness in the presence of occlusion

The implication of Section 3.2 is that for a large class of objects two regions are insufficient to determine a projective transformation uniquely. In this section we examine the case of a model composed of three regions, when one of the regions appears partly occluded. We show below that it is possible to occlude significant portions of one of the regions and still obtain a unique solution. In the analysis below we assume that the regions are ellipses and that no straight line can traverse all three regions. Furthermore, we can assume WLOG that the occluded region is a circle (because preprocessing the model with any projective transformation does not effect whether a unique solution exists). According to Theorem 2 a non-unique solution is obtained only if it is possible to contract the two ellipses inside themselves toward a pointwise-fixed line in directions emanating from a point outside the two ellipses. As shown in Section 3.2, the number of different contractions can be either one of three, according to the number of positive eigenvalues.

Consider the case that the two ellipses introduce a single contracting transformation. (It can be readily shown that it

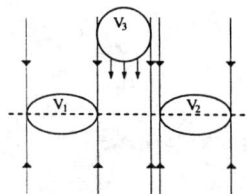

Figure 5: The effect of contracting two ellipses (V_1 and V_2) inside themselves on a third region. This figure illustrates the case that the external fixed point is at infinity. The lower half of the circle (V_3) prevents the contraction. Consequently, to destroy uniqueness the entire lower half of the circle must be occluded.

is generally impossible to have more than one contracting transformation.) Suppose that the fixed point is at infinity (in which case the contracting transformation is in fact affine). In this case we obtain the situation illustrated in Fig. 5. The contracting transformation due to the two unoccluded ellipses is not feasible because the boundaries of the third region that face the fixed line prevent the third region from contracting. Only when this side is occluded entirely will the contracting transformation become feasible and the solution cease to be unique.

To get a sense of the likelihood that occlusions may destroy uniqueness, suppose that the occluded region is a circle. Let occlusion be determined by a half-plane passing through two randomly selected points on the boundary of the circle. To construct a destructive occlusion we need to select the two points in the upper half of the circle and, in addition, select the side of the plane that includes the center of the circle. The chance of this happening (assuming uniform distributions) is 0.125. Using this model we can also estimate the expected area of occlusion that can be applied to the third region without destroying uniqueness. It can be readily shown that under this model we can on average occlude up to 93.5% of the area of the third region and still maintain uniqueness. A similar analysis, with similar results, can be applied in case the fixed point is located at a finite position.

4 Demonstration of Results

Figure 6 shows an application of our scheme to several real images. We have manually extracted regions from the images in Figure 6 (left) and used these regions to recover the projective transformation relating the two images. The top middle picture shows the result of aligning the two images using three regions, and the bottom middle shows the result of aligning the two images using only two regions. As can be seen three regions led to a fairly good alignment, indicating that the projective transformation was correctly recovered. In contrast, two regions led to a contraction of the image. Finally, on the right we used the backward constraints to align a partly occluded image (top) with an unoccluded model (top left). Four regions were used in this case, all four were partly occluded. The results of this experiment are shown in the bottom right. As can be seen, a good alignment was obtained in spite of the occlusion.

5 Conclusion

In this paper a method for recognition that uses regions to determine the pose of objects was analyzed. We considered

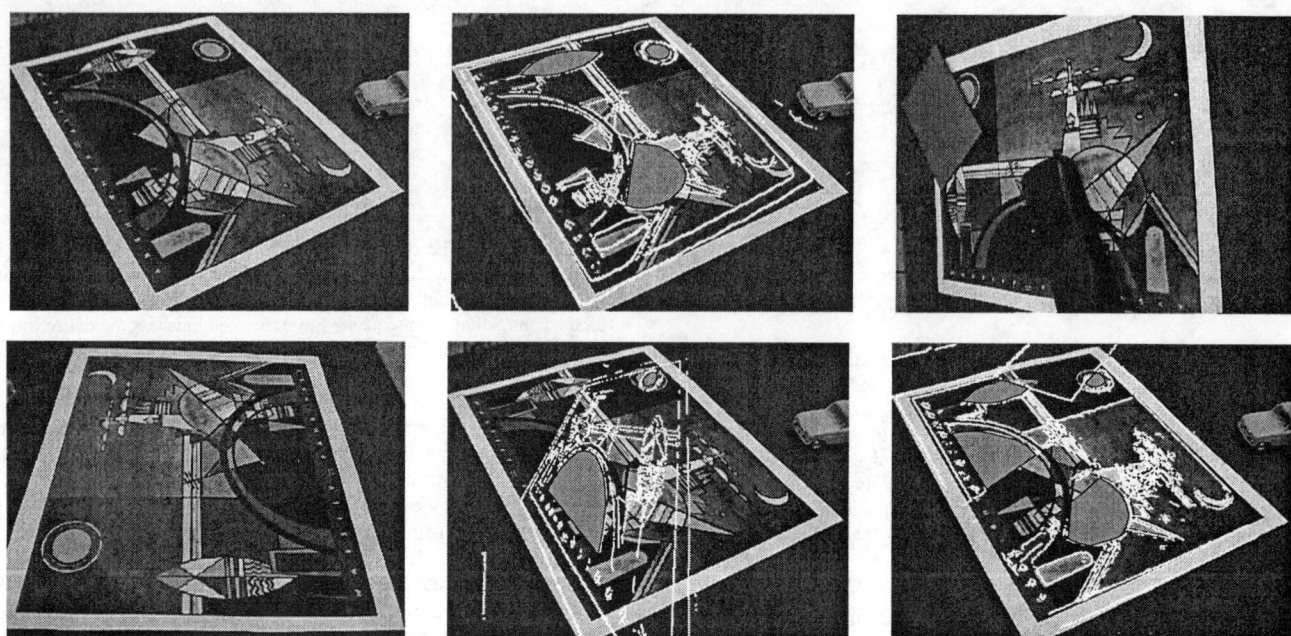

Figure 6: Two views of a drawing by Kandisky (left). Aligning the two views with the one-way constraints using three (middle top) and two (middle bottom) regions. The figures show on overlay of the two images. The gray regions represent the regions used for alignment. The top right shows an occluded view. The result of aligning this with the view in the top left, using the backward constraints, is shown on the bottom right. In this experiment we used four regions, all of which were partly occluded.

the case of planar objects undergoing projective transformations and proved that the method produces unique, correct solutions in previously unexplored situations. Our results were obtained by looking at the flow patterns of points under 2-D projective transformations in the presence of fixed points. We proved that three visible regions are sufficient to determine the transformation uniquely. In addition, by considering general pairs of triangles and ellipses we showed that two regions are often insufficient to determine the correct transformation uniquely. However, when three regions are available we showed that, depending on the model, it is possible to occlude significant portions of the area of one of the regions without destroying uniqueness. It follows directly that we can find a correct pose when many regions are matched, even if all but two are significantly occluded.

These results indicate that using only a small number regions it is possible to determine the pose of objects in the presence of significant occlusion. This is particularly interesting, because when we use the backward constraints we do not need to specify the location of occlusion. Consequently, in many situations it is not mandatory that we identify the locations of occlusion in order to determine the pose of objects in the image. The backward constraints implicitly account for these occlusions, and if sufficient information about the shape of the object appears in its non-occluded portions then the pose of the object can be recovered by solving the backward constraints.

References

[1] R. Basri and D. W. Jacobs, "Recognition using region correspondences," *IJCV*, **25**(2): 141–162, 1997.

[2] L. Brand, *Differential and difference equations*. John Wiley, 1966.

[3] S. Carlsson, "Information in the Geometric Structure of Retinal Flow Fields," *Int. Conf. on Comp. Vis.*:629–633, 1989.

[4] J. B. Conway, *A Course in Functional Analysis*. Springer-Verlag, 1990.

[5] H. S. M. Coxeter, *The Real Projective Plane*. Springer-Verlag, 1993.

[6] R. O. Duda, and P. E. Hart, *Pattern classification and scene analysis*. John Wiley and Sons, 1973.

[7] Forsyth, D., Mundy, J. L., Zisserman, A., Coelho, C., Heller, A., and Rothwell, C., 1991. "Invariant descriptors for 3-D object recognition and pose," *PAMI*, **13**(10): 971–991.

[8] Horaud, R., 1987, "New Methods for Matching 3-D Objects with Single Perspective Views," *PAMI*, **9**(3): 401–412.

[9] Hu M.K., 1962. "Visual pattern recognition by moment invariants". *IRE Trans. on Information Theory*, **8**: 169–187.

[10] D. W. Jacobs and R. Basri, "3-D to 2-D recognition with regions," *CVPR*, 547–553, 1997.

[11] K. Kanatani, *Geometric Computation for machine vision*, Oxford University Press, 1993.

[12] M. Pollefeys and L. VanGool, "A stratified approach to metric self-callibration" *CVPR*, 407–412, 1997.

[13] F. Schaffalitzky and A. Zisserman, "Geometric Grouping of Repeated Elements within Images," *Proc. 9th British Machine Vision Conference*, Southampton, 1998.

[14] A. Verri, F. Girosi, and V. Torre, "Mathematical Properties of the Two-Dimensional Motion Field: from Singular Points to Motion Parameters," *J. Opt. Soc. Am. A*, **6**(5):698–712, 1989.

[15] Weiss, I., 1993. "Geometric invariants and object recognition," *IJCV*, **10**(3): 207–231.

Empirical Evaluation of
Dissimilarity Measures for Color and Texture

Jan Puzicha, Joachim M. Buhmann
Institut für Informatik III
Universität Bonn
D-53117 Bonn, Germany

Yossi Rubner, Carlo Tomasi
Computer Science Department
Stanford University
Stanford, CA, 94305

Abstract

This paper empirically compares nine image dissimilarity measures that are based on distributions of color and texture features summarizing over 1,000 CPU hours of computational experiments. Ground truth is collected via a novel random sampling scheme for color, and via an image partitioning method for texture. Quantitative performance evaluations are given for classification, image retrieval, and segmentation tasks, and for a wide variety of dissimilarity measures. It is demonstrated how the selection of a measure, based on large scale evaluation, substantially improves the quality of classification, retrieval, and unsupervised segmentation of color and texture images.

1. Introduction

Measuring the dissimilarity between images and parts of images is of central importance for low–level computer vision. The following vision tasks directly rely on some notion of image dissimilarity: In *classification* [4, 10], a new image sample is to be assigned to the most similar of a given number of classes. A set of labeled training examples is available. *Supervised segmentation*, *i.e.*, the assignment of image regions to predefined classes, is also a classification task. In *image retrieval* [14, 1, 7, 11], the user searches a large collection of images for instances that are similar to a specified query. The search is based on perceptual similarities of attributes such as color, texture, shape, and composition. In *unsupervised segmentation* [2, 6, 5], an input image is divided into regions that are homogeneous according to some perceptual attribute. No predefined attribute classes are available in this case.

In recent years, dissimilarity measures that are based on empirical estimates of the *distribution* of feature have been developed for classification [10], image retrieval [1, 14, 11, 12] and unsupervised segmentation [2, 5]. Preliminary benchmark studies have confirmed that distribution–based dissimilarity measures

exhibit good performance in image retrieval [7, 11], unsupervised texture segmentation [5], and in conjunction with a k–nearest-neighbor classifier, color– or texture–based object recognition [14, 10]. However, most of these empirical evaluations provide only incomplete and partial information. They either pit one favorite dissimilarity measure against a small number of others, or they provide merely anecdotal evidence, or they only expose a small portion of the space of the parameters that the various dissimilarity measures depend on. Some benchmark studies [7, 11] are more systematic, but apply to generic measures, and do not elucidate strengths and weaknesses of the various dissimilarity measures for the specific tasks of classification, retrieval, or unsupervised segmentation.

In this paper, we report on the results of a systematic comparison of nine different families of dissimilarity measures for color and texture. The plots in this paper summarize over 1,000 hours of CPU time, spent in an exhaustive exploration of a rather large space of parameters. First, in sections 2 and 3, we review and categorize distribution-based dissimilarity measures, showing strengths and limitations of each with respect to the different vision tasks mentioned above. Next, in section 4, we propose a methodology for the quantitative comparison of color and texture dissimilarity measures. A major contribution here is a statistically sound procedure to establish ground truth, against which the various dissimilarity measures can be compared. This section also explains the principles we adhered to in order to enforce fairness in our comparisons. Finally, section 5 provides quantitative comparison results as a function of several parameters such as number of histogram bins, query detail, size of the response to a query, and dimensionality of the feature space. Comparisons are tailored to the specific requirements of classification, retrieval, and segmentation. The results are interpreted in order to explain which measure works best for which task. We found no all-around winners or losers, but rather different tools for different tasks.

In this section we describe the color and texture feature spaces that we use in this paper, and our representation of distributions in these spaces.

Color: For human color perception it is sufficient to represent all colors by a three dimensional space [16]. We use the CIE $L^*a^*b^*$ color space which was designed using psychophysical experiments to be *uniform*, in that the perceived differences between individual nearby colors correspond to the Euclidean distances between the color coordinates. Some similarity measures take advantage of the uniformity of a color space.

Texture: Over the past decades numerous approaches for the representation of textured images have been proposed [4, 2, 6, 7]. While color is a purely pointwise property of images, texture involves a notion of spatial extent: a single point has no texture. For each image point, frequency-domain texture descriptors refer instead to the frequency content in a local neighborhood of the point. *Gabor filters* are often used for texture analysis and have been shown to exhibit excellent discrimination properties over a broad range of textures [6, 7, 5]. In this paper we used the family of Gabor filter in log-polar space as derived in [7]. Dictionaries with 4, 6 and 8 different orientations over 3, 4 and 5 different scales, respectively, are employed, leading to filter banks of 12, 24 and 40 filters.

Distribution of Features: Color and texture descriptors vary substantially over an image or image part[1], both because of inherent variations in surface appearance and as a result of changes in illumination, shading, shadowing, foreshortening, etc. Thus, the appearance of a region is best described by the *distribution of features*, rather than by individual feature vectors. Histograms can be used as non–parametric estimators of empirical feature distributions. However, for high-dimensional feature spaces a regular binning often results in poor performance: coarse binning dulls resolving power, while fine binning leads to statistically insignificant sample sizes for most bins. A partial solution is offered by *adaptive binning*, whereby the histogram bins are adapted to the distribution. The binning is induced by a set of *prototypes* $\{\vec{c}_i\}$ and the corresponding Voronoi tessellation. Adaptive histograms are formally defined by

$$f(i;I) = \left| \left\{ \vec{x} : i = \arg\min_j \|\vec{I}(\vec{x}) - \vec{c}_j\| \right\} \right| \quad (1)$$

Here $\vec{I}(\vec{x})$ denotes the feature vector at image location $\vec{x}$. The histogram entry $f(i;I)$ corresponds to

---

[1]In the following, we restrict the notation to complete images I for convenience. However, the adaptation to image regions as needed for segmentation is straight forward.

prototypes can be determined by a vector quantization procedure, e.g. K–means [8].

For small sample sizes it may be better to estimate solely *marginal histograms*. While information about the *joint occurrence* of feature coefficients in the different dimensions is lost, bin contents in the marginals may be significant where those in the full distribution would be too sparse. Formally, the marginal histograms of the coefficients in feature dimension r are given by

$$f^r(i;I) = \left| \left\{ \vec{x} : t^r_{i-1} < I^r(\vec{x}) \leq t^r_i \right\} \right| . \quad (2)$$

Here, bin i is defined as the feature interval $(t^r_{i-1}, t^r_i]$ of dimension r. The *cumulative histogram* for marginal histograms is defined as

$$F^r(i;I) = |\{ \vec{x} : I^r(\vec{x}) \leq t^r_i \}| . \quad (3)$$

3. Dissimilarity Measures

In the following, $D(I, J)$ denotes a dissimilarity measure between the images I and J. A superscript $D^r(I, J)$ indicates that the respective measure is applied only to the marginal distributions along dimension r. We distinguish the following four categories of dissimilarity measures:

Heuristic histogram distances have been proposed mostly in the context of image retrieval:
(i) The *Minkowski-form distance* $\mathcal{L}_p$ is defined by:

$$D(I, J) = \left(\sum_i |f(i;I) - f(i;J)|^p \right)^{1/p} . \quad (4)$$

For example, the $\mathcal{L}_1$ distance has been proposed for computing the dissimilarity scores between color images [14], and the $\mathcal{L}_\infty$ was used for texture dissimilarity [15]. *Histogram Intersection* (HI) as proposed in [14] provides a generalization of $\mathcal{L}_1$ to partial matches.
(ii) The *Weighted–Mean–Variance* (WMV) has been proposed in [7]. This distance is defined by

$$D^r(I, J) = \frac{|\mu_r(I) - \mu_r(J)|}{|\sigma(\mu_r)|} + \frac{|\sigma_r(I) - \sigma_r(J)|}{|\sigma(\sigma_r)|} , \quad (5)$$

where $\mu_r(I), \mu_r(J)$ are the empirical means and $\sigma_r(I), \sigma_r(J)$ are the standard deviations of the distributions. $\sigma(\cdot)$ denotes an estimate of the standard deviation of the respective entity. For texture–based image retrieval this measure, based on a Gabor filter image representation, has outperformed several parametric models. [7]

Non–parametric test statistics provide a sound basis for probabilistic procedures that test the hypothesis

Symmetric	yes	yes	yes	yes	no	yes	yes	yes
Triangle inequality	valid	valid	valid	invalid	invalid	invalid	see text	see text
Computational complexity	medium	low	medium	medium	medium	medium	high	high
Exploits ground distance	no	no	yes	no	no	no	yes	yes
Individual binning	no	yes	no	no	no	no	no	yes
Multiple dimensions	yes	yes	no	yes	yes	yes	yes	yes
Partial matches	see text	no	no	no	no	no	no	yes
Non-parametric	yes	no	yes	yes	yes	yes	yes	yes

Table 1. Characteristics and advantages of the different distribution–based dissimilarity measures.

that two empirical distributions have been generated from the same underlying true distribution.

(i) The *Kolmogorov–Smirnov distance* (KS) has originally been proposed in [2] for image segmentation. It is defined as the maximal discrepancy between the cumulative distributions,

$$D^r(I, J) = \max_i |F_r(i; I) - F_r(i; J)| \qquad (6)$$

and has the desirable property to be invariant to arbitrary monotonic feature transformations.

(ii) A *statistic of the Cramer/von Mises type* (CvM) is also defined based on cumulative distributions:

$$D^r(I, J) = \sum_i (F_r(i; I) - F_r(i; J))^2 \ . \qquad (7)$$

(iii) The χ^2–*statistic* is given by

$$D(I, J) = \sum_i \frac{\left(f(i; I) - \hat{f}(i)\right)^2}{\hat{f}(i)}, \text{ where} \qquad (8)$$

$\hat{f}(i) = [f(i; I) + f(i; J)]/2$ denotes the joint estimate.

Information–theoretic divergences measure how compact one distribution can be coded using the other one as the codebook. Here we examine two special cases:

(i) The *Kullback–Leibler divergence* (KL) suggested in [10] as an image dissimilarity measure is defined by

$$D(I, J) = \sum_i f(i; I) \log \frac{f(i; I)}{f(i; J)} \ . \qquad (9)$$

(ii) The *Jeffrey–divergence* (JD) is defined by

$$D(I, J) = \sum_i f(i; I) \log \frac{f(i; I)}{\hat{f}(i)} + f(i; J) \log \frac{f(i; J)}{\hat{f}(i)} \ .$$

In contrast to the KL–divergence, JD is symmetric and numerically more stable when comparing two empirical distributions.

Ground distance measures are based on perceptually meaningful distance measures between individual features. Employing this *ground distance* may improve

the dissimilarity measure between two distributions. To some extent, the notion of ground distance is used by measures like the Kolmogorov–Smirnov distance and the statistic of the Cramer/von Mises type, which are based on the cumulative histograms. However, these measures are defined only in one dimension and cannot exploit the ground distance in the full feature space.

(i) The *Quadratic Form (QF)* distance [3] incorporates cross-bin information via a similarity matrix $\mathbf{A} = [a_{ij}]$ where a_{ij} denote similarity between bins i and j.

$$D(I, J) = \sqrt{(\vec{f_I} - \vec{f_J})^T \mathbf{A}(\vec{f_I} - \vec{f_J})} \ , \qquad (10)$$

where $\vec{f_I}$ and $\vec{f_J}$ are vectors that list all the entries in $f(i; I)$ and $f(i; J)$ respectively. We refer to [9] for more details including efficient implementations.

(ii) The *Earth Movers Distance (EMD)* [12] is based on the minimal cost to transform one distribution to the other. If the cost of moving a single feature unit in the feature space is the ground distance, then the distance between two distributions is given by the minimal sum of the costs incurred to move all the individual features. The EMD can be defined as the solution of a transportation problem which can be solved by linear optimization:

$$D(I, J) = \frac{\sum_{i,j} g_{ij} d_{ij}}{\sum_{i,j} g_{ij}} \qquad (11)$$

where d_{ij} denotes the dissimilarity between bins i and j, and $g_{ij} \geq 0$ is the optimal flow between the two distributions such that the total cost $\sum_{i,j} g_{ij} d_{ij}$ is minimized, subject to the following constraints:

$$\sum_i g_{ij} \leq f(j; J) \ , \qquad \sum_j g_{ij} \leq f(i; I) \ ,$$
$$\sum_{i,j} g_{ij} = \min (f(j; I), f(i; J)) \ , \qquad (12)$$

for all i and j. The denominator in (11) is a normalization factor that permits matching parts of distributions with different total mass. If the ground distance is a metric and the two distributions have the same amounts of total mass, the EMD defines a metric. As a key advantage of the EMD each image may specific distribution. When marginal histograms are used, the dissimilarity values obtained for the individual dimensions must be combined into a joint overall dissimilarity value. In [11] the Minkowski norms $D(I,J) = (\sum_r (D^r(I,J))^p)^{1/p}$ were investigated, including the limiting case $p = \infty$ utilized in [2]. Based on their results $p = 1$ is used in the sequel.

3.1. Properties

Table 1 compares the properties of the different measures. KS, CvM and WMV are defined only for marginal distributions. Metric dissimilarity measures enable more efficient indexing algorithms for image retrieval, since the triangle inequality entails lower bounds that can be exploited to substantially alleviate the computational burden. For the χ^2, KL, JD the triangle inequality does not hold, while for the QF and the EMD it holds only for specific ground distances. All the evaluated measures are symmetric except the HI and the KL divergence. A useful property for image retrieval is the ability to handle *partial matches*, i.e. to compute the dissimilarity score only with respect to the most similar image part [12]. The ability for partial matching is of minor importance for the other applications. Only the HI and the EMD allow for partial matches directly. Computational complexity is an important consideration. For applications such as image retrieval, it is important to differentiate between online and off-line complexity. Especially for the WMV the standard deviations can be computed in advance and the dissimilarity scores for a new query can be evaluated efficiently. The computational complexity of the EMD is the highest among the evaluated measures, as for each dissimilarity calculation a linear optimization is necessary. However, while using the EMD on large histograms is prohibitive for certain applications, its ability to represent different images by a different binning often yields good results even with small number of bins, and consequently less computation. In our experiments we have limited the number of bins for the EMD to 32 bins, while for the other dissimilarity measures we used up to 256 bins.

4. Benchmark Methodology

Any systematic comparison of dissimilarity measures should conform at least to the following guidelines:
(i) A meaningful *quality measure* must be defined. Different tasks usually entail different quality measures. The subdivision into classification, retrieval, and segmentation makes it possible to define general-purpose quality criteria for each task.

variety of *parameters* that can affect the behavior of each measure. These parameters include the size of the images, queries and statistical samples; the number of neighbors in a k-nearest-neighbor classifier and the number of bins in a histogram; the shape of the bins and their detailed definition; and, for texture, the dimensionality of feature space. A fair comparison in the face of this variability can be achieved by giving every measure the best possible chance to perform well.
(iii) Processing steps that affect performance independently of each other ought to be evaluated separately in order to both sharpen insight and reduce complexity. For instance the effect of different image representations can be understood separately from those of different dissimilarity measures. Also, for segmentation, the grouping procedure can be evaluated separately [5].
(iv) *Ground truth* should be available which is a set of data for which the correct solution of a particular problem is known. Collecting ground truth is arguably the hardest problem in benchmarking, because the data should represent a broad range of possible applications, the "correct solution" ought to be uncontroversial, and the ground-truth data set should be large enough for a statistically significant performance evaluation. In the following, we summarize our choice of ground truth for color and texture.

Color: Defining ground truth to measure color similarity over a set of color images is difficult. Our approach was to create disjoint sets of randomly sampled pixels from an image and to consider these sets as belonging to the same class. While for large sets of pixels within a class the color distributions of their pixels will be very similar, for small sets the variations are larger, mimicking the situation in image retrieval where images of *moderate* similarity have to be identified. From a database of 20,000 color images comprising the Corel Stock Photo Library, we randomly chose 94 images. This is the same number of images as in the texture case, so that we can compare the results from the two modalities. We defined set sizes of $4, 8, 16, 32, 64$ pixels, and for each image we obtained 16 disjoint sets of random samples in all sample sizes. For each of the five set sizes, this resulted into a ground-truth data set of $16 \times 94 = 1504$ samples in 94 different classes, one class per image. For the QF and the EMD that employ a ground distance, we use

$$a_{ij} = \exp(-\alpha \|\vec{c_i} - \vec{c_j}\|) \text{ and } d_{ij} = 1 - a_{ij} \quad (13)$$

as the measure of similarity and dissimilarity of bins i and j, where $\|\vec{c_i} - \vec{c_j}\|$ is the $\mathcal{L}_2$ distance between the bin centers in the CIE $L^* a^* b^*$ color space (see section 2). The exponential map limits the effect of large distances, which otherwise dominate the result. This

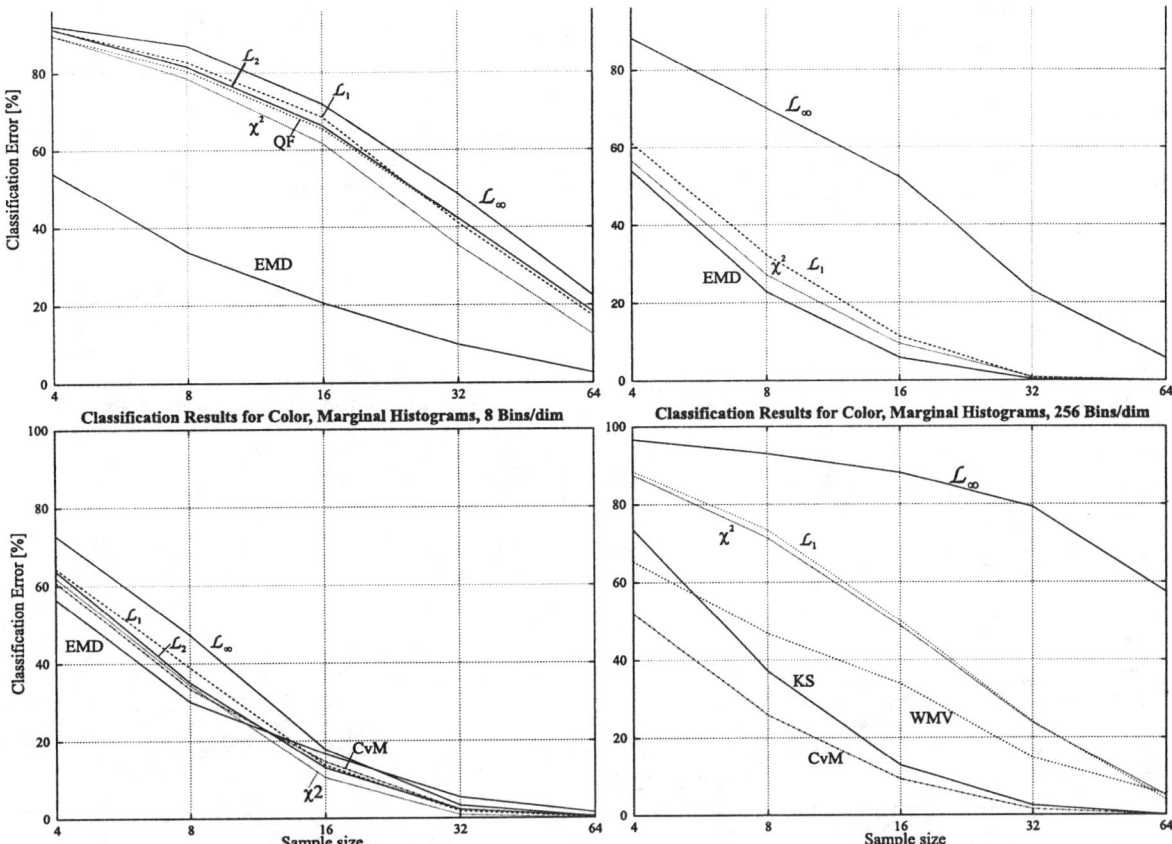

Figure 1. Classification results for the *color* database for different sample sizes and different binning. For each result, an optimal value $k \in \{1, 3, 5, 7\}$ for the k–nearest neighbor classifier has been chosen.

agrees with results from psychophysics [13]. Here we set α to half the standard deviation of all the feature values in the database. This makes closeness a relative notion, and was found empirically to give good results.

Texture: In our benchmark study we concentrated on textured images from the Brodatz album as they are widely accepted within the texture research community and provide a joint database which is commonly available. To define ground truth each image is considered as a single, separate class. This is questionable in a few cases, which are circumvented by a pre–selection of images. We selected 94 Brodatz textures *a priori* by visual inspection. We excluded the textures d25, d30, d31, d39-d45, d48, d59, d61, d88, d89, d91, d94, d97 due to missing micro–pattern properties. That is, those textures are excluded where the texture property is lost when considering small image blocks. From each of the Brodatz images we extracted sets of 16 random, non–overlapping blocks sizes 8×8, 16×16, ..., 256×256 pixels[2]. For each sample size this resulted in a ground truth data set of $16 \times 94 = 1504$ samples in 94 different classes, just as

for color. For the QF and the EMD we again employ (13), with the only difference that $\|\vec{c_i} - \vec{c_j}\|$ is defined as the $\mathcal{L}_1$ distance between the Gabor responses. Unlike with color, where the $\mathcal{L}_2$ distance has a solid psychophysical justification, for texture it is not clear how to relate the different (normalized) dimensions, so we simply sum them.

Performance Evaluation for classification, retrieval, and segmentation. For *classification*, a k–NN classifier is used, with k having the values 1, 3, 5, and 7. We use only odd values to reduce the chances of ties. As a performance measure we use the average misclassification rate in percent applying a leave–one–out estimation procedure.

For *image retrieval*, performance is usually measured by *precision* and *recall*. Precision is defined as the number of relevant images retrieved relative to the total number of retrieved images, while recall measures the number of relevant images retrieved, relative to the total number of relevant images in the database. Since our goal is to compare the different methods and not to measure performance of a retrieval system, we only plot the precision vs. the number of retrieved images.

---

[2]For a sample size of 256×256 we only extracted 4 samples per class because of the limited size of the original image.

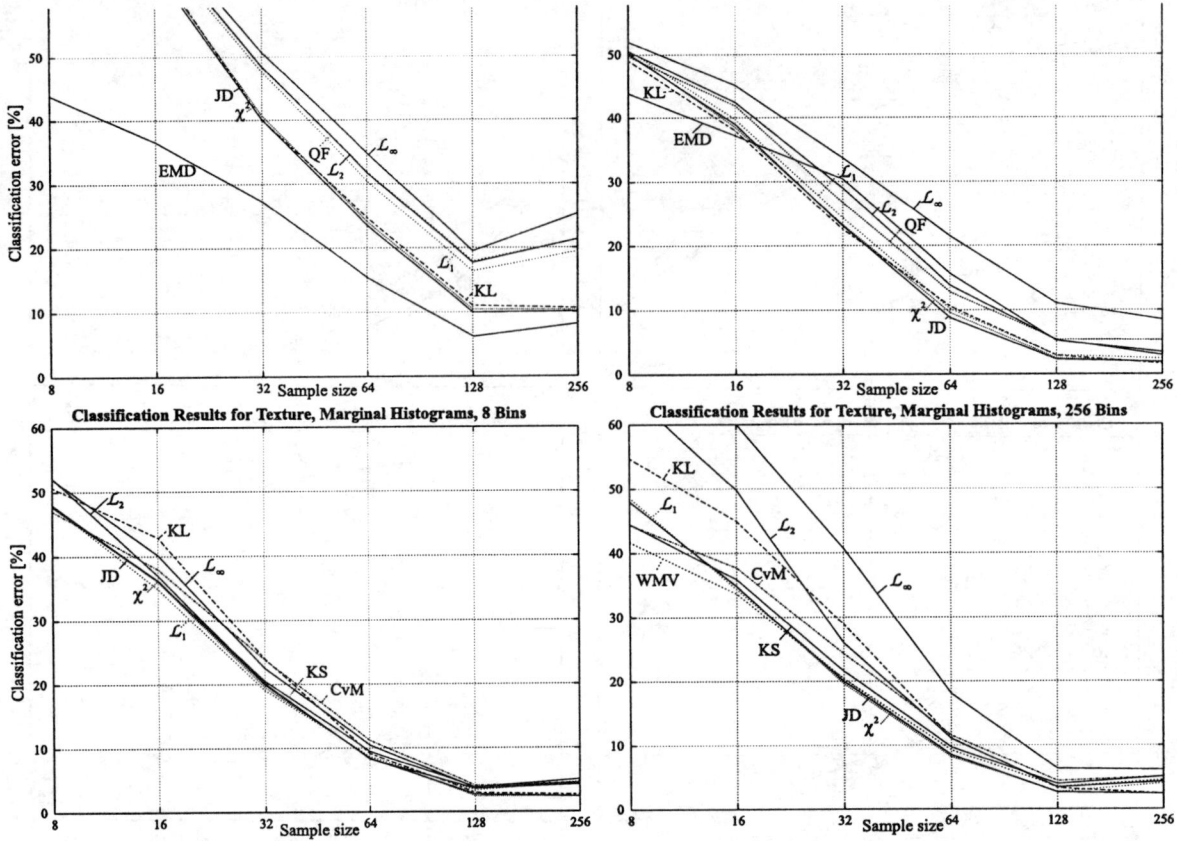

Figure 2. Results for *texture* classification for different sample sizes and different binning. In each case, the best possible k and the best number of filters has been chosen.

For *unsupervised texture segmentation* we followed the approach of [5] and used a database of random mixtures (512×512 pixels each) containing 100 entities of five Brodatz textures each (see Figure 4). Segmentations are computed on a regular sub-grid of size 128×128 by assigning each site to one out of K segments. For each site, a local histogram is extracted to estimate the local feature distribution. We compute marginal histograms which are proportional to the Gabor filter wavelength [6]. For the multivariate histograms, the binning has been adapted to the specific image. Each local histogram is then compared with 80 randomly selected images sites using the dissimilarity measure. To compute an optimal segmentation we implemented the approach of [5] which groups image sites with a high average similarity to obtain a segmentation. As a performance measure we report the average median classification error evaluated over 100 images, where each site is labeled according to the majority rule of corresponding pixels. In addition, we report the percentage of images with more than 20% errors. We consider these failures as structural segmentation errors with typically entire textures being misclassified.

5. Results and Interpretation

Classification The classification performance has been estimated in a leave–one–out procedure for all combinations of parameters $k \in \{1, 3, 5, 7\}$, number of bins $\in \{4, 8, 16, 32, 64, 128, 256\}$ [3]. In the texture case, we tried three different filter banks with $12, 24$ and 40 filters, respectively. The experiments resulted in an enormous amount of information, computed in over 1,000 CPU hours. Due to limitations in space, we present here only the main results, and plot a few informative cuts from the high-dimensional parameter space. The classification results are summarized in Figure 1 (color) and Figure 2 (texture). We plot the classification error of the dissimilarity measures as a function of the sample size both for the full distribution (top) and for the marginal cases (bottom). The results are further separated into two cases: small histograms with 8 bins (left), and large histograms with 256 bins (right). An exception to these histogram sizes is the EMD which uses locally adapted histograms. As

---

[3]For EMD because of computational limitations and the additional information carried by the local binning, we used only number of bins $\in \{4, 8, 16, 32\}$.

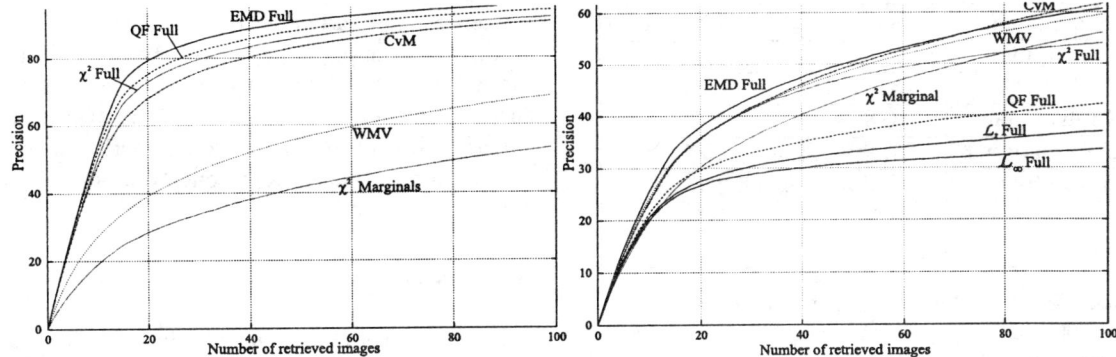

Figure 3. Precision curves in [%] for selected similarity measures. Left: color retrieval for a sample size of 16. Right: textured image retrieval for a sample size of 8 × 8.

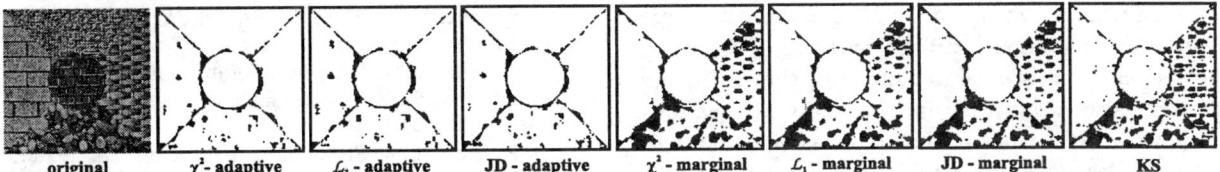

| original | χ^2 - adaptive | $\mathcal{L}_1$ - adaptive | JD - adaptive | χ^2 - marginal | $\mathcal{L}_1$ - marginal | JD - marginal | KS |

Figure 4. Examples of segmentation results with $K = 5$ clusters for the different similarity measures under consideration. Misclassified image sites are depicted in black.

discussed in Section 3, these contain more information than fixed histograms. For a fair comparison, we use 4 bins for the small histogram case for the EMD (in contrast to 8 bins), and 32 bins for the large histogram (in contrast to 256 bins). The following main conclusions can be drawn.

(i) Two regimes can be distinguished based on the sample size:

For small sample sizes, the WMV measure performs best in the texture case (last plot in figure 1). This behaviour is explained by the fact that WMV only estimates the means and variances of the marginal distributions. These aggregate measurements are less sensitive to sampling noise. The WMV competes less satisfactorily on color since histograms can be more reliably estimated in this case. The measures which are based on cumulative distributions (KS and CvM) and which thus incorporate ground distance information also perform well using marginal distributions. The EMD performed exceptionally well with full distributions, even for the hard case of small histograms where other measures scored poorly. This is explained by the local binning that provides additional information, not available to the other measures.

For large sample sizes, the classical χ^2 test statistic and the divergence measures perform best. Jeffrey's divergence behaves more stably than the KL–divergence, as expected. The χ^2–statistic and JD yield nearly identical results. The $\mathcal{L}_1$ does best from the class of heuristic measures.

(ii) For texture classification, marginal distributions do better than the multidimensional distributions ex-

cept for very large sample sizes (256×256). This is explained by the fact that the binning is not well adapted to the data, since it is fixed for all 94 texture classes. The EMD with its local adaptation does much better in this case. For color, multivariate histograms perform better with the EMD performing best, since local histograms can be more reliably estimated even for small sample sizes. We conclude that marginal distributions or measures that can use adaptive representations of the distributions should be used for large feature spaces.

(iii) The maximally allowed number of bins performs best for multidimensional histograms. More bins might result in an increased performance, up to a point where close features fall in separate neighboring bins, but also result in a prohibitive run–time behavior. Only for the EMD, the local adaptation allows to represent the distribution with a small number of bins which is an advantage if storage complexity is an issue. For marginal histograms, the binning details play a negligible role.

For the texture case, usually 12 Gabor filters have been sufficient. However, for small sample sizes additional filters *implicitly* provide more samples which results in a better performance. We conclude that a small number of features is sufficient to distinguish a large number of texture classes.

Image Retrieval As we saw in the results for classification, the EMD, WMV, CvM, and KS performed very well for the small sample sizes, while JD, χ^2, and KL usually performed better for the larger sample sizes. This is confirmed by the retrieval results

$\mathcal{L}_1$ marginal	8.2%	12%
χ^2 marginal	8.1%	13%
JD marginal	8.1%	12%
KS marginal	10.8%	20%
CvM marginal	10.9%	22%
$\mathcal{L}_1$ full	6.8%	9%
χ^2 full	6.6%	10%
JD full	6.8%	10%

Table 2. Errors by comparison with ground truth over 100 randomly generated images with $K = 5$ textures, 512×512 pixels and 128×128 sites.

depicted in Figure 3. Small sample size is closer to image retrieval, where similar images can have large variability, but should still be retrieved. Therefore, for better recall of a large number of similar images (fewer false negatives), the first class of measures performs better, while for better precision with a few, very similar images (fewer false positives), the second class of measures will probably perform better.

Unsupervised Segmentation As a major difference in segmentation the binning can be adapted to the image at hand. This leads to an increased accuracy in representing multidimensional distributions. Consequently, adaptive multivariate binning significantly outperforms marginal histograms in the unsupervised segmentation task. This is illustrated in Figure 4 for an example image and confirmed by the benchmark results on the database with 100 images presented in Table 2. χ^2, JD and $\mathcal{L}_1$ exhibit very similar performance both with marginal and multidimensional histograms. The best performance was achieved by χ^2 on adaptive multivariate histograms with a median error of 6.6% as compared to 10.8% for the Kolmogorov–Smirnoff test which was utilized in [2]. Thus, employing the benchmark results to select a proper dissimilarity measure substantially improves the quality of unsupervised segmentation. For segmentation, the EMD suffers from its high computational complexity and has, therefore, been excluded from the experiments.

6. Conclusion

In this paper, a thorough quantitative performance evaluation has been presented for distribution–based image dissimilarity measures. No measure exhibits best overall performance, but the selection rather depends on the specific task. While marginal histograms and aggregate measures are best for large feature spaces and small samples, multivariate histograms perform very well for large sample sizes. Multivariate histograms are especially effective if the number of classes to be distinguished is small or the binning can

sequence, multivariate histograms performed best for color classification and color retrieval as well as texture segmentation. If storage space is an important issue, the EMD is especially attractive since it allows superior classification and retrieval performance with a much more compact representation, but at a higher computational cost.

References

[1] M. Flickner et al. Query by image and video content: The QBIC system. *IEEE Computer*, pages 23–32, Sept. 1995.

[2] D. Geman et al. Boundary detection by constrained optimization. *IEEE Trans. PAMI*, 12(7):609–628, 1990.

[3] J. Hafner et al. Efficient color histogram indexing for quadratic form distance functions. *IEEE Trans. PAMI*, 17(7):729–736, 1995.

[4] R. Haralick, K. Shanmugan, and I. Dinstein. Textural features for image classification. *IEEE Trans. Systems, Man and Cybernetics*, 3(1):610–621, 1973.

[5] T. Hofmann, J. Puzicha, and J. Buhmann. Textured image segmentation in a deterministic annealing framework. *IEEE Trans. PAMI*, 20(8), 1998.

[6] A. Jain and F. Farrokhnia. Unsupervised texture segmentation using Gabor filters. *Pattern Recognition*, 24(12):1167–1186, 1991.

[7] B. Manjunath and W. Ma. Texture features for browsing and retrieval of image data. *IEEE Trans. PAMI*, 8(18):837–842, 1996.

[8] N. M. Nasrabad and R. A. King. Image coding using vector quantization: A review. *IEEE Trans. on Communication*, 36(8):957–971, August 1988.

[9] W. Niblack et al. Querying images by content, using color, texture, and shape. In *SPIE Conference on Storage and Retrieval for Image and Video Databases*, volume 1908, pages 173–187, April 1993.

[10] T. Ojala, M. Pietikäinen, and D. Harwood. A comparative study of texture measures with classification based feature distributions. *Pattern Recognition*, 29(1):51–59, 1996.

[11] J. Puzicha, T. Hofmann, and J. Buhmann. Nonparametric similarity measures for unsupervised texture segmentation and image retrieval. In *Proc. CVPR'97*, pages 267–272, 1997.

[12] Y. Rubner, C. Tomasi, and L. J. Guibas. A metric for distributions with applications to image databases. In *IEEE International Conference on Computer Vision*, pages 59–66, Bombay, India, January 1998.

[13] R. N. Shepard. Toward a universal law of generalization for psychological science. *Science*, 237:1317–1323, 1987.

[14] M. Swain and D. Ballard. Color indexing. *International Journal of Computer Vision*, 7(1):11–32, 1991.

[15] H. Voorhees and T. Poggio. Computing texture boundaries from images. *Nature*, 333:364–367, 1988.

[16] G. Wyszecki and W. S. Stiles. *Color Science: Concepts and Methods, Quantitative Data and Formulae.* John Wiley and Sons, New York, NY, 1982.

Vision and Learning

Error Detection and DEM Fusion Using Self-Consistency*

Howard Schultz, Edward M. Riseman, Frank R. Stolle
Computer Science Department
University of Massachusetts
Amherst, MA 01003
USA
{hschultz,riseman,stolle}@cs.umass.edu

Dong-Min Woo
School of Electrical Engineering
Myongji University
South Korea
dmwoo@wh.myongji.ac.kr

Abstract

The ability to efficiently and robustly recover accurate 3D terrain models from sets of stereoscopic images is important to many civilian and military applications. Our long-term goal is to develop an automatic, multi-image 3D reconstruction algorithm that can be applied to these domains. To develop an effective and practical terrain modeling system, methods must be found for detecting unreliable elevations in digital elevation maps (DEMs), and for fusing several DEMs from multiple sources into an accurate and reliable result.

This paper focuses on two key factors for generating robust 3D terrain models, (1) the ability to detect unreliable elevations estimates, and (2) to fuse the reliable elevations into a single optimal terrain model. The techniques discussed in this paper are based on the concept of using self-consistency to identify potentially unreliable points. We apply the self-consistency methodology to both the two-image and multi-image scenarios. We demonstrate that the recently developed concept of self-consistency can be effectively employed to determine the reliability of values in a DEM. Estimates with a reliability below an error threshold can be excluded from further processing. We test the effectiveness of the methodology, as well as the relationship between error rate and scene geometry by processing both real and photo-realistic simulations.

* Sponsored by Grants from:
  National Science Foundation (EIA-9726401)
  National Fish and Wildlife Foundation (98-089)

1 Introduction

There is a substantial body of research in two-image stereo reconstruction [3][8], and a smaller but growing body of work on multi-view stereo[1][4]. These methods have been loosely divided into two categories, feature matching and texture matching. Independent of these classifications 3D reconstruction algorithms can be divided into image space methods[2][8] in which the matching occurs without regard to the physical characteristics of the surface; and object-space matching in which the images must be consistent with the geometry and physical properties of the surface[1][4]. Each of these techniques share a common goal of identifying elements (features [5][6][11], patterns [8][12]) across two or more views of a scene. Unfortunately, there are a variety of mechanisms that will cause any of these techniques to fail locally – a flawed imaging mechanism (e.g., dropouts, dust, thermal noise), poorly modeled optical properties (e.g., using a Lambertian reflectance model for asphalt or water), occlusions (across varying image viewpoints), and/or problematic texture patterns (e.g., repetitive patterns, linear features that align with epipolar lines).

Because it is impossible to take into account all of the problems, a robust 3D reconstruction system should

Army Research Office (DAAD19-99-1-0016)
Defense Advanced Research Projects Agency
(DACA76-97-K-0005)

contain a mechanism for identifying and removing blunders. The techniques discussed in this paper are based on the concept of using self-consistency measures, first introduced by Leclerc, Luong and Fua [10], to identify unreliable points in a distribution. The main focus of their work was to obtain a quality measure for correspondence algorithms without relying on any ground truth. Their algorithm obtained a probability distribution by counting the number of corresponding image points for each object point that is consistent with the viewing geometry within a specified error limit. In a closely related application [9], they extend their work to detect changes in terrain by applying the concept of self-consistency to elevations. We extend the idea of this work to detect unreliable elements in a digital elevation map (DEM) generated from stereoscopic image pairs, and to fuse multiple DEMs. In our case, multiple pairs of images of the same site are processed using a hierarchical texture matching system.

In our application domain of environmental monitoring, aerial images are used to produce highly accurate DEM which are used to produce geo-referenced maps of biomass, ground cover classes, etc. Our input data are sequences of overlapping digitized aerial photographs (or more recently, high-quality digital video). Our 3D terrain modeling system produces a single, accurate geo-referenced DEM from multiple images (typically 3-12). We are utilizing an automatic stereo reconstruction algorithm that employs a hierarchical, texture matching scheme to generate DEMs from pairs of images that must be fused to form a large mosaic. The fusion process serves several purposes, including improving the accuracy by averaging redundant elevation estimates, detecting and removing outliers, and estimating the geospatial uncertainty. The key to a reliable fusion process is the use of self-consistency measures to identify and remove unreliable elevation estimates.

Of prime interest to us is the automatic detection of matching errors related to variables of the scene geometry. In particular we are interested in reconstructing the shape of the terrain from images which may have been taken from widely varying viewpoints. As the separation between the camera positions increases, elevation estimates become more precise [8]. At the same time, widely separated viewpoints result in a substantial perspective distortion between images, and increases the likelihood of encountering occlusions, which increase the chances of generating false matches. Even when viewing a surface from nadir, local variations in surface slope may result in highly distorted surface elements. In addition, aerial survey lenses often have a wide field-of-view [13] (typically 90°), which will increase the perspective distortion near the image edges. This tradeoff between increased accuracy versus increased error rate must be taken into account when designing a terrain modeling system.

This problem will be mitigated when multiple images are processed from different viewpoints. If a surface patch is highly distorted or obscured in one view, it may be clearly visible in another. Thus, as the number of views increase it is more likely that a correct match can be found for any particular surface patch, and it becomes imperative to detect unreliable elevation estimates, particularly when processing images taken at oblique viewing angles or when fusing multiple DEMs.

The methodology described in this paper for detecting errors in DEMs by self-consistency can be applied to both the two-image and multi-image scenarios. When only two images are available, two DEMs can be generated by reversing the roles of the reference and target images in the matching process. We will demonstrate that self-consistency measures can be effective employed to determination of the reliability of values in a DEM, which can then be excluded from further analysis. We will test the effectiveness of the methodology as well as the relationship between error rate and scene geometry by processing multiple overlapping views of a real terrain, as well as synthetic images of a realistic, 3D terrain model.

2 Photo-realistic simulation

Any comprehensive analysis and evaluation of a dense array of elevations estimates generated from images requires a dense array of ground truth. The typical use of a few ground control points spread out over an entire scene is simply not sufficient to compute meaningful statistics. Unfortunately, even with a technologically advanced system measurement system, such as an airborne scanning laser range mapping system or IFSAR (interferrometric synthetic radar), a high-resolution dense array of elevation spread out over several square kilometers would require an enormous effort.

To facilitate the analysis of the techniques described in this paper, we develop a method of generating pseudo ground truth through photo-realistic synthetic images. The process begins with a digital elevation map (DEM) and an ortho-image, which may come from an independent source (e.g., DFED or USGS digital ortho-quads), or which may have been generated from aerial images using a 3D reconstruction algorithm. We begin by treating the DEM and ortho-image as if they were precise, error-free representations of the terrain. Next, a ray tracing program is used to generate photo-realistic, synthetic images of the terrain from any viewpoint. The synthetic views then serve the function of real images.

Clearly pseudo ground truth and synthetic images are not a completely satisfactory substitute for real data. Nevertheless, the method does provide means for generating otherwise unobtainable ground truth samples, and furthermore, it generates expected types of errors due to perspective distortion, and occlusion that will occur in real data. The images used to generate the pseudo ground truth were extracted from six 9 inch × 9 inch aerial images of a desert area near 29 Palms California[1]. Four of the images were taken so that a section of the terrain was visible in each image. This set of four overlapping images (one of which is shown in Figure 1) is the basis of the data presented in this paper.

The pseudo ground truth were generated from two of the four overlapping images. The choice of which two images to use was arbitrary. This DEM will undoubtedly contain some anomalies (deviations from the actual physical world). Because these anomalies become part of the pseudo ground truth and are correctly manifested in the synthetic images, they will not affect the quality of our experiments. The pseudo ground truth covered an area of 157.5m × 368.4m, with a ground sampling distance of approximately 0.35m.

To test the validity of the simulation procedure, we synthesized the images that were not used to generate the pseudo ground truth DEM, and then compared the synthesized images to the real ones. In other words, starting with four overlapping images, labeled A, B, C, D, we generated a DEM from images A and B (denoted by Z_{AB}). We then synthesized two images labeled C′ and D′ which had the same camera parameters as images C and D. A simple analysis of visual inspection, as well image differencing showed a remarkable similarity between the real and synthesized images. This has reasonably convinced us that the DEMs generated from the photo-realistic simulated data will be valuable in test the self-consistency algorithms. Figure 1 show one of the four original images, a small 400 × 400 pixel region of the original image, and the corresponding region of the synthetic image.

3 Self-consistency

At the heart of our method is an expectation of consistency between DEMs when the computation is accurate. In addition, we rely on the observation that for many 3D reconstruction algorithms [7] two DEMs can be generated for a single image pair. We consider the class of image matching algorithms that generate a dense array of disparities $\mathbf{D}_{AB}(i,j)$ such that the pixels (i,j) in image A and the pixels $(i+\mathbf{D}_{AB}(i,j), j)$ in image B are projections of the same surface elements. In this notation image A is the reference image and image B is the target image. By reversing the roles of images A and B we can generate a second disparity map $\mathbf{D}_{BA}(i,j)$ such that the pixels (i,j) in image B and the pixels $(i+\mathbf{D}_{BA}(i,j), j)$ in image A are projections of the same surface elements. Because of the

<hr />

[1] This data set was make available by the Army Topographic Engineering Laboratory

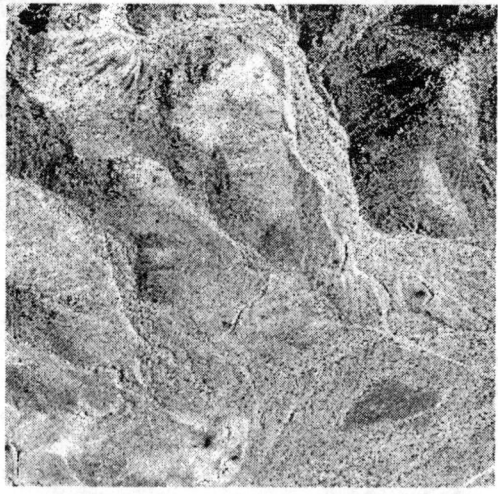

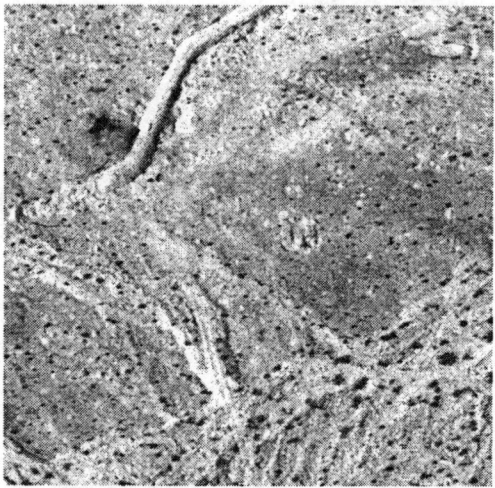

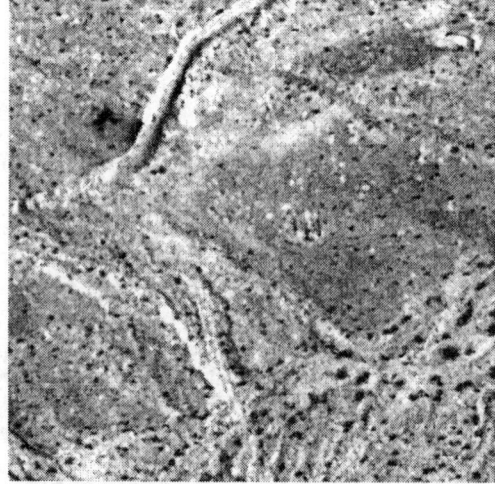

Figure 1. One of the original images (top); a small 400 x 400 pixel region taken from the original image (middle); the same region taken from the photo-realistic synthetic image (bottom).

nonlinear and adaptive manner in which disparity maps are usually computed, it is generally the case that $\mathbf{D}_{AB}$ and $\mathbf{D}_{BA}$ do not produce the same set of elevations.

Our analysis is based on testing the consistency of a pair of DEMs generated from a pair of overlapping images. By comparing reference-target duality in DEMs, inconsistency becomes a means of detecting errors. We denote the elevations recovered from images A and B by Z_{AB}, where the first subscript is the label of the reference image and the second subscript is the label of the target image. Without loss of generality, Z_{AB} may be written as the sum of the actual surface Z^* and a geospatial error term δ_{AB}. Thus, for any two overlapping images A and B, the two recovered surface models are

$$Z_{AB} = Z^* + \delta_{AB}$$
$$Z_{BA} = Z^* + \delta_{BA}$$

Taking the difference of the two computed elevation maps gives an expression that is independent of the surface structure.

$$Z_{AB} - Z_{BA} = \delta_{AB} - \delta_{BA} \qquad (1)$$

The left hand side of Equation 1, which is very similar to self-consistency described in [10], depends only on images A and B. The right hand side is the difference between the geospatial errors, which requires ground truth to evaluate. Currently, we are developing a comprehensive model that expresses the conditional probability density function (PDF) of the geospatial errors to self-consistency distribution. As a first step, we will examine methods based on statistics derived from the distribution self-consistency.

We begin by assuming that the distribution of geospatial error measures δ_{AB} and δ_{BA} are comprised of two distinct populations:

1. Errors associated with correct correspondences, which we refer to as *inliers*. These errors result from small uncertainties in camera orientation, digitization, numerical roundoff, etc. Inliers are modeled by a zero-mean, normally distributed random process with a standard deviation (s.d.) in object space that corresponds to approximately one pixel registration error in image space.

2. *Outliers* which arise from false matches. These errors have a very broad distribution which may span hundreds of pixels in image space with correspondingly large errors in object space.

A simple test for separating the two populations can be devised by taking the s.d. of both sides of Equation 1,

$$\sigma(Z_{AB} - Z_{BA}) = \sigma(\delta_{AB} - \delta_{BA}) \qquad (2)$$

This formula may be applied locally (e.g., within an $n \times m$ window), globally, or conditionally (e.g., as a function of incidence angle). Assuming that the distribution of δ_{AB} and δ_{BA} are identical, Equation (2) can be rewritten as

$$\sigma(Z_{AB} - Z_{BA}) = A\sigma(\delta) \qquad (3)$$

where A is a function, that depends on several factors, including the local slope of the terrain, the scene geometry and the processing scheme. In the simplest case, when δ_{AB} and δ_{BA} are samples from an uncorrelated, normally distributed random processes, the function A reduces to a constant equal to $\sqrt{2}$, and Equation 3 can be rewritten as

$$\sigma\left(Z_{AB} - Z_{BA}\right) = \sqrt{2}\sigma(\delta)$$

Although this simple case cannot be applied to most situations, it is important to observe that large values of the geospatial set-consistency are likely to be associated with corresponding large geospatial errors, which in turn are associated with false matches. In other words, we expect that the distribution of the object space self-consistency measure will mimic the geospatial error distribution.

A method of determining the s.d. of a population containing a mixture of inliers and outliers was developed that reduces the influence of outliers. This was necessary because the inlier population is expected to have a zero mean and a s.d. that is fraction of a meter, whereas the outlier population is expected to have values on the order of several meters. A few outliers, therefore, will drastically affect the computation of the s.d. of the entire population. To minimize the influence of the tails of the distribution, which we expect to be dominated by outliers, standard deviations were computed by fitting the histogram to a Gaussian plus a constant of the form

$$h_{\max} \exp-\left[\frac{(z_i - z_0)^2}{2\sigma^2}\right] + h_0 \qquad (4)$$

where z_i are the histogram values, and the peak value ($h_{\max}$), the floor (h_0), the mean (z_0), and standard deviation (σ) are parameters of the fit. If the population was normally distributed, there would be no need to compute σ using Equation 4. Instead σ could be found by evaluating the standard computational formula

$$\sigma = \frac{1}{n-1}\sqrt{\sum_i (z_i - z_0)^2}$$

With outliers present in the population, the curve fitting technique reduces the influence of non-Gaussian distributions in the tails.

The outlier threshold for the analysis presented in this paper was set to 2σ. It must be understood that whatever method is used to determine a threshold, the resultant reliability cannot be considered exact. Some of the values marked as reliable may not be, and vice versa, for two reasons:

- In general, the self-consistency distribution is not isomorphic with the geospatial error distribution. As pointed out above, a more comprehensive formulation is need to precisely predict the statistics of the geospatial errors from the self-consistency distribution (planned future work).

- It is possible, although very rare, that a false match will produce the same results when the reference and target images are reversed. In fact, we were not able to find any errors of this type in our data.

Although we do not offer an objective method for setting the outlier threshold, one can easily determine if the threshold is set too low or too high by checking the number of rejected points. Furthermore, we observed that the fusion results are fairly insensitive to the outlier threshold, and we were able to achieved similar results with σ set to values between 2 and 4. We chose a conservative threshold (i.e., a low value) to ensure that the DEM computed for the real data had as few unreliable elevations contributed to the fused DEM as possible. The 2σ cutoff threshold was selected because it resulted in a complete recovery for the real data, although some DEM elements in the simulated data set did not have any reliable points (note: these points could be filled in by interpolating the fused DEM).

To test the procedures we compared the s.d. of the self-consistency ($Z_{AB} - Z_{BA}$), the percent of detected inliers, the s.d. of the geospatial errors ($Z_{AB} - Z^*$), ($Z_{BA} - Z^*$), and ($\frac{1}{2} \cdot (Z_{AB} + Z_{BA}) - Z^*$) as a function of various off-nadir view angles θ for cameras A and B. The s.d. of the geospatial errors were computed by evaluating the standard computational formula for all elevation estimates less than the 2σ threshold.

The results are summarized in Table 1, and a plot of the histogram and the fitted distribution curve for $b/h = 0.277$ are shown in Figure 2. For the data summarized in Table 1, h_{max} was at least two order of magnitude greater than the outlier floor h_0, and the total extent of the histogram tails was approximately ± 60m, which was much greater than width of the fitted distribution σ. The real data were all taken with the camera looking approximately straight down. For the simulated data, however, we were able to place the cameras in any position. This allowed us to study the affects of viewing geometry on the performance of the algorithm.

Inspection of Table 1 shows that the trend is for the standard deviation of the geospatial errors to decrease with increasing base-to-height ratio (b/h) and for the number of outliers to increase with increasing b/h. As mentioned in Section 1, this is the expected trend based on standard stereo geometry [7]. The last column shows the standard deviation of the geospatial error measured relative to the average of the two retrieved DEMs.

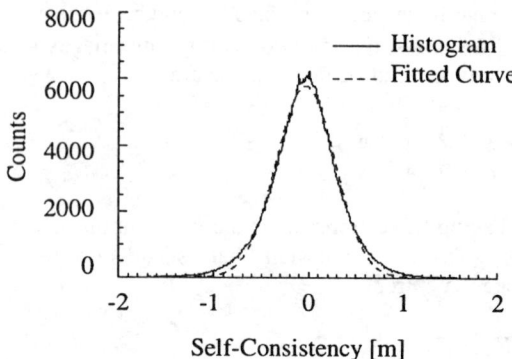

Figure 2. Self-consistency distribution for image pair 3

4 Fusing multiple DEMs

The method of using self-consistency measures to detect unreliable elevation estimates can applied to the problem of fusing multiple generated from several overlapping images. The basic principle is to identify outliers (unreliable elevations estimates) and then compute a weighted average of all reliable points. We employed the following two-pass algorithm:

- Given a set of n images where n is greater than 2, compute the set of order dependent DEMs and self-consistency distributions. For the four overlapping images discussed above (labeled A,B,C,D), 12 DEMs (Z_{AB}, Z_{BA}, Z_{AC}, Z_{CA}, ..., Z_{CD}, Z_{DC}) and six self-consistency distributions ($Z_{AB} - Z_{BA}$), ($Z_{AC} - Z_{CA}$), ..., ($Z_{CD} - Z_{DC}$) can be computed.

- For each DEM pair compute an outlier threshold by (i) fit the formula in Equation 4 to the histogram of the self-consistency distribution, (ii) set the threshold to a predetermined multiple of the s.d. of the fitted function, and (iii) assign summation weights (planned future work).

- Mark as unreliable all elements in the DEM with a self-consistency measure greater than the threshold.

Table 1. Self-consistency and geospatial error statistics as a function of the base-to-height ratio (b/h) and the angle between the optic axis and vertical (θ) for images A and B. $\sigma(Z_{AB}-Z_{BA})$ is the standard deviation of the self-consistency distribution; % inliers is the percent of all elevations where $|Z_{AB}-Z_{BA}| < 2\sigma(Z_{AB}-Z_{BA})$; the last three columns are the standard deviations of the difference between the pseudo ground truth Z^*, and Z_{AB}, Z_{BA} and average of Z_{AB} and Z_{BA}. All standard deviations are in meters.

B/h	θ_A	θ_B	$\sigma(Z_{AB}-Z_{BA})$	% Inliers 2σ cutoff	$\sigma(Z^*-Z_{AB})$	$\sigma(Z^*-Z_{BA})$	$\sigma(Z^*-\overline{Z})$
0.277	0°	15°	0.451189	91.90	0.332601	0.244706	0.213685
0.293	15°	30°	0.486813	92.50	0.344480	0.330056	0.260698
0.575	15°	-15°	0.311553	91.36	0.163137	0.213822	0.131443
0.868	-15°	30°	0.203503	89.40	0.157535	0.194275	0.152326
1.230	30°	-30°	0.167713	84.24	0.155302	0.188295	0.155993

- For each element in the DEM grid, compute the average of reliable elevation estimates $\overline{Z}$.

- An optional step would be to compute an interpolated value for all elements without any reliable elevations. This option was not in the examples presented in this paper.

- Re-apply the threshold test to the difference between the fused DEM $\overline{Z}$ and the unreliable elements. If any of the differences are less than the outlier threshold, re-label the point as reliable. This step is necessary because some of the unreliable matches occur in $\mathbf{D}_{AB}$ and not $\mathbf{D}_{BA}$ (or visa versa).

- Update the fused DEM by including the newly relabeled elevation estimates.

This fusion algorithm was applied to two data sets – the set of four overlapping images, and the photo-realistic simulated data (see Figure 1). For the simulated data we were able compare the results to an absolute reference. The results generated from the simulated data are shown in Figure 3, and the results from processing the real data are shown in Figure 4. The simulated data covered a significantly narrower region than the real data. This reduction in the size occurred because the image matching algorithm cannot process data along the boarder of the image; and the synthesized images are computed only for regions where a DEM exists.

For the simulated data set, 99.54% of the DEM elements had at least one reliable point (the missing elements show up in Figure 3 as small black flakes), and the overall accuracy, measured by the standard deviation of the difference between the pseudo ground truth and the fused DEM (i.e., $\sigma(Z^* - \overline{Z})$) was 0.169m (the ground sampling distance was 0.35).

Our methodology involves automatic determination of a reliable set of elevation estimates for each value in each DEM. Therefore, there will be a varying number of contributions to the final elevation at each point in the $2k \times 2k$ fused DEM. This is graphically displayed by gray value in Fig. 4, which shows in gray value the number of elevation estimates used (varying from 0 to a maximum of 12. About 98% of the points had 10 or more reliable values contributing, and only 215 points of the 4 million had 3 or less values (157 with no estimates). Most of these cases were isolated, and median filtering would achieve reasonable estimates for many of them.

Of course, for the real data we were not able to compute the accuracy of the retrieval. However, we did find that the algorithm found at least one reliable element in 99.99% of the scene. In addition, there were no apparent anomalies in the fused DEM. That is, the appearance of the ortho-image seemed consistent with the terrain everywhere in the scene. Our qualitative inspection consisted of checking the relationship between objects such as rocks and ditches to their shadows, and checking to see if streams (or in this case dry streambeds) flow down hill everywhere

5 Conclusions

We successfully applied the notion of self-consistency to the specific task of improving the generation of DEMs using dual symmetric stereo processing on pairs of images from a subset of overlapping aerial images. The photo-realistic simulation results shows an ability to detect almost all outliers by using a conservative threshold to mark reliable elevation estimates in dual DEMs from a pair of images. There is a significant decrease in the residual errors of the model compared to individual DEMs generated without regard to self-consistency. Experimental results are in good correlation with theoretical predictions. The strategy for fusion of the multiple DEMs can be further improved and this will be investigated in the future.

There is a significant computational overhead associated with this technique. It can be justified in cases where a very accurate DEM is important, such as for off-

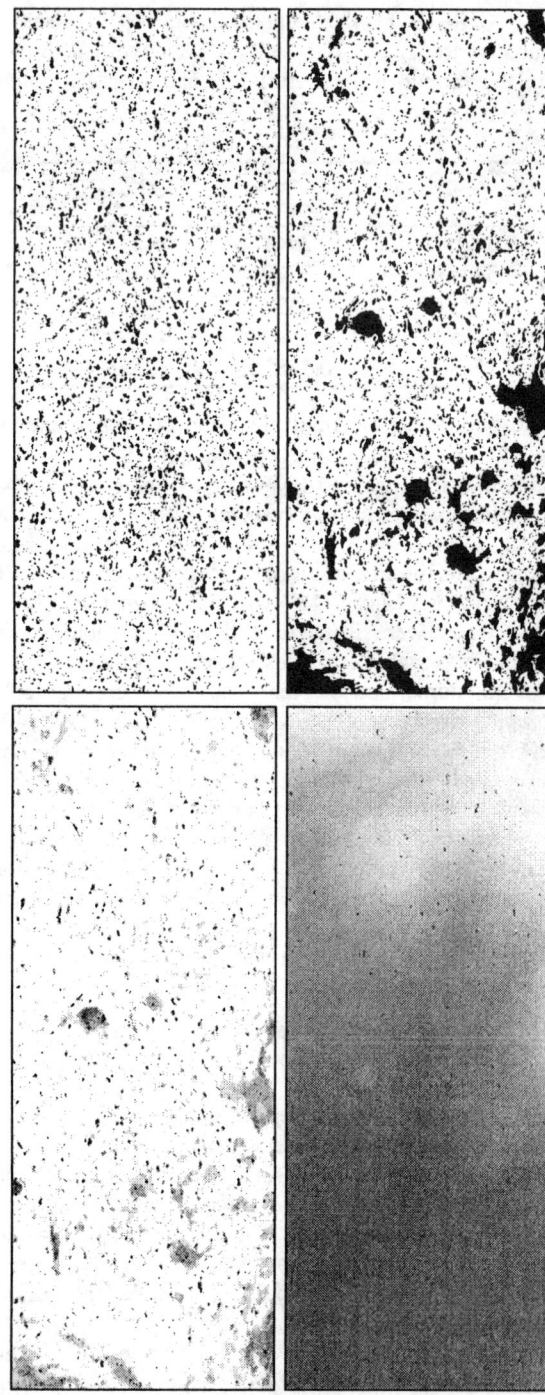

Figure 3. The inlier mask for $\theta_A=0°$ and $\theta_B=15°$ (top-left); inlier mask for $\theta_A=-30°$ and $\theta_B=+30°$ (top-right); an image of the number of samples used to compute the fused DEM, black corresponds to $n=0$ and white corresponds to $n=10$; the fused DEM, the black flecks are elements with no elevation estimates ($n=0$).

road autonomous driving. The work presented is the first step in a more comprehensive attempt to apply the notions of geospatial uncertainty and self-consistency in order to generate near-optimal elevation models. The focus of our ongoing work will be on extending the technique to investigating the value of self-consistency measures among real and across synthetic imagery. This will require a better model for the propagation of errors and weighting the contributions from the different sources.

From our experimental results, we conjecture that most of the benefit of the fusion process derives from a relatively small subset of the data. In the future, we will conduct studies that will give one the ability to select, from the available images, the optimal/minimal subset that conforms to a given error tolerance.

References

[1] Agouris, Peggy and T. Schenk, Automated Aerotriangulation Using Multiple Image Multipoint Matching, Photogrammetric Engineering and Remote Sensing, Vol. LXII, No. 6, June 1996, pp. 703-710.

[2] Ayache, N., and B. Faverjon, "Efficient Registration of Stereo Images by Matching Graph Description of Edge Segments," *Int'l J. Computer Vision,* pp. 107-131, 1987.

[3] Aschwanden, P. and W. Guggenbuehl, "Experimental Results From a Comparative Study on Correlation-Type Registration Algorithms," *Robust Computer Vision,* Foerstner and Ruwiedel, eds., pp. 268-289, Wichmann, 1993.

[4] Fua, P. and Y.G. Leclerc, "Taking Advantage of Image-Based and Geometry-Based Constraints to Recover 3-D Surfaces," *Computer Vision and Image Understanding,* vol. 64, no. 1, pp. 111-127, 1996.

[5] Grimson, W.E.L., "Computational Experiments With a Feature Based Stereo Algorithm," *IEEE Trans. Pattern Analysis and Machine Intelligence,* vol. 7, no. 1, pp. 17-34, January, 1985.

[6] Hoff, W., and N. Ahuja, "Surface From Stereo: Integrating Feature Matching, Disparity Estimation and Contour Detection," *IEEE Trans. Pattern Analysis and Machine Intelligence,* vol. 11, pp. 121-136, 1989.

[7] Horn, Berthold K. P., <u>Robot Vision</u>, MIT Press, Cambridge, MA.., 1986.

[8] Kanade, T. and M. Okutomi, "A Stereo Matching Algorithm With an Adaptive Window: Theory and Experiment," IEEE Trans. Pattern Analysis and Machine Intelligence, vol. 16, no. 9, pp. 920-932, Sept. 1994.

[9] Leclerc, Y.G., Q.T. Luong, and P. Fua, "A Framework for Detecting Changes in Terrain," *IEEE Trans. Pattern Analysis and Machine Intelligence,* vol. 20, no. 11, pp. 1143-1160, November 1998.

[10] Leclerc, Y,G., Q.T. Luong, et al., "Self-consistency: A novel approach to characterizing the accuracy and reliability of point correspondence algorithms," *DARPA Image Understanding Workshop*, Monterey, CA, Morgan Kauffman, 1998.

[11] Medioni, G. and R. Nevatia, "Segment-Based Stereo Matching," *Computer Vision, Graphics, and Image Processing,* vol. 31, pp. 2-18, 1985.

[12] Schultz, H., "Terrain Reconstruction from Widely Separated Images", Proc. SPIE, Volume 2486, pp. 113-123, Orlando, FL, April, 1995.

[13] Slama, Chester C. (Editor), Manual of Photogrammetry, 4ed., American Society of Photogrammetry, Falls Church, VA., 1980.

[14] Witkin, A., D. Terzopoulos, and M. Kass, "Signal Matching Through Scale Space," *Int'l J. Computer Vision,* pp. 133-144, 1987.

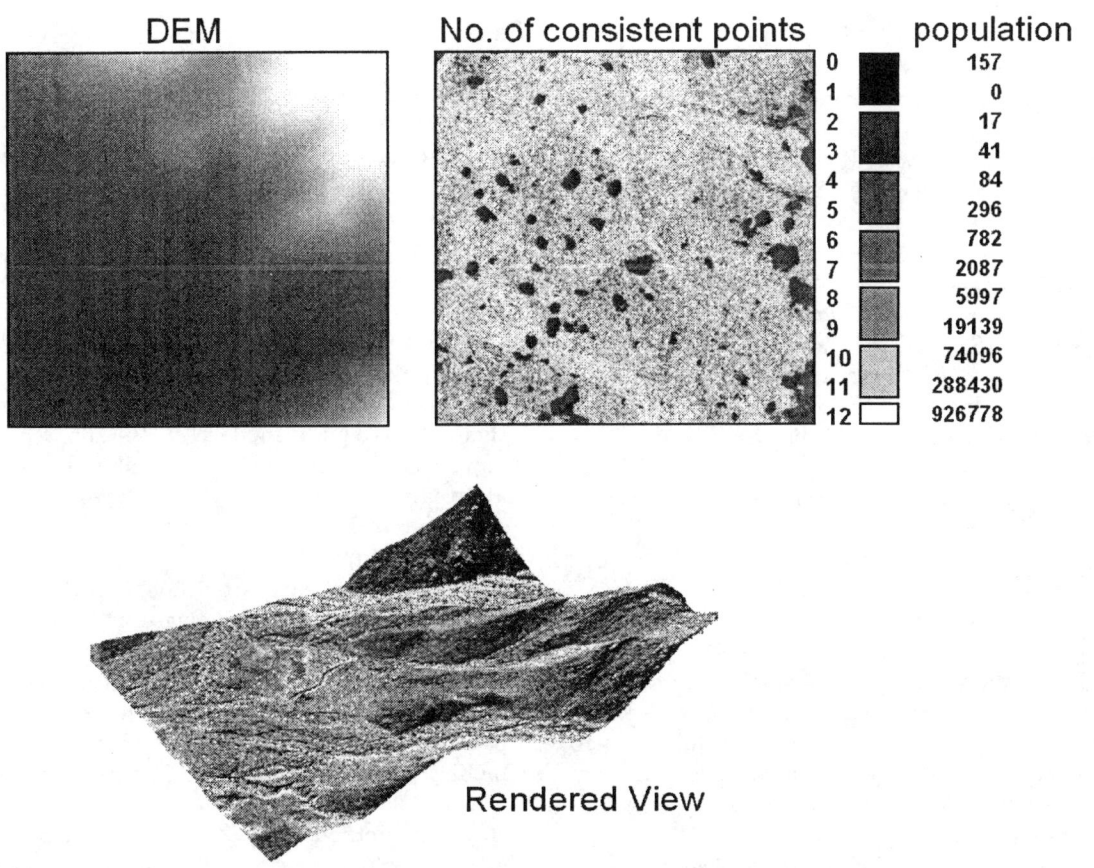

Figure 4. DEM fusion from the four real images. The DEM (top-left), a map of the number of consistent elevation estimates (top-right), the ortho-image draped over the DEM (bottom).

Learning low-level vision

William T. Freeman and Egon C. Pasztor
MERL, a Mitsubishi Electric Res. Lab.
201 Broadway, Cambridge, MA 02139
freeman, pasztor@merl.com

Abstract

We show a learning-based method for low-level vision problems–estimating scenes from images. We generate a synthetic world of scenes and their corresponding rendered images. We model that world with a Markov network, learning the network parameters from the examples. Bayesian belief propagation allows us to efficiently find a local maximum of the posterior probability for the scene, given the image. We call this approach VISTA–Vision by Image/Scene TrAining.

We apply VISTA to the "super-resolution" problem (estimating high frequency details from a low-resolution image), showing good results. For the motion estimation problem, we show figure/ground discrimination, solution of the aperture problem, and filling-in arising from application of the same probabilistic machinery.

1 Introduction

We seek machinery for learning low-level vision problems, such as motion analysis, inferring shape and albedo from a photograph, or extrapolating image detail. For these problems, given *image* data, we want to estimate an underlying *scene*. The scene quantities to be estimated might be projected object velocities, surface shapes and reflectance patterns, or missing high frequency details.

Low-level vision problems are typically underconstrained, so Bayesian [3, 23, 37] and regularization techniques [31] are fundamental. There has been much work and progress (for example, [23, 25, 15]), but difficulties remain in working with complex, real images. Typically, prior probabilities or constraints are made-up, rather than learned. A general machinery for a learning-based solution to low-level vision problems would have many applications.

A recent research theme has been to learn the statistics of natural images. Researchers have related those statistics to properties of the human visual system [28, 2, 36], or have used statistical methods with biologically plausible image representations to analyse

and synthesize realistic image textures [14, 8, 41, 36]. These methods may help us understand the early stages of representation and processing, but unfortunately, they don't address how a visual system might *interpret* images, i.e., estimate the underlying scene.

We want to combine the two research themes of scene estimation and statistical learning. We study the statistical properties of a synthetically generated, *labelled* world of images with scenes, to learn how to infer scenes from images. Our prior probabilities can then be rich ones, learned from the training data.

Several researchers have applied related learning approaches to low-level vision problems, but restricted themselves to linear models [21, 16], too weak for many applications. Our approach is similar in spirit to relaxation labelling [33, 22], but our Bayesian propagation algorithm is more efficient and we utilize large sets of labelled training data.

We interpret images by modeling the relationship between local regions of images and scenes, and between neighboring local scene regions. The former allows initial scene estimates; the later allows the estimates to propagate. We train from image/scene pairs and apply the Bayesian machinery of graphical models [29, 5, 20]. We were inspired by the work of Weiss [38], who pointed out the speed advantage of Bayesian methods over conventional relaxation methods for propagating local measurement information. For a related approach, but with heuristically derived propagation rules, see [34].

We call our approach VISTA, Vision by Image/Scene TrAining. It is a general machinery that may apply to various problems. We illustrate it for estimating missing image details, and estimating motion.

2 Markov network

For given image data, y, we seek to estimate the underlying scene, x (we omit the vector symbols for notational simplicity). We first calculate the posterior probability, $P(x|y) = cP(x, y)$ For this analysis, we ignore the normalization, $c = \frac{1}{P(y)}$, a constant over x. Under two common loss functions [3], the best scene estimate, $\hat{x}$, is the mean (minimum mean squared error, MMSE) or the mode (maximum a posteriori, MAP) of the posterior probability.

In general, $\hat{x}$ can be difficult to compute [23] without approximations. We make the Markov assumption: we divide both the image and scene into patches, and assign one node of a Markov network [13, 29, 20] to each patch. Given the variables at intervening nodes, two nodes of a Markov network are statistically independent. We connect each scene patch to its corresponding image patch, and to its nearest neighbors, Fig. 1. Solving a Markov network involves a *learning* phase, where the parameters of the network connections are learned from training data, and an *inference* phase, when the scene corresponding to particular image data is estimated.

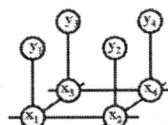

Figure 1: Markov network for vision problems. Observations, y, have underlying scene explanations, x.

For networks without loops, the Markov assumption leads to simple "message-passing" rules for computing the MAP and MMSE estimates [29, 39, 20]. Writing those estimates for x_j by marginalizing (MMSE) or taking the argmax (MAP) over the other variables gives:

$$\hat{x}_{j\,MMSE} = \int_{x_j} x_j dx_j \int_{\text{all } x_i,\ i \neq j} P(x,y)dx \quad (1)$$

$$\hat{x}_{j\,MAP} = \begin{array}{c}\text{argmax}\\ [x_j]\end{array} \begin{array}{c}\text{argmax}\\ [\text{ all } x_i,\ i \neq j\ ]\end{array} P(x,y) \quad (2)$$

For a Markov random field, the joint probability over the scenes x and images y can be written as [4, 13, 12]:

$$P(x,y) = \prod_{\text{neighboring } i,j} \Psi(x_i, x_j) \prod_k \Phi(x_k, y_k), \quad (3)$$

where we have introduced pairwise compatibility functions, Ψ and Φ, described below. The factorized structure of Eq. (3) allows the integrals and argmax operations of Eqs. (1) and (2) to pass through to the compatibility function factors with the appropriate arguments. For a network without loops, the resulting expression can be computed using repeated, local computations [29, 39, 20], summarized below: the MMSE

estimate at node j is

$$\hat{x}_{j\,MMSE} = \int_{x_j} x_j \Phi(x_j, y_j) \prod_k L_{kj} dx_j, \quad (4)$$

where k runs over all scene node neighbors of node j. We calculate L_{kj} from:

$$L_{kj} = \int_{x_k} \Psi(x_k, x_j) \Phi(x_k, y_k) \prod_{l \neq j} \tilde{L}_{lk} dx_k, \quad (5)$$

where $\tilde{L}_{lk}$ is L_{lk} from the previous iteration. The initial $\tilde{L}_{lk}$'s are 1. After at most one iteration per x_i of Eq. (1), Eq. (4) and (5) give Eq. (1). The MAP estimate equation, Eq. (2), yields analogous formulae, with the integral of Eq. (5) replaced by $argmax_{x_k}$, and $\int_{x_j} x_j$ of Eq. (4) replaced by $argmax_{x_j}$. For linear topologies, these propagation rules are equivalent to well-known Bayesian inference methods, such as the Kalman filter and the forward-backward algorithm for Hidden Markov Models [29, 26, 38, 20, 11].

Finding the posterior probability distribution for a grid-structured Markov network with loops is computationally expensive and a variety of approximations have been proposed [13, 12, 20]. Strong empirical results in "Turbo codes" [24, 27] and recent theoretical work [39, 40] provide support for a very simple approximation: applying the propagation rules derived above *even in a network with loops*. Table 1 summarizes results from [40]: (1) for Gaussian processes, the MMSE propagation scheme will converge only to the true posterior means. (2) Even for non-Gaussian processes, if the MAP propagation scheme converges, it finds at least a local maximum of the true posterior probability.

2.1 Learning the compatibility functions

One can measure the marginal probabilities relating local scenes, x_i, and images, y_i, as well as neighboring local scenes, x_i and x_j. Iterated Proportional Fitting (e.g., [18]) is a scheme to iteratively modify the compatibility functions until the empirically measured marginal statistics agree with those predicted by the model, Eq. (3). For the problems presented here, we found good results by using the marginal statistics measured from the training data, without modifications by iterated proportional fitting. Based on a factorization described in [10, 9], for a message from scene nodes j to k, we used $\Psi(x_j, x_k) = \frac{P(x_j, x_k)}{P(x_k)}$ and $\Phi(x_j, y_j) = P(y_j | x_j)$. We fit the probabilities with mixtures of Gaussians.

An alternate method, which we find gives comparable results, not shown here, is to use scene and image

Belief propagation algorithm	Network topology	
	no loops	arbitrary topology
MMSE rules	MMSE, correct posterior marginal probs.	For Gaussians, correct means, wrong covs.
MAP rules	MAP	Local max. of posterior, even for non-Gaussians

Table 1: Summary of results from [40], assuming convergence of belief propagation.

patches with spatially overlap their neighbors. We assume a Gaussian noise penalty on the multiple observations of the same pixels in the overlap region, yielding $\Psi(x_k, x_j) = \exp^{-(d_k - d_j)^2/2\sigma^2}$, where d_k and d_j are the corresponding values of the scenes described at nodes k and j in their region of common support, and σ is a penalty parameter.

2.2 Probability Representation

Inspired by the success of [17, 8], we use a sample-based representation for inference. We describe the posterior probability as a set of weights on scenes observed in the training set. Given an image to analyze, for each node we collect a set of 10 or 20 "scene candidates" from the training data which have image data closely matching the local observation. We evaluate the posterior probability only at those scene values. The propagation algorithms, Eq. (5) and (4) then are discrete matrix calculations. This simplification focuses the computation on only those scenes which render to the observed image data.

3 Super-resolution

For the super-resolution problem, the input *image* is a low-resolution image. The *scene* to be estimated is a higher resolution image. A good solution to this problem would allow pixel-based images to be handled in a relatively resolution-independent manner. Applications could include enlargment of digital or film photographs, upconversion of video from NTSC format to HDTV, or image compression.

At first, the task may seem impossible—the high resolution data is not there. However, we can see edges in the low-resolution image that we know should remain sharp at the next resolution level. Furthermore, based on the successes of recent texture synthesis methods [14, 8, 41, 36], we might expect to handle textured areas well, too.

Others [35] have used a Bayesian method, making-up the prior probability. In contrast, the Markov network learns the relationship between sharp and blurred images from large amounts of training data, and achieves better results. Among the non-Bayesian methods, fractal image representation [32] (Fig. 8c) only gathers training data from the one image, while selecting the nearest neighbor from training data

[30] misses important spatial consistency constraints (Fig. 4a).

We apply VISTA to this problem as follows. By blurring and downsampling sharp images, we construct a training set of blurred and sharp image pairs. We linearly interpolate each blurred image back up to the original resolution, to form an input *image*. The *scene* to be estimated is the high frequency detail missing from the blurred image, Fig. 2a, b. We then take two image processing steps to ease the modeling burden: (1) we bandpass filter the blurred image, because we believe the lowest frequencies won't predict the highest ones; (2) we normalize both the bandpass and highpassed images by the local contrast [19] of the bandpassed image, because we believe their relationship is independent of local contrast, Fig. 2c, d. We undo this normalization after scene inference.

We extracted center-aligned 7x7 and 3x3 pixel patches, Fig. 3, from the training images and scenes. Applying Principal Components Analysis (PCA) [6] to the training set, we summarized each 3-color patch of image or scene by a 9-d vector. From 40,000 image/scene pair samples, we fit 15 cluster Gaussian mixtures to the marginalized probabilities, assuming spatial translation invariance. For efficiency, we pruned frequently occurring image/scene pairs from the training set.

Given a new image, not in the training set, from which to infer the high frequency scene, we found the 10 training samples closest to the image data at each node (patch). The 10 corresponding scenes are the candidates for that node. We evaluated $\Psi(x_j, x_k)$ at 100 values (10 x_j by 10 x_k points) to form a compatibility matrix for messages from neighbor nodes j to k. We propagated the probabilities by Eq. (5).

To process Fig. 5a, we used a training set of 80 images from two Corel database categories: African grazing animals, and urban skylines. Figure 4a shows the nearest neighbor solution, at each node using the scene corresponding to the closest image sample in the training set. Many different scene patches can explain each image patch, and the nearest neighbor solution is very choppy. Figures 4b, c, d show the first 3 iterations of MAP belief propagation. The spatial consistency imposed by the belief propagation finds plausible and

  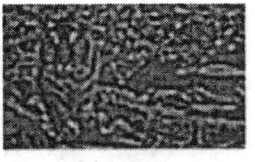 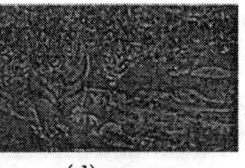

(a) input   (b) desired output   (c) image   (d) scene

Figure 2: We want to estimate (b) from (a). The original image, (b) is blurred, subsampled, then interpolated back up to the original resolution to form (a). The missing high frequency detail, (b) minus (a), is the "scene" to be estimated, (d) (this is the first level of a Laplacian pyramid [7]). The low frequencies of (a) are removed to form the input bandpassed "image". We contrast normalize the image and scene by the local contrast of the input bandpassed image, yielding (c) and (d).

Figure 3: Training data samples for super-resolution problem. The large squares are the *image* data (mid-frequency data). The small squares above them are the corresponding *scene* data (high-frequency data).

consistent high frequencies for the tiger image from the candidate scenes. Figure 5 shows the result of applying this method recursively to zoom two octaves. The algorithm keeps edges sharp and invents plausible textures. Standard cubic spline interpolation, blurrier, is shown for comparison.

Figure 6 explores the algorithm behavior under different training sets. The estimated images properly reflect the structure of the training worlds for noise, rectangles, and generic images. Figure 8 depicts in close-up the interpolation for image (a) using an ideal training set of images taken at the same place and same time (but not of the same subject) (d), and a generic training set of images (e) (Fig. 7 shows the training sets). Both estimates look more similar to the true high resolution result (f) than either cubic spline interpolation (b) or zooming by a fractal image compression algorithm (c). Edges are again kept sharp, while plausible texture is synthesized in the hair.

4 Motion Estimation

To show the breadth of the VISTA technique, we apply it to the problem of motion estimation. The *scene* data to be estimated are the projected velocities of moving objects. The *image* data are two successive image frames. Because we felt long-range interactions were important, we built Gaussian pyramids (e.g., [19]) of both image and scene data, connecting patches to nearest neighbors in both scale and position.

Luettgen et al. [26] applied a related message-passing scheme in a multi-resolution quad-tree network to estimate motion, using Gaussian probabilities.

While the network did not contain loops, its structure generated artifacts along quad-tree boundaries, artificial statistical boundaries of the model.

To show the algorithm working on simple test cases, we generated a synthetic world of moving blobs, of random intensities and shapes. We wrote a tree-structured vector quantizer, to code 4 by 4 pixel by 2 frame blocks of image data for each pyramid level into one of 300 codes for each level, and likewise for scene patches.

During training, we presented approximately 200,000 examples of irregularly shaped moving blobs of a contrast with the background randomized to one of 4 values. For this vector quantized representation, we used co-occurance histograms to measure the compatibility functions, see [10].

Figure 10 shows six iterations of the inference algorithm (Eqs. 4 and 5) as it converges to a good estimate for the underlying scene velocities. The same machinery we applied to super-resolution leads to, for this problem, figure/ground segmentation, aperture problem constraint propagation, and filling-in (see caption). The resulting inferred velocities are correct within the accuracy of the vector quantized representation.

5 Summary

We described an approach we call VISTA–Vision by Image/Scene TrAining. One specifies prior probabilities on scenes by generating typical examples, creating a synthetic world of scenes and rendered images. We break the images and scenes into a Markov network, and learn the parameters of the network from

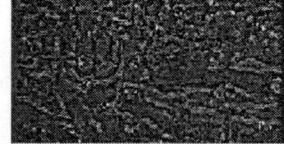

(a) Nearest neighbor   (b) belief prop., iter. 0   (c) belief prop., iter. 1   (d) belief prop., iter. 3

Figure 4: (a) Nearest neighbor solution. The choppiness indicates that many feasible high resolution scenes correspond to a given low resolution image patch. (b), (c), (d): iterations 0, 1, and 3 of Bayesian belief propagation. The initial guess is not the same as the nearest neighbor solution because of mixture model fitting to $P(y|x)$. Underlying the most probable guess shown are 9 other scene candidates at each node. 3 iterations of Bayesian belief propagation yields a probable guess for the high resolution scene, consistent with the observed low resolution data, and spatially consistent across scene nodes.

(a) 85 x 51 input   (b) cubic spline   (c) belief propagation

Figure 5: (a) 85 x 51 resolution input. (b) cubic spline interpolation in Adobe Photoshop to 340x204. (c) belief propagation zoom to 340x204, zooming up one octave twice.

the training data. To find the best scene explanation given new image data, we apply belief propagation in the Markov network, an approach supported by experimental and theoretical studies.

The intuitions of this paper–propagate local estimates to find a best, global solution–have a long tradition in computational vision [1, 33, 15, 31]. The power of the VISTA approach lies in the large training database, allowing rich prior probabilities and rendering models, and the belief propagation, allowing efficient scene inference.

Applied to super-resolution, VISTA gives results that we believe are the state of the art. Applied to motion estimation, the same method resolves the aperture problem and appropriately fills-in motion over a figure. The technique may apply to related vision problems as well, such as line drawing interpretation, or distinguishing shading from reflectance.

Acknowledgements We thank Y. Weiss, E. Adelson, A. Blake, J. Tenenbaum, and P. Viola for helpful discussions. Thanks to O. Carmichael and J. Haddon for verifying the method of overlapping patches for computing compatibility functions.

References

[1] H. G. Barrow and J. M. Tenenbaum. Computational vision. *Proc. IEEE*, 69(5):572–595, 1981.

[2] A. J. Bell and T. J. Senjowski. The independent components of natural scenes are edge filters. *Vision Research*, 37(23):3327–3338, 1997.

[3] J. O. Berger. *Statistical decision theory and Bayesian analysis.* Springer, 1985.

[4] J. Besag. Spatial interaction and the statistical analysis of lattice systems (with discussion). *J. Royal Statist. Soc. B*, 36:192–326, 1974.

[5] T. Binford, T. Levitt, and W. Mann. Bayesian infernce inmodel-based machine vision. In J. F. Lemmer and L. M. Kanal, editors, *Uncertainty in artificial intelligence.* Elsevier Science, 1988.

[6] C. M. Bishop. *Neural networks for pattern recognition.* Oxford, 1995.

[7] P. J. Burt and E. H. Adelson. The Laplacian pyramid as a compact image code. *IEEE Trans. Comm.*, 31(4):532–540, 1983.

[8] J. S. DeBonet and P. Viola. Texture recognition using a non-parametric multi-scale statistical model. In *Proc. IEEE Computer Vision and Pattern Recognition*, 1998.

[9] W. T. Freeman and E. Pasztor. Markov networks for low-level vision. Technical report, MERL, a Mitsubishi Electric Research Lab., 1999. http://www.merl.com/reports/TR99-08/.

[10] W. T. Freeman and E. C. Pasztor. Learning to estimate scenes from images. In M. S. Kearns, S. A. Solla, and D. A. Cohn, editors, *Adv. Neural Information Processing Systems*, volume 11, Cambridge, MA, 1999. MIT Press. See also http://www.merl.com/reports/TR99-05/.

[11] B. J. Frey. *Graphical Models for Machine Learning and Digital Communication.* MIT Press, 1998.

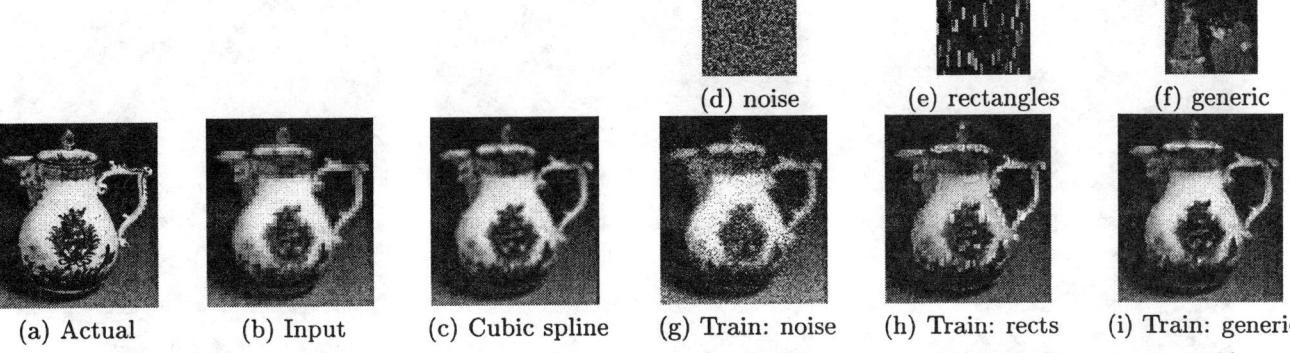

(d) noise   (e) rectangles   (f) generic

(a) Actual   (b) Input   (c) Cubic spline   (g) Train: noise   (h) Train: rects   (i) Train: generic

Figure 6: Effect of different training sets. (a) was blurred, and subsampled by 4 in each dimension to yield the low-resolution input, (b). Cubic spline interpolation to full resolution in Adobe Photoshop loses the sharp edges, (c). We recursively zoomed (b) up two factors of two using the Markov network trained on 10 images from 3 different "worlds": (d) random noise, (e) colored rectangles, and (f) a generic collection of photographs. The estimated high resolution images, (g), (h), and (i), respectively, reflect the statistics of each training world.

images from "picnic" training set   images from "generic" training set

Figure 7: Sample images from the 10 images in the "picnic" and "generic" training sets. Sharp and blurred versions of these images were used to create the training data for Fig. 8d and e.

[12] D. Geiger and F. Girosi. Parallel and deterministic algorithms from MRF's: surface reconstruction. *IEEE Pattern Analysis and Machine Intelligence*, 13(5):401–412, May 1991.

[13] S. Geman and D. Geman. Stochastic relaxation, Gibbs distribution, and the Bayesian restoration of images. *IEEE Pattern Analysis and Machine Intelligence*, 6:721–741, 1984.

[14] D. J. Heeger and J. R. Bergen. Pyramid-based texture analysis/synthesis. In *ACM SIGGRAPH*, pages 229–236, 1995. In *Computer Graphics* Proceedings, Annual Conference Series.

[15] B. K. P. Horn. *Robot vision*. MIT Press, 1986.

[16] A. C. Hurlbert and T. A. Poggio. Synthesizing a color algorithm from examples. *Science*, 239:482–485, 1988.

[17] M. Isard and A. Blake. Contour tracking by stochastic propagation of conditional density. In *Proc. European Conf. on Computer Vision*, pages 343–356, 1996.

[18] T. Jaakola. Machine learning seminar notes, 1999. http://www.ai.mit.edu/people/tommi/class/ud-est.ps.

[19] B. Jahne. *Digital Image Processing*. Springer-Verlag, 1991.

[20] M. I. Jordan, editor. *Learning in graphical models*. MIT Press, 1998.

[21] D. Kersten, A. J. O'Toole, M. E. Sereno, D. C. Knill, and J. A. Anderson. Associative learning of scene parameters from images. *Applied Optics*, 26(23):4999–5006, 1987.

[22] J. Kittler and J. Illingworth. Relaxation labelling algorithms–a review. *Image and Vision Computing*, (11):206–216, 1985.

[23] D. Knill and W. Richards, editors. *Perception as Bayesian inference*. Cambridge Univ. Press, 1996.

[24] F. R. Kschischang and B. J. Frey. Iterative decoding of compound codes by probability propagation in graphical models. *IEEE Journal on Selected Areas in Communication*, 16(2):219–230, 1998.

[25] M. S. Landy and J. A. Movshon, editors. *Computational Models of Visual Processing*. MIT Press, Cambridge, MA, 1991.

[26] M. R. Luettgen, W. C. Karl, and A. S. Willsky. Efficient multiscale regularization with applications to the computation of optical flow. *IEEE Trans. Image Processing*, 3(1):41–64, 1994.

[27] R. McEliece, D. MackKay, and J. Cheng. Turbo decoding as as an instance of Pearl's 'belief propagation' algorithm. *IEEE Journal on Selected Areas in Communication*, 16(2):140–152, 1998.

[28] B. A. Olshausen and D. J. Field. Emergence of simple-cell receptive field properties by learning a

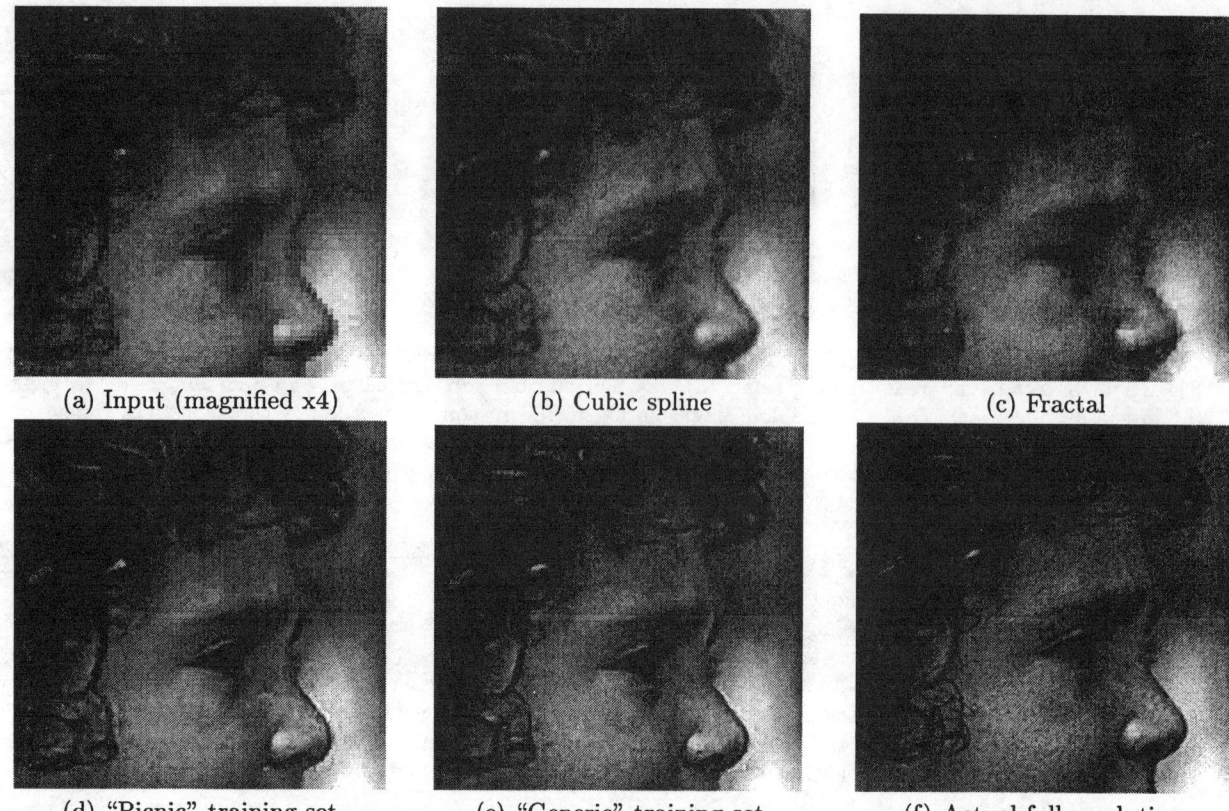

(a) Input (magnified x4)	(b) Cubic spline	(c) Fractal
(d) "Picnic" training set	(e) "Generic" training set	(f) Actual full-resolution

Figure 8: (a) Low-resolution input image. (b) Cubic spline 400% zoom in Adobe Photoshop. (c) Zooming luminance by public domain fractal image compression routine [32], set for maximum image fidelity (chrominance components were zoomed by cubic spline, to avoid color artifacts). Both (c) and (d) are blurry, or have serious artifacts. (d) Markov network reconstruction using a training set of 10 images taken at the same picnic, none of this person. This is the best possible fair training set for this image. (e) Markov network reconstruction using a training set of *generic* photographs, none at this picnic or of this person, and fewer than 50% of people. The two Markov network results show good synthesis of hair and eye details, with few artifacts, but (d) looks slightly better (see brow furrow). Edges and textures seem sharp and plausible. (f) is the true full-resolution image.

sparse code for natural images. *Nature*, 381:607–609, 1996.

[29] J. Pearl. *Probabilistic reasoning in intelligent systems: networks of plausible inference*. Morgan Kaufmann, 1988.

[30] A. Pentland and B. Horowitz. A practical approach to fractal-based image compression. In A. B. Watson, editor, *Digital images and human vision*. MIT Press, 1993.

[31] T. Poggio, V. Torre, and C. Koch. Computational vision and regularization theory. *Nature*, 317(26):314–139, 1985.

[32] M. Polvere. Mars v. 1.0, a quadtree based fractal image coder/decoder, 1998. http://inls.ucsd.edu/y/Fractals/.

[33] A. Rosenfeld, R. A. Hummel, and S. W. Zucker. Scene labeling by relaxation operations. *IEEE Trans. Systems, Man, Cybern.*, 6(6):420–433, 1976.

[34] E. Saund. Perceptual organization of occluding contours generated by opaque surfaces. In *Proc. IEEE Computer Society Conf. on Computer Vision and Pattern Recognition*, Ft. Collins, CO, 1999.

[35] R. R. Schultz and R. L. Stevenson. A Bayesian approach to image expansion for improved definition. *IEEE Trans. Image Processing*, 3(3):233–242, 1994.

[36] E. P. Simoncelli. Statistical models for images: Compression, restoration and synthesis. In *31st Asilomar Conf. on Sig., Sys. and Computers*, Pacific Grove, CA, 1997.

[37] R. Szeliski. *Bayesian Modeling of Uncertainty in Low-level Vision*. Kluwer Academic Publishers, Boston, 1989.

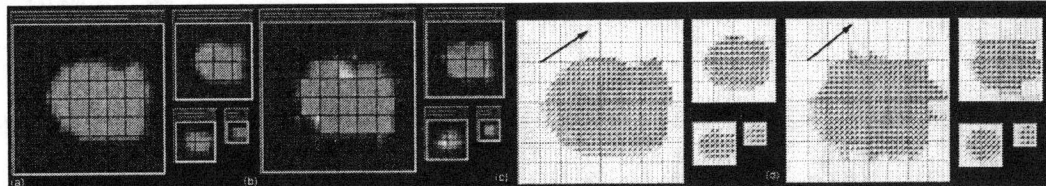

Figure 9: (a) First of two frames of image data (in Gaussian pyramid), and (b) vector quantized. (c) The optical flow scene information, and (d) vector quantized. Large arrow added to show small vectors' orientation.

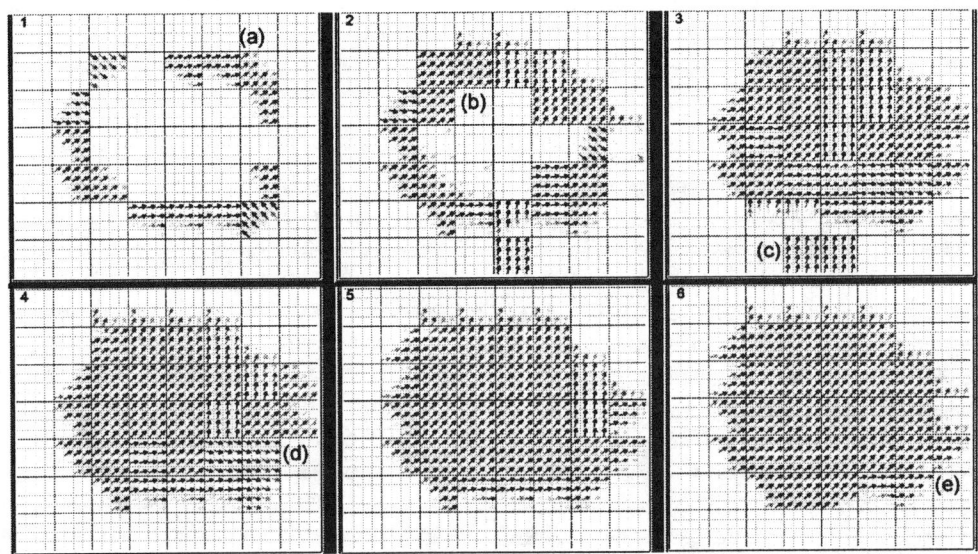

Figure 10: The most probable scene code for Fig. 9b at first 6 iterations of Bayesian belief propagation. (a) Note initial motion estimates occur only at edges. Due to the "aperture problem", initial estimates do not agree. (b) Filling-in of motion estimate occurs. Cues for figure/ground determination may include edge curvature, and information from lower resolution levels. Both are included implicitly in the learned probabilities. (c) Figure/ground still undetermined in this region of low edge curvature. (d) Velocities have filled-in, but do not yet all agree. (e) Velocities have filled-in, and agree with each other and with the correct velocity direction, shown in Fig. 9.

[38] Y. Weiss. Interpreting images by propagating Bayesian beliefs. In *Adv. in Neural Information Processing Systems*, volume 9, pages 908–915, 1997.

[39] Y. Weiss. Belief propagation and revision in networks with loops. Technical Report 1616, AI Lab Memo, MIT, Cambridge, MA 02139, 1998.

[40] Y. Weiss and W. T. Freeman. Correctness of belief propagation in Gaussian graphical models of arbitrary topology. Technical Report UCB.CSD-99-1046, Berkeley Computer Science Dept., 1999. www.cs.berkeley.edu/~yweiss/gaussTR.ps.gz.

[41] S. C. Zhu and D. Mumford. Prior learning and Gibbs reaction-diffusion. *IEEE Pattern Analysis and Machine Intelligence*, 19(11), 1997.

Transformed Component Analysis:
Joint Estimation of Spatial Transformations and Image Components

Brendan J. Frey
Computer Science, University of Waterloo
Beckman Institute, University of Illinois

Nebojsa Jojic
Beckman Institute, University of Illinois
at Urbana-Champaign

Software available at www.cs.uwaterloo.ca/~frey

Abstract

A simple, effective way to model images is to represent each input pattern by a linear combination of "component" vectors, where the amplitudes of the vectors are modulated to match the input. This approach includes principal component analysis, independent component analysis and factor analysis. In practice, images are subjected to randomly selected transformations of a known nature, such as translation and rotation. Direct use of the above methods will lead to severely blurred components that tend to ignore the more interesting and useful structure. In previous work, we introduced a clustering algorithm that is invariant to transformations [1]. In this paper, we propose a method called *transformed component analysis*, which incorporates a discrete, hidden variable that accounts for transformations and uses the expectation maximization algorithm to jointly extract components and normalize for transformations. We illustrate the algorithm using a shading problem, facial expression modeling and written digit recognition.

1 Introduction

Many popular ways of modeling images use a linear combination of vectors to represent each input. Principal components analysis (PCA, a.k.a. "eigen-*whatever*") is a way of representing a class of images using a small set of component vectors in the vector space of image pixel intensities [2]. An image can be described by a linear combination of these components plus some distortion. The first principal component is the direction in which the projected training data has greatest variance, the second principal component is the direction of greatest variance *after* the first component is subtracted off, and so on.

A different technique that is gaining in popularity is independent component analysis (ICA), which tries to find components such that when the training data is projected on these components, the component activities are independent (not just uncorrelated) [3]. ICA has been used for blind separation and deconvolution.

Factor analysis (FA) [4] is a generative model that is similar in spirit to PCA. A *generative model* is trained to generate patterns that look similar to the training data and the representation of an input is the posterior distribution over some hidden variables. In a FA model, the distribution over a small set of real-valued hidden variables is a zero-mean unit-covariance Gaussian and the distribution over the inputs given the hidden variables is also Gaussian, with a diagonal covariance matrix and a mean given by a linear combination of the hidden variables. A factor analyzer can be fit to training data using the EM algorithm [5].

In practice, data is often subjected to randomly selected transformations of a known nature, such as translation and rotation in images. In these cases, direct application of the above methods will produce severely blurred components that mostly account for the transformations and ignore the more interesting and useful structure.

We propose a method called *transformed component analysis*, which incorporates a discrete, hidden variable that accounts for transformations and uses the expectation maximization algorithm to jointly extract components and normalize for transformations. After illustrating the algorithm using a toy problem and facial expression modeling, we give results on classifying images of written digits and compare the components found by transformed component analysis with the components found by PCA and FA.

2 The Transformed Component Analyzer (TCA)

A transformed component analyzer (TCA) is a probability model that specifies how the linear combination of a set of component vectors is transformed in different ways to model input patterns. The component activities (amplitudes) $\mathbf{y}$, which form a subspace representation of an image, are assumed to be independent and Gaussian:

$$p(\mathbf{y}) = \mathcal{N}(\mathbf{y}; \mathbf{0}, \mathbf{I}), \tag{1}$$

where $\mathbf{I}$ is the identity covariance matrix. A latent image $\mathbf{z}$ is produced by combining these components linearly using a "factor loading matrix" $\mathbf{\Lambda}$, offsetting the resulting image by an image mean $\boldsymbol{\mu}$ and then adding independent Gaussian noise to each pixel:

$$p(\mathbf{z}|\mathbf{y}) = \mathcal{N}(\mathbf{z}; \boldsymbol{\mu} + \mathbf{\Lambda}\mathbf{y}, \boldsymbol{\Phi}), \qquad (2)$$

where $\boldsymbol{\Phi}$ is a diagonal covariance matrix.

We assume the image produced by the subspace model is further transformed to obtain the observed image. Although real-valued transformations (*e.g.*, rotation) are common, real-valued latent variables introduce complicated integrals (instead of summations) into the EM learning algorithm. So, we will assume there is a fixed set of possible transformations and that this set is specified beforehand. Also, the algorithm is simplified by assuming that the vector of pixel values for the transformed image is obtained by multiplying the vector of pixel values for the latent image by a *sparse* matrix. This permits a broad class of transformations, including translation, scale, in-plane rotation and out-of-plane rotation.

Let $\ell \in \{1, \dots, L\}$ index the set of L transformations represented by matrices $\mathbf{G_1}, \dots, \mathbf{G_L}$. The probability density of the vector of pixel values $\mathbf{x}$ for the image corresponding to transformation ℓ and latent image $\mathbf{z}$ is

$$p(\mathbf{x}|\ell, \mathbf{z}) = \mathcal{N}(\mathbf{x}; \mathbf{G}_\ell \mathbf{z}, \boldsymbol{\Psi}), \qquad (3)$$

where $\boldsymbol{\Psi}$ is a diagonal covariance matrix that specifies the noise on the observed pixels.

The variances $\boldsymbol{\Phi}$ of the pixels in the latent image are quite different from the variances $\boldsymbol{\Psi}$ of the pixels in the observed image. The noise modeled by $\boldsymbol{\Phi}$ coheres to the latent image during transformations. In contrast, $\boldsymbol{\Psi}$ models noise in the observed pixels and this noise does not depend on the transformation.

The translation, scale, rotation, *etc.* corresponding to each ℓ are selected ahead of time so that the set of transformations effectively covers the range of possible transformations in the data and at the same time is small enough to keep the learning time reasonable. Transformation ℓ has a prior probability $P(\ell) = p_\ell$, which may be fixed to be uniform or learned from the training data.

The joint distribution over the observed image, the transformation index, the latent image and the subspace representation is

$$p(\mathbf{x}, \ell, \mathbf{z}, \mathbf{y}) = p(\mathbf{y})P(\ell)p(\mathbf{z}|\mathbf{y})p(\mathbf{x}|\ell, \mathbf{z})$$
$$= p_\ell \mathcal{N}(\mathbf{y}; \mathbf{0}, \mathbf{I})\mathcal{N}(\mathbf{z}; \boldsymbol{\mu} + \mathbf{\Lambda}\mathbf{y}, \boldsymbol{\Phi})\mathcal{N}(\mathbf{x}; \mathbf{G}_\ell \mathbf{z}, \boldsymbol{\Psi}). \quad (4)$$

In this generative model, the subspace representation, transformation index and latent image are unobserved variables. Generating an image from a TCA consists of drawing a subspace representation from $p(\mathbf{y})$, drawing a latent image from $p(\mathbf{z}|\mathbf{y})$, drawing a transformation index from $P(\ell)$ and then drawing an image from $p(\mathbf{x}|\ell, \mathbf{z})$.

The number of parameters in a TCA is roughly equal to the number of parameters in a standard factor analyzer and the number of "parameters" used in PCA. In Sec. 3, we show how the ML estimate of this model can be obtained using the EM algorithm.

2.1 Inferring the likelihood for an image and the responsibilities of the transformations

For a given image, it is useful to know how appropriate each transformation is for matching the image to the transformed components (the "responsibility" of the transformation) and overall how well the components match the image (the likelihood).

The responsibilities are the posterior probabilities of the transformation indices,

$$P(\ell|\mathbf{x}) = p(\mathbf{x}, \ell)/p(\mathbf{x}), \;\; p(\mathbf{x}) = \sum_{\ell=1}^{L} p(\mathbf{x}, \ell), \qquad (5)$$

where $p(\mathbf{x})$ is the likelihood. Both the responsibilities and the likelihood can be easily computed from $p(\mathbf{x}, \ell)$.

To obtain $p(\mathbf{x}, \ell)$, we integrate out the component activities $\mathbf{y}$ and the latent image $\mathbf{z}$:

$$p(\mathbf{x}, \ell) = \int_{\mathbf{z}} \int_{\mathbf{y}} d\mathbf{z}d\mathbf{y}p(\mathbf{x}, \ell, \mathbf{z}, \mathbf{y})$$
$$= p_\ell \mathcal{N}(\mathbf{x}; \mathbf{G}_\ell \boldsymbol{\mu}, \mathbf{G}_\ell (\mathbf{\Lambda}\mathbf{\Lambda}' + \boldsymbol{\Phi})\mathbf{G}_\ell' + \boldsymbol{\Psi}), \quad (6)$$

where " $\prime$ " indicates transpose. Each transformation ℓ has a corresponding mean image $\mathbf{G}_\ell \boldsymbol{\mu}$ and covariance matrix $\mathbf{G}_\ell (\mathbf{\Lambda}\mathbf{\Lambda}' + \boldsymbol{\Phi})\mathbf{G}_\ell' + \boldsymbol{\Psi}$.

For an N-pixel image, K components and L transformations, the responsibilities and the likelihood for an image can be computed in $\mathcal{O}(LKN)$ time, if we assume $|\mathbf{G}_\ell (\mathbf{\Lambda}\mathbf{\Lambda}' + \boldsymbol{\Phi})\mathbf{G}_\ell' + \boldsymbol{\Psi}| \approx |\mathbf{G}_\ell (\mathbf{\Lambda}\mathbf{\Lambda}' + \boldsymbol{\Phi})\mathbf{G}_\ell'|$. This corresponds to assuming the image noise is significantly lesser than the variability introduced by the transformed components (*i.e.*, the image structure).

2.2 Inferring the subspace representation

For a given image $\mathbf{x}$, the posterior distribution over the component activities is given by

$$p(\mathbf{y}|\mathbf{x}) = \sum_{\ell=1}^{L} p(\mathbf{y}|\mathbf{x}, \ell)P(\ell|\mathbf{x}), \qquad (7)$$

where $P(\ell|\mathbf{x})$ is the responsibility of transformation ℓ from above. Given ℓ, the TCA is a multinomial Gaussian model, so $p(\mathbf{y}|\mathbf{x},\ell)$ is Gaussian and the above posterior is a mixture of Gaussians, where each Gaussian corresponds to a different transformation.

In contrast with the single point representation obtained from PCA and ICA, TCA gives a set of weighted points. The weight for point ℓ is $P(\ell|\mathbf{x})$ and the corresponding estimate is

$$\mathrm{E}[\mathbf{y}|\mathbf{x},\ell]=\beta_\ell\Lambda'\Phi^{-1}[\Omega_\ell\mathbf{G}'_\ell\Psi^{-1}\mathbf{x}-(\mathbf{I}-\Omega_\ell\Phi^{-1})\mu], \quad (8)$$

where

$$\Omega_\ell = \mathrm{COV}(\mathbf{z}|\mathbf{x},\mathbf{y},\ell) = (\Phi_c^{-1} + \mathbf{G}'_\ell\Psi^{-1}\mathbf{G}_\ell)^{-1},$$
$$\beta_\ell = (\mathbf{I} + \Lambda'\Phi^{-1}\Lambda - \Lambda'\Phi^{-1}\Omega_\ell\Phi^{-1}\Lambda)^{-1}. \quad (9)$$

To compare the subspace representations of two images, the two corresponding sets of weighted points can be compared. Alternatively, the MAP point (the point with the highest weight) can be selected for each image and a Euclidean distortion can be measured.

3 Transformed Component Analysis using the EM Algorithm

In this section, we describe an iterative expectation maximization (EM) algorithm [5] for estimating the maximum likelihood parameters of a transformed component analyzer. We refer to this procedure as transformed component analysis (TCA). The EM algorithm consists of an E-step, which accumulates statistics that are sufficient for estimating the model parameters, and an M-step, which updates the model parameters using the sufficient statistics. Each iteration increases the likelihood of the training data.

Notation: $\mathrm{diag}(\mathbf{A})$ is the vector containing the diagonal elements of matrix $\mathbf{A}$; $\mathrm{diag}(\mathbf{a})$ is the diagonal matrix whose diagonal equals the vector $\mathbf{a}$; $\mathbf{a} \circ \mathbf{b}$ is the element-wise product of vectors $\mathbf{a}$ and $\mathbf{b}$.

3.1 Expectation step

The sufficient statistics for the M-Step are computed in the E-Step during a single pass through the training set. Before making this pass, the following matrices are computed:

$$\Omega_\ell = \mathrm{COV}(\mathbf{z}|\mathbf{x},\mathbf{y},\ell) = (\Phi_c^{-1} + \mathbf{G}'_\ell\Psi^{-1}\mathbf{G}_\ell)^{-1},$$
$$\beta_\ell = (\mathbf{I} + \Lambda'\Phi^{-1}\Lambda - \Lambda'\Phi^{-1}\Omega_\ell\Phi^{-1}\Lambda)^{-1}. \quad (10)$$

For each case during the pass through the training set, $P(\ell|\mathbf{x}_t)$, $\mathrm{E}[\mathbf{y}|\mathbf{x}_t,\ell]$ and $\mathrm{E}[\mathbf{y}|\mathbf{x}_t] = \sum_\ell P(\ell|\mathbf{x}_t)\mathrm{E}[\mathbf{y}|\mathbf{x}_t,\ell]$ are first computed as described in Sec. 2.1.

For each ℓ, we then compute

$$\mathrm{E}[\mathbf{z}|\mathbf{x}_t,\ell]=\mu + \Omega_\ell\mathbf{G}'_\ell\Psi^{-1}(\mathbf{x_t} - \mathbf{G}_\ell\mu)$$
$$+\Omega_\ell\Phi^{-1}\Lambda\beta_\ell\Lambda'\Phi^{-1}\Omega_\ell\mathbf{G}'_\ell\Psi^{-1}(\mathbf{x_t} - \mathbf{G}_\ell\mu) \quad (11)$$

and obtain the following expectation:

$$\mathrm{E}[\mathbf{z}-\Lambda\mathbf{y}|\mathbf{x}_t]=\sum_{\ell=1}^{L} P(\ell|\mathbf{x}_t)(\mathrm{E}[\mathbf{z}|\mathbf{x}_t,\ell]-\Lambda\mathrm{E}[\mathbf{y}|\mathbf{x}_t,\ell]). \quad (12)$$

Two other expectations,

$$\mathrm{E}[(\mathbf{z}-\mu)\circ(\mathbf{z}-\mu)|\mathbf{x}_t,\ell]$$
$$= (\mathrm{E}[\mathbf{z}|\mathbf{x}_t,\ell]-\mu)\circ(\mathrm{E}[\mathbf{z}|\mathbf{x}_t,\ell]-\mu)$$
$$+ \mathrm{diag}(\Omega_\ell) + \mathrm{diag}(\Omega_\ell\Phi^{-1}\Lambda\beta_\ell\Lambda'\Phi^{-1}\Omega_\ell), \quad (13)$$

and

$$\mathrm{E}[(\mathbf{z}-\mu)\mathbf{y}'|\mathbf{x}_t,\ell]$$
$$= (\mathrm{E}[\mathbf{z}|\mathbf{x}_t,\ell] - \mu)\mathrm{E}[\mathbf{y}|\mathbf{x}_t,\ell]' + \Omega_\ell\Phi^{-1}\Lambda\beta_\ell, \quad (14)$$

are used to compute the expectation,

$$\mathrm{E}[(\mathbf{z}-\mu-\Lambda\mathbf{y})\circ(\mathbf{z}-\mu-\Lambda\mathbf{y})|\mathbf{x}_t] = \sum_{\ell=1}^{L} P(\ell|\mathbf{x}_t)$$
$$\cdot \{\mathrm{E}[(\mathbf{z}-\mu)\circ(\mathbf{z}-\mu)|\mathbf{x}_t,\ell] + \mathrm{diag}(\Lambda\beta_\ell\Lambda')$$
$$- 2\mathrm{diag}(\Lambda\mathrm{E}[(\mathbf{z}-\mu)\mathbf{y}'|\mathbf{x}_t,\ell]')$$
$$+ (\Lambda\mathrm{E}[\mathbf{y}|\mathbf{x}_t,\ell])\circ(\Lambda\mathrm{E}[\mathbf{y}|\mathbf{x}_t,\ell])\}. \quad (15)$$

The following expectations are also computed:

$$\mathrm{E}[(\mathbf{x_t}-\mathbf{G}_\ell\mathbf{z})\circ(\mathbf{x_t}-\mathbf{G}_\ell\mathbf{z})|\mathbf{x_t}] = \sum_{\ell=1}^{L} \mathbf{P}(\ell|\mathbf{x_t})$$
$$\cdot \{(\mathbf{x_t}-\mathbf{G}_\ell\mathrm{E}[\mathbf{z}|\mathbf{x_t},\ell])\circ(\mathbf{x_t}-\mathbf{G}_\ell\mathrm{E}[\mathbf{z}|\mathbf{x_t},\ell])$$
$$+ \mathrm{diag}(\mathbf{G}_\ell\Omega_\ell\mathbf{G}'_\ell)$$
$$+ \mathrm{diag}(\mathbf{G}_\ell\Omega_\ell\Phi^{-1}\Lambda\beta_\ell\Lambda'\Phi^{-1}\Omega_\ell\mathbf{G}'_\ell)\}, \quad (16)$$

$$\mathrm{E}[(\mathbf{z}-\mu)\mathbf{y}'|\mathbf{x}_t] = \sum_{\ell=1}^{L} P(\ell|\mathbf{x}_t)\mathrm{E}[(\mathbf{z}-\mu)\mathbf{y}'|\mathbf{x}_t,\ell], \quad (17)$$

$$\mathrm{E}[\mathbf{y}\mathbf{y}'|\mathbf{x}_t] = \sum_{\ell=1}^{L} P(\ell|\mathbf{x}_t)(\beta_\ell + \mathrm{E}[\mathbf{y}|\mathbf{x}_t,\ell]\mathrm{E}[\mathbf{y}|\mathbf{x}_t,\ell]'). \quad (18)$$

3.2 Maximization step

We use $\langle\cdot\rangle = \frac{1}{T}\sum_{t=1}^{T}(\cdot)$ to indicate a statistic computed by averaging the above expectations over the training set and "~" to denote the updated parameters:

$$\tilde{\mu} = \langle\mathrm{E}[\mathbf{z} - \Lambda\mathbf{y}|\mathbf{x}_t]\rangle, \quad (19)$$
$$\tilde{\Phi} = \mathrm{diag}(\langle\mathrm{E}[(\mathbf{z}-\mu-\Lambda\mathbf{y})\circ(\mathbf{z}-\mu-\Lambda\mathbf{y})|\mathbf{x}_t]\rangle), \quad (20)$$
$$\tilde{\Psi} = \mathrm{diag}(\langle\mathrm{E}[(\mathbf{x_t}-\mathbf{G}_\ell\mathbf{z})\circ(\mathbf{x_t}-\mathbf{G}_\ell\mathbf{z})|\mathbf{x}_t]\rangle), \quad (21)$$
$$\tilde{\Lambda} = \langle\mathrm{E}[(\mathbf{z} - \mu)\mathbf{y}'|\mathbf{x}_t]\rangle\langle\mathrm{E}[\mathbf{y}\mathbf{y}'|\mathbf{x}_t]\rangle^{-1}, \quad (22)$$
$$\tilde{p}_l = \langle P(\ell=l|\mathbf{x}_t)\rangle. \quad (23)$$

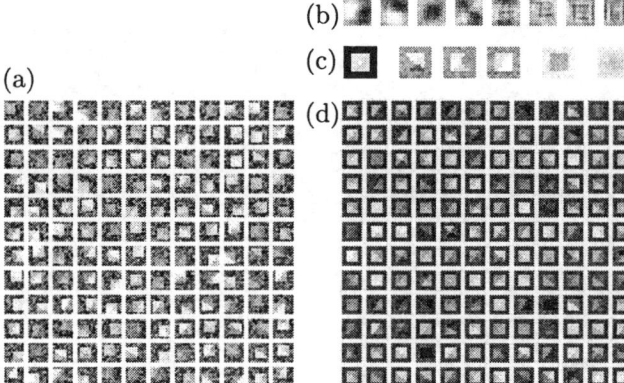

(a)

(b)

(c)

(d)

Figure 1: (a) Noisy images of a pyramid at different locations and under different lighting conditions. (b) The first 8 scaled principal components. (c) The mean, components, and noise deviation of a TCA with 3 components, after 10 iterations of EM. (d) Examples simulated from the TCA, without noise and without transformations.

In order to avoid overfitting the noise variances, it is sometimes useful to set the diagonal elements of Φ and Ψ that are below some ϵ equal to ϵ.

4 Learning shape and lighting representations from noisy unaligned images of an object

Fig. 1a shows a training set of 144 9×9 noisy images of a uniformly colored pyramid (gray) at randomly selected positions and illuminated by parallel light rays with randomly selected angle and intensity. A cluttered background was simulated by randomly selecting pixel values from a uniform distribution.

The first 8 principal components of the training data, scaled by the standard deviation of the projected data, are shown in Fig. 1b. It appears the components implement a multiresolution approximation to model shifts of the object.

We trained a TCA with 3 components and 81 transformations implementing 9 horizontal and 9 vertical shifts using 10 iterations of the EM algorithm. To initialize the parameters, the mean and variance of each pixel was first computed from the training data. The parameters were then initialized to random values, using the mean and variance as a 1st order guide. The transformation probabilities p_ℓ were set equal.

Fig. 1c shows the mean latent image μ, the 3 columns of Λ (shown as 3 images), the latent image noise Φ (shown as an image where the pixel intensity is equal to 4 times the standard deviation) and the observed image noise Ψ. The mean clearly shows

Figure 2: Imperfectly aligned images of faces with different expressions.

that the outline of the object has been determined and that the uniform coloring has been determined (except at the point of the pyramid). Linear combinations of the 3 components produce different lighting conditions (see the following paragraph) which implies that the 3-element *rows* of Λ are proportional to the object surface normals, up to some rotation in 3-dimensional space. The variance map for the latent image shows that the model predicts low variance for pixels belonging to the object, but high variance for other pixels (the background clutter). Finally, the variance map for the observed image accounts for the small amount of noise that is present in the images.

The TCA can be simulated in a noise-free transformation-free fashion, by drawing a subspace representation from $p(\mathbf{y})$, computing $\mathbf{z} = \mu + \Lambda\mathbf{y}$ and then computing $\mathbf{x} = \mathbf{G}_1\mathbf{z}$. Fig. 1d shows 144 examples simulated in this way. These "fantasies" show that the TCA can simulate the different lighting conditions.

5 Learning a subspace representation of facial expressions from imperfectly aligned images

Fig. 2 shows a training set of 100 16×24 images of automatically aligned faces with different expressions. The accuracy of the face detection algorithm used to align the images is +/-2 pixels in each direction.

(a)

(b)

(c)

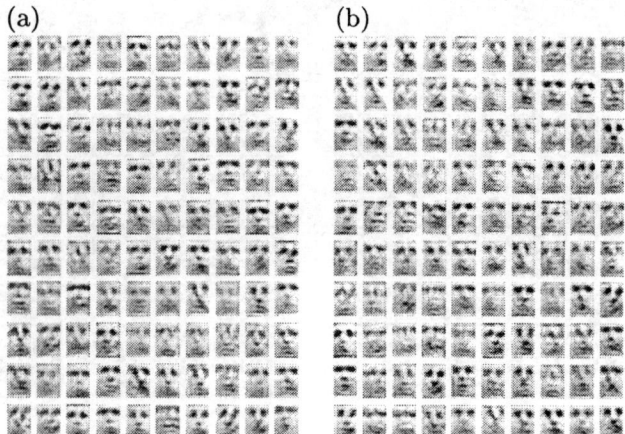

(a)   (b)

Figure 3: (a) The mean and first 10 scaled principal components of the face data. (b) The mean, 10 components and noise deviations found by FA (TCA with only the identity transformation). (c) The mean, 10 components and noise deviations found by TCA.

Fig. 3a shows the mean of the training data and the first 10 principal components, scaled by the standard deviation of the projected data. The first 5 components obviously account for vertical, horizontal and diagonal shifts in the data and the remaining components are very blurred.

Fig. 3b shows the parameters for a FA model (a TCA with only the identity transformation) trained using 70 iterations of EM. The parameters were initialized using the mean and variance of each pixel in the training data. The sum of the two images on the far right of Fig. 3b gives the variance map for FA. In contrast to PCA, different components represent similar amounts of energy (variance). This is because FA does not find a preferred set of basis vectors (factors) for the subspace. Like PCA, FA finds very blurred components.

We trained a TCA with 10 components and 25 transformations implementing 5 horizontal and 5 vertical shifts using 70 iterations of the EM algorithm. The parameters were initialized using the mean and variance of each pixel in the training data. The transformation probabilities p_ℓ were set equal.

Fig. 3c shows the mean, components and variance maps. Unlike PCA and FA, TCA extracts clear components. The first component appears to expose some teeth, the second component appears to raise the eyebrows, raise the upper lip and expose a "tongue", and so on. The components found by TCA are unique up to a unitary transformation, so each component often includes more than one feature. A further processing step can be applied to find a unitary transformation that produces components with spatially localized energy.

To see how well the PCA subspace represents the data, we can draw a subspace point from an axis-aligned Gaussian with variances determined from the projected training data, and then use the principal components to map the point to image space. 100 ex-

Figure 4: Examples of the face data simulated using (a) the PCA subspace and (b) the factor analyzer.

Figure 5: Examples of the face data simulated using the TCA model.

amples simulated in this manner are shown in Fig. 4a. Although the "faces" do appear to be shifted around the field of vision, they are also severely blurred. Fig. 4b shows examples simulated using the FA model, without adding sensor noise. They appear similar to the examples simulated using the PCA model.

Fig. 5 shows 100 examples of images simulated using the TCA, without the latent image and observed image noise and without randomly selected transformations. The images are much clearer than those simulated using the PCA subspace and the factor analyzer. The expressions in the training set are reproduced and the model also generates novel realistic expressions that are not present in the training set, such

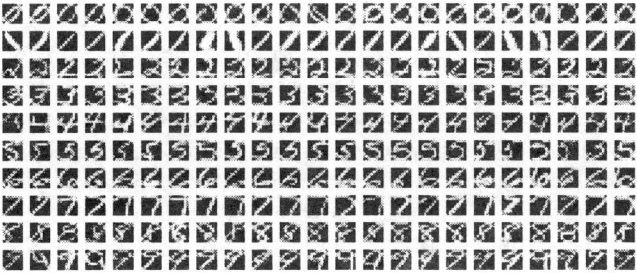

Figure 6: Example images from the training set of handwritten digits show a wide variety in writing style.

(a)

(b)

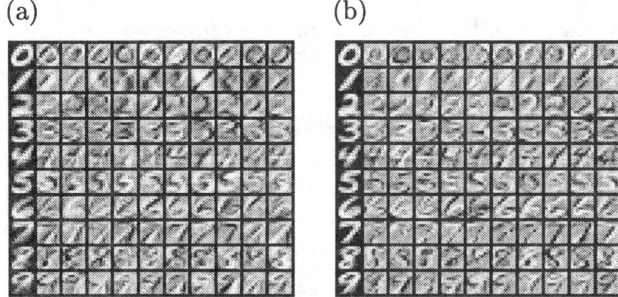

Figure 7: The means and components learned by (a) FA and (b) TCA applied to 200 images of each handwritten digit. Pixels for the means are colored using the same scale as the training images; pixels for the components are colored using intermediate gray to represent 0.

as the one in the 5th column of the 1st row and the one in the 1st column of the 3rd row.

6 Using shear transformations to improve handwritten digit recognition

Fig. 6 shows 230 images of handwritten digits taken from envelopes mailed by people in Buffalo [6]. A wide variety of handwriting styles are evident. The original images were affinely transformed to fit snugly in an 8 × 8 gray level image. Although this preprocessing helps to normalize for uniform scaling in the horizontal and vertical directions, it does not normalize for local scaling (*e.g.*, some 8s have smaller loops than others) or for shearing (*e.g.*, the vertical stroke of the 7 is at different angles).

For each class of digit, we trained a 10 component factor analyzer on 200 images using 30 iterations of EM. The parameters of each factor analyzer were initialized using the mean and variance of each pixel in the respective class. Fig. 7a shows the means and components found by FA and Fig. 8a shows images

(a)

(b)

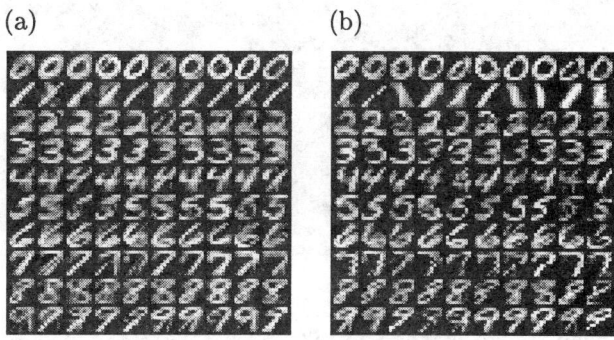

Figure 8: Images simulated from (a) the FA models and (b) the TCA models.

simulated from the trained models, without adding noise.

Some components account for interesting variability in writing style, but many clearly account for simple spatial transformations. For example, most of the components for 7 simply negate the vertical stroke in the image mean and produce a new vertical stroke at a different angle.

Shearing is a simple spatial transformation to model using a sparse matrix. Using 30 iterations of EM, we trained one TCA on each class of 200 digits using 29 transformations that included horizontal shearing plus horizontal translations. The first row of images in Fig. 9 shows how the 29 transformations modify a contrived pattern. Some transformations are quite severe and erase a large number of pixels, so in this experiment the transformation probabilities, p_ℓ, were learned. The parameters were initialized using the mean and variance of each pixel in the training set.

Fig. 7b shows the means and components found by TCA. The 2nd component for 7 models the accent on the nose of the 7; the 3rd component for 7 rounds out the angle in the upper right. These features are not clearly represented in the components found by FA. Fig. 8b shows digits simulated from the TCA models, without adding noise onto the latent image and the observed image. These images show a greater variation in style and fewer inappropriate artifacts than the images simulated from the FA model.

The 10 bottom rows of images in Fig. 9 show the means and corresponding sheared and translated images from the TCA models. Those transformed images whose average expected responsibilities were less than 0.01 in the training set are dimmed. A wide variation in writing style is captured by the transformations. For example, whereas FA uses components to model the different angles of vertical strokes in images of the

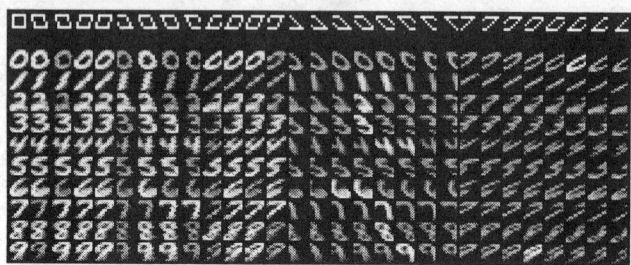

Figure 9: The sheared and translated versions of the mean image learned by TCA for each class of digit. The first row of images uses a contrived pattern to illustrate the 29 shearing and translation transformations that were used by TCA. Those versions whose average expected responsibilities were less than 0.01 in the training set are dimmed.

Table 1: Handwritten digit recognition rates, for a training set of 2000 8×8 images and a test set of 1000 images.

Method	Error rate
k-nearest neighbors	7.6%
Factor analysis	3.2%
Transformed component analysis	2.7%

digit 7, TCA models the different angles using the transformations. This allows TCA to use its components to model more subtle variations in writing style, such as the accent on the nose of the 7.

6.1 Improvement in recognition rate

We performed FA (20 components) and TCA (20 components) on 200 training cases from each class of handwritten digit using 50 iterations of EM. The noise variances were not allowed to drop below 10^{-2} to prevent overfitting a pixel that happens to always be off in the training data. Bayes rule was then used to classify 1000 test patterns. The results are summarized in Table 1 and compared with a standard feedforward method, k-nearest neighbors, where k was chosen using leave-one-out cross validation. TCA has a lower error rate than the other two methods.

The probability of each transformation p_ℓ in TCA was learned and we believe there was some overfitting. For example, some of the sheared image means in Fig. 9a that are faded (have average responsibilities less than 0.01) are good generalizations. We are currently running experiments that regularize p_ℓ and we are also running experiments to find the performance of support vector machines on this data.

7   Summary

We introduced a technique called "transformed component analysis" (TCA), that can jointly learn components from data and normalize for transformations. We explored transformations for translation and shearing, but the method can be applied to other transformations, such as rotation, scale and warping. When applied to noisy images of a uniformly colored pyramid at randomly selected positions and illuminated by parallel light rays with randomly selected angle and intensity, TCA is able to extract representations of shape and lighting, despite a significant level of background clutter. TCA also found a clear representation of facial expression from imperfectly aligned images, whereas PCA and factor analysis (FA) found severely blurred components. By including shearing transformations in the TCA model, we showed that handwritten digit recognition performance was improved over FA and that the images simulated from the TCA model contained greater variation in style and fewer inappropriate artifacts than the images simulated from FA.

Acknowledgements

We used grants from CITO (28838), NSERC (RGPIN-217657-99), NSF (IRI-9634618, CDA-9624396) and the Beckman Foundation.

References

[1] B. J. Frey and N. Jojic, "Estimating mixture models of images and inferring spatial transformations using the EM algorithm," in *Proceedings of the IEEE Conference on Computer Vision and Pattern Recognition*, June 1999, pp. 416–422.

[2] I. T. Jolliffe, *Principal Component Analysis*, Springer-Verlag, New York NY., 1986.

[3] A. J. Bell and T. J. Sejnowski, "An information maximization approach to blind separation and blind deconvolution," *Neural Computation*, vol. 7, pp. 1129–1159, 1995.

[4] B. S. Everitt, *An Introduction to Latent Variable Models*, Chapman and Hall, New York NY., 1984.

[5] D. Rubin and D. Thayer, "EM algorithms for ML factor analysis," *Psychometrika*, vol. 47, no. 1, pp. 69–76, 1982.

[6] J. J. Hull, "A database for handwritten text recognition research," *IEEE Transactions on Pattern Analysis and Machine Intelligence*, vol. 16, no. 5, pp. 550–554, 1994.

Mean Shift Analysis and Applications

Dorin Comaniciu   Peter Meer

Department of Electrical and Computer Engineering

Rutgers University, Piscataway, NJ 08854-8058, USA

{comanici, meer}@caip.rutgers.edu

Abstract

A nonparametric estimator of density gradient, the mean shift, is employed in the joint, spatial-range (value) domain of gray level and color images for discontinuity preserving filtering and image segmentation. Properties of the mean shift are reviewed and its convergence on lattices is proven. The proposed filtering method associates with each pixel in the image the closest local mode in the density distribution of the joint domain. Segmentation into a piecewise constant structure requires only one more step, fusion of the regions associated with nearby modes. The proposed technique has two parameters controlling the resolution in the spatial and range domains. Since convergence is guaranteed, the technique *does not* require the intervention of the user to stop the filtering at the desired image quality. Several examples, for gray and color images, show the versatility of the method and compare favorably with results described in the literature for the same images.

1 Introduction

Low level computer vision tasks are misleadingly difficult and often yield unreliable results, since the employed techniques rely upon the correct choice by the user of the tuning parameter values. Today, it is an accepted fact in the vision community that the execution of low level tasks should be task driven, i.e., supported by independent high level information. To be able to successfully complement this paradigm, the low-level techniques must become more autonomous. In this paper we propose such a technique for image smoothing and for segmentation.

The *mean shift estimate* of the gradient of a density function and the associated iterative procedure of mode seeking have been developed by Fukunaga and Hostetler in [6]. Only recently, however, the nice properties of data compaction and dimensionality reduction of the mean shift have been exploited in low level computer vision tasks (color space analysis [3], face tracking [1]).

In this paper we describe a new application based on the theoretical results obtained in [4]. We show that high quality edge preserving filtering and image segmentation can be obtained by applying the mean shift in the combined spatial-range domain. The methods we developed are conceptually very simple being based on the same idea of iteratively shifting a fixed size window

to the average of the data points within. Details in the image are preserved due to the nonparametric character of the analysis which does not assume a priori any particular structure for the data.

The paper is organized as follows. Section 2 discusses the estimation of the density gradient and defines the mean shift vector. The convergence of the mean shift procedure is proven in Section 3 for discrete data. Section 4 defines the processing principle in the joint spatial-range domain. Mean shift filtering is explained and filtering examples are given in Section 5. The proposed mean shift segmentation is introduced and analyzed in Section 6.

2 Density Gradient Estimation

Let $\{\mathbf{x}_i\}_{i=1\ldots n}$ be an arbitrary set of n points in the d-dimensional Euclidean space R^d. The *multivariate kernel density estimate* obtained with kernel $K(\mathbf{x})$ and window radius h, computed in the point $\mathbf{x}$ is defined as [12, p.76]

$$\hat{f}(\mathbf{x}) = \frac{1}{nh^d} \sum_{i=1}^{n} K\left(\frac{\mathbf{x} - \mathbf{x}_i}{h}\right). \tag{1}$$

The optimum kernel yielding minimum mean integrated square error (MISE) is the Epanechnikov kernel

$$K_E(\mathbf{x}) = \begin{cases} \frac{1}{2}c_d^{-1}(d+2)(1 - \mathbf{x}^T\mathbf{x}) & \text{if } \mathbf{x}^T\mathbf{x} < 1 \\ 0 & \text{otherwise} \end{cases} \tag{2}$$

where c_d is the volume of the unit d-dimensional sphere [12, p.76].

The use of a differentiable kernel allows to define the estimate of the density gradient as the gradient of the kernel density estimate (1)

$$\hat{\nabla} f(\mathbf{x}) \equiv \nabla \hat{f}(\mathbf{x}) = \frac{1}{nh^d} \sum_{i=1}^{n} \nabla K\left(\frac{\mathbf{x} - \mathbf{x}_i}{h}\right). \tag{3}$$

Conditions on the kernel $K(\mathbf{x})$ and the window radius h to guarantee asymptotic unbiasedness, mean-square consistency, and uniform consistency are derived in [6].

For the Epanechnikov kernel (2) the density gradient estimate (3) becomes

$$\hat{\nabla} f(\mathbf{x}) = \frac{1}{n(h^d c_d)} \frac{d+2}{h^2} \sum_{\mathbf{x}_i \in S_h(\mathbf{x})} [\mathbf{x}_i - \mathbf{x}]$$

$$= \frac{n_{\mathbf{x}}}{n(h^d c_d)} \frac{d+2}{h^2} \left(\frac{1}{n_{\mathbf{x}}} \sum_{\mathbf{x}_i \in S_h(\mathbf{x})} [\mathbf{x}_i - \mathbf{x}] \right) \quad (4)$$

where the region $S_h(\mathbf{x})$ is a hypersphere of radius h having the volume $h^d c_d$, centered on $\mathbf{x}$, and containing $n_{\mathbf{x}}$ data points. The last term in (4)

$$M_h(\mathbf{x}) \equiv \frac{1}{n_{\mathbf{x}}} \sum_{\mathbf{x}_i \in S_h(\mathbf{x})} [\mathbf{x}_i - \mathbf{x}] = \frac{1}{n_{\mathbf{x}}} \sum_{\mathbf{x}_i \in S_h(\mathbf{x})} \mathbf{x}_i - \mathbf{x} \quad (5)$$

is called the *sample mean shift*. Using a kernel different from the Epanechnikov kernel results in a weighted mean computation in (5).

The quantity $\frac{n_{\mathbf{x}}}{n(h^d c_d)}$ is the kernel density estimate $\hat{f}(\mathbf{x})$ computed with the hypersphere $S_h(\mathbf{x})$ (the uniform kernel), and thus we can write (4) as

$$\hat{\nabla} f(\mathbf{x}) = \hat{f}(\mathbf{x}) \frac{d+2}{h^2} M_h(\mathbf{x}), \quad (6)$$

which yields

$$M_h(\mathbf{x}) = \frac{h^2}{d+2} \frac{\hat{\nabla} f(\mathbf{x})}{\hat{f}(\mathbf{x})}. \quad (7)$$

The expression (7) was first derived in [6] and shows that an estimate of the normalized gradient can be obtained by computing the sample mean shift in a uniform kernel centered on $\mathbf{x}$. The mean shift vector has the direction of the gradient of the density estimate at $\mathbf{x}$ when this estimate is obtained with the Epanechnikov kernel.

Since the mean shift vector always points towards the direction of the maximum increase in the density, it can define a path leading to a local density maximum, i.e., to a mode of the density (Figure 1).

The *mean shift procedure*, obtained by successive

- computation of the mean shift vector $M_h(\mathbf{x})$
- translation of the window $S_h(\mathbf{x})$ by $M_h(\mathbf{x})$,

is guaranteed to converge, as it will be shown in the next section.

3 Convergence

Let $\{\mathbf{y}_k\}_{k=1,2\ldots}$ denote the sequence of successive locations of the mean shift procedure. By definition we have for each k=1,2...

$$\mathbf{y}_{k+1} = \frac{1}{n_k} \sum_{\mathbf{x}_i \in S_h(\mathbf{y}_k)} \mathbf{x}_i, \quad (8)$$

where $\mathbf{y}_1$ is the center of the initial window and n_k is the number of points falling in the window $S_h(\mathbf{y}_k)$ centered on $\mathbf{y}_k$.

The convergence of the mean shift has been justified as a consequence of relation (7), (see [2]). However, while it is true that the mean shift vector $M_h(\mathbf{x})$ has

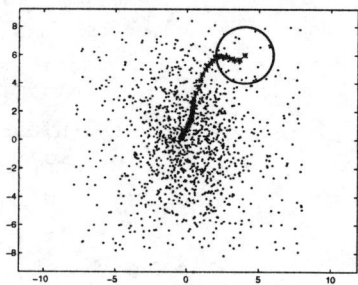

Figure 1: Successive computations of the mean shift define a path leading to a local density maximum.

the direction of the gradient of the density estimate at $\mathbf{x}$, it is not apparent that the density estimate at locations $\{\mathbf{y}_k\}_{k=1,2\ldots}$ is a monotonic increasing sequence. Moving in the direction of the gradient guarantees hill climbing only for infinitesimal steps. The following theorem asserts the convergence for discrete data.

Theorem 1 *Let* $\hat{f}_E = \left\{ \hat{f}_k(\mathbf{y}_k, K_E) \right\}_{k=1,2\ldots}$ *be the sequence of density estimates obtained using Epanechnikov kernel and computed in the points* $\{\mathbf{y}_k\}_{k=1,2\ldots}$ *defined by the successive locations of the mean shift procedure with uniform kernel. The sequence is convergent.*

Proof Since the data set $\{\mathbf{x}_i\}_{i=1\ldots n}$ has finite cardinality n, the sequence $\hat{f}_E$ is bounded. Moreover, we will show that $\hat{f}_E$ is strictly monotonic increasing, i.e., if $\mathbf{y}_k \neq \mathbf{y}_{k+1}$ then $\hat{f}_E(k) < \hat{f}_E(k+1)$, for all $k = 1, 2 \ldots$.

Let n_k, n'_k, and n''_k with $n_k = n'_k + n''_k$ be the number of data points falling in the d-dimensional windows (Figure 2) $S_h(\mathbf{y}_k)$, $S_h'(\mathbf{y}_k) = S_h(\mathbf{y}_k) - S_h''(\mathbf{y}_k)$, and $S_h''(\mathbf{y}_k) = S_h(\mathbf{y}_k) \bigcap S_h(\mathbf{y}_{k+1})$.

Without loss of generality we can assume the origin located at $\mathbf{y}_k$. Using the definition of the density estimate (1) with the Epanechnikov kernel (2) and noting that $\|\mathbf{y}_k - \mathbf{x}_i\|^2 = \|\mathbf{x}_i\|^2$ we have

$$\begin{aligned}
\hat{f}_E(k) &= \hat{f}_k(\mathbf{y}_k, K_E) \\
&= \frac{1}{nh^d} \sum_{\mathbf{x}_i \in S_h(\mathbf{y}_k)} K_E\left(\frac{\mathbf{y}_k - \mathbf{x}_i}{h} \right) \\
&= \frac{d+2}{2n(h^d c_d)} \sum_{\mathbf{x}_i \in S_h(\mathbf{y}_k)} \left(1 - \frac{\|\mathbf{x}_i\|^2}{h^2} \right). \quad (9)
\end{aligned}$$

Since the kernel K_E is nonnegative we also have

$$\hat{f}_E(k+1) = \hat{f}_{k+1}(\mathbf{y}_{k+1}, K_E) \geq$$

$$\geq \frac{1}{nh^d} \sum_{\mathbf{x}_i \in S_h''(\mathbf{y}_k)} K_E\left(\frac{\mathbf{y}_{k+1} - \mathbf{x}_i}{h} \right)$$

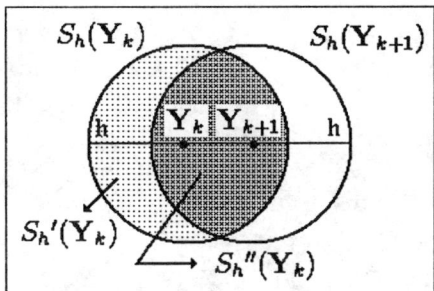

Figure 2: The d-dimensional windows used in the proof of convergence: $S_h(\mathbf{y}_k)$, $S_h'(\mathbf{y}_k)$, and $S_h''(\mathbf{y}_k)$. The point $\mathbf{y}_{k+1}$ is the mean of the data points falling in $S_h(\mathbf{y}_k)$.

$$= \frac{d+2}{2n(h^d c_d)} \sum_{\mathbf{x}_i \in S_h''(\mathbf{y}_k)} \left(1 - \frac{\|\mathbf{y}_{k+1} - \mathbf{x}_i\|^2}{h^2}\right). \quad (10)$$

Hence, knowing that $n_k' = n_k - n_k''$ we obtain

$$\hat{f}_E(k+1) - \hat{f}_E(k) \ge \frac{d+2}{2n(h^d c_d)h^2}$$

$$\left[\sum_{\mathbf{x}_i \in S_h(\mathbf{y}_k)} \|\mathbf{x}_i\|^2 - \sum_{\mathbf{x}_i \in S_h''(\mathbf{y}_k)} \|\mathbf{y}_{k+1} - \mathbf{x}_i\|^2 - n_k' h^2\right], \quad (11)$$

where the last term appears due to the different summation boundaries.

Also, by definition $\|\mathbf{y}_{k+1} - \mathbf{x}_i\|^2 \ge h^2$ for all $\mathbf{x}_i \in S_h'(\mathbf{y}_k)$, which implies that

$$\sum_{\mathbf{x}_i \in S_h'(\mathbf{y}_k)} \|\mathbf{y}_{k+1} - \mathbf{x}_i\|^2 \ge n_k' h^2. \quad (12)$$

Finally, employing (12) in (11) and using (8) we obtain

$$\hat{f}_E(k+1) - \hat{f}_E(k) \ge \frac{d+2}{2n(h^d c_d)h^2}$$

$$\left[\sum_{\mathbf{x}_i \in S_h(\mathbf{y}_k)} \|\mathbf{x}_i\|^2 - \sum_{\mathbf{x}_i \in S_h(\mathbf{y}_k)} \|\mathbf{y}_{k+1} - \mathbf{x}_i\|^2\right]$$

$$= \frac{d+2}{2n(h^d c_d)h^2} \left[2\mathbf{y}_{k+1}^T \sum_{\mathbf{x}_i \in S_h(\mathbf{y}_k)} \mathbf{x}_i - n_k \|\mathbf{y}_{k+1}\|^2\right]$$

$$= \frac{d+2}{2n(h^d c_d)h^2} n_k \|\mathbf{y}_{k+1}\|^2. \quad (13)$$

The last item of the relation (13) is strictly positive except when $\mathbf{y}_k = \mathbf{y}_{k+1} = 0$.

Being bounded and strictly monotonic increasing, the sequence $\hat{f}_E$ is convergent. Note that if $\mathbf{y}_k = \mathbf{y}_{k+1}$ then $\mathbf{y}_k$ is the limit of $\hat{f}_E$, i.e., $\mathbf{y}_k$ is the fixed point of the mean shift procedure.

4 Processing in Spatial-Range Domain

An image is typically represented as a 2-dimensional lattice of r-dimensional vectors (pixels), where r is 1 in the gray level case, 3 for color images, or $r > 3$ in the multispectral case. The space of the lattice is known as the *spatial* domain while the gray level, color, or spectral information is represented in the *range* domain. However, after a proper normalization with σ_s and σ_r, global parameters in the spatial and range domains, the location and range vectors can be concatenated to obtain a *spatial-range* domain of dimension $d = r + 2$.

The main novelty of this paper is to apply the mean shift procedure for the data points in the joint spatial-range domain. Each data point becomes associated to a point of convergence which represents the local mode of the density in the d-dimensional space. The process, having the parameters σ_s and σ_r, takes into account simultaneously both the spatial and range information.

The output of the mean shift filter for an image pixel is defined as the range information carried by the point of convergence. This process achieves a high quality, discontinuity preserving spatial filtering. For the segmentation task, the convergence points sufficiently close in the joint domain are fused to obtain the homogeneous regions in the image.

The proposed spatial-range filtering and segmentation are described in the sequel with results shown for both gray level and color images. The perceptually uniform $L^*u^*v^*$ space has been used to represent the color information, while for the gray level cases only the L^* component has been considered.

5 Filtering

Let $\{\mathbf{x}_j\}_{j=1 \dots n}$ and $\{\mathbf{z}_j\}_{j=1 \dots n}$ be the d-dimensional original and filtered image points in the spatial-range domain. The upperscripts s and r will denote the spatial and range parts of the vectors, respectively. The original data is assumed to be normalized with σ_s for the spatial part and σ_r for the range.

Mean Shift Filtering

For each $j = 1 \dots n$

1. Initialize $k = 1$ and $\mathbf{y}_k = \mathbf{x}_j$.
2. Compute $\mathbf{y}_{k+1} = \frac{1}{n_k} \sum_{\mathbf{x}_i \in S_1(\mathbf{y}_k)} \mathbf{x}_i$, $k \leftarrow k+1$ till convergence.
3. Assign $\mathbf{z}_j = (\mathbf{x}_j^s, \mathbf{y}_{conv}^r)$.

The last assignment specifies that the filtered data at the spatial location of $\mathbf{x}_j$ will have the range components of the point of convergence $\mathbf{y}_{conv}$. The number of points in the window $S_1(\mathbf{y}_k)$ of radius 1 and centered on Y_k is n_k. The unit radius of the window is due to the normalization.

5.1 Arithmetic Complexity

In a practical implementation the lattice structure of the spatial domain is used for the efficient search of the points $x_i \in S_1(y_k)$. This search can obviously be limited to a rectangular window of size 2×2 in the normalized space, which corresponds to $(2\lfloor \sigma_s \rfloor + 1)^2$ image pixels, where $\lfloor \cdot \rfloor$ is the down-rounded integer.

By denoting with k_c the mean number of iterations to convergence, the arithmetic complexity of mean shift filtering is about $k_c(2\lfloor \sigma_s \rfloor + 1)^2$ flops per image pixel.

5.2 Normalization Constants

The value of σ_s is related to the spatial resolution of the analysis while the value of σ_r defines the range (color) resolution.

An asymptotically optimal (in the MISE sense) gradient estimate is obtained when the distribution in the joint space is normal. The radius of the searching window is a function of the number of data points n [11, p.152]. In our case, however, the data is far from being normal. Therefore, no theoretical constraints can be imposed on the values of σ_s and σ_r, which are task dependent and in practical settings their choice should incorporate a top-down, knowledge driven component.

A challenging issue not considered in this paper is the adaptive definition of the normalization constants. To take into account the nonstationarity of the input adaptive kernel estimation techniques were proposed in the statistical literature [14], however for less complex data. Beside exploiting a priori information (often available for low level vision) robust image understanding methods can also be helpful.

5.3 Experiments

Mean shift filtering with $(\sigma_s, \sigma_r) = (8, 4)$ has been applied to the often used 256×256 gray level *cameraman* image (Figure 3a), the processed image being shown in Figure 3b. The regions containing the grass field have been almost completely smoothed while details such as the tripod and the buildings in the background were preserved.

The entire processing time was a few seconds on a standard laptop with a 233 MHz *Pentium II* processor. We used a Java implementation of the algorithm. The mean number of iterations necessary for convergence was very low, around 3, due to the relatively small number of data points falling in the searching window.

To illustrate the effectiveness of the filtering process, the region marked in Figure 3a is represented in three dimensions in Figure 4a. In Figure 4b the mean shift paths associated with each pixel from the central plateau and the line are shown. Note that the convergence points (black dots) are situated in the opposite direction relative to the edge, while the shifts on the line

(a)

(b)

Figure 3: *Cameraman* image. (a) Original. (b) Mean shift filtered $(\sigma_s, \sigma_r) = (8, 4)$.

remain on it. As a result, the filtered data (Figure 4c) shows clean quasi-homogeneous regions.

A second filtering example is given in Figure 5b. The original, 512×512 color image *baboon* has been processed with a mean shift filter having $(\sigma_s, \sigma_r) = (16, 16)$. While the texture of the fur has been cleaned, the details of the eyes and the whiskers remained crisp.

5.4 Comparison to Bilateral Filtering

We note here two important differences between the mean shift and bilateral filtering proposed by Tomasi and Manduchi [15]. Both methods are based on the same principle, the simultaneous processing of both the spatial and range domains. However, while the bilateral filtering uses a static window in the two domains, the mean shift window is *dynamic*, moving in the direction of the maximum increase in the density gradient. Therefore, the mean shift filtering has a more powerful adaptation to the local structure of the data.

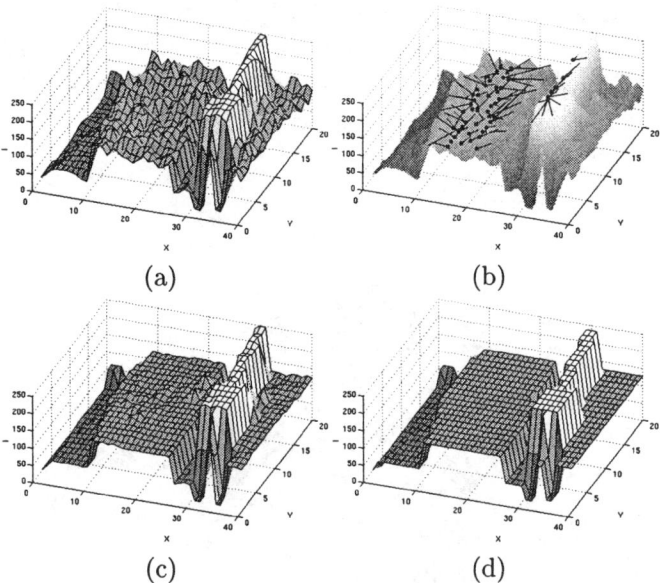

(a)   (b)

(c)   (d)

Figure 4: A 40×20 window from the image *cameraman*. (a) Original data (rotated and flipped over for better visualization). (b) Mean shift paths for the points in the central and top (white) plateaus. (c) Filtering result $(\sigma_s, \sigma_r) = (8, 4)$. (d) Segmentation result (see Section 6 for details).

In addition, the filtering iterations proposed in [15] do not have a stopping criterion. After a sufficient number of iterations, the processed image collapses to a flat surface. The same observation is valid for other adaptive smoothing techniques [9, 10]. The process defined by mean shift is run till convergence and maintains the structure of the data.

6 Segmentation

The mean shift segmentation in the spatial-range domain has the same simple design as the filtering process. Again, we assume the input data to be normalized with (σ_s, σ_r). Let $\{\mathbf{x}_j\}_{j=1\ldots n}$ be the original image points, $\{\mathbf{z}_j\}_{j=1\ldots n}$ the points of convergence, and $\{L_j\}_{j=1\ldots n}$ a set of labels (scalars).

Mean Shift Segmentation

1. For each $j = 1 \ldots n$ run the mean shift procedure for $\mathbf{x}_j$ and store the convergence point in $\mathbf{z}_j$.
2. Identify clusters $\{\mathbf{C}_p\}_{p=1\ldots m}$ of convergence points by linking together all $\mathbf{z}_j$ which are closer than 0.5 from each other in the joint domain.
3. For each $j = 1 \ldots n$ assign $L_j = \{p \mid \mathbf{z}_j \in \mathbf{C}_p\}$.
4. Optional: Eliminate spatial regions smaller than M pixels.

The first step of the segmentation is a filtering process. However all the information about the d-

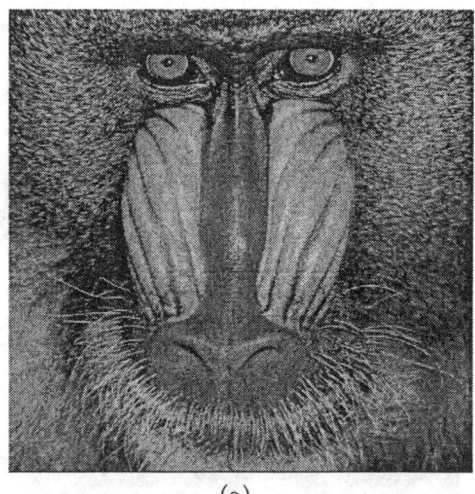

(a)

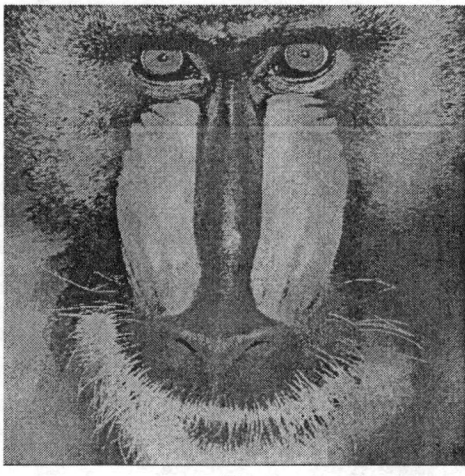

(b)

Figure 5: *Baboon* image. (a) Original. (b) Mean shift filtered $(\sigma_s, \sigma_r) = (16, 16)$.

dimensional convergence point is stored now in $\mathbf{z}_j$, not only its range part. Note also that the number of clusters m is controlled by the parameters (σ_s, σ_r).

The arithmetic complexity of the segmentation is similar to that of the mean shift filtering, its first step being the most computationally expensive.

6.1 Experiments

We employed the algorithm described above with $(\sigma_s, \sigma_r, M) = (8, 7, 20)$ to segment the 256×256 gray level image *MIT* (Figure 6a). The segmentation is presented in Figure 6b with the associated contours in Figure 6c. Compare the result in Figure 6 with the segmentations of the same image through clustering [3, Figure 4] or using Gibbs random field [8, Figure 7].

Returning to the *cameraman* image, Figure 7 shows the reconstructed image after the regions corresponding to the sky and grass were replaced with white. Observe the preservation of the details. The mean shift segmen-

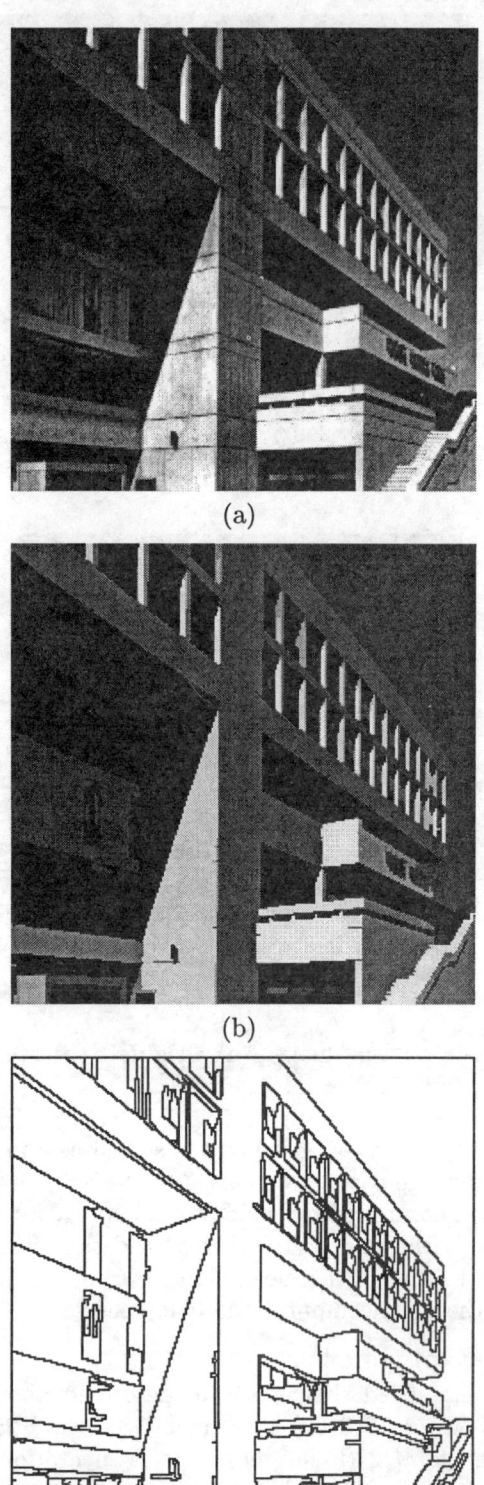

(a)

(b)

(c)

Figure 6: *MIT* image. (a) Original. (b) Segmented $(\sigma_s, \sigma_r, M) = (8, 7, 20)$. A number of 225 homogeneous regions are identified. (c) Corresponding contours allow the delineation of the walls, sky, steps, inscription on the building, etc.

tation has been applied with $(\sigma_s, \sigma_r, M) = (8, 4, 10)$. Figure 4d shows the segmentation (with the same parameters) of the selected rectangular window in Figure 3a.

Figure 7: Segmentation with $(\sigma_s, \sigma_r, M) = (8, 4, 10)$ and reconstruction of the *cameraman* image after the elimination of regions representing sky and grass.

The segmentation with $(\sigma_s, \sigma_r, M) = (16, 7, 40)$ of the 512×512 color image *lake* is shown in Figure 8b. Compare this result with that of the multiscale approach in [13, Figure 11]. Finally, one can compare the contours of the color image *hand* presented in Figure 9 with those from [16, Figure 15] obtained through a complex global optimization.

6.2 Discussion

It is interesting to contrast the mean shift segmentation with those based on the attraction force field [13] and edge flow propagation [7]. While all the three methods employ a vector field to detect regions in the spatial domain, only the mean shift based segmentation has strong statistical foundations. Our method associates the current pixel with a mode of the density located in its neighborhood (measured in both spatial and range domains).

The attraction force field defined in [13] is computed at each pixel as a vector sum of pairwise affinities between the current pixel and all other pixels. No theoretical evidence of the existence of such a force field is given.

The edge flow in [7] is obtained at each location for a given set of directions as the magnitude of the gradient of a smoothed image. The quantization of the edge flow direction, however, may introduce artifacts. Recall that, by contrast, the direction of the mean shift is dictated solely by the data.

(a)

(b)

Figure 8: *Lake* image. (a) Original. (b) Segmented $(\sigma_s, \sigma_r, M) = (16, 7, 40)$.

7 Conclusions

This paper suggests that effective image analysis can be implemented based on the mean shift procedure. The nonparametric estimation of the density gradient in the spatial-range domain is a useful tool for bottom-up computer vision tasks such as edge preserving filtering and segmentation. The methods we proposed can be easily extended to the processing of other low level image features like the texture or optical flow.

Acknowledgment

This research was supported by the NSF under the grant IRI-9530546.

References

[1] G.R. Bradski, "Real Time Face and Object Tracking as a Component of a Perceptual User Interface", *IEEE Workshop Applications of Comp. Vis.*, Princeton, 214-219, 1998.

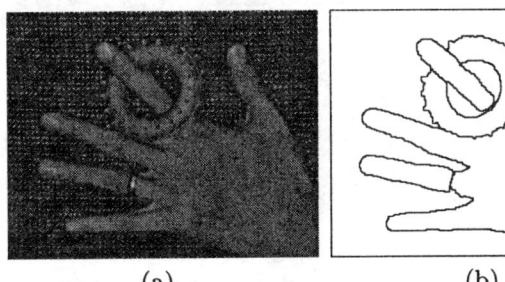

(a)   (b)

Figure 9: *Hand* image. (a) Original. (b) Contours $(\sigma_s, \sigma_r, M) = (16, 19, 40)$.

[2] Y. Cheng, "Mean Shift, Mode Seeking, and Clustering", *IEEE Trans. PAMI*, vol. 17, 790-799, 1995.

[3] D. Comaniciu, P. Meer, "Robust Analysis of Feature Spaces: Color Image Segmentation", *IEEE Conf. Comp. Vis. and Pattern Recogn.*, Puerto Rico, 750-755, 1997.

[4] D. Comaniciu, P. Meer, "Distribution Free Decomposition of Multivariate Data", *Pattern Anal. and Applications*, vol. 2, 22-30, 1999.

[5] P.F. Felzenszwalb, D.P. Huttenlocher, "Image Segmentation Using Local Variation", *IEEE Conf. Comp. Vis. and Pattern Recogn.*, Santa Barbara, 98-103, 1998.

[6] K. Fukunaga, L.D. Hostetler, "The Estimation of the Gradient of a Density Function, with Applications in Pattern Recognition", *IEEE Trans. Info. Theory*, vol. IT-21, 32-40, 1975.

[7] W.Y. Ma, B.S. Manjunath, "Edge Flow: A Framework of Boundary Detection and Image Segmentation", *IEEE Conf. Comp. Vis. and Pattern Recogn.*, Puerto Rico, 744-749, 1997.

[8] T.N. Pappas, "An Adaptive Clustering Algorithm for Image Segmentation", *IEEE Trans. Signal Process.*, vol. 40, 901-914, 1992.

[9] P. Perona, J. Malik, "Scale-Space and Edge Detection Using Anisotropic Diffusion", *IEEE Trans. PAMI*, vol. 12, 629-639, 1990.

[10] P. Saint-Marc, J.S. Chen, G.G. Medioni, "Adaptive Smoothing: A General Tool for Early Vision", *IEEE Trans. PAMI*, vol. 13, 514-529, 1991.

[11] D.W. Scott, *Multivariate Density Estimation*, New York: Wiley, 1992.

[12] B.W. Silverman, *Density Estimation for Statistics and Data Analysis*, New York: Chapman and Hall, 1986.

[13] M. Tabb, N. Ahuja, "Multiscale Image Segmentation by Integrated Edge and Region Detection", *IEEE Trans. Image Process.*, vol. 6, 642-655, 1997.

[14] G.R. Terrell, D.W. Scott, "Variable Density Estimation", *The Annals of Statistics*, vol. 20, 1236-1265, 1992.

[15] C. Tomasi, R. Manduchi, "Bilateral Filtering for Gray and Color Images", *Int'l Conf. Comp. Vis.*, Bombay, India, 839-846, 1998.

[16] S.C. Zhu, A. Yuille, "Region Competition: Unifying Snakes, Region Growing, and Bayes/MDL for Multiband Image Segmentation", *IEEE Trans. PAMI*, vol. 18, 884-900, 1996.

Higher Order Statistical Learning for Vehicle Detection in Images

A.N. Rajagopalan   Philippe Burlina   Rama Chellappa*
Center for Automation Research
University of Maryland
College Park, MD - 20742, USA.

Abstract

The paper describes a scheme for detecting vehicles in images. The proposed method approximately models the unknown distribution of the images of vehicles by learning higher order statistics (HOS) information of the 'vehicle class' from sample images. Given a test image, statistical information about the background is learnt 'on the fly'. An HOS-based decision measure then classifies test patterns as vehicles or otherwise. When tested on real images of aerial views of vehicular activity, the method gives good results even on complicated scenes. It does not require any a priori information about the site. However, it is amenable to augmentation with contextual information. The method can serve as an important step towards building an automated roadway monitoring system.

1. Introduction

Detection of vehicles in images represents an important step towards achieving automated roadway monitoring capabilities. It can also be used for monitoring activities in parking lots. The challenge lies in being able to reliably and quickly detect multiple small objects of interest against a cluttered background which usually consists of trees and buildings. In recent works, the concept of site-model-based image exploitation has been used for the detection of prespecified vehicles in designated areas as well as the detection of global vehicle configurations in aerial imagery [1, 2]. The approach consists of maintaining a geometric functional model of the site of interest. Before an acquired image can be processed, it needs to be registered with respect

to the site. In [3], an attentional mechanism based on the characterization and analysis of spectral signatures using context information is described. Moon *et al.* [4] use a simple geometric edge model in conjunction with contextual information for detecting vehicles from aerial images of parking areas. However, the method is sensitive to low illumination and/or acquisition angles. There is an increasing interest in the vision community to detect and track vehicles from video data. These approaches usually extract foreground objects from the background using frame differencing or background subtraction. The foreground objects are then classified as vehicles or otherwise using some matching criterion such as the Hausdorff measure [5] or trained neural networks [6, 7]. Although the work described in this paper deals with static images, it can be extended to video data.

The vehicle detection scheme presented in this paper uses higher order statistics (HOS) of the images of vehicles to get a better approximation to their unknown distribution. Training data samples of vehicles are first clustered and the statistical parameters corresponding to each cluster are estimated. Clustering is based on an HOS-based decision measure which is obtained by deriving a series expansion for the multivariate probability density function in terms of the Gaussian function and the Hermite polynomial. Given a test image, the background information is learnt 'on the fly'. Detection is then performed by searching the test image for patches of vehicles at all points in the image and across different scales. A vector of difference measurements of the test pattern with respect to each of the clusters is computed using the HOS-based closeness measure. A simple thresholding scheme then determines whether the test pattern belongs to the class of vehicles or not. The HOS-based measure has good discriminating capability and the results are quite encouraging. No pre-processing operations are carried out on the vehicle patterns.

---

*This work is partially supported by the ARL Federated Laboratory on Advanced Sensors Consortium under contract DAAL-01-96-2-0001.

2. HOS-Based Decision Measure

In this section, we derive a series expansion for a multivariate probability density function (p.d.f) in terms of the Gaussian function and the Hermite polynomial. An HOS-based decision measure is then derived from this expansion.

Let the random vector $\underline{X} = [X_1 \ X_2 \ \ldots X_N]^T$ and $\underline{X} \sim N(\underline{0}, I)$. If $\underline{t} = [t_1 \ t_2 \ \ldots t_N]^T$, then the moment generating function of $\underline{X}$ is given by $\Phi(\underline{t}) = E\left[\exp\left(\underline{t}^T \underline{X}\right)\right]$. Since these random variables are statistically independent, $\Phi(\underline{t}) = \exp\left(\frac{1}{2}\underline{t}^T\underline{t}\right)$. Therefore, $E\left[\exp\left(\underline{t}^T \underline{X} - \frac{1}{2}\underline{t}^T\underline{t}\right)\right] = 1$. Replacing $\underline{t}$ by $\underline{t} + \underline{s}$, we get

$$E\left[\exp\left(\underline{t}^T \underline{X} - \frac{1}{2}\underline{t}^T\underline{t}\right)\exp\left(\underline{s}^T\underline{X} - \frac{1}{2}\underline{s}^T\underline{s}\right)\right] = \exp\left(\underline{t}^T\underline{s}\right).$$

Expanding this equation in Taylor series, we obtain

$$E\left[\sum_{m,n=0}^{\infty}(\underline{t}^{\otimes n})^T \frac{\overline{H}_n(X)}{n!}\frac{\overline{H}_m^T(X)}{m!}(\underline{s}^{\otimes m})\right] = \sum_{m,n=0}^{\infty}\frac{1}{n!}(\underline{t}^{\otimes n})^T I_{q_n q_m}(\underline{s}^{\otimes m}),$$

where $\otimes$ represents the tensor product and $\underline{t}^{\otimes n} = \underbrace{\underline{t} \otimes \underline{t} \otimes \ldots \otimes \underline{t}}_{n \text{ times}}$. The matrix $I_{q_n q_m} = O_{q_n q_m}$ for $n \neq m$ and $I_{q_n q_m} = I_{q_n}$ for $n = m$, where $O_{q_n q_m}$ is the zero matrix with q_n rows and q_m columns while I_{q_n} is the identity matrix of dimension q_n. The vector $\overline{H}_n(\underline{x})$ is given by

$$\overline{H}_n(\underline{x}) = \left[(\underline{D_t}^{\otimes n})\exp\left(\underline{t}^T\underline{x} - \frac{1}{2}\underline{t}^T\underline{t}\right)\right]_{\underline{t}=0}$$

and $\underline{D_t} = \left[\frac{\partial}{\partial t_1} \ \frac{\partial}{\partial t_2} \ \ldots \ \frac{\partial}{\partial t_N}\right]^T$. The dimensions of $\overline{H}_n(\underline{x})$ and $\overline{H}_m(\underline{x})$ are given by q_n and q_m, respectively. By equating the coefficients of $\underline{t}$ and $\underline{s}$ on both sides, we obtain the important orthogonality relation

$$E\left[\underline{H}_n(X)\underline{H}_m^T(X)\right] = I_{p_n p_m} . \quad (1)$$

Note that the expectation is w.r.t $N(\underline{0}, I)$. In (1), $\underline{H}_n(\underline{x})$ is a vector whose elements are given by the product $\left(\prod_{i=1}^N \frac{H_{k_i}(x_i)}{\sqrt{k_i!}}\right)$ for all permutations of k_i, $i = 1, \ldots N$, such that $\sum_{i=1}^N k_i = n$. The dimensions of the vectors $\underline{H}_n(\underline{x})$ and $\underline{H}_m(\underline{x})$ are given by p_n and p_m, respectively. The term $H_{k_i}(x_i)$ is the Hermite polynomial of order k_i and is defined as $H_{k_i}(x_i) = \left[\frac{\partial^{k_i}}{\partial t_i^{k_i}}\exp\left(t_i x_i - \frac{1}{2}t_i^2\right)\right]_{t_i=0}$. Similarly, one can derive

an orthogonality relation in terms of $N(\underline{\mu}, R)$ as

$$E\left[\underline{H}_n\left(R^{-\frac{1}{2}}(\underline{X} - \underline{\mu})\right)\underline{H}_m^T\left(R^{-\frac{1}{2}}(\underline{X} - \underline{\mu})\right)\right] = I_{p_n p_m} .$$

Let $\underline{Y} = R^{-\frac{1}{2}}(\underline{X} - \underline{\mu})$ and $\underline{y} = R^{-\frac{1}{2}}(\underline{x} - \underline{\mu})$. If $\underline{X}$ has mean $\underline{\mu}$ and covariance R, then using the above orthogonality relation, the multivariate probability density function $f(\underline{x})$ can be written as

$$f(\underline{x}) = N(\underline{\mu}, R)\left(1 + \sum_{n=3}^{\infty} E\left[\underline{H}_n^T(\underline{Y})\right]\underline{H}_n(\underline{y})\right) . \quad (2)$$

We define the HOS-based closeness measure as $-\log f(\underline{x})$. It is interesting to note here that when $f(\underline{x})$ is Gaussian, the HOS-based decision measure neatly reduces to the normalized Mahalanobis distance.

3. Vehicle Detection

In this section, we propose an HOS-based vehicle detection scheme that finds vehicles by searching an image for square patches of different views of the vehicle at all points of the image and across different scales.

We use a statistical distribution-based model for detection. It is to be expected that the joint density function for the class of vehicles is unlikely to be well-modeled by a strict/simple Gaussian fit $N(\underline{\mu}, R)$. Since only a finite number of moments would be computable in practice, the unknown p.d.f. is approximated up to its mth order joint moment using (2) as

$$f(\underline{x}) = N(\underline{\mu}, R)\left(1 + \sum_{n=3}^{m} E\left[\underline{H}_n^T(\underline{Y})\right]\underline{H}_n(\underline{y})\right) , \quad (3)$$

where $\underline{Y} = R^{-\frac{1}{2}}(\underline{X} - \underline{\mu})$ and $\underline{y} = R^{-\frac{1}{2}}(\underline{x} - \underline{\mu})$. Thus, higher order statistics are used to get a better approximation to $f(\underline{x})$. The corresponding HOS-based finite order decision measure is given by

$$-\log N(\underline{\mu}, R)\left(1 + \sum_{n=3}^{m} E\left[\underline{H}_n^T(\underline{Y})\right]\underline{H}_n(\underline{y})\right) . \quad (4)$$

3.1. Clustering using HOS

We model the distribution of vehicles by fitting the data samples of vehicles with multi-dimensional clusters. The idea of using multi-dimensional clusters to model the p.d.f may be traced back to the works in [8, 9]. Traditional k-means clustering algorithms based on the Euclidean or the Mahalanobis distances [10, 11] work satisfactorily under Gaussian assumptions. However, if the actual distribution of the data is non-Gaussian, then traditional k-means may fail to yield satisfactory results. Hence, we propose a clustering algorithm that uses higher order (> 2) statistics for improved clustering. The closeness measure that we use for clustering is given by (4).

The Clustering Algorithm

1. Obtain k initial pattern centers from the image database of vehicles. Divide the data set into k clusters by assigning each data sample to the nearest pattern center in Euclidean space.

2. Initialize the joint moments (second and onwards up to order m) of all k clusters.

3. Recompute pattern centers to be the centroids of the current data partitions.

4. Using the current set of k pattern centers and their higher order moments, recompute data partitions by re-assigning each data sample to the nearest cluster using the HOS-based decision measure defined in (4). If the data partitions remain unchanged or if the maximum number of inner-loop (i.e steps 3 and 4) iterations have been exceeded, proceed to step 5. Otherwise, return to step 3.

5. Re-compute the moments (second and onwards up to order m) of all k clusters from their respective data partitions.

6. Using the current set of k pattern centers and their cluster moments, recompute data partitions by re-assigning each data sample to the nearest cluster using the HOS-based measure. If the data partitions remain unchanged or if the maximum number of outer loop (i.e steps 3 to 6) iterations have been exceeded, proceed to step 7. Otherwise, return to step 3.

7. Return the current set of k pattern centers and their joint moments (up to order m), for each cluster.

It was found, after some experimentation, that six clusters were adequate for our purpose.

3.2. Classification

We describe two methods for classifying vehicles. Both the methods use the HOS-based decision measure for classification. However, the first method does not use the background information in the test image while the second method incorporates dynamic background learning while testing. The two methods are compared to demonstrate the advantages of learning the background scene. As would be shown, the second method yields better overall detection rate while simultaneously reducing the number of false matches.

Method 1: (No Background Learning)
In this method, given a test image, vehicle detection is performed by searching the image for square patches of vehicles at all points in the image and across different scales. A vector of difference measurements of the test pattern with respect to each of the vehicle clusters is computed using the HOS-based closeness measure. The minimum difference value is then determined and simple thresholding is used to decide whether the test pattern belongs to the class of vehicles or not.

Method 2: (Dynamic Background Learning)
The background information can be used to improve the performance of the vehicle detector algorithm. This can be done by first learning the background dynamically as follows. Initially, the test image is scanned at its highest resolution for square patches that are not vehicles. As non-vehicles usually far outnumber the vehicles in a given test image, we use a loose threshold to classify non-vehicles based on the already available statistical knowledge of the vehicles. Since the background usually constitutes a major portion of the test image, one can obtain a sufficient number of samples that are not vehicles. The non-vehicle patterns are next distributed into six clusters using the HOS-based closeness measure and the statistical parameters corresponding to each of the six clusters are estimated.

Finally, the test image is again searched for square patches of vehicles but now at all points in the image and across different scales. A vector of difference measurements of the test pattern is computed with respect to each cluster (six corresponding to vehicles and six corresponding to the background) using the HOS-based closeness measure. If the minimum difference value corresponds to that of a vehicle cluster and is less than a specified threshold, the test pattern is declared as a vehicle, else not. The above modified condition helps to reduce the false patterns considerably. Knowledge about the background allows us to relax the threshold which in turn leads to an improvement in the vehicle detection rate while simultaneously keeping down the number of false matches. It must be noted that the above condition could lead to a few misses when some of the vehicles look quite like the background.

4. Experimental Results

We present results on the performance of the proposed HOS-based vehicle detection systems with and without background learning. The training set consisted of about 500 grey-scale patterns of vehicles (cars here), each of dimension 16×16 pixels only. The methods were then tested on real images that were aerial views of vehicular activity on roadways captured with a stationary camera. The training set was distinct from the test set. As a compromise between accuracy of representation and computational complexity, we choose

$m = 3$ (in (3) and (4)) for our experiments.

Figures 1 and 2 show the output results corresponding to these methods for some test images. Multiple boxes represent detection at different scales. For computational speedup, test patterns were evaluated every fourth pixel along the rows as well as the columns. Hence, the boxes are sometimes not exactly centered about the target. Although the figures are self-explanatory, for the purpose of comparison, a quantitative breakdown of the performance of the methods is also tabulated. Considering the complexity of the problem which lies in detecting very small objects against a cluttered background, we note that both the methods are able to detect vehicles reasonably well in all the images. Even those with non-frontal views are detected. However, there are some misses; these include vehicles that were smaller than the chosen window size and hence could not be reliably detected. For the calculations in Table 1, vehicles that were much smaller than the training image size set were not taken into consideration. We note that the average detection rate for

System	Vehicles	Detected	False Alarms
Method 1	90	56	40
Method 2	90	66	13

Table 1. Performance comparison.

Method 1 is about 62%. However, the method suffers from quite a number of false alarms. This is due to the fact that it completely ignores information about the background scene. On the other hand, the scheme described in Method 2 which incorporates dynamic background learning clearly outperforms Method 1. It has a higher average detection rate (about 73%) and only one-third of the false alarms as compared to Method 1. Clearly, dynamic background learning enhances performance significantly.

5. Conclusions

We have described a scheme for vehicle detection against a cluttered background. The proposed method (Method 2 in the paper) uses higher order statistics of data samples of vehicles to get a better approximation to the distribution of the image patterns of vehicles. The background is learnt dynamically while testing. An HOS-based decision measure is used for classification. The scheme gives good results, even on fairly complicated scenes. The method can also detect non-frontal views. It may be possible to improve the

performance further by using contextual information.

We are currently working on extending this scheme to video. The vehicle detection rate is expected to improve significantly due to the motion information that is available in video data.

Acknowledgment: The authors gratefully acknowledge the Montgomery County Department of Public Works and Transportation from whose website (http://www.dpwt.com/jpgcap/camintro.html#routes) the aerial images were downloaded.

References

[1] R. Chellappa, Q. Zheng, L. Davis, C. Lin, X. Zhang, C. Rodriguez, A. Rosenfeld and T. Moore, "Site model based monitoring of aerial images", in *Proc. DARPA Image Understanding Workshop*, (Monterey, CA), pp. 295-318, 1994.

[2] P. Burlina, V. Parameswaran and R. Chellappa, "Sensitivity analysis and learning strategies for context-based vehicle detection algorithms", in *Proc. DARPA Image Understanding Workshop*, pp. 577-583, 1997.

[3] P. Burlina, R. Chellappa and C.L. Lin, "A spectral attentional mechanism tuned to object configurations", *IEEE Trans. Image Processing*, vol. 6, pp. 1117-1128, Aug. 1997.

[4] H. Moon, R. Chellappa and A. Rosenfeld, "Performance analysis of a simple vehicle detection algorithm", in *Proc. Fed. Lab. Symposium on Advanced Sensors*, (College Park, MD), pp. 249-253, Feb. 1999.

[5] D.H. Huttenlocher and R. Zabih, "Aerial and ground-based video surveillance at Cornell university", in *Proc. DARPA Image Understanding Workshop*, (Monterey, CA), pp. 77-83, Nov. 1998.

[6] T. Kanade, R.T. Collins and A.J. Lipton, "Advances in cooperative multi-sensor video surveillance", in *Proc. DARPA Image Understanding Workshop*, (Monterey, CA), pp. 3-24, Nov. 1998.

[7] A.J. Lipton, H. Fujiyoshi and R.S. Patil, "Moving target classification and tracking from real-time video", in *Proc. DARPA Image Underst anding Workshop*, (Monterey, CA), pp. 129-136, Nov. 1998.

[8] T. Poggio and K. Sung, "Finding human faces with a Gaussian mixture distribution-based face model", in *Proc. Asian Conf. on Computer Vision*, (Singapore), Springer Verlag, Eds. S. Z. Li, D. P. Mittal, E. K. Teoh and H. Wan, 1995, pp. 437-446.

[9] K. Sung and T. Poggio, "Example-based learning for view-based human face detection", *IEEE Trans. Pattern Anal. Machine Intell.*, vol. 20, pp. Jan. 98.

[10] A. K. Jain and R. C. Dubes, *Algorithms for Clustering Data*, Prentice-Hall Inc., Englewood Cliffs, 1988.

[11] R. O Duda and P. E. Hart, *Pattern Classification and Scene Analysis*, John Wiley & Sons Inc., 1973.

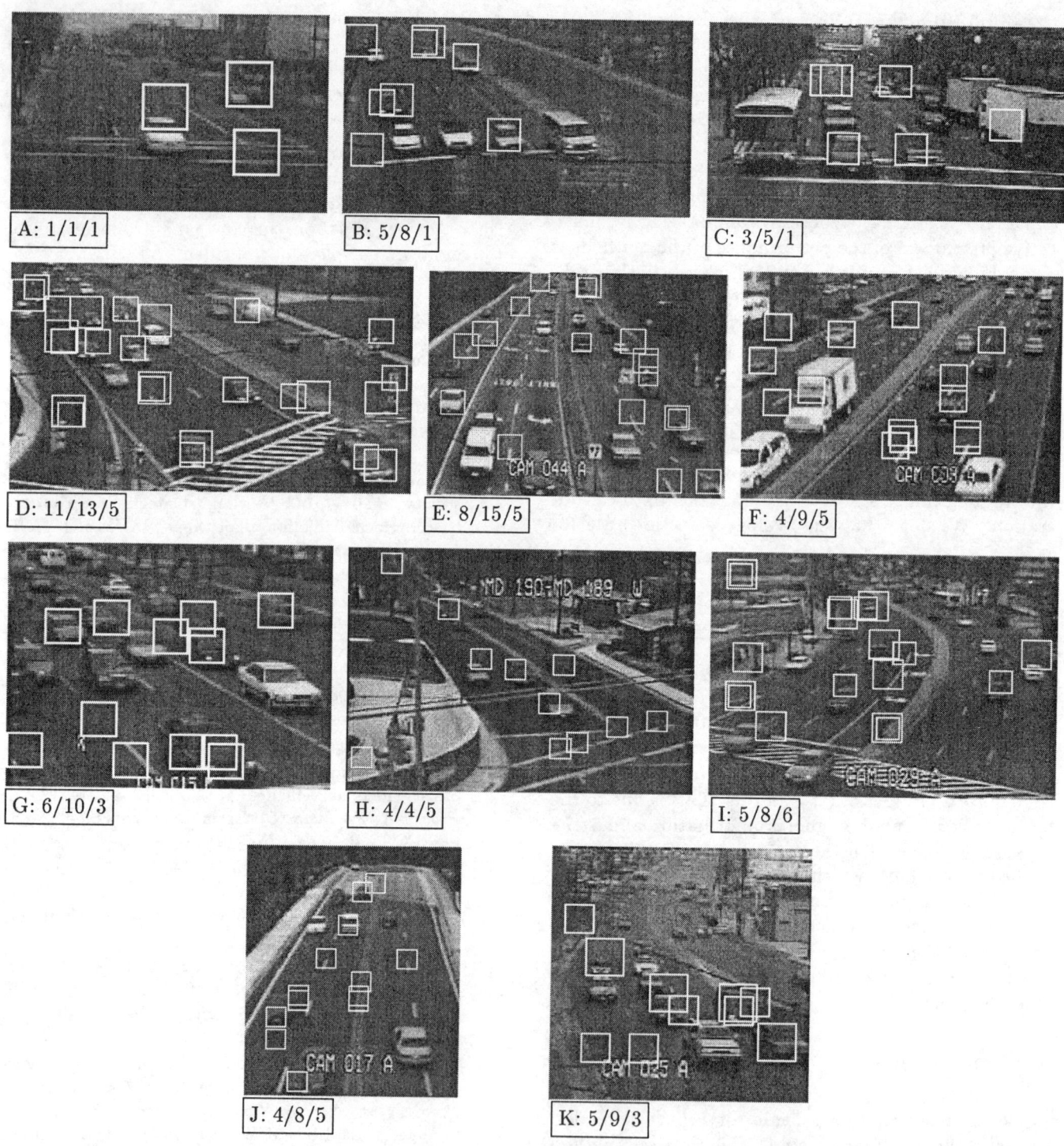

Figure 1. Results of the HOS-based vehicle detection scheme without any background learning. Multiple boxes represent detection at different scales. Below each image, three values are given: they correspond to the number of vehicles detected, the number of vehicles present in the image, and the number of false alarms, respectively. Vehicles that are much smaller than the training image are ignored in the calculations.

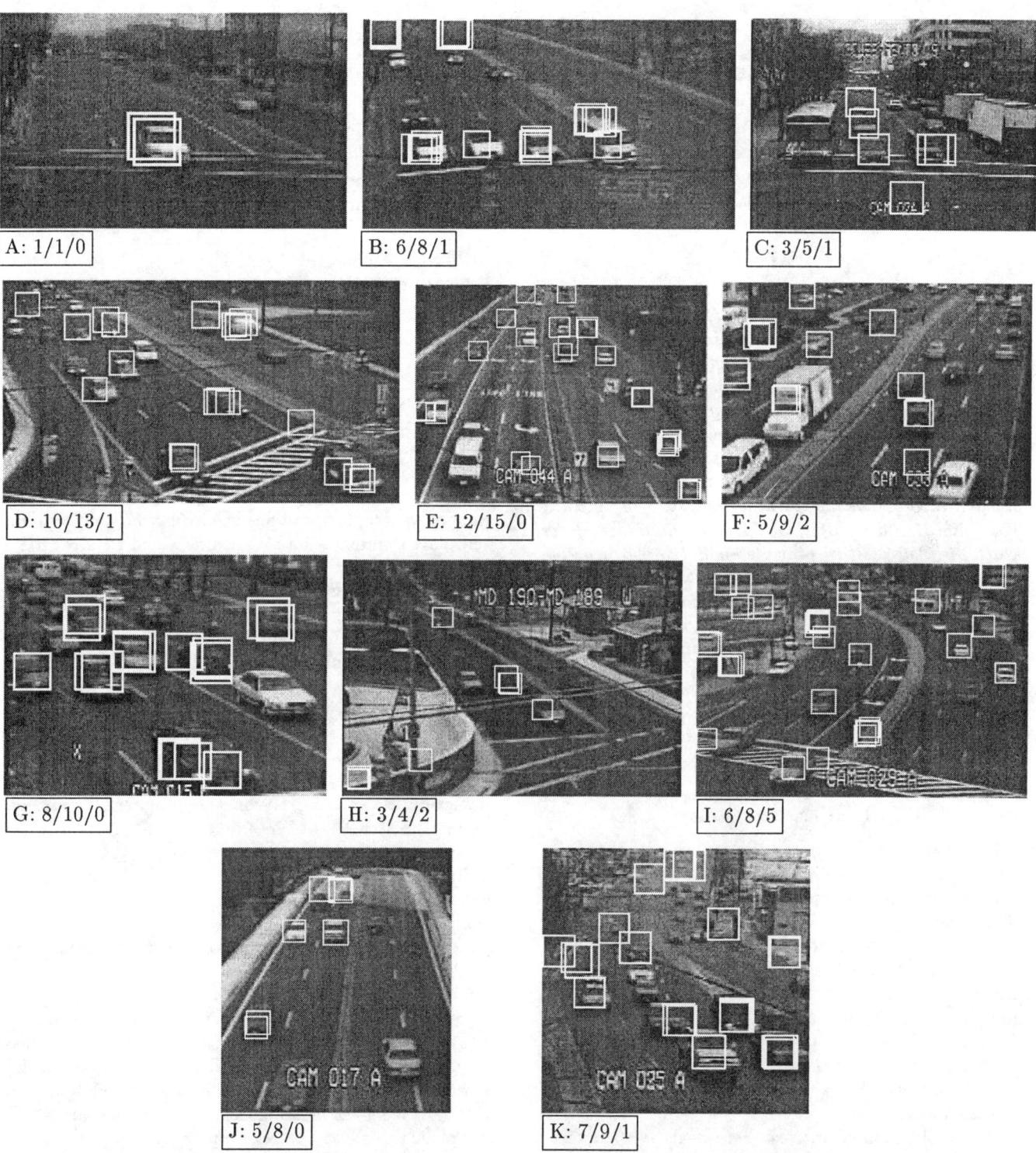

Figure 2. Results of the HOS-based vehicle detection scheme with dynamic background learning. Multiple boxes represent detection at different scales. Below each image, three values are given: they correspond to the number of vehicles detected, the number of vehicles present in the image, and the number of false matches, respectively. Vehicles that are much smaller than the training image are ignored in the calculations.

Learning-Based Object Detection in Cardiac MR Images

Nicolae Duta[1], Anil K. Jain[1], and Marie-Pierre Dubuisson-Jolly[2]

[1]Department of Computer Science and Engineering, Michigan State University
{dutanico, jain}@cse.msu.edu, http://web.cse.msu.edu/~dutanico
[2]Imaging and Visualization Department, Siemens Corporate Research, Princeton

Abstract

An automated method for left ventricle detection in MR cardiac images is presented. Ventricle detection is the first step in a fully automated segmentation system used to compute volumetric information about the heart. Our method is based on learning the gray level appearance of the ventricle by maximizing the discrimination between positive and negative examples in a training set. The main differences from previously reported methods are feature definition and solution to the optimization problem involved in the learning process. Our method was trained on a set of 1,350 MR cardiac images from which 101,250 positive examples and 123,096 negative examples were generated. The detection results on a test set of 887 different images demonstrate an excellent performance: 98% detection rate, a false alarm rate of 0.05% of the number of windows analyzed (10 false alarms per image) and a detection time of 2 seconds per 256 × 256 image on a Sun Ultra 10 for an 8-scale search. The false alarms are eventually eliminated by a position/scale consistency check along all the images that represent the same anatomical slice.

I. Introduction

The goal of this study is to automatically learn the appearance of flexible objects in gray level images. Our working definition of appearance is that it is the *pattern* of gray values in the object of interest and its immediate neighborhood. The learned appearance model can be used for object detection: given an arbitrary gray level image, decide if the object is present in the image and find its location(s) and size(s). Object detection is typically the first step in a fully automatic segmentation system for applications such as medical image analysis [1–3], industrial inspection, surveillance systems and human-computer interfaces.

The application of interest here deals with detecting the left ventricle in short axis cardiac MR images. There has been a substantial amount of recent work in studying the dynamic behavior of the human heart using non-invasive techniques such as magnetic resonance imaging [4, 5]. In order to provide useful diagnostic information, a cardiac imaging system should perform several tasks such as segmentation of heart chambers, identification of endocardium and epicardium, measure-

ment of the ventricular volume over different stages of the cardiac cycle, measurement of the ventricular wall motion, etc. Most approaches to segmentation and tracking of heart ventricles are based on deformable templates, which require specification of a good initial position of the boundary of interest. This is often provided manually, which is both time consuming and requires a trained operator.

The main objective of this paper is to automatically provide the approximate scale/position (given by a tight bounding box) of the left ventricle in 2-D cardiac MR images. This information is needed by most deformable template segmentation algorithms which require that a region of interest be provided by the user. This detection problem is difficult because of the variations in shape, scale, position and gray level appearance exhibited by the cardiac images across different slice positions, time instants, patients and imaging devices (see Fig. 1).

We make a distinction between the algorithms designed to detect specific structures in medical images and general methods that can be trained to detect an arbitrary object in gray level images. The dedicated detection algorithms rely on the designer's knowledge about the structure of interest and its variation in the images to be processed as well as on the designer's ability to code this knowledge. On the other hand, a general detection method, would necessitate very little, if any, prior knowledge about the object of interest. The specific domain information is usually replaced by a general learning mechanism based on a number of training examples of the object of interest. Among the domain specific methods for ventricle detection in cardiac images, one can mention Chiu and Razi's mutiresolution approach for segmenting echocardiograms [6], Bosch *et al.*'s dynamic programming based approach [7], and Weng *et al.*'s algorithm based on learning an adaptive threshold and region properties [5]. Most general learning strategies are based on additional cues like color or motion or rely extensively on object shape. As far as we know, the few systems that are based only on raw gray level information have only been applied to the detection of human faces in gray level images [8–12]. We want to emphasize the difference between *object detection* and *object recognition* [13, 14]. The *object recognition* problem [13] typically assumes that a

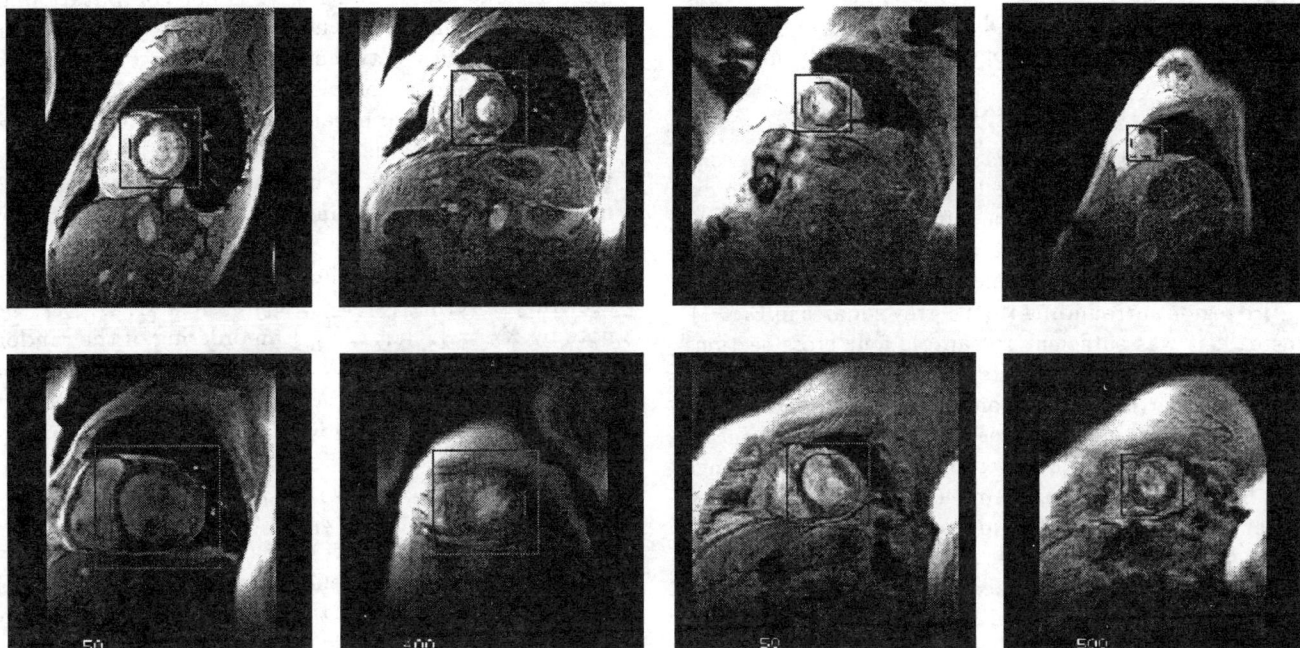

Fig. 1. Several examples of 256 × 256 gradient echo cardiac MR images (short axis view) showing the left ventricle variations as a function of acquisition time, slice position, patient and imaging device. The left ventricle is the bright area inside the square. The four markers show the ventricle walls (two concentric circles).

test image contains one of the objects of interest on a homogeneous background. The problem of object detection does not use this assumption and, therefore, is considered to be more difficult than the problem of isolated object recognition [14].

Most general-purpose detection systems essentially utilize the following detection paradigm: several windows are placed at different positions and scales in the test image and a set of low-level features is computed from each window and fed into a classifier. Typically, the features used to describe the object of interest are the "normalized" gray-level values in the window. This generates a large number of features (of the order of a couple of hundred), whose classification is both time consuming and requires a large number of training samples to overcome the "curse of dimensionality". The main difference among these systems is the classification method: Moghaddam and Pentland [8] use a complex probabilistic measure, Rowley *et al.* [9] use a neural network while Colmenarez and Huang [10] use a Markov model.

One of the main performance indices used to evaluate such systems is the detection time. Most detection systems are inherently very slow since for each window (pixel in the test image), a feature vector with large dimensionality is extracted and classified. A novel way to perform the classification (called *Information-based Maximum Discrimination*) is introduced by Colmenarez and Huang [10]: the pattern vector is modeled by a

Markov chain and its elements are rearranged such that they produce maximum discrimination between the sets of positive and negative examples. The parameters of the optimal Markov chain obtained after rearrangement are learned and a new observation is classified by thresholding its log-likelihood ratio. The main advantage of the method is that the log-likelihood ratio can be computed extremely fast, only one addition operation per feature is needed.

We propose to modify and adapt the Maximum Discrimination method [10] for left ventricle detection in MR cardiac images. The ventricle variations shown in Fig. 1 suggest that the ventricle detection problem is even more difficult than face detection. Our proposed method differs from that of Colmenarez and Huang in two significant ways:

1. Definition of the instance space. In [10] the instance space was defined as the set of 2-bit 11 × 11 non-equalized images of human faces. In our case, the ventricle diameter ranges from 20 to 100 pixels and a drastic subsampling of the image would loose the ventricle wall (the dark ring). On the other hand, even a 20 × 20 window would generate 400 features and the system would be too slow. Therefore, we used only four profiles passing through the ventricle (see Fig. 2) subsampled to define a total of 100 features.

2. Solution to the optimization problem. An approximate solution to a Traveling salesman type problem is computed in [10] using a minimum spanning tree algo-

rithm. Since the quality of the solution is crucial for the learning performance, we believe simulated annealing to be a better choice for our optimization problem.

II. Mathematical model

In order to learn a *pattern*, one should first specify the instance (feature) space from which the pattern examples are drawn. Since the left ventricle appears as a relatively symmetric object with no elaborate texture, it was not necessary to define the heart ventricle as the entire region surrounding it (the grey squares in Fig. 1). Instead, it was sufficient to sample four cross sections through the ventricle and its immediate neighborhood, along the four main directions (Fig. 2(a)). Each of the four linear cross sections was subsampled as to contain 25 points and the values were normalized in the range 0-7. The normalization scheme used here is a piece-wise linear transformation that maps the average gray level of all the pixels in the cross sections to a value 3, the minimum gray level is mapped to a value 0 and the maximum gray value is mapped to 7. In this way, a heart ventricle is defined as a feature vector $x = (x_1, ..., x_{100})$, where $x_i \in 0..7$ (Fig. 2(b)). We denote by Ω the instance space of all such vectors.

A. Markov Chain-based discrimination

We regard an observation as the realization of a random process $X = \{X_1, X_2, .., X_n\}$, where n is the number of features defining the object of interest and X_i's are random variables associated with each feature. We introduce two probabilities P and N over the instance space Ω:

$P(\mathbf{x}) = P(X = \mathbf{x}) = \text{Prob}(\mathbf{x} \text{ is a heart example})$, and
$N(\mathbf{x}) = N(X = \mathbf{x}) = \text{Prob}(\mathbf{x} \text{ is a non-heart example})$.

Since P and N can only be estimated from the training set which might be noisy, it is possible that $P(\mathbf{x}) + N(\mathbf{x}) \neq 1$. In what follows, P and N will be treated as two independent probabilities over Ω. For each instance $\mathbf{x} \in \Omega$, we define its log-likelihood ratio $L(\mathbf{x}) = log \frac{P(\mathbf{x})}{N(\mathbf{x})}$. Note that $L(\mathbf{x}) > 0$ if and only if $\mathbf{x}$ is more probable to be a heart than a non-heart, while $L(\mathbf{x}) < 0$ if the converse is true.

The Kullback divergence between P and N can be regarded as the average of the log-likelihood ratio over the entire instance space [15]:

$$H_{P||N} = \sum_{\mathbf{x} \in \Omega} P(\mathbf{x}) log \frac{P(\mathbf{x})}{N(\mathbf{x})}. \qquad (1)$$

It has been shown that the Kullback divergence is not a distance metric. However, it is generally assumed that the larger $H_{P||N}$ is, the better one can discriminate between observations from the two classes whose

distributions are P and N. It is not computationally feasible to estimate P and N taking into account all the dependencies between the features. On the other hand, assuming a complete independence of the features is not realistic because of the mismatch between the model and the data. A compromise is to consider the random process X to be a Markov chain, which can model the dependency in the data with a reasonable amount of computation.

Let us denote by S the set of feature sites with an arbitrary ordering $\{s_1, s_2, .., s_n\}$ of sites $\{1, 2, .., n\}$. Denote by $X_S = \{X_{s_1}, ..., X_{s_n}\}$ an ordering of the random variables that compose X corresponding to the site ordering $\{s_1, s_2, .., s_n\}$. If X_S is considered to be a first-order Markov chain then for $\mathbf{x} = (x_1, x_2, .., x_n) \in \Omega$ one has:

$P(X_S = \mathbf{x}) = P(X_{s_1} = x_1, ..., X_{s_n} = x_n) =$
$= P(X_{s_n} = x_n | X_{s_{n-1}} = x_{n-1}) \times ... \times$
$\times P(X_{s_2} = x_2 | X_{s_1} = x_1) \times P(X_{s_1} = x_1)$.

Therefore, the log-likelihood ratio of the two distributions P and N under the Markov chain assumption can be written as follows:

$L^S(\mathbf{x}) = log \frac{P(X_S = \mathbf{x})}{N(X_S = \mathbf{x})} =$

$= log \left(\frac{P(X_{s_1} = x_1)}{N(X_{s_1} = x_1)} \prod_{i=2}^{n} \frac{P(X_{s_i} = x_i | X_{s_{i-1}} = x_{i-1})}{N(X_{s_i} = x_i | X_{s_{i-1}} = x_{i-1})} \right) =$

$= \sum_{i=2}^{n} log \frac{P(X_{s_i} = x_i | X_{s_{i-1}} = x_{i-1})}{N(X_{s_i} = x_i | X_{s_{i-1}} = x_{i-1})} + log \frac{P(X_{s_1} = x_1)}{N(X_{s_1} = x_1)} =$

$= L^{s_1}(x_1) + \sum_{i=2}^{n} L^{s_i || s_{i-1}}(x_i, x_{i-1}). \qquad (2)$

The Kullback divergence of the two distributions P and N under the Markov chain assumption can be computed as follows:

$H_{P||N}^S = H_{P||N}(X_{s_1}, ..., X_{s_n}) =$

$= \sum_{(x_1,..,x_n) \in \Omega} P(X_{s_1} = x_1, ..., X_{s_n} = x_n) log \frac{P(X_{s_1}=x_1,...,X_{s_n}=x_n)}{N(X_{s_1}=x_1,...,X_{s_n}=x_n)}$

$= \sum_{(x_1,..,x_n) \in \Omega} P(X_{s_1} = x_1, ..., X_{s_n} = x_n) log \left(\frac{P(X_{s_1}=x_1)}{N(X_{s_1}=x_1)} \right.$

$\left. \prod_{i=2}^{n} \frac{P(X_{s_i}=x_i|X_{s_{i-1}}=x_{i-1})}{N(X_{s_i}=x_i|X_{s_{i-1}}=x_{i-1})} \right) = \sum_{i=2}^{n}$

$\left(\sum_{(x_i, x_{i-1})} P(X_{s_i} = x_i, X_{s_{i-1}} = x_{i-1}) log \frac{P(X_{s_i}=x_i|X_{s_{i-1}}=x_{i-1})}{N(X_{s_i}=x_i|X_{s_{i-1}}=x_{i-1})} \right)$

$+ \sum_{x_1} P(X_{s_1} = x_1) log \frac{P(X_{s_1}=x_1)}{N(X_{s_1}=x_1)} =$

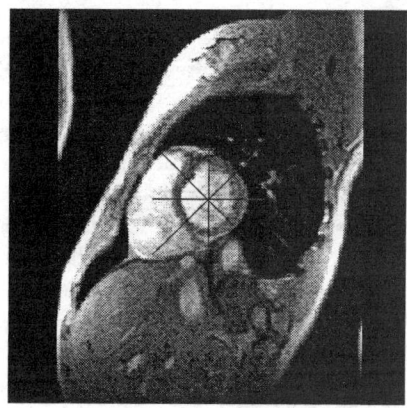
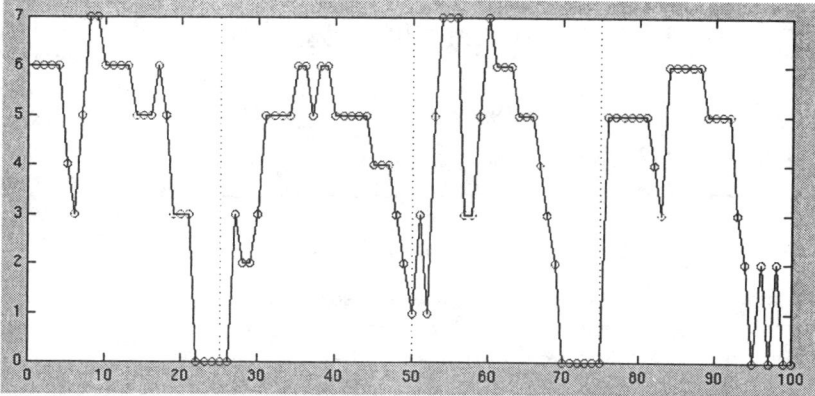

Fig. 2. The feature set defining a heart ventricle. (a) The four cross sections through the ventricle and its immediate surroundings used to extract the features. (b) The 100-element normalized feature vector associated with the ventricle in (a).

$$= H_{P||N}(X_{s_1}) + \sum_{i=2}^{n} H_{P||N}(X_{s_i}||X_{s_{i-1}}). \tag{3}$$

III. Most discriminant Markov chain

One can note that the divergence $H^S_{P||N}$ defined in Eq.(3) depends on the site ordering $\{s_1, s_2, .., s_n\}$ because each ordering produces a different Markov chain with a different distribution. The goal of the learning procedure is to find a site ordering S^* that maximizes $H^S_{P||N}$ which will result in the best discrimination between the two classes. The resulting optimization problem, although related to, is more difficult than the Traveling salesman problem since:

1. It is asymmetric (the conditional Kullback divergence is not symmetric, i.e. $H_{P||N}(X_{s_i}||X_{s_{i-1}}) \neq H_{P||N}(X_{s_{i-1}}||X_{s_i})$).

2. The salesman does not complete the tour, but remains in the last town.

3. The salesman starts from the first town with a handicap ($H_{P||N}(X_{s_1})$) which depends only on the starting point.

Therefore, the instance space of this problem is of the order of $n \times n!$, where n is the number of towns (feature sites), since for each town permutation one has n starting possibilities. It is well known that this type of problem is $NP-complete$ and cannot be solved by brute-force except for a very small number of sites. Although for the symmetric Traveling salesman problem there exist strategies to find both exact and approximate solutions in a reasonable amount of time, we are not aware of any heuristic for solving the asymmetric problem involved here. However, a good approximate solution can be obtained using simulated annealing [16]. Even though there is no theoretical guarantee to find an optimal solution, in practice, simulated annealing does almost always find a solution which is very close to the optimal (see also the discussion in [16]). Comparing the

results produced by the simulated annealing algorithm on a large number of trials with the optimal solutions (for small size problems), we found that all the solutions produced by simulated annealing were within 5% of the optimal solutions.

Once S^* is found, one can compute and store tables with the log-likelihood ratios such that, given a new observation, its log-likelihood can be obtained from $n-1$ additions using Eq.(2).

The learning stage, which is described in Algorithm 1, starts by estimating the distributions P and N and the parameters of the Markov chains associated with *all* possible site permutations using the available training examples. Next, the site ordering that maximizes the Kullback distance between P and N is found, and the log-likelihood ratios induced by this ordering are computed and stored.

Algorithm 1: Finding the most discriminating Markov Chain

• Given a set of positive/negative training examples (as preprocessed n-dimensional feature vectors).

1. For each feature site s_i, estimate $P(X_{s_i} = v)$ and $N(X_{s_i} = v)$ for $v = 0..GL - 1$ (GL = number of gray levels) and compute the divergence $H_{P||N}(X_{s_i})$.

2. For each site pair (s_i, s_j), estimate $P(X_{s_i} = v_1, X_{s_j} = v_2)$, $N(X_{s_i} = v_1, X_{s_j} = v_2)$, $P(X_{s_i} = v_1|X_{s_j} = v_2)$ and $N(X_{s_i} = v_1|X_{s_j} = v_2)$ for $v1, v2 \in 0..GL - 1$ and compute $H_{P||N}(X_{s_i}||X_{s_j}) =$

$$= \sum_{v_1,v_2=0}^{GL-1} P_X(X_{s_i} = v_1, X_{s_j} = v_2) ln \frac{P_X(X_{s_i}=v_1|X_{s_j}=v_2)}{N_X(X_{s_i}=v_1|X_{s_j}=v_2)}$$

3. Solve a traveling salesman type problem over the sites S to find $S^* = \{s_1^*, ..., s_n^*\}$ that maximizes $H_{P||N}(X_S)$.

4. Compute and store $L(X_{s_1^\bullet} = v) = ln\frac{P(X_{s_1^\bullet}=v)}{N(X_{s_1^\bullet}=v)}$ and

$L(X_{s_i^\bullet} = v_1 \| X_{s_{i-1}^\bullet} = v_2) = ln\frac{P(X_{s_i^\bullet}=v1|X_{s_{i-1}^\bullet}=v2)}{N(X_{s_i^\bullet}=v1|X_{s_{i-1}^\bullet}=v2)}$ for $v, v_1, v_2 \in \{0..GL-1\}$.

IV. Classification procedure

The detection (testing) stage consists of scanning the test image at different scales with a constant size window from which a feature vector is extracted and classified. The classification procedure using the most discriminant Markov chain, detailed in Algorithm 2, is very simple: the log-likelihood ratio for that window is computed as a sum of conditional log-likelihood ratios associated with the Markov chain ordering (Eq.(2)). The total number of additions used is at most equal to the number of features.

Algorithm 2: Classification
- Given S^*, the best Markov chain structure and the learned likelihoods $L(X_{s_1^\bullet} = v)$ and $L(X_{s_i^\bullet} = v_1 \| X_{s_{i-1}^\bullet} = v_2)$.
- Given a test example $O = (o_1, ...o_n)$ (as preprocessed n-dimensional feature vector).

1. Compute the likelihood $L_O = L(X_{s_1^\bullet} = o_{s_1^\bullet}) + \sum_{i=2}^{n} L(X_{s_i^\bullet} = o_{s_i^\bullet} \| X_{s_{i-1}^\bullet} = o_{s_{i-1}^\bullet})$.

2. If $L_O > T$ then classify O as heart else classify it as nonheart.

Here T is a threshold to be learned from the ROC curve of the training set depending on the desired (correct detect - false alarm) trade-off. In order to make the classification procedure faster, one can skip from the likelihood computation the terms with little discriminating power (associated Kullback distance is small).

V. Experimental results

A. Training Data

A collection of 1,350 MR cardiac images from 14 patients was used to generate positive training examples. The images were acquired using a Siemens Magnetom MRI system. For each patient, a number of slices (4 to 10) were acquired at different time instances (5 to 15) of the heart beat, thus producing a matrix of $2D$ images (in Fig. 4, slices are shown vertically and time instances are shown horizontally). As the heart is beating, the left ventricle is changing its size, but the scale factor between the end of diastolic and the end of systolic periods is negligible compared to the scale factor between slices at the base and the apex of the heart.

On each image, a tight bounding box (defined by the center coordinates and scale) containing the left ventricle was manually identified. From each cardiac image, 75 positive examples were produced by translating the manually defined box up to 2 pixels in each coordinate and scaling it up or down 10%. In this way, a total of 101,250 positive examples were generated. We also produced a total of 123,096 negative examples by uniformly subsampling a subset of the 1,350 available images at 8 different scales. The distributions of the log-likelihood values for the sets of positive and negative examples are shown in Fig. 3. They are very well separated, and by setting the decision threshold at 0, the resubstitution detection rate is 97.5% with a false alarm rate of 2.35%.

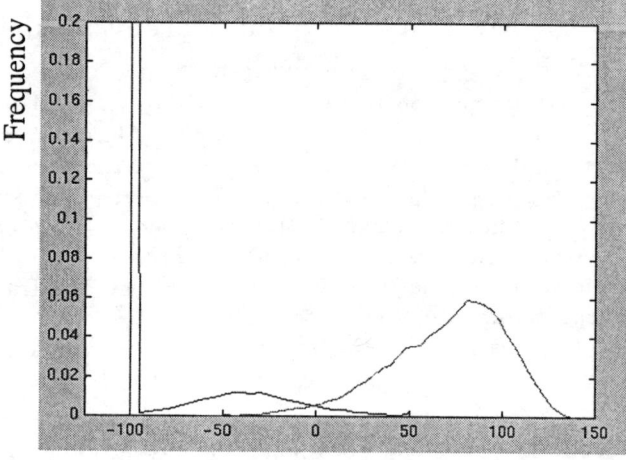

Log-likelihood ratio

Fig. 3. The distribution of the log-likelihood ratio for heart (right) and non-heart (left) examples computed over the training set.

B. Test Data

We tested our algorithm on a dataset of 887 images (size 256×256) from 7 patients different from those used for training. Each image was subsampled at 8 different scales and scanned with a constant 25×25 pixel window using a step of 2 pixels in each direction. This means that, at each scale, a number of windows equal to a quarter of the number of pixels of the image at that scale was used for feature extraction and classification. All positions that produced a positive *log-likelihood ratio* were classified as hearts. Since several neighboring positions might have been classified as such, we partitioned them into clusters (a cluster was considered to be a set of image positions classified as hearts that had

Resubstitution detection rate	97.5%
Resubstitution false alarm rate	2.35%
Test set size (# of 256 × 256 images)	887
Test set detection rate	98%
Test set false alarms per image	10
Test set false alarm rate/windows analyzed	0.05%
Detection time/image (Sun Ultra 10)	2 sec

TABLE I

PERFORMANCE OF THE LEFT VENTRICLE DETECTION ALGORITHM.

a distance smaller than 25 pixels to its centroid). At each scale, only the cluster centroids were reported, together with the *log-likelihood ratio* value for that cluster (a weighted average of the *log-likelihood ratio* values in the cluster).

It was not possible to choose the best scale/position combination based on the *log-likelihood* value of a cluster. That is, values of the *log-likelihood* criterion obtained at different scales are *not comparable*: in about 25% of the cases, the largest *log-likelihood* value failed to represent the real scale/position combination. Therefore, we report *all* cluster positions generated at different scales (an average of 11 clusters are generated per image by combining all responses at different scales). Even if we could not obtain a single scale/position combination per image using this method, the real combination was among those 11 clusters reported in 98% of the cases. Moreover, the 2% failure cases came only from the bottom most slice, where the heart is very small (15-20 pixels in diameter) and looks like a homogeneous grey disk. We suspect that these situations were rarely encountered in the training set, so they could not be learned very well. The quantitative results of the detection task are summarized in Table I. The false alarm rate has been greatly reduced by reporting only cluster centroids.

We could select the best hypothesis by performing a consistency check along all the images that represent the same slice: our prior knowledge states that, in time, one heart slice does not modify its scale/position too much, while consecutive spatial slices tend to be smaller. By enforcing these conditions, we could obtain complete spatio-temporal hypotheses about the heart location. A typical detection result on a complete spatio-temporal (8 slice positions, 15 sampling times) sequence of one patient is shown in Fig. 4).

VI. Conclusion

In order to detect the left ventricle in MR cardiac images, we have proposed a new approach based on learning the ventricle gray level appearance. The method has been successfully tested on a large dataset and shown to be very fast and accurate. The detection results can be summarized as follows: 98% detection rate, a false alarm rate of 0.05% of the number of windows analyzed (10 false alarms per image) and a detection time of 2 seconds per 256 × 256 image on a Sun Ultra 10 for an 8-scale search. The false alarms are eventually eliminated by a position/scale consistency check along all the images that represent the same anatomical slice.

Acknowledgments

This work was supported by a grant from Siemens Corporate Research, Princeton.

References

[1] L. H. Staib and J. S. Duncan. Boundary finding with parametrically deformable models. *IEEE Trans. Pattern Anal. and Machine Intelligence*, 14(11):1061–1075, 1992.

[2] N. Ayache, I. Cohen, and I. Herlin. Medical image tracking. In *Active Vision*, A. Blake and A. Yuille (Eds.), 1992. MIT Press.

[3] T. McInerney and D. Terzopoulos. Deformable models in medical image analysis: a survey. *Medical Image Analysis*, 1(2):91–108, 1996.

[4] D. Geiger, A. Gupta, L. Costa, and J. Vlontzos. Dynamic programming for detecting, tracking, and matching deformable contours. *IEEE Trans. Pattern Anal. and Machine Intelligence*, 17(3):294–302, 1995.

[5] J. Weng, A. Singh, and M. Y. Chiu. Learning-based ventricle detection from cardiac MR and CT images. *IEEE Trans. Med. Imaging*, 16(4):378–391, 1997.

[6] C. H. Chiu and D. H. Razi. A nonlinear multiresolution approach to echocardiographic image segmentation. *Computers in Cardiology*, pages 431–434, 1991.

[7] J. G. Bosch, J. H. C. Reiber, Burken G., J. J. Gerbrands, A. Kostov, van de A. J. Goor, M. Daele, and J. Roelander. Developments towards real time frame-to-frame automatic contour detection from echocardiograms. *Computers in Cardiology*, pages 435–438, 1991.

[8] B. Moghaddam and A. Pentland. Probabilistic visual learning for object representation. *IEEE Trans. Pattern Anal. and Machine Intelligence*, 19(7):696–710, 1997.

[9] H. Rowley, S. Baluja, and T. Kanade. Neural network-based face detection. *IEEE Trans. Pattern Anal. and Machine Intelligence*, 20(1):23–38, 1998.

[10] A. Colmenarez and T. Huang. Face detection with information-based maximum discrimination. In *Proceedings of CVPR-'97*, pages 782–787, San Juan, Puerto Rico, 1997.

[11] Y. Amit, D. Geman, and K. Wilder. Joint induction of shape features and tree classifiers. *IEEE Trans. Pattern Anal. and Machine Intelligence*, 19:1300–1306, 1997.

[12] A. L. Ratan, W. E. L. Grimson, and Wells W. M. Object detection and localization by dynamic template warping. In *Proceedings of CVPR '98*, pages 634–640, Santa Barbara, CA, 1998.

[13] S. K. Nayar, H. Murase, and S. Nene. Parametric Appearance Representation. In *Early Visual Learning*, pages 131–160, S. K. Nayar and T. Poggio (Eds.), 1996. Oxford University Press.

[14] T. Poggio and D. Beymer. Regularization Networks for Visual Learning. In *Early Visual Learning*, pages 43–66, S. K. Nayar and T. Poggio (Eds.), 1996. Oxford University Press.

[15] R. M. Gray. *Entropy and Information Theory*. Springer-Verlag, Berlin, 1990.

[16] E. Aarts and J. Korst. *Simulated Annealing and Boltzmann Machines: a Stochastic Approach to Combinatorial Optimization and Neural Computing*. Wiley, Chichester, 1989.

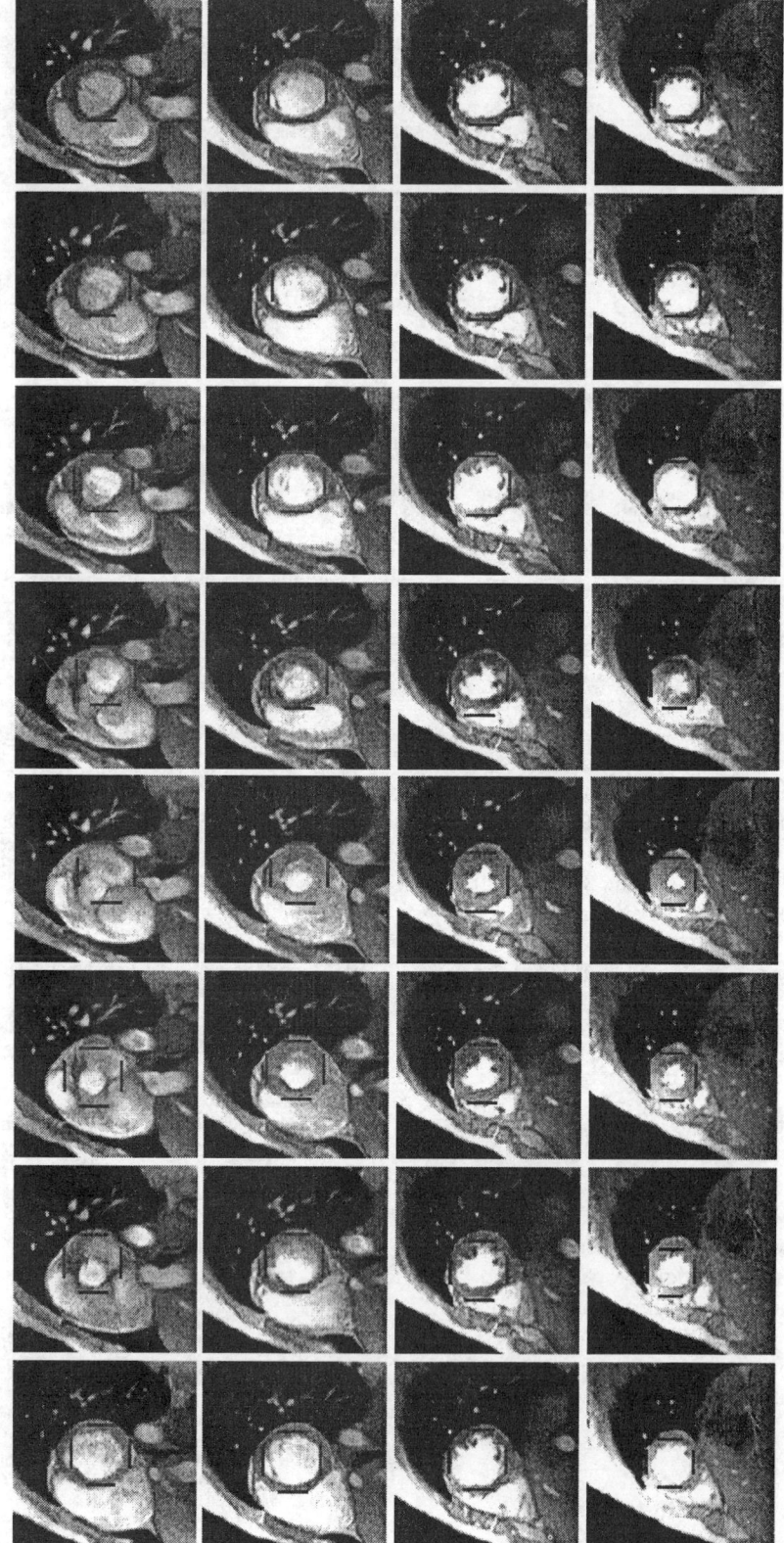

Fig. 4. Results of the detection algorithm on a complete spatio-temporal image sequence.

Learning and Evaluating Visual Features for Pose Estimation

Robert Sim and Gregory Dudek
{simra,dudek}@cim.mcgill.ca
Centre for Intelligent Machines
McGill University
3480 University St., Montreal, Canada H3A 2A7

Abstract

We present a method for learning a set of visual landmarks which are useful for pose estimation. The landmark learning mechanism is designed to be applicable to a wide range of environments, and generalized for different approaches to computing a pose estimate. Initially, each landmark is detected as a local extremum of a measure of distinctiveness and represented by a principal components encoding which is exploited for matching. Attributes of the observed landmarks can be parameterized using a generic parameterization method and then evaluated in terms of their utility for pose estimation. We present experimental evidence that demonstrates the utility of the method.

1 Introduction

In this paper, we develop an approach to vision-based robot localization by learning a set of image-domain *landmarks* in the robot's environment. The landmarks are learned from a representative set of images obtained during an initial exploration of the environment. No *a priori* assumptions are made about the scene, but rather the landmarks are initially obtained as the maximal responses to a local measure of distinctiveness in the image. In this sense we take an approach that mimics the process of visual attention. This paper extends previous work [8, 9] by considering the learning problem in broader detail, and by evaluating a variety of landmark attributes for their utility. We also present an evaluation of the experimental results which can lead to improved exploration strategies.

Our method is based on three main ideas:

1. using an attention-like model to efficiently detect recognizable characteristics of the environment;

2. using linear subspace methods to recognize features, interpolate between them, and reconstruct

incomplete data; and

3. using an optimal estimator to combine pose estimates from different sources, even within a single view.

We will elaborate on each of these ideas throughout the paper. Section 2 presents a discussion of related work on the problem of pose estimation. Section 3 presents an overview of the method. The approach that we take towards landmark detection and matching is discussed in Section 4. Section 5 presents an approach for determining landmark utility. We also examine the types of landmark attributes which can be employed for pose estimation. Section 6 provides some experimental results. The paper concludes in Section 7 with a discussion of the results.

2 Previous Work

Many early solutions to the pose estimation problem assume that the problem of landmark detection, and sometimes even recognition is easily solved [11]. In practice, however, it is often difficult to reliably extract unique landmarks from sensor data. In response to this issue, several methods rely on domain-dependent features or strict assumptions about the sensor (see, for example [7]). Alternatively, a number of authors have developed methods which avoid the use of explicit image features, but rather define implicit landmarks in a Bayesian framework [2], or through linear discrimination techniques, such as principal components analysis (PCA) [3, 6]. It has also been noted that under appropriate circumstances image recovery can be reduced to linear interpolation from suitable models [5]. While these techniques have demonstrated good results for the pose estimation and face and object recognition problems, the encoded features are often difficult to interpret. Furthermore, many of these methods are based on global charac-

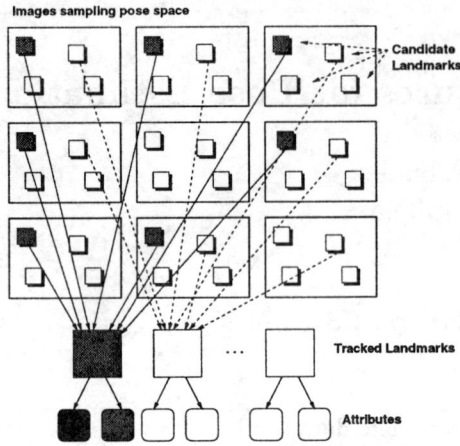

Figure 1: The offline training method.

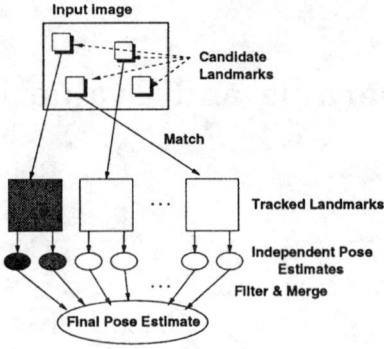

Figure 2: The online pose estimation phase.

teristics of the image and hence they tend to fail in the presence of outliers.

Our approach attempts to overcome these difficulties by avoiding any domain-dependent assumptions concerning the sensor data, and by exploiting local, rather than global, image properties.

3 Overview of the Method

In this section we present an overview of our approach to vision-based pose estimation. In this context, the method consists of two distinct phases; an initial, off-line *learning* or *exploration* phase, and an on-line pose estimation phase. In the initial off-line phase a set of landmarks is extracted from image data and grouped for future recognition. A set of attributes of the learned groups, otherwise known as *tracked landmarks*, are encoded using a generic parameterization method, which is later exploited for characterizing the landmark as a function of camera position. The on-line phase, which is employed whenever the pose of the camera is required, consists of detecting and classifying landmarks from the current view, and thereby computing a pose estimate from the attributes of the observed landmarks. The method is depicted in Figures 1 and 2 and described below.

- Off-line learning phase. (Figure 1):

  1. **Exploration:** Images are collected sampling a range of poses in the environment.

  2. **Detection:** *Landmark candidates* are extracted from each image using a model of visual attention.

  3. **Matching:** *Tracked landmarks* are extracted by tracking visually similar candidate landmarks over the configuration space.

  4. **Parameterization:** The tracked landmarks are parameterized on the basis of a set of computed landmark attributes (for example, position in the image, intensity distribution, edge distribution, etc), and then measured in terms of their *a priori utility* for pose estimation.

  5. The set of sufficiently useful tracked landmarks is stored for future retrieval.

- On-line pose estimation (Figure 2):

  1. When a position estimate is required, a single image is acquired from the camera.

  2. Candidate landmarks are extracted from the input image using the same model of visual attention used in the off-line phase.

  3. The candidate landmarks are matched to the tracked landmarks learned in the off-line phase.

  4. A position estimate is obtained using each computed attribute for *each* matched candidate landmark.

  5. A final position estimate is computed by merging the individual estimates of the observed candidates.

4 Visual Landmarks

In order to extract potential landmarks from an image, we employ a statistical measure of local image content. Good candidates include saliency measures such as edge density or local symmetry, or the output of a matched filter. We formulate our *landmark detector* as a filter that extracts local maxima from the edge-density map of the image. In this sense, landmark candidates represent regions of the image which are out of the ordinary. This concept has been employed by Bourque and Dudek for the purposes of exploration and environment representation [1]. Figure 3 shows the results obtained from running the landmark detector on an image obtained in our lab. The landmarks are superimposed on the original intensity image, and the computed density function. Further details of the landmark detection algorithm are provided in [9, 8].

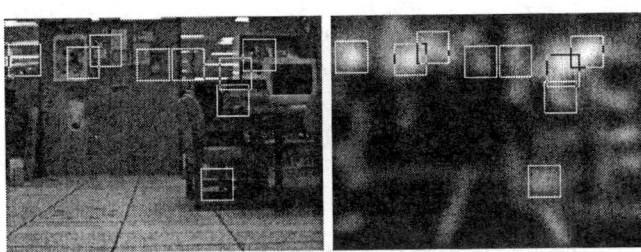

Figure 3: Detected Landmarks in an Image.

4.1 Tracking

A landmark represents the basic feature which we can employ for pose estimation, which is accomplished by computing a characterization of attributes of the landmark as a function of the camera's position. In order to achieve this characterization, however, the stability of a landmark must be established by tracking the landmark over a set of poses.

Our technique for landmark tracking operates as follows. As each training image is obtained, its landmark candidates are extracted, and matched to a selected set of landmark *prototypes*. The prototypes themselves are instances of previously observed landmark candidates. The set of landmark candidates (each of which is an observation taken from a different view) that match to a particular prototype, including the prototype itself, constitute a *tracked landmark*.

The task of landmark matching, or *recognition*, is achieved using principal components analysis (PCA) [12, 3, 4]. For the purposes of matching, we represent a landmark by the subspace encoding of the intensity distribution in the neighbourhood of the candidate. The subspace itself is computed from the intensity distributions of the set of prototypes to which we are matching. Further details of the tracking algorithm can be found in [9].

A *tracked landmark* and its derived attributes constitute the essential modelling primitive that is used for subsequent correspondence and position estimation. Figure 4 shows a typical tracked landmark (representing one of the posters on the door in Figure 3). Each thumbnail image corresponds to the landmark as detected in the image taken at the corresponding grid position in pose space. Grid positions with no corresponding thumbnail image indicate positions in the pose space where no landmark candidate was found that matched the prototype.

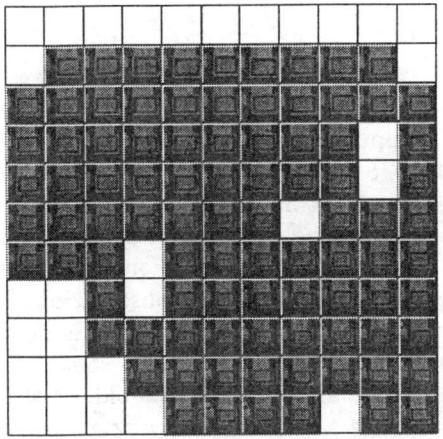

Figure 4: A typical landmark set.

5 Landmark Parameterization

Our goal is to learn a set of landmarks in order to estimate unknown parameters (that is, the pose of the camera $\mathbf{q}$) of future observations of the landmarks. Let us assume for the moment that the exploration phase yields a tracked landmark $T = \{l_1, l_2, \ldots, l_n\}$ constituting a set of observations of the landmark, each taken from a different pose $\mathbf{q}$. Furthermore, consider a set of attributes $A_i = \{\mathbf{a}_1, \mathbf{a}_2, \ldots, \mathbf{a}_m\}$ that can be computed from the image neighbourhood of the landmark. Examples of possible attributes are the intensity or edge distributions of the image in the neighbourhood of the landmark, or the position of the landmark in the image.

Clearly, when we observe T from the pose $\mathbf{q}$,

$$\mathbf{a}_j = F_{(T,j)}(\mathbf{q}) \qquad 1 < j < m \qquad (1)$$

That is, each computed attribute of T is a function $F_{(T,j)}(\cdot)$ of the pose of the robot. Note that $F_{(T,j)}(\cdot)$ is observable by simply making observations of T from different poses. In the sequel we will drop the subscript j for simplicity; however the reader should be aware that a range of attributes can be computed from a single observation, and that each will have its own generating function.

For an attribute **a** computed from an observation of T, the problem of generating a pose estimate is equivalent to that of inverting $F_T(\cdot)$. However, since different poses could lead to the same computed value for **a**, $F_T(\cdot)$ is not invertible and in general the problem is *ill-posed*. Rather, let us assume that we have a method for computing a pose estimation function $F_T^\dagger(\cdot)$ from T such that

$$\mathbf{q} \approx F_T^\dagger(\mathbf{a}). \qquad (2)$$

That is, we can use our exploratory observations of T to compute a *pseudo-inverse* of $F_T(\cdot)^1$ that can be applied to observations in order to generate approximate pose estimates. In previous work, we have presented a method for computing a pseudo-inverse using a linear least squares reconstruction from the space spanned by the training observations T[9]. The reader may refer to those works for further details. For alternative approaches, one might choose to employ bilinear interpolation in the manifold, or a non-linear technique, such as a neural network.

5.1 Landmark Utility

We are interested in evaluating each $F_T^\dagger(\cdot)$ in such a way that we can measure the the utility of each T, and of each attribute for computing a pose estimate. This is achieved using *cross validation* [13]. Cross validation operates by considering each training observation $l_i \in T$ (observed from the known pose $\mathbf{q}_i$) as an input to the function $F_{T_i}^\dagger(\cdot)$, which is computed from the modified tracked landmark $T_i = T - l_i$ and measuring the error

$$\mathbf{e}_i = \mathbf{q}_{l_i} - F_{T_i}^\dagger(\mathbf{a}), \qquad (3)$$

We define the utility U_T of $F_T^\dagger(\cdot)$ as the mean and covariance of the distribution of the observed errors:

$$U_T = \{\mu, C\} \qquad (4)$$

Where μ represents the average or systematic error inherent in $F_T^\dagger(\cdot)$, and C represents the covariance, or distribution of errors in $F_T^\dagger(\cdot)$. The benefit of computing U_T is twofold: when we compute a pose estimate for an observed landmark, we can use μ to correct for systematic error, and then associate C with the result in order to represent the uncertainty of the estimate. Note that $F_T^\dagger(\cdot)$, and hence U_T is computed solely from an attribute of T, and hence is a quantity that can be

---

¹The use of the term pseudo-inverse is intended to reflect that $F_T^\dagger(\cdot)$ approximates the inverse of $F_T(\cdot)$. It is not necessarily the pseudo-inverse in the strict linear algebraic sense.

computed in the training phase. Note also that we are assuming that the error is Gaussian in nature, which may not always be the case.

In taking this approach, we can measure the quality of the training data and improve it if necessary, before we ever perform the on-line process of estimating pose. For example, at each pose **q** in the training phase, we can compute a measure of reliability

$$R_\mathbf{q} = \sum_{T_i \in \Lambda, \mathbf{a}_j \in A} \frac{1}{|C_{T_i, \mathbf{a}_j}|} \qquad (5)$$

where Λ is the set of tracked landmarks which are observed from pose **q**, and A is the set of computable attributes, and $|C_{T_i, \mathbf{a}_j}|$ is the determinant of the covariance obtained from U_{T_i} for attribute $\mathbf{a}_j$. Clearly, larger values of R should lead to more reliable pose estimates. Figure 5 plots R as a function of pose for the scene depicted in Figure 3. In this plot, the orientation of the camera is fixed to face in the negative y direction while the robot moves over a 2m by 2m pose space. Note that the reliability is particularly for small values of y. This is due to the fact that images in that region of the pose space change dramatically under small changes in pose, leading to difficulty in tracking the landmarks.

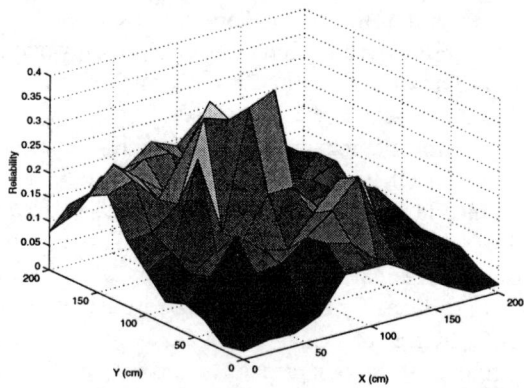

Figure 5: *A-priori* training reliability R as a function of pose. The camera faces in the negative y direction.

5.2 Pose Estimation

Pose estimation involves extracting landmarks, matching them to the learned landmarks and generating pose estimate for each of the computed attributes for each match using equation 2. The final step then combines the estimates from the different landmarks and attributes to obtain a final pose estimate. In order to combine the estimates, we employ the approach used by Smith and Cheeseman for combining estimates with associated error models [10]. In this method, U_T is employed as an error model for T. Prior to merging, however, outlier detection is performed by finding the median position estimate $\hat{\mathbf{X}}_m$, and computing a median covariance, $\mathbf{C}_m$ from the set of estimates and their associated covariances. The coefficients of $\mathbf{C}_m$ define an ellipsoidal region of the pose space, the scale of which is controlled by the user, centred at $\hat{\mathbf{X}}_m$, within which predictions can be considered to be acceptable. Figure 6 depicts a set of position estimates (the set of all diamonds), the median estimate (the ellipse) and those estimates which are considered acceptable for merging, (the solid diamonds).

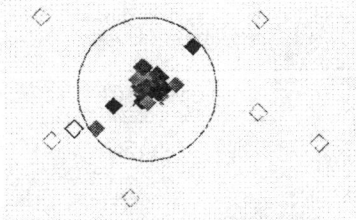

Figure 6: A set of filtered predictions.

In the following section, we will demonstrate the utility of the method.

6 Experimental Results

Our technique has been tested using a variety of different environments. In particular, we have obtained results for three different scenes, the results of which are tabulated in Table 1. In all three scenes, the pose of the camera is constrained to a single orientation as images of the scene are collected. We have demonstrated a method for recovering the orientation of the camera, even when the method is trained at a single orientation [9].

Figure 7: Scenes I and II.

	Scene		
	I	II	III
Training Samples	121	256	122
Test Samples	20	100	53
Tracked Landmarks	26	136	53
Sample Spacing S (cm)	1.0	2.0	20.0
Mean error μ_e (cm)	0.067	0.38	7.5
Std. deviation σ_e (cm)	0.04	0.3	5.0
Accuracy $\frac{\mu_e}{S} \cdot 100\%$	6.7%	19%	37.5%

Table 1: Experimental Results

Scene I (Figure 7-a) is a constrained environment in which the ground-truth position of a camera mounted on the end-effector of a gantry robot can be measured with high accuracy. The scene itself is a simple construction using a set of objects, and images are taken at 1 cm intervals over a 10cm by 10cm pose space. Scene II (Figure 7-b) employs the same robot for a slightly more complicated scene, and images are collected at 2.0cm intervals over a 30cm by 30cm pose space. Scene III employs a camera mounted on a mobile robot for which the ground truth pose of the robot can be measured to an accuracy of about 0.5cm and $1°$. The scene itself is that depicted in Figure 3. Training images are collected at 20cm intervals over a 2.0m by 2.0m pose space. The experimental results for each scene are produced in Table 1. Each column records the number of training samples, the number of test inputs (randomly sampling the pose space), the number of tracked landmarks, the space S between nearest samples in the training sets, the mean error μ_e and standard deviation in error σ_e for the set of test inputs. Finally, the last line expresses the quality of results in terms of μ_e as a percentage of S.

Figure 8 presents the set of estimates obtained for the test images obtained for Scene III, plotted against their ground-truth. Each 'x' represents the estimate generated for the image taken from the corresponding 'o'. Recall that each pose estimate was generated without any prior knowledge of the robot position. As such, the accuracy is highly satisfying.

6.1 Evaluating Attributes

Table 2 summarizes the quality of the attributes that are employed for pose estimation for the three scenes. For any given tracked landmark, the image position, intensity distribution and edge distribution of the landmarks are each used to generate a separate

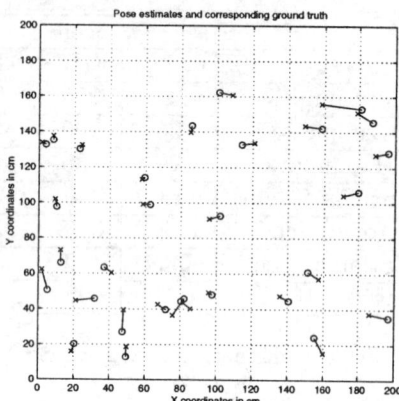

Figure 8: The set of pose estimates obtained for the laboratory environment shown in Figure 3 (Scene III).

Attribute	Scene		
	I	II	III
Image Position	1.476	0.3580	2.986
Intensity Distribution	0.6205	0.5923	21.17
Edge Distribution	4.599	2.031	29.81

Table 2: *A priori* Attribute Uncertainty

pseudo-inverse and *a priori* utility. Tabulated are the square-roots of the mean determinants of the utility covariance over all tracked landmarks. Therefore, the smaller the value, the more reliable the attribute is. It is interesting to note that, in general, the geometric position of the landmark in the image is a reliable indicator of position. This trend is violated in Scene I, however, where the motion of the camera is small enough that quantization errors interfere with the pose estimation procedure. Also note that the edge distribution tends to fare poorly. This is most likely due to the highly nonlinear variation in the edge distribution as a function of camera pose.

7   Conclusions

This paper has presented a method for *learning* a set of landmarks from a set of views of the environment in order to obtain accurate pose estimates. Candidates for landmarks are detected as local maxima of a measure of distinctiveness. Landmark candidates are then grouped into *tracked landmarks*; sets of candidates which correspond to the same visual region of the environment, as observed from different viewpoints. A function $F_T(\cdot)$ is computed that can generate pose estimates for future observations which match the tracked landmark T. The utility of each

$F_T(\cdot)$ is measured in order to determine the quality of the training data and the expected confidence in subsequent pose estimates. Online position estimation is performed by detecting candidates and matching them to the tracked landmarks. Each match is used to generate a pose estimate from the corresponding $F_T(\cdot)$, and the set of estimates are combined using robust statistics. The experimental results indicate that the method performs well for a variety of environments.

References

[1] Eric Bourque and Gregory Dudek. Automated image-based mapping. In *Proceedings of the IEEE Conference on Computer Vision and Pattern Recognition–Workshop on Perception of Mobile Agents*, pages 61–70, June 1998.

[2] F. Dallaert, W. Burgard, D. Fox, and S. Thrun. Using the condensation algorithm for robust, vision-based mobile robot localization. In *Proceedings of the IEEE Conference on Computer Vision and Pattern Recognition (CVPR)*, Ft. Collins, CO, June 1999. IEEE Press.

[3] S.K. Nayar, H. Murase, and S.A. Nene. Learning, positioning, and tracking visual appearance. In *Proceedings of the IEEE International Conference on Robotics and Automation*, pages 3237–3246, San Diego, CA, May 1994.

[4] A. Pentland, B. Moghaddam, and T. Starner. View-based and modular eigenspaces for face recognition. In *Proc. IEEE Conference on Computer Vision and Pattern Recognition*, pages 84–90, Seattle, WA, June 1994. IEEE Press.

[5] T. Poggio and T. Girosi. Networks for approximation and learning. In *Proceedings of the IEEE (special issue: Neural Networks I: Theory and Modeling)*, volume 78, pages 1481–1497, 1990.

[6] F. Pourraz and J. L. Crowley. Continuity properties of the appearance manifold for mobile robot position estimation. In *Proceedings of the 2nd IEEE Workshop on Perception for Mobile Agents*, Ft. Collins, CO, June 1999. IEEE Press.

[7] J. Shi and C. Tomasi. Good features to track. In *Proc. IEEE International Conf. Computer Vision and Pattern Recognition (CVPR)*. IEEE Press, 1994.

[8] R. Sim and G. Dudek. Learning environmental features for pose estimation. In *Proceedings of the 2nd IEEE Workshop on Perception for Mobile Agents*, Ft. Collins, CO, June 1999. IEEE Press.

[9] R. Sim and G. Dudek. Learning visual landmarks for pose estimation. In *Proceedings of the IEEE International Conference on Robotics and Automation(ICRA)*, Detroit, MI, May 1999. IEEE Press.

[10] Randall C. Smith and Peter Cheeseman. On the representation and estimation of spatial undertainty. *International Journal of Robotics Research*, 5(4):56–68, 1986.

[11] K.T. Sutherland and W.B. Thompson. Inexact navigation. In *Proceedings of the IEEE*, pages 1–7, 1993.

[12] Matthew Turk and Alex Pentland. Face processing: Models for recognition. *Mobile Robotics IV*, Nov. 1989.

[13] Grace Wahba. Convergence rates of 'thin plate' smoothing splines when the data are noisy. *Smoothing Techniques for Curve Estimation*, pages 233–245, 1979.

A Pattern Classification Approach to Dynamical Object Detection

Constantine Papageorgiou   Tomaso Poggio

Center for Biological and Computational Learning & Artificial Intelligence Laboratory

45 Carleton Street, E25-201

Cambridge, MA 02142

{cpapa,tp}@ai.mit.edu

Abstract

Current systems for object detection in video sequences rely on explicit dynamical models like Kalman filters or hidden Markov models. There is significant overhead needed in the development of such systems as well as the a priori assumption that the object dynamics can be described with such a dynamical model. This paper describes a new pattern classification technique for object detection in video sequences that uses a rich, overcomplete dictionary of wavelet features to describe an object class. Unlike previous work where a small subset of features was selected from the dictionary, this system does no feature selection and learns the model in the full 1,326 dimensional feature space. Comparisons using different sized sets of several types of features are given. We extend this representation into the time domain without assuming any explicit model of dynamics. This data driven approach produces a model of the physical structure and short-time dynamical characteristics of people from a training set of examples; no assumptions are made about the motion of people, just that short sequences characterize their dynamics sufficiently for the purposes of detection. One of the main benefits of this approach is that transient false positives are reduced. This technique compares favorably with the static detection approach and could be applied to other object classes. We also present a real-time version of one of our static people detection systems.

1 Introduction

Object detection in video sequences is an area of fundamental importance for many areas of image processing. For a face recognition based access system, the face must first be detected before it is recognized; for autonomous navigation, obstacles and landmarks need to be detected and subsequently classified; detecting different classes of objects is paramount for indexing into image and video databases. The basic problem we tackle can be formulated as follows: how can we reliably detect a certain class of objects in video sequences of unconstrained, cluttered scenes? As a testbed for our system, we will be focusing primarily on people detection.

There are two basic angles this problem could take: static images or video sequences. If we would like to detect objects in static images, the problem becomes a pure pattern classification task; the system must be able to differentiate between the objects of interest and "everything else". If, on the other hand, the problem is to detect objects in video sequences, there is a richer set of information available, namely the dynamical information inherent in the video sequence. For a general purpose system that does not make limiting assumptions about the objects, we cannot, however, exclusively rely on *motion* information per se; what if the particular scene is of a group of people standing at a bus stop? A system that relies on motion to detect people would clearly fail in this case.

What we need is a technique that uses a model that is rich enough to both a) describe the object class to the degree that it is able to effectively model any of the possible shapes, poses, colors, and textures of the object, and b) harness the dynamical information inherent in video sequences, without making any underlying assumptions about the actual dynamics of the objects.

To achieve these goals, we will use a learning-based approach. The system will automatically learn what constitutes a person and their dynamics. We will appeal to previous work, where we have described a system for object detection in static images [16] [14] [17] that has shown a high degree of performance. This system can be characterized as a learning-based approach that uses a rich, overcomplete dictionary of wavelet features. It makes no assumptions on the scene structure and does not use any motion or tracking information.

Unlike the previous systems which reduced the dimensionality of the learning task through a feature selection step, the system we describe here does not do any feature selection. Instead, the entire set of features ($O(10^3)$) are used to train a support vector machine (SVM) classifier that can effectively handle high-dimensional feature spaces populated by small data sets. We provide an empirical comparison of how using classes of features that are qualitatively different, as well as different numbers of these features, lead to detection systems with significantly different performance.

We modify this approach to represent dynamic information by extending the static representation into the time domain. One of the most important factors motivating the extension of the classification into the time domain is that for the static system, false positives often appear, but are typically transient. With this new representation, the system will be able to learn certain dynamical characteristics of people, motion or no motion. The system will learn what a person looks like and what constitutes valid dynamics over short time sequences, without the need for explicit models of either shape or dynamics. The only assumption we make is that short sequences characterize the motion of people sufficiently for the purposes of detection. We show that this technique indeed reduces the false positive rate.

2 Related work

Much of the previous work in object detection and recognition in video sequences has focused on people detection. Here, we review some of the work relevant to this paper.

[20] [11] use simple geometrical models and motion to detect and analyze people. [9] and [18] develop systems using 3D cylindrical models and the latter also uses kinematic motion data.

[22] describe a system for the real-time tracking of the human body that uses a maximum a posteriori approach to segment a body into blobs and tracks the blobs, but assumes that the camera and background are fixed and that there is a single person in the image. [1] uses a combination of probabilistic approaches, Kalman filters, and hidden Markov models to segment and recognize different human motions.

[13] describe a system that tracks multiple people in video and automatically detects a face for each person found in the images. [6] present a system for real time detection and tracking of people; here, they assume knowledge of the background.

To track moving objects, [7] use clusters of consistent color; however, an initial manual labeling step is required. This system has been combined with a time delay neural network to detect and recognize pedestrians [8].

[4] present a system for recognizing actions based on time-weighted binarized motion images taken over relatively short sequences; the system is not used for detection, however.

All these systems have succeeded to varying degrees but have relied on the following restrictive features:

- explicit modeling of the domain;

- stationary camera and a fixed background;

- assume person is moving

- make assumptions about the scene structure;

- implement tracking of objects, not detection of specific classes.

This work will overcome these problems by describing an example-based approach that learns to recognize patterns in short video sequences and avoids the explicit use of motion and segmentation. An important characteristic of our system will be that, even though it uses dynamical information for detection, it makes no assumptions about the underlying dynamics – there is no explicit model.

3 The static detection system

The object detection system we develop does not undergo any feature selection steps. This is in contrast to previously reported results [16] [14] [17] where a small subset of features was extracted from a large feature dictionary. In this section we give an overview of the system

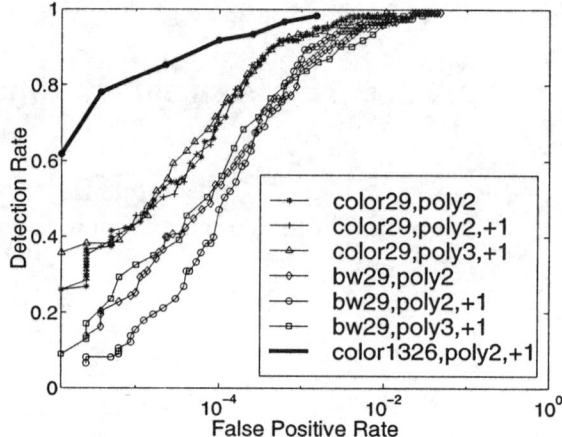

Figure 1. ROC curves for different detection systems. The detection rate is plotted against the false positive rate, measured on a logarithmic scale. The false detection rate is defined as the number of false detections per inspected window.

and highlight the increased accuracy when compared to systems doing feature selection. In addition, we present results of using different qualitative classes of features.

3.1 Representation

One of the key issues in the development of an object detection system is the representation of the object class. The patterns are 128×64 RGB images where the people have been aligned in the center of the images and can be in many different poses: frontal, rear, side walking, side standing. Typical images of people show a great deal of variability in the color, texture, and pose as well as the lack of a consistent background. Our challenge is to develop a representation that achieves high inter-class variability with low intra-class variability.

To motivate our choice of representation, we can start by considering several traditional representations. Pixel-based and color region-based approaches are likely to fail because of the high degree of variability in the color and the number of spurious patterns. Traditional fine-scale edge based representations are also unsatisfactory due to the large degree of noise in these edges.

The representation that we use is an overcomplete dictionary of Haar wavelets in which there is a large set of features that respond to local intensity differences at several orientations. We present an overview of this representation here; details can be found in [12] [19] [16] [14].

For a given pattern, the wavelet transform computes the responses of the wavelet filters over the image. Each of the three oriented wavelets – vertical, horizontal, and diagonal – are computed at several different scales allowing the system to represent coarse scale features all the way down to fine scale features. In our system for people detection, we use the scales 32×32 and 16×16. In the traditional wavelet transform, the wavelets do not overlap; they are shifted by the size of the support of the wavelet in x and *y*. To achieve better spatial resolution and a richer set of features, our transform shifts by $\frac{1}{4}$ of the size of the support of each wavelet, yielding an overcomplete dictionary of wavelet features. This results in a 1,326 dimensional feature vector for each pattern, which is used as training data for our classification engine.

There is certain *a priori* knowledge embedded in our choice of the wavelets. First, we use the absolute values of the magnitudes of the wavelets; this tells the system that a dark body on a light background and a light body on a dark background have the same information content. Second, we compute the wavelet transform for a given pattern in each of the three color channels and then, for a wavelet of a specific location and orientation, we use the one that is largest in magnitude. This allows the system to use the most visually significant features.

3.2 Support vector machine classification

Support vector machines (SVM) is a technique to train classifiers that is well-founded in statistical learning theory; for details, see [21] [3]. One of the main attractions of using SVMs is that they are capable of learning in *sparse, high-dimensional spaces* with very few training examples. SVMs accomplish this by minimizing a bound on the empirical error and the complexity of the classifier, at the same time.

This concept is formalized in the theory of uniform convergence in probability:

$$R(\alpha) \leq R_{emp}(\alpha) + \Phi\left(\frac{h}{\ell}, \frac{-log(\eta)}{\ell}\right) \quad (1)$$

with probability $1 - \eta$. Here, $R(\alpha)$ is the expected risk, $R_{emp}(\alpha)$ is the empirical risk, ℓ is the number of training examples, and h is the VC dimension of the classifier that is being used. This leads us directly to the principle of structural risk minimization, whereby we can attempt to minimize at the same time both the actual error over the training set and the complexity of the classifier; this will bound the generalization error as in Equation 1. It is exactly this technique that support vector machines approximate.

This controlling of both the training set error *and* the classifier's complexity has allowed support vector machines to be successfully applied to very high dimensional learning tasks; [10] presents results on SVMs applied to a 10,000 dimensional text categorization problem and [15] show a 283 dimensional face detection system. We will make use of this property of being able to apply SVMs to very high dimensional classification problems when we describe our dynamic object detection technique later in this paper.

Using the SVM formulation, the classification step for a pattern **x** using a polynomial of degree two is as follows:

$$f(\mathbf{x}) = \theta\left(\sum_{i=1}^{N_s} \alpha_i y_i (\mathbf{x} \cdot \mathbf{x}_i + 1)^2 + b\right) \quad (2)$$

where N_s is the number of support vectors – training data points that define the decision boundary – and α_i are Lagrange parameters.

3.3 Detecting people in new images

To detect pedestrians in a new image, we shift the 128×64 detection window over all locations in the image. This will only detect pedestrians at a single scale, however. To achieve multi-scale detection, we incrementally resize the image and run the detection window over each of these resized images. This brute force search over the image is quite time consuming; several methods can be used to reduce the computation (see Section 5).

3.4 Feature comparison

In Section 3.1, we discussed the characteristics of the class of features the system extracts. Here, we provide empirical results which show that using all the features leads to a higher-performing system than if the dimensionality of the representation is reduced using feature selection.

To determine the performance of a detection system, it is necessary to analyze a full ROC curve that shows the tradeoff between accuracy and the rate of false positives. The system is trained over a database of 1,848 positive patterns and 7,189 negative patterns. We emphasize that our ROC curves are computed over an *out-of-sample* test set gathered outdoors and over the Internet. Figure 1 compares the ROC curves of several different incarnations of our system. They are as follows:

- color processing with 29 features using a homogeneous polynomial of degree two

- color processing with 29 features using a polynomial of degree two

- color processing with 29 features using a polynomial of degree three

- grey-level processing with 29 features using a homogeneous polynomial of degree two

- grey-level processing with 29 features using a polynomial of degree two

- grey-level processing with 29 features using a polynomial of degree three

- color processing with all 1,326 features using a polynomial of degree two

From the ROC curve, it is clear that most of the impact on performance comes from the class of features that are used; the complexity of the classifier is not as significant. As expected, using color features results in a more powerful system. The curve of the system with *no feature selection* is clearly superior to all the others. This indicates that for the best accuracy, using all the features is optimal. When classifying using this full set of features, we pay for the accuracy through a slower system. It may be possible to achieve the same performance as the 1,326 feature system with fewer that the entire set of features; this is an open research question.

Figure 2. Example image sequences that are used to train our dynamic detection system.

4 The dynamic detection system

As stated in the introduction, our goal is to develop a detection system for video sequences that makes as few assumptions as possible; we do not want to develop an explicit model of the shape of people or outwardly model their possible motions in any way.

We would like a technique that implicitly generates a model of both the shape and valid dynamical characteristics of people at the same time from a set of training data. This should be accomplished without assuming that human motion can be approximated by a linear Kalman filter or that it can be described by a hidden Markov model or any other dynamical model. The only assumption we will make is that five consecutive frames of an image sequence contain characteristic information regarding the dynamics of how people appear in video sequences. From a set of training data, the system will learn exactly what constitutes a person and how people typically appear in these short time sequences.

Instead of using a single 128×64 pattern from one image as a training example, our new approach takes the 128×64 patterns at a fixed location in five consecutive frames, computes the 1,326 features for each of these patterns, and concatenates them into a single 6,630 dimensional feature vector for use in the support vector training. We use images $t-4, t-3, t-2, t-1, t$ where the person is aligned in the center of the image at t. Figure 2 shows several example sequences from the training set. The full training set is composed of 1,379 positive examples and 3,822 negative examples.

The extension to detecting people in new images is straightforward; for each candidate pattern in a new image, we concatenate the wavelet features computed for that pattern to the wavelet features computed at that location in the previous four frames. The full feature vector is subsequently classified by the SVM.

We emphasize that it is the implicit ability of the support vector machine classification technique to handle small sets of data that sparsely populate a very high-dimensional feature space that allows us to tackle this problem.

In developing this type of representation, we expect that the following dynamical information will be evident in the training data and therefore encapsulated in the classifier:

- people usually display smooth motion or are stationary

- people do not spontaneously appear or disappear from one frame to another

- camera motion is usually smooth or stationary

One of the primary benefits derived from this technique is that it extends this rich feature set into the time dimension and is able to both detect people at high accuracy, while reducing transient false positives that would normally appear when using the static detection system.

This is purely a data-driven pattern classification approach to dynamical detection. We compare this approach to the static detection system, trained with the individual images corresponding to frame t in each of the sequences, so there are 1,379 positive and 3,822 negative 1,326 dimensional feature vectors as training for the static detection system. Both the static and dynamic systems are tested on

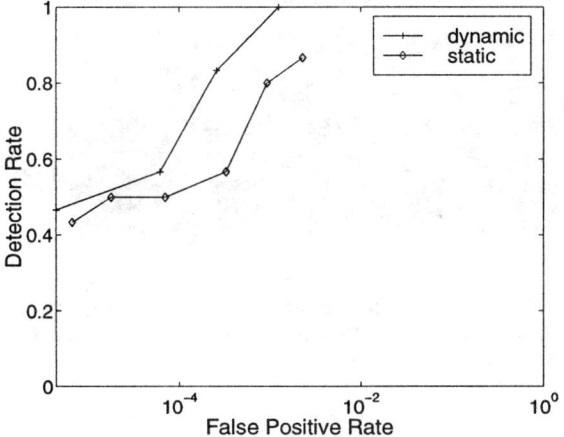

Figure 3. ROC curves for the static and dynamic detection systems. The detection rate is plotted against the false positive rate, measured on a logarithmic scale. The false positive rate is defined as the number of false detections per inspected window.

the same out-of-sample sequence. Figure 3 shows the ROC curves for the two systems. From the ROC curves, we see that the system that has incorporated dynamical information performs better than the system that uses only static patterns. This is more impressive in light of the fact that the dynamic system is doing its classification in a 6,630 dimensional space with only 5,201 training examples.

It is important to note that our features are not the 3D wavelets in space and time; what we have done is taken a set of 2D wavelet features spread through time and used these to develop our model. One extension of our system that we would like to pursue is to use 3D wavelets as features. Such a system would learn the dynamics as a set of displacements and therefore may generalize better.

5 A real, real-time system

As an alternative to dynamic detection strategies, we can use a modified version of our static detection system to achieve real-time performance. This section describes a real, real-time application of our technology as part of a larger system for driver assistance; the combined system, including our people detection module, is currently deployed "live" in a DaimlerChrysler S Class demonstration vehicle. The remainder of this section describes the integrated system.

5.1 Speed optimizations

Our original unoptimized static detection system for people detection in color images processes sequences at a rate of 1 frame per 20 minutes; this is clearly inadequate for any real-time automotive application. We have implemented optimizations that have yielded several orders of magnitude worth of speedups.

subset of 29 features: Instead of using the entire set of 1,326 wavelet features, we use just 29 of the more important features that encode the outline of the body. This changes

the 1,326 dimensional inner product in Equation 2 into a 29 dimensional dot product.

reduced set vectors: From Equation 2, we can see that the computation time is also dependent on the number of support vectors, N_s; in our system, this is typically on the order of 1,000. We use results from [2] to obtain an equivalent decision surface in terms of a small number of synthetic vectors. This method yields a new decision surface that is equivalent to the original one but uses just 29 vectors.

gray level images: Our use of color images is predicated on the fact that the three different color channels (RGB) contain a significant amount of information that gets washed out in grey level images of the same scene. This use of color information results in significant computational cost; the resizing and Haar transform operations are performed on each color channel separately. In order to improve system speed, we modify the system to process intensity images.

5.2 Integration with the DaimlerChrysler Urban Traffic Assistant

The DaimlerChrysler Urban Traffic Assistant (UTA) is a real-time vision system for obstacle detection, recognition, and tracking [5]. The system uses stereo vision to detect and segment obstacles and provides an estimate of the distance to each obstacle. We can use this information as a *focus of attention* mechanism for our people detection system. Using the knowledge of the location and approximate size of the obstacle allows us to target the people detection system to process relatively small regions for just a few sizes of people.

The combined system runs at more than 10 Hz. Furthermore, the portion of the total system time that is spent in our pedestrian detection module is 15 ms per obstacle. An analysis of how much time is taken by each portion of the pedestrian detection module shows that the smallest amount of time is being spent in the SVM classification. This bodes well for improving the performance. We should be able to use a much richer set of features than the 29 that are currently used – perhaps on the order of a few hundred features – without significantly degrading the speed of the system.

6 Conclusion

We have described a new technique for object detection in video sequences. This technique is purely data driven and makes no explicit assumptions on the dynamics or motion of people, just that short sequences characterize the dynamics sufficiently for the purposes of detection; in this manner, we avoid the need for an explicit underlying model of human motion and implicitly derive the model from a set of training data.

The core method uses training data that is in the form of high dimensional feature vectors that are generated from an overcomplete dictionary of Haar wavelets. Using traditional classifier training techniques would most likely result in overfitting such a high dimensional set, so we use a support vector machine classifier which controls the training error *and* complexity of the classifier. We have shown that the system learns in the presence of noisy features and performs better with the full set of features than when the dimensionality is reduced through a feature selection step.

Figure 4. Processing the "Downtown Ulm" sequence with the people detection system for video sequences. The system uses no explicit dynamical model; it learns the shape and some dynamical characteristics of people through a pure pattern classification approach. Using this technique achieves high detection accuracy while eliminating transient false positives.

To do detection is video sequences, with one of the primary goals being to reduce the rate of false positives, we extend the static representation directly to the time domain. In an out-of-sample test, this dynamical detection method compares quite well with a static detection system. The system learns the important characteristics of the physical structure and dynamics of people as they appear in video sequences; in this manner, we have completely avoided the need for explicit shape or motion models. Since it is purely a learning-based approach, we expect that this same architecture could be applied to other object classes.

References

[1] C. Bregler. Learning and Recognizing Human Dynamics in Video Sequences. In *Computer Vision and Pattern Recognition*, pages 568–574. IEEE Computer Society Press, 1997.

[2] C. Burges. Simplified Support Vector decision rules. In *Proceedings of 13th International Conference on Machine Learning*, 1996.

[3] C. Burges. A Tutorial on Support Vector Machines for Pattern Recognition. In U. Fayyad, editor, *Proceedings of Data Mining and Knowledge Discovery*, pages 1–43, 1998.

[4] J. Davis and A. Bobick. The Representation and Recognition of Human Movement Using Temporal Templates. In *Computer Vision and Pattern Recognition*, pages 928–934. IEEE Computer Society Press, 1997.

[5] U. Franke, D. Gavrila, S. Goerzig, F. Lindner, F. Paetzold, and C. Woehler. Autonomous driving goes downtown. *IEEE Intelligent Systems*, pages 32–40, November/December 1998.

[6] I. Haritaoglu, D. Harwood, and L. Davis. W4: Who? when? where? what? a real time system for detecting and tracking people. In *Face and Gesture Recognition*, pages 222–227, 1998.

[7] B. Heisele, U. Kressel, and W. Ritter. Tracking Non-rigid, Moving Objects Based on Color Cluster Flow. In *Computer Vision and Pattern Recognition*, 1997.

[8] B. Heisele and C. Wohler. Motion-Based Recognition of Pedestrians. In *Proceedings of International Conference on Pattern Recognition*, 1998. (in press).

[9] D. Hogg. Model-based vision: a program to see a walking person. *Image and Vision Computing*, 1(1):5–20, 1983.

[10] T. Joachims. Text Categorization with Support Vector Machines. Technical Report LS-8 Report 23, University of Dortmund, November 1997.

[11] M. Leung and Y.-H. Yang. Human body motion segmentation in a complex scene. *Pattern Recognition*, 20(1):55–64, 1987.

[12] S. Mallat. A theory for multiresolution signal decomposition: The wavelet representation. *IEEE Transactions on Pattern Analysis and Machine Intelligence*, 11(7):674–93, July 1989.

[13] S. McKenna and S. Gong. Non-intrusive person authentication for access control by visual tracking and face recognition. In J. Bigun, G. Chollet, and G. Borgefors, editors, *Audio- and Video-based Biometric Person Authentication*, pages 177–183. IAPR, Springer, 1997.

[14] M. Oren, C. Papageorgiou, P. Sinha, E. Osuna, and T. Poggio. Pedestrian detection using wavelet templates. In *Computer Vision and Pattern Recognition*, pages 193–99, 1997.

[15] E. Osuna, R. Freund, and F. Girosi. Training support vector machines: An application to face detection. In *Computer Vision and Pattern Recognition*, pages 130–36, 1997.

[16] C. Papageorgiou. Object and Pattern Detection in Video Sequences. Master's thesis, MIT, 1997.

[17] C. Papageorgiou, M. Oren, and T. Poggio. A general framework for object detection. In *Proceedings of International Conference on Computer Vision*, 1998.

[18] K. Rohr. Incremental recognition of pedestrians from image sequences. *Computer Vision and Pattern Recognition*, pages 8–13, 1993.

[19] E. Stollnitz, T. DeRose, and D. Salesin. Wavelets for computer graphics: A primer. Technical Report 94-09-11, Department of Computer Science and Engineering, University of Washington, September 1994.

[20] T. Tsukiyama and Y. Shirai. Detection of the movements of persons from a sparse sequence of tv images. *Pattern Recognition*, 18(3/4):207–13, 1985.

[21] V. Vapnik. *The Nature of Statistical Learning Theory*. Springer Verlag, 1995.

[22] C. Wren, A. Azarbayejani, T. Darrell, and A. Pentland. Pfinder: Real-time tracking of the human body. Technical Report 353, MIT Media Laboratory, 1995.

Control in a 3D Reconstruction System using Selective Perception[*]

Maurício Marengoni, Allen Hanson, Shlomo Zilberstein, and Edward Riseman
Paper Number: 596
Computer Science Department
University of Massachusetts
Amherst, MA 01003
marengon,hanson,shlomo,riseman@cs.umass.edu

Abstract

This paper presents a control structure for general purpose image understanding that addresses both the high level of uncertainty in local hypotheses and the computational complexity of image interpretation. The control of vision algorithms is performed by an independent subsystem that uses Bayesian networks and utility theory to compute the marginal value of information provided by alternative operators and selects the ones with the highest value. We have implemented and tested this control structure with several aerial image datasets. The results show that the knowledge base used by the system can be acquired using standard learning techniques and that the value-driven approach to the selection of vision algorithms leads to performance gains. Moreover, the modular system architecture simplifies the addition of both control knowledge and new vision algorithms.

1 Introduction

An Image Understanding (IU) system should be able to identify objects in 2D images and to build 3D relationships between objects in the scene and the viewer. A large number of image understanding systems developed so far are dedicated to aerial image interpretation. One of the problems with aerial image interpretation systems is the management of uncertainty. Uncertainty in this case arises from a variety of sources, such as the type of sensor, weather conditions, illumination conditions, season, random objects in the scene, and the inherent uncertainty in the definition of common objects.

Object recognition in aerial images is one important step towards 3D reconstruction of a scene, but

automating the recognition process in a real world application is not an easy task. Consider the image tiles from aerial images presented in Figure 1. The tile on top contains a building, which is easy to identify by its door and rooftop. The recognition of the three objects marked in the bottom tile is not as simple, and more detailed comparisons and measurements may be required to identify them correctly.

Figure 1: Different types of regions extracted from aerial images

Since an interpretation of an image can be viewed as a correspondence between image features and the identifying object classes, it is clear that the descriptive vocabulary of the system must be reflected in the set of features extractable from the image. Thus the image features must form the primitive descriptions of the objects in the knowledge base. Since every feature has at least one operator for measuring it, the control problem we address in this paper is this: given a general purpose system and a specific interpretation problem within the domain of the system, how do we effectively select the features to measure or, more generally, which algorithms to apply, and in what order. Furthermore, because there is a significant amount of inherent ambiguity in the interpretation process, an interpretation system must include a sufficiently rich

[*]Funded by the National Council for Scientific Research-CNPq, Brazil grant number 260185/92.2, by the APGD-DARPA project contract number DACA76-97-K-0005, and by Army Research Office, contract number DAAG55-97-1-0188

set of relations among features as well as flexible mechanisms for manipulating uncertain hypotheses until there is a convergence of evidence.

In this paper we show how to use Bayesian networks and utility theory to build a control structure for a general purpose image understanding system. We also address the knowledge engineering issue by demonstrating that it is possible to learn the Bayesian network structures from fairly coarse training information. Ascender II, an IU system for fully automated Aerial Image Interpretation, is used as a testbed to address these questions:

- How can the results of a visual operators and their associated uncertainties be combined in order to classify a particular image region?

- How can the hierarchical structure of objects be exploited in order to construct an incremental classification process?

- Can the construction of the knowledge base be simplified (or fully automated) for a particular application using both human expertise and machine learning techniques?

- Can performance be improved by using a disciplined approach to operator selection?

The next section presents an abbreviated summary of related work previous work. Section 3 introduces the Ascender II system and presents its control structures, specifically how operators are ordered given the current knowledge. Section 4 shows how to learn the structures used for control. Experimental results are presented in Section 5 and conclusions plus future direction of this work are outlined in Section 6.

2 Background

One popular approach in the 1980's to the general Image Understanding problem was knowledge-directed vision systems. A typical knowledge-directed approach to image interpretation seeks to identify objects in unconstrained two-dimensional images and to determine the three-dimensional relationships between these objects and the camera by applying object- and domain-specific knowledge to the interpretation problem. A survey of this line of research in computer vision can be found in [6], [5], and [4].

Typically, a knowledge-based vision system contains a knowledge base, a controller, and knowledge sources (or visual operators). In most of these systems the controller and the vision algorithms are combined into a single system. Problems common to most of the knowledge-directed vision systems include: control

for vision procedures was never properly addressed as an independent problem [5], the system's structure did not facilitate entry of new knowledge [4], and the knowledge engineering task was formidable [5]. These are some of the issues that are addressed in this paper.

Bayesian networks have been successfully used in systems required to combine and propagate evidence for and against a particular hypothesis. Vision systems have been developed using Bayesian networks for knowledge representation and as a basis for information integration, e.g. Rimey [15], Binford [13] and Krebs [10] (for indoor applications), and Kumar [11] (for aerial image interpretation).

3 Value-driven control of a vision algorithms

The Ascender II system was designed for aerial image interpretation, particularly for the 3D reconstruction of urban areas. The system is divided into two independent parts - the reasoning subsystem and the visual subsystem - running under different operating systems on different machines, as shown in Figure 2. One advantage of this design is that changes in the reasoning subsystem, or in the visual subsystem, can be made independently.

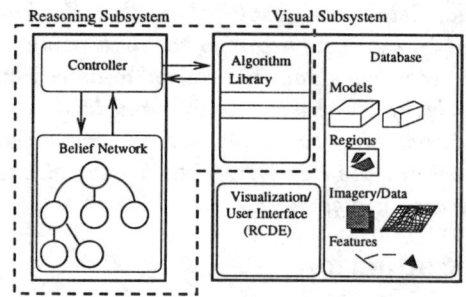

Figure 2: Process overview. Decisions are based on current knowledge about the site. Vision algorithms, stored in the visual subsystem, gather evidence about the site through focus of attention regions (FOAs), update the knowledge base, and produce geometric models.

Although the initial effort has focused primarily on recognizing and reconstructing buildings from aerial images, Ascender II has been designed as a general purpose vision system. The system has a set of focus-of-attention regions as input. These regions can be extracted from aerial images automatically (using a system such as Ascender I [3]), manually, or interactively (using cues from other sources such as maps or other classified images). The system's goal is to automatically select vision algorithms, recognize objects in the scene, and reconstruct these objects in 3D.

The system's knowledge base is composed of a set of Bayesian networks organized hierarchically. The networks are used to integrate information from different sources, and to label a region based on information provided by the visual operators. Each level of the hierarchy represents object classes at a specific scale [9]. The hierarchy leads to a system capable of performing incremental classification. The classification process is refined until the hierarchy reaches its finest level, or until the system exhausts all resources available. The Bayesian networks were developed using the HUGIN system [1].

The first set of networks were developed manually; two of the five networks used in the system are presented in Figure 3 and 4. The root node corresponds to the focus of attention region at a specific level of detail. All leaf nodes correspond to visual operators, and all internal nodes correspond to features that can be measured in the image. The probability table associated with the links between a feature node and an operator node reflects the reliability of the operator in retrieving the value of the feature; a link between the root node and the internal nodes represent relationships between object classes and feature values. The probability tables related to these links reflect the probability that a feature has a certain value given that the region is a certain object class, or:

$$P(Feature = k | Region = Object\_1)$$

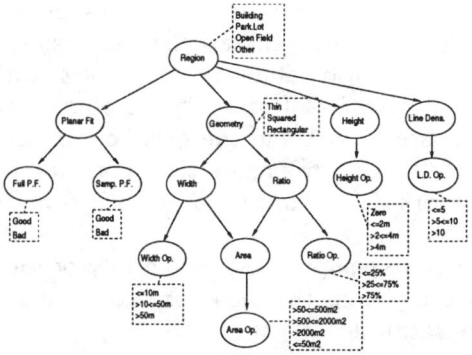

Figure 3: The level 0 hand-crafted network determines if a region belongs to one of the possible object classes (Building, Parking Lot, Open Field, or Other).

A set of experiments have been performed to compare alternative evaluation measures for operator selection. The first of these, called uncertainty distance [14], represents the difference between the value of the maximum belief in a node and the value of the belief

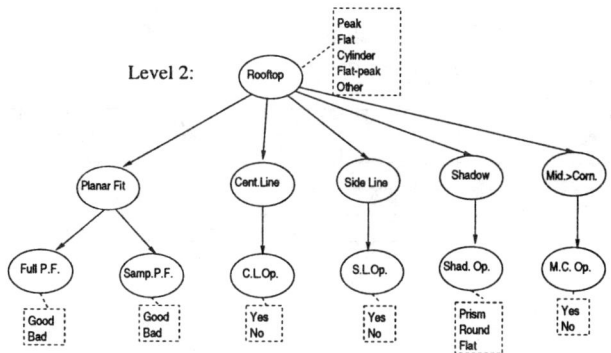

Figure 4: The level 2 hand-crafted network used to determine the type of rooftop (Peaked, Flat, Flat-Peak, Cylinder, or Other), once a single building is detected.

if the node had a uniform distribution. Given a network, the system computes the uncertainty distance for all nodes that have a correspondent IU process and selects the node with the minimum uncertainty distance. This was shown empirically to be equivalent to entropy as an evaluation measure. We have also shown that using uncertainty distance leads to a system which uses significantly less resources (operators) than an exhaustive strategy yet achieves comparable performance [14].

The work presented here uses the same system architecture, but it employs utility theory for selecting the operators to apply[12]. Utility theory is a probabilistic technique for decision making and it fits well in a Bayesian network system. Utility theory selects the decision that has the highest expected utility. In the discussion that follows, we use the following notation:

- $R_j \stackrel{\text{def}}{=}$ region R belongs to Class j.

- $DR_j \stackrel{\text{def}}{=}$ the decision that region R is identified as Class j.

- $E \stackrel{\text{def}}{=}$ all the evidence collected so far.

- $F_m \stackrel{\text{def}}{=}$ feature F is discretized in m states.

The expected utility (EU) of each decision is computed using the probability that a region belongs to a class j, $P(R_j|E)$, and the utility of deciding that a region is in class i given that the region belongs to class j, $U(DR_i|R_j)$, [12]:

$$EU(DR_i|E) = \sum_{j=1}^{N} U(DR_i|R_j) * P(R_j|E)$$

The current utility of the decision is defined as the maximum value among each of the expected utilities:

Table 1: The table shows all utilities for the level 0 network in the Ascender II system.

Decide	Class			
	Building	Park. Lot	Open Field	Other
Building	1	0	0	0
Parking Lot	0	1	0	0
Open Field	0	0	1	0
Other	0	0	0	1

$$max(EU(DR_i|E))$$

The best decision is defined as the decision α which gives the maximum expected utility:

$$\alpha = argmax_i(EU(DR_i|E))$$

In our problem domain the system has to decide the most likely identity (e.g. label) of a region. Assume that there are K features that can be measured in the region, the measurements are not completely reliable, and the measurements help in deciding about the region's label.

The region's prior probabilities and the conditional probability tables relating features with labels are stored in the Bayesian networks. The utility tables storing the values $U(DR_i|R_j)$ are not hard to define and can be adjusted by the user of the system to reflect specific goals for the classification process [12]. The utility tables used here are all similar, with ones on the diagonal and zeros in all other entries (see Table 1). In this case, only the correct labels are accepted.

Features are selected based on the value of information [8] associated with each feature. This value is computed as follows: for each feature currently available compute the expected utility of the system given that information about the feature is known.

$$EU(DR_i|E, F_m) = \sum_M P(F_m) * max_i(EU(DR_i|E, F_m))$$

Now, compute the value of information of each feature as follows:

$$VI(F_m) = EU(DR_{\alpha'}|E, F_m) - EU(DR_\alpha|E) \quad (1)$$

and select the feature with the highest value of information. Intuitively, the value of information measures the expected improvement in the utility of the best decision, once the result of an operator becomes available.

Figure 5 shows a generic Bayesian network that will be used to illustrate how feature selection is performed

in the Ascender II system. The first step is to compute the system's utility before extracting any information about the features. Each decision has an expected utility $U(Dec_i) = EU(DR_i|E)$; the expected utilities of the decisions can be calculated by multiplying the matrix of utilities by the column vector of beliefs from the root node, as shown in Figure 5. The system's utility is the maximum value among the utilities of the decisions.

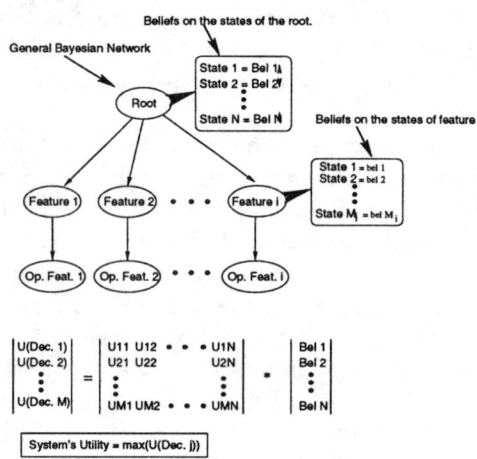

Figure 5: A generic Bayesian network for the Ascender II system

The next step is to compute the value of information of each feature. This is performed by computing the expected utility of each feature as follows: assume feature "i" has "M" states, $state_1, state_2, \cdots, state_M$; each state in feature "i" has a corresponding belief, $bel_1, bel_2, \cdots, bel_M$. These beliefs correspond to the current expectation about the outcome of feature "i". Set the outcome of feature "i" to $state_1$ (make the belief of $state_1 = 1$ and the belief of all other states equal to 0), and propagate the information through the network. This will change the beliefs in the states of the root node. Use this new set of beliefs in the root node to compute the new utility of the system. When completed, the value of information is found from equation 1.

4 Learning the models for the control structure

The knowledge engineering necessary to design a efficient Bayesian network (structure and probability tables) is a time consuming task, even for small networks such as those currently used in the Ascender II system. This has been one of the main criticisms of Bayesian networks.

Algorithms for learning Bayesian networks from

data have been developed [7, 2]. Cheng's algorithms [2] are based on statistical measures over pairs of random variables. The algorithms perform conditional independent tests using mutual information, and conditional mutual information given a third variable, and use these tests to define causality. Cheng's algorithms were used to learn the structure and the probability tables for the networks in the Ascender II system.

The data used for learning was collected from 3 different well-known data sets (Ft. Hood, Ft. Benning and Avenches); overall, 79 regions were selected representing a mix of objects drawn from buildings, parking lots, grassy fields, etc. All regions were presented to a set of 6 human subjects, and the subjects were asked to estimate the state of each feature in the feature set (features were coarsely quantized to facilitate the human task). This information was compiled and used to learn a Bayesian network representing the task domain.

Note that the structures as learned contain only the node representing the region plus the nodes representing all the features. The operator nodes (along with their reliability tables) were added manually after the learning phase was complete. If the true value of each feature is known, the tables representing the operator's reliability can also be learned from the data.

The learned networks corresponding to Figures 3 and 4 are shown in Figure 6 and 7. The general structure is completely different, although some of the substructures were preserved. Also, the learned networks are generally more densely connected.

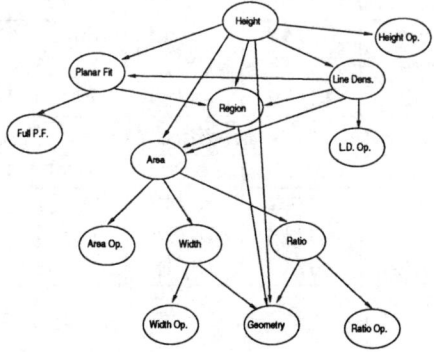

Figure 6: The level 0 learned network determines if a region belongs to one of the possible object classes: Building, Parking Lot, Open Field, or Other.

The networks learned from data are limited to the objects present in the training data. For instance, the data used to learn the networks had only peak-and flat-roofed buildings. Thus the feature *Rooftop* in Figure 7 has only states for *Peak* and *Flat* roofs, and

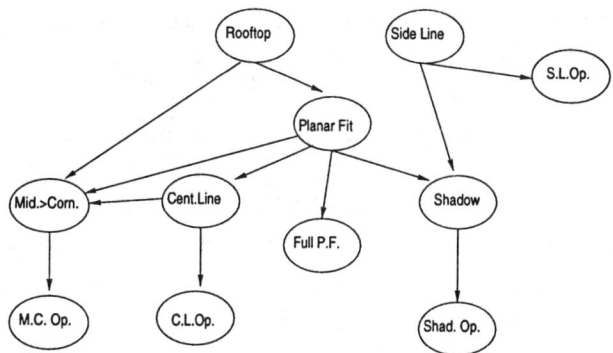

Figure 7: This level 2 learned network is called after a single building is detected. It is used to determine the building's rooftop type (Peak or Flat).

not the more general structure as in the hand-crafted networks presented in Figure 4.

5   Results

A set of experiments were performed on the Fort Hood data set (7 views with known camera parameters and corresponding digital elevation map DEM) shown in Figure 8, on the Avenches data set (1 view and a DEM) shown in Figure 9, on the Fort Benning data set (2 views and a DEM) shown in Figure 10, and on the ISPRS Flat data set (2 views and a DEM) show in Figure 11. These data sets are an effective test suite because they have different numbers of images, different resolutions and different numbers of objects in each class.

The first experiment was designed to show that a more disciplined approach to feature selection leads to a more efficient system. The experiment provides a comparison between the system using uncertainty distance (Basic System) and the system using utility theory (System A). Both systems used the hand-crafted networks. The results in terms of classification and number of operators used are presented in Tables 2 and 3.

Table 3 shows that the overall classification obtained by the two selection processes is about the same. Table 2 shows that the selection of operators is more efficient using utility theory (10% fewer operators). This result confirms the intuition that a selection methodology using utility theory would choose more effective operators, thus classifying regions faster.

The second set of experiments was designed to demonstrate the performance of the system using the learned networks on the same data sets used for training. Although the regions used in the these experi-

Table 2: Total number of calls to visual operators for all data sets for all classes.

Decision process	Number of Operators
Utility Theory	430
Uncertainty Distance	475

ments are the same as the ones used for learning, there are two major differences that have to be considered:

1. During the experimental phase the features were computed algorithmically from the image data by a visual operator. The results do not necessarily correspond to the outcome given by humans in the learning phase.

2. The values of the features computed by the visual operator were entered into the operator's node and were attenuated by the operator's reliability during the propagation.

First, the networks and probability tables (including prior probabilities) as learned from the data (System B) was applied in the 3 data sets (Ft. Hood, Avenches and Ft. Benning). Because the prior probabilities learned from data reflect the exact frequency of each object class, the system should react faster to feature values retrieved and it would not be a fair comparison to System A. So a second test was performed where the prior beliefs for each object class were changed in the networks to reflect the same prior probabilities used in the hand-crafted networks (System C). The results obtained for these two experiments are shown in Tables 4 and 5.

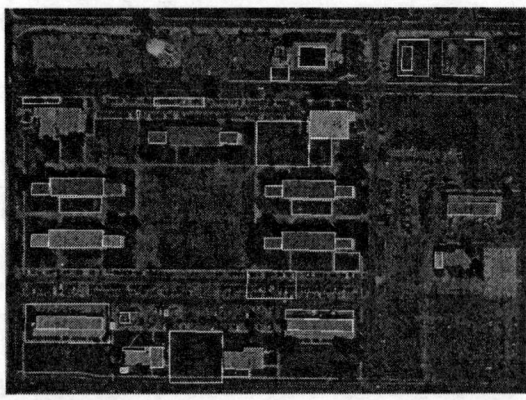

Figure 8: The input regions from the Fort Hood data set. These regions were obtained by running the original Ascender I system constrained to detect two-dimensional building footprints.

The numbers shown in Table 5 are similar to the numbers presented in Table 3. Thus, the system using

Table 3: Summary of the recognition process for different data sets using the hand-crafted networks. In each case the number of objects correctly identified is shown, followed by the total number of objects evaluated by the system.

Uncertainty Distance - Basic System				
Data set	Overall	Level 0	Level 1	Level 2
Fort Hood	34/42	36/42	22/24	21/21
Avenches	12/18	15/18	12/13	5/7
Fort Benning	17/19	18/19	17/18	17/18
Utility Theory - System A				
Data set	Overall	Level 0	Level 1	Level 2
Fort Hood	35/42	37/42	23/25	21/21
Avenches	13/18	16/18	12/13	5/7
Fort Benning	16/19	18/19	17/18	16/17

Table 4: Total number of calls to visual operators for all data sets for all classes.

Decision process	Number of Operators
Learned Networks	322
Learned + Modified Priors	400

Table 5: Summary of the recognition process for different data sets using the learned networks.

Learned Networks - System B				
Data set	Overall	Level 0	Level 1	Level 2
Fort Hood	33/42	34/42	20/21	20/20
Avenches	16/18	18/18	15/15	7/9
Fort Benning	15/19	18/19	17/18	15/17
Learned Networks + Modified Priors - System C				
Data set	Overall	Level 0	Level 1	Level 2
Fort Hood	34/42	35/42	20/21	20/20
Avenches	13/18	16/18	12/14	6/7
Fort Benning	16/19	18/19	17/18	16/17

Table 6: Summary of the recognition process for the Flat data sets using the hand-crafted and the learned networks with utility theory.

Flat Data Set					
System	Overall	Level 0	Level 1	Level 2	Operators
Hand-crafted	22/30	23/30	21/21	13/14	170
Learned	26/30	27/30	21/21	13/14	162

Figure 9: The input regions from the Avenches data set. The regions were obtained by running the Ascender I system.

Figure 10: The input regions from the Fort Benning data set. These regions were obtained by a combination of polygons extracted using Ascender I and polygons extracted from SAR data.

Bayesian networks learned from data generates classifications very similar to the system using the hand-crafted networks. However, "System B" was able to classify the regions using 32% fewer operators than the "Basic System". "System C" used 15% fewer operators than the "Basic System". The fact that "System C" used more operators than the "System B" was expected because the distributions of beliefs over the object classes were more uniformly distributed in "System C" than in "System B", thus "System C" requires more exploratory calls before deciding about a region.

The third experiment was designed to show that the structure and relationships among features learned from data is robust enough to be applied to a different data set. In this experiment, the hand-crafted system using utility theory was compared to the learned system applied to the Flat data set. In both systems the

Figure 11: Set of regions extracted by hand from the Flat data set.

Figure 12: 3D reconstruction on the Fort Benning data set.

prior beliefs were adjusted accordingly. The results over 30 regions are shown in Table 6.

The number of operators used by the system using the learned networks is slightly smaller (5%), but the larger number of relationships between the features in the learned networks allowed better performance of the system on the new data set (87% correct classifications against 73% for the system with the hand-crafted networks).

One example of the 3D reconstruction that can be obtained using the Ascender II system is presented in Figure 12. The maximum error between the reconstructed buildings and the CAD models hand-crafted for the buildings in the Fort Benning data set is less than 1.2 meters.

6   Conclusions and Future Work

The overall performance of the Ascender II system using utility theory or uncertainty distance is above 80% in terms of classification. When utility theory and value of information is used, the system selects operators more efficiently and is able to identify objects faster.

The knowledge base in Ascender II is based on Bayesian networks. Evidence from different sources are combined in the Bayesian networks and each contributes to the region classification.

We have also shown that the networks can be learned from data. The system using the learned networks had a better performance either in terms of the number of operators required to correctly classify the regions, or in terms of the percentage of regions correctly classified. The data used to learn the networks have to be representative of all objects classes desired in the system. The learned networks are robust enough to be applied in a different data set with a simple adjustment of prior beliefs for the object classes.

The hierarchical structure leads to a system capable of performing incremental classification. The current system can be adjusted to behave as an anytime system, where resources, such as number of operators or processing time, can be limited and the overall performance optimized for the resources available.

Another possible extension of this system is related to temporal reasoning. If a 3D reconstruction of a site is available and a new image is obtained for the same area, how can the information previously computed be used to drive the system in order to detect changes and to reconstruct the new site efficiently.

References

[1] Andersen, S., Olesen, K., Jensen, F., and F., J. Hugin - a shell for building bayesian belief universes for expert systems. In *Proceedings of the 11th International Congress on Uncertain Artificial Intelligence* (1989), pp. 1080–1085.

[2] Cheng, J., Bell, D., and Liu, W. Learning bayesian networks from data: An efficient approach based on information theory. Tech. Rep. -, Department of Computer Science - University of Alberta, 1998.

[3] Collins, R., Cheng, Y., Jaynes, C., Stolle, F., Wang, X., Hanson, A., and Riseman, E. Site model acquisition and extension from aerial images. In *Proceedings of the Interartional Conference on Computer Vision* (1995), pp. 888–893.

[4] Crevier, D., and Lepage, R. Knowledge-based image understanding systems: a survey. *Computer Vision and Image Understanding 67(2)* (1997), 161–185.

[5] Draper, B., Hanson, A., and Riseman, E. Knowledge-directed vision: control, learning, and integration. *Proceedings of the IEEE 84(11)* (1996), 1625–1637.

[6] Haralick, R., and Shapiro, L. *Computer and Robot Vision*. Addison-Wesley, 1993.

[7] Heckerman, D. A tutorial on learning with bayesian networks. Tech. Rep. MSR-TR-95-06, Microsoft Research, March 1995.

[8] Howard, R. Information value theory. *IEEE Transactions on Systems, Science and Cybernetics SSC-2(1)* (1966), 22–26.

[9] Jaynes, C., Marengoni, M., Hanson, A., and Riseman, E. 3d model acquisition using a bayesian controller. In *Proceedings of the International Symposium on Engineering of Intelligent Systems, Tenerife, Spain* (1998), pp. 837–845.

[10] Krebs, B., Burkhardt, M., and Korn, B. A task driven 3d object recognition system using bayesian networks. In *Proceedings of the International Conference on Computer Vision, Bombay, India* (1998), pp. 527–532.

[11] Kumar, V., and Desai, U. Image interpretation using bayesian networks. *IEEE Transactions on Pattern Analysis and Machine Intelligence 18(1)* (1996), 74–77.

[12] Lindley, D. *Making Decisions: Second Edition*. John Wiley and Sons, 1985.

[13] Mann, W., and Binford, T. An example of 3-d interpretation of images using bayesian networks. *DARPA Image Understanding Workshop* (1992), 793–801.

[14] Marengoni, M., Jaynes, C., Hanson, A., and Riseman, E. Ascender ii, a visual framework for 3d reconstruction. In *Proceedings of the International Conference on Vision Systems, Las Palmas, Spain* (1999), pp. 469–488.

[15] Rimey, R., and Brown, C. Task-oriented vision with multiple bayes nets. In *Active Vision*, A. Blake and A. Yuille, Eds. The MIT Press, 1992.

 # Shadow Puppetry

Matthew Brand

MERL — a Mitsubishi Electric Research Laboratory

Cambridge, MA 02139

Abstract

The mapping between 3D *body poses and* 2D *shadows is fundamentally many-to-many and defeats regression methods, even with windowed context. We show how to learn a function between* paths *in the two systems, resolving ambiguities by integrating information over the entire length of a sequence. The basis of this function is a configural and dynamical manifold that summarizes the target system's behavior. This manifold can be modeled from data with a hidden Markov model having special topological properties that we obtain via entropy minimization. Inference is then a matter of solving for the geodesic on the manifold that best explains the evidence in the cue sequence. We give a closed-form maximum* a posteriori *solution for geodesics through the learned density space, thereby obtaining optimal paths over the dynamical manifold. These methods give a completely general way to perform inference over time-series; in vision they support analysis, recognition, classification and synthesis of behaviors in linear time. We demonstrate with a prototype that infers* 3D *from monocular monochromatic sequences (e.g., back-subtractions), without using any articulatory body model. The framework readily accommodates multiple cameras and other sources of evidence such as optical flow or feature tracking.*

1. Dynamical Manifolds

A dynamical manifold is a locus of all possible system pose and velocity configurations, typically embedded in a higher-dimensional measurement space such as images. Actual system histories are trajectories on this manifold. In figure 1 we illustrate a 4D manifold and an embedding in a 6-space. Embeddings are often highly nonlinear; the manifold may curl over and self-intersect. Usually we have far too few samples to support an estimate of the manifold's global geometry or of any function that might unfurl it.

Inference is a search for a most probable sequence of events (path on the manifold) that best explains a sequence of observables. In this paper we propose learning all the relevant knowledge from synchronized observations of a system's true state and some cue signal—measurements of another system that approximately co-evolves with our system of interest. Our goal is to model the target system's dynamical manifold by estimating a continuous probability distribution from observed trajectories, then learn a mapping from paths taken by the cue system to paths over the target system's manifold. This framework will support traditional vision tasks such as recognition, classification, and pose estimation, plus a novel one: synthesis.

2. Representation

To model a manifold we want to identify neighborhoods where the relationship of position to velocity is roughly linear, fit a regression to each neighborhood, then probabilistically "glue" together these fittings into a smoothly-interpolating piecewise linear approximation. As figure 1R shows, these linearized neighborhoods can describe highly curved system behavior. We will describe each neighborhood with a multivariate Gaussian p.d.f. The covariance matrix does a double service, specifying how pose and velocity covary, and, implicitly, neighborhood extent and blending functions. This piecewise linear approximation is simpler than previously proposed schemes (e.g., [7]) and will lead to closed-form solutions for all quantities of interest.

Because the manifold is dynamical, the "glue" between neighborhoods must describe how quickly the system passes from neighborhood to neighborhood; this is conveniently expressed as a matrix of transition probabilities.

This manifold approximation is essentially a hidden Markov model (HMM), with each neighborhood Gaussian being the output of a hidden state, and a transition topology specially matched to the dynamical structure of the manifold. But estimated HMMs are typically very poor models for our purposes because conventional training techniques [1, 16] are extremely suboptimal with regard to placement of the Gaussian outputs (discovery of neighborhoods). Moreover, they rarely improve on the modeler's nearly-blind guess about connectivity, e.g., a full transition matrix will let every neighborhood pass directly to every other neighborhood, almost certainly violating

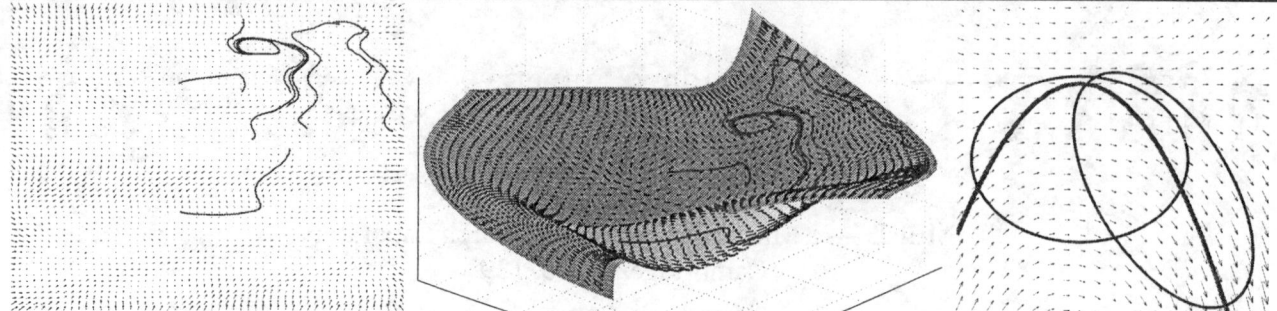

Figure 1. LEFT: 2D vector field schematic of a 4D dynamical manifold and its embedding in a 6D measurement space (MIDDLE). Arrows indicate most likely velocity at each point; contours signify actual observed system trajectories. RIGHT: Two neighborhoods in which velocity covaries linearly with position. The ellipses represent $\{x, y\}$ iso-density contours of two 4D $\{x, y, \dot{x}, \dot{y}\}$ Gaussians whose positional covariances σ_{xy} roughly delineate these neighborhoods and whose covariances $\sigma_{x\dot{y}}, \sigma_{y\dot{y}}$ (not shown) capture the local position/velocity relations. The parabola is an example piecewise quadratic trajectory that is neighborhood-consistent. See §1-2.

the manifold's topology. No modeler would expect a random walk on an estimated HMM to have the same long-term structure as the time-series in the training set. Yet that is what we require of a good manifold model. To overcome this problem we use a recently developed learning procedure based on entropy minimization. This gives fast, monotonic algorithms that produce highly structured and accurate models, free of over-fitting (§3). Entropy minimization shifts Gaussians to neighborhoods of narrow covariance, (where linear relations between dimensions tend to be stronger), minimizes their overlap, and restructures the transition matrix to reflect the topology of the manifold.

With some additional estimation (§4), we can use this model to infer a target system's hidden state from clues contained in another co-evolving *cue* signal (§5). E.g., we can infer a figure's 3D orientation from a sequence of silhouettes. The algorithm optimally integrates information over time, using clues from either end of the sequence to disambiguate mappings at the other end, if necessary.

From there we can synthesize actual *signals* that are maximally faithful to both the target system and to the observed evidence. In particular, we give a closed-form solution for the most probable trajectory on the dynamical manifold given a time-series of the co-evolving signal (§6). This works even if the target system is more complex and exhibits behaviors not found in the cue system.

Altogether these methods yield a general framework for learning functions that map between *paths*, in contrast to the classic regression task of learning mappings between *points*. These methods provide path-consistent inference and the full use of context along the path to resolve ambiguities at any point. In §7 we incorporate some visually important invariances and show how to synthesize 3D animations from 2D image sequences. All algorithms are linear in the length of the time-series; the per-frame

computation costs are fixed and the implementation runs close to real-time in interpreted Matlab code.

3. Learning by entropy minimization

We outline the entropy minimization framework here and refer readers to [3, 4] for details and derivations. We begin with a dataset $\boldsymbol{X}$ and a hidden-variable probabilistic model whose structure and parameters are specified by the vector $\boldsymbol{\theta}$. In conventional training, one guesses the sparsity structure of $\boldsymbol{\theta}$ in advance and merely re-estimates nonzero parameters to maximize the likelihood $P(\boldsymbol{X}|\boldsymbol{\theta})$. In entropic estimation, we simultaneously learn $\boldsymbol{\theta}$'s size, sparsity structure, and parameter values by minimizing the three entropies

$$\boldsymbol{\theta}^* = \underset{\boldsymbol{\theta}}{\arg\min}\left[H(\boldsymbol{\omega}) + D(\boldsymbol{\omega}\|\boldsymbol{\theta}) + H(\boldsymbol{\theta})\right], \quad (1)$$

where $H(\boldsymbol{\omega})$ is the entropy of the data's expected sufficient statistics and can be interpreted as the expected cost of coding the data relative to the model; $D(\boldsymbol{\omega}\|\boldsymbol{\theta})$ is the cross-entropy between the sufficient statistics and the model and measures the expected cost of coding aspects of the data not captured by the model; and $H(\boldsymbol{\theta})$ is an entropy measure on the model itself and, depending on its formulation, can be interpreted either as the entropy of the distribution or the expected coding costs of the model itself, in which case it can be shown to be a continuous approximation of the expected Kolmogorov complexity of the parameters $\boldsymbol{\theta}$ [2].

Minimizing eqn. 1 is equivalent to maximizing the Bayesian posterior probability with an entropic prior,

$$\boldsymbol{\theta}^* = \underset{\boldsymbol{\theta}}{\arg\max}\left[P(\boldsymbol{\theta}|\boldsymbol{X}) \propto P(\boldsymbol{X}|\boldsymbol{\theta})\, e^{-H(\boldsymbol{\theta})}\right]. \quad (2)$$

Given a factorizable model such as an HMM, the maximum *a posteriori* (MAP) problem decomposes into a separate equation for each independent parameter $\theta_i \in \boldsymbol{\theta}$, each having its own entropic prior. Iterative MAP estimation therefore minimizes the expected coding length associated with each factor of the likelihood function. Entropy minimization sharpens each of these component distributions, which has the effect of sparsifying both the parameter vector and the expected sufficient statistics that describe the data. This is in the spirit of MML/MDL/BIC, but avoids approximations and paradoxes that arise from parameter-counting heuristics. Sparse models are desirable because they are resistant to overfitting, and, if sufficiently low entropy, can be read as explanations of the data, rather than mere fittings.

For spread parameters such as the Gaussian covariance K over N samples $\{x_1, ..., x_n\}$, the entropic prior $|K|^{-1/2}$ favors minimum volume covariances; the estimator is

$$\hat{K} = \frac{\sum_i^N x_i x_i^\top}{N + Z}. \qquad (3)$$

For conditional probabilities and more generally for multinomial densities over N alternatives, the entropic prior $\theta^\theta = \prod_i^N \theta_i^{\theta_i}$ favors near-deterministic odds; the estimator is given by the fix-point

$$\hat{\lambda} = \frac{1}{N} \sum_i^N \frac{\omega_i}{\theta_i} + Z \log \theta_i + Z, \qquad (4)$$

$$\hat{\theta}_i = \frac{-\omega_i/Z}{W(-\omega_i e^{1-\lambda/Z}/Z)}, \qquad (5)$$

where ω is a vector of sufficient statistics (e.g., event counts); W is the Lambert inverse function satisfying $W(x)e^{W(x)} = x$; and Z is negative temperature term. Exponentiating the prior by Z and letting the temperature $T = 1 - Z$ decay to zero, we obtain deterministic annealing within expectation-maximization (EM), thereby speeding learning and turning EM into a quasi-global optimizer. Annealing is an example of extending the prior, in this case by adding $-T \cdot H(\theta)$. One may also modify or even replace the prior with cross-entropy terms: Use $\pm D(\theta \| \theta')$ to stay near or far from a reference distribution θ'; if θ' is the previous EM estimate then this conserves information gained in successive iterations of EM; if $\theta' = \mathcal{U}$ (uniform distribution), $-D(\theta \| \mathcal{U})$ gives a MaxEnt prior while for many distributions $+D(\mathcal{U} \| \theta)$ gives sparsifying conjugate priors (e.g., for multinomials, Dirichlet with exponents $\alpha = \frac{1}{2}$, which coincides with Jeffreys' $J(\theta)$). Any or all of these may be used as per the modeler's prior beliefs[1]. For multinomials, the system of equations $\forall_i \partial P(\theta | X)/\partial \theta_i = 0$ will typically yield a log-linear of the form $\log f(\theta_i)^n + bf(\theta_i) = g(x)$, for which we derived a general identity that gives MAP estimators:

$$\theta_i = f^{-1}\left(\frac{n}{b} W\left(\frac{b}{n} e^{g(x)/n}\right)\right) \qquad (6)$$

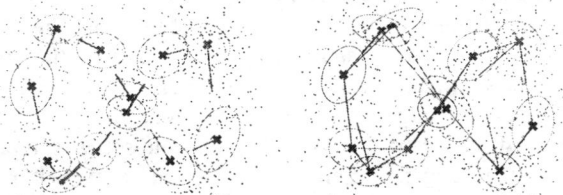

Figure 2. HMMs estimated entropically (LEFT) and conventionally (RIGHT) from identical initial conditions and projected onto the $\{x, y\}$ figure-eight training data (gray dots). Each cross and ellipse indicates the Gaussian mean and covariance of a hidden state (neighborhood); half-arcs point to transitionable states. See the last paragraph of §3.

In [3] we show how these estimators are applied to variety of probabilistic models, yielding fast code-length minimizing learning algorithms; the case of HMMs is extensively treated in [4]. MAP re-estimation gradually extinguishes excess parameters and maximizes the information content of the surviving parameters. It is also possible to speed up parameter extinction by trimming (zeroing) parameters when the gain the prior exceeds the loss in the likelihood; for the basic entropic prior this is easily diagnosed when $\partial H(\theta)/\partial \theta_i > \partial \log P(X | \theta)/\partial \theta_i$, or when a parameter affects uncertainty more than fit. Starting with a random over-complete model (containing an exponential number of embedded sub-models), entropic estimation whittles away components of the model that are not in accord with the hidden structure of the signal. This allows us to learn the proper size[2] and sparsity structure of a model. Entropic estimation of HMMs often recovers a finite-state machine quite close to the data-generating mechanism.

Figure 2 shows two HMMs estimated from very noisy samples of a system that orbits in a figure-eight. The true system is a 2D manifold (phase and its rate of change) embedded in a 4D measurement space (observed 2D position and velocity); the HMM approximates this manifold with neighborhoods of locally consistent curvature in which velocity covaries linearly with position. Note that even though the data is noisy and has a continuation ambiguity where it crosses itself, the entropically estimated HMM recovers the deterministic structure of the system. The conventionally estimated HMM gets "lost" at the crossing, bunching states at and after the ambiguity and leaving many of them incorrectly over-connected, thus allowing multiple circuits and reversals on either loop as well as numerous small circuits on the crossing and on the lobes. It is the additional precision of entropic models that makes them viable as manifold models.

---

[1]$\exp[-H(\theta)]$, Dirichlet $\alpha < 1$, and $J(\theta)$ priors have similar sparsifying properties and probably should not be used together.

[2]Note that there is no "correct" number of states for a continuous signal, but if there is insufficient data to support the parameters associated with many states, some will be automatically removed.

4. Observing a 2nd (cue) signal

For puppetry, we associate features of the *cue* signal to hidden states (neighborhoods) on the *target* HMM (manifold). This allows us to infer a sequence of target neighborhoods from a cue signal. Forward-backward analysis [16] of time-series sampled from the target system gives us an HMM θ plus an occupancy matrix $\gamma_{s,t}^X \doteq p_\theta(s_t|x_1,...,x_T) = p$(hidden state s explains training frame t). Using $\gamma_{s,t}^X$, we estimate a second set of output means and covariances such that each HMM state also observes the synchronized time-series sampled from the cue system:

$$\hat{\mu}_s' = \langle z_t \rangle_{\gamma_{s,t}^X}, \tag{7}$$

$$\hat{\Sigma}_s' = \langle (z_t - \mu_s')(z_t - \mu_s')^\top \rangle_{\gamma_{s,t}^X}. \tag{8}$$

This effectively produces a new HMM that has the dynamics of the target system but is driven by the cue signal.

5. Analysis of novel cue data

Given a new cue signal $Z = \{z_1, z_2, z_3, ...\}$, we apply the Viterbi algorithm [8] to the cue HMM to find the most likely sequence of target system hidden states $\mathcal{S}^Z = \{s(1), s(2), \ldots, s(T) \doteq \mathrm{argmax}_i \psi_{i,T}^Z\}$. Here $\psi_{i,T}^Z \doteq p$(most likely sequence ending with state i), given by the recursion $\psi_{i,t}^Z = [\max_j P_{i|j} \psi_{j,t-1}^Z] \, \mathcal{N}(z_t; \mu_i', K_i')$, where $\mathcal{N}(z_t; \mu_i', K_i')$ is the Gaussian probability of z_t given mean μ_i' and covariance K_i'; $P_{i|j}$ is a state transition probability. The recursion begins at $\psi_{i,1}^Z = P_i \, \mathcal{N}(z_1; \mu_i', K_i')$, where $P_i \doteq \langle \gamma_{i,t}^X \rangle_t$. This takes $O(TP)$ time for T frames and P non-zero HMM transition parameters.

Readers familiar with HMMs will note that the number of possible state sequences is exponential in the number of time steps. The Viterbi sequence, while most likely, may only represent a small fraction of the total probability mass; there may be billions of slightly different state sequences that are nearly as likely. If this were the case, the Viterbi sequence would be a very poor representation of the observed signal, and any calculations downstream would suffer. One may also use forward-backward analysis to obtain a new occupancy matrix $\gamma_{s,t}^Z$ that contains *all* the information that the HMM can extract from the cue signal, since it integrates over all possible sequences. In the next section we show that for low-entropy models, the Viterbi and forward-backward analyses are equivalent.

6. Synthesis of target trajectories

For synthesis, we seek a short, smooth trajectory that passes through regions of high probability density in target space at the right time—a constrained geodesic. Prior approaches to geodesics in density spaces typically involve maximizing an objective function having a likelihood term plus penalty terms for excess length and/or kinkiness and/or point clumpiness. The user must choose a parameterization and weighting for each term. This leads to variational techniques that are often approximate [19], iterative, and computationally expensive (e.g., [18]), and the results can be plagued by suboptimal local extrema.

Our inclusion of velocity constraints within the target Gaussians makes the geodesic problem well posed and amenable to a closed-form solution. The result is a smooth trajectory that is most consistent with the target dynamics and with the state sequence computed from the cue signal.

The HMM's output Gaussians together with its hidden state probabilities $\gamma_{s,t}^Z$ define a mixture of Gaussians over trajectory-space; we seek the optimal trajectory $Y^* = \{y_1, y_2, y_3, ...\} = \mathrm{argmax}_Y \, p_\theta(Y|\gamma_{s,t}^Z)$. Let $[\mu_i, \dot{\mu}_i]$ be the mean position and velocity for state i, and $K_i = \begin{bmatrix} K_i^{xx} & K_i^{x\dot{x}} \\ K_i^{\dot{x}x} & K_i^{\dot{x}\dot{x}} \end{bmatrix}^{-1}$ be a full-rank covariance matrix relating position and velocity across all dimensions. The mixture probability is

$$p_\theta(Y|\gamma_{s,t}^Z) \doteq \prod_t \left[\sum_c \gamma_{s,t}^Z \mathcal{N}(\tilde{y}_{s,t}; K_s) \right] \mathcal{N}_P(\dot{y}_t; K_P), \tag{9}$$

where the vector $\tilde{y}_{s,t} \doteq [y_t - \mu_s; (y_t - y_{t-1}) - \dot{\mu}_s]$ is the mean-subtracted target position and velocity at time t; and $\mathcal{N}_P(\dot{y}_t)$ is an optional Gaussian prior on velocities, usable for smoothing. We lower-bound with the log-sum inequality, obtaining

$$p_\theta(Y|\gamma_{s,t}^Z) \geq e^{-\frac{1}{2}(\sum_t [\sum_s \gamma_{s,t}^Z \tilde{y}_{s,t} K_s^{-1} \tilde{y}_{s,t}^\top] + \dot{y}_t K_P^{-1} \dot{y}_t^\top + c)}. \tag{10}$$

Solving for the mode of eqn. 10 leads to a block-tridiagonal system of linear equations. For T frames and $D \doteq \dim(y_t)$ dimensions, it can be LU-decomposed and solved in time $O(TD^3)$ [10, §4.3.1].

It is not unusual for eqn. 9 to be a mixture of $O(10^{5+})$ Gaussians; eqn. 10 essentially fits a single Gaussian around $p_\theta(Y|\gamma_{s,t}^Z)$ and thereby gives the approximate posterior mean. How good is this strategy? Note that the bound in eqn. 10 tightens as the entropy $H(\gamma_{s,t}^Z) \doteq \langle -\log \gamma_{s,t}^Z \rangle_{\gamma_{s,t}^Z} \to 0$ because the mixture becomes sparse, with a single Gaussian dominating each time frame. At $H(\gamma_{s,t}^Z) = 0$, the joint $p_\theta(Y|\gamma_{s,t}^Z)$ *is* a single Gaussian; so the bound and its solution are both exact. It is entropy minimization that makes eqn. 10 viable, by concentrating the probability mass on the Viterbi sequence, so that $H(\gamma_{s,t}^Z) \approx 0$. This licenses an even faster way to compute a MAP trajectory directly from the Viterbi sequence $s(1), ..., s(T)$:

$$Y^* \approx \mathrm{argmax}_Y \log \prod_t \mathcal{N}(\tilde{y}_t; K_{s(t)}) \mathcal{N}_P(\dot{y}_t; K_P)$$

$$= \mathrm{argmin}_Y \frac{1}{2} \sum_t \tilde{y}_t K_{s(t)}^{-1} \tilde{y}_t^\top + \dot{y}_t K_P^{-1} \dot{y}_t^\top + c. \tag{11}$$

HMM entropically estimated from noisy data

Geodesic calculated from random walk on the HMM

Figure 3. ABOVE: An entropically estimated HMM projected onto training data as in figure 2. BELOW: A trajectory generated via eqn. 12 from a random walk on the HMM's hidden states. (Irregularities are largely due to variations between state dwell-times in the random walk.) See §6.

where $\tilde{y}_t \doteq [y_t - \mu_{s(t)}; (y_t - y_{t-1}) - \dot{\mu}_{s(t)}]$. Eqn. 11 is optimized by solving the sparse system of linear equations:

$$\begin{bmatrix} K_{s(t)}^{xx} + K_{s(t)}^{\dot{x}x} \\ K_{s(t)}^{x\dot{x}} + K_{s(t)}^{\dot{x}\dot{x}} \\ K_{s(t+1)}^{x\dot{x}} + K_{s(t+1)}^{\dot{x}\dot{x}} \\ K_{s(t+1)}^{x\dot{x}} \\ K_{s(t+1)}^{\dot{x}\dot{x}} \\ K_P^{-1} \end{bmatrix}^{\perp} \begin{bmatrix} y_t - \mu_{s(t)} \\ y_t - y_{t-1} - \dot{\mu}_{s(t)} \\ y_t - y_{t+1} \\ \mu_{s(t+1)} \\ \dot{\mu}_{s(t+1)} \\ y_t - y_{t-1} \end{bmatrix} = 0,$$

(12)

where $K_i^{x\dot{x}} \doteq (K_i^{x\dot{x}} + K_i^{\dot{x}x})/2$ and $\perp$ signifies block-transpose $\left(\begin{bmatrix} A B \\ C D \end{bmatrix}^{\perp} \doteq \begin{bmatrix} A C \\ B D \end{bmatrix} \neq \begin{bmatrix} A^{\top} C^{\top} \\ B^{\top} D^{\top} \end{bmatrix} \right)$. Since the system is inherently smooth, we usually drop the prior and the last row of eqn. 12.

These methods trivially generalize to HMMs where each state's emission function is a mixture of Gaussians. By scaling the velocity terms, one may also solve for the trajectory at arbitrary sampling rates; in the infinite limit this gives the mode associated with the path integral $\langle Y \rangle_{p_\theta(Y | \gamma_{s,t}^z)}$.

In experiments comparing the MAP solution (eqn. 11) with the posterior mean solution (eqn. 10), we found that with maximum likelihood HMMs eqn. 11 and eqn. 10 gave rather different results, both mediocre. In contrast, with minimal-entropy HMMs, eqn. 11 and eqn. 10 gave nearly identical trajectories of very high quality.

Figure 3 illustrates with a trajectory calculated from a random walk on an HMM model of the figure-eight manifold. Increasing the number of HMM states improves the quality of the synthesized trajectory, provided there is sufficient data to support estimates of the additional parameters. (Entropic estimation will automatically remove insufficiently supported parameters.)

7. 3D animation from 2D images

3D pose recovery was originally approached as model-fitting through time [12]; with the advent of video frame-rate computing it has evolved into model-guided tracking [11, 9, 13, 17, 6, 15, 20]. All approaches assume a carefully constructed kinematic model with reduced degrees of freedom (DOFs) and a favorable initialization; most must contend with singularities, costly per-frame optimizations, and potentially troublesome Taylor-series approximations. Some high-quality results have been obtained from short sequences, but it is worth noting that these methods are incremental and require high-resolution images: A bad image or pose estimate can pollute all later estimates; there is no use of hindsight to correct early estimates. In addition, multiple camera views are usually needed to calculate depth and resolve occlusions. A notable model-free alternative uses small concatenations of *observed* 3D poses as a linear basis set for "unprojecting" 2D tracking data [14].

Here we explore the viability of inferring 3D action from noisy low-resolution silhouette sequences of the sort obtained via foreground extraction. This is rather more difficult than inferring 3D from 2D tracking data because silhouettes are inherently less informative and considerably more ambiguous. On the other hand, silhouettes can be more reliably computed over long time spans, and our method can handle the additional noise and ambiguity by integrating evidence forwards and backwards over time.

The input is a monocular monochromatic silhouette sequence. The output is the 3D sequence whose projections best explain the input and whose poses and motions are most consistent with the behavior seen in the training set. As Bayesian inference, the output will be a blend of prior experience (training) and present evidence, *not* a metric pose recovery—though we believe the results would be quite close to metric given a reasonably large training set that adequately spans the space of body motions.

We found that we can obtain reasonable results even with a very small data set of highly atypical motions and poses: We obtained five sequences from a motion-capture WWW site[3], trained on four ("cossack dance," "whirling dervish," "rampage and hurl," "abominable snowman") and used the resulting model to infer the 3D structure from random-viewpoint 2D renderings of the fifth ("thief") as well as from real-world video. The 800-frame training set consists of $\{x, y, z\}$ motion-capture data for 37 body markers, mainly joint positions, with roughly 30 statistically significant kinematic DOFs.

7.1. Handling translation, scale, and rotation

We took the four 3D training sequences, removed variations due to whole-body translation, rotation, and scale changes, and estimated a manifold-approximating HMM.

[3]Biovision, http://www.biovision.com/samples.

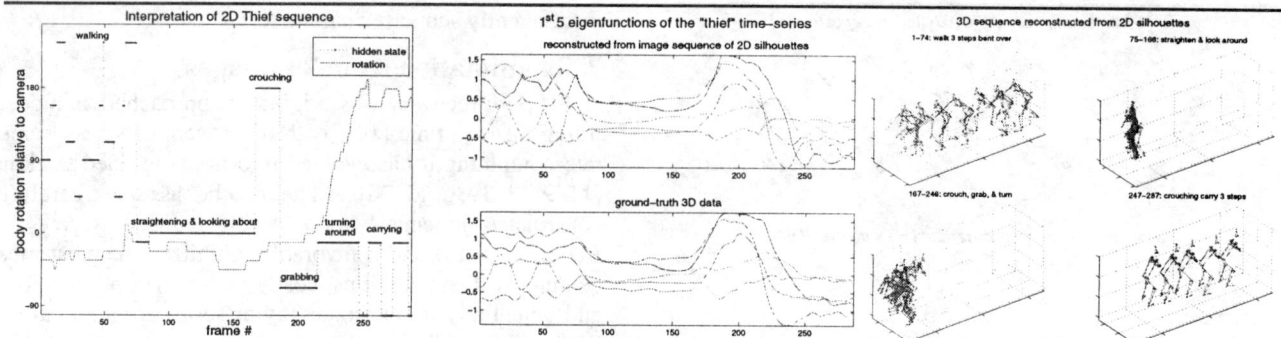

Figure 4. LEFT: A hidden-state analysis of a 2D rendering of the ground-truth test sequence, factored into pose and orientation information. MIDDLE: Eigenfunctions of the inferred and ground-truth 3D data match surprisingly well, even though training and test sets are rather dissimilar. RIGHT: A 120° view of 3D poses inferred from a 2D silhouette sequence observed by a camera at 326°. The division into activities derives from the system's analysis at left. See §7.2.

The HMM was initialized with all states fully connected and random parameter values. Training removed roughly 90% of the transitions; the internal Markov model had an entropy rate of 0.4941 and a perplexity (average branching factor) of 1.6391—a very unambiguous model. This HMM gives a simple probabilistic finite-state machine model of full-body motor control.

To handle rotations around the gravity axis, we replicated this HMM once for each view, re-estimating the output distributions of each view-specific HMM to cover an appropriately rotated version of the 3D data and its 2D "projection"—in these experiments a descriptive vector consisting of 10 scale-invariant central moments calculated from the silhouette of a rendered "tin-man" (e.g., 𝟙𝟙𝟚𝟙𝗄𝗄). We linked together all view-specific HMMs in the following manner: If $P_{i|j}$ is the probability of transitioning into state i from state j in the original HMM, and state i' is the ith equivalent state in a duplicated HMM observing data rotated by ϕ, then $P_{i'|j} = P_{i|j}\mathcal{V}(\phi; 0, \sigma^2)$, where $\mathcal{V}(\phi; \mu, \sigma^2) \propto e^{\cos(\phi-\mu)/\sigma^2}$ is a circular von Mises density with small variance σ^2 estimated from data. The resulting Cartesian-product HMM had 32 states × 32 views = 1024 states.

Note that this monocular 2D-to-3D architecture easily accommodates multiple views: E.g., for cameras viewing at $0°, 15°$, and $30°$, each view-specific HMM hidden state simply observes the product of its own Gaussian and those of equivalent states viewing 15° and 30° degrees beyond it. Similarly, other sources of evidence (e.g., feature tracking) can be exploited by estimating additional cue Gaussians on appropriately rotated projections as per §4.

7.2. Inferred vs. ground-truth data

In the ground-truth test sequence a "thief" walks forward in a crouch, stands tall, looks left and right, bends down to grab something, then turns around and scurries back carrying the loot with both hands. This is a challenging sequence because silhouettes give no indication whether the figure is walking toward or away from the camera, even if local temporal context is used. (Worse yet, the HMM only observes translation- and scale-invariant moments.) In order to correctly infer that the thief's walk and scurry are in opposite directions, the system will have to propagate orientation constraints across the intervening 170 non-walking frames.

We shadow-rendered the "thief" sequence from several random viewpoints, computed moments, contaminated them with 5% white noise, then performed a Viterbi analysis to obtain the most likely hidden state sequence. Figure 4L shows the resulting interpretation of a 326°-view shadow sequence (0° is head-on; 90° is profile). The system correctly infers the camera viewing angle and changes in body orientation throughout the sequence. In addition, the graph shows how the sequence breaks into actions and rhythmic cycles of states (walking, carrying).

The geodesic for this Viterbi sequence gives a synthesized 3D sequence that agrees well with the original (unseen) 3D data. Figure 4M shows the first 5 principal components of the synthesized trajectory, and figure 4R depicts the inferred 3D structure. The main difference between the inferred and ground-truth 3D is that walking is now more stooped and the shoulders roll slightly, consistent with the sequence in the training set that most resembles normal walking ("abominable snowman"). The accuracy of the inferred 3D improves as the number of states in the model increases, up to the limit of the maximum number of states supported by the training data (in this case, about 42).

7.3. Synthesis from image sequences

Here we analyze two low-resolution image sequences: One was graciously provided by a nearby lab also pursuing 3D recovery; the other was found on the WWW[4]. In sequence A, an individual jumps and twirls 360° in the air. In sequence B, an individual approaches and removes a package from a high perch, switches hands, and then strolls

---

[4]IrAll sequence, U. Maryland, http://www.umiacs.umd.edu.

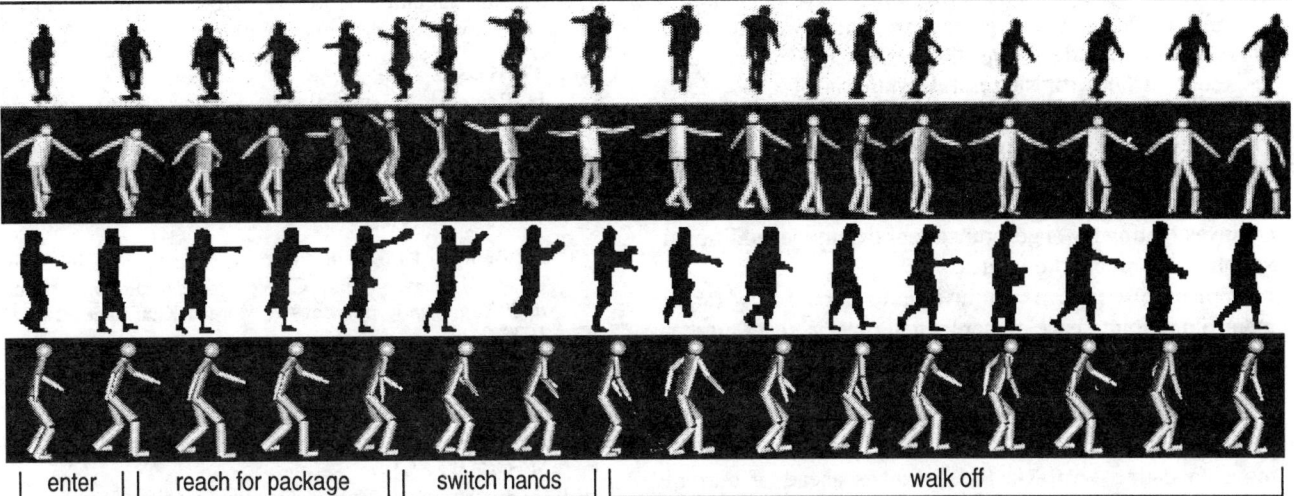

| enter | reach for package | switch hands | walk off |

Figure 5. ABOVE: Frames from a jump-and-twirl-360° sequence and the corresponding inferred 3D structure. BELOW: Every 12th frame from a grab-and-stroll sequence and the corresponding inferred 3D structure. In both examples the inferred 3D is qualitatively correct but not pose-for-pose accurate: The system exploits learned dynamics to successfully resolve image ambiguities, but often substitutes nearby poses where the training set contains no plausible near-matches to the observed silhouette. See §7.3.

away swinging the package. We background-subtracted the sequences and used morphological dilation and erosion to obtain a single silhouette per frame. Sequence A features rapid changes in aspect and occlusion, motion blur, and ambiguity w.r.t. the direction the figure is facing. Each profile-view silhouette in sequence B has four independent ambiguities (which arm/leg is foreground/forward), and all limbs disappear periodically in occlusions. In addition, limbs are amputated in many frames by back-subtraction errors and erosions. In both sequences the figure is less than 70 pixels high with limbs as narrow as 2 pixels. To the best of our knowledge, there are no other existing techniques that can extract fully articulated 3D from these shadow sequences; moreover we are led to believe that even the raw images from the "twirl" sequence are too low-resolution and fast-changing for current tracking-based techniques to succeed. These sequences also pose significant challenges for our approach, mainly because the training set contains very few of the poses in either sequence.

We computed a time-series of moments from the resulting silhouettes and inferred 3D using the same model as in §7.2. Despite their dissimilarity from the training set, the system infers 3D sequences that are action-for-action consistent with the video (figure 5). The system correctly recovers the jump, twirl, and landing in sequence A, but reconstructs the 3D with arms akimbo and a wide-legged landing, which is closer to the examples of turning observed in the training set. The figurine synthesized from sequence B reaches when the human reaches, puts its hands together when the human does, and walks as the human does. But again there are noticeable differences in posture, largely because the closest poses and motions in the training set

come from the monster sequences. We were pleasantly surprised to see that the system slightly straightened out the poses in sequence B interspersing occasional erect-posture hidden states from the dance sequences. We also noticed that when the system knows of no dynamically correct region of pose space that matches a silhouette, it substitutes a pose that is more likely to match the legs than the arms. This is probably due to the facts that (1) legs are more dynamically constrained, and (2) image moments are less sensitive to the arms' comparatively small surfaces. It should be mentioned that these were first-run results; we made no attempt to tune the system to the problem since, from a learning perspective, we are interested in testing the HMM-geodesic approach in its most generic form.

8. Discussion

Our learning-based approach has the following advantages: It makes sense of highly ambiguous sensing with extensive use of hindsight and foresight, and can incorporate any kind of evidence. It is fully trainable and makes no assumptions about jointedness, rigidity, or degrees of freedom in the target system. There are no singularities and the computational costs are fixed. It is fully Bayesian and exact. Finally, the results are guaranteed to be consistent with the configural and dynamical behavior in the training set.

This is a two-edged sword: With evidence as weak as image moments, the learned prior will dominate the reconstruction. Although our prototype shows reasonably good generalization away from its rather odd and limited training set, it is clear that improvements will require an expanded training set containing more "normal" poses and motions. Our experience in other machine learning domains is that entropic estimation scales well to large training sets, still delivering the low-entropy models that are required here for successful synthesis of geodesics[5]. However, more varied data will require more states in order to adequately populate the presumably high dimensional manifold of body movement. Present results indicate fair generalization from a sparse population of states, and we are investigating HMM generalizations that model additional variation without adding states.

It may also prove worthwhile to model the target manifold in joint-space rather than in raw $\{x, y, z\}$ marker position-space; a geodesic calculated in joint-space may yield kinematically better generalization away from the training examples. We are also interested in exploiting the HMM to make a running prediction of how the body will move (and thus be tracked) 1-5 frames ahead of current visual processing.

9. Summary

Inferring 3D body pose from highly ambiguous image sequences (e.g., shadow-plays) requires extensive use of context to resolve ambiguities. We framed this problem as one of learning a mapping between histories (paths) rather than configurations (points). We took a pure learning approach, estimating a basis for this mapping by learning a concise probabilistic model of the body's high-dimensional dynamical manifold. Entropy minimization yields extremely parsimonious and topologically accurate probabilistic models, making this approach viable even with very limited and atypical training data. For 2D-to-3D inference, we used translation- and scale-invariant moments as evidence and folded inference about rotations (around the gravity axis) into the learned model. We gave a closed-form MAP solution for constrained geodesics through the learned density space that yields the optimal target trajectory with respect to any sequence of evidence. The resulting system can infer qualitatively correct 3D action and orientation from low-resolution monocular shadow sequences with full turns and heavy occlusion, propagating information forwards and backwards through time over hundreds of frames to resolve multiple ambiguities per frame. The computational costs are fixed and reasonable; the system makes no kinematic or rigidity assumptions; and the framework can trivially incorporate other sources of evidence including tracking and multiple cameras.

10. Acknowledgments

Thanks to Jon Yedidia, who prepared the data for training; to Michael Leventon, who originally collected the training data and wrote software to manipulate and render

it; and to Bill Freeman, who originally raised the possibility of 2D-to-3D without articulatory models.

References

[1] L. Baum. An inequality and associated maximization technique in statistical estimation of probabilistic functions of Markov processes. *Inequalities*, 3:1–8, 1972.

[2] M. Brand. The entropic prior is the continuous and computable analogue of the universal prior. *(in reviews)*, 1998.

[3] M. Brand. Pattern discovery via entropy minimization. In D. Heckerman and C. Whittaker, editors, *Artificial Intelligence and Statistics #7*. Morgan Kaufmann., January 1999.

[4] M. Brand. Structure discovery in conditional probability models via an entropic prior and parameter extinction. *Neural Computation*, 11(5):1155–1182, July 1999.

[5] M. Brand. Voice puppetry. In *Technical proceedings, SIGGRAPH99*, 1999.

[6] C. Bregler and J. Malik. Tracking people with twists and exponential maps. In *CVPR98*, pages 8–15, 1998.

[7] C. Bregler and S. Omohundro. Nonlinear manifold learning for visual speech recognition. In *ICCV95*, pages 494–499, 1995.

[8] G. Forney. The Viterbi algorithm. *Proceedings of the IEEE*, 6:268–278, 1973.

[9] D. Gavrila and L. Davis. Towards 3-D model-based tracking of humans in action. In *AIU96*, pages 264–279, 1996.

[10] G. H. Golub and C. F. van Loan. *Matrix Computations*. Johns Hopkins, 1996. 3rd edition.

[11] L. Goncalves, E. Bernardo, E. Ursella, and P. Perona. Monocular tracking of the human arm in 3D. In *CVPR98*, pages 403–410, 1995.

[12] D. Hogg. A program to see a walking person. *Image Vision Computing*, 20, 1983.

[13] I. Kakadiaris and D. Metaxas. Model-based estimation of 3D human motion with occlusion based on active multi-viewpoint selection. In *CVPR96*, pages 81–87, 1996.

[14] M. E. Leventon and W. T. Freeman. Bayesian estimation of 3D human motion from an image sequence. Technical Report TR98-06, Mitsubishi Electric Research Laboratories, July 1998.

[15] D. Morris and J. Rehg. Singularity analysis for articulated object tracking. In *CVPR98*, pages 289–296, 1998.

[16] L. R. Rabiner. A tutorial on hidden Markov models and selected applications in speech recognition. *Proceedings of the IEEE*, 77(2):257–286, Feb. 1989.

[17] K. Rohr. Recognition of human movements based on explicit motion models. In *MBR97*, page Chapter 8, 1997.

[18] L. Saul and M. Jordan. A variational principle for model-based interpolation. Technical report, MIT Center for Biological and Computational Learning, 1996.

[19] D. R. Smith. *Variational Methods in Optimization*. Dover, Mineola, NY, 1998.

[20] C. R. Wren and A. P. Pentland. Dynaman: Recursive modeling of human motion. *Image and Vision Computing*, 1999. To appear. Also available as MIT Media Lab Vision and Modelling TR-451.

---

[5]For example, we have used a subset of the methods presented here to infer facial motions from audio signals, training with 4000 datapoints and synthesizing sequences equally long, with deviations from ground-truth facial motion averaging less than 0.5% of the size of the face [5].

Direction Diffusion

Bei Tang and Guillermo Sapiro
Electrical and Computer Engineering
University of Minnesota
Minneapolis, MN 55455
guille@ece.umn.edu

Vicent Caselles
Informatics and Mathematics
University of the Illes Balears
07071 Palma de Mallorca, Spain

Abstract

In a number of disciplines, directional data provides a fundamental source of information. A novel framework for isotropic and anisotropic diffusion of directions is presented in this paper. The framework can be applied both to regularize directional data and to obtain multiscale representations of it. The basic idea is to apply and extend results from the theory of harmonic maps in liquid crystals. This theory deals with the regularization of vectorial data, while satisfying the unit norm constraint of directional data. We show the corresponding variational and partial differential equations formulations for isotropic diffusion, obtained from an L_2 norm, and edge preserving diffusion, obtained from an L_1 norm. In contrast with previous approaches, the framework is valid for directions in any dimensions, supports non-smooth data, and gives both isotropic and anisotropic formulations. We present a number of theoretical results, open questions, and examples for gradient vectors, optical flow, and color images.

1 Introduction

In a number of disciplines, directions provide a fundamental source of information. Examples in the area of computer vision are (2D, 3D, and 4D) gradient directions, optical flow directions, surface normals, principal directions, and color. In the color example, the direction is given by the normalized vector in the color space. Frequently, this data is available in a noisy fashion, and there is a need for noise removal. In addition, it is often desired to obtain a multiscale-type representation of the direction, similar to those obtained for gray-level images [24, 26, 27, 39]. Addressing these issues is the goal of this paper.

An $I\!R^n$ direction defined on an image in $I\!R^2$ is given by a vector $I(x, y, 0) : I\!R^2 \to I\!R^n$ such that the Euclidean norm of $I(x, y, 0)$ is equal to one, that is, $\sqrt{\sum_{i=1}^n I_i^2(x, y, 0)} = 1$, where $I_i(x, y, 0) : I\!R^2 \to I\!R$ are the components of the vector. The notation can

be simplified by considering $I(x, y, 0) : I\!R^2 \to S^{n-1}$, where S^{n-1} is the unit ball in $I\!R^n$. This implicitly includes the unit norm constraint. (Any vector can be transformed into a direction by normalizing it.) When smoothing the data, or computing a multiscale representation $I(x, y, t)$ of a direction $I(x, y, 0)$ (t stands for the scale), it is crucial to maintain the unit norm constraint, which is an intrinsic characteristic of directional data. [1] That is, the smoothed direction $\hat{I}(x, y, 0) : I\!R^2 \to I\!R^n$ must also satisfy $\sqrt{\sum_{i=1}^n \hat{I}_i^2(x, y, 0)} = 1$. Or, $\hat{I}(x, y, 0) : I\!R^2 \to S^{n-1}$. The same constraint holds for a multiscale representation $I(x, y, t)$ of the original direction $I(x, y, 0)$. This is what makes the smoothing of directions different from the smoothing of ordinary vectorial data as in [32, 38]: The smoothing is performed in S^{n-1} instead of $I\!R^n$.

Directions can also be represented by the angle(s) the vector makes with a given coordinate system, denoted in this paper as *orientation(s)*. In the 2D case for example, the direction of a vector (I_1, I_2) can be given by the angle θ that this vector makes with the x axis (we consider $\theta \in [0, 2\pi)$): $\theta = \arctan(I_2/I_1)$. There is of course a one-to-one map between a direction vector $I(x, y) : I\!R^2 \to S^1$ and the angle θ. Using this relation, Perona, [26], transformed the problem of 2D direction diffusion into a 1D problem of angle or orientation diffusion (see also the comment in Section 3 below). Perona then proposed PDE based techniques for the isotropic smoothing of 2D orientations; see also [20, 37] and the general discussion of these methods in [26]. [2] Smoothing orientations in-

---

[1] In this work we do not explicitly address the problem where the direction smoothing depends on other image attributes (see for example [25]), the analysis is done intrinsically to the directional, unit norm, data. When other attributes are present, we process them separately or via couple PDE's, e.g., [35]. If needed, the unit norm constraint can be relaxed using a framework similar to the one here proposed.

[2] As Perona pointed out in his work, this is just one example

stead of directions solves the unit norm constraint, but adds a periodicity constraint. Perona showed that a simple heat flow (Laplacian or Gaussian filtering) applied to the $\theta(x, y)$ image, together with special numerical attention, can address this periodicity issue. This approach applies only to small changes in θ, that is, smooth data, and thereby disqualifying edges. The straightforward extension of this to S^{n-1} would be to consider $n-1$ angles, and smooth each one of these as a scalar image. The natural coupling is then missing, obtaining a set of decoupled PDE's.

In this work we follow the suggestion in [7] and directly perform diffusion on the direction space, extending to images representing directions the by now already classical results on diffusion of images representing gray values [2, 24, 27, 31, 32, 38, 37]. That is, from the original unit norm vectorial image $I(x, y, 0) :$ $\mathbb{R}^2 \rightarrow S^{n-1}$ we construct a family of unit norm vectorial images $I(x, y, t) : \mathbb{R}^2 \times [0, \tau) \rightarrow S^{n-1}$ that provides a multiscale representation of directions. The method intrinsically takes care of the normalization constraint, eliminating the need to consider orientations and develop special periodicity preserving numerical approximations. Discontinuities in the directions are also allowed by the algorithm. The approach follows results from the literature on harmonic maps in liquid crystals, and $I(x, y, t)$ is obtained from a system of coupled partial differential equations that reduces a given (harmonic) energy. Energies giving both isotropic and anisotropic flows will be described. Due to the large amount of literature in the subject of harmonic maps applied to liquid crystals, a number of relevant theoretical results can immediately be obtained.

Before presenting the details of the framework for direction diffusion here proposed, let's resume its main unique characteristics: 1. It includes both isotropic and anisotropic diffusion; 2. It works for directions in any dimension; 3. It supports non-smooth data; 4. It is based on a substantial amount of existing theoretical results that help to answer a number of relevant computer vision questions.

---

of the diffusion of images representing data beyond flat manifolds. Extensions to this work, using intrinsic metrics on the manifold can be found in [8, 33]. In [8], the authors explicitly deal with orientations and present the L_1 norm as well as many additional new features, contributions on discrete formulations, and connections with our approach. The work [33] does not deal with orientations or directions. In [30] the authors also mention the minimization of the L_1 norm of the divergence of the normalized image gradient (curvature of the level-sets). This is done in the framework of image denoising, without addressing the regularization and analysis of directional data or presenting examples. None of these works uses the classical and "natural" harmonic maps framework as we do in this paper.

2 The general problem

Let $I(x, y, 0) : \mathbb{R}^2 \rightarrow S^{n-1}$ be the original image of directions. That is, this is a collection of vectors from $\mathbb{R}^2$ to $\mathbb{R}^n$ such that their unit norm is equal to one, i.e., $\| I(x, y, 0) \| = 1$, where $\| \cdot \|$ indicates Euclidean length. $I_i(x, y, 0) : \mathbb{R}^2 \rightarrow \mathbb{R}$ stands for each one of the n components of $I(x, y, 0)$. We search for a family of images, a multiscale representation, of the form $I(x, y, t) : \mathbb{R}^2 \times [0, \tau) \rightarrow S^{n-1}$, and once again we use $I_i(x, y, t) : \mathbb{R}^2 \rightarrow \mathbb{R}$ to represent each one of the components of this family. Let's define the *component gradient* ∇I_i as $\nabla I_i := \frac{\partial I_i}{\partial x} \vec{x} + \frac{\partial I_i}{\partial y} \vec{y}$, where $\vec{x}$ and $\vec{y}$ are the unit vectors in the x and y directions respectively.

From this, $\| \nabla I_i \| = \left(\left(\frac{\partial I_i}{\partial x} \right)^2 + \left(\frac{\partial I_i}{\partial y} \right)^2 \right)^{1/2}$, gives the absolute value of the component gradient. The *component Laplacian* is given by $\Delta I_i = \frac{\partial^2 I_i}{\partial x^2} + \frac{\partial^2 I_i}{\partial y^2}$. We are also interested in the *absolute value of the image gradient*, given by $\| \nabla I \| := \left(\sum_{i=1}^{n} \left(\frac{\partial I_i}{\partial x} \right)^2 + \left(\frac{\partial I_i}{\partial y} \right)^2 \right)^{1/2}$.

Having this notation, we are now ready to formulate our framework. The problem of *harmonic maps in liquid crystals* is formulated as the search for the solution to

$$\min_{I : \mathbb{R}^2 \rightarrow S^{n-1}} \int \int_{\Omega} \| \nabla I \|^p \, dxdy, \qquad (1)$$

where Ω stands for the image domain and $p \geq 1$. This variational formulation can be re-written as $\min_{I : \mathbb{R}^2 \rightarrow \mathbb{R}^n} \int \int_{\Omega} \| \nabla I \|^p \, dxdy$, with $\| I \| = 1$.

This is a particular case of the search for maps I between Riemannian manifolds (M, g) and (N, h) which are critical points of the *harmonic energy*

$$E(u) = \int_M \| \nabla_M I \|^p \, \mathrm{dvol}M, \qquad (2)$$

where $\| \nabla_M I \|$ is the length of the differential in M. In our particular case, M is a domain in $\mathbb{R}^2$ and $N = S^{n-1}$, and $\| \nabla_M I \|$ reduces to the absolute value of the image gradient. The critical points of (2) are called *p-harmonic maps* (or simply *harmonic maps* for $p = 2$). This is in analogy to the critical points of the Dirichlet energy $\int_{\Omega} \| \nabla f \|^2$ for real valued functions f, which are called *harmonic functions*.

The general form of the harmonic energy with $p = 2$ was successfully used for example in computer graphics to find smooth maps between two given (triangulated) surfaces (normally a surface and the complex plane); e.g. [14, 21, 41]. In this case, the search is indeed for the critical point, that is, for the harmonic map between the surfaces. This can be done for example via finite elements [21]. In our case, the problem is different. We already have a candidate map, the original image of directions $I(x, y, 0)$, and we want to compute a multiscale or regularized version of it. That is, we are not (just) interested in the harmonic map between the domain in $I\!R^2$ and S^{n-1} (the critical point of the energy), but are interested in the process of computing this map via partial differential equations. More specifically, we are interested in the gradient-descent type flow of the harmonic energy (2). This is partially motivated by the fact that diffusion equations for gray-valued images can be obtained as gradient descent flows acting on real-valued data; see for example [4, 27, 31, 40]. Isotropic diffusion is just the gradient descent of the L_2 norm of the image gradient, while anisotropic diffusion can be interpreted as the gradient descent flow of more robust norms acting on the image gradient.[3]

For the most popular case of $p = 2$, the Euler-Lagrange equation corresponding to (2) is a simple formula based on Δ_M, the Laplace-Beltrami operator of M, and $A_N(I)$, the second fundamental form of N (assumed to be embedded in $I\!R^k$) evaluated at I; e.g., [15, 34]: $\Delta_M I + A_N(I)\langle \nabla_M u, \nabla_M u \rangle = 0$. This leads to a gradient-descent type of flow, that is,

$$\frac{\partial I}{\partial t} = \Delta_M I + A_N(I)\langle \nabla_M u, \nabla_M u \rangle. \qquad (3)$$

In the following sections, we will present the gradient descent flows for our particular energy (1), that is, for M being a domain in $I\!R^2$ and N equal to S^{n-1}.[4] We concentrate on the cases of $p = 2$ (isotropic) and $p = 1$ (anisotropic). The use of $p = 2$ corresponds to the classical heat flow from the linear scale-space theory [24, 39], while the case $p = 1$ corresponds to the *total variation* flow studied in [31].

Most of the literature on harmonic maps deals with $p = 2$ in (2) or (1), the linear case. Some more recent results are available for $1 < p < \infty$, $p \neq 2$, and very

---

[3]Since we have an energy formulation, it is straightforward to add additional data-dependent constraints to the minimization process. In this case we might indeed be interested in the critical point of the modified energy, which can be obtained as the steady-state solution of the corresponding gradient descent flow. Since the goal of this paper is to describe the general framework for direction diffusion, we will not add these type of constraints in the examples in §5. These constraints are normally closely tied to both the specific problem and the available information about the type of noise present in the image. In [8, 26], data-terms are added.

[4]For data like surface normals and principal directions, M is a surface in 3D and the general flow (3) is used. This flow can be implemented using classical numerical techniques to compute ∇_M and Δ_M on triangulated or implicit surfaces. Results on the multiscale analysis of directions defined on surfaces instead of $I\!R^2$ are reported in a companion paper (part of this work is in collaboration with S. Osher).

few results deal with the case $p = 1$. A number of theoretical results, both for the variational formulation and its corresponding gradient descent flow, which are relevant to the multiscale representation of directions, will be given in the following sections as well.

3 Isotropic diffusion

It is easy to show that for $p = 2$, the gradient descent flow corresponding to (1) is given by the set of coupled PDE's:[5]

$$\frac{\partial I_i}{\partial t} = \Delta I_i + I_i \parallel \nabla I \parallel^2, \ 1 \leq i \leq n. \qquad (4)$$

This system of coupled PDE's defines the isotropic multiscale representation of $I(x, y, 0)$, which is used as initial data to solve (4). (Boundary conditions are also added in the case of finite domains.)

The first part of (4) comes from the variational form, while the second one comes from the constraint. As expected, the first part is decoupled between components I_i, and linear, while the coupling and nonlinearity come from the constraint.

For $p = 2$, we have the following important results from the literature on harmonic maps:

Existence: Existence results for harmonic mappings were already reported in [16] for a particular selection of the target manifold N. Struwe [34] showed, in one of the classical papers in the area, that for initial data with finite energy (as measured by (2)), M a two dimensional manifold with $\partial M = \emptyset$ (manifold without boundary), and $N = S^{n-1}$, there is a unique solution to the general gradient-descent flow. Moreover, this solution is regular with the exception of a finite number of isolated points and the harmonic energy is decreasing in time. If the initial energy is small, the solution is completely regular and converges to a constant value. (The results actually holds for any compact N.) This uniqueness results was later extended to manifolds with smooth $\partial M \neq \emptyset$ and for weak solutions [18]. Recapping, there is a unique weak solution to (4) (weak solutions defined in natural spaces, $H^{1,2}(M, N)$), and the set of possible singularities is finite. These solutions decrease the harmonic energy. The result is not completely true for M with dimension grater than 2, and this was investigated for example in [10]. Global weak solutions exist for example

---

[5]If $n = 2$, that is, we have 2D directions, then it is easy to show that for $I(x, y) = (\cos \theta(x, y), \sin \theta(x, y))$, the energy in (1) becomes $\int \int_\Omega (\theta_x^2 + \theta_y^2)^{p/2} dx dy$. For $p = 2$ we then obtain the linear heat flow on θ ($\theta_t = \Delta \theta$) as the corresponding gradient descent flow, as expected from the results in [26]. This is of course directly derived from the theory of harmonic maps. When the data is not regular, the direction and orientation formulations are not necessarily equivalent.

for $N = S^{n-1}$, although there is no uniqueness for the general initial value problem [13]. Results on the regularity of the solution, for a restricted suitable class of weak solutions, to the harmonic flow for high dimensional manifolds M into S^{n-1} have been recently reported [11, 17]. In this case, it is assumed that the weak solutions holds a number of given energy constraints.

Singularities in 2D: If $N = S^1$, and the initial and boundary conditions are well behaved (smooth, finite energy), then the solution of the harmonic flow is regular. This is the case for example for smooth $2D$ image gradients and $2D$ optical flow.

Singularities in 3D: Unfortunately, for $n = 3$ in (4) (that is $N = S^2$, $3D$ vectors), smooth initial data can lead to singularities in finite time [9]. Chang *et al.* showed examples where the flow (4), with initial data $I(x,y,0) = I_0(x,y) \in C^1(D^2, S^2)$ (D^2 is the unit disk on the plane) and boundary conditions $I(x,y,t)|_{\partial D^2} = I_0|_{\partial D^2}$, develops singularities in finite time. The idea is to use as original data I_0 a function that covers S^2 more than once a in certain region. From the point of view of the harmonic energy, the solution is "giving up on" regularity in order to reduce energy.

Singularities topology: Since singularities can occur, it is then interesting to study them [5, 22, 29]. For example, Brezis *et al.* studied the value of the harmonic energy when the singularities of the critical point are prescribed (the map is from R^3 to S^2 in this case).[6] Qing characterized the energy at the singularities. A recent review on the singularities of harmonic maps was prepared by Hardt [22]. (Singularities for more general energies are studied for example in [28].) The results there reported can be used to characterize the behavior of the mulstiscale representation of high dimensional directions, although these results mainly address the shape of the harmonic map, that is, the critical point of the harmonic energy and not the flow. Of course, for the case of M being of dimension two, which corresponds to (4), we have Struwe's results mentioned above.

4 Anisotropic diffusion

The picture becomes even more interesting for the case $1 \leq p < 2$. Now the gradient descent flow corresponding to (1), in the range $1 < p < 2$ (and formally for $p = 1$), is given by the set of coupled PDE's:

$$\frac{\partial I_i}{\partial t} = \operatorname{div}\left(\| \nabla I \|^{p-2} \nabla I_i\right) + I_i \| \nabla I \|^p, \;\; 1 \leq i \leq n. \tag{5}$$

---

[6]Perona suggested to look at this line of work to analyze the singularities of the orientation diffusion flow.

This system of coupled PDE's defines the anisotropic multiscale representation of $I(x,y,0)$, which is used as initial datum to solve (5). In contrast with the isotropic case, now both terms in (5) are non-linear and include coupled components.

The case of $p \neq 2$ in (2) has been less studied in the literature. When M is a domain in $I\!\!R^m$, and $N = S^{n-1}$, the function $v(X) := \frac{X}{\|X\|}$, $X \in I\!\!R^m$, is a critical point of the energy for $p \in \{2, 3, ..., m-1\}$, for $p \in [m-1, m)$ (this interval includes the energy case that leads to (5)), and for $p \in [2, m - 2\sqrt{m-1}]$ [22]. For $n = 2$ and $p = 1$, the variational problem has also been investigated in [19], where the authors addressed, among other things, the correct spaces to perform the minimization (in the scalar case, $BV(\Omega, I\!\!R)$ is used), and the existence of minimizers. Of course, we are more interested in the results for the flow (5), and not just in its corresponding energy. Some results exist for $1 < p < \infty$, $p \neq 2$, showing in a number of cases the existence of local solutions which are not smooth. To the best of our knowledge, the case of $1 \leq p < 2$, and in particular $p = 1$, has not been fully studied for the evolution equation, and this is part of our future plans.

5 Examples and concluding remarks

Although advanced specialized numerical techniques to solve (1) and its corresponding gradient-descent flow, have been developed, e.g., [1], as a first approximation we can basically use the algorithms developed for scalar isotropic and anisotropic diffusion without the unit norm constraint, e.g., [31], to implement (4) and (5) [12]. Although these equations preserve the unit norm, numerical errors might violate the constraint. Therefore, between every two steps of the numerical implementation of this equations we add a renormalization step [12] (new developments by S. Osher and L. Vese might overcome this step).

For the examples we show below, a number of visualization techniques are used: 1. *Arrows.* Arrows indicating the vector direction are very illustrative, but can be used only for sparse images and they are not very informative for dense data like gradients or optical flow. 2. *HSV color mapping.* We use the HSV color map (applied to orientation) to visualize whole images of directions while being able to also illustrate details like small noise. 3. *Line integral convolution (LIC) [6].* LIC is based on locally integrating at each pixel, in the directions given by the directional data, the values of a random image. The LIC technique gives the general form of the flow, while the color map is useful to detect small noise in the direction (orientation) image.

Figure 1 shows a number of toy examples to illustrate the general ideas introduced in this paper, as well as examples for color image denoising. The first row shows, using LIC, an image with two regions having two different (2D) orientations on the left (original), followed by the results of isotropic diffusion for 200, 2000, and 8000 iterations (scale-space). Note how the edge in the directional data is being smoothed out. The horizontal and vertical directions are being smoothed out to converge to the diagonal average. This is in contrast with the results for anisotropic diffusion, as shown in the next two rows. The second row shows the result of removing noise in the directional data. The original noisy image is shown first, followed by the results with isotropic and anisotropic smoothing. Note how the anisotropic flow gets rid of the noise (outliers) while preserving the rest of the data, while the isotropic flow also affects the data itself while removing the noise. Note that since the discrete theory developed in [26] applies only to small changes in orientation, theoretically it can not be applied to the images we have seen so far, all of them contain sharp discontinuities in the directional data (and the theory is only isotropic). The third row deals with 3D directions. In this case, we interpret the vector as RGB coordinates, and use color to visualize them. We show the original image followed by the results of isotropic and anisotropic diffusion. Note how the colors, and then the corresponding directions, get blurred with the isotropic flow, while the edges in direction (color) are well preserved with the anisotropic process. We can use this to process real color images. That is, we separate the color direction from the color magnitude, and use the harmonic flows to smooth the direction (chromaticity), and standard scalar filters to smooth the magnitude (brightness), This gives very good color image denoising results, as shown in the last two rows (original, noise, and reconstructed respectively). See [35] for additional examples, comparisons with the literature, and details.[7] (Other directional filters for color denoising, based on vectorial median filtering, can be found for example in [7, 36].)

Figure 2a shows results for optical flow. The first figure on the first row shows a frame of the famous Yosemite movie. Next, in the same row, we show from left to right the original optical flow direction (computed using [3], stopping at early annealing stages to have enough noise for experimentation), the result of the isotropic flow, the result of the anisotropic flow,

and the result of the isotropic flow for a large number of iterations. The HSV color map is used. In the next row, we use LIC to visualize again the three middle figures of the first row. In the third row, arrows are used to show a blown-up of the marked region corresponding to the isotropic flow for 20, 60, and 500 iterations. Note how the noise in the optical flow directions is removed.

Figure 2b deals with 90 degrees rotated gradient directions in a fingerprint image. After the raw data for the image is shown, we use the color map visualization technique to present a number of steps (scale-space) of the isotropic flow. This is followed by arrows for a blown-up of the marked region (last row, from left to right, original, 20 steps, and 200 steps respectively). Note in the arrows images how the noise is removed and the main orientation for the fingerprint is obtained.

We observe then that the theory of harmonic maps provides a fundamental framework for directional diffusion in particular and diffusion on general manifolds in general. A number of questions remain open. First of all, we need to perform a complete analysis of the harmonic energy and gradient descent flow for $p = 1$, the anisotropic case. From the practical point of view, it will be interesting to carry out a formal analysis that compares the results obtained from image denoising followed by direction computation (e.g., gradients) with those obtained while computing the directions in the noisy image and then smoothing them with the technique presented in this paper. We are also interested in including the harmonic energy as a regularization term in more general variational problems, as the general optical flow framework, and in using the theory of harmonic maps for other image processing, computer vision, and graphics applications.

Acknowledgments

This work was motivated by the smoothing of vector-valued images, separating the vector into its direction and magnitude. GS thanks Prof. Robert Kohn from the Courant Institute, NYU, for encouraging him to think again about filtering vectorial images. GS also wants to thank Prof. Kobi Rubinstein from the Technion, Israel Institute of Technology, for pointing out very relevant literature on harmonic maps, Prof. Stan Osher, Prof. Tony Chan, Prof. Jianhong Shen, and Prof. Luminita Vese from UCLA for sharing their ideas on orientation/direction diffusion, Prof. David Heeger from Stanford University and Prof. Victoria Interrante from the University of Minnesota for pointing out references on vector visualization, Prof. Pietro Perona for helping with the color mapping visualization technique, and Brian Cabral and Casey Leedom, both from SGI, for the LIC software. Although this

---

[7]Due to the lack of color proceedings, the performance of this scheme can only be judged from the electronic version of the paper.

work was originally motivated by the smoothing of general vector-data, after making the connection with direction diffusion, Perona's work [26] was very influential and inspiring. The optical flow data was obtained using the software developed by Dr. Michael Black from Xerox PARC. This work was partially supported by the TMR European project "Viscosity solutions and their applications," reference FMRX-CT98-0234, the European Network PAVR FMRXCT960036, a grant from the Office of Naval Research ONR-N00014-97-1-0509, the Office of Naval Research Young Investigator Award, the Presidential Early Career Awards for Scientists and Engineers (PECASE), a National Science Foundation CAREER Award, the National Science Foundation Learning and Intelligent Systems Program (LIS), and NSF-IRI-9306155 (Geometry Driven Diffusion).

References

[1] F. Alouges, in J.M. Coron *et al.*, Editors, *Nematics*, Nato ASI Series, Kluwer, Netherlands, pp. 1-13, 1991.

[2] L. Alvarez, P. L. Lions, and J. M. Morel, *SIAM J. Numer. Anal.* **29**, pp. 845-866, 1992.

[3] M. Black and P. Anandan, *Proc. ICCV*, Berlin, Germany, pp. 231-236, May 1993.

[4] M. Black, G. Sapiro, D. Marimont, and D. Heeger, *IEEE Trans. Image Processing* **7:3**, pp. 421-432, 1998.

[5] H. Brezis, J. M. Coron, and E. H. Lieb, *Communications in Mathematical Physics* **107**, pp. 649-705, 1986.

[6] B. Cabral and C. Leedom. *Proc. SIGGRAPH*, 1993.

[7] V. Caselles, G. Sapiro, and D. H. Chung, *Proc. IEEE-ICIP*, Japan, October 1999.

[8] T. Chan and J. Shen, "Variational restoration of non-flat image features: Models and algorithms," *UCLA CAM-TR*, May 1999.

[9] K. C. Chang, W. Y. Ding, and R. Ye, *J. Differential Geometry* **36**, pp. 507-515, 1992.

[10] Y. Chen, *Math. Z.* **201**, pp. 69-74, 1989.

[11] Y. Chen, J. Li, and F. H. Lin, *Comm. on Pure and App. Mathematics* **XLVIII**, pp. 429-448, 1995.

[12] R. Cohen, R. M. Hardt, D. Kinderlehrer, S. Y. Lin, and M. Luskin, in J. L. Ericksen and D. Kinderlehrer, Editors, *Theory and Applications of Liquid Crystals*, pp. 99-121, Springer-Verlag, New York, 1987.

[13] J. M. Coron, *Ann. Inst. H. Poincaré, Analyse Non Linéaire* **7:4**, pp. 335-344, 1990.

[14] M. Eck, T. DeRose, T. Duchamp, H. Hoppe, M. Lounsbery, and W. Stuetzle, Computer Graphics (SIG-GRAPH '95 Proceedings), pp. 173-182, 1995.

[15] J. Eells and L. Lemarie, *Bull. London Math. Soc.* **10:1**, pp. 1-68, 1978; and **20:5**, pp. 385-524, 1988.

[16] J. Eells and J. H. Sampson, *Am. J. Math.* **86**, pp. 109-160, 1964.

[17] M. Feldman, *Comm. in Partial Differential Equations* **19**, pp. 761-790, 1994.

[18] A. Freire, *Calc. Var.* **3**, pp. 95-105, 1995.

[19] M. Giaquinta, G. Modica, and J. Soucek, *Cal. Var.* **1**, pp. 87-121, 1993.

[20] G. H. Granlund and H. Knuttson, *Signal Processing for Computer Vision*, Kluwer, Boston, MA, 1995.

[21] S. Haker *et al.* "Conformal surface parametrization for texture mapping," *ECE-University of Minnesota Technical Report*, January 1999.

[22] R. M. Hardt, *Bulletin of the American Mathematical Society* **34:1**, pp. 15-34, 1997.

[23] R. M. Hardt and F. H. Lin, *Communications on Pure and Applied Mathematics* **XL**, pp. 555-588, 1987.

[24] J. J. Koenderink, *Biological Cybernetics* **50**, pp. 363-370, 1984.

[25] T. Lindeberg, *Scale-Space Theory in Computer Vision*, Kluwer, The Netherlands, 1994).

[26] P. Perona, *IEEE Trans. IP* **7**, pp. 457-467, 1998.

[27] P. Perona and J. Malik, *IEEE Trans. PAMI* **12**, pp. 629-639, 1990.

[28] L. M. Pismen and J. Rubinstein, in J.M. Coron *et al.*, Editors, *Nematics*, Nato ASI Series, Kluwer Academic Publishers, Netherlands, pp. 303-326, 1991.

[29] J. Qing, *Comm. in Analysis and Geometry* **3:2**, pp. 297-315, 1995.

[30] L. I. Rudin and S. Osher, *Proc. IEEE-ICIP* **I**, pp. 31-35, Austin, Texas, 1994.

[31] L. I. Rudin, S. Osher, and E. Fatemi, *Physica D* **60**, pp. 259-268, 1992.

[32] G. Sapiro and D. Ringach, *IEEE Trans. IP* **5**, pp. 1582-1586, 1996.

[33] N. Sochen, R. Kimmel, and R. Malladi, *IEEE Trans. IP* **7:3**, pp. 310-318, 1998.

[34] M. Struwe, *Comment. Math. Helvetici* **60**, pp. 558-581, 1985.

[35] B. Tang, G. Sapiro, and V. Caselles, "Color image enhancement via chromaticity diffusion," pre-print, March 1999.

[36] P. E. Trahanias, D. Karakos, and A. N. Venetsanopoulos, *IEEE Trans. IP* **5**, pp. 868-880, 1996.

[37] J. Weickert, *Zeitscgr. Angewandte Math. Mechan.* **76**, pp. 283-286, 1996.

[38] R. T. Whitaker and G. Gerig, in B. ter Haar Romeny, Ed., *Geometry Driven Diffusion in Computer Vision*, Boston, MA, Kluwer, 1994.

[39] A. P. Witkin, *Int. Joint. Conf. Artificial Intelligence*, pp. 1019-1021, 1983.

[40] Y. L. You, W. Xu, A. Tannenbaum, and M. Kaveh, *IEEE Trans. IP* **5**, pp. 1539-1553, 1996.

[41] D. Zhang and M. Hebert, *Proc. CVPR '99*, Colorado, June 1999.

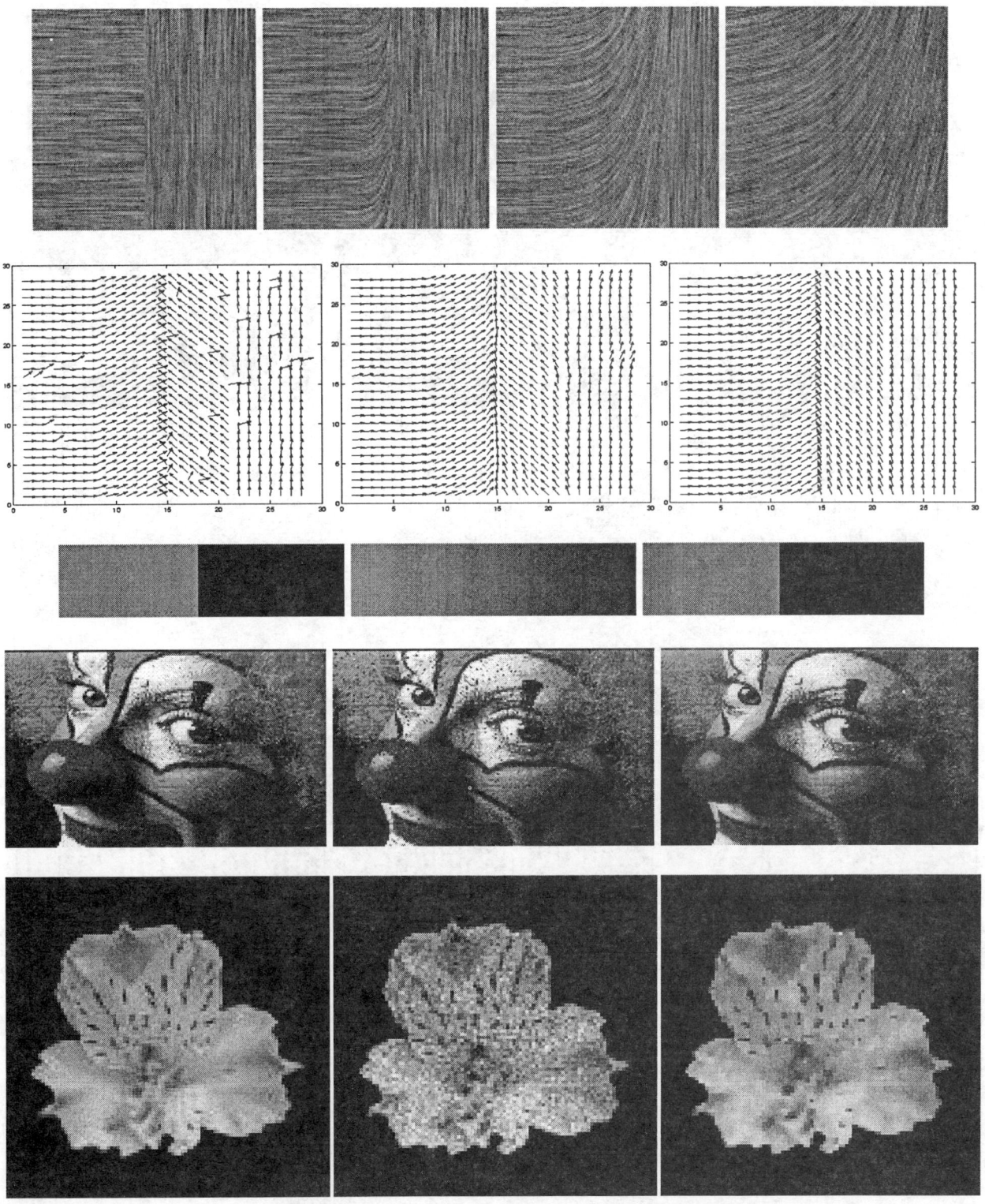

Figure 1: *Examples illustrating the ideas in this paper. See text for details.*

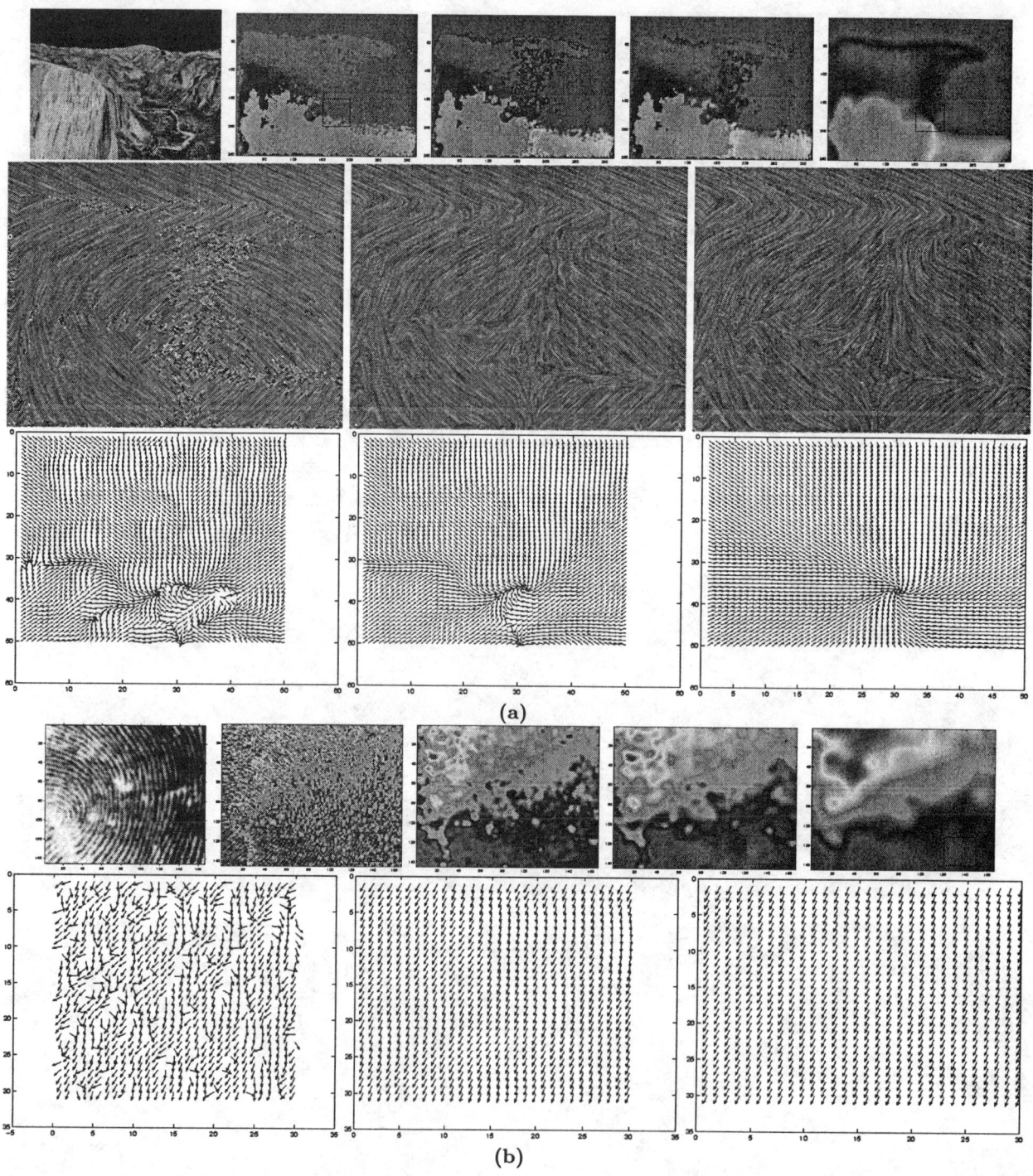

Figure 2: *Optical flow (a) and gradient (b) direction examples. See text for details.*

Semantic Organization of Scenes using Discriminant Structural Templates

Antonio B. Torralba and Aude Oliva
LIS-INPG
Grenoble, France.
torralba,oliva@lis-viallet.inpg.fr

Abstract

In this paper, we present a procedure for organizing real world scenes along semantic axes. The approach is based on the output energies of linear discriminant filters that take into account, or not, spatial information.

We introduce three semantic axes along which pictures are ordered. The main semantic axis computes the degree of naturalness of a scene. Then, urban pictures are evaluated according to their degree of verticalness and natural scenes, according to their degree of openness. We observe the emergence of typical scene categories such as beach, mountain, skyscrapers, city center, etc., along the axes.

1 Introduction

Human observers recognize complex visual scenes in a single glance, in spite of the numerous of objects they contain, with different colors, shadows, textures, etc. To resolve it, the visual system automatically extracts a global information about the main structure of the scene, ignoring most of details and objects information [4-6].

In this paper, we introduce a computational procedure that extracts a global structural information from complex scenes. Common to recent studies about scene recognition [1-4,10-11] is the classification into exclusive classes. However, when dealing with a very large database, exclusive classification may increase irrelevant classification rate as most of scenes are ambiguous in terms of category. Our approach proposes several structural attributes that allow to organize continuously scenes along semantic axes [7]. The structural attributes are computed from the output energies of linear filters. By computing a global structural attribute for each scene (e.g. a city skyline is vertically structured, a coast is horizontally structured), we observe that scenes belonging to the same category (e.g. city center, skyscraper, forest, mountain, etc.) are grouped together whereas ambiguous scenes in terms of category (tall buildings in a center area; rocky valley with trees) are located between semantic zones.

To explore computation of the "main structure" of a scene, the next sections details two kinds of optimal filters: a global filter computed over the whole image and a spatial variant filter.

2 Semantic Axes

This paper details two level of semantic axes that represents attributes of the main structure of a scene:

1) The first semantic axis represents the *degree of naturalness* of a scene. This axis goes from man-made environments to natural landscapes. Ambiguous pictures in terms of "artificiality" (as a farm in a field) are likely to be projected around the center of the axis.

2) The second semantic axis depends on the organization provided by the first axis. Natural scenes are represented according to their *degree of openness*, from panoramic scenes (e.g. coast, beach) to closed environments (e.g. forest, mountain). Degree of openness of artificial urban scenes is estimated according to their quantity of horizontal and vertical lines. This axis goes from vertical to horizontally dominant scenes (from highways to tall buildings).

3 Computation of structural attributes

Main orientations and spatial frequency distributions of the main structure of a scene are encoded in its power spectrum. We show that the power spectrum contains relevant information for the evaluation of the semantic axes.

3.1 Image Power Spectrum

The power spectrum of an image is computed by taking the squared magnitude of its Fourier Transform:

$$\Gamma(f_x, f_y) = |FT\{i(x,y)\}|^2 \qquad (1)$$

where $i(x,y)$ is the intensity distribution of the image along the spatial variables x and y. FT is the Fourier Transform, f_x and f_y are the spatial frequencies. Power spectrum, $\Gamma(f_x, f_y)$, encodes the energy density for each spatial frequency and orientations over the whole image.

3.2 Discriminant Spectral Templates

A Discriminant Spectral Template (DST) is represented by a set of low-level features (here orientation and spatial frequency distributions) encoding the structure which is discriminant between two scene categories. For example, panoramic scenes versus textured scenes (forests) are discriminated by opposing vertical spectral components (axe f_y) versus other orientations, see Fig. 1.b.

A structural discriminant feature, u, is computed per picture by using a DST as follows:

$$u = \iint \Gamma(f_x, f_y)\, DST(f_x, f_y) df_x\, df_y \qquad (2)$$

u is a weighted integral of the power spectrum of the image. $DST(f_x, f_y)$ is the weighted function that describes how each spectral component contributes to the structural attribute.

Fig. 1 shows several examples of $DSTs$ that extract structural attributes. The dark and white pixels correspond respectively to the negative and positive values. These graphical representations allow an easy understanding of the way that scene organization is performed: as an illustration, look at the Naturalness DST (Fig 1.a). Artificial components are represented by the dark zones describing a cross form, but only at medium and high spatial frequencies. This means that a scene picture will be labeled as an artificial environment whether its power spectrum mostly matches the dark zones of the DST. The white part corresponds to a natural structure: it is composed with more oblique elements from low to high spatial frequencies and a vertical spectral component only at low spatial scale (the "horizon" scenes). Performances of the DSTs are presented in the section 4.

3.3 Learning

A supervised learning stage is used to determine the DST associated to each semantic axis.

In order to represent DSTs in a low dimensional space, we decompose it into a set of functions $G_n(f_x, f_y)$ that do not need to be orthogonal. In this paper, we use gaussian envelopes which correspond to Gabor filters:

$$DST(f_x, f_y) = \sum_{n=1}^{N} d_n\, G_n(f_x, f_y)^2 \qquad (3)$$

The coefficients d_n show how weighting each Gabor filter in order to build $DSTs$. The coefficients d_n will be

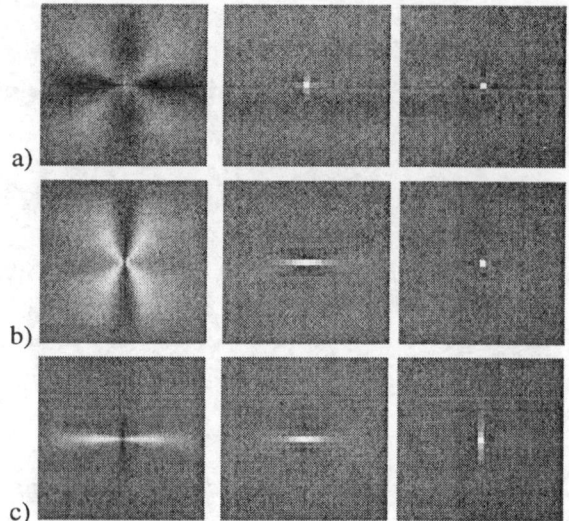

Figure 1. The left-hand column shows the 3 DSTs. The middle and right-hand columns show h_- and h_+. a) artificial vs. natural. b) open vs. closed natural scenes. c) horizontal vs. vertical artificial scenes.

determined by the learning stage. By replacing eq. (3) into eq. (2), we obtain the next equation:

$$g_n = \iint \Gamma(f_x, f_y)\, G_n(f_x, f_y)^2\, df_x\, df_y \qquad (4)$$

where g_n are the output energies for the N Gabor filters used as basis for the DST. We can compute u for each image from these energies as:

$$u = \sum_{n=1}^{N} d_n\, g_n \qquad (5)$$

Here, we sampled the power spectrum with $N = 70$ Gabor filters from high spatial frequencies (1/3 cycles/image) to low spatial frequencies (1/72 cycles/image). But no differences are when using different reasonable values of N.

In the learning step, each image is represented by a vector of features $\mathbf{x} = \{g_n\}$, g_n being the output energies of a set of Gabor filters.

Several methods can be used to determine the coefficients d_n. The method presented here consists in finding to opposed sets of images that can be described with unambiguous semantic attributes. As an illustration, consider the artificiality of a scene. The first group will be composed of images containing only man-made structures and the second one will contain only natural landscape images. The DST must at best separate these two groups. The parameters of the DST, d_n, can be learnt by applying Linear Discriminant Analysis [8, 9] which looks for the parameters giving the best classification rate. Two matrices are fundamental when applying the discriminant analysis. The covariance matrix: $\mathbf{T} = E[(\mathbf{x} - \mathbf{m})(\mathbf{x} - \mathbf{m})^T]$. $\mathbf{m} = E[\mathbf{x}]$ is the mean vector of features. The between-class scatter matrix is defined as: $\mathbf{T}_b = (\mathbf{m}_1 - \mathbf{m})(\mathbf{m}_1 - \mathbf{m})^T + (\mathbf{m}_2 - \mathbf{m})(\mathbf{m}_2 - \mathbf{m})^T$. $\mathbf{m}_1$ and $\mathbf{m}_2$ are the mean vectors of the feature vectors of the two classes. The between-class scatter matrix measures the distance between the centers of the two classes. The discriminant analysis determines the discriminant projection vector that maximizes the distance between the two classes after projection [1]. The discriminant projection vector corresponds to the vector $\mathbf{d} = \{d_n\}$ as defined in the previous section. The discriminant vector is the eigenvector of the matrix $\mathbf{T}^{-1}\mathbf{T}_b$ with the largest eigenvalue. As only two groups per semantic axis are defined, only one eigenvalue is different from zero. Therefore, only one discriminant projection vector can be defined. The discriminant projection vector is given by: $\mathbf{d} = \mathbf{T}^{-1}(\mathbf{m}_1 - \mathbf{m}_2)$. The inversion of $\mathbf{T}$ may be ill-conditioned when the number of examples is not larger enough. In that case we use classic regularization techniques (principal components or adding a perturbation to the matrix $\mathbf{T}$. There is no difference in the resulting organizations).

Once the learning is done, we compose DSTs using the equation (3). After that, projection of one image into the semantic axis does not require the computation of any Gabor filters. The computational steps for obtaining the structural feature (and, therefore, the position of the image along the semantic axis) are: 1) *Prefiltering*: We divided the image intensity at each pixel by an estimation of the local variance in order to reduce illuminant variations. 2) *Power spectrum computation*. 3) *Structural feature computation*: using equation (2). All this procedure requires only global and simple computations on the image yielding to a very efficient algorithm that gives structural information about the scene. The left-hand side of Fig. 1 shows three global DSTs. The first one organizes images from artificial to natural scenes. The second one organizes natural landscapes from open to closed scenes and the third one organizes artificial areas from horizontally to vertically structured scenes.

3.4 Scene Discriminant Filters

The output energy of a filter with transfer function $H(f_x, f_y)$ can be computed as:

$$E = \int\int \Gamma(f_x, f_y) \, |H(f_x, f_y)|^2 \, df_x \, df_y \qquad (6)$$

This expression is similar to eq. (2) used to compute the structural feature u. However, as the squared magnitude of

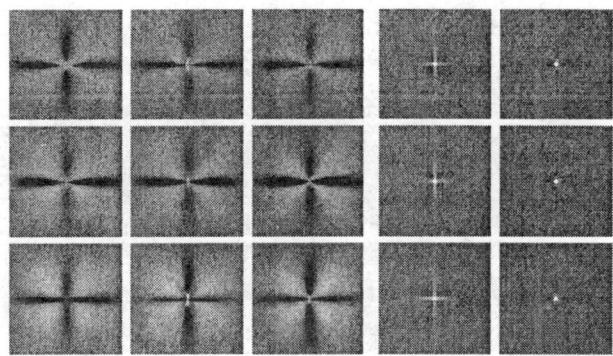

Figure 2. Spatial variant DST for Artificial versus Natural scenes. The 9 templates at the left-hand side are the local DSTs. At the right hand side we show the filters h_- and h_+.

the transfer function of a filter cannot have negative values, the DST function cannot be implemented by a unique filter. In fact, it can be implemented by computing the difference between the output energies of two filters [2]. In such a case, we can compute u as the difference between two energies as $u = E_+ - E_-$, where E_+ and E_- are respectively the output energy of two filters with transfer functions H_+ and H_-. In such a case, we obtain:

$$u = \int\int \Gamma(f_x, f_y) \, (|H_+(f_x, f_y)|^2 - |H_-(f_x, f_y)|^2) df_x \, df_y$$

This expression allows us to write the DST as:

$$DST = |H_+|^2 - |H_-|^2 \qquad (7)$$

With this expression, it is possible to obtain positive and negative values for the DST. Several functions H_+ and H_- give the same resulting DST. Here, we use:

$$|H_+(f_x, f_y)|^2 = \sum_{n=0}^{N} p(d_n) \, G_n(f_x, f_y)^2 \qquad (8)$$

and

$$|H_-(f_x, f_y)|^2 = \sum_{n=0}^{N} p(-d_n) \, G_n(f_x, f_y)^2 \qquad (9)$$

where $p(x) = x$ if $x > 0$ and $p(x) = 0$ if $x < 0$. d_n are the components of the discriminant projection vector computed in the learning stage. These equations give the magnitude of the two filters. As the phase can be freely chosen, we chose null phase filters.

---

[1]Reduction of the data can be performed before applying the discriminant analysis. However such an operation does not improve the results as the standard deviations of the Gabor energy outputs are very similar for the configuration chosen here.

[2]It must be noted that although scene category discrimination is possible using an unique filter, it will yield to poorer results than using two filters. Using more than two filters will not improve results.

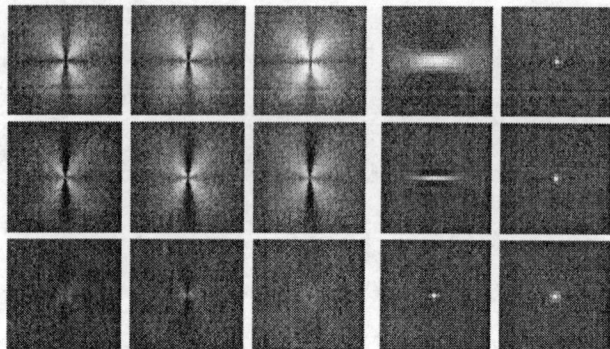

Figure 3. Spatial DST for Open vs. Closed natural scenes.

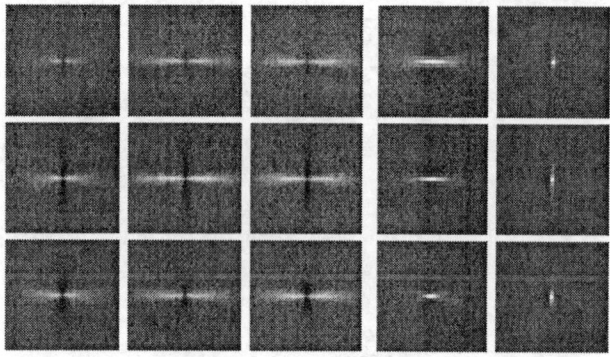

Figure 4. Spatial DST for Horizontal vs. Vertical artificial scenes.

If we compute the output of the two filters by convolution with the respective impulse responses $o_+(x,y) = i(x,y) * h_+(x,y)$ and $o_-(x,y) = i(x,y) * h_-(x,y)$, the structural semantic feature can be obtained as:

$$u = \iint |o_+(x,y)|^2 \, dx \, dy - \tag{10}$$

$$\iint |o_-(x,y)|^2 \, dx \, dy = E_+ - E_-$$

The impulse responses of these two filters are Receptive Fields that best discriminate between two groups of images and that allow a continuous organization of scenes. Fig. 1 shows the impulse responses of both filters for the three DSTs introduced in this paper.

DST (see Fig. 1) computed in the Fourier domain, is equivalent to convolve the image with two spatial invariant filters and computing the difference of their total output energies. The two impulse responses $h_+(x,y)$ and $h_-(x,y)$ reveal the spatial features that are discriminant between the two opposite sets of images. For artificial vs. natural scenes we see a cross impulse response vs an isotropic (slightly

oblique) impulse response (Fig. 1.a). For open vs. closed natural scenes we find an horizontal edge detector vs. an isotropic impulse response (Fig. 1.b). For Horizontal versus vertical artificial environments, the impulse responses are an horizontal vs. a vertical edge detector (Fig. 1.c).

Here, we ask about the relevance of using spatial variant filters despite of global filters. In fact, we can imagine that for some categories of scenes, the main structural components may vary in function of their position in the image. Such an operation may be critical for performing comparison task between similar scenes. For example, for open natural environments, we can expect to have an horizon in the middle center with texture at the bottom and sky at the top. However, closed environments may present texture everywhere in the image with sometimes oblique shapes at the top. Spatial variant filters are expected to take these spatial differences into account for improving ordering performances along the axes.

To investigate this point, we divide images (256x256 pixels) in 9 overlapped windows (128x128 pixels) from left to right and from top to bottom. We compute the power spectrum of each window, $\Gamma_i(f_x, f_y)$, and we compute a structural feature which is a composition of the 9 DSTs and the 9 power spectra:

$$u = \sum_{i=1}^{9} \left(\iint \Gamma_i(f_x, f_y) \, DST_i(f_x, f_y) df_x \, df_y \right) \tag{11}$$

The 9 DST_i are obtained by the same learning procedure as for the global DST. Differences in the shapes of the 9 DSTs will reveal different statistics of the discriminant orientations and spatial frequencies. Figure 2, 3 and 4 show the 9 DSTs. It must be emphasized that both Global DST and Spatial DST compute eventually an unique semantic feature. We can look at the impulse responses of the two discriminant filters H_+ and H_- for each DST_i. The first observation is that the DSTs vary only from top to bottom whatever the semantic axis. This means that spatial variant filters depend only on the vertical spatial variable y and not on x. This is an expected result as both artificial and natural environments have a layered structure from top to bottom (main structures, object attributes and positions differ from top to bottom but not from left to right). Another interesting result is that when discriminating between artificial and natural scenes, the 9 DSTs are highly similar. In that case, the spatial arrangement of dominant orientations carries very low information for making the difference between artificial and natural scenes. A global measure of dominant orientations over the image gives enough structural information to resolve this categorization. On the contrary, computations of *degree of openness* (Fig. 3) and *degree of verticalness* (Fig. 4) is improved by spatially variant filters.

Artificial...   ... Natural

Open ...   ... Closed

Horizontal expanded...   ... Enclosed ...   ... Vertical expanded

Figure 5. Organization of a sample of real-world scenes pictures along the semantic axes. From top to bottom: Artificial to natural scenes, open to closed natural scenes and horizontally to vertically expanded artificial scenes (at the middle of this axis are enclosed urban areas).

4 Semantic Ordering Procedure

In this section, we project scenes never learnt along the three semantic axes and provide elements of comparison between the Global DST and the spatially variant DST. We worked with gray-level pictures of 256x256 pixels size (from the Corel image database, Web pictures and personal pictures). The image database contains 2600 images (1500 natural scenes, 800 artificial scenes and 300 scenes containing both natural and artificial elements).

4.1 Ordering along the Artificial to Natural axis

The classification rate (obtained by cross-validation) for artificial and natural scenes is similar, using Global DST (92%) or Spatial DST (91%). The top line of Fig. 5 displays a sample of images revealing the organization along the Artificial to Natural axis (using the Spatial DST). Ambiguous images containing both man-made and natural structures are mainly located around the center of the axis.

4.2 Ordering along the Open to closed axis

This semantic axis organizes natural scenes from panoramic areas to closed and bounded natural environments. The classification rate is 94% with Global DST and 97% with Spatial Variant DST.

The middle line of Fig. 5 shows the continuous organization along the natural semantic axis (using 1500 natural scenes). We observe an interesting ordering: from open

a)

b)

c)

d)

Figure 6. Similar natural scenes, using Global DST (a,c) and spatial DST (b,d).

scenes with panoramic views (coast, beach, desert), progressively filled in with mountains (valley, mountain), until textural scenes (forest, waterfalls). Of course, some scenes categories may be mixed along the axis (coastline, desert and beach zones may overlap), but the addition of color information definitively disambiguates the semantic status of the scene [3].

---

[3] Performances using DST and color information is detailed in a manuscript in preparation by the two authors.

Figure 7. Similar artificial scenes, using Global DST (a,c) and spatial DST (b,d).

In order to compare performances of the two structural DST, we evaluated the ability to retrieve similar images to a given prototype. Results are shown on Fig. 6, using a beach and a valley as prototypes (left-hand side). When using the Global DST, the retrieved images have the same degree of openness but the boundary elements can change. When using the spatial variant DST, the retrieved images look slightly more similar.

4.3 Ordering along the horizontal to vertical axis

This axis organizes artificial scenes along the horizontal to vertical axis (Fig. 5, bottom). Both Global DST and spatial variant DST give the same performances (98%) when classifying prototypical urban images in horizontal- vs. vertical structured scenes. Three semantic zones emerge: highways scenes, center and city street zones, then city buildings and skyscrapers. Fig. 7 shows a sample of performances of both structural features in a retrieving task. Both results show very good performances knowing that images are retrieved by a unique structural feature (either Global DST, either Spatial DST).

5 Conclusion

In this paper, we introduced three semantic axes and computation of original filters (Discriminant Spectral Templates), optimum for the task at hand. Even if it is obvious that a few more axes would allow a precise classification, we observe that only two structural attributes, *degree of naturalness* and *degree of openness* of a scene, allow the emergence of semantic categories. Moreover, this procedure is very efficient for providing a low cost computational

method, as once DSTs are built, computation of image coordinates along the axes needs only few operations. Finally, we observe that performances are almost equivalent for the global and the spatially variant filters, highlighting the relevance of a coarse and global encoding of the main structure of the scene for its recognition.

References

[1] M. M. Gorkani and R. W. Picard. Texture orientation for sorting photos "at a glance". Proc. Int Conf. Pat. Rec., Jerusalem, 1994, Vol I, pp. 459-464

[2] P. Lipson, E. Grimson, and P. Sinha. Configuration based scene classification and image indexing. In IEEE Computer Society Conference on Computer Vision and Pattern Recognition. Puerto Rico, 1997, pp 1007-1013 (IEEE Computer Society Press)

[3] F. Liu and R. W. Picard. Periodicity, directionality and randomness: Wold features for image modeling and retrieval. IEEE transactions on Pattern Analysis and Machine Intelligence 1996; 18:722-733

[4] A. Oliva. Perception de Scenes [Scene Perception]. PhD dissertation, Institut National Polytechnique de Grenoble, France; May 1995.

[5] A. Oliva and P.G. Schyns. Coarse blobs or fine edges? evidence that information diagnosticity changes the perception of complex visual stimuli. Cognitive Psychology 1997; 34:72-107

[6] A. Oliva and P.G. Schyns. Diagnostic color blobs mediate scene recognition. Cognitive Psychology, in press

[7] A. Oliva, A.B. Torralba, A. Guerin-Dugue and J. Heraut. Global semantic classification using power spectrum templates. The Challenge of Image Retrieval,(CIR99). Electronics Workshops in Computing series, Springer-Verlag. Newcastle, 1999

[8] B. D. Ripley. Pattern recognition and neural networks. Cambridge University Press, 1996

[9] D. L. Swets and J. J. Weng. Using discriminant eigenfeatures for image retrieval. IEEE Trans. On Pattern Analysis and Mach. Intell.1996; 18:831-836

[10] M. Szummer and R. W. Picard. Indoor-outdoor image classification. In IEEE intl. workshop on Content-based Access of Image and Video Databases, 1998.

[11] A. Vailaya, A. Jain and H. J. Zhang. On image classification: city images vs.landscapes. Pattern Recognition 1998; 31:1921-1935

— Notes —

— *Notes* —

— *Notes* —

— *Notes* —

— *Notes* —

— *Notes* —

— *Notes* —